(back cover)

ENCYCLOPEDIA OF
PUBLIC ADMINISTRATION
AND
PUBLIC POLICY

ENCYCLOPEDIA OF
PUBLIC ADMINISTRATION
AND
PUBLIC POLICY

edited by

Jack Rabin

The Pennsylvania State University at Harrisburg
Middletown, Pennsylvania, U.S.A.

VOLUME 1: A–J
PAGES 1–678

MARCEL DEKKER, INC.　　　　　　　　　　NEW YORK • BASEL

ISBN
Volume 1:   0-8247-0946-2
Print/Online: 0-8247-4240-0
Online: 0-8247-0945-4

This book is printed on acid-free paper.

Headquarters
Marcel Dekker, Inc.
270 Madison Avenue, New York, NY 10016
tel: 212-696-9000; fax: 212-685-4540

Eastern Hemisphere Distribution
Marcel Dekker AG
Hutgasse 4, Postfach 812, CH-4001 Basel, Switzerland
tel: 41-61-260-6300; fax: 41-61-260-6333

World Wide Web
http://www.dekker.com

The publisher offers discounts on this book when ordered in bulk quantities. For more information, write to Special Sales/Professional Marketing at the headquarters address above.

Current printing (last digit):
10 9 8 7 6 5 4 3 2 1

PRINTED IN THE UNITED STATES OF AMERICA

To my wife

ENCYCLOPEDIA OF PUBLIC ADMINISTRATION AND PUBLIC POLICY

List of Contributors

Stephen C. Adams / *Florida Department of Environmental Protection, Tallahassee, Florida, U.S.A.*

Robert Agranoff / *Indiana University, Bloomington, Indiana, U.S.A.*

Patricia M. Alt / *Towson University, Towson, Maryland, U.S.A.*

David N. Ammons / *The University of North Carolina at Chapel Hill, Chapel Hill, North Carolina, U.S.A.*

A. Hunter Bacot / *The University of North Carolina at Charlotte, Charlotte, North Carolina, U.S.A.*

Larry Bakken / *Hamline University, St. Paul, Minnesota, U.S.A.*

Irene J. Barnett / *Kent State University, Kent, Ohio, U.S.A.*

John R. Bartle / *University of Nebraska at Omaha, Omaha, Nebraska, U.S.A.*

C. Fred Baughman / *University of Central Florida–Daytona Beach, Daytona Beach, Florida, U.S.A.*

Roger J. Beck / *Southern Illinois University Carbondale, Carbondale, Illinois, U.S.A.*

Julia Beckett / *University of Akron, Akron, Ohio, U.S.A.*

Jane Beckett-Camarata / *Kent State University, Kent, Ohio, U.S.A.*

Christina M. Bellon / *California State University, Sacramento, Sacramento, California, U.S.A.*

J. Edwin Benton / *University of South Florida, Tampa, Florida, U.S.A.*

Evan M. Berman / *University of Central Florida, Orlando, Florida, U.S.A.*

Curtis R. Berry / *Shippensburg University, Shippensburg, Pennsylvania, U.S.A.*

Bradley J. Best / *Buena Vista University, Storm Lake, Iowa, U.S.A.*

Lisa B. Bingham / *Indiana University, Bloomington, Indiana, U.S.A.*

Frayda S. Bluestein / *The University of North Carolina at Chapel Hill, Chapel Hill, North Carolina, U.S.A.*

Keith Boeckelman / *Western Illinois University, Macomb, Illinois, U.S.A.*

R. Wayne Boss / *University of Colorado at Boulder, Boulder, Colorado, U.S.A.*

Cynthia J. Bowling / *Auburn University, Auburn University, Alabama, U.S.A.*

James S. Bowman / *Florida State University, Tallahassee, Florida, U.S.A.*

Dana Burr Bradley / *The University of North Carolina at Charlotte, Charlotte, North Carolina, U.S.A.*

Paul J. Brennan / *Austin Peay State University, Clarksville, Tennessee, U.S.A.*

Gene A. Brewer / *The University of Georgia, Athens, Georgia, U.S.A.*

Raymond Brown / *University of Oregon, Eugene, Oregon, U.S.A.*

Mary Maureen Brown / *The University of North Carolina at Charlotte, Charlotte, North Carolina, U.S.A.*

Judith R. Brown / *Governor's Office of Planning and Budget, Atlanta, Georgia, U.S.A.*

William P. Browne / *Central Michigan University, Mount Pleasant, Michigan, U.S.A.*

James A. Buford, Jr. / *Ellis-Harper Management, Auburn, Alabama, U.S.A.*

Beverly S. Bunch / *University of Illinois at Springfield, Springfield, Illinois, U.S.A.*

Terry F. Buss / *Florida International University, Miami, Florida, U.S.A.*

Thomas Buttross / *The Pennsylvania State University at Harrisburg, Middletown, Pennsylvania, U.S.A.*

Kathe Callahan / *Rutgers, The State University of New Jersey, Newark, New Jersey, U.S.A.*

David G. Carnevale / *University of Oklahoma, Norman, Oklahoma, U.S.A.*

Jered B. Carr / *Wayne State University, Detroit, Michigan, U.S.A.*

Keith Carrington / *St. John's University, Jamaica, New York, U.S.A.*

Paul J. Castellani / *University at Albany, State University of New York, Albany, New York, U.S.A.*

Piper S. Charles / *The University of North Carolina at Charlotte, Charlotte, North Carolina, U.S.A.*

D. S. Chauhan / *Bowling Green State University, Bowling Green, Ohio, U.S.A.*

Keon S. Chi / *The Council of State Governments, Lexington, Kentucky, U.S.A.*

Rupert F. Chisholm / *The Pennsylvania State University at Harrisburg, Middletown, Pennsylvania, U.S.A.*

Cristina E. Ciocirlan / *The Pennsylvania State University at Harrisburg, Middletown, Pennsylvania, U.S.A.*

Cal Clark / *Auburn University, Auburn, Alabama, U.S.A.*

Charles K. Coe / *North Carolina State University, Raleigh, North Carolina, U.S.A.*

Jerrell D. Coggburn / *University of Texas at San Antonio, San Antonio, Texas, U.S.A.*

Stephen E. Condrey / *University of Georgia, Athens, Georgia, U.S.A.*

Alethia H. Cook / *The University of Akron, Akron, Ohio, U.S.A.*

Peter L. Cruise / *California State University, Chico, Chico, California, U.S.A.*

Dennis M. Daley / *North Carolina State University, Raleigh, North Carolina, U.S.A.*

Glenn A. Daley / *RAND Graduate School, Santa Monica, California, U.S.A.*

Mark R. Daniels / *Slippery Rock University of Pennsylvania, Slippery Rock, Pennsylvania, U.S.A.*

Patria de Lancer Julnes / *Utah State University, Logan, Utah, U.S.A.*

Peter deLeon / *University of Colorado at Denver, Denver, Colorado, U.S.A.*

Dwight V. Denison / *New York University, New York, New York, U.S.A.*

Victor S. DeSantis / *Bridgewater State College, Bridgewater, Massachusetts, U.S.A.*

Laurent Dobuzinskis / *Simon Fraser University, Burnaby, British Columbia, Canada*

Brian E. Dollery / *University of New England, Armidale, New South Wales, Australia*

Amy K. Donahue / *University of Connecticut, Storrs, Connecticut, U.S.A.*

Melvin J. Dubnick / *Rutgers, The State University of New Jersey, Newark, New Jersey, U.S.A.*

Larkin S. Dudley / *Virginia Polytechnic Institute and State University, Blacksburg, Virginia, U.S.A.*

William Duncombe / *Syracuse University, Syracuse, New York, U.S.A.*

Robert F. Durant / *University of Baltimore, Baltimore, Maryland, U.S.A.*

Dan Durning / *University of Georgia, Athens, Georgia, U.S.A.*

Carol Ebdon / *University of Nebraska at Omaha, Omaha, Nebraska, U.S.A.*

Richard C. Feiock / *Florida State University, Tallahassee, Florida, U.S.A.*

Patrick Fisher / *Monmouth University, West Long Branch, New Jersey, U.S.A.*

H. Edward Flentje / *Wichita State University, Wichita, Kansas, U.S.A.*

Esther M. Forti / *Medical University of South Carolina, Charleston, South Carolina, U.S.A.*

Scott R. Furlong / *University of Wisconsin–Green Bay, Green Bay, Wisconsin, U.S.A.*

Gerald T. Gabris / *Northern Illinois University, DeKalb, Illinois, U.S.A.*

James A. Gazell / *San Diego State University, San Diego, California, U.S.A.*

Stuart C. Gilman / *Ethics Resource Center, Washington, District of Columbia, U.S.A.*

Anna C. Goldoff / *John Jay College of Criminal Justice, New York, New York, U.S.A.*

Robert T. Golembiewski / *The University of Georgia, Athens, Georgia, U.S.A.*

Ray Gonzales / *Rutgers, The State University of New Jersey, Newark, New Jersey, U.S.A.*

Lawrence S. Graham / *University of Texas, Austin, Texas, U.S.A.*

Cole Blease Graham, Jr. / *University of South Carolina, Columbia, South Carolina, U.S.A.*

Roger Green / *Florida Gulf Coast University, Fort Myers, Florida, U.S.A.*

Ian Greene / *York University, Toronto, Ontario, Canada*

Daphne Greenwood / *University of Colorado at Colorado Springs, Colorado Springs, Colorado, U.S.A.*

A. Gunasekaran / *University of Massachusetts Dartmouth, North Dartmouth, Massachusetts, U.S.A.*

Krishan M. Gupta / *University of Massachusetts Dartmouth, North Dartmouth, Massachusetts, U.S.A.*

Joan E. Pynes / *University of South Florida, Tampa, Florida, U.S.A.*

Hal G. Rainey / *The University of Georgia, Athens, Georgia, U.S.A.*

F. Stevens Redburn / *U.S. Office of Management and Budget, Washington, District of Columbia, U.S.A.*

Christine M. Reed / *University of Nebraska at Omaha, Omaha, Nebraska, U.S.A.*

B. J. Reed / *University of Nebraska at Omaha, Omaha, Nebraska, U.S.A.*

Tari Renner / *Illinois Wesleyan University, Bloomington, Illinois, U.S.A.*

Rupert G. Rhodd / *Florida Atlantic University, Davie, Florida, U.S.A.*

Norma M. Riccucci / *University at Albany, State University of New York, Albany, New York, U.S.A.*

Mark D. Robbins / *University of Connecticut, Storrs, Connecticut, U.S.A.*

Donijo Robbins / *Grand Valley State University, Grand Rapids, Michigan, U.S.A.*

Gary E. Roberts / *The University of Memphis, Memphis, Tennessee, U.S.A.*

Julie W. Robinson / *Tuscaloosa Research and Education Advancement Corporation, Tuscaloosa, Alabama, U.S.A.*

Julia E. Robinson / *J. Robinson Enterprises, Inc., Boise, Idaho, U.S.A.*

Bruce D. Rogers / *Tennessee State University, Nashville, Tennessee, U.S.A.*

John A. Rohr / *Virginia Polytechnic Institute, Blacksburg, Virginia, U.S.A.*

Mark Carl Rom / *Georgetown University, Washington, District of Columbia, U.S.A.*

Jeffrey A. Rosen / *The Ohio State University, Columbus, Ohio, U.S.A.*

David H. Rosenbloom / *American University, Washington, District of Columbia, U.S.A.*

Herbert J. Rubin / *Northern Illinois University, DeKalb, Illinois, U.S.A.*

Marilyn Marks Rubin / *John Jay College of Criminal Justice, The City University of New York, New York, New York, U.S.A.*

Irene Rubin / *Northern Illinois University, Dekalb, Illinois, U.S.A.*

Mark R. Rutgers / *Leiden University, Leiden, The Netherlands*

Alan L. Saltzstein / *California State University, Fullerton, Fullerton, California, U.S.A.*

Grant T. Savage / *The University of Alabama, Tuscaloosa, Alabama, U.S.A.*

E. S. Savas / *Baruch College, City University of New York, New York, New York, U.S.A.*

George Schmelzle / *Indiana University Purdue University, Fort Wayne, Indiana, U.S.A.*

Sally Coleman Selden / *Lynchburg College, Lynchburg, Virginia, U.S.A.*

James R. Simmons / *University of Wisconsin–Oshkosh, Oshkosh, Wisconsin, U.S.A.*

Bill Simonsen / *University of Connecticut, Storrs, Connecticut, U.S.A.*

Richard G. Sims / *Institute on Taxation and Economic Policy, Washington, District of Columbia, U.S.A.*

Barbara Sims / *The Pennsylvania State University at Harrisburg, Middletown, Pennsylvania, U.S.A.*

Douglas R. Snow / *Suffolk University, Boston, Massachusetts, U.S.A.*

Nancy McCarthy Snyder / *Wichita State University, Wichita, Kansas, U.S.A.*

Catherine L. Staples / *Randolph-Macon College, Ashland, Virginia, U.S.A.*

Robert M. Stein / *Rice University, Houston, Texas, U.S.A.*

G. Ross Stephens / *University of Missouri–Kansas City, Kansas City, Missouri, U.S.A.*

Ronald M. Stout, Jr. / *New York State Judiciary, Latham, New York, U.S.A.*

Thomas C. Sutton / *Baldwin-Wallace College, Berea, Ohio, U.S.A.*

James H. Svara / *North Carolina State University, Raleigh, North Carolina, U.S.A.*

Travis K. Taylor / *Alfred University, Alfred, New York, U.S.A.*

Jon C. Teaford / *Purdue University, West Lafayette, Indiana, U.S.A.*

Matthew Tedesco / *University of Colorado at Boulder, Boulder, Colorado, U.S.A.*

Morton J. Tenzer / *University of Connecticut, Storrs, Connecticut, U.S.A.*

Fred Thompson / *Willamette University, Salem, Oregon, U.S.A.*

Marcela Tribble / *Florida International University, Miami, Florida, U.S.A.*

James L. True / *Lamar University, Beaumont, Texas, U.S.A.*

Montgomery Van Wart / *Texas Tech University, Lubbock, Texas, U.S.A.*

Eran Vigoda / *University of Haifa, Haifa, Israel*

Vera Vogelsang-Coombs / *Cleveland State University, Cleveland, Ohio, U.S.A.*

William R. Voorhees / *Arizona State University, Tempe, Arizona, U.S.A.*

Joe L. Wallis / *University of Otago, Dunedin, New Zealand*

Kenneth F. Warren / *Saint Louis University, St. Louis, Missouri, U.S.A.*

William L. Waugh, Jr. / *Georgia State University, Atlanta, Georgia, U.S.A.*

Jeffrey A. Weber / *The Pennsylvania State University at Harrisburg, Middletown, Pennsylvania, U.S.A.*

Marcie Weinstein / *Towson University, Towson, Maryland, U.S.A.*

Jonathan P. West / *University of Miami, Coral Gables, Florida, U.S.A.*

Richard D. White, Jr. / *Louisiana State University, Baton Rouge, Louisiana, U.S.A.*

Russell L. Williams / *Florida State University, Tallahassee, Florida, U.S.A.*

Katherine G. Willoughby / *Georgia State University, Atlanta, Georgia, U.S.A.*

Matthew Woessner / *The Pennsylvania State University at Harrisburg, Middletown, Pennsylvania, U.S.A.*

John D. Wong / *Wichita State University, Wichita, Kansas, U.S.A.*

E. J. Woodhouse / *Rensselaer Polytechnic Institute, Troy, New York, U.S.A.*

John Abbott Worthley / *Seton Hall University, South Orange, New Jersey, U.S.A.*

David A. Yalof / *University of Connecticut, Storrs, Connecticut, U.S.A.*

Thomas E. Yatsco / *U.S. Department of Health & Human Services, Washington, District of Columbia, U.S.A.*

Jong-In Yoon / *The University of Georgia, Athens, Georgia, U.S.A.*

Peter C. Young / *University of St. Thomas, Minneapolis, Minnesota, U.S.A*

Nikolaos Zahariadis / *University of Alabama at Birmingham, Birmingham, Alabama, U.S.A.*

Stephen J. Ziegler / *Washington State University, Pullman, Washington, U.S.A.*

Cyrus Ernesto Zirakzadeh / *University of Connecticut, Storrs, Connecticut, U.S.A.*

Contents

Preface

This venture serves a number of objectives. First, it provides the reader with entries concerning the salient theories, issues, and concepts within the broad fields of public administration and public policy. Each entry is a coherent article, rather than a short paragraph.

Second, this encyclopedia is the first attempt in our field at providing its subject matter both in hard copy and on the Internet. Thus, the work becomes a "living thing," and plans are to supplement the work quarterly with the goal of incorporating future entries—published both electronically and in future printed supplements.

Third, this work serves as a gateway into our vast field, giving the reader both an introduction to the various subjects and references to additional bodies of knowledge.

Fourth, the encyclopedia supplements and complements the Public Administration and Public Policy Book Series (published by Marcel Dekker, Inc.), now over 25 years old. With over 100 volumes published, and another 40 books under contract, it is the largest book series in our field. Within the book series reside approximately 30 Handbooks—bibliographic treatises with in-depth knowledge on a given topic. Finally, the book series is supplemented by the *International Journal of Public Administration*, also over 25 years old, and published in 14 issues annually.

I commend Marcel Dekker, Inc., for its longtime commitment to our field—a dedication crowned by this encyclopedia. I also express my gratitude to the contributing editors as well as to all the authors. Lastly, I thank all faculty and students who have supported our various endeavors for over a quarter of a century.

Jack Rabin

Accountability and Ethics: Reconsidering the Relationships

Melvin J. Dubnick
Rutgers, The State University of New Jersey, Newark, New Jersey, U.S.A.

INTRODUCTION

The relationship between ''accountability'' and ''ethics'' has long been a concern among students of public administration. Accountability has traditionally been regarded as the means used to control and direct administrative behavior by requiring ''answerability'' to some external authority. It has deep roots in American constitutional history, and can be linked to the principles implicit in the Magna Carta as well as to our system of checks and balances. In public administration, ethics has most often been associated with standards of responsible behavior and integrity.

Issues about the relationship between the two were central to the Friedrich–Finer debate of the early 1940s— one of two debates that set the intellectual agenda for the field of public administration during the Cold War era (the other being the debate between Herbert Simon and Dwight Waldo).[1] In a 1940 essay,[2] Friedrich argued that the traditional means (e.g., oversight and control) for holding administrators accountable were ineffective and unnecessary. It was reasonable, he contended, to defer to the judgment of administrators whose sense of professional responsibility and loyalty could be trusted when they carried out public policy in the national interest. In response, Finer[3] reasserted the widely held view that, despite the greater sense of professional responsibility among today's administrators, democracy still requires enhanced public control and direction of administrative agents.

That exchange was—and remains—the classic expression of the conventional relationship between ethics and accountability in public administration.[4–7] Fundamental to that view is the assumption that the commitment of modern administrators to conduct themselves responsibly (i.e., ethically, in accord with ''democratic morality'') was not sufficient to ensure that the will of the people would be carried out. Accountability, in the form of external (i.e., democratic) constraints and controls, was also necessary. Accountability mechanisms were required to render the decisions and behavior of public officials responsible, not merely in the legal, political, or bureaucratic senses of that term, but also morally.[8–10] Ethical behavior, in short, required the presence of external accountability mechanisms in their various forms.

Does accountability foster ethical or morally responsible behavior? Despite considerable scholarship devoted to the examination of efforts to control the bureaucracy through various accountability mechanisms,[11–20] the existence or effectiveness of the accountability–ethics relationship has yet to be systematically examined. A growing body of work on accountability implies that it has a significant impact on administrative behavior,[21–31] but none of these studies directly address how accountability affects the ethical standards and strategies adopted by administrators.

BARRIERS TO ANALYSIS

The barriers to such an analysis have been conceptual and methodological. Conceptually, both ''accountability'' and ''ethical behavior'' have lacked the ''sharpness'' and clarity[32] required for analytical purposes. The concept of accountability has been characterized as expansive[33] and chameleon-like[34] as applied in both theory and practice, and the appropriate meaning of ethical behavior has long been the subject of heated debate between utilitarians and deontologists (among others).[35,36] The lack of progress in conceptualization, however, can be attributed to the institutional bias and normative ambiguity fostered by our methodological approaches to both terms. Accountability and ethical behavior are rarely perceived in behavioral terms outside the institutional contexts that preoccupy students of public administration. As a result, accountability becomes associated with certain institutional forms of oversight and ethical behavior becomes tangled in discussions of codes and legalisms. Also important has been the inability of analysts to put aside the normative ''baggage'' that accompanies the use of such value-laden terms as ''accountable'' and ''ethical'' when describing human behavior.[32]

We can overcome these barriers by adopting a ''middle range'' or ''concrete theory'' perspective[37–40] that allows us to reconceptualize both accountability and ethical behavior as ''social mechanisms''—that is, in Robert Merton's terms ''social processes having designated consequences for designated parts of the social structure.''[41] Applying this approach, we assume a sociological (rather than institutional) view of accountability. The sociological view stresses the forms and functions of accountability as processes (mechanisms) that affect social actors as *situated pressures for account-giving behavior*. In this article, we focus on four general types of mechanisms that demand account-giving responses: answerability; blameworthiness; liability; and attributability.

Similarly, we regard ethical behaviors as social mechanisms constituted as norms and standards of behavior generated as partial responses to the pressures created by accountability mechanisms. In contrast to both Kantian and utilitarian views of ethics that rely on the existence of a priori knowledge or some universal standard, we assume a more naturalistic[42] and pragmatic perspective that stresses the functional role of ethics in dealing with social dilemmas.[43–45] Our focus is on the development and nurturing of ethical behaviors and strategies in response to major forms of sociological accountability.

THE SOCIOLOGICAL PERSPECTIVE

Three Approaches to Accountability

Analytically, the concept of accountability can be approached in three ways: historically; institutionally; and sociologically. Historically, the term itself has distinctly Anglican and feudalistic roots, and has only recently emerged as a universal standard of governance.[46] Mechanisms similar to the modern concept of accountability, however, do have ancient roots in Athenian democracy.[47,48] More than historical curiosities, both the Anglican and Athenian views of accountability offer insights into modern accountability and provide standards by which to assess the various approaches that emerge from sociological analyses. For our purposes, however, we focus attention on those views derived from the contemporary study of social relationships.

Institutional perspectives approach accountability as formalized means of feedback and control established with governance structures of states and corporate entities.[49] This view covers a range of phenomena, from constitutions to financial reporting standards, and has been the dominant perspective in the study of bureaucratic accountability.[4,6,19]

Sociological perspectives focus attention on accountability as a type of social act that is part of a larger class of social processes or mechanisms dealing with the need to repair or overcome damaged relationships resulting from "unanticipated or untoward behavior."[50] That group of mechanisms includes confessing to the action or seeking forgiveness,[51] subjecting oneself to punishment or retribution,[52,53] engaging in "good works" to make amends for the damage done or seeking the restoration of

one's good name,[54] and associated behaviors that stand as substitutes for (or complements of) giving an account of one's behavior.

Giving of Accounts

Specifically, the social "giving of accounts" occurs when one must justify or provide excuses for the action that resulted in the faux pas or untoward act that is the focus of attention.[50] One is essentially not denying either active or passive involvement in the particular indiscretion, but is engaging in an effort to explain why one ought not to be held either fully or partly responsible. Justification involves accepting responsibility for the act, but denying the immorality or untowardness of the behavior's consequences. Excuses, in contrast, do not deny the negative consequences of the acts in question, but argue that the account giver had no choice but to act badly and was therefore not responsible.[50,55] In this sense, an individual is "accountable" to the extent that there exists an expectation[56] within the community that they would provide an explanation for any act regarded as worthy of account giving.

While standing as a distinct type among the class of associate mechanisms related to repairing damaged relationships, account giving may also serve as a necessary complement to the other forms. The expectation to provide a justification or excuse for one's actions may include a demand for an accounting, even if the individual confesses to the act, apologizes, and submits to punishment or undertakes restitution. Consider the case of Scott Waddle, commander of the submarine U.S.S. Greeneville that collided with a Japanese vessel, the "Ehime Maru," south of Hawaii on February 9, 2001. The incident, which led to nine deaths, was the subject of a military court of inquiry; by April, Commander Waddle had accepted "full responsibility and accountability" for the accident and made several widely publicized apologies. But in this instance, and others like it, the public admission of guilt and expression of regret and apologies did not preclude the requirement for an accounting of what took place. Thus, with each public appearance, Commander Waddle had to relive the incident and provide an account of why he acted as he did.

In contrast, there are some acts of omission or commission considered so despicable that no amount of excuses or justifications would be acceptable. For example, Adolph Eichmann, Albert Speer, and other Nazis offered defenses of their actions based on accounts that they were just "following orders," carrying out their civic and legal "duties," or (in the case of Speer) unaware of what was taking place despite their prominent roles in the German war effort.[57,58] No account giving in the form of excuses or justifications was perceived as acceptable.

Typology of Account-Giving Mechanisms

With its focus on actions taken in response to social expectations, the sociological perspective can generate a useful typology of account-giving mechanisms. Expectations relevant to providing an explanation for one's behavior can be viewed along two dimensions. First, the expectations can be related to specific actors or can focus on situations. Second, the expectations setting or environment can be highly structured and relatively stable or emergent and subject to fluctuation. Table 1 illustrates the resulting forms of socially relevant accountability emerging from relating these two dimensions.

In the following sections, I describe the distinctive features of the resulting four types of account-giving mechanisms and discuss the relevant literature associated with each. I also briefly consider the implications of each for generating ethical behavior mechanisms among those being held accountable. As we see, accountability and ethics are closely related both analytically and empirically.

TYPE A: ACCOUNTABILITY-AS-ANSWERABILITY

Demanding Answers

Role-specific expectations for account giving are those found in highly structured social relationships where the tasks and obligations of individuals are either clearly articulated (i.e., formalized) or so "institutionalized" (in the sense of "regularized") that they are perceived as inherent to the position a person is occupying.[59,60] We label this form of accountability "answerability" to stress the idea that persons who fall in this category are expected to respond to calls for giving an account upon demand. In short, that expectation comes with their role. This conceptualization of accountability is among the most commonly used, and has been central to contemporary studies of democratic and organizational accountability.[22,61]

Within democratic theory,[62,63] accountability-as-answerability indicates a relationship between the governors and the governed, involving mechanisms requiring the former to inform the latter of actions taken on their behalf (i.e., in their "interest"), and allowing the latter to judge and take action against the former based on that

information. The specific mechanisms involved range from accountability through elections[64] and mediated procedures (e.g., a "vote of no confidence" in parliamentary systems)[65] to the creation and strengthening of "horizontal" institutions (e.g., courts and ombudsman offices).[49] Accountability-as-answerability has also played a central role in classical and contemporary organization theory, where the central problem has been to develop mechanisms (e.g., chain of command, limited span of control) and related strategies for creating and sustaining cooperative social systems.[66–69]

Answerabilty Research

There have been several streams of research associated with accountability-as-answerability mechanisms, each applying a distinct model of the social relationship involved and generating a different picture of the ethical implications of answerability. One stream models answerability as a relationship between accountable individuals and the audience to which they must provide the account. In a series of articles published in the 1980s, Teltock and his colleagues found that being told one must provide a justification for a decision had a significant influence on the individual's approach to each decision.[70–73] Moreover, individuals put in such situations were motivated to seek the approval of their perceived audiences, leading Tetlock to develop an "accountability theory" emphasizing the view of answerable individuals as "intuitive politicians . . . whose primary goal is to protect their social identities in the eyes of the key constituencies to whom they feel accountable."[74]

In contrast, a principal agent theory stream provides a contractual context within which answerability mechanisms and relationships are used to overcome the inherent "moral hazard" and "selection" problems principals face when relying on an agent.[75–78] Here, the answerability mechanisms are regarded as structural responses to dilemmas created by the effort of rational principals attempting to control rational agents, each pursuing their own self-interest.

A third research stream, that of the "new institutionalism," regards organized behavior as dominated by rules and institutional norms, and would treat answerability as part of that rule structure.[79–81] The accountable individual is a rule follower whose actions are governed by what March and Olsen have termed, the "logic of ap-

Table 1 Types of accountability

Expectations	Structured	Emergent
Related to persons	Type A: Answerability	Type B: Blameworthiness
Related to situations/events	Type C: Liability	Type D: Attributability

propriateness.'' Under this logic, accountability-as-answerability is dominated by three questions: what kind of situation is this?; who am I (i.e., what is my identity or role)?; and what is the rule I should follow given my identity and the situation?[82]

Answerability Ethics

The three perspectives on accountability-as-answerability present us with alternative models of the accountable actor, and thus imply three models of ethical behavior mechanisms. The ethics of Tetlock's intuitive politician are driven by the psychological need to be accepted by the ''audience''—in the case of elected officials, the electorate or the people, and in the case of a public administrator, the client, supervisor, or stakeholder. This can result in an approach that judges the ethicality of actions on the basis of their strategic value.[83] The ethics of the rational self-interested agent is shaped by individuals' calculations of what actions will best suit their interests, regardless of whether those interests are focused on the accumulation of power, the accumulation of wealth, or some other goal.[84,85] The rule followers' ethics are primarily shaped by role expectations and the individual's social identity—a fact that leads them to select the most ''appropriate'' action among alternatives based on assessments of what best fits that identity and set of expectations.

What these three ethical roles share is a reliance on exogenous signals or structures. The intuitive politician is constantly monitoring the audience for signals about appropriate behavior, whereas the rational agent is engaged in ongoing calculations about that behavior that will provide the best payoff. The rule follower, in the meantime, is always engaged in balancing the expectations associated with their social identity with the demands of the situation. All three look outward as they make their ethical choices, and all three reflect a concern for the consequences of their actions. In that sense, Type A accountability tends to make administrators rely on various forms of ethical mechanisms stressing the consequences of their actions vis-à-vis the expectations of those to whom they are answerable. This stress on consequences will, in turn, lead to the adoption of ethical strategies drawn from teleological schools of ethics,[86] providing logical support to the various models of bureaucratic behavior applied or implied in many positive, political, and organizational theories. Among positive theories of bureaucratic behavior, mechanisms rooted in utilitarian ethics (act, rule, and motive) are the assumed position for administrator actions. Similarly, political theories of bureaucratic behavior emphasize mechanisms that enhance the influence and power of agencies, whereas organization theories focus on the

striving for autonomy, security, and resources. Implied in these models is a set of ethical strategies closely linked to Type A accountability.

TYPE B: ACCOUNTABILITY-AS-BLAMEWORTHINESS

Status-Based Accountability

Although accountability is most often thought of in terms of answerability, it is not always applied to persons in specific and defined roles. Blameworthiness as a form of accountability involves a shift in focus from specific roles and contractual obligations as an agent to one's perceived social status and membership in some group that has status. Whereas role identifies what tasks and functions you perform, status implies power and influence within the organization.[87] Put briefly, one is held accountable not because of one's tasks or formal responsibilities, but because of one's relative social position or identification with a certain group. Thus, you are held accountable because you are regarded as socially, if not organizationally, blameworthy.[88]

In its most extreme form, Type B accountability involves ''scapegoating''—that is, imposing blameworthiness on a group simply by characterizing it as the source of the undesirable condition.[89,90] It is, in Peter Gay's words, the construction of a ''convenient Other'' upon whom one can visit the blame for any problem—and against whom we can target our anger and aggression.[91]

But accountability-as-blameworthiness can also take less extreme forms. In military organizations, for example, those at the highest echelons of any unit are deemed blameworthy and accountable for events that occur on their ''watch.'' This form of accountability differs from mere answerability, which is related to whether one is performing one's specific role. Here, the primary issue is one's status as the commanding officer that is most important.

A relevant case is that of Rear Admiral Husband E. Kimmel, Commander-in-Chief of the Pacific Fleet at the time of the Japanese surprise attack on Pearl Harbor on December 7, 1941. There is no question that the devastation wrought by Japan's forces was causally responsible for the damages suffered on that ''day of infamy.'' Yet, both Admiral Kimmel and Lieutenant General Walter Short, who was Commanding General of the local Army contingent, were officially blamed and sanctioned for the state of ''unreadiness'' at Pearl Harbor on the morning of the infamous attack, and their careers were ended despite their potential value as commanders in the war that followed.[92] Similarly, in a statement issued in July 1997, then Secretary of Defense William Cohen held Brigadier General Terryl Schwalier "personally accountable" for the lax force protection that led to the death of 19 American service personnel at the Khobar Towers bombing a year earlier.[93] The facts in both cases indicated that there was more blame to go around than that visited on Kimball, Short, or Schwalier, but that is not the way accountability operates in the military. "In the military," observed Judith Shklar, "responsibility has to be personalized at the highest level of the organization since its system of command is built on the principles of obedience and reliance.... We cannot afford to be philosophically discriminating when our security depends on maintaining the principles of hierarchical responsibility for victory and defeat, especially the latter" (p. 63).[94]

Blameworthiness in Public Service Cultures

While accountability-as-blameworthiness is an accepted part of military culture [and can be found in some organizations that model themselves after the military, (e.g. some police forces)], it is rarely evident in other formal organization contexts. However, it is a pervasive presence in the extraorganizational contexts of public service. Our government and its agents operate in a culture where officials are implicitly held blameworthy for possible misfortunes, regardless of causal responsibility.[88,94] A hurricane is an act of nature, but government meteorologists will be held accountable for forecasting its exact point of impact as well as expected intensity, and local emergency preparedness offices will be blamed if proper steps were not taken to deal with the storm's impact. In the aftermath of the September 11, 2001 attacks on the World Trade Center and the Pentagon, issues were raised about the competence and culpability of the U.S. intelligence community as well as security at America's airports. Within 2 weeks of those tragic events, the media began to castigate the policies of the U.S. Immigration and Naturalization Service for its inability to track aliens who remained in the country illegally. Like other public sector agencies, they were blameworthy; unlike others, they were called into account for their implied role in facilitating the devastating attack.

What is involved in this form of accountability comes close to what is traditionally termed "moral responsibility." As Marion Smiley notes, in both its Christian and Kantian forms, moral responsibility implied the existence of some higher or external authority. Under those forms, blameworthiness was a matter of whether one was in a position to violate the norms of those universal standards that constituted morality. But in discussing accountability-as-blameworthiness, we are focused on the social construction of blameworthiness and the social practice of blaming.[95] We are blameworthy as a result of our status within a community (e.g., the mayor) or organization (e.g., the general), not due to any specific task responsibilities or actual authority. We are blameworthy because we are members of a group whose members are regarded as blamable (e.g., bureaucrats, politicians), not because anyone in that group could really be an effective causal agent.

Type B Ethical Responses

The ethics of those facing Type B accountability is necessarily pragmatic in the broadest sense of that term and can take three forms beyond the mere passive acceptance of one's fate as a blameworthy actor. First, accountability-as-blameworthiness can be approached instrumentally. Faced with the social reality of blameworthiness, the accountable individual should use the situation to deal with the challenges within that context. The heads of agencies that have been subjected to severe criticism for past performance can use the opportunity to strengthen the organizations' future capacities. In response to their experiences as field-level soldiers in Vietnam, the officers who rose through the military's ranks from the mid-1970s to the 1980s developed ethical strategies that literally transformed the role of the armed forces in U.S. policy as well as the way the military was perceived by the public and perceived itself.[96] An equally dramatic transformation of the ethical and operational norms of the Federal Emergency Management Agency (FEMA) took place under James Lee Witt, who assumed his position in April 1993 in the wake of severe criticism for FEMA's handling of recent disaster relief efforts.

A second approach is to assume a commitment to a deontological moral standard[97] that would meet with widespread approval within the community or organization. The call for public administrators to focus on "service" rather tan "steering,"[98] to engage in the pursuit of the "public interest,"[10,99] to adopt a professional standard of social equity,[100,101] or to "refound" itself in the regime values of the constitution[102,103] are part of this effort to fill the moral void implied by the condition of blameworthiness.

The third approach is to engage in an "identity shift" by dissociating oneself from the blameworthy status or group. Under the view of social constructivism, just as certain groups are regarded as blameworthy, so other groups are inherently praiseworthy. In lieu of a tag such as "bureaucrat" or government employee, one can stress a professional identity such as city planner, park ranger, or law enforcement official. These identity shifts, in turn, have implications for the type of accountability and ethical standards to which one is subject. Of course, as social constructions, the blameworthiness of these identities can vary from place to place and over time. Police officers in a small midwestern town will face a different set of community expectations than their peers in New York or Los Angeles; similarly, the status and perception of an FBI agent in the 1990s was quite different from that of the 1950s.

Common among these three Type B responses is the establishment of credibility for public administrators as autonomous ethical actors. The post-Vietnam era commanders focused on establishing and articulating basic rules for the use of military force—rules that sometimes led them to openly resist putting U.S. personnel in harm's way when other options were available. The military professionalism represented by the likes of George Patton were replaced by the model provided by Colin Powell and his cohort who served and suffered as field officers during the Vietnam War. The call for the public service professional to give priority to general ethical commitments is also a step toward asserting an ethically autonomous position, as is the effort to create a distinct professional identity among the public service professions. Each of these is a means toward the realization of Carl Friedrich's model of the responsible administrator.

TYPE C: ACCOUNTABILITY-AS-LIABILITY

Law-like Situations

In contrast to accountabilities based on the expectations related to persons, Types C and D accountabilities focus on the structure of the situation in which actors operate. Although posited as distinct types, accountability-as-liability and accountability-as-attributability would more appropriately be described as forms found at opposite ends of a continuum. At one end are highly structured contexts in which expectations are well defined and clear to all; at the other extreme are situations so vaguely defined that they are almost devoid of stable expectations. Our current focus, Type C accountability, falls on the "highly structured" section of that range.

As implied in its name, accountability-as-liability is closely associated with a legalist view of the world in which actions are guided and assessed according to rules that carry sanctions for noncompliance.[104] Unlike answerability (Type A), where expectations for accountability derive from the actor's institutional role or organizational position, liability stresses the requirements of the structured situation. The nature of that structure can vary from the strictures of legal requirements backed by state sanctions to implicit contracts between two parties that carry with them rewards for compliance and/or sanctions for violations. At the core of these mechanisms is the idea that law, in a general sense, is an effective way to establish and maintain order and control.[105,106]

In a strictly formal sense, accountability-as-liability would be limited to shaping one's actions according to the "letter of the law"—that is, doing what is required by law and avoiding those actions prescribed under law. For Type C accountability, however, the concept of law is much broader, taking on the characteristics of both an institutional setting (i.e., the "rule of law")[107,108] and a context for social relationships.[109–112]

Issues of Liability

The relationships between Type C and other forms of accountability are quite complex for two related reasons. First, ours is an "organizational society" where individuals are constantly identified by their role or status. It is rare to find a structured situation where one is completely without some role identity. Accountability-as-liability, however, tends to focus on the act and its consequences rather than on the actors or their status-derived blameworthiness. In its most stringent form, Type C accountability seeks out the actors who "did the deed" (who were directly, causally responsible) rather than the individual "in charge" or playing some other relevant role. Thus, an individual in a supervisory role/status would not be held accountable *unless* there was both evidence and willingness to link that person to the untoward activity.

For example, in the case of the infamous 1969 My Lai massacre, the U.S. Army believed that it had to treat the event as a legal case; in so doing, it found its ability to hold people accountable severely limited. Taking the legal liability route, the Army charged Lieutenant William Calley with the premeditated murder of at least four civilians. Several others in command positions at the scene of the massacre (which involved at least 175 to 200 deaths) were initially charged, but it was later decided to drop those charges in all but one additional case due to "insufficient evidence"—a standard reflecting the legal nature of the accountability approach being applied. The exception was Captain Ernest Medina, Calley's immediate superior officer, who was also brought to trial and charged with murder. However, there was a difference. The murder charges against him were not for specific acts of premeditated killing (although evidence indicates that he killed at least four civilians at My Lai); rather, he was charged with 102 murders under a provision of military law that allowed prosecution of those with command responsibility. He was court-martialed and acquitted of those charges. Thus, although the military could have (and did in many cases) hold many more persons blameworthy under its Type B accountability approach (and subject to organizational sanctions), it held only Calley legally liable for four of approximately 200 deaths and sentenced him to 20 years in prison. By focusing on liability, in other words, and not pursuing specific counts of premeditated murder again Medina and others, the military was unable to fulfill the need for accountability-as-liability.

This leads to the second issue associated with Type C accountability—the problem of collective responsibility.[113] Just as the legal system has difficult dealing with collective responsibility,[114] liability-based accountability systems are constantly challenged by the ''many hands'' problem.[115] As Dennis Thompson noted, typical solutions to this problem include applying ''hierarchical'' or ''collective'' forms of responsibility, and he finds both wanting. In their place, he advocates applying ''personal responsibility'' approach based on some weak causal connection between an individual and the event. In terms of the present framework, that would mean shifting from Type C to either Type A or Type B accountability—a move that raises issues regarding the integrity and fairness of any sanctions that might be imposed. Such an approach does not deal with the complex situations where even a weak causal link cannot be proven. In such cases, even the legal system has had to modify its standards by allowing liability to rest almost entirely on an individual possible ''fault'' rather than cause.[116]

As with its legal equivalent, the inherent problems of accountability-as-liability are many.[117–120] Nevertheless, it is an approach to accountability that is extremely important in public administration. A central factor shaping Type C accountability for public administrators has been the judicial treatment of two issues—administrative discretion and administrative immunity. Historical shifts in the judiciary's handling of administrative discretion and delegation of authority cases[121,122] have altered the jurisdictions and tasks of administrative agencies to such a degree (some have argued) that we have witnessed a de facto constitutional transformation of the American republic.[123] The courts' willingness to lift the cover of sovereign immunity over the past several decades[124,125] has been as significant in its impact on accountability, exposing administrators to legal actions and making it urgent for them to become more ''constitutionally competent.''[126]

As significant has been the general impact on public administration of the legalistic mindset fostered by these developments. Almost every area of public management has shown signs of deference to the ''lawyer's'' perspective, and an abandonment of the administrator's view of the world.[127] The very act of entering the public service places one in a distinctive legal relationship to the state,[128] and efforts to assure public employee integrity through Type C approaches have been pervasive and often counterproductive for the day-to-day operations of government.[129]

Law-like Ethics

The ethics related to Type C accountability have their roots in distinct and conflicting concepts of law. Two approaches emerge from debates among philosophers regarding the nature of law, while a third is derived from the analogical reasoning used in the practice of law.

In the philosophy of law, a major division exists between those who assume laws to be human artifacts without any inherent moral value (the *positivist* school) and those who assess laws in terms of their relation to a higher law standard (the *natural law* school). Each school generates numerous ethical positions, but for our purposes we offer them in caricature as the positivist *ethics of obligation* and the naturalist *ethics of conscience*. As applied by those who are held accountable, the ethics of obligation calls for adherence to the explicit rules that define a situation. Here, we find the ethics of neutral competence that has been so central to the norms of American public administration.[130–133] The ethics of conscience, in contrast, is manifest in efforts to have public administrators adhere to some ''higher standard'' when engaged in the enforcement or implementation of the law. Here, again, we find various standards from ''regime values'' and ''public interest'' to ''social equity'' and ''justice-as-fairness.''[100,134–136]

A third ethical approach relevant to Type C accountability comes from the practice of law. Sunstein[137] offered the term ''analogical reasoning'' to describe the type of thinking that takes place in legal practice. It is reasoning that focuses on applying laws and rules to specific cases based on how that law or rule has been applied in the past to similar (although not identical) cases. Sunstein highlighted four features of analogical reasoning. First, it is based on the norm of ''principled consistency''—that is, the need to provide some principle to ''harmonize seemingly disparate outcomes.'' Second, there should be a focus on the details of the case, letting the facts shape the decision. Third, analogical reasoning avoids the application of any ''deep or comprehensive theory'' that might overwhelm the facts of the case. Finally, this form of reasoning produces and applies standards that should be at a ''low or intermediate level of abstraction.'' In public administration, the ethics of ''constitutional competence'' advocated by Rosenbloom and Carroll[125,126] operates at this analogical level by focusing on the need for public service employees to become familiar with their place and responsibilities within the U.S. constitutional system through relevant cases.

The common thread holding these Type C ethical strategies together is their commitment to determining what is ethical through a reasoning process—one guided by rules, the second by a higher standard, and the third through analogy. In contrast to the stress on consequences (generated by Type A account giving) and blame avoidance (through Type B), the ethical approaches of Type C accountability rely on ethical behavior mechanisms that call for an actor to engage in a certain type of reasoning that fosters consideration of procedural requirements, legal standards, or precedent.[138]

TYPE D: ACCOUNTABILITY-AS-ATTRIBUTABILITY

Relevance of Nonwork Expectations

Accountability-as-attributability brings into consideration those arenas of social life where the rules and roles of public administration are *seemingly* irrelevant, but are potentially quite important in the environment of accountability of public sector workers. It involves those contexts where the fact that an individual holds a certain position in an organization, or that one is subject to rules and constraints in the workplace, is of little or no consequence *most of the time*. It is the context of the ''nonwork domain'' where one lives a ''private life'' distinct from the public life of the government job, or so it seems. In reality, accountability pressures spillover into the private lives of all employees, both public and private.

In the nonwork domain, one is subject to accountability standards that are broader in scope, more diverse, and constantly subject to change over time and from place to place. The sources of those standards are other social actors in the domain who regard an action or behavior as requiring an accounting by some actor. In short, they *attribute* an action or behavior to an individual and would *expect* an accounting if they were in a position to demand one. This attributing behavior is regarded by social psychologists as part of our standards means for making sense of, and dealing with, the world.[139–141] From the perspective of ''attribution theory'' research, this form of attribution is subject to ideological, cultural, and stereotypical bias,[142,143] as well as situational determinism.[144] In addition, attributions tend to be unstable and malleable by changing conditions such as information or expectations.[72,145,146] The shortcomings of such attributions, however, have not diminished their relevance.

Being of ''Suspect'' Character

The link between specific instances of attribution and our Type D accountability emerges when those attributions lead to the perception of individuals as being of suspect character given the actions attributed to them. Thus, an individual seen emerging in a disheveled state daily from a local bar might be regarded as a ''drunk,'' and someone cited by police for speeding might be characterized as a reckless driver. An attributed behavior becomes a character attribute, and it is the fact that we are subject to such characterizations that can make us Type D accountable. Individuals whose actions in private life are found to be questionable or potentially embarrassing to their employer are likely to find themselves being held accountable for those actions, despite their irrelevance to the employees' tasks or functions.

This is especially true for those who hold public office. In the private sector, the relevance of Type D accountability pressures is likely to depend on numerous factors, including (but not limited to) one's position and status in the organization and the nature of the nonwork behavior that triggers the concern. Is the individual a highly visible employee whose offense affects the public image of the business? Was the behavior so offensive that the presence of the individual will result in significant losses in sales or productivity unless action is taken?

Exposure to this form of accountability is unavoidable, and yet students of management have paid little attention to it.[147,148] Scholars have long acknowledged the intermingling of social and personal factors. They were central to the work of the human relations school and played an important role in Barnard's classic analysis of executive management.[66,149] Interest in the relationship of family life to work has produced a stream of research in sociology and organization studies,[150,151] including the examination of strategies developed to deal with the boundaries between work and nonwork.[152,153] There is also research focused on the nonwork lives of public sector workers, in particular.[154–156] But, with few exceptions,[157] little of this research considers the link between personal life and accountability.

Uniqueness of Public Office Holding

The rules that protect one's private life from public intrusions do not necessarily apply to those in public offices. Although modern society might proffer the ''principle of uniform privacy'' as a desirable standard for its citizens, for public office holders it is the ''principle of diminished privacy'' that is more likely to be applied. There are various reasons for this, including the perceived necessity to know more about the behavior of those who wield power over us, as well as expectations that public officials must achieve a higher standard of conduct in their private affairs than ordinary citizens.[158]

Of course, accountability-as-attributability is not limited to those who hold public office. What kind of accountability is involved? Some take the form of formal constraints on the private, nonwork lives of government employees. Hatch Acts, conflict-of-interest legislation, and related policies are designed explicitly to deal with the perceived dangers of having civil servants too actively engaged in politics or private business enterprises.[128,159–161] Other examples are found in managerial strategies to offset the potentially adverse impact of private preferences. The possibility that employees or their families might grow too attached to local communities (''going native'') has led some agencies to establish personnel transfer policies to minimize the influence of nonwork factors.[162] Concern for an agency's reputation or public image is also used as a rationale for holding employees accountable for their private behavior and lifestyles. Private behavior has been regarded as grounds for adverse personnel actions, even if the behavior had little or nothing to do with the position of workplace.[163] As significant, the courts have held that the ''perception'' of questionable private behavior can be used to take action against a public employee.[164]

Type D Ethical Strategies

The ethical responses to Type D accountability pressures are likely to require that the individual accept the linkages between one's personal and professional/work lives. Two assumptions are at work here. First is the assumption that individuals accepting a public office do so with the expectation that they will be subject to diminished privacy and greater scrutiny of their behavior. Second is the fact that, in today's complex social world, efforts to carve out a private space free from the intrusions of work or public life is all but impossible. At least some aspects of the behavior attributed to individuals in their personal lives are relevant to how they will be viewed in their working lives, and vice versa. This fact of modern social life means that the ethical demands of work life often overlap or intrude into the ethics of personal life, a phenomenon that has been at the center of many of the most popular and influential studies of American social dynamics since the 1950s.[165–168] The result is the blurring of the lines between one's personal and work life ethics.

Thus, the individual must constantly contend with an existential conflict between ethical demands generated by one's role expectations, perceived blameworthiness or

liability, and those related to one's standing as an autonomous private individual or citizen. In some cases, the solution would be an ethical position that subordinates at least some of one's personal autonomy to the demands emerging from Types A, B, or C accountability. Accepting the limits on one's citizenship rights is the price paid under certain Hatch Act provisions, just as forest rangers accept the order to move their families to the next assignment station. As significant is the choice to subordinate one's private tastes and behavior to the demands imposed by one's job or status.[169,170]

A more positive stance has been articulated by Terry Cooper in his calls for a ''citizenship ethics,'' which he later presents as the ''responsible administrator'' model.[171,172] Subordination of the personal is replaced with a commitment to continuously reflect on one's life as a public administrator. Implied is the idea that one can achieve self-actualization through such an ethical stance, an idea that traces back to ancient ethics and its emphasis on ethics as a means for achieving the good (e.g., happiness) in oneself (in contrast to the modern focus on achieving the good for others).[173]

At a more general level, the response to Type D accountability might be the adoption of a virtue or character ethics approach. In an environment where standards and rules are ambiguous or unstable, it would be reasonable to assume that a consistent adherence to some higher standards of personal conduct (e.g., to be trustworthy, honest, benevolent, caring) would provide some protection from the whims of accountability-as-attribution. Some have articulated this in terms of being a person of ''good character.''[174] It can also involve the a commitment to act virtuously on and off the job as the situation requires,[175–179] or at least to avoid falling prey to the ''ordinary vices'' that plagued us in both our private and public existence.[180]

The ethical path selected in response to Type D accountability pressures has implications for the general orientation of the individual toward the other forms of accountability. Deference to the intrusions of accountability-as-attributability is most closely associated with the norm of political neutrality that characterizes mainstream American public administration. A ''citizenship ethics'' is likely to complement the effort to promote

Table 2 Accountability–ethics relationships

Accountability type	Ethical strategies based on		
A: Answerability	Intuitive politician	Rational agent	Rule follower
B: Blameworthiness	Instrumental	Higher moral standard	Identity shift
C: Liability	Positivist obligation	Naturalist conscience	Analogical reasoning competence
D: Attributability	Subordination	Citizenship ethics	Virtue/character ethics

competency-centered ethics, while implied in the virtue/character ethics approaches is a view of public administrators as more actively engaged autonomous ethical agents who understand their moral obligations.[181]

CONCLUSION

Among the various issues raised by the Friedrich–Finer debate, those focused on accountability–ethics relationships are at once the most significant and least explored. Despite the lack of explicit attention to that relationship in the public administration literature, there are obviously considerable resources that can be brought to bear on this topic. Through the reconceptualization of the key terms in that relationship, this essay opens the door to a more thorough examination of the relevant issues.

Such an examination would begin with a further elaboration and empirical validation of the associations summarized in Table 2. If those posited relationships are validated, the implications for our understanding of administrative behavior can be significant. By focusing on accountability and ethical norms and standards as social mechanisms, we can start to reexplore the "black box" of "contingent" administrative behavior that has been so central to public administration scholarship since Herbert Simon began to model the administrative decision maker in the 1940s. Relying on social mechanisms in lieu of models and positive theory assumptions about bureaucratic behavior, we are able to consider various forms of reasoning and "reasons" that help to shape administrative choices and behavior.[37,182]

There are also potential implications for those concerned with institutional design and administrative reform. Reformers who advocate greater accountability, for instance, typically put forward suggestions that create or enhance answerability mechanisms. A more fully elaborated "theory" of the relationship between accountability and ethical strategies would help us to assess the potential impact of alternative forms of answerability and to explain the success or failure of various reforms. The same logic could be useful in highlighting the source of current problems. What might otherwise be perceived as an arbitrary abuse of discretionary authority, for example, might be due to the absence of (or an indifference to) Type C accountability mechanisms.

REFERENCES

1. Dubnick, M.J. *Demons, Spirits, and Elephants: Reflections on the Failure of Public Administration Theory*; American Political Science Association: Atlanta, GA, September 1–4.

2. Friedrich, C.J. Public Policy and the Nature of Administrative Responsibility. In *Public Policy: A Yearbook of the Graduate School of Public Administration*; Friedrich, C.J., Mason, E.S., Eds.; Harvard University Press: Cambridge, MA, 1940; 3–24.

3. Finer, H. Administrative responsibility in democratic government. Public Adm. Rev. **1941**, *1* (4), 335–350, Summer.

4. Burke, J.P. *Bureaucratic Responsibility*; Johns Hopkins University Press: Baltimore, MD, 1986.

5. Harmon, M.M. *Responsibility as Paradox: A Critique of Rational Discourse on Government*; Sage: Thousand Oaks, CA, 1995.

6. Gruber, J.E. *Controlling Bureaucracies: Dilemmas in Democratic Governance*; University of California Press: Berkeley, CA, 1987.

7. McSwite, O.C. *Legitimacy in Public Administration: A Discourse Analysis*; Sage Publications: Thousand Oaks, CA, 1997.

8. Appleby, P.H. *Morality and Administration in Democratic Government*; Louisiana University Press: Baton Rouge, LA, 1952.

9. Gilbert, C.E. The framework of administrative responsibility. J. Pol. **1959**, *21*, 373–407, (August 3).

10. Marx, F.M. Administrative ethics and the rule of law. Am. Polit. Sci. Rev. **1949**, *43* (6), 1119–1144.

11. Aberbach, J.D. *Keeping a Watchful Eye: The Politics of Congressional Oversight*; The Brookings Institution: Washington, D.C., 1990.

12. Balla, S.J. Administrative procedures and political control of the bureaucracy. Am. Polit. Sci. Rev. **1998**, *92* (3), 363–373, September.

13. Calvert, R.L.; McCubbins, M.D.; Weingast, B.R. A theory of political control and agency discretion. Am. J. Polit. Sci. **1989**, *33* (3), 588–611.

14. Harris, J.P. *Congressional Control of Administration*; Brookings Institution: Washington, D.C., 1964.

15. Hood, C.; James, O.; Scott, C. Regulation of government: Has it increased, is it increasing, should it be diminished? Public Adm. **2000**, *78* (2), 283–304.

16. Kettl, D.F. Micromanagement: Congressional Control and Bureaucratic Risk. In *Agenda for Excellence: Public Service in America*; Ingraham, P.W., Kettl, D.F., Eds.; Chatham House: Chatham, NJ, 1992; Chapter 5.

17. Light, P.C. *Monitoring Government: Inspectors General and the Search for Accountability*; Brookings Institution: Washington, D.C., 1993.

18. McCubbins, M.D.; Schwartz, T. Congressional oversight overlooked: Police patrols versus fire alarms. Am. J. Polit. Sci. **1984**, *28* (1), 165–179 February.

19. Rosen, B. *Holding Government Bureaucracies Accountable*, 2nd Ed.; Praeger Publishers: New York, 1989.

20. Wood, B.D.; Waterman, R.W. *Bureaucratic Dynamics: The Role of Bureaucracy in a Democracy*; Westview Press: Boulder, CO, 1994.

21. Behn, R.D. *Rethinking Democratic Accountability*; Brookings Institution Press: Washington, D.C., 2001.

22. Caiden, G.E. The Problem of Ensuring the Public Accountability of Public Officials. In *Public Service*

Accountability: A Comparative Perspective; Jabbra, J.G., Dwivedi, O.P., Eds.; Kumarian Press: West Hartford, CT, 1988; 17–38.

23. Deleon, L. Accountability in a 'Reinvented' government. Public Adm. **1998**, *76*, 539–558, Autumn.

24. Dubnick, M.J.; Romzek, B.S. *American Public Administration: Politics and the Management of Expectations*; Macmillan: New York, 1991.

25. Dubnick, M.J.; Romzek, B.S. Accountability and the Centrality of Expectations in American Public Administration. In *Research in Public Administration*; Perry, J.L., Ed.; JAI PRESS: Greenwich, CT, 1993; 37–78, Chapter 2.

26. Kearns, K.P. *Managing for Accountability: Preserving the Public Trust in Public and Nonprofit Organizations*; Jossey-Bass: San Francisco, CA, 1996.

27. Romzek, B.S. Accountability of congressional staff. J. Public Adm. Res. Theory **2000**, *10* (2), 413–446.

28. Romzek, B.S.; Dubnick, M.J. Accountability in the public sector: Lessons from the Challenger tragedy. Public Administration Review **1987**, *47* (3), 227–238.

29. Romzek, B.S.; Dubnick, M.J. Issues of Accountability in Flexible Personnel Systems. In *New Paradigms for Government: Issues for the Changing Public Service*; Ingraham, P.W., Romzek, B.S., Eds.; Jossey-Bass: San Francisco, CA, 1994; 263–294.

30. Romzek, B.S.; Dubnick, M.J. Accountability. In *Defining Public Administration: Selections from the International Encyclopedia of Public Policy and Administration*; Shafritz, J.M., Ed.; Westview Press: Boulder, CO, 2000; 382–395.

31. Romzek, B.S.; Ingraham, P.W. Cross pressures of accountability: Initiative, command, and failure in the Ron Brown plane crash. Public Adm. Rev. **2000**, *60* (3), 240–253.

32. Kaplan, A. *The Conduct of Inquiry: Methodology for Behavioral Science*; Chandler Publishing Co.: Scranton, PA, 1964.

33. Mulgan, R. 'Accountability': An ever-expanding concept? Public Adm. **2000**, *78* (3), 555–573.

34. Sinclair, A. The chameleon of accountability: Forms and discourses. Account. Organ. Soc. **1995**, *20* (2/3), 219–237.

35. Beu, D.; Buckley, M.R. The hypothesized relationship between accountability and ethical behavior. J. Bus. Ethics **2001**, *34* (2), 57–73.

36. Garofalo, C.; Geuras, D. *Ethics in the Public Service: The Moral Mind at Work*; Georgetown University Press: Washington, D.C., 1999.

37. Elster, J. *Nuts and Bolts for the Social Sciences*; Cambridge University Press: New York, 1989.

38. Elster, J. A Plea for Mechanisms. In *Social Mechanisms: An Analytical Approach to Social Theory*; Hedström, P., Swedberg, R., Eds.; Cambridge University Press: Cambridge, 1998; 45–73.

39. Hedström, P.; Swedberg, R. Social Mechanisms: An Introductory Essay. In *Social Mechanisms: An Analytical Approach to Social Theory*; Hedström, P., Swed-

berg, R., Eds.; Cambridge University Press: Cambridge, 1998; 1–31.

40. Lane, R. *Political Science in Theory and Practice: The 'Politics' Model*; M.E. Sharpe: Armonk, NY, 1997.

41. Merton, R.K. *Social Theory and Social Structure*; Free Press: New York, 1968, 1968 enlarged.

42. Harman, G. *The Nature of Morality: An Introduction to Ethics*; Oxford University Press: New York, 1977.

43. LaFollette, H. Pragmatic Ethics. In *The Blackwell Guide to Ethical Theory*; LaFollette, H., Ed.; Blackwell: Oxford, UK, 2000; 400–419.

44. Flanagan, O. Ethics Naturalized: Ethics as Human Ecology. In *Mind and Morals: Essays on Cognitive Science and Ethics*; May, L., Friedman, M., Clark, A., Eds.; MIT Press: Cambridge, MA, 1996; 19–43, Chapter 2.

45. Putnam, R.A. The Moral Impulse. In *The Revival of Pragmatism: New Essays on Social Thought, Law, and Culture*; Dickstein, M., Ed.; Duke University Press: Durham, NC, 1998; 62–71.

46. Dubnick, M. Clarifying Accountability: An Ethical Theory Framework. In *Public Sector Ethics: Finding and Implementing Values*; Charles Sampford, N.P., Bois, C.-A., Eds.; The Federation Press/Routledge: Leichhardt, NSW, Australia, 1998; 68–81, Chapter 5.

47. Roberts, J.T. *Accountability in Athenian Government*; University of Wisconsin Press: Madison, WI, 1982.

48. Elster, J. Accountability in Athenian Politics. In *Democracy, Accountability, and Representation*; Przeworski, A., Stokes, S.C., Manin, B., Eds.; Cambridge University Press: Cambridge, UK, 1999; 253–278.

49. *The Self-Restraining State: Power and Accountability in New Democracies*; Schedler, A., Diamond, L.J., Plattner, M.F., Eds.; Lynne Rienner Publishers: Boulder, CO, 1999.

50. Scott, M.B.; Lyman, S.M. Accounts. Am. Sociol. Rev. **1968**, *33* (1), 46–62 February.

51. Tavuchis, N. *Mea Culpa: A Sociology of Apology and Reconciliation*; Stanford University Press: Stanford, CA, 1991.

52. Minow, M. *Between Vengeance and Forgiveness: Facing History after Genocide and Mass Violence*; Beacon Press: Boston, 1998.

53. Borneman, J. *Settling Accounts: Violence, Justice, and Accountability in Postsocialist Europe*; Princeton University Press: Princeton, NJ, 1997.

54. Benoit, W.L. *Accounts, Excuses, and Apologies: A Theory of Image Restoration Strategies*; State University of New York Press: Albany, 1995.

55. Sykes, G.M.; Matza, D. Techniques of neutralization: A theory of delinquency. Am. Sociol. Rev. **1957**, *22* (6), 664–670.

56. Cava, A.; West, J.; Berman, E. Ethical decision-making in business and government: An analysis of formal and informal strategies. Spectrum **1995**, *68* (2), 28–36.

57. Arendt, H. *Eichmann in Jerusalem: A Report on the Banality of Evil*; Penguin Books: New York, 1976, revised.

58. Sereny, G. *Albert Speer: His Battle with Truth*; Knopf: New York, 1995.

59. Turner, R.H. The role and the person. Am. J. Sociol. **1978**, *84* (1), 1–23July.

60. Biddle, B.J. Recent developments in role theory. Annu. Rev. Sociology **1986**, *12*, 67–92.

61. Schedler, A. Conceptualizing Accountability. In *The Self-Restraining State: Power and Accountability in New Democracies*; Schedler, A., Diamond, L.J., Plattner, M.F., Eds.; Lynne Rienner Publishers: Boulder, CO, 1999; 13–28.

62. Held, D. *Models of Democracy*, 2nd Ed.; Stanford University Press: Stanford, CA, 1996.

63. *Representation*; Pitkin, H.F., Ed.; Atherton Press: New York, 1969.

64. Fearon, J.D. Electoral Accountability and the Control of Politicians: Selecting Good Types Versus Sanctioning Poor Performance. In *Democracy, Accountability, and Representation*; Przeworski, A., Stokes, S.C., Manin, B., Eds.; Cambridge University Press: Cambridge, UK, 1999; 55–97.

65. Laver, M.; Shepsle, K.A. Government Accountability in Parliamentary Democracy. In *Democracy, Accountability, and Representation*; Przeworski, A., Stokes, S.C., Manin, B., Eds.; Cambridge University Press: Cambridge, UK, 1999; 279–296.

66. Barnard, C.I. *The Functions of the Executive*; Harvard University Press: Cambridge, MA, 1968.

67. March, J.G.; Simon, H.A. *Organizations;* John Wiley and Sons: New York, 1958.

68. McMahon, C. *Authority and Democracy: A General Theory of Government and Management*; Princeton University Press: Princeton, NJ, 1994.

69. McGregor, D. *The Human Side of Enterprise*; McGraw-Hill: New York, 1960.

70. Tetlock, P.E. Accountability and the perseverance of first impressions. Soc. Psychol. Q. **1983**, *46* (4), 285–292, December.

71. Tetlock, P.E. Accountability and complexity of thought. J. Pers. Soc. Psychol. **1983**, *45* (1), 74–83.

72. Tetlock, P.E. Accountability: A social check on the fundamental attribution error. Soc. Psychol. Q. **1985**, *48* (3), 227–236, September.

73. Tetlock, P.E.; Kim, J.I. Accountability and judgment processes in a personality prediction task. J. Pers. Soc. Psychol. **1987**, *52* (4), 700–709.

74. Tetlock, P.E.; Skitka, L.; Boettger, R. Social and cognitive strategies for coping with accountability: Conformity, complexity, and bolstering. J. Pers. Soc. Psychol. **1989**, *57* (4), 632–640.

75. Miller, G.J. *Managerial Dilemmas: The Political Economy of Hierarchy*; Cambridge University Press: Cambridge, UK, 1992.

76. Eisenhardt, K.M. Agency theory: An assessment and review. Acad. Manage. Rev. **1989**, *14* (1), 57.

77. Waterman, R.W.; Meier, K.J. Principal-agent models: An expansion? J. Public Adm. Res. Theory **1998**, *8* (2), 173–202.

78. Moe, T.M. The Politics of Structural Choice: Toward a Theory of Public Bureaucracy. In *Organization Theory: From Chester Barnard to the Present and Beyond Expanded*; Williamson, O.E., Ed.; Oxford University Press: New York, 1995; 116–153.

79. March, J.G.; Olsen, J.P. The new institutionalism: Organizational factors in political life. Am. Polit. Sci. Rev. **1984**, *78* (3), 734–749, September.

80. March, J.G.; Olsen, J.P. *Democratic Governance*; Free Press: New York, 1995.

81. March, J.G.; Olsen, J.P. *Rediscovering Institutions: The Organizational Basis of Politics*; Free Press: New York, 1989.

82. March, J.G. *A Primer on Decision Making: How Decisions Happen*; Free Press: New York, 1994.

83. Paul, J.; Strbiak, C.A. The ethics of strategic ambiguity. J. Bus. Commun. **1997**, *34* (2), 149–159.

84. Bøhren, Øyvind. The agent's ethics in the principal-agent model. J. Bus. Ethics **1998**, *17*, 745–755.

85. Brehm, J.; Gates, S. *Working, Shirking, and Sabotage: Bureaucratic Response to a Democratic Public*; University of Michigan Press: Ann Arbor, 1997.

86. Scheffler, S. *The Rejection of Consequentialism: A Philosophical Investigation of the Considerations Underlying Rival Moral Considerations*; Claredon Press: Oxford, UK, 1994, revised.

87. Stryker, S.; Macke, A.S. Status inconsistency and role conflict. Annu. Rev. Sociology **1978**, *4*, 57–90.

88. Dubnick, M.J. In *Public Service Ethics and the Cultures of Blame*, Fifth International Conference of Ethics in the Public Service, Brisbane, Australia, August 5–9, 1996.

89. Douglas, T. *Scapegoats: Transferring Blame*; Routledge: London, UK, 1995.

90. Girard, R. *The Scapegoat*; Johns Hopkins University Press: Baltimore, 1986.

91. Gay, P. *The Cultivation of Hatred: The Bourgeois Experience, Victoria to Freud*; W. W. Norton. and Co.: New York, 1993.

92. Cohen, E.A.; Gooch, J. *Military Misfortunes: The Anatomy of Failure in War*; Vintage Books: New York, 1991.

93. Cohen, W.S. *Personal Accountability for Force Protection at Khobar Towers*, Department of Defense, Office of the Secretary of Defense, Washington, D.C., July 31; http://www.defenselink.mil/pubs/khobar/index.html.

94. Shklar, J.N. *The Faces of Injustice*; Yale University Press: New Haven, CT, 1990.

95. Smiley, M. *Moral Responsibility and the Boundaries of Community: Power and Accountability Fom a Pragmatic Point of View*; University of Chicago Press: Chicago, 1992.

96. Woodward, B. *The Commanders*; Simon and Schuster: New York, 1991.

97. Chandler, R.C. Deontological Dimensions of Administrative Ethics. In *Handbook of Administrative Ethics*; Cooper, T.L., Ed.; Marcel Dekker: New York, 1994; 147–156.

98. Denhardt, R.B.; Denhardt, J.V. The new public service: Serving rather than steering. Public Adm. Rev. **2000**, *60* (6), 549–559.

99. Huddleston, M.W. The Carter Civil Service Reforms: Some implications for political theory and public administration. Polit. Sci. Q. **1981–1982**, *96* (4), 607–621.

100. Frederickson, H.G. *The Spirit of Public Administration*; Jossey-Bass Publishers: San Francisco, 1997.

101. *Toward a New Public Administration: The Minnowbrook Perspective*; Marini, F., Ed.; Chandler Publishing: Scranton, PA, 1971.

102. Wamsley, G.L.; Bacher, R.N.; Goodsell, C.T.; Kronenberg, P.S.; Rohr, J.A.; Stivers, C.M.; White, O.F.; Wolf, J.F. *Refounding Public Administration*; Sage Publications: Newbury Park, CA, 1990.

103. *Refounding Democratic Public Administration: Modern Paradoxes, Postmodern Challenges*; Wamsley, G.L., Wolf, J.F., Eds.; Sage Publications: Thousand Oaks, CA, 1996.

104. Shklar, J.N. *Legalism: Law, Morals, and Political Trials*; Harvard University Press: Cambridge, MA, 1986.

105. Pound, R. *Social Control Through Law*; Transaction Publishers: New Brunswick, 1997.

106. Schuck, P.H. *The Limits of Law: Essays on Democratic Governance*; Westview Press: Boulder, CO, 1999.

107. Ingram, P. Maintaining the rule of law. Philos. Q. **1985**, *35* (141), 359–381.

108. von Hayek, F.A. *The Constitution of Liberty*; Regnery: Chicago, 1972.

109. Fuller, S.R.; Edelman, L.B.; Matusik, S.F. Legal readings: Employee interpretation and mobilization of law. Acad. Manage. Rev. **2000**, *25* (1), 200–216.

110. Minow, M. *Making All the Difference: Inclusion, Exclusion, and American Law*; Cornell University Press: Ithaca, 1990.

111. Minow, M. *Not Only for Myself: Identity, Politics and the Law*; The New Press: New York, 1997.

112. Weber, M. *Economy and Society: An Outline of Interpretive Sociology, Volume 1*; University of California Press: Berkely, CA, 1978.

113. *Individual and Collective Responsibility*, 2nd Ed.; French, P.A., Ed.; Schenkman Books: Rochester, VT, 1997, rev.

114. Stone, C.D. *Where the Law Ends: The Social Control of Corporate Behavior*; Harper Torchbooks: New York, 1975.

115. Thompson, D.F. Moral responsibility of public officials: The problem of many hands. Am. Polit. Sci. Rev. **1980**, *74*, 905–916, (December 4).

116. Thomson, J.J. Remarks on causation and liability. Philos. Public Aff. **1984**, *13* (2), 101–133.

117. Huber, P.W. *Liability: The Legal Revolution and Its Consequences*; Basic Books: New York, 1988.

118. *Foundations of Tort Law*; Levmore, S.X., Ed.; Oxford University Press: New York, 1994.

119. Lieberman, J.K. *The Litigious Society*; Basic Books: New York, 1981.

120. Howard, P.K. *The Death of Common Sense: How Law is Suffocating America*; Random House: New York, 1994.

121. Horwitz, R. Judicial review of regulatory decisions: The changing criteria. Polit. Sci. Q. **1994**, *109* (1), 133–169.

122. Stewart, R.B. The reformation of American administrative law. Harvard Law Rev. **1975**, *88*, 1669–1813.

123. Lowi, T.J. *The End of Liberalism: The Second Republic of the United States*, 2nd Ed.; W. W. Norton and Co.: New York, 1979.

124. Rosenbloom, D.H. *Public Administration and Law: Bench V. Bureau in the United States*; Marcel Dekker: New York, 1983.

125. Rosenbloom, D.H. Public administrators' liability: Bench V. Bureau in the contemporary administrative state. Public Adm. Q. **1987**, *10* (4), 373–386, Winter.

126. Rosenbloom, D.H.; Carroll, J.D.; Carroll, J.D. *Constitutional Competence for Public Managers: Cases and Commentary*; F. E. Peacock Publishers: Itasca, IL, 2000.

127. Dimock, M.E. *Law and Dynamic Administration*; Praeger Publishers: New York, 1980.

128. Rosenbloom, D.H. *Federal Service and the Constitution: The Development of the Public Employment Relationship*; Cornell University Press: Ithaca, NY, 1971.

129. Anechiarico, F.; Jacobs, J.B. *The Pursuit of Absolute Integrity: How Corruption Control Makes Government Ineffective*; University of Chicago Press: Chicago, 1996.

130. Kaufman, H. Emerging conflicts in the doctrines of public administration. Am. Polit. Sci. Rev. **1956**, *50* (4), 1057–1073, December.

131. Lockard, D. The city manager, administrative theory and political power. Polit. Sci. Q. **1962**, *77* (2), 224–236.

132. Finer, H. Better government personnel: America's next frontier. Polit. Sci. Q. **1936**, *LI* (4), 569–599.

133. Rourke, F.E. Responsiveness and neutral competence in American bureaucracy. Public Adm. Rev. **1992**, *52* (6), 539–546, November/December.

134. Marshall, G.S.; Choudhury, E. Public administration and the public interest: Re-presenting a lost concept. Am. Behav. Sci. **1997**, *41* (1), 119–131, September.

135. Rohr, J.A. *Public Service, Ethics, and Constitutional Practice*; University Press of Kansas: Lawrence, KS, 1998.

136. Rohr, J.A. *Ethics for Bureaucrats: An Essay on Law and Values*, 2nd Ed.; Marcel Dekker: New York, 1989.

137. Sunstein, C.R. *Legal Reasoning and Political Conflict*; Oxford University Press: New York, 1996.

138. Raz, J. *Practical Reason and Norms*; Princeton University Press: Princeton, NJ, 1990.

139. Forsyth, D.R. The functions of attributions. Soc. Psychol. Q. **1980**, *43* (2), 184–189, June.

140. Crittenden, K.S. Sociological aspects of attribution. Annu. Rev. Sociology **1983**, *9*, 425–446.

141. Howard, J.A. A social cognitive conception of social structure. Soc. Psychol. Q. **1994**, *57* (3), 210–227, September.

142. Howard, J.A.; Pike, K.C. Ideological investment in cognitive processing: The influence of social statuses on attribution. Soc. Psychol. Q. **1986**, *49* (2), 154–167.

143. Al-Zahrani, S.S.A.; Kaplowitz, S.A. Attributional biases in individualistic and collectivistic cultures: A comparison of Americans with Saudis. Soc. Psychol. Q. **1993**, *56* (3), 223–233.

144. Holloway, S.D.; Fuller, B. Situational determinants of causal attributions: The case of working mothers. Soc. Psychol. Q. **1983**, *46* (2), 131–140.

145. Yarkin-Levin, K. Anticipated interaction, attribution, and social interaction. Soc. Psychol. Q. **1983**, *46* (4), 302–311.

146. Tetlock, P.E. The influence of self-presentation goals on attributional reports. Soc. Psychol. Q. **1981**, *44* (4), 300–311, December.

147. Cozzetto, D.A.; Pedeliski, T.B. Privacy and the workplace. Rev. Public Pers. Adm. **1996**, *16* (2), 21–31.

148. Cozzetto, D.A.; Pedeliski, T.B. Privacy and the workplace: Technology and public employment. Public Pers. Manage. **1997**, *26* (4), 515–527.

149. Roethlisberger, F.J. *Management and Morale*; Harvard University Press: Cambridge, MA, 1941.

150. Cohen, A. An examination of the relationships between work commitment and nonwork domains. Human Relat. **1995**, *48* (3), 239–263.

151. Bielby, D.D. Commitment to work and family. Annu. Rev. Sociology **1992**, *18*, 281–302.

152. Kanter, R.M. *Men and Women of the Corporation*; Basic Books: New York, 1977/1993.

153. Kirchmeyer, C. Managing the work–nonwork boundary: An assessment of organizational responses. Human Relat. **1995**, *48* (5), 515–536.

154. Romzek, B.S. Personal consequences of employee commitment. Acad. Manage. J. **1989**, *32* (3), 649–661.

155. Johnson, C.M.; Duerst-Lahti, G. Private lives and public work: Professional careers in state civil service. Rev. Public Pers. Adm. **1991**, *12* (1), 14–32.

156. Romzek, B.S. Work and nonwork psychological involvements: The search for linkage. Adm. Soc. **1985**, *17* (2), 257–281.

157. Dworkin, T.M. It's my life—leave me alone: Off-the-job employee associational privacy rights. Am. Bus. Law J. **1997**, *35* (1), 47–103.

158. Thompson, D.F. *Political Ethics and Public Office*; Harvard University Press: Cambridge, MA, 1987.

159. Thruber, K.T. Big, little, littler: Synthesizing hatch act-based political activity legislation research. Rev. Public Pers. Adm. **1993**, *13* (1), 38–51.

160. Roberts, R.N. Conflict of interest regulation, employees' rights, and the constitution. Public Adm. Q. **1992**, *16* (3), 344–367Fall.

161. Rosenbloom, D.H. The public employment relationship and the Supreme Court in the 1980s. Rev. Public Pers. Adm. **1988**, *8* (2), 49–65.

162. Kaufman, H. *The Forest Ranger: A Study in Administrative Behavior*; Johns Hopkins University Press: Baltimore, MD, 1967.

163. Lewis, G.B. Lifting the ban on gays in the civil service: Federal policy toward gay and lesbian employees since the cold war. Public Adm. Rev. **1997**, *57* (5), 387–395.

164. Stark, A. The appearance of official impropriety and the concept of political crime. Ethics **1995**, *105* (2), 326–351.

165. Bellah, R.N.; Madsen, R.; Sullivan, W.M.; Swidler, A.; Tipton, S.M. *Habits of the Heart: Individualism and Commitment in American Life*; University of California Press: Berkeley, CA, 1985.

166. Bellah, R.N.; Madsen, R.; Sullivan, W.M.; Swidler, A.; Tipton, S.M. *The Good Society*; Alfred A. Knopf: New York, 1991.

167. Whyte, W.H. *The Organization Man*; Doubleday Anchor: Garden City, NY, 1956.

168. Coleman, J.S. *The Asymmetric Society*; Syracuse University Press: Syracuse, NY, 1982.

169. Hummel, R.P. *The Bureaucratic Experience: A Critique of Life in the Modern Organization*, 4th Ed.; St. Martin's Press: New York, 1994.

170. Denhardt, R.B. *In the Shadow of Organization*; The Regents Press of Kansas: Lawrence, KS, 1981.

171. Cooper, T.L. *An Ethic of Citizenship for Public Administration*; Prentice Hall: Englewood Cliffs, NJ, 1991.

172. Cooper, T.L. *The Responsible Administrator: An Approach to Ethics for the Administrative Role*, 4th Ed.; Jossey-Bass Publishers: San Francisco, 1998.

173. Annas, J. Ancient ethics and modern morality. Philos. Perspect. **1992**, *6*, 119–136.

174. Luke, J.S. Character and Conduct in the Public Service: A Review of Historical Perspectives and a Definition for the Twenty-First Century. In *Handbook of Administrative Ethics*; Cooper, T.L., Ed.; Marcel Dekker: New York, 1994; 391–412.

175. Hart, D.K. The virtuous citizen, the honorable bureaucrat, and 'Public' administration. Public Adm. Rev. **1984**, *44* (Special Issue), 111–120, March.

176. Hart, D.K.; Smith, P.A. Fame, fame-worthiness, and the public service. Adm. Soc. **1988**, *20* (2), 131–151, August.

177. Frederickson, H.G.; Hart, D.K. The public service and the patriotism of benevolence. Public Adm. Rev. **1985**, *45* (5), 547–553.

178. Frederickson, H.G.; Hart, D.K. Patriotism, Benevolence, and Public Administration. In *The Spirit of Public Administration*; Jossey-Bass Publishers: San Francisco, 1997; 195–208.

179. Hart, D.K. Administration and the Ethics of Virtue: In All Things, Choose First for Good Character and then for Technical Expertise. In *Handbook of Administrative Ethics*; Cooper, T.L., Ed.; Marcel Dekker: New York, 1994; 107–123.

180. Shklar, J.N. *Ordinary Vices*; Belknap/Harvard University Press: Cambridge, MA, 1984.

181. Bovens, M. *The Quest for Responsibility: Accountability and Citizenship in Complex Organisations*; Cambridge University Press: Cambridge, England, 1998.

182. *Social Mechanisms: An Analytical Approach to Social Theory*; Hedström, P., Swedberg, R., Eds.; Cambridge University Press: Cambridge, 1998.

Accounting, Financial

Mozaffar Khan
University of Toronto, Toronto, Ontario, Canada

INTRODUCTION

It is said that to truly understand a culture one must be proficient in its language. Financial accounting is the language of business. Just as linguistic constructs (or words) are used to articulate our unobservable thoughts to listeners, so also are financial accounting constructs used to communicate summary information to a firm's external stakeholders about the economic activities of the firm. Similarly, just as linguistic rules guide how we meaningfully string together words, so also do financial accounting rules govern what, when, where, and how information is summarized and transmitted to outsiders to best convey the firm's economic fundamentals.

The set of financial accounting rules is commonly referred to as generally accepted accounting principles (GAAP). There are two kinds of GAAP in the United States—GAAP for business and GAAP for government. The latter defines accounting standards for the various federal, state, and local governments and agencies. The primary rule-making body for business accounting standards in the United States is the Financial Accounting Standards Board (FASB), which derives its authority from the Securities and Exchange Commission. The primary governmental accounting standard setter in the United States is the Governmental Accounting Standards Board (GASB). Both the FASB and the GASB are arms of the Financial Accounting Foundation.

FINANCIAL ACCOUNTING FOR BUSINESS

The FASB's Conceptual Framework of Accounting is a collection of overarching objectives and principles that informs its promulgation of rules and serves to impose internal consistency on the set of rules. According to this framework, a primary objective of financial statement reporting is to provide information to investors, creditors, and other external stakeholders that is useful in helping them assess the amounts, timing, and uncertainty of the firm's future cash flows. Four of the primary desired qualitative characteristics of useful financial statement information are held to be relevance, reliability, comparability, and consistency. Relevant information is that which is timely, facilitates prediction, and updates prior information. Reliable information is that which is faith-

fully represented, neutral, verifiable, and conservative. Comparability requires that the financial statements be presented in a uniform format, using standard accounting rules, across companies. Consistency requires that a given company have accounting policies, choices of accounting method, and format of financial statement presentation that are consistent over time.

The Business Financial Statement Reporting Environment

Considerable complexity is introduced into the financial statement reporting environment by the fact that it consists of multiple parties whose interests are not necessarily aligned with each other. This problem is addressed in the principal–agent theory, which examines the conflict of interest between the principal or owner of a business and the agent or manager hired to run the business. Typically, because the agent is involved in the day-to-day operation of the firm and the principal is not, the agent has more information than the principal about the future prospects of the firm. This information asymmetry gives agents the opportunity to further their own interests at the expense of those of the principal. In the financial reporting context, managers (who are the agents) may seek to release only self-serving information to investors and creditors (who are the principals). This is known as the adverse selection or hidden information problem, and its existence hinders the achievement of the financial reporting objective assumed in the Conceptual Framework of Accounting (the provision of useful information to investors and creditors). Thus, accounting rules have to be designed to mitigate the adverse selection problem.

Another principal–agent problem arises from the fact that efforts exerted by agents in discharging their responsibilities are not fully and directly observable by principals, thereby giving agents the opportunity to shirk. This is known as the moral hazard or hidden effort problem. Because firm performance is driven by various factors other than managerial effort, it is not possible for the owner to fully infer managerial effort after observing firm performance ex post. Consider a firm that has high performance in a given year despite low managerial effort and low performance in another year despite high managerial effort. If managerial compensation is tied to firm performance, the manager gains ex post at the owner's

DOI: 10.1081/E-EPAP 120010722

expense in the first instance and the owner gains ex post at the manager's expense in the second instance. Ex ante however, neither party knows who is going to gain. The point here is that it is important to both the owner and the manager that performance measures are highly correlated with managerial effort so that effort may be reasonably inferred from performance. The implication for financial reporting is that accounting rules governing performance measurement should be designed to mitigate the moral hazard problem.

Both adverse selection and moral hazard result from information asymmetry. This asymmetry cannot be completely eliminated and can only be reduced at some cost. For example, an owner may devise elaborate monitoring and reporting schemes, but these would be neither perfect nor inexpensive. Financial accounting rules are therefore also designed to balance reporting costs with reporting benefits.

Business Financial Accounting Research

Financial accounting theory is rooted in economic theory. Theoretical financial accounting research involves building economic models that help understand, explain, predict, and control the financial accounting environment. These models may also guide the design of new accounting rules.

Empirical financial accounting research uses econometric methods to test theoretical models. It also tests whether new accounting rules better capture a firm's economic fundamentals. Typically, accounting researchers assume that capital markets are semi-strong form efficient, that is, that all publicly available information is reflected in the current stock price. If a new accounting rule allows financial statements to portray more accurately the underlying economic position of the firm then it should be useful to investors and creditors in making rational investment decisions. Thus, the establishment of the new rule should bring new information to the market and, given market efficiency, should lead to revised market expectations of the amounts, timing and uncertainty of future cash flows. These revised expectations can lead to any of three testable effects: they may lead to abnormal stock returns, abnormal trading volume and/or abnormal stock price volatility. The presence of any of these effects then is held to be evidence of the decision usefulness of the new accounting rule.

Selected Topics in Business Financial Accounting Research

Voluntary disclosure

This literature examines why managers issue forecasts of quarterly or annual earnings per share (EPS) and other-

wise reveal to the securities markets private information about the firm's future prospects when they are not mandated to do so by SEC disclosure rules. Four suggested motives and reasons for voluntary disclosure are legal liability, adverse selection, expectations adjustment, and transactions cost. In the following discussion, news refers to private EPS information relative to current public expectations of future EPS (e.g., bad news refers to private management information that actual EPS will be substantially below what the market expects, while no news refers to information that actual EPS will be very close to expected EPS, either from above or below). Under the legal liability argument, managers who suppress bad news may be successfully sued by investors for the loss suffered once actual performance is realized and disclosed in the future, and the stock price plummets. Thus, managers are expected to preemptively disclose only bad news prior to the mandated earnings announcement date to mitigate their legal liability. Under the adverse selection hypothesis, managers preemptively disclose only self-serving or good news to immediately boost the price of their firm's stock. The expectations adjustment hypothesis posits that managers preemptively disclose both good and bad news, but not no news, to "correct" the market's expectations. The assumption is that the market does not like negative surprises (or bad news) on earnings announcement dates and that the firm is better off revealing positive surprises (or good news) as early as possible. Finally, the transactions cost hypothesis argues that a firm's managers will disclose all private information to investors to lower investors' information costs in acquiring that firm's stocks and to increase investor confidence in the firm. This in turn will translate into a lower cost of capital for the firm.

The empirical evidence is mixed as to which motive best explains voluntary disclosure, but the transactions cost hypothesis appears to be the weakest of the four. For more information, see Refs. [1–3].

Positive accounting theory (PAT)

GAAP often allows managers some discretion in their choice of accounting method (first in, first out vs. last in, last out for inventory, straight line vs. accelerated method for depreciation, etc.). Given discretion, why do firms make the choices they do? Note that an accounting policy simply determines how an economic event is portrayed. It does not change the economics of the event. Inspired by positive economics and motivated by agency theory, PAT attempts to explain firms' accounting policy choices. In other words, it attempts to explain why certain economic events are accounted for in the manner they are. It argues that a firm can be viewed as a web of contracts between multiple parties (managers, investors, creditors, regulators, consumer groups), with each party seeking to achieve its interests over, and perhaps at the expense of, those of others.

For example, consider the conflicts in the manager–stockholder relationship. If managers are compensated based on reported earnings, then they will choose income-increasing accounting policies so that their compensation will increase despite the fact that there has been no change in the economic value of the owners' equity in the firm. Another conflict arises when outside investors attempt a takeover of the firm. Although their offer may be in the best interests of the current stockholders, it may be rebuffed by managers if they fear that they will be displaced by the new owners.

Consider, too, the conflict in the creditor–stockholder relationship. Managers, acting on behalf of stockholders, may attempt to circumvent financial limits stipulated in the debt indenture to avoid triggering a technical default. For example, if the indenture calls for the firm to maintain a certain minimum level of return on assets, then managers may opportunistically make accounting policy choices that increase reported income or decrease average total assets when they are in danger of falling below the specified minimum.

Finally, firms are also believed to have a latent social contract with society. If an industry or firm finds itself reaping excess or abnormally high profits, then it may attract the scrutiny of governmental regulators or consumer groups. For example, if firms in the oil industry rake in excess profits when the price of gasoline is high, then they may be suspected of price gouging. Positive accounting theory predicts that such firms will attempt to depict earnings as being lower than they are and will thus make accounting choices that decrease reported earnings to avert attention.

Empirical research has found evidence of accounting choices broadly consistent with those predicted by PAT. For more information, see Refs. [4–6].

Earnings management (EM)

This literature examines whether managers opportunistically manipulate reported earnings up or down. For example, if current earnings performance is poor, then managers may "borrow" earnings from future periods to increase current reported earnings to acceptable levels, or if current earnings are exceptional, then they may "store" some earnings to use in future periods. The motive for this may be to meet market expectations or to maximize their bonus. Another example of EM is a "big bath"—a new chief executive officer (CEO) may have the management team aggressively record write-offs and other charges in the current year so that good performance is easier to achieve in future years. In effect, the new CEO "cleans

house," knowing that a huge loss in the current year will be blamed on the predecessor and good performance in future years will be self-attributed. Earnings management may also occur when a domestic industry petitions the federal government for import relief. This industry may manage its reported earnings down to bolster its claims of damage from foreign competitors and their products.

This literature assumes that managers believe that capital markets are fixated on the reported earnings figure and that the market is unable to fully detect EM. If managers believed otherwise, then they would not engage in EM because doing so would be futile. Clearly, managers would like to manipulate earnings surreptitiously. The literature therefore generally assumes that EM occurs through the manipulation of accrual accounts because this is the least easily detected.

Empirical researchers have attempted to identify specific instances of EM to prove that the phenomenon exists in reality. For any given firm, only its total accruals are observable or identifiable. The managed portion of total accruals cannot be identified from financial statements. Typically, the researcher will specify a statistical model that generates the expected level of "normal" total accruals in any given year. The difference between expected accruals and actual total accruals is the "abnormal" accrual for that year. Abnormal accruals are held to represent the manipulated portion of total accruals. This decomposition of observable total accruals into its unobservable normal and abnormal components is heavily dependent on the mechanism that is assumed to generate "normal" accruals. Thus, findings of abnormal accruals constitute evidence of EM only insofar as the normal accrual-generating model is correctly specified. For more information, see Refs. [7] and [8].

Anomalies

As mentioned previously, a key maintained hypothesis in financial accounting research is that capital markets are efficient. The anomalies literature attempts to debunk this hypothesis by investigating instances where market efficiency is apparently violated, that is, where public information that is marginally useful in predicting a firm's future performance is apparently not incorporated in stock prices. The typical approach adopted by researchers is to use some public information to develop a trading strategy that yields excess or risk-adjusted returns. The implication then is that this information could not have been incorporated in stock prices and that the markets are inefficient. For example, certain financial statement information may be used to predict which firms will experience robust performance and which will experience poor performance. Next, a long position may be taken in the first set of firms and an off-setting short position in the second set of firms, under the assumption that the stock price will rise in response to strong realized but unanticipated performance and decline if performance turns out to be poor. If markets are efficient, then future performance implied by all current public information should be anticipated in the current stock price and there should be no stock price reaction once performance is realized as anticipated. However, if the market is not efficient with respect to some information, then the previous trading strategy should yield positive net returns.

Another example of an anomaly is the postearnings announcement drift. It is observed that the stock price of firms that announce robust earnings performance tends to drift upward for an appreciable period of time after the earnings announcement date, and a similar downward drift is observed for firms announcing poor performance. The anomaly here is that this phenomenon is a documented empirical regularity; that is, there continues to persist this period of time over which price movements are predictable. Consider a firm announcing poor current earnings. If investors are aware of the drift phenomenon, then they should immediately short the stock once earnings are announced. The stock price will drop immediately as a result, and no drift will occur thereafter. However, this does not happen. The drift phenomenon continues to be observed.

A third example of an anomaly would be an abnormal stock return response to an accounting method change. In efficient markets, an accounting method change should generate no abnormal returns because it merely changes the way an economic event is accounted for, or depicted, and does not change the underlying event itself.

One explanation for these anomalies is that researchers who have developed hypothetical trading strategies to exploit apparent market inefficiencies have not taken transactions costs or short-selling constraints into account. The costs incurred in searching for mispriced securities and buying or selling them can be substantial, and may offset the marginal benefit of engaging in such activity. Another explanation is that risk factors may not be fully controlled for. For example, market efficiency would call for abnormal returns in response to an accounting method change if this change also leads to a change in the firm's risk.

It is important to note that market inefficiency does not imply investor irrationality. An ostensible profit opportunity may not be exploited if the mispriced stock is available only in limited quantities or if the transactions costs are prohibitive even though the stock is available in unlimited quantities.

Although significant evidence of apparent market inefficiency has been tendered, it has not been as unassailable as to warrant abandonment of the assumption of market efficiency, especially in the absence of refutable alternative hypotheses. For more information, see Ref. [9].

Earnings response coefficient (ERC)

In an efficient market, a firm's stock price changes only in response to revised investor expectations about the amounts, timing, and uncertainty of its future cash flows. One stimulus for expectation revision is unanticipated earnings. Faced with an earnings surprise, investors try to assess how long they can expect the unanticipated portion of earnings (termed the earnings innovation) to persist. This persistence assessment is then fed into an asset valuation model, such as the discounted cash flow (DCF) model, to yield a new price. The earnings persistence is a parameter of the firm's time series of earnings. Typically, a pure random walk is held to be a reasonable description of a firm's time series of annual earnings, implying that all earnings innovations are permanent. Given this, and assuming a one-to-one link between earnings and cash flows, the DCF model simply prices a stock with a dollar earnings innovation as the current stock price, plus a dollar, plus the value of a dollar in perpetuity.

The ERC is the marginal stock price change in response to a $1 earnings innovation. For example, given the previous assumptions, and a discount rate of 10%, the ERC should be $1 + 1/0.1 = 11$. Empirical ERC estimates have been substantially lower, however, spawning a large literature attempting to explain this attenuation. One explanation is that a portion of the supposedly unanticipated earnings was actually previously anticipated by market participants, so that the earnings innovation or surprise is measured with error. Attenuation due to measurement error in the earnings surprise can be mitigated by using a reverse regression econometric design. Another explanation for the observed attenuation is that a portion of the unanticipated earnings may be transitory; that is, it may have resulted from one-time gains or losses rather than from continuing operations. However, empirical ERC estimates have been shown to remain attenuated, even when transitory items are removed from reported earnings. Finally, it has been argued that the marginal investor response to losses is lower than that to profits because losses have less information content than profits about the future prospects of the firm. Losses are less informative than profits because losses are not expected to occur in perpetuity. They can also be less informative as a result of the application of the conservatism principle of accounting, under which managers are quicker to recognize foreseeable losses than to recognize foreseeable gains. Reported gains are a lot more certain than reported losses. For more information, see Ref. [10–13].

FINANCIAL ACCOUNTING FOR GOVERNMENT

The goals and accounting environments of government and business differ. These factors lead to differences between GAAP for government and GAAP for business.

Although the goals of business are typically to maximize return on investment, the goals of government as recognized by GASB are twofold—accountability to citizenry and promoting the common welfare. These give rise to the external financial reporting objectives of the GASB. One objective is to demonstrate accountability. This implies providing information that is useful in assessing accountability, including such information as whether there was intergenerational shifting of resources. For example, will some current-year services be funded partly by future-year citizens, or are some future-year benefits funded by current-year citizens? Another objective is to report on current operating results by revealing the sources and uses of revenues. A third objective is to report on the entity's financial condition in terms of its long-term financial viability. Finally, a fourth objective is to report on long-lived physical and nonfinancial assets, and their future service potential.

The Governmental Financial Accounting Environment

In setting accounting standards, the GASB is mindful of certain characteristics that are peculiar to the governmental accounting environment. One salient characteristic of this environment is that decision making within a governmental entity is far more political, because of its public nature, than decision making within a corporate entity. In addition, governments have to balance the needs of diverse constituents who often have conflicting notions of the common good. Another characteristic is the use of fund accounting by governments. A fund is its own fiscal and accounting entity, set up to ensure availability of resources for a specific purpose. The monies from a given fund can only be applied toward the designated purpose of that fund. Usually, the General Fund is the only unrestricted fund in a government entity. Although separate financial reporting for each fund is no longer required, each fund still has to maintain its own books. Yet another characteristic is that governmental budgets are legal documents in that they often carry the force of law. They cannot be altered once passed. They are also public documents because they are products of the public intent as revealed through public hearings and dialog. This is in contrast to corporate budgets that have the discretionary flexibility to respond to changing conditions through the fiscal year and that are secret for competitive reasons.

A fourth characteristic is that some entity may be affiliated with a governmental entity, yet offer private services. The conflict here is whether to follow government or business GAAP. For such entities, the compliance hierarchy is GAAP for government first, then GAAP for business, followed by other sources of accounting standards such as experts, common practice, and the accounting literature. A fifth characteristic is that resources are often transferred from one level of government to another, requiring intergovernmental accountability. For more information, see Refs. [14] and [15].

Governmental Accounting Research

Research in this area examines diverse questions, such as performance measurement, the impact of incentives, the impact of politics and the tenure of elected officials, discretionary accounting practices, and the accounting and auditing impact of intergovernmental revenue sharing, to name a few.

A prominent issue in governmental accounting today is whether to move toward accrual-based accounting as is required for businesses by business GAAP. Governmental accounting today typically follows a modified accrual method, thereby hiding such future liabilities as past service (or pension) costs.

CONCLUSION

Financial accounting is a vast and vibrant field. Accounting practice (both for business and for government) is constantly evolving to meet changing needs, and accounting research is gaining rigor in theory as well as sophistication in empirical methods. It is impossible to understand the culture and environment of financial management without understanding financial accounting.

REFERENCES

1. Ajinkya, B.B.; Gift, M.J. Corporate managers' earnings forecasts and symmetrical adjustments of market expectations. J. Acc. Res. **1984**, *22* (2), 425–444.
2. Lang, M.; Russell, L. Cross-sectional determinants of analyst ratings of corporate disclosures. J. Acc. Res. **1993**, *31* (2), 246–271.
3. Scott, W.R. *Financial Accounting Theory*, 2nd Ed.; Prentice-Hall Canada Inc.: Scarborough, Ontario, 2000.
4. Press, E.G.; Weintrop, J.B. Accounting-based constraints in public and private debt agreements: Their association with leverage and impact on accounting choice. J. Account. Econ. **1990**, *12* (1–3), 65–95.

5. Watts, R.L.; Zimmerman, J. *Positive Accounting Theory*; Prentice Hall: Englewood Cliffs, NJ, 1986.

6. Zmijewski, M.E.; Hagerman, R.L. An Income Strategy Approach To The Positive Theory Of Accounting Standard Setting/Choice. J. Account. Econ. **1981**, *3* (2), 129–149.

7. Dechow, P.M.; Sloan, R.G.; Sweeney, A.P. Detecting earnings management. Account. Rev. **1995**, *70* (2), 193–225.

8. Jones, J.J. Earnings management during import relief investigations. J. Acc. Res. **1991**, *29* (2), 193–228.

9. Ou, J.A.; Penman, H.P. Financial statement analysis and the prediction of stock returns. J. Account. Econ. **1989**, *11* (4), 295–329.

10. Collins, D.W.; Kothari, S.P. An analysis of intertemporal and cross-sectional determinants of earnings response coefficients. J. Account. Econ. **1989**, *11* (2/3), 143–181.

11. Das, S.; Lev, B. Nonlinearity in the returns-earnings relation: Tests of alternative specifications and explanations. Contemp. Account. Res. **1994**, *11* (1-II), 353–379.

12. Easton, P.D.; Zmijewski, M.E. Cross-sectional variation in the stock market response to accounting earnings announcements. J. Account. Econ. **1989**, *11* (2/3), 117–141.

13. Hayn, C. The information content of losses. J. Account. Econ. **1995**, *20* (2), 125–153.

14. Chan, J.L. The Governmental Environment: Characteristics and Influences on Governmental Accounting and Financial Reporting. In *Handbook of Governmental Accounting and Finance*; Apostolou, N.G., Crumbley, D.L., Eds.; John Wiley & Sons, 1988.

15. Johnson, W.L.; Goodwin, G.L. State and Local Government Accounting Principles. In *Handbook of Governmental Accounting and Finance*; Apostolou, N.G., Crumbley, D.L., Eds.; John Wiley & Sons, 1988.

FURTHER READING

Ball, R.; Brown, P. An empirical evaluation of accounting income numbers. J. Acc. Res. **1968**, *6* (2), 159–178.

Beaver, W.; Lambert, R.; Morse, D. The information content of security prices. J. Account. Econ. **1980**, *2* (1), 3–28.

Skinner, D.J. Why firms voluntarily disclose bad news. J. Acc. Res. **1994**, *32* (1), 38–60.

Achieving Productivity Through Budgeting

Gerald J. Miller
Rutgers, The State University of New Jersey, Newark, New Jersey, U.S.A.

Donijo Robbins
Grand Valley State University, Grand Rapids, Michigan, U.S.A.

INTRODUCTION

Budgets serve many purposes, all of which can promote productivity. The budget serves as a plan, a means of control, a motivation device, and a process for accountability. At its narrowest, a budget is a plan that estimates proposed expenditures for a given period, usually for a year or a ''fiscal'' year, and relates planned spending to an estimate of revenues needed to finance the plan. The budget also acts as a control device, directing that only the amount specified in the budget be spent in the way the budget dictates. In this sense, budgets control the amount of scarce resources fed into the governmental system, as well as the size and nature of the programs within the budget. Budgets offer incentives, implying a contract in which a set amount of performance or results is exchanged for a certain amount of resources. Finally, budgets improve the accountability of government to citizens by making budget decision making public. That is, government budgets reveal to the public the amount of money spent, with what results, and often why it was spent.

BUDGETING AND PRODUCTIVITY

Budget designers create a process that forces managers to consider different programs, often in competition within and between government departments. Managers commonly employ a simple economic idea—that any alternative must be judged in terms of other alternatives. Budgeting for productivity involves analysis, and proponents of analysis argue that explicit or systematic examination of alternative policies allows the public to hold its public officials accountable for performance.

Budget designers have productivity concerns in mind. In narrow terms, productivity may refer to economic efficiency, a surplus of the goods or services produced over the resources used in their production. Closely akin to this idea are two others: achieving the highest levels of effectiveness for a given investment and choosing the least costly investment that will yield a given level of performance. These often translate through budgets into managerial plans, controls, and incentives for more innovative programs and greater performance.

Another view of productivity holds that budgets should steer government agencies to spending on projects with large, durable returns on investment. Budgets can favor productivity by encouraging choice and favoring alternative investments that have larger returns for the public resources committed to projects, agencies, and activities.

Political leaders make ultimate budget decisions. Political decisions are often based on the geographic distribution of spending and log rolling in which political leaders trade support for each other's favored spending plans. Compromise-driven politics tend to dampen any resolve to increase the effectiveness or efficiency in government programs. Much more emphasis gets placed on maintaining the existing distribution of budget resources, thereby making innovative choices seem irrelevant to the process.

Given all the effort to make the budgeting process favor more productive programs, politics still overshadows economic efficiency as the basis for budget decisions. Thurmaier's research supports this.[1] He suggested that ''conflicts between political and economic imperatives are handled subtly in practice, but it appears that economic and technical calculations are subordinated to prior political determinations.''

Since the era of modern budgeting began in the early twentieth century, government budgets have undergone various reforms. First, the line item budget was a rudimentary way of recording and balancing expenditures and revenues; as such, the line item budget produced accountability. Early performance budgeting was a method of going one step beyond the line item budget by classifying items by function and determining the efficiency of the budgeted expenditures. Functional spending revealed how much revenue was needed to produce a certain level of program production. Next, there was program budgeting, which combined planning and budgeting, and promoted the economic analysis of allocation choices. Zero base budgeting decentralized decision making in an effort to redirect funds from existing programs to new programs. Finally, performance base budgeting attempts to tie the

Encyclopedia of Public Administration and Public Policy
DOI: 10.1081/E-EPAP 120010908

allocation of resources in budgets to the improvement in program performance, the achievement of results, and the success of efforts to realize strategic outcomes.

The success of these reforms has not been impressive. Few have lasted beyond the administration of the executive who instituted them, or they have lasted in only a single department. Although many contextual factors may have led subsequent administrations to seek other methods of budgeting, most reforms have failed to combine a sharp sensibility for both productivity and politics. One former analyst for the legislative branch observed that the "failure of [reform] efforts ... are largely a result of an inability to account for politics. No set of budget techniques can substitute for political decisions about who wins and who loses."[2]

PRODUCTIVITY-ORIENTED SPENDING DECISIONS

If the conceptual linkage between productivity and budgeting is stronger than that revealed in the practice of budgeting, efforts attempt to narrow the difference. These greater efforts have rested in the major and minor modifications of productivity improvement and budget practices; productivity-friendly and budget-friendly reforms may bridge the gap between the concepts and the practices of productivity improvement and budgeting. Productivity-friendly elements refer to reducing the budget process' outright exclusion of productivity goals. Budget-friendly elements empower productivity programs to work inside budget routines.

Productivity-Friendly Budget Elements

Budgeting serves many purposes for decision makers. Lauth[3] warned of the pitfalls of using budgeting as the handmaiden for productivity improvement. The budget is simply too cumbersome to help, he said. Rather, the budget can be made less hostile and more friendly to the ideas underlying productivity improvement. Three major groups of efforts narrow the differences between management and politics: technical modifications, support for measurement, and incentives.

Technical modifications

Small, technical modifications could overcome some of the barriers between budgeting and productivity. For example, many opportunities for cost savings through transfers among budget categories and line items within the fiscal year are forbidden without legislative approval. To illustrate, purchases or repairs may be deferred due to this restriction, forcing more costly ones later. Budgeted

personnel lines are seldom able to be converted to any other object class or vice versa. Thus, consultants may be allowed for many times the expense of a fully trained, permanent employee. Finally, central finance offices often pull back from productive line units salary savings due to attrition, unpaid leads, or other temporary absences. The department is shackled to lower-level performance—fewer people to do the same amount of work—without the opportunity to use the same salary savings to reward employees for what might be a temporary bulge in workload.

Support for measurement

Productivity and budgets often stand at arms length when the performance-to-budget dollar measurements became complicated or numerous. In truth, agreement about valid measures of public sector work performance only exist on the input side, such as dollars given to school districts. Many blame time limits, training gaps, and primitive computing capability for the lack of development in the other areas, whereas others blame the incoherence in the organization segregation and information flows between program evaluation and budgeting.

In one of the clearest insights into the operation of budget offices, Grizzle[4] dispeled much doubt about the ability to solve these problems. She found that many efforts to create time and develop information would involve negligible amounts of the central budget office's work year and little cost.

Her view is that measurement problems could be less considerable and more mythical than believed, if measurement were merely a technical problem, not a problem that becomes politicized. When measurement is a political problem, it becomes one of several behavior problems for which budget officers blame incentives.

Incentives

The motivation to perform productively gets caught in the cross-currents produced by budgets. There are, first of all, incentives to misrepresent information in budgeting, thereby confusing the measurement problem further.[5] Organization, program, and job survival become the ultimate goals when decision makers outside the organization threaten budget reallocations. The incentive for change and innovation has often come from making those inside the organization both responsible for and rewarded for reallocation.

Just as there are incentives to misrepresent, there are incentives to work in less than the most productive ways. Incentive pay is the best known antidote. The availability of funds and careful design of incentives for individuals is important. Group incentive plans are another variation.

As reported by the U.S. General Accounting Office in 1983,[6] for example, North Carolina state employees could propose programs for which they would be rewarded as a group, with a quarter of the savings, if greater productivity were realized. The state budget office chose those for which documentation might provide clear assessments of savings. Strong political support for such incentive programs must exist. In the North Carolina case, Lauth[3] reported, the legislature terminated the program in less than 10 years because the program did less to reduce costs than it did to induce group incentives.

Budget-Friendly Productivity Elements

At another level, the productivity program can profit by major changes in the budget system. The budget system itself has been changed, in this case to one of two major systems, an expenditure control budget and a target base budget. Short of wholesale system change, retained savings plans remove the biggest disincentive to productivity improvement, the transfer of budget surpluses to the central treasury at the end of the fiscal year. Still short of a savings plan, calculating mechanisms may be added to budget systems. Finally, research on policy and program outcomes suggests that more effort in this direction may hold considerable promise.

First developed in California cities in the 1970s, expenditure control budgeting (ECB) has five elements, according to Herzik.[7] First, the system relies on a base budget figure adjusted for population and prices level changes. Second, ECB base budgets assume existing service levels and require explicit approval of changes. Third, departments create retained savings plans, developed through productivity plan-induced savings, to finance changes in service levels or increases in programming. Fourth, central budget offices permit departments to carry forward savings realized in a fiscal year. Fifth, ECB relies on line item control of spending.

The most important aspects of ECB are selection of a base year and maintenance of department head interest in service delivery innovation. Base years may be different for agencies because, at any time, some have unique expenditures, such as capital projects, and others do not. Careful scrutiny prevents one department's base budget from being inflated, creating unfairness.

Second, a department normally having considerable political clout and able to gain bigger budgets to meet service demands may feel unfairly treated under ECB. Because all expansion must be paid out of savings, the department resists. Top management action to force attention to innovation consists of making the sole route to expansion the production of savings.

Target base budgeting[8,9] relies on excellent revenue forecasting to establish a target. Given that accuracy, central budget offices allocate a target figure to departments within which existing service delivery costs must fit. New programs must pass muster separately in budget requests.

The existing services or target budget, even though revenue driven, force priority setting and often innovations. Rubin pointed out that the targets are assigned as a percentage of the base budget for a department. The targets "may be less than the department's base, by a percent that varies from year to year, and may vary from department to department."[8] The target is protected, however, in that it is often an appropriated lump sum, with review of productivity or performance goals and not spending proposals, allowing various trade-offs and transfers within departments, between lines, between programs, and even between operating and capital budgets.

The unprotected or new budget requests to expand services to compete with those of other departments. The list of a department's projects is submitted in priority order. All lists get substantial scrutiny from budget examiners, Rubin stated. These lists force detailed scrutiny to the margin, making target base budgeting rational but not comprehensive.

Although ECB explicitly mandates retained savings and target base budgeting creates savings that may be reallocated, such savings plans may exist independently of a budget system. Klay[10] reviewed these savings plans and described two types—conditional appropriations and discretionary savings plans.

Klay[11] proposed that legislatures give state agencies direct incentives to innovate by appropriating the agency's funds in two parts—one unconditionally and the other conditionally. The legislature would authorize a part of an agency's program on the condition that the agency generate savings in its unconditionally appropriated program. If the agency is given appropriations for normal service delivery and the highest-priority program expansions in its unconditional appropriation, the legislature might also allow the agency to use savings on lower-priority expansions. The legislature might actually premise supplemental appropriations, especially when revenues are underestimated, on the generation of savings.

To retain some leverage over agencies, especially when the agencies that generate savings are not agencies that central budget offices or legislatures consider to be well managed, finance officers might distribute savings, at their discretion, when productivity goals are met. Klay[10] argued that also giving these same well-managed agencies their savings would provide substantial incentives. Discretionary savings plans might also be used in cases where several agencies competed in supplying essentially the same or similar services. Many pointed out the productivity potential of interagency competition, especially among agencies such as city governments, school boards, county governments, and independent districts, which perform some similar services. State oversight agencies, which have some control over the subnational governments, might retain discretion to reward those that produce the service most efficiently or that develop the greatest level of innovation. The ability to use retained savings might provide an incentive, and merger of service providers might aid in gaining effort toward either efficiency or innovation.

Ultimately, budget-friendly productivity elements must include outcome measures. Providing equitable incentives across agencies may instill a will to innovate, be efficient, or attain goals. Attitudes may portray the perceived needs of association members, organization customers, or agency clients. Allocation, however, demands an unbiased measure of achievement to which incentive programs may urge effort and against which attitudes may be viewed and balanced. To force budget-friendly performance decisions, therefore, there must exist outcome measures and a system to monitor work with these measures and evaluate performance itself.

Fisk[12] warned of the difficulty in finding outcome measures and suggested three basic types of measures, operational, immediate, and consequential. Operational measures are those that describe the internal efficiency of an agency, including, for example, the number of reports produced, audits completed, and equipment downtime. Such measures help in the day-to-day management of an agency, but, strictly speaking, they are not productivity measures, as are immediate and consequential measures.

Immediate measurements are those that depict the final organizational output divided by the resources used to produce it or its inputs. For example, tons of garbage collected per employee hour provides a ratio, a technical efficiency measure. The shortcomings of these measures relates to their lack of power to explain why an organization collects garbage—is garbage collection a public health matter or a issue of aesthetics?—or how well we are doing it. Knowing that we are collecting garbage for public health reasons tells managers what priority to assign kinds of garbage and, therefore, where to go to collect it.

A consequential measure is one Fisk said that[12] ''addresses the issue of a program's impact on society and whether the program makes optimum use of resources to achieve its goals.'' Knowing that an organization collects garbage to protect the health of the public can provide an avenue to explore, as above, the kinds of garbage to collect and where to go to collect the garbage. Other examples of consequential measures include deaths prevented per employee hour for a fire department and jobs created per employee hour for an economic development project. These measures directly relate organization members, customers, and clients to the organization's work.

Although immediate and consequential measures form the bulk of traditional performance measurement in government agencies, relating them is an effort of more recent vintage. Swiss[13] used the concept of ''output chains'' to show that budget-friendly productivity elements can be both valid and highly relevant to managers. That is, chains relate the question, ''Did we perform the job without wasting resources?'' to the other question, ''Did the job achieve the desired result?'' In our fire department example, we would establish first the number of fires fought (internal efficiency), then the cost per fire fought or fire fought per employee hour (immediate measures), and finally deaths prevented per fire or per employee hour (the number of reasonably foreseeable deaths without any fire action minus the actual number of deaths divided by the number of employee hours).

Finally, the measure of input used in immediate and consequential measures has traditionally been related to labor productivity. Labor costs dominate budgets, are relatively easy to calculate, are readily available in existing datasets, and have private sector data available for comparison. Simply, labor productivity reveals hours paid.

Because budgets, organization structures, and systems of work are based implicitly on output chains, making these chains explicit demands considerable work but relates technical efficiency measures based on labor productivity to immediate measures to consequential measures and then, most important, provides feedback. Feedback systems that use the outcome measures have budget consequences. Simply, the system should reveal the overall performance of a given program or organization and answer the questions raised about whether results are achieved.

What the measures emphasize may or may not jibe with the organization's goals, with fairness, or with the budget's emphasis. Consider lessons for social welfare entitlement programs learned from one past program initiative[14,15] and the budgeting process connected with it. Measures were developed for overpayments and ineligible recipients. The system was monitored and state agencies administering the program sanctioned when their rates substantially exceeded federal standards. Yet, the system did not ferret out those underpaid or those who were eligible but not receiving benefits. Truly, the organization's goals were minimized and unfairness increased, and the initiative forced displacement of the long-term economic goals of budget policy.

The initiative also splintered efforts to evaluate the program and guide its development in a budget-friendly way. First, the effort to evaluate the program went in two directions: one political to buttress the claim that the program had eliminated welfare cheats, and the other economic to justify the use of transfer payments to provide income floors—a safety net—for the young, the disabled, and the poor. Second, the initiative failed to guide budget-friendly productivity efforts. The initiative, as many who oppose it now look back and see, failed to discourage dependency. It did nothing to offer alternatives to transfer payments, more or less emphasizing greater spending in the future as transfer payment dependency reached future generations.[16] Moreover, the initiative's implicit budget policy became cost centered. Cost-centered budgeting, generally, rewards projects that cost little, whatever their productivity value. Cost-centered budgeting leads eventually to zero-sum gaming where increased spending in one area means decreased spending in others and where deferred maintenance (keeping destitute or needy individuals whole) supports new projects.

CONCLUSION

A budget is a plan, a set of controls, a potentially large set of incentives, and a means of holding governments accountable for both what work is done and how much the work costs. Productivity and budgets would seem to be self-reinforcing and dynamic in encouraging innovation and performance. Many attempts have occurred over the years to change the format of the budget to make the conceptual linkage between productivity and budgeting stronger in practice. Many agree that these reforms succeeded in some ways, but failed to survive the politics of budgeting. Further, less ambitious efforts also exist to produce a politically acceptable connection. These efforts include approaches that lead budgeting to include productivity-friendly elements and ideas by change budgets to focus on productivity concerns.

REFERENCES

1. Thurmaier, K. Decisive decision making in the executive budget process: Analyzing the political and economic propensities of central budget bureau analysts. Public Adm. Rev. **1995**, *55*, 448–460.

2. Joyce, P.G. Using performance measures for federal budgeting: Proposals and prospects. Public Budg. Finance **1993**, *13* (4), 3–17.

3. Lauth, T.P. Budgeting and Productivity in State Government: Not Integrated but Friendly. In *Performance-Based Budgeting*; Miller, G.J., Hildreth, W.B., Rabin, J., Eds.; Westview: Boulder, CO, 2001; 191–202.

4. Grizzle, G. Linking Performance to Funding Decisions: What Is the Budgeter's Role? *Performance-Based Budgeting*; Miller, G.J., Hildreth, W.B., Rabin, J., Eds.; Westview: Boulder, CO, 2001; 203–214.

5. Jones, L.R.; Euske, K.J. Strategic misrepresentation in budgeting. J. Public Adm. Res. Theory **1991**, *1*, 437–460.

6. U.S. General Accounting Office. *Increased Use of Productivity Measurement Can Help Control Government Costs*; U.S. Government Printing Office: Washington, D.C., 1983.

7. Herzik, E.B. Improving budgetary management and fostering innovation: Expenditure control budgeting. Public Prod. Manage. Rev. **1991**, *14*, 237–248.

8. Rubin, I.S. Budgeting for our times: Target base budgeting. Public Budg. Finance **1991**, *11*, 5–14.

9. Wenz, T.; Nolan, A. Budgeting for the future: Target base budgeting. Public Budg. Finance **1982**, *2*, 88–91.

10. Klay, W.E. Management Through Budgetary Incentives. In *Performance-Based Budgeting*; Miller, G.J., Hildreth, W.B., Rabin, J., Eds.; Westview: Boulder, CO, 2001; 215–227.

11. Klay, W.E. A legislative tool to encourage agency efficiency. Public Prod. Rev. **1978**, *3* (1), 23–31.

12. Fisk, D. *Measuring Productivity in State and Local Government*; Bulletin 2166, U.S. Department of Labor, Bureau of Labor Statistics, U.S. Government Printing Office: Washington, D.C., 1983; 2.

13. Swiss, J.E. *Public Management Systems: Monitoring and Managing Government Performance*; Prentice-Hall: Englewood Cliffs, NJ, 1991.

14. Danziger, S. *Approaching the Limit: Early Lessons from Welfare Reform*; Joint Center for Poverty Research Conference: Chicago, 2000.

15. Randall, R. Presidential power versus bureaucratic intransigence: The influence of the Nixon Administration on welfare policy. Am. Polit. Sci. Rev. **1979**, *73*, 798–800.

16. DeParle, J. To Moynihan, welfare dependency signals new ill. N. Y. Times **December 9, 1991**, *141*, A13.

Acquiring Resources Through Price Negotiation

Rupert G. Rhodd
Florida Atlantic University, Davie, Florida, U.S.A.

INTRODUCTION

Public and private firms, seeking to acquire goods, generally do so through vertical integration or outsourcing. Whereas a vertical chain of production is the coming together of firms at various stages in the production of a good, outsourcing is that situation in which a firm gets an input to deliver a good or service from an external firm. With vertical integration, benefits like reduction in transaction and coordination costs, continuity of supply, the nonsharing of proprietary rights, and greater control over the quality of inputs are often realized.

Organizing production through vertical integration means that firms are organized into business units. The implication from this is that measuring the performance of the individual units requires that a "transfer price" be established for the goods and services exchanged. With a transfer price, total profits can be reallocated among firms in the business unit, and this could impact the business unit's overall profit. Supplying goods through vertical integration may, therefore, not encourage least-cost production by an individual firm because of subsidies by more profitable firms within the integrated business unit. There are, however, certain standard pricing methods by which goods can be transferred. If there is a competitive external market for the good in question, the product can be transferred at the "external market price." If there is no external market or if for some reason the market price does not truly measure the opportunity cost of producing the good, the "marginal production cost" could be used to determine the transfer price. Because the marginal production cost is the cost of producing the last unit, it is said to represent the value of resources foregone to produce the last unit. Some firms in an integrated unit have also made use of "full-cost transfer prices," because it is felt that marginal cost of production focuses on variable cost and omits fixed cost. This method is simple, is easily implemented, and is the most popular of the pricing mechanisms used by firms in an integrated unit.[1]

PRICE NEGOTIATION AND MARKET CONDITIONS

Price negotiation can assist in the transfer of goods between firms in an integrated unit and also in the acquisition of goods through outsourcing. In an integrated unit, the price at which goods are transferred is aptly labeled the "negotiated transfer price," because it is determined by negotiation between the units. A negotiated price between firms in a business unit is expected to maximize the combined profits of the negotiating firms. The selling firm will not negotiate a price below its production cost, and the acquiring firm will not pay a price above that for which it can buy the product for elsewhere. The reference to purchasing a good at a price not higher than that for which it can be purchased elsewhere indicates that the market plays an indirect role, and serves more as a reference point for the determination of a negotiated transfer price. Because it is possible for two firms in an integrated unit to negotiate a transfer price without at the same time agreeing on the quantity to be transferred at that price, there is no guarantee that the negotiated price will maximize the business unit's value. There is also the possibility of a long, drawn-out, and time-consuming process which, when converted to a monetary value, could increase the cost of acquiring goods and services.

For the public sector in the United States, goods and services are acquired mostly through outsourcing. There are many reasons why, in recent times, the public sector and the private sector have increasingly sought to acquire goods and services through outsourcing. Among them are heightened competition between supply firms and the reduction in cost that competition causes, flexible production techniques and the willingness of producers to satisfy demand, and improved communications and the relative ease with which goods and services can be obtained from outside agents and within a short time frame. The extent to which firms are expected to benefit by acquiring goods and services through outsourcing rather than through vertical integration depends on the price paid for the outsourced goods and services.

Encyclopedia of Public Administration and Public Policy
DOI: 10.1081/E-EPAP 120016944

When firms seek to acquire goods and services through outsourcing, the cost of these goods and services are determined in either the "spot" market, where the price is determined by market conditions, or the price is determined through negotiation, especially where there are long-term contracts.[a] Buying goods in the spot or competitive market could be advantageous as compared to a noncompetitive or negotiated situation, because it could easily be argued that because competitive firms do not make surplus profit over the long-run period, the market-determined price tends to be lower than a negotiated price. However, even with the benefit from purchasing goods on the spot market, purchasing agents in private sector and procurement officers in the public sector have used negotiation and long-term contracts with a few vendors to acquire goods and services. There seems to be the feeling that through negotiation, there is more control over price, quality, and delivery. Although this may be true for quality and delivery, the negotiated price is more dependent on the skillfulness of the parties "at the negotiator table" and the conditions in the market.

Negotiation, in general, differs from a ball game or a war where only one side wins and the other side loses. In successful negotiations, both sides win something, giving rise to a "win–win" situation. When procurement officers or purchasing agents seek to acquire goods and services through negotiation, the objectives of negotiation are to obtain the quality specified, to obtain a fair and reasonable price, and to get the vendor to perform the contract on time. Although all three objectives are important, budgetary restrictions of public-sector agencies and private firms cause most attention to be paid to obtaining goods and services at a fair and reasonable price. Even though mention is often made of securing goods and services at the "right price," this concept has more to do with fairness than profitability of the firm needing the goods or service (buyer) and the firm supplying the goods or service (seller). The "right price" is said to be that which is fair to both buyer and seller.[2] And even with this definition, the "right price" is not static, because firms are able (within limits) to adjust their asking and offering prices, which could vary with conditions in the market.

In the United States, we find the three forms of competition that are discussed in any elementary microeconomics textbook. At one extreme, there is the idealist form of perfect competition characterized by "atomistic" competition in which a large number of sellers trade a homogeneous good. This form of competition is also characterized by the availability of low cost of accurate information and the ability of firms to freely enter and leave the industry.

At the other extreme of the competitive spectrum is monopoly, where one firm controls the supply and hence the price of the product. Some reasons for the establishment of monopolies include the control of specific assets, production requiring large output and the realization of economies of scale, the availability of excess capacity and the ability to increase production at will, precommitment contracts, licenses and patents, and pioneering brand advantages.

Between the two extremes are conditions of imperfect competition, where the number of sellers of a heterogeneous or homogenous good can be large or small. Under this market form, the supplier has some control over "brand" price. Studies have shown that in the United States, most goods are traded under conditions where there is some freedom to adjust price, and this would imply conditions of imperfect competition (see Ref. [2], for list of these studies). We accept the conclusions of these studies as true, but we also believe that tightly budgeted expenditures and the encumbering of funds for future expenditure cause the government sector to secure goods under varying conditions of competition. To get the biggest "bang for the buck," government procurement is forced into markets where the price will be "right" or most beneficial to the agency.

GOVERNMENT PROCUREMENT: IMPLICATIONS FOR NEGOTIATION

Pricing of Goods

One of the tips given for conducting successful negotiation is "do your homework." For government agents, this includes having knowledge of the product and market. Regarding the procurement of goods, one would be more inclined to believe that if quality and quantity are easily ascertained, pricing issues involving government procurement, would be at a minimum. If this is so, the situation boils down to whether pricing should be based on full cost, marginal cost, or some method to benefit the government agency as well as the firm supplying the good.

In the most competitive market, substitute goods are differentiated by design, wrapping, or other such features. The market has a large number of sellers with the individual seller forced to sell at "near equal" prices. Furthermore, to remain in this market, suppliers must be efficient. We could, therefore, infer from this that suppliers in this market will sell to government agencies at the lowest possible price, that the goods will be of the highest value, and that price is a true indicator of quality.

---

[a]Long-term contracts could be in the form of long-term supply and distribution contracts, franchise contracts, leasing contracts, or strategic alliances.

Intense competition forces manufacturers to make their products intrinsically different, and this gives room for different negotiated prices between suppliers and the government, as components such as service and delivery are included in the price. Also, as the number of producers and sellers in the market declines, there will be more pricing issues. The heterogeneous nature of these markets will require more effort by government agencies to determine quality and similarity of prices. If procurement personnel is limited, government agencies could be forced to accept the seller's words, with the negotiated price more beneficial to the seller.

Pricing of Services

Research indicates that employee's compensation as a percentage of noncapital direct expenditure is between 30 to 40% at the state and local levels and 15 to 20% at the federal level. Economic theory proposes that labor should be paid according to its marginal revenue product, which is the marginal product of labor expressed in dollar value. This approach is only useful in the public sector, where the output of labor is easily determined and where the government can determine the quality of the output. If quality and quantity are not easily determined, there is room for a negotiated wage rate. Many factors can determine the negotiated wages, these including union representation, skill of labor, demand by the public sector, and wage rate in other sectors of the economy.

There is also the additional issue of what price should the government pay labor when productivity of labor and wages in the other sectors of the economy increase faster than in the public sector. This issue is important, because depending on the policy chosen, the supply of labor in the public sector could decline, efficiency could fall, and the average cost of services in the public sector could increase. Here again, negotiations are important. To reduce the above problems, the negotiated price of labor should be close to that offered in the more efficient private sector. Furthermore, because jobs in the public sector tend to be more secure and with the likelihood of more generous benefits, paying labor a rate close to that paid in the more efficient private sector could attract labor from the private sector and improve the efficiency of labor in the public sector.

Even with the analysis outlined above, we understand that each procurement project is unique and complex and thus defies the use of a general rule or policy. We also believe that for each purchasing organization, the regulations and the rules are different. These complicate the procurement process. In the end, the procurement approach used and the manner in which it is implemented, will determine the success or failure of government's projects. Because of the dynamic nature of today's market, it is imperative that government agencies continue their vigilance on procurement procedures.

REFERENCES

1. Brickley, J.; Smith, C.; Zimmerman, J. *Managerial Economics and Organizational Architecture*; McGraw-Hill: 2001; 448.
2. Dobler, D.; Burt, D.; Lee, L., Jr. *Purchasing and Materials Management: Text and Cases*, 5th Ed.; McGraw-Hill, pp. 242, 244.

Activity-Based Costing in the Public Sector

Thomas Buttross
*The Pennsylvania State University at Harrisburg,
Middletown, Pennsylvania, U.S.A.*

George Schmelzle
Indiana University Purdue University, Fort Wayne, Indiana, U.S.A.

INTRODUCTION

This article is meant to provide the reader with a general understanding of activity-based costing (ABC), and its uses and benefits in the public sector. Some of the limitations of ABC are also covered.

ABC is designed to provide information for strategic decisions. Applying this model to the public sector, ABC can provide information on the cost of providing government services for strategic decisions, such as determining the affordability of providing discretionary government services (e.g., picking up yard waste); setting user fees, both internally between agencies and externally, for billable government services (e.g., water and waste water services); and determining whether to outsource government services (e.g., trash pickup).

Activity-based management (ABM) takes the ABC model to the next logical step, providing information for operational decisions (i.e., for cost management aimed at improving day-to-day operations). For example, instead of outsourcing trash pickup, the governmental entity might use the activity-based information to improve the government operation to the point where it is competitive with the private sector. The combined use of ABC and ABM is so common that many writers refer to the combined models as one—ABCM (activity-based cost management).

Activity-based budgeting (ABB) takes the model to its third logical step. Once the organization knows the cost of providing various services, it can budget the level of services it wants to provide and determine the amount of resources required to provide that level of services. Given scarce resources, the level of services is likely to exceed the available resources, even after additional sources of funds have been considered. Reductions of funds can then be logically tied to reductions of particular services. For example, if recycling pickup costs $2 per house per pickup, the cost savings of reducing pickups from once per week to once every two weeks can be determined. Viewed from the opposite angle, the effect of cutting resources available for recycling pickup in half on the frequency of pickups can be more clearly determined.

ADVANTAGES OF ABC

Activity-based costing has several advantages:

1. It provides understandable information—people intuitively understand activities, and how activities consume resources and raise the cost of cost objects.
2. It reduces arbitrary cost allocations by charging resources to the activities that consume them and charging activities to the cost objects that consume them, where possible.
3. It identifies activities that highlight departmental interdependencies, which can reduce functional suboptimization.
4. It provides cost driver information for managers and employees to remove costs on existing services or avoid costs on new services.
5. It provides data for other improvement initiatives (e.g., total quality management).
6. It improves budgeting by tying the budget to the actual work that is done.

CAVEATS REGARDING ABC

Activity-based costing is not a panacea; ABC models tend to address cost only, at a strategic level too general to satisfy operational needs. Operational improvement information comes from the addition of ABM and requires the addition of noncost performance measures to the model.

Even ABCM does not lead to improvements. People must use the data to make improvements. If the ABC system indicates that governmental trash pickup is more costly than the private sector, it will continue to be more costly unless the governmental garbage entity uses ABM information to reduce the cost of providing that service.

Encyclopedia of Public Administration and Public Policy
DOI: 10.1081/E-EPAP 120010726

Activity-based costing, ABM, and ABB are not one-time efforts, which is another way of saying that they are costly in terms of time and money. If ABC indicates that the cost of providing a service is too high and that service is reengineered to be less costly, then a new ABC model needs to be constructed to determine the new cost of providing that service.

Finally, there are problems caused by generally accepted accounting principles (GAAP). Under GAAP, a cost incurred in 1 year, but related to several years, may be expensed in the year incurred. For example, a major training program for newly installed software may be expensed when incurred, making it less likely to be reflected in the cost of future activities that benefited from the training. Conversely, a cost delayed, such as maintenance, will not be reflected in the accounting records until incurred, making it unlikely to be reflected in the current activities that benefited from the use of the asset.

MODEL AND TERMINOLOGY

The CAM-I Cross

To understand ABC systems, it is instructive to examine the CAM-I Cross. The vertical portion of the cross, the cost assignment view, is ABC, whereas the horizontal portion, the process view, is ABM (Fig. 1).

As the cost assignment view shows, resources are consumed by activities and activities are consumed by cost objects. From another perspective, cost objects require the performance of certain activities, and those activities require the use of certain resources. Each part is discussed in turn.

Activities (Tasks and Processes)

Activities are at the center of ABC. They are a series of tasks (work steps) performed by an organization yielding a useful aggregation. To be useful, the aggregation needs to be neither too broad nor too narrow. For example, "provide unemployment benefits" would probably be too broad. Such aggregations of activities are called processes. "Hand blank benefits form to next person in line" would be too narrow. Such narrow parts of activities are called tasks or work steps. "Process unemployment-benefits application," "authorize benefits payment," and "issue benefits check" might be proper aggregations.

Because activities represent work done by the organization, they should be defined by an action verb followed by a noun, with an adjective in the middle optional. Where only one type of application is processed (or where every application processed requires the same level of resources), "process application" is an understandable activity name. Where different applications are processed, more descriptive names such as "process unemployment-benefits application" are warranted.

There are various ways to identify activities (e.g., storyboarding and activity dictionaries) but their discussion is beyond the scope of this article.

The CAM-I ABCM Model
AKA The CAM-I Cross

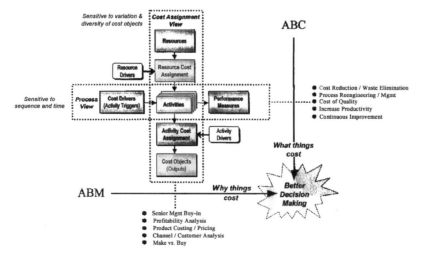

Fig. 1 The CAM-I Cross. (©1990 CAM-I. Used with permission.)

Resources

Resources are economic elements used by an organization (e.g., labor, equipment, utilities). Although the model refers to resources, the cost of resources is what appears in the model. So, while labor is a resource consumed by activities, the salaries, which represent the cost of the labor, are reflected in the ABC computations.

To process unemployment benefits applications, the entity will use resources such as labor, equipment, utilities, and office supplies. The cost of these resources can be found in the accounting records and needs to be charged to the activity that consumed the resources.

Cost Objects

Cost objects are the reason that organizations perform activities. They are simply objects for which management desires a cost. Examples include products, customers (individual recipients of benefits or selected groups of benefit recipients, such as laid-off workers from a particular employer), and services.

Cost objects cause activities (e.g., provision of unemployment benefits requires the provider to process unemployment-benefits applications, authorize benefits payment, and issue benefits checks). The activities caused by a particular cost object should be charged to that cost object.

Resource Drivers

Resource drivers are used to charge the cost of resources to activities. In some cases, a resource is used for only one activity and, therefore, can be traced to the activity. If employees spend 100% of their time processing unemployment-benefits applications, then the employees' salaries can be charged in total to that activity. However, cost assignment (allocation) becomes necessary when employees spend time on multiple activities.

Resource drivers (first-stage drivers) are used to assign resource costs to activities. They represent a measure of the quantity of resources consumed by an activity. As examples, labor and fringe benefits of an employee can be assigned based on the percentage of time the employee spends "processing unemployment-benefits application" and "authorizing benefits payment," and equipment rent or depreciation can be assigned based on the percentage of time the equipment is used for different activities.

There are various ways to identify resource drivers (e.g., labor logs, questionnaires, interviews of employees and supervisors, observation, physical measurement for items like square footage) but their discussion is beyond the scope of this article.

Activity Drivers

Activity drivers (second-stage drivers) are factors that are used to assign activity costs to cost objects. They represent a measure of the quantity of activity cost consumed by the cost object. There should be a cause-and-effect relationship with the cost driver. For example, assume that we are processing unemployment benefits for two companies, Company X and Company Y, and we want to assign the cost of this processing to each company. In this case, the activity driver might be "number of claims processed." If we process twice as many claims for Company X as Company Y, then twice as much cost for this activity should be charged to Company X.

Activity drivers exist at various levels: unit, batch, product or service, customer, facility, and organization sustaining are common categories.

Cost Drivers

Cost drivers are the root causes of costs. Identifying cost drivers can help an organization to improve processes or reduce costs by eliminating or reducing the nonvalue-added activities and by performing value-added activities more efficiently.

Again, consider the processing of unemployment claims. Assume that the agency has a policy that requires a supervisor to review each unemployment-benefits application that is processed, before payments can be made. The policy requiring the supervisor to look at each processed claim would be a cost driver. The related work step or task—the supervisor actually reviewing each claim—would be included in the activity "authorize benefits payment." By eliminating this policy, the cost of performing this activity would be reduced. Another cost driver of both "process unemployment-benefits application" and "authorize benefits payment" is the design of the unemployment-benefits application. A poorly designed document will increase the time required to input/review the information and increase the likelihood of errors, thereby increasing the processing and authorization costs. Redesigning a problematic claim form can reduce the cost of these activities.

There are multiple cost drivers associated with most activities. The cost of the activity "process unemployment-benefits application" is driven by many factors, including the number of claims processed, the completeness of the information supplied by the claimant, the training and experience of the agency employees processing the documents, the design of the form, and the time of day when processing occurs. The identification of significant cost drivers is critical to ABM.

As a final note, cost driver is not a synonym for activity driver. There is only one activity driver for a par-

Table 1 Estimated overhead costs using record-keeping categories

Overhead only	Estimated cost
Salaries	$150,000
Fringe benefits	30,000
Building rent	70,000
Building utilities	10,000
Small tools and supplies	15,000
Equipment depreciation	160,000
Equipment insurance	3,000
Equipment maintenance	17,000
Gasoline	45,000
Total	$500,000

Table 3 ABC overhead activities

ABC overhead activities	Estimated costs
Schedule pickups/cuts	$40,000
Set up equipment (for pickups/cuts)	100,000
Drive routes (and pickups/cuts)	270,000
Dispose of leaves and branches	50,000
Total	$460,000

ticular activity, but there are multiple cost drivers. In the case of "process unemployment-benefits application," one of the cost drivers—the number of claims processed—is likely to be used as the activity driver. There are even situations where the chosen activity driver is not one of the cost drivers. If one remembers that cost drivers are what causes cost to appear in the activity cost pool, whereas activity drivers are a measure of the consumption of the activity cost pool by cost objects, the difference between the two types of drivers is understandable.

Performance Measures

Performance measures determine how effective an organization is at performing activities. These measures describe how effective the organization is at performing the work (the activities) in the organization, along with an indication of whether the activities that are being performed meet the needs of the organization's internal and external customers. Performance measures can be either financial or nonfinancial in nature. There are four categories of performance measures: time, quality, cost, and productivity.

An organization that processes unemployment claims might be interested in the "number of claims processed

per hour" (a performance measure that is measuring time), the "number of claims that were error free" (a performance measure that is measuring quality), "the cost per claim filed" (a performance measure that is measuring cost), or "total number of claims filed during the week" (a performance measure that is measuring productivity).

Also note that performance measures for one group can be cost drivers for another. Take the use of "number of claims that were error free" as a performance measure for the activity "process unemployment-benefits application." Errors in processing applications increase the cost of the subsequent activity—"authorize benefits payment"—because such errors require correction before authorization can occur. They can also decrease the performance of the "authorize benefits payment" activity because they decrease the number of authorizations that can be completed in a given amount of time. In other words, errors in "process unemployment-benefits application" are a cost driver for the downstream activities.

EXAMPLE

The following example helps to clarify the discussion.

The City of Kendallville performs two lawn services for its taxpayers. It picks up leaves after residents rake them into the street, and it cuts the branches of trees that

Table 2 Traditional cost allocation

Traditional cost allocation	Picking up leaves (4 DLH)	Cutting trees (5 DLH)
Direct labor (@ $7 per DLH)	$28	$35
Service overhead (@ $227 per DLH)	908	1,135
Totals per pickup/cutting	$936	$1,170

Table 4 Activity data

ABC overhead activities	Picking up leaves	Cutting trees	Total
Schedule pickups/cuts[a]	30	100	130
Set up equipment (for pickups/cuts)[b]	5	80	85
Drive routes (and pickups/cuts)[c]	35,000	30,000	65,000
Dispose of leaves and branches[d]	50,000	100,000	150,000

[a]Number of trips scheduled.
[b]Number of setups.
[c]Number of miles driven.
[d]Pounds dumped.

Table 5 Overhead rates per unit of activity

Activity	Estimated overhead cost/ Estimated total activity	Overhead per activity
Schedule pickups/cuts	$40,000/130 trips	$307.69 per trip
Set up equipment (for pickups/cuts)	$100,000/85 setups	$1,176.47 per setup
Drive routes (and pickups/cuts)	$270,000/65,000 miles	$4.15 per mile
Dispose of leaves and branches	$50,000/150,000 pounds	$0.33 per pound

are close to street signs and power lines. Except for a few smaller items, the same equipment is used for both services. Picking up leaves is done three times per year, whereas cutting trees is done twice per year.

Kendallville is divided into 100 neighborhoods. Thus, picking up leaves is done 300 times and cutting trees is done 200 times. For each neighborhood, it takes 4 hours to pick up the leaves of the residents, and 5 hours to cut the branches. The city currently has a traditional cost system in which direct labor hours are used to assign overhead cost to these two services.

Table 1 shows the estimated overhead using record-keeping categories.

The predetermined overhead rate of $227 per direct labor hour is determined by dividing the budgeted overhead cost of $500,000 by the budgeted 2200 direct labor hours. (The budgeted direct labor hours represent 300 occurrences of picking up leaves times 4 hours per neighborhood plus 200 occurrences of cutting trees times 5 hours per neighborhood.)

Table 2 shows the cost of each service for one neighborhood.

The City of Kendallville is considering the implementation of an ABC system to cost these two services. The city manager has collected the following information.

First, the city determined that, of the $500,000 in service overhead, $10,000 of the small tools and supplies represents saw blades and such, which can be directly traced to cutting trees. In addition, $30,000 of the salaries represents payments to an external consultant who reviews the neighborhoods and determines where tree cutting will be necessary. This $40,000 will be directly traced to the tree-cutting cost object ($40,000/200 cuttings = $200 per cutting), whereas the remaining $560,000 will be assigned (allocated) using ABC.

Table 3 presents the activities that were determined to be the cause of the remaining $460,000 in overhead costs. Table 4 presents estimated activity data.

The following activity data was estimated (Table 4).

Because picking up leaves is determined by the seasons, scheduling of 10 neighborhoods at one time is possible. So, 300 pickups need only 30 trips scheduled. Also, because the pickups occur close together in time, few equipment changeovers are required between pickups. Tree cutting, however, is not restricted by the seasons and is done is small batches of neighborhoods, as need is identified by an external consultant.

Table 5 displays the overhead rates computed for each specific activity. With these overhead rates, Table 6 presents the assignment of overhead to services. The as-

Table 6 Assigning overhead to services

Activity	Picking up leaves		Cutting trees	
Schedule pickups/cuts	30 trips × $307.69 per trip	$9,231	100 trips × $307.69 per trip	$30,769
Set up equipment (for pickups/cuts)	5 setups × $1,176.47 per setup	5,882	80 setups × $1,176.47 per setup	94,118
Drive routes (and pickups/cuts)	35,000 miles driven × $4.15 per mile	145,250	30,000 miles driven × $4.15 per mile	124,500
Dispose of leaves and branches	50,000 pounds disposed of × $0.33 per pound	16,500	100,000 pounds disposed of × $0.33 per pound	33,000
Totals (assigned $459,250, instead of $460,000 due to rounding)		$176,863		$282,387
Service overhead per pickup/cutting	$176,863/300 pickups	$590	$282,387/200 cuttings	$1,412

Table 7 ABC cost allocation

ABC cost allocation	Picking up leaves (4 DLH)	Cutting trees (5 DLH)
Direct labor (same as traditional above)	$28	$35
Directly traced service overhead (computed earlier)		200
Service overhead per pickup/cutting	590	1,412
Totals	$618	$1,647

signed overhead is then used to compute the service cost using ABC (Table 7).

In this example, the ABC rates of $618 per pickup and $1647 per cutting indicate that the traditional system rates of $936 and $1170, respectively, are overcosting the leaf removal service and undercosting the tree-cutting service. This information would be useful if, for example, the local utility reimburses the city for much of the tree-cutting service.

CONCLUSION

With activity-based costing information, a public entity can make strategic decisions regarding what discretionary government services to offer, what user fees to charge internally as well as to consumers for billable government services, and whether to in source or out source public services. With the addition of activity-based management, the governmental entity can make decisions involving the management of its costs that will improve the efficiency of its operations. Finally, with the addition of activity-based budgeting, the public entity can determine which services it can afford to provide to members of the community based on available resources, and how much it can save from curtailing various services in times of scarcity.

FURTHER READING

Brimson, J.A.; Antos, J. *Activity-Based Management for Service Industries, Government Entities, and Nonprofit Organizations*; John Wiley & Sons, Inc.: New York, 1994.

Brian, F. Marked improvements. Gov. Exec. **2000**, *32* (3), 86–88.

Carter, T.L.; Sedaghat, A.M.; Williams, T.D. How ABC changed the post office. Manage. Account. **1998**, *79* (8), 28–32.

Harvey, M. Indianapolis speeds away. J. Bus. Strategy **1998**, *19* (3), 41–46.

Kline, J.J. ABC, SPC, SEA: Alphabet soup or quality synergy. Gov. Account. J. **2000**, *49* (1), 40–45.

LaPlante, A.; Alter, A.E. U. S. Department of Defense: Activity-based costing. Computerworld **1994**, *28* (44), 84.

May, M. An activity-based approach to resource accounting and budgeting in government. Manage. Acc. (Lond.) **1995**, *73* (7), 27.

Simpson, W.K. Activity-based: Costing, management and budgeting. Gov. Account. J. **1996**, *45* (1), 26–28.

Turney, P.B.B. *Common Cents: The ABC Performance Breakthrough*; Cost Technology: Beaverton, OR, 1993.

Williams, C.; Ward, M. Is ABCM destined for success or failure in the federal government? Public Budg. Finance **1999**, *19* (2), 22–36.

Williams, C.; Ward, M. The ABC's of government reinvention: Can activity-based costing reinstill public trust in government? Penn. Times **1997**, *20* (12), 1.

Administrative Discretion

Kenneth F. Warren
Saint Louis University, St. Louis, Missouri, U.S.A.

A

INTRODUCTION

Administrative discretion refers to the degree of latitude or flexibility exercised by public administrators when making decisions or conducting any agency business. The chief source of administrative discretion comes from legislative bodies that have drafted vague laws. These skeletal statutes essentially allow public administrators the discretionary power to interpret laws as they see fit, as long as their discretionary interpretations do not contradict specific statutory provisions. Public administrators are normally not hesitant to exercise broad discretionary power because the reviewing courts tend to routinely defer to agency discretion (i.e., expertise), and also are specifically prohibited by statute from reviewing any agency action precluding judicial review or committed to agency discretion by law [Section 700 of the Administrative Procedure Act (APA) of 1946, as amended, United States Code: Title 5].

DISCRETIONARY BEHAVIOR IN THE CONTEXT OF FORMAL VS. INFORMAL AGENCY ACTIONS

Public administrators can follow relatively formal or informal procedures. In reality, agency actions are not wholly formal or informal, but a blend of the two. That is, formal action would consist of decision-making processes going solely by the book, whereas procedural steps are meticulously followed to reach decisions. However, because the APA or other laws or rules always permit administrators some administrative discretion when making decisions, even under the most structured or formal decision-making situations, total adherence to formal procedures would be both impossible and undesirable.

Actually, only about 10% of administrative behavior can be legitimately classified as formal.[1] A formal agency action usually consists of those actions by administrators that fall well within prescribed (usually written) procedures, as dictated by statutes, court rulings, and/or agency rules and regulations. Formal administrative action, in contrast to informal administrative action, is characterized by the limited role an administrator's discretion can play in determining what procedures can be

followed and what decisions can be reached as the result of following specified procedures. One clear example of formal agency behavior can be seen when agencies conduct elaborate, trial-like formal evidentiary hearings where relatively strict rules of procedure are followed. Agency rule making can also be quite formal if administrators follow the elaborate provisions for making rules as required in Sections 556 and 557. Generally speaking, under the APA, informal action refers to any administrative action or inaction (e.g., a decision not to act) that does not involve a trial-like hearing. Formal rule making requires a trial-like hearing and is governed by Sections 556 and 557 of the APA, whereas informal rule making, which does not require a formal hearing, is governed by Section 553 or not by the APA at all. Likewise, adjudications that require a formal trial-like evidentiary hearing are considered formal, whereas adjudications that occur without a trial-like hearing are considered informal.

However, it would be futile to try to classify administrative actions into neat categories of either formal or informal because, in practice, administrators interchange formal and informal procedures. The point is that informal administrative actions are characterized by a broader use of administrative discretion than are formal administrative activities. As the formal–informal agency action continuum in Fig. 1 illustrates, the more agency actions are controlled by administrative discretion, the more informal the agency action is. Conversely, the more formal the procedural codes (e.g., statutes, rules, court orders) that dictate agency actions, the more formal the agency action is. Of course, agency actions would never, in practice, be completely controlled by formal procedural codes or totally dominated by an administrator's discretion. The extreme ends in the continuum only represent the theoretical extremes. Although at times one may not perceive any evidence that an administrator's discretionary decisions are being modified by prevailing legal sanctions, in reality sane administrators are always cognizant of the need to submit somewhat to environmental pressures to conform to expected patterns of behavior. Systems theory, popular in the social sciences, conveys that it would be unrealistic to believe that administrators could expect to survive in office for long by totally ignoring prevailing legal and professional sanctions when employing their discretionary powers. An appropriate response to systemic

Encyclopedia of Public Administration and Public Policy
DOI: 10.1081/E-EPAP 120010934

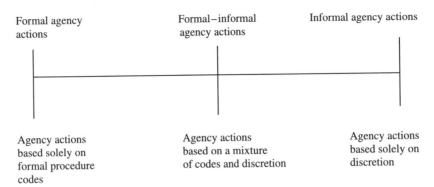

Formal agency actions	Formal–informal agency actions	Informal agency actions
Agency actions based solely on formal procedure codes	Agency actions based on a mixture of codes and discretion	Agency actions based solely on discretion

Fig. 1 Discretion's role in formal–informal agency actions.

demands would entail keeping the use of discretion within at least minimally tolerable bounds. However, this is not to suggest that administrative discretion is not abused. In fact, social scientists and legal scholars have devoted considerable attention to studying abuses of discretion and how to control them. Yet, it is maintained that the vast majority of discretionary acts by our public administrators are reasonable because they are guided by numerous legal, ethical, and professional standards of conduct forced upon them by the system in which they function. Even when reviewing court cases involving the use of discretion, one finds most allegations of discretionary abuse rest on technical legal arguments, that is, on whether an administrator acted within or outside their discretionary authority, as defined by specific statutes or rules.

EXPANDING ON THE MEANING OF ADMINISTRATIVE DISCRETION

Discretionary actions by administrators are informal administrative acts, even though they may be within an administrator's formal authority. According to Kenneth C. Davis, perhaps the most authoritative source on the concept of administrative discretion, public administrators have discretion whenever the effective limits on their power leave them free to make choices among possible courses of action or inaction.[2] To Davis, it is important to stress, as it is implied above, that discretion is not limited to what is authorized or what is legal, but includes all that is within the *effective* limits on the officer's power.[3] Davis added that the specific phraseology he employs to describe discretion is necessary because a good deal of discretion is illegal or of questionable legality.[3]

Davis stated that the lifeblood of the administrative process is informal discretionary action.[4] Further, he emphasized that informal discretionary power is enormous, especially when compared with an administrator's quite limited formal powers.[4] It is appropriate to mention here that political scientists, in reference to presidential

powers, have for many decades acknowledged that president's informal powers are many times greater than their formal powers, as sanctioned by the Constitution, various statutes, and court decisions.[5,6] Scholars have noted that, although vague and general, statutes and constitutional provisions give rise to discretionary power, but they do not effectively control or limit discretion. Consequently, willful administrators, including presidents, can use their discretionary authority, to make themselves far more powerful than their creators, the Constitutional framers and legislators, probably originally intended.[1]

When examining the breadth of informal discretionary power, it is easy to understand why it is said to be the lifeblood of the administrative process. Informal discretionary powers include such positive functions as initiating, prosecuting, negotiating, settling, contracting, dealing, advising, threatening, publicizing, concealing, planning, recommending, and supervising.[1] But the most awesome discretionary power is the omnipresent power to do nothing.[1] That is, administrators may simply decide not to initiate, prosecute, negotiate, settle, contract, deal, and so on. These negative discretionary powers, in practice, provide administrators with more discretionary clout than positive discretionary powers, because it is far more difficult to check the former than the latter. That is, action, simply because it is action, is easier to control than inaction because checks are designed mostly to cope with abusive action, not abusive inaction.

For those interested in the problems of implementing public policies, the above has obvious implications. Through failing to act, or acting feebly, administrators can use their discretionary powers to help ensure the failure of certain duly authorized public programs under their jurisdiction that they disfavor. Although courts have ruled that administrators are not free to use their discretionary authority to block the implementation of programs authorized by Congress or to prevent persons from receiving their statutory entitlements, strong-willed administrators may nevertheless have their way in most instances, especially because forcing administrators to comply with statutory demands through court action is so difficult.[7] As Davis and Pierce concluded: "Judicial review of agency action can never be more than a partial solution to the problem of discretion."[1] "Federal agencies take millions of actions every year. It is unrealistic to expect courts to identify or deter each occasional case in which agencies abuse their discretion."[4,8] Besides, courts work too slowly, frequently acting after the damage has been done (after administrators have achieved their purpose).

When we think of the discretionary power of administrators, we probably think in terms of how administrative officials may employ their broad discretion to say yes or no to certain major program proposals. For example, in *D.C. Federation of Civic Associations v. Volpe*, 459 F.2d 1231 (1971), John Volpe, then Secretary of Transportation, used his discretion to approve construction of the Three Sisters Bridge, a controversial project vehemently opposed by many civic associations and environmentalists. Although Volpe's decision essentially constituted an abuse of discretion in the eyes of Judge Bazelon, the *Volpe* case served, inter alia, to demonstrate the vast discretionary powers administrators possess to make final decisions, thus likely determining the fate of major public programs. It is true that administrators possess great discretionary powers in making final decisions, but Davis holds that administrators' interim decisions may actually carry more weight than their final decisions.[4] Interim actions may be more subtle, but they can nevertheless make or break programs. In essence, interim decisions determine what steps, if any, should be taken to reach some end. Of course, an administrator's interim decisions play a significant role in determining the possible ends that will result. Typically, agency administrators use their discretion to make interim decisions in response to such key questions as: Should we investigate the X Company? Should we institute an investigation proceeding? Should we make it a prosecutory proceeding? Or should we make it somewhat one and somewhat the other, allowing its nature to change as it progresses? Should we give X a chance to escape by agreeing to comply? Or should we make an example of X? Should we start a cease-and-desist order proceeding, or should we recommend a criminal prosecution to the Department of Justice?[4]

Such interim questions appear to be endless. Yet, how each question is answered may make a big difference to, say, Company X, as X may be vitally affected at every step. Even if it is found guilty of nothing, the investigation may cost half a million dollars. Or its license worth

millions of dollars may be jeopardized. Adverse publicity may cripple its business.[9–11] Discretionary interim decision making may also play a critical role in determining the fate of public policies. In *Implementation*, Jeffrey Pressman and Aaron Wildavsky held that success in implementing public policy programs depends heavily on whether administrators make the vital discretionary interim decisions that permit programs to pass the crucial clearance points necessary for program survival.[3] In sum, dramatic final actions by public agencies may make frontpage news headlines ("Fed hikes interest rates against Bush's wishes"), but the daily, routine, nonnewsworthy interim decisions ("Fed decides to discount Labor Department's 2002 projection on unemployment") are largely responsible for preventing such agency headline stories from ever occurring.

Thus far, administrative discretion has been defined in the context of substantive decision making, but the scope of informal discretion extends much further. Says Davis: "Discretion is not limited to substantive choices but extends to procedures, methods, forms, timing, degrees of emphasis, and many other subsidiary factors."[3] Actually, because administrative law focuses on procedural due process, administrative law scholars and the courts are not so much interested in what substantive choices were made, but in how discretion was used by administrators in making their choices. Fig. 2 illustrates how administrators can ideally exercise their discretion in resolving an administrative problem. This simple model conveys that to resolve an administrative problem, administrators would first have to employ discretion, acknowledge the problem, discover the relevant facts, and then use discretion to search for those applicable laws, rules, and so on, that would settle the matter. But this ideal conceptualization is grossly complicated in reality. In the real world, administrators may use their discretionary powers to deny that a problem even exists. This action in itself must be regarded as a powerful exercise of discretion.

Thus, even if administrators acknowledge the existence of the problem, discretion may be used to define it in a particular way. Naturally, the discretion to define the problem in various ways provides administrators with the flexibility to arrive at different possible solutions. In addition, administrators can employ their discretion to determine what facts are relevant and what laws, rules, and so on, are pertinent. Of course, the discretion to include and exclude facts that are perceived as relevant or irrelevant allows administrators the opportunity to apply

| Administrative problem | Discovery of relevant facts | Application of relevant laws, rules, etc., to facts | Responsible administrative decision |

Fig. 2 Simplistic, ideal exercise of discretion.

or not to apply various laws, rules, and so forth, because the facts of a situation obviously determine what laws and rules should be applied.

CONCLUSION

Discretionary decisions are also clouded by administrators past experiences, present environmental demands, politics, and personal values. Regarding police discretion, Joel Samaha commented: "Discretion creates an enormous gap between what law books say and what law officers actually do, because class, race, economics, and politics influence discretion."[12] Uncertainty also plays an intervening role. A decision as to what is desirable may include not only weighing desirability, but also guessing about unknown facts and making a judgment about doubtful law, and the mind that makes the decision does not necessarily separate facts, law, and discretion. Furthermore, the term discretion may or may not include the judgment that goes into finding facts from conflicting evidence and into interpreting unclear law; the usage is divided.[13] In sum, discretionary decisions are complicated informal administrative actions that involve factors and processes that are extremely difficult to pinpoint and assess. It is partly for these reasons that abuses of administrative discretion are hard to prove, especially if bad faith must be shown to substantiate the charge that administrators abused their discretionary authority when reaching a decision.[14]

REFERENCES

1. Davis, K.C.; Pierce, R.J., Jr. *Administrative Law Treatise,* 3rd Ed.; Little, Brown, and Co.: Boston, 1994; Vol. 1, p. 22; Vol. 3, chapt. 17; p. 105.

2. Mashaw, J.L. *Due Process in the Administrative State*; Yale University Press: New Haven, 1985; 12–28.

3. Davis, K.C. *Discretionary Justice: A Preliminary Inquiry*; Greenwood: Westport, CT, 1980; 4–5. This book is a reprint of his classic work first published by University of Illinois Press (Urbana, 1969).

4. Davis, K.C. *Administrative Law: Cases-Text-Problems*; West Publishing Company: St. Paul, MN, 1977; 440–447.

5. Koenig, L.W. *The Chief Executive,* 5th Ed.; Harcourt Brace Jovanovich, Publishers: New York, 1986; especially chap. 1.

6. Thomas, N.C.; Pika, J.A.; Watson, R.A. *The Politics of The Presidency,* 3rd Ed.; Congressional Quarterly Press: Washington, D.C., 1994; pp. 23–37, 434–453.

7. For a discussion of such court rulings see, Warren, K.F. A special deconcentration: A problem greater than school desegregation. Adm. Law Rev., **Fall 1977**, *29*, 577–99.

8. Pierce, R.J., Jr.; Shapiro, S.A.; Verkuil, P.R. *Administrative Law in Process,* 3rd Ed.; Foundation Press: New York, NY, 1999; 132–139.

9. Pressman, J.; Wildavsky, A. *Implementation*; University of California Press: Berkeley, 1973; chaps. 1–3.

10. Mazmanian, D.A.; Sabatier, P.A. *Implementation and Public Policy*; Scott, Foresman: Glenview, IL, 1983; especially chaps. 1–3.

11. Durant, R.F. EPA, TVA and pollution control: Implications for a theory of regulatory policy implementation. Public Adm. Rev. **July/August 1984**, *44*, 305–313.

12. Samaha, J. *Criminal Law,* 2nd Ed.; West Publishing Company: St. Paul, MN, 1987; 14.

13. See, for example, the court's arguments in defense of the broad use of discretion in *United States v. International Telephone Corp. and Hartford Fire Insurance Co.*, 349 F.Supp. 22 (1972). It is not as necessary to prove bad faith today because good faith cannot be used as a defense when constitutional rights are violated by public officials.

14. Samaha, J. Some Reflections on the Anglo-Saxon Heritage of Discretionary Justice. In *Social Psychology and Discretionary Law*; Abt, L.E., Stuart, I.R., Eds.; Van Nostrand Reinhold: New York, 1979; 4.

Agricultural Policy

William P. Browne
Central Michigan University, Mount Pleasant, Michigan, U.S.A.

INTRODUCTION

Agricultural policy was once synonymous with farm (and ranch) public policy, the actions of U.S. government to modernize and industrialize producers of food and fiber commodities away from subsistence agrarianism. Thus, agricultural policy has been categorized as economic policy, or sector support. Today this is a misleading description. The evolution of modernizing agricultural policy touches myriad domestic social and international affairs matters through a formidable Agricultural Establishment. Issues of hunger, food safety and nutrition, trade, world food needs, environmental degradation, soil and water conservation, farm worker status and protection, rural poverty, and rural development are each institutionally central to contemporary agricultural policy.

POLICY INNOVATION: THE CREATION OF AN AMERICAN AGRICULTURAL ESTABLISHMENT

Public policies to benefit from American food and fiber producers understandably predate the formation of the Republic.[1] Farmers and what they produced were assets deserving of attention. That should hardly be surprising since both British sovereigns and constitutional lawmakers governed lands dominated and hopefully stabilized by farmers and ranchers once the wilderness trail blazers and adventurers passed through. The early Americas were truly low-density rural societies, characterized by small, family-controlled farms, except in the South where large plantation owners shared space with generally small-scale growers, often tenants.[2]

Policy debates over improving the status of farmers flourished for 20 years prior to the Civil War; farm prosperity was of obvious value to national growth. Resolution of these debates proved impossible due to national geographic divisions. With the outbreak of war and with a shaken northern electorate, otherwise divided Republicans quickly coalesced to pass popular legislation intended to keep their party in congressional control.[3] Southern congressional members who had withdrawn from Washington were no longer an obstacle to public policy that assisted small landowners. In 1862, four significant acts were passed: the first Homestead Act, to provide tracts of federal land to new small-scale settlers; the Morrill Act, which deeded federal lands to the states for use in capitalizing state "land grant" colleges of agriculture and mechanics; the establishment of the U.S. Department of Agriculture (USDA), as a small agency to identify and promote proper seeds and plants to growers who lacked both funds and horticultural knowledge; and the Railroad Act, which subsidized railroad expansion and, incidentally, brought means of transportation for farm supplies to the West and farm products to the East.

Although these distinctive policy innovations were administratively unplanned by politically troubled lawmakers and rarely seen by any contemporaries as an integrated approach to agrarian modernization, they proved to be just that.[4] New federal and state institutions were being created to serve an ever-expanding cadre of American family farmers. Science and discovery were being put in motion through the creation of public sector experts who could bring applied knowledge to farmers.

Expertise and administrative outreach were facilitated throughout the remainder of the nineteenth century, in no small part because so many farmers were not commercially viable. The states were building their land grant colleges and creating state departments of agriculture to promote farming and ranching. Because so few farmers availed themselves of educational services, many state institutions employed extension administrators to work personally with farmers, usually housing these case workers within county governments.[5]

The federal government responded similarly. Legislation created federal agricultural experiment stations in 1893, locating them within the states and usually adjacent to land grant colleges. These nonintegrated institutions were to engage applied science even further, conducting research specifically on local agricultural problems and local farm failures. The Black land grants were created in 1890, to bring science, education, and outreach to large numbers of unserved southern farmers. The USDA was given full cabinet status in 1889, after intensive farm lobbying. Thus, an ever-growing department could represent its increasing number of programs on an equal footing with those of military, foreign affairs, public lands, and economic policy makers. Finally, in 1914, the

Encyclopedia of Public Administration and Public Policy
DOI: 10.1081/E-EPAP 120012940

federal government passed an extension act to ensure a national farm outreach policy and join federal agricultural institutions to those of the states and counties in a highly decentralized process.

By World War I, two lasting innovations of general policy importance to the development of modern public administration had occurred. First, an unprecedented network of federal institutions had been created in a laissez-faire American government. Big government, fostering expertise and promoting applied science was in place; its institutions provided a mélange of policy for federal lawmakers to oversee, fund, reconsider, and recast into the twenty-first century. Second, what public administration scholars refer to as "picket-fence federalism" was in practice on a large scale. The plight of American farmers, chronically plagued by low prices and extensive supplies of their products, became a joint undertaking of all three levels of American government. No level was truly "in charge." Agricultural specialists emerged at each level, maintained an ongoing dialog with one another, relied on often shared field administrators to demonstrate institutional worth, and provided mutual support both administratively and politically. It was little wonder that, in the 1950s, economist Theodore Shultz looked back at this maze of public institutions and pro-farm sector policies and almost admiringly labeled it the "Agricultural Establishment".[6]

POLICY EFFECTS, POLICY EVOLUTION

The concept of Establishment unwittingly communicates the impression of a favored elite; and, surely, agricultural institutions brought elitism to American farming. Farmers who were better prepared, better funded, and more likely to join in local organizations were also more likely to gain educations for themselves and family members, pay attention to agricultural field administrators, and employ applied science and its technology.[4] As a consequence, larger-scale farmers gained the most from publicly assisted technological adaptation as early innovators. They then produced greater amounts of commodities, did so at lower costs, and at least for the short term gained profits even with low prices. Smaller-scale, less-positioned farmers did not, bringing poverty, economic failure, and farm exits. Larger-scale neighbors having excess capital assets in turn purchased their lands. The ongoing demise of the subsistence, peasant farmers of America led to the emergence of commercial farm elites who made use of Establishment resources.

Agricultural policy prior to and just after 1900 provided more than field administration services to producers. A regulatory era ensued. Substantive legislation provided opportunities to those who could and would take them, which again disproportionately meant farm elites. Policies to federally fund irrigation and drainage were established, as were programs for land improvement to facilitate production. Both farmer associations and marketing cooperatives were subsidized. Local farm bureaus were encouraged to form with institutional assistance. Loans and credit were extended to cooperatives. The cooperatives were freed from antitrust laws and assisted in marketing safe products. The net effect was to give agricultural producers special marketing and political status and, more important, lower their cost of production due to federal contributions.

The legacy of such opportunistic policy lingers on. The USDA still supports and regulates cooperatives. Food handlers are inspected. Water projects, loan programs, and farm credit remain consequential components of agricultural policy, in part because of strong state government advocacy. The USDA's Forest Service provides roads through national forests to subsidize lumber companies. Public policy makers, accordingly, struggle to supervise and reshape the allocation of policy set in motion over 100 years ago. They engage these evaluative struggles with the same institutional supporters who promoted farm assistance in its beginning, agricultural field administrators with their local farm connections and technological interests.[7] Thus, administrative components of agricultural public policy serve as advocates of both continued and reformulated service and regulatory policy, much as did the many patronage appointees in agriculture in the nineteenth century. While that early generation of agricultural experts capitalized on their political contacts at home and in Washington, modern field administrators more fully embrace the expert guise of home state economists, horticulturalists, agronomists, and nutritionists. The single constant is that a locally and professionally fragmented array of field administrators sets much of the agenda and dominates many of the debates over future agricultural policy.

THE CREATION OF MARKET POLICY: THE MAJOR CONCERN

Agriculture enjoyed several years of good production and high prices in the early twentieth century, through World War I. The transition to commercial agriculture flourished as a result, solidifying cooperation between producers and field administrators. However, commercial producers, often indebted by expansion, were ill prepared for a postwar fall off in demand and the unavoidable collapse of prices. Agricultural depression began in 1920, predating general economic collapse by 10 years. Both agricultural institutions and newly strong farmer organizations became advocates of direct government intervention in the farm economy, displacing the emphasis on more and better farm services and regulation.

It was not until 1933 that policy makers responded to grassroots demands and moved to directly subsidize farmers by intervening in the marketplace of production and sales. That action, which was intended to raise prices by limiting production, set in motion a complex series of policies that would essentially drive agricultural policy throughout the century. The policy vehicles were the Agricultural Adjustment Acts of 1933 and 1938, along with the Soil Conservation and Domestic Allotment Act of 1936.[8]

The featured program types that evolved from this legislation included marketing orders, which licensed agreements by commodity cooperatives to hold exclusive sales rights to their sorts of products by negotiating pricing and trade practices; production controls, either mandatory or voluntary, which limited grower planting in return for financial payments; direct supports, payments made by the federal government to landowners, for cutting back production or some other contribution to policy, such as constructing soil conservation projects; and loan guarantees, which provided preproduction loans to farmers at guaranteed rates and allowed producers to voluntarily forfeit crops to government if commodity prices fell below loan rate levels.

Four other consequential and lasting features were introduced into agricultural policy by these programs. First, it was increasingly logical to wrap the many service, regulatory, and market policies of agriculture into one extensive renewable bill, called an omnibus act. These farm bills allowed policy makers to oversee and recast policy in cycles that concentrated attention to agriculture's many details. Second, local (mostly county) and state farmer-operated committees were established to rule on producer eligibility for the previous programs. Third, policies were set by individual commodity, with no general allocation scheme and the omission of numerous products. Fourth, the largest payments and benefits accrued to the largest producers, the most commercially able farmers. Only by rewarding the largest producers would these growers cut significant sums of production and effect prices. Small-scale farmers and their small cuts in production would negligibly influence prices. Of course, this policy rewarded those who had found favor with institutional administrators. Moreover, programs for the rural poor, for small farms, and for tenants were strongly resisted by administrators and given diminished attention in the New Deal and beyond.

Agricultural policy, through 2002, saw a confusing mix of these programs recurring, coming and going, and being constantly readjusted from one omnibus farm bill to another. Variances in crop prices, partisan politics, con-

gressional control, and interest group strength heavily affected changes. For example, after the House and Senate agricultural committees lost control, Congress passed the Federal Agriculture Improvement and Reform Act (FAIR) as the 1996 farm bill. This act was directed by congressional leaders who had little contact with agricultural professionals.[3] Their intent was to phase out intervention and all commodity support programs by 2002, letting the marketplace then set prices.[9] That act provided large direct payments as phase-outs to farmers over a 7-year period; it was later supplemented with increased emergency direct payments from 1998 through 2001. In 2002, with farm prices again depressed, Congress, with the committees once more in control, reversed FAIR and reinstituted commodity programs. A review of price policy effectiveness was scheduled for 2008. Market intervention in farm incomes and pricing thus have been the central but far from only concern of federal policy makers for over three-quarters of a century.

AN EXPANDED AGRICULTURAL POLICY AGENDA

Even if market intervention, or price policy, remains the central concern of federal officials, that focus is difficult to maintain. Trade-offs are necessary. As farm voters diminish in number, as the comparative economic contribution of agriculture shrinks, and as nonfarm citizens expect greater federal attention to other issues of food and fiber production, agricultural officials expand their policy agenda. Omnibus farm bills and the already extensive base of agricultural institutions make that possible, through simple accommodation.[10]

The regulatory era of agricultural policy instituted programs to inspect meat-packing plants, set standards for food processing, and protect against manipulative pricing and food contamination by middle market businesses that brought products to consumers. Current policies extend these efforts and bring federal agencies into a review of emerging citizen worries, such as pesticide contamination and genetically engineered crops. Thus, much of the ongoing work of agricultural policy agencies is evolutionary in detail and politically responsive to shifting public opinion.

As are all public agencies, however, agricultural officials are often charged with having less than total loyalty to new agenda items and nontraditional clientele. Often, new legislation must be initiated to legitimize agency actions and overcome resistance. Omnibus farm bills have been expansive; statutes grew in length from a few dozen pages in the 1960s to over 700 in 1990. These have added important dimensions to what was once economic policy.[11]

In 1964, the provision of food stamps to low-income Americans for use in making retail purchases was made a "permanent" agricultural agency responsibility. Supplemental assistance to low-income children and mothers followed in later years, as did a renewed USDA emphasis on nutrition. The 1973 Agriculture and Consumer Protection Act responded to twin political realities: inflation and consumers. Basic price program features were remixed to provide more direct payments to farmers, keep food prices low, and expand production with overseas markets in mind. After 1973, both consumer matters and international trade became ever more important components of agricultural policy, particularly in efforts to determine which user preferences increased product sales. Environmental advocates turned considerable attention to the farm bill in 1985, notably in preserving prairies and wetlands. As that bill passed, it was clear that environmental interests had attached themselves to existing soil and water programs and became long-term partners in policy making. Irrigation use, the release of genetically engineered products, safe food, erosion, and groundwater contamination all became ongoing issues. In sum, a variety of social causes, all of which intermingle, are now enmeshed in the economics of commercial farming and food production.

CONCLUSION

Today's U.S. agricultural policy should be understood as general social policy, taking place in a global economy. In that economy, America is a huge food exporter and gigantic food importer. Agricultural policy in that context struggles with three problems: continued fostering of U.S. commercial production by large-scale farms, developing commercially viable producers of organic and sustainable farms that satisfy noneconomic public food wants, and integrating often poorly informed social values about food safety and health into economic policies of production and trade. Integration is the critical challenge: integrating sound trade practices that ensure worldwide environmental standards in producing safe foods; integrating USDA and other agricultural institutions with the interrelated policies of the Food and Drug Administration and the Environmental Protection Agency; and integrating organic and sustainable producers, as favored by the public, into a dominant system of large-scale producers and into the commercially directed Agricultural Establishment.

REFERENCES

1. Benedict, M.R. *Farm Policies of the United States, 1750–1950*; Twentieth Century Fund, 1953.
2. Cochrane, W. *The Development of American Agriculture: A Historical Analysis*; University of Minnesota Press, 1979.
3. Scheingate, A.D. *The Rise of the Agricultural Welfare State: Institutions and Interest Group Power in the United States, France, and Japan*; Princeton University Press, 2001.
4. Browne, W.P. *The Failure of National Rural Policy: Institutions and Interests*; Georgetown University Press, 2001.
5. Baker, G.L. *The County Agent*; University of Chicago Press, 1939.
6. Schultz, T.W. *The Economic Organization of Agriculture*; McGraw-Hill, 1953.
7. Hallberg, M.C. *Policy for American Agriculture: Choices and Consequences*; Iowa State University Press, 1992.
8. Bowers, D.E.; Rasmussen, W.D.; Baker, G.L. *History of Agricultural Price Support and Adjustment Programs, 1933–84*; Agricultural Information Bulletin, Economic Research Service, U.S. Department of Agriculture: Washington, DC, 1984; Vol. 485.
9. Orden, D.; Paarlberg, R.; Roe, T. *Policy Reform in American Agriculture: Analysis and Prognosis*; University of Chicago Press, 1999.
10. Browne, W.P. *Private Interests, Public Policy, and American Agriculture*; University Press of Kansas, 1988.
11. Browne, W.P. *Cultivating Congress: Constituents, Issues, and Agricultural Policymaking*; University Press of Kansas, 1995.

Allocation Formula in Budgeting

Patricia Moore
Kean University, Union, New Jersey, U.S.A.

INTRODUCTION

Allocation by formula is one of the decision rules used in the United States by budgeters to allocate scarce resources in the public sector. Other rules include budget allocation in terms of existing base plus a fair share of the increment or decrement, top-down containment rules and targets and relative merit.[1] Mikesell described an allocation formula as a quantitative mathematical equation used to distribute grant funds to eligible recipients.[2] Wildavsky suggested that allocation formulas for public-sector program expenditures evolved out of recurrent budget processes.[3] Usually, an allocation formula is specified in legislation, but sometimes it is provided by regulation.

In the Western world, the underlying theory surrounding formula allocation seems to be a calculative logic that formulas are sensitive to the concerns of democratic government. These concerns include equity, efficiency, and effectiveness of service provision on behalf of the (voting) population. In the United States, prior to World War II, budget allocations were often based on historical precedent or negotiation; however, since that time, federal and state governments have progressively shifted in favor of distributing aid to states and localities by formulas.[4] This shift to formula allocation may have dampened the political problems naturally arising from the annual competitive budget appropriation process in Congress at the federal and state levels of government.[5]

A good allocation formula should be free from perverse manipulations, open to review, and should distribute resources equitably across governmental units. Moreover, it should be understandable, equitable, adequate, and predictable. It should also be reasonable in reporting requirements, fiscally accountable, and politically acceptable.[6] Grizzle[1] suggested that the design of an allocation formula should give primary consideration to program objectives, operational measures of objectives, data availability, and simple methods.

Although formulas can be used to direct funds to individual service providers, historically, they have been directed at aggregations of service providers: state governments, hospitals, counties, municipalities, and school districts. In the United States, formulas are frequently used to determine allocation levels for various intergovernmental fund transfers, such as general revenue sharing, block grants, and categorical grants.[7] While formulas are used to allocate resources for many different governmental functions, they are most widely used in education, health, housing, and commerce.[8]

WHY ARE ALLOCATION FORMULAS USED WIDELY IN BUDGETING?

Formula allocation is appealing in public budgeting, because it has several advantages. Formula allocation makes justification for budget requests easier. It also has an appearance of neutrality and rationality, because a formula allocation is expressed as a mathematical equation. Using a precise mathematical formula can make the allocation plan less controversial and, therefore, more politically acceptable. ''A multitude of (redundant) statistical variables may be politically necessary to rationalize a program, to at least give the appearance of responding to special circumstance.''[9]

Furthermore, allocation formulas allow for greater precision and accuracy and thus save legislative time and energy in arguing about the intended appropriation. Allocation formulas provide local government a reasonable assurance of the general level of funding they are to expect; thus, they keep planning from being chaotic. Another advantage of formula allocation is that it suggests consistency and fairness. When the objective is equalization, allocation formulas seem to be an effective instrument for redistributing public resources. Their transparency and stability tend to reduce the possibility of manipulation, therefore, facilitating equity.

A well-designed allocation formula simplifies program administration, reduces paperwork, as well as provides state and local governments a reasonable degree of fiscal certainty. In addition, formula allocations reduce the discretion of federal administrators in the review process, allowing public administrators to insulate themselves from political pressures.

TECHNICAL NATURE OF ALLOCATION FORMULAS

The typical allocation formula has a complex structure entailing the identification of several variables. For example, the United States Department of Agriculture

Encyclopedia of Public Administration and Public Policy
DOI: 10.1081/E-EPAP 120010986

allocates funds to school districts for their Breakfast Program using the following formula:

$$M = NAP_1*NPB + NAP_2*NFB + NAP_3*NRB$$

$$+ (NPB + NFB + NRB)*0.06 + AD$$

M = The amount of federal funds given the school district.

NAP_1 = A National Average Payment.

NAP_2 = A National Average Payment prescribed for free breakfasts.

NAP_3 = A National Average Payment for reduced priced breakfasts.

NRB = Number of reduced priced breakfasts.

NFB = Number of free breakfasts.

Allocations to school districts are calculated by multiplying the number of paid breakfasts served to eligible children during the fiscal year by a National Average Payment (NAP); multiplying the number of breakfasts served free to eligible children by a NAP prescribed by the Secretary of Agriculture for free breakfasts; and multiplying the number of reduced price breakfasts served to eligible children by a NAP prescribed by the Secretary for reduced priced breakfasts. School districts also receive an additional six cents for every breakfast served. Schools with a high percentage of needy children and high breakfast costs may receive additional payments.[10]

In adopting allocation formulas, the United States Congress commonly uses measures that closely represent at least one of the following characteristics of the recipient government: "need," "capability," and "effort."[11] Kreps and Slater suggested that few allocation formulas include all three measures, however, more than half include a measure of need. "Need" often refers to the population to be served, while "capability" refers to the ability of a jurisdiction to meet the defined need from local or state funds. "Effort" refers to the actual amounts of local or state revenues available for the need. One common measure of "capability" is per capita income. School districts often use per pupil property values as a measure of "need," while per pupil expenditures is frequently used to measure "effort."

TYPES OF ALLOCATION FORMULAS

Formulas may be demand driven or resource constrained.[1] The main characteristic of a demand-driven formula is that allocations are driven by the need of the different units, e.g., school districts, states, or municipalities. It is mainly used to stimulate action by the recipient government as much as possible. Demand-driven formulas

are more appropriate when policy makers value controlling agency behavior more than agency spending.[12] One of the disadvantages of a demand-driven formula is its unpredictability in terms of the level of total spending that will result. Medicaid in the states and the federal government shares an example of a demand-driven formula. Total spending depends on the number of people entitled to have their medical care paid for by the government, those who apply for help, and the basket of services for which the states reimburse health care providers.

On the other hand, resource-constrained formulas place a limit on the resources available for a specific purpose. Each unit's allocation is determined by its percentage of the total appropriation. An example of a resource-constrained formula is the equation used to allocate resources to the airline industry in the aftermath of the September 11, 2001, attack on the World Trade Center in New York City. According to the Air Transportation Safety and System Stabilization Act, the federal funding formula was based on each carrier's share of the industry's flying capacity, measured in available seat miles.[13] Specifically, the allocation for each airline was the total aid provided by the federal government multiplied by the percent of the industry's total flying capacity, i.e., number of seats multiplied by total miles. This formula determined what fraction of the total appropriation each airline received. When controlling spending is more important, the resource-constrained funding formula is more likely to be effective in containing spending than demand-driven formulas.[12] The main difference between the two is that demand-driven formulas may not have funding ceilings but resource-constrained formulas do.

WEAKNESSES OF ALLOCATION FORMULAS

Allocation formulas are often incredibly complex.[14] Frequently, they require a bewildering combination of mathematical calculations, i.e., addition, multiplication, subtraction, squaring, and even quadratic equations that all too frequently produce unsatisfactory results. Quite often, they are not clearly understood by policy makers, program designers, or even the statisticians. Mathematical models, from which policy makers derive allocation formulas, fail, even with the best available data, to produce the desired allocation pattern, because models generally represent an oversimplification of the real world.

Although proponents of allocation formulas suggest that predictability is one of their strengths (especially when compared with policy makers' caprice), in many instances, public administrators find they cannot predict the results the formula will produce. Also, often, the formula or model does not reflect the complexity of natural and social phenomena. Unpredictability, as a result, cripples long-term planning and budgeting at all levels of government. This inability to plan, ironically, makes for poor policy execution because of the simplicity of the models and formulas.[4]

It is not an easy task to design a formula that closely approximates congressional intent; however, the job gets more difficult when the legislature does not make the goals and objectives of a particular program clear. As one might expect, a decision to adopt a specific formula involves a series of distinct prior choices. An inappropriate decision at any of these steps in the process may lead to a formula, which results in skewed allocations. Generally, in the United States, Congress does not legislate the use of direct measures in the mathematical formula, so statisticians have the arduous task of finding measures that adequately operationalize legislative intent. Quite often, this is not achieved.

A central dilemma for formula allocation is that while it simplifies justifications for budget requests, it frequently presents difficulties in reconciling various policy objectives. For instance, the U.S. Department of Transportation Highway Funding Formula attempts to meet a relatively large number of objectives, some of which are in conflict with one another. For example, one objective is to return funds to the states. At the same time, the program must address national goals and deal with "externalities," which often require redistributing resources from one state to another.[15]

PROBLEMS RELATING TO DATA SOURCE

Allocation formulas rely on data that need to be reliable and valid. But frequently, bias and corruption in the gathering and use of data create serious problems, which might not be easily corrected. For instance, the U.S. Department of Transportation developed a formula for allocating aid to the airline industry in the aftermath of the September 11, 2001, attack on the World Trade Center in New York City. Larry's Flying Service, one of the 112 airlines that recently received federal aid claimed that it was too honest to get its "fair share."[16] In other words, it suspected that other airlines might not have submitted valid data.

Another concern with formula allocation is that irrelevant or outdated factors often undermine the funding calculations for certain services. For example, the formula for apportioning federal highway funds among states is derived from a complicated set of calculations. The U.S. General Accounting Office (GAO) described the formula as cumbersome, relying on factors and data, which, in some cases, are outdated and irrelevant.[17]

In many cases, allocation measures are selected solely on the basis of of familiarity, plausibility, and ease of administration. One measure that is frequently used is per capita. States in the northeast tend to have an advantage when formulas are based on per capita, because they are more densely populated. Those in the south tend to fare better when the formula requires units of $1000 of personal income. On the other hand, states in the west topped distribution figures when the formula relied on a percentage of local general revenue.[18]

Furthermore, allocation formulas frequently require census data; however, census data have problems. Census data tend to undercount persons living in rural areas, ghetto areas, and large cities. Critics of the use of census data maintain that large numbers of Hispanics, African Americans, American Indians, and Asians are frequently missed by the census, with the undercount resulting in a loss of federal funds to minorities. But, others argue that the debate over the significance of the undercount has been highly distorted, even misleading.[18]

In terms of the fiscal stakes, the GAO 1998 study found that only 0.5% of the $185 billion distributed by the federal government was affected by the overall undercount.[18] The reason suggested is that population is only one of several factors in most federal grant formulas, and many programs designed to help distressed communities actually reduce funding when population increases. Even when grant increases are pegged to population gains, the critical factor for a given jurisdiction is not merely its absolute population, but its population relative to other jurisdictions—a result that can obviously hurt as well as help minorities.

However difficult it may be to understand and evaluate the performance of a formula, the task of foreseeing and assuring good performance is even more difficult.[11] There seems to be three issues. First, the formula may require data that cannot be updated frequently. Policy makers often argue that the formula makes allowances for the data. But often, the degree of distortion caused by the use of obsolescent data cannot be estimated precisely at the time allocations are made. Second, data, which can be updated, may depart from their historical behavior and from their assumed stable relationships with other variables. Third, the social or economic problem to which the program is directed may evolve in such a way that the measure chosen may no longer be the most relevant measure available.

CONCLUSION

Allocation formulas reflect political and economic relationships among federal, state, and local governments. They are effective and convenient tools used to translate congressional intent. When used correctly, they give a predictable framework for government organizations to use to meet needs through goal setting, careful planning, control, oversight, and review. Formula allocation generally guarantees funds to state and local governments based on economic or demographic factors outlined in the formula. Citizens tend to be accepting of allocations that are based on formulas, because they have an aura of objectivity and fairness. Nevertheless, their effectiveness can be severely hampered by data that are stale, inaccurate, and irrelevant.

REFERENCES

1. Grizzle, G. Five Issues in Budgeting and Financial Management. In *Handbook of Public Administration*; Rabin, J., Bartley, H., Miller, G., Eds.; Marcel Dekker Publishers: New York, 1989; 197–206.

2. Mikesell, J. *Fiscal Administration: Analysis and Applications for the Public Sector*; Harcourt Brace Publishers: Orlando, FL, 1999.

3. Wildavsky, A. *The Politics of the Budgetary Process*; Little Brown: Boston, MA, 1979.

4. Fessler, W. *The Politics of the Administrative Process*; Chatham House Publishers: New Jersey, 1996.

5. Dugdale, P. The better practice program funding formula. Aust. J. Public Adm. **1997**, *56* (3), 65–67.

6. Parish, T. *Removing Incentives for Restrictive Placements. Fiscal Issues in Special Education*; CSEF Policy Paper 4, US Department of Education: Washington, DC, 1995, ED.377608.

7. Bowman, A.; Kearney, R. *State and Local Government*; Houghton Mifflin Company: Boston, MA, 2002.

8. U.S. General Accounting Office. *Federal Funding 2001*; (http://financenet.gov).

9. Spencer, B. Technical issues in allocation formula design. Public Adm. Rev. **1982**, *42*, 524–529.

10. General Service Administration, Office of Government Policy (M), Office of Acquisition Policy (MV), Government Information System Division (MVS), and Federal Domestic Assistance Catalog Staff. *11.553 School Breakfast Program*; www.cfda.gov.

11. Kreps, J.; Slater, C. *Report on Statistics for Allocation Formulae*; Statistical Policy Working Paper, Federal Committee on Statistical Methods: Washington, DC, 1978 (NTIS PB86-211521/AS).

12. Cothran, D. Some sources of budgeting accountability. Public Budg. Finance **1986**, *6*, 45–62.

13. United States Public Law 107-42, Washington, DC, September 22, 2001.

14. Parry, D. *The Highway Trust Fund Uses a Complicated Allocation Formula EconomicResearch Service*; Agriculture Information Bulletin, USDA: Washington, DC, August 1999; 3. http://www.ers.usda.gov/publications/aib753b.

15. Parry, D. *The Highway Funding Has Been Criticized*; Agriculture Information Bulletin, Economic Research Service, USDA: Washington, DC, August 1999; 4–5. http://www.ers.usda.gov/publications/aib753-1.

16. O'Donnell, J. Airline bailout grants. USA Today, Money Sec. B **November 6, 2001**.

17. U.S. General Accounting Office. Highway Funding Alternatives for Distributing Federal Funds. In *Report to Congressional Committees*; November, 1995, GA1.13:RCED-96-6 ([0546-D(MF)].

18. Skerry, P. *Race, Group Identity and the Evasion of Politics*; Brookings Institution Press: Washington, DC, 2000.

Annexation

Jered B. Carr
Wayne State University, Detroit, Michigan, U.S.A.

Richard C. Feiock
Florida State University, Tallahassee, Florida, U.S.A.

INTRODUCTION

Annexation is the legal process whereby municipalities add land, and usually population, to their boundaries. In some instances, these actions enable the provision of entirely new services to the territories annexed; in others, they enable higher levels of already existing services; and yet in others, the level and mix of public services do not change, but the responsibility for providing these services is transferred from another jurisdiction such as a township, county, or special district government to a municipal government.

Although annexation involves the extension of the entire institution of municipal government, it is the expansion of city services that typically receives the most attention. It is difficult to overstate the central role service provision plays in annexation. Annexation is a process that, in many instances, proceeds literally property by property, as services are exchanged for city residence. As the most tangible benefit offered to suburban residents, city services are an inducement used by the city to encourage suburban property owners to join the city. Consequently, annexation issues revolve around service provision and the revenues necessary to pay for them. In some instances, municipal boundary expansion may result in one jurisdiction seizing another's revenue base. When officials from other local governments oppose annexation proposals, it is usually because of the effect of these annexations on their jurisdiction's ability, real or perceived, to fund current and future service levels.

Given the central role of service provision in annexation, the fiscal impact of these actions are critical. However, current research has shown that the fiscal impact of annexation is not well understood.[1] Few local governments have the time and resources to undertake comprehensive fiscal analyses of annexation activities. Moreover, studies show that annexation is not necessarily a "winner take all" process.[1] Annexation can be fiscally advantageous for both, one, or neither community. Conventional wisdom holds that annexation is fiscally beneficial to the annexing municipality and fiscally disastrous for the government losing the territory. However, in practice, the fiscal impact of annexations is far more complex.

Despite the key roles that service provision and financing play in municipal annexation, the racial and income disparities present in communities also influence annexation patterns. Numerous accounts have chronicled the ways in which annexation has been used to intentionally alter the racial composition of cities, and conversely, how cities have refrained from annexing areas comprised largely of racial minorities or low-income populations.[2] Importantly, the full effects of municipal annexation on the racial composition of a community may become obvious only when annexations are viewed on a cumulative basis.[3,4]

KEY STAKEHOLDERS IN ANNEXATION

Three stakeholders are most often at the center of municipal annexation activity: municipal officials, suburban residents, and the officials of other local governments. In some instances, city residents and state legislators may also become important players in these actions. Whether these stakeholders choose to become involved in a proposed annexation depends on the incentives created by the characteristics (e.g., land area, population demographics, land use) of the specific parcel considered for annexation; by how revenue sources and functional responsibilities are distributed among the local governments in the area; and by how difficult state annexation laws make their participation in the action. The role played by state laws in affecting the participation of the different stakeholders is discussed in detail in the next section.

Municipal Officials

Municipal officials in cities experiencing population growth and urbanization on their periphery will often view boundary expansion through annexation as desirable. The thinning and sorting of population that goes on in most urban areas works to diminish the revenue capacity of

DOI: 10.1081/E-EPAP 120010837

central cities, while also increasing the demand and need for public services in these cities. The availability of cheaper land, new housing, lower densities and suburban amenities encourage population dispersion and distribution throughout the metropolitan area. Deterioration of neighborhoods, decreased personal safety, and the widespread apprehension regarding low-income and minority group members all help to push affluent citizens to new residences in areas lying outside the city. Annexation is often seen as an important instrument by which municipal officials can maintain the city's economic base.[5]

Despite the attractiveness of annexation to municipal officials, whether it makes fiscal sense for a city is often unclear. Annexation may appear to be in the long-term fiscal interests of cities by expanding the property tax base and increasing revenues from user fees, utility charges, and sales taxes. Yet, in the short term, annexation can result in tremendous capital costs for the extension of services to new residents. Thus, while the annexed area may provide a fiscal surplus, it may also constrain policy options in the short run and affect the ability of a city to undertake other initiatives for years to come.[6] Even in the longer term, annexation may not prove to be in the fiscal interests of the annexing municipality. For instance, annexation may capture revenues from increased commercial development of the periphery of the municipality, but along with these gains may come increased costs from traffic congestion, and infrastructure provision and maintenance.[1]

State revenue-sharing programs are often an important motivating factor behind municipal expansion, especially where revenue distribution is linked to population or the location of revenue generation. Consequently, city officials may seek to annex territory less for its value in terms of property tax base than for the intergovernmental revenues attached to the area's population and the sales or income tax potential of its businesses.

The extension of municipal boundaries may reduce the costs of service provision borne by current city residents in two different ways. First, the additional customers provided through annexation may lead to lower unit costs produced by economies of scale. Second, annexation expands the base of taxable property that can be tapped to support municipal services. City residents may also see annexation as a way to achieve fiscal equivalence in the wider community. The city's infrastructure and services often directly or indirectly affect residents of bordering unincorporated areas. Thus, annexation can be a means to bring property owners into the municipality who were previously benefiting from these services at no cost.

However, annexed residents also have the right to participate in municipal elections. Adding a pool of new voters to the city can be controversial, and some city residents may oppose a proposed annexation because of its potential effect on municipal elections. In contrast, race has also been cited as the motivation behind the annexing of white suburban residents. In these instances, city officials have been accused of using annexation to add white population to a city that is nearing a majority-minority status.[2] Empirical analyses of state annexation patterns have linked reductions in the number of Black elected office-holders to aggressive annexation by communities.[4]

Suburban Residents

The incentives of suburban residents are less clear than those of city officials. Annexation can be a way to satisfy unmet service demands in these areas, and thus may be viewed as a means to expand the scope and quality of public services and to increase property values. However, while suburban residents may benefit from the extension of most services and infrastructure, they may instead prefer lower tax and service levels.[6] Also, suburban residents may resist annexation because they want to maintain the status quo of benefiting from city services and infrastructure at no cost. For example, suburbanites enjoy the benefits of the city's cultural amenities and physical infrastructure at no cost. In addition, some city services have regional effects, such as economic development and urban planning. Annexation can prevent suburban residents from exploiting the central city by imposing marginal costs without full repayment in terms of taxes, fees, or charges.

Even where suburban residents do not seek to "free ride" on city taxpayers, they may still resist annexation because they oppose having to share in the costs of redistributive services that they see as primarily benefiting inner-city residents. Ostensibly, city officials are motivated to add properties that cost less to support in services than they generate in tax revenue. This logic is usually apparent to suburban residents as well. Thus, the city must be able to convince them that services through the city will cost less than their other options.

Finally, for a variety of reasons, people within suburban areas and cities sort themselves in many ways. Members of different income groups tend to congregate to form relatively homogeneous communities, both inside and outside of cities. Suburban residents may resist annexation to preserve the "character" of their community, which they may define in various ways. Numerous anecdotal accounts exist of suburban residents resisting annexation to a city with substantial minority or poor populations. In other instances, opposition may be based on preserving area qualities, such as the rural nature of the neighborhood or low-density development.

Officials from Other Local Governments

The way that officials from local governments outside the annexing city view annexation depends greatly on how functional responsibilities have been divided among the local governments in the community. Conventional wisdom suggests annexation is a zero-sum game and that the other local governments in the region will always see expansion by neighboring jurisdictions as a threat to their own long-term viability. This is not always the case. In some instances, the annexation of the property displaces a service provider, such as a township, county, or special district government. The other local government may strongly oppose annexation to the city because the other government may suffer a loss of revenue from property and/or sales taxes. For example, opposition by county officials is more likely where county governments have made a significant commitment to providing municipal-level services to the unincorporated areas of the county.[7] However, in other instances, annexations may involve the acquisition of territory not previously receiving the services in question. The municipal expansion simply adds another layer of government with fundamentally different responsibilities to the property and no government is displaced. In this situation, other local governments may even support annexation to the city.

STATE STATUTORY REGIMES

State restrictions on local government powers are embodied in Dillon's Rule, which holds that local governments are "creatures of the state." As such, local government authority has to be granted by the state constitution or by legislative acts.

For states, the fundamental question is whether annexation is a technical exercise of matching political jurisdictions to service delivery boundaries, an exercise in political association, or a little of both. State legislatures have generally decided that it is a little of both, although they have balanced these two roles in different ways. The different ways that states have resolved this balance has been effectively captured by the Frank Sengstock's classification of annexation laws.[8] This five-part typology groups state annexation laws in terms of where the key decision-making authority is placed. It effectively answers the question: Of the three stakeholder groups described in the previous section, which one holds the balance of power to authorize annexations? Generally, each stakeholder has a role in the proceedings, but state law puts one in the favored position where their consent is required for annexation to occur. Given that this diverse set of actors may have different preferences for jurisdictional lines, the inclusion or exclusion of particular actors is expected to have important consequences for annexation activity.[9]

Regardless of whether it is explicitly stated, all state statutory regimes begin with the presumption that municipalities will generally seek to expand their boundaries. Some states provide municipalities with the authority to expand their boundaries essentially at will, trusting that city officials will not abuse this discretion and expand only where necessary to ensure efficient and equitable service delivery for the population in the area. Other state legislatures do not display the same level of confidence in municipal governments and require cities to obtain the permission of property owners before expanding. Yet others require that a third party make the decision, apparently trusting neither of the directly affected parties to rise above their own narrow interests on this issue.

Municipal Determination

In these states, municipal governments are authorized to extend their boundaries by the unilateral action of their governing bodies, typically by passing a municipal ordinance annexing the territory. States typically permit unilateral action only if the territory to be annexed meets specific requirements for urban character, such as contiguity, density, or extent of subdivision.[10] Some states also require that annexation be addressed in a comprehensive plan or overall strategy for annexation. Finally, states that allow unilateral annexation often stipulate that municipalities must produce service plans setting out the timetable for extension of services to the annexed territory.

Popular Determination

Under this approach, the affected electorate or property owners have the right to vote to determine if a municipal boundary change will take place. This approach is rooted in the philosophy that property owners should be able to choose the jurisdiction in which they live, not the other way around. Electors and property owners can grant approval by initiating annexation with a petition signed by a majority of electors and/or property owners in the territory to be annexed, by referendum, or by written permission filed subsequent to a muncipality's decision to pass an annexation ordinance or resolution.[10] In a few cases, a majority of electors and/or property owners have the power to veto an annexation action by petition or by filing written objections.[10]

Among popular determination states there are differences with regard to who may vote in annexation referenda. Generally, only the electorate and/or property owners within an area proposed for annexation are allowed to vote on a proposed action. However, in some states, the electors of the municipality may also vote. In a few states, the electors of the diminished territory, typically a county or township government, are also empowered to vote on the action. Referenda commonly require only a simple majority for approval. In cases where the electors of the city are empowered to vote, the two elections and results are usually considered separately, and double majorities are required to approve annexation. Importantly, many states also have provisions that permit annexation to occur without a referendum of property owners. In those instances where a super-majority of electors or property owners initiate annexation, all referenda requirements are generally waived. Depending on the state, a super-majority of 75% or 100% may be required to avoid the referendum provision.[10]

Judicial Determination

The final three categories represent different approaches to empowering third parties to approve annexations. The first of these third parties is the judiciary. In some states, courts are empowered to determine if an annexation may proceed, using guidelines and criteria established by the legislature. However, court review is usually limited to procedural or statutory compliance issues. Legislative guidelines usually do not empower courts to assess substantive issues, such as the prudence or equity of annexation, or to consider adverse fiscal impact on other local governments.[10]

Legislative Determination

The second third party authorized to approve annexations is the state legislature. Because legislatures have the power to create annexation statutes, this is more accurately viewed as the legislature simply retaining this authority. This approach is found most often in states that are highly urbanized and therefore possess little remaining unincorporated territory. For example, the states of New England typically do not have general statutes outlining the process for annexing unincorporated territory, because they lack unincorporated territory. Annexation in these states requires deannexing property from one municipality and annexing it to another.[10] In addition, in states where annexation procedures are too burdensome or nonexistent, municipal boundary changes may be made by special act of the state legislature.

Importantly, this approach provides a forum for other local government officials to participate in these decisions. Although the entire legislature must act on the annexation proposal, typically these local bills will not be put before the entire body until a consensus within the local delegation is achieved. The local delegation is unlikely to act, and therefore annexation will not occur, where there is conflict among the local governments about the proposed annexation.

Quasilegislative Determination

Finally, some states use independent, nonjudicial boards or tribunals to determine whether a proposed municipal annexation will occur. This approach provides for a more direct role by other local governments in annexation policy. Most states that use this approach provide for local commissions that consist of various local officials from within a county or group of counties. A few states have state boards with members appointed by the governor.[10]

PATTERNS OF ANNEXATION ACTIVITY ACROSS THE STATES

State annexation laws affect annexation patterns by providing incentives and disincentives for participation by key stakeholder groups.[7] The specific procedural constraints outlined in these laws make some options harder to achieve than others because some provisions necessitate the coordination of greater numbers of people. For example, rules requiring referenda and majority approval by property owners and/or city residents impose collective action barriers to effecting annexation as proponents must circulate petitions and/or get their supporters to the polls. In contrast, where state law permits boundaries to be extended by the unilateral action of municipal officials, no collective action is required. The need to act collectively to expand municipal boundaries means that those groups better able to organize and sustain these actions will be favored in the process. Consequently, local boundaries will often be drawn to match the preference of those groups that have an advantage under the procedure. Table 1 provides a listing of municipal annexation activity ranked by state.

Annexation as Strategic Action

Despite the widespread usage of the Sengstock typology to classify annexations laws, state annexation regimes often do not fit into a single Sengstock classification, but instead have elements of two or more different types.[10] For instance, many states permit annexation to be initiated by municipalities and property owners.[10] Multiple state procedures create opportunities for stakeholders to manage the scope of conflict. As E.E. Schattschneider recognized in 1960, the outcome of any conflict is determined by the extent to which the audience becomes involved in it.[11] "Every change in the number of participants is about something, that the newcomers have sympathies or antipathies that make it possible to involve them. By definition, the intervening bystanders are not neutral" (Ref. 11, p. 4).

Studies show that procedural constraints such as referenda, which are expected to raise the costs of collective action and therefore reduce annexation activity, have instead increased the likelihood of these actions.[7] One explanation for this finding is that because many states have created multiple procedures for municipal annexa-

Table 1 Municipal annexation activity ranked by state, 1990–1999

State	Total actions	State	Population annexed	State	Housing units	State	Area (sq. mi.) annexed
IL	9,973	NC	315,370	NC	113,490	MT	1,153.96
NC	4,763	TX	312,969	WA	85,525	CA	783.61
FL	4,123	WA	220,663	TX	80,013	TX	776.51
AL	3,816	IN	95,767	IL	40,867	FL	677.61
SC	3,620	IL	95,142	IN	35,093	AZ	608.53
GA	3,411	MS	69,811	TN	34,952	NC	520.03
TN	2,888	MO	68,244	OR	28,060	WA	475.72
TX	2,819	OR	67,941	FL	26,993	IL	417.66
WI	2,792	TN	66,326	MO	26,276	AL	259.97
MO	2,572	CA	54,974	NE	17,451	TN	250.58
OR	2,193	FL	51,036	AZ	16,499	MN	238.78
CA	2,164	AZ	43,670	MS	15,482	IN	223.68
OH	2,026	SC	43,604	CA	14,371	MO	204.90
IN	1,915	NE	43,280	SC	13,621	AR	195.40
CO	1,792	LA	36,516	GA	13,237	GA	193.82
KS	1,499	AL	33,652	CO	13,176	MS	191.34
MN	1,452	GA	32,696	AL	11,669	CO	183.48
WA	1,415	CO	30,757	LA	11,568	OH	174.48
IA	1,190	MN	24,937	OH	8,932	WI	162.40
ID	1,095	OH	22,183	UT	7,979	UT	149.60
UT	1,002	UT	21,147	AR	7,883	AK	138.46
AR	932	AR	20,602	KY	7,469	SC	135.98
KY	931	KS	18,283	ID	6,390	KY	109.16
LA	863	KY	18,152	MN	6,330	SD	107.01
MI	732	ID	16,395	KS	5,833	OK	105.78
NE	716	WI	11,206	WI	4,430	IA	100.80
OK	681	OK	10,347	OK	4,060	NV	95.06
AZ	609	VA	10,111	IA	3,201	KS	89.99
MT	602	IA	8,044	MD	2,907	LA	83.86
NV	460	NV	4,944	MT	2,256	NM	68.13
SD	440	NM	4,600	NM	2,038	OR	62.18
MD	320	SD	4,317	VA	2,037	ID	53.93
ND	302	MI	4,070	SD	1,775	VA	47.58
NM	291	WV	3,964	WY	1,350	NE	38.21
WY	257	MD	3,615	NV	1,332	MI	34.87
WV	180	WY	3,561	WV	1,315	MD	19.33
NY	167	MT	3,497	NY	1,298	WY	18.54
DE	160	NY	3,022	MI	1,274	WV	17.52
MS	84	ND	1,509	ND	822	ND	14.62
VA	77	AK	1,395	DE	605	NY	8.17
AK	21	DE	1,276	AK	443	DE	6.88
PA	10	PA	2	PA	1	PA	0.13
NJ	3	NJ	0	NJ	0	NJ	0
CT	0	CT	0	CT	0	CT	0
HI	0	HI	0	HI	0	HI	0
ME	0	ME	0	ME	0	ME	0
MA	0	MA	0	MA	0	MA	0
NH	0	NH	0	NH	0	NH	0
RI	0	RI	0	RI	0	RI	0
VT	0	VT	0	VT	0	VT	0

Source: State annexation data compiled from the U.S. Census Bureau's Boundary Adjustment Survey.

Table 2 Municipal annexation activity per action ranked by state, 1990–1999

State	Average population	State	Average housing units	State	Average area annexed (sq. mi)
MS	831.08	MS	184.31	AK	6.59
WA	155.92	WA	60.44	MS	2.28
VA	131.31	TX	28.38	MT	1.92
TX	111.02	AZ	27.09	AZ	1.00
AZ	71.71	VA	26.45	VA	0.62
AK	66.43	NE	24.37	CA	0.36
NC	66.21	NC	23.83	WA	0.34
NE	60.45	AK	21.10	TX	0.28
IN	50.01	IN	18.33	SD	0.24
LA	42.31	LA	13.40	NM	0.23
OR	30.98	OR	12.80	AR	0.21
MO	26.53	TN	12.10	NV	0.21
CA	25.40	MO	10.22	MN	0.16
TN	22.97	MD	9.08	FL	0.16
AR	22.11	AR	8.46	OK	0.16
WV	22.02	KY	8.02	UT	0.15
UT	21.10	UT	7.96	KY	0.12
KY	19.50	NY	7.77	IN	0.12
NY	18.10	CO	7.35	NC	0.11
MN	17.17	WV	7.31	CO	0.10
CO	17.16	NM	7.00	WV	0.10
NM	15.81	CA	6.64	LA	0.10
OK	15.19	FL	6.55	TN	0.09
ID	14.97	OK	5.96	OH	0.09
WY	13.86	ID	5.84	IA	0.08
FL	12.38	WY	5.25	MO	0.08
KS	12.20	OH	4.41	WY	0.07
SC	12.05	MN	4.36	AL	0.07
MD	11.30	IL	4.10	MD	0.06
OH	10.95	SD	4.03	KS	0.06
NV	10.75	KS	3.89	WI	0.06
SD	9.81	GA	3.88	GA	0.06
GA	9.59	DE	3.78	NE	0.05
IL	9.54	SC	3.76	ID	0.05
AL	8.82	MT	3.75	NY	0.05
DE	7.98	AL	3.06	ND	0.05
IA	6.76	NV	2.90	MI	0.05
MT	5.81	ND	2.72	DE	0.04
MI	5.56	IA	2.69	IL	0.04
ND	5.00	MI	1.74	SC	0.04
WI	4.01	WI	1.59	OR	0.03
PA	0.20	PA	0.10	PA	0.01
NJ	0.00	NJ	0.00	NJ	0.00
CT	0.00	CT	0.00	CT	0.00
HI	0.00	HI	0.00	HI	0.00
ME	0.00	ME	0.00	ME	0.00
MA	0.00	MA	0.00	MA	0.00
NH	0.00	NH	0.00	NH	0.00
RI	0.00	RI	0.00	RI	0.00
VT	0.00	VT	0.00	VT	0.00

Source: State annexation data compiled from the U.S. Census Bureau's Boundary Adjustment Survey.

tion, those that seek annexation are able to strategically select the arena (i.e., annexation procedure) in which they are most likely to be successful. In other words, they are able to choose the annexation path of least resistance, given their resources and objectives. Most often, the path of least resistance is annexation on a small scale.

For example, many states have created provisions that enable annexation to occur without referenda if all the property owners in the targeted area agree to the annexation.[10] These procedures enable municipal officials to exclude city residents, county officials, and all the other suburban property owners in the immediate area from the annexation decision. Consequently, efforts by municipal officials to manage the scope of conflict have led cities to annex literally property owner by property owner. Although large-scale annexations do occur, they are comparatively rare. Not only do annexations effected under these procedures exclude other stakeholders, but also because of their small scale, these actions also go relatively unnoticed in the wider community.

The fact that annexation proponents act strategically underscores the importance of thinking about municipal annexation not only in terms of measures of scale, such as population and territory annexed, but also in terms of the frequency of these actions (Table 2). An overly narrow focus on measures of scale has led scholars to mistakenly conclude that the annexation law in a state is more restrictive than it really is in practice. This occurs because they see the requirements for referenda as making annexation nearly impossible, yet many of the annexations occurring in the state circumvent the more restrictive provisions.

MUNICIPAL ANNEXATION RESEARCH: KEY QUESTIONS FOR THE TWENTY-FIRST CENTURY

All parties, whether city officials, suburban residents, or interested third parties, have various mechanisms at their disposal to achieve their service delivery objectives. In previous years, suburban residents could obtain municipal-level services only by joining a municipal government, either through annexation to an existing municipality or through the formation of a new city government. Many states now empower counties and special districts to offer services directly competing with municipal governments. Similarly, municipal governments once had to annex suburban properties to provide services to them, but now many states permit municipal governments to provide services to properties beyond their borders.[12] Thus, annexation policy must be understood within this broader context of multiple service providers.

More recently, concern over sprawl has led to renewed calls for regional government in our urban areas. An-

nexation has long been seen as a means of achieving regional government, but its role in urban sprawl is unclear. Is annexation a solution to sprawl, an outgrowth of sprawl, or a cause of sprawl? Moreover, what role has the movement by state legislatures toward annexation laws that give property owners greater control over annexation outcomes had on urban sprawl?[10] Has the movement toward smaller annexations been positive or negative with regard to urban sprawl? This change has coincided with a more general movement aimed at providing suburban property owners with more choices in service provision. What role has the increased use of special districts and county government to provide suburban infrastructure and services played in determining annexation patterns and encouraging sprawl? The answers to these questions will be central to the debate over the role municipal annexation does and should play in the governance of our communities during the next few decades.

REFERENCES

1. Edwards, M. Annexation: A 'winner-take-all' process? State and Local Government Review **1999**, *31* (3), 221–231.
2. Murphy, T.P. Metropolitan reorganization and black political power. Urban Interest **1979**, *1* (2), 29–34.
3. Feiock, R.C.; Carr, J.B. *African Americans and the Political Economy of Municipal Annexation*; American Political Science Association, San Francisco, August, 30, 1996.
4. Feiock, R.C.; Carr, J.B. *Lines and Color: The Role of Race in Local Government Annexation Decisions*; American Political Science Association, Washington, DC, August, 29, 1997.
5. Liner, G.; McGregor, R.R. Institutions and the market for annexable land. Growth and Change **1996**, *27*, 55–74, , Winter.
6. Clingermayer, J.C.; Feiock, R.C. *Institutional Constraints and Policy Choice: An Exploration of Local Governance*; State University of New York Press: Albany, 2001.
7. Carr, J.B.; Feiock, R.C. State Annexation 'constraints' and the frequency of municipal annexation. Polit. Res. Q. **2001**, *54* (2), 459–470.
8. Sengstock, F.S. *Annexation: A Solution to the Metropolitan Area Problem*; University of Michigan Law School: Ann Arbor, 1960.
9. Feiock, R.C.; Carr, J.B. Incentives, entrepreneurs, and boundary change: A collective action framework. Urban Aff. Rev. **2001**, *36* (3), 382–405.
10. Palmer, J.; Lindsey, G. Classifying state approaches to annexation. State and Local Government Review **2001**, *33* (1), 60–73.
11. Schattschneider, E.E. *The Semisovereign People: A Realist's View of Democracy in America*; Holt, Rinehart and Winston: Fort Worth, 1960.
12. Krane, D.; Rigos, P.; Hill, M. *Home Rule in America: A Fifty State Handbook*; CQ Press: Washington, DC, 2001.

Appearance of Impropriety

Stuart C. Gilman

Ethics Resource Center, Washington, District of Columbia, U.S.A.

INTRODUCTION

One of the most controversial concepts in public service ethics is the notion of the appearance of impropriety. Whereas few would question the evil of impropriety in carrying out one's public duties, many have great difficulty with the modifier "appearance." After all, some might argue, cannot any action be falsely perceived? Does not the appearance standard leave anyone open to attacks by the most excessive elements of the community? Is not appearance an excuse for subjective extremism? Even if all these questions are answered affirmatively, reality for those who serve the public is that the appearance of impropriety is a critical standard by which to evaluate public officials. Yet, at the end of the day, it might be the most important standard by which to judge the actions of public officials.

Appearance standards are not limited to public administrators, but also extend to legislators and judges. In fact, many professional associations, such as the American Society for Public Administration, the International City/County Managers Association, and the Association of Government Accountants, have codes that have appearance as one element. Recently, the appearance of impropriety has even be raised for private-sector companies whose multiple business lines seem to conflict with each other (e.g., public auditing companies and their consulting firms).

Appearance standards are all derived from the English Common Law Standard of the Common Man Rule, or in its modern incarnation the Prudent Person Rule:

> Historically known as the prudent or reasonable man rule, this standard does not mandate an individual to possess exceptional or uncanny investment skill. It requires only that a fiduciary exercise discretion and average intelligence in making investments that would be generally acceptable as sound.[1]

The Prudent Person Rule provides a model test: Would a reasonable person armed with all the facts conclude that an action or inaction was inappropriate?

TOWARD A DEFINITION

Appearance of a conflict of interest, *appearance of the loss of impartiality*, and *appearance of impropriety* often are used interchangeably. Although some might claim that it is valuable to refine the differences among them, for our purposes these concepts are synonymous. A claim can be made that conflicts of interest are a subset of impropriety; however, in applied, practical cases it is almost impossible to support the distinction. Andrew Stark has argued that appearance of impropriety can either take "a factual or a normative caste (or sometimes both). Either (a) it *looks* like the official did something wrong or (b) the official did something that *looks* wrong" (Ref. 2, p. 328). In other words, an official's action is questioned; however, no law was broken and no broadly agreed-on mores were violated. Instead, people feel there should have been a law against the action (or result), or it should be defined as an actually improper action (or result).

On a number of levels such judgments seem unfair. They are prejudiced (decided before the facts are actually known) and also seem to smack of ex post facto laws (laws made after the action). Following Stark's argument, in civil matters such standards of legal fairness are excessive because they assume protections inherent in criminal prosecutions (e.g., innocence until proven guilty). In the vast majority of cases, appearance issues do not rise to criminal standards. Most often, they are punished either politically or administratively, with the most extreme penalty being removal from office. In addition, we assume that public officials will be held to superrogatory standards, thereby justifying the public's trust.

Another argument against an appearance standard is that it rests on knowing one's intention. Former Senator Alan Cranston, reprimanded by the U.S Senate for his role in the Keating Five Case, claimed that no one knew what he was thinking when he acted.[3] The only real person who can judge is the senator himself. "You were not there. I was. And I know that what I knew at the time...convinced me that my [actions] were appropriate."[4] However, there are always mixed motives in anyone's actions. Simply saying the behaviors were not viewed as intended is not enough. Therefore, as Dennis

Encyclopedia of Public Administration and Public Policy
DOI: 10.1081/E-EPAP 120005561

Thompson pointed out, "because appearances are often the only window that citizens have on official conduct, rejecting the appearance standard is tantamount to denying democratic accountability."[4]

In a democracy, it seems reasonable to hold public officials to standards that average citizens might not apply for their own behavior. An official has an obligation to do the "right thing" and also to sustain the confidence of the people in governmental institutions. It is important that officials not do one or the other, but do both. This is the double standard to which most democracies hold their officials. It might be argued that this is true of all types of government. Because information is arguably the one most jealously guarded resource in non-democratic societies, it is almost impossible for citizens to find out about impropriety, much less distinguish between real impropriety and its appearance.

WHY IS "APPEARANCE" A PROBLEM?

Unlike other unethical actions, "appearance" issues seem to violate the usual regulatory standards of clarity and objectivity. However, if we understand appearance not in its juridical form, but as a way of clarifying values, it seems to take on a wholly different character. Where a law, regulation, or rule would emphasize a "bright-line" test of whether you violated the precept, a values approach requires balancing various principles and interests. So, for example, under a regulatory regime a senior official might be limited to a $25 gift each year from a single source. If an individual receives 1000 gifts worth $25 or less, it would not violate the rule. However, a reasonable claim can be made that the individual would have violated the *spirit* of the rule. In this sense, the notion of spirit is the view that there are essential values that are a predicate to the rule itself. In this case, individuals seem to be intentionally exploiting the rule for their own benefit and, even more egregiously, consciously circumventing the letter of the law in a way that seems to be purposely abusive.

An additional dimension of appearance is that it is dynamic, often varying with historical tides, scandals, and changing societal mores. For example, the press and public often ignored sexual peccadilloes in the nineteenth century when "affairs of the heart" seemed to be part of the privilege of the ruling class. Well into the twentieth century, both Franklin Roosevelt and Dwight Eisenhower were purported to have long-term relationships with mistresses. Today, the slightest hint of such a relationship would be front-page news.

Other issues that now seem to be clear impropriety, in other historical contexts, seemed to be a mere appearance problem. As late as the early twentieth century, George

Washington Plunkitt could claim that the Tammany Hall Democrats were more ethical than the Philadelphia Republicans. Although the Republicans had stolen the zinc roofs from poor houses to enrich themselves, the Democrats only took advantage of buying land (and making a profit) when they knew some public project, such as a building or bridge, might be built on it. Plunkitt used these examples to distinguish between *honest* and *dishonest* graft.[5]

The impact of these actions, even if legal at the time, can have a devastating impact on the public confidence in government. Public confidence is always fragile in democracies. Inevitably, revolutions, military coups, and other methods of destroying democratic institutions are justified by the lack of confidence in public institutions. In this way, a reasonable claim can be made that appearance of impropriety can have a far more pernicious impact, because collectively a series of unrelated appearance issues can undermine the most robust democratic institutions. This "death by a thousand cuts" by the appearance of impropriety can lay claim to the destruction of untold numbers of political regimes since the 1800s.

GENERAL RULES

Notions of "conduct unbecoming a civil servant" or "conduct that leads to embarrassment of the service" are some of the more general rules used by government. Without mentioning the word appearance, these general rules can often give wide latitude when it comes to enforcement against actions that are perceived as unethical. However, they are often criticized as overly broad and as license to carry out political or personal vendettas against an individual or a group of individuals. In Great Britain, the Nolan Committee on Standards in Public Life created a series of standards based on either "actual or apparent" violations. These broad principles of behavior expected from government officials include *selflessness*, *integrity*, *objectivity*, *accountability*, *openness*, *honesty*, and *leadership*. Although these are aspirational in terms of any enforcement capability of the committee, they are capable of being administratively enforced within ministries or departments.

In the United States, the courts have supported agency actions against employees for activities that appear to be improper, yet do not violate a specific law. One of the clearest examples comes from the federal court case *Wild v. U.S.*[6] At the time, the executive branch was operating under the Lyndon Johnson's *Executive Order 11222* (1965), which allowed each department or agency to develop its own specific standards of conduct, based on the model standards found in the executive order. The U.S. Department of Housing and Urban Development (HUD) had such a set of standards that forbid employees from undertaking activities that could appear to conflict with their jobs.

Lawrence Wild was an employee of HUD who had been dismissed for violating HUD's code of conduct. Among other elements, the code prohibited the appearance of official impropriety. Wild had violated this norm through his ownership of private rental units. These were so badly deteriorated that local newspapers noted his official position as a manager with HUD and as a landlord of slum dwellings:

> In his defense, Wild had argued that as a matter of fact, the newspaper's impressions were inaccurate: he had either demolished or rehabilitated that vast majority of units in question, and had plans to do the same with the remainder. And in any case, Wild urged, as a normative proposition the appearance standard is "so vague as to fail to provide adequate notice" as to what kind of "off-duty conduct places [an official's] job on the line" (Ref. 2, pp. 326–327).

The court recognized that the point of the appearance standard is to make certain conduct, not forbidden by regulation, a grounds for removal from federal service.

The appeals court went further in its opinion by arguing that whether an employee actually engaged in misconduct is not as important as whether *he could be perceived of having done so*. The appearance norm itself "adequately conveys its concern that an employee not conduct himself in a way likely to bring public obloquy on HUD."[6] As the court concluded, the irony of Wild moonlighting as a slum lord while serving as a professional employee of HUD should have allowed him to conclude that his actions would have reduced the public's confidence in the department.

This case illustrates both the appearance of impropriety and some of the appearance concept's fundamental problems. The case allows us to distinguish between actual behavior and the perception of behavior. The perception that an official of an agency committed to upgrading the quality of housing bought slum dwellings was enough for the court to argue that HUD had legitimately fired Wild. Whether his personal actions were ethical, the mantle he carried as a HUD official required him to consider not only his own personal actions, but also the impact of those actions on the public's confidence in his agency's work.

Even if one accepts this as a reasonable line of argument, it is obvious that there are extraordinary impositions on an official's civil liberties and personal freedom. Many government officials are attracted to their agencies because of a passionate interest a particular policy arena: environment, forestry, children's health, etc. One can easily imagine the many circumstances that would lead to appearance issues. Yet, the potential of apparent conflicts of interest might prevent a public employee from buying stock in a particular pharmaceutical company that deals with children's health issues, purchasing public forest land, or even accepting payment for giving speeches against the current government air pollution policies.

As with all exercises in clarifying values, the dilemma with the appearance standard is that there is a constant balancing of ethical principles. One can imagine cases where the upholding of a fundamental value trumps the issue of appearance. In a hypothetical example, an official responsible for disease prevention in prisons might be an advocate for provision of contraceptives to prevent AIDS. This disease is rampant in the prison system, with hundreds of inmates infected and dozens dying each year. In this particular state, state law bans purchase of such contraceptives by the state. The employee could create a nonprofit organization to provide contraceptives free of charge and become a spokesperson for that group. Perhaps a newspaper accuses this employee of coercing inmates into using contraceptives forbidden by the state and therefore encouraging homosexual sex among inmates. Under the Wild standard, a judge could find it reasonable to fire this person because it would "bring public obloquy" on the prison system.

SPECIFIC RULES

Attempting to clarify the concept of appearance of impropriety, numerous governments codified the concept in the 1990s. Although this is true for a number of federal, state, and local governments, as well as Canada and Australia, the paradigm case is the executive branch of the U.S. federal government. In 1989, then President George H. W. Bush issued *Executive Order 12674*, which articulated 14 general principles of government conduct, including "employees shall endeavor to avoid any actions creating the appearance that they are violating the law or the ethical standards promulgated pursuant to this order."[7] In the executive order, President Bush further ordered the U.S. Office of Government Ethics (OGE) to promulgate regulations to clarify and allow for enforcement of these standards, including appearance.

The regulations appear in Subpart E of the regulations (5 CFR 2635.501–503) entitled *Impartiality in Performing Public Duties*.[8] There are two detailed provisions that deal with different aspects of avoiding "an appearance of a loss of impartiality." The first issue focuses on appearance issues that would be created by personal or business relationships. For this, the OGE used the traditional English Common Law Standard (5CFR2635.501) "an employee should not participate . . . if he determines that a reasonable person with knowledge of the relevant facts would question his impartiality in the matter.'' The guidance actually provides a ''test'' (2635.502) for an employee who is unsure of how to answer the question of appearance by detailing types of relationships, as well as types of actions that would constitute an appearance of impropriety. This expands the prohibition against actual conflicts of interest in the criminal statutes (18 USC 208) that forbids actions that would benefit an employee, his or her spouse, or their minor children. In effect, this regulation extends the appearance of a conflict of interest to any member of the employee's household or someone with whom the employee has a personal relationship (e.g., parent, lover, uncle, sister, companion, personal friend). Interestingly, it also allows an independent source (authorization by an agency designee) to use an additional series of factors related to the impact on the agency to make an appearance determination. For the executive branch of the federal government, this determination would be usually made by the ethics official in the agency.[9]

The regulation also provides several vignettes to illustrate how to apply the regulation, for example:

> An employee of the Internal Revenue Service is a member of a private organization whose purpose is to restore a Victorian-era railroad station and she chairs its annual fund raising drive. Under the circumstance, the employee would be correct in concluding that her active membership in the organization would be likely to cause a reasonable person to question her impartiality if she were to participate in an IRS determination regarding the tax-exempt status of the organization.

What the regulation attempts to do is to provide some guidance to evaluate the circumstance oneself. If that does not resolve the question, the regulation provides a set of standards through which an independent, third party can make a determination.

The second part of the regulation deals with the appearance problem of receiving extraordinary payments (defined as that is $10,000 or more in value) from a private organization when joining the government. In effect, there is a 2-year disqualification (from the date of receipt of the payment) from dealing with any specific matter before the government in which a prior employer has an interest. Unlike the first section of the appearance standard that involves various tests and balancing of interests, this second standard suggests a clear-cut standard of appearance.

THE FIDUCIARY RESPONSIBILITY

It is worthwhile noting that appearance of impropriety or losses of impartiality are not isolated to the public service.

There are many notable examples in the nongovernment arena where chief executive officers, as well as others, have been fired because of acts that appeared improper or unethical. Indeed, there is a fiduciary responsibility in publicly traded companies to stockholders and other stakeholders. However, there is a significantly broader sense of fiduciary responsibility for public servants, and this is often ignored when one analyzes appearance problems in public service.

There are several dimensions to the breadth of fiduciary responsibilities for public servants, including the constitutional undergirding of public service, the limits to privacy, and the growth of transparency. Most constitutional regimes put extraordinary constitutional obligations on public employees. For instance, in the United States, all public employees (including the vast majority of state and local officials) take an oath to uphold the Constitution. They do not swear to support their immediate supervisor, the head of the agency, or the president. Rather, they swear to uphold a document that begins ''We the people...''. Although this oath takes many forms, it is worthwhile noting the similarity in most ethics regimes as reported to the Organization for Economic Cooperation and Development (OECD).[10]

Although privacy concerns are a growing arena for constitutional debate in many countries, one of the few areas of contraction can be found in terms of public servants. In the United States, the use of public financial disclosure is an obvious example of the importance of appearance over the value of privacy for public servants. Currently, the OGE accounts for more than 20,000 public financial disclosure forms in the executive branch of the federal government alone. Because ethics officials review these forms and actions to eliminate real or apparent conflicts of interest, they must be taken before they are permanently filed. Available to anyone on request, the primary purpose of the forms is to eliminate any appearance problem. The growth of disclosure systems since the early 1990s, as noted in the OECD report mentioned previously, is nothing short of remarkable. This is true worldwide, including countries as diverse as Argentina, South Africa, and Slovakia. It is also true in most states in the United States and provinces in Canada.[11]

Some of these systems are confidential and not public. Confidential systems also rely on the citizen's faith in the independence and objectivity of offices reviewing such disclosures. The Canadian Ethics Counsellor is responsible for reviewing financial disclosure and eliminating conflicts.[12] In a recent address, the Ethics Counsellor, Howard Wilson, commented that Canadians had faith in his office, and the Canadian people's respect for privacy would never put up with a public disclosure system for their public officials. One wag responded that the Canadian system was simply one scandal away from public disclosure.

Transparency, or the general openness of government, is another major force expanding fiduciary responsibility. From procurement to contracting, and from hiring personnel to making major policy decisions, government transparency is designed to not only eliminate impropriety, but also to eradicate the appearance of impropriety. Perhaps the best legal example of this is the Freedom of Information Act. Although many in the media complain about redacted or denied documents, the law places severe limitations on what an agency can keep out of public scrutiny. Generic requests can place overwhelming claims on an agency's personnel and time. For example, one request from a conservative nongovernment organization for any document with the name ''Hillary Rodham Clinton'' required a search of every paper file, electronic file, and e-mail. The search, gathering, review, and release, all under legal supervision, took hundreds of personnel hours of labor for what was little more than a fishing expedition. Whatever one thinks of such processes, they are a stark testament to the broad fiduciary responsibilities to which we hold public servants.

CONCLUSION

The appearance of impropriety is both a vexing and illuminating concept. It is vexing because, although it appeals to fundamental values, it also undermines fairness. It is illuminating because it points to the extraordinary set of responsibilities of public servants, and the growing expectations around those responsibilities held by the public. In a sense, the appearance of impropriety is the leading edge of the organic expansion of public service ethics. Impropriety acts as a sort of tidewater mark, to which laws and regulations ultimately rise. Dennis Thompson called this phenomena mediated political corruption.[4] Appearance of impropriety rises to inform and define the definition of political corruption. For this reason, understanding the shape and volatility of the appearance of impropriety is vital for political leaders and the public service, in general.

As Judge Frank Nebeker, then Director of the U.S. Office of Government Ethics, wrote in an opinion excoriating former Reagan Attorney General Ed Meese:

Avoiding criminal conduct is not the mark of public service. The duties imposed by non-criminal standards are far harder to discharge. They may even be strange and seem overly restrictive to some joining the government for the first time . . . [But] the vast majority of officers and employees are hard working and loyal individuals who make every effort to adhere to the high ethical standards the public has a right to expect from them and that they expect from themselves.[13]

Therefore, although the appearance standard has a legal foundation, only emphasizing jurisprudence would ensure that we would miss its political weight and importance. The appearance standard is also grounded in political values and is an expression of democratic accountability. The basis of appearance is the notion that civic employees are servants of the public, and therefore must do everything in their power to assure citizens that government officials are working for the *public* good.

REFERENCES

1. Prudent Person Rule. In *West Encyclopedia of American Law*; Farmington Hills, March, 1998.
2. Stark, A. The appearance of official impropriety and the concept of political crime. Ethics **January 1995**, *105*.
3. The Keating Five case involved accusation against five U.S. Senators had illicitly used their influence to help Charles Keating, a savings and loan financier whose default significantly contributed to the Savings-and-loan disaster of the 1980s.
4. Thompson, D. Mediated political corruption: The case of the Keating Five. Am. Polit. Sci. Rev. **June 1993**, *87* (2), 376.
5. Riordan, W. *Plunkitt of Tammany Hall: A Series of Very Plain Talks on Very Practical Politics*; Putnam: New York, 1963. (Originally published in 1905).
6. *Wild v. U.S. 692 F. 2nd 112*; 1982.
7. George H.W. Bush Administration *Executive Order 12674*; 1989.
8. Although the Bush administration promulgated the initial executive order, two years later when asked to review the regulations balked at the title ''Appearance of Impropriety'' and instead compromised on the word ''Impartiality''.
9. In the administrative structure of the ethics system in the executive branch of the U.S. government, each department and agency must (under the Ethics in Government Act of 1978) appoint a Designated Agency Ethics Official (DAEO) who works conjointly with the U.S. Office of Government Ethics. In turn, many DAEOs have large staffs that provide guidance to employees. See www.usoge.gov for a detailed description of this program.
10. OECD. *Trust in Government*; PUMA: Paris, 2000.
11. See www.cogel.org.
12. Canadian Ethics Counsellor. Available at: http://strategis.ic.gc.ca/SSG/oe00001e.html.
13. 88X1. *Informal Advisory Opinions of the U.S Office of Government Ethics*; Washington, D.C.

Attractors, Strange Attractors and Fractals

David Ogula
Valley Stream, New York, U.S.A.

INTRODUCTION

The conduct of complex dynamic systems has been the focus of research across disciplines. The intense scrutiny of such systems has led to the unearthing of such fascinating features as attractors, strange attractors, and fractals. Examining the behavior of dynamic systems provides a sense of the direction in which the system is headed, as well as allows us to determine patterns of behavior in systems that are otherwise unpredictable. The study of complex systems, of which attractors and fractals are a component, has provided the basis for a better understanding of the nature of chaos and turbulence.

Attractors provide an understanding of the behavioral results of a complex dynamic system, while strange attractors depict the gyrations between chaos and turbulence; that is, the notion that unstable motions result in a geometrically strange object. Fractals, on their part, make it possible for us to measure and define shapes in infinite detail.

The following review provides a basic understanding of some of the well-known attractors, fractals, and associated types. It also correlates with attractors, complex behavioral patterns, observable in organizations.

ATTRACTORS

The literature on chaos theory shows that chaotic systems manifest specific bounds that are peculiar to each system. Such systems are known as attractors. Simply stated, an "attractor" is a state into which a system settles. Chaotic systems are known to dissipate, which means that in the long term, such a dissipative dynamical system may settle into an "attractor."[1] Attractors and associated types such as strange attractors, describe the long-term conduct of a dynamical system.

Although there is still some controversy among researchers as to the appropriate definition of an "attractor," most scholars accept the definition of an "attractor" as "a set in the phase space that has a neighborhood in which every point stays nearby and approaches the attractor as time goes to infinity."[1] An attractor could also be described as "...a model representation of the behavioral results of a system." The attractor is not a force of attraction in the system, it simply provides a sense of the direction in which the system is headed, based on rules of motion in the system.[2] Others define an attractor as "a set for which a positive measure of initial conditions in a neighborhood are asymptomatic to the set."[1]

Nonlinear systems have a wide array of attractor types—point attractor, cyclic attractor or oscillating attractor, etc. The point attractor and cyclic attractor manifest when a system's behavior repeats itself in precisely the same manner. A point attractor behaves like a free-falling object that comes to rest at a point—the point of attraction. Thus, a steady behavioral state corresponds to a fixed-point attractor, where all trajectories beginning from the appropriate "basin-of-attraction" eventually meet at a single point. Fixed-point attractors are said to be the only possible form of attractor in linear dissipative systems.[3] On the other hand, a cyclic attractor or oscillating attractor behaves like a yard security light that comes on or goes off according to the amount of daylight.

According to Merry, attractors can also be simple linear systems, which can be calculated precisely. Such calculations are obtainable in organizational behavior. However, organizational behavior that displays such characteristics is more typical of mechanical systems and could apply to individuals only if they are treated as machines. Merry describes five distinct behavioral stages of organizational experience, comparable to the different stages in a person's life. Organizations experience progression from growth to maturity, through crisis, and transforms in much the same way as do people.[4]

In the first two stages, organizational behavior is repetitive, meaning that organizational behavior repeats itself in exactly the same way. The behavior of the organization (point attractor), repeats itself like a pendulum that comes to rest at the same point or like a thermostat that maintains the temperature between two points (cycle attractor).

The study of adaptive systems has shown that organizations go through different stages of order and chaos. That is to say, organizational behavior mirrors a cyclical stage, where the organization's behavior changes and repeats itself, passing through cycles of complex forms—the cyclic attractor.

In the third stage, which corresponds to the dissipative stage, change occurs in organizations in ways that cause it

Encyclopedia of Public Administration and Public Policy
DOI: 10.1081/E-EPAP 120010681

to break apart, causing entirely new structures to emerge. The organization at this stage is seen as a dynamic system capable of reconfiguring itself.[5] In Kiel's view, this dynamic instability allows the organization to alter its basic structures as it responds to pressures for change.[5]

At stage four, instability in the behavior of the organization becomes more pronounced. Bifurcation and strange attractors occur—a stage where organizational behavior bifurcates into a wide array of forms. Bifurcation denotes uncertainty, unpredictability, and reduction in the ability to control. The progression of change is "from similar, uniform behavior to a variety of different behaviors...there is a division of dissimilar behavioral patterns." The notion here is that people will react differently to similar circumstances. Even when people are exposed to similar situations, their behavior breaks into a wide range of possibilities. Evidence of this can be seen in individuals, departments, and teams in organizations. Differences in behavior can be caused by a small change in organizational action. For example, the introduction of a simple work procedure such as setting a specified time for turning in employee time records, in a week, can create far more complicated reactions from employees. Furthermore, disciplinary action taken by management against one employee may be a signal for other employees to take their duties more seriously, or it may reduce morale, cause anxiety, or create an atmosphere of insecurity.

Although such organizational behavior is unpredictable, it is possible to delineate the pattern that is the framework of the dynamics of such behavior over time. For instance, there are situations in which one may be aware that a company's property may be subject to theft but cannot predict when or by whom (Ref. 4, pp. 6–8). With regard to property damage suffered by the Verizon corporation during the August 2000, workers' strike, company management may have been aware that its telephone cables may be sabotaged, but they could not have been able to predict when and by whom, specifically. Merry reinforces this point, stating that in much organizational behavior that falls within this stage, the organizational behavior and relationships are based on a chaotic pattern strange attractors. One can know that a major transformation is going to take place in the organization, but it is impossible to foretell exactly how it will affect your team or work. He notes that, though at first glance, chaotic behavior seems to be the antithesis of organizational behavior, a second look shows that the variety and irregularity allow resilience and creativity, which are necessary for organizational learning—a condition necessary for an organization to survive.[4]

In the fifth behavioral stage, the organization moves from "chaos to a new order." This stage is referred to as that of "deep chaos." At this stage, the limits of the behavioral process disappear, and randomness becomes the order of events. However, it should be noted that in adaptive systems, deep chaos is a transitional phase in the system, where the old order breaks and disintegrates, allowing a new order to emerge, which replaces the old. Merry notes that "complex systems reach this state after internal gradients have turned into deep cleavages and external perturbations have agitated the system beyond a critical point."[4] The state of the former Soviet Union in its last stages of break up, and in a far more catastrophic way, the breakup of Tito's Yugoslavia, illustrate this state.

Notwithstanding the complex nature of attractors, its and related concepts such as strange attractors, basin boundaries, period-doubling, bifurcations, and the like, can easily be understood by those who have no mathematical or scientific background.[6] Another example of an attractor is a limit cycle, which is a periodic orbit that attracts. Limit cycles attract as well as repel.

Attractors also produce basin boundaries. When two or more attractors are present, basin boundaries occur. Attractors in complex dynamic systems have their basins similar to a river with a watershed basin that empties into it, and each basin has it own boundary.[7] It is common for basin boundaries to have unstable chaotic sets. The basin boundaries are pairs that separate different basins and easily reveal unstable chaotic pairs, which wind up as basin boundaries with intricate fractal structures.[8]

The boundary between two or more attractors in a dynamical system serves as a portal of a kind that seems to govern so many ordinary processes. One behavior that becomes evident when the system settles is that of a chaotic attractor (or an attractor that is chaotic). On the other hand, other systems can wind up as a "steady-state" nonchaotic behavior but with several steady states. Where the initial condition is specified with precision, it becomes difficult to decide in which basin it lies, especially in cases where the boundaries are fractals (Ref. 7, p. 233). The complicated structure of basin boundaries makes it difficult to predict long-term behavior.

STRANGE ATTRACTORS

Strange attractors are a class of fractals that depicts the long-term behavior of dissipative dynamical systems. Although all strange attractors are fractals, not all fractals originate from strange attractors. When initial conditions are drawn to a special type of attractor, that attractor is called strange attractor.[9] Strange attractors describe the gyrations between turbulence and order. A strange attractor is said to emerge in the realm of chaos, where everything is supposed to fall apart—instead, order emerges and not chaos (Ref. 10, p. 117). Chaos and strange attractors require nonlinearity. The term "strange attractors" was introduced by David Ruelle and Floris Takens in their presentation, "On the Nature of Turbulence," in 1970. They remarked that when periodic motion goes unstable, the typical product will be a geometrically strange object.[11] When applied to organizations, it becomes evident that even organizations often exhibit a pattern of behavior that is difficult to predict. They exhibit a pattern of behavior that can be described as chaotic and can take the form of the strange attractor, with gyrating or irregular twists and turns that give it the name of "strange." But, such "behavior does have a pattern that throughout time can be identified and the form does have boundaries that set limits to behavior."[4]

Researchers have used computers programs to simulate the evolution of strange attractors. These computer programs can display each moment of a system's chaotic behavior as a point of light on the screen and enable one to observe how the system evolves. When observing such systems on a computer screen, one would see that the system twists and meanders unpredictably across the screen, hardly appearing in the same spot again. But, as one observes, this chaotic behavior knits into a pattern, and order emerges on the screen. The result is that the chaotic movements of the system have formed into a shape, which is a "strange attractor," and what appears on the screen could be described as the order inherent in chaos (Ref. 10, p. 116). On the whole, strange attractors evoke feelings of wonder and astonishment for most people who watch them.

There are various well-studied strange attractors, the most famous of which is Lorenz's attractor. This attractor emerged from the study of equations used in the prediction of weather.

Ed Lorenz, in his 1963 presentation, determined that simple systems of three differential equations can have complicated attractors. The Lorenz attractor, which has the shape of butterfly wings, graphically illustrates the notion of sensitive dependence as a representation of chaos. Lorenz demonstrated that his attractor was chaotic, because it exhibited sensitive dependence. Moreover, his attractor was also "strange," which made it a fractal.[11] The term strange attractor generally refers to most chaotic attractors. However, some argued that the term "strange attractor" should be reserved for attractors that are "geometric" strange, e.g., fractals. There are instances in which chaotic attractors are not strange.[12]

FRACTALS

Fractals deal with shapes of infinite detail. They can be used to illustrate geographical boundaries of a nation, the bifurcation or dividing of a river's delta, cloud formations, and so on. A fractal "allows us to define and measure accurately the property of roughness."[13]

Benoit Mandelbrot, who has conducted extensive research on fractals, defines a fractal as "a rough geometric shape that can be subdivided in parts, each of which is a reduced size of the whole."[14] Mandelbrot introduced the term fractal as a means of dealing with the problems that arise while studying scale in the real world.[15] While exploring the iteration of complicated process equations with mathematical tools such as sines, square roots, etc., Mandelbrot devised a set of complex mathematical objects that became known as the Mandelbrot set.

To Benoit Mandelbrot, a fractal is a way of coping with problems of scales. He described a fractal as "any curve or surface that is independent of scale—a property described as *self-similarity*," which implies that any portion of the object, if magnified, "would appear identical to the whole."[15] Self-similarity is an even arrangement across scale. Its images are identifiable everywhere, in culture, in the reflection of a person standing between two mirrors, or in the sketching of fish eating a smaller fish. It entails patterns within patterns. Objects that display self-similarity exhibit details in such fine scale as well as produce constant measurements (Ref. 7, p. 103).

The notion of self-similarity in fractals is a way of "seeing" infinity, which could easily be illustrated as iterations of a scaling process as shown in Fig. 1, or by taking the middle of an equilateral triangle and attaching a new triangle that is one-third in size with identical shape. This will increase the number of points in the object thus formed, from three to six. When the process is repeated by attaching a smaller triangle, the points increase from six to 12 and so on to infinity. The resulting shape is similar to a snowflake.

Fractal shapes such as those shown in Fig. 1 and the well-known Koch curve, show self-similarity in that any portion of the object will look identical to the whole when enlarged. While Euclidean one-dimensional lines fill or occupy no space, the outline of the above shape or the Koch curve, which has a finite length crowding into finite area, fills space. In fact, a fractal literally means self-similarity (Ref. 7, pp. 98–100).

The pioneering work of Mandelbrot and others gained wide acceptance over time, leading to the application of fractals in describing shapes, scales, and dimensions. Mathematicians, engineers, and other scholars began using fractals to graphically illustrate the capacity for "self-reference"—a key concept in the study of complex dynamic systems. In such systems, instead of spinning off in different directions, each part of the system maintains harmony with itself and with all other parts of the system

a.   b.   c.   d.

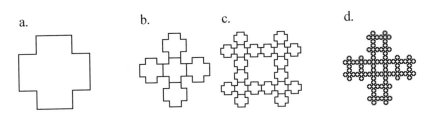

Fig. 1 Illustrates self-similarity by a simple iteration of a cross-shaped object. Each segment of the object from b to d will look identical to a, if magnified. *Constructed by David Ogula* ©.

as it changes, maintaining a deep relationship between individual activity and the whole.

In recent years, there has been tremendous interest in the field of fractals. They have been applied to complex physical shapes from mathematical shapes, to illustrations in the social sciences, management and administration, and even the sound of music. Some musical artists are currently using fractals to generate basic melodies in their compositions.[16]

One of the key concepts in the study of fractals is that of "fractal dimension," which provides a way to measure the roughness of fractal curves. As more scholars studied fractal dimensions, they began to wonder about the dimension of coastlines, mountains, and national boundaries. Mandelbrot, on his part, argued that any coastline is, in a sense, infinity or, in another sense, depends on the length of the measuring instrument.

Fractal dimension can be viewed as a way of measuring qualities that apparently have no clear definition, i.e., the degree of roughness or irregularity of an object.[8]

Fig. 2 The fractal nature of a shoreline, showing the degree of irregularity of the Eastern coastline of the United States. *Constructed by David Ogula* ©.

The dimension of a fractal curve is a number that characterizes the way in which the measured length between given points increases as scale decreases. There is evidence that fractals have also been used to store photographic quality images in a tiny fraction of the space ordinarily needed.[17] Thinking of fractal dimensions makes one wonder how the twists and turns of a coastline could be measured (Fig. 2). For example, one begins to wonder how long is the coastline of Britain, or how long is the coast of the Eastern United States from Maine to the Florida panhandle.

If we directly measure the eastern coastline of the United States, we would find discrepancies with existing estimates of the length of the coastline. The eastern seaboard of the United States, like most shorelines and national boundaries, goes up and down, with rocks, hills, cracks, and curves. A measuring device that is straight and hard like a ruler would give a value of length different from another device that is made of material that can bend and curve over such uneven surfaces. Thus, "fractals can be characterized by the way in which representation of their structure changes with changing scale."[16]

Another concept in the study of fractals is Fractal Geometry, which deals with "geometric forms used for building man-made objects"—made up of "lines, planes, rectangular volumes, arcs, cylinders, spheres, etc." These objects originate from Euclidean geometry, and they "can be classified as belonging to an integer dimension, either 1, 2, or 3."[14]

As the literature on fractals shows, there are different types of fractals, but fractals are not just necessarily curves. There are important differences between fractal curves and the ideal curve that is normally applied to natural processes.

REFERENCES

1. Meiss, J.D. *What is An Attractor*; 1995–2000 [2.8]; http://amath.colorado.edu/appm/faculty/jdm/faq.html (accessed Sept. 16, 2000).
2. Conveney, P.; Highfield, R. *Frontiers of Complexity*; Fawcett: Columbine, 1995.

3. Ilachinski, A. Fractals 1996 (http://www.cna.org/isaac/Glossb.htm#fractalss (accessed Sept. 11, 2000).

4. Merry, U. *Nonlinear Organizational Dynamics: The Scientific Revolution*; http://pw2.netcom.com/~nmerry/art2.htm (accessed Jan. 10, 1998).

5. Kiel, L.D. *Managing Chaos and Complexity in Government*; Jossey-Bass: San Francisco, 1994; 9–15.

6. Lorenz, E.N. *The Essence of Chaos*; University of Washington Press: Seattle, 1993; ix, 5.

7. Gleick, J. *Chaos, Making a New Science*; Penguin Books: New York, 1988; 95–235.

8. Grebogi, C.; Ott, E.; Yorke, J.A. Chaos, strange attractors, and fractal basin boundaries in nonlinear dynamical systems. Science **1987**, *238*, 585.

9. Sprott, C.J. *Strange Attractors—Creating Patterns in Chaos*; The University of Wisconsin: Madison, WI, 1999; 5–7.

10. Wheatley, M.J. *Leadership and the New Science—Discovering Order in a Chaotic World,* 2nd Ed.; BK Publishers: San Francisco, 1999; 117.

11. Meiss. *What is a Strange Attractor* [2.12]; http://amath.Colorado.edu/appm/faculty/jdm/faq-[2].html (accessed Sept. 16, 2000).

12. Elert, G. *Strange Attractors*; 1997–2000; http://hypertextbook.com/chaos/21.shtml (accessed Oct. 6, 2000).

13. Ramsden, S. *Fractals, Feedback and Chaos—A Brief History*; http://online.anu.edu.au/ITA/ACAT/contours/docs/fractals-history.html (accessed Sept. 11, 2000).

14. Burke, P. *An Introduction to Fractals*; 1991; http://astronomy.swin.edu.au/pbourke/fractals/fracintro/ (accessed Sept. 6, 2000).

15. Green, D. *Fractals and Scale*; 1995; http://life.csu.edu.au/complex/tutorials/tutorial3.html (accessed Sept. 15, 2000).

16. Swickape. *Fractals, Chaos and Music*; http://www.geocities.com/SoHo/Square/7921/Math.html (accessed Sept. 15, 2000).

17. Connors, M.A. *Exploring Fractals*; 1994–1997; http://www.math.umass.edu/~mconnors/fractals/intro.html (accessed Sept. 21, 2000).

Auditing

Jean Harris
The Pennsylvania State University at Harrisburg, Middletown, Pennsylvania, U.S.A.

Ann Pushkin
West Virginia University, Morgantown, West Virginia, U.S.A.

INTRODUCTION

Auditing is fundamental to providing assurance that information is creditable, and creditable information is fundamental for accountability. An audit is an examination. Although there are many types of audits, this explanation is primarily about financial statement and financial-related audits of state and local governments. In these audits, assertions are examined on a test basis, and accounting principles and estimates are assessed. Based on the collection and evaluation of evidence, the auditor renders an opinion about the financial statements and, for governments, sometimes issues additional reports. Fair presentation of financial statements is judged relative to established criteria set forth in generally accepted accounting principles (GAAP). For many governments, additional reports address the adequacy of internal controls and compliance with policies, contractual agreements, grant provisions, regulations, and statutes.

AUDITS

Purpose of Audit and Types of Opinions

A financial statement audit provides assurance that an entity's financial statements are presented fairly. The financial statements are prepared and owned by the entity being audited or auditee, and embody the assertions of that entity. By applying appropriate audit processes and observing auditing standards, the auditor evaluates the auditee's assertions relative to established criteria. From the assurance provided by the auditor of fair presentation, the users of reports may hold the auditee accountable.

From conducting an audit, the auditors may disclaim an opinion on the financial statements or issue one of three types of opinions: unqualified, qualified, or adverse. An opinion is disclaimed when an auditor does not have sufficient evidence to express an opinion. An unqualified opinion indicates that financial statements are fairly presented in accordance with GAAP. If an entity's record of financial performance is poor, it may receive an unqualified opinion if its financial statements fairly reflect its poor financial performance. Many rules guide the distinction between a qualified opinion and an adverse opinion. In general, a qualified opinion indicates that, except for a deviation from GAAP, the financial statements taken as a whole are presented fairly. An adverse opinion indicates the financial statements taken as a whole lack of fair presentation.

Responsibility for Fraud

To reach an opinion, the auditor must plan and execute a financial audit to obtain reasonable assurance that management's assertions are free of material misstatement, whether due to error or fraud. Even when audits are executed in accordance with due professional care, there are no guarantees that all fraud will be discovered, particularly when management sets out to deceive the auditor, and others. However, if an allegation of fraud has been made, a fraud audit should be performed; this is a separate type of engagement from a financial audit.

Concept of Entity

The concept of entity is central to financial reporting and auditing. The bounds of entity establish the activities reported in financial statements. State and local governments are familiar reporting entities. The financial statements of a governmental reporting entity include the activities of the primary government, such as a city, and of component units that have financial accountability to the primary government, such as a city school board. All the activities reported in general purpose financial statements (GPFS) are subject to examination under a financial statement audit.

Reporting entities and accounting entities may have different bounds. Any entity for which a distinct set of financial statements is prepared is an accounting entity. Thus, a discretely presented component unit or a fund, such as the general fund, is an accounting entity. In

Encyclopedia of Public Administration and Public Policy
DOI: 10.1081/E-EPAP 120010728

contrast, the GPFS of a reporting entity may include data from many accounting entities.

A reporting entity's GPFS may be issued separately or as part of the entity's comprehensive annual financial report (CAFR). Supplemental and statistical information in the CAFR, that is additional to the financial statements, is not subject to audit.

AUDIT ACTIVITIES

Differences Between Auditing and Accounting

Although financial statement auditors must understand accounting, it is the reporting entity that is responsible for its accounting and preparation of its financial statements in accordance with GAAP. For state and local governments, the primary authoritative bodies for promulgating GAAP are the Governmental Accounting Standards Board and the Financial Accounting Standards Board.

Because auditors assess the fair presentation of financial statements, they must have a sound knowledge of GAAP. But unlike accountants, auditors also must have a strong knowledge of auditing standards and procedures that set forth the means for conducting an audit.

Types of Audits

Generally accepted governmental auditing standards (GAGAS) address two types of audits: financial audits and performance audits. Financial audits include financial statement and financial-related audits. Financial statement audits pertain to the fair presentation of financial position, results of operations, and cash flow in conformity with GAAP. In contrast, financial-related audits pertain to the disclosure of information, adherence to compliance requirements, and suitability of internal controls.

Performance audits include economy and efficiency audits and program audits. The objectives of an economy and efficiency audit are to assess the economical and efficient acquisition, protection, and use of resources; to

identify inefficient and uneconomical practices; and to determine if the entity has complied with relevant laws and regulations. In contrast, the objectives of a program audit are to evaluate the extent to which desired results and benefits are achieved, to assess the effectiveness of operations, and to determine compliance with applicable laws and regulations.

Performance audits are directed to evaluating efficiency and economy of programs or to evaluating the effectiveness of program results. Thus, auditees are frequently selected on the bases of potential for saving costs or improving results. Legislative bodies often have agencies that perform performance audits at the request of members or committees. At the federal level, the General Accounting Office (GAO) serves this function. In addition, the GAO includes standards for performance audits in *Government Auditing Standards* (Yellow Book). Table 1 shows the ways that performance audits differ from financial statement and financial-related audits.

Audits in Public and Private Sectors

Public sector refers to governments at all levels. Audited financial statements and information, along with the independent external auditor's report, contribute to the accountability imposed on government officials for the resources entrusted to them. Public officials, legislators, creditors, and citizens use the audited information and audit reports to determine whether government assets are properly accounted for and have been expended in compliance with relevant laws and regulations. Also, in the public sector, performance audits indicate whether government organizations, programs, and services are achieving their purposes and are operating economically and efficiently. Accordingly, information and audit reports for public sector auditing have a much broader scope than in the private sector. Results of both financial audits and performance audits in the public sector are available to the public.

Most large organizations have an office or department of internal audit. Internal auditors are employed by the

Table 1 Performance audits

Performance audits	Financial statement and financial-related audits
Audits are preformed at irregular intervals.	Audits are performed annually.
Assertions may be vague or undefined.	Assertions are well defined.
A broad range of evidence is considered.	Well-defined types of evidence are sought.
The focus tends to be program specific.	Financial statements reflect the entity as a whole.
Auditors tend to have diverse educational backgrounds with strong knowledge of programs.	Auditors tend to have strong backgrounds in accounting.

Source: From Ref. [3].

auditee, and generally report, by separate channels, to the highest level of management or administration within the auditee's organization. Internal auditors are expected to maintain an objective perspective and to provide assurance regarding the reliability of systems and data within the auditee' organization to its top officials. In contrast, external auditors work for public accounting firms or for special audit agencies, such as the office of a State Auditor or, at the federal level, the GAO. Internal and external audit functions are linked. The presence of an internal audit function serves as an internal control to enhance the reliability of information. Thus, a strong internal audit operation tends to reduce the level of assessed risk and accordingly reduces the amount of audit resources required to conduct an external audit.

Private sector refers to business entities. However, the only businesses required to have financial statement audits by external independent auditors are those businesses that trade securities on an organized stock exchange and are regulated by the Securities and Exchange Commission (SEC). These businesses are called public companies because their stock trades on an exchange that is open to the public. Hence, the term, public companies, has a meaning distinct from public sector governmental entities. Likewise in the professional designation, certified public accountant (CPA), public refers to holding one's self out to render services to the public rather than being an employee of a public sector governmental entity. Results of financial statement audits of public companies within the private sector are public information and are used primarily by current and potential stockholders, financial analysts, creditors, and customers for business decision making. Regardless of sector, financial statement audits attest to the fair presentation of information rather than to the quality of management's decisions or the soundness of an investment.

Conduct of Audits

There are three basic phases in a financial audit—the planning stage, the execution of the plan along with evaluation of results, and report writing. Developing an audit plan is an extremely complex task requiring knowledge of prior audits and a thorough understanding of the auditee's operation and environment. With this knowledge, the auditor assesses the inherent or business risks associated with the auditee and structures an audit plan based on assessed risk.

In addition, the plan addresses any uncorrected recommendations made by the auditor in prior years for known material findings. Once the initial plan is established, the auditor executes the plan and documents all evidence as a basis for drawing conclusions. As the audit progresses, each piece of new evidence is evaluated with

respect to the audit objectives of the relevant procedure. Such evidence is compared with other evidence and conclusions drawn in preceding audit procedures. When this comparison produces conflicting evidence, resolution of the conflict may require an expansion of the initial audit plan. Thus, auditing is a reiterative process. When all steps in the plan are completed and the auditor is satisfied with the sufficiency and competency of the evidence to support conclusions, a report is written and communicated to the auditee.

SINGLE AUDITS

Purpose

Any government or nonprofit organization that expends over a threshold amount in federal awards from more than one program must have a single audit. The single audit is not distinct from a financial statement audit, but is an extension to it. Thus, the organizationwide single audit serves as a basis of opinion on financial statements and as a basis for judging that federal awards are used in an appropriate manner in accordance with contractual and legal requirements.

The single audit approach was adopted as a way to improve financial management, conduct uniform audits, promote efficient and effective use of audit resources, and ensure reliable audits. Rather than being audited on a grant-by-grant basis for each separate grant, recipients are subject to a single organizationwide audit. This one single audit satisfies all federal agencies. Thus, the duplication of having many agencies separately auditing a common recipient on a grant-by-grant basis is avoided.

Standards and Reports

Single audits are conducted in accordance with generally accepted auditing standards, GAGAS, and single audit standards. Table 2 indicates the standards, the standard setters, and primary source of guidance issued by standard setters. The American Institute of CPAs (AICPA) is a private national professional organization, the Office of Management and Budget (OMB) is a federal executive agency, and the GAO is a federal legislative agency. In addition to its roles in establishing GAGAS and conducting other activities, the GAO is responsible for audits of the financial statements of federal agencies.

Under the rules for a single audit, six reports must be issued in addition to the auditor' basic opinion on the financial statements. The term, financial-related auditing, refers to the work that supports the additional reports required by a single audit. In contrast to the opinion on financial statements that is directed to the financial

Table 2 Auditing standards

Standards	Standard setter	Source of guidance
GAAS[a]	AICPA[c]	*Statements on Auditing Standards* (SASs); AICPA: New York, 2001.
		Audits of States and Local Governmental Units (audit guide); AICPA, New York, 1998.
GAGAS[b]	GAO[d] Comptroller General of the United States	*Government Auditing Standards* (Yellow Book); GAO: Washington, DC, 1994.
Single audit standards	OMB[e]	*OMB Circular No. A-133, Audit of States Local Governments, and Non-Profit Organizations*; OMB: Washington, DC, 1997.

[a]GAAS, generally accepted auditing standards.
[b]GAGAS, generally accepted governmental auditing standards.
[c]AICPA, American Institute of Certified Public Accountants.
[d]GAO, General Accounting Office.
[e]OMB, Office of Management and Budget.
Source: From Ref. [4].

statements taken as a whole, the additional reports required in a single audit tend to be directed to major federal financial assistance programs. The extra reporting requirements of the single audit focus on the adequacy of internal controls and compliance with contractual, regulatory, and statutory requirements. Internal controls refer to the plans, procedures, and actions of an entity to ensure compliance with its policies, and with regulations and laws to which it is subject; to enable the evaluation of operations and personnel; to ensure reliable data; and to protect its assets. Although a single audit does not require testing for illegal acts, the auditor must report any illegal acts that are discovered. The auditing standards that apply to specific reports are shown in Table 3.

The Office of Management and Budget first implemented the concept of the single audit in 1979. Subsequently, it was adopted by statute with enactment of the Single Audit Act of 1984 and then amended in 1996.

Single audits are administered by OMB, which issues circulars that provide guidance for performing audits. By statue, single audits must be conducted in accordance with GAGAS of GAO. Periodically, GAO issues amendments that are codified as part of its *Government Auditing Standards* (Yellow Book).

REGULATION OF AUDITS

Public Interest in Regulation

The strong public interest in auditing derives partially from a lack of direct economic exchange and, in a governmental setting, partially from the need for stewardship over public funds. In the acquisition of audit services, there is no direct exchange between the auditor and the external user of audit reports. It is the auditee who

Table 3 Single audit reports

| Focal report | Applicable standards | | |
	GAAS[a]	GAGAS[b]	Single audit standards
Financial statements	X	X	X
Entity's internal control structure		X	X
Entity's compliance with laws and regulations		X	X
Schedule of expenditures of federal awards			X
Internal controls over federal financial assistance			X
Major federal financial assistance program			X
Compliance schedule of prior audit findings			X

[a]GAAS, generally accepted auditing standards.
[b]GAGAS, generally accepted government auditing standards.
Source: From Ref. [4].

employees and pays the auditor rather than the external users of reports. Thus, to accept the creditability of audit report, the user must have a high level of confidence in the auditors, the standards they observe, and the procedures they employ. The public interest in stewardship is evidenced by the many single audit requirements that emphasize compliance with policies, regulations, and statutes. Report users who are dissatisfied with the work of an auditor may make their dissatisfaction known to the auditee, pursue a complaint with a state board of accountancy or federal oversight agency, or bring suit against the auditor in court. For a discussion of the role of auditing in society, see *The Audit Society*.[2]

Stakeholders

There are many stakeholders with an interest in government audits. Two of the primary stakeholders are parties who participate in the municipal bond markets and federal agencies that disburse funds to auditees. Present and potential investors in municipal bonds are concerned about the receipt of bond interest and ultimate repayment of bond principal. These investors rely heavily on the judgment of bond raters who review financial statements, audit reports, and a lot of other information in making their evaluations. Federal agencies are concerned that federal funds expended by state and local governments are spent in appropriately authorized ways. Other stakeholders with an interest in financial information and audit reports include public administrators, legislators, taxpayers, and citizens, in general.

Role of Independence

Independence of the auditor is critical to the audit. The independent auditor must be independent with respect to financial connections and to managerial decision making. In particular, the independent auditor must not be involved with the auditee in a way that enables the auditor to make managerial decisions that subsequently are examined under audit. If the auditor is not independent from the auditee in mental attitude and in appearance, the creditability of the audit report and of the audited financial information is so severely damaged that neither the report nor financial statements may be regarded as legitimate.

The core of all independence requirements is that the external auditor be financially independent from the auditee and not involved in managerial decision making for the auditee. Auditors must comply with rules, regulations, and laws adopted by various authorities. These authorities include the GAO, state boards of accountancy that license CPAs, the AICPA, and the SEC. As required by GAGAS, CPAs and other professionals who audit under the Single Audit Act must be free from personal and external impairments with the auditee, and must maintain both an independent mental attitude and independence in appearance.

Additional independence requirements apply to CPAs. When CPAs are performing an audit or other attest engagement with respect to financial statements, they must comply with the laws and regulations of the relevant state with regard to independence of the auditor from the auditee. For CPAs who are members of the AICPA, they must also comply with its rules regarding independence. When a CPA audits a business that is under the regulatory authority of the SEC, the CPA is said to practice before the SEC. To practice before the SEC, CPAs must show that they are in good standing with their state board of accountancy and in compliance with SEC rules regarding independence.

QUALIFICATIONS AND CERTIFICATION OF AUDITORS

Education of Auditors

Independent audits of financial statements may be performed by CPAs or by persons employed by independent audit agencies of governments. Most independent auditors have a Bachelor's degree in accounting or its equivalent. Maintaining a license as a CPA generally requires the completion of continuing professional education (CPE) on an annual basis. Specific CPE requirements are imposed for all auditors who participate in single audits.

Certification of Auditors

All CPAs are certified and licensed by state boards accountancy. The requirements for certification vary among the states and may be obtained from the National Association for State Boards of Accountancy or a state board of accountancy. To be certified, an auditor must meet an educational requirement to take the CPA exam and pass the CPA exam. Many states have gone beyond requiring a bachelor's degree to require a minimum of 150 credit hours to sit for the CPA exam. An additional requirement for licensing is to obtain relevant experience of a certain type and duration. Maintaining a license then requires the completion of CPE.

Oversight and Peer Review

Auditors conducting a single audit must provide federal oversight officials with access to their working papers that document the conduct of the audit. To ensure and promote quality work, members of the AICPA who have clients regulated by the SEC are subject to the peer review processes of the AICPA. In addition, some states require a peer review for licensing of CPAs.

TRENDS IN AUDITING

Influence of Information Systems

In today's environment, most financial information and statements are produced using complex electronic information systems. Thus, auditors must assess the reliability of these systems before accepting evidence from such systems as a basis for an opinion on the fair presentation of financial statements. That is, the validity of substantive evidence can be only as reliable as the system that produces such evidence. Effective systems must have physical and logical access controls to programs and data, processing controls, change controls, maintenance policies and procedures, and authoritative oversight. Accordingly, financial auditors must be technologically competent with respect to computerized financial systems and frequently must be able to engage information systems auditors to conduct effectiveness tests of system controls. Evidence on the effectiveness of the system will guide the financial auditor in planning the audit and in gathering substantive evidence on which to base an opinion on the fair presentation of financial statements.

Continuous Audits

Continuous audit refers to procedures and practices employed on a continual basis throughout the year that are intended to provide ongoing assurance to decision makers about the quality of information they are receiving. Traditional financial statement audits are performed annually with much of the audit work done after the auditee has prepared a set of financial statements. On completion of the audit, a report or set of reports are issued at one point in time about one set of annual financial statements. In today's environment, the annual audit supplies a small part of the total information available to decision makers. However, most of the other information available to decision makers is not audited by independent auditors and is not regulated by authoritative bodies. Accordingly, regulators and standard setters believe that there is a demand for more timely information than that provided by the annual audit of annual financial statements. In addition, decision makers most likely will expect independent external auditors to provide continuous assurances on both financial and nonfinancial data and on the effectiveness of the systems that produce the continuous flow of information. For more information about this new approach to auditing, see *Continuous Auditing*.[1]

RESEARCH METHODS AND ISSUES

Methods

Various methods are employed in the conduct of auditing research. Subjects tend to be auditors, auditees, and users of audit reports. Data are often collected from subjects by means of experiments, surveys, and interviews. Other rich sources of data are archival stores of financial statements, audit opinions, regulatory reports to the SEC, and stock and bond market information. Much research centers around one or more hypotheses that reflect a possible association between or among variables. It is common to employ statistical methods in testing for associations.

Issues

The relationships suggested by hypotheses often connect auditing to the disciplines of psychology, economics, and

Table 4 Auditing-related web sites

Abbreviation	Name	Web site
AAA	American Accounting Association	www.AAA-edu.org
AGA	Association of Government Accountants	www.agacgfm.org
AICPA	American Institute of CPAs	www.aicpa.org
FASB	Financial Accounting Standards Board	www.fasb.org
GAO	General Accounting Office	www.gao.gov
GASB	Governmental Accounting Standards Board	www.gasb.org
IIA	Institute of Internal Auditors	www.theiia.org
NASACT	National Association of State Auditors, Comptrollers and Treasurers	www.nasact.org
NASBA	National Association of State Boards of Accountancy, Inc.	www.nasba.org
NYSSCPAs	New York State Society of CPAs	www.nysscpa.org
OMB	Office of Management and Budget	www.omb.gov
SEC	Securities and Exchange Commission	www.sec.gov

finance. Some of the dominant questions in auditing research are as follows: What variables influence the behavior and/or judgment of auditors, of personnel and directors of the auditee, or of audit report users? What is the nature of the market for audit and other assurance services? What variables influence market pricing, the quality of audit services, and the response of financial markets to audit opinions? How effective are various audit procedures, regulatory processes, and management practices within auditing firms? Many accounting-related professional and academic periodicals publish auditing research. *Auditing: A Journal of Practice and Theory* (American Accounting Association), an academic journal, disseminates auditing research exclusively. Four important practitioner journals are *The CPA Journal* (New York State Society of CPAs), *Internal Auditor* (Institute of Internal Auditors), *The Journal of Accountancy* (AICPA), and the *Journal of Government Financial Management* (Association of Government Accountants).

Influence of Internet

The Internet has affected the performance of audits, expanded research resources, and introduced new means to improve the proficiency of auditors. Using the Internet during the conduct of audits, auditors may rapidly exchange information among themselves and with the auditee. Government policies, programs, and publications may be researched using the Internet. Many academic and professional periodicals are available electronically and may be searched easily. As a means of resolving problems, auditors may participate in discussion groups and listservs. One issue relating to the information via the Internet is whether the source is reliable and verifiable. Another issue is the confidentially of transmission for certain information. Auditing-related web sites are listed in Table 4.

REFERENCES

1. Canadian Institute of Chartered Accountants (CICA). *Continuous Auditing*; CICA: Toronto, 1999.
2. Power, M. *The Audit Society*; Oxford Univ. Press: Oxford, 1997.
3. Granoff, M.H. *Government and Not-for-Profit Accounting*, 2nd Ed.; John Wiley & Sons, Inc.: New York, 2001.
4. American Institute of CPAs (AICPA). *Audits of State and Local Governmental Units*; AICPA: New York, 1998.

Benchmarking in Public Administration and Public Policy

A. Gunasekaran
Krishan M. Gupta
University of Massachusetts Dartmouth, North Dartmouth, Massachusetts, U.S.A.

INTRODUCTION

Changing markets, globalization of economies, technological pressures, and competitive positions are necessitating the need for innovative management practices not only in the private sector, but also in the public sector and its administration. Due to heightened public awareness and also as a matter of good public policy, public sector organizations are being increasingly challenged to achieve the highest levels of performance. Although the definition of performance may be difficult to establish for the public enterprises, they are increasingly expected to perform better, and to deliver more to their various stakeholders and constituents with lesser resources.

Since the 1980s, the private sector for-profit enterprise management has changed significantly, thanks in part to the various modern management practices, such as strategic management, Just-In-Time (JIT), business process reengineering, lean and agile manufacturing, total quality management (TQM), and benchmarking (BM). With a time lag, public enterprises have also implemented these strategies and techniques for improving their performance and efficiency.

Benchmarking is becoming an increasingly popular tool for transferring best practices into the public sector. It has also been used effectively as a tool to control and scrutinize the mission effectiveness and the underlying generic service processes of nonprofit public enterprises (PEs). It facilitates a radical change in the organizational culture, and supports continuous and sustained efforts toward improvement. It is a positive and proactive process; however, it can easily turn into a negative and reactive process, especially for the PEs, if the controlling authorities use BM for measuring performance alone.

The main significance of BM lies in its ability to identify and unearth the best practices, from anywhere and anyone. The key emphasis is on learning from others and not trying to reinvent the wheel. Openness and ability to adapt and change are the major ingredients of the BM process.

Market-based economy is generally accepted as the appropriate model for global and national economic development. However, the public sector organizations will continue to deliver critical services and play a significant role in any economy. Just like the private sector, the PEs are equally driven by the concerns of cost, efficiency, and responsiveness toward their stakeholders. However, unlike the private sector, it is difficult to identify suitable measures of performance in PEs. Further, dependence on public-funded, fixed, short-term budgets creates its own peculiarities and political imperatives. Nonetheless, BM in the public sector has proved to be equally, if not more, successful. Considering the importance of BM in PEs, this article attempts to review some of the literature with the objective of understanding the major issues in performance improvement and discussing the application of BM in PEs. A framework for BM in PEs has also been outlined. It is hoped that this article will serve as background work for further research in this area.

BM AND PEs

American Productivity and Quality Center (APQC) defines BM as "the process of identifying, understanding, and adapting outstanding practices from organizations anywhere in the world to help your organization improve its performance".[1] Camp[2] defined BM as "the continuous process of measuring products, services, and practices against the toughest competitors or those companies recognized as industry leaders. [It is a] search for the industry best practices that will lead to superior performance." Thus, the BM process is focused on continuous performance improvement by identifying, understanding, and adapting the best practices both inside and outside the organization.

Benchmarking improves overall efficiency of the organization. A typical large business enterprise can have significant payback within the first year of BM.[3] It integrates easily into the strategic management of the organization through its emphasis on continuous improvement of quality and learning culture. BM facilitates the organization in achieving its strategic objectives and makes them more knowledge based. It forces organizations to move away from internal performance measurement and toward adaptation and learning. Although BM is well integrated with TQM and continuous improvement, it does not conflict with the other ongoing efforts of performance improvement.

The continuous process of documenting and sharing BM efforts promotes the core value of learning and openness necessary for continuous improvement and growth. Further, it forces organizations to become more outward looking and to seek new challenges with the spirit of overcoming new challenges. It improves the overall competitiveness of the organization not only by making its business processes more efficient, but also by actively promoting the learning and continuous improvement culture, which is much needed in the rapidly changing environments. Exposure to the outside world and interaction with BM partners also helps PEs to identify new areas of opportunities, improve their overall mission effectiveness, and achieve cost reduction and efficiency.

Benchmarking is equally applicable to different service processes within any organization—profit or nonprofit, private or public. The approach has been successfully applied in manufacturing, sales, service, training, and educational organizations. In the private sector, top managers are always aware of the environment and are constantly comparing (consciously or unconsciously) their organizational performance with others. Benchmarking formalizes this process for PEs and changes the primary management focus from "outcomes" to the enablers of the outcomes. In the public sector, BM has been used successfully as a tool for measuring organizational performance, bringing in the best managerial practices, and learning from other organizations. However, there remain some skepticism and resistance to organizational change, along with a certain level of mistrust in the public sector about the ready adaptability of private sector management practices to the PEs.[4]

It is quite likely that the industry best practice may not be easily revealed due to transaction and other search costs. Only relative or local optimum benchmarks may be established to bridge the perceived gaps in performance.[4] Benchmarking can also be achieved against well-established industry practices, instead of searching for the external best practices. For example, DIN ISO 9000-9004, quality awards, and Citizen Charters can be equally effective in BM in PEs. Quality award competitions promote superior performance by fostering innovation and quality. The generic administrative practices of participating agencies become more transparent and open to public scrutiny, thereby forcing them to strive for superior performance. Citizen Charters, quite popular in Europe, focus on the idea of accountability in PEs. They are used for assessing and rewarding quality in PEs. It is a quality checklist having the sanction and authority of the state with the stated objective of im-

proving the delivery of public service to the citizens. However, BM is considered a superior approach as compared with the traditional target-setting approach for managing performance.[2]

The BM process is a paradigm shift requiring a sea-change in the organization's practices, culture, and structure. The focus is on adaptation, not on adoption or mere imitation. The classic example in BM is that of Henry Ford, who adapted the Chicago slaughterhouse practices to develop the assembly line approach for automobile manufacturing. It is most effective when applied as a tool of continuous improvement within the context of a larger change initiative.

Although an easy case can be made for growing "managerialism" in the public sector, with the stated goal of transferring the best managerial approaches/practices of the private sector to the public sector, it may not be all that easy. It is easy to apply bottom-line and customer-driven approaches in the management of private business enterprises. However, similar measures for PEs are difficult to identify. Even the customer satisfaction approach may be questionable in some cases. Here, the uniqueness of BM stands out. The private sector is driven by competition, and BM introduces an element of cooperation with the BM partners. Yet, in the context of PEs, BM introduces an element of competition—they are forced to compare themselves with others and to improve.

IMPLEMENTATION OF BM PROJECTS

Total commitment, support, and understanding of the top management for BM is the most critical ingredient for successful implementation of the BM process. Besides providing support to the BM team and encouraging involvement at all levels, top management also needs a good understanding of internal business processes and the process of BM itself.

Benchmarking becomes more powerful when combined with change initiatives and used as a tool for continuous improvement. It has yet to become a core value in itself for the organization. However, there is a clear understanding that the best practice is a moving and ever-evolving target. There is no single best—it is relative and contextual.[5]

Benchmarking requires an organizational culture that encourages openness to new ideas and eagerness to seek best ideas from any source. It requires active willingness to seek BM partners within and outside your own industry. Obviously, it is a two-way street and requires openness to share your own practices with your partners. In terms of attitude, the BM approach can be summed up as, "We want to meet and beat the best known performance in any process."

Adequate time and resources need to be allocated for BM projects. However, there has to be a strict cost–benefit analysis at every stage to ensure significant positive contributions and to not waste resources on marginal issues. Not everything can be benchmarked, and the PEs have to choose carefully the areas for BM process.

Like any implementation barriers, BM has its own impediments during the course of performance measurements and identifying best practices. Some of them include inertia and resistance to change, cost, response time, temptation to copy, focusing on performance measurement rather than the processes and practices that result in superior performance, lack of involvement by top management, and organizational structure and culture that punishes mistakes made while innovating. Lack of adequate support, time, and resources are identified as primary obstacles in successful implementation of BM.[1]

A FRAMEWORK FOR BM IN PEs

Performance measurement in the public sector is more difficult than in the private sector because simple concepts of financial measurements cannot be applied. It is not feasible to apply the usual measures of profitability to the public sector. At the same time, it is equally difficult to operationalize the concept of "consumer satisfaction." The problem of scarce resources in public sector administration necessitates a certain degree of insensitivity to consumer demands. In other words, consumer satisfaction cannot be the only, or dominating, dimension in performance measurement in the public sector.[4]

Technology, globalization, competition, and collaboration have completely transformed business processes in the public sector. This calls for a different approach to BM for PEs in terms of its responsiveness to mission objectives. The BM champions also have to take advantage of the possibilities offered by technology in terms of communication, conferencing, and search. However, at the same time, one has to be careful about the reliability of the search results because the barriers to entry in the information dissemination are much lower. Further, by carefully defining and limiting the scope of the project, BM can deliver quicker results.

An effective way to control cost is to select only a few processes at a time for BM. One need not benchmark all the areas at once. The step-by-step approach will also help to leverage the experience and results gained from the initial phases.

Under the present environment, there is a greater need for analyzing the service processes before launching a BM project. First, the process of internal service process mapping itself will reveal several ideas that can make the process more efficient. Second, a thorough understanding of the internal service processes will reduce the total project time by focusing on core service processes.

Mission Effectiveness

The goal of any PE is to fulfill its mission or charter, whereas the business enterprises seek profitability. Therefore, the key performance metric for a PE at the strategic level is *mission effectiveness*.[6] This concept can be compared with the strategic competitiveness in the corporate sector. The mission effectiveness for the PEs is not fixed, it is relative and contextual. The mission and underlying sub-missions may change their tone and dominance, depending on the political and social pressures on the PEs.

Political Issues

The existence of a business enterprise is solely determined by its economic performance. However, for a PE, its existence is often determined by a political process, which in turn depends on various sociopolitical factors at a given time. Further, some public agencies in the area of public safety or law and order might even receive a higher dose of resources, even when not able to provide the expected deliverables. Thus, the life of a PE may be much more dependent on its sociopolitical relations with its environment than on improved or worsened performance. At the same time, public pressures and fiscal constraints may impose certain performance targets (Citizen Charters in Europe) on PEs. However, BM is considered to be a better approach to manage performance than the traditional target-setting approach.

Cost Reduction and Efficiency

Profitability measures, so common in business enterprises, cannot be readily applied to the PEs. However, some financial measures such as cost reduction and efficiency can be used to establish best practices. Efficiency measures can also be financial or nonfinancial. For example, capacity utilization ratios, total passenger journeys per year per staff hours, and so on, can be used to measure efficiency of a metropolitan mass transit system.

Thus, if performance is the factor for the viability of a PE, effectiveness and efficiency of its operations are the key indicators to be examined and improved. While it may be relatively easier to set up metrics and subject them to BM for generic support functions, it may not be so easy to set up metrics for mission-specific effectiveness and to benchmark them. When faced with internal or external targets and imprecise measures of effectiveness, measures of economic efficiency and cost reductions will dominate the BM performance metric.

Customer Satisfaction

It seems easy to select customer service as one area that may be common to PEs enterprises. Both should strive for better customer service. However, "even here there is a difference, because the definition of customer is different in the two cases."[6] Besides, the concept begs the question—who is the customer? The user of the service or the ones funding the PE (the taxpayer)? Further, even if the consumer of the service is accepted as the customer, it may be optimal to allow a certain amount of dissatisfaction as part of the mission.[4] For example, it may be desirable to leave the recipients of public dole a little bit dissatisfied with the service to coax them away from systemic dependence on public welfare.

Stakeholders

In the case of business enterprises, business owners can easily be identified as the primary stakeholders. However, for PEs, it is difficult to identify one major group of stakeholders. By definition, PEs exist for the public good. Taxpayers and founders of the PEs, regulators, legislators, and the general public have a stake in successful mission accomplishment. The various stakeholders may not have a unified vision for the PE and its mission, thereby making the exercise of performance measurement and BM extremely fractious.

Open Information

In business enterprises, information is often protected due to the fear of losing the competitive advantage through the loss of intellectual property. Among PEs, generally, it is easier to secure cooperation and open communication. However, the information may still be guarded due to legal, security, and safety concerns.

Uniqueness

For a business enterprise, being unique can be a success factor. However, because competition is generally not an issue for PEs, sameness and economies of scale are more important than being different from others.

Club v. Out-of-the-Box Approach

Because competition is usually not an issue for PEs, it is easier to form "innovation rings" or consortia of similar PEs to foster innovation and to learn from each other. The managers are more comfortable sharing the information

with each other in such clubs. The knowledge transfer is easier due to the shared language and technologies.

However, such clubs can easily degenerate into mutual back-scratching clubs trying to establish excuses for their poor performance. A certain amount of "soldiering" can also take place. Nonetheless, such clubs can help to quickly establish in-class best practices.

Out-of-the box or "world-class" out-of-the-class BM processes can be helpful in establishing the best practices at a global level. This approach is especially useful when establishing best practices for generic business processes.

Information Technology

Information Technology is both the enabler and enforcer for BM. Advances in information technology (IT) and communication technology have lowered the costs for identifying and transferring best practices and monitor their implementation. The IT advances can assist in readily evaluating the impact on all aspects of an organization, both in detailed and aggregated levels. Knowledge management tools, such as Enterprise Resource Planning (ERP) systems, will continue to evolve and provide management even better controls over the service processes.

However, in the case of PEs, IT can become a stumbling block due to the lack of adequate investment in IT, inability to attract and retain the right kind of personnel, and the need to constantly upgrade and reconfigure. Often, IT can become a hinderance rather than a facilitator of BM. Sometimes, IT itself can become a key area for BM for the PEs.

GENERIC STEPS FOR BM IN PEs

Jarrar and Zairi list six major steps in BM for transferring the best practices—searching, evaluating, validating, implementation, review, and routinizing.[5] Some of the major aspects that one should consider in BM practices include top management involvement, team, BM partners, networking, consultants, proactive approach, change champions, cost–benefit analysis, and continuous improvement.

The following are generic steps that can be used in the BM process in PEs:

1. *Choose the core service processes that need to be benchmarked.* The related question is "how do the selected processes fit into the overall mission of the organization from the stakeholders' perspective?" Senior management support and understanding of the process is critical to BM. However, in the case of PEs, this may be problematic because the locus of real power may lie outside the organization.

2. *Select a team with well-defined scope and team leader.* The team should have adequate influence throughout the organization. Because the power structure in PEs is generally more centralized and most of the authority is concentrated at the top level, it is imperative that some members of the top management join this team to provide support and leadership to the project. This kind of highly visible team composition is also essential for post-BM activities. In short, the team has to become the change champion.

3. *The team scope should include a timeline for deliverables.* This issue becomes even more relevant in today's fast-changing, quick-response environment. The team should be fully responsible for training, providing assistance and guidance, and transferring and sharing the knowledge within the organization. The team may also need adequate training and resources to carry out the process.

4. *Time and resources have been identified as primary challenges to BM; adequate budgeting is necessary.* Innovative funding techniques that involve different agencies and partnership with the private sector may be necessary. The organizational culture in PEs is different from the corporate sector—it is generally more bureaucratic and resistant to change. Therefore, the BM may not be able to deliver immediate short-term returns.

5. *Engage an outside consultant.* If there is not enough in-house expertise or understanding of the issues involved in BM then it may be necessary to engage an outside consultant who has a proven track record of BM in similar areas.

6. *Analyze and understand the core service process thoroughly before looking elsewhere.* This analysis itself will reveal significant insights into the current operations and help to improve the service process. Benchmarking essentially relates both inside and outside the organization.

7. *Adopt a strict protocol (Code of Conduct) for sharing information and proprietary knowledge with the BM partners.* This is critical not only for satisfying the concerns of your potential BM partners but also to avoid any potential antitrust, ethical, or legal issues. Well-established and tested protocols are readily available, and can be easily modified and adapted to meet the specific needs.

8. *Identify potential BM partners within or outside the industry.* It is not always necessary to work with the best-in-class performing organizations. One can also learn from less-than-the-best performing organizations.

9. *Establish an open communication link with your potential BM partners.* If the potential BM partners believe that a partner is trying to steal their ideas, then there will be no positive response. Networking through professional and trade organizations can be extremely valuable in this process.

10. *Identify core areas of service that need to be improved through BM.* Develop a few key performance measures and a suitable metric that can be used for the BM process. This metric will have to be developed in close cooperation with the BM partners.

11. *Identify the best practices in the key performance measures from BM partners.* Here, the focus should be on understanding the underlying processes that lead to the best practices. The team should distill the best practices for adaptation by the organization. Mere imitation or copying does not work.

12. *Perform a cost–benefit analysis to see if it is worthwhile to adapt such practices.*

13. *Share the results and the knowledge gained through this exercise throughout the organization on a formal basis.* Organizations involved in BM generally miss out on the opportunity to take full advantage of the potential gains, in learning and changing the culture, that can arise from sharing the knowledge gained in BM.

14. *Adapt, implement, and monitor the identified improvements in the service processes.*

15. *Perform periodic followup to evaluate the impact of improvements initiated by BM.* The evaluation should include achievement of financial and strategic objectives. Such a followup will help to further improve the process by internal BM. It will also help to leverage the BM process throughout the organization by promoting the learning culture—the fundamental focus of BM.

Benchmarking is not merely a process of measuring the best performance. The primary focus has to be on identifying business practices that lead to superior performance, and determining how such practices can be adapted and emulated within the organization in a cost-effective manner. In other words, learn from examples set forth by others.

CONCLUSION

The research clearly indicates that BM has earned its place as a management tool and will continue to be used in the future.[1,3,5] It is a fundamental process that promotes learning and change, thereby improving the overall efficiency and mission effectiveness of PEs.

Benchmarking is the most economical method to improve productivity and efficiency of any organization.

76

However, it requires a sustained long-term continuous effort and cannot be a quick fix. The growth in the academic and practitioner literature in BM is indicative of its momentum and potential.

Application of BM in the PEs requires careful fine-tuning, specifically in the involvement of top management, identification of measures of mission effectiveness, and a commitment to a continuous and sustained effort toward service process improvement. The organizational culture, time, and resources can become major stumbling blocks. Certain PEs might even enjoy a limited amount of monopolistic powers due to their political right to exist and may not have any incentive to improve.

Benchmarking in PEs is a viable management practice with considerable potential for making a significant improvement in the performance in an economical manner without reinventing the wheel.

REFERENCES

1. American Productivity and Quality Center. *Benchmarking: Final Report*; APQC: Colorado Springs, CO, 1997.
2. Camp, R. *Benchmarking: The Search for Best Practices that Lead to Superior Performance*; ASQC Quality Press: Milwaukee, WI, 1989.
3. *Benchmarking: Leveraging Best-Practice Strategies*; American Productivity and Quality Center. http://www.bettermanagement.com (accessed April 2002).
4. Kouzmin, A.; Loffer, E.; Klages, H.; Korac-Kakabadse, N. Benchmarking and performance measurement in public sectors. Int. J. Public Sect. Manag. **1999**, *12* (2).
5. Jarrar, Y.; Zairi, M. Internal transfer of best practice for performance excellence: A global survey. Benchmarking: Int. J. **2000**, *7* (4).
6. Arveson, P. *Translating Performance Metrics From the Private Sector to the Public Sector*; http://www.balalancedscorecard.org/metrics/translating.html (accessed April 2002).

BIBLIOGRAPHY

American Productivity and Quality Center: http://www.apqc.org.

Benchmarking in Practice (Journal); American Productivity and Quality Center.

Benchmarking: Int. J.

Berman, E.M. *Productivity in Public and Nonprofit Organizations*; Sage: London, 1998.

Bogan, C.E.; English, M.J. *Benchmarking for Best Practices*; McGraw Hill Inc.: New York, 1995.

Bruder, K.A.; Gray, E.M. Public-sector benchmarking: A practical approach. Public Manag. **1994**, *76*, S9–S16, , September.

European Center for Total Quality Management. *Benchmarking: A Global Survey*; ECTQM Report Series, Bradford, 2000.

Loffler, E. A Survey on Public Sector Benchmarking Concepts. In *Quality, Innovation and Measurement in the Public Sector*; Hill, H., Klages, H., Loffler, E., Eds.; Peter Lang: Frankfurt, 1996; 137–159.

Walsh, K. Quality and public services. Public Adm. **1991**, *69* (4).

Biomedical Ethics, Public Policy and

John Abbott Worthley
Seton Hall University, South Orange, New Jersey, U.S.A.

B

INTRODUCTION

Developments in medical technology during the latter part of the twentieth century revitalized the field of biomedical ethics. As we enter the twenty-first century, broad availability and application of this powerful technology is now bringing the biomedical ethics dialog foursquare into the public policy-making forum. The issues being deliberated are both organizational and clinical.

THE NATURE OF BIOMEDICAL ETHICS PUBLIC POLICY DISCOURSE

The clinically related issues for public policy fundamentally revolve around one of the oldest questions of bioethics: should we do everything that we can do? Specific attention-getting issues include human cloning, stem cell research, fertility technology, euthanasia, and abortion.[1] Technology has largely set the agenda. In November 2001, a Worcester, Massachusetts, company announced that it had cloned human embryos. Now that we can do it, should the polity permit, encourage, proscribe, or limit the cloning of human cells? Scientists tell us that human cells harvested from embryos offer significant pathways to healing spinal cord injuries and dementia. Should we fund stem cell research aimed at curing such disabilities and diseases? Or should issues of fetal life prevail? At the end of the twentieth century, a 63-year-old woman was successfully fertilized in vitro through frozen embryo transfer. She gave birth to a 6-pound girl. Should senior citizen women be legally denied fertility therapy? Or, should the issue not even enter the public policy forum? Largely based on the availability of sophisticated pharmaceuticals, Holland in Europe as well as Oregon in America have developed regulations for hastening the death of terminally ill citizens through the use of such drugs. Should public policy ban ''mercy killing'' or continue to develop regulatory procedures for applying technology to painful end-of-life circumstances?

Advocates on all sides are lobbying to have these kinds of questions addressed in the public policy-making process. As a result, for example, in the fall of 2001, the U.S. House of Representatives passed legislation, supported by the sitting president, banning all human cloning. In January 2002, a Presidential Council on Bioethics was appointed to advise the government on cloning and other issues. Organ selling and transplantation, as well as issues of nutrition and hydration for the terminally ill, are among other subjects being addressed. The ethics of abortion, of course, has had a significant place on the public policy agenda for some time.

Organizational issues have entered the forum more recently prompted by social and economic developments.[2] Socially, the professional role of medical professionals has changed and social attitudes toward them have followed. Physicians have become powerful lobbyists, corporate officers of health care organizations, and more group based than individual oriented. Nurses have unionized, entered managerial positions, and become more powerful in the health care enterprise. Not surprisingly, societal perspectives on these professionals have evolved. Deference to medical paternalism has diminished. Physicians are more routinely subject to legal processes for malpractice. Consumers have become more alert to self-serving inclinations of physicians and less tolerant of medical hubris. As a result, discussion of truth-telling, confidentiality, conflict of interest, and informed consent has proliferated and public policies on these matters have been developed.

Economically, the escalated cost of health care has impelled debate on issues of resource allocation, fiduciary competence, insurance configurations, and compliance with standards and regulations. Is it ethical within the reality of limited resources to duplicate health care services in defined geographic areas? Is it ethical to close an emergency room or a maternity ward to realize economies of scale within local communities? How should health care resources—needed by all but sufficient for only some—be distributed? How should such decisions be made? Should insurers be required to offer certain coverages and prohibited from some denials of coverage? Should health care providers be monitored for strict compliance with standards and penalized criminally, as well as financially, for noncompliance? Should these questions be addressed privately or within the political process? Should answers become a matter of public policy? These are some of the concerns that have come to the fore in shaping modern bioethics discourse within the public policy context.

Encyclopedia of Public Administration and Public Policy
DOI: 10.1081/E-EPAP 120011078

FUNDAMENTAL QUESTIONS

The public policy debate over these and other issues revolves around a few fundamental, timeless, and profound questions. The clinically focused debate inevitably centers on questions about human life. When does human life begin? What, in fact, constitutes human life? When does human life end? Should society directly intervene in the beginning and ending of life, or should society leave it to more natural processes? The abortion public policy-making experience, for example, is grounded in the question of when human life begins. The conclusion that life begins at conception leads to a public policy position to ban all abortion. The conclusion that viable life begins at the third trimester of pregnancy leads to a public policy position to fund abortion within limits and regulations. The conclusion that human life begins at birth leads, of course, to less restrictive abortion policy proposals. Perspective on the nature of human life enters the debate when prenatal screening reveals anomalies such as genetic defects. When deformities and abnormalities are viewed as a diminution of human life, policy proposals permitting late-term abortion tend to emerge. When a child is born in great distress, perspective on the end of life spawns views on policy for intervention or nonintervention.[3]

Euthanasia policy dialog is largely rooted in conceptions of the nature of human life. Those who see a certain level of brain function as essential tend to seek policies permissive of euthanasia actions in situations such as a persistent vegetative state. Those who view the ''human soul'' as the essential factor seek proscriptive policies. Those who view physical well-being, such as freedom from continuous and severe pain, as essential to human life tend to propose less restrictive public policies. The emergence of technology for human cloning, of course, is now bringing the question of the nature of human life to another level of discernment.

The organizationally focused debate centers on questions of conflicting interests. Should the health care interest of each individual person be the chief concern of bioethics, or should the interest of society as a whole be primary? If both interests are viewed as essential, what should policy be when the interests conflict? How do we honor the dignity of every person and still maintain the viability of the community? Because the health care resources of the polity are less than the full health care needs of all the individuals who form the community, how should allocation of the limited resources be directed? Should the finite health care resources be allocated on cost–benefit principles of economics, on power and influence principles of politics, or on philosophical principles of the greatest good with the least harm? Who should make the decisions? Ethics committees organized

within health care enterprises? Medical experts organized through their professional societies? Politicians elected by the masses? Jurists organized in legal systems? Insurers organized capitalistically and regulated governmentally? Philosophers organized academically? These are basic questions today and increasingly the public policy-making process is being used as an arbiter for framing answers. Implicit in the discussion is a disconcerting issue—in policy decisions involving bioethics, whose judgment should prevail? The patient's? The health care provider's? The jurist's? The ethicists? Or the judgment of the polity through the public policy-making process?

AN EXAMPLE OF BIOETHICS AND PUBLIC POLICY

Current developments in human cloning and stem cell research, because they are markedly bringing the fields of bioethics and policy making into the public arena, provide rich fodder for better understanding the expanding intersection of biomedical ethics with the public policy process. This technology now enables society to produce human life outside normal reproductive processes. The fundamental question is whether society should now use this new, profound capability or proscribe, limit and/or regulate its application. The debate is spawning new insights on the nature of human life as well as refining understanding of life's beginnings and endings.[4] For example, because cloning and stem cell research entail destruction of some embryos the issue of protecting innocent human life is a hallmark of the discourse. Scientists are, therefore, active in clarifying distinctions of biological reality. Some are noting that parthenogenetically activated eggs used in stem cell research cannot result in human birth and, therefore, do not fit into the notion of ''conception.'' Others, while accepting the scientific distinction, disagree with the conclusion. They argue that these embryos are potential human life, and therefore are sacred and deserving of protection. Perspective on the issue of the beginning of human life is, in effect, expanded from the idea of conception to the notion of potentiality. The public policy of protecting life is thus challenged.

The issue of the ending of human life is similarly germane in this dialog around cloning and stem cell research. Is human life unnaturally ended when embryos are destroyed in the process of cloning? For those who judge in the affirmative public policy concerning homicide comes into play. Of course, implicit in this dialog is the question of just what constitutes human life. Some ethicists see a significant distinction between eggs produced artificially from parthenotes and those embryos fertilized naturally. From this sense of the nature of humanity, these ethicists are arguing for public policies that prohibit the sale of human gametes but do not prohibit parthenogenetic cloning per se. Similarly, other ethicists distinguish individuality from personhood. They observe scientifically that the early embryo (called a blastocyst) is not individualized until about 2 weeks into its developmental process. At that point, they note, the organism has the human genome but lacks personhood. Extraction of stem cells for medical or therapeutic purposes can then be distinguished from cloning for reproductive purposes. Based on this sense of human life, they argue for public policies that ban reproductive cloning but allow medical cloning.

This dialog on cloning also illustrates the tension between the interests of individuals and that of the community. The interests of the polity in defining and defending human life can easily lead to policies that conflict with the interests of individuals, who want reproductive assistance. Moreover, cloning and stem cell therapy are expensive. Should limited public health care funds be spent in these dramatic areas that benefit relatively few individuals, or would they more ethically be devoted to preventive health care needs that benefit the community as a whole? Public budgetary policies face this question.

Additional organizational issues arise when public policy in this area focuses on regulation and limits on research. Would it be managerially possible to develop, monitor, and enforce such restrictions within ethical standards of competence and compliance? As cloning technology continues to evolve, these kinds of questions confront public policy with increasing insistence.

CONCLUSION

The subject of biomedical ethics will accelerate its expansion on the public policy-making agenda as the first decade of the twenty-first century unfolds. Continuing and increasing resource limitations auger a higher level of intensity in the area of managerial and organizational policies. Who should get how much health care and when, as well as where should they get it? These will be focal questions for policy makers. Technological advances are also likely to soar presenting fundamental questions in ever-challenging ways to bioethicists and public policy makers alike. Responses in the form of new public policies arguably will reshape society in some fundamental aspects. Bioethical analysis will be essential.

REFERENCES

1. Loewy, E. *Textbook of Healthcare Ethics*; Plenum Press, 1996.
2. Worthley, J. *Organizational Ethics in the Compliance Context*; Health Administration Press, 1999.
3. Arras, J.; Steinbock, B. *Ethical Issues in Modern Medicine*; Mayfield, 1998.
4. Shannon, T. Human cloning. America **2002**, *186* (5), 15–18.

Budget Execution and Management Control

L. R. Jones
Jerry McCaffery
Naval Postgraduate School, Monterey, California, U.S.A.

Fred Thompson
Willamette University, Salem, Oregon, U.S.A.

INTRODUCTION

Once funds have been appropriated for spending in the sequence of budget formulation, negotiation, and enactment, budgets then must be executed as planned and authorized.[1] However, budgets also must be responsive to changing circumstances during the period of spending execution. All organizational entities employ management control systems with imbedded incentives, sanctions, and a myriad of rules to control spending and the budget execution process. Agreed upon authority relationships, institutional roles and responsibilities, job performance criteria, rules and regulations, incentives and motivational structures, and intra-organizational arrangements comprise the management control systems to provide accountability in an effort to stimulate decision making that results in efficient and effective use of funds.[2] Various levers of management control are used in the private sector to achieve organizational objectives.[3] In the public sector, these levers of control are employed by elected officials and, more typically as a result of delegation, by budget control agents and agency managers in budget execution. Control systems and controls have important consequences for how managers behave—this is the explicit purpose of these systems and levers. In budget execution, rules may be designed to tightly control what money is spent on before it is spent (ex ante controls). Alternatively, controls may be applied after the fact, focused on measuring, rewarding, and sanctioning the results of managerial action after spending has occurred (ex post controls). Correctly designed control systems help to stimulate efficient use of resources and development and use of appropriate reporting systems. Conversely, inappropriate control systems and controls tend to create budget execution procedures and processes that are simultaneously over-controlled and out of control. Where budget execution controls are inappropriate for what is demanded of them and do not report correct information in a timely manner, they will fail to stimulate efficient spending decisions and management behavior and, paradoxically, may create or exacerbate waste, fraud, and other forms of funding misuse.

DESIGNING THE SYSTEM

Critical choices must be made in designing the appropriate budget execution management control system. The successful design should fit the objectives of control and the nature of the entity to be controlled. For example, increasing costs and homogeneous outputs imply one kind of design, while decreasing costs and heterogeneous outputs imply another. The purpose of the analysis of budget execution and management control provided here is to improve understanding of control dynamics, incentives, disincentives, and the behavior of the various participants in the budget execution and management control process. Our analysis focuses most closely in this regard on the roles of central executive branch budget agency controllers, agency budget officials, and program managers.

The other purpose served by this analysis is to ask whether there is cause to change budget execution and management control processes, as they now operate in many, if not most, public-sector organizations. If so, what direction should change take? The analysis delineates alternative types of control applied in executing budgets and the rationale for employing these different methods. A distinction is drawn between budget execution control intended to influence the behavior and performance of managers of government programs from controls applied to affect independent private-sector firms that contract to deliver goods or services to the public on behalf of government. The central theme of this analysis is that budget execution and management control system design should fit the objectives of control and the nature of the entity to be controlled.[4]

Perhaps the most challenging task in budgeting is to execute well, so that the best program outcomes are achieved with some degree of efficiency and a genuine

Encyclopedia of Public Administration and Public Policy
DOI: 10.1081/E-EPAP 120010970

concern for the proper use of public funds. Budget execution skill is required to respond to inevitable contingencies that arise to complicate the implementation of programs in the manner planned and according to the commitments made in budget formulation. Accountability and management control must be maintained, and employees must be motivated to perform to high standards. At the same time, uncertainty must be accommodated, as budgets are executed to meet the demands of the real world—demands that often cannot be anticipated and budgeted accurately in advance. While the highly visible politics of budget formulation and enactment garner the attention of the media and of budget negotiators and critics, it is only in the phase of budget execution that performance, outputs, and outcomes are obtained. In our assessment of budgeting, we must not lose sight of the fact that it is consumption (use) of assets in attempt to achieve the objectives of organizations and governments that matters most if our goal is to learn to spend and manage better.

BUDGET EXECUTION AND MANAGEMENT CONTROL ISSUES

Budget execution typically is highly regulated to control what program managers may and may not do. Controllers are driven by the objective of insuring that budget appropriations in total and by legally segregated account are not overspent by programs.[4] However, controllers also must be concerned with underexecution. Department and agency budget officers and program managers do not want to underspend and thereby lose claim to resources in the following year. Central executive budget office controllers do not want programs to execute without good cause, so that money not used in the manner justified in budget formulation may be withdrawn from program managers. Executive controllers want to be able to withdraw funds from programs to protect the integrity of the appropriation process and to reallocate money to areas where it will be spent efficiently in response to client demand. For these reasons, budget execution typically is monitored and controlled carefully by agency budget staff and central executive budget controllers. Often, execution is also monitored closely by legislative oversight committees and their staffs out of a desire to insure that legislative will is implemented faithfully, and to make sure that benefits are distributed to the clients targeted in the appropriation process.[4] Because the electoral fortunes of legislators are tied to some degree to the public perception that they are solving the problems and meeting the demands of their constituents, legislators have considerable interest in budget execution control.

BUDGET EXECUTION TECHNIQUES

Among the techniques used to control budget execution, variance analysis is probably the most familiar. Controllers and budget officials in government program offices monitor the differences between projected and actual revenues and expenses in total and by account. They monitor revenue and expense rates against allotment controls by quarter, month, week, and day—temporal control generally is required by the allotment process. Other variables monitored are purpose of expense relative to budget proposal and appropriation rationale, and location of revenues and expenses by unit and, at times, by geographical location. Monitoring of actual revenue and expense rates as well as program output and demand, where measurable, is done to compare current spending to proposals made in the budget for the next year that is under negotiation at the same time as the fiscal year budget is expended. Comparisons are made to historical revenue and spending trends, in some instances, to better understand how current programs are performing. Budget execution monitoring and control are particularly important toward the end of the fiscal year for reasons stated above, to avoid over- and underexpenditure relative to appropriation.

BUDGET EXECUTION MANAGEMENT CONTROL CHOICES

Research in public finance has paid considerable attention to budget formulation but has tended to ignore budget execution.[5–7] The reasons for this oversight are understandable. Government budgets are formulated in public, and the issues debated during this stage of the public spending process are dramatic and crucial. On the other hand, budgets are executed in private, and the issues raised in their execution are often mundane. Because of this selective attention, observers and participants in the public spending process understand program analysis far better than controllership. Consequently, the conduct of program analysis has come to be guided by a fairly coherent set of professional standards. There is agreement on what is good analysis and what is good accounting practice. Although the design and operation of control systems can profoundly influence governmental performance, budget execution controllership is not guided by a coherent set of professional standards. Without appropriate performance standards, budget officers cannot be held accountable for performance of this function. Consequently, control systems are not designed to optimize the quality, quantity, and price of goods and services purchased with public money, but "to facilitate the controller's [other] work."[4]

EX ANTE AND EX POST
CONTROLS DEFINED

The choice of whom to subject to controls and when to execute those controls is not easy. The control system designer has at least four options. First, the subject may be an organization or an individual. Second, controls may be executed before or after the subject acts. The former may be identified as ex ante and the latter as ex post controls.[8] Ex ante controls are intended to prevent subjects from doing wrong things or to compel them to perform well. Necessarily, they take the form of authoritative commands or rules that specify what the subject must do, may do, and must not do. Subjects are held responsible for complying with these commands, and the controller attempts to monitor and enforce compliance. In contrast, ex post controls are executed after the subject decides on and carries out a course of action and after some of the consequences of the subject's decisions are known. Because bad decisions cannot be undone after they are carried out, ex post controls are intended to motivate subjects to make good decisions. Subjects are held responsible for the consequences of decisions, and the controller attempts to monitor consequences and rewards or sanctions accordingly. The control system designer may choose between four distinct design alternatives: individual responsibility, ex ante or ex post, and organizational responsibility, ex ante or ex post.

PURPOSES OF EX POST CONTROLS

Ex post financial controls are used to reveal demand. They are executed after operating decisions have been made, after asset acquisition and use decisions have been carried out, and after output levels have been monitored. Their subject may be a free-standing organization, such as a private contractor or a quasi-independent public entity, or an individual manager subordinate to the controller, such as a responsibility center or program manager within a government agency.

In a free-standing organization, the structure of authority and responsibility within the organization is assumed to be an internal matter. The controller establishes a price schedule and specifies minimum service quality standards or a process whereby these standards are to be determined. This price or cost schedule may entail all sorts of complex arrangements, including rate, volume and mix adjustments, and default penalties. Where one organization can optimally supply the entire market, the controller may grant it a monopoly franchise, for example, in garbage collection for a small town or neighborhood. The significant characteristic of this approach is that a unit price cost schedule remains in effect for a specified time period.[9–11] This means that the government's financial liability will depend on the quantity of service provided and not on the costs incurred by the organizations supplying the service.

Where this budget control system design is employed, for example, where a municipality purchases gasoline at the spot-market price or where states commit to pay free-standing organizations such as a university a fixed price for performing a specific service such as enrolling students or treating heart attacks, or where the Air Force buys F-16s for a fixed price, the controller must rely upon interorganizational competition to provide sufficient incentives to service suppliers to produce efficiently and make wise asset acquisition and use decisions. If interorganizational competition is effective, those organizations that do not produce cost-effectively will not survive.

However, even where the declining marginal cost of the service in question makes monopoly appropriate, ex post controls can still be employed. This is done in businesses and business-like public-sector enterprise organizations by holding managers responsible for optimizing a single criterion value, subject to a set of constraints.[4] A prevalent approach through which this control system design is employed at the federal level is the revolving fund.[12,13] In this circumstance, the controller gives the manager the authority to make spending decisions and to manage cash flow for an extended period of time, e.g., for one year or more. For example, the manager is given the authority to make spending decisions to acquire and use people and assets, subject to output quality and quantity constraints determined by customers, and is held responsible for supplying agreed upon outputs while minimizing costs.

THE LOGIC OF EX POST CONTROL

Large private-sector firms produce comprehensive operating reports describing the performance of responsibility centers and programs, but their budgets seldom are detailed. The logic of ex post control is that the purpose of the budget is to establish performance targets that are high enough to elicit from the organization's managers their best efforts. Such budgets might contain only a single number for each responsibility center—an output quota, a unit-cost standard, a profit, or a return-on-investment target.

Under this approach to budget control, the structure of authority and responsibility within the organization is of interest to the financial controller. The effectiveness of this design depends on the elaboration of well-defined objectives, accurate and timely reporting of performance in terms of objectives, and careful matching of spending authority and responsibility. Its effectiveness also depends upon the clarity with which individual reward schedules are communicated to responsibility center managers and the degree of competition between alternative management teams. Finally, under this approach, the financial liability of government depends on the costs incurred in providing the service and not merely on the quantity or quality of the service provided.

PURPOSES OF EX ANTE CONTROLS

In contrast to ex post budget controls, ex ante controls are demand concealing. Their distinguishing attribute is that the controller retains the authority to make or exercise prior review of spending decisions. Ex ante financial controls are executed before public money is obligated or spent, and they govern the service supplier's acquisition and use of assets. Examples of ex ante financial controls include object-of-expenditure appropriations, apportionments, targets, position controls, and fund and account controls that regulate spending by account and the kind of assets that can be acquired by governmental departments and agencies. Such controls also govern the behavior of private contracting entities that supply services to government or to clients on behalf of governments.

Execution of ex ante controls requires assessment of the consequences of asset acquisition decisions. This consideration may be implicit, as it is in the execution of the traditional line-item budget and basic-research contracts, or explicit, as in the execution of performance and program budgets and systems development contracts. It is often influenced by information on current and past performance, but consideration of the consequences of spending decisions is always prospective in nature.

The logic of ex ante control is that constraining managerial discretion is the first purpose of budget execution. Because the degree of constraint will depend upon the detail of the spending plan, as well as the degree of compliance enforced by the controllers, these budgets need to be highly detailed. A department or agency budget must identify all asset acquisitions to be executed during the fiscal year and make it clear who is responsible for implementation.

Under ex ante budget control, service-supplying organizations must be guaranteed an allotment of funds in return for continuously providing a service for a specified period. The service provider will assume some responsibility for managing output levels or delivery schedules, service quality, or price to the government customer. Government is directly responsible for all legitimate costs incurred in the delivery of services, regardless of the actual quantity or quality of the services provided.

ENFORCING EFFICIENCY WITH EX ANTE CONTROLS

Where a manager seeking to increase a budget is subject to tight ex ante controls, the controller can enforce efficiency during the budget period by requiring affirmative answers to the following questions:

1. Will a proposed change permit the same activity to be carried out at a lower cost?
2. Will higher priority activities be carried out at the same cost?
3. Will proposed asset acquisitions or reallocations of savings support activities that have a higher priority than those presently carried out?

When operating managers are faced with these criteria, they respond appropriately. Controllers approve most changes in spending plans proposed by operating managers because only mutually advantageous changes will be proposed in most circumstances.

WHEN TO DELEGATE EX ANTE CONTROLS

When line-item or lump-sum appropriations have a comparative advantage, to say that ex ante controls are a necessary means of reinforcing the controllers' bargaining power should not imply that tight ex ante controls always must be administered by them. Under certain conditions, authority to spend money, transfer funds, fill positions, etc., may be delegated to subordinate managers. The threat of reimposition of ex ante controls will be sufficient to insure that the manager's behavior corresponds to the controllers' and elected officials' preferences. In order for such delegation to take place, the following conditions must be present:

1. Reimposition of controls must be a credible threat.
2. The gain to the manager from delegation must more than offset the associated sacrifice in bargaining power; the manager of an agency in the stable backwaters of public policy has little to gain from relief from ex ante controls if the price of such relief is a change in business as usual.
3. Controllers must be confident that their monitoring procedures, including postaudit, will identify violations of "trust."

Clearly, all long-term relationships with private contractors and government goods and service suppliers rely to some degree on ex ante controls. Even the operation of fixed-price contracts requires prior specification of product quality standards and delivery schedules. But, flexible-price, cost-plus type contracts and appropriated budgets require considerably higher levels of reliance on ex ante controls and also on monitoring and enforcing compliance. And, the cost of tightly held budget execution control is high.

ACCURATE RECORDS AND EFFICIENCY

At the least, adoption of the budget execution control systems described herein means that controllers must take steps to ensure that suppliers fairly and accurately recognize, record, and report their expenses. This, in turn, requires careful definition of costs and specification of appropriate account structures, accounting practices and internal controls, direct costing procedures, and the criteria to be used in allocating overheads. Still, accurate accounting does not guarantee efficiency. Even where the service supplier's financial and operational accounts completely and accurately present every relevant fact about the decisions made by its managers, they will not provide a basis for evaluating the soundness of those decisions. This is because cost accounts can show only what happened, not what might have happened. They do not show the range of asset acquisition choices and trade-offs the supplier considered, let alone those that should have been considered but were not.

APPROPRIATE DESIGN OF BUDGET CONTROL SYSTEMS

Under line-item or lump-sum budgets and flexible-price contracts, asset acquisition decisions must be made by the contractor, but the contractor cannot be trusted completely to make them efficiently. Consequently, the contractor must be denied some discretion to make managerial decisions. The fundamental question is, how much must be denied? To what extent should government officials or their controller agents regulate, duplicate, or replace the contractor's managerial efforts?

This question must be addressed, because oversight is costly in terms of monitoring and reporting costs, and also because of the benefits sacrificed due to failure to exploit the contractor's managerial expertise. The controller and the government official will seldom be more competent to make asset acquisition decisions than the contractor. The answer to this dilemma is that controllers and officials should do the minimum necessary, given the incentives faced by and the motivations of the contractor. Still, at times, the minimum necessary is a great deal. This de-

cision depends on circumstance and the controller's skill in exploiting the opportunities created by the contractor's response to institutional constraints. In other words, all long-term relationships between government officials and contractors must rely on incentives, even those governed by lump-sum budgets and flexible-price contracts. The difference is that when these control system designs are employed, the incentives are deeply embedded in the process of budget and contract execution.

Budget execution management control should be matched to circumstances: increasing costs and homogeneous outputs imply one kind of design, while decreasing costs and heterogeneous outputs imply another. However, what we observe in practice is that this match is not always achieved. Controllers tend to rely on monopoly supply and ex ante controls.[14–17] This combination cannot be appropriate for every service to which it is applied. Evidence can be marshaled to show that a variety of services might be performed satisfactorily by competing organizations, including in air traffic controls,[18] custodial services and building maintenance,[19,20] day-care centers,[19] electrical power generation,[19] fire protection services,[21,22] forest management,[23] management of grazing lands,[24] hospitals and health care services,[25] housing,[26] postal services,[25] prisons and correctional facilities,[25] property assessment,[27] refuse collection,[28,29] security services,[25] ship and aircraft maintenance,[19,30] urban transit,[25] and wastewater treatment.[25] Furthermore, even when controllers eschew monopoly supply, they frequently fail to fully exploit the benefits of competition. In New York City, for example, the municipal social services agency acquires child-care services for its clients from public and private day-care centers. Public centers are subject to the full panoply of ex ante controls associated with lump-sum appropriation budgets, and private centers are subject to those associated with flexible-price contracts.

DEPARTMENT OF DEFENSE PRACTICES

To cite another example, Department of Defense (DoD) policy often has restricted the use of flexible-price contracts to situations characterized by considerable procurement risk, e.g., in R&D projects. In other contracts, the degree of incentive is supposed to be calibrated to project risk. The first ship in a multiship construction program is supposed to be constructed under a cost-plus-fixed-profit contract, while later editions are supposed to be built under fixed-price contracts, on the assumption that experience permits the contractor to manage to a narrower range of cost outcomes and to assume a greater share of the risk burden. It may be observed that while DoD generally makes the proper transition from cost-plus to award-fee contracts as it moves from design to prototype development, it may not make the transition to a fixed-price contract for downstream production.[31] To be consistent with the logic advanced here, selection of defense system production suppliers should be reduced to a question of cost and price search. Acquisition should be based upon fixed-price contracts, awarded by competitive bidding. Where production volume is sufficient, DoD should try to maintain long-term contractual relations with two or more producers, as multisourcing permits price search at each negotiation of the relationship between DoD and its suppliers.[32] Nevertheless, winning a contract to develop a weapons system continues to be tantamount to winning subsequent production contracts in a high proportion of cases. Finally, not only do controllers tend to subject government agencies and contractors to a wide array of ex ante controls, they often hold them to tight output, quality, and service delivery schedules. Performance targets that can be met all of the time are not very ambitious.

CAUSES OF BUDGET AND MANAGEMENT CONTROL MISMATCH

What accounts for mismatches between how budgets are controlled in practice and the approach advanced here, which relies on a more sophisticated set of controls dependent on analysis of cost structure (increasing or decreasing) and type of output (homogeneous or heterogeneous)? One explanation is ignorance of consequences on the part of the controllers and elected officials. Also, some of the empirical data required to employ the control criteria outlined here are often unavailable. The most critical gap in this knowledge is how costs vary with output. Definitions and measurements of service outputs and activities are often inadequate. Insufficient effort has been made to correct this situation in most public organizations. Of the two tasks, getting knowledge about the shape of cost functions is the more difficult. But if we first answer the question, "Cost to do what?," this knowledge can be derived deductively in a manner similar to the methods used in cost accounting and conventional price theory. Cost and supply analysis can yield highly useful information about marginal and average costs. Finally, experimentation with funding and output levels will increase our knowledge of service supply and cost functions.[33–35]

The kind of information called for here requires a high level of analytical sophistication in budget execution and system design, a skill that staff responsible for executing budgets may lack. Indeed, even if controllers had good information on cost and service supply functions, some

might not know how to use it. Their experience tends to orient them to the administration of the traditional line-item, object-of-expenditure budget. Effective administration of a lump-sum or line-item appropriation requires no more than a modicum of arithmetical ability combined with a substantial amount of horse sense and bargaining savvy. However, matching control systems design to circumstances requires a practical understanding of applied microeconomics and financial and managerial accounting. Controllers often fail to understand the ideas outlined here or how to implement alternatives to the line-item appropriations budget—where to exercise judgment and where to exercise specific decision rules. This is demonstrated by the persistent attempt of controllers to employ techniques devised for use within organizations, such as standard costs based on fully-distributed average historical costs, to establish per-unit prices for public organizations such as hospitals and universities.

OBSTACLES TO REFORM

Absence of knowledge of options and objectives is not a satisfactory explanation for controller decisions to resist reform. Such problems can be corrected, and incompetence may be weeded out. If a better match between control system design and circumstances would have a substantial payoff, why has this situation not been corrected? One answer regarding the implementation of reform is as follows.

A large part of the literature on budgeting in the United States is concerned with reform. The goals of the proposed reforms are couched in similar language–economy, efficiency, improvement, or just better budgeting. The President, the Congress and its committees, administrative agencies, even the citizenry are all to gain by some change. However, any effective change in budgetary relationships must necessarily alter the outcomes of the budgetary process. Otherwise, why bother? Far from being a neutral matter of "better budgeting," proposed reforms inevitably contain important implications for the political system, that is, the "who gets what" of governmental decisions.[36]

If controllers and elected officials empowered to determine the methods used in executing budgets are rational (we understand that politics often compromises rationality as we define it from a management perspective), this quote implies that they have a strong interest in maintaining the status quo. To explain the persistent mismatch between budget execution control system designs and practice, it is necessary to determine who benefits from the status quo and, therefore, who will oppose the adoption of a more appropriate type of control.[37]

Members of Congress, state legislators, city council members, and any politician with a constituency worth cultivating would appear to lose as a result of reforms proposed. As the collective holders of the power of the purse, legislators clearly have the authority to order budgets to be executed in almost any way they like, including the power to delegate this authority to controllers. Efficiency implies an exclusive concern with the supply of goods and services to the citizenry, with some indifference as to the means used to supply the goods or even to the identity of the suppliers. However, legislators are frequently as concerned about where public money is spent and who gets it, as they are with what it buys.[38–41] Line-item appropriations in general, and object-of-expenditure budgets in particular, are ideally suited to the satisfaction of legislative preferences with respect to how public money is spent, where it is spent, and who gets it.

REFERENCES

1. McCaffery, J.L.; Jones, L.R. *Budgeting and Financial Management in the Federal Government*; Information Age Press: Greenwich, CT, 2001.
2. Jones, L.R.; Thompson, F. *Public Management: Institutional Renewal for the Twenty-First Century*; JAI-Elsevier Science Press: Stamford, CT, 1999.
3. Simons, R. *Levers of Control*; Harvard Business School Press: Boston, MA, 1995.
4. Anthony, R.; Young, D. *Managerial Control in Non-Profit Organizations*; Irwin, 1984; pp. 20, 21, 288, Chaps. 7–9.
5. Simon, H., et al. *Centralization vs. Decentralization in Organizing the Controller's Department*; The Controllership Foundation: New York, 1954.
6. Schick, A. Control patterns in state budget executions. Public Adm. Rev. **1964**, *24*, 97–106.
7. Schick, A. Contemporary Problems in Financial Control. In *Current Issues in Public Administration,* 2nd Ed.; Lane, F., Ed.; St. Martin's Press: New York, 1982; 361–371.
8. Demski, J.; Feltham, G. *Cost Determination*; Iowa State University Press: Ames, 1967.
9. Goldberg, V. Regulation and administered contracts. Bell J. Econ. **1976**, *7*, 426–428.
10. Thompson, F. How to stay within the budget using per-unit prices. J. Policy Anal. Manag. **1984**, *4/1*.
11. Thompson, F.; Fiske, G. One more solution to the problem of higher education finance. Policy Anal. **1978**, *3/4*.
12. Bailey, M. Decentralization Through Internal Prices. In *Defense Management*; Enke, S., Ed.; Prentice-Hall: Englewood Cliffs, NJ, 1967; 337–352.
13. Beckner, N.V. Government efficiency and the military: Buyer–seller relationship. J. Polit. Econ. **1960**, *68*.
14. Thompson, F.; Zumeta, W. Controls and controls: A reexamination of control patterns in budget execution. Policy Sci. **1981**, *13*, 25–50.
15. Pitsvada, B.T. Flexibility in federal budget execution. Public Budg. Finance **1983**, *3/2*.
16. Draper, F.; Pitsvada, T. Limitations in federal budget execution. Gov. Account. J. **1981**, *30*, 3.
17. Fisher, L. *Presidential Spending Power*; Princeton University Press: Princeton, NJ, 1975.
18. Poole, R. Air traffic control: The private sector option. Herit. Found. Backgrounds **1982**, *216*.
19. Bennett, J.; DiLorenzo, T. Public employee labor unions and the privatization of public services. J. Labor Res. **1983**, *4*, pp. 42, 43.
20. Blankart, C.B. Bureaucratic Problems in Public Choice: Why Do Public Goods Still Remain Public? In *Public Choice and Public Finance*; Roskamp, R., Ed.; Cufas: New York, 1979; 155–167.
21. Poole, R. Fighting fires for profit. Reason **1976, May**.
22. Smith, R.G. Feet to the fire. Reason **1983, May**, 23–29.
23. Hanke, S. The privatization debate. Cato J. **1982**, 656.
24. Hanke, S. Land Policy. In *Agenda*; Howill, R., Ed.; Heritage Foundation: Washington, DC, 1983; Vol. 83, 65.
25. Hanke, S. Privatization: Theory, Evidence, Implementation. In *Control of Federal Spending*; Harris, R., Ed.; Academy of Political Science, 1985; 106–110.
26. Weicker, J. *Housing*; American Enterprise Institute: Washington, DC, 1980; 80.
27. Poole, R. *Cutting Back City Hall*; University Books, 1980; 164.
28. Savas, E.S. Policy analysis for local government. Policy Anal. **1977**, *3*, 49–77.
29. Bennett, J.; Johnson, M. Public v. private provision of collective goods and services. Public Choice **1979**, *4*, 55–63.
30. Bennett, J.; Johnson, M. *Better Government at Half the Price: Private Production of Public Services*; Caroline House, 19XX.
31. Thompson, F.; Jones, L.R. *Reinventing the Pentagon*; Jossey-Bass: San Francisco, 1994.
32. Jones, L.R.; Bixler, G.C. *Mission Financing to Realign National Defense*; JAI Press: Greenwich, CT, 1992.
33. Wildavsky, A. *Budgeting: A Comparative Theory of the Budgetary Process*; Little Brown: Boston, 1975; 118–119.
34. Larkey, P. *Evaluating Public Programs: The Impact of General Revenue Sharing on Municipal Government*; Princeton University Press: Princeton, NJ, 1979.
35. Cothran, D. Program flexibility and budget growth. West. Polit. Q. **1981**, *34*, 593–610.
36. Wildavsky, A. Political implications of budget reform. Public Adm. Rev. **1961**, *21*, 183–190.
37. Zimmerman, J. The municipal accounting maze: An analysis of political incentives. J. Account. Res. **1977**, *21*, 107–144.
38. Arnold, D. *Congress and the Bureaucracy*; Yale University Press: New Haven, CT, 1979.
39. Ferejohn, J. *Pork Barrel Politics*; Stanford University Press: Stanford, CA, 1974.
40. Fiorina, M. *Congress: Keystone of the Washington Establishment*; Yale University Press: New Haven, CT, 1977.
41. Shepsle, K.; Weingast, B. Political preferences for the pork barrel. Am. J. Polit. Sci. **1981**, *25*.

FURTHER READING

Barton, D. Regulating a monopolist with unknown costs. Econometrica **1982**, *50*.

Breton, A.; Wintrobe, R. The equilibrium size of a budget maximizing bureau. J. Polit. Econ. **1975**, *83*, 195–207.

Cheung, S.N.S. The contractual nature of the firm. J. Law Econ. **1983**, *25*.

Coase, R. The nature of the firm. Economica **1937**, *4*.

Fox, R. *Arming America: How the U.S. Buys Weapons*; Harvard University Press: Cambridge, MA, 1974.

Hofsted, G.H. *The Game of Budget Control*; Van Gorcum, 1967.

Holstrom, B. Moral hazard and observability. Bell J. Econ. **1979**, *10*.

Meyerson, R.B. Incentives compatibility and the bargaining problem. Econometrica **1979**, *47*.

Mirlees, J. The optimal structure of incentives and authority within an organization. Bell J. Econ. **1976**, *7*.

Mitnick, B. The theory of agency: The policing "paradox" and regulatory behavior. Public Choice **1977**, *30*.

Morgan, J. Bilateral monopoly and the competitive output. Q. J. Econ. **1949**, *63*.

Peck, M.; Scherer, F. *The Weapons Acquisition Process: An Economic Analysis*; Harvard Business School: Cambridge, MA, 1962.

Scherer, F. *The Weapons Acquisition Process: Economic Incentives*; Harvard Business School: Cambridge, MA, 1964.

Stark, R. On Cost Analysis for Engineered Construction. In *Auctions, Bidding, and Contracting*; Englebrecht-Wiggins, R., Shubik, M., Stark, R., Eds.; New York University Press: New York, 1983.

Stark, R.; Varley, T. Bidding, Estimating, and Engineered Construction Contracting. In *Auctions, Bidding, and Contracting*; Englebrecht-Wiggins, R., Shubik, M., Stark, R., Eds.; New York University Press: New York, 1983; 121–135.

Thompson, F. Utility maximizing behavior in organized anarchies. Public Choice **1981**, *36*.

Wildavsky, A.; Hammann, A. Comprehensive versus incremental budgeting in the Department of Agriculture. Admin. Sci. Q. **1956**, *10*, 321–346.

Williamson, O. *The Economics of Discretionary Behavior*; Prentice Hall: Englewood Cliffs, NJ, 1964.

Williamson, O. *Markets and Hierarchies*; Free Press: New York, 1975.

Budget Reform

Jerry McCaffery
Naval Postgraduate School, Monterey, California, U.S.A.

INTRODUCTION

Budget reform involves restructuring the budget process to provide better information so that decision makers can make better resource allocation decisions. Reforms have focused on process improvements such as program budgeting, performance budgeting, and zero-based budgeting, and desired outcomes such as balanced budgets and mechanisms to produce them. After an examination of the meaning of budget reform and its historical context, this article discusses how the concepts of planning, management, and control form core elements of all budget systems, but are emphasized differently in different budget systems and reforms.

MEANING OF BUDGET REFORM

Budget reform has been hampered because government budgeting itself is not simple. In sending his proposal to create an executive budget system to Congress in 1912, President Taft said, "The Constitutional purpose of a budget is to make government responsive to public opinion and responsible for its acts" (Ref. 1, p. 19). The proposal further noted that a budget served numerous purposes, from a document for Congressional action, to an instrument of control and management by the President, to a basis for the administration of departments and agencies. Since then, the multiple purposes for budgeting have been well recognized.[2] As long as a multiform definition of budget is acceptable, defining budget is relatively easy. Considering budget reform is much more difficult. What is budget reform? Budget reform involves reshaping the budget and the budget process so that money is spent more efficiently, effectively, and wisely. Ultimately, budget reform might result in the more efficient application of public expenditures to public needs. In 1940, V.O. Key[3,4] suggested that the critical question for budget decision makers was how to supply the answer to the fundamental question, "On what basis shall it be decided to allocate x dollars to activity A instead of activity B?" Key argued that this was fundamentally a political question, and how one answered that question was dependent on the one's values.[5] If the answer to Key's question is no clearer now than it was in the 1940s,

it is also clear that budget practitioners before and after Key believed that improving the elements of the decision process was useful (For example, some researchers have found that budget type influences budget discussion, i.e. program budgets provoke more programmatic discussion. See Refs. 6 and 7).

EARLY AMERICAN PATTERNS: PREHISTORY

Budget reform has a rather extensive history. Early American budgetary patterns were both part of and separate from their predominantly English colonial heritage. They were part of that heritage in that the American colonies inherited English historical experience with gradual imposition of limits on the power of the monarch and the gradual expansion of legislative power. They were separate from this legacy in that the American revolutionaries carefully tried to avoid anything that smacked of giving power to an executive; having rid themselves of one king, they had no taste for another. In the turmoil during and after the American Revolution, two giants emerged on stage almost simultaneously. The reforms of William Pitt the Younger reshaped British budgetary practices (Wildavsky calls Pitt a pivotal figure in British budgetary history. See Ref. 8), while in the new United States Alexander Hamilton almost single-handedly created a budgetary system and practice for the new American nation.

As Chancellor of the English Exchequer from 1783 to 1801, Pitt faced a heavy debt load as a result of the American Revolution. Pitt consolidated a maze of customs and excise duties into one general fund from which all creditors would be paid, reduced fraud in revenue collection by introducing new auditing measures, and instituted double-entry book-keeping procedures. Moreover, Pitt established a sinking fund schedule for amortization of debt, requiring that all new loans made by government impose an additional 1% levy as a term of repayment. Pitt raised some taxes and lowered others to reduce the allure of smuggling. This model encompassed a royal executive with varying degrees of strength and a legislative body attempting to exert financial control over the Crown by requiring parliamentary approval of

Encyclopedia of Public Administration and Public Policy
DOI: 10.1081/E-EPAP 120010974

sources of revenue and expenditure. Approval was provided through appropriations legislation and ultimately made administrative officials accountable to Parliament.

Hamilton's problems were different from Pitt's, but equally serious. After the Revolutionary War, the colonies departed from English tradition when they created fiscal systems that virtually excluded the executive, vesting power in various legislative arrangements. As a result of their distaste for central government, the powers of the first Congress established under the Articles of Confederation were weak. Their fear of creating a new monarch was evident in the manner in which powers were delegated to both the legislative and executive branches. The colonists were also averse to a system of national taxation. Taxation imposed a special hardship on the colonies because hard coinage was scarce and bills or letters of credit were used irregularly.

In 1789, as the first Secretary of Treasury, Alexander Hamilton strongly influenced development in this period (For an excellent biography of Hamilton, see Ref. 9). Initially, Hamilton set to establish the credit of the new government. His first two reports to Congress urged funding the national debt at full value, the assumption by the federal government of all debts incurred by the states during the Revolutionary War, and a system of taxation to pay for the debts.[a] Strong opposition arose to these proposals, but Hamilton's position prevailed after he made a bargain with Thomas Jefferson, who delivered southern votes in return for Hamilton's support for locating the future nation's capital on the banks of the Potomac. Hamilton's third report to Congress proposed a national bank, modeled after the Bank of England. In a few short years, Hamilton submitted four major reports to Congress, gaining acceptance of three that funded the national debt at full value, established the nation's credit at home and abroad by creating a banking system and a stable currency, and developed a stable tax system based on excise taxes to fund steady recovery from the debt and to provide for future appropriations. Hamilton's role in establishing a system for debt management, securing the currency, and providing a stable revenue base make him the founding father of critical elements of the American budgeting system.

FIRST EFFORTS AT REFORM

As early as 1800, civilian agency budgets were presented in carefully detailed object-of-expenditure form, whereas

military expenditures tended to be appropriated as lump sums not unlike specific program categories. Early debate on budget development focused on enhancing flexibility and program accomplishments rather than on strict agency accountability in the arguments over the merits of lump sum versus line item appropriations, over the merits of allowing for executive discretion in spending money to execute programs as opposed to requiring that agencies follow explicit legislative directions constrained by line item appropriations. However, for most of the nineteenth century, government functions were few and simple, and were supported by equally simple budget structures and procedures. Tyler and Willand noted that by 1900, the United States was the "only great nation without a budget system" (Ref. 10, quoting Ref. 11).

Debate about form and content of the federal budget accelerated as a result of local government reforms implemented in New York City and elsewhere from the mid-1870s through the beginning of the twentieth century, and culminated in Congressional enactment of the Budget and Accounting Act of 1921. The stimuli for passage of this act may be found in the deficits incurred in World War I and the various reform movements rising in local governments as a reaction to egregious examples of boss rule and political corruption in the late 1870s and after. It also had a national background. Irene Rubin[12] suggested that some part of federal reform came from efforts to oversee the railroads at the end of the nineteenth century. Railroads were big and important to the public for carrying goods and passengers. With the expansion of railroads and the acquisition of one railroad by another, it was not always easy to tell if a railroad was making a profit or, indeed, if it were solvent. This meant it was also difficult to tell if the rates that were set for freight and passengers were fair. Thus, in the 1880s, the Interstate Commerce Commission was put in the position of regulating rates, but to do this it had to develop better accounting tools in consultation with the railroads. Once these procedures had been implemented for railroads—considered to be the largest, most complex, and most sophisticated of private corporations—government was then urged to make similar improvements for its own operations. Thus, reformers had rather clear ideas about what they were against and what they were for. Nevertheless, Rubin suggested that business leadership in budget reform has been overstated, and that it was government officials and academics who invented and modified public budgeting in the United States, while business methods have historically been given more credit than they deserve (Ref. 12, p. 444).

In the 1900s, reform efforts were continued by Frederick Cleveland at the New York Bureau of Municipal Research and by President Taft's Commission on Economy and Efficiency in 1912. Long before the federal

---

[a] Hamilton's program was outlined in four reports: Reports on the Public Credit of January 14, 1790 and December 13, 1790; The Report on a National Bank, December 14, 1790 and The Report on Manufactures, submitted to Congress on December 5, 1791.

government passed the Budget and Accounting Act of 1921, many American cities had passed local budget reform acts that prevented city councils from appropriating money outside the confines of a budget. As early as 1899, the National Municipal League drafted a model municipal charter that incorporated a budget system under the direct supervision of the mayor (Ref. 1, p. 13). Passage of the 1921 Act was an important point in the development of the executive budget power, giving the president the power to organize the executive budget process and to create a staff agency to compile, analyze, and make recommendations to Congress about agency budgets. The power of the executive over the budget process would grow steadily for the next 50 years as the functions of the federal government expanded under the impress of the Great Depression and Presidents Hoover and Roosevelt in the 1930s, World War II, and the social service revolution of the 1960s. These trends resulted in dramatic changes in the nature of the federal budget. From 1950 to 1990, federal government spending shifted from favoring discretionary expenditures with more than one-half of the annual budget spent on defense, to mandatory expenditures with more than one-half being spent on social security, health, and welfare programs. This made tools and processes related to discretionary expenditure less important than those aimed at analyzing, predicting, and controlling mandatory expenditures (see Refs. 13–15), and ensured that the search for better budget processes and tools would continue.

In the United States, twentieth-century budget reform spread from the local level to state and national levels. Although the influence of state and local reforms on national patterns has varied, state and local governments have remained a vital force for reform. Smaller and with a less complicated mechanism than the federal government, subnational governments faced less inertia and were more flexible in adopting reform elements and discarding them for something better. States and certain large cities must be seen as first adopters; the wise student of innovation will always find something of interest occurring there. Recently, states have been involved with target-based budgeting, performance budgeting, and performance measurement and accountability (see Refs. 16–19). Federal adoption of a particular state reform may be seen as mainstream acceptance of that reform; state adoption of a federal pattern often comes as an attempt to increase the synchronization between state and federal patterns in order for the state to extract more money from the federal budget.

Evaluation of the history of reform has been mixed. Irene Rubin argued that budget reforms are much more widely adopted than is generally recognized. The benefits tend to be oversold and when exaggerated outcomes do not seem to appear, many participants lose interest and deem the reform a failure, regardless of whether it leaves real improvements in the budget process.[20] Forrester and Adams cited the paucity of successful reforms and warned that budget reform requires attention to the organizational context, and that the objectives and execution of a reform must match the dynamic objectives and needs of the organization and be cognizant of the organizational culture.[21] Notwithstanding that reform is neither linear nor certain, the last 100 years indicate reform efforts have a certain irrepressibility.

MODERN REFORMS OF PROCESS AND OUTCOME

Reforms have involved both process and outcome. Much of the history of budget reform involved finding ways to present budget information to decision makers in a more meaningful way so that better decisions can be made about how to allocate scarce resources. These reforms have included performance budgeting, program budgeting, zero-based budgeting. Planning–programming–budgeting (PPB) and various systems focused on target- or mission-based budgeting. Some reforms have focused on the budget process itself, in the belief that better staff or a more timely process would provide a better budget process. Paramount among these sorts of reforms are the Budget and Accounting Act of 1921, and the Congressional Budget Reform and Impoundment Act of 1974.

Dissatisfaction with budget outcomes, usually in respect to growing deficits, has resulted in a different type of budget reform basically attempting to mandate outcomes (e.g., deficit reduction or balanced budgets). Examples of this kind of budget reform at the federal level include in the Gramm–Rudman–Hollings (GRH) Acts of 1985 and 1987, and the Budget Enforcement Acts of 1990 and 1993, with their spending caps and pay-as-you-go requirements, and several attempts at a Constitutional Balanced Budget Amendment. These efforts were not without some adverse consequences. Attempts to meet the GRH targets often involved optimistic estimates of spending and revenues, and certain gimmicks such as shifted paydays, which probably did more to damage the budget process than reform it, especially because few if any of the GRH targets were met. With the Budget Enforcement Act of 1990, the United States shifted from a deficit control approach to a spending cap approach. This was a looser discipline, but it was used throughout the 1990s, being reenacted in the Balanced Budget Agreement of 1997 for the 5-year period out to 2002. For discretionary accounts this meant tight discipline, often at or below a growth rate equal to that of inflation. Both Congress and the President seemed to move toward supplemental appropriations and emergency spending designations to escape some of this discipline.

In terms of process, the spending cap focus appeared to put more emphasis on the beginning of the budget process, and it is arguable that the 1990s saw the full fruition of the Congressional Budget Reform and Impoundment Control Act of 1974. The budget committees and the budget resolution became important forces in the budget process because they were used by both parties, but especially the Republicans, to seek new notions of the shape and size of the federal government. This new role was to be a diminished one, with power and programs being pushed toward more innovative and effective state and local governments, or even toward the private sector. New national security concerns occurring with the terrorist attacks of 2001 may lead to a reevaluation of this position. Providing for the common defense and responding to a great crisis has always been the role of the central government.

PLANNING, MANAGEMENT, AND CONTROL

In 1964, Allen Schick offered an analytic framework for budget reform that has withstood the test of time; its insights remain as penetrating and relevant now as they were then,[22,23] and its explanations just as powerful. Schick said that every budget system comprised elements of planning, management, and control, and that different budget systems arranged and emphasized those elements differently. Planning involved the determination of objectives, the scrutiny of alternative courses of actions, and the selection of programs. Management involved programming of approved goals into specific goals and activities, designing programs to carry out those activities and providing staffing and resources to carry out those designs. Control involved the process of ''binding'' operating officials to the policies and plans set by their superiors, through the appropriation and budget execution process, and through budget control procedures such as position controls, limits on staffing, and transfer authority, purchase requisition, procurement, and travel procedures, capital outlay procedures, and pre- and post-audit processes.

Schick observed that planning, management, and control were not equally emphasized in budget systems because time was a scarce commodity in the budget process and participants had to choose which of these elements to maximize. In addition, Schick concluded that different budget systems inherently emphasize one of these elements over another. Consequently, the observer can examine different budget systems for different characteristics, but these characteristics cluster around concepts of control, management, and planning. For example,

control-oriented budget systems focus on line item budget systems, value the skills of accountants, focus on inputs (e.g., dollars, personnel), and are focused most heavily on budget execution. In contrast, management-oriented budget systems focus on the preparation stage of budgeting, are dominated by managers rather than accountants, focus on the units of work to be done (e.g., cases to be cleared, miles of highway to be built), and seek efficiency and effectiveness, rather than legally correct expenditure patterns. Budget systems that focus on planning were the most broad-gauge and focus on the prepreparation stage of budgeting (e.g., What is good policy? What should government do to bring about good policy?), emphasize benefit–cost analysis and the skills of economists and systems analysis, rather than managers or accountants, to work out streams of future benefits and costs. A planning-focused system in its insistence on supporting policy with dollars was the most generalized and difficult system to operate in Schick's paradigm.

As a practical matter, Schick was concerned with explaining the differences between the early version of the PPB system then in use in the Department of Defense and the powerful analysis of nondefense spending offered by Aaron Wildavsky under the rubric of incrementalism, where the future is controlled by the past and departs modestly from it as budgets change by increments from year to year. Under PPB, Schick suggested that change would occur from the top down, rather from the bottom up. PPB systems would implement change as a result of comprehensive policy-making procedures, rather than an aggregation of individual decisions made year by year. PPB would be rational. Incrementalism would be experiential, and rely heavily on feedback and course correction procedures as a counterbalance to the lack of rationality and foresight. Although incremental budgeting would result in information and budgets building up from the bottom, PPB systems would result in a downward flow of budget decisions resulting from choices about policy.

After a brief governmentwide trial in the 1960s PPB was again limited to defense, not because defense is well suited to certain analytical skills or benefit–cost analysis logic, but because the existence of a threat drives everything. In defense, the critical budgetary questions each year are ''what is the threat?'', ''how has it changed from last year?'', and ''what will we need to meet this threat 5 years from now.'' PPB allows for these questions to be answered centrally in a unifying scenario and for subsequent decisions to flow down through the organization in response to that scenario. In most years, the defense budget is an incremental system, in the same sense that federal nondefense budgets are incremental. However, occasionally, the threat situation changes dramatically. When that happens, the planning and budgeting system must reflect those changes. After the fall of the Berlin Wall and the collapse of the USSR, the threat situation for the United States changed dramatically. It was obvious that U.S. defense spending could now be lower, but efforts to articulate a new threat situation and a response to it took almost a decade and were not really resolved by the time of the terrorist attack in September 2001, although the defense establishment was downsized by about one-third during that period. Nonetheless, PPB remains alive and well in the Department of Defense because the defense budget must attempt to ascertain long-term threats, as well as to perfect the mix of current and future assets that will meet that threat. PPB is especially well suited to plan to meet threats to the United States by designing force structure (e.g., number of troops, tanks) and managing a stream of resources to fund each year what is necessary to meet the threat this year and in the future. In most years, PPB outcomes appear and may be incremental, reflecting an incremental change in the threat situation. No reason exists why PPB could not be used in the health or aging areas, except that it is an expensive system to use and it does tend to surface the total cost of packages that political decision makers would perhaps prefer to ignore until they need to be resolved in a climate of emergency.

Philip Joyce suggested that an understanding of the history of budget reform can be organized around Schick's concepts; thus, he divides U.S. budget history into four periods.[24,25] The early period (1873–1937) is characterized by weak executive power, little central control, and idiosyncratic processes. Reformers sought to emphasize central control and to bring sound business practices to government, while focusing on increasing economy and efficiency. Joyce asserted that perhaps the single greatest outcome of this period was the Budget and Accounting Act of 1921, with its creation of the Bureau of the Budget and the establishment of the General Accounting Office to audit the results of federal spending and report to Congress. Joyce suggested the second period lasted from 1937 to 1960; this period emphasized management, thanks to the various challenges faced by the federal government with the Great Depression of the 1930s and World War II and its aftermath. Early efforts at performance budgeting were a key element of this period.

Joyce suggested that 1960 to 1985 was the third period of budget reform. Here, the emphasis was on planning for outcomes with program budgeting and PPB systems. During this period, reforms sought to move beyond efficiency and management to comprehensive program decisions based on notions of comprehensive and rational decision making. Zero-based budgeting, another variant of comprehensive budgeting, also enjoyed a brief popularity. These systems failed to displace incremental patterns based on line item budgeting,[26,27] although they

did leave a legacy biased toward more analysis in the budget process. In 1974, the Congressional Budget Reform Act gave Congress its equivalent to the Office of Management and Budget in the Congressional Budget Office, and provided a highly capable source for budget estimation and appropriation scorekeeping. The budget resolution and the budget committees also helped Congress assume some comprehensive planning functions for the budget at the start of its budget process. Joyce suggested that these comprehensive reforms were only partially successful, but that they did leave a legacy favoring greater analysis, and zero-based budgeting, with its concentration on levels of effort around the budget base, has led to target-based budget systems at state and local levels. Joyce noted that the period after 1985 was mostly occupied with deficit reduction measures with GRH I and II and the various Budget Enforcement or Balanced Budget Acts, as well as a resurgence of performance-based budgeting focused on evaluating the results of government spending with the Government Performance and Results Act of 1993. Rubin[28] argued that two additional emphases should be added to Schick's framework to represent trends from 1970 through the 1990s—prioritization and accountability. This is a useful clarification, but if prioritization is understood to be a primary emphasis in planning and accountability in control, then Schick's framework may stand.

OBSERVATIONS

Schick's powerful analytical construct helps us to think about current budget reform efforts. Clearly, the Chief Financial Officers Act of 1990 is a control mechanism. It is focused on budget execution, fiduciary concerns, and correct and appropriate spending of budgetary funds. With its emphasis on auditable financial statements for the federal government and individual agencies, it is concerned that dollars of input be spent for correct and appropriate purposes; that fraud, waste, and misuse funds be avoided; and that the public be able to trust their government to faithfully administer budgets within the parameters in which they have been passed. The Government Performance and Results Act of 1993, however, clearly emphasizes the management aspects of budgeting, with its emphasis on outputs and outcomes, and their costs. It pushes beyond the propriety of control aspects to efficiency and effectiveness, and even beyond with an emphasis on outcomes—for example, measurably more justice or measurably less poverty. With linkage to strategic planning efforts, it also moves toward a planning orientation and one that has rather widespread input to it.

Schick's analysis is also a caution about the difficulty of budget reform. For example, reforms that emphasize one element usually impair another; increased control usually means decreased management. Thus, balancing these concepts is important. Finally, while no magic formula for a good budget process has been discovered, despite strenuous efforts, modern American budgeting at the federal level is remarkably accessible to its citizens. In a democracy, much should be made of this. Moreover, budget reformers remain remarkably persistent about ensuring that government should act as a wise fiduciary agent, that decisions reflect attempts to get the most value from the dollars spent, and that government target important and achievable ends. There is much to praise in these efforts.

REFERENCES

1. Burkhead, J. *Government Budgeting*; John Wiley & Sons: New York, 1956.
2. Wildavsky, A. *The Politics of the Budgetary Process*; Little, Brown: Boston, 1964. Revised editions in 1974, 1979 and 1984. Also, Caiden, N. and Wildavsky, A. *The New Politics of the Budgetary Process*. Little, Brown: Boston, 1988, 1992.
3. Key, V.O., Jr. The lack of budgetary theory. Am. Polit. Sci. Rev. **1940**, *34*, 1137–1144.
4. Wildavsky, A. Political implications of budgetary reform: A retrospective. Public Adm. Rev. **1992**, *52* (6), 594–603.
5. Jones, L.R. Changing how we budget: Aaron Wildavsky's perspective. J. Pub. Budg. Account. Financ. Manag. **1997**, *9* (1), 46–71.
6. Grizzle, G. Does budget format govern actions of budget-makers? Public Budg. Finance **1986**, *6*, 60–70.
7. Pettijohn, C.; Grizzle, G. Structural budget reform: Does it affect budget deliberations? J. Pub. Budg. Account. Financ. Manag. **1997**, *9* (1), 26–45.
8. Wildavsky, A. *A Comparative Theory of Budgetary Processes*; Little, Brown: Boston, 1975; 272. The best recognized biography on Pitt is J. Holland Rose, William Pitt and National Revival, London: G. Bell and Sons, 1911. See also J.H. Rose, William Pitt and the Great War, London: G. Bell and Sons, 1911; and J.H. Rose, Pitt and Napoleon, London: G. Bell and Sons, 1912.
9. Miller, J.C.; Hamilton, A. *Portrait in Paradox*; Harper: New York, 1959.
10. Tyler, C.; Willand, J. Public budgeting in America: A twentieth century retrospective. J. Pub. Budg. Account. Financ. Manag. **1997**, *9* (2), 182–219.
11. Buck, A.E. *Public Budgeting: A Discussion of Budgetary Practice in the National, State and Local Governments of the United States*; Harper: New York, 1929; 10.
12. Rubin, I. Who invented budgeting in the United States? Public Administration Review. **September/October 1993**, *53* (5), 438–444.
13. Schick, A. *The Capacity to Budget*; Urban Institute Press: Washington, D.C., 1990; 86.
14. White, J. Entitlement budgeting vs. bureau budgeting. Public Adm. Rev. **1998**, *58* (6), 113–134.
15. Schick, A. From the old politics of budgeting to the new. Public Budg. Finance **1994**, *14* (1), 135–144.
16. Douglas, J.W. Redirection in Georgia: A new type of budget reform. Am. Rev. Public Adm. **1999**, *29* (3), 269–289.
17. Lee, R.L., Jr.; Burns, R.C. Performance measurement in state budgeting: Advancement and backsliding from 1990 to 1995. Public Budg. Finance **2000**, *20* (3), 38–54.
18. Willoughby, K.G.; Melkers, J.E. Implementing PBB: Conflicting views of success. Public Budg. Finance **2000**, *20* (1), 105–120.
19. Melkers, J.E. The state of the states: Performance-based budgeting requirements in 47 out of 50. Public Adm. Rev. **1998**, *58* (1), 66–74.
20. Rubin, I. Budget theory and budget practice: How good the fit? Public Adm. Rev. **1990**, *50*, 179–189See also Ref. [10].
21. Forrester, J.; Adams, G. Budgetary reform through organizational learning: Toward an organizational theory of budgeting. Adm. Soc. **1997**, *28* (4), 466–488.
22. Schick, A. The road to PPB: The stages of budget reform. Public Adm. Rev. **1966**, *26* (4), 243–258.
23. Schick, A. The road from ZBB. Public Adm. Rev. **1978**, *38* (2), 177–180.
24. Joyce, P. Budget Reform. In *International Encyclopedia of Public Policy and Administration*; Shafritz, J., Ed.; Westview Press: Boulder, CO, 1998; 276–281.
25. Grafton, C.; Permaloff, A. Budgeting Reform in Perspective. In *Handbook on Public Budgeting and Financial Management*; Rabin, J., Lynch, T., Eds.; Marcel Dekker: New York, 1983; 89–124.
26. Wildavsky, A. A budget for all seasons? Why the traditional budget lasts. Public Adm. Rev. **1978**, *38* (6), 501–509.
27. White, J. (Almost) Nothing new under the sun: Why the work of budgeting remains incremental. Public Budg. Finance **1994**, *14* (1), 113–134.
28. Rubin, I. Budgeting for accountability: Municipal budgeting in the 1990's. Public Budg. Finance **1996**, *16* (3), 112–132Summer.

Budgetary Analysis and Economics

John R. Bartle
University of Nebraska at Omaha, Omaha, Nebraska, U.S.A.

INTRODUCTION

The discipline of economics offers the potential to apply a systematic and rational approach to public budgeting. In particular, the concept of economic efficiency can be used to identify the goods and services that a private market does a good job of distributing, and also those goods and services for which it does not perform well. This analysis can help to answer one of the primary questions in budgeting—"What should government do?"—and provides a clear justification for the answer. Further, economic methods such as cost–benefit analysis can provide answers to more specific budgetary questions, such as "Which program should be funded?", "How beneficial is the program?", and "When will the benefits and costs of the program be realized?" At the same time, there are some limitations with the application of economics to budgeting.

ECONOMIC EFFICIENCY AND GOVERNMENT

Markets are economically efficient if firms are producing output at the minimum cost and if those consumers who value the goods the most get them. When this is not the case, a market failure exists. Market failures can exist for several reasons, specifically public goods, externalities, monopoly, and information problems in the market. When a market failure exists, the private market will not be efficient. From an economic viewpoint, this provides the central justification for government supply of certain goods or services, as appropriate government action can correct the market inefficiency. Richard Musgrave referred to this rationale as the allocative role of government.[1] For example, pollution is an undesirable by-product of the production of many desired goods, such as steel. People near the factory would be willing to pay to have the pollution reduced, but find it difficult to organize to do so. The government can correct the market failure by taxing polluting firms for the cost to society of their emissions. This tax induces the firm to internalize the external costs into their production decisions. They may continue to pollute, but typically will do so at a lower level. It is argued that without some

government intervention into this market, the externality will continue and the market will remain inefficient. In this manner, the government can make the economy more efficient. The same is true of the other types of market failures, and is one of the justifications for programs such as national defense and food safety (public goods); zoning and antinuisance ordinances (externalities); antitrust litigation and price regulation (monopoly); and public pensions and health care regulation (information problems).

In 1960, Ronald Coase pointed out that the presence of a market failure should not necessarily lead to the conclusion that government should intervene.[2] In the pollution example, it might be possible for the residents of the community to organize themselves in some other fashion to negotiate with the polluting firm. How possible this is depends on the transaction cost of their mobilization and collective action. Coase's point provided one of the intellectual justifications for the subsequent privatization movement. More generally, just as markets can fail to be efficient, so can governments. Therefore, the appropriate comparison in the face of any inefficiency is between the two institutions of the market and government, and further between the various service provision arrangements possible. Some possible arrangements are direct government provision, intergovernmental agreements, contracts, franchises, vouchers, and voluntary action. This perspective ties these economic concepts to the public administration literature on policy implementation and service provision in a way that can help the student and practitioner of public administration to conceptualize the rationale for action and the range of alternatives in providing services. In turn, this shapes the "big picture" of the budget, as well as the options a budget official may consider.

Musgrave's other two roles for government are stabilization and distribution.[1] Stabilization refers to macroeconomic concerns about issues such as unemployment, inflation, international trade, monetary policy, and interest rates. The distribution role refers to concerns about the distribution of income and other resources among members of society. Of course, one might add to these roles. But he made it clear that other concepts besides economic efficiency are relevant in determining government programs and budgets.

Encyclopedia of Public Administration and Public Policy
DOI: 10.1081/E-EPAP 120010978

Arthur Okun advanced the argument that in many policy decisions, there is a trade-off between efficiency and equity.[3] For example, in health care, a pro-efficiency viewpoint would argue for reliance on the private market with little or no interference by the government. Those who valued the services highly and could afford them would get them with little interference, and producers would have incentives to respond to consumers through the market. However, those who could not afford treatment might have to go without. A pro-equity argument might deemphasize the private market as a basis for health service provision in favor of public provision or arrangement of health services, ensuring access and coverage to all. However, this strategy would likely require higher taxes, limit provider incentives, and create nonprice forms of rationing that might be troubling. Okun advocated balancing these two social goals of efficiency and equity. Although he realized that this balance was difficult to strike is difficult in practice, many economists see it as a useful construct for policy decisions.

FISCAL FEDERALISM

The concept of economic efficiency can also help to sort out which level of government (national, state/provincial, or local) should provide which services. Wallace Oates pointed out that some goods are local public goods (e.g., public safety), whereas others are more appropriately supplied at the state, regional, or national level.[4] Local public goods are characterized by a smaller scope of impact. For example, fire safety in Boston is important to residents of that city and perhaps in other nearby cities, but not to Chicago. The efficiency criterion would dictate that citizens of Boston should decide what level of fire protection they want and the amount they are willing to pay for it. Because Bostonians' decisions have little or no cost and benefit on people outside that area, the correspondence principal would dictate that the geographic area of the benefit and the taxes to support the service should coincide. If tastes for public services and tax levels vary among communities, then this implies that levels of service will not be and should not be uniform. Further, because different goods have different spatial distributions of costs and benefits, a federal system has the potential to be more efficient than a centralized system, as it better allows for local variation.

POSITIVE AND NORMATIVE APPLICATIONS OF ECONOMICS TO BUDGETING

A positive theory attempts to explain "what is," whereas a normative theory attempts to explain "what should be." Economic theories can be either positive or normative. A common criticism of the economic perspective of government action is that it is not a good positive model; many of the decisions about programs and public spending are political and do not follow this or any other prescribed theory about what government should do. For example, despite the fact that it does not address any market failure, education is provided publicly in many nations. Indeed, education is currently the largest functional area of spending among all governments in the United States.[5] Further, the structure of American government often makes it difficult to enact efficient policies. The institutions of constitutional separation of powers, bicameralism, and federalism require that any policy proposal receive majority approval among many different political bodies. This tends to produce policies that have a broad distribution of benefits and a vague distribution of costs. Efficient policies, however, tend to have explicit and visible linkages between costs and benefits. Thus, as a general rule, the policies emanating from U.S. governments are not particularly likely to meet the strict standard of efficiency. This may be less true of unified governments, such as parliamentary systems.

Economists have produced a number of positive models relevant to government budgeting. The best known is the median voter model, which assumes that in each polity a single individual is the decisive voter. The preferences, income, and prices faced by this individual then help to predict their vote and, in turn, the government's budget. A great number and variety of articles have been published on this model, with mixed conclusions [for a review, see Kearns and Bartle[6]]. Despite some problems with this model, it does demonstrate the attractive traits of positive economic models. They are testable and relatively simple, and can be used to describe, explain, and predict government behavior.

Normatively, it is often argued that the economic perspective is flawed. There are many different angles that this argument takes, but a common one is that it is undemocratic. If a majority of the citizens want to tax themselves to provide a program that they want, then this alone is a sufficient justification, whether or not there is a market failure. Certainly this criticism has merit, yet it does seem that the efficiency rationale serves as one good reason—among many—for justifying government programs. The efficiency rationale is grounded in the utilitarian justification of achieving the greatest satisfaction possible for all individuals given social resources available. Although utilitarianism has its limits as a guiding social principle, most economists are comfortable with it because it maintains the focus of policy on the individual and allows individuals to make their own decisions. Philosophies that put the government first and the individual second tend toward collectivism. As with most normative debates, there are compelling arguments on either side.

COST–BENEFIT ANALYSIS

Most programs entail gains for some and losses for others. A vexing problem is how to resolve these distributional consequences, yet still be assured that the program is in the social interest. Economists have contributed three decision rules to attempt that answer this question [for a detailed discussion, see Gramlich[7]]. The strictest test is the "Pareto rule," which states that a program should be undertaken if it makes at least one person better off and no one worse off.[8] Conceptually, this is appealing, but practically it is of limited help because few programs leave no one worse off. A second test is the "Kaldor–Hicks rule," which states that a program should be undertaken if those benefiting from it could compensate those hurt by it and still be better off. The winners need not actually compensate the losers; this test is conceptual rather than actual.[9,10] The third, and least strict, test is the fundamental rule of cost–benefit analysis (CBA)—do all projects with a positive net present value of benefits minus costs. (Present value is a method for adjusting economic values over time so that dollar values of costs or benefits realized at different times may be compared.) These three tests guide decision makers in selecting programs with distributional consequences. The strictness of the standards of these tests is important because it affects which programs will be selected, with the fewest programs passing the Pareto rule, and the most passing the CBA rule.

Once a market failure is identified and service provision arrangement is chosen, several other operational decisions need to be made about the design and scope of the program. Cost–benefit analysis has been applied to budgeting to guide decisions about the advisability and design of programs, as well as a means to justify expenditures. In deciding about whether to adopt a program, CBA would recommend its adoption if the net value is positive and recommend against it if it is negative. If there are several competing programs and one were able to pick only one of them, CBA would recommend selecting the program with the highest net benefit. If one were trying to determine the total amount that should be spent on a collection of programs, CBA would recommend doing all those that had a positive net benefit and none of those that did not. Although the decision rule is simple and the application flexible, CBA does require care in identifying what values should be included; how they should be measured; how risk, timing, and uncertainty are dealt

with; and the discount rate used to recognize the time value of money.

Although it is becoming more popular, CBA is not routinely used in most agencies. It requires advanced technical skills, and the details of the analysis can be difficult to explain. Further, many noneconomic considerations come into play in decisions about public spending. Despite this, the growing demand for accountability in the public sector and the business-like "bottom line" that a CBA can deliver has recently made this approach more attractive to administrators, policy makers, and the public.

AN APPLICATION TO THE BUDGETARY PROCESS

In a classic piece, Verne Lewis argued that the economic approach of marginal analysis could be productively applied to public budgeting.[11] He suggested a budgetary process where, in addition to their appropriation requests, each agency would also detail how their request would change if the appropriation were, for example, 10% to 20% lower or higher. This would present decision makers with packages of programmatic decisions meant to facilitate, if not force, a comparison both among programs and between public and private spending. The goal of such an approach is to compare the relative value of programs in accomplishing social goals and to make the opportunity cost of budgetary decisions readily apparent. This recognizes the basic economic insight that it is the marginal or additional unit that determines the value of a good or service.

The approach Lewis described foreshadowed many budget reforms that have been implemented (e.g., target-based budgeting, zero-based budgeting, program budgeting), as well as institutional arrangements (e.g., the U.S. Congressional Budget Act of 1974, which in part attempted to present Congress with explicit decisions of this type). Studying these reforms illustrates the strengths and weaknesses of the application of basic economic principles to public budgeting. Some governments incorporate these principles into their process of budgeting, although clearly political, and other considerations are relevant and often more important.

It is therefore apparent that any thoughtful practitioner of budgeting should be aware of these principles of economic analysis as both a theoretical foundation and an analytical tool that can be used. Certainly, other valuable perspectives differ in their fundamental premises and normative approach to public budgeting [see e.g., Wildavsky,[12]] and so the practitioner may not embrace the economic approach. However, it will continue to be relevant to this central function of government.

REFERENCES

1. Musgrave, R.A. *The Theory of Public Finance: A Study in Public Economy*; McGraw-Hill: New York, 1959; 3–27.
2. Coase, R.H. The problem of social cost. J. Law Econ. **1960**, *3*, 1–44.
3. Okun, A.M. *Equality and Efficiency: The Big Tradeoff*; The Brookings Institution: Washington, 1975.
4. Oates, W.E. *Fiscal Federalism*; Harcourt Brace Javonovich: New York, 1972; 3–20.
5. U.S. Census Bureau. *Statistical Abstract of the United States: 1999*; Economics and Statistics Administration, U.S. Department of Commerce: Washington DC, 1999; 312.
6. Kearns, P.S.; Bartle, J.R. The Median Voter Model in Public Budgeting Research. In *Evolving Theories of Public Budgeting*; Bartle, J.R., Ed.; Elsevier Science Ltd.: Oxford, UK, 2001; 83–100.
7. Gramlich, E.M. *A Guide to Benefit–Cost Analysis,* 2nd Ed.; Prentice Hall: Englewood Cliffs, NJ, 1990; 30–33.
8. Pareto, V. *Manual of Political Economy, 1971 Translation of 1927 Edition*; Augustus M. Kelley: New York, 1906; 261.
9. Kaldor, N. Welfare propositions of economics and interpersonal comparisons of utility. Econ. J. **1939**, *49*, 549–552.
10. Hicks, J.R. The valuation of the social income. Economica **1940**, *7*, 105–124.
11. Lewis, V.B. Toward a theory of budgeting. Public Administration Rev. **1952**, *12*, 43–54.
12. Wildavsky, A. Political implications of budgetary reform. Public Administration Rev. **1961**, *21*, 183–190.

Budgetary Balance and Deficit Controls

William R. Voorhees
Arizona State University, Tempe, Arizona, U.S.A.

INTRODUCTION

Budgets are generally considered to be in balance when an organization's inflow of economic resources is equal to its outflow of economic resources. When an organization allocates resources beyond those currently available, a deficit occurs and additional resources must be collected in future periods reducing future opportunities. In its simplest form, budgetary balance is expressed by the budgetary equation:

Revenues = Expenditures

In a neat and tidy world, this equation would serve us well; however, in the real world, the equation is seldom as simple as it appears. Economic stability, political ideology, fiscal management skills, and fiscal policy will all influence whether a budget is in balance. Even when the budgetary equation appears to be in balance, it may be so only after an application of "smoke-and-mirror gimmickry," such as accelerating revenues from or delaying expenditures to subsequent periods. When the budgetary equation is not in balance, surpluses or deficits are the result.

There are two basic categories of budget deficits: cyclical and structural. Cyclical deficits are the result of downturns in the economy. When downturns occur, expenditures are prone to increase while revenues decrease, often resulting in a cyclical deficit. Structural deficits, however, are the result of permanent deficits resulting from the expenditure or revenue structures making up the budget.

CYCLICAL DEFICITS

When considering the budgetary equation and balance, it is necessary to understand how forecast accuracy affects each side of the budgetary equation. On the revenue side, forecasts are generally accurate in the United States, with states normally having less than a 2% error in their revenue forecasts. The problem arises with the inability to forecast turning points in the economy in time for inclusion in the budget. Turning points represent the peaks and valleys of a cyclical economy and because most revenues are conditional on the state of the economy, the

accuracy of the revenue forecast is affected when an economy turns. Because estimating turning points is extremely difficult, governments are often faced with revenue shortfalls when the economy turns downward. Likewise, when the economy begins a growth period after an economic downturn, revenues will often exceed forecasts resulting in excess revenues.

The behavior of expenditures during cyclical changes presents officials trying to maintain a balanced budget with equally challenging problems. During periods of economic downturns, expenditures will generally increase due to mandatory spending. Entitlements such as food stamps, unemployment relief, and welfare will increase during economic downturns as more of the population find themselves unemployed or working for lower wages. These additional expenditures create additional fiscal stress at exactly the time when revenues are falling. As workers lose jobs and wages fall, revenues derived from income and consumption taxes are affected correspondingly.

Recissions and Supplemental Budgets

The primary tools that governments have to fight cyclical imbalance are recissions and the supplemental budget. Recissions are cuts to the budget after the budget has been passed. Because governmental expenditures are in reality, planned activities of the government, a recission can present severe disruptions to government operations. Often, because expenditure commitments have already been made, recissions may not come from programs that either politicians or citizens want cut.

Recissions result in budgetary cutbacks that can come in several forms, including line item reductions, across-the-board departmental reductions, or programmatic reductions. Line item reductions may result in hiring and salary freezes, early retirement, unpaid furloughs, layoffs, reduced maintenance on equipment and fixed assets, and elimination of new equipment purchases.[1] Departmental cuts may be across the board, with each department required to contribute a fixed percentage. Across-the-board cuts, where all departments bear an equal burden, are often contrary to optimal budget allocation and result in both high- and low-priority programs being cut equally. However, programmatic cuts fall

Encyclopedia of Public Administration and Public Policy
DOI: 10.1081/E-EPAP 120010972

on specific programs, especially those that are allocated large amounts of funds and that are not federally funded, mandated, or supported by earmarked funds.[2]

In the case of an upturn in the economy and excess revenues, supplemental budgets can be appropriated after the original budget has been passed. Supplemental budgets allow lawmakers to add additional dollars to the budget through additional expenditures or tax expenditures. Supplemental appropriations may fail to provide optimal resource allocations, and they often have limited citizen and legislative participation in the allocation of the additional resources.[3]

Stabilization Funds

To mitigate the problems of forecasting, many states have adopted reserve funds to maintain budgetary balance. Typically, these funds go by several names, including rainy day funds, contingency funds, and stabilization funds. Although any of these funds can be used to smooth out revenue shortfalls and higher expenditures due to economic fluctuations, only stabilization funds are used specifically for that purpose.

Three features—fund-sized, funding mechanisms, and fund expenditure—identify the structure of a stabilization fund. The most common suggestion for fund size at the state level is a 5% reserve.[4] In reality, some states seem not to have set target amounts for their funds, whereas other states have statutes controlling and limiting fund size. In 1998, most states with stabilization funds had balances between 2% and 14%.[5]

The second feature, funding mechanisms, can vary from predefined constitutional requirements to no requirements at all. For example, South Carolina requires a 5% balance in the fund and, if the fund is less than the 5% amount, a minimum of 1% must be added each year until the 5% minimum is achieved.[6]

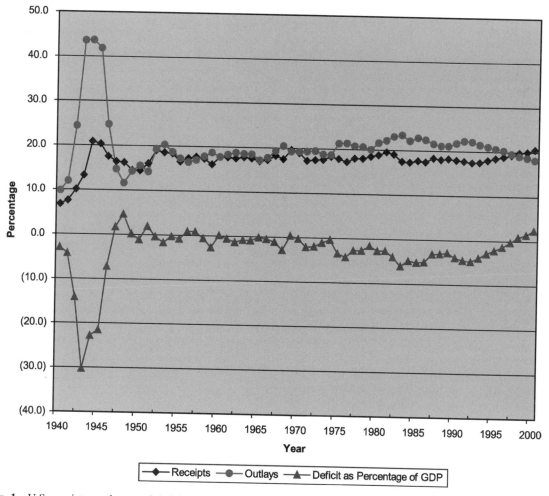

Fig. 1 U.S. receipts, outlays, and deficits/surpluses as percentage of GDP. (From the United States FY 2002 Budget.)

Finally, fund withdrawal varies considerably among states with some states using a formula approach that is triggered in times of fiscal distress; other states withdrawal funds after either a majority or supermajority vote of the legislative; and, in still other states, the executive need only declare a need to use stabilization funds.[7]

At the municipal level, few cities have opted to implement stabilization funds for economic smoothing. Interestingly, those cities most sensitive to economic cycles are no more likely to establish stabilization funds than the least sensitive. In fact, those municipalities least dependent on cyclical revenue are most likely to institute such funds.[8]

STRUCTURAL DEFICITS

Structural deficits are the result of permanent deficits resulting from the expenditure and/or revenue structures of a government's budget. Whereas cyclical deficits disappear during economic growth cycles, structural deficits can only be corrected by permanently reducing expenditures or increasing revenues. Because of balanced budget requirements and debt limitations, state and local governments generally have fewer problems with structural deficits than the federal government. Fig. 1 shows the federal government deficits as a percentage of the gross domestic product (GDP). It is useful to consider the deficit in respect to the GDP to offset economic growth trends. In looking at the figure, a structural deficit is clearly apparent from 1975 to 1995, although some might argue that a structural deficit existed even prior to 1975.

Process Controls at the State Level

A primary means of controlling budgetary balance is through controls on the budgetary process. Such process controls may require specific reports or budgetary formats, allow for executive veto of budgetary items, or consist of laws that mandate a balanced budget. Budgetary formats may or may not place emphasis on the budgetary balance aspect of the appropriations process. Formats such as zero-based budgeting place a stronger emphasis on budgetary balance with their built-in

mechanism for identifying potential budgetary cuts. In addition to traditional budgets, some states are now requiring tax expenditure budgets that aid in identifying revenue reductions that may lead to budgetary imbalance if other actions are not taken to increase other revenues or decrease expenditures.

The executive veto has often been suggested as a primary tool of the executive in maintaining budgetary balance at the state level. Even when the executive fails to exercise a veto, the threat of the veto may prevent the legislature from adding appropriations they know the executive has threatened to veto.

Several forms of the veto exist, including the popular line item veto. The traditional line item veto permits the executive to delete one or more budget lines. In some states, the item veto is extended to allow the executive to change the wording of the legislation. Currently, only the governor of one state has no veto power, whereas 42 states allow a line item veto, 40 allow an item veto of appropriations, 14 allow veto of selected words, and 3 allow the governor to veto and change the wording of an appropriations bill.[9] It should be noted that veto power was given to the U.S. president in 1995 with passage of the Line Item Veto Act, but was rescinded in 1998 when the Supreme Court ruled it unconstitutional. The effect of the line item veto power was considered to be miniscule during the short time the president had the authority.[10]

Other controls may take the form of laws that require states to have budgetary balance. These laws may set requirements at different points in the budgetary process such as submission of a balanced budget by the executive, passage of a balanced budget by the legislature, or a requirement for the executive to sign a balanced budget. Often, these requirements are written into the state's constitution, which generally requires a supermajority to modify. Statutory requirements may also be used by states to implement balanced budget requirements; however, in times of fiscal stress, statutory requirements are more easily circumvented.

Some states also have laws that require the state to achieve balance at year end (Table 1). In a survey conducted by the General Accounting Office (GAO), it was found that 39 out of 49 states required budgetary balance at year end. At the same time, it was found that 21 of

Table 1 Balance budget requirements in the states

	States with balance requirements[a]	Constitutional	Statutory
Governor must submit balanced budget	44	32	26
Legislature must pass balanced budget	40	33	18
Governor must sign balanced budget	35	30	17

[a]Several states have both statutory and constitutional requirements. States are counted only once.
Source: NASBO, Budget Processes in the United States, 1999.

those 49 states were allowed to carry over deficits to the following years. The same GAO report suggests that year-end budgetary balance is often "more of a perception than a legal requirement".[11] For instance, in the state of Massachusetts, the law is written such that the budget may be balanced through the use of loans.[12]

For states that do have budgetary balance requirements, the funds covered by the requirements may not always specify which funds fall under the requirement. The focus of balance regulations is usually directed at governmental operations and the general fund. Unlike the federal government, capital funds at the state level are generally excluded from budgetary balance requirements. Less clear is the manner in which fiduciary and enterprise funds are affected under balance requirements. In the case of enterprise funds, bond covenants may necessitate budgetary balance.

Process Controls at the Federal Level

At the federal level, the U.S. Congress has passed several pieces of legislation to control deficits. The first major effort by Congress to control deficit spending was the Anti-Deficiency Act of 1870, which prevented agencies from obligating more funds than appropriated and then submitting "coercive deficiency" requests to Congress to pay their obligations.

The Budget and Accounting Act of 1921 was the second major effort by Congress to control budgetary expenditures. This act centralized fiscal processes by codifying the president's budget and creating both the Bureau of the Budget and the GAO. The result of the Budget and Accounting Act of 1921 was to shift substantial budgetary power and responsibility from the Congress to the executive branch of government.

In 1974, Congress passed the Congressional Budget and Impoundment Control Act, establishing the Budget Committees in both the House and the Senate. It also modified the budgetary process in Congress by requiring a Budget Resolution at two different points in the budgetary process, a tax expenditure analysis, a current services budget presentation by the president, and the creation of the Congressional Budget Office. It was the intent of Congress to create a budgetary process that both enhanced their control over the budget, and integrated revenue and appropriation decisions.

Persistent deficits of the late 1970s and early 1980s caused by increased budget complexity due to the growth of entitlements and multiyear spending, a structural imbalance due to the lost revenues of the Economic Recovery Tax Act of 1981, and increased budget vulnerability with respect to incorrect estimates and forecasts prompted Congress to once again address the budgetary process with attempts to limit expenditures.[13] In 1985

and again with modifications in 1987, Congress enacted the Balanced Budget and Emergency Deficit Control Act (Gramm–Rudman–Hollings) with the intent of lowering the deficit and ultimately balancing the budget. This legislation attempted to bring more fiscal discipline to the budgetary process by establishing new deadlines and deficit targets. If the deficit target was exceeded by more than $10 billion, then automatic cuts or sequestration would be implemented. Sequestration required that the president make across-the-board spending cuts that were evenly divided between both domestic and defense programs to achieve the deficit targets. Because debt interest and most entitlement programs were either totally or partially exempt from budgetary reductions, the bulk of the reductions under sequestration came from discretionary appropriations. It was believed that the sequestration process would be so distasteful that Congress would attempt to avoid it at all cost. What was not anticipated was that Congress would devise means through the use of delayed appropriations and other "smoke-and-mirror gimmickry" to avoid the consequences of sequestration.

The deficits continued, forcing Congress to revisit the problem of budgetary balance in 1990 by passing the Budget Enforcement Act (BEA). The BEA created three categories of spending—domestic, defense, and international aid—with each category having separate deficit targets. The breach of a spending target in any single category would result in sequestration for programs in that category only and, if appropriations for one category fell below the target, the difference between the target and the appropriation could only be used for deficit reduction. This was to create a unique problem with defense appropriations in 1992. Due to the dissolution of the Soviet Union, defense spending realized a peace dividend, which spurred many legislators to proposed using the defense reductions for spending in the other two categories; however, by law, these categories were walled off preventing movement of funds from one category to another. After a protracted battle in Congress, the walls held and the reductions in defense spending were applied to deficit reduction.[14]

In addition, BEA required that increases in direct spending or revenue reduction be financed on a pay-as-you-go basis (PAYGO) and prohibited any net change in the deficit. In effect, this requirement tied new spending to either tax increases or cuts in other expenditures, making new expenditures unlikely.

The Omnibus Reconciliation Act of 1993 revised and extended spending caps and significant reductions were realized in the budget between 1992 and 1997, with the budget deficit decreasing from $290.4 billion to $20 billion in 1997. The Balanced Budget Act was passed in 1970, requiring a balanced budget in the year 2002. This act once again revised and extended discretionary spending limits and PAYGO requirements, and made permanent a 5-year horizon for budget resolutions.[15] With the Balanced Budget Act of 1997 in place along with strong revenues from a thriving economy, the budget was balanced the following year, well ahead of the 2002 deadline.

CONCLUSION

The budgetary process is faced with two forms of deficits: cyclical deficits that are a result of the economic cycle, and structural deficits that are a result of the permanent imbalance between the institutional structures designed to raise resources and those design to use resources. Cyclical deficits are often solved through recissions and cutback management techniques. Structural deficits have been found to be more difficult to solve because they tend to pit various groups of resource consumers against each other over the long run. Governments have implemented various budgetary processes in attempts to control deficits, sometimes successfully and often to no avail. Often, the legislation was focused on integrating the revenue and expenditure decision-making processes. In the end, however, budgetary balance is probably best achieved through a combination of not only a strong economy and reasonable process controls, but also the political will of the groups competing for resources.

REFERENCES

1. Lee, R.; Johnson, R. *Public Budgeting Systems,* 6th Ed.; Aspen: Gaithersburg, MD, 1998; 140–144.
2. Lauth, T. Reductions in the FY 1992 Georgia Budget: Responses to a Shortfall. In *Case Studies in Public Budgeting and Financial Management*; Khan, A., Hildreth, B., Eds.; Kendall Hunt: Dubuque, IA, 1996.
3. Forrester, J.; Mullins, D. Rebudgeting: The serial nature of the municipal budgetary process. Public Adm. Rev. **1992**, *52* (5), 467–473.
4. National Conference of State Legislatures. *State Budget Actions in 1984*; National Council of State Legislatures: Denver, CO, 1984.
5. National Association of State Budget Officers. *The Fiscal Survey of States*; National Association of Budget Officers: Washington, DC, 1998.
6. National Association of State Budget Officers. *Budgeting Amid Fiscal Uncertainty: Stabilization Funds and Other Strategies*; National Association of Budget Officers: Washington, DC, 1985.
7. National Association of State Budget Officers. *Budget Stability: A Policy Framework for States*; National Association of Budget Officers: Washington, DC, 1995.
8. Wolkoff, M. An evaluation of municipal rainy day funds. Public Budg. Finance **1987**, *7* (2), 52–63.
9. National Association of State Budget Officers. *Budget Processes in the United States*; National Association of Budget Officers: Washington, DC, 1999.
10. Joyce, P. The federal line item veto experiment: After the Supreme Court ruling, what's next? Public Budg. Finance **1998**, *18* (4), 3–21.
11. United States General Accounting Office. *Balanced Budget Requirements: State Experiences and Implications for the Federal Government*; United States General Accounting Office, 1993; 16.
12. Mikesell, J.L. *Fiscal Administration: Analysis and Applications for the Public Sector,* 5th Ed.; Harcourt Brace College Publishers: New York, 1999; 124.
13. Leloup, L.; Graham, B.; Barwick, S. Deficit politics and constitutional government: The impact of Gramm–Rudman–Hollings. Public Budg. Finance **1987**, *7* (1), 83–103.
14. Doyle, R.; McCaffery, J. The Budget Enforcement Act in 1992: Necessary but not sufficient. Public Budg. Finance **1993**, *13* (2), 20–37.
15. Leloup, L.; Long, C.; Giordano, J. President Clinton's fiscal 1998 budget: Political and constitutional paths to balance. Public Budg. Finance **1998**, *18* (1), 3–32.

Budgeting, Line Item and Object-of-Expenditure Controls

Suzanne Leland
University of North Carolina at Charlotte, Charlotte, North Carolina, U.S.A.

INTRODUCTION

A line item budget is a traditional budget format that uses object classifications by broad categories to present proposed expenditures. Primarily used for the purpose of financial control, the categories in a line item budget consist of lists of expenditures that are logical, and contain items such as personnel, travel, equipment, or supplies. A line item budget provides simple, but limited information beyond the cost of specific categories of expenditures or appropriations in order to ensure accuracy and control. In a household budget, an example of a line item would be the amount of household income spent on clothing, but the list of expenditures would not detail the particular items purchased for each family member.

LINE ITEM BUDGET FORMATS

When governments solely rely on the line item format, the budgetary process is said to be best characterized as ''incremental'' because it typically calls for the last completed fiscal year, the current year, and the forthcoming fiscal year, including funds, organizational units, and objects of expenditure.[1] Although budget battles appear to be controversial matters, the outcome is seldom a little more than the prior year's budget using this process. This often leads to the gradual increase in expenditures, and can lead to mounting debt and deficits overtime. Despite criticisms of the incremental nature of budgeting via the line item process, this method of budgeting does provide a sense of stability from year to year. The stability of the line item budgetary process is valued by lawmakers and administrators because they often rely on budgetary projections for political decision making.[2]

According to Wildavsky's theory of incrementalism, budgetary decision making is driven by department heads.[1] Therefore, each year only the increments from an already existing and well-defined base are examined by policy makers. From this point of view, governmental budgeting is considered to be an annual repeated process that results in the bargaining between individuals who know one another through budgetary activities. This theory most adequately describes what happens when a government uses a line item budget, but does not accurately describe other methods of budgeting used in government. For example, the theory of incrementalism could not take into account or explain entitlement programs such as social security, which over time squeezed out other categories of expenditures in the federal budget. Nor could Wildavksy's theory of incrementalism account for top-down budgeting processes when bureaus and departments were bypassed or when cutbacks took place.[3]

OBJECT OF EXPENDITURES

Technically, a budget following a line item format is a detailed financial plan developed according to governmental accounting based on object of expenditure classifications. Objects of expenditures (or objects of expense) are detailed categories of goods and services that are purchased by an organization, such as supplies, travel, equipment, or personnel services. Each object-of-expenditure classification is a form of accounting that attempts to limit expenditures by the organization. Normally, objects of expenditures are divided by departments or divisions within the organization that serve as appropriation guides to personnel.

USE OF LINE ITEM BUDGETS

The line item budget format is especially useful for purposes of financial control and is the simplest budget format to link to governmental accounting systems. The format of a line item budget is straightforward, readable to citizens, and can easily be converted to accounting systems. For these reasons, this form of budgeting is now common across public and nonprofit organizations in the United States.

The first widespread use line item budget in the United States came about as part of the reform movement that was aimed at cleaning up municipal corruption in the early part of the twentieth century and the move to make government more efficient like business. The focus of the reform movement was on gaining financial control, and the budget reform preferred was the line item format.[4]

For local governments, line item budgeting is closely associated with the introduction of city manager forms of

Encyclopedia of Public Administration and Policy
DOI: 10.1081/E-EPAP 120010967

government. The reformers at this point in time were keen on introducing "efficiency" measures into government administration, and accountability to the public for how and why taxes were spent.[4]

Due to the advantages of the line item format, approximately 51% of U.S. local governments still use some form of line item budgets.[5] Governments can incorporate the line item budgeting format in one of two ways. First, a government may use the line item format primarily to present their budgets to elected officials and the public. Second, and more common, the local government uses this format as a supporting document or to supplement to another format. Typically, in the case of the latter, the more comprehensive the budget format, the more varied and numerous the formats and systems for classifying data.

At the federal level, line item budgeting is associated with the first wave of budget reforms in the United States. The move to centralize the federal budgeting process was culminated in the passage of the Budget and Accounting Act of 1921. This law established the Bureau of the Budget (BOB) as the central agency in charge of the federal budgetary process. Along with the BOB, the act created the congressional Governmental Accounting Office to scrutinize federal expenditures. Gradually, after the passage of this act through the 1930s, the federal budgetary process became more detailed. Categories were narrowly defined so that expenditures were attached to line items to link expenditures to specific programs.

It is important to note that while line item budgets do not preclude planning or the aim of achieving objectives, they are primarily concerned with controlling and confirming the budgetary process to set aggregate spending limits. A well-designed budget format should provide a general statement of financial status, inform stakeholders of the cost of achieving agency goals, simplify operational procedures with well-classified expenditures, and serve as a means to evaluate objectives. The traditional line item format alone does not adequately meet these requirements and works best when used by governments in a supplemental manner to other budgetary formats such as performance-based budgeting.

REFERENCES

1. Wildavsky, A. *The Politics of the Budgetary Process*; Little Brown: Boston, 1964.
2. Pitsvada, B.; Draper, F. Making sense of the federal budget the old fashioned way—Incrementally. Public Adm. Rev. **1984**, *44* (5), 401–407.
3. Rubin, I. Aaron Wildavsky and the demise of incrementalism. Public Adm. Rev. **1989**, *49*, 78–81 (January/February).
4. Rubin, I.; Stein, L. Budget reform in St. Louis: Why does budgeting change? Public Adm. Rev. **1990**, *50*, 420–427 (July/August).
5. Lee, R.; Johnson, R. *Public Budgeting Systems*, 6th Ed.; Aspen Publications: Gaithersburg, MD, 1998; 120.

Budgeting, Performance-Based

Julia E. Melkers
Georgia State University, Atlanta, Georgia, U.S.A.

INTRODUCTION

Using performance data in the budgetary process means integrating information about outcomes and impacts in decisions about the allocation of funds where the goal is to be able to allocate financial resources using performance information to make a more informed decision. Performance measures are generally established at the agency level, oftentimes with input from executive and legislative budget offices. Ideally, performance measures are developed for both internal use by agency staff as well as use for external reporting, including use in the budget process. Improved accountability is the primary rationale for the push to performance-based budgeting at all levels of government. An important thrust of current budget reform efforts is to develop structures that improve communication both within and between government and citizens. This activity is referred to as performance-based budgeting (PBB).

OVERVIEW

Simply put, PBB is a recently revived phenomena in budget reform that involves the integration of performance measures and data representing agency activities in the budget decision-making process. Although it seems innate that aspects of performance will be included in decisions about the allocation of resources, this is often not the case. In recent years, however, governments and nonprofit organizations are moving away from a line item approach and adopting performance budgets, where a link is established between allocated funds and what an organization will achieve with those funds. Line item budgets encourage decision-making processes that focus on individual items in a short-term framework with little or no explanatory information. Performance budgeting efforts take a broader approach, encouraging a long-term perspective with an emphasis on what will be achieved in the future.[1]

TERMINOLOGY

With the trend toward the use of performance measures in budgetary processes, PBB has become increasingly popular in this era of budget reform and government reinvention. However, what may described as PBB, is actually a more diverse set of requirements, blending various aspects of current public management trends, including outcome measurement, performance measurement systems, strategic planning, and benchmarking. Although PBB may be the most common term to refer to this process, the actual terminology varies a great deal as organizations and governments design the process and "make it their own." In fact, these variations are reflected in the performance-based requirements used in different governments and organizations. Some state and local governments refer explicitly to PBB, "performance-budgeting," "results-based budgeting," or "outcome-based budgeting system." Others, however, are more descriptive, indicating that certain performance-related elements be included in the budgetary process. Here, they may use terms such as "program performance reports," "performance measures," "outcome measures," and "performance standards and measures." These differences, however, are simply a matter of language. The essence of these different requirements does not vary—each indicates that performance measures be actively incorporated in the budgetary process. Specifically, these performance budgeting initiatives involve:

- Identification of broad performance measures for selected organizations (programs/departments/agencies), with an emphasis on outcomes.
- Linking of outcome measures to organizational activities and their respective budgets.
- Targeting performance levels and budget levels together.

LEGISLATIVE AND ADMINISTRATIVE REQUIREMENTS

The use of performance data in budget processes and budget decision making is increasingly becoming the norm in public and nonprofit organizations. Governments are not only *encouraging*, but *requiring* the integration of performance data in the budgetary process. In 1993, the Government Performance and Results Act (GPRA) was passed, requiring the establishment and use of performance measures in federal agencies. One of the stated

Encyclopedia of Public Administration and Public Policy
DOI: 10.1081/-E-EPAP 120010968

purposes of the act is to "improve congressional decision-making by providing more objective information on achieving statutory objectives, and on the relative effectiveness and efficiency of Federal programs and spending." More specifically, as noted in Section 1115 of the act, the role of performance measures in the budget process are stated as follows:

In carrying out the provisions of section 1105(a)(29), the Director of the Office of Management and Budget shall require each agency to prepare an annual performance plan covering each program activity set forth in the budget of such agency. Such plan shall—

1. establish performance goals to define the level of performance to be achieved by a program activity;
2. express such goals in an objective, quantifiable, and measurable form unless authorized to be in an alternative form under subsection (b);
3. briefly describe the operational processes, skills and technology, and the human, capital, information, or other resources required to meet the performance goals;
4. establish performance indicators to be used in measuring or assessing the relevant outputs, service levels, and outcomes of each program activity;
5. provide a basis for comparing actual program results with the established performance goals; and
6. describe the means to be used to verify and validate measured values.

The tone set by the GPRA is reflected in many similar state and local PBB requirements. At the state level, all but three states (*Arkansas*, *Massachusetts*, and *New York*) have legislative or administrative requirements for the integration of performance data in the budget process, with most of these requirements established in the 1990s (Melkers and Willoughby, 1998).[5] One state (Missouri) established PBB by executive order. States that are best known for the development and use of performance measures in the budget process include Texas, Oregon, Minnesota, and Florida. A similar trend toward the use of performance measurement information in the budget process is taking place in local governments, with many municipal and county governments requiring performance measurement with an intent to use it in the budgetary process.

In earlier budget reforms, integrating performance information in the budget process was viewed as a linear process. Research shows, however, that decision makers consider a range of factors in budgetary decisions.[2,3] Today's reform, however, acknowledges the complexity of not only public programs, but also of the budget process itself.[4,5] For example, in the state of Washington, the budget guidelines are clear that performance data

inform, but do not drive, budgetary decision making. Instead, the actual budget or policy decision involves performance measures, but is also affected by a variety of other factors, such as financial realities, stakeholder requirements, competing priorities, public sentiment, organizational capacity, and public sentiment.

SELECTING APPROPRIATE PERFORMANCE MEASURES FOR THE BUDGET PROCESS

The Government Finance Officers Association (GFOA) recommends a useful list of characteristics for performance measures that are used in budgetary processes. They suggest that financial, service, and program performance measures be developed and used as an important component of decision making and incorporated into governmental budgeting. Specifically, they state that performance measures should:[6]

- Be based on program goals and objectives that tie to a statement of program mission or purpose.
- Measure program results or accomplishments.
- Provide for comparisons over time.
- Measure efficiency and effectiveness.
- Be reliable, verifiable, and understandable.
- Be reported internally and externally.
- Be monitored and used in decision-making processes.
- Be limited to a number and degree of complexity that can provide an efficient and meaningful way to assess the effectiveness and efficiency of key programs.

In an ideal performance budgeting process, output measures are included to show the level of work accomplished, but efficiency and effectiveness measures are most relevant and may be most informative in the budgeting process where decision makers are looking for links to actual funds. Taking output, outcome, and efficiency measures together gives policy makers a full view of activities completed, the cost and value of the outputs and outcomes, and what has actually been accomplished with the actual expenditures. In the current state of government reform, helping government to become more efficient is an important focus. In this same vein, as performance measures are introduced in the budgetary process, they are important for identifying the relative efficiency of services. Efficiency measures are important in the budget process because they help to answer the question, "How much output is there for a given input?" This type of information is especially important in making fiscal decisions because they provide information on the cost of providing services and when linked to output measures, provide information on the cost of obtaining given outputs.

The rationale behind performance budgeting processes is that better resource allocation decisions will occur with the use of information that indicates how well an entity is performing. For many governments, this performance is linked to agency or program goals and objectives. Therefore, performance budgeting should indicate how well an agency or program is meeting those goals an objectives. It is imperative that performance measures in the budgeting processes are not limited to measures of outputs, but that include actual outcomes.

Although it seems straightforward to select certain categories of measures most useful for budgetary decision making, it is not a uncomplicated process. Along with challenges relating to the identification and selection of performance measures, there are three important challenges in the selection of measures for budget processes:

- Nature of the budget cycle.
- Perspective and attention span of policy makers.
- Pressure to demonstrate macroresults.

Typically, most budget cycles are on an annual basis, with some governments adopting a biennial budget. Because of this relatively short time frame, integrating performance measures in budget process means selecting measures that can show some change within that time-frame. Measures cannot be so global to not be meaningful within the budgetary calendar. One problem with measuring outcomes within the budgeting cycle is that the outcomes of most government and nonprofit programs and services occur in a much longer timeframe. This is perhaps the greatest challenge in integrating performance measures in the budgetary process. Because of this challenge, it is important to identify interim or intermediate outcomes that show progress toward or a contribution to the ultimate projected outcome. In addition, performance targets or goals may also be shown to provide a context for the performance information.

Another important challenge is that policy makers and others involved in the budget process typically have to review budgets and measures for numerous programs and departments. Further, these individuals will have varying levels of familiarity with the individual budgetary entities. For this reason, it is important to include only key measures in the budget process. More detailed measures are more appropriate for the departmental level. For example, in Florida, the guidelines for their performance budgeting initiative, PB^2 (performance-based program budgeting), note that measures of broad program results appear in the budget documents, while detailed output and outcome measures are maintained and used at the agency level. Similarly, in Washington State, the guidelines stress that key, summary measures appear in the budget documents, but must also link to the agency strategic plan. Further,

they note that the focus should be on developing a core set of useful and verifiable indicators, rather than on a large quantity of indicators.

In addition, there may be pressure from policy makers to identify measures that reflect macrolevel policy goals in a government, such as ''lower infant mortality rate'' or ''healthier society.'' However, it is important that performance measures in the budget should be tied to activities and results that the agency can affect. It is important then that interim measures be selected that show progress toward those larger policy goals where performance may be linked to agency strategy and goals.

As performance measures are integrated in the budget process, guidelines for their selection, reporting format, and use are important to ensure consistency across government, but also to inform stakeholders about the changes and related requirements associated with the new process. In some cases, such as in the state of Florida, there are elaborate review procedures of the measures themselves to ensure consistency and quality of measures across agencies. In most cases where performance measures are required in the budget process, general guidelines are provided indicating the types of measures that are to be included.

IMPLEMENTING PERFORMANCE BUDGETING

Implementing performance budgeting means changing the way that agencies submit budget requests as well as changing the way that policy makers make decisions.[7] The formalization of PBB requirements provides a framework or process so that performance data are considered in the budgetary process. For many systems, this requires a complex reworking of existing processes.

Because most governments have not been collecting performance data as a regular activity, implementing performance budgeting means not only refining the budget process, but also developing a parallel or concurrent process where performance measures are identified, and data collected and reported to fit with the existing budget cycle. Thus, implementing performance budgeting often means initiating performance measurement activities in the first place. Many governments that have adopted performance budgeting processes have done so in a multistage process, where different programs or agencies are selected to pilot the use of performance measures in the budget process before the process is implemented governmentwide.[5] Adopting a performance budgeting system in this way is important because it allows for learning, adaptation, and integration with existing systems. For example, the state of Florida implemented its

PB^2 initiative over several years, adding new departments and programs each budget cycle. An important advantage of a pilot process is that, as new agencies or departments or programs begin performance budgeting, they are able to look at and communicate with other entities within their government as examples.

An important fiscal issue arises in this implementation process. If performance measures are meant to be used in budgetary decision making, what happens when programs or agencies do not meet their targets? For state governments, a handful provide explicit guidelines for actual agency attainment, or nonattainment of goals and objectives as part of their legislated performance budgeting requirements. These are guidelines that offer rewards to public managers to strive for and attain the performance goals that they have identified in their strategic planning or other process. Research has summarized and compiled the different variations that guidelines have taken in the states.[8,9]

CONCLUSION

Overall, there is little evidence to show that performance data are affecting actual budget appropriations. This is not surprising or disturbing because the implementation of performance budgeting is still in the early phases for many governments. However, integrating performance data in the budget process can help decision makers to make better, more informed decisions along the way.[10] Specifically, performance data are useful for helping decision makers in a number of areas:

- Understanding the activities and objectives of funded programs by viewing summary measures of performance.
- Understanding changes in performance over time compared with budgetary changes.

- Having more meaningful dialogs with public managers about agency activities, goals, and performance.
- Identifying poorly performing and high-performing programs and departments.
- Justifying fiscal decisions using evidence rather than anecdotes or impressions.

REFERENCES

1. *Performance Based Budgeting*; Miller, G.J., Hildeth, W.B., Rabin, J., Eds.; ASPA Classics Volume, Westview Press: Boulder, CO, 2001.
2. Grizzle, G. Does budget format really govern the actions of budget makers? Public Budg. Finance **1986**, *6* (1), 60–70.
3. Stanford, K.A. State budget deliberations: Do legislators have a strategy? Public Administration Review **1992**, *52* (1), 16–26.
4. Joyce, P.G. Using Performance Measures for Budgeting: A New Beat, or is it the Same Old Tune? In *New Directions for Evaluation*; Jossey-Bass Publishers: San Francisco, 1997; Vol. 75.
5. Melkers, J.; Willoughby, K. The state of the states: Performance-based budgeting in 47 out of 50. Public Administration Review **1998**, *58* (1), 66–73.
6. Tigue, P.; Strachota, D. *The Use of Performance Measures in City and County Budgets*; Government Finance Officers Association (GFOA): Chicago, IL, 1994.
7. Forrester, J.P.; Adams, G.B. Budgetary reform through organizational learning: Toward an organizational theory of budgeting. Adm. Soc. **1997**, *28* (4), 466–488.
8. Melkers, J.; Willoughby, K. Budgeters views of state performance budgeting systems: Distinctions across branches. Public Administration Review **2001**, *61* (1), 52–62.
9. Willoughby, K.; Melkers, J. Implementing PBB: Conflicting views of success. Public Budg. Finance **2000**, *20* (1), 105–120.
10. Broom, C.A.; McGuire, L.A. Performance-based government models: Building a track record. Public Budg. Finance **1995**, *15* (4), 3–17.

Budgeting and Public Choice

John R. Bartle
University of Nebraska at Omaha, Omaha, Nebraska, U.S.A.

INTRODUCTION

Public choice theory applies the logic of microeconomics to politics and public affairs, and generally assumes rationality and self-interested behavior among citizens and public officials in the choices they make by and for the public. The persons most closely associated with public choice theory are James Buchanan and Gordon Tullock.[1] Buchanan described the genesis of the theory as being a specification of the Constitutional and other rules for making choices by and for the public, as well as an investigation of their consequences, in the tradition of the original designers of the U.S. Constitution. Buchanan explained:

> Tullock and I considered ourselves to be simply taking the tools of economics, looking at something like the structure of American politics in the way James Madison had envisioned it. That is, it was clearly not a majoritarian democracy, which would be the parliamentary model (which was the ideal, at that time especially, of all the political scientists), rather it was a sort of a constitutional structure. We were the first to start analyzing the Constitution from an economic point of view. There were other people who analyzed particular voting rules, like majority voting, but we put that in a constitutional structure and provided an argument for choices among voting rules. We concentrated on that. So, in a sense, I considered us to be simply writing out in modern economic terms more or less Madison's framework of what he wanted to do, as opposed to anything new and different. It turned out that nobody had looked at it in that way.[2]

Public choice theory has had an important influence on governments across the world, as several advisors to conservative governments were scholars who helped to develop this perspective, or were influenced by it. As a result, it has been a controversial perspective. Public choice theory is relevant to many other areas of public affairs and political science (e.g., voting, international relations, macroeconomic policy); however, this article focuses on the influence of this perspective on public budgeting theory and practice.

RELEVANCE TO PUBLIC BUDGETING

Public choice theory deals with many topics relevant to public budgeting, but unlike most of the study of government budgeting, takes a deductive theoretical approach to these topics. In public choice theory, budgetary actors are usually assumed to be acting in their self-interest rather than in the interests of their agency or the public interest. Rather than focusing on "how to" topics that are the main substance of public budgeting texts, public choice looks at the incentive structure within institutions, and attempts to predict outcomes either on a solely theoretical level, or to compare these predictions with empirical findings. Public choice theory usually does not take the descriptive approach that most budgeting literature does, but rather seeks to theorize, test, and refine its theories.

Public choice denies the notion that government is a "benevolent despot" that will act to correct market failures and make distributional judgments in an even-handed way. From this perspective, one "ceases to see government as standing apart from the economy adjusting, correcting, and fine-tuning the economy. Rather, one sees it as being thoroughly enmeshed in the economy".[3] It is argued that this is a better way to understand why certain government policies exist, such as price controls, price supports, tax preferences, government-sponsored monopoly, and transfers to business and the nonpoor.

Despite many differences, public choice and the study of budgeting have much in common. John Forrester pointed out that both perspectives have similar interests in the choices that governments make. That is, both focus on the actions of budgetary actors, both have similar definitions of bureaucratic success (the rate of budgetary increase), both accept the value of economical government, and both accept the argument that administration and politics are not separate.[4]

Early writings in public choice tended to come from the conservative side of the political spectrum and often clashed with mainstream public administration. Many public servants and their teachers had a visceral reaction against public choice writings about "greedy bureaucrats," the public choice rejection of Wilsonian principles

Encyclopedia of Public Administration and Public Policy
DOI: 10.1081/E-EPAP 120011042

of public administration, and the rejection of the notion of the "public interest."[5] As a result, there was initially a deep rift between the perspectives. However, since then, many public choice theorists have emerged that are less ideological, and many public administration scholars have come to see some value in public choice models. In particular, because public choice has launched many empirical studies that have carefully tested propositions from public choice theory, as well as public administration, there have been some productive attempts to bridge the gap and to see how the two perspectives can strengthen each other.

GOVERNMENT SUPPLY AND AGENDA MANIPULATION

Perhaps the best-known public choice model in public administration is William Niskanen's model of public good supply.[6] Niskanen hypothesized that agency heads will seek to maximize their budget. In doing so, they are constrained by the fact that they must deliver a certain level of services to their political sponsor. A conflict arises where the sponsor, unlike the agency head, is unable to observe the "production process" whereby inputs are turned into outputs. All sponsors know is that for x dollars, y output is produced. A self-interested agency head, Niskanen argued, would exploit this information advantage and supply more output than demanded. This in turn increases the agency's budget, which is in the interests of the agency head, but not those of the sponsor (nor, presumably, the public). This is wasteful because the level of output provided is higher than the efficient level, so that marginal social costs are greater than marginal social benefits. The agency head in a sense is empire building by controlling the information the political sponsor receives. In a later piece, Niskanen modified his model to assume that agency heads maximize their utility, rather than their budget, and that utility is based on the discretionary budget and the output of their bureau.[7] This adds another possible outcome, that the output level is efficient, but that it is done inefficiently.

Niskanen's model generated a vast array of work, either testing his hypotheses or questioning the logic of his model. For the more practical purposes of public budgeting, it has had three important contributions. First, it was the first explicit model of government supply, which enabled a more complete modeling of public goods demand and production. Second, it demonstrated the importance of agenda control. For instance, in some cases, budgets have to be approved by referendum rather than by a vote of the elective body. Theories such as

Niskanen's can be developed and tested to see if budgetary outcomes are different when the process of approval is different. Third, it was one contribution that helped to provide a theoretical justification for the move to limit government size. In the political arena, this contributed to the success of many of the tax and spending restrictions in U.S. states, and also in the central governments of the United States during the Reagan Administration and the United Kingdom during the Thatcher administration. Indeed, Niskanen himself was on Reagan's Council of Economic Advisors.

CONSTITUTIONALISM

Along with Niskanen, the work of James Buchanan and his coauthors provided the intellectual foundation of the movement to increase the constitutional restrictions on government fiscal practice. This work is of fundamental importance to understanding movements, such as Proposition 13 in California, and similar limitations on democratic governments. Brennan and Buchanan made the standard economic assumptions about humans—that they are rational and self-interested—and asked what constitutional arrangement an actor will agree to before the establishment of the government.[8]

Brennan and Buchanan argued that people will fear that any majority will act as a tyrant and use the coercive powers of the state to fund inefficient projects to the benefit of the majority, or simply to use the tax and transfer system to effectively steal from the minority. Although the actor might be able to be part of the majority and therefore benefit from this redistribution, they might not; and if they are risk averse, they will choose a safer arrangement. Because of this concern, they argued, the rational actor choosing the fiscal rules of the constitution will limit both the constitutional procedures for considering policy and the allowable range of fiscal outcomes to limit the revenue-raising potential of the state. These limitations form the basis for a fiscal constitution that may narrowly constrain the actions of the government. The constitutional procedures they suggest are super-majority votes, multiple levels of approval, clearly defined property rights with application of due process in the protection of property, uniformity in taxation, and constitutional restrictions to balance the budget. The fiscal outcome restrictions suggested are limitations on tax rates, constraints on the breadth of tax bases, earmarking of revenues for specific expenditures, and restrictions on debt issuance and money creation.

Some of these constraints have been in place since the Magna Carta or the founding of the U.S. republic, whereas others are hotly debated topics in seats of government throughout the world. If nothing else, this public choice model forces us to rethink the fiscal rules of the game for any government. Not only is Buchanan's perspective relevant in these important current debates, but it also challenges the fundamental approach of contemporary public finance analysis and many of its most basic policy recommendations. For example, it is typically recommended that in order to serve the goals of efficiency and equity, tax bases should be broad with few "loopholes." This public choice perspective argues the opposite, as broad tax bases only make it easier for government to increase its revenue. In the words of Joe Stevens, rather than assuming that the state is a "good fairy," this approach sees the state as the "wicked witch," seeking to increase its power with little regard for the welfare of the citizens.[9] Although this approach rubs many public administration scholars the wrong way, it is congruent with the views of some American citizens, and probably a roughly accurate description of the practices of some despotic governments both in history and in the current day.

SIZE AND GROWTH OF GOVERNMENT

Since the early 1900s, government has grown in most nations, and sometimes at a high rate. What explains this? Several theories have been examined. In 1977, Buchanan looked at two views of government—"government by the people" and "government against the people"— and summarized the findings at that time.[10] The first model, a benign theory of the state, hypothesized that this growth is attributable to factors such as population growth, urbanization, the growth of the service economy, the income elasticity of demand for public goods, and Baumol's "productivity paradox." He wrote that one-half to two-thirds of the growth in government could be attributed to these factors. The unexplained gap suggested that a more pernicious model of government may explain the trends. His "government against the people" view suggested that other factors might explain part of this growth: the voting of bureaucrats for larger government; the profit-seeking activities of elected officials; and "fiscal illusion," the phenomenon that the full cost of government services is hidden or not understood by voters. Buchanan concluded that the motivational structure of government is probably the cause of this unexplained growth in government.

Later, Mueller reviewed several research articles speaking to this question. The range of factors is suggestive of the breadth of scholarship in this area. They include both good and bad reasons for government growth, specifically urbanization, income growth, the price elasticity of demand of public goods, the expansion of suffrage over time, changes in the distribution of income, voting of public employees and welfare recipients, interest groups, bureaucracy, and fiscal illusion. For some factors there is some supportive evidence, but overall he concluded that, "little consensus exists in what the key determinants of the growth of government are."[11]

Some public choice theorists have concluded from this research that there is a good case for fiscal limitations of the sort that Buchanan suggested. These limitations may be constitutional, procedural, or statutory limits on government growth or tax rates. Recent reforms in the United States, such as a proposed constitutional amendment to require a balanced federal budget; the statutory budget rules passed by Congress in the 1980s and 1990s; state tax, expenditure, and debt limits on local governments; and state restrictions on local revenue sources, in part speak to these concerns. Although both theory and empirical findings do not clearly support these steps, they may provide a plausible argument that is often advanced by fiscal conservatives.

RENT SEEKING

Economic rents are surpluses that cannot be competed away, for example, the return from an asset that is unique and in high demand, such as a parcel of property with a favorable location. Rent seeking is "attempting to use the political process to allow a firm or group of firms to earn economic rents in excess of their opportunity costs,"[12] or one firm or a group of firms acting to obtain special treatment by the government at the expense of others. Although firms might compete in the economic market for sales and profits, they may also compete in the political market for restrictions that enable them to receive rents. They might do so in legal ways, such as lobbying or campaign contributions, or illegal ways such as bribery, intimidation, or kickbacks. There are numerous examples of market restrictions that might lead to rents: regulatory protection, patents, zoning, exclusive licenses, occupational licensing, and academic tenure. Not only might these uncompetitive practices lead to economic inefficiencies, but also the competition among businesses and individuals for these rights would be wasteful. A casual look at lobbying practices in most governments suggests that this phenomenon is an issue. Evidence from research on campaign contributions is supportive of this assertion.[13]

Government budgets are susceptible to rent-seeking behavior on the part of officials and interest groups. Constitutional economists would urge that the scope of action allowed to the state should be restricted so there will be little opportunity to extract rent by use of the apparatus of government. This might be done through requiring super-majorities for passage of such legislation, or simply by abolition of regulatory bodies that might be prone to this behavior. Others who may not be true believers in public choice theory might agree for the need for structural defenses of the public treasury against rent seekers. Many public administration scholars suggest that a strong code of ethics can accomplish the same result. It is hard to generalize about which solution is best, but it is worth noting that both the public choice and public administration approaches to the study of government recognize this problem.

CONCLUSION

Public choice theory has had an important influence on both practice and thinking about government budgets. Its validity in explaining behavior within agencies and patterns of change in the public sector is open to question; however, public choice advocates are energetic examiners of their theoretical speculations, so inquiry in this area continues to advance the ideas. Public choice has generally been seen in opposition to orthodox public administration, although as Forrester pointed out, this need not be. In fact, the public choice view of government sees numerous actors with varying motives, in competition with each other, some scrupulous and some not. This is more congruent with what we know about politics than the ''benevolent despot'' view of the state. Both for polemic and scholarly reasons, practitioners and scholars in public administration need to understand public choice theory and follow its development.

REFERENCES

1. Buchanan, J.M.; Tullock, G. *The Calculus of Consent: Logical Foundations of Constitutional Democracy*; The University of Michigan Press: Ann Arbor, MI, 1962.
2. Woodrow ''James Buchanan'' (Interview). In *Fedgazette (Federal Reserve Bank of Minneapolis)*; September 1995. http://woodrow.mpls.frb.fed.us/pubs/region/int959.html. Accessed January 16, 2002.
3. Levy, J.M. *Essential Microeconomics for Public Policy Analysis*; Praeger Publishers: Westport, CT, 1995; 95.
4. Forrester, J.P. Public Choice Theory and Public Budgeting: Implications for the Greedy Bureaucrat. In *Evolving Theories of Public Budgeting*; Bartle, J.R., Ed.; Elsevier Science Ltd.: Oxford, UK, 2001; 101–124.
5. Golembiewski, R.T. *Public Administration as a Developing Discipline*; Marcel Dekker Inc.: New York, 1977; 157–201.
6. Niskanen, W.A. *Bureaucracy and Representative Government*; Aldine-Atherton: Chicago, 1971.
7. Niskanen, W.A. Bureaucrats and politicians. J. Law Econ. **1975**, *18*, 617–643.
8. Brennan, G.; Buchanan, J.M. *The Power to Tax: Analytical Foundations of a Fiscal Constitution*; Cambridge University Press: Cambridge, 1980.
9. Stevens, J.B. *The Economics of Collective Choice*; Westview Press: Boulder, CO, 1993; 174.
10. Buchanan, J.M. Why Does Government Grow. In *Budgets and Bureaucrats: The Sources of Government Growth*; Borcherding, T.E., Ed.; Duke University Press: Durham, NC, 1977; 3–18.
11. Mueller, D.C. *Public Choice II*; Cambridge University Press, 1989.
12. Stevens, J.B. *The Economics of Collective Choice*; Westview Press: Boulder, CO, 1993; 187.
13. Mueller, D.C. *Public Choice II*; Cambridge University Press, 1989; 242–243.

Budgeting, Target-Based

B. J. Reed
University of Nebraska at Omaha, Omaha, Nebraska, U.S.A.

INTRODUCTION

Target-based budgeting (TBB) has become an increasingly common approach to the budgeting, particularly for local governments. It is a method of budgeting that identifies overall expenditures for an agency or unit based on the estimated revenue available to government. It allows control to be imposed at the executive or legislative levels while allowing decentralization and flexibility at lower levels of the organization. TBB is particularly useful when state and local governments have needs to control spending but also face turbulent and unpredictable demands for services.

WHAT IS TBB?

In most cases, the expenditure "target" for each unit of the organization under TBB is determined by the budgeting or finance office under the direction of the chief administrative officer and the policy board for that organization. This target is based on the strategic priorities or direction of the agency as well as the estimated availability of revenue.[1] These expenditure ceilings are set well in advance of departments preparing their budgets and are not negotiable. Usually, a percentage of the total budget is set aside for contingencies as well as for discretionary spending. The discretionary spending allows for organizationwide priorities and may include departmental requests beyond those funded within the targets set for each unit.

Targets can be set a few different ways. One is to simply divide proportionately historical expenditures by department. For example, if public safety historically has take 35% of a city's expenditures, their target would be 35% of the revenue available after contingencies, discretionary allocations, and one-time expenditures have been determined. Rubin referred to this as the "constant services or maintenance of effort budget."[2] Another approach would be to combine historical spending patterns with strategic priorities of the government. If the elected officials determined that neighborhood development was to become a key focus for the city, targets for departments involved in neighborhood development could be adjusted upward. However, in most cases, such strategic emphases would be included within the discretionary portion of the budget rather than in adjusting the targets for each agency.

Target budgeting is designed to centralize overall expenditure patterns among departments, while maximizing discretion within each agency about how to spend those dollars. Although some service deliveries within departments are mandated by law, other activities are discretionary. Units can determine within the target provided what they believe to be the most important, and what personnel and operating expenditures are necessary to carry out these services and activities.

If the target provided is above the historical dollars provided to the agency, discretion increases. However, if targets are at or below previous targets, discretion is reduced. Departments with high mandated activities may be at a competitive disadvantage relative to units with fewer mandated service levels. County health departments may be mandated by the state to carry out inspections of restaurants, so some expenditures will have to be dedicated to this activity within the target set by the county commissioners. Similarly, departments with access to external funding through fees, grants, or donations may be able to shift expenditures covered by such revenue sources rather than having them covered by tax-based revenue set as part of the budget process. Also, because some tax revenue is earmarked for particular purposes, some departmental targets may be adjusted to reflect trends in revenue generation in these areas. County road departments may have revenue generated through gasoline taxes because such revenue has to be used for the construction or reconstruction of roads, while county health departments may receive revenue generated through inspection fees. Such earmarking must be taking into consideration as the chief executive and budget office develop targets for each department.

Linking targets to revenue forecasts is a tricky business, but is essential to making TBB work. Revenue forecasts must be set early enough to ensure time for target expenditures to be set and departmental responses to be developed. Forecasting property tax receipts may be quite easy because past patterns are good predictors of future revenue. Predicting sales or income tax is much more difficult because they are based on underlying economic conditions and consumer confidence rather than

Encyclopedia of Public Administration and Public Policy
DOI: 10.1081/E-EPAP 120010985

on mandatory fee payments. White suggested that forecasts be set at least 6 to 8 months in advance.[1]

Target-based budgeting is different from lump sum budgeting (LSB), which assumes no line item discipline within the agency or departmental budget. It also does not necessarily involve setting target ceilings for expenditures based on forecasted revenue. Target-based budgeting can be combined with LSB to create only a ceiling on expenditures. In this case, the department has total discretion to shift funds between personnel and operating line items as long as they remain within the target ceiling. Target-based budgeting can also be linked to specific line items. In such cases, permission would be required for shifts among personnel or operating categories once the target budget has been established.

Target-based budgeting is also different from zero base budgeting (ZBB), which requires extensive development of budget scenarios within each department through the development of "packages" of services and the costs associated with each of those packages. Target-based budgeting is much less paper and time intensive because it only requires departments to provide overall requests as they might typically do in more traditional budget processes as long as they do not exceed the ceiling.

The amount set aside for contingencies or discretionary spending is determined by the chief administrator and the policy board, and is likely to range from 10% to 15% of the overall revenue projected for the agency. Agencies can also pass down the contingency estimates to each individual department but this will require targets to be adjusted for expenditure predictability. Public works departments, for example, may require greater contingencies for such things as salt, sand, and overtime due to inclement weather than would be true in a department such as human resources or planning. The amount set aside for discretionary spending increases the ability of policy boards to set priorities but it also decreases the flexibility and discretion at the unit level. Policy makers must be willing to allow 85% to 90% of

the budget to be decentralized to individual units. However, the remaining 10% to 15% can be ranked to meet overall organizational priorities. Table 1 provides an example developed by Wenz and Nolan about how the process would work.[3]

HISTORY AND USE

According to Rubin,[4] the first mention of TBB was a case study of Berkeley, California, in the 1920s. Although the exact term was not used, the process used in Berkeley was similar to what we think of as target budgeting. In this case, each department was provided a "maximum amount" to spend during the fiscal year, while providing supplemental requests in priority order to the city manager.

Some form of TBB has been practiced since the 1920s. The emergence of ZBB in the 1970s in Georgia, and later at the federal level, provided a new twist on target budgeting. However, the enormous complexity and paper work requirements of ZBB made it fall from favor even when TBB was continuing to be used throughout the United States.

As noted earlier, most documented uses of TBB have been in city and county governments. Cincinnati, Tampa, Rochester, Phoenix, Salina, Kansas, and Douglas County, Nebraska, have all used the target budgeting approach. In Cincinnati, the city council developed decision criteria to allocate discretionary funds centrally once the target budgets had been established. The criteria included such things as maintenance of the city's infrastructure, legal mandates, agency capacity, employment potential for the private sector, environmental impact, preventive maintenance, and support for long-range plans.[5]

Rochester developed a target for each unit, but subtracted all one-time costs that occurred in the previous fiscal year and the addition of new one-time costs for the coming fiscal year. Phoenix along with many of the other cities used some form of performance measures either at

Table 1 Calculation of targets

Total operating fund budget	$151,840,000
Recreation department budget	7,956,740
Proportion of total operating fund budget	$(7,956,740)/(151,840,000) = 0.0524$
Total projected operating fund budget resources	153,850,000
Less 10% discretionary reserve	15,340,000
Net projected total operating fund resources[a]	138,510,000
Recreation department target	$0.0524 \times \$138,510,000 = \$7,258,200$

[a]The projected $138 million did not involve certain expenses, such as fringe benefits, that were not included in the target.
Source: from Ref. [3].

the unit level or individual level in conjunction with TBB. Outcome measurement is seen as an important linkage to target budgeting.[6] Salina, Kansas, closely tied its TBB efforts to strategic planning with the city council developing performance goals that help to direct strategic priorities for the city.[1]

STRENGTHS

Target-based budgeting has several benefits. First, target budgeting can be carried out without extensive burdens on departments. It requires some analysis, but not the extensive kinds of detail that other budget approaches require. Second, it can provide constructive policy involvement by elected officials, but leave considerable discretion to unit managers. The target budgeting approach allows prioritization of a percentage of the budget at the policy level, while delegating decisions for most of the funding to the unit level. This mix of centralized and decentralized decision making often creates a healthy balance in the budget process. Third, by having the targets set by revenue estimates, TBB avoids much of the expenditure haggling that occurs with other budget approaches. Departments know the parameters they will be working within and this predictability can improve management decisions throughout the fiscal year. Finally, the ability to identify discretionary funds that can be used to reallocate toward priorities of the organization allows chief executives and policy boards the ability to have substantial affects on meeting agency goals.

WEAKNESSES

Target-based budgeting must have the total support of the policy board and the chief executive. Pressure will exist to vary the targets set, and it is likely that some departments will attempt to manipulate the process in other ways. Only strong support by organizational decision makers will make the process work. Conversely, government officials must avoid the temptation to micromanage decisions made at the departmental level. The true incentive for unit managers is the discretion to control budgetary allocations. Target budgeting without such discretion ties the hands of managers, and reduces support and incentives to innovate and produce efficiencies that benefit the entire organization.

Revenue projections must be as accurate as possible. The whole basis of TBB is that ceilings are set based on proportionate allocation of known revenue. Inaccurate forecasting can undermine the entire approach. Although improvements can result with TBB, the process is still likely to be an incremental one. To some extent, this is

determined by how the discretionary dollars are allocated across the agency. Placing substantial portions of the revenue into new initiatives can result in substantial changes. This is not common. If the culture is developed where innovation is supported, nonincremental change may be possible at all levels of the organization. However, TBB does not guarantee that such chance will occur.

Target-based budgeting works well with general fund tax dollars. It does not work as well with departments that generate substantial dollars externally through fees or external grants or donations. Public utilities are not good candidates for TBB because most of their resources are based on customer payments. In this case, these units operate through self-funded activities. Another complexity of TBB is sorting through tax revenues that are earmarked for particular activities within departments. Public works departments who receive earmarked funding of gasoline or cigarette taxes rely on different allocation and forecasting processes than those departments that depend exclusively on property, sales, or income taxes.

CASE STUDY OF TBB

The University of Nebraska (NU) system operates under a modified target budgeting approach. As a result of a state Supreme Court decision, the Nebraska Unicameral Legislature (NUL) is required to provide NU with funding in a ''lump sum'' based on revenue forecasts without the ability to earmark funding for specific purposes. The University of Nebraska submits line item detail to NUL in the late summer or early fall of each year. Nebraska Unicameral Legislature approves the budget in May or early June and, based on revenue forecasts, developed by a state forecasting board. The governor can approve the recommendations of NUL or line item veto elements that are oppositional. Nebraska Unicameral Legislature can then sustain or override the governor's vetoes. Once approved, the university has total discretion in how those tax dollars are spent beginning July 1 of each year.

Once NUL and the governor have acted, the elected Board of Regents in conjunction with the president of NU allocates target lump sum budgets to each of the four campuses of the system. Certain campuswide expenditure priorities are identified by the top administrators of each campus and funding is set aside for these priorities. At The University of Nebraska at Omaha, however, the vast majority of funding is allocated in the form of ''target'' amount to each unit on the campus. Certain assumptions are built into these target allocations. These are initial established as NU prepares its budget for submission to the state and are revised based on final action taken. Estimates are made for personnel and operating based on existing lines and previous state-funded operating expenditures. Any increases in personnel costs or fringe benefits are added to the targeted amount for each unit.

Once this target budget is established, unit directors have complete discretion in shifting dollars between established personnel and operating line items as long as they remain within the overall budget target established at the beginning of each fiscal year. In reality, the amount of discretion is a function of changes in personnel status within the unit. If all personnel lines are filled, discretion becomes almost nonexistent because most assumptions concerning operating budgets are considerably below actual need. However, if personnel lines are open and remain unfilled, discretion increases substantially.

Each unit is charged a ''tax'' by NU, based on legislative assumptions about the number of open lines that will exist within each campus and unit each year. These charges are passed down to each unit in proportion to their overall personnel budget, irrespective of the number or dollars associated with actual open positions. In some cases, these charges can be offset during the fiscal year by allocations made centrally for such things as equipment requests, funding for part-time instructors, and so forth. However, the allocation of such funds remains at the discretion of upper-level administrators and may or may not materialize depending on priorities that exist at a campuswide level. Unit discretion will also vary based on how many external dollars can be generated from grants, fees, and endowment support. Units with significant revenue generated from such sources have much greater discretion than units without such revenue streams.

Budget and finance offices for the campus track line item expenditures to compare with estimated expenditures, but their primary focus is the bottom line expenditure budget for each major unit. If expenditures by month in total begin to exceed estimated expenditures, they notify the manager in charge of a unit to ensure that total expenditures are in line with budgeted amounts. Overages within individual line items are genrally not an area of concern because of the discretion available to each unit manager to shift funds as needed. If total unit expenditures appear to be exceeding the proposed budget, unit managers must identify additional revenue sources that will be provided to cover these overages.

CONCLUSION

Target-based budgeting is a little-recognized but extensively used approach to public budgeting. It provides both executive control and decentralized flexibility. Advantages include reduced bureaucratic reporting and procedural systems, increased policy involvement by elected officials, and reduced conflict over expenditure decisions. Problems with the approach are often associated with limited support by elected officials and chief executives, lack of accurate revenue forecasting, and extending the approach beyond general fund tax dollars to units generated substantial dollars externally.

As the previous case study demonstrates, TBB can work effectively if it is designed to accommodate the governmental structure in which it operates. As with any budgeting approach, failure is likely unless that budgeting approach fits within the organizational environment.

REFERENCES

1. White, J. *Target-Based Budgeting: A New Approach to an Old Activity*; Kansas Government Journal, August, 1994. http://www.co.saline.ks.us/Budget/TBB.htm (accessed June 2001).
2. Rubin, I. Target-Based Budgeting. In *Defining Public Administration: Selections From The International Encyclopedia of Public Policy and Administration*; Weston Press: Boulder, CO, 2000; 369.
3. Wenz, T.W.; Nolan, A.P. Budgeting for the future: Target based budgeting. Public Budg. Finance **1992**, *2* (2), 88.
4. Rubin, I. Target-Based Budgeting. In *Defining Public Administration: Selections From The International Encyclopedia of Public Policy and Administration*; Weston Press: Boulder, CO, 2000; 368–369.
5. Wenz, T.W.; Nolan, A.P. Budgeting for the future: Target based budgeting. Public Budg. Finance **1992**, *2* (2), 90.
6. Rubin, I. Budgeting for our times: Target base budgeting. Public Budg. Finance **1991**, *3* (11), 5–13.

FURTHER READING

Koehler, F.U.; Reed, B.J. Target Budgeting in Lincoln County. In *Public Budgeting and Financial Management*; Khan, A., Hildreth, B.W., Eds.; Kendall/Hunt: Deubuque, IA, 1994; 101–112.

Budgets and Accountability

Jonathan Justice

Rutgers, The State University of New Jersey, Newark, New Jersey, U.S.A.

INTRODUCTION

From one perspective, public budgets and budgeting processes may be viewed as being, first and foremost, instruments of accountability. A century of budget and financial reporting (or ''accounting'') reforms in the United States have been aimed largely at making budgeting a more effective means of holding users of resources accountable to others. As reformers and other students of budgeting have learned, budget processes, formats, and distribution are important factors in determining whether, to whom, and for what public organizations and administrators are actually accountable in their use and application of resources, and budget design choices often involve trade-offs. Considerable progress has been made toward making public budgets more accountable, however, and continued progress seems likely.

ACCOUNTABILITY AND BUDGETS

Accountability in the conventional organizational or managerial, instrumental sense provides a means for one person or group (the principal) to manage the behavior of another person or group (the agent) as it relates to some expectation of performance. It relies on the prospect of postperformance sanctions and/or rewards, applied after an examination of the results of the agent's behavior, as an efficient way to provide incentives for the agent to satisfy the principal's expectations. Key elements in accountability, then, are the principal–agent relationship, the stipulation of expectations, the account that enables comparison of actual with desired behavior and outcomes, and the application and effects of sanctions.

For accountability to be effective, it is generally presumed that all four elements must be in place and recognized by all parties. There must be a principal–agent relationship and a delegated task or responsibility such that the parties are able to establish a relatively unambiguous (and feasible) set of expectations for the agent's performance. There must be an account of the agent's performance through observation by the principal, reporting by the agent or other means, that enables the principal to verify accurately and reliably whether performance satisfied those expectations. There must also be at least the potential for sanctions to be applied in the event that performance is not satisfactory.

What is a budget, and what is its relationship to accountability? Most of us are familiar with the idea that a budget is a constraint on resource use, a prohibition against spending more than a certain amount. For example, a household may have a weekly grocery budget, which stipulates an upper limit on the amount of money that can be used each week to purchase groceries. We can see that even this simple household example introduces budget functions beyond simple economy of resource consumption. It also specifies a particular purpose to which the resource may be consumed (groceries), and a period of time over which the resource will be employed toward the stipulated purpose. A budget, then, is also a plan. It identifies the goods we propose to purchase or produce and the time during which we propose to do so, and it links those elements to the requisite resources.

We can say that a public organization's budget conveys a set of *expectations* about the organization's use, as *agent,* of resources provided to it by an executive, a legislature, or the general public, as *principal.* Further, typical budget processes require an *account*, in the form of a review after the end of the budget period of the extent to which actual resource use and performance conformed to the initial expectations or plan. Budget appropriations enacted by legislatures have the force of law, and budgets established within organizations carry hierarchical authority, so that, at least in principle, *sanctions* are potentially available in the case of unacceptable deviations from expectations. Budgets are instruments of accountability, and the history of budget reform is a history of efforts to make budgets more accountable.

EARLY BUDGET REFORMS: ACCOUNTABILITY FOR ECONOMY AND EFFICIENCY

In the United States, early twentieth-century Progressive reformers were concerned with, among other things, developing ways in which budgets could be used as means to make the bureaucracy more accountable to elected executives and governments more accountable to

Encyclopedia of Public Administration and Public Policy
DOI: 10.1081/E-EPAP 120010976

an engaged citizenry. In New York City, the Bureau of Municipal Research (BRM) built on the image of business as the model of efficiency to suggest that citizens regard themselves as shareholders in a ''business'' of government, and so ''mind their own business'' by in effect holding government accountable through scrutiny of its performance. Efforts included a 1908 budget exhibit, visited by over 60,000 people, ''that used photographs, charts, and models to show how the city spent its $143,500,000 budget.''[1] Here, then, was an attempt to enhance budgetary accountability by generating greater attentiveness by the public, as principal, to a comprehensible account of how local government, as agent, was using resources. In keeping with a focus on economy and efficiency, the BRM highlighted some instances of apparent waste in the form of unnecessary expenditures or overly high prices paid.

A concern with accountability, particularly for economy and efficiency, may also be seen in the early proposals for and adoption of an executive budget process by the federal government. The reformers emphasized a hierarchical, control-oriented model of accountability, aimed at replacing a decentralized legislature-dominated process with a centralized, executive-centered one. Replacing a multitude of disparate agency budgets with a consolidated federal budget would make for more comprehensive and comprehensible statements of expectations (plans) and accounts of past performance by the government as a whole, reporting to the president, Congress, and the public. The executive-centered format provided a single agent for the public and the legislature to hold accountable, while empowering that agent to be a stronger principal to government departments.

As adopted in 1921, federal budget reform provided for a unified budget, establishing a chain of budgetary accountability up through the executive branch, thence to Congress and the public. In recognition of the unavoidable complexity of large budgets, cost estimates, and revenue projections, specialized agencies were created to advise Congress and the president. The need for special expertise suggests there is a tradeoff, then, between a centralized and comprehensive approach to large budgets, and their direct accessibility to the nominal principals in the accountability relationship. The use of a line item, or object-of-expenditure, budget format, in keeping with the contemporaneous emphasis on economy and expenditure control, also represents a tradeoff. This format focuses attention on resource inputs and their application to specific efforts, but does little to highlight the relationship of inputs to results or to expectations concerning the desired outcomes of agency spending.

The 1920s and 1930s in the United States also saw increasing recognition of the importance of financial accounting practices for the accountability of businesses to their shareholders. The continuing development of generally accepted accounting principles (GAAP) to date represents an effort to ensure that financial reports (accounts) provided by business management are substantively meaningful, accurate, and comparable to one another. This responds to the potential for loss of accountability when the accounts given by agents are incorrect or incomprehensible to principals, whether due to well-intentioned mistakes or to opportunism on the part of agents. Generally accepted accounting principles have subsequently also been developed for nonprofit and government applications.

INCREMENTAL BUDGETING, EXPERTISE, AND PROFESSIONAL ACCOUNTABILITY

After World War II, the federal budget process settled into a routine that has been described as ''incremental''.[2] The incrementalist account of budgeting emphasizes the insularity and regularity of the process, and describes a system of continually increasing budgets, negotiated with little conflict, among a small number of insiders in Congress and the Executive branch. Like the ''iron triangle'' described by mid-century policy literature, this system seems largely unaccountable to the public. It confines the communication of expectations and accounts to a relatively small decision-making elite, and appears to provide little in the way of public participation or strong central direction for economy, efficiency, and effectiveness.

As the size and complexity of the U.S. public sector continued to grow, however, budget reformers rose to the occasion, proposing a number of alternative budget models, processes, and formats, all with implications for the how, for what, and to whom of budget accountability. Along the way, tax revolts, business cycles, and budget deficits and surpluses have stimulated and structured the public, the reformers, public officials, and other participants.

Although this is not immediately apparent from the incrementalist account, mid-twentieth century budget reform proposals, such as the recommendations of the 1949 Hoover Commission, had emphasized managerial accountability for performance of delegated policy tasks.[3] Proposals for the use of functional, rather than object-of-expenditure, budget formats reflected an idea that administrators should be accountable to their superiors and legislators for delivering specified results or meeting performance targets. Budgets built on functional accounts targeted specified quantities of outputs, given specified unit costs and allocations of funds for each functional category. The highly ambitious planning–

programming–budgeting system (PPBS) reform of the 1960s aimed at using budgets as an instrument of managerial accountability, but with a vastly inflated sense of what expert administrators could be responsible for. In common with the contemporaneous enthusiasm for the developing ''policy sciences,'' PPBS sought to extend the scope of managerial responsibilities to also include policy planning and design.

The PPBS reform of the 1960s acknowledged the intimate relationship between the form used for budget presentation and the nature and content of the accounts given by agents to their principals. Taking advantage of emerging innovations in computer technology, PPBS facilitated the integration and ''cross-walking'' of budget data among line item, activity-based, and program or policy-based presentation formats.[3] Conceivably, such an approach would facilitate holding administrators accountable for economy, efficiency, effectiveness, and equity, as information could be made available on their plans and performance with respect to avoiding excess or nonsanctioned spending, producing the expected outputs and activities, and directing resources to the appropriate social purposes. This last charge, however, presses against the limits of the conventional model of accountability, which emphasizes the performance of delegated tasks by an agent rather than the stipulation by the agent of the values of the principal. The planning–programming–budgeting system never really took root outside the U.S. government, and did not last long even there. Numerous arguments have been advanced for the failure of the PPBS reform, but we might suspect that part of the cause might be related to its step away from the familiar model of accountability for resource use.

Another short-lived reform, zero base budgeting (ZBB), similarly sought to integrate some level of policy choice with budgeting, by requiring administrative agencies to identify and rank their programmatic priorities. ZBB aimed at achieving administrative accountability for economy and efficiency by facilitating a chief executive's ability to identify and cut low-priority activities, and efficiency and effectiveness by identifying ''packages'' of activities and outputs to be achieved in return for specified levels of resource input. In principle, ZBB could use professional expertise to produce a clear set of choices among competing public expectations, for which administrators and elected officials could then be held accountable. Zero base budgeting, like PPBS, was highly demanding procedurally and was never fully implemented. Subsequent budget reforms, many of which appear to be more enduring, have been less ambitious regarding the scope of budgeting and accountability, emphasizing the task performance-related aspects of efficiency and effectiveness, and striving to keep administrators accountable to their hierarchical and legislative superiors.

DEVELOPMENTS AND CONTINUING ISSUES

Activity-based costing (ABC) and the use of ''cost center'' accounting for support services and program activities are techniques meant to facilitate managerial accountability, by identifying in detail the application of resources by administrators and the results of resource consumption. In theory, managerial or elected principals can use this information, by itself and in comparison with information from comparable administrative units, to demand more cost-effective performance from their subordinates. Under some schemes of internal or public–private producer competition, sanctions might include loss of responsibilities and the attendant budget allocations, or even termination of an administrative unit. Potentially, then, ABC and related managerial accounting techniques in budgeting can provide strong managerial accountability.

These accounting techniques often complement performance-based budgeting (PBB) schemes, which are increasingly popular with state and local governments in the United States. Performance-based budgeting links budgeting to performance measurement, making it possible in principle for administrative units to be held accountable by citizens, legislators, and elected executives for efficiency and effectiveness in the performance of tasks and delivery of activities and outputs. The integrated presentation of performance targets and resource allocations in statements of expectations and in accounts of performance makes it possible for agents to be held accountable for economy, efficiency, and effectiveness by means of a single accountability mechanism. Although this has great promise as a tool for accountability within units of government or other public organizations, it may be less useful as an instrument of accountability to external constituencies and the general public. The form in which expectations and accounts are presented tends not to be readily accessible (i.e., both available for inspection and easily understood) to external principals. This may be true of most detailed budget formats and processes, and efforts to hold public organizations accountable often use broader forms of expectation specification, accounts, and sanctions. Examples might include ''tax revolts'' in many U.S. states, President Reagan's effort to ''cut off'' Congress's ''allowance'' with his 1981 tax cut, and various deficit reduction and ''cutback management'' measures undertaken by public agencies throughout the 1980s and (most of the)1990s.

In these instances of tax ''reform'' and cutbacks, aggregate spending ''accounts'' that failed to meet political expectations of more public service for less money were responded to through sanctions in the form of reduced (or at least more slowly expanding) resource levels for public organizations. This highlights a long-recognized paradox of public budgeting incentives, which is an important additional challenge to accountable public budgeting: the question of sanctions. In the accountability model, the prospect of retrospectively suffering penalties for misfeasance and the cautionary example of penalties administered to other agents who failed to meet expectations are meant to serve as a means of regulating the conduct of a self-interested agent. In public sector budgeting, the key form of material sanction is budget reduction. This leads to some perverse incentives. First is the ''use-it-or-lose-it'' motive to spend a unit's full allocation regardless of need to avoid future budget reductions as the penalty for spending too *little* in the current period. Second is the likelihood that output reductions may follow budget reductions, with the result that sanctions can prove no less injurious to the principal than to the agent. Third, the fear of electoral or employment-affecting sanctions may encourage officials to avoid accountability by working to make revenue increases invisible to the public.

PROSPECTS

This quick review indicates both that a primary use of budgets in the public sector is as instruments of accountability for the employment of public resources toward achieving public ends, and that this use is subject to numerous challenges and tradeoffs. Detailed and complex presentations of budgetary information are valuable for managerial or hierarchical accountability within public organizations, but may be impenetrable to nonspecialists. This can have the consequence (sometimes intended, we might at times suspect) of discouraging political accountability, when accounts are inaccessible to legislators and political constituencies, and are presented in forms incommensurate with the ways in which political expectations are formulated. Attempts at broad political accountability and sanctions, in turn, can potentially lead to diminished organizational effectiveness with adverse consequences for principals as well as for agents. Holding agencies accountable for economy by cutting their budgets broadly might preclude holding them responsible for effectiveness. Aggregate or general presentations of budgets may be more accessible to the public, thus enhancing political accountability. However, they may be less useful as managerial tools, thus reducing potential administrative accountability.

Are trade-offs and suboptimality of budget accountability inevitable? Our review of past reforms and evolving technologies of budgeting suggest that many improvements have already occurred and that more may be expected. Although it appears unlikely that the inherent conflicts among market, political, administrative, professional, and legal bases of accountability can be eliminated, there is good potential for approaching the work of budgeting in a way that increasingly facilitates the application of each model of accountability. Central to this are opportunities for improving the clarity of budget presentations, the comparability of budgets and accounting among similar entities, the accessibility of and attentiveness to budgets by the public, and their representatives and the complementarity of multiple accountabilities.

The low cost and increasing processing and storage capacity of contemporary computers has made possible the implementation of cost accounting methodologies that enable budgets and financial reports to be generated quickly and reliably in various formats, using the same underlying data elements. Cost accounting-based information can be generated to serve managerial needs, line item formats, and PBB or target-based budgeting formats for legislators' appropriation-related purposes, and GAAP-compliant financial reports for other reporting purposes. Integration with larger and longer-term performance plans and performance measurement schemes can serve political accountability and policy determination needs. At the federal level, the newly created Federal Accounting Standards Board is charged with developing GAAP for the federal government, and the recently adopted Government Performance and Results Act mandates the integration of strategic planning, performance measurement, and annual agency budgets. Success, however, will require overcoming significant challenges of implementation and political will.

At the state and local levels, there are a number of opportunities for complementarity of different accountabilities. The work of specialized professional associations, such as the Government Finance Officers Association, involves setting professional standards for the management of public budgeting and finance, and encouraging accountability among their members for adhering to those standards. There is some evidence that administrators have internalized certain norms they believe to be responsive to the general public interest.[4] However, in certain circumstances, the attempt to be accountable to political expectations can still conflict with norms of professional accountability for prudence.[5] Staff organizations and public interest ''watchdog'' groups concerned with all levels of government and the nonprofit sector employ specialists to examine public organization's budgets and accounts on behalf of nonspecialist legal and political principals, and to enforce professional and bureaucratic accountability.

Thoughtful experimentation with different budget formats and forms of dissemination can help to advance the cause of clarity and relevance of budget presentations. Interactive budget presentations might take advantage of the Internet or freestanding information kiosks to enable citizens and their representatives to examine multiple presentations of budgets and financial reports at their own discretion and in accordance with their own expectations for public organizations' priorities and performance. In the U.S. nonprofit sector, an ingenious collaboration of the U.S. Internal Revenue Service, the Urban Institute and Philanthropic Research, Inc. (Guidestar), has made the standardized (and therefore comparable across organizations) IRS-990 financial reports and other budget data for charitable organizations available over the Internet (this and other information can be accessed at http://www.guidestar.org/ or http://nccs.urban.org/). The fruits of ongoing efforts at budget benchmarking by state and local governments could be used in a similar fashion, through standardization of categories and widespread public dissemination. Comparability of budgets and performance measures across organizations helps attentive principals know what they can reasonably expect from their agents. As the popularity of the BRM's 1908 budget exhibit illustrated, experimentation with alternative formats and media can identify ways to overcome the all-too-common reluctance of nonspecialists to examine budgets through effective presentation.

REFERENCES

1. Schachter, H.L. *Reinventing Government or Reinventing Ourselves: The Role of Citizen Owners in Making a Better Government*; State University of New York Press: Albany, NY, 1997.
2. Wildavsky, A.; Caiden, N. *The New Politics of the Budgetary Process*, 3rd Ed.; Longman: New York, 1997.
3. Schick, A. The road to PPB. Public Administration Rev. **1966**, *26*, 243–258.
4. McCue, C. The risk-return paradox in local government investing. Public Budg. Finance **2000**, *20* (3), 80–101.
5. Kearns, K.P. Accountability and entrepreneurial public management: The case of the orange county investment fund. Public Budg. Finance **1995**, *15* (3), 3–21.

Bureaucracy, Economic Theories of

James R. Simmons
University of Wisconsin–Oshkosh, Oshkosh, Wisconsin, U.S.A.

INTRODUCTION

Economic theories of bureaucracy begin with the assumption that people who act in a self-interested way in the marketplace are the same people who vote, run for office, and are employed in the public sector. Government officials and civil servants are portrayed as acting to advance their own private agendas in the name of the "public interest." The primary implication drawn from this perspective is that the collective political process fails because participants are responding to incentives other than those assumed by conventional theory. Economic reasoning promises a logical deductive model of how public agencies behave with clear directions for policy analysis and simple normative recommendations for reform.

Classical management theory envisioned public sector bureaucracy as a modernizing form of organization that would ensure precision, speed, reliability, clarity, efficiency, and regularity in the provision of high-quality goods and services. In contrast, modern political economists have developed theories of bureaucracy, which see in these same hierarchical structures institutions that foster self-serving behavior that corrupts the natural functioning of markets and mask the political pursuit of private gain by those who manipulate them. Self-interest in the private sector is said to produce optimal outcomes. However, in all government agencies, this same motivation generates command-and-control monopolies operated by an intrusive, problem-finding elite that overemploys, overpays, overbuilds, and overproduces. Thus, whenever possible, the reliance˘ on the public sector should be reduced and market forces restored.

HISTORY

Much of the prescription for the model organization comes down to us from the writings of Max Weber. In Weber's bureaucratic world, public employees are rational professionals who follow the routines and duties of the agencies for which they work. Their values are expected to be limited to the neutral pursuit of their organization's objectives or official norms, while their status is derived from their training, title, and job performance. Although organization theory has been dominated by adherents of the Weberian perspective, modern political economists have developed a competing diagnosis of bureaucracy that emphasizes public failure in the absence of market discipline. This literature on public bureaucracy can be traced back to Ludwig von Mises and Frederick Hayek. However, neither their works is a recognizable economic account because there is little abstract modeling in either contribution. Formal theorizing about government is best represented by contemporary authors such as Anthony Downs, Gordon Tullock, Vincent Ostrom, and William Niskanen.

Economic theories of bureaucracy begin with the assumption that people who act in a self-interested way in the marketplace are the same people who vote, run for office, and are employed in the public sector. Government officials and civil servants are portrayed as acting to advance their own private agendas in the name of the "public interest." The primary implication drawn from this perspective is that the collective political process fails because participants are responding to incentives other than those assumed by conventional theory. Economic reasoning promises a logical deductive model of how public agencies behave with clear directions for policy analysis and simple normative recommendations for reform.

The distinguishing feature of economic theory is its concentration on a narrow conception of individuals as inherent utility maximizers. This account of what bureaucrats want is a direct analogy of the standard neoclassical assumption that the managers and owners of private firms maximize profits, because their compensation is tied to performance (materialistic motivation) and because high profits safeguard management against aspiring underlings or potential hostile external takeover bids that would jeopardize their positions (survival motivation). But because public bureaucracies are "nonprofit organizations," what do bureaucrats maximize?

The basic answer (apart from Downs) has been that officials maximize the size of their agency, the size of their budget, or their job satisfaction. Some theorists have suggested that size is assessed primarily in terms of size. Bureaucrats from larger, well-financed agencies will have greater visibility, enhanced reputations for influence, and higher status among their peers. Compa-

Encyclopedia of Public Administration and Public Policy
DOI: 10.1081/E-EPAP 120010894

rative budget increases across departments are seen as an indicator of winners and losers in the ecological competition for resources. Bureaucrats in larger agencies control more patronage and have a greater capacity to influence events or overcome resistance. Size also creates organizational slack and excess capacity that allows officials to more easily meet unusual risks or crises whenever they occur.

In addition, maximizing behavior is critical for an agency's survival in two ways. The organization's budget is allocated to it by a "sponsor"—a single, dominant collective entity such as a chief executive, a department secretary, or a committee of the legislature. Sponsors expect to be routinely presented with proposals for increased funding. During the budgetary process, attention will concentrate on the marginal increments being sought. If no such increase is requested, the funding body is likely to become suspicious or disoriented and these procedures become inoperative. Completely static or reduced budget requests are likely to be interpreted as evidence of the bureau's stagnation or loss of initiative.

Senior bureaucrats seek funding expansion as a balm that facilitates agency operations. In large or growing agencies, contentious or incompetent officials can be moved sideways into sinecures. Also, the costs of reorganization can be more easily absorbed and wage demands or staff resistance to change can be more easily bought off. Budget maximization facilitates the hiring of skilled staff, and improves wage and promotion prospects. Client groups also value top officials who expand programs because this will enhance their own agendas. They will even cooperate by mobilizing public support for the agency's policies, especially where key clients are well-organized interest groups.

The economic account says little explicitly about the internal operations of government agencies. Most writers assume that institutional and functional variations among government departments simply do not matter. They generally adopt the view of bureaus as command-and-control organizations run in a top-down manner. This contrasts starkly with markets (which they prefer) that they claim operate as decentralized preference systems. In addition, proponents employ a unitary theory of the firm that treats both private corporations and public agencies as if they are run by a single management team so that they can focus on their aggregate behavior vis-à-vis other actors. The basic differential in the behavior of these "firms" is explained by the profit driven "bottom line" of business and the less measurable "public interest" service imperatives of government.

Similar to other organizations, bureaus have an inherent tendency to expand, but with fewer than the normal constraints on their capacity to do so. Agency growth helps in the retention and promotion of personnel, and it enables leaders to acquire more power, income, and prestige. It reduces internal conflicts, facilitates economies of scale, helps to insulate top officials from social pressures, and strengthens the agency's ability to survive. Larger agencies are also in a better position to manipulate their environment than are small ones. If top officials do not have to pay the costs of adding more personnel, they will be inclined to increase the size of the organization indefinitely because each new member adds incrementally to their total direct action capabilities.

Most economic analyses of bureaucracies posit a fundamental dichotomy between two basic ways of coordinating social activities in industrialized societies— markets and command structures. Anthony Downs labeled this contrast the "*law of hierarchy.*" Coordination of large-scale activities without markets requires a hierarchical authority structure. This law results directly from the limited capacity of each individual, as well as the existence of ineradicable sources of individual conflict. In particular, the general self-interest axiom implies that actors will not cooperate unless compelled to do so by an effective command structure. Yet, this ultra-Weberian picture of government agencies is qualified by more stress on an underling's self-centered inclination to resist the demands of their superiors.

Max Weber looked for alternative mechanisms of administrative coordination through the inculcation of a common organizational culture or strong ideology that guides and justifies operations. Yet, economists view all such mechanisms as simply devices for defending collective interests, not as methods to ensure accountability. Bureaus develop ideologies, they argued, to rationalize their activities and insulate them from external scrutiny or criticism. All agencies develop peculiar cultures that enhance member identification with their activities. But none of these devices can substitute for authoritative guidance. Employing ideology to guide detailed policy making risks ossification that inhibits creative responses to new problems or circumstances. The strengthening of agency culture will exacerbate the inherent tendency toward organizational rigidity.

For one organization to monitor another or to coordinate the activity of multiple agencies also requires hierarchical interorganizational relations to overcome resistance from staff in the subordinate bureaus. The law of countercontrol combined with the stress on hierarchy produces duplication because any attempt to control one large organization tends to generate another new bureau. Of course, controlling organizations need not become as large as implementing agencies. But the law does mean that contrasts between "line" and "staff" organizations often become blurred as supervisory agencies absorb increasing resources. A continuous spiral is likely as top-down control efforts are followed by subordinate agency evasion, which, in turn, produces renewed attempts to secure control.

In addition, strong internal pressures push monitoring bureaus to extend their control over subordinate agencies. The logic is that by placing one agency in a supervisory position over another promotes an "ever-expanding control" whereby the quantity and detail of reporting required by monitoring bureaus tends to rise steadily over time, regardless of the amount or nature of the activity being monitored. Agencies can also be significantly affected by their suppliers, by clients (interest groups or firms that benefit from their activities), and by those entities whose behavior they regulate. A "territorial drive" in all bureaus leads them to define core functions central to their organization's mission and the more peripheral activities that surround this basic core and are used to insulate it from erosion or attack.

Most economic analyses of bureaucracies view them as uniformly hierarchical organizations for two reasons. First, early authors in the field posited a fundamental contrast between organizations run in a centralized command mode and markets, which are viewed as decentralized preference systems. "In the absence of profit goals, bureaus must be centrally managed by the pervasive regulation and monitoring of the activity of subordinates (von Mises)." For many polemicists, such as Hayek, it became axiomatic that government agencies in the West were comparable in their operation with the bureaucracies of communist states, particularly in their reliance on centralized planning and management systems. Second, methodological assumptions carried over from the neoclassical theory of the firm invariably included an undifferentiated management team that makes unitary rational decisions and is capable of centralized control over the organization.

By collapsing all nonmarket mechanisms of coordination into voting or command and control, economists exclude other potentially important options, such as

* Incremental agreements that "balance interests"
* Behavior modification that alters motives
* Interactive "mutual adjustment"
* Participation, delegation, and salesmanship
* Voluntary cooperation between self-interested actors
* Nonhierarchical "kinship" systems of "mutual service"
* Persuasion through logic, charm, and reasoned argument
* Economic and ideological hegemony by a dominant class
* Consensus and accommodation among multiple stakeholders

This unitary control orientation rejects or ignores any solidaristic behavior, public interest orientation, or altruistic values by public sector managers or employees.

Within this general framework, only Downs provides a complex, pluralistic perspective of motivation in the public sector. Unless economic theorists can show why these options do not function or will not work, their propositions about behavior in bureaus become tautological, claiming only that "hierarchical organizations must be run hierarchically."

Variations in institutional form and function will produce differences in agency behavior and influence. Moreover, relationships between agencies are qualitatively different from the relationships between ranks, sections, or groups of actors within one relatively unified institution. These two propositions will seem obvious to a political scientist, but apparently not to those who write public choice accounts. Using simply specified parameters (e.g., perfect competition, oligopoly, or monopoly), economists can move easily from their analysis of how one enterprise behaves in a market to conclusions about the behavior of the industry as a whole. Within this tradition, writers seem bound to the claim that once they understand how "the bureau" works, they have also ipso facto discovered how the entire state apparatus works. Aggregate behavior across bureaus is typically described only in passing. Economic theorists usually concentrate their efforts on demonstrating why distortions in the behavior of public agencies stimulate their growth.

The conclusion they draw is that the most important government problem is the unnecessary and continuous expansion of its bureaucracy. From this perspective, the most corrupting impact of the behavior of top public officials is their tendency to exploit their positions to increase the size of their agencies so that they become much larger, less accountable, and more expensive than they need to be. This general proposition that government bureaus are continuously expanding monopolies leads directly to reform proposals that emphasize encouraging public entrepreneurship and the promotion of competition between bureaus. Thus, political economists favor such diverse measures as bonuses for bureau heads from the savings they uncover, breaking up large centralized agencies into regional entities, allowing bureaucratic duplication in the provision of public goods, and privatizing or contracting out many governmental activities.

Classical management theory envisioned public sector bureaucracy as a modernizing form of organization that would ensure precision, speed, reliability, clarity, efficiency, and regularity in the provision of high-quality goods and services. In contrast, modern political economists have developed theories of bureaucracy, which see, in these same hierarchical structures, institutions that foster self-serving behavior that corrupts the natural functioning of markets and that masks the political pursuit of private gain by those who manipulate them. Self-interest in the private sector is said to produce optimal outcomes, but in all government agencies this same motivation generates command-and-control monopolies operated by an intrusive, problem-finding elite that overemploys, overpays, overbuilds, and overproduces. Thus, whenever possible, the reliance on the public sector should be reduced and market forces restored.

FURTHER READING

Buchanan, J. Social choice, democracy, and free markets. J. Polit. Econ. **1954**, *LXII*, 114–123, April.

Buchanan, J. Why Does Government Grow? In *Budgets and Bureaucrats*; Borcherding, T., Ed.; Duke: Durham, 1977.

Downs, A. *Inside Bureaucracy*; Rand: Prospect Heights, 1967.

Downs, A. *An Economic Theory of Democracy*; Harper & Row: New York, 1957.

Downs, A. Why the government budget is too small in a democracy. World Polit. **1960**, *XII*, 541–563, July.

Friedman, J. *The Rational Choice Controversy*; Yale: New Haven, 1995.

Green, D.; Shapiro, I. *Pathologies of Rational Choice Theory*; Yale: New Haven, 1994.

Hayek, F. *Individualism and Economic Order*; Chicago: Chicago, 1948.

Knott, J.; Miller, G. *Reforming Bureaucracy*; Prentice-Hall: Englewood Cliffs, 1987.

Knott, J.; Baybrooke, R. *A Strategy of Decision*; Free Press: New York, 1965.

Mitchell, W.; Simmons, R. *Beyond Politics*; Westview: Boulder, 1994.

Niskanen, W. *Bureaucracy and Representative Government*; Aldine: Chicago, 1971.

Ostrom, V. Public choice. Public Adm. Rev. **1971**, *31* (2), 203–216.

Ostrom, V. *The Intellectual Crisis in American Public Administration*; Alabama: Tuscaloosa, 1974.

Savas, E. *Privatization*; Chatham House: Chatham, 1987.

Stevens, J. *The Economics of Collective Choice*; Westview: Boulder, 1993.

Tullock, G.; McKenzie, R. *The New World of Economics*; Irwin: Homewood, 1975.

Tullock, G. *Toward a Mathematics of Politics*; Michigan: Ann Arbor, 1967.

Tullock, G. *The Politics of Bureaucracy*; Public Affairs: Washington, DC, 1965.

von Mises, L. *Bureaucracy*; Yale: New Haven, 1944.

Weber, M. *Essays in Sociology*; Oxford: New York, 1968.

Weber, M. *Theory of Social and Economic Organization*; Free Press: New York, 1966.

Bureaucracy, Perspectives on

Larkin S. Dudley
Virginia Polytechnic Institute and State University,
Blacksburg, Virginia, U.S.A.

INTRODUCTION

A brief encyclopedia entry cannot capture the vast cornucopia of themes and studies that surround the concept of bureaucracy. To introduce some of the bureaucratic literature pertinent to public administration, this entry restricts itself to the following themes: the historical context of bureaucratic scholarship, characteristics of the organizational form, public bureaucracies in their political environment, public bureaucracies in an economic framework, and the case against and for bureaucracy.

THE STUDY OF BUREAUCRACY: HISTORICAL CONTEXT

The term bureaucracy is believed to have its origin as a reference to a cloth covering the desks of French government officials in the eighteenth century.[1] Early usage referred to an official workplace (bureau) in which individual activities were routinely determined by explicit rules and regulations. From a plethora of conceptions, such as a synonym for civil service to a pejorative term for inefficient and corrupt systems, the usage that has dominated the social sciences is bureaucracy as a form of organization.

The work of Karl Marx and Alexis de Tocqueville documented the historical trend toward increasing bureaucratization throughout modern Western Europe. However, most link the term and tradition of study of bureaucracy to the intellectual legacy of Max Weber, who conducted his studies at the turn of the nineteenth century, but whose work was not available widely to English-speaking scholars until later translations in the 1940s.[2] Weber's conception of bureaucracy is understandable in terms of his focus on the legitimatization of power in societies, including Chinese, Egyptian, Roman, Prussian, and French administrative systems.[3]

In Weber's analysis, the bureaucratic form of administration reflected one way in which power could be legitimated. Weber argued that power was the ability to direct others' behavior, regardless of whether those being directed believed it was proper and acceptable.[4] Autho-

rity, however, represented power believed to be proper by those whose activities were being directed, that is, the legitimate use of power. Three different types of authority were then identified: traditional, charismatic, and legal–rational.[4] Under a system of traditional authority, the use of power is believed to be legitimate because of belief in the time-honored traditions and patterns of behavior. Charismatic authority, however, is imbued in individuals who exhibit exceptional or heroic characteristics. Rational–legal authority derives from belief in the legitimacy of law, including the belief that rules and the authority of officials to perform mandated duties are legitimate. Thus, the legal authorization of individuals to behave in a certain manner (e.g., the use of coercion) is a crucial dimension under rational–legal authority.

According to Weber's historical analysis, distinctive types of administrative systems are associated with each type of authority. Rational–legal systems of authority stress impersonal rules and regulations, exemplified in modern rationalistic bureaucracy.[5] However, the Weberian model of bureaucracy has often been misunderstood and erroneously explained. One source of the confusion is that Weber conceived of his model of bureaucracy as an "ideal type."[1,6] Ideal in this sense does not mean desirable, but instead means a simplification of many features to more clearly understand the essence of a construct. Weber understood that actual bureaucratic organizations may exhibit only some of these characteristics or may possess them in varying degrees. The construct identifies a bureaucracy by a certain structure and certain characteristics, but the outer meaning of the construct would be determined by the context, being neither necessarily a pejorative nor exalted term outside the context in which it is embedded.

CHARACTERISTICS OF BUREAUCRACY

In the Weberian model of bureaucracy, the importance of rules is paramount. Rules become the basis for decisions, displacing individual judgment, and the means to efficiently achieve specific organizational goals. Weber himself was skeptical of bureaucracy and even pessimistic that the bureaucratization of societies would

Encyclopedia of Public Administration and Public Policy
DOI: 10.1081/E-EPAP 120010952

devour the relationships connected to our values. Following Weber,[2] distinguishing characteristics of bureaucracies include:

1. *Division of labor*: A clearly defined division of labor with specialization and training for assigned tasks.
2. *Hierarchy*: Authority relations are hierarchically ordered with definite limited areas of responsibility for superordinate and subordinate personnel.
3. *Rationality of rules*: Explicit rules are designed to ensure uniformity of performance and treatment, displacing emotional and personal decision making.
4. *Technical expertise*: Individuals are recruited and promoted on the basis of technical expertise and competence, rather than on personal relationships or luck.
5. *General rules*: Prior publication and general imposition of rules were believed to replace administrative systems of unpredictable arbitrary decisions.
6. *Written documentation*: Official records become important because documentation would make it possible to trace actions and have them inspected by others.
7. *Full and continuous employment*: Career expectations are to be fulfilled within the organization in a full-time capacity. This assumes that fulfillment of one's duty will be the highest priority, thus assuring that clients' legitimate needs will be met if at all possible. In addition, full and continuous employment contributes to the ability to develop an impersonal and impartial relationship among organization members and with those outside the bureaucracy.

Although Weber certainly saw bureaucratic organizations in relationship to their social, political, and economic environments, the most prevalent study of bureaucratic structure has tended to follow his discussion of bureaucratic characteristics. As David Nickinovich[7] summarized, one focus of study has been the internal characteristics of bureaucracy (e.g., how organizational structure is related to technology and worker productivity, how individuals are integrated within organizations, how the characteristics of bureaucracy identified by Weber may be interrelated). In this tradition, scholars have attempted to empirically assess the extent to which bureaucratic organizations exhibit bureaucratic properties or have interrelated dimensions. Other scholars, such as Ralph Hummel,[8] articulated one of Max Weber's theses that humanistic values are too easily lost within the bureaucratic ethos.

One example of later work that combines a focus on the relationship between organizational structure of bureaucracy and how operators, managers, and executives understand their duties is that of James Q. Wilson.[9] He

also furthers our understanding of the differences in private and public bureaucracies, particularly pointing out the importance of the political context in which bureaucracies operate, a subject to which we next turn.

PUBLIC BUREAUCRACIES IN THEIR POLITICAL ENVIRONMENTS

Three important themes relate the study of public bureaucracies to the political environment and political structures of which they are a part. First is the theme of bureaucratic politics, where bureaucracies are seen as important actors in policy decisions. Second is that of the control of the political system over bureaucratic choices and performance; and third is that of the relationship of bureaucracy and democracy, particularly in terms of being representative and responsive.

Two important works more than a decade apart illuminated the importance of the bureaucracy in relation to its political environment. In 1973, the bureaucratic politics approach was singled out by Graham Allison[10] as one of several lenses to view the Cuban Missile Crisis. Allison's ability to probe the relationship of bureaucratic processes and interests to the making of foreign policy challenged a view of rational policy making determined by a monolithic entity that is goal directed and intentional. Instead, as summarized by Allison, the bureaucratic politics model sees policy making as being influenced by many players who act in terms of various conceptions of national, organization, and personal goals in the politics of negotiation and bargaining. The public bureaucracies involved in foreign policy were seen as having their own interests of budgets, power, prestige, and access to the White House that they sought to enhance and protect. Players in the process were viewed as having relative influence in terms of personality and skill, and in terms of where they were hierarchically in the chain of command.

The influence of the political system on bureaucracy is a different theme, one exemplified in the publication of James Q. Wilson's *Bureaucracy, What Government Agencies Do and Why They Do It* in 1989.[9] Wilson stressed the need to understand the political context. He argued that much of what agencies do is defined from the outside in—by the political structure and culture in which agencies operate. Through several chapters on the relationship of the bureaucracy to the presidency and to Congress, Wilson carefully laid out the difficulties with a political system that asked agencies to serve a multitude of ends and a variety of masters. He noted that public officials and operators must often manage situations over which they have little control, on the basis of a poorly defined mission and in the face of a complex array of growing constraints.

Finally, the theme of bureaucracy within a democracy has been undertaken by many serious scholars of public administration.[11] One manifestation of that theme has been the interest of scholars in both the normative and empirical study of representative bureaucracy for more than 45 years.[12] This interest is premised on the idea that insofar as the personnel in a public bureaucracy reflect those of its jurisdiction in characteristics such as race, ethnicity, and gender, the bureaucracy will be more responsive. Authors argue that, through ensuring that all politically significant interests and values are represented in the formulation and implementation of policies and programs, the pubic interest will be better served. A second idea has been that of bureaucratic responsiveness. Scholars have examined the extent to which decisions made in public bureaucracies reflect the preferences of elected officials, interest groups, and private citizens.[13] This idea has become even more pronounced in literature using an economic framework in the following section.

BUREAUCRACY IN AN ECONOMIC FRAMEWORK

The 1980s and 1990s brought increased attention to economic-based approaches to describe within a different framework some of the themes of bureaucratic politics and the relationship of the bureaucracy to its political environment.[14] Economic theory has stressed that rather than a focus on workers hired for their skills and controlled through authority, as in the traditional concept of bureaucracy, workers are self-interested. The most noted economic approach, principal-agent theory, views organizations as relationships between a principal, who has a job to be done, and an agent, who agrees to do the job in exchange for compensation.[15] In such relationships, principals and agents alike seek their self-interest. Although the approach focuses on the driving force of self-interest, it also helps to explain organizational pathologies. For example, information asymmetries plague relationships so that principals may not know if they have selected the best agents or be able to tell when agents' work matches the terms of contracts.

Agency theory has influenced both the theories of bureaucratic outcomes and theories of institutional choice. The bureaucratic-outcome approach questions the traditional theme of bureaucratic politics that emphasizes how bureaucracies resist change.[16] Instead, principal-agency theory suggests that bureaucracies can be viewed as agents for the principals' (elected officials) wishes. Thus, part of the research focus has been on the prin-cipals' design of incentives and sanctions to enhance their control. As such, principal agency theory maintains elected leaders in the presidency and Congress can and do shape bureaucratic behavior in systematic ways.

Building also upon agency theory and the bureaucratic politics tradition, scholars identified as working within institutional choice theory also emphasize the relationships among agents in the regulatory bureaucracy and their political principals (e.g., legislators, presidency, interest groups). However, they attempt to model these interactions formally to illustrate how bureaucracies are acted upon, as well as how they perform as actors.[17] As such, these scholars argue that the design of bureaucracy does not promote efficiency, but instead is the result of rules that are the result of political forces. Thus, organizations reflect the power of political interests. As Donald Kettl[14] explained, these political interests are understood as selecting among organizational options for the improvement of results, thus giving the approach the name of institutional choice.

Even more formal models, often within a game theory approach, have emphasized modeling the relationships between bureaucrats and the rest of the system as a bargaining process. Conflicting arguments about the relationships between bureaucrats and the rest of the system include one argument that the bureaucracy exploits its information advantages over politicians leading to bureaucratic budgets too large, bureaucrats too numerous, and bureaucratic output too abundant, as in the work of William Niskanen.[18] Others contend that information asymmetries may actually favor politicians who can control the behavior of bureaucrats.

THE CASE AGAINST AND FOR BUREAUCRACY

A final theme in this brief overview of bureaucracy is that most academic treatments of bureaucracy contain not so hidden biases. Most studies are highly critical, according to Charles T. Goodsell,[19] who surveys the many kinds of criticism by grouping them under three broad categories. The first group of criticisms Goodsell reviews are those that focus on unacceptable performance, including arguments of general distrust of public ownership, fear of budget maximization, and the rigidity of bureaucratic forms that produces goal displacement along with other pathologies. A second theme Goodsell sees is the accusation that bureaucracies mobilize dangerous political power; that is, they may be totalitarian or, at the least, elitist in distorting the democratic political process. Finally, Goodsell notes that many academics condemn bureaucracy for its oppressive qualities. In other words, bureaucracies are portrayed as treating humans, at a minimum, in a callous manner and are often seen as crushing employees and clients. Finally, Goodsell states that a considerable literature has now emerged that attempts to assess bureaucratic performance and power in a democracy in a balanced fashion, pointing out the many positive contributions of bureaucracy as well.

CONCLUSION

Scholarship on bureaucracy will continue to develop somewhat around the themes surrounding the internal characteristics of bureaucracy, particularly concerning structure and performance. However, as is true of organizational theories in general, more literature will focus on how bureaucracy affects and is affected by its environment, particularly its political environment in the case of public bureaucracies. One can speculate that research will also highlight the changing role of bureaucracies in a networked and globalized world.

REFERENCES

1. Bendix, R. Bureaucracy. In *International Encyclopedia of the Social Sciences*; Sills, D.L., Ed.; Crowell, Collier and Macmillan, Inc.: New York, 1968.
2. Weber, M. Bureaucracy. In *From Max Weber: Essays in Sociology*; Gerth, H.H., Mills, C.W., Eds.; Oxford University Press: New York, 1946.
3. Weber, M. *The Religion of China; Confucianism and Taoism*; Free Press: Glencoe, IL, 1951.
4. Weber, M. *Max Weber on Law in Economy and Society*; Rheinstein, M., Ed.; Harvard University Press: Cambridge, MA, 1954.
5. Turner, J.; Beeghley, L.; Powers, C. *The Emergence of Sociological Theory*, 4th Ed.; Wadsworth Publishing Company: Belmont, CA, 1998; 137–188Mouzelis, N.P. *Organization and Bureaucracy: An Analysis of Modern Theories*; Aldine Publishing Company: New York, 1979.
6. Hummel, R. Bureaucracy. In *International Encyclopedia of Public Policy and Administration*; Shafritz, J., Ed.; Westview Press: Boulder, CO, 1998.
7. Nickinovich, D. Bureaucracy. In *Encyclopedia of Sociology,* 2nd Ed.; Borgatta, E., Montgomery, R.J.V., Eds.; MacMillan Reference: New York, 2000; 229–236.
8. Hummel, R.P. *The Bureaucratic Experience,* 2nd Ed.; St. Martin's Press: New York, 1982.
9. Wilson, J.Q. *Bureaucracy, What Government Agencies Do and Why They Do It*; Basic Books, 1989.
10. Allison, G.T. *Essence of Decision*; Little, Brown: Boston, 1971, Art, R.J. Bureaucratic politics and american foreign policy: A critique. Policy Sci. **1973**, *4*, 467–490; Bendor, J.; Hammond, T. Rethinking Allison's models. Am. Polit. Sci. Rev. **1992**, *86*, 301–322.
11. For example, see the scholarly works of D. Waldo, H. Kaufmann, and P. DeLeon.
12. Greene, V.; Selden, S.C.; Brewer, G. Measuring power and presence: Bureaucratic representation in the American States. J. Public Adm. Res. Theory **2001**, *11*, 379July.
13. Verba, S.; Nie, N.H. *Participation in America: Political Democracy and Social Equality*; Harper and Row: New York, 1972; Bendor, J.; Moe, T.M. An adaptive model of bureaucratic politics. Am. Polit. Sci. Rev. **1985**, *79*, 755–774.
14. Kettl, D.F. Public administration at the millennium: The state of the field. J. Public Adm. Res. Theory **2000**, *10*, 7Jan.
15. Williamson, O.E. *Markets and Hierarchies: Analysis and Antitrust Implications*; Free Press: New York, 1975.
16. Wood, B.D.; Waterman, R.W. The dynamics of political control of the bureaucracy. Am. Polit. Sci. Rev. **1991**, *85*, 801–828.
17. Moe, T.M. The Politics of Structural Choice: Toward a Theory of Public Bureaucracy. In *Organization Theory; From Chester Barnard to the Present and Beyond*; Williamson, O.E., Ed.; Oxford University Press: New York, 1995.
18. Niskanen, W.A. *Bureaucracy and Representative Government*; Aldine: Chicago, 1971.
19. Goodsell, C.T. *The Case for Bureaucracy: A Public Administration Polemic,* 3rd Ed.; Chatham House Publishers, Inc.: Chatham, NJ, 1994.

Bureaucratic Agencies, Evolution of Delegation of Authority/Power to

Scott R. Furlong
University of Wisconsin–Green Bay, Green Bay, Wisconsin, U.S.A.

INTRODUCTION

Throughout the history of the United States, there has been an evolution in the role that the federal government plays in our daily lives. For much of our history, this role was somewhat limited. Many point to Article I, section 8 of the Constitution, the enumerated powers section, in describing much of what the federal government did. These powers include, for example, the power to lay taxes, regulate commerce, coin money, and many others. This evolution of the role of the federal government has also occurred within the executive branch itself. The role of the bureaucracy in our daily lives is much different than it was 200 years ago, or even 50 years ago. The expanded role of the federal government, specifically the bureaucracy, are interconnected and have been facilitated by the idea of delegation of authority in the United States. This article examines the evolution of delegation of authority or power, especially since the 1940s and how this evolution has had a major impact on public policy making in the United States.

ISSUES OF DELEGATION OF AUTHORITY

Delegation of authority or power is simply the Congress providing the bureaucracy with lawmaking powers that are typically held by itself. Congress, for various reasons, has decided that most of the specifics in policy making should be left to the agencies to develop and has increasingly written their statutes in such a way as to provide agencies with expanded authority. This delegation raises numerous issues that political and legal scholars have been debating for years.

One of the primary arguments against delegation of authority concerns the constitutional issue of separation of powers. According to this major component of the Constitution, power is to be divided among the three branches of government. The legislative branch would be responsible for law making, the executive branch for executing the law, and the judicial branch for interpreting the law. Much of what Congress delegates to bureaucratic agencies is ''law-making'' power. In other words, when agencies develop regulatory policy that

dictates or prevents some forms of behavior, that is, in a sense, law making. In addition, these same agencies are often given the primary responsibility to interpret and adjudicate challenges against their policies and thus have judicial power as well. Many consider these forms of delegation to be blatant violations of the separation of power principles and thus unconstitutional.

Another issue raised, often in regards to delegation, concerns the issue of to whom the power is actually being delegated. By giving policy-making power to the executive branch agencies, Congress is actually allowing policy to be made by a branch of government that is somewhat removed from the general public and electoral politics. When Congress, or more specifically a member of Congress, votes for a law that we as citizens may not agree with, we have the option of voting against that individual in the next election. This representative role of a member of Congress is the basis of our representative democracy. When we believe that our congressperson is not representing us, we can vote for someone else. But that option is not available when someone within the bureaucracy makes a policy. Bureaucratic officials are either appointed, or more likely, were hired based on merit considerations. Voters have some minimal electoral recourse regarding an appointed official in that they could hold the president accountable for the people appointed (although unlikely). If a career official from the Occupational Safety and Health Administration (OSHA) decides to issue a regulation requiring more stringent indoor air quality in the workplace and I disagree, I do not have the option to vote for another OSHA official. There is no direct representation function and therefore no electoral consequences.

Another issue raised by those concerned about delegation of authority concerns the relationship between executive agencies and interest groups. The issue arises if one is concerned with issues of agency capture. According to capture theory, administrative agencies are beholden to those interests in which they have been created to regulate.[1,2] In other words, policies adopted by agencies are heavily influenced by the very organizations the agencies were legislated to control. If agencies are captured by the interests they should be regulating, then one has to wonder about the desirability of delegation of

Encyclopedia of Public Administration and Public Policy
DOI: 10.1081/E-EPAP 120010883

authority. As delegation increases and agencies become responsible for developing more public policy, organizations have more opportunities to dictate the terms of these policies, especially if it is a captured agency. Critics of delegation argue that this provides advantages to the best-organized groups, and not what might be the best public policy.[3] Others state that delegation eliminates accountability of our elected leaders.[4]

A potential example of a captured agency was the Civil Aeronautics Board (CAB), which was responsible for the setting of airline rates for the industry. Yet, many believed that the CAB was basically carrying out the desires of the airline industry itself and not necessarily protecting consumers from monopolistic-type practices. This issue was one of the reasons that the CAB was disbanded when deregulation occurred in the airline industry in the 1970s.

Of course, positive issues are also associated with the delegation of authority that many scholars recognize. One of the primary arguments in support of delegation is that Congress is delegating policy making to the experts in the field.[5] These agency officials can develop, use, and understand the best information (science, economic, risk, etc.) available in the making of the policy. In addition, agency bureaucrats, unlike members of Congress, should be further removed from the political interests associated with policy making because they do not have to worry about reelection.

Another argument made by those supporting delegation relates to the simple time and resource constraints faced by our elected leaders to be able to develop specific policies. Given the growth of the federal role in our daily lives, it would be difficult, if not impossible to expect our elected leaders to be able to develop the vast amount of policy necessary in our daily lives. Of course, this might be an argument in support of a major deemphasis of the role of the federal government, but that is perhaps a topic for another article. It is unlikely that we will see that type of reduction in the role of the federal government at any time.

WHY DELEGATION OF AUTHORITY

An important question to ask when discussing delegation of authority is why would Congress willingly abdicate its lawmaking powers and give it away to the bureaucracy. According to the Constitution, Congress is the lawmaking branch of government, which means that it has certain authority in our system of government. Why would Congress as an institution be so willing to share this authority with another branch?

Morris Fiorina[6] discussed two major theories as to why Congress may be so willing to delegate authority to the bureaucracy—the "good government" and the "shift-the-responsibility" models of delegation. Under the "good government" model, Congress delegates for various reasons associated with the making of better public policy. Delegation allows policy to be made by, theoretically, nonpolitical actors that are experts in the field. Because they are not beholden to constituents through elections or the campaign money provided by special interests, the bureaucracy does not have to be concerned about these outside influences in policy development. They can select the most rational policy and not worry about the political fall out.

In addition, people working within the bureaucracy are careerists and have much information and expertise in the specific policy area. Therefore, Congress delegates to take advantage of this expertise in policy development. We do the same in our daily lives. We seek out doctors, auto mechanics, and electricians to do certain jobs that they are trained to do. Should we do anything less with the development of our nation's policies? The final element of the "good government" model is that the bureaucracy may have more discretion and flexibility to make changes to a policy given changing circumstances. Congress can write a vague law and allow the agency to apply it to the appropriate situations. As technology, science, or the economic conditions change, the bureaucracy can make changes to a policy more easily, and typically more quickly, than the legislature. These reasons would then support the delegation of authority because the end result should be a better-construed policy whose interpretation can be readjusted as necessary.

Fiorina's other model, the "shift-the-responsibility" model, appears to be a pessimistic view of why Congress delegates policy-making power to the bureaucracy. Under this scenario, Congress delegates for numerous reasons. One reason is that Congress does not have the necessary time and resources to develop specific laws, so they pass general laws and allow agencies to fill in the details, which may be quite extensive. Legislators would rather not spend time on the details of policy for many reasons. First, more conflict will likely arise between colleagues in hashing out the details of a policy. It is sometimes relatively easy to agree on the broad ideas or goals of a policy (e.g., a policy to improve air quality), but how the nation gets to that goal will generate a lot of conflict. In other words, the devil is in the detail. Second, working on the details of legislation will take more time and effort. Delegation allows Congress to potentially pass more legislation because they let agencies work out the specifics of policy, thus freeing congressional time and resources. In addition, they can use the time to do other congressional duties, such as constituent service, to help in their reelection goals.

Politically, the "shift-the-responsibility" model is also rational for members of Congress. By delegating decision making to agencies, Congress can avoid the responsibility of making a "bad" decision. The ultimate decisions that will affect citizens will come out of the bureaucracy through regulations or other administrative policy tools. People may complain about these decisions, but Congress can shield itself from these complaints by basically passing the buck to the bureaucracy. Not only can Congress avoid responsibility for these decisions, but they are also in a position to take advantage of the bad decision and make some political points. Complaints about a policy decision will come to a member of Congress, who can then look into the decision for a constituent through their casework networks. This member of Congress can serve their constituent by fixing this problem created by the agency decision and then claim credit for being a responsive legislator. These behaviors and activities by members of Congress follow closely with Mayhew's[7] premises discussed in *Congress: The Electoral Connection*, as well as Fiorina's[8] in *Congress: Keystone of the Washington Establishment*.

Between these two models for why Congress may delegate to the bureaucracy, there are many potential reasons why they are so willing to abdicate their power and responsibilities in policy making. Of course, varying situations may lead to different reasons as to why Congress delegates authority to the bureaucracy. In some cases, a lack of information and a need to use the experts available in an agency might represent a good and perhaps appropriate decision to delegate. In other cases, delegation may occur simply because members of Congress cannot agree on the specifics of a policy; therefore, they pass a general policy direction and give the agencies the responsibility of actually making law. Whatever the reason, delegation is accepted by many as a fact of life in today's governmental system. Congress has given agencies broad discretionary authority to make policy that affects are daily lives, but it has not always been that way. Delegation of authority has gone through some evolution, especially since the 1930s.

EVOLUTION OF DELEGATION

The best way to discuss the evolution of delegation is to start with the definition of the delegation doctrine. The doctrine states that "congressional delegations of power are constitutional so long as they are accompanied by sufficient standards or guidelines so that the executive branch's exercise of legislative power is not unbridled".[9] Note that the doctrine does not prohibit delegation of power, but rather states that delegations need to occur with "sufficient standards or guidelines," in other words, rules by which an agency is governed in its use of the delegation. For a large part of our nation's

history, the courts upheld the delegations that Congress provided to bureaucratic agencies due to the standards provided. However, the New Deal era ushered in a tremendous expansion of federal government agencies and responsibilities that brought the delegation issue to a head. This expansion of government authority is most directly tied to the enumerated power of regulating commerce among the states. Because so many of our goods and services are transported between state borders, now more than ever, but even in the early-1900s, Congress could use this power to govern many activities.

The Supreme Court became involved in the issue of delegation during the New Deal, specifically in the ruling of three separate cases, in which the court ruled that the congressional delegation was unconstitutional. The three cases, *Panama Refining Co. v. Ryan*,[10] *A.L.A. Schechter Poultry Corp. v. United States*,[11] *and Carter v. Carter Coal Co.*,[12] examined the issue of congressional delegation. In *Panama Oil*, the court ruled that the delegation that authorized the president to prohibit interstate shipments of contraband oil was overly broad. The court ruled in the *Schechter* case that there were not clear policy directives from the legislature in the issuance of "codes of fair competition" for particular industries. The issues were similar in *Carter Coal*, with the additional concern that the delegation had, in effect, been made to committees of industry representatives and not government officials.[13] In general, the court was very concerned about the vagueness of these delegations and the amount of authority provided to nonlegislative personnel to make policy.

This time period was also one of the last times where the court ruled so conservatively on the delegation doctrine. President Roosevelt, whose policies these court rulings were overruling, attempted to increase the size of the Supreme Court in response to the court actions. His hope was to add additional justices, with beliefs similar to his own, to the current slate of justices to get more favorable rulings in the future. Although Roosevelt's court-packing scheme failed, a strong message was sent to the court. Some justices shifted their voting, and others retired, giving Roosevelt the opportunity to fill those vacant positions.[14]

Since these three cases, the court has been much more accepting of congressional delegations of power, and in many cases, these delegations have been much broader and with less guidelines than the ones in the New Deal cases. The gradual acceptance of delegation made it clear that administrative agencies would play a much larger role in the development of public policy. This was not lost on Congress, which in 1946 passed the Administrative Procedure Act as one tool to control the expanding power of agencies brought on by delegation and the use of the rule-making process.

The 1960s and 1970s saw another large increase in federal government involvement as Congress passed a wide range of regulatory laws focused on areas of public health, safety, and the environment. Laws such as the Clean Air Act, Consumer Product Safety Act, and the Occupational Safety and Health Act all delegated a tremendous amount of policy-making authority to the administrative agencies responsible for carrying out these laws. The vagueness and lack of guidelines associated with these laws is quite telling in the delegation controversy. For example, the Occupational Safety and Health Act directs the Secretary of Labor to issue regulations that requires employers to protect their workers "to the extent feasible" from harm in the workplace. This delegation provides OSHA with a wide range of options in which to interpret and implement the law. In the Supreme Court case of *Industrial Union Department, AFL-CIO v. American Petroleum Institute*,[15] otherwise known as the *Benzene* case, this form of delegation was called into question by one of the justices in the majority. Justice Rehnquist believed that the statute represented an unconstitutional delegation of authority to the secretary. He restated his position in another case involving an OSHA rule, *American Textile Manufacturers Institute v. Donovan*.[16] Although, the concern over a overly broad delegation was not the basis of the Supreme Court's ruling on these cases, the issue of what constituted an appropriate delegation was once again being raised by the court.

The election of Ronald Reagan and then George H. Bush also led to the appointment of more conservative Supreme Court justices that would likely be more receptive to the idea of the nondelegation doctrine. Although those opposing broad delegations of power to agencies would perhaps have reasons to cheer when you examine the current Supreme Court, it has to date not gone so far as to reinstate the nondelegation doctrine and has also upheld congressional delegations. The court continues to follow a principle in administrative law that if Congress does not speak clearly about a particular policy, then a wide latitude is provided to agencies in their interpretation and implementation of the law. Such was the case in *Chevron U.S.A., Inc. v. NRDC*,[17] where the court allowed for the Environmental Protection Agency's interpretation of what constituted a stationary source, as discussed in the Clean Air Act. However, if Congress is clear on issues of agency jurisdiction, then Congress has the last word.

This last point was the issue in a Supreme Court case *Food and Drug Administration v. Brown and Williamson Corp.*,[18] where the Food and Drug Administration (FDA) attempted to regulate tobacco products under the authority granted to it by the Food, Drug, and Cosmetic Act. The court ruled that Congress was clear in de-

veloping the jurisdiction of the FDA in that it did not have the authority to regulate tobacco. Although the basis of the ruling is not specifically an issue of undue delegation, it is clear that the result of the ruling limited the FDA's authority in interpreting a statute as they see fit. In fact, news accounts of this court ruling explicitly discussed the issues of delegation and agency power in their reporting and also referenced another court case concerning the role of delegation more specifically.

This second case dealt with the EPA's ability to set clean air standards under the authority granted to it by the Clean Air Act. Upon challenge, a DC Circuit Court of Appeals struck down the agency's ozone and small airborne particle standards under the nondelegation doctrine. The appeals court believed that EPA lacked any criteria in developing their standards and thus raised the issue of unbridled discretion. This ruling by the appeals court brought the issue of the nondelegation doctrine explicitly to the forefront on the debate. In addition, it raised some very real substantive concerns regarding environmental policy making, as well as other regulatory policy making within other agencies, because of the nature of many of the regulatory laws passed by Congress that had similar levels of nonspecificity. Although it appeared that the Supreme Court might have been ready to implement the nondelegation doctrine more thoroughly upon an appeal based on pass rulings and opinins, it did not do so. The Supreme Court ruled, unanimously, in *Whitman v. American Trucking Associations*[19] that EPA's standard-setting authority was not an unconstitutional delegation of power. In fact, one of the strongest supporters of the nondelegation doctrine, Justice Scalia, wrote the opinion of the court stating, "Even in sweeping regulatory schemes we have never demanded, as the Court of Appeals did here, that statutes provide a 'determinate criterion' for saying 'how much of the regulated harm is too much.[19]'" Although the question of what might be considered unbridled delegation may still exist, the Supreme Court still seems very willing to accept the idea of broad delegations of authority to administrative agencies and to rely on agency expertise in regards to general language such as "an adequate margin of safety."

CONCLUSION

This article examines the issue of congressional delegation of authority from various perspectives. It explored the issues surrounding delegation, reasons why Congress has chosen to delegate power to the bureaucracy, and also the evolution of delegation within the United States. It is clear that congressional delegation is a way of life in today's society.

Agencies are very much involved in the policy-making business due to the level of broad delegation provided them by Congress. In fact, Stewart[20] argued that such broad delegation is necessary for them to do their job adequately. This delegation provides the bureaucracy with the power to develop policy through administrative procedures. Although Lowi[3,21] argued that these delegations and the use of the administrative process to make policy gives interest groups undue influence, Stewart[22] countered by saying that interest representation is fundamental to our modern bureaucracy. Increased participation by these interests allows the agency personnel to understand what alternatives are desired. The conflict that occurs between interests ultimately leads to an agency policy.

The debate over delegation of authority will likely continue. In fact, in the *Whitman v. American Trucking Associations* case, Justice Thomas wrote in a separate opinion that he would be open to consider other non-delegation challenges. So, the court has not yet closed the door on this important constitutional and policy-making question. Therefore, we can expect to see further evolution of the delegation issue in the future.

REFERENCES

1. Berstein, M.H. *Regulating Business by Independent Commission*; Princeton University Press: Princeton, NJ, 1955.
2. Stigler, G.J. The theory of economic regulation. Bell J. Econ. Manage. Sci. **1971**, *2*, 3–21no. 1 (spring).
3. Lowi, T. *The End of Liberalism: The Second Republic of the United States,* 2nd Ed.; W.W. Norton: New York, 1979.
4. Schoenbrod, D. *Power without Responsibility: How Congress Abuses the People Through Delegation*; Yale University Press: New Haven, 1993.
5. Rourke, F. *Bureaucracy, Politics, and Public Policy,* 3rd Ed.; Little Brown: Boston, 1984.
6. Fiorina, M. Legislative choice of regulatory forms: Legal process or administrative process. Public Choice **1982**, *39*, 33–66.
7. Mayhew, D. *Congress: The Electoral Connection*; Yale University Press: New Haven, 1974.
8. Fiorina, M. *Congress: Keystone of the Washington Establishment*; Yale University Press: New Haven, 1977.
9. Cann, S.J. *Administrative Law,* 3rd Ed.; Sage Publications: Thousand Oaks, CA, 2002.
10. Panama Refining Co. v. Ryan. 1935. 293 U.S. 388.
11. A.L.A. Schechter Poultry Corp. v. United States. 1935. 295 U.S. 495.
12. Carter v. Carter Coal Co. 1936. 298 U.S. 238.
13. Gellhorn, E.; Levin, R.M. *Administrative Law and Process in a Nutshell*; West Publishing: St. Paul, 1997.
14. Kerwin, C.M. *Rulemaking: How Government Agencies Write Law and Make Policy*; Congressional Quarterly Press: Washington, D.C., 1999.
15. Industrial Union Department, AFL-CIO v. American Petroleum Institute. 1980. 448 U.S. 607.
16. American Textile Manufacturers Institute v. Donovan. 1981. 452 U.S. 490.
17. Chevron U.S.A., Inc. v. NRDC. 1984. 467 U.S. 837.
18. Food and Drug Administration v. Brown and Williamson Corp. 2000. 529 U.S. 120.
19. Whitman v. American Trucking Associations. 2001. 531 U.S. 457.
20. Stewart, R.B. Beyond delegation. Am. Univers. Law Rev. **1987**, *36*, 323–343.
21. Lowi, T. Two roads to serfdom: Liberalism, conservatism and administrative power. Am. Univers. Law Rev. **1987**, *36*, 295–322.
22. Stewart, R.B. The Reformation of American Administrative Law. Harvard Law Rev. **1975**, *88*, 1667–1711.

Bureaucratic Discretion and Political Control and Influence

Scott R. Furlong
University of Wisconsin–Green Bay, Green Bay, Wisconsin, U.S.A.

INTRODUCTION

Delegation of authority is predominant in our democratic society today. Congress, when writing laws and policies, has given the bureaucracy leeway in developing policies and regulations that interpret these statutes. Political scientists often refer to this leeway as bureaucratic discretion—the amount of control that bureaucratic agencies have in making public policy. Another chapter in this book discusses the potential issues surrounding delegation of authority, but one of the primary issues regards the ability of our elected leaders to control and influence the policy making of our unelected bureaucrats. This is an issue primarily because of the information asymmetries that arise between the bureaucracy and the elected leaders of Congress and the President. Left unchecked, many believe that the bureaucracy can use information advantages to set policy that is not what our elected institutions and, ultimately, the general public desire.

This essay discusses some of the primary elements used by our elected leaders in their attempts to maintain control or to influence the decisions of agencies. Within the political arena, these controls can be placed into three major categories: administrative procedures, scientific and economic decision rules, and political oversight.[1] Elected officials use these controls to influence bureaucratic agencies in their decisions, even though these agencies have an informational advantage. While these tools are presented as separate entities, it is important to recognize that, in many cases, they are interrelated. For example, a presidential directive that requires agencies to conduct a cost–benefit analysis on their regulatory activities is a procedural requirement to use a type of economic analysis or decision rule.

ADMINISTRATIVE PROCEDURES

Administrative procedures have been one of the primary ways in which our elected leaders have attempted to control and influence bureaucratic policy making. As bureaucratic policy making became more prevalent in the mid-twentieth century, our lawmakers recognized the po-tential concerns and began to develop some statutory requirements to ensure a sense of fairness and participation when dealing with issues of bureaucratic discretion. The major result of this activity was the passing of the Administrative Procedure Act (APA) in 1946. This was an important law because of the procedures required that ensured that bureaucratic agencies could not regulate out of control. Some of the major components of the law were as follows: 1) granting the right to seek judicial review to "any person suffering legal wrong because of agency action, or adversely affected or aggrieved by agency action within the meaning of the relevant statute";[2] and 2) setting administrative procedures for how agencies would conduct rule making and adjudication. These two parts of the APA limited what agencies could do and allowed elected leaders and general citizens to be part of the administrative process. Agencies, in general, must follow certain procedures when developing policy, which will limit their discretion. The threat of judicial review also will make agencies think seriously about their policies and the possible impacts on individuals.

A large amount of agency policy making occurs through the rule-making process, and specifically through informal or notice-and-comment rule making. The APA requires three minimum steps when agencies conduct informal rule making. First, they must provide notice of a proposed policy. This typically occurs in the *Federal Register*. Second, agencies must provide an opportunity for interested parties to comment on these proposals. Finally, agencies must consider the comments before issuing the final regulation, which is again published in the *Federal Register*.

Kerwin[3] comments that the core elements put forth in the APA are information, participation, and accountability, and these are basic to our democracy. Information is crucial to a democratic system and to decision making in general. The APA requires that notice be provided to the public when a rule is being developed and when it becomes final. Participation is another important element in democratic decision making. In the case of the APA, agencies must allow for the submission of written comments to any rule being developed. Finally, as mentioned earlier, the provision of judicial review ensures some element of accountability that we typically associate with the electoral process—in other words, if we as a society are not happy with our policies coming out of Congress, then we can elect someone different. While these elements are not full protections against unbridled bureaucratic discretion, they provide a minimum level of criteria that all agencies must follow. In a number of cases, our elected institutions and the agencies have developed even more stringent administrative requirements to facilitate bureaucratic control.

As Congress increased the level of regulatory policy making in the 1970s, additional procedural elements to help control bureaucratic discretion were also provided. One concrete example of this was the passage of the National Environmental Protection Act in 1969, which required environmental impact statements for all federally funded projects expected to impact the environment. Other examples have included minimum public comment periods when conducting informal rule making, requirements for public hearings, and the maintenance of a rule-making docket.[1]

While these procedures may appear to be mundane and neutral, the writings of McCubbins, Noll, and Weingast[4] suggest that they are anything but. According to "McNollGast," these procedures provide political principals, in this case Congress, with the necessary tools to help monitor and perhaps influence the activities of bureaucratic agencies. In addition, interest groups with similar parochial interests will benefit from these procedures. The passing of the National Environmental Protection Act provides such an example. Organizations and politicians were interested in affecting programs from a number of different policy areas, and this procedural law gave them entrée and influence into these decisions. Requiring longer public comment periods provides similar benefits to organizations that may have had difficulty responding to a solicitation of comments from an agency in a short period of time.

So, administrative procedures have been an important tool in controlling bureaucratic discretion and influencing agency decision for a number of years. These procedures establish boundaries as to how much leeway agencies have in making decisions and can also push agencies to make decisions in a certain direction. In addition, they establish procedural protections to address the potential dangers to delegation of authority.

ECONOMIC AND SCIENTIFIC DECISION RULES

Another popular tool used in influencing agency decision making is the use of economic and scientific decision rules. This has been especially true in those policy areas

dependent upon a large amount of technical or economic expertise, such as health, safety, and environmental policy making. Examples abound in this area of discretionary control. According to Bryner,[1] statutory requirements that impose "best available" technology for pollution sources or that require agencies to focus on the hazards at hand, regardless of the costs involved, are ways that technical analyses are used to limit agency discretion. A similar requirement by the Reagan Administration stated that agencies had to show that the benefits of the rule outweighed the cost imposed before issuing a regulation. Another way of limiting discretion is by using of science advisory boards that must review agency decisions prior to issuing policies.

One of the more common forms of analysis used, especially in recent history, has been some form of economic analysis. Typically, presidents have issued executive orders requiring agencies to conduct one type of analysis or another to justify the policies at hand. These types of analyses began in earnest during the Carter Administration, which required rules to discuss economic consequences of their alternatives. It was the Reagan Administration, though, that took the use of economic analysis to a new level.

Upon taking office, President Reagan issued Executive Order 12291, which was the most direct requirement for economic analysis of agency rules. Under the order, agencies were required to conduct regulatory impact analyses that showed that the potential benefits to society would outweigh the potential costs; the regulatory objective chosen would maximize net benefits; and among a series of alternatives, the one involving the least net cost to society would be chosen. The Office of Management and Budget was given the responsibility of overseeing this requirement placed upon agencies. Requiring such analyses, and dictating how they were to be used, limited the agencies' decision-making discretion by dictating the information they had to use when regulating in their policy area. Certain categories of policies were exempt from the decision-rule criteria included in the executive order (e.g., certain statutes do not allow cost to enter into the decision-making process). Even so, the writing was "on the wall" for agencies. Even for policies that were exempt from the benefit–cost decision rule, agencies collected economic data and information, and they were important elements of the regulatory proposals.

OVERSIGHT

The final major way that elected institutions can influence agency policy making is through a variety of oversight techniques. Oversight is typically associated with a function performed by the legislative branch, and in fact, oversight is usually discussed as those activities performed by Congress to ensure that the bureaucracy is following through on congressional intent. For purposes of controlling agency behavior, though, one can also consider the President as overseeing the bureaucracy as well. Oversight demonstrates the interesting situation of an agency having multiple principals, or in other words, these agencies must respond to two different "bosses." On the one hand, Congress provides statutory and budget authority to the agencies, but on the other, the President is the head of the executive branch and ultimately the top of the bureaucratic hierarchy. Agencies need to somehow respond to both actors.

Presidential Oversight

The President has a number of tools at his disposal to try to control and influence agency policy making. In some cases, these tools are based on constitutional powers, and in others, they have evolved as the powers of the presidency have evolved. The most common and well-known tool that a president can use is his appointment power. According to Article II of the Constitution, the President has the power to appoint officials to government offices. One typically thinks of the President appointing a secretary to a cabinet office such as the Secretary of Transportation, but these appointments are much more extensive. A president, will want to appoint officials with similar ideological views in order to improve the chances of a certain agenda being followed by an agency. Ideally, such an official might be considered an extension of the president in the policy arena in question. President Reagan was especially successful in the use of his appointment power, placing people such as James Watt into the Department of Interior and Ann Gorsuch into the Environmental Protection Agency. These individuals shared Reagan's conservative beliefs in regards to the government being too involved in regulating business. If an appointee fails to follow the presidential agenda, the president can remove that person in favor of someone more likely to follow the president's views.[a] Presidents are often concerned that their appointees will "go native," meaning that they will take on the views of their agencies rather than the administration. This appoint-

ment power provides a tool for which the president may guard against this concern.

Another tool that a president can use is to reorganize agencies or agency functions. Restructuring agencies internally, or a series of agencies, has the effect of emphasizing or de-emphasizing particular areas of policy. So, for example, President Carter's splitting off of the Department of Education from what was once the Department of Health, Education, and Welfare focused attention on this area of policy. Likewise, President Nixon's reorganization of many agencies to create the Environmental Protection Agency was an attempt to highlight this policy arena. A related organizational tool that presidents have used relates more to internal reorganization so that agency heads have more control over enforcement activities.[1] Different interpretations of compliance and the strictness of the related penalties, where there is some discretion, will influence agency activities and impact the policy area. If regulated entities believe that agency enforcement activities will decrease or that the penalties will be less, then there is an incentive to perhaps not spend the resources necessary to comply with the policy.

Another tool at the president's disposal is the use of the budget. Because the president and his economic staff initiate the budget process, they can send signals to agencies about policy direction. In addition, agency budgets are submitted to the Office of Management and Budget (OMB) for their review of the dollars and the related programs. OMB will not look favorably on agency programs that are not within the framework of the administration's agenda. OMB will likely suggest or dictate changes that influence agency policy making.

One final, but particularly valuable, form of presidential oversight and influence is the actual presidential management of rule making and regulatory policy. In some cases, rule-making management has been the result of executive orders issued by presidents over the past 30 years (e.g., Reagan's Executive Order 12291). In other cases, organizational structures within the executive branch have provided presidents (or their designates) with the ability to influence these agency actions (e.g., President George H. Bush's Council on Competitiveness).

There have been a number of executive orders issued in recent history that have been directly aimed at influencing agency rule-making behavior and outcomes. Many of these historically have dealt with the economic side of rule-making activities. In other words, President Ford required inflationary impact statements for each major rule, and I have already mentioned President Reagan's executive order requiring benefit–cost analysis. These executive orders required the gathering and consideration of economic data in rule development and passage, but other executive orders have focused on

---

[a]Presidential removal of agency officials is allowed for executive departments but not for commissioners working for independent regulatory commissions, because commissioners serve for fixed terms and cannot be removed due to personal differences in policy direction [see *Humphrey's Executor v. United States*, 1935;[5] and *Wiener v. United States*, 1958[6]].

different types of information. Executive Order 12612 required agencies to conduct a "federalism assessment" of their rules. Other executive orders required agencies to consider the impact of their policies on families, the judiciary process, and private property rights.[3] These types of requirements serve at least two purposes for presidents wanting to influence agency policy making. First, they may slow the rule-making activity in general, because agencies must collect and consider additional information. For the Reagan Administration, this was an important goal. Second, agencies now must use additional pieces of data to make their decisions, and the data being required affects the type of decision being made.

Upon taking office, President Clinton also issued an executive order concerning rule making and associated analysis. Executive Order 12866 superseded Reagan's 12291 but kept many of the same principles. In essence, Clinton's executive order attempted to decrease the amount of conflict between agencies and the OMB by decreasing the number of rules needing to be reviewed, opening up the process more for public scrutiny, and allowing agencies to consider other areas besides benefit–cost analysis. Still, this executive order continues the trend of presidents using tools to get more involved in agency policy making.

Presidents have also centralized their management structures in recent history, which has led to their ability to influence agency policy. The OMB under the Reagan Administration is the best example of this centralization. OMB's Office of Information and Regulatory Affairs had the ability, theoretically, to review almost every rule making coming out of the executive agencies. These reviews, provided by the authority of Executive Order 12291, gave OMB access to all agency rule-making decisions. While Executive Order 12291 was clear in stating that OMB reviewed these regulations and did not have to approve them prior to their issuance, politically, agencies wanted the go-ahead from OMB prior to publishing the regulation in the *Federal Register*. Executive Order 12498 was another tool of presidential management that required agencies to provide OMB with a yearly calendar of regulatory activities, and hence, giving OMB the ability to see the upcoming agency agenda and to attempt to influence the agenda or the policies within that agenda. Executive review is now an accepted part of the regulatory process, and although President Clinton decreased the role of OMB in terms of the number of regulations reviewed, it is clear that no president will ever eliminate this form of review now that it has been created.

Presidents have used other managerial tools to help them control and influence agency policies. For example,

President Carter created the Regulatory Analysis Review Group (RARG) to help improve the quality of regulatory analysis. President Reagan created the Vice President's Task Force on Regulatory Relief to consider the impacts of regulations on certain sectors of the economy.[3] President George H. Bush, perhaps adopting from his past role as head of such a task force, created the Council on Competitiveness, which was chaired by Vice President Quayle, to act as another level of regulatory review for selected, major-impact rules. All of these ad hoc councils and groups provided presidents with another tool with which they could attempt to influence agency rules, but not without some controversy. The Council on Competitiveness, for example, was harshly criticized for its lack of openness and secret meetings. Critics charged that the group was violating the APA and other procedural protections when having their discussions.[7] Of course, it did not help when it was revealed that the interest groups that appeared to have entrée into the Council happened to be strong financial and electoral supporters of the Bush Administration.

As you can see, the president has a number of formal and informal tools to help influence and control agency policy making. These tools have become more prevalent during the past 30 years with the growth of the administrative presidency. During this growth, presidents have taken their role as the chief administrative officer very seriously.

Congressional Oversight

Congress also has a series of tools available to influence and control agency policy making. From the congressional standpoint, oversight is important, because it is their way of ensuring that the policies coming from the agencies are consistent with the statute initially passed. Scholars have paid much more attention to the area of congressional oversight vis-à-vis presidential oversight. Given the other duties of Congress and the personal preferences of the members, many believe that there is not much time left for congressional oversight. Others have found oversight to be prevalent, if not by the congressional members, then by the committee and personal staff of the members.[8,9] Still others may argue that we may need to think about what types of activities constitute oversight.[10]

Congress has many oversight tools at its disposal. One of the more common is the use of a committee or subcommittee hearing. These hearings can examine a number of different elements regarding agency activity or programs, such as whether the programs are working correctly, the budgetary issues surrounding the program, or even the efficiency of the program. While it is typical to think of oversight as occurring after the fact, it is important to recognize that committees may call hearings in order to give direction or preferences of ongoing policies. In either case, Congress has the ability to send signals to an agency about what its members would like to happen in a policy area.

Another form of this type of oversight is when Congress asks for an investigation or evaluation of an agency or its programs. The General Accounting Office (GAO) will often conduct such a study and then report to the committee or subcommittee that made the request. This investigation will provide more detailed information about the program that Congress will focus upon in another committee hearing with the agency.

Much congressional oversight occurs informally. Members and their staff may make phone calls, have meetings, or provide some passing commentary to agency personnel. Of course, these forms of oversight are outside of public scrutiny and can always be backed up by other, more formal, oversight tools.

Agencies will respond to oversight due to many of the formal tools discussed earlier, in addition to some others. As discussed in the presidential oversight section, budget power is shared between the President and Congress, and so Congress may turn toward the budget as a way of influencing agency policy. Increases or decreases in agency budget could send strong signals to agencies in regard to the policies they are implementing. Of course, Congress' legislative power provides, in many ways, the ultimate form of oversight. The initial enabling statute that provides agencies with their statutory authority can influence and control agency behavior. The earlier section on administrative procedures discussed some of the procedural requirements Congress has placed within certain statutes. Congress has also used statutory deadlines as a way to force agency action by a certain date. And "hammers"—provisions that take effect if an agency fails to act by a certain date—have been used. A more specific piece of legislation will also dictate certain policy directions. Theoretically, if unhappy with an agency policy, Congress can attempt to pass a law that overrules the agency.

This last comment about overruling an agency policy brings up the issue of the legislative veto. For a number of years, Congress included in some statutes the ability to veto or disallow an agency action before it went into effect. The Supreme Court in *Immigration and Naturalization Service v. Chadha*[11] ruled the legislative veto unconstitutional due to separation of powers and bicameralism violations. The legislative veto was a potentially powerful management tool that Congress created, because it allowed broad authority to be delegated to administrative agencies but still provided Congress the ability to stop an action with which it was uncomfortable.

Since the Supreme Court's ruling in *Chadha*, Congress has attempted to recapture some of its ability to prevent agency policy with which it disagrees. In 1996, Congress passed the Congressional Review Act (CRA) as a way to circumvent some of the concerns stated in the Court's ruling. The CRA provides Congress with oversight ability, not with a legislative veto, but rather with a "report-and-wait" provision. A report-and-wait provision is one in which the agency provides Congress its proposed action and gives Congress the opportunity to review the action before it becomes effective and to pass legislation barring its effectiveness if Congress is dissatisfied with the agency action.[12] The CRA states that Congress can bar the effectiveness of an agency action with the passage of a joint resolution presented to the President for signature. The CRA had not been invoked until the election of George W. Bush as president, when Congress used it to review and prevent regulatory actions passed during the waning days of the Clinton Administration. It would appear that the only time this act might be used to stop an action would be during this transition phase, or if there was a large majority within Congress not from the president's political party. Symbolically though, a member of Congress may threaten to invoke the law as a way of pressuring an agency decision.

CONCLUSION

Many are concerned about the issue of bureaucratic discretion and the ability of agencies to develop policy. In many ways, the primary issue is that unelected bureaucrats are making policy, and they are not beholden to the people of the United States through an electoral process. In addition, information asymmetries provide an advantage to the specialized agencies compared to the elected leaders who tend to be generalists. But, as this article has discussed, our elected leaders have traditionally had a number of avenues in which to control these unelected officials, and over the past 50 years, have developed additional ways to influence agency policy.

Administrative procedures, economic and scientific decision rules, and statutory requirements are a priori tools available to give direction to agency decisions as they are being made. In the event these fail to persuade agencies, there are a number of post hoc mechanisms available to Congress and the President to bring an agency or its policies in line after the fact. Will every agency policy receive the ultimate amount of scrutiny from the political principals? No, but we should have some assurance that those areas especially important to the elected leaders and their constituency groups will be adequately monitored and changed if necessary.

REFERENCES

1. Bryner, G.C. *Bureaucratic Discretion: Law and Policy in Federal Regulatory Agencies*; Pergamon: New York, 1987.
2. *Administrative Procedure Act of 1946*; 551–7065 U.S.C.
3. Kerwin, C.M. *Rulemaking: How Government Agencies Write Law and Make Policy,* 2nd Ed.; CQ Press: Washington, D.C, 1999.
4. McCubbins, M.D.; Noll, R.G.; Weingast, B.R. Administrative procedures as instruments of political control. J. Law Econ. Organ. **1987**, *3* (2), 243–277(Fall).
5. *Humphrey's Executor v. United States*; 1935; 295U.S. 602.
6. *Wiener v. United States*; 1958; 357U.S. 349.
7. Friedman, B.D. *Regulation in the Reagan-Bush Era: The Eruption of Presidential Influence*; University of Pittsburgh Press: Pittsburgh, 1995.
8. Foreman, C.H. *Signals from the Hill: Congressional Oversight and the Challenge of Social Regulation*; Yale University Press: New Haven, 1988.
9. Aberbach, J.D. *Keeping a Watchful Eye: The Politics of Congressional Ovesight*; Brooking Institution: Washington, D.C.
10. McCubbins, M.D.; Schwartz, T. Congressional oversight overlooked: Police patrol versus fire alarms. Am. J. Polit. Sci. **1984**, *28*, 165–179.
11. *Immigration and Naturalization Services v. Chadha*; 1983; 462U.S. 919.
12. Korn, J. *The Power of Separation: American Constitutionalism and the Myth of the Legislative Veto*; Princeton University Press: Princeton, 1996.

Bureaucratic Politics

Gene A. Brewer

The University of Georgia, Athens, Georgia, U.S.A.

B

INTRODUCTION

Bureaucratic politics occurs when bureaucrats, who are nonelected government officials, enter the political arena and try to influence or shape the policy-making process. In most cases, this process is characterized by conflict and bargaining as multiple actors vie for control of the same policy space. Most theories of bureaucratic politics portray bureaucrats as self-interested and self-serving individuals who steer policy decisions in directions that protect and advance their personal interests and those of their employing agencies.

THE RISE OF BUREAUCRATIC POLITICS

Politics and administration have always been messily intertwined, but this fact has not always been clear. The rise of bureaucratic politics in the United States is a good case in point. During the Progressive era, the academic field of public administration was born, and government was reformed on the premise that politics and administration are separate spheres. However, this make-believe separation became strained and was finally rejected in the 1940s when the nation experienced two successive crises of global magnitude: the Great Depression and World War II. The scope and severity of these crises required the best efforts of political leaders and public administrators working in tandem. Thereby, scholars and practitioners discovered that politics and administration are one, and that this can be a good thing.

Since then, two broad streams of research have spotlighted the relationship between bureaucratic agencies and other participants in the policy-making process. The first stream of research has investigated the relationship between bureaucratic agencies, client groups, and special interests, while the second has focused on the relationship between bureaucratic agencies and overhead political actors such as the president and Congress. These two streams of research are described in more detail below.

Bureaucratic Agencies, Client Groups, and Special Interests

In the post-war years, scholars described bureaucratic politics as a process in which officials and agencies become "captured" by client groups and other special interests. For example, David E. Lilenthal explained that organizing and managing the Tennessee Valley Authority (TVA) was essentially a political enterprise, and Phillip Selznick described how TVA cultivated political constituencies to accomplish its mission and ensure its survival.[1,2] Selznick labeled this process "cooptation"—a Faustian-type bargain in which agencies receive political support from client groups and special interests by giving them a voice in the agency's decision-making process.

These types of alliances often turned into "iron triangles"—cooperative relationships between an agency, legislative committee, and interest group. The opportunities for quid pro quo in such a relationship are obvious, as members of the legislative committee receive political support from the pressure group, while providing favorable legislation and funding to the agency. These iron triangles seemed ironclad: they dominated specific policy areas to the extent that even presidents could not penetrate them.

In the 1960s and early 1970s, economic deregulation and liberalizing social changes in American society made iron triangles and agency capture theories seem somewhat outdated. Hugh Heclo observed that iron triangles were giving way to "issue networks," which he described as loose alliances between agencies and other parties interested in a particular policy or issue.[3]

Bureaucratic Agencies and Overhead Political Actors

Meanwhile on the political front, there was growing concern over the president and Congress's ability to control the bureaucracy. This concern was exacerbated during periods of divided government, which prevailed after 1968. For example, the Nixon Administration feared that liberal bureaucrats would side with Congressional Democrats and sabotage Nixon's conservative policy agenda. Thus, the administration mounted an aggressive campaign to regain political control of the bureaucracy.[4] Their strategies included applying litmus tests to presidential appointees and weakening the career civil service by bending merit system rules.[5] This battle for control of the bureaucracy grew fiercer in the Carter and Reagan Administrations. President Carter secured passage of the Civil Service Reform Act of 1978, making the bureaucracy more accessible and vulnerable to overhead political control.

Encyclopedia of Public Administration and Public Policy
DOI: 10.1081/E-EPAP 120010868

President Reagan seized this opportunity to protect and advance his conservative policy agenda: he significantly increased the number of political appointees, further politicized the appointments process, and instituted policy reforms that weakened the career service in most regulatory, social service, and central management agencies.[6]

Scholarship on bureaucratic politics increasingly reflected this concern about bureaucratic control. Researchers from several different academic fields began applying the principles of neoclassical economics to the problem. Most of these treatments suggested that bureaucrats and their agencies were on a feeding frenzy, acting in their self-interest rather than the public interest.[7] One particular application—principal–agent theory—has become quite influential in recent years.[8] Studies using this framework have shown that elected officials can exert control over bureaucratic outputs, but that doing so is costly and time-consuming. Excessive overhead political control seems to breed bureaucratic inefficiency.[9]

In the United States, politics and administration have always been intermingled, and bureaucratic politics has always been an important part of the policy-making process. This fact was made clear in the 1940s, when elected officials and bureaucrats worked together to rescue the nation from economic bankruptcy and despotism. Ironically, scholarship on bureaucratic politics has become increasingly disconnected from this heroic era.

SCOPE OF BUREAUCRATIC INFLUENCE

According to James Q. Wilson and John J. DiIulio Jr., three features of the American political system make American bureaucracy distinctive. These features also promote bureaucratic politics: first, political authority over the bureaucracy is shared between the executive, legislative, and judicial branches; second, agencies at the federal, state, and local levels often share functions; and third, the American political system is adversarial in nature. In this highly charged political environment, bureaucratic politics is likely to thrive.[10]

Most observers agree that bureaucrats' preferences are important, and that their behaviors are consequential. Yet the extent of bureaucratic influence in the policy-making process is not always clear. Francis E. Rourke contends that bureaucratic influence has declined in recent years. He says the main culprits are divided government, transformed constituencies, and increased policy volatility.[11] Robert F. Durant disagrees in part. He provides numerous examples showing that bureaucratic influence is alive and well in some quarters, and he concludes that it is highly variable. Durant lists more than a dozen factors that affect the degree of bureaucratic influence. These

factors include individual and organizational attributes, type of constituents, and variables describing the policy arena and political environment.[12] Both authors are probably correct. Bureaucratic influence has declined in recent years, but it remains quite potent in certain situations and may reassert itself in the future.

SOURCES OF BUREAUCRATIC POWER

Bureaucrats exercise considerable discretion in the modern democratic state. This fact is inevitable and desirable. It is inevitable because administration is about exercising discretion. Even if bureaucrats choose to be neutral, they are electing a course of action with sure and important consequences. Bureaucratic discretion is desirable, because elected officials need help. Bureaucrats have the expertise to provide this help, and they are strategically situated. That is, they work in close proximity to the problems elected officials face and the people they serve.

Bureaucrats also wield considerable influence in the policy-making process. They make many decisions in their own right and work behind the scenes to influence others. In fact, bureaucratic influence is found in every stage of the policy-making process. Bureaucrats help set policy agendas, frame issues, formulate alternatives, calculate costs and benefits, secure funding, make decisions, and implement those decisions. Furthermore, bureaucrats are involved in policy evaluation and provide crucial feedback to policy makers.

Political scientist Norton E. Long once explained that "power is the lifeblood of administration."[13] To be effective, bureaucrats must enter the political arena and take an active role in the policy-making process. The bureaucracy is a political institution just like the president, Congress, and the Supreme Court. Kenneth J. Meier explained: "It must build political support for its actions, and it uses that political support to interact with other political institutions to make public policy."[14]

There are many other sources of bureaucratic power. In the American political system, governing coalitions come and go. Yet the bureaucracy is relatively permanent. Bureaucrats administer programs and execute laws that are the cumulative legacy of past and present governing coalitions. Thus, the bureaucracy has a vivid institutional memory that spans several hundred years of self-government. Its stability and permanence, and the continuity it provides, are primary sources of bureaucratic power.

Francis E. Rourke emphasized the ability of bureaucrats to mobilize political support and lend professional expertise.[15] James Q. Wilson contended that bureaucratic power is dependent on the type of task an agency performs and the ease of monitoring its operations and activities.[16]

Kenneth J. Meier provided yet another view. He explained that resources and autonomy are the two principal sources of bureaucratic power, and that this power can be enhanced or diminished by the type of policy environment, level of political and public support, specialized knowledge, cohesion of bureau personnel, and skill of bureau leadership.[14] In sum, there are many sources of bureaucratic power, and its exercise is situation-dependent.

BUREAUCRATIC MOTIVES AND THE "AGENCY VIEW"

An important part of bureaucratic politics is the belief that officials are motivated primarily by self-interest and tend to promote their agency's view on most policy issues. The notion that individuals and their employing agencies have similar interests comes from Mile's Law: where you sit determines where you stand. Bureaucrats want to keep their jobs, advance their careers, and increase their budgets. Their agencies are likely to have similar goals: they want to maintain their current staffing levels, extend their jurisdiction and reach, and increase their budgets.

Another reason bureaucrats tend to have an agency orientation is that they spend most of the their careers in a single agency. After years of indoctrination and investment in the agency, they naturally come to embrace its cause.

So far, the study of bureaucratic politics has been dominated by the assumption that bureaucrats are self-interested and self-serving, and that their agencies are similarly motivated. One of the most promising avenues for future research is to relax this assumption and recognize other important motives. These motives may include the desire to perform meaningful public service and to protect the public interest.

AN EXAMPLE: THE CUBAN MISSILE CRISIS

In his classic study of the Cuban Missile Crisis, Graham T. Allison examined the decision-making processes of the United States and Soviet governments during the tense international standoff that occurred in October 1962.[17,18] Allison used three "conceptual lenses": the rational, organizational process, and bureaucratic politics models. Thus, his study is particularly enlightening because it compares and contrasts the bureaucratic politics model with the two other models.

Summary of Events

The Cuban Missile Crisis was the most dangerous U.S.–Soviet confrontation of the Cold War. After the U.S.-sponsored Bay of Pigs incursion failed to depose Cuban Premier Fidel Castro, relations between the two nations steadily worsened. In October 1962, a U.S. reconnaissance flight discovered that the Soviet Union was secretly building ballistic missile launch sites in Cuba—approximately 100 miles from the Florida coastline. President John F. Kennedy was informed on the morning of October 16, and he immediately called the first of a series of meetings with his top advisors. After several days of gut-wrenching deliberations, Kennedy decided to impose a naval blockade on Cuba. He simultaneously warned Soviet Premier Nikita Khrushchev that any missile launches from Cuba would prompt a full-scale U.S. retaliatory attack against the Soviet Union. Khrushchev called the naval blockade "an act of aggression which pushes mankind toward the abyss of a world nuclear war." On October 24, Soviet ships carrying missiles to Cuba approached the quarantine line. After several tense hours, the Soviet vessels turned back averting a direct military confrontation. Soon afterward, Khrushchev ordered the missile sites dismantled and the missiles removed from Cuba. Thus, the 13-day crisis ended.

The Rational Actor Model

The rational actor model assumes that states are unitary actors, and that they make rational decisions. Two types of rationality are possible: procedural and substantive. Procedural rationality focuses on the decision-making process. This process consists of the following steps: defining the problem, searching for alternatives, estimating the costs and benefits of each alternative, and finally, selecting the best option. In contrast, substantive rationality focuses on the result. The preference of the decision maker can be inferred from the outcome, as all actions are viewed as intentional.

In the present case, Kennedy and his advisors tried to utilize the rational model. They searched for alternatives and identified several: an Army invasion of Cuba; an Air Force attack on the missile sites; a naval blockade to prevent missiles from entering Cuba; a State Department diplomatic protest; and simply ignoring the situation because it did not change the overall balance of power. Each alternative was evaluated against a set of criteria that included potential loss of American lives; monetary cost; probability of starting a nuclear war; domestic political fallout; and others. After careful study, Kennedy decided that the most prudent course of action was his twin response: a naval blockade of Cuba and the threat of massive retaliation against the Soviet Union. Thus, viewing the decision-making process through the rational model lends important insights.

The Organizational Process Model

Next, Allison considered the organizational process model. All large organizations develop bureaucratic structures and decision rules to avoid uncertainty and improve their decision-making ability. These structures and rules represent organizational learning from past successes and failures, and they provide continuity in the event of employee turnover. That is, bureaucratic organizations use decision rules and link decision-making power to offices rather than particular individuals.

The main difference between the rational and organizational models is in how the decision-making process is depicted. The rational model assumes that individuals go through the lengthy process of winnowing down alternatives and arriving at the one-best-solution. The organizational process model counters that rules—often referred to as standard operating procedures (SOPs)—guide decision making. Many participants with different preferences are involved, but they usually unite behind the SOP.

Allison provided the following example. President Kennedy ordered a naval blockade to prevent the Soviets from shipping more missiles into Cuba. Defense Secretary Robert McNamara wanted to draw the quarantine line close to the Cuban coast. He felt that a ''tight blockade'' would reduce the chances of a U.S.–Soviet confrontation. However, the Navy's SOP called for a more relaxed 500-mile quarantine line. Such a line would serve several purposes for the Navy. It would increase their chances of intercepting ships headed for the coast and give them ample space to maneuver away from hostile naval forces and thwart air attacks from the mainland. Even though McNamara ordered the Navy to implement a tight blockade, they did not heed his order. The type of blockade was determined by the Navy's SOP. Thus, the organizational process model provides important insights about the decision-making process.

The Bureaucratic Politics Model

The bureaucratic politics model (Fig. 1) emphasizes that many officials are involved in policy decisions, and their preferences are derived from their organizational backgrounds. The Secretary of the Army will stress the Army's position in interexecutive bargaining, while the Secretaries of the Navy and Air Force will represent their respective service branches. Hence, the decision-making process involves multiple actors with different preferences, and it is marked by conflict and bargaining. The participants engage in a ''tug-of-war'' to pull policy toward their preferred outcome. Allison called the final decision a ''resultant.''[19,20]

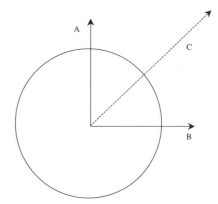

Fig. 1 The bureaucratic politics model of decision making. In the bureaucratic politics model, the decision-making process is characterized by conflict and bargaining. The participants engage in a ''tug-of-war'' trying to steer policy in the direction they prefer. Imagine two participants with equal power tugging in different directions (lines A and B). The outcome is what Allison called the ''resultant'' (line C).

During the Cuban Missile Crisis, many different groups were involved in the White House decision-making process: the Defense Department, State Department, Joint Chiefs of Staff, Central Intelligence Agency, and others. These actors had different preferences, largely because of their formal roles and agency ties. Furthermore, some had more influence than others. For example, Attorney General Robert F. Kennedy was highly influential because he was President Kennedy's younger brother and close confidant.

An intense tug-of-war ensued. Defense Secretary McNamara originally proposed a ''do nothing'' option, but the President deemed this response politically unacceptable. A hard-line coalition led by the Service Chiefs, former Secretary of State Dean Acheson, and others emerged and pushed for a surgical air strike. McNamara opposed this option and countered by proposing a naval blockade. He convinced the Attorney General and Presidential Counsel Ted Sorenson to support his plan. In the end, this moderate coalition prevailed.

Allison said the decision-making process was a bargaining game, and the participants knew it. They formed strategic coalitions and entered the fray. The outcome was a political result hammered out by these coalitions. Allison explained that even when an outcome is mostly the triumph of one individual or group, bureaucratic politics may help explain the context and inner workings that made the victory possible.[18]

In conclusion, the rational model assumes that states are unitary actors with fixed preferences. Officials acting for the state try to maximize the state's utility by making decisions rationally. The organizational process model

	Rational Model	Organizational Process Model	Bureaucratic Politics Model
No. of Actors	One	Many	Many
No. of Preferences	One	Many (United)	Many (Divergent)
Decision-Making Process	Rational	According to Rules and Procedures	Via Conflict and Bargaining
Outcomes	Intentional	Pre-Determined	Resultant
Major Drawbacks	Hard to Attain	Not Very Flexible	Hard to Predict

Fig. 2 Comparison of Allison's three models of decision making.

assumes that each organization has unique preferences and that decisions are made according to predetermined bureaucratic routines called SOPs. The bureaucratic politics model assumes that decision makers have a unique set of preferences derived from their positions in government, and that the decision-making process is a tug-of-war between these individuals. Overall, the bureaucratic politics model seems more plausible than the other two models because it conveys the dynamism and "real politik" of the policy-making process.

Fig. 2 summarizes the key differences between these models.

In the end, Allison is not advocating one best approach. He suggests using a variety of conceptual lenses.

CRITIQUES OF BUREAUCRATIC POLITICS

Theories of bureaucratic politics are limited for several reasons. First, Mile's Law does not always hold true. Officials are not always self-interested and self-serving, and they do not always promote their agency's view on important policy issues. Second, the model does not lend itself to making predictions. Third, bureaucratic politics raises the important question of bureaucratic accountability in democratic government.

How can we be sure that bureaucrats, who are non-elected government officials, will subordinate their self-interest and act in the public interest? This question is the Achilles heel of modern-day public administration, and it seems to defy any simple answer.[21] Most contemporary thinkers contend that a combination of internal and external control mechanisms is the best strategy. Accord-

ingly, bureaucrats are urged to act responsibly, and they are monitored by overhead political officials.

CONCLUSION

The term bureaucratic politics has several different meanings in the literature. These meanings vary from the narrow decision-making model described by Graham T. Allison to the broader, more encompassing notion of bureaucratic influence on policy making described by political scientists Francis E. Rourke, James Q. Wilson, and Kenneth J. Meier. Another stream of scholarship portrays bureaucrats and their agencies as threats to the public interest. Thus, this portrayal casts a negative light on bureaucratic politics. Overall, these various perspectives have several things in common. They all acknowledge that bureaucrats have a significant amount of discretion, and that these officials are active participants in the policy-making process.

Accordingly, bureaucratic politics emphasizes that bureaucrats, who are nonelected government officials, enter the political arena and try to influence or shape the policy-making process. These officials are assumed to be self-interested and likely to promote their agency's view on specific policy issues. That is, they are expected to protect and advance their own interests when engaged in inter-executive or inter-agency competition. As a result, theories of bureaucratic politics suggest that policy outcomes are the result of conflict and bargaining rather than the more rational or incremental processes described elsewhere.

REFERENCES

1. Lilenthal, D.E. *Democracy on the March*; Harper and Row: New York, NY, 1944.
2. Selznick, P. *TVA and the Grass Roots*; University of California Press: Berkeley, CA, 1949.
3. Heclo, H. Issue Networks and the Executive Establishment. In *The New American Political System*; King, A., Ed.; American Enterprise Institute: Washington, DC, 1978; 87–124.
4. Lynn, L.E., Jr. The Reagan Administration and the Renitent Bureaucracy. In *The Reagan Presidency and the Governing of America*; Salamon, L.M., Lund, M.S., Eds.; The Urban Institute Press: Washington, DC, 1984; 339–370.
5. White House Personnel Office The Malek Manual. In *Classics of Public Personnel Policy*; Thompson, F.J., Ed.; Moore Publishing Co., Inc.: Oak Park, IL, 1979; 159–187.
6. Nathan, R.P. *The Administrative Presidency*; John Wiley: New York, NY, 1983.

7. Niskanen, W.A., Jr. *Bureaucracy: Servant or Master?* Institute of Economic Affairs: London, 1971.

8. Perrow, C. *Complex Organizations: A Critical Essay,* 3rd Ed.; Random House: New York, NY, 1986.

9. Wood, B.D.; Waterman, R.W. *Bureaucratic Discretion: The Role of Bureaucracy in a Democracy*; Westview Press: Boulder, CO, 1994.

10. Wilson, J.Q.; DiIulio, J.J., Jr. *American Government: Institutions and Policies,* 8th Ed.; Houghton Mifflin Company: Boston, MA, 2001.

11. Rourke, F.E. American bureaucracy in a changing political setting. J. Public Adm. Res. Theory **1991**, *1* (2), 111–129.

12. Durant, R.F. Whither bureaucratic influence?: A cautionary note. J. Public Adm. Res. Theory **1991**, *1* (4), 461–476.

13. Long, N.E. Power and administration. Public Adm. Rev. **1949**, *9* (3), 257–264.

14. Meier, K.J. *Politics and the Bureaucracy: Policymaking in the Fourth Branch of Government,* 3rd Ed.; Brooks/Cole Publishing Co.: Pacific Grove, CA, 1993; 1.

15. Rourke, F.E. *Bureaucracy, Politics, and Public Policy*; Little, Brown and Co.: Boston, MA, 1969.

16. Wilson, J.Q. *Bureaucracy: What Government Agencies Do and Why They Do It*; Basic Books: New York, NY, 1989.

17. Allison, G.T. *Essence of Decision*; Little, Brown: Boston, MA, 1971.

18. Allison, G.T.; Zelikow, P. *Essence of Decision: Explaining the Cuban Missile Crisis,* 2nd Ed.; Addison-Wesley: New York, NY, 1979.

19. Allison, G.T.; Halperin, M.H. Bureaucratic Politics: A Paradigm and Some Policy Implications. In *Theory and Policy in International Relations*; Tanter, R., Ullman, R.H., Eds.; Princeton University Press: Princeton, NJ, 1972; 40–78.

20. Rousseau, D.L. *Bureaucratic Politics Module*; 2000. Available online: http://www.polisci.upenn.edu/psci150/modules/bur/index.htm.

21. Waldo, D. *The Administrative State*; Ronald Press: New York, NY, 1948.

Burnout in Public Agencies

Robert T. Golembiewski
The University of Georgia, Athens, Georgia, U.S.A.

INTRODUCTION

A favorite metaphor involves efforts to add tension to a system to energize it, which requires fine-tuning short of that point at which the system becomes overloaded and "snaps." In this elemental sense, organizations are like rubber bands propelling a spitball. Increase the loading on the band by extending it, *but not too far*, and the missile will go further and faster. Apply too much loading, and the rubber band will just pop into two or more pieces, and that may sting the shooter rather than provide momentum for the projectile.

Some such metaphor underlies most downsizing or rightsizing. For example, a system is seen as having too many human resources, or the wrong kinds, and the goal is to eliminate some employees while increasing the workload of those who remain. All too often, however, the human system may be deteriorated in the process (e.g., Ref. [1]).

This common elemental fine-tuning strategy is not guaranteed to "work," far from it, in fact. Guidelines exist for seeking that magical middle ground, where systems become more energized (e.g., Ref. [2]) and also avoid the breaking point. Failure can be costly, nonetheless, and perhaps is so in the majority of cases. Witness violence at the work site, which seems more and more a hallmark of our age. Frequently, these outbursts can be traced to a person or persons under stress, tragically beyond the point at which they "snap," or "go around the bend," emotionally speaking. In the most dramatic form, someone turns gunfire on fellow workers, on specific targets as well as those unlucky enough to be in the wrong place at the wrong time.

The burnout literature takes us a substantial distance toward isolating such "breaking-points" in practice, although we are not yet there. In the opinion of this author, and he has a clear vested interest (e.g., Ref. [3]), the "phase model of burnout" is the farthest along of several possible developmental models. A few details suggest the nature and range of support for this view.

PHASE MODEL OF BURNOUT

After a decade of development, the phase model permits a number of confident generalizations. In turn, six points will receive emphasis below:

- Conceptually, we have a solid idea of how to define a dimension reasonably labeled "burnout."
- Operationally, for extensive purposes, we know how to measure the incidence and severity of burnout.
- Tactically, the phases of burnout are associated with a long list of undersized and undesirable outcomes, both personal and individual.
- Burnout seems to persist over extended periods of time.
- The incidence of burnout, as seen in various contrasts, seems to fall in the range of bad to worse.
- In general, incidences of burnout do not seem to vary robustly and regularly, in public versus business contexts.

Normal Definition of Burnout Subdomains

Most observers generally agree that burnout is comprised of three subdomains. Following Maslach,[4,5] individual burnout is contributed to by the following:

- High scores on items relating to *depersonalization* or the tendency to think of individuals as things or objects rather than as sensitive, valuing beings.
- Low scores on *personal accomplishment* (*reversed*), which is tapped by items relating to how well a person does on work tasks as well as on how worthwhile these tasks are seen to be.
- High scores on *emotional exhaustion*, with items relating to the emotional slack available to individuals—as coping skills and attitudes are discounted by the stressors an individual experiences at a particular point in time.

Encyclopedia of Public Administration and Public Policy
DOI: 10.1081/E-EPAP 120010854

Operational Definition of Phases

Items from the MBI (or Maslach Burnout Inventory) are used to estimate the three subdomains, scores on which for each individual are differentiated as high versus low using norms based on the population of a large public agency[3] operating under substantial stressors and strain. A median-cut on each subdomain is utilized to make the high versus low distinction.

Beyond this point, a single decision rule applies: depersonalization is seen as more virulent than personal accomplishment, and both are seen as less determinative of burnout than emotional exhaustion. Overall, each individual is assigned to one of the eight phases in Fig. 1. Note that the high versus low assignments are based on norms from 1500 respondents in a U.S. federal agency high levels of strain.

Note that one significant point that the model does not imply is that progression to full burnout must take the path I → II... → VIII for individuals. Rather, however one arrives at a specific phase, the model predicts that worsening conditions for individuals will be associated regularly with I versus II, II versus III, III versus IV, and so on.

Indeed, there seem to be two basic flight paths to advanced burnout. In *chronic onset*, the basic pattern seems to be I → II → IV → VIII. In *acute onset*, various flight paths may exist. Thus, a person suddenly losing a beloved mate might quickly advance I → V. Beyond that point, continued growing might be variously reflected in advancing burnout. For example, a person might adapt by losing interest in work, in which case, the flight path becomes I → V → VII and might then extend to VIII. Alternatively, that person might try to "lose self in work," in which case, the pathway would be I → V → VI, ultimately with a possible extension to VIII. Recovery could variously work its way back through (perhaps) phase I, in the cases of chronic and acute onset.

In sum, the burnout phases progress from least advanced → most advanced, or phase I → VIII, but not in a simple and sovereign progression. In sum, an VIII strongly tends to objectify personal relationships, believes self to be doing poorly on a task with little socially redemptive value, and experiences only a slight positive

balance, if not an actual deficit, in the stressors experienced as contrasted with coping skills and attitudes for dealing with them.

The overall results, in North America and worldwide, suggested that their distribution needed close attention.[6] Only Phases I → VIII are regularly and robustly associated with a broad range of worsening conditions, phase by phase. In addition, 40% or more of all employees are assigned to Phases VI → VIII, which indicates a large proportion of "burned-out" individuals.

Phases as Breaking Points

The phases do not provide a map of the specific point when strain becomes "too great," but the model nonetheless has tolerable utility. Table 1 suggests the point in contrasting the consequences of high versus low burnout, generally defined as phases I–III versus VI–VIII, respectively. Perhaps most notably, differences on virtually all variables are regular; thus, Phase I covariants are more desirable than those of Phase II, Phase II covariants are more desirable than those for Phase III, and so on for all paired comparisons. These mean differences for phases not only fall in the same directions, but they are also statistically-different in far more cases than one would expect.

Note that this general pattern of associations is all but universal, although variations in intensity exist that may reflect local conditions. The generalizations in Table 1 come from many studies in which those in Phase I were better off than those in II, those in II better than in III, and so on. To illustrate, the pattern is virtually the same in North American populations as well as those in 20-plus other nation states for which data are available.[6] To a similar effect, the pattern is much the same for archival data as for self-reports. For example, those in Phase I spend the least on medical insurance; those in VIII spend the most; and the other phases have spending that progresses quite regularly through the phases.[3]

Of great significance, both theoretic and practical, note that the high profile in Table 1 has a familiar character. Quite directly, that profile is like that associated with Participative Management or Industrial Humanism. This profile suggests that burnout is a centroid—the phases

Phases of Burnout

	I	II	III	IV	V	VI	VII	VIII
Depersonalization	Lo	Hi	Lo	Hi	Lo	Hi	Lo	Hi
Personal accomplishment (reversed)	Lo	Lo	Hi	Hi	Lo	Lo	Hi	Hi
Emotional exhaustion	Lo	Lo	Lo	Lo	Hi	Hi	Hi	Hi

Fig. 1 Phase model assignments.

Table 1 Illustrated conditions characteristic of extremes of burnout

Least-advanced phases of burnout are characterized by:		Most-advanced phases of burnout are characterized by:
High	Participation in work decisions	Low
High	Involvement	Low
Low	Spending on medical insurance	High
Low	Physical and emotional symptoms	High
High	Performance evaluation	Low
High	Cohesiveness	Low
High	Autonomy at work	Low
High	Trust in management	Low
High	Trust in fellow employees	Low
High	Supervisory support	Low
Low	Family dislocation	High

seem related to many aspects of nature relevant to management. This feature implies that the phases are a source of great leverage in planned change, once we understand them sufficiently to induce the effects we desire.

Virulence of Phases

The phase model is the only one that permits an estimate of how many people have which degrees of burnout. And, the overall message is alarming. On a large and growing panel of variables, self-reports and "objective" or "hard" variables, that is to say, persons in the progressive phases experienced diminishing and deteriorating conditions. Thus, those in Phase I reported the fewest or least severe symptoms of mental or physical illness, to illustrate; and those in VIII have the poorest record. In between, even more revealing, II are significantly worse off than Is; IIIs tend to report greater deficiencies than Is; and so on.

One example of the common pattern of relations will serve to illustrate the correlation of the phases with relevant variables. Consider physical symptoms, for example (e.g., Ref. [3]). The 19 Michigan physical symptoms—from sweaty palms to chest pains[7]—covary directly with the phases. For example, a national sample of respondents reflected this familiar pattern when

compared to symptoms arrayed by the phases: those in Phase I had a small fraction of each symptom reported by the national panel; those in Phase VIII had five to 15 times to the incidence of symptoms reported by the national panel; and those in other phases fell in regular order.

The general sense of it is like a stepladder: as the phases vary, regularly and robustly, so do the conditions experienced by people tend to worsen or deteriorate. Table 1 provides useful illustration of these stable patterns of effects. As is almost universally true, all variables reflect such a good and bad pattern as burnout varies I → VIII.

Generalization About Incidence

The usual reservations about accumulating research apply, but the news is dominantly bad about the phase model, if not shocking. Several generalizations applied to a panel of studies of incidence that numbered over 100 work sites from almost 20 nations, altogether including about 50,000 respondents.

First, overall, the United States and Canada report the least incidences of advanced phases along with New Zealand, but the base is high. In sum, over 24,000 cases reflect this distribution by phases among North American nonpublic work sites:[6]

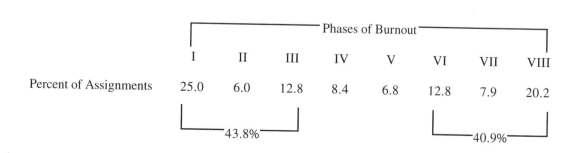

Second, the most favorable distribution of phases observed so far had over 22% in the three most advanced phases in any organization of any size ($N = 406$). Even this distribution will seem troubling to most observers.

Third, as a gross generalization, the global incidence seems worse. Roughly, about 10% more cases fell in the three most advanced phases; and 10% less are assigned to Phases I–III.[6]

To be sure, the sampling of global work sites is not necessarily as representative as all non-North American work settings. So the generalization may have to be updated as the panel of national work sites is enlarged.

Fourth, there seem to be few outliers. Thus, phase data for New Zealand are substantially more attractive than for other non-North American settings, which is consistent with all other observations using various operational measures. Even this outlier estimate promises no bed of roses, however. To illustrate several recent estimates of the distribution of phases in six New Zealand work sites generated the following pattern:

Details on several of the New Zealand sites are conveniently available.[8]

In sum, such estimates suggest that burnout poses serious issues even in New Zealand, a "good" environment for burnout. Had the distribution shown related to a physical disease like measles, for example, it would be interpreted as a pandemic, or far beyond "epidemic" status. Even "pandemic" might be too mild to label what exists, even in North America or New Zealand.

Arenas and Burnout Differences

Despite common opinion, public agencies do not appear to be markedly worse off in the matter of burnout than businesses. Available data do not permit a fine-tuned conclusion on the point, especially because most public agencies for which incidence data are available come from North American contexts, i.e., the United States and Canada.

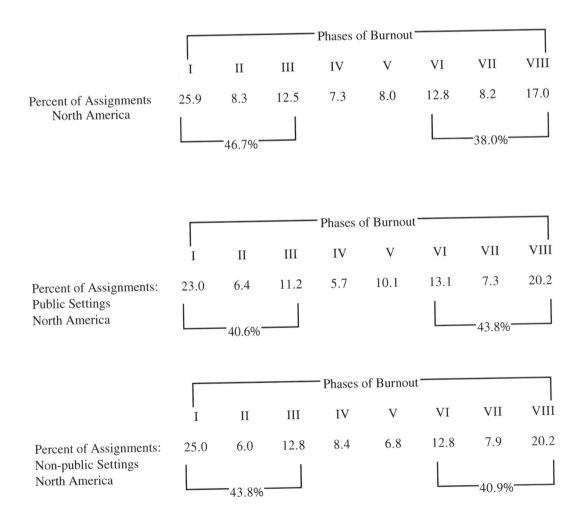

Basically, the public sector seems to suffer about the same, or perhaps a tad more, than available business work settings. To suggest the point, 9656 employees in 24 North American public-sector settings demonstrated this distribution in the eight phases of burnout,[6] contrasted with 63 North American nonpublic settings (N = 24080).

Overall, this summary suggests no better or worse situation in public versus business employment.

CONCLUSION

These perspectives on the phase model of burnout are usefully placed in several broader contexts: a half-dozen-plus generalizations seem appropriate at this general level of analysis. A much longer and detailed list has been developed (e.g., Ref. [2]).

1. Globally, it seems safe to conclude that we have a burnout problem, of substantial dimensions in many cases, and even worse in some work settings.
2. One set of items, the Maslach Burnout Inventory, is the most dominant instrument for assessing burnout. The phase model uses the MBI, essentially. Overall, the MBI items seem to tap three subdomains: depersonalization, personal accomplishment, and emotional exhaustion.
3. One basic disagreement exists among MBI users. The phase model assumes for testing that the three MBI subdomains tend to build to the most extreme burnout. Depersonalization builds with negative consequences on personal accomplishment. High levels of these two can lead to emotional exhaustion.

   The major opposed view is that of Maslach and her supporters (e.g., Leiter and Maslach, 1999). The interest begins with heightening levels of emotional exhaustion, which if accompanied by high depersonalization, will generate decrements in personal accomplishment.

   It is too early to make a decision concerning these two views. They may reflect different target phenomena, e.g., the full burnout sequence for the phases, and a basic focus on advanced burnout eruptions by Maslach and her supporters. For extreme cases, this distinction does not matter much, but practical and especially theoretical advances will occur once the issue is resolved.
4. Applications to ameliorate burnout stand in need of further development, to be sure, but the phase model has supported several successful efforts to reduce burnout. Thus, Golembiewski and his associates[3] report designs for three type of situations: when

burnout is rooted in interaction, policies and procedures, or in structure.[9]

5. Evidence suggests that burnout will become an even greater problem over time, although this certainty is not appropriate. We are definitely in an era of downsizing or rightsizing, to suggest the point, and burnout predictably increases in work sites affected by adverse personnel actions (e.g., Ref. [3]). Evidence establishes that advanced burnout seems characteristic of people against whom adverse personnel actions have been taken.
6. Institutional and policy linkages seem to influence burnout, but as of today, there has been no concerted effort to confront them (e.g., Ref. [3]). For example, burnout seems most advanced among working single parents, especially mothers (e.g., Ref. [10]), and one can envision supports in public policy for such subgroups.

   The apparently high costs, both personnel and organizational, associated with advanced burnout suggest the value of attention to such linkages. However, no vigorous study of the economic costs of burnout now exists, as far as this author knows. The dour inventory of burnout covariants suggests these economic costs will be substantial; and those covariants also imply high social and economic costs.
7. Advanced burnout has been tracked in expected ways in its impact on a substantial panel of variables, but much work remains to be done. Consider only two points. Thus, most measures of burnout effects have relied on self-reports, i.e., on what are often labeled "soft data." Work with objective or hard measures (absence rates, costs of production, turnover, and so on) is growing. But, more attention to such data is necessary.

In addition, increases in burnout are reasonably enough associated with the outbursts of violence at work that seem to be stage-center so often these days. Testing of such linkages has not yet been made directly. Advancing burnout has been all but conclusively associated with affective states that seem related to violence. These states include depression, hostility, and a broader range of nonpsychotic conditions that would warrant therapeutic interactions (e.g., Ref. [3]). However, the specific linkages to outbursts of violence have not yet been made.

REFERENCES

1. Hager, G. Worker output plunges—productivity falls, labor costs soar. USA Today **May 9, 2001**, 1A.

2. Golembiewski, R.T. Next stage of burnout research and applications. Psychol. Bull. **1999**, *84*, 441–446.

3. Golembiewski, R.T.; Boudreau, R.A.; Munzenrider, R.F.; Luo, H. *Global Burnout*; JAI Press: Greenwich, CT, 1996; pp. 83–128, 160, 239–244.

4. Maslach, C.; Jackson, S.E. *Maslach Burnout Inventory*; Consulting Psychologists Press: Palo Alto, CA, 1982.

5. Maslach, C.; Jackson, S.E. *Maslach Burnout Inventory*; Consulting Psychologists Press: Palo Alto, CA, 1986.

6. Golembiewski, R.T.; Boudreau, R.A.; Sun, B.C. Estimates of burnout in public agencies worldwide. Public Adm. Rev. **1999**, *58*, 59–63.

7. Quinn, R.F.; Staines, G.I. *The 1977 Quality of Employment Survey*; Survey Research Center, University of Michigan: Ann Arbor, MI, 1979.

8. Boudreau, R.A.; Everett, A.M.; Golembiewski, R.T. Burnout in New Zealand. J. Health Human Resour. Adm. **1999**, *23*, 37–43.

9. Golembiewski, R.T.; Rountree, B.H. System Redesign in Nursing, II: Action Planning and Its Effect on Worksite Stakeholders. In *Current Topics in Management*; Rahim, M.A., Golembiewski, R.T., Mackenzie, K., Eds.; JAI Publishers: Greenwich, CT, 1999; 197–211.

10. Ellay, D.; Anderson, K.S. An exploratory analysis of burnout among dual income and single income families. J. Health Human Resour. Adm. **1991**, *13*, 457–469.

11. Golembiewski, R.T.; Munzenrider, R.F. *Phases of Burnout*; Praeger: New York, 1998.

12. Leiter, M.P.; Maslach, C. Six areas of worksite: A model of the organizational causes of burnout. J. Health Human Serv. Adm. **1999**, *21*, 472–489.

Capital Budgeting

Jane Beckett-Camarata
Kent State University, Kent, Ohio, U.S.A.

INTRODUCTION

Capital budgeting is the process of determining need and acquiring, constructing, improving, or purchasing capital assets. For our purposes, a capital asset is any large resource (e.g., land or buildings) that has benefits that extend more than 1 fiscal year. Capital assets are budgeted for in a capital budget. The capital budget is an integrated physical and financial plan for improvements. The capital budget is also the authorization for funding and acquisition of capital assets and must be approved by the legislative body.[1] The capital budget plays a critical role in most public organizations since the life of capital assets usually extends beyond 1 year. When used in conjunction with the strategic plan, master plan, capital improvements plan (CIP), and debt management plan, the capital budget provides a way of systematically and efficiently acquiring and funding capital expenditures. Capital budgets are used extensively by state and local governments. The federal government currently uses elements of the capital budgeting process and it too is moving toward using a capital budget.

THE CAPITAL BUDGET PLANNING AND DECISION PROCESS

State and local governments are recognizing the importance of planning for capital improvements and tying capital improvements to the overall goals of the community through strategic planning and capital budgeting. The connection between strategic planning, capital improvements planning, and capital budgeting is important because such a connection has a potential positive influence on economic development and offers a way of increasing fiscal capacity. Inadequate planning can result in unnecessary expenditures of public funds.

The key parts of capital budget planning and decision-making process are

- Strategic plan
- Master plan
- CIP
- Debt management plan

The capital budget planning and decision process model is outlined in Fig. 1.

Strategic Plan

For those state and local governments who have and use a strategic plan, the goals, objectives, and strategies outlined in the plan indicate how jurisdictions intend to fulfill their mission and address critical issues including capital needs. The strategic plan should be the basis for identifying capital requirements. The master plan should flow naturally from the strategic plan.

Master Plan

Most state and local governments are required to have a have a master plan. A master plan delineates current and future land use, and guides land and physical plant use. Master plans may contain, for example, site and utility drawings.

CIP

The CIP is a catalog of capital projects selected for funding for the next 5 to 10 years. Capital projects have an impact on future operating budgets. Each CIP should contain estimates for operating and maintaining the capital improvement after it is completed. The cost estimates include any expenses in connection with maintaining the improvement as well as costs of additional activities or new programs that will be using the new or expanded land/space.

The CIP identifies the needs of the state or local government and ranks the projects in priority order. The primary difference between the capital budget and the CIP is that the capital budget is a legal document that appropriates funding for specific projects. The CIP is important for capital planning for any local government, even if there are not a lot of large-scale projects.[2] In addition to shaping thinking about future capital assets needs, the CIP compels decision makers to review, compare, and assign priorities to projects. If the capital and operating budgets are combined, the first year of the CIP is then included as the capital portion of the annual budget.

Encyclopedia of Public Administration and Public Policy
DOI: 10.1081/E-EPAP 120010975
Copyright © 2003 by Marcel Dekker, Inc. All rights reserved.

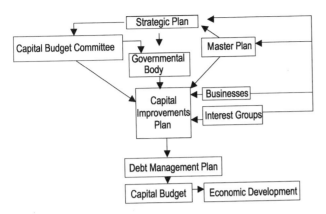

Fig. 1 The capital budget planning and decision process model.

The CIP is a "rolling list" of capital projects. The first year of the CIP becomes the capital budget. Each year the CIP is updated (second year of the plan and a new year is added), and revenue and expenditure estimates are revised for the remaining period. An effective CIP consists of both an administrative process to identify the location, scale, and timing of needed capital projects and a fiscal plan to provide for funding those projects. Producing a CIP is more efficient than conducting a new search each year for capital projects or capital equipment purchases.

If a state or local government has an existing capital budget, why does it also need a CIP? The capital budget represents the first year of the CIP. The capital budget is a legal document that authorizes specific projects during the following fiscal period. The capital budget lists only the projects and equipment to be carried out or purchased during the fiscal year. A CIP lists projects and equipment purchases that are expected and scheduled over a period of 5 years or more. CIP requires state/local governments to look ahead, see what their capital needs are, and plan for future projects. What are the population trends? Will more schools, prisons, or roads be necessary? How will such projects be funded? Will funding the projects require a bond referendum? Large and expensive projects such as roof replacement may need to be completed in segments, to hold down annual costs. The out years of the CIP are not binding and are therefore subject to change.

The typical CIP is a multiyear projection that forecasts spending for all anticipated CIPs. Buying land for parks, airports, retention ponds, and public buildings is much less expensive when the population is small, and the land can be held in a relatively undeveloped state until needed. Long-term planning for water and sewer lines can also be helpful. For example, if projecting ahead discloses that future population estimates exceed current water produc-

tion capacity, planning may be needed to expand and protect the watershed, build aqueducts, drill wells, or lay pipe to reach surface water. Such projects may require more than a 5-year planning range.

Many capital proposals come from the departments, for example, public works (street improvements), utilities (water, wastewater, sanitation), and planning (as part of the master plan). Citizen complaints are a second source of requests for capital spending, although these may be funneled through departments or council members. Community-based interest groups can also be an important source of proposals for projects. Proposals also come from members of the business community and elected officials. Normally, the cost of these proposals far exceeds available financing.

Decision making on capital assets that go into the CIP is not simple and can be aided greatly if there are clear, detailed answers to the following questions:

1. How many citizens will be harmed or inconvenienced if the project is not constructed? Which citizens?
2. Adequacy of existing facilities to meet current and projected program demand.
3. Will the project add to the property value of the area, thus increasing the value of state/city property and receipts from property taxes? How much of an increase will be realized?
4. What services will be initiated, expanded, or improved because of this project?
5. What is the impact on those services?
6. Will the project increase the efficiency of performance? How much and where? What cost savings will result? Will the project reduce the cost of performance for a particular service? How much and where?
7. Will the project provide a service required for economic growth and development of the municipality/state?
8. Is the estimated cost of the improvement within the city's/state's ability to pay?
9. How the project fits the approved strategic plan and master plan?

Ultimately, priorities have to be decided and decisions have to be made. Sometimes analytical techniques such as cost–benefit analysis are useful, but judgment is also used. Some communities use a point system to establish priorities. One scale used is:

1. Urgent (highest priority)
2. Essential
3. Necessary
4. Desirable
5. Acceptable
6. Deferrable (lowest priority)[3]

WHO USES CAPITAL BUDGETS?

Many state and local governments separate capital expenditures from operating expenditures. Eighty-four percent of state governments separate capital expenditures from operating expenditures,[4] 40% of counties[5] separate capital expenditures from operating expenditures, and 71% of cities[6] separate capital expenditures from operating expenditures. The federal government does not have a "full-scale" capital budgeting process. Funding for most federal capital assets is provided in annual appropriations under discretionary caps.

State and local governments use capital budgets because it improves decision efficiency since capital assets can be financed either by revenue raised currently (taxes, charges, grants, etc.) or by borrowing on the promise to repay from future revenues. If operating and capital expenditures are combined, capital assets appear more expensive relative to operating expenditures, even though they will be used over a number of years. Capital budgets are financed, but not necessarily balanced; operating budgets are balanced.[7]

WHO IS INVOLVED IN THE CAPITAL BUDGET PROCESS?

Because capital expenditures represent a considerable financial outlay, who participates in the process is important to the success of the capital budgeting process. The main participants in the capital budgeting process are the government unit's (state or municipality) departments, a Capital Improvement Committee, a budget and/or finance department, legislative bodies, individual politicians, citizens, interest groups, and planning commissions.

The most traditional approach to formally soliciting citizen input into the capital budgeting process has been to form a capital budget planning committee. In the past, the committees have been made up of large, politically important interest groups in the municipality. Elected officials are becoming more sensitive to the need to increase the diversity of these committees for both equity and economic reasons.[8] Some governments have also moved outside merely soliciting input from one citizen committee to broader representation, such as formally soliciting suggestions for capital improvement priorities from several citizen advisory boards representing different planning areas.[9] Providing citizen input into the capital budgeting process may potentially provide the foundation for public support if a bond referendum is necessary.

The traditional informal approach is that which takes place through informal political bargaining in the capital budgeting process. Politics are an integral part of the capital budget process because elected officials must be perceived as being responsive to the electorate.

There are high power stakes in project selection. For example, the location of a new highway and its major intersections can produce windfalls for property owners whose land borders the project. Professional staff can examine campaign promises for political priorities relevant to the capital budget.[1] For example, the mayoral campaign may have promised downtown renewal, council members may have promised downtown renewal, and council members may have promised to revitalize the neighborhoods or to improve the physical plant of a school. Appointed officials usually have some priorities, such as adequate funding of maintenance projects and compliance with state and federal mandates.

INVENTORY OF ASSETS

Decisions to add a public facility or make extensive repairs can be made on the basis of understanding the needs of the community or the state and the resources available. The best approach to identifying the resources is to inventory the existing public facilities. The next step is to catalog the proposed public facilities. The key data in the capital register include:

1. Location of the proposed facility
2. Year of construction
3. Cost priority
4. Project description
5. Financing schedule
6. Prior or sunk costs
7. Projection of future-related funding requests
8. Operating costs
9. Savings in operating and maintenance costs

DEFERRED MAINTENANCE

In addition to cataloging the existing capital assets, they also must be evaluated to project repair, renewal, or replacement needs that will preserve their ability to support the mission or activities that they were assigned to serve.[10] Condition assessment is critical to a capital budgeting program. To perform such an assessment requires both a useful database of existing conditions and the implications of such conditions for future performance.[11] Condition assessment, cost estimating, and other asset management approaches are important individual strategies within a capital maintenance program. This is especially true where the highest priority is not acquisition of new assets but maintenance of old ones.

Maintenance of capital assets is becoming an increasingly important subject because many public organizations must manage what they have and keep assets in service long after their "useful life" has expired. The challenge is to avoid deferral of necessary expenditures for maintenance, referred to as "deferred maintenance." Deferred maintenance can lead to asset failure that in turn can lead to replacement and extensive rehabilitation needs that are much more expensive than would have been the case if the assets had been kept in regular working condition. Many public organizations have poorly developed methods of measuring and costing deferred maintenance and its potential affects, and condition assessment is inconsistent. Because condition assessment is a prerequisite for deferred maintenance reporting, failure in condition assessment can lead to deferred maintenance.[12]

COST ANALYSIS

Most state and local governments have limited resources, as well as legal political restrictions on their ability to raise revenue. For these reasons, a limited number of capital items can be acquired during any one period of time. Priorities have to be made to fund those that are considered to be the most important. Some combination of economic analysis, such as cost–benefit analysis, citizen input, and the political agenda, are factors that determine importance. A combination of quantitative, qualitative, and political is preferable. The key is to match available revenue sources with a wide-ranging set of expenditure options and to match expenditure options to revenue availability.

Cost–benefit analysis can be used to compare capital improvements. Not all proposed capital expenditures are associated with their cost relative to their benefits. Many decisions are made on other bases. State and local governments would not spend the level of resources they currently do on such things as hazardous waste disposal sites if it were not required by the federal government. Also, some decisions are made on the basis of equity rather than cost. For example, providing mass transit in low-use areas may not make economic sense. If these areas are also populated by low-income citizens, however, eliminating such facilities simply because they are not economical is often rejected by government agencies responsible for such facilities on the basis of equity.

FUNDING SOURCE IDENTIFICATION

Only a limited pool of resources is available to fund all the requested projects. The challenge is to identify the full range of resources available, both current and borrowed, and to determine how these funds can be used to meet the needs with the highest priorities. The resources usually considered are:

- Pay-as-you go financing—costs are paid directly from current income, such as taxes, fees and user charges, and interest earnings
- Grants from other governments
- Debt financing—tapping external funds through the issuance of debt in the capital market
- Public/private ventures, including privatization

Most governments find that current revenues are inadequate to fund all the projects in their capital plan. For this reason, a well-structured CIP should include a review of all financial resources that are available to meet current and future capital needs. The mix of financing methods that will be used to fund a CIP is likely to be one of the most important decisions made in developing and executing a CIP. In the case of debt financing, amortization rates and repayment schedules are determined by the parameters established by the mix of financing tools used. Each method of financing has advantages and disadvantages, and each is viewed in the context of its applicability and its effect on the government's overall spending levels and fiscal health.

DEBT MANAGEMENT PLAN

Rating agencies look favorably on state and local governments that assess affordability in managing debt. Debt capacity recognizes that state and local governments have limits to capacity to issue debt at a given credit level. As a general policy, a local government should decide whether to pursue a pay-as-you-go or a pay-as-you-use strategy. The pay-as-you-go approach relies on current revenues to pay for capital improvements; the pay-as-you-use approach relies on general obligation debt to pay for capital outlays. Using pay-as-you go financing, current taxpayers bear the burden of financing improvements and future residents reap the benefits. As long as the repayment of the debt does not exceed the life of the asset, a pay-as-you-use strategy may be more equitable than pay-as-you-go. However, debt funding of capital projects does have some obstacles. State law may require a voter referendum to obtain citizen approval for issuing bonds, and that approval may be difficult to obtain. Some local governments may face legal limits on the amount of debt that can be backed by the full faith and credit of the local government.

With the pay-as-you-go approach, intergenerational equity is violated. This means that those who benefit from the use of the capital asset are not necessarily the ones who finance the asset. For example, if taxpayers in a community use money from current revenues to build a swimming pool, the beneficiaries of the swimming pool may not be the same as those who put their tax dollars toward building it because some, for example, may move away. This in inequitable because they helped build a facility they have never had a chance to use.

The pay-as-you-use approach provides for intergenerational equity because it helps spread the costs of the capital asset over a number of years, which makes acquisition or replacement more feasible in the majority of cases. It avoids great fluctuations in expenditures and revenues. It also provides for intergenerational equity by allowing those paying taxes or user fees for a particular capital expenditure to have access to that asset.

The issue with the pay-as-you-use approach is that financing a capital asset might exceed the useful life of that asset. In other words, an asset should not be financed for 10 years if the asset will need to be replaced in 5 years. That type of borrowing can place the organization in a financially difficult position of using current revenues to pay for capital assets that no longer exist.

The debt management plan should deal with issues such as:

- What type of bond repayment guarantee to offer investors
- How much borrowing to allow
- What to do if actual expenditures are higher or lower than the funding set aside for the projects

To a certain extent, selecting funding sources for capital projects is a matter of piecing together the funds that are available in any one year. For example, a project may be funded from a mix of current revenues, state or federal grants, bond proceeds, intergovernmental contributions (e.g., from a county or from other communities benefiting from the improvement), reimbursements, and builder contributions. Improvements to utility services may be financed through grants, the sale of revenue bonds, and service charges levied on users.

Whatever the mix of funding sources for capital projects, there are underlying policy issues that must be dealt with—preferably through an explicit debt policy statement. A policy statement protects the operating budget from excessive debt service and sets a limit on the amount (and type) of borrowing.

THE CAPITAL BUDGET

The capital budgeting cycle consists of capital budget planning, development, council/legislative budget review, and capital budget execution. The operating and capital budgets may be prepared separately during the fiscal year, or they may be prepared concurrently. During the capital improvements planning stage, CIPs are proposed. Next the capital improvement requests are prioritized based on the strategic plan goals (if a strategic plan is used) and availability of funds. During the capital budget development stage, departments submit their capital requests. The budget office refines each project budget and scope to determine if they are appropriate. This phase concludes with the highest-priority projects being included in the capital budget.

The beginning stages in the capital budget process become the link between the strategic plan and the CIP. With capital budgets, an ongoing problem exists, as with all public decisions concerning resource allocations, that is, how to fund capital priorities. When planning capital improvements, the question is "on what basis shall capital asset decisions be made to promote long-term (capital) activity A instead of short-term (operating) activity B?" The most difficult decision faced by policy makers is choosing which capital assets to acquire or replace. State and local governments usually have finite resources, and have legal and political restrictions on their ability to raise revenue. For these reasons, a limited number of capital items can be acquired during any time period. Priorities must be set to fund projects that are seen as most important. No matter how the various projects are ranked, rated, or prioritized, the funding of capital items is dependent on adequate revenue. An important difference between the capital budget and the operating budget is the method of financing. The process of developing a separate capital budget helps public decision makers to choose between funding specific individual capital assets or projects while staying within a total resource threshold.

What are some of the justification for including items in the capital budget?

- Essential public purpose
- Long useful life
- Infrequent and expensive

Unique Characteristics of Capital Budgets

Local and state governments have two types of budgets: capital and operating. The difference between the budgets is that the operating budget funds recurring activities, whereas the capital budget funds large nonrecurring expenditures for capital assets. Capital budgets are different from operating budgets in two ways. First, capital and operating financing sources are different. Capital budget items are normally paid out of one-time, earmarked sources such as debt proceeds and grants. Segregating capital expenditures helps to ensure that revenues budgeted for capital items are indeed spent for those purposes.

Second, capital and operating budgets decision-making processes are different. Preparing a capital budget involves using information obtained from the CIP. One way to help the capital budget decision-making process is to include a definition of a capital improvement/asset in the capital budget policy statement. Everything in the operating budget occurs within a fiscal year; capital projects, however usually take years to plan and implement. For example, road repairs may be defined as operating or as capital, or road repair projects intended to last less than a few years may be defined as capital. Whatever the definition, it should be used consistently, and the legal and policy implications of any deviation from this definition should be explored before a change is implemented. Unlike an operating appropriation, which is usually limited to 2 years' duration, a capital expenditure appropriation routinely may be retained, carried over from year to year, and spent until the project is completed.

Capital projects ordinarily require extensive planning reviews and site preparation. Any major change in a capital project can only be done at considerable expense. However, an amendment or revision in an operating budget can normally be during the current year. Capital projects usually have to be in sequence. For example, a street-resurfacing project may be preceded by replacement of water and sewer lines. Capital spending tends to be uneven because capital projects are often grouped in clusters. Operating expenditures tend to be relatively even throughout the year. Finally, capital projects normally require change orders and require closer monitoring of project performance, whereas actual operating expenditures are assessed against expected expenditure outlays (Table 1).

There is usually some discretion in determining what expenses relate to the operating budget and capital budget.[2] For example, if a police squad car is leased, is it part of the operating budget? One method for handling ambiguities relating to categorizing capital assets is to divide them into two types: ongoing departmental capital and large capital projects. Ongoing departmental capital includes furniture, office equipment such as computers and photocopiers, and minor remodeling. For departmental capital, the criterion of lasting a year or more and costing more than some minimum number of dollars is appropriate. In the case of motor vehicles, it is simpler to categorize all expenditures for passenger vehicles as either capital or operating, rather than to distinguish between automobiles that will last more than 1 year and those that will last less. For large capital projects, whatever labor and supplies are used can be considered part of the capital costs. The result may not be perfect, but it is clear and useful. The important point is to develop policies appropriate to the circumstances and then apply these policies consistently to avoid the potential of a lower bond rating or even to a qualified audit opinion.

The capital budget appropriates funds for the projects in the first year of the CIP and recommends the authorization of necessary bond issues. This legislative authority does not extend to the remaining years of the CIP, thereby necessitating an annual update of the plan.

After the proposed capital budget expenditures are approved, appropriated funds are allotted for expenditures as the capital project progresses through the various stages. Usually, funds are allotted so that preliminary site drawing work can begin. Awards are made from submitted bids, and the facility is constructed and/or lands purchased. To access the remaining appropriated funds, formal written justification needs to be submitted.

Table 1 Capital budget decision categories

Acquisition consists of obtaining any interest in real property, including improvements of any kind on the acquired land, except certain utility easements. All acquisitions are subject to the capital improvements process.

New construction is a single undertaking involving construction of one or more facilities. It includes 1) construction of or site work for a new facility; 2) any addition, expansion, or extension to a structure that adds to its overall exterior dimensions; and 3) complete replacement of a facility. If a new construction project meets one or more of the following criteria, it is subject to the capital budget process:

◆ It creates additional building space of 5000 square feet or greater.
◆ It has a total project cost of $250,000 or greater.
◆ It is acquired through a lease with options to purchase or any other alternative financing approach.

Improvements are a complete and usable change to an existing facility or structure. Improvements are a complete and usable change to an existing facility or structure. Improvements include 1) alteration or conversion of interior space and other physical characteristics; 2) renovation to a facility or its infrastructure; 3) restoration of a facility or structure; and 4) major repairs to restore a facility or system. If an improvement costs $500,000 or more, it is subject to the capital process.

Equipment is a tangible resource of a permanent or long-term nature used in an operation or activity. No precise criteria exist to help to determine whether equipment is an operating or capital expense.

Source: From Ref. [13].

In addition, capital appropriation balances are normally reappropriated at the end of each fiscal year until the project is completed.

CONCLUSION

The capital budget plays a critical role in most public organizations because the life of capital assets usually extends beyond 1 year. In capital budgeting, planning and careful action is essential. When used in conjunction with the strategic plan, master plan, CIP, and debt management plan, the capital budget provides a way of systematically and efficiently acquiring and funding capital expenditures. State and local governments are beginning to integrate strategic planning, master planning, capital improvement planning, and debt management. Capital budgets are used extensively by state and local governments because they improve decision making as capital assets can be financed either by revenue raised currently (taxes, charges, grants, etc.) or by borrowing on the promise to repay from future revenues. Decisions to add a capital asset such as a public facility or to make extensive repairs to an existing facility should be made on the basis of understanding the needs of the community and the resources available. The capital improvement planning process is becoming less political. Some local governments have moved away from simply soliciting input from one citizen committee to broader citizen representation by formally soliciting suggestions for capital improvement priorities from several citizen advisory boards representing different planning areas.

REFERENCES

1. Bland, R.L.; Rubin, I.S. *Budgeting: A Guide for Local Government*; International City/County Management Association: Washington, 1997.
2. Bland, R.; Nunn, S. The impact of capital spending on municipal operating budgets. Public Budg. Finance **1992**.
3. Lynch, T. *Public Budgeting in America*; Prentice Hall: Englewood Cliffs, 1995.
4. Hush, L.W.; Peroff, C. The variety of state capital budgets: A survey. Public Budg. Finance **1988**, *8*, Summer.
5. Halachmi, A.; Sekwat, A. Strategic capital budgeting and planning: Prospects at the county level. Public Budg. Financ. Manag. **1997**, *8* (4), Winter.
6. Forrester, J.P. Municipal capital budgeting: An examination. Public Budg. Finance **1993**, Summer.
7. Mikesell, J. *Fiscal Administration: Analysis and Application*; Harcourt Brace: Forth Worth, 1999.
8. MacManus, S.A. Democratizating the capital budget planning and project selection process at the local level: Assets and liabilities. Public Budg. Finance **1996**, *8* (3).
9. Griffin, M.; Hester, J. Freenets: Cities open the electronic door. Gov. Finance Rev. **1990**, *6*.
10. Rugless, J. Condition assessment survey/capital asset management. Facilit. Eng. J. **1993**, *21* (3).
11. Gordon, C. The fables and foibles of federal capital budgeting. Public Budg. Finance **1998**, *18* (3), Fall.
12. U.S. General Accounting Office. *Deferred Maintenance Report: Challenges to Implementation*; 1998; GAO/AIMD-98-42.
13. Darr, D. The benefits of long-range capital planning—The Virginia experience. Public Budg. Finance **1998**, *18* (3), Fall.

Capital Markets

Kenneth A. Kriz
University of Nebraska at Omaha, Omaha, Nebraska, U.S.A.

Peter J. Kiedrowski
Wells Fargo, Minneapolis, Minnesota, U.S.A.

INTRODUCTION

When people need to purchase a car, a house, or other things of value, they usually turn to a bank to borrow the money necessary to complete the purchase. The money is capital—financial resources available to purchase something of value. One can say that the market for residential mortgage capital, for example, consists of (mostly) individual borrowers and bank or finance company lenders. The borrowers need the capital to finance the purchase of homes.

The term capital markets refers to the informal meeting of buyers and sellers of capital. We use the term informal, because most often, there is no particular meeting place for buyers and sellers (in contrast, the New York Stock Exchange is a formal market for the buying and selling of stocks listed on the Exchange). More likely, the parties meet through an intermediary such as a broker or dealer of municipal securities. Through the exchange of securities, such as bonds for cash, municipalities are able to raise funds to invest in infrastructure, to carry out economic development activities, or to carry out any number of functions related to the exercise of government authority.

Municipal capital markets are large in a financial sense. At mid-year 2001, the municipal market comprised $1.6 trillion of debt outstanding.[1] More than $240 billion in long-term municipal securities were sold in 2000.[2] They are also large in an economic sense. Many of the important facets of American life—schooling, transportation, recreation—would not be the same without the influence of the capital markets, both as a provider of capital and as a source of financial discipline for issuers.

In this article, we will sketch the dimensions of the municipal capital markets. We will first define the demand side of the market, detailing who is buying capital, why they buy it, and what they exchange for the purchase of capital. Then we turn our attention to the supply side and describe who provides capital in the municipal market.

THE DEMAND SIDE OF THE MUNICIPAL CAPITAL MARKETS

The primary purchasers of municipal capital are state and local governments and their affiliated agencies and authorities. These organizations buy capital by selling municipal securities, most often in the form of bonds. A bond is considered a debt instrument—a loan for a defined period of time at a specified interest rate. In exchange for capital, the government organization issues a certificate, or bond, that states the interest rate to be paid and when the loaned funds are to be returned (maturity date).

State Governments

State governments borrow to build infrastructure where the benefits of that infrastructure accrue to residents of the state as a whole. As of 1997, state governments had almost half a trillion dollars ($454.5 billion) of debt outstanding.[3] On a per capita basis, that is an average of $1697 in state debt outstanding. However, there is tremendous variation in the per capita amount of state debt outstanding. Dividing the nation into nine somewhat arbitrary regions (and excluding Alaska, Hawaii, and the District of Columbia), Northeastern states have an average of $4386 in debt outstanding, and Middle Atlantic states have an average of $2779. Without those regions included, per capita debt outstanding drops to an average of $1290. The majority of states fall near this lower average. Southwestern and Southeastern states have average per capita debt burdens that are much lower than in other regions.

Nearly three-quarters of state debt outstanding (73.7%) in 1997 was ''nonguaranteed'' debt, while the other one-quarter was ''full faith and credit.'' Full faith and credit debt is issued with the full backing of the issuing jurisdiction. That jurisdiction pledges that it will use all resources at its disposal to pay back bondholders. This implies that the government will raise taxes if necessary to repay the holders of debt. Nonguaranteed debt lacks

Encyclopedia of Public Administration and Public Policy
DOI: 10.1081/E-EPAP 120010732

such a pledge. An example would be a city that issues debt to finance a new stadium. If the city issues full faith and credit debt (most often called general obligation or GO debt), regardless of the financial outcomes of the stadium, citizens of the city are responsible to repay the debt, usually through payment of property taxes to the city. By contrast, if the city issues nonguaranteed debt and the stadium is not profitable, citizens are not held responsible for repaying bondholders.

There is some variation among states in the use of nonguaranteed versus full faith and credit debt. Nine states (Idaho, Indiana, Iowa, Kansas, Kentucky, Nebraska, North Dakota, South Dakota, and Wyoming) have no state issued full faith and credit debt outstanding, and one (Colorado) has full faith and credit debt representing less than 1% of their total outstanding debt. At the other end of the spectrum, four states (Connecticut, Georgia, Nevada, and Washington) have more than 60% of their outstanding debt in the form of full faith and credit debt. With some exceptions, the heaviest users of nonguaranteed debt are Midwest and Great Plains states, while the heaviest users of full faith and credit debt are in New England, the Southeast, and the Pacific Northwest.

The largest category of debt outstanding for states is industrial development bonds (IDRBs). These nonguaranteed bonds account for 42.6% of all state debt outstanding (they also account for 49% of debt issued by states in 1997). State and local governments issue IDRBs to finance improvements of private businesses. The business then makes some form of regular payment to the governments who pass them through to bondholders. The difference between what state and local governments pay in interest on debt outstanding and what the private business would pay is a subsidy to the business; the subsidy is offered in order to encourage capital investment in an area. Again, there is substantial variation in the use of IDRBs. IDRBs represent more than three-quarters of the debt outstanding of seven states (Alaska, Idaho, Montana, Nebraska, North Dakota, South Dakota, and Wyoming). Kansas has no IDRBs outstanding, and in Arizona and Texas, IDRBs account for less than 10% of debt outstanding. With the exception of Kansas, the heaviest users of IDRBs are Great Plains, Great Lakes, and Rocky Mountain states. Southeast and Southwest states use relatively less IDRBs.

The second largest category of debt outstanding for states is debt incurred for higher education purposes. It accounts for 11.3% of state debt outstanding. Florida has the largest per capita debt outstanding for higher education—$541 or 49.5% of total debt outstanding. Other states with large per capita debt outstanding for higher education are Alabama, Indiana, and New York. Georgia and Wisconsin, by contrast, have no outstanding debt for higher education purposes.

The Relationship Between State and Local Borrowing

When discussing local government debt issuance, it is most useful to divide the local sector into different types of issuers, such as school districts or special districts. This is because each type of issuer has distinct reasons for borrowing. However, before we move to different types of issuers, we make a general observation about local government borrowing as a whole. The amount of borrowing that local governments make seems to be inversely related to the amount that the state borrows (formally, a regression of local government debt outstanding on state government debt outstanding produces a negative and significant coefficient).

There are at least two explanations for this phenomenon, one structural and the other market based. The structural explanation holds that in some states, borrowing for certain activities is effectively reserved for one level of government. One example of this is IDRBs. New Hampshire has the second highest per capita amount of state IDRB debt outstanding, while at the same time having no local IDRB debt outstanding. Massachusetts has the fifth highest level of state IDRB debt outstanding and the 48th lowest level of local IDRB debt. In these states, borrowing to subsidize private business development has (explicitly or perhaps only implicitly) been designated a state function. On the other end of the continuum of state/local responsibility, the examples are Kansas with zero state IDRB debt has the sixth highest local IDRB debt outstanding, and Florida, with the 47th highest level of state IDRB debt and the ninth highest level of local IDRB use. In these states, local governments bear the burden of financing economic development through borrowing. So, there seems to be some evidence supporting a structural explanation of the relationship between state and local borrowing (furthermore, a regression of local IDRB debt outstanding on state IDRB debt outstanding also yields a negative and significant coefficient).

The market-based explanation is based on the notion of market segmentation. Instead of one large market for municipal capital, there are actually multiple segmented markets, at least one for each state and potentially more for different types of securities. The interest rate that an issuer must offer in order to sell bonds is based not only on prevailing interest rates and on the default risk of an issue, but also on the amount of demand for municipal capital.[a] In states where the state government issues debt

---

[a]For more on segmented markets, see Hendershott, Patric H.; Kidwell, David S. The impact of relative security supplies: A test with data from a regional tax-exempt bond market. *Journal of Money, Credit and Banking* **1978**, *10* (3), 337–347.

quite often, the increased demand may bid up interest rates. This forces the local issuer to sell bonds at higher interest costs or to forego borrowing. While it would be nearly impossible to test this explanation directly, the market segmentation hypothesis has held up quite well in empirical tests.

Local Governments

Local governments are large issuers of municipal bonds. As of 1997, local governments had $750 billion in debt outstanding. As mentioned above, there are several types of local government issuers, each with a unique set of needs for municipal capital. We will consider four types of issuers: counties, cities (along with townships with borrowing authority similar to cities), special districts, and school districts.

There is large variation in the amount and type of debt issued by U.S. counties. In total, counties had $163 billion in debt outstanding, or about 21% of the local total. The average per capita county debt outstanding for states was just over $610. But the standard deviation of per capita county debt is almost as large as the mean. The range of county debt is from essentially no debt outstanding (in Vermont, the figure is less than one cent per capita) to over $2000 per person in two states (in Maryland and Nevada). In eight states (Maryland and Nevada, as well as Florida, Kansas, Kentucky, Mississippi, North Carolina, and Tennessee), county debt outstanding is equal to or greater than state debt. However, in most of the remaining 42 states, state debt far outpaces county debt. County debt issuance tends to be highest in the Middle Atlantic, Southeast, Southwest, and Western states. The Midwest ranks far below the other regions, and there is little county debt outstanding in New England states.

IDRBs are by far the largest reason for counties borrowing. Counties had $62.4 billion in IDRBs outstanding in 1997, or about 38% of their total debt outstanding. In six states (Arkansas, Kentucky, North Dakota, Oklahoma, West Virginia, and Wyoming), IDRBs comprise over 85% of total county debt outstanding. In per capita terms, the largest state concentrations of county IDRB use are in the Middle Atlantic, Mideast (Ohio, Kentucky, West Virginia), Southeast, Midwest, and Upper Great Plains (North Dakota, Wyoming) states. States in the Pacific Northwest and Great Lakes regions have relatively little county IDRB debt outstanding. Four states in New England (Maine, Vermont, New Hampshire, and Massachusetts) have no county IDRB debt outstanding. The next largest amount of county debt outstanding (about $8.3 billion) is for elementary and secondary (K–12) education. Most of the debt outstanding in this category is

concentrated in four states (Maryland, North Carolina, Tennessee, and Virginia). ·

Cities are by far the largest issuers of local debt. As of 1997, cities and townships had $302.2 billion in debt outstanding. On a per capita basis, that amounts to about $1100 per person. Again, there is some variation in city borrowing but not as much as with counties. Alaska, New York, Minnesota, and Colorado cities all have more than $2000 in per capita city debt outstanding, while Idaho, Maryland, Mississippi, South Carolina, and West Virginia each have less than $400 per capita. The heaviest city borrowers are located in the upper Midwest, lower Great Plains, and Southwest regions.

The largest reason for city borrowing is to provide utility services to residents. Cities had $64.7 billion in outstanding utility debt, or about 21% of total city debt outstanding. Cities in the Southwest and West Coast regions tend to have more debt outstanding than in other regions. Most of the utility debt outstanding is for water and electric utilities. Within the general category of utilities, water utilities are 69% of the debt outstanding, electric utilities comprise 29% of the debt outstanding, and gas utilities the remaining 2%. The Southwest, Rocky Mountain, and Southeast regions have the most debt outstanding for water utilities, while the West Coast, Southwest, lower Midwest (Iowa, Nebraska, Missouri, and Arkansas), and Mideast (Kentucky and Tennessee) regions have the most electric utility borrowing. Most utility debt (81%) is nonguaranteed. City water utilities are most often run on a fee-for-service basis. The fees provide a dedicated revenue stream that can be leveraged with bond issuance to provide increased water system capacity.

The other major area of borrowing by cities is once again for industrial development. But, there is marked variation of city borrowing in this area. In 18 states, less than 10% of debt outstanding is IDRBs. However, in 10 states, more than one-third of borrowing is for industrial development. Also, there appears to be no geographic pattern to city use of IDRBs. The states with the heaviest use are spread throughout each geographic region.

There is surprising variation in the amount that school districts borrow to fund capital investment in K–12 education. School districts across the United States had $105 billion in outstanding debt in 1997, or about $393 per capita. School districts in 11 states had more than $500 per capita in outstanding debt, led by Nevada, Minnesota, and Pennsylvania with more than $900 per capita. Conversely, 10 states had outstanding school district debt of less than $200 per capita, with five states (Connecticut, Indiana, Massachusetts, Rhode Island, Tennessee, and Virginia) having less than $100 per capita outstanding. However, these figures are somewhat misleading. In these states, other government types borrow to fund capital investment in K–12 education. In Indiana, school districts are considered separate special districts. In Connecticut, Massachusetts, and Rhode Island, cities and townships borrow for this purpose. Finally, in Tennessee and Virginia, counties carry the bulk of K–12 debt. Once the borrowing by all types of government for K–12 education is taken into account, only one state, North Dakota, has less than $200 per capita in outstanding K–12 debt.

The final category of borrower that we consider here is the special district. Special districts have more debt outstanding in aggregate than do school districts—$179 billion in 1997. The purposes for which special districts issue debt are diverse. The largest category of debt outstanding is for electric utilities. Just over $51 billion of special district debt for this purpose was outstanding in 1997. Once again, variation is high in electric utility debt. Seventeen states have no special district electric utility debt outstanding, and 25 have less than $10 per capita outstanding. However, nine states have more than $300 per capita outstanding, and three states (Nebraska, Utah, and Washington) top $1000 per capita. Another large category of special district debt outstanding is for water utilities. The heaviest issuers of special district water utility debt are in the Southwest and Rocky Mountain regions.

In sum, the demand side of municipal capital markets shows a wide variety of issuers issuing debt for divergent purposes. These issuers may be in competition with each other for scarce municipal capital. We next turn to the supply side of the market for municipal capital.

THE SUPPLY SIDE OF MUNICIPAL CAPITAL MARKETS

Who provides capital to state and local governments? The suppliers (buyers of municipal securities) have changed over time. In 1980, commercial banks were the largest buyers of municipal securities, holding 37% of outstanding debt; individual investors through direct holdings, mutual funds, and fiduciary accounts held 34%; property and casualty insurance companies held 22%; and other organizations held 7%. By 2000, the individual investor became the largest owner of municipal securities. Individuals owned 71% of municipal debt outstanding in 2000, either directly, through mutual funds (which grew from 2% in 1980 to 31% in 2000), or in fiduciary accounts. Property and casualty insurance companies owned another 12% in 2000. Commercial banks fell to 7%, and other organizations rose to 10%.

Individuals

Individuals buy municipal securities most often because the interest paid on the securities is in general not included in the calculation of income on federal income tax returns. The size of these "tax preferences," and how they impact various buyers of municipal securities, is often the driving force behind the supply of financial capital. The Sixteenth Amendment to the U.S. Constitution (which created the provision for the federal income tax) does not authorize tax exemption of municipal securities directly; rather Congress must provide it and budget for its effects annually. The original authorizing federal income tax legislation contained a specific exemption for interest on municipal securities. There have been various attempts over the years to tax municipal securities interest, although there have been none in recent years, and the constitutionality of the proposals has been hotly contested. In 1986, South Carolina contested the right of Congress to require that municipal bonds be in registered or book entry form to be exempt from federal income taxes (Congress had done away with the right to hold bond certificates, with their negotiable bearer coupons, due to concerns about the sale of coupons outside of the normal coupon interest redemption). The U.S. Supreme Court ruled against the state of South Carolina on that issue, and also ruled that Congress had the right to tax municipal bond interest if it chose to do so. Congress could also change major provisions of the federal income tax (for example, create a flat-rate structure) that would diminish or eliminate the tax preferences of municipal securities.[4] In most states, the interest from municipal securities issued within the state is also exempt from state and local taxes. In addition, interest income derived from securities of the territories of the United States is free from federal, state, and local income taxation in all 50 states.

An example of the tax reduction for individuals helps to illustrate the advantages of municipal securities over taxable debt securities. Assume a couple with an income of $155,000 (which puts them in the 36% federal income tax bracket) files a joint return. They have $30,000 to invest and are considering two possible investments: a tax-exempt municipal bond yielding 5% and a taxable corporate bond yielding 7.5%. If the couple invested in the municipal bond, they would annually earn $1500 and pay no federal taxes on that interest. The taxable bond would provide the couple $2250 annually, but they would have to pay $810 in federal income taxes on that interest every year, so their after-tax earnings would be $1440 (or $60 less than the municipal bond). The tax-exempt bond would be an even better investment in a state that had an income tax and exempted municipal bond interest from taxation. Market participants often speak of the "taxable-equivalent yield," which is the interest rate an investor would have to earn on a taxable bond to equal a municipal bond with a specific interest rate. (In our above example, the couple would have a taxable-equivalent yield of

7.8125% for a 5% municipal bond, taking into account only federal tax consequences of the investment decision.)

There are other tax provisions that are important to individuals as they consider municipal securities. One of these is the taxation of capital gains. While the interest on municipal securities is exempt from the federal income tax, any gains or losses realized from selling municipal securities are treated as taxable securities sales and are subject to the capital gains tax, either short or long (depending on whether held for longer than 12 months before sale). Capital losses may be applied to capital gains to offset the capital gains tax, however.

Another provision for individuals is that certain types of municipal bonds are taxable, and certain types are subject to the federal alternative minimum tax (AMT is a set of provisions that restricts the amount of tax-free income that can be derived by an investor). Private activity municipal securities (such as IDRBs) and certain refunding bonds (which in combination account for over 10% of all municipal bonds issued) are included in the calculation of the AMT. A further complicating provision is that for some individuals, a greater portion of their social security benefits can be taxed if they have tax-exempt interest. There are also special tax provisions for buying original issue discount bonds (bonds sold at prices far below their face value, for instance, a $5000 face value bond sold at $2000), bonds at a premium (bonds selling above face value), and bonds with a market discount (bonds sold below face value but not by as much as original issue discount bonds. Individuals may not borrow to buy municipal bonds, and annual municipal interest must be reported on their federal income tax returns.

Property and Casualty Insurance Companies

Property and casualty insurance companies also own municipal securities in order to take advantage of tax preferences. These companies need tax-exempt income as their business fluctuates. In years of poor insurance underwriting results, they have less need for municipal securities with their tax exemption in their insurance portfolio, because they can offset their net income with the underwriting losses. In good underwriting years, they need the municipal income from their insurance portfolio to be tax exempt to maximize after-tax profit. Property and casualty insurance companies tend to favor long-term bonds and revenue bonds in order to increase the annual interest. In 1999, 24% of the assets outstanding of these insurance companies were in municipal securities.

Commercial Banks

Commercial banks own municipal securities for tax exemption as well. As noted above, their share of mu-

nicipal capital supply dropped over 20 percentage points from 1980 to 2000. The Tax Reform Act of 1986 removed many of the tax incentives for commercial banks, and the ones remaining were difficult for large commercial banks to utilize.

Commercial banks still utilize municipal securities for two purposes. First, they can buy bank-qualified municipal securities into their bank portfolio, and the carrying cost is tax deductible. Bank-qualified municipal securities are general obligation bonds for public purposes of jurisdictions (or revenue bonds issued for nonprofit organizations within their boundaries) that offer no more than $10 million dollars in securities annually. Small banks utilize these bonds more than the large banks, because of their size. Second, banks will actually make loans to governmental units. This helps fulfill their requirements under the Community Reinvestment Act. Also, government loans are more attractive in credit markets, where there are few opportunities to extend credit with reasonable risk to businesses. Commercial banks tend to favor short-and medium-term securities that better match the maturities of their bank portfolios. In 1999, only 2% of commercial banks' assets were in municipal securities.

Other Organizations

The other organizations purchasing municipal securities are small companies, large pension funds, and hedge funds. Small companies that are owned by an individual may choose to use municipal securities for their tax-exempt nature. The case with large pension and hedge funds is quite different. These organizations actually monitor the municipal markets for discontinuities between rate patterns on municipal bonds and taxable treasury securities. They believe that the municipal market will tend to the norm, and they hope to capture gains on temporary discrepancies in prices from the actual value of the bond (this technique of exploiting temporary mispricing between different types of bonds is called arbitrage). Municipal futures and options can be used for leveraged-hedging (providing some insurance against falling bond or stock prices) and speculation. Futures are securities that pay a holder the difference between the actual price of the bond or bond index and some future price. Options are rights to buy or sell a bond or an index at a specific price at some future date.

Other Factors Important to the Buyers of Municipal Bonds

For all municipal securities investors, the provisions of each individual bond will also determine their attractiveness beyond their tax preference. A security's stated interest rate, call features (calls are options that the bond issuer puts in the bond indenture that allow the issuer to redeem the bond at a given point in time at a specified price), source of repayment, credit rating, liquidity, maturity, general economic conditions, securities, market conditions, and the perceived credit quality and sector of the jurisdiction influence demand.

CONCLUSION

In short, many institutions and individuals comprise the municipal securities market: Governments and associated special districts demand municipal capital by issuing municipal debt. The buyers of that debt, including individuals by themselves and through mutual funds, insurance companies, banks, and other organizations, purchase the bonds for tax preferences and as part of their overall investment strategy. Purchasing the bonds provides capital to governments for economic development, education, basic public services, and for other capital-intensive purposes.

REFERENCES

1. Board of Governors of the Federal Reserve System. *Trends in the Holdings of Municipal Securities*; http://www.bondmarkets.com/Research/munios.shtml (accessed 20 August 2001).
2. Thomson Financial Services. *Short-and Long-Term Municipal Issuance*; http://www.bondmarkets.com/Research/issuance.shtml (accessed 20 August 2001).
3. U.S. Census Bureau. *State and Local Government Finances: 1997 Census of Government*; http://www.census.gov/govs/www/estimate97.html (accessed 18 July 2001).
4. *South Carolina v. Baker*. 485 US 505.

Cash Management for State and Local Governments

Dwight V. Denison
New York University, New York, New York, U.S.A.

INTRODUCTION

Cash is the lifeblood of a public organization. Without cash, it becomes difficult, if not impossible, to provide goods and services. Governments without adequate cash cannot buy garbage trucks, maintain bridges, pay teachers' salaries, or operate social programs. On the other hand, cash not actively employed in providing government services should be prudently invested and earning interest revenues.

The day-to-day operations of governments generate and consume cash. Cash receipts arise from tax, fee, grant, and interest collections. Cash disbursements occur with vendor payments, employee salaries, finance charges, and capital expenditures. Cash must be obtained through borrowing during a cash deficit. Excess cash balances provide the opportunity for investment revenue. Comprehensive cash management is comprised of four primary components: cash forecasting, cash mobilization, investment, and bank relations. Each component is vital in fostering good fiscal health.

CASH FORECASTING

Cash management insures that cash inflows are adequate to meet cash outflows. To do so requires an ability to forecast the arrival and amount of cash receipts and disbursements. The timing of cash receipts is classified as certain, forecastable, or unpredictable cash flows. Certain flows are known in advance of when they occur. Examples of certain cash expenditures include contract salaries and interest payments. Forecastable cash flows can be estimated with reasonable accuracy using statistical methods and professional judgment. Examples of forecastable cash flow include sales tax collections and pension fund disbursements. Unpredictable cash flows arise from unanticipated events such as a lawsuit settlement or severe weather damage.

Governments usually forecast the operating cash deficit or surplus on at least a monthly basis through a cash budget. The cash budget tracks cash receipts and disbursements while taking into account the collection cycle of receivables and payment schedules. Monthly cash bud-

gets help to identify financing needs and to determine investment strategies. Daily cash balances can be monitored on a daily basis to determine opportunities for investing idle cash balances. Adams and Harrison[1] discuss common techniques for forecasting cash balances.

CASH MOBILIZATION

Cash mobilization is the process of maximizing cash balances by decreasing the time it takes to collect cash owed to the government and by deferring disbursements. Unless efforts are made to mobilize cash, cash balances may be insufficient to meet disbursements. Furthermore, aggressive cash mobilization potentially increases the idle cash balances available for investment.

The first aspect in cash mobilization is to monitor the accounts and taxes receivable to the government. An aging schedule can be used to track delinquent tax payments and help determine appropriate collection efforts. Governments usually promote timely tax payments by imposing charges on delinquent accounts. In cases of nonpayment, liens are frequently imposed. As an additional incentive, some governments offer a discount if the payment is received prior to the due date. Governments should regularly monitor the billing and collection processes to find ways to promote timely payments and reduce delinquency.

Larger governments often take steps to reduce collection float. Collection float is the time it takes for the funds to become available in government bank accounts once the payment has been submitted. Collection float is the total time it takes to transmit the payment from the payer to the government (transmission or mail float), plus the time it takes for the government to process the payment (process float), plus the time it takes for the payment to clear in the bank account (clearing float). To illustrate, consider that a citizen remits a property tax payment on June 1. It takes 2 days by mail to reach the revenue department and 1 day for the revenue department to process and deposit the check. Then, the check takes 1 day to clear before the funds become available for the government to spend. The collection float in this case is 4 days. Every day of collection float represents lost interest re-

Encyclopedia of Public Administration and Public Policy
DOI: 10.1081/E-EPAP 120010740

venue to the government, for if the cash were available, it could be invested.

While it is impractical to expect that collection float could be completely eliminated, there are several techniques that governments employ to reduce collection float. Payment of taxes is primarily done via check, but some governments have implemented electronic transfers directly from one bank account to another through the Automated Clearing House (ACH). Electronic transfers between accounts reduce the mail and clearing floats. In the prior example, electronic transfer would reduce the collection mail float by at least 3 days. ACH transfers are recommended for transferring large payments between governments and are also convenient for smaller reoccurring payments.[2]

Lockbox services are provided by banks to expedite the deposit of remitted checks, and if strategically located geographically, will also reduce mail float. In a basic lockbox service, the bank empties a P.O. box, deposits checks to the appropriate account, and forwards the documentation to the government. Many state and local governments significantly reduce collection float through the use of lockboxes.

The second aspect of cash mobilization requires that governments pay current obligations without incurring unintended fees or charges. Generally, obligations are not prepaid unless there are compensating incentives or discounts; otherwise, the cash could remain invested and generating interest. Vendors usually impose late charges if a payment is not received by the due date. Governments should avoid paying late charges unnecessarily but may consider late payment as an alternative to borrowing to meet a temporary cash deficit.

Governments may utilize float to detain cash outflows and increase idle cash balances. Disbursement float is the collection float in reverse. Governments can increase disbursement float by increasing mail float or clearing float. For example, there are generally 2 to 3 days of disbursement float on employees' wage checks before the balance posts to the government's bank account. In practice, excessive actions to extend disbursement float may result in late payments and jeopardize relationships with suppliers. Actions to extend clearing float, such as remote disbursement, are opposed by the Federal Reserve System.

Electronic transfers (ACH) have several benefits for disbursements. Electronic transfers are immediate, meaning the cash can be held until just prior to the due date. Electronic transfers can reduce paperwork and administration and therefore may be more cost effective than printed check disbursements. Moreover, supplier relationships are enhanced, because ACH transfers reduce their collection float.[2]

The third aspect of cash mobilization is concentrating cash into pools that make it easier to invest. Banks offer a number of services for concentrating cash into pools that preserve the legal restrictions for accounting on the separate funds. Two common services are the sweep account and the zero balance account. In a sweep account, the bank transfers the balance at the end of the day from each individual account to a central account, where the money can be invested overnight. The next morning, the appropriate balance is returned to the originating account. The zero balance account operates on the reverse principle. Individual account balances are zero, with the combined balances being held in a central account. Once a draft is presented to an individual account, the draft is honored, and the appropriate amount is transferred from the central account to bring the account balance back to zero.

Cash pooling makes forecasting daily cash needs easier, because pooled cash flows become less volatile and are more predictable than the cash flows of each component fund. As a result, concentrating cash balances also benefits investment aspects of cash management.

INVESTMENT

Cash not actively employed in providing government services should be invested and earning interest revenues. Investment revenues are increasingly important to governments with restricted tax revenues. Because higher rates of return are generally compensation for assuming greater risk in the portfolio, the public has been increasingly concerned about the regulation of government investment practices. Public concern in the oversight of government investment practices is warranted, because loss of tax dollars, potential default on debt, or even bankruptcy, can result from irresponsible investment.

The basic investment objectives considered when investing idle cash balances include liquidity, security, and return. Liquidity refers to the ability to transform the investment into cash. Liquidity is an important priority when investments may need to be converted to cash to meet unanticipated cash disbursements. Security refers to the credit and market risk associated with the investment. All investments carry some degree of risk, but certain classifications of investments are more vulnerable to loss. For example, securities issued by the U.S. Treasury have a low risk of default and are therefore called "risk-free," while noninvestment-grade corporate bonds have a much higher probability of default. The return or yield from investments is the interest revenue that provides additional cash into government coffers. Investment returns may include direct interest payments or gains that result from securities purchased at a discount. Investment returns also include inflows of dividend payments and capital gains from mutual funds and stocks.

The investment objectives of liquidity, security, and yield typically conflict. In general, investment alternatives with higher risk generate higher yields. Under normal market conditions, higher yields are also associated with investments of longer maturity, as illustrated in the typical yield curve. Thus, aggressive maximization of yields often requires the sacrifice of security and liquidity.

Governments should establish investment goals through a written investment policy.[3] Each government prioritizes the basic investment objectives based on cash flow characteristics, organizational goals, and various external factors, including legal, regulatory, and economic environments. Money market securities vary with respect to liquidity, security, and yields, and therefore, the securities held in a portfolio are screened to ensure compliance with the investment policy and to make sure investment objectives are met. A listing and description of common money market securities is presented in Table 1.

Permissible Assets

Security of principal is crucial for government organizations, because investment default results in the loss of public funds and invokes political and fiscal repercussions. Consequently, all states constrain to some degree the investment of idle cash to permissible investment assets that meet a minimum standard of security. In a recent survey, all but five of the states reported administrative statutes influencing the permissible assets in which the state treasurer could invest public funds. Furthermore, 14 of the states also had constitutional restrictions in addition to state statutes regulating permissible assets.[4]

Municipalities are also subject to legal restrictions when investing idle cash. Based on a survey of cities with over 200,000 in population, state statutes are the source of restrictions in 76% of the responding cities, and 6% of the municipalities are subject to state constitutional restrictions on permissible assets. In addition, municipal law dictates permissible assets for 41% of the surveyed cities.[5]

It is important to emphasize that the basic investment objectives of liquidity, security, and yield are constrained by permissible assets. As presented in Table 1, 94% or more of the states permit the purchase of repurchase agreements and U.S. Treasury and agency obligations. Other investments commonly allowed are certificates of deposits issued by state banks and commercial paper. Repos, U.S. Treasury and agency obligations, and CDs comprise

the core of permissible assets. Other assets like banker's acceptances and commercial paper are now more permissible than 15 years ago.[6]

Arbitrage

Investment of tax-exempt bond proceeds is regulated by the Internal Revenue Service (IRS). The IRS is concerned most with arbitrage of tax-exempt bond issues. In this context, arbitrage occurs when proceeds of tax-exempt bond issues are invested to generate investment revenue from securities bearing higher taxable yields. The difference between the investment revenue and the interest payment on the bond is a cash subsidy that comes at the expense of the federal government. The rules defining arbitrage can be tedious, but generally, arbitrage is not a concern if the proceeds are used in a timely manner to construct buildings or purchase other capital assets.[7] Minor arbitrage infractions require cash payments to the IRS equal to the subsidy. Egregious arbitrage threatens the tax-exempt status of the bond issue.

Investment Strategy

The investment objectives of security, liquidity, and yield are accomplished through the investment strategy. The investment strategy employed by the portfolio management may vary among the different types of cash balances. The nature of the idle cash balances invested by state governments can be classified into three types: temporary surplus, long-term surplus, and pooled surplus. A temporary surplus results from the lag between revenue collections and expenditure disbursements in the general, special-revenue, capital, and enterprise funds. A temporary cash surplus will be expended within the year, and therefore, liquidity is crucial. Long-term cash balances held by the state for a year or longer are often associated with the trust, pension, or debt service funds. A long-term investment horizon provides more flexibility in the investment strategy to increase yields without compromising security. Pooled surplus results from the pooling of cash balances from separate funds or even multiple governments. The characteristics of pooled surpluses are different in nature than the comprising temporary or long-term funds, because pooling can increase the stability and predictability of the cash flows.

Cash-flow characteristics also have a great deal of influence on the strategies utilized in managing the investment of idle cash balances. Government funds with more certain cash flows may be managed more aggres-

Table 1 Description and permissibility of select money market securities

Security	Description	Percent of states where permissible
Bankers acceptances (BA)	BA is a negotiable draft payable at a specified future date where a bank guarantees payment at maturity. BAs are used to make payment easier in the movement of goods, particularly international trade. The credit risk of a BA depends on the accepting bank. BAs are highly liquid and are bought and sold at a discount from par. ($25,000–$1,000,000 denomination)	78%
Commercial paper (CP)	CPs are unsecured short-term obligations (1 to 270 days) of a corporation usually sold at a discount from the par value. There is a strong secondary market, and the credit risk depends on the creditworthiness of the issuing corporation. (usually $100,000 denomination)	90%
State investment pools	This is a money market fund operated by a state government for municipal and county investors. Pools provide good liquidity and diversification at substantially lower minimum investment requirements.	60%
Negotiable and nonnegotiable certificates of deposit (CD)	Financial institutions issue certificates of deposit for maturities generally up to 1 year but may have maturities up to 5 years. The liquid (negotiable) aspects of the CD depend on the reputation of the issuing bank. Negotiable CDs are normally denominated in $100,000 per round lot with interest paid semiannually or at maturity. Nonnegotiable CDs can be purchased at much lower denominations, but there is no secondary market. Some states also require that CDs be obtained from banks within the state.	In state 88%; National 48%
Repurchase agreements (repo)	Repos are a collateralized transaction, where a securities dealer agrees to sell securities (usually U.S. Treasury or agency obligations) to the investor and then repurchase the securities at a predetermined price on some future date. The investor receives a fixed rate of interest as compensation for the exchange. Repos require $100,000 to $1 million to initiate and are negotiated between dealer and investor and are therefore difficult to sell on a secondary market. However, the maturities are overnight to 90 days and, therefore, are highly liquid. The risk of repos depends on the counter party and the market value of the collateral.	98%
U.S. treasury bills, notes, and bonds	These are highly liquid securities that are direct obligations of the U.S. Government, and therefore, are considered credit risk-free. T-bills have short maturities and are purchased at a discount. Notes and bonds are longer-term securities that generally pay semiannual interest and are vulnerable to market risk if sold before maturity.	96%
U.S. agency bonds	These are low-risk securities issued by U.S. Agency corporations (Fannie Mae, Freddie Mac, Sallie Mae, Ginnie Mae). They are issued in denominations of $1000 and $5000 with maturities usually more than a year, and therefore, they are vulnerable to market risk.	94%

(Continued)

Table 1 Description and permissibility of select money market securities (*Continued*)

Security	Description	Percent of states where permissible
State/local government obligations	State and local governments issue general obligation securities that are backed by the full faith and credit of the government and therefore have a low risk of default. Securities can be short-term notes or bonds with longer maturities. Revenues bonds have more credit risk, as the underlying collateral is a pledged revenue source. Interest on these securities is generally exempt from federal income tax and may be exempt from the state income tax.	70%
Corporate notes/bonds	These offer fixed income security that obligates the corporation to make scheduled payments to the bondholder. They vary in maturity and denomination and are vulnerable to credit and market risks.	68%
Corporate stocks	These are an equity instrument that constitutes an ownership share in a corporation and therefore may exhibit high financial risk. Stock share prices fluctuate widely with the market. There exists a strong secondary market for the stock of many publicly traded firms, but they are considered too risky by most organizations for short-term investment.	Domestic 32%; Foreign 22%
Derivatives	Derivatives are financial securities, where the market value depends on an underlying market indicator. For example, STRIPS are the principal portion of Treasury Bonds sold at a deep discount (zero coupon bond) that are extremely vulnerable to market risk.	14%

Permissibility percentages are calculated from NAST.[14,15]

sively to enhance yield without unduly compromising liquidity and security. On the other hand, funds with unpredictable cash flows require a more liquid strategy to ensure the availability of funds on demand.

Investment strategies may also be influenced by the expertise of the state's investment staff and the ability to consolidate cash balances and manage risk. Investment strategies are generally classified as active or passive, depending on assumptions about market efficiency. An efficient market is one in which a security's price reflects all public information. This is important, because in an efficient market, it would be futile to devote time searching for underpriced bargains or avoiding overpriced lemons. A passive investment strategy assumes market efficiency. Therefore, there is no effort to play the market in order to enhance returns. The goal of a passive investment strategy is to maximize coupon income through a buy and hold approach. On the other hand, an active investment strategy assumes the portfolio can outperform the market by searching for undervalued securities and incorporating expectations about future market conditions. For example, a portfolio manager may purchase a 5-year treasury note with the expectation that interest rates are declining, and the note can be sold in 30 days at

a capital gain. For more on investment strategies, see Ramsey and Hackbart.[8]

Prudent Person

Many states and municipalities are implementing a prudent person rule. The prudent person rule emphasizes preservation of capital and discourages speculative transactions by requiring that the government's funds be invested with the same discretion and care that a reasonably well-informed person would use to manage their own affairs.[9] The advantage of the prudent person rule is that the portfolio manager is held legally accountable for speculative investing, without the governing board being overly concerned that the investment policy may not delineate the permissibility of every new financial market innovation or derivative. Still, the prudent person rule does not excuse a legislative body or governing board of its oversight responsibilities.

Local Government Investment Pools

Local government investment pools are increasingly popular for investing idle cash from state and local governments. Investment pools generally operate as a mutual fund, with investors purchasing a share of the portfolio. Total portfolio returns are distributed to the investors proportional to the number of shares. The advantage of investment pools is that the governments can obtain greater diversification at lower investment minimums. There are 30 local government investment funds operated through states for a combined portfolio worth more than $143 billion, with more than 16,000 participating governments nationwide.[10]

Outsourcing

Governments are increasingly outsourcing investment functions; nearly 65% of the cities responding to a 1999 survey utilized an external investment manager or consultant. While municipalities can delegate investment selection, the municipality remains responsible for the safety and liquidity of governmental funds. This does not mean, however, that the investment advisor does not have due diligence in adherence to investment policies and acting prudently. The Government Finance Officers Association (GFOA) has produced guidelines on the contracting of services that underscore the issues of investment priorities and permissible assets.[11]

BANK RELATIONS

Bank relationships are vital to effective cash management. While banks provide core services like checking

and savings accounts, banks are also expanding the range of cash management services available. Table 2 lists a range of services that banks provide to help the cash mobilization and investment efforts of governments. For an in-depth description of specific bank services, see Harrell[12] and Redlin.[13]

Banks do not provide services for free. Banks recoup the costs of these services through fees or compensating balances. The cost of compensating balances to a government is the foregone interest revenue. The decision to utilize banking services should consider the costs and benefits of the arrangement, keeping in mind that the charges for specific services often vary from bank to bank. As with any outsourcing, contracts should detail the services provided and specify fees and other compensation.

CONCLUSION

Cash is the lifeblood of a public organization, and cash management ensures the vitality of the organization. The four primary components of cash management are cash forecasting, cash mobilization, investment, and bank relations. Cash management must be adapted to meet the needs of a specific public organization. For some organizations, the fundamentals of cash management discussed here may be a sufficient foundation in forming effective cash management processes. Most, however, will need to explore the cash management components in more detail through the references and additional study. As long as governments continue to bolster nontax revenues and feel the pressure to improve fiscal efficiency, cash management will play a vital role in public administration.

Table 2 Types of cash management services offered through banks

Collection services	Disbursement services
• Electronic (ACH) collections	• Electronic (ACH) payments
• Wire transfers	• Wire transfers
• Preauthorized checks	• Concentration and zero-balance accounts
• Lockbox services	• Controlled disbursement accounts
• Armored car services	• Account reconciliation
• Night deposit	• Check imaging and digital archiving
• Coin counting services	
Credit services	Investment services
• Revolving line of credit	• Certificates of deposit
• Letter of credit	• Money market instruments
• Short-term notes	• Custodial arrangements for repurchase agreements
• Leasing	• Overnight sweep accounts
• Community and economic development lending	

REFERENCES

1. Adam, P.S.; Harrison, W.A. *Essentials of Cash Management*, 6th Ed.; Treasury Management Association: Bethesda, MD, 1998; Chapter 11.
2. McAndrews, J. The automated clearinghouse system: Moving toward electronic payment. Bus. Rev. **1994**, 15–23 (July/August).
3. Government Finance Officers Association. *Recommended Practices for State and Local Governments*; Government Finance Officers Association: Chicago, IL, 2001; 44, May.
4. National Association of State Treasurers. *State Treasury Activities and Functions*; National Association of State Treasurers: Lexington, KY, 2001; 44, Table 20.
5. Denison, D.V. How conservative are municipal invest-

ment practices in large cities. Munic. Finance J. **2002**, *23* (1).

6. Denison, D.V. *States' Investment of Idle Cash Balances*; Association for Budgeting and Financial Management National Conference: Washington, DC, 1998, November.

7. Golembiewski, P.; Bornholdt, G.; Jones, T. *Allocation and Accounting Regulations For Arbitrage Bonds*; http://www.irs.ustreas.gov/plain/bus_info/eo/topics.html (referenced June 2001).

8. Ramsey, J.R.; Hackbart, M.M. Public Funds Management: Current Practices and Future Trends. In *The Handbook of Municipal Bonds and Public Finance*; Lamb, R., Leigland, J., Rappaport, S., Eds.; New York Public Institute of Finance: New York, 1993.

9. Miller, G.; Larson, M.C.; Zorn, W.P. *Investing Public Funds*, 2nd Ed.; Government Finance Officers Association: Chicago, IL, 1998; 44.

10. National Association of State Treasurers. *State Treasury Activities and Functions*; National Association of State Treasurers: Lexington, KY, 2001; 76.

11. Government Finance Officers Association. *Recommended Practices for State and Local Governments*; Government Finance Officers Association: Chicago, IL, May 2001; 59–61.

12. Harrell, R. *Banking Relations*; Government Finance Officers Association: Chicago, IL, 1986.

13. Redlin, B.M. Cash management technology for small governments. Gov. Finance Rev. **1999**, *15* (4), 55–57.

14. National Association of State Treasurers. *State Treasury Activities and Functions*; National Association of State Treasurers: Lexington, KY, 2001; 59, Table 28.

15. National Association of State Treasurers. *State Treasury Activities and Functions*; National Association of State Treasurers: Lexington, KY, 2001; 78, Table 38.

Citizen Participation in the Budget Process: Exit, Voice, and Loyalty

Carol Ebdon
University of Nebraska at Omaha, Omaha, Nebraska, U.S.A.

INTRODUCTION

Various methods enhance citizen participation in the budget process. Even though empirical evidence is sparse, participation appears to be beneficial when it educates citizens in the complexities and costs of government services, and may help to reduce distrust of government. There is still little evidence, partly due to methodological difficulties, that participation actually changes budget outcomes, although several cases and anecdotal stories support the notion that there is some effect.

In spite of the perceived benefits of participation, opportunities are still not prevalent. This is particularly true early in the budget process, when public opinion would conceivably have the greatest impact on decision making. To move beyond education to true two-way dialog regarding the budget is not easy, due to structural and cost barriers, difficulties in gaining input from numerous representative citizens, and conflicts in the roles and attitudes of both administrators and elected officials.

PARTICIPATION MECHANISMS

Researchers looking at general participation mechanisms have found that it is most beneficial when it occurs early in the process and when it is two-way deliberative communication, rather than simply one-way information sharing.[1] In the case of the budget process, then, this requires more than the ubiquitous public hearing that is usually held at the end of the process, just before final adoption by the legislative body. Citizens also have a voice in direct voter referenda, which are often required for governments to increase taxes or to issue general obligation debt. Again, though, referenda usually occur at the end of the process, and voters may not be well informed about the potential consequences of their actions.

Citizen surveys can be used early in the budget process to determine service satisfaction levels, needs, and priorities. For example, the city of Auburn, Alabama, used surveys prior to budget development; citizens re-

viewed a list of city services and were asked to which they would give the highest priority in the upcoming budget.[2] Surveys can show officials citizen satisfaction levels, responses may represent views of the public at large, and if used consistently over time can show important trends in opinions. However, appropriate question design is important, and surveys may not reflect the intensity of a respondent's opinion.[3] In addition, cost is a factor, and the responses may not be well thought out.[4]

Public meetings may also be used to discuss budget issues during or prior to budget development. These forums provide citizens the opportunity to voice their opinions and can provide for two-way communication early in the process. However, attendance is often low and may not represent the community as a whole, and participants may have insufficient knowledge for effective input.[3] Some communities use public meetings in an intensive way for a broad "community visioning" process to plan for the future or allow citizens to work through options related to major issues.[5] A Minnesota school district superintendent used a public deliberation process to cut $2.4 million from the budget after significant state aid reductions. The process lasted 4 months, beginning with recommendations from teachers, administrators, staff, and students, followed by reviews and cost analyses. Over 2000 citizens then attended public meetings held throughout the district to discuss the alternatives. The superintendent finally reviewed 4000 recommendations; her final choices were approved unanimously by the board of education.[6]

Citizen advisory committees are another participatory mechanism applied to the budget process. These may be used during budget preparation, as a review of the proposed budget, or may deal with specific programs, such as the Capital Improvement Program, Community Development Block Grant funds, or social service agency funding. Advisory committees allow members to develop expertise in an area, so that input may be broader and more in-depth than that received through surveys or public meetings. However, these mechanisms can require more effort and time on the part of both city administrators and participants, and may not be representative of

Encyclopedia of Public Administration and Public Policy
DOI: 10.1081/E-EPAP 120010988

the community.[3] A study of advisory committees in New Jersey municipalities found that committees were perceived as effective when the appointment process was democratic, and the committee had clearly stated goals and objectives.[7]

Some communities use several types of participatory mechanisms in conjunction with each other. Eugene, Oregon, in the face of severe fiscal stress, developed a deliberative process, with a series of input methods, including public meetings, a budget-balancing exercise, and citizen surveys with varying levels of service cost information provided.[4] Hillsborough County, Florida, combines a series of public hearings during budget consideration with community meetings throughout the year, advisory committees, and surveys.[8] The benefits of one method can offset disadvantages of another.

FREQUENCY OF USAGE

To what extent is input sought in the budget process? Participation in budgeting is apparently relatively low in local governments, which is where most surveys have been conducted. One study found extensive use of public hearings and budget summary documents across various local government types, but little usage of other methods; larger jurisdictions (over 100,000) were more likely to use these tools than smaller ones.[9] A 1996 International City/County Management Association (ICMA) survey of managers in council-manager cities also found larger cities more likely to use participation, but the overall levels were not high. Only 18% of respondents hold community meetings for budget development input, and 32% receive formal recommendations from citizen groups during city council consideration of the budget. The most-used methods in these cities were those that simply provide information to the public, rather than seeking input.[10]

A study based on interviews with 28 midwestern city budget directors found that only 21% have used participation mechanisms during development of the budget proposal. Approximately one-third use input from surveys or strategic planning sessions that are not directly budget related, whereas another one-third allow input for allocation of specific funds, such as the Community Development Block Grant (CDBG). Many of these cities focus their efforts on improving communication of the proposed budget to the public, rather than encouraging citizen input.[11]

A citizen participation survey of chief administrative officers in cities with populations over 50,000 found that 96.9% hold public hearings, 81.6% use citizen advisory boards, 52.9% use citizen surveys, and 56.5% use citizen focus groups. When asked about participation in specific functions, 46.2% reported active involvement by citizens in the budgeting function (as compared with 93.9% for zoning and planning, 87.1% for parks and recreation, and 72.5% for policing and public safety). Again, larger cities reported more participation.[12]

Overall, then, there is some movement toward increasing citizen input in the budget process, but it is stronger in larger cities than smaller jurisdictions. Also, much of the participation effort remains at the end of the process, rather than during budget development, and with attempts to improve communication and education of citizens.

EFFECTS OF PARTICIPATION

Measuring the usage of participatory mechanisms is easier than determining the actual effects of citizen input. Empirical evidence, beyond anecdotes and individual perceptions of effectiveness, is limited. Survey respondents believe that citizen input affects budget decisions; in the earlier mentioned study of budget directors, 77% of respondents agreed that input definitely influenced decisions.[11] Citizen survey priorities also appeared to affect capital spending decisions in Auburn, Alabama.[2] The Eugene, Oregon, city council acted on the budget strategies identified through their deliberative process.[4] A case study of participation in two cities, however, found little evidence of decision-making effects.[13] We cannot conclusively state the effects of participation on budget decisions, though, without knowing what would have happened in the absence of citizen input.

Decision making is not the only possible benefit from participation. ''For administrators, those benefits can include better information on service needs, more services for the dollar, and better feelings about their work. For citizens, the gains can include services better suited to their needs, a more accessible and responsive public bureaucracy, and more positive feelings about themselves and government''.[3]

Much of the work in this area stresses the advantages of educating the public in budget complexities and providing people an opportunity to be heard.[11] Information may affect citizen perceptions. For example, the city of Dayton, Ohio, uses community boards to improve neighborhoods; with their support, the city has not lost a tax election in 20 years.[14] In studies of the Eugene case, the amount of budgetary information provided to citizens, as well as the citizen's use of services, affected their revealed preferences.[4]

This increased openness may increase public trust in and support for government. Wang found that managers perceived the use of general participatory mechanisms to be associated with increased public trust in government, although this was not the case for specific functions such as budgeting.[12] In addition, input can provide officials with information on where they need to better market and communicate their proposals. For example, in the Auburn surveys, the areas considered to be high priorities to city council were not seen this way by the public, so the council improved publicity and communication regarding the importance of these projects.[2]

OBSTACLES

The literature centers around three primary sources of obstacles to citizen participation. The first is the public itself. There are various "publics," not one homogenous whole; some people want to be active, for different reasons, whereas others do not, and still others could possibly be reached with some effort.[5] Lack of knowledge and time, apathy, and perceptions that their opinions are unwanted often lead to low and nonrepresentative participation levels.[11]

Second, structuring budget participation to be meaningful and effective is difficult. As noted earlier, different methods have distinct advantages and disadvantages; public hearings that are accessible to everyone often are less useful for two-way communications and for educating citizens than are advisory committees or prioritization exercises with smaller groups of people. Timing is also an issue. Opportunities for budget input are often placed at the end of the process, although it would presumably have more of a chance to affect decisions if it occurred earlier. Finally, some mechanisms are very costly, requiring considerable effort on the part of both citizens and public officials.[6]

Third, public administrators and elected officials may resist increased citizen input. Expert professional administrators may feel better able to make decisions on complex issues.[3] Research has found that finance officers are interested in participation, but that they would rather have it be initiated by elected officials than administrators.[5] Some elected officials, though, believe that they already have ample ways to find out what citizens want and believe that formalized group mechanisms are unnecessary given the increased access that citizens have to individual elected officials through e-mail, etc.[15]

EXIT, VOICE, AND LOYALTY

Albert O. Hirschman, in his book *Exit, Voice, and Loyalty*,[16] suggested that members of an organization (or customers of a firm) can use some combination of these three mechanisms to respond to declines in product/service quality. In some cases, this decline may arouse

primarily voice from the members/customers, while the organization may actually be more sensitive to exit (or vice versa), so will not take appropriate actions to halt the decline. Therefore, institutional mechanisms are important to have greater congruency between the member's response and the organization's sensitivity. In the current case, then, giving citizens greater opportunities to express their "voice" by participation in the budget process can help to provide valuable signals to governments regarding organizational performance, which may both reduce the level of outmigration from the jurisdiction and allow the government to "fix" the problems. If people believe that voice will be effective, they may postpone exit, especially if they have loyalty to the organization.

As noted earlier, serious concerns in this area revolve around the frequently low levels of participation and the potential that participants are not representative of the community. In some sense, Hirschman suggested, that may be positive rather than negative. It is better to have a mix of "alert" and "inert" customers/organizational members. In this way, sufficient numbers of citizens use voice to let the organization know that there are quality concerns, but the quiet public gives the organization time to address the issues before massive exit. Also, with limited use of voice, citizens retain "reserves" of resources to be used in extreme cases when they are most needed. In addition, in some cases, the "captive customers" for whom exit is the most difficult may actually have the greatest incentive to use voice to get the organization to pay attention.

Hirschman also discussed potential difficulties with the voice option. Voice can be overdone, to the point where protests may actually hinder rather than help organizational operations. In addition, the most quality-conscious constituents, rather than the "captive customers" may be more likely to use voice rather than exit in the short term. This can lead to class cleavages and more organizational sensitivity to the elite. If, however, the organization listens too much to the "captive customer" with loud voice and ignores individuals who are exiting as a result of dissatisfaction, the organization may face greater problems in the long run. The issue of representation, then, is an important one.

Hirschman's work sheds valuable light on the relationship between quality and price, and the potential response of customers/citizens to quality decline. However, determining the quality of government services is complex. The correlation between an individual's perception of government performance and their willingness to pay for services has been found to be strong for many people. However, there are also groups of individuals who are either willing to pay even though they believe performance to be low, or vice versa.[17] In addition to the value of citizens using voice to signal dissatisfaction, governmental officials may be able to use their own voice to provide more information to citizens regarding the true cost of services, and can use performance data to convince some that government performance is better than commonly perceived. Hence, the efforts by many jurisdictions to increase opportunities to educate citizens in budget issues.

The greatest challenge in applying Hirschman's thesis is that he concludes that it is difficult, if not impossible, to find a stable optimal mix of exit and voice. "Once members have a slight preference for, say, voice over exit, a cumulative movement sets in which makes exit look ever less attractive and more inconceivable. As a result, voice will be increasingly relied on by members at a time when management is working hard to make itself less vulnerable to it."[16] For this reason, organizations may have to go through cycles with exit and voice alternating as dominant mechanisms. This suggests the difficulty in institutionalizing budget participation mechanisms that will be optimally effective in the long run, because officials will become less sensitive to voice over time and may eventually simply pay lip service to citizen demands.

CONCLUSION

The citizen participation literature has focused on the voice option, without specifically addressing the role of citizen exit from the community. To what extent do citizens leave a community due to dissatisfaction with service quality or taxation levels? Does citizen participation actually reduce or delay the degree of exit? These are questions that require future research.

Efforts to enhance citizen input will undoubtedly continue to gain momentum, and we will hopefully accrue more hard evidence of the effects of participation. Mechanisms can be designed to provide congruence between citizens' need for voice and government officials' sensitivity to this voice. However, we also need to heed Hirschman's warning that officials will not be sensitive to voice forever, and the pendulum may need to shift toward a greater sensitivity to citizen exit from the community at some point.

REFERENCES

1. King, C.S.; Feltey, K.; Susel, B.O. The question of participation: Toward authentic public participation in public administration. Public Adm. Rev. **1998**, *58* (4), 317–326.
2. Watson, D.; Juster, R.; Johnson, G. Institutionalized use of citizen surveys in the budgetary and policy-making processes: A small city case study. Public Adm. Rev. **1991**, *51* (3), 232–239.
3. Thomas, J.C. *Public Participation in Public Decisions*; Jossey-Bass Publishers: San Francisco, 1995.
4. Simonsen, W.; Robbins, M.D. *Citizen Participation in Resource Allocation*; Westview Press: Boulder, CO, 2000.
5. Miller, G.J.; Evers, L. Budgeting structures and citizen participation. J. Pub. Budg. Account. Financ. Manag. **2002**, *14* (2), 233–272.
6. Roberts, N. Public deliberation: An alternative approach to crafting policy and setting direction. Public Adm. Rev. **1997**, *57* (2), 124–132.
7. Callahan, K. The utilization and effectiveness of citizen advisory committees in the budget process of local governments. J. Pub. Budg. Account. Financ. Manag. **2002**, *14* (2), 259–319.
8. Johnson, E.R. Recommended budget practices: Incorporating stakeholders into the process. Gov. Finance Rev. **1998**, *14* (4), 15–18.
9. O'Toole, D.E.; Marshall, J.; Grewe, T. Current local government budgeting practices. Gov. Finance Rev. **1996**, *12* (6), 25–29.
10. Ebdon, C. The relationship between citizen involvement in the budget process and city structure and culture. Public Prod. Manage. Rev. **2000**, *23* (3), 383–393.
11. Ebdon, C. Beyond the public hearing: Citizen participation in the local government budget process. J. Pub. Budg. Account. Financ. Manag. **2002**, *14* (2), 273–294.
12. Wang, X. Assessing public participation in U.S. cities. Public Perform. Manage. Rev. **2001**, *24* (4), 322–336.
13. Ebdon, C.; Franklin, A. Searching for a role for citizens in the budget process. **2001**, Working paper.
14. Gurwitt, R. A government that runs on citizen power. Governing **1992**, *6*, 48–54(December).
15. Franklin, A.; Ebdon, C. Aligning priorities in local budgeting processes. J. Pub. Account. Financ. Manag., forthcoming.
16. Hirschman, A.O. *Exit, Voice, and Loyalty*; Harvard University Press: Cambridge, MA, 1970; 125.
17. Glaser, M.A.; Hildreth, W.B. Service delivery satisfaction and willingness to pay taxes. Public Prod. Manage. Rev. **1999**, *23* (1), 48–67.

City Government

Jon C. Teaford
Purdue University, West Lafayette, Indiana, U.S.A.

INTRODUCTION

City government has adapted markedly to the changing demands of exploding urban populations. Throughout U.S. history there has been a strong deference to grassroots authority, and this has ensured local governments a major role in public policy developments. In the nineteenth century, city leaders offered a growing list of services to urban dwellers while facing complaints about corruption. Reform-minded citizens of the late nineteenth and early twentieth centuries revised the structures of local rule and invented new schemes of municipal government. Suburbanization in the twentieth century produced a fragmentation of local authority as metropolitan residents migrated to myriad suburban municipalities, and thereby avoided the taxes and social problems of older central cities.

HISTORY

Since the first European settlement of North America, there have been city governments. The earliest municipal corporations were patterned after European models. During the Middle Ages and early modern era, European cities acquired charters from the crown that granted them a degree of self-government and certain immunities from royal interference, as well as valuable commercial privileges. These European municipal corporations largely existed to promote and regulate trade, and to protect the interests of artisans and merchants. Similarly, the first North American city governments operated under royal charters that authorized them to regulate local trade activities and bestowed certain lucrative privileges on the municipal corporations. The corporation of Albany, New York, enjoyed a monopoly on the fur trade, and New York City was granted ownership of all tidal lands surrounding Manhattan Island and profited from a monopoly on local ferry service.[1]

During the eighteenth century, city functions expanded as fire protection, street lighting, and the regulation of such nuisances as stray livestock assumed new importance. Moreover, the American Revolution shifted responsibility for the granting of charters from the crown to the state legislatures. During the nineteenth century, the legislatures granted virtually any petition for a municipal charter and eventually adopted general incorporation laws to free themselves from the burden of enacting hundreds of charters. Municipal incorporation became a right rather than a privilege. Any locality of a few hundred residents could establish itself as a municipal corporation.

This pattern of permissive incorporation reflected the emerging American deference to grassroots rule. Generally, if local voters wanted to incorporate or annex their property to an existing city, it was their business and the state governments would allow them to determine their own destinies. State legislatures did interfere with city governments, and sometimes ignored the petitions of mayors and city councils. But interference usually arose at the behest of some local faction seeking a favor; it did not necessarily express the state's interest in systematic central control. If a locality requested a charter amendment or authorization to exercise a new power and there was no organized opposition at the local level to the request, then the legislature would generally approve the petition. In the United States, local governments were means by which the people of a locality could express and fulfill their needs. In contrast, throughout most of the world, local government was a means by which the central authorities could administer localities, and ensure the order and safety of the populace. This contrast between top-down authority and grassroots rule continued to differentiate American city government from local government elsewhere in the world.

During the nineteenth century, the largest cities in America and Europe expanded their functions and developed bureaucracies. In 1829, the creation of a uniformed, full-time police force in London, supplanting the earlier constable–night watch system, set an example for cities throughout the English-speaking world. Between 1840 and 1870, the major American cities established professional, full-time police and firefighting forces, the largest of which included thousands of men by the close of the nineteenth century. The growing cities also constructed great water supply systems and expansive sewerage networks. Moreover, by the end of the nineteenth century, New York City, Philadelphia, and Chicago could each boast of thousands of acres of public parkland rivaling the great urban preserves of London and Paris.[2]

Encyclopedia of Public Administration and Public Policy
DOI: 10.1081/E-EPAP 120010831

Accompanying these developments in the United States was a growing chorus of complaints about corruption and incompetence in city government. The native-born elites resented the rise of immigrant voters and politicians in the nineteenth-century city, and they were ever ready to expose any malfeasance of an Irish politician or police officer. Although city government provided unprecedented services, the newspapers and native-born commentators could point to some notorious examples of corruption in their indictments of city government. Thus, by the close of the nineteenth century, American city government was widely criticized and deemed a failure by many influential observers.

REFORM

The prevailing late-nineteenth-century American obsession with corruption in city government was to have a profound influence on twentieth-century municipal development. Demands for administrative reform dominated the municipal dialog of the early twentieth century, and there was persistent tinkering with the structure of city rule to achieve the honesty and efficiency supposedly lacking in the government of America's great cities. The goals of honesty and efficiency were to determine the reform agenda of the twentieth century.[3]

Beginning in the 1880s, civil service reform was a favorite of American good-government advocates, and gradually an increasing proportion of city employees enjoyed the protection of a civil service system. Consequently, the patronage power of city politicians declined, and demands for professionalism in government eroded the clout of party leaders. This was especially evident in police departments. Whereas nineteenth-century police forces were often tools of the politicians, and appointment and promotion were political favors, in the twentieth century, police reformers sought to cleanse departments of political influence and ensure a nonpartisan professionalism.[4]

Meanwhile, reformers sought to limit the power of neighborhood-based ethnic politicians by curbing the authority of ward-elected city councils and enhancing the authority of the mayors. This contrasted markedly with developments in Canada and Great Britain, where city council committees remained the dominant policy-making element of city government and the mayor was largely a ceremonial figurehead. Suspicion of plebeian, neighborhood representatives led to a strong mayor structure in the United States with the executive, elected by the city's voters at large, exercising veto authority and broad appointive powers.[5]

Another reform intended to ensure honesty and efficiency in American municipal government was the adoption of at-large election of city council members. To eliminate ward representation and destroy the power of the supposedly venal ward politicians, municipal reformers advocated that all elected officials be chosen by the city electorate at large. Consequently, an increasing number of cities abandoned ward representation, or at least provided for mixed councils with some members chosen by neighborhoods and others by the citywide electorate.

To further improve city administration, Americans experimented with two new forms of rule: commission government and city manager rule. Originating in Galveston, Texas, in 1901, the commission plan placed all executive and legislative authority in the hands of a small board of commissioners elected at large.[6] During the 1910s, the city manager plan superseded the commission scheme on the reform agenda. Under manager government, the city council remained in charge of basic policy making, but implementation of that policy and the administration of city services was the responsibility of the city manager. This manager was ideally a nonpartisan professional appointed by the council to ensure expert administration. The early city managers were often engineers with a devotion to efficiency and an expert knowledge of public works.[7] Whereas commission government lost favor, the city manager plan was adopted in municipalities throughout the United States and in Canada as well. By the close of the twentieth century, more American municipalities operated under the manager plan than under the mayor–council scheme.[8]

During the late nineteenth and early twentieth centuries, the tradition of deference to the locality was reinforced through the adoption of home rule measures. Viewing the state legislature as a channel through which corrupt local interests could obtain their selfish ends, good-government reformers in the United States sought to close this avenue to nefarious gain. Home rule provisions in state constitutions forbid state lawmakers to legislate on questions solely of local concern, and authorized cities to draft their own charters and charter amendments that would take effect subsequent to approval by the city electorate.[9]

LATE TWENTIETH-CENTURY DEVELOPMENTS

During the second half of the twentieth century, the reform mentality remained influential in the United States, although some questioned the merits of the structural and administrative changes of earlier years. The number of American cities adopting manager rule continued to increase. The new breed of managers often were graduates of university city management programs, not simply engineers with some background in the planning and administration of public works. Moreover, an increasing number of mayor–council cities were hiring chief administrative officers to assume charge of municipal administration without compromising the strong mayor's policy-making or appointive powers. In other words, these officers provided administrative expertise, but unlike city manager municipalities, the mayor was not reduced to a ceremonial figure, presiding over council meetings and cutting ribbons.

Not all elements of the reform agenda survived unscathed. At-large election of city councils came under attack, especially because it seemed to deprive ethnic minorities—who dominated a single neighborhood but were outnumbered citywide—of their fair share of council representation. Thus, there was some shift back to district representation, but at-large elections survived in many municipalities.

Meanwhile, the municipal bureaucracy became more entrenched, and police forces grew increasingly hostile to any civilian interference that threatened their professional independence. Amid the racial disorder of the 1960s, many observers called for civilian review boards to judge charges of police brutality. But such reforms made little headway, and elected officials often seemed impotent when faced with resistance from the city bureaucracy. Militant action by municipal employee unions in the 1960s and 1970s made this quite evident. Despite tight municipal budgets and citizen complaints about city employees, mayors and councils often had to concede cash and favors to the powerful municipal employee unions.

City leaders in the United States did, however, enjoy some new sources of revenue that helped to alleviate money worries. Before World War II, city governments depended overwhelmingly on property taxes for their revenues. Since the 1940s, state legislatures have granted cities the authority to levy a range of new taxes, weaning them from their overwhelming dependence on the property tax. In 1939, Philadelphia became the first American city to levy a municipal income tax, and numerous other large cities were to follow Philadelphia's example in the following decades. Similarly, municipal sales taxes proved a boon to many cities. In addition, during the 1960s and 1970s, federal aid to cities rose as Washington financed a larger share of the local government burden. Beginning in the late 1970s, however, the federal share began to decline, and Uncle Sam's short-lived interest in city government waned.[10] The federal government's program of general revenue sharing with municipalities lasted only 14 years, from 1972 to 1986. Federal budget woes and declining political interest in a perceived urban crisis doomed prospects for federal munificence.

The aging central cities of the Midwest and the Northeast especially needed additional funding. Ringed by independent suburban municipalities, these cities could not annex additional territory. As well-to-do residents and lucrative businesses moved beyond their boundaries, these cities watched their tax bases erode. Metropolitan reformers claimed that the answer to this problem was the creation of some form of metropolitan government that would distribute the burdens of governance more equitably throughout the urban region. Other nations had experimented with metropolitan governments. As early as 1888, the British parliament created the London County Council to assume certain areawide functions in the London region without destroying the many existing borough and city governments that continued to exercise local responsibilities. In 1953, the Ontario parliament established a metropolitan structure for Toronto, comprising the central-city municipality and surrounding suburban municipalities. The municipalities performed specified local functions, while the overarching metropolitan government was allocated regional duties. Political scientists praised the Toronto scheme as a model for American metropolitan reform, but in the United States overarching metropolitan bodies with authority over a range of functions were not a realistic option. In Great Britain, Canada, and much of the rest of the world, the central government could impose reform schemes on localities without winning prior approval from the voters in those localities. No popular referendum preceded the adoption of metropolitan government in Toronto. In the United States, however, the long-standing deference to grassroots opinion generally prevented the states from forcing their will on the localities and supplanting existing patterns of fragmented rule with metropolitan federations abridging the autonomy of area municipalities. Special-purpose metropolitan authorities did develop in the United States. Existing city governments were willing to abdicate responsibility for a single function such as water supply or sewerage, but Americans did not embrace metropolitan behemoths designed to largely supersede city rule.[11]

CONCLUSION

At the close of the twentieth century, then, the American tradition of deference to local autonomy survived in marked contrast to the pattern of central control over local government found elsewhere in the world. In the United States, Canada, and Europe, the forces of professional city administration remained unabated. This was evident in the continuing popularity of the city manager plan in the United States and the increased reliance on chief administrative officers in American mayor–council cities and in European municipalities as well. Given rising concern about such regional problems as urban sprawl and wasteful land-use patterns, it remains unclear to what extent American city governments will retain their autonomy, or whether city governments will yield power to regional authorities or confront greater interference from state lawmakers.

REFERENCES

1. Teaford, J.C. *The Municipal Revolution in America: Origins of Modern Urban Government 1650–1825*; University of Chicago Press: Chicago, 1975.
2. Teaford, J.C. *The Unheralded Triumph: City Government in America, 1870–1900*; Johns Hopkins University Press: Baltimore, 1984.
3. Schiesl, M.J. *The Politics of Efficiency: Municipal Administration and Reform in America: 1880–1920*; University of California Press: Berkeley, CA, 1977.
4. Fogelson, R.M. *Big-City Police*; Harvard University Press: Cambridge, MA, 1977.
5. Griffith, E.S. *The Modern Development of City Government in the United Kingdom and the United States*; Oxford University Press: London, 1927.
6. Rice, B.R. *Progressive Cities: The Commission Government Movement in America, 1901–1920*; University of Texas Press: Austin, 1977.
7. Stillman, R.J. *The Rise of the City Manager: A Public Professional in Local Government*; University of New Mexico Press: Albuquerque, 1974.
8. Renner, T.; DeSantis, V.S. Municipal form of government: Issues and trends. Munic. Year Book **1998**, *65*, 30–41.
9. McBain, H.L. *The Law and Practice of Municipal Home Rule*; Columbia University Press: New York, 1916.
10. Teaford, J.C. *The Rough Road to Renaissance: Urban Revitalization in America, 1940–1985*; Johns Hopkins University Press: Baltimore, 1990.
11. Hamilton, D.K. *Governing Metropolitan Areas: Response to Growth and Change*; Garland Publishing: New York, 1999.

Civic Duty

Vera Vogelsang-Coombs
Cleveland State University, Cleveland, Ohio, U.S.A.

Larry Bakken
Hamline University, St. Paul, Minnesota, U.S.A.

INTRODUCTION

This article discusses the civic duty of public administrators, based on legal, ethical, and practical interpretations of democratic citizenship. Civic duty refers to the rights, obligations, feelings, and habits of a citizen. A citizen has membership in a democratic state. A state is an independent country with defined territory. A state compels obedience from all who reside in its geographic domain because its sovereign commands absolute power internally. The sovereign's institutions promote a country's permanent interests—law and order, social stability, long-term prosperity, and national security. The relationship between a state and citizens is two-way. The state provides protection to citizens. In exchange, citizens accept the duty to obey the sovereign, to fulfill the requirements of citizenship, and to defend the state from external aggression. Adult residents who are not citizens do not enjoy the full protection or the rights therein of a state.

A democratic state is one in which the "demos"—the people collectively—are the sovereign; its defining characteristic is self-governance. In America, the founders vested the new country's sovereignty in the citizenry. The founders believed that citizens, as differentiated from a king's subjects, could govern themselves, because they could regulate themselves (Ref. 1, pp. xvii–xviii). Citizens regulate themselves when they are faithful to the duties associated with the status of citizenship. Citizenship takes two forms: legal citizenship and ethical citizenship; ethical citizenship has two subclasses—national citizenship and democratic citizenship. The meaning of civic duty is dynamic because the American state embeds the norms of citizenship in changing political institutions, legal rules, and democratic culture. American democracy involves citizens in the roles of private individual, political participant, and officeholders. Officeholders can have three identities: 1) political representatives, i.e., elected officials or lawmakers; 2) public administrators, i.e., bureaucrats or the civil service; and 3) and independent judges. In this analysis, we will limit our discussion to citizenship and the civic duties of the public administrator. The following discussion explains each row of Table 1 in turn.

LEGAL CITIZENSHIP AND LIMITED GOVERNMENT

Democratic government sets the foundation for legal citizenship. American government is a form of liberal democracy. Liberal democracy rests on the principle of limited government. This principle assumes that the citizens voluntarily surrender part of their absolute power as sovereign to government so that government can make decisions for the state. In exchange for the people's grant of some sovereign power, liberal democracy functions according to a constitution or charter. In America, the Constitution is written and sets the reciprocal relationship between individual citizens and democratic government. Besides enumerating the powers that the people have surrendered to government, the Constitution also lists the restraints on government. Its significance is that it is the supreme law of the land. All who reside in America are subject to it, including the popularly elected president, the head of state. The U.S. Constitution uses three other legal devices to protect citizens from government. First, it establishes a federal republic with dual sovereigns. Federalism means that two distinct governments exist that derive their powers directly and independently from the sovereign people: the national government and states. The Constitution assures a republican form of government in every state and at the national level. Citizens of one state enjoy the privileges of citizenship in every other state. It also guarantees to protect states from external invasions and domestic violence. Second, the Constitution secures citizens' civil rights and liberties. The U.S. Bill of Rights, constitutional amendments, and federal laws express these protections. Liberties, such as free speech, are inalienable and are immune from the arbitrary exercise of governmental power. Neither government nor a citizen can repudiate them or transfer them to another

Encyclopedia of Public Administration and Public Policy
DOI: 10.1081/E-EPAP 120010936

Table 1 Citizenship, liberal democracy, and civic duty

Types of citizenship	Characteristics of liberal democracy	Norms for citizenship	The civic duty of public administrators
Legal citizenship	Limited government	Personal responsibility	The higher standard of conduct
National citizenship (ethical citizenship)	Good government	Caring for public interests	Office as public service
Democratic citizenship (ethical citizenship)	Potential responsiveness	The civic culture	Citizenship as office

person. Third, the Constitution authorizes the principle of reserved powers. Amendment X gives to the states or the people the powers that the Constitution has not explicitly granted to the national government or withheld from the states.

Pluralism and Civil Society

Liberal democracy presupposes the existence of a pluralist civil society. A pluralistic society divides a democratic state's power into open and competing groups instead of concentrating it in a ruling elite. Pluralism creates a civil society. Civil society is broader than government, giving citizens a private (social) life and a political life. Citizens get a unique identity by pursuing personal interests, including family life, in private (nongovernmental) associations. The premise is that only citizens can define their interests. Self-interested citizens advance their interests by joining groups of similarly minded individuals. Pluralism assumes that a check on group power occurs as self-interested individuals shift their allegiances from group to group in response to changing perceptions of their own interests.[2] Citizens' groups align with others in the political arena to advocate for policy preferences and to achieve favorable outcomes. Politics is the mechanism for aggregating and converting individual preferences into collective decisions. In theory, this conversion takes place in the competitive processes of responsible parties and within a set of legal rights and political rules.[3] Backed by political authority, these collective choices compel obedience.

Civic Duty and Personal Responsibility

Citizens in liberal democracy can assume the identity of a private citizen, a political participant, or an officeholder. All have a duty to be responsible. Personal responsibility for private citizens means that individuals voluntarily restrain their behavior. They choose to restrict themselves not to interfere with others' private lives, liberties, and interests. In exchange, responsible citizens have the right to expect others to do the same. Furthermore, citizens'

private lives have legal protections. Democratic government has a duty to avoid arbitrary intrusions into the citizenry's private affairs and can only do so reluctantly after following due process. Personal responsibility also means that citizens have a civic duty to participate in democratic political processes. Political participation is necessary, because the legitimacy of democratic government depends on it. It allows the citizenry to show consent. Showing consent legitimates democratic government's use of the state's power. Citizens show consent indirectly by voting for political representatives who, in turn, conduct the "people's business." Voting depends on three principles. First, citizens stand as political equals. Second, liberal democracy holds open and free elections at regularly scheduled intervals. Third, democratic government has an obligation to count each citizen's vote. Personal responsibility for elected officials means that they encourage pluralistic participation, grant access to citizen groups, broker exchanges among competing interests, and enforce contracts. Political representatives grant the right to exercise limited discretion to public administrators so that democratic government can listen and respond to legitimate group interests. Elected officials control administrative discretion by organizing government agencies into hierarchies and through legislative oversight. The electorate has the power to replace democratic government if the voters perceive officeholders as unresponsive or even to change the Constitution.

The Higher Standard of Conduct

In democratic theory, the position of a free and autonomous citizen is the most esteemed identity. Citizens who serve in government must surrender more rights and democratic freedoms to government. The democratic sovereign restricts the conduct of officeholders because of its distrust of concentrated political authority. Therefore, some actions of private citizens are illegal if done by political representatives or public administrators. The restrictions of office translate into a higher standard of conduct. Legislative codes, conflict of interest statutes, and criminal sanctions operationalize this higher standard. In exchange for discretionary authority, public administrators must follow the rules of their office. Legal requirements exist for public administrators to carry out their office with political impartiality and professionalism. They have a duty to respect election outcomes, to support democratic processes, and to act as rule-abiding trustees (Ref. 4, pp. 154–155). Administrators must submit to sanctions if a legislative review finds that they have failed to discharge these duties properly. Impartiality and professionalism counteract the partisanship and ideologies of popularly elected officials. One school of thought frees public administrators from legal restraints, obliging them to disobey evil-minded elected officials in times of crises. If nefarious elected officials capture the state's absolute power and present their unconstitutional activities as those of the democratic sovereign, then dictatorship happens, as in Nazi Germany. According to March and Olsen, public administrators in similar situations must actively thwart the wishes of iniquitous political officials (Ref. 4, pp. 86–89).

NATIONAL CITIZENSHIP AND GOOD GOVERNMENT

The legal foundations of citizenship are incomplete. Citizens who possess legal and civil rights in a pluralist society do not automatically feel political allegiance to their country.[5] To stimulate national citizenship, the American founders vested the sovereignty of the new country in the political community, not the electorate. This political community encompasses the nationwide body of citizens as they interact informally and formally in social, religious, economic, cultural, and community associations in their localities.[6] By vesting sovereignty in the national political community, the founders broadened the idea of citizenship to include an ethical dimension. Ethical citizenship refers to the moral beliefs, values, fraternal feelings, habits, and reciprocal commitments of individuals that guide their lives. Whereas legal citizenship is expressed in laws and rules, ethical citizenship is in standards that most people acknowledge but are not codified. Ethical citizenship is always a matter of voluntary behavior and is subject to different interpretations by different people.

The founders rooted the political community in a culture of ''good government.'' Political culture refers to the citizenry's attitudes about the style of democratic governmental operations.[7] Good government, as opposed to perfect government, is based on legitimacy that extends beyond electoral popularity. This means that democratic government must defend its legitimacy on higher (normative) values. It is not enough for govern-

ment to appear good; its actions must be good. To make government's actions ''good,'' officeholders are bound to justify publicly and receive approval from the democratic sovereign (not just the electorate).[8] In obtaining prior approval, officeholders determine whether their proposed actions are ethically appropriate, i.e., have wide community support. For March and Olsen, the ethic of appropriateness means that government acts consistently with cultural and political norms.[4] This ethic reassures the democratic political community that officeholders will not act arbitrarily nor for purely private interests. The actions of good government strengthen the democratic sovereign's confidence in those to whom it has entrusted the state's power.

Civic Duty and Caring for Public Interests

Membership in the political community gives citizens a public life besides a private life. In public life, citizens actively maintain public purposes, based on a perception of national solidarity and a sense of a common destiny. For Norton Long, a precondition of legal citizenship is that citizens have a sense of ''*moi commun*''.[9] Communal feelings stir in citizens, he says, if ''a public thing'' quite literally exists for which they feel responsible. For John Dewey, this public thing emerges when citizens rediscover the ''public and its interests''.[10] A political community of citizens, he says, cares for public interests. To care for public interests, citizens must engage each other to discern common needs. This task requires citizens to reflect and to distinguish between the special case (their own interests) and the general case (the interests of others). In other words, citizens use moral reasoning to perceive the difference between public interests and private interests. According to Dewey, people create private interests when they join voluntarily, and only those people involved in a transaction experience the direct or indirect consequences of those interactions. Public interests are not fixed. They emerge when individuals as a group are seriously and indirectly harmed by the consequences of transactions in which they have not engaged. Although citizens may disagree, their open discussions about public interests allow the political community to search for remedies.

Caring for the public gives diverse citizens a common ethical identity. Public spirit awakens this identity in citizens. The civic virtue of private citizens is the source of public spirit. Public-spirited citizens participate in public life when they perceive that the personal advantage of each member of the community is consistent with working for the good of all. Alexis de Tocqueville called this disposition of American citizens ''the principle of self interest rightly understood'' (Ref. 11, pp. 129–132).

Citizens live this principle daily in small acts of self-restraint, not through great sacrifices. Such daily actions, said de Tocqueville, gradually draw individuals through their habits in the direction of the national political community. Virtuous citizens, acting on this principle, voluntarily help others. In place of doing it themselves, they willingly give up additional personal resources to sponsor community programs aimed at serving the poor and at improving society. De Tocqueville said that this public role for private citizens is based on custom, not law. This custom binds together the nation, allowing diverse citizens in the political community to lead a good life. For Dewey, public life is a good life. A good or high-quality common life emerges only if a democratic state is a good state. A good state comes into existence when trustees of the public (lawmakers and public administrators) systematically care for public interests. In the good state, citizens have greater liberty and security in their private affairs because they are relieved from the waste of negative struggle and needless conflict (Ref. 10, pp. 71–72). Its community-based processes, by promoting reflection, moral reasoning, and open discourse, civilize humanity, allowing citizens to show empathy, tolerance, and generosity (Ref. 4, p. 60).

Office as Public Service

For Dewey, the public is vital to the creation of government. Government is the public organized to carry out the functions of the state in a way that strengthens bonds among citizens. The sovereign political community connects the power of the democratic state to care for public interests through government officials. It gives them the use of the democratic state's power to regulate the conjoint actions of individuals and groups that cause a public interest to emerge. Different issues create different public interests. As trustees of the public and its interests, public administrators hold the office of a public servant. The duty of public servants is to recognize the dynamics and the consequences of individuals "acting as a public." According to March and Olsen, the political community's discussions about public interests should guide and restrain public servants' actions. By listening to these discussions, public servants will get an idea about what governmental actions are acceptable to the larger political community on moral grounds. These discussions reveal the issues that government should avoid or remove from the policy agenda because of a lack of wide acceptance. By withdrawing these issues temporarily, public servants help to prevent the polarization of the community. Moreover, the influence of community discussions on public servants allows the democratic sovereign to civilize government.

Ethical Maturity

This task of public service requires ethically mature officeholders. Ethically mature public servants, said Stephen K. Bailey, appreciate the reality of self-interest and its impact on motivating behavior, both public and private:

> . . .Public service is the capacity to harness private and personal interests to public interest causes. Those who will not traffic in personal and private interests (if such interests are within the law) to the point of engaging their support on behalf of causes in which both public and private interests are served are, in terms of moral temperament, unfit for public responsibility (Ref. 12, p. 47).

Ethically mature public servants, said Bailey, possess three moral qualities: optimism, courage, and fairness tempered by charity. Optimism allows public servants to see possibilities in shifting political priorities so that they can perform the functions of government without becoming cynical. Optimistic public servants are motivated to better society and to improve the quality of human life. Cynical officials who perceive humankind as unworthy of such efforts are the ultimate source of corruption in a free society. Courage overcomes the forces of private relations, especially friendship, and provides a degree of neutrality to override requests for special favors. Ethical courage means that public servants are willing to decide even with inadequate information. Ethical courage is meaningless unless it enables public servants to act justly. Fairness tempered by the virtue of charity promotes justice. Charitable public servants discipline themselves by controlling persistent inner claims for personal recognition, power, and status. Charity is also a source of visions for the "good society" without which government, said Bailey, becomes "a sullen defense of existing patterns of privilege" (Ref. 12, p. 52). Fairness compensates for the subjective nature of all decision making. Fairness is necessary because of administrative discretion. Fair-minded public servants control their discretion by balancing flexibility and consistency in their decisions. As Bailey pointed out, public administrators who never deviate are rigid and lack compassion; those who deviate too much are subversive. The ethical compromises of mature administrators allow them to act with enough consistency and flexibility to survive and succeed in public service.

CHALLENGES TO NATIONAL CITIZENSHIP

At the end of the twentieth century, scholars have identified at least five challenges to national citizenship in America. First, Robert Putnam argued that American life lacks communal solidarity. Instead of a "nation of joiners" with a vibrant public life, Americans are "bowling alone," and their civic life has all but disappeared (Refs. 11, pp. 114–118, 13). Second, scholars have identified a societal malaise: widespread alienation of citizens from government. For example, Evan Berman's national survey identified three sources of citizen discontent: 1) government officials whom citizens perceive as indifferent or hostile to their needs; 2) poor service delivery; and 3) governmental processes that exclude citizens.[14] Third, the emergence of the welfare state has significantly undermined the citizen–government relationship. Specifically, Don Eberly said that Americans have assumed problematic identities as clients, customers, consumers, and claimants of government:

> The provision of public assistance to tens of millions of Americans is often accompanied by the subtle message that recipients are hopelessly trapped in conditions that require the permanent help of advocates, interest groups and government workers. It produces a mindset that dwarfs citizenship for the poor and the non-poor alike. It leaves the poor feeling justified in doing little to reclaim control of their lives and the non-poor feeling no obligation to intervene with neighborly aid (Ref. 1, p. xxix).

Fourth, in a comprehensive study of citizenship, Rogers Smith found that liberal democracy is not the core meaning of the American civic identity.[15] Clashing traditions and popular politics have excluded most Americans from enjoying full citizenship. Fifth, Chester Newland argued that a pervasive system of spoils at the national level excludes most of the public administration community from important matters of governance (Ref. 16, pp. 45–56). This exclusion undermines the capacity of American democracy to function adequately or to achieve social change. Some fixes to these problems of national citizenship, such as Benjamin Barber's "strong (grassroots) democracy," aim at weakening liberal democratic institutions and basic protections.[17] A more constructive approach is not to deny democratic liberal traditions. It draws the norms of ethical citizenship from the operations of successful liberal democracies. If democracy is to endure, then pragmatic realism must temper the idealistic notions of citizenship.[18]

DEMOCRATIC CITIZENSHIP AND POTENTIAL RESPONSIVENESS

E.E. Schattschneider provided a realist's view of democratic citizenship. The most damage to the democratic cause comes from idealists who attribute a "mystical, magical omnipotence" to the people (Ref. 19, pp. 135–136). This attribution takes no heed of what the democratic system can do. Involving 280 million people directly in all aspects of governance is physically impossible. Instead, he assumed that democratic citizens were moral equals: Each person is a precious and unique human. Morally equal citizens have potential involvement. Potentially involved citizens become active in public affairs because of a democratic dynamic: conflict is contagious. Different public issues activate different citizens. If only 0.10% of the citizenry mobilizes around an issue, then the latent force of the remaining citizens is 999 greater than that of the activists. Schattschneider's point is that any estimate of citizen participation based on the number of original activists is fatuous. Potentially involved citizens are not neutral spectators. Public issues succeed or fail because the original activists mobilize or exclude the spectators. The balance of citizen involvement in any public issue, he said, is not fixed until *everyone* is involved (Ref. 19, pp. 4–5).

From this analysis, Schattschneider recasted the meaning of citizenship. He made its characteristics consistent with what most citizens can and are willing to do in public life. He said that the role of democratic citizens is the same as in private relationships: People take advantage of what other people know and judge results. In public affairs, citizens rely on government leaders and organizations, or their responsible opposition, to give them choices about policy alternatives. These choices must allow citizens the potential to participate in meaningful ways. In this democratic system, the sovereign people "act through the government." This system satisfies citizens only if it meets the condition of "potential responsiveness." Potential responsiveness in a democracy, said Hannah Pitkin, requires citizens to have: "...access to power rather than its actual exercise...There need not be a constant activity of responding, but there must be a constant condition of responsive*ness*, of potential readiness [of government] to respond".[20] If citizens perceive potential responsiveness in the democratic system, then they feel that they can initiate action or trust leaders to do the right thing. Citizens accept governmental authority despite their lack of awareness of what government is doing most of the time. These beliefs are a part of the democratic civic culture.

The Civic Culture

According to Gabriel Almond and Sidney Verba, the civic culture shapes the norms for citizens and their relationships to each other and to their democratic government.[21] Their comparative analysis of five democracies, though drawn in 1963, remains the classical formulation. It showed that stable democracies have democratic civic cultures. They described the American civic culture as mixed. Citizens' activity in public life combines involvement and activity with passivity and noninvolvement. They take on and balance the duties of three identities: the influential activist, the passive governmental subject, and the parochial (family-oriented, private) person. Almond and Verba found that the norms of trust and confidence from citizens' social interactions transfer to their political relationships and temper them. They also found that the interactions of citizens and government showed a cyclical pattern. In normal times, most citizens are quiescent. They are uninterested in what decision makers do, but officeholders can act only within legal and ethical bounds. If an issue becomes salient, then citizens will increase their involvement with government, making demands on elected officials and public administrators. If government officials make appropriate adjustments, then the importance of politics will lose saliency for mobilized citizens, and they will withdraw from active participation. This cycle allows a democratic system to change slowly and humanely. If issues become and remain intense, then they destabilize a democracy.

Almond and Verba's research showed that the cycle of political participation strains neither people nor liberal democracy. The reason is that the civic culture controls decision makers without checking them so tightly as to render democratic government ineffective. The check and balance occur for four reasons. First, democratic government officials subscribe to the belief in the influence potential of citizens. Second, government decision makers anticipate citizens' reactions even if citizens are not active or making demands on them. Third, government officials and citizens are part of the same political community. They share the same civic culture that exposes them to the same democratic values. Fourth, public and private life are not opposites in the civic culture. The democratic culture mixes the personal, social, and political identities of citizens. It socializes government officials to uphold a continuum of public–private relationships that flourish legitimately in the political community.

Citizenship as Office

Terry Cooper formulated an ethic of citizenship for democratic public administration. He assumed that citizenship underpins all normative relationships in the political community. Citizenship, in his conceptualization, is the public office of virtuous individuals in the political community. Public administrators are citizens first. They are virtuous citizens "employed *as* one of us to work *for* us".[22] In office, they are fiduciary citizens. Acting as trustees for the political community, virtuous administrators make citizens part of the administrative role. Efficient service delivery and law enforcement are their penultimate obligations. Their ultimate duty is to build and contribute to community life by sharing the sovereign's power, upholding civic values, and pursuing long-term interests. The authority relationships of virtuous administrators are both vertical and horizontal. They look at popularly elected politicians and to the citizenry for direction. For Cooper, the ultimate loyalty of virtuous administrators belongs to the citizenry because the citizenry's authority is that of the sovereign. The sovereign's authority transcends loyalty to specific elected officials or particular governmental agencies.

Virtuous administrators use transformational leadership practices to facilitate (or awaken) the involvement of citizens in public affairs. They combine their professional expertise and civic values in a way that gives citizens new and meaningful opportunities to participate in governance and for self-reflection (Refs. 16, p. 53 and 55, 23). Their practices stimulate positive changes in individuals, institutions, and the community (Ref. 4, p. 55). "Coproduction," "indirect administration," and "transparent decision making" are three examples of such practices. Coproduction, for Charles Levine, meant that virtuous administrators involve active citizens as partners in allocation decisions regarding service delivery.[24] For Cooper, virtuous administrators engage in indirect administration by subordinating their technical expertise to active community leaders. They engage in policy deliberations by working through and respecting existing communities and their associations and authorities. Cooper said that administrators are justified to shed their neutrality and to act as policy advocates if their judgments are consistent with their roles as fiduciary citizens. Transparent decision making, said Carol Lewis, establishes the ethical credibility of public administrators.[25] It is necessary because most administrative decisions take place without the physical presence of citizens. Credible administrators, she said, "go on record." By going on record, they publicly justify their decisions. This practice socializes them to account for their decisions even if citizens will not judge the results for years.[26] Besides enhancing governance and enriching community life, these practices develop the character of democratic citizens.

Political Socialization

The development of democratic citizenship is a task of political socialization. Political socialization is concerned with the "personal and social origins of political outlooks".[27] It is the process through which citizens orient themselves to the political community, democratic government, and the civic culture. Political socialization begins early and is lifelong. It takes place in the family, peer groups, public schools, workplaces, and in political processes, although the quality of these experiences will vary. A liberal education is a vehicle for building citizenship in young adults. This broad education allows young people to reflect carefully about the human condition. It encourages them to use this learning to shape their lives as moral citizens and civilized human beings.[28] Socialization also takes place in university-based Master of Public Administration (MPA) programs and through the associations of professional administrators, such as the American Society for Public Administration (ASPA) and the International City/County Management Association (ICMA). Finally, virtuous administrators socialize citizens. Their transformational practices connect citizens and democratic government. Virtuous administrators teach citizenship, using the experience of the political community.

CONCLUSION

Underpinning this analysis of citizenship and civic duty is the relationship between elected officials and public administrators. It touches on a fundamental political question: What is the proper balance between representative institutions and the civil service in a liberal democracy? Answers to this question are political as much as matters of law, ethics, and best practice. The terms associated with civic duty—the "common good," "the public interest," "ethical maturity," and "the virtuous administrator"—are political terms. Political terms have ambiguous meanings, because no consensus exists on their definitions. This definitional ambiguity accommodates multiple interpretations of civic duty. For example, citizen-centered norms of civic duty prevail in the literature at the end of the twentieth century. Embedded in these norms is the following proposition: The citizen is supreme in governance, despite what legitimate elected officials want public administrators to do. This is an explosive proposition. It implies that the ultimate duty of the public administrator is to enable citizens to realize their view of the public interest. In effect, those professional administrators, through their citizenship identity, are preeminent over elected officials in democratic governance. As a political proposition, one can place this view at an extreme point on a definitional scale of civic duty. Given this conceptual placement, one can see why this interpretation of civic duty is controversial and is likely to elicit reactions. Moreover, political shifts in a changing environment are inevitable, and they will lead people to challenge the prevailing conventions. For example, before the terrorists attacked America on September 11, 2001, national citizenship was a minor identity for Americans (Refs. 1, p. xx, 4, p. 72, also see the section on Challenges to National Citizenship in this article). Putnam's "bowling alone" metaphor

captures the view that civic duty was irrelevant in American society. After the attacks, national citizenship has become a primary identity for many Americans. In the catastrophe's wake, the definition of civic duty has tipped to the other extreme. New interpretations have placed the preferences of elected officials as preeminent in American governance. These views contain another controversial political proposition: The ultimate duty of public administrators is to enable elected officials to realize their view of the public (i.e., national) interest. It implies that the public interest is whatever elected officials say it is. Our point is that the question of civic duty, as a political question, is one that a liberal democracy can never resolve once and for all. Inherent in the literature on civic duty are different and successive political interpretations of "who should govern."

INTERNET RESOURCES

The National Civic League is the oldest civic organization in the country; see www.ncl.org. The National Association of Schools of Public Affairs and Administration is the accrediting body of MPA programs; see www.naspaa.org. The American Political Science Association has formed a Civic Education Network; see www. apsanet.org/CENnet. This network has a list of more than 60 civic organizations; see www.apsanet.org/CENnet/ organizations. Its list of teaching and research resources is found at www.apsanet.org/CENnet/resources.

REFERENCES

1. Eberly, D.E. The Quest for a Civil Society. In *Building a Community of Citizens: Civil Society in the 21st Century*; Eberly, D.E., Ed.; University Press of America: Lanham, MD, 1994.
2. Shafritz, J.M. Pluralism. In *The HarperCollins Dictionary of American Government and Politics,* 1st Ed.; Harper Collins Publishers: New York, 1993; 354–355.
3. Lowi, T.J. *The End of Liberalism*; W.W. Norton: New York, 1979.
4. March, J.G.; Olsen, J.P. *Democratic Governance*; The Free Press: New York, 1995; 154–155.
5. Heywood, A. *Political Ideas and Concepts, An Introduction*; St. Martin's Press: New York, 1994; 156.
6. Hult, K.M.; Walcott, C. *Governing Public Organization: Politics, Structures, and Institutional Design*; Brooks/Cole Publishing: Pacific Grove, CA, 1990.
7. Shafritz, J.M. Political Culture. In *The HarperCollins Dictionary of American Government and Politics,* 1st Ed.; Harper Collins Publishers: New York, 1993; 362.
8. Madison, J. Federalist Paper #49. In *The Federalist Papers*; New American Library: Mentor Book, New York, 1788/1961; 313–317.

9. Long, N.E. An Institutional Framework for the Development of Responsible Citizenship. In *The Polity*; Press, C., Ed.; Rand-McNally: Chicago, 1962; 184.

10. Dewey, J. *The Public and Its Problems*; Swallow Press: Chicago, 1927.

11. de Tocqueville, A. *Democracy in America*; Bradley, P., Ed.; Vintage Books–Random House: New York, 1838/1945; Vol. II; 129–132.

12. Bailey, S.K. Ethics and the Public Service. In *Combating Corruption/Encouraging Ethics*; Richter, W.L., Burke, F., Doig, J.W., Eds.; American Society for Public Administration: Washington, D.C., 1964/1990; 47.

13. Putnam, R. Bowling alone: America's declining social capital. J. Democr. **1995**, *6* (1), 65–78.

14. Berman, E. Dealing with cynical citizens. Public Adm. Rev. **1997**, *57* (2), 105–112.

15. Smith, R.M. *Civic Ideals: Conflicting Visions of Citizenship in U.S. History*; Yale University Press: New Haven, 1997.

16. Newland, C.A. Public executives: Imperium, sacerdotium, collegium? Bicentennial leadership challenges. Public Adm. Rev. **1987**, *47* (1), 45–56.

17. Barber, B. *Strong Democracy: Participatory Politics for a New Age*; University of California Press: Berkeley, 1984.

18. Baldwin, H.W. Warfare and Civilization. In *The Peloponnesian War*; Bantam Books: New York, 1960; 8Thucydides; 4th Printing, Introductory Essay.

19. Schattschneider, E.E. *The Semi-Sovereign People: A Realist's View of Democracy in America;* Reissued Ed.; The Dryden Press: Hinsdale, IL, 1975; 135–136.

20. Pitkin, H.F. The Concept of Representation. First Paperback Ed.; UCLA Press: Berkeley, CA, 1972; 233.

21. Almond, G.A.; Verba, S. *The Civic Culture: Political Attitudes and Democracy in Five Nations*; Princeton University Press: Princeton, NJ, 1963; 5.

22. Cooper, T.L. *An Ethic of Citizenship for Public Administration*; Prentice-Hall: Englewood Cliffs, NJ, 1991; 139.

23. Burns, J.M.G. *Leadership*; Harper and Row: New York, 1978; 434.

24. Levine, C.H. Citizenship and Service Delivery: The Promise of Coproduction. In *Democracy, Bureaucracy, and the Study of Administration*; Stivers, C., Ed.; Westview Press: Boulder, CO, 2001; 280–300.

25. Lewis, C.W. *The Ethics Challenge in Public Service: A Problem-Solving Guide*; Jossey-Bass Publishers: San Francisco, CA, 1991; 58.

26. Thompson, D.F. *Political Ethics and Public Office*; Harvard University Press: Cambridge, MA, 1987; 113.

27. Dawson, R.E.; Prewitt, K.; Dawson, K.S. *Political Socialization,* 2nd Ed.; Little, Brown and Co.: Boston, 1977; 1.

28. Gray, H. The Aims of Education. In *The Aims of Education*; Boyer, J.W., Ed.; The University of Chicago Press: Chicago, 1987/1997; 63–79.

Civil Disobedience

Matthew Tedesco
John Harris
University of Colorado at Boulder, Boulder, Colorado, U.S.A.

INTRODUCTION

An act of civil disobedience involves a violation of law with the intent of effecting a change in current policy, regarded as unjust by the citizens taking action. Important issues involved in civil disobedience include fidelity to the state, publicity of the disobedient act, the permissibility of violence in civil disobedience, and the acceptance of punishment on the part of the protesters. Civil disobedience was first explicitly discussed in detail by Henry David Thoreau, and later refined by activists such as Martin Luther King, Jr. and Mohandas Gandhi, and theorists such as John Rawls and Ronald Dworkin; however, its first important treatment is offered by Socrates, the ancient Greek philosopher, as presented in Plato's *Crito* and *Apology*.

KEY FIGURES AND IDEAS

As a matter of policy, it may appear strange for political theorists to attempt to justify a citizen's refusal to obey the law. One might think that if the government is, for the most part, just, then the citizens under the authority of the government always have a duty to obey the laws. Socrates (469–399 b.c.e.) appears to advocate just this position in the *Crito* when he stated, "...one must not give way or retreat or leave one's post, but both in war and in courts and everywhere else, one must obey the commands of one's city and country, or persuade it as to the nature of justice."[1] It would appear that Socrates thought that one ought to obey the government regardless of what it commands. This is, in part, because Socrates thought that the laws of the state provided so much for him that he owed a debt of gratitude, and thus, fidelity to the law compeled Socrates to go so far as to give his life if necessary. However, in the *Apology*, Socrates appears to have said something quite different. Here, Socrates proclaimed before the court of Athens that, "...I will obey the gods rather than you, and as long as I draw breath and am able, I shall not cease to practice philosophy...."[2] This example, taken from antiquity, shows that even Socrates, a man who eventually killed himself because he was commanded to do so by the laws, thought that there are some laws that one should not obey. Even if we accept, as Socrates appeared to, that there are some laws that should be disobeyed, the question then becomes what differentiates an act of civil disobedience from a simple violation of the law, and when, if ever, is civil disobedience justified.

Modern interest in civil disobedience was rekindled by Henry David Thoreau. His essay "Resistance to Civil Government" (later known as "Civil Disobedience") was first published in 1849,[3] and it served as an important influence on prominent social and political activists in decades to follow. In it, Thoreau addressed his reasons for refusing to pay a poll tax over the course of several years, an act of defiance that landed him briefly in jail until, to his consternation, an associate paid it for him and procured his release. Thoreau was primarily concerned with the evil of slavery, and specifically, the way in which his tax dollars causally implicated him in it—supporting the government that supported slavery. Thoreau took no issue with the imediate direction of taxes, such as his highway tax, in that paying it made him simply a "good neighbor." Furthermore, while Thoreau strongly disagreed with slavery, he did not think that any person's duty was to be devoted to combating serious wrongs. Crucially, Thoreau considered it every person's duty to make sure that a role, even indirect, in supporting serious wrongs was not played. It is this crucial causal link that led Thoreau to take action—in his case, refusing to pay the tax that indirectly attached him to the wrong.

Thoreau was explicit in his endorsement of breaking the law in actions of civil disobedience; even if these actions come at some substantial cost to the agent, these costs are simply outweighed by the importance of removing oneself from blameworthiness in the wrong being protested. He specifically acknowledged that this cost might include imprisonment or loss of property, along with other harassments. This is not to say, however, that he endorsed acceptance of punishment and, by extension, the legitimacy of government; he simply was at the mercy of something stronger than him.

Thoreau, then, introduced several important components to contemporary understandings of civil disobedience, including the moral requirement of action, likely

Encyclopedia of Public Administration and Public Policy
DOI: 10.1081/E-EPAP 120012956

illegal, by private citizens, and the acknowledgment of the inevitability of punishment. In general, a key feature of Thoreau's presentation of civil disobedience is that it is in many ways indistinguishable from outright revolution. Thoreau blurs any distinction here by speaking explicitly and approvingly of revolution and "war with the State" within the essay, including the permissibility of bloodshed. This conflation can be contrasted with prominent advocates of civil disobedience in the twentieth century, beginning with Mohandas K. Gandhi.[4]

Gandhi is perhaps most famous for endorsing and engaging in nonviolent civil disobedience (an approach that Thoreau clearly did not advocate). Gandhi was primarily concerned with the British rule of India and sought through civil disobedience to achieve independence for his nation. For Gandhi, civil disobedience was merely a part of the broader movement of what he called *Satyagraha*, often described in English as something like "truth-force."

Gandhi offers two primary, related reasons for preferring nonviolence to violence in acts of civil disobedience. The first concerns the nature of the action. That is, violent action, even taken in the service of some supposed greater good, is still by definition violent, and so evil. This evil cannot be eradicated, given the way it is contained within the act, and thus, the outcome of the action, while good, can only be temporary. Because violent action is by definition evil, while nonviolent action is untainted by anger and hatred, Gandhi offers a second reason for preferring nonviolent action: it is more effective. That is, because the pressure exerted on the state by nonviolent civil disobedience is grounded in "goodwill and gentleness," it will more effectively and lastingly accomplish its ends than will violent action.

Another key element of Gandhi's discussion of civil disobedience was the notion of "self-purification" that the protester is required to first undergo. As Gandhi presents it, this self-purification is a deep and profound preparation, whereby the protester acknowledges the nature of the protest and what actions must be taken because of it. Like Thoreau, Gandhi acknowledges the hardships the protester is likely to endure; unlike Thoreau, Gandhi believed that these hardships must be voluntarily accepted. This voluntary acceptance and emphasis on nonviolence are two of Gandhi's most important contributions toward a contemporary understanding of civil disobedience.

Martin Luther King, Jr. took up these elements in addressing civil disobedience in relation to the civil rights movement in the United States. In King's "Letter From Birmingham City Jail,"[5] he echoes many of the key elements of civil disobedience presented by Gandhi before him. In advocating nonviolence as the appropriate means of civil disobedience, King explained that it is right because of its nature as a moral act, and because this moral foundation makes the act more effective in making the issue a focal point of public awareness. Like Gandhi, he advocated acceptance of the punishment, also calling the process "self-purification" and advocating this acceptance via workshops concerning appropriate behavior in civil disobedience. It was this acceptance of the state's reaction to civil disobedience that placed him willingly in jail, from where he wrote this famous letter.

King went further than Gandhi in making explicit the reasoning behind accepting the punishment of the state following civil disobedience. While Thoreau advocated violence and outright revolution in objecting to the state, King acknowledged the narrower focus that distinguished civil disobedience from revolution. That is, for King, it was not the state that needed to be toppled in the face of injustice, but rather the specific elements of law. In just this way, King preserved the notion of fidelity to the state that revolution denied. King mirrored the natural law tradition in drawing this distinction, explicitly citing Augustine's famous line that "an unjust law is no law at all." King took great care to point out the distinction between just and unjust laws, noting that he was solely targeting the latter.

Through Thoreau, Gandhi, and King, then, the notion of civil disobedience was importantly refined. Thoreau's primary concern was addressing the moral duty of the private citizen to be critical of the state through civil disobedience, while acknowledging the reaction that this protest would certainly elicit. Gandhi stressed the acceptance of this reaction, and crucially emphasized nonviolent activity as the proper means of civil disobedience. King echoed Gandhi in these important refinements, adding a more detailed discussion of the manner in which civil disobedience targets specific laws of the state while preserving fidelity to the state, recognizing its legitimacy in spite of its endorsement of some unjust laws.

Contemporary philosophers and theorists, notably John Rawls and Ronald Dworkin, contributed to our understanding of civil disobedience by continuing to refine how it is defined. Rawls, in his book *A Theory of Justice*,[6] argued that an adequate theory of civil disobedience would define and differentiate it from other forms of disobedience and specify the conditions under which civil disobedience is justified. An adequate theory also will explain the role that civil disobedience will play within the political system.

Civil disobedience, according to Rawls, involves a number of important features that serve to distinguish it from other forms of political action or protest. First, for Rawls, civil disobedience is an essentially political act, and thus is done openly and publicly. By engaging in civil disobedience, one hopes to bring a claim of injustice to the attention of the populace. Because civil disobedience is political, one must appeal to those political principles that are widely accepted by the members of that society. Civil disobedience is an appeal to the majority and its sense of justice, and by engaging in civil disobedience, one hopes to show the majority that the policy or law in dispute is inconsistent with the society's shared political values.

This public, political appeal must be nonviolent, because it is the final appeal to the society to have one's claim of injustice addressed. Like Gandhi and King, Rawls thought that civil disobedience should be nonviolent, because it will be more effective in accomplishing one's goals. Violence or violation of another's civil liberties, Rawls argued, could obscure the justness of the claim that one hopes to bring before the majority.

Further, Rawls shared King's conviction that nonviolence expresses one's fidelity to the law, and insofar as civil disobedience is a means of altering rather than replacing the current political system, nonviolence is an important way of expressing such fidelity. Rawls explained that, while civil disobedience is done with the hopes of changing the laws, it necessarily involves the violation of laws. One need not violate the law that is being protested, but nonetheless, the civilly disobedient act is an act that violates the law. Thus, according to Rawls, civil disobedience is defined as ''...a public, nonviolent, conscientious yet political act contrary to law usually done with the aim of bringing about a change in the law or policies of the government.''[6]

Rawls contrasted civil disobedience with conscientious refusal. Conscientious refusal is the violation of laws or administrative orders because the laws or orders violate one's personal convictions. One may, for instance, refuse to obey a certain law because to do so would violate a strongly held religious belief. This is conscientious refusal, not civil disobedience as Rawls understood it. Civil disobedience and conscientious refusal are distinguished by a variety of features. For instance, conscientious refusal is not a public act. That is, it is not intended to address the majority's sense of justice. In fact, when engaged in conscientious refusal, one may wish that the disobedience remain unknown to the general population and the government. Further, conscientious refusal is not necessarily based on the shared political principles of the society. Conscientious refusal is not necessarily a political act and thus may be grounded in one's personal moral, religious, or philosophical convictions.

Rawls argued that civil disobedience is justified when three conditions are satisfied. First, civil disobedience is appropriate only when there are substantial and clear injustices. Rawls thought that the most serious injustices will involve violations of liberty as opposed to economic injustices. Second, civil disobedience should generally be a last resort for bringing about political change. Before

resorting to civil disobedience, one should exhaust all other options that may redress the injustice. That is, all other appeals to the majority as well as legal appeals have failed to resolve the problem, and thus, the only remaining option to rectify the injustice is civil disobedience. Finally, Rawls argued that one must not disobey if this will threaten the existence of the state. Rawls explained that for civil disobedience to be justified, it must not threaten the stability of the government. Because civil disobedience is intended to bring about improvements within the government, individuals must be certain they are not threatening its existence by raising the objection. If the government or society is particularly unstable at the time, or a number of other people or groups are engaging in civil disobedience, then this is good reason to wait until the society is stable enough to address another claim of injustice.

According to Rawls, civil disobedience will play the role of a stabilizing device within the state. Rawls claimed that, much like free and regular elections or a judiciary empowered to interpret the constitution, civil disobedience will play an important role in preserving the integrity of the legal or political system. Here, again, one can see the distinctively political role that Rawls reserved for civil disobedience. Civil disobedience is just another part of the system of checks and balances within Rawls's theory of justice. The legal philosopher, Ronald Dworkin, disagrees with Rawls and King on this account, and sees no reason to limit civil disobedience only to cases of political protest.

While Dworkin and Rawls's accounts of civil disobedience were similar, the two philosophers disagreed in a number of important respects. In his book *A Matter of Principle*,[7] Dworkin argues that when one's morals, conscience, or integrity forbid obedience to a law or policy, then that person need not attempt to alter the law by other methods before refusing to obey. Such instances of what Dworkin called ''integrity-based civil disobedience'' justify one's refusal to obey, because when people violate their morals, conscience, or integrity in order to obey a law, they suffer immediate, irreparable harm by doing so. Thus, Dworkin broke from Rawls insofar as Rawls insisted that civil disobedience must be one's last resort. For Dworkin, one is justified in disobeying if the law requires a significant compromise of that person's moral, religious, or philosophic beliefs.

This is contrasted with justice-based civil disobedience which, according to Dworkin, is disobedience intended to challenge an unjust political policy or program. In those instances in which people object to the law because they have a justice-based complaint, Dworkin argued that they must first attempt to exhaust all other political avenues for bringing about the desired change before resorting to civil disobedience.

Additionally, Dworkin, unlike Rawls, did not consider publicity to be an essential feature of civil disobedience. Some instances of civil disobedience, for instance, dodging the draft or ignoring slave laws, are best accomplished covertly. People may wish to be arrested and charged with a crime to bring their cause to the attention of the majority. But, in order to be an act of civil disobedience, an individual need not have to be charged with a crime or be publicly violating the laws that the individual deems objectionable.

CIVIL DISOBEDIENCE AND PUBLIC POLICY IN THE UNITED STATES

The civil rights movement of the mid-twentieth century in the United States offers no shortage of illustrations of civil disobedience in practice, and through them, we can evaluate their relation to public policy. Perhaps one of the more famous cases begins with Rosa Parks, who, on December 1, 1955, violated segregation laws in Montgomery, Alabama, by refusing to yield her seat to White passengers boarding a bus after her. Her subsequent arrest touched off a year of monumentally important social upheaval, culminating in the November 13, 1956, decision by the U.S. Supreme Court declaring bus segregation laws unconstitutional. This set the stage for further pivotal features of the civil rights movement, including the national prominence of Dr. Martin Luther King, Jr., the protests in Birmingham in 1963, and the Civil Rights Act of 1964.

Immediately following the arrest of Rosa Parks, the African-American citizens of Montgomery, led in part by Dr. King and his associates, launched a bus boycott that would last for months. In lieu of buses, participants in the boycott took taxis, engaged in car pools, or even walked, maintaining a solidarity that would inform and inspire the civil rights movement. All of these actions, however, stood in violation of existing anti-boycott laws, and led to the arrests of 89 African-American leaders, including King. When this tactic failed, local officials turned to less scrupulous means in an attempt to undermine the boycott. Fabricated violations led to indiscriminate arrests of African-Americans; those awaiting carpools were charged with crimes ranging from illegal hitchhiking to loitering. Laws were passed with the clear purpose of undermining the boycott; African-American taxi drivers, who had taken to charging African-Americans a lesser fare in order to support the boycott, were prohibited from doing so. The city then attacked the car pools as a public nuisance interfering with private enterprise, a charge affirmed by local courts on November 13, 1956. This last step would have been devastating for the movement, had it not been for the Supreme Court's decision that day agreeing with a lower federal court's opinion that the segregation laws were unconstitutional—a case originating from Rosa Parks' refusal to pay the fine demanded of her for refusing to surrender her seat nearly a year earlier.

Montgomery, then, saw acts of civil disobedience against bus segregation laws and antiboycott laws, first by Rosa Parks and then by the African-American community participating in the bus boycott. These acts all challenged existing laws that were clearly unjust and did so while maintaining the nonviolence described and practiced by King, among others. While official local response was frequently disgraceful, the federal judicial response saw through the moral bankruptcy of the laws and local officials in question and supported the Montgomery African-American community.

With regard to public policy, it is worth noting one of the two ways that acts of civil disobedience seek to effect change: through judicial review. That is, while acts of civil disobedience most often seek to generally raise public awareness of a wrong, change is most frequently brought about by two avenues: through judicial review or through legislative action. For law enforcement officials, such as the police responding to cases of civil disobedience, response options are likely quite limited; insofar as civil disobedience involves violation of law, law enforcement officials cannot themselves change policy. They must simply enforce the laws impartially. Acts of civil disobedience, however, are aimed beyond law enforcement at the laws being enforced. These acts seek to set a course of judicial review underway or to raise awareness such that lawmakers will respond through legislation. When Rosa Parks' lawyers advised her to decline to pay her fine, their purpose was to pursue a legal challenge that would impact public policy via judicial decision. Importantly, the civil rights movement set in motion in part by Parks' action led to the Civil Rights Act of 1964, illustrating the legislative avenue of change.

This example of civil disobedience allows a clear evaluation of official response, precisely because of the way in which the protesters were plainly supported by justice and morality. In retrospect, we see clearly not only that the laws were unjust, but also that local law enforcement was in the wrong in administering punishment partially and arbitrarily. Looking beyond the civil rights movement, other cases where we are less clear about the moral standing of protesters and those they are protesting are also available, such as those involving protest against nuclear power and weaponry.

Perhaps one of the most famous movements against the development of nuclear power occurred during the late 1970s in Seabrook, New Hampshire. In 1977, a group calling themselves the Clamshell Alliance occupied the construction site of the Seabrook nuclear power plant. During the protest, the New Hampshire police arrested over 1400 members of the Clamshell Alliance. Refusing to post bond of $1500, the protesters were in prison for 2 weeks until the charges were dropped, and they were released.

The Alliance not only brought attention to the antinuclear power movement, but also helped further develop techniques of civil disobedience. The Clamshell Alliance had no centralized leadership, but instead, it was composed of smaller support groups or cells. Without centralized leadership, decisions had to be made democratically, and this was at times a slow process; however, the advantage was that there was no figurehead, and thus those who opposed the movement had no clear target to attack. Decentralized group organization was adopted by a number of other groups whose members sought to resist nuclear power in their communities.

There have also been a number of civilly disobedient actions taken against nuclear weapons and their production. On September 9, 1980, eight people entered the General Electric Nuclear Missile Re-entry division in King of Prussia, Pennsylvania. While in the factory, the eight poured bottles of their own blood on documents and hammered on, and thus destroyed, two nose cone casings for nuclear warheads. This group, whose members called themselves the plowshares eight (alluding to a biblical passage that references beating swords into plowshares), was convicted of burglary, conspiracy, and criminal mischief. In February of 1984, the Pennsylvania Superior Court overturned the conviction of the plowshares eight. The appellate process continued, but the plowshares eight were never sent back to prison. This act started what has since become known as the plowshares movement.

The plowshares movement has continued to draw attention to the nuclear weapons debate by engaging in similar acts of civil disobedience. Similar to those committed by the plowshares eight. For instance, the group that came to be known as the minuteman III plowshares was clearly influenced by the actions of the plowshares eight. On August 6, 1998, the 53rd anniversary of the bombing of Hiroshima, Japan, activists Daniel Sicken and Sachio Ko-Yin entered a nuclear silo in Weld County, Colorado. Sicken and Ko-Yin poured blood and stenciled a broken rifle, the international symbol of disarmament, onto the concrete cap of the silo. They then hammered on the tracks used to slide the concrete cap back so that the missile may be launched. After bending the tracks and breaking the anchoring bolts that hold the tracks in place, the two men sat down on the concrete cap and waited to be arrested. Sicken and Ko-Yin were later convicted of sabotage, conspiracy, and destruction of government property, and were sentenced to 41 months and 30 months in prison, respectively.

The prosecution and subsequent conviction of Sicken and Ko-Yin highlight a further matter of public policy related to civil disobedience. There is a great deal of disagreement about what is the appropriate governmental response to acts of civil disobedience. While most of the theorists and activists discussed here hold that those who violate the law must accept their resulting arrest willingly, it does not follow from this that the government should prosecute all those arrested. In fact, most will agree that the intentions and purposes of the individuals who engage in civil disobedience clearly distinguish them from common criminals. What is unclear, however, is whether the appropriate legal response to the common criminal is, for these reasons, inappropriate for the individual who engages in civil disobedience.

In his book, *The Morality of Civil Disobedience*,[8] Robert T. Hall presented a number of possible legal responses to civil disobedience. The options discussed by Hall can be divided into three separate categories: one may refuse to prosecute any case of civil disobedience, one may prosecute selectively, or one may prosecute all cases.

The first possibility, advocated by legal philosopher Hugo A. Bedau,[9] is to attach a rider to all laws stating that anytime a person violates a law in an act of civil disobedience or conscientious refusal, that person should not be prosecuted for the legal violation. The value of such a proviso is that the government would protect an important form of political or social expression.

Ronald Dworkin[10] argued that civil disobedience does not necessitate legal action or the drastic legal protection suggested by Bedau. Instead, Dworkin argues, whether an act of civil disobedience should or should not be prosecuted is a matter of prosecutorial discretion. For instance, if the violation of law associated with a particular act of civil disobedience did not harm anyone, then the prosecutor may have good reason to refuse to press the case against the individual who broke the law. In cases that involve harm, be it to persons or institutions, or the destruction of property, the prosecutor may then have a compelling reason to press the case against the individual. It is important to note that Dworkin believes no special actions or arrangements need to be made for cases of civil disobedience, prosecutorial discretion is already a feature of the legal landscape.

Another possibility is to allow a jury to address the problem of civil disobedience. That is, if the jury feels that the defendant was justified in violating the law, then they may acquit, despite the fact that they believe the defendant is genuinely guilty of a violation of the law. Allowing the jury to decide the issue may include the complication of forcing the courts to allow testimony regarding the defendant's motivations for violating the law as part of the defense, but this should not be an insurmountable problem. Indeed, motives already play an integral role in legal actions. However, within the United

States, the legal system has typically sought to limit the extent of jury nullification rather than extend it.

CONCLUSION

While the appropriate legal response to civil disobedience remains a significant problem for scholars and administrators, there can be no doubt that progress has been made in refining its definition and justification. Thoreau provides one of the first sustained discussions of civil disobedience. His argument for one's obligation to violate laws, when those laws contribute to injustices, helped lay the theoretical foundation for a more precise understanding of civil disobedience. Gandhi and King built on this foundation and helped permanently establish nonviolence as a necessary component of civil disobedience. Further, Gandhi and King agree with Thoreau that one must accept the consequences for violating the law. However, they differed from Thoreau in that they believe that by accepting the punishment, one reveals a general attitude of fidelity to the law, thus bolstering the moral strength of one's position. The works of Rawls and Dworkin further clarified the definition, but perhaps more importantly, both substantially clarified possible justifications for, and the role of, civil disobedience within a political system. Yet, it is not the writings but the actions of Thoreau, Gandhi, King, the Clamshell Alliance, the plowshares movement, and others like them that makes clear the

important role that civil disobedience can play in addressing injustices within a society.

REFERENCES

1. Plato. Crito; (Trans. G.M.A. Grube). In *Plato: Complete Works*; Cooper, J.M., Hutchinson, D.S., Eds.; Hackett Publishing Company: Indianapolis, 1997; 45.
2. Plato. Apology; (Trans. G.M.A. Grube). In *Plato: Complete Works*; Cooper, J.M., Hutchinson, D.S., Eds.; Hackett Publishing Company: Indianapolis, 1997; 27.
3. Thoreau, H.D. Resistance to Civil Government. In *Political Writings*; Cambridge University Press: Cambridge, 1996; 1–21.
4. Gandhi, M.K. *Selections From Gandhi*; Bose, N.K., Ed.; Navajivan Publishing House, 1957; 149–172.
5. King, M.L., Jr. Letter From a Birmingham Jail. In *Civil Disobedience*; Bedau, H.A., Ed.; Pegasus: New York, 1969; 72–89.
6. Rawls, J. A *Theory of Justice,* 2nd Ed.; The Belknap Press, 1999.
7. Dworkin, R. *A Matter of Principle*; Harvard University Press, 1985; 104–116.
8. Hall, R.T. *The Morality of Civil Disobedience*; Harper Row, Publisher, Inc.: New York, 1971; 131–151.
9. Bedau, H.A. On civil disobedience. J. Philos. **1961**, *58* (21), 653–665.
10. Dworkin, R. *Taking Rights Seriously*; Harvard University Press, 1977; 206–222.

Civil Service

J. Edward Kellough
University of Georgia, Athens, Georgia, U.S.A.

INTRODUCTION

In a general sense, the civil service is comprised of all individuals employed in government, with the exception of those in the military and those who work for the legislature and judicial branches of government. As such, civil service systems exist at every level of government and in every country. Because those who work in the civil service are charged with the responsibility for implementing and managing government operations and programs, the relationship between the civil service and political authorities at the heads of governments has always been of critical importance. Competence, responsiveness, and accountability in the civil service are issues often defined in terms of the context of that relationship. It is expected that public employees will posses the knowledge, skills, and abilities requisite for their positions; that they will be responsive to the public that they serve; and that they will be held accountable to the public and government leaders for their official actions.

THE CIVIL SERVICE SYSTEM

Early in the history of the United States, positions in the civil service were controlled largely by political authorities and were obtained primarily on the basis of political connections. At the federal level, the earliest presidents sought to guarantee that appointments went to people who were capable, but they also preferred people who held political views largely consistent with those advocated within their administrations. Eventually, as political parties became more active and more important nationally, party affiliation became a central criterion for appointment. This system, which became known as political patronage, was defended on the grounds that most jobs in government required little technical skill and that appointment on the basis of political connections would help to ensure responsiveness and accountability to the chief executive. Eventually, however, questions of competence were made subordinate to political considerations, and corruption and inefficiency were common. Patronage practices had given rise to a spoils system in which the offices of government were considered the rightful plunder of those who were victorious in the electoral process. As the parties alternated in control of the executive branch in the mid-1800s, instability, graft, and the abuse of public authority became common problems.

Significant reform of the spoils system at the federal level began with passage of the Pendleton Act of 1883. The law was passed following the assassination of President James A. Garfield by an individual who had lobbied the Garfield administration unsuccessfully for an appointment in the civil service. Garfield's assassination, along with generally declining fortunes of the Republican party, prompted the Republican majority in Congress to support the Pendleton bill. The legislation, which originally covered only approximately 10% of the federal workforce, specified that employees would obtain their jobs on the basis of their performance on open and competitive examinations designed to measure their abilities to perform the work at issue. Employees covered by the system were also protected from political abuse or removal from office solely for political reasons. As time passed, this approach to public employment, known as the merit system, was extended to cover more than 90% of the federal workforce, and today, most state and local governments have civil service systems similarly staffed on the basis of the merit principle.

Indeed, the prevalence of merit systems for public employment is such that the term civil service is often equated only with those positions filled on the basis of demonstrated ability rather than political connections. Defined in this manner, the civil service is governed by elaborate systems of rules and procedures intended to insulate public employees from undue political influence. For example, in addition to hiring, there are rules governing promotions, transfers, performance appraisal, and compensation. Politically neutral competence on the part of employees and equity or fairness in the manner in which employees are treated within the system are the core values served by the structures of rules and procedures. Obviously, such systems have the effect of constraining managerial discretion or the freedom with which managers may assign and utilize public employees. That is, in fact, the intention behind the array of civil service rules. Some observers, however, argue that greater flexibility for management is necessary to more effectively and efficiently achieve the purposes of government.

Encyclopedia of Public Administration and Public Policy
DOI: 10.1081/E-EPAP 120010769

Currently, popular civil service reform proposals are designed to bring about those greater levels of flexibility. Consistent with concepts known as the "new public management," recent reform initiatives stress reinvention, reengineering, decentralization, and deregulation of the civil service. Advocates for these approaches argue that authority for such key personnel actions within the civil service as selection, promotion, pay, and the classification of jobs should be moved from central personnel offices and placed in the various line agencies, where agency managers will be able to use that authority to better pursue organizational goals and objectives. In this way, human resources functions within the civil service could be better integrated with the planning and management control functions within public organizations. There is also a sense that by placing greater authority for the civil service in the hands of agency heads or directors, who often are political appointees, accountability from the civil service to political authority, especially executive authority, will be enhanced. While that may be the case, there may also be fewer safeguards designed to protect employees and promote equity in the public service. In effect, the great difficulty is to find a way to properly balance the legitimate need for flexibility and political control with appropriate levels of employee protection consistent with the concept of politically neutral competence. The U.S. federal civil service system has been reformed moderately in recent years to allow for greater flexibility in areas such as employee examination and selection procedures, but some state governments have pushed those reforms much further. The state of Georgia, for example, implemented a wide-ranging set of reforms in which authority over personnel policy within the state civil service has been highly decentralized. There is little empirical evidence, however, to demonstrate that the new personnel system is a significant improvement over the more traditional arrangement that had been in place earlier.

CONCLUSION

It is obvious that the civil service performs numerous essential tasks in any society. It is the means by which government services are delivered. One can generally find an extremely wide range of jobs within the civil service, ranging from skilled crafts and trades to engineers, scientists, technicians, and a host of professions from law to medicine. There are also numerous administrators skilled in organizing and managing organizational activities. Certainly, the quality of public services and even the perceived legitimacy of government are determined in large part by the quality of the civil service and the way in which it operates. Given the range of occupations and complexity, the administration and management of a civil service personnel system is not an easy task. Competent and capable employees must be recruited and selected. Jobs must be classified according the duties associated with them, and systems of compensation that are fair to employees and competitive with employers in the private sector must be devised. Employee training and development programs must also be implemented. Performance appraisal systems must be established, and policies for employee discipline must also be placed into operation. All of these personnel tasks must be accomplished in an effective manner if the civil service is to function properly.

FURTHER READING

Ban, C.; Riccucci, N.M. *Public Personnel Management: Current Concerns, Future Challenges*, 3rd Ed.; Longman: New York, 2002.

Berman, E.M.; Bowman, J.S.; West, J.P.; Wart, M.V. *Human Resource Management in Public Service: Paradoxes, Processes, and Problems*; Sage Publications: Thousand Oaks, CA, 2001.

Daley, D.M. *Strategic Human Resources Management: People and Performance Management in the Public Sector*; Prentice Hall: Upper Saddle River, NJ, 2002.

Gatewood, R.D.; Field, H.S. *Human Resource Selection*, 4th Ed.; The Dryden Press: Fort Worth, TX, 1998.

Hays, S.W.; Kearney, R.C. *Public Personnel Administration: Problems and Prospects*, 4th Ed.; Prentice Hall: Englewood Cliffs, NJ, 2002.

Ingraham, P.W. *The Foundation of Merit: Public Service in the American Democracy*; The Johns Hopkins Press: Baltimore, MD, 1995.

Ingraham, P.W.; Ban, C. *Legislating Bureaucratic Change: The Civil Service Reform Act of 1978*; SUNY Press: Albany, NY, 1984.

Kearney, R.C.; Hays, S.W. Reinventing government, the new public management and civil service systems. Rev. Public Pers. Adm. **Fall 1998**, *18*, 38–54.

Kellough, J.E.; Selden, S.C. Pay-for-performance systems in state government: Perceptions of state agency personnel managers. Rev. Public Pers. Adm. **Winter 1997**, *17*, 5–21.

Nigro, L.G.; Kellough, J.E. Civil service reform in Georgia: Going to the edge? Rev. Public Pers. Adm. **Fall 2000**, 41–54.

Shafritz, J.M.; Rosenbloom, D.H.; Riccucci, N.M.; Naff, K.C.; Hyde, A.C. *Personnel Management in Government: Politics and Process*, 5th Ed.; Marcel Dekker: New York, 2001.

Van Riper, P.P. *History of the United States Civil Service*; Row, Peterson and Company: Evanston, IL, 1958.

Civil Service Reform Act of 1978

Jerrell D. Coggburn
University of Texas at San Antonio, San Antonio, Texas, U.S.A.

INTRODUCTION

The Civil Service Reform Act of 1978 (CSRA) is considered a watershed event in the evolution of federal personnel administration. This stems from the fact that it was the first comprehensive civil service reform passed at the federal level since the Pendleton Act of 1883. The CSRA made a number of major structural changes to the federal civil service system and embraced a number of important administrative values. In so doing, the CSRA established the general framework under which federal human resource management is conducted today.

BACKGROUND

The passage of the CSRA in 1978 represented the culmination of decades of growing dissatisfaction with the federal government's personnel system. In the period between the passage of the Pendleton Act—which created the Civil Service Commission (CSC) and a merit-based personnel system for the federal government—and the CSRA, fundamental changes occurred in the scope and size of government. Throughout the twentieth century, the federal government grew in size and complexity as the problems it addressed multiplied and became increasingly intractable (e.g., poverty, civil rights). Predictably, the public began to question government's growth and cost and to associate policy failures with bureaucratic waste, laziness, and ineptitude. Such sentiment was understandable given the public's historic skepticism and distrust of the government, especially in the post-Watergate era.

Perceptions from inside the federal government were equally critical. The Pendleton Act had created a civil service system that promoted merit and politically neutral competence, but such an emphasis was not without consequence. What emerged was a professionalized federal workforce, protected from political coercion, that became resistant to political control. This created tension for presidents and their political appointees who were responsible for government performance but felt unable to control it. Similarly, federal managers felt hampered by restrictive and cumbersome personnel procedures and regulations. Employees, for their part, felt that they did not receive adequate recognition for their contributions. While a number of reforms were enacted over the years to address problems related to the civil service, they were piecemeal: as particular problems arose, the common approach was to pass legislation or to enact rules in an ad hoc fashion. Over time, however, these reforms served to create a civil service system widely perceived to be ineffective, inefficient, and unresponsive to presidential direction.

So, by the eve of the CSRA's passage, observers could agree upon a number of problems afflicting the federal personnel system, including the CSC's dual and conflicting mission (discussed below); the insularity of civil servants from political direction; excessive administrative procedures; a socially unrepresentative federal bureaucracy; and an inability to reward excellent employee performance.[1] In order to remedy the civil service's myriad problems, wholesale change was needed.[2] That wholesale change came in the form of the CSRA, which is generally considered one of President Jimmy Carter's most significant domestic policy achievements.

STRUCTURAL CHANGES

The CSRA included a host of changes to the organizational arrangements for carrying out the federal government's human resource function. Most of these structural changes were achieved through Reorganization Plan Number 2. Though Reorganization Plan Number 2 is not technically a component of the actual CSRA, it established the framework for carrying out the CSRA's provisions, so they are generally discussed as one. The most obvious structural change was the abolition of the CSC. The CSC, created by the Pendleton Act, was a three-member, bipartisan panel that represented an attempt to remove overt political control (i.e., the "spoils") over the federal personnel system. While largely successful in removing political abuses, experience showed that the CSC was pressured by its dual mission of administering the personnel function, including protecting merit principles, and serving as the president's personnel advisor. In its place, the CSRA created several administrative agencies.

Encyclopedia of Public Administration and Public Policy
DOI: 10.1081/E-EPAP 120010768

Office of Personnel Management

Under the CSRA, the Office of Personnel Management (OPM) became the main personnel management agency of the federal government. Among its mandates, OPM is responsible for making federal personnel policy, advising federal agencies on personnel-related issues, and monitoring compliance with personnel laws and regulations. In contrast to the former CSC's format, OPM is headed by a single director, appointed by and responsible to the president.

Merit Systems Protection Board

The CSRA assigned CSC's role of protecting merit principles to the newly created Merit Systems Protection Board (MSPB). The MSPB is a bipartisan, quasijudicial entity that carries out its merit protection role by hearing employee appeals and reviewing the government's personnel regulations. Additionally, the MSPB conducts research studies to ensure federal agencies' actions (including those of OPM) comply with merit principles. The MSPB's three members are appointed by the president and serve fixed, 7-year terms.

Office of Special Counsel

Within the MSPB, the CSRA created the Office of Special Counsel (OSC). The CSRA gives the OSC investigative and prosecutorial powers. In other words, the OSC has authority to investigate cases of alleged violation of prohibited personnel practices and to prosecute cases where civil service laws and regulations have been violated. OSC places special emphasis on providing protection to whistleblowers, that is, those federal employees who report violations of law, government mismanagement, or waste. The counsel is appointed by the President, with the Senate's advice and consent, and serves a 5-year term.

Federal Labor Relations Authority

The act also created the Federal Labor Relations Authority (FLRA). The "authority," as it is commonly referred to, is charged with overseeing union–management relationships, including determining bargaining units; certifying bargaining agents; and resolving labor–management impasses through its Federal Service Impasses Panel. The provision creating the authority (Title XII) was not originally contained in the CSRA as presented to Congress, but it was added later during the legislative process. Title XII is significant, because it gives statutory recognition to collective bargaining at the federal level. Prior to the CSRA, collective bargaining rights for federal employees had only been recognized in presidential

executive orders. The three members of the authority are appointed by the president (with senate approval) and serve overlapping 5-year terms.

Senior Executive Service

One of the most significant features of the CSRA was the creation of the Senior Executive Service (SES). The act envisioned the SES to be a cadre of top-tier executives, drawn from the highest levels of the federal service, serving as managerial generalists. In exchange for forgoing some protections they enjoyed under the civil service system, members of the SES are given the opportunity to compete for performance-based pay increases and bonuses (which can be as high as $20,000), to assume policy-making roles, and to develop their managerial skills through rotating assignments. Rotating assignments are also important from a political standpoint, because presidents and their political appointees (e.g., departmental or agency heads) are given flexibility to move senior career managers to the programs they deem appropriate. The basic idea for the SES is similar to Great Britain's higher civil service model that establishes "rank in the person"—members of the SES retain their rank (pay, status), even if their specific positions change.

VALUES AND CONCEPTS EMBODIED IN THE CSRA

A Foundation of Merit

In addition to the CSRA's major structural changes, the act is important for the administrative values and managerial concepts it embodies. Obviously, the act sought to improve the efficiency and effectiveness of the federal personnel system. These represent classic public administration values and are typically used to sell all sorts of administrative reform, not just civil service reform. But, in addition to these instrumental performance goals, the act reaffirmed the federal government's commitment to a number of important principles, not the least of which is the merit principle.

According to Alan K. Campbell, a chief architect of the CSRA and the first director of OPM, the merit principle was the foundation upon which the entire federal personnel function was to be based.[2] The drafters of the CSRA considered merit so important that the act codifies a statement of the merit principle at its outset (see Table 1). Accompanying this delineation was a statement of prohibited personnel practices (Table 2) which sought to clarify any ambiguity about who (anyone with personnel authority) could be held responsible for what (violating prohibited personnel practices). Together, these

Table 1 Merit system principles

- Recruiters should seek to achieve a workforce made up of qualified people from all segments of society, and selection and promotion should be based solely on merit, after fair and open competition.
- All employees and applicants should be treated fairly, without discrimination, and with proper regard for their privacy and constitutional rights.
- Equal pay should be provided for work of equal value, with appropriate consideration for the rates paid by private sector employers. Appropriate incentives and recognition should be provided for excellent performance.
- Employees should maintain high standards of integrity, conduct, and concern for the public interest.
- The federal workforce should be used efficiently and effectively.
- Retention should be based on performance, inadequate performance should be corrected, and employees who cannot or will not improve their performance to meet required standards should be separated.
- Employees should receive effective education and training in order to achieve better organizational and individual performance.
- Employees should be protected against partisan politics and may not use their offices for partisan political purposes.
- When employees legally disclose information evidencing wrongdoing (known as ''whistle-blowing''), they should be protected from reprisal.

Source: Merit System Protection Board, http://www.mspb.gov/foia/forms-pubs/intro.html#The Merit System (accessed August 2001).

provisions underscore the importance of merit as a guiding value in federal personnel under the CSRA.

Executive Control

While the act clearly reaffirmed the federal government's commitment to merit, it also represented the desire to make the federal bureaucracy more directly accountable to presidential control. The act strengthens such political accountability in a number of ways. For example, making OPM's director a presidential appointee helps to ensure that federal personnel policy will be responsive to presidential (political) priorities. Also, the structure of the SES, with career members working on a contractual basis in agencies led by presidential appointees, means that the reward and advancement of SES members depend in part on the performance assessments of these political appointees. Thus, an additional increment of political control is provided by the CSRA.

Social Representation

The CSRA reaffirmed the federal government's commitment to a socially representative workforce. This re-

affirmation came in various ways. For example, the act explicitly states the federal government's policy of having a workforce reflective of the nation's diversity. Toward that end, the act established a minority recruitment program—the Federal Equal Employment Opportunity Recruitment Program—within OPM. In addition, the CSRA shifted responsibility for enforcing nondiscrimination in the federal government to the Equal Employment Opportunity Commission. Finally, the act, as originally submitted to Congress, attempted to significantly curtail veteran's preference by limiting veteran's preference to a one-time, initial hiring preference. This was important,

Table 2 Summary of prohibited personnel practices

- Discriminating on the basis of race, color, religion, sex, national origin, age, disability, marital status, or political affiliation.
- Soliciting or considering statements concerning a person who is being considered for a personnel action unless the statement is based on personal knowledge and concerns the person's qualifications and character.
- Coercing the political activity of any person, or taking any action as a reprisal for a person's refusal to engage in political activity.
- Deceiving or willfully obstructing anyone from competing for employment.
- Influencing anyone to withdraw from competition for any position to help or hurt anyone else's employment prospects.
- Giving unauthorized preferential treatment to any employee or applicant.
- Nepotism.
- Taking or failing to take, or threatening to take or fail to take, a personnel action because of an individual's legal disclosure of information evidencing wrongdoing (''whistle-blowing'').
- Taking or failing to take, or threatening to take or fail to take, a personnel action because of an individual's exercising any appeal, complaint, or grievance right; testifying or lawfully assisting any individual in the exercise of any appeal, complaint, or grievance right; cooperating with or disclosing information to an agency Inspector General or the Special Counsel, or refusing to obey an order that would require the individual to violate a law.
- Discriminating on the basis of personal conduct that does not adversely affect the performance of an employee or applicant or the performance of others, except that an employee or applicant's conviction of a crime may be taken into account in determining suitability or fitness.
- Taking or failing to take any other personnel action if the act or omission would violate any law, rule, or regulation implementing or directly concerning the merit system principles.
- Violating a veterans' preference provision in connection with a personnel action (for purposes of disciplinary action only).

Source: Merit System Protection Board, http://www.mspb.gov/foia/forms-pubs/intro.html#Prohibited Personnel (accessed August 2001).

because granting hiring preferences to veterans, the over-whelming majority of whom are male, hampers diversification efforts. This provision, however, was dropped during congressional consideration of the act in favor of less far-reaching limitations.[3]

Decentralization

The CSRA gives OPM authority to delegate significant areas of responsibility to line agencies within the federal government. In so doing, the CSRA makes a statement about the desirability of personnel decentralization. The delegation and decentralization of examining, for example, is intended to give agencies direct control over determining employee qualifications and hiring, while freeing OPM to devote more of its energies to providing technical assistance to agencies.[4] In such an arrangement, agency managers have greater flexibility over personnel decisions and can make these decisions more quickly. It also emphasizes a service orientation for OPM instead of a centralized decision-making role.

Whistle-Blower Protection

The CSRA's inclusion of whistle-blower protections embodies at least two administrative values: employee rights and efficiency. Employee rights are bolstered by the OSC's charge to investigate cases of alleged reprisals suffered by whistle-blowers. The intent is to encourage employees to come forward with allegations of waste, mismanagement, and wrongdoing. This, in turn, will improve the efficiency of government, as these costly problems are rooted out.

Private Sector Management

Certain provisions of the CSRA represent the federal government's acceptance of private sector management models. The clearest examples of this are the act's merit pay provisions for mid-level managers (GS 13–15) and the model of executive compensation created for the SES. Both forms, which rely on individual performance evaluation, seek to increase performance by offering employees financial incentives. The logic used by the CSRA's drafters was simple: if the federal government was to become more efficient, it needed to adopt private sector techniques like performance evaluation and pay for performance.[5]

Experimentation

Finally, the CSRA provides for personnel experimentation through demonstration projects. Implicitly, this recognizes the inadequacy of synoptic, "one size fits all" approaches to personnel management. By allowing ex-perimentation with novel personnel practices, the CSRA seeks to improve personnel management while reducing the risk of applying reforms or new management practices government-wide prior to discovering their full implications.

APPRAISING THE CSRA

In general, academic treatments of the CSRA's implementation and impact have been unfavorable. At worst, the act has been described as a failure; at best, it has been said to have fallen short of its highest objectives. The act's shortcomings have been tied to its internal contradictions that reflect the tensions its designers faced, including: 1) the desire for decentralization to promote better management versus the desire for centralization to protect merit; 2) the maintainance of control through rules and regulations versus delegating authority and stressing individual accountability; 3) the desire for better management versus political responsiveness; and 4) reorganization of personnel structures to effect positive change versus revitalization of the civil service.[6] Political and economic factors have also been blamed for the act's failings. For example, implementation of significant pieces of the act occurred during the Reagan Administration. In the throes of economic stagflation, Reagan, who has never been described as a friend of the civil service, focused more on government cutbacks than on achieving the implementation objectives of the CSRA. Thus, the CSRA suffered from design and implementation problems. Specific examples of the act's problems are easy to identify.

First, consider the agencies created by the CSRA. In a survey of federal personnelists conducted by the MSPB, OPM received poor marks in key areas like technical assistance, monitoring and oversight, and policy guidance.[7] Academic researchers have been equally critical of OPM, noting that it has not modernized federal personnel management as envisioned by the CSRA and that many of the problems it was intended to remedy persist.[8] The MSPB and OSC have been criticized for not being aggressive in their efforts to protect merit and, in the case of MSPB, for favoring management in its decisions.[9] Also, the CSRA's language left unclear the relationship between the OSC and the MSPB. The tensions this created ultimately led to OSC being established as a separate, independent agency by the Ethics Act of 1989. Finally, researchers have given the FLRA credit for the timeliness and impartiality of its decisions but have also pointed out the ineffectual nature of its decisions: FLRA decisions are often overturned upon judicial review.[10] So, while the CSRA's structural changes have been effected, each of the new agencies has faced its share of operational difficulty.

Second, problems have plagued the SES. Attracted by the lure of advancement and monetary incentives, almost all of those eligible for the SES joined in the first year. Many felt betrayed when, within the year, Congress cut the number of SES members eligible for performance bonuses from 50 to 25%. Rotation in office has also proven to be troublesome. Intended to be a managerial development tool, many in the SES view reassignments as punitive measures. Early on, problems such as these resulted in low morale among SES members, rapid turnover within the SES (more than half of the original members were gone in 3 years), and a majority of SES members saying they would not recommend a career in federal government.[11] More recently, however, the SES has seen some positive developments. Resentment over pay issues was ameliorated when the Reagan administration lifted salary caps for the SES, and a 1992 MSPB survey[12] found SES members to have the highest levels of job satisfaction among all government employees. Despite this, most observers agree that the SES is one of the more disappointing aspects of the CSRA.

Finally, several other objectives of the act have achieved disappointing results. Merit pay, for example, has proven to be virtually unworkable in the federal government. The problems, which have been examined extensively by academics (for example, see Ref. [13]), center on employee perceptions about the fairness of merit pay determinations, the link between performance and pay, and the size of merit pay increases. Recognition of the problems in the merit pay for middle manager system came quickly, as Congress replaced the original system after only 3 years with the Performance Management System. This replacement system faced its own problems and was eliminated in 1993.

The act sought to afford additional protections to whistle-blowers, thus encouraging them to come forth with allegations. This objective has met with mixed success. A report by the MSPB[14] shows a decrease in the number of employees who reported witnessing wasteful activities. This would suggest that less waste has occurred over time. The same report shows that the number of employees blowing the whistle when waste was witnessed has increased over time. This again would suggest some success: fewer incidents, but a higher rate of reporting on the incidents that are observed. The problem, however, is that unacceptably high percentages (37%) of whistle-blowers report suffering reprisals for reporting the waste they observed.

The story is similar in the area of adherence to merit principles and prohibited personnel practices. As stated above, the CSRA reaffirmed the merit principle as the foundation for federal personnel management. However, alarmingly high numbers of federal employees report problems with their respective agencies' adherence to merit. For example, one-third of those responding to a 1996 MSPB survey indicated a belief that their agencies regularly fail to uphold merit in hiring and promotions, over one-third indicated their agencies do a poor job of protecting employees from personal favoritism, and one-fourth indicated their agencies do a poor job of ensuring equal pay for equal work.[15] In the area of equal employment opportunity, the same survey found a significant minority of employees who reported being denied a job or job benefit: 14% reported suffering racial discrimination, 13% reported sexual discrimination, and 11% reported age discrimination.[16] Findings such as these illustrate the difficulty of ensuring adherence to the most fundamental civil service tenets in a government of approximately 3 million employees.

Finally, experimentation through personnel demonstration projects has not lived up to expectations. This is due in part to limits placed on the number of demonstration projects that can be authorized (no more than 10 at one time), the time-consuming nature of receiving approvals to conduct the projects, and OPM passivity in encouraging agency demonstration projects.[17] Still, the demonstration projects are not without value. The China Lake Naval demonstration project, for example, experimented with the use of broad banding pay. This approach collapses pay grades into wide pay bands, thereby increasing managerial flexibility in pay administration. The positive results achieved at China Lake have helped to make broad banding a mainstay of contemporary personnel reform proposals. Even here, however, government-wide implementation remains elusive.

CONCLUSION

The CSRA held out the promise of creating a more efficient, effective, and responsive personnel system. Given all that it promised, coupled with the novelty of many of its reform components—at least as applied to the *public* sector—it is not surprising that the act has not been able to deliver on all fronts. Indeed, the continued interest in reforming the federal civil service (e.g., the Clinton Administration's National Performance Review) attests to the fact that the CSRA was not the success story proponents had hoped for. Despite its shortcomings, the CSRA retains prominence in the public administration field, because it still constitutes the broad framework for federal human resource management.

REFERENCES

1. Ingraham, P.W. The Civil Service Reform Act of 1978: Its Design and Legislative History. In *Legislating Bureaucratic Change: The Civil Service Reform Act of 1978*;

Ingraham, P., Ban, C., Eds.; State University of New York Press: Albany, NY, 1984; 13–28.

2. Campbell, A.K. Testimony on Civil Service Reform and Reorganization (March 14, 1978). In *Classics of Public Personnel Policy*; Thompson, F., Ed.; Moore: Oak Park, IL, 1979; 77–102.

3. Rosenbloom, D.H.; Berry, C.R. The Civil Servive Reform Act and EEO: The Record to Date. In *Legislating Bureaucratic Change: The Civil Service Reform Act of 1978*; Ingraham, P., Ban, C., Eds.; State University of New York Press: Albany, NY, 1984; 182–199.

4. Ingraham, P.W.; Reed, P.N. The Civil Service Reform Act of 1978: The Promise and the Dilemma. In *Public Personnel Administration: Problems and Prospects*, 2nd Ed.; Hays, S., Kearney, R., Eds.; Prentice Hall: Englewood Cliffs, NJ, 1990; 277–291.

5. Ingraham, P.W.; White, J. The design of civil service reform: Lessons in politics and rationality. Policy Stud. J. **1989**, *17* (2), 315–330.

6. Ingraham, P.W. The Design of Civil Service Reform: Good Politics or Good Management? In *The Promise and Paradox of Civil Service Reform*; Ingraham, P., Rosenbloom, D., Eds.; Pittsburgh University Press: Pittsburgh, PA, 1992; 19–36.

7. Merit Systems Protection Board. *Federal Personnel Management Since Civil Service Reform: A Survey of Federal Personnel Officials, A Report to the President and the Congress of the United States*; Merit Systems Protection Board: Washington, DC, 1989; 1–23.

8. Lane, L.M. The administration and politics of reform: The Office of Personnel management. Policy Stud. J. **1989**, *17* (2), 331–351.

9. Vaughn, R.G. The U.S. Merit Systems Protection Board and the Office of Special Counsel. In *The Promise and Paradox of Civil Service Reform*; Ingraham, P., Rosenbloom, D., Eds.; Pittsburgh University Press: Pittsburgh, PA, 1992; 121–140.

10. Rosenbloom, D.H. The Federal Labor Relations Authority. In *The Promise and Paradox of Civil Service Reform*; Ingraham, P., Rosenbloom, D., Eds.; Pittsburgh University Press: Pittsburgh, PA, 1992; 141–156.

11. Huddleston, M.W. Is the SES a higher civil service? Policy Stud. J. **1989**, *17* (2), 406–419.

12. Merit Systems Protection Board. *Working for America: An Update, A Report to the President and the Congress of the United States*; Merit Systems Protection Board: Washington, DC, July 1994; 1–42.

13. Perry, J.L. The Merit Pay Reforms. In *The Promise and Paradox of Civil Service Reform*; Ingraham, P., Rosenbloom, D., Eds.; Pittsburgh University Press: Pittsburgh, PA, 1992; 199–215, see also Gaertner, K.N.; Gaertner, G.H. Performance Evaluation and Merit Pay: Results in the Environmental Protection Agency and the Mine Safety and Health Administration. In *Legislating Bureaucratic Change: The Civil Service Reform Act of 1978*; Ingraham, P., Ban, C., Eds.; State University of New York Press: Albany, NY, 1984; 87–111.

14. Merit Systems Protection Board. *Working for America: An Update, A Report to the President and the Congress of the United States*; Merit Systems Protection Board: Washington, DC, July 1994; 1–42.

15. Merit Systems Protection Board. *Adherence to the Merit Principles in the Workplace: Federal Employees' Views, A Report to the President and the Congress of the United States*; Merit Systems Protection Board: Washington, DC, September 1997; 1–12.

16. Merit Systems Protection Board. *The Changing Federal Workplace: Employee Perspectives, A Report to the President and the Congress of the United States*; Merit Systems Protection Board: Washington, DC, March 1998; 1–41.

17. Ban, C. Research and Demonstration under CSRA: Is Innovation Possible. In *The Promise and Paradox of Civil Service Reform*; Ingraham, P., Rosenbloom, D., Eds.; Pittsburgh University Press: Pittsburgh, PA, 1992; 217–235.

Civil Service Reform and Reinvention

Jerrell D. Coggburn
University of Texas at San Antonio, San Antonio, Texas, U.S.A.

INTRODUCTION

Civil service reform and reinvention refers to the purposeful modification of governmental human resource management (HRM) systems with the goal of maximizing important administrative values. The particular modifications adopted and the values they manifest vary over time and circumstance.

THE IMPORTANCE OF ADMINISTRATIVE VALUES TO CIVIL SERVICE REFORM

In the most basic terms, civil service systems exist to meet three purposes:[1]

1. To recruit qualified workers for public sector jobs.
2. To reward and develop the public workforce.
3. To provide rules for the public workforce to meet public objectives.

The simplicity of this depiction, however, masks important tensions inherent to civil service systems. These tensions are often described by academics as resulting from a number of competing administrative values seeking expression (Several authors have discussed the importance of administrative values. For example, see Ref. 2). At different points in time, some of these values receive greater emphasis relative to others, and these shifts in emphasis are reflected in the reforms adopted. Because an emphasis on one value can come at the expense of others, there remains continual pressure for reform. Thus, civil service reform has become an enduring feature of the American political system.

David H. Rosenbloom (This discussion of administrative values draws heavily on Ref. 3) provided one framework for understanding the values contained in civil service systems. Specifically, Rosenbloom contended that public administration can be understood from three perspectives: managerial, political, and legal. Each perspective is associated with certain administrative values. The following discussion highlights these administrative values within the context of civil service reform (For complete treatments the history of American civil service reform, see Ref. 4).

Political Values

First, the political perspective emphasizes two administrative values: representativeness and responsiveness. Representativeness means that the composition of the civil service should mirror American society. This, in turn, should allow the actions undertaken by administrative agencies to reflect (or "represent") the will of the majority in the populace. This value has taken on several forms during the history of the civil service. Under George Washington, representativeness took on a geographic connotation, because having all regions of the country represented was viewed as a way to insure legitimacy and support for the federal government. Representativeness has also entailed partisan considerations. This was evident in Thomas Jefferson's efforts to balance the proportions of Republicans and Federalists within the federal bureaucracy so that they reflected the nation's partisan composition. In more recent times, the value has taken on a demographic tone, which can be seen in governments' Equal Employment Opportunity and Affirmative Action policies. Despite these variations, the general objective is the same: to have a civil service reflective of the nation.

Responsiveness is the second value associated with the political perspective. In the context of the civil service, this value means having a government that does not thwart the political will of citizens as reflected in their choice of elected officials. Essentially, this means that elected executives should have control over government's policies and programs and, by necessity, the civil servants who implement them. This value was prominent in the patronage or "spoils" systems that emerged full-blown at the federal level following the election of Andrew Jackson in 1829. Under spoils, newly elected executives fill administrative positions with political supporters, whether they are technically qualified or not. Being supporters, such individuals are likely to be sympathetic (or "responsive") to the policies of the newly elected. While the most egregious abuses of patronage have virtually vanished due to various civil service laws and court de-

Encyclopedia of Public Administration and Public Policy
DOI: 10.1081/E-EPAP 120010770

cisions,[a] the desire for responsiveness endures. For example, President Franklin Roosevelt established many "New Deal" agencies outside of the federal civil service system, President Eisenhower created a new category of federal policy-making positions (known as "Schedule C"), with appointees who were exempt from the civil service system's provisions, while the Carter Administration's Civil Service Reform Act (CSRA) of 1978 gave presidents power to make political appointments to high-ranking posts within the Senior Executive Service and to appoint the director of the Office of Personnel Management (OPM). In all of these cases, the underlying intent was the same: make the federal bureaucracy (i.e., the civil service) more responsive to presidential direction.

Managerial Values

The second perspective identified by Rosenbloom is the managerial perspective. This perspective emphasizes the values of efficiency, effectiveness, and economy. These values are to be achieved through the apolitical, business-like administration of the human resource (HR) function. As is the case with the values of the political perspective, the importance of managerial values has fluctuated over time. For example, in the late 1800s, the Progressive movement sought to remove rampant partisan abuses from the civil service. Under the spoils approach, it was not uncommon for unqualified workers to be appointed to office and then to use their positions for personal gain. Because new elections brought new rounds of patronage appointments, the activities of governmental agencies also lacked consistency and continuity. The passage of the Pendleton Act in 1883 sought to remedy this by creating a merit-based civil service system. This meant that civil servants were to be selected on the basis of competence—that is, their ability to perform the job as determined by open, competitive exams—and political neutrality. In so doing, qualified persons would be hired (efficiency and effectiveness) in a systematic fashion (efficiency and economy), and much of the abuse would be eliminated (economy). In other words, the Pendleton Act was an attempt to combat the consequences of the spoils system's emphasis on political values by establishing a civil service system emphasizing managerial values.

The Pendleton Act did not mark the end of managerial values' importance to the civil service. Indeed, the desire

to take political considerations out of the public HR equation and to make the civil service more "business-like" was a central theme in the evolution of civil service systems during the twentieth century, and it remains a salient feature today. The Classification Acts of 1923 and 1949, for example, established position classification as a key personnel function. Position classification systematically organizes government jobs according to the nature of work done and the knowledge, skills, and abilities required. Ideally, this represents an efficient way to specify what work is to be done, ensure that people doing similar work are treated similarly, establish the basis for reward, and establish career paths for civil servants. The passage of the Hatch Act at the federal level and "Little Hatch Acts" at the subnational level are also indicative of attempts to remove politics from the "administrative" questions of the civil service. In general, the desire to remove politics from civil service decisions and instead to base them on technically efficient, effective processes has been a defining characteristic of the development of recruitment, hiring, compensation, and promotion systems.[1]

Legal Values

Finally, the legal perspective emphasizes values like employee rights and equity. These values have steadily gained importance in the United States, especially since the demise of the "doctrine of privilege." This doctrine held that government employment was a privilege—not a right—and that governments could set strict conditions on public employment. Public employees, in turn, "voluntarily" agreed to these restrictions when they accepted a government position. In practice, this meant that civil servants had no recourse when they suffered an adverse personnel action (e.g., being denied a job or promotion, receiving a reprimand or demotion, being separated) for exercising rights they normally enjoyed as citizens (e.g., free speech, freedom of expression, etc.). With the fall of this doctrine by the 1970s, many of the rights and liberties public employees enjoyed as private citizens were extended into the public workplace. So, for example, an employee that blows the whistle on agency wrongdoing can no longer be dismissed for disloyalty; rather, such expression is a protected right.

Due process is another important employee right. In *Board of Regent's v. Roth*, the Supreme Court held that public employees can establish property interests in their government positions. Since the Constitution, through the fifth and 14th amendments,[b] establishes that no person can

---

[a]The Pendleton Act of 1883 eroded patronage by creating a limited merit system for the federal government. The merit system's coverage was gradually expanded over time. The Hatch Act of 1939 (as amended) places additional limits on the partisan activities of both public employers and employees. The courts have also played an important role in curbing patronage. Notable cases include *Elrod* v. *Burns* (1976), *Branti* v. *Finkel* (1980), and *Rutan* v. *The Republican Party of Illinois* (1989).

---

[b] Due process for federal government employees is established constitutionally by the 5th amendment and statutorily by the Lloyd-LaFollette Act of 1912. Due process for state and local government employees is established constitutionally through the 14th amendment.

be denied life, liberty, or *property* without due process of the law, civil service systems at all levels of government had to be modified to afford employees due process. The practical result has been the creation, in many instances, of elaborate employee grievance and appeals procedures designed to ensure the protection of these rights.

Finally, the legal perspective values the equitable treatment of all applicants and employees. In other words, similarly situated applicants or employees should be treated in a similar fashion regardless of their gender, race, age, ethnicity, religious beliefs, or physical abilities. So, for example, when the federal government's Professional and Administrative Career Examination (PACE) was found to have an adverse impact on minority applicants, the federal government was forced by the courts to take remedial action. While PACE represented an attempt to make the selection of entry-level professional and career candidates more efficient (thus, maximizing managerial values), its demise represented the importance of legal values (equity) to the civil service. As a matter of practice, civil service regulations and procedures emphasizing legal values often come at the frustration of managerial values.

Rethinking the Purposes of Civil Service

Returning to the basic purposes mentioned at the outset, the values emphasized in civil service systems have profound effects on how individuals are recruited and selected for government positions (through patronage or competence?), how employees are rewarded and developed (through political loyalty or on-the-job performance?), and how employees are directed toward meeting public objectives (through overt political direction or through elaborate position descriptions?). Thus, the basic purposes of civil service are inextricably linked to managerial, political, and legal purposes and the administrative values they encompass. Since there has yet to be an agreement on what an appropriate balance is among the various administrative values,[5] there is little question that civil service reform will continue to be a feature of the American political landscape.

THE RECENT FACE OF REFORM: CIVIL SERVICE REINVENTION

Civil service reform has proceeded in an ad hoc fashion in the United States. As particular problems have arisen, the tendency has been to enact laws, rules, and regulations designed to prevent those problems from occurring again. Typically, scant attention has been given to the cumulative effect of adding rules and regulations on top of existing rules and regulations. In many jurisdictions, this

has resulted in the creation of rigid, complex, and ineffective civil service systems (For example, see Ref. 6). Critics cite a litany of problems to illustrate this, including lengthy and bureaucratic recruitment processes that repel quality applicants; labyrinthine grievance and appeal processes that stifle managers' ability to deal with poor performers; rigid and complex classification and compensation systems that make it difficult to assign work and reward performance; and central HR offices that emphasize regulatory compliance over HR effectiveness.

It is from this general depiction of public sector HR management that the most recent civil service reform efforts have emerged, largely under the broad "reinventing government" banner. The reinvention moniker is a reference to the work of David Osborne and Ted Gaebler, whose 1992 book, *Reinventing Government*, touched off a wave of interest in administrative reform, not just of civil service, at all levels of government. In fact, many aspects of reinvention mirror administrative reform efforts in other parts of the world (for example, in Canada, New Zealand, and Great Britain). Generally, reinvention-type reforms undertaken attempt to dramatically streamline regulatory burdens while simultaneously decentralizing decision-making authority to managers in line agencies. "Let managers manage" is the common rallying cry, reflecting reformers' desire to improve the quality of services government delivers to citizens (or "customers," in reinventing lingo).

Because an effective HR function is intimately related to government's ability to perform, civil service reform has become a prominent feature of reinvention. Among the key civil service reinvention themes are deregulation, decentralization, a shift to a "service" orientation for central HR offices, and privatization.

Deregulation

In attempting to combat the abuses and corruption associated with patronage, civil service systems developed rules and procedures that emphasized merit and neutral competence. While largely successful in battling problems associated with patronage, proponents of reinvention argue that this has come at a significant cost to managerial flexibility and, ultimately, government performance. Thus, deregulation entails removing administrative rules and procedural requirements that are thought to impede performance. Deregulation can affect almost every aspect of HRM. For example, in the area of recruitment and selection, deregulation might include eliminating requirements for all job applicants in a given jurisdiction to use the same standardized application or to take a written exam. Instead, applicants might be allowed to submit résumés containing information more directly related to the jobs they are applying for. Similarly, deregulation can come into play in employee discipline and termination. As mentioned above, managers often feel constrained by the inability to effectively deal with poor performers or nonperformers. Streamlining (i.e., "deregulating") grievance and appeals procedures by consolidating reviews and relaxing management's evidentiary burdens attempts to balance employees' due process rights with government's desire to effect employment actions in a timely, efficient fashion. Finally, in compensation, deregulation might provide agency managers the freedom to set or adjust employee pay within broad pay bands based upon prevailing market wages and an employee's skill and on-the-job performance (this, as opposed to rigid classification-based pay schedules and step increases). As these examples show, deregulation attempts to remove "red tape" that is thought to undermine HR management effectiveness and efficiency.

Decentralization

Decentralization is another aspect of reinvention. It entails parceling out authority and discretion over many important HR functions from central HR offices to managers in line agencies. The basic idea is to empower managers responsible for producing programmatic results by giving them more control over HR management. For example, decentralizing hiring authority to agencies allows managers to formulate job criteria, control the evaluation of applicants, and hire qualified individuals. The rationale for this is straightforward: managers in line agencies have greater technical knowledge about their vacant positions than personnelists working in central HR offices; thus, they are in a better position to ensure the recruitment and selection process results in hires that meet their respective agencies' needs. Moreover, placing HR management authority in the hands of the agencies actually doing the hiring, promoting, training, etc., expedites these processes. In general, a decentralization strategy seeks to increase managerial authority over HR management, thereby enabling managers to utilize it as an effective performance improvement tool.

Service Orientation

This aspect of reinvention is directly related to the preceding two. Traditionally, central HR offices assumed responsibility for creating HR policy, administering various HR functions (e.g., classification, competitive exams, training, and development), and for ensuring regulatory compliance through agency oversight. Proponents of reinvention argue that these central "counterbureaucracies," as they are sometimes called, have the tendency to act as "guardians" of the merit principle and the merit system. From the reinvention standpoint, this represents a form of "goal displacement," in that the true goals of the civil service system (e.g., attracting and retaining the most qualified workforce) are obscured by an overemphasis on ensuring adherence to rules. In contrast, a service orientation would have central HR offices focus on providing assistance and advice to line agencies, as these agencies assumed increased responsibilities for the day-to-day management of HR functions within a decentralized, deregulated environment.

Privatization

A final aspect of reinventing the civil service is privatization. While there are many varieties of privatization, a common approach is for government to contractually "outsource" services to nonprofit or private (for-profit) organizations. In other words, government makes a provision for some "public" service or good, but the actual production is left to a contracted entity. Free of the civil service's regulatory burdens and armed with the ability to design service delivery, private contractors are thought to be able to provide better services at lower costs. Importantly, privatizing also sends the politically symbolic message that big government—as exemplified by the number of civil servants—is being cut. Privatization of public services like prisons and solid waste collection has been around for decades. Importantly, however, privatization is not isolated to programmatic areas. Indeed, traditional HR functions like payroll and benefits administration, workforce training and development, employee assistance programs, and employment testing have been targeted for privatization. Proponents argue that outsourcing these "housekeeping" activities frees HR offices to focus on their strategic and advisory roles.

CONTEMPORARY EXAMPLES OF REFORM AND REINVENTION

Recent examples of civil service reinvention are plentiful. At the federal level, reinvention activities were initiated under the Clinton Administration's National Performance Review (NPR). In *Reinventing Human Resource Management*, a report that accompanied the original NPR, the administration specified a number of goals for federal HR management (Table 1).

The NPR recommended a variety of specific initiatives designed to accomplish these broad reinvention objectives. In many instances, these recommendations were followed. For example, the NPR resulted in several instances of deregulation. The most visible was the elimination of the *Federal Personnel Manual*: the administration went so far as to use a wheelbarrow to ceremoniously discard it in a dumpster.[7] In another example

Table 1 Reinventing human resource management under the National Performance Review

---

Enable managers to create and maintain a quality, diverse workforce
- Create a flexible and responsive hiring system.
- Reform the general schedule classification and basic pay system.

Enable managers to empower, develop, train, reward, and discipline employees
- Authorize agencies to develop programs for improvement of individual and organizational performance.
- Authorize agencies to develop incentive reward and bonus systems to improve individual and organizational performance.
- Strengthen systems to support management in dealing with poor performers.
- Clearly define the objective of training as the improvement of individual and organizational performance; make training more market driven.

Enable employees to manage work and family responsibilities
- Enhance programs to provide family-friendly workplaces.

Hold managers accountable for adherence to principles of merit and equal opportunity
- Improve process and procedures established to provide workplace due process for employees.
- Improve accountability for Equal Employment Opportunity goals and accomplishments.
- Improve interagency collaboration and cross-training of human resource professionals.

Create a system that is self-renewing and continually improving
- Strengthen the Senior Executive Service so that it becomes a key element in the government-wide culture change effort.
- Eliminate excessive red tape and automate functions and information.
- Form labor–management partnerships for success.
- Provide incentives to encourage voluntary separations.

Source: National Performance Review. *Reinventing Human Resource Management*; Accompanying Report of the National Performance Review. National Performance Review: Washington, DC, 1993.

of deregulation, the OPM also eliminated the requirement for all federal agencies to use a standard application form (the form is known as SF-171). The NPR also accomplished decentralization—as of 1998, virtually all of the federal government's hiring authority has been decentralized to line agencies.[8]

An important question is whether the reinvention reforms initiated by the Clinton Administration will last under the administration of George W. Bush. There is early evidence that many broad reinvention themes will, in fact, be continued. In the *President's Management Agenda*, for example, President George W. Bush calls for the flattening of agencies to make them "citizen centered," for the contracting out of "commercial positions," and for agencies to more fully utilize the existing HR flexibilities already available. Additionally, the

administration will be searching for other ways "to enhance management flexibility, permit more performance-oriented compensation, correct skills imbalances, and provide other tools to recruit, retain, and reward a high quality workforce."[9]

Not all reinvention activity—or perhaps even the most impressive—has occurred at the federal level. The most far-reaching, perhaps radical,[10] reinvention has occurred at the state level. Georgia is the prime example. In 1996, under the direction of then Governor Zell Miller, the state effectively eliminated its traditional merit system. The justification for this change was classic reinvention. According to Miller, the state's merit system was outdated, overregulated, and provided cover for bad workers instead of rewarding good workers (As quoted in, see Ref. [11]). The reform adopted, Act 816, contained deregulation and decentralization components aimed at speeding hiring and disciplinary processes, providing agency managers greater HR flexibility, and reorienting the state HR office to an advisory and service role. The initial impacts are only beginning to surface, and they appear mixed. For example, there is some evidence that deregulation and decentralization have allowed cronyism and favoritism to creep back into the state's HR functions, and while most state workers in Georgia agree that the reforms have expedited certain HR processes, most do not perceive an increase in overall HR effectiveness (see Ref. 12).

Wisconsin is another state that has been widely recognized for recent civil service reforms. Responding to many of the same frustrations as Georgia, Wisconsin undertook a number of civil service reforms during the 1990s. Under the direction of Robert Lavigna, the state's merit system administrator at the time, Wisconsin instituted a number of reforms intended to improve the state's HR function. Examples include decentralizing HR authority, establishing walk-in testing procedures for some administrative positions, and creating an on-line jobs bulletin service. The state also created two specialized recruitment programs: the Critical Recruitment Program and Entry Professional Program. The Critical Recruitment Program gives agencies the flexibility to quickly hire workers in competitive areas like engineering and health care. Similarly, the Entry Professional Program eschews traditional written exams in favor of more flexible recruitment techniques so that qualified college graduates can be recruited and hired more quickly. These reforms, which incorporate reinvention themes like decentralization and deregulation, appear to have improved the civil service system in the state. Specifically, the state reports that hiring is more timely, applicant pools are better qualified, workforce diversity has improved, and HR costs have decreased (These reforms and their outcomes are described in Ref. 13).

Most recently, the state of Florida announced its intention to privatize major portions of its HR function. In September 2001, the state issued an "intent to award" for a $40 million per year contract with a private firm, Convergys, Inc. The scope of work to be performed by the contractor, as indicated in the invitation for bids issued by the state, is broad. Included are many transactional processes like advertising vacancies, assisting in employee training and development, collecting time sheets, processing new appointments, administering payroll and benefit systems, and maintaining employee personnel records.[14] Obviously, shifting these functions to a private sector provider represents a large-scale HR experiment. The rationale for conducting it is economical and political. Economically, the state figures that it can save the $80 million needed to update its antiquated personnel computer system, plus an estimated $25 million per year in personnel salaries over the 5- to 7-year life of the contract. Politically, privatizing HR represents the priorities of Governor Jeb Bush, who ran on the pledge to make Florida's government "leaner." It is worth noting that the state plans to maintain control over critical areas like employee selection, discipline, grievances, and collective bargaining. Still, the scope of the proposed outsourcing is enormous.

CHALLENGES OF REINVENTED CIVIL SERVICE

The direction that civil service reform and reinvention has taken in recent years, as exemplified above, leads to a number of important challenges. Among these are ensuring that the requisite HR management knowledge, skills, and abilities are present in central HR offices and line agencies; addressing equity issues associated with the removal of standard, centralized HR processes; and preventing the potential political abuses from materializing. How these challenges are addressed will be telling to the next, perhaps inevitable, wave of civil service reform.

HR Management Expertise

First, a decentralized personnel system means that expertise formerly found in central HR offices must now be disseminated throughout the line agencies of government. Mangers and HR generalists in these agencies must possess the knowledge, skills, and abilities needed to effectively and legally assume a range of HR responsibilities, potentially including recruitment, selection, performance appraisal, classification, compensation, and training. Some solace is offered by reinvention's call to have central HR offices move to consultative roles in which they offer advice and assistance to line agencies.

This, however, entails new knowledge, skills, and abilities on the part of those in central HR agencies, for example, they need to become skilled consultants with a breadth of HR knowledge as opposed to specialized personnel experts. If either of these necessities fails to materialize, then the effectiveness, efficiency, and perhaps legality of public HR management practices may be called into question.

Equity

A second major concern related to civil service reinvention is equity. Traditionally, a primary responsibility of central HR offices has been to ensure equity. Examples include ensuring open competitive exams, classification and compensation systems that award equal pay for equal work, and consistent procedures for employee grievances. When control is decentralized and the processes are deregulated, there remains a real possibility that similar cases will be treated in a dissimilar fashion. Such a possibility has been raised by many in the public administration community who warn that public employees have come to expect equitable treatment (See for example, Ref. 15). If civil servants experience disparate treatment as a result of where (i.e., which agency) or for whom (i.e., which manager) they work, then there will likely be a backlash that favors the reassertion of standardized, centralized controls. In other words, managerial flexibility may run into renewed demands for equity.

Politics

Finally, reinvention has to contend with the "politics problem" (For example, see Ref. 16). By removing HR rules and regulations and by decentralizing authority, a reinvented civil service is one that is more open to political and partisan abuses. As mentioned above, the historical development of the civil service placed a premium on combating such problems. When rules are relaxed or eliminated and when HR authority is decentralized, there is a greater likelihood that political officials will use their positions of control and influence to reward friends and political supporters. If and when such political favoritism or cronyism occurs, the result will likely be new calls for reform—reforms that echo traditional antipatronage themes. It is important to recall, however, that not all civil service protections are embodied in civil service laws and regulations. Indeed, the courts have placed severe limits on the ability of government officials to "clean house" on purely political grounds. Similarly, widespread fixation on government performance means that political figures have an incentive to use their HR authority to hire competent individuals who can help government "do more for less." Still, the possibilities of political intrusions into HR decision making raise the chances that reinvention will encounter difficulties.

CONCLUSION: MORE REFORM AND REINVENTION

Any description of civil service reform and reinvention must be viewed as prologue. Indeed, civil service reform has become "virtually a national pastime."[17] At this point, it is difficult to say what the full effects of civil service reinvention will be, as it will take many more years, perhaps decades, for them to materialize. However, a dynamic environment, influenced by shifting political, economic, and social forces, virtually ensures that the nature of civil service's problems will fluctuate, as will the administrative values civil service systems emphasize.

REFERENCES

1. Ingraham, P.W. *The Foundation of Merit: Public Service in American Democracy*; The Johns Hopkins University Press: Baltimore, MD, 1995.
2. Kaufman, H.F. Emerging conflicts in the doctrines of public administration. Am. Polit. Sci. Rev. **1956**, *50* (4), 1057–1073; and Thompson, F.J. Managing Within Civil Service Systems. In *Handbook of Public Administration*; Perry, J.L., Ed.; Jossey-Bass Publishers: San Francisco, 1989; 359–372.
3. Rosenbloom, D.H. Public Personnel Administration and Collective Bargaining. In *Public Administration: Understanding Management, Politics, and Law in the Public Sector,* 4th Ed.; McGraw-Hill: New York, 1998; 207–273.
4. Van Riper, P.P. *History of the United States Civil Service*; Row, Peterson and Co.: Evanston, IL, 1958; Cayer, N.J. Evolution of the Personnel System. In *Public Personnel Administration in the United States*, 3rd Ed.; St. Martin's Press: New York, 1996; 16–41; and Ingraham, P.W. *The Foundation of Merit: Public Service in American Democracy*; The Johns Hopkins University Press: Baltimore, MD, 1995.
5. Thompson, F.J. Managing Within Civil Service Systems. In *Handbook of Public Administration*; Perry, J.L., Ed.; Jossey-Bass Publishers: San Francisco, 1989; 359–372.
6. Ban, C. *How do Public Managers Manage?*; Jossey-Bass Publishers: San Francisco, CA, 1995; Jorgensen, L.; Fairless, K.; Patton, D. Underground merit systems and the balance between service and compliance. Rev. Public Pers. Adm. **1996**, *16* (2), 5–20; Cohen, S.; Eimicke, W. The overregulated civil service: The case of New York City's personnel system. Rev. Public Pers. Adm. **1994**, *14* (2), 10–27; Kettl, D.F.; Ingraham, P.W.; Sanders, R.P.; Horner, C.

Civil Service Reform: Building a Government that Works; The Brookings Institute: Washington, D.C., 1996. Several reform commissions have also singled-out civil service systems as a major source of government's performance problems, including The Volcker Commission (1989), the Winter Commission (1993), and National Performance Review (1993).
7. Gore, A. *The Best Kept Secrets in Government*; The Fourth Report of the National Performance Review; Government Printing Office: Washington, DC, 1996.
8. Ban, C. The National Performance Review as Implicit Evaluation of CSRA: Building on or Overturning the Legacy? In *The Future of Merit*; Pfiffner, J.P., Brook, D.A., Eds.; John Hopkins Press: Baltimore, MD, 2000; 57–80.
9. Executive Office of the President. U.S. Office of Management and Budget. In *The President's Management Agenda: Fiscal Year 2002*; Office of Management and Budget: Washington, DC, 2002; 13.
10. Condrey, S.E. Georgia's Civil Service Reform: A Four Year Assessment. In *Radical Reform of the Civil Service*; Condrey, S., Maranto, R., Eds.; Lexington Books: Lanham, MD, 2001; 179–194.
11. Nigro, L.G.; Kellough, E.J. Civil service reform in Georgia: Going to the edge? Rev. Public Pers. Adm. **2000**, *20* (4), 41–54.
12. Condrey, S.E. Georgia's Civil Service Reform: A Four Year Assessment. In *Radical Reform of the Civil Service*; Condrey, S., Maranto, R., Eds.; Lexington Books: Lanham, MD, 2001; 179–194; and Nigro, L.G.; Kellough, E.J. Civil service reform in Georgia: Going to the edge? Rev. Public Pers. Adm. **2000**, *20* (4), 41–54.
13. Lavigna, R. Creating a responsive personnel system. PA Times **1996**, *19* (11), 10, 14; and Lichster, J.E. Reinventing personnel systems. State Government News **1997**, *40* (8), 25, 31.
14. This information is drawn from the state of Florida's website:http://www.myflorida.com/dms/hrm/hrout/HR_Outsourcing_Project.html (accessed on September 2001).
15. Peters, B.G.; Savoie, R.J. Managing incoherence: The coordination and empowerment conundrum. Public Adm. Rev. **1996**, *56* (3), 281–290; Kellough, E.J. The reinventing government movement: A review and critique. Public Adm. Q. **1998**, *22* (1), 6–20.
16. Kellough, E.J. The reinventing government movement: A review and critique. Public Adm. Q. **1998**, *22* (1), 6–20; Ban, C. The National Performance Review as Implicit Evaluation of CSRA: Building on or Overturning the Legacy? In *The Future of Merit*; Pfiffner, J.P., Brook, D.A., Eds.; John Hopkins Press: Baltimore, MD, 2000; 57–80; and Thompson, F.J. The winter commission report: Is deregulation the answer for public personnel management? Rev. Public Pers. Adm. **1994**, *14* (2), 5–9.
17. Cayer, N.J. Merit System Reform in the States. In *Public Personnel Administration: Problems and Prospects,* 2nd Ed.; Hays, S., Kearney, R., Eds.; Prentice Hall: Englewood Cliffs, NJ, 1990; 263.

Collective Bargaining

Robert Hebdon
McGill University, Montreal, Quebec, Canada

INTRODUCTION

By permitting the formation and legal representation of unions or associations, collective bargaining processes reconcile the competing interests of managers and employees in the workplace. The potential for conflict exists in both private and public sectors—not only over economic issues but also the control of work processes. A third element of collective bargaining in a North American context is the institutionalization of disputes over disciplinary practices and the interpretation of collective bargaining agreements signed by management and unions. Thus, the goals of collective bargaining are to provide orderly and peaceful mechanisms for the resolution of disputes between management and labor over the distribution of economic rewards, the control over work processes, and the interpretation and application of collective bargaining agreements.

SCOPE

By the year 2000, over 37% of the U.S. public sector workforce were members of unions or employee associations. Collective bargaining had become entrenched as a mechanism for providing employee voice in public sector establishments at the local, state, and federal levels. Not all states, however, have collective bargaining laws. Twenty-four states have comprehensive laws that impose a "duty to bargain" on public employers for all public employees—state, teacher, police, fire, and other municipal employees (Table 1). At the other extreme, there are 11 states that have no duty to bargain in the law and five states that have no law at all (Arkansas, Colorado, Louisiana, Missouri, and West Virginia).

Differences Between Public and Private Sector Collective Bargaining

It is widely believed that the private sector model of collective bargaining is inappropriate for the public sector. Consequently, numerous important differences have emerged in the laws that govern two bargaining systems.

Scope of bargaining

Generally, public employee unions are more restricted in the scope of negotiable issues than their private sector counterparts. For example, employees of the federal government cannot bargain over wages or benefits. In the public sector, management's rights are more broadly defined to include matters of public policy.

Economic context

To some extent, public sector bargaining is insulated from the same market forces that exist in the private sector. By definition, such public goods as public health and safety are offered in a less competitive environment than in the private sector. Although the monopoly of services was seen as a bargaining advantage by public employee unions, particularly in the early years, fiscal conservatism and the privatization threat have eliminated any such advantage.

The right to strike

Unlike private sector collective bargaining, most public employee unions do not have a legal right to strike. As a matter of public policy, the services that public employees provide are viewed as too essential to permit disruptions. Strikes may threaten the health and safety of the public. Even in states where public sector strikes are legal (e.g., Pennsylvania), strikes may be stopped by injunction if they pose a threat to the health and safety of the public.

Four Decades of Bargaining

Since the 1960s, collective bargaining has gone through four distinct phases roughly corresponding to the four decades since then. The first generation represented the growth phase of employment and unions of the 1960s, the second was characterized by the taxpayer revolts of the 1970s, and the third generation in the 1980s involved greater emphasis on the performance and productivity of public services.[1] In what may be described as a period of heightened aggression against public sector collective bargaining, the 1990s represented the fourth generation

Encyclopedia of Public Administration and Public Policy
DOI: 10.1081/E-EPAP 120010785

Table 1 Legislated bargaining duty

Occupational coverage	Number of states and DC
All	24
All less state	3
Police, fire, and education	2
Education and municipal	2
Education only	5
Police and fire	4
None	11

Source: Ref. [6].

of public sector collective bargaining.[2] Since 1990, public employees have been increasingly under attack on the related fronts of job security and compensation through privatization and challenges to collective bargaining rights.

Dispute Resolution Procedures

Given that a primary goal of collective bargaining is the peaceful resolution of disputes between management and labor, we examine the evolution of dispute resolution procedures. Most public sector dispute resolution mechanisms were designed over 20 years ago to avoid strikes. The belief was that essential public employees simply could not be allowed to walk off their jobs because of the irreparable harm that might be done to the public and because "excessive" union bargaining power would result in huge wage gains in negotiations. This provided the rationale for extensive intrusions into the collective bargaining process in the public sector, in contrast to the voluntarism of private sector dispute resolution. The result was the current North American legislative patchwork of arbitration,[a] fact finding,[b] and compulsory mediation[c] (Table 2).

In recent years, public sector strikes have declined and new issues of concern have emerged, associated with such factors as wage freezes, layoffs, restructuring, contingent workers, privatization, and employee benefits. In this new environment, it is not surprising that policy makers are reassessing the necessity of these intrusive procedures that

focus on avoiding the strike outcomes, not the process for dealing with these new issues. It is entirely possible that both fact finding and arbitration will come under even more scrutiny as their costs and benefits are reevaluated. Public sector dispute resolution procedures are at the center of the assault on public sector bargaining. An important issue, for example, is the extent to which interest arbitration (a dispute resolution procedure adopted when the focus was on prohibiting strikes) is appropriate to the current environment, when the focus is on retrenchment and restructuring.

Recent Trends

Dispute resolution in the public sector adapted to meet the more extreme economic, political, and financial environment of the 1990s. Intensifying fiscal pressures and more conservative political forces combined to create the apparent need for major cost reductions and/or layoffs in many jurisdictions. Paradoxically, this crisis atmosphere created a unique opportunity for labor and management to experiment with cooperative approaches to dispute resolution. Experiments in "interest-based bargaining"[d] abound at federal, state, and local levels of government covering a wide range of occupations from blue-collar municipal employees in Wisconsin to clerical and administrative employees in the Federal Department of Labor. In Wisconsin, for example, the Wisconsin Employment Relations Commission (WERC) now offers training to the parties in "consensus bargaining," a problem-solving approach to negotiations and dispute resolution. The WERC[3] reported that it trained 25 sets of municipal negotiators (over 525 persons) in this new approach. Interest-based and problem-solving bargaining has also been employed in bargaining at the federal level. For example, the Labor Department and the American Federation of Government Employees negotiated two "major agreements" using a win–win approach (Ref. 4, p. 506; Ref. 5, p. 5). Probably the most pervasive changes in collective bargaining are occurring as a result of reform of the U.S. educational system. As teachers become increasingly involved in educational policy making, more cooperative approaches to bargaining are beginning to appear, although research indicates that this has not spelled the end of adversarial bargaining.

Although numerous strikes has remained low after the steep decline of the early 1980s, other forms of conflict

---

[a]Interest or "contract" arbitration involves the establishment of agreement provisions by a third party; grievance or "rights" arbitration deals with matters of contract interpretation during the life of the agreement.
[b]As the name implies, fact finding is a process that normally involves a formal hearing with briefs and evidence in support of the parties' positions, followed by a written public report in which the fact finder makes a nonbinding recommendation on each issue in dispute. Interest arbitration differs mainly in the private and binding nature of the arbitrator's (or board's) award.
[c]Compulsory mediation is usually an intermediate stage where a neutral third party acts as an informal facilitator. Unlike its private sector counterpart, it is often a compulsory step in the public sector.

[d]Interest-based bargaining, which has many variants (win–win, principled, consensus, mutual gains, cooperative, etc.), attempts to replace the adversarial negotiations that often accompanies collective bargaining with a more cooperative or integrative approach that emphasizes the common concerns of management and labor.

Table 2 Law by terminal resolution procedure

Procedure	Police and fire	State	Education	Municipal
Mediation	5	9	9	9
Fact finding	6	13	19	15
Arbitration	22	5	8	6

Source: Ref. [6].

such as grievance arbitrations and unfair labor practices have steadily increased in some jurisdictions. To meet this new challenge, public sector agencies have institutionalized new forms of mediation, particularly grievance mediation.[e]

The courts continue to play an inconsistent but important role in shaping dispute resolution procedures Lund and Maranto.[6] The right to strike has been extended by decisions of state supreme courts to all public employees in Louisiana (1990) and Colorado (1992), but denied in common law to public employees in West Virginia (1990). In addition, interest arbitration awards have been reviewed in the supreme courts of Iowa (1992) and New Jersey (1993), and a binding interest arbitration law was found to be unconstitutional by Nebraska's supreme court (1991).

The antigovernment mood has placed public sector collective bargaining under severe scrutiny. What appeared just a few years ago as acceptable dispute resolution methods are increasingly under assault from taxpayers, employers, and politicians. For example, the utility of interest arbitration is being questioned in Wisconsin, Iowa, New Jersey, and New York. For both fact-finding and interest arbitration, the debate focuses on the appropriate weight to be attached to the criteria of taxpayer concerns and ability to pay. This reassessment of dispute resolution procedures comes after two or three decades of experience in many states.

CONCLUSION

Despite the challenges of public sector collective bargaining since the 1960s, it remains a popular mechanism for providing employees voice in the workplace. After the growth period in the 1960s, close to 40% of public service employees at the local, state, and federal levels of government are covered by collective bargaining.

REFERENCES

1. Lewin, D.; Feuille, P.; Kochan, T.A.; Delaney, J.T. *Public Sector Labor Relations: Analysis and Readings*; Lexington Books: Lexington, MA, 1988.
2. Hebdon, R. Public Sector Dispute Resolution in Transition. In *Public Sector Employment in a Time of Transition*; Belman, D., Gunderson, M., Hyatt, D., Eds.; Industrial Relations Research Association, 1996; 85–125Ch. 3.
3. Biennial Reports. Wisconsin Employment Relations Commission: Madison, WI, **1992.**
4. McKee, J. Beyond Litigation: New Approaches to Federal Labor Relations—Let's Give Change a Chance. In *Proceedings of the IRRA Meeting, Seattle, WA*; 1993; 506. (Spring).
5. Annual Reports. Federal Labor Relations Authority: Washington, D.C., **1992** and **1993.**
6. Lund, J.; Maranto, C. Public Sector Labor Law: An Update. In *Public Sector Employment in a Time of Transition*; Belman, D., Gunderson, M., Hyatt, D., Eds.; Industrial Relations Research Association, 1996; 21–39.

---

[e]Unfair labor practices refer to complaints to a labor relations administrative agency (e.g., the National Labor Relations Board), either by a union or employer over such matters as bargaining in bad faith or interference and/or coercion in the organizing process. Grievance mediation represents the application of voluntary mediation techniques to grievance disputes as an intermediate step before formal binding arbitration.

Collective Bargaining, The Politics of

Robert Hebdon
McGill University, Montreal, Quebec, Canada

INTRODUCTION

A concern in the early period of public sector bargaining (1960 to early 1970s) was that public employee unions may have too much power, particularly political power vis-à-vis weaker interest groups.[1] Subsequent evidence, however, has not supported this fear. Most research has shown that union–nonunion wage differentials, for example, are greater in the private sector than the public sector (see Ref. 2). Nonetheless, public employee unions have exercised their right to engage in various political activities to significantly increase wages, employment levels, and departmental budgets (summarized in Ref. 3; see also Ref. 4).

Three broad questions have been the focus of early exploratory research into union political activities in the public sector. The few studies that are available examined the types of political activities at the municipal level and the considerable occupational and union variation. Second, studies examined the factors that explain the variation in type and level of political activity. Finally, some research analyzed the relationship of political action to collective bargaining. For example, do public sector unions compensate for weak bargaining laws by engaging in political action?

After reviewing some theoretical considerations, this paper will examine the nature and scope of union political action, some factors that affect levels and intensity, and the evidence on the relationship between political action and collective bargaining. The paper begins with a brief case study of union political action in New York state.[a]

A CASE STUDY OF UNION POLITICAL ACTION

The New York State Public Employees Fair Employment Act (Taylor Act) was amended in 1977 to eliminate fact-finding for police and firefighter bargaining units and to replace it with binding arbitration of disputes. The amendment provided for a 2-year sunset provision. When the 2 years was up, New York state unions and municipalities lobbied the state legislators for their respective positions. The unions, who wanted to keep arbitration, argued that arbitration contributed to labor peace and produced comparable settlements to those under fact-finding. The employers—the New York Conference of Mayors—wanted to scrap arbitration, because it increased the rate of impasse; it constituted an invasion of the authority of government; it cost a great deal; and it took away the right of the parties to say no to a settlement. For his part, the Governor wanted to keep arbitration but make it binding only on the union. The Public Employment Relations Board (PERB), the neutral agency, recommended keeping arbitration without modification. PERB argued that 2 years was not a long enough period to judge the arbitration process. The police and firefighter unions extensively lobbied the state legislators. They held face-to-face meetings, submitted briefs, appeared before select committees, etc. A compromise was finally worked out when government finally realized that the unions had the votes to renew the arbitration process. The final bill that was passed and signed by the Governor provided for a 2-year extension with minor changes to the arbitration process.

In the final analysis, the unions, employers and their organizations, neutral agencies, and the public, through their elected representatives, engaged in an intelligent debate about the merits of arbitration versus fact-finding as a dispute resolution process. It is true that this case demonstrates the exercise of considerable union political power, but it also shows that conducted in a pluralistic setting, a wide range of legitimate views were exchanged, and in the end, a reasonable outcome was achieved.

THEORETICAL CONSIDERATIONS

Freeman[6] offers a plausible explanation for the failure of public sector unions to wield excessive political influ-

[a]Based on a paper by Kochan.[5]

ence and power. While it is true that public sector unions can affect employer behavior through the political process, because they help elect executive and legislative branches, the demand for public sector labor is not necessarily more inelastic than in the private sector. Freeman suggests that the discipline of the budget, the high labor intensity of public services, and the ability of citizens to act as a constraint on public sector wages through such activities as referenda, limit the power of public sector unions. Anderson and Delaney[7] develop a conceptual framework for the study of political activities. They make a distinction between activities directed at collective bargaining and those devoted to long-run political benefits for union members generally.[b]

TYPES AND INCIDENCE OF POLITICAL ACTIVITY

In the summer of 1988, the International Cities and Counties Management Associations surveyed city managers in all U.S. cities over 10,000 population, where some of their employees were in a union or association. The 910 survey respondents provided a rare glimpse into the scope and character of union political activities in America. City managers were asked to list the number and type of union political activity over the previous 10-year period (1978–1988). Table 1 shows the breadth of coverage of political activities throughout the country. In only a few states were there no reports of union political activities (Alabama, North Dakota, and South Carolina), and in these states, there were only one or two cities reporting. In terms of the raw numbers, California, Florida, Michigan, Pennsylvania, and Texas have the highest state totals of political activities. When expressed as per city rates, the District of Columbia, Hawaii, Nevada, West Virginia, and Wyoming had the most significant levels of political action.

In Table 2, the data are broken down by occupational group (police, fire, sanitation, public works, and other) and by electoral politics (candidate endorsements, financial contributions, and manpower or in-kind support), publicity campaigns (mismanagement disclosure or publicity), state lobbying (including referendum campaigns), and total political actions.

Electoral politics is by far the most popular form of political activity across all occupational groups reported, with sanitation and firefighter unions showing the highest rates per city and police and public works

[b]For a thorough review of the literature on this topic, see Anderson and Delaney.[7]

Table 1 Political actions and dominant collective bargaining law by state 1978–1988

| State | Number of cities | Political actions | | Law[a] |
		Total	Per city	
AK	2	5	2.5	2
AL	4	0	0.00	0
AR	8	8	1.00	0
AZ	7	3	0.43	0
CA	139	259	1.86	0
CO	8	9	1.13	0
CT	40	32	0.80	1
DC	1	6	6.00	0
DE	1	1	1.00	0
FL	52	131	2.52	0
GA	3	5	1.67	0
HI	2	10	5.00	2
IA	16	30	1.88	1
ID	5	15	3	2
IL	60	37	0.62	0
IN	8	18	2.25	0
KS	9	8	0.89	0
KY	4	6	1.50	0
LA	4	7	1.75	0
MA	37	40	1.08	1
MD	8	6	0.75	0
ME	9	9	1.00	1
MI	45	85	1.89	0
MN	40	45	1.13	2
MO	16	22	1.38	0
MS	3	5	1.67	0
MT	4	11	2.75	2
NC	8	8	1.00	0
ND	1	0	0.00	0
NE	7	10	1.43	0
NH	9	5	0.56	0
NJ	64	53	0.83	1
NM	1	1	1.00	0
NV	6	21	3.50	0
NY	29	44	1.52	0
OH	45	53	1.18	0
OK	19	39	2.05	2
OR	14	23	1.64	2
PA	63	23	0.37	1
RI	7	4	0.57	1
SC	2	0	0.00	0
SD	2	2	1.00	0
TN	4	7	1.75	0
TX	44	83	1.89	0
UT	5	12	2.40	0
VA	6	9	1.50	0
WA	8	20	2.50	0
WI	25	51	2.04	1
WV	3	11	3.67	0
WY	3	10	3.33	0
Totals	**910**	**1302**		
Mean			**1.66**	

[a]*Legend:* Arbitration = 1; Right to Strike = 2; No Finality = 0. Note that in this table, the dispute resolution law is based on the dominant state public sector collective bargaining law, but in reality, it varies by occupational group in many stated.

Table 2 Union municipal political activities by occupational groups

	No. of cities	Per city rate of electoral politics	Per city rate of lobbying	Per city rate of publicity campaigns	Per city rate of total political activity
Police	804	1.84	0.84	0.59	3.27
Fire	619	2.29	1.06	0.71	4.06
Sanitation	316	2.39	1.02	0.79	4.2
Public works	679	1.85	0.84	0.62	3.31
Other	665	2.01	0.85	0.63	3.49

the lowest. In order of declining importance, lobbying and publicity campaign rates were distributed in the same manner across occupational units as electoral politics.

Overall, there were on average between 3.3 and 4.2 incidents of political activity reported by city over the previous 10-year period. It was not surprising that sanitation unions were the most politically active over this period, because they were confronting the issue of the contracting out of their services, and the collective bargaining process was ill-equipped to handle it.[8] Additionally, high levels of political activity were expected for firefighter unions local, given the rich history of the International Association of Fire Fighters as an American Federation of Labor craft union.

DETERMINANTS OF UNION POLITICAL ACTIVITIES

Anderson and Delaney[7] show that union political action is inversely related to success in bargaining and weak legislation. They also found that factors that determine union involvement in electoral politics differ from those that determine union involvement in legislative politics. Chandler and Gely[3] find that electoral politics is a complement to collective bargaining.

Hebdon and Stern[9] postulate that where the collective bargaining law fails to provide finality, there will be higher than average levels of political action. In this case, because unions cannot strike or force an agreement through arbitration, greater use of political pressure is expected. Here, publicity campaigns are more likely to be used as pressure tactics as part of the bargaining process. Bargaining laws were shown to have a negligible impact on electoral politics and state lobbying.[9] Only under final offer arbitration[c] is there a higher propensity to engage in electoral politics when compared

to right to strike laws, but this is only significant at the 10% level. The unambiguous result is the stronger propensity to conduct publicity campaigns when under a strike ban law compared to right to strike laws. The Hebdon and Stern interpretation of this finding is that unions use mismanagement threats and publicity campaigns as substitute pressure tactics for threatening or organizing a strike. In other words, laws that permit legal strikes channel conflict away from publicity campaigns against public employers to more traditional strike pressures.

Also tested was Anderson's[10] hypothesis that union political action, necessary for the introduction of the collective bargaining law, diminishes over time as the union–management relationship matures. Hebdon and Stern found no support for Anderson's[10] hypothesis that political action diminishes as the union–management relationship matures. In fact, political actions increased significantly with the age of the relationship over this 1978–1988 period.

POLITICAL ACTION AND COLLECTIVE BARGAINING

Unlike their counterparts in the private sector, public sector unions may play a direct role in electing their bosses.[11] Collective bargaining performs a political function in the sense that a system of governance is established. Unlike the private sector bargaining model, in the public sector, it takes on a multiparticipant character that includes taxpayers, unions, politicians, school boards, employer organizations, and other interest groups.

Thus, to achieve their goals, collective bargaining and political action may present strategic choices for unions in the public sector. There is some evidence from California, for example, that unions in the public sector seem to prefer political action (forming coalitions and lobbying) over industrial action and strikes.[12] This substitution of political actions for striking also appears in the work of O'Brien,[4] who showed that the political activities of police and firefighters' unions could be

---

[c]Under final offer arbitration, the arbitrator must choose the last position of management or of the union.

more important than collective bargaining in pay determination. Finally, Hebdon and Stern[9] showed that a hidden cost of strike ban laws is the redirection of conflict away from strikes to such other expressions as publicity campaigns.

REFERENCES

1. Wellington, H.H.; Winter, R.K., Jr. The Limits of Collective Bargaining in Public Employment. In *The Unions and the Cities*; The Brookings Institution: Washington, D.C., 1971; 12–32.

2. Belman, D.; Heywood, J.S. The Structure of Compensation in the Public Sector. In *Chapter in Public Sector Employment in a Time of Transition*; Belman, D., Gunderson, M., Hyatt, D., Eds.; Industrial Relations Research Association, 1996.

3. Chandler, T.; Gely, R. Toward identifying the determinants of public-employee union's involvement in political activities. Am. Rev. Public Adm. **1996**, *26* (4), 417–438.

4. O'Brien, K.M. The impact of union political activities on public-sector pay, employment, and budgets. Ind. Relat. **1994**, *33* (3), 322–345 (July).

5. Kochan, T.A. The Politics of Interest Arbitration. In *Public Sector Labor Relations: Analysis and Readings*; Lewin, D., Feuille, P., Kochan, T.A., Delaney, J.T., Eds.; Lexington Books, 1988; 76–85.

6. Freeman, R.B. Unionism comes to the public sector. J. Econ. Lit. **1986**, 41–53.

7. Anderson, J.C.; Delaney, J.T. The involvement of Canadian unions in political activities: An exploratory analysis. J. Labor Res. **1990**, *XI* (4), 361–379.

8. Hebdon, R. Contracting out in New York State: The story the Lauder Report chose not to tell. Labor Stud. J. **1995**, *20* (1), 3–29 (Spring).

9. Hebdon, R.; Stern, R. Do public sector strike ban laws really prevent conflict? Ind. Relat. (Forthcoming).

10. Anderson, J.C. Bargaining outcomes: An IR systems approach. Ind. Relat. **1979**, *18* (2), 127–143 (Spring).

11. Kearney, R.C. *Labor Relations in the Public Sector*, 2nd Ed.; Marcel Dekker: New York, 1992.

12. Johnston, P. *Success While Others Fail*; ILR Press: Ithaca, NY, 1994.

Compensation, Salary and Benefits

C

James A. Buford, Jr.
Ellis-Harper Management, Auburn, Alabama, U.S.A.

INTRODUCTION

Compensation is one of the most challenging areas of human resource management. The compensation system, consisting of pay and benefits, should attract and retain a competent workforce, build motivation and performance, and control costs.[1] Most organizations in the public sector have job-based classification systems, grant annual pay increases or ''step raises,'' and offer conventional health insurance and defined benefit retirement programs. In recent years, however, emerging approaches in delivering pay and benefits have begun to gain acceptance.[2] These include skill and competency-based pay, structures with wide grades or bands, merit pay, group incentive pay, managed care, medical savings accounts, and defined contribution retirement programs. Traditional and emerging approaches can be useful, depending on what the organization wishes to accomplish. In any case, clearly articulated strategic objectives are necessary if the compensation system is to match the unique characteristics and culture and effectively contribute to implementing the mission of the organization.[3]

JOB-BASED PAY STRUCTURES

Most public organizations use pay systems that focus on work performed in specific jobs. Once pay policies have been determined, the development of a pay system includes determining the internal value of jobs and establishing grades or classes containing jobs having approximately the same value.[4]

Evaluating Jobs

Organizations first develop an internal hierarchy of job value through a process known as job evaluation. All job evaluation techniques are based, implicitly or explicitly, on the ''universal'' factors of skill, effort, responsibility, and working conditions. These factors are also set forth in the Equal Pay Act of 1963 (discussed in a following section) as the legal standard for equal work. The most common job evaluation techniques are classification and the point method. Classification, which originated in the public sector, is a whole-job approach that involves matching jobs against classification descriptions arrayed in increasing order of difficulty and responsibility. In the point method, jobs are evaluated based on the degree to which they require factors or subfactors that measure the universal factors mentioned above. The point method is the technique of choice in the private sector and is used increasingly by public organizations such as municipalities and counties.

In evaluating jobs, organizations may use a plan containing a set of class descriptions or factors designed to cover all jobs in a single pay structure or separate plans for each job family, such as clerical, labor and trades, administrative and professional, and so on, and develop multiple pay structures. While placing all jobs in one structure implements the principle of equal pay for work of equal value (or comparable worth), many compensation professionals contend that the work content is too varied to be compared on the same factors. For example, factors that distinguish among levels of equipment operators include manual dexterity, physical effort, and working conditions. These factors rarely apply in clerical and administrative support work; rather such factors as knowledge of office technology, public contacts, and access to confidential data are more important.

Determining Grades

Jobs of approximately equal internal value are then grouped into grades (or classes) that are assigned pay ranges (discussed in a following section). The actual number of grades in a pay structure is a policy question. Specialization and upward mobility are facilitated by a relatively large number of narrow grades. Wider grades promote teamwork and lateral mobility. Some public sector pay structures contain up to 50 grades, while others contain as few as 10. The trend is to have fewer grades in all types of structures. The General Schedule (GS) of the U.S. Office of Personnel Management classifies thousands of jobs into 15 grades, which might be considered a reasonable upper limit for most public organizations.

Encyclopedia of Public Administration and Public Policy
DOI: 10.1081/E-EPAP 120010779

217

218

ALTERNATIVES TO JOB-BASED STRUCTURES

While job-based structures are still the major approach to pay in public organizations, they have come under increasing criticism in recent years. Rather than build participation and contribution to objectives, these structures are seen to be rigid and bureaucratic and to promote individual agendas and entitlement. Alternatives to traditional structures include broadbanding and skill-based pay.

Broadbanding

In broadbanding, a number of grades are consolidated into a single band with a maximum and minimum rate of pay.[5] Most organizations use four to eight bands set at logical breaks in skill or competency levels, such as clerical, technical, administrative/professional, managerial, and executive. Administration of pay to individual employees (discussed in a following section) is typically delegated to operating departments rather than centralized in the human resources department. Broadbanding is considered to be more compatible with self-directed work teams, employee empowerment, and other features of the egalitarian, process-centered organization. Fig. 1 illustrates the contrast between pay grades and bands.

Skill and Competency-Based Pay Structures

Skill-based pay structures essentially do away with job boundaries.[6] In these systems, the employee is paid for skills mastered and applied in a work situation, regardless of the tasks assigned at a particular time. Structures typically contain a block of foundation skills, a number of blocks of required or "core" skills, and additional blocks of optional skills. For example, an equipment operator might receive a pay increase for learning a required number of core skills, such as finish grading, even though most of the work consists of less difficult earthmoving tasks such as trenching, rough grading, and loading. A skill-based structure for equipment operators is shown in Fig. 2.

While skill-based structures are used mainly in hourly trade and craft work, competency-based pay extends the concept to administrative, technical, and professional work.[7] However, the term competency covers a wider range of employee attributes, such as a competency to "make effective and timely decisions." Accordingly, competencies are considerably more difficult to operationally define and build into a pay structure.

PRICING THE PAY STRUCTURE

The next activity is to price the structure by establishing a pay policy line as a basis for pay ranges with

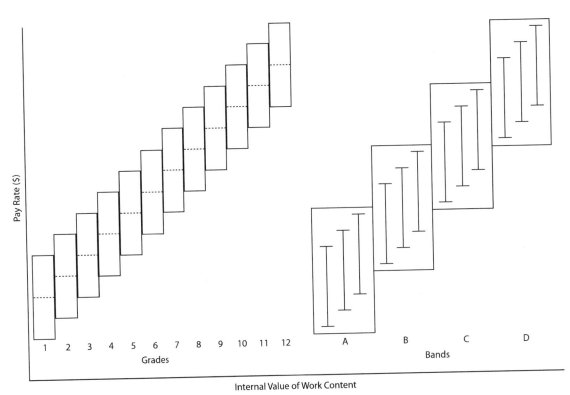

Fig. 1 Pay grades versus bands.

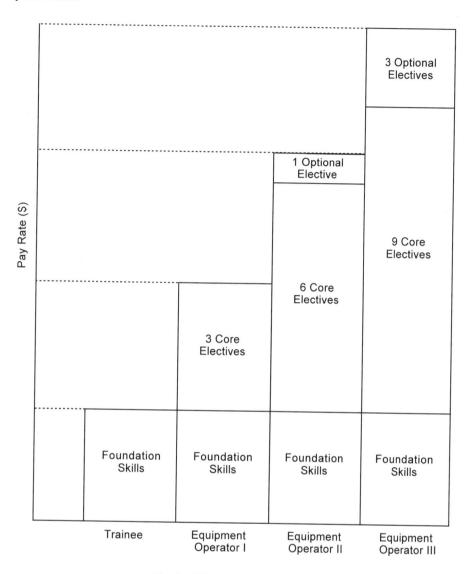

Fig. 2 Skill-based pay structure.

minimum and maximum rates of pay. In establishing ranges, the organization must consider what other employers in the relevant labor market pay for similar jobs. This information may be obtained by conducting a compensation survey or by using secondary data. In pricing the structure, organizations may establish grade midpoints that lag, match, or lead the market, depending on funding levels, strategic objectives, and policy guidance. In skill-based structures, the pay must be further allocated to various skill blocks. Because most public organizations have attractive benefits programs (discussed in a following section), the policy is typically to lag or match the market. Moreover, organizations such as units of government would encounter considerable political resistance in setting pay higher than market levels.

COMPLYING WITH LEGAL REQUIREMENTS

Employee compensation is heavily influenced by laws and regulations that emphasize fairness, sufficiency, and protection. The Fair Labor Standards Act (FLSA) establishes the minimum wage, defines maximum hours for various work periods (typically the 40-hour week), provides for overtime pay, and restricts child labor. The FLSA is enforced by the Wage and Hour Division of the U.S. Department of Labor. The Equal Pay Act (EPA) requires employers to provide equal pay for equal work, defined as that which requires equal skill, equal effort, equal responsibility, and is performed under similar working conditions. If jobs are equal, males and females may be compensated differently only if pay is based on seniority, merit, quality or quantity of production (dis-

220

cussed in the following section), or other factors based on sex. Title VII of the Civil Rights Act prohibits disparate treatment in pay based on race, sex, color, religion, and national origin, even if jobs are not equal, and addresses discrimination in the provision of benefits. The Age Discrimination in Employment Act (ADEA) extends protection to persons 40 and older. The EPA, Title VII, and the ADEA are enforced by the Equal Employment Opportunity Commission (EEOC). While these are the major laws, other federal laws and regulations apply in specific situations, and many states also have laws applying to compensation.

ADMINISTRATION OF PAY TO INDIVIDUALS

In job-based structures, pay for employees is administered within the maximum and minimum for the grade. The control mechanism is the midpoint, which represents the target level of pay for a fully trained employee performing at a satisfactory level. Fig. 3 illustrates the basic approaches to administering pay within grades.

In Panel A, the grade is divided into quartiles. In Panel B, the grade is divided into 13 steps, with each step representing a 3% increase from the previous step. In Panel C (12 steps), each step represents 3% of the midpoint rate. Most public organizations follow a step approach in administering pay within grades. Pay adjustments are designed to set pay at a level appropriate to the employee's length of service, job performance, and qualifications. The grade midpoint represents the target rate of pay for a fully trained employee performing at a satisfactory level. Recall that midpoints were set previously at or near the market rate of pay. When bands are used, organizations often establish guidelines or "shadow grades" within bands as shown in Fig. 1. Where this is the case, within-band pay adjustments are handled similarly to within-grade adjustments.

Approaches to Individual Pay Advancement

Seniority-based pay systems are common in the public sector. In these systems, employees are placed in and advance through rate ranges based on length of service

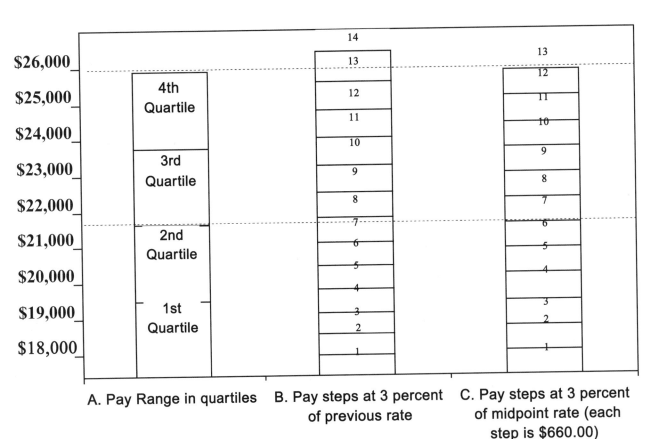

Fig. 3 Approaches to administration of pay within grades.

(the familiar annual step increase). In recent years, however, various forms of performance-based pay have gained increased acceptance.[8] Merit pay is an addition to an employee's base wage or salary in recognition of *past* contributions. A major disadvantage of merit pay is that increases are "locked in" and have a compounding effect even if performance declines. This problem is overcome by one-time incentives or bonuses, offered as an inducement for *future* performance. In this approach, pay reverts to the base rate during any period that performance does not exceed the standard, and the incentive amount is therefore "at risk." Individual incentive plans such as piecework and performance bonuses are found mainly in the private sector, although a few public organizations are beginning to implement this approach.

In skill- and competency-based structures, pay is increased when an employee has mastered a skill or competency. Often, work sample tests are used for this purpose. For example, to demonstrate the skill of finish grading, an equipment operator might be required to operate a motor grader, manipulating controls, adjusting the height and angle of the blade, and positioning the wheels to raise or lower terrain to grade marked on reference stakes.

Rewarding Group Performance

Various types of incentive plans are used to reward group or team performance. In the approach known as "gainsharing," a productivity standard based on allowable labor costs is established.[9] For example, the labor cost standard in a solid waste collection department may be $100,000 for a given month. If actual costs are $95,000 during the month, there is a "gain" of $5000. In distributing the gain, 50% is typically allocated to the work group, 25% is retained by the organization, and 25% is set aside for periods in which labor costs exceed the standard during a period. Note that in this approach, pay is at risk, as was the case with individual incentives. The procedures discussed above follow the Scanlon Plan, which is the gainsharing approach that has gained the most acceptance in the public sector.

DETERMINING EMPLOYEE BENEFITS AND SERVICES

The creation of a benefits package is the final step in designing the compensation program. As was the case with pay, strategic objectives and policies are important. Because public organizations do not typically lead the market in pay, a reasonably attractive benefits package is necessary to attract and retain employees. Certain benefits

are required by law. These include workers' compensation, unemployment compensation, and Social Security (some public jurisdictions elected not to participate and are required to offer a comparable retirement benefit). The major categories of optional benefits include retirement and savings plans, health and medical plans, payment for time not worked (paid leave and holidays), and miscellaneous benefits.

Retirement and Savings Plans

Most public organizations, especially units of government, offer defined benefit retirement plans or pensions that provide lifetime annuities of 50 to 70% of employees' preretirement earnings. Because of cost and uncertainty, many organizations have implemented or are considering defined contribution plans, similar to 401 (K) plans, which predominate in the private sector. In these types of plans, the employer cost is known up front, however, the amount that employees receive at retirement depends on the performance of the invested funds.[10]

Medical and Health Benefits

In the area of medical and health benefits, the traditional approach is to provide insurance coverage where the employees can select a health care provider (physician, hospital, clinic, etc). By the early 1990s, the premiums for this type of coverage had increased to such levels that employers began intensive efforts to control costs. By the mid-1990s, a small but growing number of public organizations had begun to implement managed care plans through health maintenance organizations or HMOs.[11] These organizations typically negotiate a flat rate and have an incentive to promote wellness rather than respond to costly medical emergencies. Under managed care, patients must use health care providers designated by the plan. Moreover, the provider has the responsibility to provide care based on cost-effectiveness, not necessarily on the needs of the patient. These and other issues have led to legislation at the state and federal levels establishing "bills of rights" for employees covered by managed care plans. Other approaches to controlling include preferred provider organizations (PPOs) and medical savings plans, which may be used in combination with traditional coverage and managed care.[12]

Other Benefits and Services

In regard to payment for time not worked, public organizations tend to give more paid time off than their counterparts in the private sector. Practically all organizations observe national holidays and others with a regional or statewide significance. Most also provide various forms of paid leave, including vacation, sick, military, jury, and so forth.

Other benefits and services often provided by public organizations include group life insurance, employee assistance programs, tuition refund programs, and credit unions.

REFERENCES

1. Buford, J.A., Jr.; Lindner, J.R. *Human Resource Management in Local Government*; South-Western: Cincinnati, 2002.
2. Risher, H. Emerging model for salary management. Public Manage. **1997**, *79* (1), 10–14.
3. Ledford, G.E., Jr.; Hawk, E.J. Compensation strategy: A guide for senior managers. ACA J. **2000**, *9* (1), 19–27.
4. Mllkovich, G.T.; Newman, J.M. *Compensation,* 6th Ed.; Irwin McGraw-Hill: Boston, 1999.
5. Abosch, K.A.; Hand, J.H. *Broadbanding Models*; American Compensation Association: Scottsdale, 1994.
6. Jenkins, G.D., Jr.; Ledford, G.E.; Gupta, N.; Doty, H.D. *Skill-Based Pay*; American Compensation Association: Scottsdale, 1992.
7. O'Neal, S. Competencies and pay in the evolving world of work. ACA J. **1996**, *4* (4), 72–79.
8. McRenolds, M.; Hopkins, J. Breaking the step-and-COLA cycle. Public Manage. **1998**, *80* (4), 10–14.
9. Risher, H. Can gain sharing help to reinvent government? Public Manage. **1998**, *80* (1), 17–21.
10. Jankowski, J.J. Defined contribution plans can be win–win solutions in the public sector. Public Manage. **1997**, *79* (4), 14–17.
11. Whitton, P. Tulsa's move to managed care. Public Pers. Manage. **1995**, *24* (2), 133–138.
12. Bond, M.T.; Hesheizer, B.P.; Hrivnak, M.W. Medical savings accounts: A health insurance option for the public sector? Public Pers. Manage. **1997**, *26* (4), 535–544.

Conflict of Interest

Russell L. Williams
Florida State University, Tallahassee, Florida, U.S.A.

INTRODUCTION

The phrase ''conflict of interest'' may appear so self-explanatory that it does not require further examination. However, thoughtful scrutiny reveals that many of the pitfalls and failures associated with public service at any level grow out of legal or ethical conflicts of interest. Some consider conflicts of interest to occur only when specific conflict of interest rules or laws are broken. Many of those laws are aimed at specific issues, such as financial disclosure, nepotism, improper use of public resources, or influence peddling. However, in the larger sense, if an individual (or group) functioning under governmental auspices, responsible for making decisions or taking actions affecting the public, places self-interest ahead of public interest in exercising authority, then a conflict of interest exists.

A LONG-STANDING PROBLEM

Arguably, the necessity to address conflict of interest problems was the engine driving the civil service reform movement that started in the late 1800s. Woodrow Wilson's canonized ''The Study of Administration,'' written in 1887, clearly recognizes that conflicts of interest form perhaps the most intractable challenge to truly improving and professionalizing public service:

> The question for us is, how shall our series of governments within governments be so administered that it shall always be to the interest of the public officer to serve, not his superior alone but the community also, with the best efforts of his talents and the soberest service of his conscience? How shall such service be made to his commonest interest by contributing abundantly to his sustenance, to his dearest interest by furthering his ambition, and to his highest interest by advancing his honor and establishing his character? And how shall this be done alike for the local part and for the national whole? If we solve this problem we shall again pilot the world.[1]

As obvious as ''this problem'' was to Wilson, it is also obvious that it was not then, and has not been to the present, wholly solved. Yet, the modern American civil service system was built on the expectation that government employees' actions are to be motivated by nonpartisan, nonself-interested behavior directed toward the benefit of the public. This expectation was manifested in the Pendleton Act of 1883. Although limited in scope, it was the first substantive effort toward ridding the federal civil service of the blatant conflicts of interest created when the norm was to hire government employees routinely on the basis of their political loyalties. Ironically, however obvious the wisdom of such a reform was to many of the people of the time, it took the impetus created by the assassination of President James A. Garfield by a disappointed office seeker who expected a reward for political service to lead to the passage of that initial template for eliminating conflicts of interest.[2]

Since the Pendleton Act, efforts have continued to eliminate situations wherein conflicts of interest can occur. Much of what is identified as reforms in ''government ethics,'' a rather general term, have come to be related to preventing conflicts of interest. This holds true even in the state and local level ''ethics in government'' initiatives that occurred in the wake of the Watergate government corruption scandal of the 1970s. Many state government ethics commissions or offices focus largely on monitoring financial disclosure statements from public servants, the presumption being that ''following the money'' reveals whether the potential for conflict of interest problems exists.

CONFLICT OF INTEREST AS A STATUTORY ISSUE

In a country devoted to the rule of law, there has been a logical effort to use laws, rules, regulations, codes of ethics, and even presidential executive orders to define and prevent conflicts of interest by those in public service. Section 201 of Presidential Executive Order 11222, signed by Lyndon B. Johnson in 1965, while not the first attempt at addressing conflict of interest issues by government employees,[3] established a standard of conduct that not only devoted three of its six provisions to matters concerning conflicts of interest, but also called at-

Encyclopedia of Public Administration and Public Policy
DOI: 10.1081/E-EPAP 120010937

tention to the need to avoid even the appearance of such conflicts (the so-called "appearance standard"):

> It is the intent of this section that employees avoid any action ... which might result in, or *create the appearance of—*
>
> 1. *Using public office for private gain.*
> 2. *Giving preferential treatment to any organization or person.*
> 3. Impeding government efficiency or economy.
> 4. *Losing complete independence or impartiality of action.*
> 5. Making a government decision outside official channels; or
> 6. Affecting adversely the confidence of the public in the integrity of the Government (emphasis added).[4]

The Ethics in Government Act of 1978, passed during the administration of President Jimmy Carter, reinforced the identification of government ethics with conflict of interest concerns. It too focused on financial disclosure as a means to ameliorate the problem. The act also established the Office of Government Ethics, giving it the responsibility to examine the financial disclosure statements of federal officials. The Ethics in Government Reform Act of 1989 served to strengthen the financial disclosure system, again with the assumption that this was crucial to reducing the potential for conflicts of interest. This approach continues to be echoed in many state and local governments by the use of laws, as well as codes of ethics or conduct.

CONFLICT OF INTEREST AS A PROFESSIONAL ISSUE

Beyond the violation of laws and rules per se, there is another aspect related to conflicts of interest that cannot be overlooked. Intrinsic to the "modern" approach to public administration espoused by Woodrow Wilson is the concept of professionalism (for a discussion of what this might entail, see Ref. 5). That is, those who seek to serve the public must treat what they do as more than a mere means to trade labor for wages. They must aspire to levels of professional standards consistent with those expected of doctors and lawyers. Recognizing this, professional associations within the field of public administration also use a statutory (i.e., rule-based) approach regarding conflicts of interest. The codes of ethics of both the American Society for Public Administration (ASPA) and the International City/County Management Association (ICMA) specifically mention the need for government workers to avoid conflicts of interest or their appearance. ICMA goes so far as to have punitive pro-

cedures in place for those found in violation of its code, including those tenets associated with conflicts of interest. In essence, avoiding conflicts of interest is instrumental to meeting the professional standards that define the practice of public administration.

CONFLICT OF INTEREST AS A MORAL ISSUE

Upon his inauguration on January 20, 2001, President George W. Bush repromulgated to all executive branch personnel 5 C.F.R. 2635, *Standards of Ethical Conduct for Employees of the Executive Branch*. Section 2635.101, titled, "Basic obligation of public service," that contains the following statement:

> Public service is a public trust. Each employee has a responsibility to the United States Government and its citizens to place loyalty to the Constitution, laws and *ethical principles* above private gain (emphasis added).[6]

This is similar in tone to words found in the *Code of Ethics for Government Service*, found in Congressional Resolution 175, adopted by both houses of the 85th Congress on July 11, 1958 and still in effect:

> Put loyalty to the *highest moral principals* and to country above loyalty to Government persons, party, or department...Uphold these principles, ever conscious that public office is a public trust (emphasis added).[7]

There is within the above excerpts a clear expectation that public service requires action that is not "merely" legally, but also morally, principled.[a] This is couched in terms of where the civil servant's loyalties must lie. While the legally defined aspects of conflicts of interest can vary from one government entity to another, the ethical aspects do not. While road maps (written laws and rules) exist that, if followed, may allow someone to claim that a specific kind of conflict of interest does not exist, it is usually not so easy to justify actions that, looked at dispassionately, show a lack of regard for the public good. In ethical terms, the government employee is expected to act deontologically. There is an underlying moral obligation to do what is best for the public

---

[a]Carol Lewis highlights a classic example of the ramifications of that expectation in her book, The Ethics Challenge in Public Service (Jossey-Bass, 1991). She relates the succinct response of George Washington to a friend who was seeking a job: "As George Washington, I would do anything in my power for you. As President, I can do nothing' (Bailey, 1964, p. 241)." The root causes and pressures of, as well as the underlying appropriate response to, conflict of interest situations have remained consistent from Washington's time until now.

as a whole. This does not leave room for the erstwhile public servant to act egoistically, placing the needs of self, whether for money, power, position, or political advantage, ahead of the public's needs. To do so is antithetical to the concept of American public service, but it is the essence of what constitutes a conflict of interest in the public sector.

THE MOST INTRACTABLE CHALLENGE

In 1887, Woodrow Wilson did not have an answer to the problems stemming from conflicts of interest. Well over a century has passed. While much has changed with the advent of special laws and codes of ethics, somehow much is still the same. Now, as then, it is easy to see why, at the appointive and elective levels of public office, conflict of interest issues create a constant and inevitable tension. No one whose position is so clearly dependent upon the support of specific individuals or groups can be wholly insulated from the pressures that will come from those expecting special treatment in return for that support. However, the danger for the "average," unelected, unappointed public servant is no less considerable, despite, for many, the protection afforded by a merit-based civil service system. Anytime an individual is faced with a situation, no matter how trivial, that places perceived personal gain at odds with the public good, there will be conflicting interests. It may be as simple as favoring a somewhat less-qualified friend over a better-qualified applicant in the hiring process for a public service job or withholding needed information from another agency in order to make oneself look good at a meeting. The ultimate intractability of the conflict of interest problem is not a function of being able to identify when such a problem exists. Imperfect as they may be, various laws, rules, and codes of ethics provide some

assistance in that matter.[b] It is in the moral realm, to have or find the strength to act in a manner that is not consistent with one's self-interest, wherein the solution to Wilson's problem is found.

REFERENCES

1. Wilson, W. The study of administration. Polit. Sci. Q. **1887**, *2* (2), 197–222.
2. Ingraham, P.W. *The Foundation of Merit: Public Service in American Democracy*; Johns Hopkins, 1995.
3. McCampbell, A.S.; Rood, T.L. Ethics in government: A survey of misuse of position for personal gain and its implications for developing acquisition strategy. J. Bus. Ethics **1997**, *16*, 1107–1116.
4. Executive Order 11222 of May 8, 1965, 30 F.R. 6469, 3 C.F.R. (1964–1965).
5. Kettl, D.F.; Ingraham, P.W.; Sanders, R.P.; Horner, C. *Civil Service Reform: Building a Government That Works*; Brookings Institution, 1996.
6. *Standard of Ethical Conduct for Employees of the Executive Branch*; 1999; 2635, 5 C.F.R.
7. Code of Ethics for Government Service, Para. 10, H. Con. Res. 175, 85th Cong., 2d Sess., 72 Stat., pt. 2, B12 (adopted July 11, 1958).

---

[b]The following websites contain many examples and gateways to various ethics laws, rules, and codes that seek to clarify what remains a complex subject:

U.S. Office of Government Ethics at http://www.usoge.gov/ (accessed December 2001).

Professions Codes of Ethics Online: Government & Military webpage of the Illinois Institute of Technology Center for the Study of Ethics at http://www.iit.edu/departments/csep/PublicWWW/codes/gov.html (accessed December 2001).

Los Angeles City Ethics Commission at http://www.cityofla.org/ETH (accessed December 2001).

Consolidated Governments

Dan Durning
University of Georgia, Athens, Georgia, U.S.A.

INTRODUCTION

In 1997, the United States had 87,451 substate governments, including 3043 counties; 19,371 cities; 16,629 townships; 34,682 special districts; and 13,726 school districts. The large number of local governments in the United States, many with overlapping jurisdictions and powers, has long concerned some experts and citizens. Their concern has largely been about multiple governments sharing a geographical area. They point out that although a metropolitan area has an interrelated economy, workforce, and social structure, its service delivery is usually spread among many different local governments. They maintain that this governmental fragmentation contributes to different pathologies that harm metropolitan areas.[1]

Other researchers have rejected the idea that governmental fragmentation causes harm. In fact, they argue, it contributes to governmental efficiency.[2] As discussed below, this disagreement has pitted public administration scholars against political economists for more than two decades. At this point, the debate about the value of governmental consolidation is far from settled. It seems certain that attempts to consolidate governments in the United States will continue into the foreseeable future, and that these proposals will be vigorously opposed.

CONSOLIDATED CITY–COUNTY GOVERNMENTS IN THE UNITED STATES

The United States has 33 consolidated city–county governments. This number is equal to slightly more than 1% of the nation's 3043 county governments. The consolidated governments can be divided into two groups: those created before World War II and those that came after the war. The pre-World War II group consists of the eight consolidations that date back to 1805, when New Orleans and Orleans Parish were consolidated. They include these consolidated governments: Nantucket Town–Nantucket County, Massachusetts (1821); Boston–Suffolk County, Massachusetts (1821); Philadelphia–Philadelphia County, Pennsylvania (1854); San Francisco–San Francisco County, California (1856); New York and five boroughs, New York (1890s); Denver–Denver County, Colorado (1902); and Honolulu–Honolulu County, Hawaii (1907). These consolidations were created by state legislation.

The post-World War II era of consolidation began in 1947, when Baton Rouge and East Baton Rouge Parish (Louisiana) were consolidated. Since then, 24 other city–county consolidations have occurred; all but two were approved in local referenda. The Indianapolis–Marion County (Indiana) consolidated government was formed by an act of the state legislature. The recently created city and county of Broomfield came through a constitutional amendment approved in 1998 by the voters of Colorado. The constitutional amendment permitted creation of a new city–county carved out of parts of the four counties in which Broomfield residents live. A list of the post-World War II consolidated governments is presented in Table 1.

This list of city–county consolidations shows two things. First, a surge in local government consolidations occurred from 1967 to 1977, when 10 mergers were completed. Among those were mergers in larger metropolitan areas such as Nashville, Tennessee; Jacksonville, Florida; and Indianapolis, Indiana. Second, no consolidations were approved in larger metropolitan areas from 1969 to 2000. Before the recent successful vote in Louisville–Jefferson County, all consolidations since 1969 had been in smaller metropolitan counties and rural counties.

Since 1947, at least 132 votes have been held on proposals to consolidate city and county governments. Voters approved fewer than one in five of the proposals. In the 1970s and 1980s, only 9 of 79 consolidation referenda (11%) resulted in a consolidated government. The number of referenda and the number of successes by decade are shown in Table 2.

The 19 failed referenda in the 1990s were in nine different states: California (Sacramento–Sacramento Co.), Florida (Gainesville–Alachua Co., Miami–Dade Co., Tallahassee–Leon Co.), Georgia [Griffin–Spalding Co. (twice), Douglassville–Douglas Co., Metter–Chandler Co., Hawkinsville–Pulaski Co., Waycross–Ware Co.], Iowa (Des Moines–Polk Co.), Kentucky (Owensboro–Daviess Co., Bowling Green–Warren Co., Ashland and Catlettsburg–Boyd Co.), North Carolina (Wilmington–New Hanover Co.), Tennessee (Knoxville–Knox Co., Clarkesville–Montgomery Co.), Virginia (Roanoke–Roanoke Co.), and Washington (Spokane–Spokane Co.).

Including the successful referenda in Kansas and Louisiana, local consolidation referenda were held during the 1990s in 11 different states. Only 16 states have legislation authorizing city–county consolidations and

Encyclopedia of Public Administration and Public Policy
DOI: 10.1081/E-EPAP 120010833

Table 1   Consolidated city–county governments in the United States

Year	City/County/State	2000 Population
1947	Baton Rouge–East Baton Rouge, Louisiana	412,852
1952	Hampton–Elizabeth City County, Virginia	146,437
1957	Newport News–Warwick County, Virginia	180,150
1960	Chesapeake–South Norfolk–Norfolk Co., Virginia	199,184
1962	Virginia Beach–Princess Anne County, Virginia	425,257
1962	Nashville–Davidson County, Tennessee	569,891
1967	Jacksonville–Duvall County, Florida	778,879
1969	Juneau–Great Juneau County, Alaska	30,711
1969	Carson City–Ormsby County, Nevada	52,457
1969	Indianapolis–Marion County, Indiana	860,454
1970	Columbus–Muscogee County, Georgia	186,291
1971	Sitka–Greater Sitka County, Alaska	8,835
1972	Lexington–Fayette County, Kentucky	260,512
1972	Suffolk–Nansemond County, Virginia	63,677
1975	Anchorage–Greater Anchorage County, Alaska	260,283
1976	Anaconda–Deer Lodge County, Missouri	9,417
1977	Butte–Silver Bow County, Montana	34,606
1984	Houma–Terrebone Parish, Louisiana	104,503
1988	Lynchburg–Moore County, Tennessee	5,740
1990	Athens–Clarke County, Georgia	101,489
1992	Lafayette–Lafayette Parish, Louisiana	190,503
1995	August–Richmond County, Georgia	199,775
1997	Kansas City–Wyandotte County, Kansas	157,882
1998	Broomfield–Broomfield County, Colorado	38,272
2000	Louisville–Jefferson County, Kentucky	693,604

Note: Except for Indianapolis–Marion County and Broomfield–Broomfield County, the years are when the referendum on consolidation took place. For Indianapolis–Marion County, the date is the year when legislation creating the consolidated government was enacted. For Broomfield–Broomfield County, the date is the year that the creation of the combined city–county of Broomfield was approved in a state referendum.

prescribing the procedures for them. In other states, state legislation or constitutional amendments are required before city and county governments can consolidate.

In addition to the 132 referenda on city–county consolidation since World War II, many studies of consolidation have been conducted. For example, in the 1990s, consolidation advocates were active in Texas, New Mexico, Nevada, and South Carolina; however, no votes on consolidation were held in those states. Sometimes, study groups cannot get the state legislation needed to move consolidation forward. Other times, they decide that the chance of a successful vote is so low that it makes no sense to continue to work on the issue. Or they may conclude that consolidation would not be in the area's best interest.

Consolidation referenda are usually hard fought. Typically, support for consolidation comes from local newspapers, business owners, chambers of commerce, and ''good government'' advocates influenced by the ideas of the progressive movement. Opposition is most likely to come from government employees, unions, suburban dwellers who do not want to be part of a larger local government, and racial minorities. When race is an issue, it usually arises

because, without consolidation, minority voters will be able to gain political control of the city government.

When referenda are held, double majorities are often required before the consolidation passes. That is, the

Table 2   Total number of referenda on city–county consolidations and the number of referenda that passed by decade

Decade	Number of referenda	Number and percent of referenda that passed
1940–1949	3	1 (33)
1950–1959	9	2 (22)
1960–1969	20	6 (31)
1970–1979	49	7 (14)
1980–1989	27	2 (8)
1990–1999	23	4 (17)
2000–2000	1	1 (100)
Totals	132	23 (17)

Source: List of referenda on city–county consolidation compiled by the author from different sources. The most complete list of referenda was published by the National Association of Counties.

merger proposal must be approved by a majority of city dwellers and by a majority of people who live outside the city or cities to be consolidated with the county government. Thus, a majority of city voters or of voters in unincorporated areas can stop consolidation. The double majority requirement has been a difficult one for consolidation advocates to overcome.

Experience shows that the defeat of a proposed consolidation does not mean that the issue will go away. The 1990 vote to merge Athens and Clarke County (Georgia) was the fourth referendum on the issue. The residents of Wilmington and New Hanover County (North Carolina) have voted four times on consolidation, and in 2001, a commission was again studying the issue. The 2000 referendum in Louisville (Kentucky) was the third vote there on that issue.

IS GOVERNMENTAL CONSOLIDATION A GOOD IDEA?

Almost every proposal to merge city and county governments creates considerable controversy. The proponents and opponents disagree about the value of consolidation. Often, they turn to research on this topic and to experts to bolster their arguments for what they want to do. They find substantial disagreements among them about the impact of governmental consolidation.

The Simple Arguments About Efficiency and Knowledgeable Citizens

For most of the twentieth century, consolidation proponents dominated the academic discussion of the topic. Proponents derived their views from the founders of public administration, including Woodrow Wilson and Frank Goodnow.[3] The pro-merger arguments were formulated and refined by leading public administration academics in the 1930s and 1940s.[4,5] The views reflected the progressive agenda that advocated such things as fewer elected officials, shorter ballots, and the professional city management.

The public administrationists argued that political fragmentation of metropolitan areas was counterproductive given the social and economic integration of the areas. They maintained that fragmentation causes nearby local governments to be inefficient, because they duplicate services and lose economies of size in service delivery. Also, they said that fragmentation causes confusion among citizens about which governments are providing them with different services, thus reducing their ability to influence policy makers. In addition, they argued that the fragmentation of governments makes impossible the area-wide planning and action needed to address some of the most important programs facing a metropolitan area.

The influence of this perspective can be seen in the recommendations for governmental consolidation and regionalism that came in the 1960s and early 1970s from the National Research Council, the Committee for Economic Development, and the U.S. Advisory Commission on Intergovernmental Relations.[6,7] Thus, as concern grew about the future of large American cities, prestigious study groups were suggesting consolidation as a cure for urban problems.

Opposition to the public administration orthodoxy developed in the late 1960s and early 1970s. It was led by political economists with a public choice perspective.[8,9] The growing influence of their views was evident in 1987, when ACIR issued a report reflecting them.[2] The theory of the political economists now holds strong currency in the academic world and has been termed the "new orthodoxy" of consolidation.[10]

Political economists reject the idea that the fragmentation of local governments is harmful. In fact, they argue, the opposite is true: the existence of many proximate local governments contributes to governmental efficiency. They maintain that fragmentation creates a type of market in which local governments compete to attract citizens by offering different packages of services and taxes.[8,9,11] In this situation, people are better able to maximize their utility by moving to the jurisdiction of the local government that has the service and tax combination that best reflects what they want. Because different people have different preferences, they are better able to find a closer match for their preference when many competing local-government tax and service packages are available. Also, political economists say that the existence of many smaller local governments enhances democracy by enabling people to influence more directly the local governments whose decisions affect them.

According to this perspective, the competition of local governments causes them to be more efficient than one large consolidated government. Also, these multiple competing governments provide citizens with valuable information on the costs of services: people can compare the costs per unit of services in neighboring cities with their own to monitor the efficiency of their government, making it more difficult for a government to overcharge for them. The political economists say that consolidated governments are inefficient also because they act as monopolists, giving power to budget-maximizing bureaucrats and unions.

The More Complex Arguments About the Value of Fragmentation and Consolidation

In the 1990s, a group of "new consolidationists" shifted the debate from concern about the economy and effectiveness of consolidation to equity and economic development issues. They pointed out the social and racial problems of central cities and suggested consolidation as a good cure. These ''new consolidationists'' have challenged the ''new orthodoxy'' of the public choice perspective of consolidation.

A leading proponent and pioneer of the new proconsolidation perspective is David Rusk, a former mayor of Albuquerque, New Mexico. In ''City Without Suburbs,'' he argued that inelastic cities contribute to problems that are at the heart of central city problems: poverty; economic, racial, and social segregation; and fiscal disparities.[12] He noted that poor and disadvantaged citizens are confined to core cities. He suggested the creation of merged city–county governments as one way to make metropolitan areas elastic, thereby better able to address the central city problems. Books by Downs and other ''New Regionalists'' also viewed city–county consolidation as a way to address the social and economic development problems of metropolitan areas.[13] From an academic perspective, Lowery[10] critiqued the ''new orthodoxy,'' finding it weak in many regards, and he formulated a theory underlying the new case for consolidation. His critique suggested that Tiebolt sorting includes not only choosing the best service and tax package but also maximizing race and class proximity. Thus, people tend to locate within governmental boundaries with people of similar race and class. As residents of small cities, they define their self-interest according to what happens within city boundaries, not the boundaries of the metropolitan areas. Thus, they view any effort to use taxes of their city to help the ailing central city as redistribution. Lowery argued that redistribution has significant transaction costs.[10]

Lowery viewed consolidation as a way to broaden the self-interest perspectives of citizens and to turn decisions to assist central cities into allocation issues, which have lower transaction costs than reallocation decisions. In this context, according to Lowery, it is much easier to ''enhance equity of social opportunities and promote economic development.''

Political economists have also been refining their arguments against city–county consolidation. They rely less on the Tiebolt model of citizen movement among competing local governments as the way efficiency is achieved in fragmented areas. Because Tiebolt's theory includes the assumption that moves within urban areas are costless, it has been subject to criticism. According to Parks and Oakerson, Tiebolt's sorting theory is not necessary to explain why fragmentation creates economic benefits.[14] The benefits can be derived through a combination of citizen voice and public entrepreneurship. They wrote that voice is amplified and access is increased when the ratio of citizens to elected officials is low. Also, they maintained that by having a multiplicity of local government, many sources of entrepreneurial initiative exist.

Also, public choice advocates have rejected the idea that metropolitan areas are a bewildering mix of unrelated governments. They view metropolitan areas as well-functioning urban economies in which complex interrelationships have been formed to insure that services are provided at the proper (that is, most efficient) levels. According to Parks and Oakerson,[14] ''Instead of textbook fragmentation, real metropolitan areas exhibit varied and complex organizations: a variety of small-, medium-, and large-provision units are linked to a variety of production units.'' They point to intergovernmental compacts, privatization, contracting for service, special districts, and functional consolidations as creating a complex web of relationships that makes a metropolitan area a functioning entity.

They suggested that instead of wasting time on city–county consolidation, reformers should concentrate on making sure that the ''local government constitution'' provides the flexibility that citizens need to govern democratically (and thus efficiently) at the local level. They defined ''local government constitution'' as the rules about the types of local government units that may be created and the rules for their creation.

Public administrationist and political economy perspectives are rejected by a third perspective on city–county consolidation. According to contextualists, these two approaches assume that local governments are all alike and that politics does not matter. This perspective suggests that the success or failure of consolidation is not preordained but depends largely on local context, including how well the local budgets and practices governments match; the potential for economies of size; the provisions in the charter that do or do not give decision makers flexibility to implement changes that would increase efficiency, effectiveness, or fairness; and the decisions of the people who are elected to the new government. This perspective insists that each proposed consolidation should be examined separately to forecast its outcomes.[15,16]

What is the Empirical Evidence About the Impacts of Consolidation?

Many anecdotal accounts of city–county consolidation and some research have found that city–county consolidations have contributed to governments that are more efficient. The preponderance of research has supported the conclusion that greater fragmentation is associated with lower government costs in large metropolitan areas.[17] However, these results do not necessarily extend to smaller and nonmetropolitan areas, as shown by the research by Chicoine and Walzer,[18] who found weak evidence that having fewer governments in a county resulted in lower per capita costs.

Similarly, anecdotal evidence and limited research have supported the view of proconsolidation advocates that consolidation contributes to more effective government. That conclusion is contested by the research of the public choice researchers. Other research has suggested that consolidation does not contribute to economic development or increased citizen participation.[19]

Taken as a whole, the body of research on consolidation does not lead to strong conclusions regarding the impacts of city–county consolidation. It is especially inconclusive about consolidation that occurs outside larger metropolitan areas—where, in fact, all but one consolidation has occurred since 1969.

There are many reasons for the difficulty in gaining conclusive research on governmental consolidations. First, few governments have consolidated, so it is difficult to make comparisons. Second, it is difficult to determine the effects of consolidation. Not all changes that occur after consolidation are caused by the consolidation. Thus, when trying to identify the impacts of consolidation on local government expenditures, a researcher must separate the effects of consolidation from the other factors that affect expenditures. The econometric research that attempts to separate impacts from other causes of change is skimpy, nonreplicated, and rarely generalizable. Third, much of the "research" has been anecdotal, and opinions about the value of consolidation may reflect the biases of the speakers. This type of research must be treated with skepticism.

THE FUTURE OF GOVERNMENTAL CONSOLIDATIONS

The success of consolidation efforts in Kansas City–Wyandotte County and Louisville–Jefferson County may encourage consolidation advocates elsewhere to try against long odds to consolidate their city and county governments. Even without those successes, it is likely that attempts to consolidate local governments would have continued.

The history of city–county consolidation has shown it to be an "evergreen issue." In cities that have voted on city–county consolidation in the past, the issue may submerge, but it rarely departs. A good example is Macon-Bibb County, Georgia, where an estimated 22 different groups have studied city–county consolidation since 1923, and voters have rejected it five times. The issue is again on the agenda. As in Macon-Bibb County, in the next 20 years, other areas will vote on consolidating local governments for the third, fourth, and fifth times. Just as referenda are rarely the last word on city–county consolidation, the issue of whether governmental consolidation is good public policy is unlikely to be resolved soon. Starting from different assumptions and holding different views of the world, public administration and political economy researchers will likely continue to conduct research with results that support their views of city–county consolida-

tion. Contextualists will continue to suggest that the only way to determine if city–county consolidation is good public policy is to look at each case individually.

REFERENCES

1. Committee for Economic Development. *Modernizing Local Governments to Secure a Balanced Federalism*; Committee for Economic Development: New York, 1966.
2. U.S. Advisory Commission on Intergovernmental Relations. *The Organization of Local Public Economies*; Government Printing Office: Washington, DC, 1987.
3. Stephens, G.R.; Wikstrom, N. *Metropolitan Government and Governance*; Oxford University Press: New York, 2000.
4. Studenski, P. *The Government of Metropolitan Areas in the United States*; National Municipal League: New York, 1930.
5. Jones, V. *Metropolitan Government*; University of Chicago Press: Chicago, 1942.
6. Committee for Economic Development. *Reshaping Government in Metropolitan Areas*; Committee for Economic Development: New York, 1970.
7. U.S. Advisory Commission on Intergovernmental Relations. *Trends in Metropolitan Government*; Government Printing Office: Washington, DC, 1977.
8. Bish, R.; Ostrom, V. *Understanding Urban Government*; American Enterprise Institute: Washington, DC, 1973.
9. Ostrom, V.; Bish, R.; Ostrom, E. *Local Government in the United States*; ICS Press: San Francisco, 1988.
10. Lowery, D. A transactions costs model of metropolitan governance: Allocation versus redistribution in urban America. J. Public Adm. Res. Theory **2000**, *10* (1), 49–78.
11. Parks, R.; Oakerson, R. Metropolitan organization and governance: A local political economy approach. Urban Aff. Q. **1989**, *25*, 18–29.
12. Rusk, D. *Cities Without Suburbs*; Woodrow Wilson Center Press: Washington, DC, 1993.
13. Downs, A. *New Visions for Metropolitan America*; Brookings Institution: Washington, DC, 1994.
14. Parks, R.; Oakerson, R. Regionalism, localism, and metropolitan governance: Suggestions from the research program on local public economies. State Local Gov. Rev. **2000**, *32* (3), 169–179.
15. Durning, D.; Nobbie, P.D. Post-transition employee perception of city–county unification: The case of Athens-Clarke County. Public Adm. Q. **2000**, *24* (2), 140–168.
16. Selden, S.C.; Campbell, R.W. The expenditure impacts of unification in a small Georgia county: A contingency perspective of city–county consolidation. Public Adm. Q. **2000**, *24* (2), 169–201.
17. Boyne, G.A. Local government structure and performance: Lessons from America? Public Adm. **1992**, *70*, 333–357.
18. Chicoine, D.; Walzer, N. *Government Structure and Local Public Finance*; Oelgeschlager, Gunn, and Hain: Boston, 1985.
19. Feiock, R.C.; Carr, J.B. A reassessment of city–county consolidation: Economic development impacts. State Local Gov. Rev. **1997**, *29* (3), 166–171.

Constitutional Constraints on the Administrations of Public Policy

Matthew Woessner
*The Pennsylvania State University at Harrisburg,
Middletown, Pennsylvania, U.S.A.*

INTRODUCTION

The Constitution of the United States, long celebrated as
the greatest political accomplishment of the Enlightenment, is often regarded with less enthusiasm by proponents of strong and efficient public administration.
Despite its many accomplishments, this political contract
was primarily an instrument of decentralization, designed
to frustrate those who might abuse the power of a strong
central government. To the extent that the Founding
Fathers constrained the new government, they also placed
burdens upon servants of the public good by creating a
complex chain of political command, establishing restrictive boundaries on federal power, and creating limits
on government use of private property. Ultimately, the
primary purpose of the Constitution was to establish domestic tranquility without unnecessarily depriving citizens of their basic liberties. The efficiency of public administration was secondary to concerns over a return
to monarchy.

To allay concerns that a new central government would
become too powerful and overrun the autonomy of the
states, the Founders placed specific limitations on federal
authority in a deliberate attempt to keep it at bay. From a
conceptual standpoint, these limitations are often described in terms of *organizational*, *jurisdictional*, and
property constraints.

From an organizational standpoint, administrators must
know from whom they are taking orders. In the American
context, the answer to this question turns out to be quite
complex. Further, administrators must be aware of the
jurisdictional limitations of their powers under a federal
system of shared political authority. The fact that an
organizational decree comes from the national government does not, in and of itself, guarantee that the directive
is legitimate. The founders designed a layered system of
authority in which the state and national governments are
given jurisdiction over specific segments of American
affairs. Understanding how this has been interpreted will
influence how and when administrators choose to act.
Finally, the power to act is often tempered by constitutional guarantees of due process and just compensation.
So even with clear directives and unambiguous jurisdic-

tion, administrators must occasionally bow to the rights of
property. Although these limitations have varied remarkably over the last century, they remain an important
consideration for any scholar of public administration.

ORGANIZATIONAL CONSTRAINTS

Organizational constraints refer to the inherent difficulties of public administration, where the chief bureaucratic
officers answer to more than one central authority. In
contrast to the classic bureaucratic model, the heads of
government agencies do not report exclusively to one
individual. Rather, department heads are, themselves,
responsible to a large number of different authorities,
including but not limited to, the President of the United
States, the Speaker of the House, the Majority Leader of
the Senate, members of governing committees, subcom-
mittees, and the Congressional membership in general.
While it is true that the President has an inordinate degree
of influence over the goals and direction of high-level
public administrators, they are, nonetheless, compelled to
consider the interests of legislators.[1]

The myth of the presidential bureaucracy stems largely from the fact that department heads serve at the
pleasure of the president. To obtain a post at the head of
a large government agency, an aspiring cabinet secretary
must demonstrate that his appointment will ultimately
serve the interests of the chief executive. Given the president's power to terminate top-level appointments, the
tenure of a department head will last only as long as he
can continue to demonstrate his usefulness. However
strong a motivating factor, the power to dismiss high-
ranking administrators does not guarantee their loyalty.
Beyond the power of appointment, administrators look to
Congress to meet their most basic needs, including the
confirmation of executive appointments, relevant statutory authorities, and agency funding.[2] To the extent
that public administrators are dependent upon the legislature, agency heads will look to Congress and the President for oversight.

From an organizational standpoint, the job of a public
administrator is further complicated by the responsibility

Encyclopedia of Public Administration and Public Policy
DOI: 10.1081/E-EPAP 120010948

to act within the bounds established by the Federal Judiciary. Although the courts do not traditionally make demands on public administrators, the process of statutory interpretation and judicial review forces judges to examine the legal basis for the actions taken at the behest of the political branches. Whenever government takes actions deemed contrary to the letter of the law or the spirit of the Constitution, administrators alter their policies in such a way as to satisfy the concerns of the courts.[3]

While useful in preventing despotism, the principles of ''checks and balances'' and the ''separation of powers'' are generally at odds with classical notions of bureaucratic organization. As a result, nimble public administrators must be capable of pursuing some public good without a single clearly-defined goal from any of the competing branches.

JURISDICTIONAL CONSTRAINTS

Jurisdictional constraints refer to the constitutional limitations placed on federal power in order to prevent the national government from infringing upon the authority traditionally left to states. Before exercising a power established by the legislature, a public administrator must know that the given authority does not conflict with an existing power granted exclusively to the state government or to the people. To do so might risk a lengthy legal battle and, ultimately, repudiation by the judiciary.

From an eighteenth century perspective, concerns over *jurisdictional constraints* were paramount in the minds of public administration, as the newly established national government was granted a narrow list of specific powers meant to provide for domestic security and to promote economic integration. In the execution of administrative power, bureaucrats looked carefully to the enumerated powers listed in Article I, Section 8, of the U.S. Constitution, as a roadmap of legitimate federal authority.

Early battles over the power of the federal government and the scope of its administrative control turned on the last line of Section 8, known commonly as the elastic clause. ''The Congress shall have Power To. . .make all Laws which shall be necessary and proper for carrying into Execution the foregoing Powers, and all other Powers vested by this Constitution in the Government of the United States, or in any Department or Officer thereof.'' For, while the Founders methodically listed the powers of the new central authority, this final directive would seem to imply that Congress could move beyond its narrowly defined charter, so as to satisfy one or more of its aforementioned responsibilities.

Early on, the federal courts were receptive to arguments in favor of an expansive federal power. In *McCulloch v. Maryland*,[4] the Supreme Court was asked to determine whether the charter of the Second Bank of the United States was constitutionally permissible under the powers outlined in Article I. According to its detractors, the federal government lacked the specific authority to charter banks and, therefore, had exceeded its constitutional mandate. Attorneys representing the United States argued that, under the elastic clause, the government was within its right to establish financial institutions for the purpose of strengthening commerce and promoting the general welfare. Writing for a unanimous court, Chief Justice John Marshal argued:

> Among the enumerated powers, we do not find that of establishing a bank or creating a corporation. But there is no phrase in the instrument which, like the articles of confederation, excludes incidental or implied powers; and which requires everything granted shall be expressly and minutely detailed.... After the most deliberate consideration, it is the unanimous and decided opinion of this court that the act to incorporate a bank of the United States is a law made in pursuance of the constitution and is part of the supreme law of the land.

Accordingly, in the exercise of federal authority, officials would, henceforth, not be limited to the enumerated powers listed in Article I, Section 8. Rather, Congress could expand the powers of the federal government to include any influence roughly tied to its responsibility, apart from those specifically forbidden by the Constitution.

Despite the Supreme Court's recognition of implied federal power in *McCulloch v. Maryland*, the states managed to retain an enormous degree of autonomy, particularly in terms of their domestic affairs. Early attempts to regulate or outlaw child labor were met with stiff resistance by a court predisposed to favor a state's right to self-determination. In *Hammer v. Dagenhart*,[5] a private citizen challenged the right of the federal government to set minimum age standards under the Federal Child Labor Act of 1915. The Supreme Court ultimately upheld the decision of the district court, which struck down the act as a usurpation of state authority. Four years later, in *Bailey v. Drexel Furniture Co.* (1922), the Supreme Court would strike down attempts to regulate child labor, this time through taxation. While the court was willing to acknowledge Congress's implied powers under the elastic clause, it was, as yet, unwilling to let loose that authority, so long as it clashed with the responsibilities of the states. This, too, would change with the further integration of state commerce and the onset of a national economic emergency in the Great Depression.

The great turning point in the battle over the scope of federal power would begin in 1932 with the election of Franklin D. Roosevelt as president. With the onset of the Depression, the Roosevelt Administration carried a popular mandate to exercise federal authority over the faltering agriculture and manufacturing sectors in an effort to jump-start the national economy. However, the federal judiciary, still accustomed to seeing economic regulations as a state prerogative, struck down a vast majority of Roosevelt's New Deal programs, arguing that congressional regulations of state commerce must be substantially related to matters of commerce between the several states. With the appointment of sympathetic justices and a threat to pack the court, the judiciary gradually relented. Arguing in *National Labor Relations Board v. Jones & Laughlin Steel Corporation*,[6] the Supreme Court conceded that, in matters of commerce, it is not sufficient that states be granted autonomy over domestic manufacturing, as disputes within those industries could affect the nation as a whole:

> When industries organize themselves on a national scale, making their relation to interstate commerce the dominate factor in their activities, how can it be maintained that their industrial relations constitutes a forbidden field into which Congress many not enter when it is necessary to protect interstate commerce from paralyzing consequences of industrial war?

In the decisions that would follow, the Supreme Court gradually expanded the power of congressional administration, using its constitutional authority over interstate commerce as the justification for intervening in any number of state-related activities.

From a practical standpoint, the importance of federal jurisdictional considerations has declined quite dramatically with the growth of a modern interstate economy. Since the court battles of the mid-1930s, the judiciary has scarcely challenged the power of federal officials to regulate state functions under the interstate commerce clause. In one notable exception, *United States v. Lopez*,[7] the Supreme Court upheld a lower court decision to strike down the Gun-Free School Zone Act of 1990. Under the act, individuals were prohibited from knowingly possessing firearms within a ''school zone.'' Stemming from an earlier decision, the U.S. Congress had grown quite accustomed to asserting its authority in matters relating to the public good under the assertion that it was regulating commerce. This case, however, provided a more difficult situation.

Congress sought to regulate local crime and education, traditionally matters of state control. In addition, the act scarcely provided any evidence that gun possession on school property was in any way related to matters of interstate commerce. Although legal scholars debate the long-term implication of *Lopez*, in striking down the law, the Supreme Court did, if only modestly, reassert the independence of state power and limit Congress' authority to regulate its internal functions.

In the modern context, the constraints of federalism are far less potent than they were when the nation was founded. Nevertheless, under the American constitutional system, administrators of public policy must come to recognize that all federal power operates with specified legal boundaries. To the extent that Congress authorizes the use of federal power outside of long-established precedent, administrators will face a daunting string of court challenges, whether or not the policies enjoy broad public support.

PROPERTY CONSTRAINTS

Property constraints refer to constitutional limitations placed on the government's administration of private resources.

It has been argued that the preservation of property rights was a major motivating factor for the American Revolution. Consequently, safeguards against unreasonable intrusion on privately held resources would eventually become a hallmark of the newfound government; buried inconspicuously within the Constitution's Fifth Amendment:

> No person shall be held to answer for a capital, or otherwise infamous crime, unless on a presentment or indictment of a Grand Jury, except in cases arising in the land or naval forces, or in the Militia, when in actual service in time of War or public danger; nor shall any person be subject for the same offence to be twice put in jeopardy of life or limb; nor shall be compelled in any criminal case to be a witness against himself, nor be deprived of life, liberty, or property, without due process of law; *nor shall private property be taken for public use, with-out just compensation.*

Originally, the protections granted under the Fifth Amendment were narrow in scope and application. The meaning, as determined by early American courts, was to prevent the outright confiscation of land by agents of the federal government. Early attempts to broaden the protection to include the mere devastation of property were met with stiff judicial resistance.[8]

From an administrative perspective, these early constraints were of little consequence in the day-to-day execution of government policies. The practice of eminent domain, while long established in common law, was rarely ever invoked. The true significance of the Constitution's *property constraints* would not become apparent until the Fifth Amendment protections were expanded beyond the physical occupation of privately held lands.

One of the first successful extensions of the Constitution's property protections came amidst preparation for the Second World War. In *United States v. Causby*,[9] a family of chicken farmers brought suit against the federal government, arguing that a newly reconstituted Air Force base had destroyed their poultry business and ruined their living space. The vibrations from the airstrip and the sound from the low-flying bombers so upset the livestock that the Causby's could not continue to raise healthy chickens. Relying on traditional notions of eminent domain, the government argued that, absent the physical occupation of their land, the air traffic alone did not justify compensation. The Supreme Court disagreed, arguing that the deprivation of one's livelihood might, under the appropriate conditions, require government compensation. In this case, the restitution was appropriate.

More recently, the courts have come to view the Constitution's *property constraints* in even broader terms, extending compensation for some environmental and zoning regulations. In *Lucas v. South Carolina Coastal Council*,[10] an oceanfront property owner brought suit against his state for its application of the Beachfront Management Act. Under the regulations, the development of his oceanfront properties would be prohibited. Arguing that the regulations were passed after he had acquired the properties, Lucas suggested that the state legislature had rendered his land worthless. Accordingly, if the state's interests in preserving the land were valid, he must be compensated. The Supreme Court ultimately agreed, ordering the state to provide for the substantial economic damage done to the property as a result of the restrictions.

The overall importance of the Constitution's property constraints is tempered by the prescribed remedy. Even in the most recent rulings, the judiciary has failed to question whether the alleged intrusion on private lands is within the government's valid police powers. Rather, the court has focused, instead, on the circumstances in which the valid use of government power is sufficiently destructive as to warrant compensation. From the perspective of the Constitution's *property constraints*, public administrators need not worry whether a given power is permissible, but rather, what are the public costs associated with any mandated compensation.

CONCLUSION

In assembling the American constitution, the Founding Fathers were forced to confront the tensions between private freedoms and the efficient administration of public resources. By fragmenting the chain of command and limiting the scope of governmental authority, they consciously elected to bias the system in favor of personal liberties.

The *organizational constraints* nested within the "separation of powers" have, to date, thwarted a dangerous consolidation of power. But these organizational safeguards serve to complicate the efficient execution of public policy by forcing administrators to accommodate conflicting political demands.

The Constitution's *jurisdictional constraints* further obscure the administration of public policy by forcing administrators to mind the complicated legal boundaries established between state and federal governments. Even with clear administrative directives, government officials are occasionally reined in by the judiciary for overstepping their constitutional responsibilities.

As if the execution of public policy were not sufficiently complicated, officials must be mindful of the *property constraints*, which compel government entities to provide compensation for the regulation of some privately held resources.

In each of the three examples, administrative efficiency is sacrificed to ensure the preservation of basic personal liberties. However problematic or politically inexpedient, their basis in constitutional law renders many notions of practical reform virtually impossible.

REFERENCES

1. Rosenbloom, D.H.; O'Leary, R. *Public Administration and Law,* 2nd Ed.; Marcel Dekker: New York, 1997.
2. Neustadt, R.E. *Presidential Power and the Modern Presidents: The Politics of Leadership from Roosevelt to Reagan*; The Free Press: New York, 1990.
3. Cooper, P.J. *Public Law and Public Administration*; Mayfield Publishing Company: Palo Alto, CA, 1983.
4. McCulloch v. Maryland 4 Wheat. 316 (1819).
5. Hammer v. Dagenhart 247 U.S. 251 (1918).
6. National Labor Relations Board v. Jones & Laughlin Steel Corporation 301 U.S. 1 (1937).
7. United States v. Lopez 514 U.S. 549 (1995).
8. Barron v. Baltimore 7 Pet. 243 (1833), 603.
9. United States v. Causby 328 U.S. 256 (1946).
10. Lucas v. South Carolina Coastal Council 505 U.S. 1003 (1992).

Constitutional Constraints on Administrative Behavior in the United States

David H. Rosenbloom
American University, Washington, District of Columbia, U.S.A.

INTRODUCTION

United States constitutional law currently places broad and substantial constraints on public administrative behavior at all levels of government. Since the 1950s, public administrators' interactions with clients and customers, coworkers, contractors, patients confined to public mental health facilities, prisoners, and individuals involved in street-level administrative regulation have become bounded by constitutional law.[1–3] Federal court decisions based on a mix of statutory, constitutional, and common law have also made public administrators vulnerable to "constitutional tort" suits, that is, civil suits for money damages to redress their violations of individuals' constitutional rights. This entry explains the legal doctrines that established and define present-day constitutional constraints on administrative behavior.

RELATIONSHIPS WITH CLIENTS OR CUSTOMERS

Prior to the 1950s, there were few effective constitutional constraints on public administrators' relationships with clients or customers. Recipients of governmental benefits were effectively unable to challenge the constitutionality of administrative conditions attached to welfare payments, public education, occupational licenses, or similar governmental "gratuities" or "largesse." Nor, for the most part, could they successfully use the Constitution's Equal Protection Clause to challenge the distribution of such benefits. Client–customer relationships were governed by the historic "doctrine of privilege." It held that the government had no constitutional duty or obligation to supply benefits, the client or customer accepted them voluntarily and without governmental coercion, the government was therefore largely free to establish the conditions on which the benefits could be received, and benefits might even be distributed in a discriminatory fashion under some circumstances.

The key to this approach was a distinction between rights and privileges. Rights are viewed as predating government and protected by the Constitution. In the Declaration of Independence's terms, they are bestowed by human's "Creator" and "unalienable." Privileges, by contrast, are interests established by the government, essentially on whatever terms it chooses. Because clients or customers have no constitutional right to the privileges offered by government, the Constitution is essentially irrelevant to the denial or withdrawal of benefits, no matter how dependent on them recipients may be. Famous examples included the denial of such things as public university education to conscientious objectors who would not join the Reserve Officers Training Corps, old-age assistance to a man who refused to live in conventional housing, a license to sell liquor to a man who exercised his privilege against self-incrimination, participation in extra curricular public high school activities by married students, bartenders' licenses to women (other than the wives and daughters of male bar owners), and licenses to practice law and medicine on account of one's political beliefs.

The doctrine of privilege predated the development of the large-scale U.S. administrative state. In the 1950s and 1960s, it came under increasing criticism as a threat to the constitutional rights of an ever-growing number of clients and customers. By the 1970s, three doctrinal developments had rendered the distinction between rights and privileges meaningless.

Equal Protection

First, the federal courts reinterpreted the Constitution's Equal Protection Clause. Logically, the doctrine of privilege should not have trumped the guarantee of equal protection of the laws. The fact there is no right to government benefits does not support the conclusion that they may be offered to members of one race but not another. Modern equal protection doctrine, beginning most clearly with public education cases culminating in *Brown v. Board of Education*,[4] prohibits the government from offering a privilege to some but not others, except in a fashion that is consonant with equal protection.

Today, equal protection has a three-tiered structure. The threshold issue is whether a government has classified by some characteristic, such as race, gender, wealth,

Encyclopedia of Public Administration and Public Policy
DOI: 10.1081/E-EPAP 120010676

residency, or age. The classification may be implicit in a policy or its implementation, rather than explicitly stated in legislation or formal regulations. However, if there is no classification, there is no equal protection issue.

Classifications based on race or ethnicity are considered "suspect" because, in view of the nation's history, it is likely that they will be used to disadvantage minorities. They are subject to strict judicial scrutiny and are constitutional only when narrowly tailored to promote a compelling governmental interest. A heavy burden of persuasion rests on the government and the courts will not be deferential to its claims. These requirements apply whether the purpose of the classification is benign, as in the case of affirmative action, or invidious as in the case of racial segregation.

Classifications based on factors that are not immutable, such as wealth and residency, are constitutional when they are rationally related to the achievement of a legitimate governmental purpose. The burden of persuasion is typically on the challenger, and the courts grant considerable deference to the government's claims. This is called "mere rationality" or "rational basis" analysis. It also applies to classifications based on age. An exception occurs if a nonsuspect classification directly interferes with the exercise of a protected constitutional right. For example, a residency requirement for welfare eligibility might abridge the constitutional right of indigents to travel and relocate across state lines. In such a case, the classification is subject to strict judicial scrutiny and must serve a compelling governmental interest in a way that is narrowly tailored or, possibly, the least restrictive of the protected constitutional rights involved.

Classifications based on gender are "quasisuspect" and face an intermediate test. They must be substantially related to the achievement of important governmental objectives. The courts may ask the government to provide an "exceedingly persuasive" justification for such classifications, many of which are legacies of earlier practices and beliefs about gender differences that society no longer supports.

Contemporary equal protection doctrine constrains administrative behavior with respect to clients and customers in a wide range of circumstances. Most obviously, it prohibits racial and ethnic discrimination in public education, housing, welfare, health, recreation, occupational licensing, and other programs, except where the government can meet the compelling governmental interest and narrow tailoring tests under strict judicial scrutiny. Invidious discrimination is likely to be justified only under the most extraordinary circumstances, if ever. Benign or remedial racial and ethnic classifications, as in affirmative action, face the same test, but it is plausible that some may serve a compelling governmental interest in a narrowly tailored fashion. Even though classifications

based on gender do not require a compelling governmental interest and narrow tailoring, it is highly unlikely that invidious discrimination against females or males will be constitutional in client–customer relationships. Theoretically, the weaker standard for gender classifications makes it easier to justify affirmative action programs for women and girls than for minorities. However, in practice, there may be no real difference. By contrast, classifications based on other factors, such as age, will most likely be constitutional unless they interfere with the exercise of another protected constitutional right.

Procedural Due Process: The "New Property"

A second doctrinal change contributing to the demise of the doctrine of privilege is called "new property" theory. This approach developed in the 1960s and 1970s. It treats individuals' governmental benefits as their own property. As such, they are covered by the Due Process Clauses of the Fifth and Fourteenth Amendments, which protect against the deprivation of "life, liberty, or property, without due process of law." Consequently, welfare benefits, public housing, public education, various occupational and other licenses, and other benefits cannot be withheld or terminated (during the period for which they were offered) without a fair procedure.

Procedural due process has a fluid structure. It requires a balancing of three factors: 1) the individual's interest in the benefit and/or the severity of the deprivation at issue; 2) the risk that procedure in place, if any, will result in an erroneous decision *and* the probable value of additional procedures in reducing errors; and 3) the government's administrative and financial interests in not using additional or alternative procedures. The underlying assumption in this formula is that, in general, the more elaborate the procedures, the lower the risk of error. Once a statute or administrative regulation establishes a new property interest, it can be withheld or terminated only in consonance with constitutional due process.

The application of procedural due process is subjective. One must weigh both the individual's and government's interests. Typically, two issues arise. First, whether the client is entitled to procedural due process prior to the termination of a benefit during the term for which it was offered. Recipients of means-tested welfare benefits, which may be vital to their survival or ability to use posttermination procedures, generally enjoy a procedural due process right to some pretermination protection against erroneous administrative decisions. An exception exists when there is no factual dispute about their continuing eligibility.

The second issue is how elaborate the procedures required by due process must be. They can range from highly informal notice and opportunity to respond, to a formal response in writing only, to the rudiments of a nonjury judicial trial with a right to counsel, presentation of evidence and witnesses, confrontation and cross-examination of adverse witnesses, a written transcript, a decision by an impartial decision maker, and a right to appeal.[5–7] In federal administrative law, an impartial decision maker is defined as one who does not have "an irrevocably closed mind." More generally, impartiality prevents those who investigated the case from making the final decision. Sometimes pre- and posttermination requirements are linked. For example, because elaborate posttermination procedures are available to social security disability recipients, only limited procedure is required before these non-means-tested benefits are cut off.

The impact of new property doctrine on administration depends on the specific context. Pre- or posttermination hearings became common in decisions regarding the termination of welfare, disability, and occupational licenses. Suspensions and expulsions from public schools are also controlled by procedural due process. It is important to remember that when benefits terminate because they were offered for a fixed term or the recipients have aged, moved, married, or otherwise changed their eligibility status, procedural due process may require nothing more than notice, if that. However, if there is a factual question about the recipient's continuing eligibility, more elaborate procedure may be required.

Unconstitutional Conditions

Reinvigoration of the "unconstitutional conditions" doctrine was the third constitutional change to undercut the doctrine of privilege. The conditions attached to governmental benefits sometimes interfere with clients' and customers' constitutional rights. For instance, a state might mandate that applicants for unemployment compensation be available for work on Saturday despite their sabbatarian religious beliefs, or that public school students recite prayers or the pledge of allegiance to the flag. The unconstitutional conditions doctrine seeks to limit the government's ability to use benefits as leverage for regulating behavior that it could not reach directly without violating individuals' constitutional rights. For instance, under the unconstitutional conditions doctrine, American governments, which lack the power to establish religion directly, cannot do so indirectly through the manipulation of benefits.

The problem public administrators and lawmakers face is knowing which conditions attached to benefits will be adjudged unconstitutional. Essentially, the courts apply a two-part test, but as in the case of procedural due process a good deal of subjectivity is involved. Specific requirements vary with the nature of the benefit and type of

condition. Conditions that gratuitously infringe on protected rights by failing to serve a significant governmental purpose or by prohibiting more than necessary to achieve a legitimate or compelling public interest are likely to be unconstitutional. Narrowly tailored conditions involving freedom of speech, association, religion, or protection from unreasonable searches must generally promote at least an important governmental interest. Under the Fifth Amendment's "Takings Clause," conditions attached to building permits must be roughly proportional to the impact the proposed development will have on legitimate governmental interests, such as traffic congestion.

Taken together, contemporary equal protection, new property theory, and the unconstitutional conditions doctrine bring constitutional law directly into the relationships between public administrators and their clients and customers. They complicate public administration by broadening the set of values that administrators and programs must protect and, sometimes, by requiring elaborate procedure. They also strengthen the role of courts and judges in this area of public administration, most notably with regard to remedying systematic violations of equal protection, as in the case of desegregating schools.

PUBLIC PERSONNEL ADMINISTRATION

The doctrine of privilege also applied to public employment. Until change began in the 1950s, a public sector job was considered a benefit or gratuity. Having voluntarily accepted it, public employees could not claim that conditions imposed violated their constitutional rights. As in the case of benefits to clients and customers, racial and gender discrimination in public employment was not controlled by the Equal Protection Clause. Until the 1950s, individuals could be denied public employment or dismissed from it essentially for any reason or no reason at all, including their speech, beliefs, religious practices, reading habits, race, gender, or membership in unions, civil rights, and other organizations.

Cases involving public employment contributed substantially to the demise of the doctrine of privilege. Constitutional constraints became important to public personnel administration as equal protection was applied to public employment, civil service jobs were considered part of the new property, and the unconditional conditions doctrine was invoked to protect public employees' First Amendment rights. However, the constitutional doctrine that constrains public sector human resources management differs from that pertaining to clients and customers.

Constitutional rights within the framework of public employment are now assessed through a "public service model." Its core premise is that the administrative values of efficiency and effectiveness are more important to governments when they act as employers than when they seek to regulate the behavior of ordinary citizens. Government, like any employer, needs greater authority over its employees than it can exercise over its clients, customers, or the general public. But there are also limits to that authority.

The public service model balances three considerations. First is the interest of the employees in exercising their constitutional rights, that is, in being free of governmental controls. Second is the government's interest in achieving some important purpose as an employer. Third is the public's interest in the way government and public administration operate. The key point in the public service model is that the public's interest may coincide with either that of the employee or the government. For example, in the realm of free speech, the public has a clear interest in affording strong constitutional protection to whistleblowing by public employees. The public is better able to asses governmental performance when public employees can freely expose illegality, gross waste, fraud, abuse, and specific and immediate dangers to public health or safety. By contrast, the public has only a minimal interest, if any, in public employees' partisan campaign speeches, routine office gossiping, or grousing about politicians and administrative higher-ups. Under the public service model, whistleblower speech is strongly protected, whereas partisan speech and speech that is of minimal or no public concern are not.

The same kind of balancing applies to public employees' free exercise of religion and association, as well as to their Fourth Amendment privacy rights and guarantee of equal protection of the laws. In assessing constraints on personnel management in these contexts, one always considers the individual's interest in exercising or retaining protected rights, the government's interests that could justify abridgments, and the public's interest. It is important that public personnelists, managers, and employees bear in mind that the governmental interest, although often stated as serving the taxpayers, is not necessarily synonymous with the public interest. Even in the context of public employment, the government's interest in cost-effective administration may not justify infringements on constitutionally protected rights. If there is no clear public interest one way or the other, then the balance is simply between the interests of the employee and the government. The employee will sometimes win because despite the importance of cost-effective administration, it is not always sufficient to justify interference with protected constitutional rights.

First Amendment Rights

Public employees enjoy broad First Amendment rights under the public service model. The major limitations on

their freedom of speech are that to enjoy constitutional protection, expressive activity must be on a matter of public concern, and speech as part of a partisan political campaign may be banned. Disruptive remarks on matters of private concern only are not protected because they serve no public interest. Restrictions on the partisan political activity of public employees are constitutionally justified by the public interest in administrative impartiality and efficiency, as well as by the protection they afford government workers against being coerced by political appointees and supervisors to support political parties and candidates.

In general, public employees' speech on matters of public concern is most vulnerable to an adverse action when it impairs discipline or harmony in the workplace, jeopardizes close working relationships, interferes with normal operations, or detracts from employees' ability to do their jobs. In balancing the interests of the government, employee, and public, attention must be paid to the nature of the employee's position in the organization. Identical remarks by those at the top and bottom of an organizational hierarchy may be treated differently. When disciplining employees for their off-the-job remarks or other protected activities, the government should be able to show a nexus between its significant interests as an employer and the conduct involved.

The public service model also broadly protects employees' freedom of association and religious freedom. Restrictions on these freedoms have to be justified by the balance among the interests of the employee, public employer, and public. Constitutional law extends extensive protection to employees' freedom of association on the premise that membership alone is not a proxy for behavior. Consequently, employees may join labor unions, employee associations, antisocial groups such as the Ku Klux Klan, and even subversive organizations. Exceptions are permissible for categories of employees whose membership in particular organizations would significantly harm the employer's or public's interests. For instance, supervisors and managers can be banned from joining labor unions representing rank-and-file employees because such membership might conflict with their hierarchical responsibilities. Employees also have the right not to join organizations and, consequently, "closed shop" labor agreements are unconstitutional in the public sector. Since the late 1970s, public employees' freedom of association has been interpreted to make job actions based on political partisanship unconstitutional unless the government can show that party affiliation related to effective job performance.

The parameters of public employees' religious freedom are less clear. The governmental employer cannot coerce employees to engage in prayer or other religious activity. Nor can it gratuitously restrict their religious expression or behavior. Because discrimination based on religion is prohibited by federal equal employment opportunity law, a public employee is ordinarily not required to refrain from wearing religious jewelry or headgear, even if other workers find it objectionable. By contrast, restrictions on religious activity might be justified when overt religious proselytizing or vocal praying at work is disruptive or otherwise interferes with the employer's legitimate interests in workplace harmony and cost effectiveness.

Fourth Amendment Privacy

Public employees retain protections against unreasonable searches and seizures even while in the public workplace. The threshold question is whether the employee has a reasonable expectation of privacy under the circumstances. That is, an expectation of privacy that society is prepared to support (according to federal judges). In the absence of such an expectation, public employers are free to search an employee's workspace, desk, files, computer, and so forth. Where there is a reasonable expectation of privacy, the governmental search must be reasonable in its inception and scope. Employees have a reasonable expectation of privacy in their body fluids, but suspicion-less drug testing is constitutionally permissible when it reasonably promotes national security, law enforcement, or public safety.

Procedural Due Process

Civil service systems generally provide public employees with new property rights in their positions. Consequently, procedural due process protects them against arbitrary, capricious, or abusive dismissal or demotion. Pretermination notice and opportunity to respond are generally required, as are more elaborate posttermination procedures. Depending on the circumstances, public employers may not be required to offer any procedural due process prior to suspending an employee without pay for wrongdoing. However, the employee should be offered a hearing of some kind within a reasonable time after the suspension takes effect. For the most part, the constitutional requirements for public employees' procedural due process are now written into civil service laws and regulations. However, once a new property right in public employment is created by the government, its termination of diminution is controlled by constitutional, rather than statutory law. Where public employees do not have civil service or tenured status, adverse actions may be "at will" only insofar as they do not violate First Amendment, Fourth Amendment, equal protection, or other constitutional rights.

Equal Protection

The three-tiered equal protection analysis previously discussed applies to public employees, as well as to clients and customers. Racial and ethnic classifications, whether benign or invidious, are subject to strict scrutiny. Thus far, the Supreme Court has not held that promoting workforce diversity is a compelling governmental interest. It has permitted benign racial classifications only as a remedy for past, proven, egregious violations of equal protection. These and other racial or ethnic classifications must be narrowly tailored. That is, they must 1) be efficacious relative to alternative remedies that avoid such classifications (such as fining a jurisdiction for violations of equal employment opportunity); 2) have a clear and logical stopping point; 3) be demographically proportionate; 4) contain waiver provisions so that the government is never forced to hire someone who is unqualified; and 5) not unduly burden the employment interests of nonminority employees.

Residency and age requirements are subject to rational basis analysis. They will be constitutional if they are rationally related to the achievement of a legitimate governmental interest. Gender-based classifications face a higher standard—they must be strongly related to the achievement of important governmental purposes.

RELATIONSHIPS WITH CONTRACTORS

Governments also face constitutional constraints when dealing with contractors. Some of these are well settled. Governments cannot engage in invidious racial, ethnic, or gender discrimination when contracting out. Contracts that establish new property interests cannot be terminated without procedural due process. In the 1990s, the Supreme Court strengthened two additional types of constraints.

First, the court unequivocally held that benign racial and ethnic classifications in governmental contracting are subject to strict scrutiny. They must serve a compelling governmental interest in a narrowly tailored fashion. This severely restricted the use of minority business set asides and other preferences. Even though the constitutional test for gender classifications is weaker, preferences for women-owned businesses will probably face the same fate, if such litigation reaches the Supreme Court.

Second, the court made it clear that contractors and those engaged in preexisting commercial relationships with governments, such as firms on a tow truck rotation list, retain First Amendment rights. Using unconstitutional conditions analysis, the court held that the Constitution protects contractors' public criticism of a government or opposition to its officials. Essentially, the same constitutional test that applies to public employees' speech is used to determine the free speech rights of contractors and others engaged in ongoing business relationships with government. A government can terminate its commercial relationship with such parties in response to their speech only if it can show that, on balance, such action is justified by the speech's detrimental impact on its ability to deliver public services.

THE MANAGEMENT OF PATIENTS IN PUBLIC MENTAL HEALTH FACILITIES

Since the early 1970s, constitutional law has required that patients confined to public mental health facilities be afforded treatment. Earlier, they were often "warehoused" indefinitely or otherwise inadequately treated. In *Wyatt v. Stickney*,[8] a federal district court held that confining such patients without treatment constitutes a violation the right to liberty under the Fourteenth Amendment. Although the decision applied directly only to the Alabama mental health system, its logic was soon adopted nationwide.

The constitutional right to treatment was eventually defined in broad terms. It includes reasonable care and safety, reasonably nonrestrictive confinement conditions, and individualized treatment (or training for the mentally disabled). Implementation requires a humane physical and psychological environment, as well as adequate staffing. In practice, this may require far-reaching architectural and medical reforms. The *Wyatt* court eventually required Alabama either to release patients or to provide the following: protection of patients' right to wear their own clothes, have physical exercise, and freedom of religious worship; no more than six patients per room; no single room with less than 100 square feet; at least one toilet for each eight patients; at least one shower or tub for each 15 patients; not less than 50 square feet per person in the dayroom; at least 10 square feet per person in the dining room; a temperature range between 68 and 83 degrees Fahrenheit; and various per-patient staffing ratios for professionals, clerical workers, and other staff.

Although judicial involvement in public mental health care was sometimes characterized as interference, eventually the American Psychiatric Association supported the right to treatment. Along with other factors, including better psychoactive drugs, crowding was reduced through deinstitutionalization and shorter stays, and the overall conditions in public mental health facilities improved substantially.

PRISON MANAGEMENT

Since the 1970s, the treatment of prisoners has also been thoroughly constitutionalized. The Eighth Amendment prohibition of cruel and unusual punishment was reinterpreted to apply to the conditions of confinement, rather than the sentence only. This required prison reforms in more than 40 states to reduce overcrowding, provide adequate medical care and safety, and guarantee inmates at least a minimal level of nutrition, hygiene, and civilized life's other necessities. The scope of what is prohibited by the Eighth Amendment changes as society progresses and standards of decency evolve. For instance, in the 1990s, prisoners gained the right to challenge subjection to second-hand tobacco smoke when it poses a risk of serious harm due to personal respiratory or other health problems.

In addition to Eighth Amendment protections, prisoners have a right to procedural due process when proposed discipline creates extraordinary hardships within the framework of normal prison life. Similarly, within the confines of what incarceration requires in practice, they have the right to free exercise of religion and to marry. The general test is whether restrictions on the prisoners' constitutional rights serve legitimate penological interests, including their impact on guards and other inmates. Prison administration has become so thoroughly infused with constitutional concerns that some prison systems engage in "constitutional audits" to assure their compliance with the latest judicial decisions.

STREET-LEVEL REGULATORY ENCOUNTERS

Public employees whose jobs require constant face-to-face regulatory interaction with the public are often called "street-level bureaucrats." The term includes police, social workers, public school teachers, public health workers, health and safety inspectors, and others who tend to work in the absence of close proximate supervision, have a great deal of discretion in dealing with members of the public, are largely self-reporting, and are often in a position to have a great positive or negative impact on the individuals with whom they deal. It is also common for street-level bureaucrats to work with heavy caseloads and inadequate resources. Their work environment may be charged with physical and/or psychological threats.

The Fourth Amendment and Equal Protection Clause are the most relevant Constitutional constraints on street-level bureaucrats' behavior. However, these controls are loose and subject to evasion.

Fourth Amendment Constraints

Fourth Amendment law is notoriously uneven and fact specific in its application. As noted earlier, it only applies to situations in which there is a reasonable expectation of privacy. The courts treat that expectation as a continuum.

On one end, individuals who are in their own homes with the windows and doors closed and curtains drawn have a great expectation of privacy. On the other, the same individuals would have a minimal expectation of privacy in their baggage when seeking to board a scheduled commercial airplane at a U.S. airport. In between, there are many gradations. In addition, some individuals have reduced Fourth Amendment protections due to their special relationship with an administrative function and its personnel. For example, public school administrators have greater leeway to search students because the schools have special custodial and tutelary responsibilities.

A distinction is usually drawn between law enforcement searches and administrative inspections. Whenever practicable, the Fourth Amendment requires law enforcement officers to seek a warrant from a judge, magistrate, or other judicial official. The warrant is issued on probable cause, which essentially means there is specific evidence that a violation of law may exist. When time or other considerations make obtaining a warrant impractical, law enforcement agents can proceed on probable cause alone. Administrative inspections of nonpervasively regulated businesses may also require warrants. However, it is not necessary to show probable cause as these may be issued when reasonably necessary for the enforcement of the statute involved. Administrative searches involving special relationships or needs, such as public school discipline, are generally governed by a reasonableness standard.

The constraints on street-level administration generated by this framework often appear inconsistent and, sometimes, close to nonexistent. For instance, a federal Occupational Safety and Health Administration (OSHA) inspector may be need a warrant to inspect a workplace, depending in part on how open the facility, or a section of it, is to the public. Similarly, a public hospital cannot engage in a law enforcement search of patients' bodily fluids without a warrant or their consent, although it apparently can draw the same fluids for diagnostic medical reasons without Fourth Amendment restriction.[9] At the same time that an OSHA inspector and public health worker may need a warrant, an individual can be arrested for any traffic infraction, however minor, and consequently subject to a legitimate personal and vehicle search. The Supreme Court has eschewed all inquiry into whether traffic stops or arrests following them are merely pretexts used by the police to search individuals and their vehicles. Even arrest for a nonjailable offense, such as not wearing a seatbelt, is permitted.[10,11]

Equal Protection Constraints

Equal protection constraints on street-level bureaucrats are less complex than Fourth Amendment requirements,

but also subject to circumvention. The threshold question for equal protection analysis is whether a government or its employees classifies individuals by some social characteristic, such as race, age, or wealth. If there is no classification, there is no equal protection issue. A "classification of one" is cognizable under equal protection, but unfair treatment of particular individuals is typically litigated under procedural due process protection against arbitrary or capricious administrative decision making.[12]

The main problem for individuals who would challenge street-level personnel's behavior on equal protection grounds is that the burden of persuasion rests on the private party to demonstrate that a government or its employees have explicitly or implicitly created a classification. Explicit invidious racial, ethnic, or gender classifications are highly unusual in contemporary public administration. Implicit classifications, based on these social characteristics, may be inferred from patterns of administrative behavior. However, establishing their existence to a court's satisfaction is difficult. This is why the Equal Protection Clause has been relatively ineffective in combating racial and ethnic profiling by law enforcement agents when there is no written or verbal evidence. Unless profiling is the only plausible explanation for the administrative behavior at issue, it may be impossible to show that an implicit classification exists. Of course, equal protection is a more effective constraint against street-level behavior that follows directly from racist, ethnically derogatory, or sexist statements.

PUBLIC ADMINISTRATORS' LIABILITY FOR CONSTITUTIONAL TORTS

There is often a gap between formal constitutional requirements and actual administrative practice. Constitutional law may be unclear or poorly communicated to administrators. Sometimes it is highly subjective or requires elaborate balancing of multiple factors. Specific constraints may seem counterintuitive to administrators or impractical due to scarce resources, including time. Furthermore, not everyone whose constitutional rights are violated has either the incentive or ability to sue the government or its employees for redress.

In a series of decisions crystallizing in the 1980s, the Supreme Court strengthened the application of constitutional constraints on administrative behavior by reinvigorating the law of "constitutional torts." The court made it far easier for individuals to sue public administrators personally in federal court for money damages for violations of their constitutional rights. It reasoned that facilitating constitutional tort suits serves both to deter breaches of constitutional law and also to compensate victims. The current standard for administrators' liability for violating constitutional rights requires that they personally factor knowledge of constitutional constraints into their decisionmaking.

Since 1982, most American public administrators potentially have been personally liable for money damages when their conduct violates "clearly established statutory or constitutional rights of which a reasonable person would have known".[13] Under this standard, knowledge of constitutional law becomes a matter of job competence. In the Supreme Court's words: "[A] reasonably competent public official should know the law governing his conduct".[13] An exception is that public administrators cannot be sued for committing constitutional torts while engaged in adjudicatory or legislative functions. There are also some technical differences in how local, state, and federal employees may be sued. However, the vast majority of public administrators are subject to suit and constitutional torts produce considerable litigation. Municipalities and their agencies are also liable to such suits when their policies directly cause violations of individuals' constitutional rights. Under limited circumstances, they can also be sued for failure to train their employees to protect constitutional rights.

CONCLUSION

During the second half of the twentieth century, the federal courts, often led by the Supreme Court, revolutionized the application of constitutional constraints to administrative behavior in the United States. Constitutional law became relevant, if not central, to administrative decisions and operations regarding clients or customers, public personnel systems, outsourcing, the treatment of patients in public mental health facilities, incarceration, and the exercise of regulatory authority in street-level encounters. The courts also vastly strengthened the opportunity for aggrieved individuals to vindicate their newfound rights through constitutional tort suits. Perhaps most important, the federal judiciary now expects public administrators at all levels of government to follow the development of constitutional law, to know how it bears upon their official functions, and to consider obeying it a central element of job competence.

REFERENCES

1. Barron, J.; Thomas, D.C. *Constitutional Law in a Nut Shell*; West: St. Paul, MN, 1999.
2. Rosenbloom, D.H.; O'Leary, R. *Public Administration and Law*, 2nd Ed.; Marcel Dekker: New York, 1997.
3. Rosenbloom, D.H.; Carroll, J.; Carroll, J. *Constitutional Competence for Public Managers: Cases and Commentary*; F. E. Peacock: Itasca, IL, 2000.
4. *Brown v. Board of Education of Topeka*. 1954. 347 U.S. 483.
5. *Goss v. Lopez*. 1975. 419 U.S. 565.
6. *Board of Curators of University of Missouri v. Horowitz*. 1978. 435 U.S. 78.
7. *Mathews v. Eldridge*. 1976. 419 U.S. 319.
8. *Wyatt v. Stickney*. 1971. 325 F. Supp. 781; 334 F. Supp. 1341.
9. *Ferguson v. City of Charleston*. 2001. U.S. Supreme Court, No. 99–936.
10. *Atwater v. City of Lago Vista*. 2001. U.S. Supreme Court, No. 99–1408.
11. *Whren v. United States*. 1996. 517 U.S. 806.
12. *Village of Willowbrook v. Olechon*. 2000. 528 U.S. 562.
13. *Harlow v. Fitzgerald*. 1982. 457 U.S. 800, p. 819.

Contracting for Social Services

Nancy McCarthy Snyder
Wichita State University, Wichita, Kansas, U.S.A.

C

INTRODUCTION

This article addresses the issues associated with growth in government contracting for human services. Interest in the contracting relationship between governments and nonprofit organizations has increased since the 1980s. Political pressure to reduce the size of government has led states and municipalities to become more dependent on nonprofits to deliver public human services. This trend has been reinforced by deinstitutionalization of disadvantaged populations. Nonprofit organizations have stepped forward to design and deliver community-based services for the elderly, the mentally ill, abused and neglected children, and the developmentally and physically disabled. As a result, nonprofits have become increasingly dependent on government.

Growth in the nonprofit sector and heavy reliance on tax-supported revenue have led to increased scrutiny and concerns about the management capacity of nonprofit agencies, particularly in human services where executive directors are typically promoted from line positions and lack training in finance and management. Therefore, the trend toward contracting raises important challenges for governments. Public officials have less control over contracted services than they do over directly produced services. This article further discusses the need for government capacity to monitor the contracting relationship and to ensure accountability for public resources.

HISTORICAL CONTEXT

The primary challenge of public finance is always resource allocation, including how the level and content of government services fits in the overall mix of public, business, and nonprofit sector production. The history of social welfare in the United States is a case study in federalism, as well as in the division of responsibilities between the public and private sectors. Relationships between governments and nonprofit social service agencies have a long tradition in the United States. At the turn of the twentieth century, it was common for local governments to fund orphanages, hospitals, and relief organizations that were operated by private organizations.

The Social Security Act of 1935 brought the federal government into the social welfare policy arena. However, the federal role was limited, with the exception of retirement insurance, to small grants to states for a few welfare programs. During the 1960s and 1970s, the federal role expanded greatly with the creation of new programs (e.g., foodstamps, Medicaid, Medicare) and large increases in existing programs (e.g., Aid to Families with Dependent Children, child care, and social services). The 1980s was marked by retrenchment in many areas of social welfare. By fiscal year 1997, social service agencies received 20% less from the federal government (as a percent of gross domestic product) than they had in 1980.[1] In addition to reducing relative spending, the federal government devolved operating responsibility for many programs to state and local governments. At the same time, major changes in policy toward services for the elderly, the mentally ill, and physically and developmentally disabled individuals resulted in the creation of community-based programs to replace institutional care. Thus, at the turn of the twenty-first century, state and local governments had considerably more responsibility for human services and turned increasingly to nonprofit organizations to deliver services.

Two major factors have increased attention to the contracting relationship between governments and nonprofits organizations. First is a general growing interest in the U.S. nonprofit sector. The overall size of the sector increased dramatically during the second half of the twentieth century, from 50,000 to approximately 1.5 million organizations, over one-third of which are "charitable" (i.e., eligible to receive tax-deductible contributions; other categories of nonprofit agencies are religious congregations, foundations, and mutual benefit organizations, such as labor unions and professional associations). Today, the nonprofit sector, broadly defined, receives revenue equal to almost 9% of gross domestic product and employs roughly 11 million people or 7% paid employment.[2] This success has led to increased scrutiny and concerns about the management capacity of nonprofit agencies,[3,4] particularly in human services where executive directors are typically promoted from line positions and lack training in finance and management. Attention to nonprofit operations has also grown because human service nonprofits have become increas-

Encyclopedia of Public Administration and Public Policy
DOI: 10.1081/E-EPAP 120011050

ingly dependent on government. By 1980, over one-half of the revenue of these agencies came from the public sector.[5]

The second trend that has stimulated interest in contracting is political pressure to reduce the size of government. For the most part, Americans have always been suspicious of the public sector, but the period from 1935 through 1980 was marked by significant expansion in all levels of government. Although the trend toward contracting with nonprofit agencies for human services predates the strong privatization ideology of the last two decades, the movement has been accelerated by the desire to limit the size and scope of government that has been evident since 1980.

THE CONTRACTING DECISION

The contracting decision involves two major questions: what services should government produce itself, and what should it contract out? Second, when it does contract services, what mechanisms should be employed to ensure effective service delivery?

Governments contract with nonprofit and for-profit agencies for services for various reasons—most often to save money, to limit the size of the public labor force, or to use specialized expertise (e.g., legal, architectural, or construction services), for which there is insufficient need for in-house production. In the case of human services, there are addition motives. Among them are to offer consumers greater choice in service providers, to minimize bureaucratic red tape that restricts or slows innovative policy, a belief that nonprofit values are more suitable to human service delivery, and a desire to avoid political blame for the failures that inevitably occur. In some jurisdictions, contracting is simply a matter of history or habit. Relationships between governments and nonprofit agencies are well established and are maintained with little thought given to their costs or advantages.

Most recently, the increase in contracting has been reinforced by ideological beliefs that markets and competition work better than governments. The traditional accountability tools employed in contracting with for-profit firms are unlikely, however, to be successful with human service nonprofits. Contracting works best when market forces are present (i.e., a demand and a supply made up of many buyers and many sellers who compete with each other). To capture competitive efficiencies, the market should be more or less perfect: balanced and complete information, no externalities, increasing costs, homogeneous products, rival consumption, etc. The more imperfect the market, the lower the potential benefits to taxpayers.

The market for human services is characterized by imperfections on both the demand and supply sides.[6] There is a often a single buyer (a monoposonist), either the state or local government, purchasing specialized services from relatively few suppliers. The problem of limited supply is particularly acute outside large urban areas. The presence of market imperfections means that government has limited alternatives, increasing its interdependence with private providers, exacerbating the problem of acquiring accurate information to make contracting decisions and raising the potential for conflicts of interest. The result is similar to a bilateral monopoly, the very antithesis of competitive efficiency. As Don Kettl pointed out: "a too enthusiastic embrace of the competitive prescription might produce the wrong medicine for a misdiagnosed disease."[6] Nevertheless, the trend toward expanded contracting is unlikely to be reversed in the foreseeable future. As a result, governments need effective tools to manage the contracting process.

ACCOUNTABILITY

When governments produce services directly, accountability to the public is assured through the electoral process and the presence of hierarchical bureaucracies that make line workers answerable to supervisors who are ultimately answerable to elected officials. When governments contract for services with for-profit firms, market competition enforces accountability for cost and service quality. Nonprofit organizations lack both political and market feedback systems to ensure accountability.

Early financing relationships between government and nonprofits involved grants with few strings attached. As government has come under increased scrutiny and demands for accountability, public officials have passed those demands on to nonprofits. Increased contracting for human services creates challenges for both governments and nonprofits to develop additional methods of assuring the public that its resources are being efficiently and effectively used. Contracts essentially substitute for markets and typically incorporate two different accountability models:[3] standards/compliance and outcomes/performance.

Standards/Compliance

The standards/compliance approach is the most commonly used method of ensuring accountability. It compares agency operations with a set of established standards. It asks questions such as: How many clients were served? Were clients accurately screened to determine eligibility for services? What services and how much of each service did they receive? Are client records complete and current? Are procedures in place to protect client confidentiality? Do employees possess the appropriate professional licenses? Are clients made aware of the agency's process for appealing a service decision? Does the agency have a governing board of at least seven members that meets at least four times per year? Are copies of last year's audit and IRS Form 990 on file?

The standards/compliance model is used extensively because it is the cheapest and most easily managed accountability tool. Standards are relatively easy to write into contracts and auditors can easily monitor and document compliance. The major disadvantage of this model is that is does not guarantee effective services. It is possible to meet all standards and not achieve program goals.

Outcomes/Performance

In recent years, funders of human services have placed greater emphasis on identifying program outcomes and measuring performance toward achievement of those outcomes. This outcomes/performance model of accountability addresses many of the weaknesses of standards/compliance techniques. It keeps agencies focused on desired outcomes, rather than on mere service levels. It starts with the underlying question of "what is this program trying to achieve?" It then asks questions such as: Is the client improving? Has the client gained knowledge or changed their behavior? Is the client avoiding negative outcomes (e.g., hospitalization, incarceration, truancy)? Is the client satisfied with the services received?

Outcomes/performance accountability has been difficult to implement. Nonprofit agencies argue that much of the work in human services is inherently unmeasurable.[7] The outcomes/performance model is also hampered by the fact that consistently effective treatments do not exist for some conditions. So even when measurable outcomes are known, dependable interventions may not be available to achieve desired outcomes. Contracting agencies are naturally resistant to being held accountable for outcomes that are not consistently achievable or when factors outside the contractors' control (e.g., judicial decisions) affect outcomes.

Because human service goals are hard to define, results hard to measure, and treatments uncertain, it becomes difficult to write meaningful quality specifications into requests for proposals (RFPs) and contracts. This creates a tendency to substitute client satisfaction or professional standards for quality. Although satisfaction is a legitimate concern, what happens if the client is satisfied, but does not appear to be improving?

Professional standards have their own set of problems, the greatest of which is cost. Although most national accrediting bodies would argue that they enforce minimal standards, they tend to have biased views of what is minimal or acceptable. Substituting professional standards for quality measures (e.g., client–staff ratios) can have the effect of forcing government to purchase a higher level of service than the public generally demands. Decision makers need to be able to distinguish a "Cadillac" from a "Chevy" in terms of service quality and allocate resources with knowledge of those distinctions. However, despite these weaknesses, outcomes/performance approaches show considerable promise for improving the effectiveness of human service programs.

Capacity Building

It has been convincingly argued[4] that overemphasis on outcomes can create problems for nonprofits and ultimately for society. As funders (United Ways and foundations, as well as governments) have become more outcomes conscious, they have moved more and more toward program funding (as opposed to general grant funding). The result is that it is increasingly difficult for nonprofits to use "profitable" programs to subsidize unprofitable ones or to fund administrative overhead.[7] Outcomes are more expensive for agencies to document and for funders to monitor. Social service agencies are generally resource poor relative to other nonprofits. In 1996, human service organizations comprised 40% of active charities (those that file IRS Form 990), but expended only 13% of the resources.[8] Many lack up-to-date computer technology, appropriate accounting systems, and generally accepted management practices.

Analysts of nonprofit reform[3,4] have begun to argue that far too little attention has been given to the potential of capacity-building in the nonprofit sector as a way to ensure accountability. They claim that effective nonprofit organizations are more important than effective programs in providing lasting social impacts. Programs do not stand alone and are a weak base for large scale social reform because client needs and the operating environment are always changing. A capacity-building model of accountability asks questions such as: Does the agency have the ability to identify changing community needs? Can the agency adapt to shifting needs and operating environments? Does the agency possess the information systems to accurately track finances and client outcomes? Does agency staff possess the managerial, financial, and technical skills to design, fund, and implement innovative programs?

The advantage of capacity building is that it institutionalizes responsiveness, learning, and innovation, and ultimately reduces the need for detailed contract monitoring. It is, however, a more expensive and long-term accountability method than either standards/compliance or outcomes/performance, requiring efforts and resources that may be beyond those of a single government.

GOVERNMENT CAPACITY

Contracting imposes significant transaction costs on both governments and nonprofits. The latter must adapt to short lead times, voluminous reporting requirements in formats that vary among funders, uncertain political climates, limited discretion, divergence from declared mission to respond to government service priorities, fragmented planning and program structures, and cost shifting resulting from demands that they supplement contracts with their own resources.[9] Both governments and nonprofits need good information systems, the full cost of which is rarely covered in contracts.

Governments incur other transactions costs that are typically not calculated in the cost of contracting. It has become a truism that "contracts do not manage themselves." It takes time and resources to effectively monitor the performance of nonprofit service providers. Particularly when employing outcomes/performance accountability, government agencies need staffs who can write detailed and specific RFP and contract specifications, identify effective rewards and penalties, and who know how to advertise and solicit bids, review proposals, resolve technical disputes, analyze costs, negotiate final[6] agreements, and monitor for service quality and costs. They need a strong mix of program expertise and contract management skills, as well as communication skills and sound judgment. Staff members with long histories of monitoring standards/compliance-type contracts often find it difficult to loosen the control necessary for successful outcomes/performance contracting.

Effective contact enforcement requires independent audits of reported outcomes. In addition to hiring individuals with the requisite skills, governments need to have sufficient internal resources to effectively manage the existing contract caseload in both program and legal departments. From a broader policy perspective, contracting makes it more difficult for government managers to develop a clear jurisdictionwide picture of services and beneficiaries, hindering effective policy planning.

The challenge for governments is to assist in capacity building in the nonprofit sector, as well as to instill best practice in nonprofit management and operations, while resisting the temptation to dictate, dismiss, duplicate, or micromanage the contracting agencies. In an era of privatization, government performance depends on contractor performance. "[G]overnment is no longer a buyer dealing at arm's length with a seller, but a partner in a virtually seamless, mutually dependent interrelationship."[6]

The most effective partnerships incorporate joint planning in identification of need, service design, and specification of performance measures. Nonprofits are more likely to embrace outcomes/performance accountability if they participate in selection of the measures and targets.

Partnerships are characterized by mutual respect for the values and demands of both parties. Public managers need to develop a deeper appreciation of the strengths of the nonprofit sector[10] while they work to teach nonprofit managers to speak the language of performance, outcomes, and accountability. Successful contracts depend more on the personal relationships between contract monitor and program director than on legal specifications. Communication and trust can overcome many technical hurdles.

POLICY ISSUES

Contracts add organizational layers between taxpayers who finance human services and the nonprofit workers who deliver the services. This inevitably increases administrative costs and hinders effective communication. It also complicates questions of accountability for public resources, and of who gets political credit for successes and blame for failures.

The recent push toward privatization is based less on clear evidence of its benefits than on ideology. Historically, human service nonprofits have developed informal networks of like-minded agencies to serve disadvantaged populations. The advent of winner-take-all contracting and the forcing of competitive "business-like" practices on individuals and organizations that are naturally noncompetitive appears to be breaking down the cooperative infrastructures that makes nonprofits so appealing as service delivery agents (i.e., values of compassion and service, responsiveness and flexibility, disregard for profit motives, willingness to assume contracts at less than full cost of production, acceptance of below-market wages, openness to sharing information).

Public sector human service systems (e.g., public welfare, mental health, developmental and physical disability services, senior services) were created in the mid-twentieth century because the private social welfare system was unable to meet public demand for serving the most difficult client populations. State and local governments are now asking nonprofit organizations to assume a larger portion of service delivery to the most needy clients. This raises questions about the sustainability of nonprofits' willingness or ability to assume public duties. It also begs the question of what is public and what is private.

CONCLUSION

Overall, contracting for human services is a public policy tool that can serve useful purposes. It is not a substitute for answering the underlying policy questions. What services should be contracted and with whom? What benefits are achieved if a government service delivery monopoly is replaced with a nonprofit monopoly? Are efforts to improve accountability forcing uniformity that undermines the diversity and flexibility of nonprofit service delivery? With what justification do governments treat nonprofit contractors different from for-profit contractors? When resources are inadequate to serve all those who are eligible, what allocation decision should be made (e.g., restricted eligibility, waiting lists)? Who should make those decisions? How thin can resources be spread before they become ineffective for clients? Is the public willing to accept the reality that there are some clients who are unlikely to improve no matter how many services are provided, or that in the best human service delivery systems, there will be occasional failure? Finally, who is ultimately responsible for caring for the hardest to serve, most vulnerable and needy populations?

REFERENCES

1. Abramson, A.J.; Salamon, L.M.; Streuerle, C.E. The Nonprofit Sector and the Federal Budget: Recent History and Future Directions. In *Nonprofits and Government: Collaboration and Conflict*; Boris, E.T., Steuerle, C.E., Eds.; The Urban Institute Press: Washington, DC, 1999; 99–139.

2. Salamon, L.M. *America's Nonprofit Sector: A Primer*, 2nd Ed.; The Foundation Center: USA, 1999.

3. Light, P. *Making Nonprofits Work*; Brookings Institution Press: Washington, DC, 2000.

4. Letts, C.W.; Ryan, W.P.; Grossman, A. *High Performance Nonprofit Organizations: Managing Upstream for Greater Impact*; John Wiley & Sons: New York, 1999.

5. Hall, P.D. *A History of Nonprofit Boards in the United States*; National Center for Nonprofit Boards: Washington, DC, 1997.

6. Kettl, D.F. *Sharing Power*; The Brookings Institute: Washington, DC, 1993; pp. 13, 201.

7. Smith, S.R.; Lipsky, M. *Nonprofits for Hire*; Harvard University Press: Cambridge, MA, 1993.

8. Boris, E.T. Nonprofit Organizations in a Democracy: Varied Roles and Responsibilities. In *Nonprofits and Government: Collaboration and Conflict*; Boris, E.T., Steuerle, C.E., Eds.; The Urban Institute Press: Washington, DC, 1999; 3–29.

9. Gronbjerg, K.A. Transaction Costs in Social Service Contracting: Lessons from the USA. In *The Contract Culture in Public Services: Studies from Britain, Europe and the USA*; Perri 6, Kendall, J., Eds.; Arena, 1997; 99–113.

10. Frumkin, P. *Balancing Public Accountability and Nonprofit Autonomy: Milestone Contracting in Oklahoma*; Harvard University: Cambridge, MA, 2001; http://papers.ssrn.com/paper.taf?abstract_id=269361

Correctional Administration, The Challenges of

Betsy A. Matthews
Eastern Kentucky University, Richmond, Kentucky, U.S.A.

INTRODUCTION

The American correctional system consists of four major components including jails, prisons, probation, and parole. These components are interdependent, working together to protect society and carry out the criminal sentence. Because corrections is a matter of public policy, its goals and activities are often dependent on which political ideology is dominant at the time.[1] As such, correctional policy has vacillated between the liberal agenda of rehabilitation and the more conservative approaches of deterrence and incapacitation. For the past 25 years, the latter has won out with ''get-tough'' policies that have contributed to unmanageable growth in the correctional population. Most of a correctional administrator's time is devoted to managing this growth and to developing practices that promote the objective and efficient allocation of resources. This article will first review the evolution of correctional policy and discuss the consequences of getting tough on crime. It will then describe four correctional trends that have emerged to manage the ever changing and growing population of offenders.

THE EVOLUTION OF CORRECTIONAL POLICY

In an effort to compete for limited resources and gain public support, correctional policies have adapted over time to reflect the prevailing political ideology. This chameleon-like shift in policy has resulted in two very different approaches to achieving the correctional goal of public safety.

The Rehabilitative Ideal

The Rehabilitative Ideal served as the basis for our criminal justice system from the early 1900s until the 1970s. It was an outgrowth of the positivist school of thought, which assumed that criminal behavior was determined by biological, sociological, and psychological factors over which people have little control. As such, the focus was on identifying and addressing these factors as a way to curb criminal behavior. The Rehabilitative Ideal involved the Progressives' plan for individualized treatment, which featured broad discretionary practices, and

reflected their abiding faith in the state to act in the best interests of the offender.[2,3] Offenders were sentenced to an indeterminate period of incarceration (e.g., 2–5 years) with their release based on their demonstrated reform.[2] Probation was introduced as an alternative to incarceration for those who did not require incarceration, and parole was instituted to facilitate an offender's reintegration to the community.

Several events throughout the 1960s and 1970s led to the dismantling of the rehabilitative agenda. In 1974, Robert Martinson published an article about what works in offender reform. In the article, Martinson reviewed 231 community- and institutional-based programs and concluded that there was no appreciable evidence that rehabilitation works to reduce the recidivism of offenders.[4] While Martinson is often credited for undermining rehabilitation, several authors speculate that the lost faith in rehabilitation was more of a reflection of the times than a careful consideration of Martinson's research.[2,5] The 1960s were turbulent times with protests against Vietnam, Watergate, the deaths at Kent State, and the emergence of the Civil Rights movement. For conservatives, these times were signs of a disintegrating moral order; for liberals they were signs of a corrupted government.[2] Both views prompted changes in the criminal justice system.

According to Cullen and Gilbert,[2] conservatives viewed rehabilitation strategies as signs of a permissive society. They believed that the criminal justice system was coddling offenders and decreasing the costs of crime by releasing offenders early. They called for determinate sentences (i.e., a fixed period of incarceration) aimed at minimizing discretion and tougher sentencing practices designed to restore social order. Liberals, believing that the government was ''using the mask of benevolence'' to inflict suffering on offenders, agreed that discretion must be limited through the use of determinate sentences. However, they wanted to reduce the length of sentences to minimize the harm caused by the coercive prison environment. In the end, punishment won out,[3] and the get-tough movement was set into motion.

The Get-Tough Movement

The get-tough movement is characterized by deterrence and incapacitative-based strategies. The concept of deter-

Encyclopedia of Public Administration and Public Policy
DOI: 10.1081/E-EPAP 120011032

rence can be traced back to the 1700s and the classical school of thought.[6,7] The classical school of thought assumes that people are rational beings who calculate the benefits of crime against the potential risks of getting caught and behave according to what will bring them the most pleasure and the least pain. Thus, according to deterrence theory, as the severity, swiftness, and certainty of punishment increases, crime will go down. Tough-on-crime policies such as mandatory sentences, truth in sentencing, and three-strikes legislation are designed to create special deterrence for the individual experiencing the punishment and general deterrence for others who observe the punishment.[8]

Incapacitation, which emerged in the early 1980s, is designed to prevent crime through the physical constraint of individuals. Advocates of incapacitation make no claims of offender reform; they simply assert that offenders will not be able to commit crimes against society while incarcerated or otherwise restrained.[9,10] Incapacitative measures are seen by many as the shortest path to public safety and thus, are popular in the American culture that is permeated by the principle of efficiency.[11] Together, incapacitative and deterrent ideologies have contributed to unmanageable growth in the U.S. correctional population.

THE CONSEQUENCES OF GETTING TOUGH ON CRIME

Unmanageable Growth

The persistence of the get-tough movement over the past 30 years has contributed to an expanded net of social control in the United States. According to the Bureau of Justice Statistics, there were 6.5 million people, or 1 in every 32 adults, under some type of correctional supervision by the year-end of 2000.[12] Of this correctional population, one-third, or 1,933,503 people, were in prison or jail, an annual increase of 5.6 percent since the year-end of 1990 and the continuation of a trend that began in 1971.

It is often assumed that the growth in the prison population reflects an increase in crime rates, but comparisons of trends have revealed that changes in the crime rates and changes in the prison populations are loosely matched over time.[13,14] Other explanations offered for the growth in prison population include the introduction of tough legislation such as mandatory sentences, truth in sentencing, and three-strikes legislation,[15-17] and the increased willingness by judges to imprison convicted felons.[18] Regardless of the cause, the increasing prison population has created overwhelming challenges for the American correctional system.

In an effort to keep pace with the growing population, states have added 351 correctional facilities in the past decade.[19] Still, many state prisons are operating at 15% above their rated capacity,[19] a situation that creates management nightmares for prison administrators. Prison crowding has been found to contribute to negative psychological and physical reactions among inmates[20] and to increased rates of violence.[21] It also limits the number and quality of vocational, educational, and counseling programs that are available to inmates,[22,23] and thus, impedes the extent to which correctional facilities can achieve the goal of rehabilitation.

Recognizing that it is impossible to build their way out of the current correctional crisis, states have instituted a range of community-based correctional options that are designed to divert low-level offenders from prison. Two of the most popular programs are intensive supervision programs (ISP) and electronic monitoring, which are typically operated by probation and parole agencies. The defining characteristics of ISPs are small caseloads (e.g., 25–40 offenders) and an emphasis on controlling offenders in the community through increased contact, drug testing, and stringent responses to technical violations.[24] Electronic monitoring involves the electronic surveillance of offenders to assure compliance with home confinement.[25] Other, less popular, options include community service, house arrest, and day reporting centers. Despite their community placement, all of these correctional options (often referred to as intermediate sanctions or alternatives to incarceration) are tough programs designed to protect the public by providing close surveillance of offenders in the community and quick responses to violations or new criminal behavior. These tough new programs were well received by the public, politicians, and practitioners because they ''shared the rhetoric of punishment but offered to accomplish crime control at a reduced cost.''[26] Their continuing popularity has contributed to an alarming growth in probation and parole populations.

By the end of 2000, approximately 4.6 million men and women were on probation or parole, representing an annual increase of 3.6% since 1990.[12] Unfortunately, state budgets have not kept pace with the growing probation and parole populations. Despite the fact that three-fourths of the correctional population is under probation and parole supervision, only about one-tenth of the correctional budget is allocated to probation and parole agencies.[27] This translates into high caseloads for officers: The national average for the number of cases per officer is 124 for probation and 67 for parole.[28] As is the case with the prison system, this type of unmanageable growth in probation and parole populations has limited the scope of services that can be provided to offenders. Without the type of meaningful treatment and supervision that is capable of promoting long-term behavioral change, significant reductions in recidivism are unlikely and the correctional system appears inadequate in its pursuit of public safety.

Lack of Credibility

Public opinion polls have repeatedly revealed that what the public wants from corrections is to be safe from crime.[29–32] Thus, in the eyes of citizens and public officials, the value of correctional policies lies in their ability to reduce recidivism and crime rates. Repeated news reports of heinous crimes committed by offenders under correctional supervision have contributed to a lack of confidence in the correctional system. Unfortunately, the results of more objective outcome studies would do little to bolster this confidence.

Recidivism rates generally refer to the proportion of offenders under correctional supervision who are arrested or convicted for a new crime. A national study of adults on probation found that 43% of probationers were rearrested for a felony within three years of their probation sentences.[33] Recidivism rates for parole are equally disheartening. According to a recent report by the Bureau of Justice Statistics, about 60% of parolees were returned to prison in 1999; 70% of those returned had been arrested or convicted for a new offense.[34]

Studies of control-oriented, intermediate sanction programs have revealed that they are no better at reducing recidivism than the more traditional probation and parole programs. As compared to control groups of offenders placed in other correctional options, participating offenders had an increase in technical violations (i.e., violations of the rules of probation/parole) but no significant differences in the rates of new arrests.[35–38] In fact, a meta-analysis of studies on these control-oriented intermediate sanctions revealed that they produced a slight increase in recidivism.[39] As a result, more offenders in these specialized programs are returned to prison, thus limiting the extent to which any diversionary effect or cost savings can be achieved.

Recidivism rates and studies, such as those cited above, show that a substantial proportion of offenders (the people most directly affected by get-tough strategies) are not deterred from future crime. Crime rates offer a better reflection of whether or not these strategies are providing a general deterrent. The two primary methods of crime measurement are the Uniform Crime Reports (UCR), which reports on crimes reported to the police, and the National Crime Victimization Survey (NCVS), which estimates crime rates based on interviews with members of a nationally representative sample of households in the United States about victimization they have experienced in the past year. According to the UCR, rates of serious crime in 2000 were 14% lower than in 1996 and 22% lower than in 1991.[40] Statistics from the NCVS reveal a similar downward trend since 1993.[41]

There are disparate views as to whether these statistics provide support for get-tough legislation. Langan, for example, sees the rising incarceration rates from 1973 to 1986 and the concomitant decline in crime rates as evidence that prisons were "responsible for sizable reductions in crime."[18] Similarly, a report by the National Center for Policy Analysis concludes that the recent reduction in crime can be attributed to an increase in "expected punishment" (i.e., an increase in the likelihood of going to prison and the median sentence length).[42]

Other research disputes the role of imprisonment and other get-tough strategies in reducing crime. For example, given Langan's contention regarding the benefits of prison, how would he explain the increase in violent crime in the wake of rising incarceration rates from 1986 to 1993?[43] Reiss and Roth report that violent crime rates remained stable despite a tripling in the average prison time served per crime.[44] Similarly, Visher examined several studies on the effect of incapacitation and concluded that despite a doubling of the prison population crime, reductions were limited to 10–30%.[45] Spokespersons for the Campaign for an Effective Crime Policy summarize the debate in a 1995 report by concluding that "clearly, imprisonment has an incapacitative effect on the individual offender. The key issue, however, is whether increased imprisonment results in an overall decrease in crime and at what cost."[46]

A review of recidivism studies and crime rates reveals little support for get-tough policies. Despite this, they persist as the basis of the American correctional system leaving correctional administrators to deal with large populations, limited resources, and a lack of public confidence. The remainder of this article will focus on measures that are being taken to overcome these obstacles.

MOVING TOWARD RATIONAL CORRECTIONAL POLICY

Keeping pace with the growing correctional populations and managing constant change is no easy task. Proposed solutions often are nothing more than stopgap approaches designed to appease a particular audience. Four recent trends, however, represent a sincere effort to find long-term answers and to interject rationality and accountability into the system. Following are brief discussions on how community justice initiatives, privatization, structured decision making, and the development of research-based intervention programs are improving services and decision making in the correctional systems.

Community Justice

Traditional correctional practices, whether rooted in rehabilitation or deterrence and incapacitation, have focused on things to be done *to* or *for* offenders.[47] One of the most persistent trends in corrections is to shift from this offender-focused model of justice to a model of community justice that "places the community and victims at the center of justice activities and efforts."[47] Toward this end, correctional agencies are redefining the way they do business. Instead of working as a closed system, in isolation from the community, they are seeking community input and developing opportunities for citizen involvement.

A common approach to involving citizens is through the use of community advisory boards. Most states have some form of citizen advisory board although the composition and functions may differ. The role of the 21-member State Advisory Board in New Jersey, for example, is to advise the Supreme Court on matters related to probation. The Community Corrections Advisory Committee in Multnomah County, Oregon, is a statutory requirement of the Community Corrections Act adopted in 1977; it helps develop the county's community corrections plans and oversee its operations. Advisory boards bring many benefits to corrections agencies including a sounding board and a set of allies for correctional personnel, diverse views and perspectives, access to private and public resources, accountability to the public, and a forum in which public officials and private citizens work together on developing opportunities and strategies for change.[48]

Another common approach to involving citizens in corrections is through restorative justice initiatives. Restorative justice is a philosophy that views crime as a violation of people and interpersonal relationships.[49] As such, it seeks to repair these relationships by: 1) providing victims with support, opportunities for input, and restitution; 2) holding offenders accountable for the harm they caused; and 3) empowering communities to develop constructive responses to crime that recognize our mutual responsibilities to one another.[50] Two of the more popular restorative justice programs include victim offender mediation (VOM) and community sentencing panels. The VOM programs provide an opportunity for the victim of a crime to meet face-to-face with the offender and a volunteer mediator to discuss how the crime has impacted their lives and to work out an agreement for restitution.[51] Community sentencing panels involve citizen volunteers in the sentencing of offenders. For example, in Minnesota, volunteers serve on a community intervention team that communicates to offenders the impact of their behavior on the local community, sets special conditions of probation, provides support to offenders, and periodically reviews offender progress.[52]

Although there is evidence to suggest that these types of programs lead to an increase in both victim satisfaction and citizen awareness of the justice process, there is little research available to ascertain the extent to which community and restorative justice initiatives are effective in controlling crime.[51] Despite this lack of evidence, and unlike other correctional initiatives, community and restorative justice have gained acceptance from both conservatives and liberals.[53] This widespread appeal and the pragmatic need to expand resources and support for correctional services is likely to sustain the movement toward a more open and inclusive system of justice.

Privatization

Complaints about ineffective practices, crowding, and rising correctional costs have led policy makers to turn to the private sector for solutions. Although private nonprofit organizations have a history of involvement in the provision of diversion and drug treatment programs for offenders in the community, it has only been since the early 1980s that private for-profit corporations have engaged in the full-scale operation of prisons.[11] There are several objections to the privatization of prisons. Most of the controversy, however, surrounds the issues of the profit motive and the right to punish and use force. It has been argued that the profit motive of private corporations will contribute to a lower quality of services in an attempt to cut corners and to lobbying for excessive use of incarceration because it is good for business.[54,55] More fundamental is the concern about granting private corporations the power to punish and use force.[56] Some authors claim that punishment is a government function and that granting this right to private corporations undermines the legitimacy of the state.[57,58]

Despite these controversies, many states are moving ahead and authorizing private corporations to engage in the full-scale operation of prisons. By the end of 2000, 5.8% of all state inmates were housed in privately operated facilities.[19] Several studies have reported that private prisons outperformed their public counterparts on several dimensions of quality (e.g., care, safety, security, order) and that they accomplished this at a reduced cost.[59–61] Camp and Gates report that these evaluations failed to statistically control for factors (e.g., age and race of inmates, staff-to-inmate ratios) that could influence the research outcomes and that their findings should be reviewed with caution.[62] Based on a comprehensive review of the available research on privatization, the Bureau of Justice Assistance concludes that: privately operated prisons function at least as well as publicly operated prisons; private prisons can reduce costs in markets that have high benefits for public employees; there is evidence to suggest that private corporations can build prisons faster and cheaper than the public sector; and the presence of private prisons has prompted public facilities to develop cost-saving strategies.[63] Although they are not overly supportive, these conclusions certainly favor the continued inclusion of the private sector in the operation of prisons.

Structured Decision Making

Shrinking resources and a demand for equitable and appropriate decision making have led to an increased interest in strategies that structure the discretion of judges and correctional personnel.[64] Sentencing guidelines and case classification systems have emerged to guide decision making in a way that minimizes disparities and reserves scarce prison resources for the most dangerous offenders.

Sentencing guidelines

The introduction of sentencing guidelines in the late 1970s represents one of the most salient efforts to interject accountability into the criminal justice system. As of the end of 1999, 18 states had implemented sentencing guidelines, 4 states were considering proposals for guidelines, and 3 states had appointed commissions to study the approach.[65] The initial aims of sentencing guidelines were to promote proportionality and reduce disparity in sentencing by prescribing a punishment that is based on the seriousness of the offense and the criminal history of the defendant rather than on extralegal factors like race and sex.[66,67] Increasingly, however, states (e.g., Minnesota, North Carolina, Utah) have included mechanisms within their sentencing guidelines for linking sentences with correctional resources.[68]

In 1994, North Carolina introduced sentencing guidelines that were based on projections of future crime and sentencing patterns, and matched sentences to the number of prison beds, probation slots, and other correctional resources. The guidelines called for shorter and community-based sentences for nonviolent, first time offenders and longer sentences for violent and career offenders. Preliminary results suggest that the plan is working with a greater percentage of serious felons serving longer than average prison terms and an increased use of nonprison punishments for less serious felons.[69] The North Carolina Legislature has demonstrated its commitment to these "capacity-based guidelines" by requiring that a fiscal impact statement accompany any recommended revisions to the guidelines.

Case classification

Whereas sentencing guidelines attempt to control judicial discretion and the inputs to correctional systems, case classification systems attempt to guide the discretion of correctional personnel themselves. Classification systems are designed to categorize offenders based on specific behavioral or psychological dimensions and to facilitate the placement of offenders into appropriate programs or facilities.[70] A well-designed classification system can minimize bias in correctional decision making and promote more efficient use of resources.

The dominant focus of case classification is on predicting offenders' risk of recidivism or their risk to institutional security.[71] The methods of risk prediction have evolved over the years from a more subjective form of clinical assessment based on professional judgment to actuarial risk assessment based on objective and standardized instruments.[64] These instruments include items that are known to be associated with recidivism or institutional misconduct (e.g., age at first arrest, prior criminal history). Although variations exist, the basic process for actuarial risk assessment is the same: Correctional personnel use information gathered from the offender's case file and/or a structured interview with the offender to assign a score on each item depending on the degree to which the risk factor is present; the individual item scores are then summed for an overall risk score; and this score is used to categorize offenders as low, medium, or high risk. Depending on the offender's categorization, s/he is placed in a minimum, medium, or maximum level of community supervision or facility. Risk assessment can assist agencies in managing offenders' risk through the application of control-oriented measures (e.g., surveillance, curfews, electronic monitoring), and, more importantly, in planning for more effective interventions to reduce the probability of recidivism or institutional misconduct.

Developing Research-Based Interventions

A quick perusal of the recidivism rates previously reported for probation and parole perpetuates the "nothing works" mentality propagated by Martinson. A closer examination of outcome studies, however, provides a more optimistic perspective on the effectiveness of correctional programming.

Over the past two decades, numerous authors have conducted literature reviews and meta-analyses to examine the effectiveness of various correctional interventions. These reviews directly challenge Martinson's conclusion that "nothing works" in correctional programming: About 60% of the studies reviewed reported a reduction in recidivism with the average reduction being 10%.[72] Even more promising, programs that met certain principles of effective intervention were shown to reduce recidivism by 30 to 50%.

The programs that have lead to the largest reductions in recidivism possess several common characteristics.[73–76] The most effective programs were conducted in the community,[75–78] included multimodal programming,[72,76,79,80] and involved the family in the offender's treatment.[79–81] Other more specific characteristics that have been identified have been referred to as "the principles of effective intervention."[73,74,82] They include:

1. Effective interventions are behavioral in nature. A well-designed behavioral program combines a system of reinforcement with modeling by the treatment provider to teach and motivate offenders to perform prosocial behaviors. Additionally, problem solving and self-instructional training may be used to change the offender's cognitions, attitudes, and values that maintain antisocial behavior.
2. Levels of service should be matched to the risk level of the offender. Intensive services are necessary for a significant reduction of recidivism among high-risk offenders, but when applied to low risk offenders, intensive services produce a minimal or negative effect.
3. Offenders should be matched to services designed to improve their specific criminogenic needs such as antisocial attitudes, substance abuse, family communication, and peer associations. Improvements in these areas will contribute to a reduced likelihood of recidivism.
4. Treatment approaches and service providers are matched to the learning style or personality of the offender. For example, high anxiety offenders do not generally respond well to confrontation;[83] and offenders with below-average intellectual abilities do not respond to cognitive skills programs as well as offenders with above average or high intellectual abilities.[84]
5. Services for high-risk offenders should be intensive, occupying 40 to 70% of offenders' time over a 3- to 9-month period.
6. The program is highly structured, and contingencies are enforced in a firm but fair way: Staff design, maintain, and enforce contingencies; internal controls are established to detect possible antisocial activities; and program activities disrupt the criminal network and prevent negative peers from taking over the program.
7. Staff relate to offenders in interpersonally sensitive and constructive ways and are trained and supervised appropriately.
8. Staff monitor offender change on intermediate targets of treatment.
9. Relapse prevention is employed in the community to monitor and anticipate problem situations, and to train offenders to rehearse alternative behavior.
10. High levels of advocacy and brokerage occur if community services are appropriate.

The research on "what works" in correctional interventions provides a powerful agenda for correctional programming, one that holds agencies accountable for achieving the bottom-line results that the public expects—a reduction in recidivism.

CONCLUSION

Years of politically motivated policies have strained the correctional system beyond its capacity. Prison crowding and large probation and parole caseloads make it nearly impossible to provide offenders with the type of supervision and services that are needed to reduce their likelihood of returning to crime. Yet that is what the public expects from corrections—to be kept safe from offenders. Knowing that their credibility depends on meeting this expectation, correctional agencies are working hard to meet the challenge. Through community justice initiatives and the privatization of prisons, correctional agencies are expanding resources and developing valuable partnerships. Through sentencing guidelines and case classification systems, correctional agencies are better equipped to allocate resources in a fair and equitable way and are able to reserve scarce prison space for the most dangerous offenders. And for the first time ever, through ongoing research, corrections agencies have a blueprint for developing programs capable of reducing recidivism. These proactive initiatives suggest that, despite the political context within which correctional agencies operate, there is hope for a more rational approach to managing state corrections policy.

REFERENCES

1. Freeman, R.M. *Correctional Organization and Management: Public Policy Challenges, Behavior, and Structure*; Butterworth Heinemann: Boston, MA, 1999.
2. Cullen, F.T.; Gilbert, K.E. *Reaffirming Rehabilitation*; Anderson Publishing: Cincinnati, OH, 1982.
3. Rothman, D.J. *Conscience and Convenience: The Asylum and its Alternatives in Progressive America*; Little, Brown and Company: Boston, MA, 1980.
4. Martinson, R. What works? Questions and answers about prison reform. Public Interest **1974**, *35*, 23–54. (Spring).

5. Cullen, F.T.; Gendreau, P. The Effectiveness of Correctional Rehabilitation: Reconsidering the "Nothing Works" Debate. In *The American Prison: Issues in Research and Policy*; Goodstein, L., MacKenzie, D.L., Eds.; Plenum: New York, 1989; 23–44.

6. Beccaria, C. *On Crimes and Punishments*; Bobbs-Merrill: Indianapolis, IN, 1963[1764].

7. Geis, G. Pioneers in criminology, VII: Jeremy Bentham (1748–1832). J. Crim. Law Criminol. Police Sci. **1955**, *46*, 160.

8. Shichor, D. Following the penological pendulum: The survival of rehabilitation. Fed. Probat. **1992**, *52* (2), 19–25.

9. Wilson, J.Q. *Crime and Public Policy*; Institute of Contemporary Studies: San Fransisco, CA, 1983.

10. Zimring, F.E.; Hawkins, G. *Incapacitation: Penal Confinement and the Restraint of Crime*; Oxford University Press: New York, 1995.

11. Schichor, D. Penal policies at the threshold of the twenty-first century. Crim. Justice Rev. **2000**, *25* (1), 1–30.

12. Bureau of Justice Statistics. National correctional population reaches new high grows by 126,400 during 2000 to total 6.5 million adults. http://ojp.usdoj.gov/bjs/abstract/ppus00.htm (accessed November 2001).

13. Clear, T.R. *Harm in American Penology: Offenders, Victims, and their Communities*; State University of New York Press: Albany, NY, 1994.

14. Zimring, F.E.; Hawkins, G. *The Scale of Imprisonment*; University of Chicago Press: Chicago, IL, 1991.

15. Parent, D.; Dunworth, T.; McDonald, D.; Rhodes, W. *Key Legislative Issues in Criminal Justice: Mandatory Sentencing*; Research in Action, National Institute of Justice: Washington, DC, 1997 (January); 1–6.

16. Tonry, M. *Sentencing Reform Impacts*; National Institute of Justice: Washington, DC, 1987; 1–113.

17. Wooldredge, J. Research note: A state-level analysis of sentencing policies and inmate crowding in state prisons. Crime Delinq. **1996**, *42* (3), 456–466.

18. Langan, P.A. America's soaring prison population. Science **1991**, *251*, 1568–1573. (March).

19. Bureau of Justice Statistics. Nation's state prison population falls in second half of 2000 first such decline since 1972. http://ojp.usdoj.gov/bjs/abstract/p00.htm (accessed November 2001).

20. Paulus, P.; McCain, G.; Cox, V. The Effects of Crowding in Prisons and Jails. In *Reactions to Crime: The Public, Courts, and Prisons*; Farrington, D., Gunn, J., Eds.; John Wiley and Sons Ltd.: New York, 1985; 113–134.

21. Gates, G.; McGuire, W. Prison violence: The contribution of crowding versus other determinants of prison assault rates. J. Res. Crime Delinq. **1985**, *22* (1), 41–65.

22. Gottfredson, S. Institutional responses to prison overcrowding. Rev. Law Soc. Change **1984**, *12*, 259–273.

23. Joyce, N.M. A view of the future: The effect of policy on prison population growth. Crime Delinq. **1992**, *38*, 357–368.

24. Fulton, B.; Stone, S.; Gendreau, P. *Restructuring Intensive Supervision Programs: Applying "What Works"*; American Probation and Parole Association: Lexington, KY, 1994.

25. Bureau of Justice Assistance. *Electronic Monitoring in Intensive Probation and Parole Programs*; U.S. Department of Justice: Washington, DC, 1989.

26. Cullen, F.T.; Wright, J.P.; Applegate, B.K. Control in the Community: The Limits of Reform. In *Choosing Correctional Interventions That Work: Defining the Demand and Evaluating the Supply*; Harland, A.T., Ed.; Sage: Newbury Park, CA, 1996; 69–116.

27. Petersilia, J. A crime control rationale for reinvesting in community corrections. Prison J. **1995**, *75* (4), 479–496.

28. Camp, C.G.; Camp, G.M. *The Corrections Yearbook 1999: Adult Corrections*; Criminal Justice Institute, Inc.: Middletown, CT, 2000.

29. Doble, J. *Crime and Punishment: The Public's Vie*; Public Agenda Foundation: New York, 1987.

30. Cullen, F.T.; Cullen, J.B.; Wozniak, J.F. Is rehabilitation dead? The myth of the punitive public. J. Crim. Justice **1988**, *16*, 303–317.

31. Tilow, N. New public opinion poll cites support for intermediate punishment programs. Perspectives **1992**, *16* (1), 44–46.

32. Applegate, B.K.; Cullen, F.T.; Fisher, B.S. Public support for correctional treatment: The continuing appeal of the rehabilitative ideal. Prison J. **1997**, *77* (3), 237–258.

33. Langan, P.A.; Cunniff, M.A. *Recidivism of Felons on Probation, 1986–1989*; Bureau of Justice Statistics: Washington, DC, 1992.

34. Bureau of Justice Statistics. *Forty-Two Percent of State Parole Discharges Were Successful*; http://ojp.usdoj.gov/bjs/abstract/tps00.htm (accessed November 2001).

35. Jolin, A.; Stipak, B. Drug treatment and electronically monitored home confinement: An evaluation of a community-based sentencing option. Crime Delinq. **1992**, *38* (2), 158–170.

36. Petersilia, J.; Turner, S. *Evaluating Intensive Supervision Probation/Parole: Results of a Nationwide Experiment*; Research in Brief, National Institute of Justice: Washington, DC, 1993 (May); 1–11.

37. Smith, L.; Akers, R. A comparison of recidivism of Florida's Community Control Program: A five-year survival analysis. J. Res. Crime Delinq. **1993**, *30* (3), 267–292.

38. Wagner, D. Reducing criminal risk: An evaluation of the high risk offender intensive supervision Project. Perspectives **1989**, *13* (3), 22–27.

39. Gendreau, P.; Little, T. *A Meta-Analysis of the Effectiveness of Sanctions on Offender Recidivism*; Department of Psychology, University of New Brunswick: Saint John, 1993. Unpublished Manuscript.

40. Federal Bureau of Investigation. *Press Release—2001—Crime in the United States*; 2000. http://www.fbi.gov/pressrel/pressrel01/cius2000.htm (accessed November 2001).

41. Rennison, C.M. *Criminal Victimization 2000: Changes 1999–2000 with Trends 1993–2000*; National Crime

Victimization Survey NCJ-187007, Bureau of Justice Statistics: Washington, DC, 2001; 1–16.

42. Reynolds, M.O. *Crime and Punishment in America: 1997 Update*; NCPA Policy Report 209, National Center for Policy Analysis: Washington DC, 1997.

43. Rand, M.R.; Lynch, J.P.; Cantor, D. *Criminal Victimization, 1973–95*; National Crime Victimization Survey NCJ-163069, Bureau of Justice Statistics: Washington, DC, 1997; 1–8.

44. Reiss, A.J.; Roth, J.A. *Understanding and Preventing Violence*; National Academy Press: Washington, DC, 1993.

45. Visher, C. Incapacitation and crime control: Does a ''lock 'em up'' strategy reduce crime? Justice Q. **1987**, *4* (4), 513–543.

46. Campaign for an Effective Crime Policy. In *What Every Policymaker Should Know About Imprisonment and the Crime Rate*; Campaign for an Effective Crime Policy: Washington, DC, 1995; 2.

47. Barajas, E., Jr. Community Justice: An Emerging Concept and Practice. In *Community Justice: Concepts and Strategies*; American Probation and Parole Association, Ed.; American Probation and Parole Association: Lexington, KY, 1998; 11–26.

48. Fulton, B.A. *Restoring Hope Through Community Partnerships: The Real Deal in Crime Control*; American Probation and Parole Association: Lexington, KY, 1996.

49. Zehr, H.; Mika, H. *Restorative Justice Signposts (Bookmark)*; Mennonite Central Committee and MCC U.S.: Akron, PA, 1997.

50. Pranis, K. Promising Practices in Community Justice: Restorative Justice. In *Community Justice: Concepts and Strategies*; American Probation and Parole Association, Ed.; American Probation and Parole Association: Lexington, KY, 1998; 37–58.

51. Kurki, L. *Incorporating Restorative and Community Justice into American Sentencing and Corrections*; Sentencing and Corrections, National Institute of Justice: Washington, DC, 1999; Vol. 3, 1–11.

52. Pranis, K. *Community Involvement in Offender Sentencing*; Minnesota Department of Corrections: St. Paul, MN, 1995. Unpublished paper.

53. Levrant, S.; Cullen, F.T.; Fulton, B.; Wozniak, J.F. Reconsidering restorative justice: The corruption of benevolence revisited. Crime Delinq. **1999**, *45* (1), 3–27.

54. Kinkade, P.T.; Leone, M.C. Issues and answers: Prison administrators' responses to controversies surrounding privatization. Prison J. **1992**, *72* (1), 57–76.

55. Bates, E. Prisons for Profit. In *The Dilemmas of Corrections: Contemporary Readings*, 4th Ed.; Haas, K.C., Alpert, G.P., Eds.; Waveland Press, Inc.: Prospect Heights, IL, 1999; 592–604.

56. Vardalis, J.J.; Becker, F.W. Legislative opinions concerning the private operation of state prisons: The case of Florida. Crim. Justice Policy Rev. **2000**, *11* (2), 136–148.

57. Durham, A.M. *Crisis and Reform: Current Issues in American Punishment*; Little, Brown: Boston, 1994.

58. Shichor, D.; Sechrest, D.K. Quick fixes in corrections: Reconsidering private and public for-profit facilities. Prison J. **1995**, *75* (4), 457–478.

59. Archambeault, W.G.; Deis, D.R. *Cost Effectiveness Comparisons of Private Versus Public Prisons in Louisiana*; Louisiana State University, School of Social Work: Baton Rouge, LA, 1996.

60. Logan, C.H. Well kept: Comparing quality of confinement in private and public prisons. J. Crim. Law Criminol. **1992**, *83* (3), 577–613.

61. Thomas, C. *Comparing the Cost and Performance of Public and Private Prisons in Arizona: An Overview of the Study and its Conclusions*; University of Florida, Center for Studies in Criminology and Law: Gainesville, FL, 1997.

62. Camp, S.D.; Gates, G.G. Private Adult Prisons: What Do We Really Know and Why Don't We Know More? In *Privatization in Criminal Justice: Past, Present, and Future*; Shichor, D., Gilbert, M.J., Eds.; Anderson Publishing: Cincinnati, OH, 2001; 283–298.

63. Bureau of Justice Assistance. *Emerging Issues on Privatized Prisons*; Bureau of Justice Assistance: Washington, DC, 2001.

64. Jones, P. Risk Prediction in Criminal Justice. In *Choosing Correctional Options That Work: Defining the Demand and Evaluating the Supply*; Harland, A.T., Ed.; Sage: Thousand Oaks, CA, 1996; 33–69.

65. Reitz, K.R. The status of sentencing guideline reforms in the U.S. Overcrowded Times **1999**, *10* (6), 9–10.

66. Lubitz, R.L.; Ross, T.W. *Sentencing Guidelines: Reflections on the Future*; Sentencing and Corrections, National Institute of Justice: Washington, DC, 2001; Vol. 10.

67. Tonry, M. *Sentencing Matters*; Oxford University Press: New York, 1996.

68. Frase, R.S. State sentencing guidelines: Still going strong. Judicature **1995**, *78* (4), 173–179.

69. Wright, R.F. *Managing Prison Growth in North Carolina through Structured Sentencing*; Program Focus Series, National Institute of Justice: Washington, DC, 1998; 1–16.

70. Van Voorhis, P. An Overview of Offender Classification Systems. In *Correctional Counseling and Rehabilitation*, 4th Ed.; Van Voorhis, P., Braswell, M., Lester, D., Eds.; Anderson Publishing: Cincinnati, OH, 2000; 81–110.

71. Clements, C. Offender classification: Two decades of progress. Crim. Justice Behav. **1996**, *23* (1), 143–212.

72. Lipsey, M. Juvenile Delinquency Treatment: A Meta-Analytic Inquiry into the Variability of Effects. In *Meta-Analysis for Explanation*; Cook, T., Cooper, H., Cordray, H., Hartman, H., Hedges, L., Light, R., Louis, T., Mosteller, F., Eds.; B. Russell Sage: New York, 1992; 83–127.

73. Andrews, D.; Zinger, I.; Hoge, R.; Bonta, J.; Gendreau, P.; Cullen, F. Does correctional treatment work? A clinically relevant and psychologically informed meta-analysis. Criminology **1990**, *28*, 369–404.

74. Gendreau, P.; Andrews, D. Tertiary prevention: What the meta-analyses of the offender treatment literature tell us

about "what works." Can. J. Criminal. **1990**, *32* (1), 173–184.

75. Izzo, R.; Ross, R. Meta-analysis of rehabilitation programs for juvenile delinquents: A brief report. Crim. Justice Behav. **1990**, *17* (1), 134–142.

76. Lipsey, M.; Wilson, D. Effective Intervention for Serious Juvenile Offenders: A Synthesis of Research. In *Serious and Violent Juvenile Offenders: Risk Factors and Successful Interventions*; Loeber, R., Farrington, D.P., Eds.; Sage: Thousand Oaks, CA, 1998; 313–345.

77. Palmer, T. The youth authority's community treatment project. Fed. Probat. **1974**, *38* (1), 3–14.

78. Whitehead, J.; Lab, S. A meta-analysis of juvenile correctional treatment. J. Res. Crime Delinq. **1989**, *26* (3), 276–295.

79. Clements, C. Delinquency prevention and treatment: A community-centered perspective. Crim. Justice Behav. **1988**, *15* (3), 286–305.

80. Palmer, T. Programmatic and Nonprogrammatic Aspects of Successful Intervention. In *Choosing Correctional Options That Work*; Harland, A.T., Ed.; Sage: Thousand Oaks, CA, 1996; 131–182.

81. Gendreau, P.; Ross, R. Revivication of rehabilitation: Evidence from the 1980s. Justice Q. **1987**, *4* (3), 349–407.

82. Gendreau, P. The Principles of Effective Intervention with Offenders. In *Choosing Correctional Options That Work*; Harland, A.T., Ed.; Sage: Thousand Oaks, CA, 1996; 117–130.

83. Warren, M. Application of Interpersonal Maturity Theory to Offender Populations. In *Personality Theory, Moral Development, and Criminal Behavior*; Laufer, W., Day, J., Eds.; Lexington Books: Lexington, MA, 1983; 23–49.

84. Fabiano, E.; Porporino, F.; Robinson, D. Canada's cognitive skills program corrects offenders' faulty thinking. Correct. Today **1991**, *53* (5), 102–108.

Council/Commission Representation

Tari Renner

Illinois Wesleyan University, Bloomington, Illinois, U.S.A.

INTRODUCTION

How well do local government legislatures (city councils and county commissions) reflect the interests, opinions, and characteristics of their communities? This article provides an overview of the empirical research on the linkage between elected local officials and constituents. Given their particular importance, the focus is primarily on the impact of varying electoral structures used to choose elected representatives.

The legislative bodies of cities and counties have a central place in the processes of popular representation, democratic governance, and accountability in their communities. Unlike their counterparts at the state and federal level, local legislatures are unicameral and rarely have to contend with a powerful separately elected executive who has veto power over their actions.[1] Legislative bodies in cities are most commonly referred to as councils, but a small number may use the titles of board, selectmen, or trustees. The most common name of county legislatures is commission, followed by council and board.

OVERVIEW

The procedures for electing representatives to city and county legislative bodies vary widely between the two types of local governments. The overwhelming majority of cities use nonpartisan elections. The latest city form of government survey by the International City/County Management Association (ICMA) puts the figure at 76%. Alternatively, the overwhelming majority of counties use partisan ballots (82% in the latest ICMA survey of county forms of government). There is also a distinct difference between the two types of local governments in the distribution of at-large, district, and so-called mixed systems. At-large systems have representatives elected from the entire jurisdiction. In contrast, district systems have legislators elected from different areas of the city or county. The mixed systems have some legislators elected communitywide (at-large) and some elected from individual districts. A clear majority of American cities use at-large elections, whereas few use districts. The latest figures from the ICMA indicate that approximately 60% of cities have at-large elections and less than 20% have district elections (the remainder report having combination

or mixed election systems). In contrast, nearly one-half of counties report having district elections and only one-fifth elect their legislatures at-large. Cities, therefore, are more likely than counties to have so-called reformed electoral systems (promoted by the structural reform movement in the late nineteenth and early twentieth centuries).

The federal Voting Rights Act prohibits the use of racially discriminatory election procedures by both state and local governments. In fact, jurisdictions with a history of discrimination, disproportionately in the South, must have any changes in their election rules and procedures "precleared" by the U.S. Justice Department or the federal district court in Washington, D.C., *before* they can go into effect. Although the most overt forms of racial discrimination are largely a thing of the past, election systems can have subtle discriminatory effects that inhibit or "dilute" minority strength. At-large elections, for example, may permit a White majority to consistently elect *all* members of a council over Black minority opponents. When faced with such a case in *City of Mobile v. Bolden*, 446 U.S., 55 (1980), the Supreme Court stated that in order for an electoral system to be overturned under the Voting Rights Act, it must be established that there was some *intent* to discriminate by those who established the structure. The demonstration that an election procedure had discriminatory consequences was not deemed by the court to be sufficient to invalidate the system. In response to this case, the 1982 amendments to Section 2 of the Voting Rights Act make it clear that laws that *result* in diluting minority representation are just as impermissible as those accompanied by discriminatory *intent*. As amended, Section 2 states that an electoral system is invalid if, based on a totality of circumstances, it is apparent that minorities will have fewer opportunities than others to participate in the electoral process and elect representatives of their choosing. The factors to be considered in making this determination include the degree of historical discrimination in the community; the degree of racially polarized block voting; racial appeals in political campaign rhetoric; the proportion of minorities elected to public office (although the Supreme Court in *Thornburgh v. Gingles*, 106 S.Ct. 2752, 1986, made it clear that minorities do not have a right to have a fixed percentage of elected positions in any legislative body); and the extent to which there is responsiveness to minorities on the part of public officials in a community. These legal changes are largely

Encyclopedia of Public Administration and Public Policy
DOI: 10.1081/E-EPAP 120010839

responsible for the decrease in the use of at-large elections by local governments in the late 1980s.[2]

The body of academic literature examining the interactive effects of local government election systems on the linkage between minority population percentages and minority representation on elected councils is quite clear. Beyond a certain population threshold (usually 15% or 20%), district and mixed systems tend to facilitate minority representation, whereas at-large systems tend to inhibit minority representation in both cites[3] and counties.[4] These systematic patterns persist despite anecdotal evidence that minorities can win in a progressive political environment with at-large elections.[5] There is also evidence that racial minorities living in communities with district elections have higher levels of political efficacy than those living in communities where councils are elected at-large.[6]

The extent to which elected councils and commissions are demographically representative of their constituencies (sharing similar distributions of race, ethnicity, gender, income, and education levels) is only one component of the broader concept of representation. Hanna Piktin[7] referred to this as descriptive representation. In addition, she identified another form—substantive representation—which refers to the extent to which the policies supported by elected representatives are in the interests of their constituencies. Eulau and Karps[8] referred to a similar type of representation as policy responsiveness. To illustrate the basic distinction between the descriptive and substantive concepts, a Hispanic commissioner who represents a majority Hispanic district might provide good descriptive representation but poor substantive representation if the commissioner voted against policies or programs that were in the best interest of their constituents.

A central question linking the two concepts is "what is the substantive effect of more equitable descriptive representation?" Some academic literature suggests that Black representatives can modestly change local hiring practices and spending priorities, whereas others suggest the change in the Black community is negligible.[9,10] Research by Zolton Hajnal,[11] however, focuses on the White community. The project concludes that Black representation in local government tends to decrease racial tension and increase White support of Black elected leadership, although White Republicans were "largely immune" from these effects.[12] "Once an African American is elected, . . . whites obtain important information about the effect black representation on their livers. They can now base their assessments on an incumbent's record rather than on stereotypes, exaggerated fears, or the incendiary predictions of white opponents."[13]

Welch and Bledsoe[6] explored two additional aspects of representation in their analysis of a national survey of city council members. These include representational focus and service representation. The former refers to whom council members or commissioners believe they should represent (a geographic area of the community or neighborhood, a racial or ethnic constituency, a partisan or ideological constituency, the city as a whole, a single issue group, a business or labor constituency, etc.). Service representation, however, refers to how commissioners or council members view their roles in providing constituency service.

Welch and Bledsoe's data on representational focus indicated that council members who are elected from districts are more likely to report that a particular geographic area or neighborhood is more important to their representation than council members who are elected at-large. The latter are, however, the most likely to report that they focus on the city as a whole or a business constituency. In service representation, the data indicate that at-large council members devote less time to constituency service or ombudsman activities than district members and are less likely to report that their constituents expect personal service. This relationship persisted even after the size of the constituency served was controlled.

In their analysis of policy or substantive representation, Welch and Bledsoe found that there were no statistically significant differences in policy attitudes between council members elected under different structures. However, councils with district elections were engaged in more conflict than those elected at-large. In addition, the nature of the conflict differed because district councils were the most likely to report that their disputes were geographically based. Predictably, the data indicated that councils elected with party labels on the ballot had more partisan conflict than those elected in nonpartisan systems. However, it appeared that partisan conflict on the council made both the partisan and nonpartisan issues more salient to the public.

In descriptive representation, Welch and Bledsoe's data indicated at-large council members tend to have higher incomes and education levels than those elected by district. This provides additional evidence to suggest that district elections facilitate council demographic diversity. Nonpartisan elections were found to result in more upper-income council members and Republicans. The partisan bias of nonpartisan systems, in favor of Republicans, has been documented in earlier academic literature.[14,15] In Welch and Bledsoe's data, however, nonpartisan elections only advantaged Republicans when they were also elected at-large. District systems, in other words, eliminated the partisan bias of nonpartisan elections.

Few, if any, city councils or county commissions can claim to be fully representative of their constituencies. Those in the least affluent stratum of society, likely to be disproportionately Democratic in political identification, are underrepresented in every type of electoral system. However, the literature demonstrates quite clearly that "some kinds of structures block representation of these groups more than do others."[16] Research on cumulative voting in American local elections by Bowler, Brockington, and Donovan[17] concluded that all plurality/majoritarian election systems tend to depress voter participation. They found that cumulative voting encourages voter mobilization and turnout.

Since the 1990s, it appears that city councils and county commissions are becoming somewhat more demographically representative of their constituencies. Susan MacManus,[18] for example, found that from 1988 to 1996, the percent of city council members who were black increased from 4.1% to 5.5%. She also found that the percentage of women increased from 15% to 21% over the same period. Women were found to be most prevalent in the largest cities with racially and ethnically diverse, and more affluent and highly educated, populations. On county commissions, the trend toward gender diversification was even stronger. In the 1988 national survey by the ICMA, only 9% of county legislators were women, compared with 29% in the organization's 1997 questionnaire. Comparable data on the racial change in county legislatures are not available because the ICMA dropped the race question from its most recent survey.

In the early 1990s, a term limits reform movement was successful in adopting their agenda through popular referendum. These reforms appear to be an effective strategy to ensure that the tenure of elected officials is limited and, therefore, that turnover is maximized. The core assumption seems to be that policy-making bodies need constant membership change to remain responsive because over time incumbents become increasingly insulated from their constituent's interests. There is, however, little empirical evidence to support this assumption in local legislatures. Data from ICMA indicate that few city council or county commission members are term limited (less than 10%), yet, there appears to be a great deal of turnover in these positions. Nearly one-half of all city council members were reported to be serving their first term.[19]

CONCLUSION

The linkage between constituents and their elected local representatives is a complex and multifaceted phenomenon. The existing academic literature has focused primarily on so-called descriptive representation, the correlation between elected officials' demographic characteristics and those of their respective constituencies.

The conditioning or interactive effects of election systems on this relationship have also received considerable scholarly attention. The available longitudinal data indicate that city councils and county commissions have experienced trends toward greater demographic representativeness over the last decade as minorities and women have increased their presence in these bodies. Comparatively little research exists, however, on the degree of substantive representation in local legislatures. There is no systematic evidence, for instance, on the congruence between constituency ideological characteristics and the roll call voting of representatives, which is common in the literature at the national level. The existence of thousands of jurisdictions and councils with various forms of record keeping means that such data would be extremely difficult, if not impossible, to collect. Future research could fill this gap by exploring the other dimensions of representation through elite surveys similar to those used by Welch and Bledsoe.[6] However, all aspects of local legislative representation need continuing scholarly attention. Comparatively high membership turnover on these councils suggests that all facets of the representation nexus will be dynamic over time.

REFERENCES

1. Renner, T.; DeSantis, V. Municipal Forms of Government: Issues and Trends. In *The 1998 Municipal Yearbook*; International City/County Management Association: Washington, 1998.
2. Renner, T. Municipal Election Processes: The Impact Upon Minority Representation. In *The 1998 Municipal Yearbook*; International City/County Management Association: Washington, 1988.
3. Welch, S. The impact of at-large elections on the representation of Blacks and Hispanics. J. Polit. **November 1990**, *52*, 1050–1076.
4. DeSantis, V.; Renner, T. Minority and Gender Representation in American County Legislatures: The Effect of Election Systems. In *United States Electoral Systems: Their Impact on Women and Minorities*; Rule, W., Zimmerman, J., Eds.; Greenwood Press: New York, 1992.
5. MacManus, S.; Bullock, C., III. Minorities and women do win at-large. Natl. Civic Rev. **May/June, 1988**, *77*, 231–244.
6. Welch, S.; Bledsoe, T. *Urban Reform and Its Consequences: A Study in Representation*; University of Chicago Press: Chicago, 1988.
7. Pitkin, H. *The Concept of Representation*; University of California Press: Berkeley, 1967.
8. Eulau, H.; Karps, P. The puzzle of representation: Specifiying components of responsiveness. Legis. Stud. Q. **August, 1977**, *2*, 233–254.
9. Mladenka, K. Blacks and Hispanics in urban politics. Am. Polit. Sci. Rev. **March, 1989**, *83*, 165–191.

10. Reed, A. The Black Urban Regime: Structural Origins and Constraints. In *Power, Community and the City*; Smith, M., Ed.; Transaction: New Brunswick, NJ, 1988.

11. Hajnal, Z. White residents, Black incumbents, and a declining racial divide. Am. Polit. Sci. Rev. **September, 2001**, *95*, 603–617.

12. Hajnal, Z. White residents, Black incumbents, and a declining racial divide. Am. Polit. Sci. Rev. **September, 2001**, *95*, 603.

13. Hajnal, Z. White residents, Black incumbents, and a declining racial divide. Am. Polit. Sci. Rev. **September, 2001**, *95*, 604.

14. Hawley, W. *Nonpartisan Elections and the Case for Party Politics*; Wiley: New York, 1973.

15. Lee, E. *The Politics of Nonpartisanship*; University of California Press: Berkeley, 1960.

16. Welch, S.; Bledsoe, T. *Urban Reform and Its Consequences: A Study in Representation*; University of Chicago Press: Chicago, 1988; 53.

17. Bowler, S.; Brockington, D.; Donovan, T. Elections systems and voter turnout: Experiments in the United States. J. Polit. **August, 2001**, *63*, 902–915.

18. MacManus, S. The Resurgent City Councils. In *American State and Local Politics: Directions for the 21st Century*; Weber, R., Brace, P., Eds.; Chatham House: New York, 1999.

19. DeSantis, V.; Renner, T. Term Limits and Turnover Among Local Officials. In *The 1994 Municipal Yearbook*; International/City County Management Association: Washington, 1994.

FURTHER READING

Karnig, A.; Walter, O. Decline in municipal voter turnout. Am. Polit. Q. **October, 1983**, *11*, 491–506.

The American County: Frontiers of Knowledge; Menzel, D., Ed.; The University of Alabama Press: Tuscaloosa, AL, 1996.

County Government

J. Edwin Benton
University of South Florida, Tampa, Florida, U.S.A.

INTRODUCTION

County governments are perhaps the oldest and most familiar units of local government in the United States. Currently, there are 3040 county governments or their equivalent[a] in 48 of the 50 states. (Rhode Island and Connecticut abolished county governments in 1842 and 1958, respectively.[b]) The number, size, and population of counties vary considerably. While the number of county governments per state ranges from three in Delaware to 254 in Texas, the geographic area of counties can be as small as 46 square miles (Hudson County, New Jersey) or as large as 89,783 square miles (North Slope Borough, Alaska). The typical county covers an area of 600 to 700 square miles. The average population served by county governments is 79,100, but this ranges from 141 in Loving County, Texas, to over 9 million in Los Angeles County, California. Around 15% of all county governments (N = 460) serve populations of 100,000 or larger, with 187 of these counties in 40 states containing 250,000 or more inhabitants. But, 72% of all American counties (N = 2204) serve populations of less than 50,000 persons, with 700 of them containing fewer than 10,000 persons. Finally, some counties (e.g., Hernando and Orange in Florida) have experienced a tremendous growth in their population (over 100% in Hernando since 1990), while the population in counties in some states, such as Iowa and West Virginia, has remained unchanged or even declined.

To better understand what county governments are and what they do, the remainder of this entry is divided into three parts: 1) a brief history of the development of counties; 2) a description of county government structure; and 3) an overview of the roles counties play as service providers.

HISTORICAL DEVELOPMENT OF COUNTY GOVERNMENTS

County governments were originally established to serve the needs of their state. From the outset, county govern-ments were viewed as instruments by which their state governments could insure the delivery of essentially state programs at the local level. The administration of public welfare and health care programs, provision of roads, bridges, and highways, operation of court systems, maintenance of law and order, supervision of elections, tax assessment and collection, and furnishing agricultural information are examples of state services or services of statewide concern for which counties are responsible. Because of the role that county governments were to play, they frequently have been referred to as political or administrative subdivisions of their state government.

In spite of this general view of the purpose and func-tioning of county governments, counties developed dif-ferently in different parts of the country. To a large extent, the powers that county governments exercise and the functions they perform today—in short, the form of county government that was created—can be traced back to the needs of the settlers of the southern, northern, and middle colonies.[2–4]

Those states that adopted the model of the Virginia colony (primarily southern states) developed a strong system of county governments. Southern colonies required a form of government that could effectively respond to the needs of a society consisting mainly of plantations, farms, and small agricultural communities. In fact, the wide geographical dispersion of the population in most southern states made the English strong county model a suitable form of local government. Therefore, county government became the primary unit of local government through which the state guaranteed the coordination and provision of many state services (e.g., welfare, health care, roads, courts, public safety) at the local level.

By contrast, counties in the northern part of the nation (New England) historically were vested with fewer po-wers and responsibilities and consequently played a much less important role in the lives of residents of these colonies (later to become states). For the most part, states in this region traditionally relied much more frequently on municipal governments and townships, and even special

---

[a]In Alaska, they are referred to as boroughs, while they are called parishes in Louisiana.

[b]At this writing, it appears that county governments in Massachusetts are being systematically eliminated. In 1997, the state abolished Middlesex County and eliminated two more counties—Hampden and Worcester—in 1998.

Encyclopedia of Public Administration and Public Policy
DOI: 10.1081/E-EPAP 120010832

districts, than on county governments to provide state services and programs to citizens at the local level. This arrangement was a result of the fact that most New England states followed the example set by the Massachusetts Bay Colony, where towns, cities, and townships were established before counties. Therefore, many of the functions and responsibilities that were assigned to counties in the southern colonies were given instead to these other units of local government. Because county governments never attained the level of importance in this region of the country as they did elsewhere, Rhode Island and Connecticut eventually abolished their county governments, and more recently, counties appear to be headed for extinction in Massachusetts.

The middle colonies of Pennsylvania, New Jersey, and New York established local governments different from those found in the southern and northern colonies. Cities and towns in New York and New Jersey, like in the New England region, were the primary units of local government. Townships also were established and played an important role. However, county governments were not only established in New York and New Jersey, but they were given substantially more responsibilities. County government in Pennsylvania developed even differently from that in New Jersey and New York. County governments in that state were intentionally established as the primary unit of local government and, hence, developed as important administrative units before cities and towns. Townships were also created in Pennsylvania to help counties in the provision of services on a level larger than the city or town but smaller than the county.

As the nation expanded westward, the other 37 states that were to eventually join the Union looked to the original 13 states for guidance when creating a system of local government. The model of the southern states, whereby counties became the central focus of local governance as well as the principal agents of service delivery, was adopted by many of the western states. The example set by the states of the Middle Atlantic region was most influential in the scheme of local governance that was created in many states in the Midwest. Here, county governments developed as important political entities, although not to the extent found in southern states. No future state, however, adopted the model set by New England states, where county governments were insignificant units of local government.

STRUCTURE OF COUNTY GOVERNMENT: TRADITIONAL VERSUS MODERNIZED

To understand the manner in which county governments are structured, one must recognize that counties are le-

gally "creatures of the state." Emphasizing this fact, the U.S. Supreme Court in the case of *Maryland v. Baltimore and Ohio Railroad* (1845) held that "the several counties are nothing more than certain portions of the territory into which the state is divided for a more convenient exercise of the power of government." Later, in *Merriam v. Moody's Executors* (1868), the Iowa Supreme Court ruled that local governments, including counties, could exercise only: 1) those powers expressly delegated to them by the state legislature via enabling legislation; 2) those powers necessary and incident to execution of the express powers; and 3) those powers absolutely necessary to discharge the express powers. These two court cases (the latter known as Dillion's Rule) reinforced the principle that county governments were essentially administrative districts of the state. Therefore, it should come as no surprise that the states historically have dictated the structure of county governments. The form of county government that resulted frequently is referred to as a traditional county commission structure.

Although traditional county commission governments may differ noticeably in their organization, they have three distinctive features in common. First, they have a governing (legislative) body usually referred to as the "county commission" (sometimes, however, it can be called the "county board," "board of supervisors," or even "board of judges"), which is comprised of anywhere from three to 50 elected members. Typically, there are three or five county commissioners elected for overlapping four-year terms. Second, although the governing board may supervise some functions, it generally shares responsibility for the administration of many county functions with a number of separately elected officials with county-wide jurisdiction (usually referred to as "row officers"), such as the sheriff, county attorney, auditor, recorder, coroner, assessor, judge, treasurer, tax collector, and clerk of the circuit court. For instance, the county commission and the elected sheriff share responsibility for the county jail, with the sheriff overseeing day-to-day operations but the commission deciding on its construction, repair, and financing. The commission usually determines the property tax rate to be imposed on property owners (subject to limitations or tax caps or ceilings in the state constitution or imposed by the state legislature). But, the tax assessor determines the value of each piece of property in the county against which the rate is to be applied. And, in some counties, a separate tax collector actually sends out the tax bills and assumes responsibility for collecting revenue, while another separately elected county official (treasurer) may maintain the county's financial accounts and write checks. Hence, responsibility for the administration of county government functions is fragmented and dispersed and generally beyond the control of one county official or county office.

A third common feature is the existence of a number of special boards or commissions that have authority over various functions, whose members may be elected or appointed by the county commissioners or may even include the county commissioners in an ex officio capacity. Generally, these include such things as welfare, library, zoning, code enforcement, and pension boards; hospital, housing, and sanitation authorities; and water, sewer, and fire districts.

Reformers historically viewed the traditional structure of county government as lacking in efficiency and political accountability. In addition, reformers have lamented the fact that very little local home rule or self-determination exists for county governments, because they are creatures of the state. This means that the local governing body is limited in its ability to respond to public expectations and the service needs of their constituency. While reformers have advocated that state legislatures grant counties greater discretion in local matters as well as give them the authority to adopt more modern governmental structures, an overwhelming majority of all counties still operate under the traditional county commission structure.

In recent years, however, counties have been granted greater discretionary authority or home rule and the opportunity to modernize their structure of government. Since the early 1900s, 36 states have relinquished substantial control over the internal affairs of counties through the grant of home rule, while another four states have given additional authority in functional and fiscal areas to their counties.[5] Moreover, some of the 12 states without home rule have granted authority through special legislation.[6]

The most common type of home rule is charter government, which is available to counties in 24 states.[6] Charter home rule permits counties to devise and adopt their own charter and basically results in greater autonomy than other types of home rule, particularly in functional and fiscal areas.[7] While around 120 of the 1307 counties eligible to adopt a charter have done so, 2920 counties (95%) remain general law counties.[6] As a general rule, urban counties and counties with more affluent, more educated, and reform-minded citizens are more likely to adopt a charter form of government.

While counties have been slow to take advantage of the opportunity to adopt home rule charters, they have been more willing to move toward greater centralization of executive and policy-making authority. To date, over 800 counties have adopted the commission–administrator form of government, and over 400 counties have opted for an elected executive form of government.[7,8] Moreover, there has been a steady movement by counties to centralize their government by abolishing or merging the elective positions of constitutional officers under the governing board. For instance, a survey of state county

associations in 1992 revealed that 19 of 41 responding states reported some kind of change in the status of elected constitutional officers.[9] Many states even permit this type of structural change, regardless of home rule or charters.[1]

These changes have coincided with the willingness of the states to permit counties greater latitude in raising revenue. Specifically, an increasing number of states have granted counties wider authority to implement sales and gas taxes and to levy a variety of fees and charges for services. At the same time, states have substantially increased the amount of state aid to counties and have demonstrated a greater willingness to share a larger proportion of their revenue receipts with counties.[1] To a large degree, it seems that financial pressures resulting from reductions in federal aid have been responsible for the willingness of states in recent years to increase state aid and shared revenues and grant expanded revenue-raising authority to counties.[1]

COUNTY SERVICES

County governments, regardless of their structure of government, provide three basic types of services—traditional, municipal-type, and regional. Traditional services (many of which are mandated) are typically some of the oldest county services and result from the fact that counties are administrative subdivisions of the state and are provided to all county residents. As such, counties are responsible for services that include public welfare, health and hospitals, highways, police, judicial and legal matters, corrections, elections, tax assessment and collection, and public buildings. Municipal-type services (sometimes referred to as ''newer'' county services) are usually provided to residents of the unincorporated area who expect the county to assure the delivery of a number of services that historically have been provided only by municipalities. These include fire protection, utilities (water, sewer, and garbage collection), libraries, and protective inspections. Like traditional services, regional services are provided to the entire county (that is, to both incorporated and unincorporated area residents). These are services (also frequently referred to as ''newer'' county services) that deal with service issues that know no political boundaries (e.g., airports, housing and urban development, sewer and solid waste disposal, parks and recreation, natural resource conservation, and transit) and, hence, require a county-wide response.

To gain a better understanding as to the role that county governments play as providers of these three types of services, it is instructive to examine county financial effort. This can be done best by comparing county expenditures over time and, where appropriate, with other units

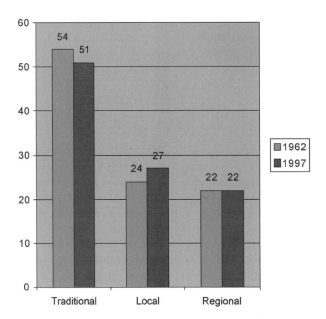

Fig. 1 County service proportions, 1962 and 1997. *Source*: U.S. Bureau of the Census, 1962 Census of Government, *Compendium of Government Finances* (Washington, D.C.: Government Printing Office, 1964), Table 48; U.S. Bureau of the Census, 1997 Census of Governments, *Compendium of Government Finances* (Washington, D.C.: Government Printing Office, 2000), Table 48.

of local governments (i.e., municipalities, townships, and special districts). The most reliable expenditure data exists for the 1962–1997-time period.

Because county governments were created to serve as administrative arms of the state, it is not surprising that counties historically have devoted the largest proportion of their fiscal resources to the provision of traditional services. As Fig. 1 indicates, counties spend over twice as much to deliver traditional services as they do for either municipal-type or regional services. In short, counties continue to be heavily involved in the provision of state services and programs at the local level. Nevertheless, it

appears that this role diminished somewhat between 1962 and 1997, while the role as providers of municipal-type services increased. The role of counties as providers of regional services showed no change between 1962 and 1997.

A comparison of the service role of counties to other local governments provides another perspective. For instance, it can be seen that county governments are the dominant providers of traditional services. In both 1962 and 1997, counties accounted for the largest proportion of all local government funds allocated to the provision of traditional services (see Fig. 2). In fact, the county

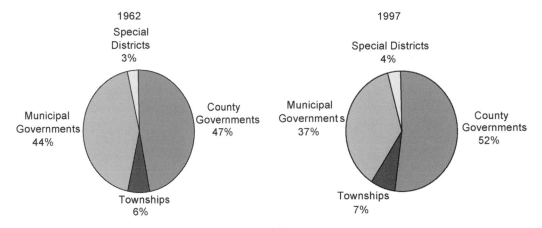

Fig. 2 Traditional service proportions, 1962 and 1997. *Source*: U.S. Bureau of the Census, 1962 Census of Government, *Compendium of Government Finances* (Washington, D.C.: Government Printing Office, 1964), Table 48; U.S. Bureau of the Census, 1997 Census of Governments, *Compendium of Government Finances* (Washington, D.C.: Government Printing Office, 2000), Table 48.

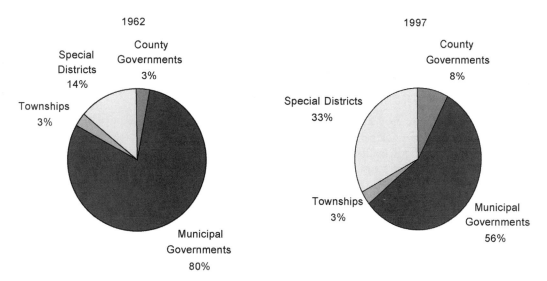

Fig. 3 Local service proportions, 1962 and 1997. *Source*: U.S. Bureau of the Census, 1962 Census of Government, *Compendium of Government Finances* (Washington, D.C.: Government Printing Office, 1964), Table 48; U.S. Bureau of the Census, 1997 Census of Governments, *Compendium of Government Finances* (Washington, D.C.: Government Printing Office, 2000), Table 48.

proportion increased from 47 to 52 between 1962 and 1997.

With regard to municipal-type services, counties tend to play a relatively minor role in their delivery when compared to municipalities and special districts (see Fig. 3). Here again, this finding comes as no surprise, because most municipal-type services (e.g., fire, utilities, protective inspections, and the like) are ones that municipalities typically have provided to their residents. Nonetheless, two important observations should be noted. First, the county government proportion increased from 3

to 8% between 1962 and 1997. Second, the special district proportion increased substantially over this same time period (that is, from 15 to 33%). This is significant, because special districts are frequently created to provide services to some or all county residents when counties are unable or unwilling to provide them. Therefore, it is reasonable to conclude that, to a certain extent, special districts assist counties in their role as providers of municipal-type services.

The greatest surprise comes from the role that county governments play in the provision of regional services. As

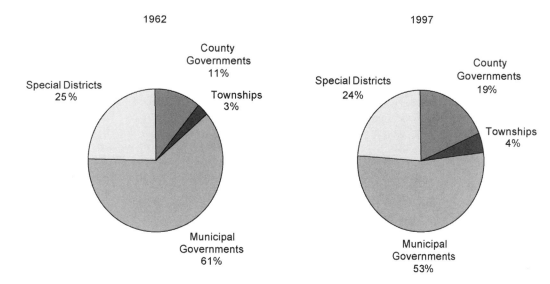

Fig. 4 Regional service proportions, 1962 and 1997. *Source*: U.S. Bureau of the Census, 1962 Census of Government, *Compendium of Government Finances* (Washington, D.C.: Government Printing Office, 1964), Table 48; U.S. Bureau of the Census, 1997 Census of Governments, *Compendium of Government Finances* (Washington, D.C.: Government Printing Office, 2000), Table 48.

the data in Fig. 4 indicates, the county government proportion of all local government spending for regional services increased noticeably from 11% in 1962 to 19% in 1997, an increase of 8%. Over the same period of time, the municipal government share decreased by 8%, while the township and special district proportion basically remained unchanged. In short, it appears that in recent years, county governments have been called upon to play a much more important role in the delivery of regional-type services at the same time that municipalities are finding it more difficult or are even unwilling to provide some of these services than they have in the past. Examples would be in the area of airports, sewer and solid waste disposal, and housing.

The role that county governments play in the provision of traditional, municipal-type, and regional services, however, varies considerably across counties. On the one hand, the service role of counties vis-à-vis municipalities, townships, and special districts is greatest among counties in the South and West regions of the country, in rapid-growth counties (particularly if most of the growth is occurring in the unincorporated part of the county), in metropolitan counties, and in counties that have adopted a charter form of government and have an appointed administrator or elected executive (that is, a reformed structure). Moreover, counties tend to play a more important role in the provision of municipal-type and regional services, where their states have assigned more functional responsibility or provided more fiscal assistance. On the other hand, the service role of counties is much less important in the New England and Middle Atlantic region, in nonmetropolitan counties, in negative and no- or slow-growth counties, and in states with the traditional commission (i.e., unreformed) form of government. In addition, a much smaller county role in the delivery of traditional and regional services is the norm for counties in which the state assigns greater functional responsibility to other local governments or distributes smaller amounts of state financial aid. In short, the role of counties as providers of the three types of services can vary significantly from region to region, from state to state, even from county to county in the same state.

CONCLUSION

In addition to being the oldest form of local government in the United States, counties are perhaps the least un- derstood. This is probably the result of the multiple expectations that we have for these units of government and the different service roles they are required to play. Although originally created to serve as administrative subdivisions of the state, they are frequently expected to provide municipal-type services to the vast numbers of unincorporated areas' residents and provide an increasing menu of services with regional implications to all county residents. In fact, county governments probably touch the lives of individuals more frequently than any other unit of government in the United States. Sometimes, counties are seen as assisting the state in the delivery of state programs and services, and at times, they are seen as trying to perform like municipalities. And, at still other times, they appear as direct providers or as coordinators of the activities of a number of local governments in efforts to deal with issues that need an area-wide or county-wide solution. In spite of the constantly changing image of counties, they have always been and are destined to continue as the cornerstone of local government in most states.

REFERENCES

1. Berman, D.R.; Salant, T.J. The Changing Role of Counties in the Intergovernmental System. In *The American County: Frontiers of Knowledge*; Menzel, D.C., Ed.; University of Alabama Press: University, AL, 1996; 19–33.
2. Benton, J.E. *Counties as Service Delivery Agents: Changing Roles And Expectations*; Praeger: New York, 2002.
3. Duncombe, H.S. *Modern County Government*; National Association of Counties: Washington, D.C., 1977.
4. Martin, L.L. American County Government: A Historical Perspective. In *County Governments in an Era of Change*; Berman, D.R., Ed.; Greenwood Press: New York, 1993; 1–13.
5. Salant, T.J. *County Home Rule: Perspectives for Decision Making*; University of Arizona: Tucson, AZ, 1988.
6. Salant, T.J. County, governments: An overview. Intergovernmental perspective. State Local Gov. Rev. **1991**, *17* (1), 5–9.
7. Blake, J.; Salant, T.J.; Boroshok, A.L. *County Government Structure: A State By State Report*; National Association of Counties: Washington, D.C., 1989.
8. International City/County Management Association. *The Municipal Year Book 2001*; International City/County Management Association: Washington, D.C., 2001.
9. Salant, T.J. *Survey of State County Associations Officials*; 1992; unpublished manuscript.

Court Administrators as Managers and Executives

Steven W. Hays
University of South Carolina, Columbia, South Carolina, U.S.A.

INTRODUCTION

Professional court administrators emerged relatively recently within the field of Public Administration. Court systems, which had always been managed primarily by judges and elected court clerks, had been slow to modernize until the introduction of these specially trained managers. Their roles are diverse, but their essential responsibility is to improve the operation of courts by freeing judges from nonjudicial duties and providing them with competent managerial infrastructures. Known by a variety of titles—such as court executive assistant, court executive officer, and judicial executive—court administrators are now common fixtures in many sizeable judicial systems in federal, state, and local government. However, they are not a universally accepted innovation in some locales. Serving at the pleasure of the presiding judge of their court systems, their duties also vary as dramatically as one might imagine within such a diverse mosaic as the American justice system.[1]

A BRIEF HISTORY OF THE PROFESSION

The development of the court administrator profession has been sporadic. Its origins can be traced to several catalysts. Most notable were the court reform movement promoted by Dean Roscoe Pound of the Harvard Law School, "good government" efforts that fostered professionalism among city managers and other civil servants, and the "crisis in the courts" that occurred during the 1960s and 1970s.[2] Court delay, backlog, and notoriously inefficient operating practices led such groups as the American Bar Association (ABA), the American Judicature Society (AJS), and various collections of judges (including the Federal Judicial Council led by Chief Justice Warren Burger) to demand improvements in the administrative capacity of courts. Spurred by federal funding—most notably the Law Enforcement Assistance Program (LEAP)—professional court managers were hired at a feverish pace during the 1960s and 1970s. A complementary trend in this regard was the creation of specialized training programs designed to prepare individuals for the unique challenges of managing judicial bureaucracies. The Institute for Court Management in Denver, Colorado, was the first program focused exclusively on honing the skills of court managers. This joint effort of the ABA and AJS was soon joined by several academic degree programs, most notably, those at the University of Southern California and at American University in Washington, D.C. By the turn of the twenty-first century, the court administrator profession had achieved a respectable degree of status inside and outside of courthouses across the nation. Every state now has a centralized Court Administrator's Office (usually as an appendage of the Supreme Court), and most urban trial courts and judicial circuits employ at least one professional court administrator and an appropriate support staff.

A MANAGEMENT PROFILE

Not only are judicial systems extremely diverse, but they are also some of the most tradition-bound institutions of government. These facts are reflected in the heterogeneity that prevails among workers who carry the title of court administrator. Most surveys reveal that court managers at the federal and state levels are attorneys, whereas lower courts more commonly employ individuals with more eclectic backgrounds. There is a strong tendency for judges to appoint people to these positions who have prior experience in quasi-legal organizations such as parole offices, law enforcement agencies, and court clerks' offices.[3] Moreover, many of today's "court administrators" are court clerks; the traditional role of court clerk, which usually involved housekeeping functions and jury management, has been expanded to include a wider array of responsibilities. Although many of these clerks are elected and therefore not known for their preentry professional qualifications, considerable numbers now enroll in training institutes and other programs intended to refine their managerial skills. About one quarter of all court administrators are actually the jurisdictions' court clerks (either elected or appointed), while most of the remaining group come from diverse occupational backgrounds. Notably, more than 70% of all court managers possess a college degree or better, suggesting that the field is becoming more professional over time.[1] However, there are still many court administrators (about 20%) whose formal education ended with a high school

Encyclopedia of Public Administration and Public Policy
DOI: 10.1081/E-EPAP 120010819

diploma. The ABA strongly endorses an elevation in the educational and professional standards for court administrators,[4] and progress is clearly being made (albeit slowly in many locations).

Organizational Considerations

Court administrators' professional lives are significantly affected by the judicial context in which they work. Courts are hierarchical organizations, just like any other public institution. This hierarchy will usually be mirrored in the court administrators' duties. Those employed by the highest court in a state (usually called the Supreme Court) typically serve at the pleasure of the Chief Justice. As "at will" employees, their job descriptions and job security will fluctuate depending upon the whims of their boss. Some are therefore integrated into high-level policy-making decisions concerning such topics as judicial assignments and budget priorities, while others may be relegated to relatively insignificant tasks such as data collection. If the Supreme Court exercises administrative responsibility over the lower courts in the state (a typical arrangement), then the state-level court administrator may have some supervisory authority over counterparts in lower courts (circuit, county, or specialized bodies such as Family Courts). Stated more directly, centrally mandated procedures and other requirements might be monitored and enforced through the state's highest court administrator. That individual usually has a support staff of professional and quasi-professional employees, including clerks, statisticians, information management experts, budgeting specialists, and the like.

As one descends the judicial hierarchy, the court administrator's role continues to be controlled (in part or completely) by the chief administrative judge of the court in which the administrator is employed. The simple fact is that court administrators always have "a boss," and that boss is a judge or a group of judges acting collectively. In the latter case, a judicial council may take responsibility for management of the judicial system, and thereby appoints the court administrator much like city councils appoint city managers. And, logically, the size and jurisdiction of the court system will directly influence the administrator's job responsibilities. Trial courts will often make jury management a central task of the court administrator, while housekeeping functions (courthouse maintenance and security) will be part of the job only when those obligations are not already assigned to someone else (e.g., an elected court clerk, a sheriff, or other local official). In sum, it is almost impossible to generalize about the specific duties and responsibilities of court administrators. There is no accepted template or approved job description; each position differs, and each is subject to dramatic change whenever there is turnover among the judges directly responsible for court management assignments.

JOB DUTIES AND RESPONSIBILITIES

As noted, the essential function of court administrators is to relieve judges of as many of their administrative burdens as possible so that they can focus on their chief obligation: hearing and deciding cases. Another implicit expectation is that the presence of a full-time manager within the court will increase the likelihood that administrative problems will be confronted head-on, and that modernization and innovation are more likely to occur. Judges are not generally regarded as being managerial gurus, so the introduction of professional managers is expected by many experts to be an essential step in improving court operations.

Consistent with these expectations, surveys of court administrators indicate that most of their efforts are focused on providing judges with a support infrastructure that handles most of the administrative minutiae, and upgrading management practices within the courthouse. The most common duties of court administrators are in the areas of personnel and financial management. They hire, fire, and supervise most of the nonjudicial staff (court reporters, deputy clerks) and are responsible for preparing and monitoring the judicial budget. While these tasks may not appear to be challenging at first glance, the reality is much different. Summoning, selecting, feeding, and paying jurors can be a huge undertaking, even in a fairly small jurisdiction. Record keeping, meanwhile, is a highly specialized and labor-intensive responsibility that requires constant attention. The number of subordinate employees necessary to manage a typical courthouse usually exceeds 75, all of whom must be hired, trained, supervised, paid, evaluated, and disciplined. Riding herd on such a labor force is a major undertaking, and one that judges (and sometimes court clerks) are more than happy to offload.

Categories of Duties

David Saari and his colleagues[1] organize the duties of court administrators around three management functions: "Operations," "Fiscal Services," and "Special Support Services." Operations include case management, calendaring, courtroom support, research, and program development. Of these, research and program development are activities that rarely, if ever, occurred before the arrival of court administrators. Over-worked judges simply did not have the time to devote to research and planning functions, so professional managers have clearly been a major asset in this regard. Under the fiscal services category, the court administrators not only assume most of the tedious burdens associated with drafting and monitoring budgets, but they also might bring new skills to the table. In particular, professionally trained managers are better able to generate new revenue sources through grant writing efforts, and they can also provide audit and accounting services that were beyond the capacity of most judges.

The "special support" category has perhaps been the area in which court managers have made their biggest contribution to judicial administration. In addition to functions that have already been mentioned, such as jury management, court administrators increasingly offer assistance in emerging "problem areas" within courts. One prime example is in the provision of language interpreters during trials. The recent influx of immigrants spurred by the collapse of the Soviet Union and related international developments has led to an incredible upsurge in trials involving non-English speakers. Sacramento County's (CA) court system, as one simple example, must provide interpreters for 91 different nationalities (including Russian, Chinese, Vietnamese, Greek, and Bulgarian). Other more recent areas of responsibility include courtroom security (this was almost a non-issue prior to the 1970s, when some judges were physically attacked by defendants) and pretrial services (such as intervention programs that permit first-time defendants to expunge their records through community service).

Of special note is the contributions that court administrators are making in the areas of information management and the introduction of new technologies. Prior to the modernization movement, courts were notorious for retaining handwritten docket books and otherwise ignoring the technological revolution that was occurring as a result of the computer age. Computerizing legal records, jury management functions, payroll, judicial calendars, and other courthouse operations has been a major preoccupation of many first- and second-generation court administrators. By upgrading the internal capacity of courts to manage their caseloads efficiently, some commentators have credited court administrators with much of the credit for reducing court delay and eliminating backlogs that once prevailed throughout the United States.[5]

JUDGES AS THE CRITICAL FACTOR IN JOB EFFECTIVENESS

For obvious reasons, much of the court management literature focuses on the relationship between judges and

their court administrators. Ultimately, the courthouse is a highly constrained environment for a professional manager. Judges are unquestionably the key figures within courts, and their level of receptivity to court administrators spells success or failure. Unless they respect the role that a professional manager might play in enhancing judicial operations, the court administrator's job can be terribly lonely and frustrating. Conversely, visionary and progressive judges can fundamentally improve their organizations' functioning by making maximum use of the managerial skills that many of today's professionals possess. But, because many judges neither understand nor trust the concept of court administrators, much additional groundwork needs to be laid before the profession achieves its true potential. A model that is espoused by many proponents is that judges and administrators govern the courthouse as a collaborative "team," yet this approach has seldom (if ever) been realized. For this reason, most court administrators continue to function as part of the judicial system's support infrastructure, but few exercise the discretion or policy-making influence associated with comparable positions in Public Administration (e.g., city managers or agency directors). This reality does not diminish the contributions that court administrators have already made, and continue to make, in modernizing judicial operations.

REFERENCES

1. Saari, D.; Planet, M.; Reinkensmeyer, M. The Modern Court Managers: Who They Are and What They Do in the United States. In *Handbook of Court Administration and Management*, 1st Ed.; Hays, S., Graham, C., Eds.; Marcel Dekker, Inc.: New York, 1993; 237–261.
2. Frank, J. *Courts on Trial: Myth and Reality in American Justice*; Atheneum: New York, 1971.
3. Berkson, L.; Hays, S. Injecting court administrators into an old system. Justice Syst. J. **1976**, *2* (1), 55–76.
4. American Bar Association. *Standards Relating to Court Organization*; ABA: Chicago, 1998.
5. Solomon, M. Fundamental Issues in Caseflow Management. In *Handbook of Court Administration and Management*, 1st Ed.; Hays, S., Graham, C., Eds.; Marcel Dekker, Inc.: New York, 1993; 369–381.

Court Technology and Information Systems

Ronald M. Stout, Jr.
New York State Judiciary, Latham, New York, U.S.A.

INTRODUCTION

A full discussion of the concepts, applications, promises, and realities of court technology and information systems would require, and indeed deserve, an extensive analysis and discussion far beyond the confines of the space possible in the *Encyclopedia* (for example, see Ref. [1]). Instead, this article will identify court functions that can be enhanced by the application of technology, the types of application software that are available in which to develop these functions, equipment and connectivity options depending upon the size and scope of the functions, and courts, design, implementation and maintenance considerations, and cautions to be exercised.

Developing technology and information systems for courts is a highly appropriate activity, because receiving, processing, and disseminating information is the method by which courts achieve their objective. From the initial filing of a case to the final postdisposition action, litigants, the bar, judges and their staffs, and the public, are entirely dependant upon timely and accurate information about the status and the substance of the case. Courts have always had information systems. Manually maintained docket books, ledgers, index cards, and file folders, combined with handwritten documents and notices are information systems. Some courts to this day continue to process information in this manner, while many more have hybrid systems that combine manual and automated components.

ENHANCEMENT OF FUNCTIONS BY TECHNOLOGY AND INFORMATION SYSTEMS

Virtually every function required by a court can benefit from the application of technology and information systems. Perhaps the first function that comes to mind when considering court information systems is case-flow management. Case-flow management, dealt with more extensively elsewhere in the *Encyclopedia*, "involves the entire set of actions that a court takes to monitor and control the progress of cases, from initiation through trial or other initial disposition to the completion of all post-disposition court work, to make sure that justice is done promptly."[2] A comprehensive case-flow management system should include the ability to:

- Record all incoming documents or actions that initiate and continue a case, including those that are filed electronically.
- Assign a case to a judge.
- Schedule all events and record the outcome of those events.
- Monitor compliance with interim and final deadlines, and produce appropriate warning notices.
- Produce scheduling and noncompliance documents (such as warrants).
- Record all fees and fines levied, collected, or delinquent, and produce appropriate documents.
- Record all individuals associated with the case, including litigants, attorneys, probation officers, and court-appointed representatives or fiduciaries, and produce appointment and termination notices.
- Allow ad hoc inquiries to determine the status of one or more cases, the schedules for any day or judge, and the cases with which one or more participants are involved.
- Produce all required statistics, including those describing case processing, judicial workload, and court assignments of attorneys and fiduciaries.

If automating case-flow management can be considered applying technology to the processing of cases, a second function that can be assisted by automation is the substance of a case. Applying automation to this function assists judges by, for example, producing substantive orders, calculating structured settlements in civil cases or child support payments based upon income and expenses, producing transcripts of judgements and criminal commitment orders. In addition, automated systems can permit electronic filing of initial and subsequent papers, answers, motions, depositions, fees, and proposed orders. The line between this function and the case-flow management function is not definitive—after all, a case-flow management function should produce warrants and commitment orders. However, automated systems can offer judges the option of selecting a wide variety of standard provisions and provide calculation power for complex financial proposals. Even orders that require

Encyclopedia of Public Administration and Public Policy
DOI: 10.1081/E-EPAP 120010823

extensive tailored provisions can benefit from the automated capture of the names of the parties, the issues, and the attorneys.

A third function is computer-assisted legal research, permitting judges and staff to conduct rapid and comprehensive legal research from their offices or from the bench. Materials available on-line include:

- Federal, state and local statutes.
- Appellate and trial court decisions and opinions.
- Treatises on specific areas of law.
- Citation checking in a draft opinion or decision.

A fourth function that can benefit from the application of technology is case conferencing and presentation. This includes:

- Telephone and videoconferencing to conduct scheduling, settlement, and pretrial conferences.
- Videoconferencing for trial testimony.
- Video display units for presentation of evidence during trial, with images of evidence displayed on screens of opposing attorneys, court clerks, the judge, and jurors.

Establishing a record of court proceedings is another function in which technology can improve efficiency and effectiveness. Software is available that:

- Instantaneously transcribes court reporters' notes, which greatly facilitates read-backs and the production of transcripts.
- Where permitted by law, electronically records court proceedings using either audio or video.

Courtroom utilization in large facilities can also benefit from technology. The demand for courtroom space in large urban settings is frequently very high. When a case in a trial settles, a trial is suspended for a significant period of time, or a case goes to a jury, the use of telephones, e-mail and even radios can notify judges and court staff of the availability of a courtroom.

Technology and information systems can also be applied to records management with great effect. Microfilm is an excellent records preservation tool but generally not a good management tool. Imaging systems that capture documents directly or in concert with microfilming systems make documents available to judges, staff, and the public, under the appropriate controls.

Technology can improve jury operations by:

- Merging mailing lists from different sources to establish the widest possible pool of potential jurors.
- Printing qualification and summoning notices.

- Tracking the response to those notices and producing corrective documents.
- Monitoring juror utilization once in the courthouse.
- Recording attendance.
- Producing documents necessary to authorize payment to jurors.

Communication within and without the court is another function ripe for the application of technology and information systems. Effective communication is essential for any organization, but particularly for the courts. The multiplicity of players in the courts makes establishing and maintaining effective communications especially difficult. This includes judges, staff, the private bar, executive branch agencies at the local, state, and federal levels, and litigants.[3] Each organization and individual may have vastly different communications capabilities, ranging from integrated information and technology systems to homes without a telephone.

Communication covers a broad area, including:

- Informing each other about events affecting the status of a case, such as motions, agreements, scheduled appearances, proposed and final orders, and settlements.
- Advising attorneys about court rules, forms, schedule of terms of court, and changes thereto.
- Providing the public with a description of the court system and the purposes and general processes of the different components of the court, hours of court, directions to the court, types of proceedings that can be brought and the forms to be used, and a directory of related agencies.

Automating administrative functions has long been practiced by the public and private sectors. Administrative functions that can be automated include:

- Preparing budgets, and submitting them to the appropriate legislative body.
- Establishing expenditure accounts based on appropriations, tracking encumbrances, expenditures, reporting balances, and providing projections.
- Issuing purchase orders, and preparing vouchers for payment.
- Maintaining inventories of accountable equipment.
- Maintaining lists of authorized position titles and their qualifications.
- Maintaining lists of positions authorized to be hired, production of vacancy reports, and turnover rates.
- Tracking employee information, including data on hiring, salary, promotions, disciplinary actions, fringe benefits, training, and separation.

- Issuing paychecks.
- Tracking the availability of judges and nonjudicial staff for assignment throughout the appropriate jurisdiction.

Many of these functions may be performed in whole or in part by local or state governmental agencies. Nevertheless, a careful review of the court's needs is advisable to determine if supplemental systems would be useful.

TYPES OF APPLICATION SOFTWARE

There are many types of software in which applications can be developed to perform the functions needed by the courts. In addition, the types of software have increasingly been bundled into ''suites'' of software that easily interact with each other. Increasingly, also, each type of software has elements of other types of software built into their design.

Database software is highly useful for developing systems to augment most court functions. A proper and comprehensive database application will identify all entities (e.g., people, places, events) and have the capability of storing all required information about those entities (e.g., names and addresses of people, court appearance dates, purposes of appearances and their outcomes, courtroom numbers, appropriations, voucher amounts, and personnel titles).

Database software programs have the capability of retrieving and presenting information in printed reports, on video display terminals, or electronically to other systems inside or outside of the courts. Data can be retrieved on a periodic or ad hoc basis. It can be tailored for any number of purposes, from providing a complete case history for a judge, to confirming a court date to a member of the public, to providing the latest court decision on a topic of interest.

Once the data is entered, it can be used for a virtually endless stream of documents, reports, and displays. Routines can be written to periodically scan records for compliance with processing dates and produce exception reports, compile statistics, and compute balances.

Word-processing programs can be used alone or in concert with database programs to produce documents for every court function. Templates can be written for standard documents, and automated messages can be built in to prompt for specific information. Alternatively, data can be automatically transferred from database programs to populate standard information, and specific information can be added to the document. Word-processing programs also have the capability of storing names, ad-

dresses, and other information in a database-like format, which can then be merged with a standard letter to produce mass mailings.

Spreadsheet programs are used primarily for manipulating numbers through mathematical formulas. Templates can be designed that are extremely useful for calculating the consequences of different proposed settlements or payments required for support payments. They can also be used for projecting expenditures under different assumptions. It is also interesting to note that relational database systems store data in tables that are, in effect, spreadsheets. Under carefully controlled design criteria, a spreadsheet can be used as a source of data in a database program, and vice versa. Finally, word-processing programs usually have a table feature, which also resembles a spreadsheet. Spreadsheets can be imported into word-processing programs as tables. This can be very useful, if, for example, a structured settlement worked out in a spreadsheet needed to be incorporated into a settlement order written in a word-processing program.

Electronic mail is an increasingly widespread communications tool capable of very quickly reaching one or more individuals or institutions. Information can be contained in the body of the message or in attached documents. In addition, most database, word-processing, and spreadsheet programs have the capability of attaching documents created by the software directly to an e-mail message.

Scanning and document retrieval software has the ability to capture images of documents filed with the court, including signatures and seals, and to retrieve those documents for printing or display on terminals. It is becoming increasingly common for database programs to be able to electronically link to document images, so that, for example, all papers that have been filed regarding a case can be retrieved while reviewing case-processing information contained in the database. In addition, scanned documents can be attached to e-mail messages.

Facsimile transmission software is available that will permit sending documents or reports that have been produced by database, word-processing, or spreadsheet software to recipients who have fax machines or computer-based fax software. In addition, scanned documents can be distributed using facsimile transmission software.

Word recognition software permits an individual to enter information into software applications by using a microphone rather than a keyboard. This software is useful for judges and staff to dictate information into a word-processing document, and for the public in responding to automated information sites.

Touch-screen software can greatly simplify accessing information from automated systems. It is typically applied to programs that present structured responses to a set of structured questions.

EQUIPMENT AND CONNECTIVITY OPTIONS

There is an ever-increasing variety of equipment available to the courts that can operate independently or be connected in a wide array of options. Manufacturers are constantly developing equipment that has increased capacity and speed, as well as new items. It is difficult to keep current with developments in this area. Consequently, this section of the article will endeavor to be as generic as possible.

Telephones, copiers, and fax machines have been part of the office and the court for so many years that we tend to overlook them as components of court technology. They should not be overlooked as vital components of court automation. As mentioned previously, telephone conferencing can be a vital part of case processing. Fax machines can be used in every aspect of communication involving case documents, including initiating cases, filing motions and supporting papers, scheduling orders and notices, and making interim and final orders. The use of copiers is obvious, and their utility can be greatly increased by placing them throughout the court facility. For example, placing a copying machine in a courtroom can increase productivity by providing instant copies of orders, documents in evidence, and other case-processing information.

The most immediately recognizable configuration of automation equipment is a desktop computer with an attached printer. Although relatively simple, desktops have become sufficiently powerful to run every type of application software performing every type of function listed above. To have e-mail, a modem would be necessary to connect to the internet. To be able to use document imaging, a scanner would be required. There are multipurpose devices that incorporate printing, faxing, scanning, and copying in one machine.

Laptop computers have the same basic capacities as desktop computers. Their advantage is that they are portable, capable of, for example, being carried from a judge's chambers into a courtroom. Their disadvantage is that they are more expensive and less powerful than desktop computers for the same price.

The next step in automated systems is the local area network (LAN). A LAN connects two or more computers and allows users to share data, application software, and devices such as printers, scanners, and modems. In addition, a LAN can have an internal e-mail system installed, as well as a system of equipment and software to establish an intranet for court judges and staff to have access to information and applications within their own environment. A LAN can also have a gateway to allow users to access the Internet without having individual modems for each computer.

A wide area network (WAN) is a LAN with users separated by distances further than can be reached by signals generated by LAN equipment. Routers or switches that convert and send signals over telephone lines are required. The features of a WAN are essentially those of a LAN, but extended beyond the reach of a LAN.

Kiosks are capable of displaying information about the courts in general, court schedules, forms to use and print out, and receiving information from the public, including court filings, pleas, and payments of fees and fines. The information provided and functions performed by these devices can be updated and modified from direct manipulation of the application software on the kiosks or "remotely" from court staff using their computers connected to a LAN or WAN. Status boards or running displays, similar to those found in airports, can also provide information to the public, and their messages can be modified from local devices or LAN- or WAN-based computers.

E-mail systems can also feed pagers, cell phones, and personal digital assistants via wireless Internet connections or through other communications systems. It is no longer necessary to be physically connected to receive information about courts, the status of a case, or a change in schedules.

DESIGNING, IMPLEMENTING, AND MAINTAINING SYSTEMS

The most challenging aspect of applying technology and information systems to the courts is determining the needs of the courts and establishing the appropriate mix of functions, software applications, and equipment and connectivity options. The most critical step in designing a system is to obtain a project sponsor for developing or improving an information system. A project sponsor should be placed high enough within the organization to be recognized as having the necessary authority to cause sufficient resources to be devoted to the effort to enable it to succeed. The project sponsor will change radically depending upon the size of the court system and the size of the project. It could range from a chief justice of a supreme court in a statewide system, to a magistrate in a rural town overseeing a two-person staff.

Once the project sponsor has been established, the court must carefully examine its resources to determine if it can reasonably design, implement, and maintain an information system. Larger court systems may well have sufficient in-house staff to undertake such an effort, while others may need consultant services. Even the largest organizations may contract with outside firms to provide guidance, support, and technical advice. Consultant services may be available from local and state governmental agencies, national organizations such as the National Center for State Courts, and the private sector. For smaller courts, the state court administrator's office can frequently provide services directly or offer guidance in selecting consultants and vendors.

An important step in starting a court automation project is to become familiar with and adhere to basic principles of project management. There are a number of different methodologies and tools available, ranging from relatively simple to highly developed. The scope of the project will help to suggest the level of project management sophistication required to bring a project in on time and within budget.[4]

Another critical step in designing information systems is to define the scope of the project. A careful definition of what functions are to be automated in which courts or offices, with a budget and timetable, and adherence to the scope definition, will help increase the probability of success. The scope should be committed to writing and signed by the project sponsor and key staff involved with the project. Any change to the scope of the project should be expressly addressed, complete with the additional time and expense required to include the change in the scope. Special attention should be given to insure that only those changes necessary to the success of the project are approved. Many requested changes can be dealt with at a later time, as a separate project.

In many instances, the court may find that it is not possible to incorporate all functions or courts in a current project. It is important that statements of scope that incorporate less than a total design include the possibility of expansion to other functions or courts in the future.

It is important that the judges and staff define the scope. They are the business experts and know what court functions would benefit the most from automated systems. While internal information technology analysts or consultants may offer advice as to the structure of the scope statement, or the time and cost implications of elements of the scope statement, the project sponsor, judges, and staff should have control of the final statement of scope.

Systems designs can range from a simple single desktop computer running a word-processing program to automate repetitive documents, to completely integrated data, voice, and imaging systems incorporating virtually all court functions with thousands of users spread over thousands of miles. Regardless of the size of the system, as with the preparation of the scope of the project, judges and court staff must be involved with the design of the system. This may require a significant amount of time,

depending upon the scope of the project. It will also require a joint effort with in-house and consultant technology staff. Court staff and technology staff must take the time to insure that the needs of the court are completely understood, while the cost and maintenance implications are clear and unambiguous. The final design, backed up by test runs of software and hardware, should be reviewed and approved by the project sponsor. Finally, it is imperative that all aspects of the design be well documented. The documentation provides the basis for corrections, modifications, and support in the future.

Implementing a new or modified system requires careful planning and patience. The system may require physical modifications, new equipment, and furniture. A certain amount of disruption of ongoing operations is inevitable, so careful coordination of court schedules, vacation plans, and backup will minimize problems. Arrangements must be made for training and intensive support after installation. Finally, last minute adjustments to the system may be required as a result of using the system in actual operations.

The assets required to maintain the system once it is installed should be included in the design phase. The need to modify the system for new requirements and correct problems will always occur. Providing for adequate maintenance is imperative, if the court's investment and operations are to be protected. Maintenance services can be provided by in-house staff or through contracts. The utility of solid systems documentation will become readily apparent at this time. However, the systems documentation must be maintained and updated by the group maintaining the system, or future efforts will be severely hampered.

CAUTIONS

One of the overriding concerns in any automated system is security. This is particularly important in court system records. Statutes and case law establish strict security requirements. Every effort should be made to incorporate appropriate security measures in the scope and design phase of a project. Judges and staff should ensure that the technical staff understand security requirements, and that they are satisfied with the security measures being described to them.

A second cautionary note is not to simply automate existing manual systems. The design phase of an automated system is an excellent opportunity to carefully review systems and procedures to insure that they are required by law, rule, good management practices, and are not redundant. Automating a confusing and unnecessarily complex system will only perpetuate past problems.

A third concern is the potential of e-mail to exacerbate the problem of ex parte communications. E-mail is widely used and can be an efficient method of communications with participants in a court case. Because it is so easily used, caution must be exercised by all parties to ensure that the contents of an e-mail message from a litigant or an attorney does not cross the line into discussing a proceeding before the court without the full knowledge of all parties.

CONCLUSION

Technology and information systems have great applicability to the processes and procedures used by the courts. Virtually every function of the courts can benefit from carefully designed automated systems. Application software is widely available to develop automated systems in the courts. The capacity of equipment and interconnectivity continues to grow.

A well-known observer of court systems noted, "The great unknown for court leaders is the ultimate effect of telecommunications and computer technology on the courts.... As information systems integrate all types of information and the court starts to become a self-aware, self-correcting system, there will be fundamental changes in time-honored court practices."[5]

In order to take advantage of the promise of technology and information systems, courts must devote the resources necessary to design systems. In addition, judges and staff must devote a significant proportion of their time to ensure that the systems meet the needs of the courts.

Technology and information systems present a great opportunity and a great challenge to the courts. To keep abreast of ever-increasing workloads and to respond to the public's demand that the courts become more efficient, courts will have to meet the challenge and take advantage of the opportunity.

REFERENCES

1. Webster, L.P. *Automating Court Systems*; National Center for State Courts: Williamsburg, VA, 1996.
2. Steelman, D.C.; Goerdt, J.A.; McMillan, J.E. *Caseflow Management: The Heart of Court Management in the New Millennium*; National Center for State Courts: Williamsburg, VA, 2000; xi.
3. Steelman, D.C.; Goerdt, J.A.; McMillan, J.E. *Caseflow Management: The Heart of Court Management in the New Millennium*; National Center for State Courts: Williamsburg, VA, 2000; 97–100.
4. Webster, L.P. *Automating Court Systems*; National Center for State Courts: Williamsburg, VA, 1996; 17–24For a comprehensive overview of the subject, see *A Guide to the Project Management Body of Knowledge*; Project Management Institute: Sylva, North Carolina, 2000.
5. Tobin, R.W. *Creating the Judicial Branch: The Unfinished Reform*; National Center for State Courts: Williamsburg, VA, 1999; 205.

Court Unification

James A. Gazell
San Diego State University, San Diego, California, U.S.A.

INTRODUCTION

Court unification is the degree to which federal and state judicial systems in America have achieved one level of trial and appellate courts administered from the top by one institution or individual. It is a facet of centralization in government—an application to one of its branches: the courts. It proceeds along a continuum from autonomous individual judges and other court officers at one end to hierarchical supervision at the other. Synonymous terms include court centralization, court modernization, court bureaucratization, and court reform. It was a structural and administrative concomitant to the development of the nation's court systems.

PREEMINENCE

Court unification has been the preeminent characteristic of judicial administration since the end of World War I. The next comparable feature has been the emergence of judicial administration as a profession in the 1970s. Although court unification started at the federal level shortly after the first World War, its preeminence has been at the state level, beginning with New Jersey in 1948, as a result of a successful campaign, led by the Chief Justice of its highest court, Arthur T. Vanderbilt. Since then, most other states followed in greatly varying degrees.

ORIGIN

In 1906, legal scholar Roscoe Pound credited the origin of court unification to the experience of the United Kingdom in the 1870s, which took this action with respect to its national court system. It eliminated levels of trial and appellate courts that had jurisdiction that overlapped, work that was duplicative and wasteful of judicial personnel, and operations that spawned long delays in the resolution of cases. He agreed with the popular aphorism that justice delayed was justice denied. Pound wanted America's state court systems (many of which encountered the same problems) to undergo an overhaul and adapt the new British model to their own circumstances. He thought these systems would become more

effective if they compressed their several levels of trial courts into one or two and established only one appellate court, standing alone or as a branch of a single trial court with comprehensive original jurisdiction. Presiding over such a structure would be one judge, empowered to make court-related rules and to assign other judges from one division of a court to another, equalizing the distribution of caseloads.

Furthermore, Pound's advocacy was one part of the Progressive Era in American history (1900–1914), which sought in part to strengthen all branches of government at the federal, state, and local levels. Pound had looked to the United Kingdom for a model suitable to fortify one branch of government: the judiciary. Progressives like him lived at a time when the business world had become increasingly centralized and bureaucratic as large corporations, monopolies, oligopolies, and trusts emerged. Their size made them effective but also, to progressives, dangerous to the public interest because of restrictions on production, exploitation of labor, unsafe products, and excessive prices. However, they were too powerful to be broken up as populists wanted. But, government might be strengthened enough for their effective regulation in the public interest. Only government had the potential to become a genuine counterweight to the growing concentration of corporate power and its increasing domination of the nation.

Effective regulation also necessitated a degree of government centralization: the creation of honest and competent government machines to fight corporate machines. Government had to be run more like a business to be more effective, as a future president, Woodrow Wilson, once wrote. The famous sociologist Max Weber saw such machines as forms of bureaucracy, which he viewed as the most effective model of organization, the one best way of organizing. In a complementary vein, management writer Frederick Taylor argued that, within bureaucracy, there was one best way of doing and supervising work.

A degree of countervailing centralization began at the level of the federal government, with the enactment of antitrust laws, the formation of independent regulatory commissions, and the strengthening of administrative capacity of the executive branch through expansion of a civil service system, budgetary control, and the develop-

Encyclopedia of Public Administration and Public Policy
DOI: 10.1081/E-EPAP 120010824

ment of the presidential staff. Government centralization slowly spread horizontally and vertically. It first extended to the legislative and judicial branches of the federal government, which sought to manage their own affairs. They sought to emulate the executive branch and to avoid becoming dependent on it. They hoped to function as a bona fide coordinate branch of the federal government, roughly equal in power. Otherwise, government by separation of powers and checks and balances would have remained mostly a concept in constitutional theory, not an operational reality. The federal legislative response largely took the form of strengthening its oversight of the federal executive branch through imposing a degree of due process on its operations through administrative procedure statutes, expanding its structure of committees and their staffing, and developing its ability to provide its own alternatives to executive budgets.

FEDERAL COURT UNIFICATION

The federal judicial response mostly took the form of persuading the other two branches to divest themselves of their traditional but increasingly onerous role of managing numerous aspects of federal judicial operations and to permit the federal judicial branch to handle its own finances, personnel, information, and rules to virtually the maximum extent permitted by the United States Constitution. Between 1891 and 1984, a series of notable structures came into existence. Some ran counter to court unification, but others fostered it. On balance, they brought a degree of centralization to the administration (but not the structure) of the federal judiciary.

Three structural developments diluted such unification:

1. In 1891, a second level of federal appellate courts— circuit courts of appeal—was established to ease the workload of the Supreme Court of the United States, generated by the population growth, urbanization, and industrialization of the nation. Furthermore, in 1925 the Supreme Court was granted virtually complete control over its docket.
2. In 1968, a second level of federal trial courts, the United States Magistrates, was also established. These courts were to decide minor criminal and civil cases and thereby enable the original level of trial courts, the federal district courts, to focus on more complex cases.
3. Various specialized appellate and trial courts were created to relieve circuit and district courts of some of their technical and complex cases but at the cost of structural fragmentation. These included the United

States Tax Court in 1942, the United States Court of Military Appeals in 1951, the United States Court of International Trade in 1980, and the United States Court of Appeals for the Federal Circuit (for bankruptcy challenges), the United States Court of Federal Claims, and the United States Tax Court, all in 1982.

However, other developments more than offset such movements toward disunification. In 1922, the Conference of Senior Circuit Judges (which became the Judicial Conference of the United States in 1948) was established to permit the federal courts to make recommendations to Congress as to what the rules governing federal judicial operations should be. Congress transferred its judicial rule-making authority to this body in stages: in 1938, for civil procedure; in 1946, for criminal procedure; in 1968, for appellate rules; and in 1975, for rules of evidence. These transfers virtually ended legislative domination of the federal judiciary. But in 1984, Congress backtracked by asserting a degree of authority over sentencing, a traditional judicial function. It established the United States Sentencing Commission and entrusted it with formulating guidelines for the courts.

In 1939, movement toward federal court unification accelerated. The Administrative Office of the United States Courts was set up, ending the actual dependence of the federal courts on the executive branch. This office allowed the federal courts to gather statistics, to prepare a judicial-branch budget, and to hire their own staffs. Before this office came into existence, these matters were handled by a federal executive branch agency, the Department of Justice, also the chief litigant in the federal courts. Moreover, a council for each of the federal judicial circuits was established to manage its own workload. Thus, the circuit council, not the Supreme Court of the United States, became the administrative model for running the federal judiciary and served to limit the degree of centralization that took place. In addition, the circuit conference was also created to enable judges within each circuit to meet periodically and keep abreast of legal and administrative developments.

Other unifying developments deserve mention. In 1967, the Federal Judicial Center was set up to become the research, development, and educational arm of the national court system. In 1971, the office of Circuit Executive was created. Each circuit chose a professional court administrator to run its operations and to allow judges to spend more time discharging their primary duty: adjudication. In 1972, the office of Administrative Assistant to the Chief Justice of the United States was set up. It was the functional equivalent of the circuit executive. In 1974, the office of District Court Executive became a reality for the nation's federal trial courts.

STATE COURT UNIFICATION

After spreading horizontally at the federal level, the quest for government centralization moved vertically after World War II, seeping down to the executive, judicial, and legislative branches of state and local governments. One reason remained the same: the widely perceived need to establish counterweights to centralization in the business world. The state executive and legislative branches roughly emulated their federal counterparts. The state courts, like their federal counterparts, sought to increase their administrative capacity to perform functions entrusted to the other two branches, to end their dependence on them, and to become a genuine coordinate branch of state government. However, unlike the federal courts, the state courts favored a degree of centralization to escape a second broad source of dependence—reliance on local governments, which handled fiscal and personnel matters affecting the courts. In practice, state courts were often appendages not only of executive and legislative branches of state governments but also the corresponding branches of county and city governments. To end such dependencies, state courts established a set of structures roughly parallel to those in the federal judiciary. But, overall, the states went beyond the federal government in pursuit of court unification, because, as legal historian Lawrence Friedman suggested, their judiciaries were more atomistic to begin with and thus provided more room for such change.

States replaced their multiple trial courts of overlapping jurisdiction with one level or two levels of trial courts. In some states, there was to be only place where all criminal and civil cases were to be filed—in short, a forum with comprehensive, original jurisdiction. In other states, there were to be two levels of trial courts modeled after the federal judiciary: a general trial court to handle major cases and courts of limited jurisdiction to handle minor matters. Moreover, 38 states have followed the federal model by creating a second appellate level.

All states established a judicial council, analogous to the Judicial Conference of the United States. It is the one body that makes policies applicable to an entire court system and reduces (but usually does not eliminate) the control of individual courts over their own operations. This structure promulgates rules regarding various aspects of court administration: finances, human resources, the assignment of judges, jury administration, the education and training of judges and court staff members, and management information systems. The judicial council selects a state court administrator, comparable to the Director of the Administrative Office of the United States Courts (one official who supervises a staff that carries out the council's policies and who serves at its pleasure). This administrator sometimes exercises close supervision over the operations of individual courts but generally leaves them with discretion within broad boundaries to handle their own business through appellate and trial court administrators. In a highly unified system, such officials are appointed by the state court administrator, subject to the approval of the judicial council. More characteristically, individual courts are permitted to make the choice within broad guidelines. Thus, judges of the individual courts or their presiding judge select their own court administrator as well as the deputies, assistants, division heads, clerks, reporters, secretaries, analysts, and planners.

The state court administrator oversees the performance of numerous judicial functions, none more important than the budgetary process. The work of this official often involves the use of a unitary judicial budget, one budget formulated for all the courts in a state, subject to legislative review, as opposed to the authority of each court to devise its own budget, subject to the same limitation. The unitary judicial budget is based on the executive budgeting model, which originated in the Progressive Era and served as a method for advancing the degree of administrative unity in federal, state, and local executive branches. Previously, individual executive branch departments, like individual courts, had prepared their own budgets and submitted them to the appropriate legislative bodies for disposition. Furthermore, unitary judicial budgeting has often gone hand in hand with still another unifying concept, state court financing. In this, all state courts submit all revenues raised through their own actions (fines, fees, and forfeitures) to one place (the state general fund) and receive their funding through appropriations from one source: the state legislature. State unitary judicial budgeting usually accompanies state court financing, but the converse is not always true. For instance, California has state court financing but not unitary judicial budgeting. The federal judiciary has both.

The state court administrator, like the Director of the Administrative Office of the United States Courts, oversees another aspect of court unification: a judicial civil service system. All court employees are under the supervision of one system, which hires, retains, promotes, transfers, demotes, fires, and retires them. Thus, courts gain control over all the people who perform judicially related duties. Previously, some employees who worked in the courts were members of the executive branch of governments. In state trial courts, for example, deputy sheriffs provided security but were county executive branch personnel. They were comparable to deputy marshalls, who performed the same function in federal courts but worked for an executive branch agency. Other court employees worked within an overall state, county, or city civil service system, which also included legislative and executive branch employees.

The state court administrator follows the federal counterpart with regard to other characteristics of court unification. First, this official exercises the authority to assign judges and court staff members across and within jurisdictions. The administrator can more effectively utilize such employees by shifting them temporarily to those jurisdictions where they are most needed—for instance, from courts with light caseloads (usually rural trial courts) to those with heavy burdens (mostly urban trial courts). Second, this official oversees the preservice and in-service education of judges and other court employees, typically offered in one place, a subdivision of the state court administrator's office. Third, the same official often supervises an integrated judicial management information system like that of the federal court system. This form of computerization links courts at the same level, courts at different levels, and all courts to the state court administrator's office. Information can be readily disseminated throughout the system. If, for instance, a court where defendants are appearing on one charge can find out where they are also wanted by another court, such as for violating bail or failing to pay fines or fees. Moreover, states have taken this form of unification a step further by not only integrating court operations but also integrating the courts with other state and local justice system agencies, such as police departments, prosecutors' offices, and probation and parole offices. So far, there is no federal counterpart.

State court unification also encompasses two other features, neither of which exists at the federal level. One is the establishment of a judicial performance commission, which represents one place where all allegations of judicial misconduct can be heard. Its decisions also exert a unifying impact on the behavior of judges, subjecting them to one set of expectations and one range of sanctions from reprimand to removal. The other is merit judicial selection. In pure form, it involves the establishment of one body—a judicial selection (or qualifications) commission, which examines the backgrounds of all possible candidates for judicial vacancies at all levels and compiles a list of what it regards as qualified individuals. All candidates must be certified by the commission. When vacancies occur, the governor is required to fill them by selecting someone only from the certified list. In one variation, the process is reversed. A governor is allowed to nominate candidates, contingent upon subsequent (rather than prior) commission approval before they can take office. The commission is not required to compile a list of qualified candidates. Instead, it handles nominees on a case-by-case basis, approving or rejecting them as it deems appropriate. In another variation, a judicial election is added and held within several years after a candidate takes office, regardless of whether there was prior or subsequent commission approval.

SKEPTICISM

The spread of court unification at the federal and state levels has taken place despite much skepticism. One source is rooted in the entrenched political sway of localism. County and city governments, for example, do not want to relinquish their budgetary oversight and concomitant financial control over trial courts in their jurisdictions. Hence, they resist unitary judicial budgeting and state court financing. They also do not want to give up control over court personnel. Thus, they fight efforts to replace elected court clerks with judicially appointed court clerks or court administrators. And, they do not want to entirely let go of their responsibility for court security. Furthermore, justices of the peace do not want their offices to be eliminated and absorbed into a unified state court system. Typically, these officials are unsalaried, lack a legal education and a license, and derive their compensation from finding defendants guilty of minor offenses and fining them. They are often so politically well-organized that their position is secured in the state constitution and therefore cannot be abolished by statute.

Another source of skepticism is more intellectual than political. Some acknowledge that, for decades, the trial courts in most states were too decentralized, too subservient to local culture and pressures, and too individualistic. They were virtually unsupervised by the highest state court and varied greatly in their performance. They needed at least a degree of court unification, although exactly what that entailed should depend on the peculiar milieu of each state or jurisdictions within it. But, to such skeptics, court unification cannot be treated as a one-size-fits-all type of remedy for judicial dysfunctions across and within states. Dogmatic fervor allegedly accompanies court unification and ignores the particular historical legal, political, economic, social, and cultural factors. A high degree of court unification may fit some environments but not others. Advocates of court unification often pursue their goal of a structurally simplified and centrally administered system despite the lack of contextual knowledge. Consequently, there is no one best way of organizing and managing court systems, regardless of the specific local circumstances. Thus, it is therefore as doctrinaire to view court unification like a law of nature as it would be to espouse decentralization under all circumstances.

CONCLUSION

This article has provided a brief description and analysis of six aspects of court unification: definition, preeminence, origin, federal courts, state courts, and skepticism.

However, most writings on the subject discuss it as if it were fundamentally a matter of structure and administration. The desired outcome is an increase in the number of case dispositions, a quicker flow of filings through trial and appellate assembly lines of judicial systems. The result is usually considered from an empirical rather than a normative perspective. There is insufficient consideration of whether the eventual upshot will be a genuinely more just court system, greater public satisfaction, and more widespread respect for the nation's potpourri of court systems. These are presumed to accrue in proportion to an increase in court unification as automatically as day follows night.

FURTHER READING

Fish, P.G. *The Politics of Federal Judicial Administration*; Princeton University Press: Princeton, NJ, 1973.

Friedman, L.W. *A History of American Law*, 2nd Ed.; Touchstone Book: New York, 1985.

Friesen, E.C., Jr.; Gallas, E.C.; Gallas, N.M. *Managing the Courts*; The Bobbs-Merrill Company, Inc.: Indianapolis, IN, 1971.

Gallas, G. The conventional wisdom of state court administration: A critical assessment and an alternative approach. Justice Syst. J. **Spring 1976**, *2* (1), 35–55.

Gerth, H.H.; Mills, C.W. *From Max Weber: Essays in Sociology*. Oxford University Press: New York, 1946.

Hays, S.W.; Graham, C.B. *Handbook of Court Administration and Management*. Marcel Dekker, Inc.: New York, 1993.

Hofstadter, R. *The Age of Reform*; Vintage Books: New York, 1955.

Pound, R. The causes of popular dissatisfaction with the administration of justice. Rep. Am. Bar Assoc. *29* (Part 1), **1906**, 395–417.

Rottman, D.B.; et al. *State Court Organization 1998*; United States Department of Justice (Office of Justice Programs, Bureau of Justice Statistics): Washington, D.C., 2000, URL: http://www.ojp.usdoj.gov/bjs/.

Saari, D.J. *American Court Management*; Quorum Books: Westport, CT, 1982.

Taylor, F.W. *The Principles of Scientific Management*; W. W. Norton and Company, Inc.: New York, 1967 (orginally published in 1911).

Tobin, R.W. *Creating the Judicial Branch: The Unfinished Reform*; National Center for State Courts: Williamsburg, VA, 1999.

Vanderbilt, A.T. *Minimum Standards of Judicial Administration*. Law Center of New York University: New York, 1949.

Wilson, W. The study of administration. Polit. Sci. Q. **June 1887**, *2*, 199–222.

Courts, Financing the

John K. Hudzik
Michigan State University, East Lansing, Michigan, U.S.A.

C

INTRODUCTION

Courts are large, complex organizations.[a] With growth in workloads and programs, judicial branch costs have increased steadily (e.g., about 250% between 1982 and 1997).[1] The emergence of performance standards (e.g., the American Bar Association (ABA) trial court standards)[2] and legislative performance expectations lead to increased scrutiny of the resource planning and management practices of courts. Pressure throughout the public sector to cut costs requires greater attention to efficiency in the judicial branch through improved practices. Perceived declines in public confidence and satisfaction with the courts require that more attention, and hence resource allocations, are given to customer services.

The growth in trial court costs places stress on local government's ability to pay. The movement toward state financing of trial courts and away from traditional forms of local financing is one consequence. Generally, larger judicial branch budgets, especially when aggregated into a single appropriation under state financing, draw greater political and public attention to how much the judicial branch costs and hence to how well it is managed. Critiques of judicial branch organization and performance have resulted in legislated reforms in the interest of greater efficiency and effectiveness. In several states, the adoption of state financing was tied to court reorganization and consolidation, performance standards, and greater controls over judicial branch allocation and expenditure decisions. Even where local financing remained the norm, increased costs brought increased supervision of expenditures by local commissioners and executives. In many jurisdictions, courts are treated as another agency of the executive branch, in direct competition with them for scarce resources, and subject to the same kinds of budget planning requirements and controls. These changes are particularly salient for U.S. trial courts.

HISTORICAL CONTEXT FOR JUDICIAL BRANCH BUDGETING AND FINANCIAL MANAGEMENT

Court reform, court unification, and unified court budgeting provide a context for understanding contemporary practice and debate over judicial branch budgeting and financial management. These terms originated in the court reform movement of the first half of the twentieth century; however, their impact has affected the reform efforts since the 1980s as well. Early reforms mainly sought to reduce variance in the number and types of trial courts and in local rules and procedures, and also sought to impose minimum standards of conduct and practice. The principal outcome was to create "one court of justice" in each state.

Besides unification and simplification, the three other components of early reforms included centralized rule making, centralized management, and centralized budgeting.[3] The Supreme Court imposed rules to be adhered to statewide, and offices of state court administrators were established to increase centralized monitoring and control. In theory, centralized budgeting offered the ultimate means for unification because state-level preparation of the judicial branch budget would permit control over resource allocations at all levels and greater accountability to statewide standards.[4]

Centralized budgeting requires state financing to be meaningful, and many see unification as being incomplete without state financing. Yet, although all states moved to establish one court of justice, principally through rule making and some features of central monitoring, few adopted state financing. Using 1979 data, one study reported that only 8 states' trial court systems were entirely or nearly entirely funded by the state; another 14 states had mixed state/local funding, with the state supplying more than half of that funding; and 28 states had mainly locally funded trial courts.[5] Since 1985, more states have moved toward state financing, most notably California in the mid-1990s, and Florida has projected to do so by 2004. However, a mixture of state and local funding remains the norm in most states, and somewhat less than one-half the states' trial court systems mostly remain locally funded.

---

[a]Portions of this article explore similar issues, although from a somewhat different perspective, to those in an article by the author in the 2002 American Bar Association's volume on the administration of justice.

Encyclopedia of Public Administration and Public Policy
DOI: 10.1081/E-EPAP 120010821

State financing does not require highly centralized allocation and expenditure control from the state capitol. It is possible (and some would say preferable) to have relatively decentralized management control systems while using state financing. This was, for example, part of the plan in the mid-1990s as California moved from mainly local to state support of trial courts.

By the 1970s, court reform acquired a new emphasis that was less oriented toward reducing variance because, for the most part, one court of justice had been achieved in the states. The new goals were increased efficiency and effectiveness through continuing consolidation and centralization. In 1967, the President's Commission on Law Enforcement and the Administration of Justice[6] awakened reform interest throughout the criminal justice system and touted rational planning, consolidation, and coordination as means for dealing with the inequities and inefficiencies spawned by a political system that devolved too much to local control. The justice system, it was argued, was fragmented and in the absence of coordination it was inefficient and ineffective.

The press, for greater efficiency and effectiveness throughout government, was reinforced by the tax-cutting fever of the 1980s and 1990s, and by economic downturns in the early 1980s and early 1990s. Improved court organization and management practices were directed toward reducing costs and improving services. The movement toward state financing was seen not only as a means to force additional reforms, but also as a way to shift the cost burden from local jurisdictions, which were increasingly unable to pay (for new staff, new programs, and for ''black hole'' areas of expenditure, such as indigent defense).

EXPENSIVE AND DIVERSE JUDICIAL BRANCH OPERATIONS

Judicial branch costs have become a significant public expense, even though they constitute less than 2% to 3% of total state expenditures. State and local trial court expenditures nationwide are in the range of $12 billion to $15 billion annually; state appellate court expenditures (intermediate and supreme) add to the total. There are over 26,000 trial and appellate judicial positions nationwide and over one-quarter of a million other key court personnel.[7] Large limited-jurisdiction urban trial courts spend over $100 million annually and, even among the smaller courts, expenditures of several million dollars per year is not unusual.

Growth in cost has been driven partly by inflationary factors, but there are other important causes. The types of programs and services offered by trial courts have broadened considerably. Multiple formats of alternative dispute resolution, pretrial diversion programs, multiple types of pre- and post-trial services, help centers for unrepresented litigants, victim-witness assistance programs, a range of postadjudication programming, and more customer-oriented services are common in courts today (and were not, even 20 years ago). Speciality courts are also much more common (e.g., mental health courts, drug courts, benches specializing in complex litigation). Growth in complex litigation such as toxic torts or class action product suits has increased the unit cost of trials on the civil side. Since the 1960s, annual caseloads have grown dramatically, and since 1988, caseloads have grown annually at an average of 5% per year. There are now nearly 1 million felony convictions[8] per year in state courts.

INTERBRANCH RELATIONS AND CHALLENGES TO JUDICIAL-BRANCH INDEPENDENCE

Increased costs have led to interbranch funding disputes. At both local and state levels, legislative and executive branches desire to manage judicial-branch line items, and program allocations have strengthened, and in some cases threaten judicial-branch independence. In addition, because most states have a mixed model of state and local funding for trials courts (including most of those states that are largely either state funded or locally funded), achieving coherency in the funding plan is challenged by inconsistencies between local and state priorities. Unitary budgeting is thereby challenged. Shifting or unclear agreements about which level of government pays for what (e.g., for court security, indigent defense, certain kinds of local programs, or shared use of local infrastructure, such as the County Clerks Office) can lead to ''playing off'' funding behaviors between levels of government.

Courts are sometimes caught between levels of government that argue over which gets to use court-generated fee and fine revenue. This revenue, generated by limited jurisdiction courts, typically produces surplus over cost, whereas the costs of general jurisdiction courts are rarely if ever covered. In the aggregate, trial courts produce insufficient revenue to meet costs; thus, pressure mounts on them to improve collection rates, tempting legislatures and executives to increase fee and fine rates.

Stormy interbranch relationships over funding led to a spate of court-ordered funding actions during the 1970s, 1980s, and 1990s. Local funding authorities were angered. Bad press, challenges to public confidence in the courts, and concerns that judges were becoming too closely involved in local politics resulted. In some states, funding disputes between trial courts and local authorities reached sufficient heat and frequency that the Supreme Court and state court administrative offices imposed mediation and cooling off periods, and required Supreme Court or state court administrator approval before a local court order for funding could be enforced.

It was hoped that state financing would remove funding disputes from the local political thicket, and it usually did. However, in some states, it merely moved disputes to the state level. In some states, unpopular court decisions (e.g., the Supreme Courts striking down legislation as unconstitutional or otherwise flawed) led to retribution by legislative or executive branches in the form of "short" appropriations, or refusal to fund certain programs or new judicial positions. State financing also did not necessarily solve the problem of unfunded mandates from the state legislature or from ballot initiatives (e.g., few, if any new funds followed to offset the impact of "three-strikes" legislation, which increased the number and cost of trials).

Interbranch funding disputes attracted sufficient national concern during the 1980s and early 1990s that the State Justice Institute funded a national conference on funding the courts in 1995. The conference was cosponsored by the National Conference of Chief Justices, the ABA, and the National Conference of State Legislatures. During a conference plenary session, the problem was defined as a basic dissonance between the underlying assumptions of branches. The judicial branch asserted that it had the constitutional responsibility to define funding levels adequate to discharging its responsibility, and the legislative branch asserted its constitutional power of the purse. As a result, separate and coequal branches of government seemed inherently adversarial.

An alternative set of behaviors and assumptions was offered as a means to restore interbranch harmony. The legislative and executive branches, it was suggested, should 1) appropriate a lump sum to the judicial branch; 2) allow the judicial branch to set priorities in allocating the lump to branch-set priorities; 3) permit the judicial branch authority to reallocate funds during the year; 4) permit the carryover of unspent funds across fiscal years as an incentive for implementing efficiencies; and 5) consult the judicial branch about effects on workload and attendant costs from proposed legislation. The qui pro quo was that the judicial branch should 1) become more managerially proactive in controlling costs; 2) improve or change practices in the interest of greater efficiency and effectiveness (e.g., by enforcing a firm continuance policy); 3) promulgate and be held accountable to performance standards; and 4) review priorities, discard nonperforming programs, and reallocate resources to more important needs. Although not directly addressing whether the size of the "lump" might be sufficient in the first place, the quid pro quo sought a balance between power of the purse and judicial independence and sought to reestablish a functioning relationship between coequal branches.

Interbranch relations remain problematic. Some state legislatures have become more engrossed in reviewing judicial branch line items, and some executives have begun to treat the judicial branch as another agency of executive branch in terms of budget submission and review. In a little over one-third of the states, the judicial branches' budgets are submitted directly to the executive branch and its review lenses; in a little less than one-half the states, they are submitted directly to the legislature (and to both simultaneously in the remainder). In states where the judicial branch retains a fair degree of budgetary discretion and avoids the worst forms of interbranch warfare, politically astute and administratively skilled state court administrators and chief justices have been essential to forging positive and regular working relationships with key legislative and executive leaders. Similar skills of presiding judges and trial court administrators are equally essential in locally funded systems. Perceived managerial competence[b] and leadership has also risen in importance; courts perceived to be well run and that meet performance expectations appear to have a better environment for negotiating budgets and are given greater latitude to manage their affairs.

PROFESSIONALIZING THE MANAGEMENT OF COURT RESOURCES

In the early 1970s, the National Advisory Commission on Criminal Justice Standards and Goals, followed by the ABA, underscored the importance of professional administrators to improving the performance of the criminal justice system, including the courts. With the blessing and active involvement of Chief Justice Warren Burger, the Institute for Court Management (ICM) was formed in the early 1970s, with the mission of creating a professional cadre of court administrators for U.S. trial courts. Phase I of ICM's core curriculum consisted of five topical areas, including budgeting. All graduates of ICM had to successfully complete the budgeting segment (along with the others). This requirement was conscious recognition that competent budgeting and financial management skills were increasingly essential in court administration.

In 1998, the National Association for Court Management published the results of its 3-year national study to identify the "core competencies" of court managers. Ten competencies were identified and "Resource Allocation, Acquisition, Budget, and Finance" was one. The study

---

[b]For twenty years, the author has informally surveyed presiding judge and court administrator attendees at executive management programs. They have been asked to identify the factors most important to favorable relations with funding authorities. In the 12–15 factors usually identified, managerial reputation of the leadership team is typically ranked within the top two or three factors.

and yet-to-be published curricular guidelines concluded the following:

> The allocation, acquisition, and management of the court's budget affect every court operation, and arguably, determine how well, even whether, courts achieve their mission in the American political system. Allocating, acquiring, and managing financial resources is a core court management competency carried about by court managers, both judicial and administrative, and other court staff.... Effective court performance requires that court leaders—the executive team—have the ability: to set priorities and to manage competing demands on existing court resources in ways that build credibility, both internally and externally; to link resource requests to fundamental court purposes; to state court needs and objectives clearly and compellingly; and to protect judicial independence and essential court functions while constructively negotiating with elected and appointed executive leaders and their staff.[9]

This quotation is striking for many reasons, but for two in particular. First, there is implicit recognition of just how important and complicated budgeting and financial management have become in the modern court system. Second, there is reinforcement of the points made during the 1995 interbranch conference about the need for constructive behaviors between the judicial and the other branches of government.

The complexity of interbranch negotiations is the new reality. It is reflected in presiding judge rules in many states that assign presiding judges formal responsibility for the sound financial management of their courts. Although the addition of professional court administrators has helped, the sometimes complicated relationship between presiding judges and their court administrators confounds attempts at sound financial management and good interbranch relationships. Most judges, including presiding judges, have not had much management experience or much if any training in management practice. In addition, it is not unusual for presiding judges to change by election or rotation every 2 years or so. Frequent changes in leadership make consistency in budget decision making and the building of stable interbranch relationships problematic. The frequent turnover in presiding judges underscores the need for continuous training opportunities in budgeting and financial management.[c]

---

[c]For an introduction to trial court budgeting, see Ref. [10]. Also, the relationship between sound financial management skills and other managerial and leadership skills was underscored by the NACM study mentioned in Ref. [9]. In that study, sound financial management was linked to relating resources to fundamental court purposes, to clear communication of purposes, and to an understanding of budget planning formats, problem solving skills, performance measurement, audit and request justification.

SHIFTS IN THE MIX OF LOCAL/STATE FUNDING

The movement toward state financing of trial courts has been underway for a number of years. By the late 1990s, nearly one-half of the states had wholly or substantially state-financed trial court systems and one-third of the states had substantially locally funded systems. The remainder were mixed with heavy components of both state and local support. Few states have full state financing (e.g., local jurisdictions almost always pay for facilities, and most locally funded systems still have state support for judges' salaries). However, the movement overall is toward greater portions of trial court budgets being supported through state appropriations.

The rhetoric for and against state financing involves numerous claims. The arguments in favor include greater equity in funding across trial courts, greater efficiency through scale, improved management quality, and more funds overall because of access to state coffers. Opponents assail proponents' claims as unsupported and predict that there will be loss of local control, more red tape, greater volatility in appropriations, simplistic formula funding, and a stifling of innovation.

Few if any of the claims on either side have been systematically researched, although there is strong anecdotal evidence that courts from the poorest jurisdictions are helped by state financing, that state financing makes it easier to temporarily shift judicial resources in a state, and that certain economies of scale are possible for programming that crosses trial court or jurisdictional boundaries (e.g., data systems).

OTHER REVENUE

As general fund appropriations fail to keep pace with perceived needs, the search for alternative sources of revenue intensifies. Fees and fines are substantial sources of court-generated revenue for both state and local jurisdictions (and for some states' trial courts directly). However, fees and fines as a direct source of budget support for court operation are inherently problematic. If courts are expected to fund their own costs through fees and fines (or perhaps even produce surplus), it is not hard to imagine how justice and entrepreneurial motives could clash. Fees set too high limit access to the judicial system, and fines levied against the poor and indigent suffer from low collection rates if no consideration is given to the ability to pay. Fine revenue is a function of both the amount of the fine and its collectability. In addition, numerous states have already raised fee schedules over the last several years, calling into question the "market's" ability to absorb greater increases.

Numerous states, when moving from local to state financing, experienced difficulties accurately predicting how much of the cost of state assumption would be offset by redirecting fee and fine revenue from the local to the state level. Part of the problem was local government resistance to losing the fee and fine revenue, even though the local jurisdiction would no longer have to fund trial courts. Compromises were sometimes reached, which left a portion of the fee and fine revenue at the local level. Another problem is that the costs of state assumption have been underestimated significantly in several states. This, coupled to shortfalls in fee and fine revenue, yield continuing controversy between the judicial and other branches of government.

Grants, principally from federal sources, such as the State Justice Institute or Office for Juvenile Justice and Delinquency Prevention, and from similar kinds of state programs are increasingly used by courts to fund innovation, special programs, or services and to provide enhancements not supported by general fund appropriations. However, grants rarely if ever provide ongoing funding, and pressure is put on court administrators to find replacement dollars for successful programs, either from other external sources or through internal reallocation. Federal reimbursement programs such as those for IV-D child support enforcement can return revenue for meeting federal objectives. Federal anticrime legislation adds potentially renewable revenue for targeted purposes (e.g., drug courts).

Other ideas for supplementing revenue include the use of volunteers, who if properly trained and assigned, supplement the personnel budget. Other ideas periodically surface such as ''cut-of-the-action'' schemes for the civil side of the docket where winners pay the courts a percentage of their ''take'' if they refuse mediation or others forms of dispute resolution, which are usually less costly than full-scale trials.

EMERGING ENVIRONMENTS
FOR ACQUIRING RESOURCES

The reality of court funding is that a new relationship is evolving between the judicial branches and the other branches, one that requires a quid pro quo, mutual responsibilities, and ongoing dialog across branch leadership on issues of court costs and financing. Regardless of promising alternative revenue sources, general fund appropriations, whether from state or local levels, will remain by far the largest source of money for funding judicial branch operations.

Courts will have to compete with other agencies of government for scarce resources. The *acquisition* of resources and the *allocation/management* of existing re-

sources will increasingly be tied. Improved practice with the view of increasing both performance and efficiency can potentially yield resources for internal reallocation, as well as improve court management reputation with funding authorities.

Priority setting in resource requests helps to focus attention on the most important of needs, and a strategic approach to priority setting can help courts to focus requests rather than to diffuse or constantly change them. Frequent shifts in funding priorities send a message of unclear leadership. Multiyear budget planning will be required for many areas of new expenditure, such as for technology and other forms of organizational change, because the costs of these can only be met over several years. This would further suggest that courts increasingly will need to ''stabilize'' their strategic expenditure priorities, thinking through not only multiyear commitments to achieving long-range objectives, but also whether proposals involving new costs (e.g., new personnel) unintentionally commit the court to additional multiyear obligations. New multiyear obligations reduce allocation flexibility by tying up ever larger amounts of money. In addition, in times of fiscal constraint, funding authorities, although generally inclined not to incur new obligations of any kind, are particularly resistant to new multiyear rather than one-time obligations. One-time or 1- or 2-year commitments are more palatable than permanent new allocations.

Interest in having line agencies self-fund or at least partially fund new initiatives is growing as a means for leveraging central resources (and vice versa). Self-funding or partnership funding requires courts to institutionalize organizational change as a means of freeing resources (e.g., by discarding low value-added programs or figuring out how to do the job differently and less expensively, such as, substituting court recorders for court reporters, or looking for partnerships with other public agencies or the private sector (e.g., in collections).

Forced efficiency reductions to court budgets by funding authorities is another reality with which court managers may have to contend. ''Efficiency'' reductions are a way for funding authorities to create policy reserves for reallocation, as well as a means to squeeze fat out of line agencies. In the process, the ongoing budget is deliberately underfunded as a means to force organizational change (typically 1% to 3% in a given year). Agencies can usually absorb these over 1 or 2 years, but over longer periods they are nearly bled to death unless fundamental change takes place either in the service mix or in how tasks are performed. Shorting budgets in the interest of creating policy reserves or in forcing efficiencies may or may not be publically announced, but are real nonetheless.

Change required to improve judicial branch efficiency and effectiveness will require a reshaping of programs and services that in some instances will require forming partnerships and effective cross-walks between the judicial and other branches of government, and between courts and other agencies of the criminal justice system. Joint commissions, interagency working groups, and standing interbranch staff analysis groups will be needed not only to review proposed legislation, but also to cooperate in meeting the costs of the many new kinds of programs that have become a more or less standard part of court programming.

REFERENCES

1. *Sourcebook of Criminal Justice Statistics 2000*; Pastore, A.L., Maguire, K., Eds.; 3–4. http://www.albany.edu/sourcebook/Sourcebook of Criminal Justice Statistics/1995/pdf/t12.pdf (accessed December 2001).
2. American Bar Association Commission on Standards of Judicial Administration. *Standards Relating to Court Organization*; American Bar Association: Chicago, 1974.
3. Berkson, L.C. The emerging ideal of court unification. Judicature **March 1977**, *60*, 372–382. Lawson, H.O.; Gletne, B.J. *Fiscal Administration in State-Funded Courts*; National Center for State Courts: Williamsburg, VA; 1981.
4. Skoler, D.L. Financing the criminal justice system: The national standards revolution. Judicature **June–July 1976**, *60*, 32–38.
5. Hudzik, J.K. Rethinking the consequences of state financing. Justice Syst. J. **1985**, *10* (2), 135–158.
6. The President's Commission on Law Enforcement and Administration of Justice. *The Challenge of Crime in a Free Society*; Commission Report: Washington, DC, 1967.
7. Rottman, D.B.; Flango, C.R.; Cantrell, M.T.; Hansen, R.; LaFountain, N. *State Court Organization 1998*; NCJ 178932, U.S. Department of Justice, Office of Justice Programs, Bureau of Justice Statistics: Washington, DC, June, 2000; 7–18. Also see, Pastore, A.L.; Maguire, K., Eds. *Sourcebook of Criminal Justice Statistics 2000*, http://www.albany.edu/sourcebook/Source book of Criminal Justice Statistics/1995/pdf/t120.pdf (accessed December 2001), 26–30.
8. *Sourcebook of Criminal Justice Statistics 2000*; Pastore, A.L., Maguire, K., Eds.; 453. http://www.albany.edu/sourcebook/Sourcebook of Criminal Justice Statistics/1995/pdf/t540.pdf (accessed December 2001).
9. NACM Professional Development Advisory Committee. Core competency curriculum guidelines: History, overview, and future uses. Court Manager **1998**, *13* (1), 6–18.
10. Tobin, R.W. *Trial Court Budgeting*; Court Management Library Series, National Center for State Courts: Williamsburg, VA, 1996.

Criminal Justice Public Policy

Barbara Sims
The Pennsylvania State University at Harrisburg, Middletown, Pennsylvania, U.S.A.

INTRODUCTION

Perhaps one of the most complex of all public institutions is the American criminal justice system. With its myriad of agencies, each with a distinct and critical role, this open-ended system projects a picture of "doing justice" as though it were a well-oiled machine. People come in contact with the system through the police, and a decision is made at the street level whether that individual will stay in the system. If an arrest is made, the offender becomes part of a process that is often referred to as "assembly line justice."[1] Developing and implementing policies up and down the justice assembly line is no easy task. One jolt to the system can send rippling effects throughout all of these agencies, leaving criminal justice administrators in the unenviable position of having to make some rather "rushed" decisions. Even when administrators know that change is coming, as opposed to unplanned changes that occur as the result of events outside the purview of criminal justice agencies (demographic changes, for example, or drastic downturns in the economy), navigating the waters of how best to make those changes, and where, is not without its problems.

As is the case with any public agency, criminal justice agencies must constantly struggle on two major fronts. First, they must contend with a public that has become increasingly more concerned about crime and wants something done about it. Second, they must walk through political mine fields when attempting any approach to the crime problem. The result is that more often than not, crime policies are based on knee-jerk reactions to the more celebrated cases (O.J. Simpson, Willie Horton, etc.) as opposed to careful projections about the consequences of actions taken. It is those cases, after all, that are in the public eye, and as such, are closely paid attention to by the people elected to serve them.

As argued by Hancock and Sharp,[2] many different groups have an interest in shaping crime policies, as it has become one of the most "popular for legislative, executive, and judicial manipulation and debate." Sometime in the decade of the 1980s, the American criminal justice system moved from one of due process and concern for the constitutional rights of individuals to a crime control model seemingly intent on incarce-

rating more individuals and for longer periods of time. The idea that "criminals" could be rehabilitated and turned into law-abiding citizens gave way to punishment as retribution, or "just desserts." Americans began to see crime as the result of a lenient criminal justice system as opposed to wayward youth in need of assistance and supervision.

With "tough on crime" the new mantra of both major political parties, complete with phrases such as "war on crime" and "war on drugs," the 1990s ushered in a time of unprecedented incarceration rates. The U.S. prison population rose from 196,429 in 1970 to 1.9 million in 1998, with the incarceration rate rising from 96 per 100,000 in 1970 to 452 per 100,000 in 1998. Compared with other countries, the United States is clearly out of step, with Japan at 42 out of 100,000 and Canada at 111 per 100,000.[3] The new policies directed at waging the war on crime, and that resulted in this exponential growth in the incarceration rate, are the subject of this article. As will be illustrated, there are other negative consequences associated with these new crime policies in addition to skyrocketing corrections budgets that most state departments of corrections cannot afford. Further, a great deal of research has produced convincing evidence of certain policies that could work to curb crime in the United States. Findings from that research are also discussed, and an argument is made for a more sensible approach to the crime problem.

PUBLIC POLICY AND CRIMINAL JUSTICE

Dye[4] defined public policy as anything that government chooses to do or not to do. Government leaders in the United States began using the "war" rhetoric when talking about crime policies beginning with President Lyndon Johnson in 1965, followed by Richard Nixon in 1969, and in 1989, President George Bush declared a war on drugs.[5] As a result, policy makers have chosen to react to America's crime problem, as Walker[5] argues, by implementing certain "crime control fads," such as "selective incapacitation," or "three strikes and you're out" legislation. These policies are in one day and seemingly out the next, and what government has not

Encyclopedia of Public Administration and Public Policy
DOI: 10.1081/E-EPAP 120011075

chosen to do is to examine with some clarity the extent to which they do, or do not, work.[5]

Problems Associated with Defining the Extent and Nature of America's Crime Problem

According to Welsh and Harris,[6] the policy process begins by clearly defining the problem at hand. In the criminal justice policy arena, the problem is crime in U.S. communities. Determining the extent of the problem, however, is not without its problems. There are three ways that are used to measure crime in the United States, none of which is problem free. Referred to as official data, the Uniform Crime Reports (UCR) consists of collected and disseminated crime statistics as reported to the F.B.I. by about 16,000 local, county, state, and federal law enforcement agencies. The major problem with UCR data is the fact that it contains only reports of crimes known to the police and for which an arrest was made. Data from the National Crime Victimization Survey (NCVS), an annual survey of 60,000 U.S. households, seeks to uncover the so-called "dark figure" of crime by identifying those crimes not known to the police. NCVS data is criticized primarily for undercounting certain crimes (sexual and domestic abuse, for example), and because it does not contain crimes associated with businesses or commercial operations. Finally, self-reported studies ask people to disclose their crime and delinquency and may fill the gap between UCR and NCVS data. Those types of offenses often missed by both, public order crimes, for example, or drug use, may be more accurately measured through self-report studies. The major problem with self-report studies, however, is the fact that even guaranteed confidentiality and complete anonymity, individuals may not fully disclose their crimes to the interviewer.

Some criminologists have sought to get around the problem of reliability and validity when it comes to measuring crime by comparing the findings from different sources. The most successful of these undertakings have come from those comparing UCR data with NCVS data. Blumstein et al.[7] for example, have found that, despite the different methodologies associated with both, similarities exist, especially for robbery and burglary. For policy makers, an awareness of the problems associated with any crime data is an important first step in the policy process.

Selective Incapacitation: Identifying and Locking Up the Career Criminal

A good example of a modern-day criminal justice policy is that of selective incapacitation, a term used to describe the process of identifying and incarcerating so-called "career criminals." Conservatives believe that if those

individuals responsible for most of the crimes, those repeat offenders for which the threat of punishment does not appear to work, can be weeded out and targeted for long prison terms, crime rates will decline. The notion of the career criminal was first examined through cohort studies, the most well-known and respected of which is that by Wolfgang et al. in 1972.[8] The authors tracked 9945 boys born in the city of Philadelphia in 1945 through their 18th birthday in 1963, using data from police reports, school records, and children and youth services. The overall finding was that the majority of all crimes (52%) associated with this birth cohort were committed by only 6% of these individuals. Approximately 627 of the 9945 individuals were identified by Wolfgang and his colleagues[8] as chronic or career criminals.

When Wolfgang et al.'s[8] results were published, crime rates had been rising. According to Walker,[5] the time was ripe for any program that promised to get tough with chronic, repeat offenders. Selective incapacitation seemed like the perfect solution. The problem, however, is how best to predict future offending. In a thorough examination of the "prediction problem," Walker[5] concluded that even if the criminal justice system could accurately identify the career criminal, the next hurdle for criminal justice policy makers would be to determine just how much crime could actually be prevented by incarcerating them. He argues that the three ways often used to predict criminal behavior might not be successful. Those three ways are: 1) the actuarial method, such as insurance companies use when predicting driving behaviors by certain groups, the young driver, for example; 2) examining prior criminal history; and 3) extensive clinical evaluations by the use of trained experts.[5]

Attempts at predicting future violent behavior

When researchers have sought to develop instruments that can be used to predict future criminal behavior, they have often worked with a sample of incarcerated individuals. Wenk et al.[9] examined closely the records of 4146 youths held by the California Youth Authority using an instrument that included information about prior criminal record coupled with the youths' histories of violent behavior and substance abuse. In this identified group of juvenile delinquents, 104 went on to become violent recidivists.[9] Through a series of psychological evaluations and interviews, Wenk et al.[9] discovered that only about half of the 104 recidivists were identified correctly. The remainder of the group were false negatives, that is to say, they were not predicted to become violent recidivists, but ultimately did. Further, 404 people who were predicted to become violent recidivists did not. Had the instrument been used with the original sample and had the goal been to selectively incarcerate those predicted to become violent recidivists, these "false positives" would have been facing incarceration for violent crimes they would never commit.

The Wenk et al.[9] study and others like it suggest that selective incapacitation is a policy that cannot succeed unless better prediction instruments can be developed to get around the problem of false negatives and false positives. In addition, prediction is further complicated by disagreement among researchers about just how much crime these so-called "career criminals" commit. As Walker[5] points out, "If the averages are low (as some suggest they are), we will not get that much payoff in terms of crime reduction."

"Gross incapacitation" versus selective incapacitation

Selective incapacitation, predicting future criminal behavior, will not work to reduce crime in the United States. The evidence suggests that the courtroom work group (attorneys, judges, jurors, etc.) is just as accurate as are prediction instruments. This means that the overall goal of this particular criminal justice policy is not feasible. Public policy is a fluid process, however, and what has happened in criminal justice is the rapid move toward "gross incapacitation," "locking up a lot of people and sending them to prison for long terms."[5] The goal of carefully selecting individuals who are likely to cause the most harm to society has fallen away.

In 1987, a report titled "Making Confinement Decisions," published by the U.S. Government Printing Office and authored by Edwin Zedlewski, purported to illustrate the public value of gross incapacitation. Using "costs to society" as his starting point, Zedlewski[10] calculated that every dollar spent on incarceration actually saves taxpayers $17. Other researchers have pointed out the problems associated with Zedlewski's formula upon which his estimates were based (for an excellent review of the subject, see Ref. [11]). Primarily, the critical problem is with his estimate of the number of crimes committed a year by criminals. Career criminals specialists cannot agree on what that figure might be, but Zedlewski chose the higher value of 187 crimes per year per criminal offender, as opposed to the more often used figure of about 18 crimes a year. Yet, policy makers relied heavily on Zedlewski's[11] calculation and continued down the path of gross incapacitation. One of the best examples of such a policy is mandatory sentencing laws, more commonly referred to as "three-strikes and you're out."

Three-Strikes Legislation

Mandatory sentences are extremely popular with the public and with elected officials. This popularity comes from, as noted above, the media play of some criminal justice cases. When 12-year-old Polly Klass was kidnapped and murdered by a twice-convicted felon named Richard Davis, out on parole at the time of the murder, the citizens of California were outraged. This outrage led to California's three-strikes law, soon followed by other states. Today, 26 states have some sort of mandatory sentencing statute. The major premise of these laws is that for the third convicted felony, offenders will receive a life sentence in a state prison.

The goal of mandatory sentencing

Just as selective incapacitation is a policy aimed at reducing crime in the United States, so is mandatory sentencing. A major step in the policy process is to ensure that the targeted population is clearly defined and that steps to reach that population are equally clear. Determinations as to the feasibility of the proposed policy are crucial prior to implementing major changes. As mentioned above, the courtroom work group works not unlike other street-level bureaucrats to put up roadblocks to the implementation of newly enacted crime policies. This use of discretion has been described by Lipsky[12] as a more important deciding factor as to how policies will be implemented than is the power of the executive or legislative branches of government, the sources of many crime policies.

Through mandatory sentencing, states are able to send a message to the public that something is being done about crime. This message meets the goal, in policy terms, of engaging in symbolic politics.[13] Once again, a public in fear of crime has been reassured that government is cracking down on felony recidivists. Interest groups, those rallying around the family of young Polly Klass for example, are able to influence state legislators. Through widespread media footage of proposed mandatory sentences, the political climate becomes ripe for such legislation, as indicated by a series of public opinion polls.

Based on an excellent analysis of the policy process as it applies to "three-strikes" legislation, Welsh and Harris[6] came to the conclusion that this law was doomed to fail because of poor planning. They posed the question, "What evidence was used to demonstrate a need for change in U.S. crime policies dealing with felony offenders?"[6] As was pointed out above, although the perception in society was that crime was rising, actually, it had been declining. Thus, instead of working to assure the public that crime was not on the rise and to educate the public about the negative consequences that sometimes come with poor planning, politicians were "too eager to cater to the perceived public will, rather than documented problems."[6]

Implementing three-strikes legislation

Welsh and Harris[6] pointed out that prior to the implementation of any policy, all parties involved in that implementation should be fully apprised of their responsibility. The policy process requires brainstorming about possible obstacles to implementation and how those obstacles will be overcome. It became clear almost immediately that mandatory sentencing laws would be met with resistance or simply ignored. Why? The answer can be found again in the manner in which employees in bureaucratic organizations apply discretion in the everyday job of doing the public's business.

Welsh and Harris[6] described the plea bargaining process, for example, and the manner in which prosecutors circumvent the law by reducing the charges. Mandatory sentencing laws give the prosecutor a tool to dangle before offenders in an effort to get them to plead guilty. Police officers may engage in more selective arrest policies, and at the federal level, it has been shown that the law has been used sparsely since its inception in 1994.[6] Walker[5] pointed out that Tennessee, New Mexico, and Colorado have not used their three-strikes law at all, and that Wisconsin only used its law once in the first two years after it was enacted.

Evaluating three-strikes laws

In the policy process, it is important to determine to what extent the goals and expected outcomes are being met. Evaluation research provides public agencies with this critical information. With three-strikes laws scarcely being used as they were intended, however, evaluating the impact of them is tenuous at best. The finding that criminal justice personnel often ignore the law or somehow get around it is the type of information that comes from what is termed "process evaluation." Unlike impact assessments that provide outcome or impact measures of the new program, process evaluation is designed to determine whether any new program was implemented the way it was intended. Clearly, the usurping of the law by the courtroom work group means that these types of sentencing structures are not being implemented the way they were intended.

First, mandatory sentences add a tremendous burden to an already-overworked criminal justice system. With more at stake, defendants who are in a district where mandatory sentencing has been fully implemented are demanding jury trials. In California, third-strike cases represent about 24% of all trials, raising court costs for local counties. Too, the increase in the number of defendants waiting in jail for their trial dates has resulted in astronomical increases in local corrections budgets. In Los Angeles, the new three-strikes law cost the county an additional $169 million in the first two years of its implementation.[5]

Another important piece of evidence from attempts to evaluate mandatory sentences is that they probably do little to bring down crime in the United States. On one hand, and as pointed out above, it is difficult to argue that such laws are tailored toward identifying an individual's propensity to commit future crime.[5] On the other hand, Walker[5] argued that under such a policy, older offenders are likely to end up in three-strikes statistics at about the time they would have naturally aged out of the crime-prone years. This means that there are more and more older people being sent to prison, and costs associated with housing the elderly inmate are quite substantial, adding even more to correctional budgets.

Welsh and Harris[6] summarized the projected effects of California's three-strikes law by stating that fully implementing this policy will:

• Triple California's prison population over the next 25 years.
• Cost an average of $5.5 billion more each year for the next 25 years.
• Corrections could consume 18% of the state's spending by the year 2002.

PROMISING APPROACHES FOR CRIMINAL JUSTICE POLICY MAKERS

The above discussion about two modern-day crime control policies was used as a backdrop for demonstrating that not unlike any other public institution, policy making in criminal justice is often driven more by symbolic politics than sound policy analysis. The nation's "war on crime" and "war on drugs" rhetoric has created "get tough" approaches targeted toward the so-called "career criminal" and major drug dealers. Much of the literature suggests, however, that these policies have failed, by not being implemented correctly or by not doing much to reduce crime rates. Instead, these policies have produced a plethora of negative backlashes against an already over-extended system. This leaves many forward-thinking and innovative criminal justice administrators thinking seriously about what *can* work to curb serious crime in local communities.

Programs such as Pennsylvania Governor Mark Schweiker's "Weed and Seed" programs, a state-sponsored offshoot of the federal government's program by the same name, are beginning to stress approaches that are founded in research. Weed and Seed programming calls for the "weeding out" of hot spots of crimes in specially targeted areas by local law enforcement, in conjunction, in some cases, with the State Police. "Seeding" programs then seek to involve community-based agencies in a joint effort to provide these targeted areas with critical resources needed to correct problems found to be conduits for crime. Terminology such as "research-based" initiatives, "blueprints for change," and "best practices" is emerging in the Weed and Seed policy arena, not only in Pennsylvania, but also in similar programs around the country.

These research-based initiatives are just that: programs that have been evaluated and found to have a positive impact on local communities and their ability to curb serious and violent criminal activity. Funding from state and federal sources is being tied to conditions placed on grant recipients to conform to specific guidelines for program implementation and future evaluation of the new programs coming on line. The balance of this chapter examines some of these programs and argues for a more "sensible" approach to the crime problem. This approach is grounded more in sound policy analysis and processes and less in symbolic politics.

Research-Based "Promising Approaches" to Curb Crime in U.S. Communities

In 1998, Lawrence Sherman and his colleagues[14] at the University of Maryland released a report to the National Institute of Justice in which they summarized a comprehensive review of evaluation research in the area of crime prevention. In the report, entitled "Preventing Crime: What Works, What Doesn't, What's Promising," Sherman et al.[14] identified seven institutional settings in which these promising approaches take place: 1) communities; 2) families; 3) schools; 4) labor markets; 5) places; 6) police agencies; and 7) other agencies of criminal justice. The authors first distinguished between the terms "practice" and "program," a distinction that is important for policy makers and practitioners. They suggest that a practice is any activity that is continuous in a particular setting, and it can only change if a new government policy restricts it or takes the place of the old practice. A program, on the other hand, is much more specific. It is a *focused effort* to affect change in a crime prevention setting. As such, unlike routine practices, actual program implementation and continuation requires a continuing source of resources. Given the amount of resources going toward crime prevention programs, it is not surprising that the Department of Justice would have a great interest in the findings from an examination of any evaluation of those programs.

The Maryland Report, as the Sherman et al.[14] study has come to be called, takes a great deal of evaluation

research and condenses it into more simple terms. At the end of each chapter, where various authors addressed those programs associated with the above-identified seven institutional settings, there is a concluding section that summarizes "what works" and "what doesn't." Beginning with the community setting, it appears that what will work to bring down crime is gang violence prevention focused on reducing gang cohesion and mentoring programs targeted toward 10- to 14 year-olds. What does not work at the community level are community mobilization efforts and gun buyback programs, both of which have received a great deal of attention and press coverage in the recent past.

Family programs identified in the Maryland Report as being promising are long-term frequent home visitation programs that have been shown to reduce child abuse, and family therapy for delinquent and predelinquent youth. In the school setting, programs aimed at improving communication about rules and behavior norms appear promising (anti-bullying programs, for example), as long as those rules are consistently reinforced. Also, comprehensive instructional programs that focus on such issues as stress management, problem solving in social settings, and self-control, and that are maintained over an extended period of time, appear promising. To bring down substance abuse by young people, behavior modification programs, in addition to the comprehensive instructional programs previously listed, are needed, according to Sherman et al.[14]

Programs that do not work in the school setting to reduce substance abuse are peer-group counseling sessions and single efforts at offering more recreation activities. Further, Sherman et al.[14] concluded that education programs based on fear arousal, moral appeal, and information dissemination will not work to bring down the use of drugs by young people.

When it comes to labor market programs aimed at reducing crime in U.S. communities, Sherman et al.[14] identified such programs as short-term vocational training programs for older male parolees. Promising approaches include intensive training programs (Job Corps, for example) for at-risk youth, prison-based vocational programs for adults, and the development of Enterprise Zones. What does not work, according to Sherman et al.[14] are subsidized work programs for at-risk youth and pretrial diversions for adult offenders (making employment training and finding a job a condition of case dismissal).

Targeting "places" and policing programs can work together to prevent crime in local communities but only under certain conditions.[14] These two approaches are often termed "situational crime prevention through problem-oriented policing." One of the more promising approaches is one in which some form of crime analysis is conducted (mapping of types of serious crimes, for example) followed by a well-designed police effort in those targeted areas. In fact, of all the studies examined in the area of policing, Sherman et al.[14] argued that none other is effective as a clearly, focused program. Simply putting more police on the streets is not going to do much to bring down serious crime. Saturated patrol may have some short-term effect, but that effect fades over time without a more focused, targeted approach.[14]

Finally, and in the area of corrections, evaluation studies point to the conclusion that the following programs can work to reduce repeat offending: prison-based therapeutic community treatment of drug-addicted offenders; structured and focused treatment programs that use multiple components; programs that allow for a substantial amount of contact between the treatment provider and the offender; and programs that address the characteristics of the client.[14] As alluded to above, programs that focus only on incapacitation, and that lock up less serious offenders for longer periods of time, are likely to be extremely expensive and to not do much to bring down serious crime.

SUMMARY AND CONCLUSIONS

This "tip of the iceberg" summary of the many studies examined in the Maryland Report suggests that there is ample evidence on which criminal justice policy makers and practitioners can rely when it comes to making critical decisions about program changes in the criminal justice system. The move toward incarcerating more individuals and for longer periods of time, while symbolically pleasing to many, may have failed as a crime prevention approach. Practices such as gross incapacitation through mandatory minimum sentences have been shown to overburden the criminal justice system while not doing much to reduce recidivism. More sensible approaches to the crime problem seem warranted, and research-based initiatives are appearing as blueprints for needed change. The question becomes, "To what extent are policy makers and practitioners willing to pay attention to such reports as those produced by Sherman and his colleagues?"

Petersilia[15] has argued that research has affected how policy makers "*think* about issues, problems, and the range of viable solutions." In her example, it is the *conceptual* use of research findings that may be more pronounced than the so-called *instrumental* use of research findings. In other words, although the effects of research on policy development may not always be measured and thus can be easily missed, the effects are there, nonetheless, and present themselves in more subtle ways. The word gets out. It may not come through an examination of peer-reviewed journal articles by criminal justice practitioners, but there is now a substantial amount of reporting of program evaluations appearing in trade journals and being posted on government web sites to support an argument that research findings are now being disseminated beyond mere academic circles. As stated above, many sources of funding are tying that funding to programs that are research based. Making use of criminal justice research in the policy process has actually begun to take place.

Criminal justice research is better preparing practitioners and policy makers to analyze the problem at hand. The policy process is informed, through the research, about the history of the problem and the outcome of previous interventions. Using the information gained in this first step of the process, goals and objectives of any new program can be determined. The process can then move toward a discussion, by key stakeholders, about the feasibility of implementing the new program, including brainstorming about any obstacles that might be faced at that point in the process. During the actual designing of the new program, the research findings add even more to the mix through assisting policy makers and practitioners in determining the target population, how clients will be selected, and even what type of staff will be needed to fill the new positions created by the program. Finally, building in an evaluation component is critical to new program development and implementation. Impact evaluations of the new program can be used then to make any necessary changes to the new program and to guide others in development and implementation of similar programs.

As Welsh and Harris[6] argued, "Rarely does planning go smoothly, and it takes willpower, a clear vision, and lots of communication to remain rooted in the planning process." They also add that "planned changed" is better than ad hoc decision making, and that it "increases the likelihood of successful interventions."[6] With the safety of the community at stake, planned changes in the criminal justice policy arena, following closely the policy analysis process as well as research-based recommendations for what will work to accomplish that goal, are most certainly called for.

REFERENCES

1. Packer, H.L. *The Limits of the Criminal Sanction*; Stanford University Press: Stanford, CA, 1968.

2. Hancock, B.W.; Sharp, P.M. *Public Policy, Crime, and Criminal Justice,* 2nd Ed.; Prentice Hall: Upper Saddle River, NJ, 2000.

3. Bureau of Justice Statistics. *Sourcebook of Criminal Justice Statistics—1998*; Government Printing Office: Washington, D.C., 1999.

4. Dye, T. *Understanding Public Policy,* 4th Ed.; Prentice Hall: Englewood Cliffs, NJ, 1981.

5. Walker, S. *Sense and Nonsense About Crime and Drugs: A Policy Guide,* 5th Ed.; Wadsworth Press: Belmont, CA, 2001.

6. Welsh, W.N.; Harris, P.W. *Criminal Justice Policy and Planning*; Anderson Publishing: Cincinnati, OH, 1999.

7. Blumstein, A.; Cohen, J.; Rosenfeld, R. Trend and deviation in crime rates: A comparison of UCR and NCS data for burglary and robbery. Criminology **1991**, *29*, 237–263.

8. Wolfgang, M.; Figlio, R.M.; Sellin, T. *Delinquency in a Birth Cohort*; University of Chicago Press: Chicago, IL, 1972.

9. Wenk, E.A.; Robison, J.O.; Smith, G.W. Can violence be predicted? Crime Delinq. **1972**, *18*, 339–402.

10. Zedlewski, E.W. *Making Confinement Decisions*; Government Printing Office: Washington, D.C., 1987.

11. Zimring, F.E.; Hawkins, G.E. The new mathematics of imprisonment. Crime Delinq. **1988**, *34*, 425–436.

12. Lipsky, M. *Street Level Bureaucracy: Dilemmas of the Individual in Public Service*; Russell Sage: New York, NY, 1980.

13. Stolz, B.A. *Criminal Justice Policy Making: Federal Roles and Processes*; Praeger: Westport, CN, 2002.

14. Sherman, L.W.; Gottfredson, D.; MacKenzie, D.; Eck, J.; Reuter, P.; Bushway, S. *Preventing Crime: What Works, What Doesn't, and What's Promising*; National Institute of Justice, Department Of Justice Programs: Washington, D.C., 1998.

15. Petersilia, J. Policy Relevance and the Future of Criminology. In *Public Policy, Crime, and Criminal Justice,* 2nd Ed.; Hancock, B.W., Sharp, P.M., Eds.; Prentice Hall: Upper Saddle River, NJ, 2000; 383–395.

Customer Service

Evan M. Berman
University of Central Florida, Orlando, Florida, U.S.A.

INTRODUCTION

Customer service is the activity of identifying and satisfying the needs of customers. In public organizations,
the term "customer" is broadly used to include program
clients, external customers of public organizations, internal customers (for example, employees who depend on the
service of other employees in the same public organization), and citizens. The term "customer service" is sometimes also used to connote a standard, such as in the
statement: "The customer service in this public agency is
world class." Customer service is currently viewed as
essential to maintaining sound stakeholder relations.

RECENT DEVELOPMENT OF CUSTOMER SERVICE IN THE PUBLIC SECTOR

Although customer service is arguably as old as public
administration, the importance of providing customer service by U.S. public organizations dramatically increased
in the mid-1980s. This increased emphasis followed that
of U.S. corporations in the late 1970s and early 1980s,
during which period U.S. corporations lost market shares
to Japanese and other foreign firms. These firms had
innovated a new approach to product development based
on the rapid utilization of customer feedback. The new
approach, based on a management philosophy called
"Total Quality Management" (TQM; see below) resulted
in products with superior reliability and more user-
oriented features. American firms quickly and successfully copied the new management philosophy that emphasized customer service in an effort to counter the
advantage that foreign rivals enjoyed. Later, this new
management philosophy was widely adopted by other
organizations; TQM was broadly introduced into the federal government during the late 1980s, and local and
state governments followed in the early 1990s.

In broader context, the period of the late 1970s and
early 1980s is seen as a nadir in stakeholder trust toward
American private and public institutions. Trust in the
federal government reached a record low in the early
1980s. Whereas in the mid-1960s about 62% of respondents answered the question: "How often do you trust
the federal government to do what is right?" with "most

of the time" or "some of the time," by the early 1980s,
this percentage had dropped to about 18%. It is probable
that concerns in the late 1970s and early 1980s of high
unemployment, high inflation, two energy crises, and
deceit by elected officials (for example, Watergate) contributed to broad public distrust, as did poor service to
program clients and citizens. State and local governments
enjoyed a higher level of trust but were not immune from
public apathy and cynicism. With 20/20 hindsight, the
turn to customer service in the public sector can be
viewed as an effort to address causes of citizen distrust
that were narrowly related to program quality and service. The mantra "to run government as a business"
(that is, borrowing management practices from the private sector) regained importance as a dominant ideology
in the late 1980s. Although some critics regarded the
customer service emphasis as a blind adoration of capitalist values and as inconsistent with the fiduciary and
political responsibilities of government, most observers
believed that an increased orientation toward customer
service was long overdue in government, as it had been
in business.

Customer service is an integral part of TQM. This
management orientation emphasizes meeting customer
needs through a comprehensive strategy that encompasses
empowerment, process analysis and improvement, customer service, partnering and performance measurement,
and benchmarking.[1] Although initially organizations attempted to implement TQM as a coherent management
strategy, today it is widely regarded as a management
philosophy that encompasses a broad range of specific
strategies, among which is customer service. As a management philosophy, the core values of TQM are to 1)
identify, meet, and exceed the needs of customers (and
other stakeholders); 2) strive to produce services right the
first time (that is, reduce errors that upset stakeholders
and cause rework and increased costs); 3) use systematic
analysis to evaluate and improve services delivery; and
4) consistently support workers in their efforts to improve quality and meet customer needs. TQM invites
managers to think broadly about customer service and
needs and to develop innovative approaches to improve
service delivery. Many applications of TQM begin with
emphasizing meeting and exceeding customer expectations, in part by focusing on customer complaints. Hence,

Encyclopedia of Public Administration and Public Policy
DOI: 10.1081/E-EPAP 120010869

customer service is usually the first strategy in TQM efforts. Other strategies that affect customer satisfaction are discussed below.

Generally, the principles of establishing a customer service strategy involve addressing the following questions: 1) How do our long-term plans serve the needs of our customers?; 2) What specifically do customers expect from us?; 3) How can we exceed their expectations?; 4) Are we exceeding customer expectations?; 5) What can we do to further improve upon our satisfaction of customer expectations?; and 6) Do we have the capacity to meet our customer service goals? Regarding the latter, is the commitment of managers and employees as well as technology infrastructure, consistent with our customer service goals? If not, how can we improve?

THE IMPORTANCE OF ORGANIZATIONAL CULTURE

Widespread agreement exists that customer service outcomes reflect an organization's values, that is, the daily expectations and practices of organizational members as they deal with customers and plan their work. All organizations have expectations for how staff should deal with customers; they vary with regard to these expectations, including the extent that customer service is viewed as being important. At issue are not generally espoused values such as "we value our customers highly," but rather the specific guidelines that all employees and managers are given as they go about their daily work. The specifics matter, because general statements provide little guidance and assurance in the face of specific daily challenges. Some examples of specific customer service values that are found in organizations are the following:

- We always stay focused on resolving the customer's problem or need.
- We value changing what or how we do it to increase customer satisfaction.
- We want our customers to think good things about us.
- We use policies and procedures as guides to resolving requests or complaints, not as excuses for saying "no."
- We try to provide the entire service as soon as possible; at a minimum, we provide a concrete result within 24 hours.
- We always address customers with dignity, respect, and calm.
- Whatever you do, do not be the source of any customer complaint.
- We acknowledge and reward superior customer service in ways that matter to our employees and managers.

Agreement also exists that top managers play a crucial role in making customer service an important organizational value. Organizational values usually face competing challenges from other values, such as being responsive to elected officials, getting along with others in the organization (not rocking the boat), and respecting rules and policies. One role of top management is to clarify the importance of customer service, for example, "our customers vote for our elected officials, who are our bosses," in relationship to other competing values. When customer service is made an important priority, top management will also have to resolve, or provide a process for resolving, various issues that come up as staff attempt to achieve customer service, such as unclear or contradictory rules or agency practices. Top managers need to be consistent in these clarifications and in their support for others who deal with these clarifications.

Another role is ensuring that specific customer service values are ingrained throughout the organization. Broad-scale commitment is necessary, because customers come in contact with a broad number of employees. Also, employees often depend on other employees to satisfy the needs of "their" customers, thus, all employees must work in concert to achieve customer satisfaction. The job of top management is to ensure that organizational values relating to customer service are driven deep into every nook and cranny of the organization, affecting the actions and thought processes from the highest managers to the lowest-ranking employee. To this end, top management must ensure that the structure of rewards and expectations promotes its values with regard to customer service. Typically, middle managers and supervisors become accountable for ensuring that these values receive broad-scale support in their units. Training is usually part of instilling these values at lower levels (see further). Managers can also be asked to lead by example. Continuing top management support appears to be critical, even after work groups have embraced it. In short, top management plays an important role in shaping customer service actions of organizational members.

CHALLENGES TO ACHIEVING CUSTOMER SERVICE IN THE PUBLIC SECTOR

Organizations that begin on the path toward improved customer service often face a number of issues. An important top management task is to acknowledge these issues and to assist in clarifying them for others. First, many authors have noted differences between private and public sector "customers." Individuals often wear different hats as they interact with governments. Citizens expect something different from government than only easy access to its services, and these different roles are sometimes seemingly at odds: for example, as citizens, many residents value speed limit enforcement in their neighborhoods, but as motorists, they might not value enforcement. Public organizations must acknowledge these different roles and accommodate the differences or assist others such as elected officials in doing so.[2] Also, the fact that individuals play different roles does not preclude improvement in their interactions with public agencies.

Second, in some public organizations, customers are involuntary, such as regulated businesses, taxpayers, and inmates. The paradox is presented that it may be impossible for regulators to satisfy the regulated, when their requests are denied, and actions are monitored. According to Bruce McClendon,[3] surveys show that customer satisfaction has little to do with whether a request is approved; it is more strongly affected by whether employees are knowledgeable, respectful, and creative in finding solutions, and whether services are accessible, accurate, consistent, timely, and dependable. Explanations need to be given for how and why requests are granted or denied. The physical appearance of service areas is also a factor. It seems reasonable that inmates might be approached in a similar way; for example, they might be told why a request cannot be immediately granted.

Third, customer service is consistent with orientations toward empowerment, sometimes more than is customary in some organizations. It is obvious that "one size does not fit all," thus employees will need to use a little ingenuity in dealing with customer requests. Empowerment means holding employees and managers accountable for results; rather than using rules and regulations to stipulate how service is to be provided, agencies may do better by providing a few stipulations as to what cannot be done (or which may require supervisory review), and a mix of general principles that aid in providing a high level of customer service. This approach gives employees considerable latitude in meeting customer needs, but it also implies the possibility of inappropriate actions that might be taken. How managers specify the latitude and responsibility of employees, and how they deal with customer service failures (for example, through punishment or as learning opportunity) greatly shapes employee orientations toward customer service efforts.

Fourth, customer service requires attention to resources and rewards. It is sometimes alleged that public agencies have inadequate resources for training and insufficient flexibility for monetary rewards that might shape behavior. Rather, the resources required for training are quite minimal, though they are higher when investments are made in information technology as well. Reinforcement of employee and manager customer service behavior need not involve (many) monetary resources. A consensus

exists that monetary rewards matter less in shaping behavior than immediate and consistent feedback; public acknowledgement (for example, in staff meetings) for tasks well done can be provided. In addition, formal approaches may be considered, such as incorporating customer service criteria in performance appraisal criteria, though these are seldom sufficient in the absence of informal approaches to instill and maintain strong customer service values.

CUSTOMER SERVICE TRAINING

Employees need to be told what actions are expected of them. Thus, training is usually part of an effort to increase customer service. Training usually begins with identifying the need for customer service, assessing current customer service outcomes and practices, specific organizational values and practices, applications to specific situations relevant to employees, and formulating an implementation or follow-up plan that discusses how change will be monitored, improved, and rewarded. Customer service training involves basic principles as well as advanced applications.

The basic principles of customer service are that it is about achieving real results for customers and the organization; it involves more than a slogan or merely putting on a friendly smile, although the latter may be part of the improvement. Customer service is attitude and expected behaviors that should always be present. The above values clarify specific attitudes and expectations that may be expected of employees. They involve matters of direct interaction (for example, how phone calls are transferred), as well as willingness to change the way that services are provided (for example, electronic acceptance of applications, whereas previously, only in-person or hard copy applications were accepted).

The basic principles include a four-step process of personal interactions with customers: open, interact, ask for an expression of satisfaction, and conclude. Examples in role playing are provided that help staff develop ways of dealing with customers that have a wide range of conditions, such those that are indecisive, irate, overly insistent, angry, violent, as well as those that are within a normal comfort zone in dealing with public agency personnel. These applications should be relevant to the actual jobs of employees. Basic training sometimes also includes a site visit or film of an organization that is known for excellence in customer service.

Advanced training involves the steps for creating customer service teams in departments, which are tasked with recommendations for improving customer satisfaction, and implementing specific proposals.[4] Training involves a range of practical steps that such teams should take, as well as challenges that may stem from resistance or apathy. Advanced training also involves the development and use of a customer satisfaction survey. Although they are increasingly used, voluntary surveys are distinguished from systematic (or scientific) surveys. Voluntary customer surveys are completed at the initiative of the customer; although they are not generalizable to all customers, they do provide an early warning signal to managers about problems that may need to be addressed. Scientific surveys use a representative sample of customers; such surveys are generalizable, and are used for benchmarking customer service satisfaction.

MEASURING CUSTOMER SERVICE OUTCOMES

Organizations are increasingly measuring the level of their customer service:[5]

1. Customer and citizen surveys are used to measure perceptions of customer service and program outcomes.
2. Objective measures, such as performance measures, are used track performance in areas relevant to customers.
3. Trained observers are used to observe conditions against customer service standards.
4. Other methods, such as tracking customer complaints or compliments or conducting focus groups, are also used.

Scientific surveys are increasingly used in public administration to obtain the perceptions of a representative sample of citizens or program clients. Such surveys typically include such questions as ''Have you had contact with any (our office) employees during the last 12 months?,'' and, if yes, ''Thinking about your recent experiences with _____, please tell me whether you strongly agree, agree, disagree or strongly disagree with the following statements:''

• The employees were helpful.
• The employees treated me with respect.
• The employees were friendly.
• The service was provided without mistakes.
• The service was provided in a timely manner.
• The service experience exceeded my expectations.

Responses to such items help assess average customer satisfaction. In many cities and counties, it may be found that more than half of residents have had some contact with an official from the jurisdiction, that most residents have only one or two interactions, and that the perceived level of customer service during those interactions significantly affects overall perceptions of the jurisdiction. It thus follows that customer service is of great importance. Of course, surveys are also used to assess perceptions about the overall functioning of programs and policies.

Systematic surveys are not usually designed to provide much insight into the reasons for high or low levels of customer satisfaction; they usually only provide a valid snapshot of the current performance. Focus groups and customer comment cards can shine light on the causes of customer satisfaction. Customers can identify specific program features that are irritants to them, hence, suggesting or implying alternative courses of action for improvement. Although these source of information are not generalizable, they stimulate insight and, hence, possible action.

Performance measurement is increasingly used and often involves collecting objective data about program activities and outputs. For example, an emergency response program might measure the number of calls acted on within the first 2 minutes of receipt, the average time it takes for a response team to appear at location, the percentage of response teams that show up exceeding a standard time, the number of dispatched teams that did not involve emergency, and so on. Many of these administrative data are related to customer satisfaction, and continuous improvement is likely to affect customer satisfaction.

Trained observers are not always widely used, but they, too, can help assess customer service outcomes. For example, parks programs often used trained observers to rate the appearance of their facilities in ways that are relevant to customer satisfaction. Role playing is also used to assess customer interactions, such as at service request counters, toll booths, and telephone response centers.

DESIGNING PROGRAMS AND SERVICES WITH THE CUSTOMER IN MIND: SOME EXAMPLES

In recent years, public organizations have found many ways to improve customer satisfaction. In most instances, this involved redesigning the ways in which services are delivered, as well as the manner in which customers and citizens are addressed. Even basic operations such as answering citizen requests are redesigned. In many agencies, a standard is now set that calls are answered on or before the fourth ring, and that a ''warm'' hand-off is used when transferring calls; no longer are callers transferred to voice mail boxes. Standards are also set for resolving caller queries, such as immediately or within 24 hours for most calls. Fairfax

County, VA has implemented software that tracks the status of citizen requests.

Agencies have also redesigned their services to better meet the needs of citizens, often through information technology. Sometimes, this has required rethinking of the business that they are in. For example, the U.S. Internal Revenue Service (IRS) has reshaped itself from an agency that only attempts to maximize revenue to one that now aims to ensure that citizens pay the correct amount of taxes; taxpayers can call the IRS for advice on ways to reduce their tax burden. The IRS has also improved the way it deals with tax refunds. To satisfy its customers, the IRS has an electronic system, whereby taxpayers call to learn whether their Income Tax Returns have been received, when they will be processed, and when a check has been issued for any refund that is claimed.

Transportation agencies have also increased their customer orientation. The Orlando-Orange County Expressway Authority operates over 80 miles of toll roads in Orange County (Florida). It was among the first of such agencies to use an electronic system for collecting tolls, thus reducing traffic backups at toll booths during rush hour and allowing users of the electronic to drive through toll booths without stopping. This saves users many minutes in their commute. It is now considering expanding the use of its electronic payment device for such alternative uses as parking. Other agencies are also inquiring about the feasibility of providing users with real-time updates of traffic situations and alternative routing.

Many jurisdictions are now investing in their Internet web site to improve their delivery of services. On many sites, citizens are now able to download a wide range of forms that they might need, such as for regulatory inspections or enrollment. They are also able to electronically submit these forms, through e-mail or by on-line completion of them. Governments are also beginning to use their Internet sites for e-commerce, such as for paying parking fines or providing user fees for services. They are also able to order government products on-line, such as special reports and T-shirts and mugs. In short, agencies are increasingly rethinking how they can satisfy and exceed the expectations of citizens, through what they do and how they do it.

REFERENCES

1. Berman, E. *Productivity in Public and Nonprofit Organizations: Strategies and Techniques*; Sage, 1998.
2. Leon, L.; Denhardt, R. The political theory of reinvention. Public Adm. Rev. **2000**, *60* (2), 89–97.
3. McClendon, B. Customer service for regulators. Public Manage. **1996**, *78* (5), 19–22.
4. Otey, D. Citywide customer satisfaction in Peoria. Public Manage. **2001**, *83* (1), 15–18.
5. Epstein, P. Measuring the Performance of Public Services. In *Public Productivity Handbook*; Holzer, M., Ed.; Marcel Dekker, 1992; 161–194.

Data Integrity

Theo Edwin Maloy

West Texas A&M University, Canyon, Texas, U.S.A.

INTRODUCTION

Data integrity is the assurance that information can only be accessed or modified by those authorized to do so. Integrity measures include controlling the physical environment of networked terminals and servers, restricting access to data, and maintaining rigorous authentication practices. Data integrity can also be threatened by environmental hazards, such as heat, dust, and electrical surges.

Physical measures to protect data integrity include making servers accessible only to network administrators; keeping transmission media, including cables and connectors, covered and protected to ensure that they cannot be tapped; and protecting hardware and storage media from power surges, electrostatic discharges, and magnetism.

Network administration measures to ensure data integrity include maintaining current authorization levels for all users; documenting system administration procedures, parameters, and maintenance activities; and creating disaster recovery plans for power outages, server failure, and virus attacks.[1]

PHYSICAL AND ENVIRONMENTAL SECURITY

Alternative processing methods for critical functions should be available in case local area network services are disrupted for extended periods:

- Servers should be located in a physically secure area accessible only to the network administrators.
- Where every workstation may be used as a server, all devices should be under supervision when in use and should be physically secured when not in use.
- Transmission media should be covered and protected to ensure unauthorized personnel or devices cannot tap them. Transmission media should be physically secured in conduits, trenches, or ducts to prevent electronic eavesdropping.
- Hardware and storage media should be protected from excessive dust, dirt, heat, and moisture. Hardware and storage media should be protected from power surges, electrostatic discharges, and magnetism. There should be an uninterruptible power supply attached to the server.

- Combustible materials should not be stored near network equipment, and fire and smoke detectors should be installed near network equipment. Carbon dioxide fire extinguishers should be located near network equipment.
- Power cords should be covered to ensure they are not a hazard. Cables and connectors should be installed in accordance with organization standards and the National Electrical Code and the National Fire Protection Code.
- Sensitive, confidential, or critical documentation, files, and software should be stored in a fireproof safe when not in use.
- Interconnection device access should be disabled after hours.

NETWORK OPERATING SYSTEMS

Access to network operating system software, files, and commands should be controlled and appropriately restricted:

- Each node attached to the network should be uniquely identified.
- The network should provide the ability to log and to audit network activity when a security threat has been identified.
- The network should provide the ability to produce reports on network utilization and on audited events.
- Access privileges granted to read, modify, create, and delete files should be limited to only what is necessary. Data should be available only to users authorized to access that data.
- Access privileges granted to execute only, read, update, create, and delete programs and applications should be limited to only what is necessary. Access to utility programs should be controlled, and their use should be monitored. Each authorized user should be uniquely identified.
- The network should authenticate by password each authorized user. Users should be able to change their passwords and should be required to change their passwords at a predefined interval. Passwords associated with special privileges, such as the administrator's login, should be changed more frequently.

Encyclopedia of Public Administration and Public Policy
DOI: 10.1081/E-EPAP 120010798

Passwords should not be displayed and should be passed on the network in a secure format. A specific number of unsuccessful login attempts should result in the suspension of the login ID.

- Users should be automatically logged out or the workstation should be locked after a period of nonuse to prevent unauthorized access.
- Access to data or files classified as sensitive, confidential, or critical should be controlled appropriate to their classification. All sensitive data transmitted over the network should be encrypted if encryption is available.
- An audit trail of all station additions and deletions should be maintained.
- For authorized personnel, security tables and files should be easy to maintain. Additions and changes to the security tables and files should be effective immediately.
- The software should provide the ability to delegate administration of some functions and some users in such a way that the subadministrator can be assigned responsibility for those portions of the security tables and files that directly affect his or her organizational unit.
- Adequate network administration resources, including manuals and vendor support, should be available.

DATA AND SOFTWARE BACKUP

Regular backups of production software should be performed, with backup devices kept in a secured location, protected from environmental hazards and unauthorized use. Periodic backup copies of the entire system should be made, as well as selected backup copies of specific files as needed. Backup procedures should be documented, and external labels should be used to identify the contents of backups. Data sensitivity and security should be monitored during recovery from a backup and should be reinstated once recovery is complete. Alternative processing methods for critical functions should be available in case local area network services are disrupted for extended periods.

NETWORK ADMINISTRATION

Managers and supervisors within the departments using the local area network should understand the importance of security, and should communicate that importance to departmental personnel:

- Network administrators should be trained, and a backup administrator should be identified.

- Access privileges for transferred or terminated employees or employees on leave should be reviewed and adjusted.
- Network administration functions should be limited to specific users and to specific network nodes.
- A current inventory of workstation and file server hardware and software should be maintained.
- Users should be aware of the license and contract restrictions that affect their use of the local area network. Copyrighted software and documentation should not be copied, and concurrent access to single-user software should not be allowed on the local area network.
- Users should be informed about their responsibilities for equipment, software, data security, and copyrighted material.
- Requests to develop or change programs and files should be approved by authorized personnel.
- Adequate documentation of system administration procedures, parameters, and maintenance activities should be maintained.
- Contact information should be available for vendors or others who have agreed to provide network maintenance.
- A disaster recovery plan should be in place that lists symptoms, possible causes, preventative measures, and recovery steps for power outages, server failures, tape backup unit failures, application software failures, network operating system upgrade failures, cabling failures, client failures, and virus attacks.
- Procedures should be in place to ensure that all modifications to routing tables and translator tables are properly authorized, that such changes are made only by authorized personnel, that changes are tested prior to implementation, and that an adequate audit trail exists to document all modifications.
- Procedures for changing or updating existing programs and files should be established and maintained. Vendor-supplied software changes and updates should be tested, installed, and distributed where appropriate.
- Users should be informed of changes such as new versions of software changes and the effects of those changes, and users should be informed about any restrictions on using hardware and software for personal use.

COMMUNICATION CONTROLS

Access to interconnection devices including gateway servers, routers, and bridges, should be limited to authorized users. Monitoring systems should be in place to detect unauthorized access attempts. Interconnection device access should terminate automatically if unauthorized use is detected and should be disabled after hours. Access to the communication devices' configuration files and tables should be restricted to authorized network administrators.[2]

PUBLIC ADMINISTRATORS' SPECIAL CONSIDERATIONS

Governmental agencies and private organizations that use public agencies' data must assure their customers, including individuals, firms, and other governmental entities, that the confidentiality and privacy of information they electronically collect, maintain, use, or transmit is secure. Information security is especially important when information can be directly linked to an individual or firm. Confidentiality is threatened not only by the risk of improper access to electronically stored information but also by the risk of interception during electronic transmission of the information.

Many government records require access signatures, but there is no national standard for security or electronic signatures. Each governmental entity must define its own security requirements. To satisfy the legal characteristics of a written signature, an electronic signature must identify the signatory individual, assure the integrity of a document's content, and provide strong and substantial evidence that will make it difficult for the signer to claim that the electronic representation is not valid.

Public Administrators should establish data integrity standards that conform to these generally desirable principles:

1. Improve system efficiency and effectiveness by leading to cost reductions or improvement of service from electronic transactions.
2. Meet the needs of the user community, particularly individuals, firms, and other governmental agencies.
3. Be consistent and uniform with other private and public sector data standards, including data element definitions and codes and their privacy and security requirements.
4. Have low additional development and implementation costs relative to the benefits of using the standard.
5. Be supported by an American National Standards Institute-accredited standards-developing organization or other private or public organization that will ensure continuity and efficient updating of the standard over time.
6. Have timely development, testing, implementation, and updating procedures to achieve administrative simplification benefits faster.

7. Be technologically independent of the computer platforms and transmission protocols used in electronic health transactions, except when they are explicitly part of the standard.
8. Be precise and unambiguous but as simple as possible.
9. Keep data collection and paperwork burdens on users as low as is feasible.
10. Incorporate flexibility to adapt more easily to changes in the infrastructure (including new services, organizations, and provider types) and information technology.

A master data dictionary providing for common data definitions should be developed and maintained. Data element definitions should be precise, unambiguous, and consistently applied. The transaction-specific reports and general reports from the master data dictionary should be readily available to the public. At a minimum, information presented will include data element names, definitions, and appropriate references to the transactions where they are used.

Security Standards

A security standard is a set of requirements with implementation features that individuals, firms, and governmental agencies must include in their operations to assure that electronic information remains secure. The standard need not address the extent to which a particular entity should implement the specific features. Each affected entity should assess its own security needs and risks and devise, implement, and maintain appropriate security to address its requirements. These measures must be documented and kept current.

There is no recognized single standard that integrates all the components of security (administrative procedures, physical safeguards, technical security services, and technical mechanisms) that must be in place to preserve information confidentiality and privacy as defined in the law. There are numerous security guidelines and standards in existence today, focusing on the different techniques available for implementing the various aspects of security.

There are several concepts on which a standard should be based:

1. The standard must be comprehensive. A standard must address all aspects of security in a concerted fashion.
2. The standard must be technology neutral. Because security technology is changing quickly, there should be flexibility in choosing technical solutions. A standard dependent on a specific technology or tech-

nologies would not be flexible enough for future advances.

3. The standard must be scalable. The standard must be implemented by all the affected entities, from the smallest firm to the largest government agency. A single-sized approach would be neither economically feasible nor effective in safeguarding data.[3]

Outsourcing and Privatization

Insourcing and outsourcing, usually called privatization in the public sector, describe a multitude of information technology options available in the marketplace. Total outsourcing is the decision to transfer assets, leases, staff, and management responsibility for information technology service delivery to a single third-party vendor that represents more than 80% of the information technology budget. Total insourcing is the decision to retain management and provision of more than 80% of the information technology budget internally. Selective sourcing is the decision to source selected information technology functions from external providers while providing between 20 and 80% of the information technology budget internally.

General outsourcing can be divided into selective, value-added, and cooperative outsourcing. Selective outsourcing is when one area of information technology, such as data center operations, is chosen to be turned over to a third party. Value-added outsourcing is when an area of information technology activity is turned over to a third party thought to be able to provide a level of support or service that adds value to the activity that could not be cost-effectively provided by the internal information technology group. Cooperative outsourcing is when a third-party provider, public or private, jointly performs some targeted information technology activities with the internal information technology department.

Information technology research has produced three major findings:

1. Conflicting stakeholder expectations place information technology managers in the precarious position of providing Rolls Royce service at a Chevrolet price. In general, senior management perceives the entire information technology function as a utility, and therefore, sets the information technology agenda to be cost minimization. Agencies and end users perceive that information technology critically contributes to operations, and therefore, sets the information technology agenda to be service excellence. Information technology managers are frustrated, because senior managers and users set conflicting agendas for information technology, expecting information techno-

logy managers to deliver Rolls Royce service at a Chevrolet price.

2. The published literature portrays an overly optimistic view of information technology outsourcing. The optimism exists, because reports are made during the honeymoon period when clients first sign an outsourcing contract, and clients and vendors possess high outsourcing expectations. Second, the literature only reports projected savings, not actual savings. Third, public reports underrepresent outsourcing failures, because few managers wish to advertise a mistake. Therefore, the literature misrepresents the spectrum of outsourcing experiences by focusing on the success stories.

3. Organizational members initiated outsourcing evaluations for a variety of reasons. Financial reasons included cutting costs, improving cost controls, and restructuring the information technology budget. Business reasons included returning to core competencies and devolving organizational and management structures. Technical reasons included improving technical services, gaining access to new technical talent, providing access to new technologies, and focusing the internal information technology staff on core technical activities. Political reasons included reacting to the efficiency imperative, acquiring or justifying additional resources, reacting to the positive outsourcing media reports, reducing uncertainty, eliminating a burdensome function, and enhancing personal credibility.

4. Successful sourcing evaluations compared vendor bids against a newly submitted internal bid, not against current information technology performance. When vendors submit bids that indicate savings, managers must question how the vendor proposes to reduce costs and not just attribute savings to economies of scale. In many cases, vendor bids were based on efficient managerial practices such as standardization, consolidation, centralization, and tighter controls—practices that internal information technology managers may be able to replicate if empowered to do so. Implementing cost savings measures required information technology managers to adopt policies that may not be readily agreed to by the agency units or by the agency's clientele.

5. Internal information technology departments possess superior cost advantages from some information technology cost drivers. Outsourcing vendors have an inherent data center operating cost advantage over small information technology departments, but they are comparable to large information technology departments. Internal information technology departments have comparable hardware purchase volume discounts with outsourcing vendors, but small depart-

ments have an inherent disadvantage. Internal information technology departments and outsourcing vendors have comparable software licensing costs. Internal departments have inherent advantages on agency expertise and organizational, marketing, and transaction costs. Outsourcing vendors have inherent advantages on technical expertise, research and development, and opportunity costs.

6. When managers decide to outsource, detailed contracts are more likely to be successful than relational contracts. Vendors are not partners unless profit motives are shared, and the profit motive is not prominent in the public sector. Many public and nonprofit organizations used vendors to satisfy their information technology needs for hardware and software upgrades, installation and maintenance of area networks, staff training, expert solutions, data management of payroll and accounting, and general consultation about technology and available options. Many governments have learned that the small software firms lack the staying power to improve upon or even support their products beyond the first few years. These problems show that choosing a vendor and consultant must be done carefully and with objectivity. Choosing a vendor begins with a needs assessment that should be based on multiple users and experts.

System maintenance contracts require great detail with regard to software development and enhancement, purchasing procedures, the expertise of service personnel, staff training, and responsibilities with regard to system reliability and security. Access, data integrity, and the protection of information assets are important, because public and nonprofit organizations increasingly rely on their information systems for operations and decision making, and because information technology systems are increasingly subject to the threat of viruses, hackers, and sabotage.[4] Outsourcing vendors and information technology suppliers compound the data integrity issues and vulnerabilities, especially when hardware or software is removed from the public administrator's or the agency's control.

REFERENCES

1. http://searchDatabase.techtarget.com/sDefinition/ 0,,sid13_gci518970,00.html (accessed October 2001).
2. http://www.itd.umich.edu/cgi-bin/otfdoc?ID=r1099 (accessed October 2001).
3. http://www.radcs.com/SESSpr.html (accessed October 2001).
4. Lacity, M.C.; Hirschheim, R. Information Technology Outsourcing: What Problems are We Trying to Solve? In *Rethinking Management Information Systems: An Interdisciplinary Perspective*; Currie, W., Galliers, B., Eds.; Oxford University Press: New York, 1999; 326–360.

Data Mining as a Decision-Making Aid

William J. Mead
Consultant, White Plains, New York, U.S.A.

INTRODUCTION

Data mining (DM) is a relatively new concept by which it has become possible and feasible to dig through huge collections of data looking for previously unrecognized trends or patterns. The resulting information can potentially be highly useful. The name is a clever takeoff on mining for precious metals or gems, where it is necessary to laboriously plow through masses of rubble to find a few pieces of material of great value.

Data mining is also called "knowledge discovery in databases," although some workers in this field draw slight distinctions between this and data mining. The definitions have not been standardized or universally agreed upon.

Most organizations, such as government agencies, commercial and industrial businesses, health care facilities, educational institutions, etc., generate large volumes of data in the course of conducting day-to-day operations. These data come from a variety of sources, examples of which include the following: in business situations, from order processing, inventory control, production planning and billing; in financial institutions, from customer account transactions; in the telecommunications industry, from keeping track of billions of phone calls and Internet connections for billing purposes; in health care, for patient records and responses to medications and procedures; in educational institutions, for student records; in government, from such things as tax receipts and expenditures, and the activities in various agencies.

For many years, computer mainframes and personal computers have been grinding out data, much of which has gone to inactive storage. But, within the past decade, it has been realized that by going back and carefully studying these banks of data, interesting and useful knowledge can sometimes be obtained. Software has been developed for this specific application, and many stunning successes have been reported. This has resulted in the evolutionary development and commercialization of more sophisticated data mining tools using applications of statistical analysis, modeling, artificial intelligence, and neural networks. As favorable results were made known, many agencies, firms, and ins-

titutions picked up interest in the concept, and more software firms became involved in developing improved data mining tools. It is said that there are now more than 100 firms offering such software, consulting, and seminars.[1]

As pointed out by Simon,[2] data mining is a highly useful technique to use to help gain deeper insight into the overall picture and general trends described by the data. However, these methods can also uncover patterns that have no real-world meaning or use, so human judgment remains a critical factor. This is sometimes overlooked in the glowing reports of successes with data mining—it is indeed a good tool but not necessarily a panacea.

THE APPLICATION OF DATA MINING TO DECISION-MAKING

As mentioned by Cratochvil,[3] the whole point of data mining is to reveal hidden information as an aid for prompt and effective decision-making. Action results from the knowledge obtained through the data mining process by discovering nonobvious patterns in existing collections of data. This process is a tool that can be of immense importance to decision makers.

In public administration, data mining or knowledge discovery can be helpful to aid auditors in detecting faulty tax returns, by establishing efficient profiles of non-compliant taxpayers by using models created from historical information. This can help identify the tax returns worth investigating, out of the millions filed. This has proven far more efficient than the previous somewhat hit-and-miss techniques of selecting the returns to be audited.[4]

In some instances, the operation of court systems has been improved by "mining" the profiles of potential jurors. Similarly, data mining has proved useful in helping establish the relative toxicity of chemicals released into the air, and in predicting the effectiveness of new drugs and medical tests, both of which have obvious regulatory applications.

Encyclopedia of Public Administration and Public Policy
DOI: 10.1081/E-EPAP 120011039

Data mining is useful also in isolating the factors involved with fraud and abuse in social assistance programs, Medicare and Medicaid, and procurement. Digging into historical records to detect patterns can prove far more efficient in controlling fraud and recouping money than the previously used human intuition methods of approaching these topics.[5]

Government departments and agencies can use data mining techniques to help determine how well programs under their jurisdiction are really performing. Law enforcement agencies have made effective use of data mining to find patterns and trends in crime, to help resolve open cases, to target repeat offenders, and to take steps to help prevent crimes. Data mining is also useful in analyzing and predicting traffic flows and growth. These techniques can also be used to help assure that government programs and services are more accessible to the public, and to develop and monitor programs to help meet the needs of stakeholders in the communities served. These are merely a few examples of the potential usefulness of data mining in public management.

There are interesting uses of data mining in commerce and industry, such as determining buying habits of consumers, tracking the effectiveness of advertising, credit risk assessment, and many others. One application that many of us have encountered is the ability of credit card companies, and telephone companies, to detect unusual activity on a specific account, which enables them to quickly contact the holder of the card in question to see if the use was really authorized or if the card had been misappropriated.

DATA WAREHOUSING

Most information systems are designed to facilitate day-to-day operations. However, as pointed out by Gupta,[6] it is impractical to keep data in operational systems indefinitely. Moreover, the sheer volume of data generated by organizations and agencies makes it difficult at best to effectively extract, analyze, and identify previously unrecognized relationships and trends in historical information. Operational databases usually are not designed for long-term storage of data, or for easy access for queries. As a result, it is now common practice to transfer consistent, cleaned, organized data from operational systems into special archives called data warehouses designed and maintained for historical queries and for data mining.

Straightforward answers to simple or complex questions can often be obtained from archived data through the employment of what are called query tools, the most conventional of which is called structured query language

(SQL). This is defined in American National Standard ANSI X3-135-1992 entitled *Database Language SQL*, and the international standard ISO/IEC 9075:1992 entitled *Information Technology-Database Languages-SQL*.[7,8] A query defines a set of rules to find the desired information. SQL is a way to communicate directly with a database. The user can specify the type of information that is wanted and can also control which set or sets of data that are to be accessed. Moreover, through SQL, the database can be modified by adding or deleting records, or by creating or modifying tables or other views of information contained within the database.

Beyond the types of questions for which SQL is useful, data warehouses also allow more sophisticated techniques to find otherwise hidden knowledge and patterns through data mining. Query tools and data mining tools are complementary, both employed to extract useful information from archives of historical data but in different ways for different purposes.

Data warehouses can be fed not only from the output of mainframe computers but also from files and spreadsheets generated on desktop and laptop personal computers. Obviously, the design of the data warehouse must take into account the sources of input and the ways the stored information is likely to be used. A variety of hardware and software exists for building, maintaining, managing, and using data warehouses. Also, a wealth of literature exists on data warehousing.[a]

According to Siegel,[14] making data warehousing integral to an organization's daily operational fabric tends to be far more difficult than designing and building the system. Effective data warehousing requires a considerable amount of training on the part of all involved.

In summary, data warehouses serve two goals, one of decision support through ready access to historical information via query tools, and the other the possibility of recognizing otherwise hidden patterns and trends in the accumulated data via data mining.

ONLINE ANALYTICAL PROCESSING (OLAP)

One of the several tools used in data mining is termed on-line analytical processing (OLAP). OLAP is a category of software that permits the use of ''multidimensional'' databases, i.e., it permits a wide variety of ways of looking at accumulated data to help give meaning and reduce confusion. For example, the dimensions might be

---

[a]Examples of books on data warehousing include Refs. [9–13].

time, location, the weather at various points in time, who was on duty, or other such factors that might be significant. OLAP facilitates navigating through large and complex databases. A spreadsheet is considered to be two dimensional, having rows and columns. However, more complicated scenarios of data can be considered as cubes composed of cells of information. In the language of OLAP, it is possible to view "cubic" data in many ways, by "drilling down" from higher to lower levels, by "slice and dice" techniques, by pivoting or rotating the cube, etc. These methods of viewing historical accumulated data enable complex queries involving multiple but interacting variables, for effective decision support.[15] Similarly, OLAP allows decision-makers to ask "What if" questions of the data. There are many vendors of software for variations on the OLAP theme, all of which enable great flexibility in complex analysis of information stored in data warehouses.

VISUAL DATA MINING

It has long been known that seeing data graphically presented allows better and faster comprehension than looking at rows and columns of numbers. Tufte[16] said that graphical presentations were used long before the advent of computers, dating back to the 1700s, when statistical graphics and Cartesian coordinates were originated. Such graphics as scatterplots, histograms, time-series charts, bar charts, line graphs, pie charts, Pareto charts, boxplots, control charts, and many other versions of two-dimensional representations of data have been and continue to be used to get away from what many consider to be boring tabular presentations. Many of these presentations are easy to achieve on computers. Data maps have also been used extensively for powerful presentation of facts.

The way the data are presented can impact the ease with which decisions are made. At the same time, however, graphical presentations can deliberately or inadvertently mislead the decision maker through deceptive distortions of scale and other visual tricks.

The use of color can make graphical presentations more interesting and can focus attention on important features. Color can also be used to emphasize a point or to identify recurring themes.

One of the major purposes of data mining is to detect unexpected trends and relationships. The human eye and brain are excellent at recognizing patterns, so the use of graphics with data mining is an entirely logical step. As pointed out by Thearling,[17] useful relationships between variables that are nonintuitive are the jewels data mining

hopes to locate, and visualization techniques can greatly aid this process.

Visualizing the data mining models is also a good way to help the decision maker understand and trust the complex models involved. Within the past few years, software developers have come up with many approaches to showing the results of data mining in interesting and helpful graphic presentations. Some of these tools enable the user to manipulate the variables to better demonstrate the concepts under consideration. Lawler[18] added that not only can complex patterns be easily spotted, but also, an aesthetically pleasing image can help spark the creativity and curiosity of viewers otherwise unmoved by simply seeing pages of numbers. In addition, visual data can help stimulate discussions and communication between individuals and groups, which can even help bridge gaps when people from different disciplines or different parts of an organization are jointly involved in decision making and problem solving.

In some instances, vivid three-dimensional images of data mining results are possible, yielding a virtual-reality environment. As Eliot[19] said, visualization presents the data landscape in a natural and intuitive form, making full use of the human capacity to absorb and interact with complex images.

CONCLUSION

Due to the incredible increase in computing power and the accumulation of large quantities of data over recent years, combined with the development of specialized software making data mining feasible, this has become an evolving tool for decision support that has great possibilities in a number of different types of applications. However, data mining requires establishing a well-designed "data warehouse," which is time consuming and costly to properly set up and maintain. Moreover, because human involvement is required in the interpretation of what is unearthed, considerable training and experience is needed. The successes of data mining are sometimes overstated and exaggerated, making it difficult to determine whether (in any specific circumstances) it is truly worth the effort and the money. But, the possible benefits can indeed be real, making this a topic worthy of careful consideration.

REFERENCES

1. http://www.acm.org/sigkdd/charter.html (accessed August 2001).

2. Simon, H. A data mining primer. Today's Chem. Work **March 2001**, 17–21.

3. Cratochvil, A. *Data Mining Techniques in Supporting Decision Making*; http://cs.unimaas/nl/~kuper/scripties/andac (accessed August 2001).

4. ftp://ftp.spss.com/pub/web/wp/TAXWP-1000.pdf (accessed August 2001).

5. http://www.spss.com/industries/government/fraud.htm (accessed August 2001).

6. http://system-services.com/dwintro.asp (accessed August 2001).

7. http://www.ora.com/reference/dictionary/terms/S/Structured_Query_Language.htm (accessed August 2001).

8. http://www.cs.unibo.it/~ciaccia/COURSES/RESOURCES/SQLTutorial/sqlch1.htm.

9. Mattison, R.; Alask, R. *Data Warehousing: Strategies, Technologies, and Techniques*; McGraw-Hill: New York, 1996.

10. Inmon, W.H. *Building the Data Warehouse*; John Wiley & Sons: New York, 1996.

11. Agosta, L. *The Essential Guide to Data Warehousing*; Prentice Hall: New York, 1999.

12. Inmon, W.H.; Hackathorn, R.D. *Using the Data Warehouse*; John Wiley & Sons: New York, 1994.

13. Watson, H.J.; Gray, P. *Decision Support in the Data Warehouse*; Prentice Hall: New York, 1997.

14. Siegel, P. Data warehousing. Chem. Eng. **2001**, 55, April.

15. http://dssresources.com/glossary/olaptrms.html (accessed August 2001).

16. Tufte, E.R. *The Visual Display of Quantitative Information*; Graphics Press: Cheshire, CT, 1998.

17. http://www3.shore.net/~kht/text/dmviz/modelviz.htm (accessed August 2001).

18. Lawler, A. New imaging tools put the art back into science. Science **2001**, 292, 1044.

19. http://www.labs.bt.com/library/archive/btej_v14_1/part1.htm (accessed August 2001).

Debt Affordability

Bill Simonsen
Mark D. Robbins
University of Connecticut, Storrs, Connecticut, U.S.A.

Raymond Brown
University of Oregon, Eugene, Oregon, U.S.A.

INTRODUCTION

Municipal bonds are an important way that state and local governments finance their infrastructure improvements. An understanding of how much the government can afford to pay for debt and how much debt it can safely carry is a crucial element in capital and debt planning. The purpose of this article is to describe and analyze the different ways that local governments can measure how much debt they can afford.

BACKGROUND

Debt affordability assessments are intertwined with capital improvement programs (CIP) and debt policy formulation. A CIP is a financial plan that includes an analysis, prioritization, implementation, and financing of infrastructure and other capital needs. The CIP is a multiyear plan that prioritizes and identifies capital projects (as compared to the capital budget, which is the annual spending plan). Governments may have multiple CIPs, each with a different time horizon. The CIP ''provides for an orderly and routine method of planning and financing a government's required capital improvements.''[1] Borrowing via the municipal bond market is the primary form of capital financing, and planning for it is a key ingredient to a CIP.

Municipal borrowings are generally called municipal bonds, even though some are not technically bonds (e.g., certificates of participaton). Municipal bonds are often retired over 15, 20, or even 30 years. The municipal market is very large, with from $300 billion to $400 billion sold each year. With this much debt, even small interest rates savings can have a substantial financial impact. The potential financial impact on future generations adds salience to municipal debt decisions. Therefore, debt policies that provide a set of guiding princi-

ples for management decision making are important to the CIP. The Government Finance Officers Association (GFOA) and others have espoused the use of debt policies as an important management tool for state and local governments.

''A carefully crafted debt policy can enhance a government's credit quality and improve access to both taxable and tax-exempt credit markets.''[2] Debt policies include such items as when to use a request for proposals; the appropriate conditions for competitive or negotiated sales; proper disclosure procedures; and including citizens in the decision process through public meetings, a vote, or other means, etc.

Larkin and Joseph[2] advocated that a government's debt policy should begin with a comprehensive review of affordability. As Larkin and Joseph pointed out, just as when homebuyers make a selection on which home they want based on how much they can afford on a monthly basis, governments need to have a good understanding of debt affordability prior to forecasting needs and issuance. Debt affordability analysis is conducted by calculating a series of ratios and comparing them with established standards that provide guidance about the amount of debt the government can afford. Fig. 1 shows how the CIP, the debt policy, and the debt affordability analysis relate: a debt policy is an important part of a CIP, while debt affordability analysis is an important part of a debt policy.

Debt Affordability and Municipal Credit Analysis

Debt affordability analysis is closely related to the municipal credit analysis conducted by bond-rating agencies. Bond-rating agencies seek to determine the riskiness of the debt based upon a government's ability to call forth and manage its resources, while governments need to understand how much debt they can comfortably

Encyclopedia of Public Administration and Public Policy
DOI: 10.1081/E-EPAP 120010733

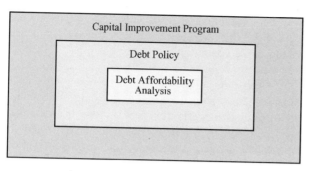

Fig. 1 The relationship between capital improvement programs, debt policies, and debt affordability analysis.

issue. The bond-rating agencies assess the following four factors to determine credit quality of municipal tax-backed debt:

- *Economy.* Analysis of economic factors consists of an examination of the current and projected future economic profile. This includes analysis of the breadth and depth of the local economy. Measures include trends in unemployment rates; business diversification and industry concentration; trends in the issuance of building permits; and the mix of residential, commercial, and industrial property. Demographic trends such as population growth or decline are also examined. In addition, wealth indicators are analyzed, such as per capita or personal income trends, property value per capita, percent below poverty level, and household income.
- *Financial Condition.* A key to the analysis of fiscal condition is the flexibility of the financial environment. Are revenues limited? What percent of expenditures is mandates or otherwise fixed? Are tax rate adjustments implemented as needed, or do rate increases tend to be traumatic events that are only implemented after reaching crisis conditions? Some broad factors indicative of financial condition are compliance with generally accepted accounting principles (GAAP); diversity and stability of revenue sources; a trend of operating surpluses; and fund balance as a percent of revenues.
- *Debt Position.* Analysis of debt position focuses on the structure and security of the bonds in the context of future borrowing needs and the resources available to pay the current and future debt service. Analysis of debt position is key to debt affordability analysis.
- *Administrative Factors.* The rating agency, Fitch IBCA, views management as a crucial component when evaluating the creditworthiness of a community as they report having seen management salvage,

as well as exacerbate, difficult financial situations. "In its future rating assignments, Fitch IBCA will place greater and more specific weight on management practices, both good and bad, that are employed by issuers in running their financial operations."[3] Past management performance, in balancing budgets, managing capital needs, etc., is examined. Appropriate capital improvement programs, accurate capital and operating budgets, and prudent investment policies are indicators of sound management practices.

Debt affordability is generally understood in terms of tax-supported debt. A separate type of analysis is conducted for debt backed by other forms of security. General obligation bonds, lease bonds paid from general revenues, certificates of participation, special assessment bonds, and tax-increment bonds are forms of tax-backed securities.

Measuring Debt Affordability

Three key notions comprise debt affordability analysis: 1) ratio calculation; 2) comparison to norms or standards; and 3) forecasting. We will discuss each of these notions in turn.

Ratio calculation

The GFOA recommends that "issuers undertake an analysis of their debt capacity prior to issuing bonds."[4] The purpose of such a suggestion, according to the GFOA, is that a comprehensive and routine analysis ensures that the government will know all new debt issued is affordable, there is balance between current and future capital needs, and there is the ability to pay for them.[4] The GFOA suggests that a comprehensive debt analysis should contain the following:

- Measures of the debt service obligation.
- Evaluation of trends relating to the government's performance (revenues, expenditures, and unreserved fund balance).
- Measures of debt burden on the community.
- Statutory or constitutional limitations on debt issuance.
- Market factors affecting tax-exempt interest costs (interest rates, market receptivity, and credit rating).[4]

Other obligations to consider include unfunded pension liabilities and capital leases.

More specifically, typical measures of debt affordability include the following:

Debt service. Debt service consists of principal and interest payments. It is usually stated in terms relative to total revenues or expenditures.

Direct debt (or net direct debt). Direct debt is a measure of a municipality's debt paid for by its general revenues including taxes. Bonds that are self-supporting by means other than taxes, such as user fees or charges, are not included in direct debt. As mentioned earlier, tax increment bonds, special assessment bonds, and certificates of participation are included in direct debt, as they are backed by taxes or general revenues.

Using these measures, a variety of ratios can be calculated to put these figures into relative, comparable, terms to other governments. Some of the common ratios are listed below:[a]

Debt per capita. Debt per capita is a measure of total indebtedness divided by the population. This standardizes the debt by the population size of the government—ten million dollars might be a lot of debt for Mansfield Connecticut, but a small amount for New York City.

Debt as a percentage of real market value. Debt as a percentage of the real market value is derived by dividing the direct debt by the real market value of all taxable property within the jurisdiction. Because property taxes are typically a primary source of revenues, this is an important measure, as it highlights a municipality's ability to support its current, and future, debt through the taxing of its property.

Debt as a percentage of personal income. This statistic compares the debt outstanding to a measure of community wealth. This measure is limited in that personal income statistics are often unavailable for smaller jurisdictions.

Annual debt service as a percentage of general and debt service fund expenditures. This measure identifies the portion of the general and debt service funds that goes to debt service.

Annual debt service as a percentage of operating expenditures. This concept is broader than the last, as it includes expenditures from all operating funds, such as the general fund, special revenue funds, and debt service funds.

Impact of the debt on the tax rate. This measures the portion of the tax rate that is dedicated to servicing tax-supported debt.

Impact of the debt on the average household. This statistic measures the monetary burden on the average household in the community.

It is important to also include overlapping debt when calculating the principal amount outstanding. Overlapping (or sometimes underlying) debt is the tax-supported principal owed by other governments that overlap (or underlie) the geography of the jurisdiction conducting the debt affordability analysis. For instance, if it is a city conducting the analysis, the overlapping debt would include the proportionate debt of the county, school districts, and special districts. Overlapping debt is calculated as follows:

$$OD = \frac{MV_O}{MV_T} * TD$$

where:

OD = Overlapping debt.
MV_O = Market value of the overlapping property.
MV_T = Total market property value of the overlapping government(s).
TD = Tax-supported debt outstanding for the overlapping government(s).

The notion behind overlapping debt is that the taxpayers of a jurisdiction are responsible for the debt of all their governments, not just the one conducting the debt affordability analysis. Debt as a percentage of market value that includes overlapping debt is called debt burden.

Table 1 summarizes the different statistics that typically can be used to measure debt affordability.

Table 1 Debt affordability statistics

Debt service
Direct debt
Debt per capita
Debt per capita including overlapping debt
Debt as a percentage of real market value
Debt as a percentage of real market value including overlapping debt (also called debt burden)
Debt as a percentage of personal income
Debt as a percentage of personal income including overlapping debt
Debt service as a percentage of general and debt service fund expenditures
Debt service as a percentage of operating expenditures
Impact of the debt on the tax rate.
Impact of the debt on the average household

---

[a]This section draws significantly from Ref. 4, pp. 15–18.

Comparison to norms or standards

The debt statistics and ratios are difficult to interpret on their own. Is a debt burden of 5% high, low, or moderate? Is a debt per capita of $5000 a lot, or just a little? It helps to interpret the statistics by comparing them to some norm or standard. Examples of standards are rules of thumb, medians, and benchmarks.

Rules of thumb are industry standards for certain ratios. Some rules of thumb standards used by Standard and Poor's[5] are as follows:

* Debt per capita (including overlapping debt) is low if it is below $1000, moderate between $1000 and $2500, and high above $2500
* Debt burden is low if less than 3%, moderate from 3 to 6%, and high if over 6%.
* Debt service as a percent of operating expenditures is low if 5% or less, moderate if 10%, and high if over 15%.

Debt statistics outside of the range of the rules of thumb are not necessarily dangerous, because governments have different service responsibilities. For instance, a fire district with volunteer firefighters may have a high debt service as a percent of operating expenditures, because there are very low labor costs.

Medians can help refine government's understanding of its debt position. Medians are generally calculated by population and government type, e.g., median debt burden for counties with a population from 100,000 to 249,999. In the past, Moody's Investors Service published medians for selected debt statistics, but they no longer do so.

Another way to refine the debt affordability analysis is to compare debt statistics with those of similar governments, or benchmarks. While the use of benchmarks can provide important comparison information, there are two basic difficulties with this approach. First, no two communities are exactly alike, so the choice of comparable governments must be done carefully. Important characteristics to match when choosing comparison governments are population, revenue mix, service responsibilities, bond rating or credit quality, and whether the laws governing the use and issuance of debt are comparable.

Second, ratios are not consistently measured across organizations. Some governments deduct funds set aside for principal payment from the outstanding debt prior to calculating ratios. For instance, some governments calculate ratios based only on general obligation debt and ignore other tax-supported debt. One of the reasons for this is that state statutes or constitutions often define the way debt is to be calculated for the purpose of state debt limits. These calculations generally exclude lease debt, COPs, or any debt considered self supporting. This may

be appropriate for this purpose, but provides an inadequate and incomplete view of the debt picture for debt affordability analysis.

Forecasting future capacity

Much of the value of debt affordability analysis is to estimate how much debt a government can afford to issue into the future. Estimating debt affordability into the future requires multiyear projections for the debt statistics. This consists of forecasts of the information that are part of the ratios, along with projections of future capital needs, such as the following:

* Population.
* Operating revenues.
* Operating expenditures.
* Real market value of property.
* Personal income (if available).
* The size of the potential issues (annual dollar amounts to be issued).
* Debt maturity schedules.
* Type of debt service structure; (level debt service, equal principal, other)
* Interest rate schedule.

Different scenarios can be modeled, given different capital expenditure requirements or debt issuance structures. Constant annual growth rates applied to a base year is the way many of these parameters were estimated by Miranda and Picur[4] for the city of Pittsburgh. Sometimes the baselines for the ratios, such as revenues, expenditures and real market value, are forecasted for other budgeting purposes.

There is uncertainty anytime projections are made. With this in mind, it is often prudent to include sensitivity analysis for varying rates of growth for the relevant factors. Once the forecasts are accomplished, the government can decide whether it can afford to pay for the debt issuance, or if the capital program needs to be scaled back. In this way, the debt affordability analysis provides important information for the government's CIP. Spreadsheet programs, such as Excel, are well suited for this future analysis.

CONCLUSION

In many ways, deciding upon debt affordability criteria is an art and not a science. Ratios can be calculated, but they need to be interpreted to be useful. Benchmarks can provide an indication of what constitutes high, or low, ratios for key debt statistics. However, because there are multiple ratios, it is possible to be low for some, but high on others. In this case, the government must decide whether that is acceptable, or whether efforts must be made to lower the troublesome ratios.

Ratios or benchmarks alone do not tell the whole story. Other factors, such as strong economics or history of strong management, may offset high ratios. That is, a wealthy or diverse tax base and a history of sound management practices may provide a government with a better chance to withstand and recover from problems despite poor ratios.

Debt affordability analysis is an important part of a debt policy, which in turn, is an important part of a capital improvement program. Debt affordability analysis, debt policies, and capital improvement programs are an important part of any government's financial planning.

REFERENCES

1. Joseph, J.C. *Debt Issuance and Management: A Guide for Smaller Governments*; Government Finance Officers Association: Chicago, IL, 1994; 5.
2. Larkin, R.; Joseph, J.C. Developing formal debt policies. Gov. Finance Rev. **1991**, 7 (4), 11–14.
3. Larkin, R.C. *Impact of Management Practices on Municipal Credit*; Fitch IBCA: New York, 2000; 1.
4. Miranda, R.A.; Picur, R.D. *Benchmarking and Measuring Debt Capacity*; Government Finance Officers Association: Chicago, IL, 2000; pp. 5, 6.
5. Standard & Poor's Public Finance Ratings Criteria. 2000; 29. Downloaded 9/5/01 from http://www.standardandpoors.com/ResourceCenter/RatingsCriteria/PublicFinance/index.html#a.

Debt Issuance

Beverly S. Bunch
University of Illinois at Springfield, Springfield, Illinois, U.S.A.

D

INTRODUCTION

Debt issuance occurs when a government borrows money and agrees to repay the money with interest at a later time. This practice is similar to when an individual borrows money to pay for a house and then makes monthly mortgage payments.

State and local governments borrow money for a variety of purposes. One of the major uses of debt is to finance large capital projects, such as the construction of a street, a public building, or a water treatment plant. Using debt to finance these types of projects allows the costs of the project to be spread over time rather than being paid in a single year. This can help make a project more affordable and allow the government to avoid large fluctuations in tax rates. The use of debt also helps facilitate intergenerational equity in that there is a closer match between those who use the facility over time and those who pay for the facility.

Some governments also issue debt when there is a mismatch between the timing of revenues and expenditures. For example, a government may not receive the majority of its tax revenues until the third month of the year; however, expenditures, such as payroll, will have to be made prior to that time. The government may borrow funds to pay for its expenditures and then repay the debt when the tax revenues arrive. This type of debt is referred to as tax anticipation notes (TANS) or tax and revenue anticipation notes (TRANs), if other types of revenues also are used to repay the debt.

Historically, some governments have issued debt to address a deficit situation in which revenues are less than spending. However, this practice is not considered financially prudent, because future generations have to pay for services that were provided in the past. Investors also may be reluctant to lend funds to a government that is having financial difficulties.

Governments may also issue debt to finance a loan program, such as a housing mortgage program or a student loan program. In this case, the government issues debt and then uses the money to make loans to private individuals or organizations. The government uses the funds from the loan repayments to repay the original debt.

TYPES OF DEBT

State and local government debt can be classified in a variety of ways. One form of classification is based on the length of time the debt is outstanding. Short-term debt typically refers to debt that will be repaid in one year or less, while long-term debt refers to debt that will be outstanding for a longer time period, often 20 years. Short-term debt is referred to as notes, while long-term debt is called bonds.

Another way to categorize debt is based on the security associated with debt. The most secure type of debt is general obligation debt, which is guaranteed by the full-faith-and-credit of the government. This means that investors legally can require the government to utilize its taxing authority to generate sufficient funds to repay the debt. In contrast, revenue bonds are secured solely by a specified revenue source, such as water user charges or tolls collected on a toll road. Because revenue bonds do not have the full-faith-and-credit backing of the government, they tend to have higher interest rates than general obligation bonds. However, many governments find revenue bonds attractive for the financing of projects that are expected to be self-sustaining.

Another way to classify governmental debt is by the purpose for which the bond proceeds will be used. Public purpose debt is used to finance infrastructure that will be owned by the government, such as public roads or buildings. Alternatively, a state or local government can issue private activity debt on behalf of a private organization or group of individuals who will be the primary beneficiaries from the bonds or will have primary responsibility for generating the funds to repay the bonds. Examples of private activity debt include housing mortgage revenue bonds, student loan bonds, and industrial development bonds.

Governments may issue debt to refinance existing debt. These bonds are referred to as refunding bonds, while debt issued to finance new projects is referred to as new money bonds. Similar to the refinancing of a house mortgage, a government may refinance debt when interest rates are significantly lower than when the debt was originally issued. A government also may choose to refinance debt when it wants to change some feature of the debt, such as the timing of the principal repayments or the legal requirements associated with the debt.

TAX-EXEMPT STATUS OF DEBT

Most debt issued by state and local governments is tax exempt. This means that the interest payments made to investors are not subject to federal and, in some cases, state income taxes. As a result, investors are willing to lend funds to state and local governments at lower rates than if the interest was taxable. This feature of the federal income tax code results in significant interest savings to state and local governments.

The federal government has imposed a number of constraints to avoid abuse of the tax-exempt provision. One of the major provisions relates to restrictions on arbitrage earnings. Arbitrage is the difference between the interest rate paid on the bonds and the interest rate earned on the borrowed money until it is spent. The federal government also has imposed a state cap on the amount of tax-exempt private activity bonds that can be issued each year within each state.

Some governments issue taxable debt when they want to finance a project or program that does not satisfy the eligibility requirements for tax-exempt debt.

VOTER REFERENDUMS AND DEBT LIMITS

Most state and local government general obligation debt is subject to approval by the voters and also may be subject to some form of legal debt limitation. At the local level, the limit may be imposed by the state government or a local charter. For example, some states restrict the amount of local debt outstanding to a specified percentage (e.g., 5%) of the taxable property value within the jurisdiction. At the state level, a constitutional or statutory debt limit may restrict the amount of debt to a particular dollar amount or to a specified percentage of state revenues. Alternatively, the debt limit may indicate the maximum percentage of general revenues that can be used to repay the debt.

Revenue bonds usually are not subject to voter approval requirements or debt limitations, because they are not backed by the taxing power of the government.[1] A special type of revenue bond, called a lease revenue bond, also is not usually subject to voter approval and debt limitations, even though the debt may ultimately be repaid with tax revenues. With this type of debt, a government utilizes a separate agency or a nonprofit entity to issue bonds that are used to acquire or construct a facility to be used by the government. The facility is then leased to the government, and the agency or nonprofit entity uses the lease payments to repay the bonds. The lease revenue bonds typically include a nonappropriation clause that allows the government to terminate the lease if funds are not appropriated for the lease payments. As a result of this clause, most state and local governments' laws do not legally classify lease revenue bonds as long-term debt.[2]

STRUCTURE OF DEBT SERVICE

Debt service refers to the payment of principal and interest on bonds. The structure of debt service addresses issues such as the timing of principal and interest payments and the process by which interest rates are set.

Most government debt is structured as serial bonds, in which a portion of the principal is repaid each year over the life of the debt. The interest rate on serial bonds varies by maturity (the date on which the principal is repaid to investors), with the shortest-term series usually having lower interest rates than the longer-term series. Some governments also issue term bonds, in which the principal is due in one or two lump sum payments in the final years the bonds are outstanding. Throughout the life of the term bonds, the government makes interest payments and transfers funds into a sinking fund to generate sufficient funds for the eventual repayment of the principal. Governments also may issue bonds that are a combination of serial and term bonds.

Government bonds are usually structured as level debt service or level principal payments.[3] Level debt service is similar to how mortgage payments are structured in that the total amount of principal and interest paid each period is equal. The advantage of a level debt service structure is that it provides stability in the budget, because the same amount is due each year. In contrast, under a level principal structure, the amount of principal repaid each period is equal, and the debt service payments decrease over time.

Bonds can be structured with fixed-rate interest rates or variable-rate interest rates. With fixed rates, the interest rate on each serial payment is set at the time the bonds are issued, while with variable rates, the rates typically vary over the life of the bonds. In the latter case, the interest rates can be tied to some type of market index and are reset at specified internals, such as daily, weekly, monthly, or annually.

Bonds also may be structured with a call option, which allows a government the option of repaying the debt prior to maturity. This may be helpful for a government that would like to be able to refund bonds in the future to take advantage of lower interest rates. However, the inclusion of a call option typically results in a slightly higher interest rate on the original bonds.

DEBT ISSUANCE PROCESS

Professional Advisors

State and local governments typically receive assistance in the debt issuance process from a team of professionals, including a financial advisor, a bond counsel, and underwriters.

The role of the financial advisor is to assist the state or local government throughout the debt issuance process. This may include helping the government decide what type of debt to issue, how much debt to issue, and the necessary steps to obtain the appropriate legal approvals. The financial advisor also may help the issuer structure the debt and prepare the official statement. The official statement is a document for investors that describes the bond issue and the financial condition of the government issuing the bonds. The financial advisors also may assist in selecting the other team members, obtaining a bond rating, and evaluating whether bond insurance is financially advantageous.

The bond counsel helps the government ensure that all legal provisions related to the issuance of debt are followed. This includes making sure that the debt is legally authorized, drafting legal documents, obtaining the necessary approvals, and helping the government adhere to all relevant legal procedural provisions. The bond counsel also is responsible for evaluating and certifying that the debt satisfies the legal requirements for being considered tax exempt.

The role of the underwriters is to identify investors willing to lend the government money. The underwriter purchases the bonds from the government and then sells them to investors. In a negotiated sale (explained below), underwriters may also be involved in many of the same types of activities as the financial advisor.

Method of Sale

Bonds typically are sold through competitive bid or a negotiated sale. In a competitive bid sale, underwriters or groups of underwriters called syndicates submit concealed bids specifying an interest rate for each serial maturity of the bonds. The bonds are then awarded to the underwriter or syndicate who submitted the bid that will result in the lowest overall interest cost for the government.

The bonds are typically awarded based on the calculation of the true interest cost—the TIC. The TIC takes into account the amount of interest paid, as well as the timing of those interest payments. Some governments used to (and some still do) award bonds on the basis of the net interest cost (NIC), which is based on the total interest payments but does not take into account the

timing of the interest payments. The TIC is preferred over the NIC, because the TIC takes into account the time value of money.[4]

In a negotiated sale, an issuer selects an underwriter or syndicate well in advance of the sale date to help the issuer with the marketing and sale of the bonds. The issuer negotiates with the underwriter or syndicate to determine the underwriter's spread, which is the underwriter's compensation, and an interest rate for each maturity in the series. After an underwriter or syndicates purchases a government's bonds, the underwriter then sells the bonds to investors.

There has been an ongoing debate regarding whether it is better for a government to sell bonds through competitive bid or through a negotiated sale. Some professionals believe that the competitive bid process is more likely to result in a lower interest cost, especially for bonds that are "plain vanilla."[5] This means that the issuer is known in the market and that the bonds do not have a complicated structure or security. Competitive bid also has an appearance of fairness, in that the bonds are awarded through a sealed bid process to the underwriters that submit the bid with the lowest interest cost.

However, in some cases, critics note that a negotiated sale may be preferable. With a negotiated sale, the underwriters know in advance of the actual sale that they will be awarded the bonds and, therefore, may be more willing to invest in presale marketing of the bonds. If they are able to find investors for most of the bonds prior to the setting of the interest rates, they may be less inclined to incorporate a risk component into the negotiated interest rates.[6] Negotiated sales also allow underwriters flexibility in structuring the bonds (such as maturity schedules and call features) and in selecting a sale date depending on the condition of the market. In a competitive bid sale, the structuring of the bonds and sale date have to be decided and announced in advance. Another potential advantage is that a negotiated sale tends to allow a government more flexibility in pursuing policy objectives, such as making bonds available to citizens as investments or facilitating participation by locally-owned businesses or minority- or women-owned businesses.[7]

However, the increased discretion in selecting an underwriter for a negotiated sale raised some concerns about the relationship between underwriters' contributions to political campaigns and the awarding of bonds by elected officials who received those funds. In response, the Municipal Securities Rulemaking Board established Rule G-37, which states that municipal securities brokers and dealers generally are prohibited from engaging in municipal securities business with an issuer within 2 years after having made a contribution to that official.

Bond Ratings

Most governments that sell bonds in the national market obtain a bond rating prior to the sale. A bond rating is the assignment of a grade by a private bond rating firm as to the creditworthiness (risk of default) associated with a particular bond issue. The bond rating firms utilize grades ranging from AAA to C. Higher-rated bonds typically receive lower interest rates than lower-rated bonds due to the lower perceived probability of a default.

Analysts for the bond rating companies assess the structure of the particular bond issue and the financial security backing the bond. For a general obligation bond, the bond rating analyst also addresses the issuer's managerial capabilities, debt burden, financial and operational factors, and the economic conditions of the government's jurisdiction. For a revenue bond, the bond rating analyst considers other factors such as the coverage ratio (the ratio of net revenues to annual debt service) and the structure of a reserve fund to pay for debt service if sufficient revenues are not available.

Bond Insurance

In some cases, a government may find it advantageous to purchase bond insurance from a private company. In exchange for an insurance premium, the bond insurance company agrees to pay the debt service if the government is unable to make the payments. For insured bonds, the bond rating is based on the bond rating for the private bond insurance company rather than the government issuing the debt. Historically, the major municipal bond insurance companies have been rated AAA, the highest bond rating. In assessing whether bond insurance is prudent, the government should weigh the cost of the insurance premium versus the present value of the expected decrease in interest costs associated with a higher bond rating.

Use of Technology

Governments are beginning to increase their use of technology for activities related to the issuance of municipal bonds. Recently, some governments have sold their bonds through a bond auction held on the Internet. This has allowed governments to try innovative features such as selling serial bonds maturity-by-maturity rather than on an all-or-none basis and selling bonds directly to large institutional investors. The City of Pittsburgh, one of the pioneers in this area, notes that it has obtained significant savings by using the Internet for bond sales.[8]

DISCLOSURE

State and local governments that issue debt are obligated to provide investors with relevant and timely information about the bonds and the financial condition of the government. Although there have been few government bond defaults, situations such as the Washington Public Power Supply System bond default in the 1980s and the financial difficulties of Orange County, California, in the 1990s, have drawn increased attention to the importance of having appropriate disclosure.[9]

The Government Finance Officers Association (GFOA), which is a membership organization of state and local budget and finance officials, has established *Disclosure Guidelines* to assist state and local governments with the disclosure of appropriate information related to the issuance of debt. The Securities and Exchange Commission Rule 15c2-12 also requires underwriters of state and local government bonds to adhere to certain reporting requirements. In addition, some governments are utilizing their web sites to make relevant information available to investors before and after the sale of bonds. The latter is especially important, because many state and local government bonds are traded in a secondary market after the initial sale.

REFERENCES

1. Petersen, J.E.; McLoughlin, T. Debt Policies and Procedures. In *Local Government Finance: Concepts and Practices*; Petersen, J.E., Strachota, D.R., Eds.; Government Finance Officers Association: Chicago, 1991; 263–292.
2. Aguila, P.R., Jr.; Petersen, J.E. Leasing and Service Contracts. In *Local Government Finance: Concepts and Practices*; Petersen, J.E., Strachota, D.R., Eds.; Government Finance Officers Association: Chicago, 1991; 321–338.
3. Robbins, M.D.; Simonsen, B.; Jump, B., Jr. Maturity structure and borrowing costs: The implications of level debt service. Munic. Finance J. **2000**, *21* (3), 40–63.
4. Mikesell, J.L. *Fiscal Administration: Analysis and Applications for the Public Sector*, 5th Ed.; Harcourt Brace College Publishers: Fort Worth, 1999; 533–584.
5. Simonsen, W.; Kiltredge, W.P. Competitive versus negotiated municipal bond sales: Why issuers choose one method over the other. Munic. Finance J. **1998**, *19* (2), 1–29.
6. California Debt Advisory Commission. *Competitive Versus Negotiated Sale of Debt*; Issue Brief; California Debt Advisory Commission; September 1992; Vol. 1.
7. Bunch, B.S. Increasing women and minority participation in municipal debt issuance: An analysis of Texas' experiences. Munic. Finance J. **1997**, *18* (3), 1–20.
8. Hennigan, P. Municipal bond sales via the internet: The story of Pittsburgh's electronic auction. Gov. Finance Rev. **1998**, *14* (4), 23–27.
9. Fairchild, L.M. Are federal disclosure requirements beneficial for the municipal bond market? Munic. Finance J. **2000**, *21* (3), 65–82.

Decision Making in Administrative Organizations, Theories of

James S. Guseh

North Carolina Central University, Durham, North Carolina, U.S.A.

INTRODUCTION

Decision making is the process of choosing from among alternative courses of action. It is both an objective and subjective process. The objective process involves setting goals and formulating an efficient process for attaining the goals. The subjective process may involve the values of decision makers, which may lead to the acceptance of a satisfactory rather than an optimum solution. Decision making is central in public administration because it is one of the core managerial functions in organizations. How decisions are made, what criteria are used, what costs are involved, and who benefits are some of the important questions that characterize the decision-making process. Thus, how managers are judged depends on the decisions they make.[1]

There are various theories or models of decision making. This article focuses on the five dominant models of decision making: the classical, bounded-rationality, incremental, mixed scanning, and garbage-can. An emerging model of decision making, known as win-win analysis, which seems to address some of the limitations of the other models, is also discussed. The analysis includes the approaches utilized by each model, the criticisms, and other dimensions of the process.

THE RATIONAL MODEL

The rational model of decision making also known as the classical or economic model, has held a prominent place in the literature in public administration. The model is derived from economic theory that people seek to maximize utility and pursue their self-interests. The model is based on the assumption that people are economically rational and attempt to maximize outputs for a given input or minimize input for a given output in an orderly and sequential process. Political economist Anthony Downs presents the economic analysis of the rational model as follows:

> Economic analysis thus consists of two major steps: discovery of the ends a decision maker is pursuing and

analysis of which means of attaining them are most reasonable, i.e., require the least input of scarce resources.... Thus, whenever economists refer to a "rational man" they are not designating a man whose thought processes consist exclusively of logical propositions, or a man without prejudices, or a man whose emotions are inoperative. In normal usage all of these could be considered rational men. But the economic definition refers solely to a man who moves toward his goals in a way which, to the best of his knowledge, uses the least possible input of scarce resources per unit of valued output.[2]

Although the steps involved have been outlined in various ways by different authors, the essential elements involved the following steps:

1. Identify the problem to be solved.
2. Establish the evaluation criteria for problem resolution.
3. Propose the various alternatives for solving the problem.
4. Analyze the likely consequences of each.
5. Compare and evaluate the results of each alternative
6. Choose the best alternative.
7. Implement the chosen alternatives.
8. Evaluate the results.

Details of each step can be addressed as separate topics but are not discussed in this article.

Although, in actuality, the decision-making process is rarely this orderly, the rational model has had a significant influence on decision making in bureaucracy. For example, it is reported to have been applied in some form by President John F. Kennedy's administration to address the Cuban Missile Crisis in 1962.[3] It has also been employed in addressing many urban problems in American cities such as Cleveland, Dallas, Dayton, Forth Worth, Long Beach, Philadelphia, Phoenix, Pittsburgh, San Antonio, San Francisco, Virginia Beach, Roanoke, and Greensboro, to name but a few.[1]

Despite its widespread application in organizations, the rational model has been challenged since the late 1950s. One of the leading critics of this model is Nobel laureate Herbert Simon. While the rational decision of the clas-

Encyclopedia of Public Administration and Public Policy
DOI: 10.1081/E-EPAP 120010888

sical model assumes that the decision maker is completely informed about both the organizational goals and all possible alternatives and acts to maximize utility, the administrative decision maker can rarely approximate the kind of rationality assumed by the classical economic model. Rarely can an administrator count on full knowledge of the situation, including the consequences of the various alternatives. According to Simon:

> It is impossible for the behavior of a single, isolated individual to reach any high degree of rationality. The number of alternatives he must explore is too great, the information he would need to evaluate them so vast that even an approximation to objective rationality is hard to conceive. Individual choice takes place in an environment of ''givens''—premises that are accepted by the subject as bases for his choice; and behavior is adaptive only within the limits set by these ''givens.''[4]

Thus, Simon put forth a more realistic model of decision making known as the bounded-rationality model.

THE BOUNDED-RATIONALITY DECISION-MAKING MODEL

This model represents the decision maker as an ''administrative man'' with limited information processing ability. According to Simon, the decision maker's ability to analyze the alternatives and objectives is limited or bounded to varying degrees. He explains the concept as follows:

> When the limits to rationality are viewed from the individual's standpoint, they fall into three categories: he is limited by his unconscious skills, habits and reflexes; he is limited by his values and conceptions of purpose, which may diverge from the organizational goals; he is limited by the extent of his knowledge and information. The individual can be rational in terms of the organization's goals only to the extent that he is *able* to pursue a particular course of action, he has a correct conception of the *goal* of action, and he is correctly informed about the conditions surrounding his action. Within the boundaries laid down by these factors, his choices are rational—goal-oriented.[5]

Unlike the ''economic man'' of the classical economic model who seeks to maximize, the ''administrative man'' seeks to ''satisfice,'' i.e., find satisfactory solutions rather than maximize. While the economic man seeks rationality, the administrative man recognizes the limits of his capability for rational behavior. The administrative man is content with a simplified and incomplete view of the world that can never, because of human limita-

tions, approximate the complexity of the real world. Simon highlights the characteristics of the administrative man as follows:

> First, because he satisfices rather than maximizes, administrative man can make his choices without first examining all possible behavior alternatives and without ascertaining that these are in fact all the alternatives. Second, because he treats the world as rather ''empty,'' and ignores the ''interrelatedness of all things (so stupefying to thoughts and action), administrative man is able to make his decisions with relatively simple rules of thumb that do not make impossible demands upon his capacity for thought.[6]

Thus, while the administrative man cannot achieve the ideal behavior of the classical economic man, he does the best with what he has. He is willing to settle for an adequate solution in contrast to an optimal one.[7]

The steps in the bounded-rationality model are as follows:[8]

1. Identify the problem to be solved or goal to be defined
2. Determine the minimum level or standard that all acceptable alternatives will have to meet
3. Choose one feasible alternative that will resolve the issue.
4. Appraise the acceptability that will resolve the issue.
5. Determine if it meets the minimum levels that have been established.
6. If the alternative is not acceptable, identify another and put it through the evaluation process.
7. If the alternative is acceptable, implement it.
8. After implementation, determine how easy (or difficult) it was to discover feasible alternatives, and use this information to raise or lower the minimum level of acceptability on future problems of a similar nature.

How accurate is the bounded-rationality model? Empirical studies have shown that the model is very accurate.[9,10] A comparison of the classical economic model and the bounded-rationality model shows that the latter presents a more realistic view of decision making.

INCREMENTAL MODEL

Political scientist Charles Lindblom has also criticized the rational model. He argues that the rational model suffers from a number of limitations, such as:[11]

1. Human intelligence or problem-solving capacity is too limited to encompass all of the options and

potential outcomes of the alternatives generated by the synoptic approach.

2. Information is not adequate to assess all options accurately.
3. Comprehensive analysis requires too much time.
4. Comprehensive analysis is too expensive.
5. Facts and values cannot be neatly separated as required by the comprehensive approach.

Lindblom offers another theory of decision making, variously called incrementalism, muddling through, and successive limited comparisons. Incrementalism, in contrast to the rational model,

> stresses decision making through a series of limited, successive comparisons with a relatively narrow range of alternatives rather than a comprehensive range; it uses the status quo, not abstract goals, as the key point of reference for decisions. Incrementalism focuses primarily on short-term rather than long-term effects, on the most crucial consequences of an action rather than on all conceivable results, and on less formalized methods of measuring costs and benefits.[12]

The essential elements of this model include the following:[11,13]

Goals are not isolated and determined before analysis begins. Goal determination and analysis are closely intertwined, even simultaneous. The means often affect the ends, and vice versa.

Decision makers usually consider only a limited number of alternatives—ordinarily only those that differ marginally from existing policy.

All consequences, even of the more restricted options, are not evaluated. All consequences cannot be known, and the time and effort required for comprehensive assessment normally is unavailable.

Since means and ends are inseparable, problem redefinition is continuous; analysis is never-ending, and policy is never made once and for all but remade endlessly.

Lindblom has presented several arguments to support this model. Errors resulting from employing incremental changes from the status quo may not have serious implications and may be easier to correct. Politically, incremental solutions are easier to agree upon since this change may fall somewhere between extreme positions, thereby getting plurality support. Lindblom further maintains that making continual incremental adjustments in both the problem definition and proposed solutions is a reasonable and effective method of solving problems and making decisions.

Like the rational model, the incremental model has also come under attack. Two of the leading critics, Yehezkel Dror and Amitai Etzioni, have identified serious shortcomings of the model, and the latter has proposed an alternative model of decision making. According to Dror, the incremental changes may not address real-world problems, such as a declaration of war that may require innovative solutions that are bolder than those of the incremental approach. Thus, the incremental approach does not facilitate or provide a basis for organizational motivation or change but instead facilitates the maintenance of the status quo. According to Dror, incrementalism works best when[14]

The results of present policies are satisfactory.

There is a high degree of continuity in the nature of the problems.

There is a high degree of continuity in available means for dealing with the problem.

Expanding on Dror's criticisms, Amitai Etzioni argues that the incremental approach fails to distinguish between fundamental and nonfundamental decisions. He suggests that the incremental approach is suitable for nonfundamental matters but not for fundamental ones where a wider perceptual horizon is needed.[15] Etzioni has proposed an alternative approach to decision making, known as mixed scanning.

MIXED SCANNING

This approach combines the best features of both the rational and incremental approaches to decision making. As Etizioni describes decision making:

> Fundamental decisions are made by exploring the main alternatives the actor sees in view of his conception of his goals, but—unlike what rationalism would indicate—details and specifications are omitted so that an overview is feasible. Incremental decisions are made but within the context set by fundamental decisions (and fundamental reviews). Thus, each of the two elements in mixed-scanning helps to reduce the effects of the particular shortcomings of the other; incrementalism reduces the unrealistic aspects of rationalism by limiting the details required in fundamental decisions, and ... rationalism helps to overcome the conservation slant of incrementalism by exploring longer-run alternatives.[15]

According to Etzioni, one of the instances in which this models applies is in the court system. With many cases to decide, lower courts tend to apply the incremental approach by maintaining or slightly deviating from the status quo. When cases are appealed, higher courts tend to analyze issues in more detail, using the rational approach in order to make fundamental and (sometimes bold) decisions.

Despite this example of when this model is applied, the major criticism is that it provides few guidelines for how and when it should be employed.

THE GARBAGE-CAN MODEL

While the approaches to decision making discussed earlier may suggest that organizations make decisions under conditions of much certainty and knowledge, Michael Cohen, James March, and Johan Olson have examined decision making under conditions of unclear organizational setting. That is, there are circumstances in which organizations have "goals that are unclear, technologies that are imperfectly understood, histories that are difficult to interpret, and participants who wander in and out."[12] Cohen et al. have termed these conditions as "organized anarchies." Such organizations operate under conditions of pervasive ambiguity, with so much uncertainty in the decision-making process that traditional theories of coping with uncertainty do not apply.[12] Thus, they consider an organization as "a collection of choices looking for problems, issues and feelings looking for decision situations in which they might be aired, solutions looking for issues to which they might be the answer, and decision makers looking for work."[16] According to March et al., decision making in these circumstances is not regarded as a crisis or transitory. Instead, it is regarded as "characteristic of any organization in part," and is "particularly conspicuous in public, educational, and illegitimate organizations (Ref. [7] citing Michael D. Cohen, James G. March, and Johan P. Olsen, "People, Problems, Solutions and the Ambiguity of Relevance," in Ambiguity and Choice in Organizations, pp. 24–37, ed. James G. March, and Johan P. Olsen. Bergen, Norway: Universitetsforlaget)." Decision making under these conditions is referred to as the "garbage-can theory of organizational choice."

The garbage-can model views:

> a choice opportunity as a garbage can into which various problems are dumped by participants. The mix of garbage in a single can depends partly on the labels attached to the alternative cans; but it also depends on what garbage is being produced at the moment, on the mix of cans available, and on the speed that garbage is collected and removed from the scene.[17]

Which problems get attached to which solutions is a major issue. This is largely determined by chance—by what participants with what goals happened to be on the scene, by when the solutions or the problems entered, and so on."[7] Although the model may seem bizarre or pathological when compared to the traditional rational decision making model, "it does produces decisions under conditions of high uncertainty: that is some solutions do get attached by some participants to some problems."[7]

According to Cohen and March, decision making in this model is made in three ways:[18]

By oversight, without any attention to existing problems and with a minimum of time and energy

By flight (or avoidance), postponement, or buck-passing

By resolution, which occurs generally [on] when flight is severely restricted or when problems are relatively minor or uncomplicated.

In terms of application, this model seems to describe the decision-making processes by college and university presidents as follows:

> Opportunities for choice in higher education can easily become complex "garbage cans" into which a striking variety of problems, solutions, and participants may be dumped. Debate over the hiring of a football coach can become connected to concerns about the essence of a liberal education, the relations of the school to ethnic minorities, or the philosophy of talent (Ref. [7] citing Michael D. Cohen, James G. March, and Johan P. Olsen, "People, Problems, Solutions and the Ambiguity of Relevance," in Ambiguity and Choice in Organizations, pp. 24–37, ed. James G. March, and Johan P. Olsen. Bergen, Norway: Universitetsforlaget).

Despite the unstable environment or unusual nature of organized anarchies, leaders in these organizations can still improve their performance in decision making. Scott suggests that:

> By carefully timing issue creation, by being sensitive to shifting interests and involvement of participants, by recognizing the status and power implications of choice situations, by abandoning initiatives that have become hopelessly entangled with other, originally unrelated problems, by realizing that the planning function is largely symbolic and chiefly provides excuses for interaction, leaders in organized anarchies can maintain their sanity and, sometimes, make a difference in the decision made.[7]

In light of recent developments in many public organizations, this model of decision making may provide the most appropriate perspective from which to understand the complexity of government decision making in the twenty-first century.[12]

WIN-WIN POLICY ANALYSIS

In each of the models of decision making discussed, there seems to be some trade-off among the alternative choices. For example, in the rational model, all decision makers involved may not agree on the evaluation criteria. The policy alternative selected may not be the choice of some decision makers. Thus, the evaluation criteria selected can determine the policy alternative that is chosen. In the case of the incremental model, the incremental choice tends to be a compromise, whereby all major sides have to give up something to gain something.

An emerging decision-making model that seems to address the win-lose phenomenon in these models of decision making by presenting a win-win policy is referred to as win-win policy analysis or super-optimizing solutions. Although the model received initial treatment in the 1980s by various researchers, Stuart Nagel has expanded upon the model since the 1990s through various world-wide applications.[19,20]

Win-win analysis is defined as formulating policies that exceed the best initial goals of expectations of all major groups involved in the policy dispute.[20] The groups could be conservatives, liberals, and political parties. A win-win or super-optimum solution is different from a compromise. While in a compromise situation all sides lose something and gain something in order to arrive at an agreement, a win-win analysis is "capable of achieving conservative goals more than the conservative policies"[19,20] and simultaneously capable of achieving the liberal goals more than the liberal policies. Win-win analysis has applications in any field of public policy, such as economic, social, political, legal, or environmental.

Nagel provides the basic steps in the win-win policy analysis and various ways to facilitate the development of win-win solutions. There are five basic steps to win-win policy analysis:

1. What are the major goals of conservatives, liberals, or other major groups who are disputing what policy should be adopted for a given policy problem?
2. What are the major alternatives of those groups for dealing with the policy problem?
3. What are the relations between each major alternative and each major goal? In their simplest form, these relations can be expressed in terms of a minus sign (relatively adverse relation) and plus sign (relative conducive relation), and a zero (neither adverse nor conducive relation)
4. What new alternative there is might be capable of
   a) achieving the conservative goals even better than the conservative alternative and
   b) simultaneously capable of achieving the liberal goals even more than the liberal alternative? Whatever new alternative meets these two criteria is a win-win alternative or a super-optimum solution.
5. Is the proposed win-win alternative capable of getting over various hurdles that frequently exist. These hurdles may be, in random order, political, administrative, technological, legal, psychological, and economic.

There are various ways of facilitating ideas for win-win solutions, such as

1. Expand the resources available so that both liberal and conservative goals can be achieved.
2. Modify the liberal alternatives so they also achieve the conservative goals, and/or modify the conservative alternatives so they also achieve the liberal goals.
3. Redefine the problem to emphasize goals, rather than alternatives.
4. Fully combine alternatives that are not mutually exclusive.
5. Make use of a mind-stimulating matrix that shows goals on the column, alternatives on the rows, and scores or directions of relations in the cells. Have an empty row at the bottom of the matrix for inserting words and data on possible win-win solutions.

CONCLUSIONS

Decision making is important in administrative organizations. Although the various models of decision making discussed have their strengths and limitations, they provide insights into organizational decision making. Moreover, since the choices made can have positive or negative implications for the organizations, the type or mode of decision making employed is important. Given the importance of decision making in organizations, more research is needed to improve organizational decision making.

REFERENCES

1. Morgan, D.R.; England, R.E. *Managing Urban America*, 4th Ed.; Chatham House Publishers: Chatham, 1986; pp. 116, 121.
2. Downs, A. *An Economic Theory of Democracy*; Harper & Row: New York, 1957; 4.
3. Allison, G. *Essence of Decision: Explaining the Cuban Missile Crisis*; Little, Brown: Boston, 1971.

4. Simon, H. *Administrative Behavior*, 3rd Ed.; Macmillan: New York, 1976; 79.

5. Simon, H.A. *Administrative Behavior*, 3rd Ed.; The Free Press: New York, 1976; 241.

6. Simon, H.A. *Administrative Behavior: A Study of Decision-Making Process in Administrative Organization*, 2nd Ed.; The Free Press: New York, 1957; xxvi.

7. Scott, W.R. *Organizations: Rational, Natural, and Open Systems*, 3rd Ed.; Prentice Hall: Englewood Cliffs, NJ, 1992; pp. 45, 297–299.

8. Hodgetts, R.M. Organizational Behavior: Theory and Practice; Macmillan: New York, 1991; 374.

9. *A Behavior Theory of the Firm*; Cyert, R.M., March, J.G., Eds.; Prentice-Hall: Englewood Cliffs, NJ, 1963.

10. Clarkson, G.P.E. A Model of Trust Investment Behavior. In *A Behavior Theory of the Firm*; Cyert, R.M., March, J.G., Eds.; Prentice-Hall: Englewood Cliffs, NJ, 1963; 253–267.

11. Lindblom, C.E. *The Intelligence of Democracy*; Free Press: New York, 1965; 138–143.

12. Milakovich, M.E.; Gordon, G.J. *Public Administration in America*, 7th Ed.; Bedford/St. Martin's: Boston, 2001; pp. 202, 227, 228, note 51.

13. Lindblom, C.E. The science of muddling. Public Adm. Rev. **Spring 1959**, *19*, 79–88.

14. Dror, Y. Muddling through—'science' or inertia? Public Adm. Rev. **September 1964**, *24*, 154.

15. Etzioni, A. Mixed scanning: A 'third approach to decision making'. Public Adm. Rev. **December 1967**, *27*, 385–392.

16. Cohen, M.D.; March, J.G.; Olsen, J.P. A garbage can model of organizational choice. Adm. Sci. Q. **1972**, *17*, 2.

17. Cohen, M.; March, J.; Olsen, J. *Organization Theory*; Brooks/Cole: Pacific Grove, CA, 1989; 263, as quoted in Harold Gortner, Julianne Mahler, and Jeanne Nicholson.

18. Cohen, M.; March, J. *Leadership and Ambiguity*; McGraw-Hill: New York, 1974; 83–84.

19. Nagel, S. *Super-Optimum Solution and Win-Win Policy: Basic Concepts and Principles*; Greenwood Publishers/Quorum Books: Westport, CT, 1997.

20. Nagel, S. *Policy-Analysis Methods and Super-Optimum Solutions*; Nova Science: New York, 1994.

Decision Making, Incrementalism and Transformational Change

D

Keith Carrington
St. John's University, Jamaica, New York, U.S.A.

INTRODUCTION

Before the publication of Herbert Simon's text, *Administrative Behavior*, in 1957,[1] most scholars showed little interest in decision making at the low levels in organizations. This surprisingly was due to the influence of the politics-administration dichotomy, which caused the focus to be on decision making at the highest level in organizations where policy was formulated. Simon's work, however, adjusted the focus when he asserted that decision making constituted the core of administration, and that the process was the same throughout the organization.[2]

Decision making is one of most frequently discussed topics in public administration. The quest to understand the decision-making process is not new, and the process of "deciding" has frustrated many decision makers. Public sector managers are inundated with decision-making models. Despite these models and a proliferation of literature, no one model has been proffered as the "one best" method. Notwithstanding, the models, each with its strengths and weaknesses, present an array of choices for public managers.

DECISION MAKING: A DEFINITION

Starling[3] defined decision making as the process of "selecting from various alternatives one course of action." Starling further postulated that the decision process involves several distinct steps: 1) identifying the problem; 2) gathering facts; 3) making the decision; and 4) implementing and evaluating the decision.[3] An essential component in the definition is the final step, which emphasizes that the decision-making process does not conclude with the selection of a particular course of action. Simon[4] reinforced this point when he stated, "the process of decision does not come to an end with the general purpose of an organization has been determined. The task of 'deciding' pervades the entire administrative organization quite as much as does the task of 'doing'."

The development of an ideal decision-making model with universal application seems impractical. Hence, public sector managers utilize various models to select a particular course of action. This paper will address a few decision-making models.

DECISION-MAKING MODELS

There are several decision-making models, each based on a variety of premises and assumptions. The *Essence of Decision*[5,6] provides frameworks for explaining decision making. Using three models, Rational Actor (Model I), Organizational Process (Model II), and Government Process (Model III), the authors outlined approaches to decision making by using the Cuban Missile Crisis to illustrate their application.

MODEL I: THE RATIONAL ACTOR MODEL

Stevenson et al.[7] described the Rational Actor Model as a prescription that tells decision makers how to "decide." This model is based on two assumptions: all information is available to the decision maker, and the decision maker would maximize the decision to benefit the organization.[8] The central concepts of the Classical Model are:

1. *Goals and objectives*: The rational decision maker ranks all possible sets of consequences in terms of his or her values and objectives.
2. *Alternatives*: The decision maker must choose among a set of available alternatives.
3. *Consequences*: To each alternative, there is a set of consequences or outcomes to be considered.
4. *Choice*: The decision maker selects the alternative with the highest payoff function.[9]

The behavior of the actor—an individual, agency, or group—is intentional, goal seeking, and value maximizing. The decision maker employs rigor, purposiveness, and consistency—among goals and objectives.[9] The comprehensive rationality component of this model infers

Encyclopedia of Public Administration and Public Policy
DOI: 10.1081/E-EPAP 120010680

that the decision maker has the ability to consistently rank and review all alternatives and their consequences and then choose the alternative that achieves the highest utility.

MODEL II: THE ORGANIZATIONAL PROCESS MODEL

The Organizational Process Model's premise is that government decisions stem from the output of several agencies that provide information and advice. This model proffers decision making as less deliberate and the function of government's "vast conglomerate of semi feudal, loosely allied organizations each with a substantial life of its own," functioning according to standard patterns of behavior.[9] Each organization is given individual aspects of a problem to attend to.

This model emphasizes that the organization's major concern is to operate within the framework with a set of constraints negotiated through various components of the organization. This helps them reduce uncertainty in the environment and set out those alternatives that are immediate, available, and related to the problem at hand. According to Allison and Zelikow,[9] the decision-making process then can be understood with knowledge of the organizations' operations.

MODEL III: GOVERNMENT PROCESS MODEL

Allison's Governmental Politics Model stipulates that decisions are made through bargaining among individuals and groups with diverse interests and varying degrees of power to support those interests. Decisions reached are sometimes a result of compromise and the power and skill of proponents and opponents. Politics plays a major role in decision making. Decisions are made through the involvement of many actors who focus on many problems, numerous goals, some of which are personal, and by "pulling and hauling that is politics."[9]

CRITICISMS OF ALLISON'S MODELS

The Classical Model appears to be oversimplified. It ostensibly makes unrealistic demands on the decision maker, who, according to Simon, must have "powers of prescience and capacities for computation resembling those usually attributed to God."[5] In fact, decision makers experience considerable stress in attempting to deal with their limited cognitive abilities. President Warren G. Harding articulated the cognitive stress in the following statement:

John, I can't make a damn thing out of this tax problem. I listen to one side and they seem right, and then God! I talk to the other and they seem just as right, and there I am where I started. I know somewhere there is a book that would give me the truth, but hell, I couldn't read the book. I know somewhere there is an economist that knows the truth, but I don't know where to find him, and haven't the sense to know him and trust him when I did find him God what a job.[10]

The cookie-cutter approach of the prescriptive classical model epitomizes logic, focus, and rationality, which, misleadingly, may convey the idea that the approach guarantees successful decision making. However, the model does not enjoy widespread use. According to the article, *The Wisdom of Solomon*,[11] rational decision-making techniques are used "less than 20% of the time."

Models II and III have several weakness. According to Bendor and Hammond,[12] the two models are "sufficiently ambiguous that it is difficult to discern the models' defining properties." Model III depicts decision making as a process involving many actors engrossed in "pulling and hauling." At the end of this process, one group triumphs over the others. Przeworski[13] reminds us that during these political discussions, "reasons and facts are exhausted...issues are decided by voting, which is an imposition of one will upon a resisting will ... Politics is an antagonistic relationship between 'us' and 'them'...". This approach to decision making creates winners and losers. Although the process produces a decision that may be based on a mixture of alternatives, it might be a patchwork decision that can have disastrous consequences.

Bendor and Hammond[12] articulated that the three models unquestionably have several important methodological points. However, the lessons learned from the models may lack foundation and, in some cases may be incorrect. Finally, it seems that the models do not provide good frameworks for low-level decision makers.

THE ADMINISTRATION MODEL

The Administration Model was proposed by March and Simon[14] as a descriptive model that explains how decision makers actually make decisions. A decision maker using this model defines the problem in terms of his or her understanding of the situation, and does not consider all information, alternatives, and their consequences. This model may require decision makers to follow steps similar to those of the classical model, such as generating alternatives and reflecting on their consequences. However, there is no impractical quest to glean all information. Instead, the decision maker collects relevant information based on a definition of the situation.[15] Simon[16] stated that there are limits to a decision maker's cognitive ability, and it is this bounded rationality that forces them to satisfice rather than optimize.[14]

THE INCREMENTAL MODEL

Lindblom's[17] Incremental Model offers another approach to decision making. Lindblom suggests that incrementalism is more likely used in practice. This method of decision making involves making sequential (incremental) decisions. Successive limited comparisons may be the most appropriate approach when problems are complex. Using the incremental model, the decision maker goes through the following steps:

1. An objective is established.
2. Few alternatives immediately relevant are outlined and then compared.
3. Select an alternative. This would be a combination of the choice among values and the choice among the instruments for achieving the objective.

With this approach, the decision maker focuses on incremental values and analyzes only those demonstrating the differences between the alternatives. According to Lindblom,[17] the decision maker's "need for information on values or objectives is drastically reduced . . . and his capacity for grasping, comprehending, and relating values to one another is not strained beyond the breaking point." The decision maker expects to have partial success with this decision, so he or she would expect to repeat the process endlessly, as they will be building on what has already been done. A major advantage of incrementalism is that it safeguards against errors, as the previous steps would have informed the decision maker of the possible consequences of similar steps.

Tarter and Hoy[18] state that the incremental model has the following five distinctive features:

1. Means–ends analysis is inappropriate, because objectives and alternatives emerge simultaneously.
2. Good solutions are those upon which decision makers agree regardless of objectives.
3. Options and outcomes are dramatically reduced by considering only alternatives similar to the current state of affairs.
4. Analysis is limited to differences between the existing situation and proposed alternatives.
5. The incremental method eschews theory in favor of successive comparisons of concrete, practical alternatives.

The authors believe that incrementalism simplifies decision making, which does not make it whimsical.

Incrementalism is not without its critics. True[19] articulates that despite incrementalism's widespread use, it has several flaws. They include the model's failure to provide comprehensive explanation of the expectations from policy and budget decisions; it says little about competition; it lacks a method to differentiate between incremental change and nonincremental change; it does not offer an understanding of value conflicts in the three levels of government when there is disagreement about who gets what; and it only gives a partial description of what really happens.

Lindblom[17] stated that the model had several imperfections; for example, the model did not have built-in safeguards for the relevant values; and that several important policies might be overlooked, because steps taken earlier may not point in their direction. Despite the shortcomings, incrementalism has remained the dominant model used to understanding government decision making since its introduction in the mid-1960s.[20]

TRANSFORMATIONAL CHANGE

Why would an organization choose to change its operations, and what factors would determine the type of change an organization should undertake? This question can be answered in a variety of ways. Most organizations do not voluntarily change their operations; and change does not occur by chance. Instead, organizational change occurs in response to some phenomenon from within or outside the organization or both. Organizations may undergo change to deal with inertia, chart a new course for the organization to follow, introduce new technology or handle some unexpected outcome. In addition, shrinking budgets, increased demands for improved services, and pressure from clientele may force management to do things differently to deliver better quality services.

Organizations are susceptible to many factors, as they do not operate in a stable, protected environment shielded from internal and external pressures. Notwithstanding, many organizations resist change because management may see the system as being stable. According to Kiel,[21] "When change is desired, demanded, or inevitable, changing such a stability creates wrenching situations for employees and management."

Management scholars no longer associate order, stability, and consistency with the operations of organizations. In fact, according to Kiel,[21] public organizations operate in a nonlinear and dynamic system full of surprises. Consequently, in response to turbulence in the organization's environment, an organization may be forced to change.

Jurow[22] defines transformational change as "doing something different by creating new structures and new processes to fit a new objective." It necessitates a change in the status quo and the creation of new frameworks unmistakably different from what existed previously. The typical view of organization transformation theorists is that the process is a "holistic, ecological, humanistic approach to radical, revolutionary change in the entire context of an organizational system."[23] Some theorists believe that organizations do not deliberately implement transformational change and that the change may be crisis-driven and necessary for the organization's survival.[24] However, some organizations may change, because it is rational to do so. Dyck[25] found that transformational changes based on value-rationality and not the status quo were the most likely to be implemented.

The literature on organizations provides different theories on how organizational change takes place. However, Sastry[26] postulates, "Despite the important theoretical and practical implications of understanding organizational change, the organizational processes involved in transformational change have not been fully explored." Porras and Robertson[27] concur and articulate that the theories' failure to fully explain the dynamics of the planned change is a major weakness of the field.

It is difficult to disagree that theories have not fully explained the implications of organizational change. However, Kiel[21] articulates several principles drawn from nonlinear dynamics that can provide public managers with insights into the dynamics of transformational change. There are three essential processes in transformational change. First, there will be fluctuations within the organization, and they should not be viewed as negatives, because these fluctuations can drive and energize the change process in the organization. The unusual behaviors that occur within the organization encourage the search for new problem-solving methods and service provision.

Second, managers should be aware that there would be instability within the organization. This, however, should serve as a prerequisite to change, thereby allowing the appropriate responses to environmental demands. Managers must exercise caution when dealing with instability, as only a certain level is required to realize the potential for change.

The third essential process in transformational change is disorder. This element is critical, as it facilitates the exploration of several possibilities that may lead to new operating procedures or new structures or both.

Like any other process, transformation change may fail to have the intended impact on the organization. Backer[28] identifies management's failure to address the human side of the organization as a major factor. Managers shepherding transformation change in organizations must involve all employees in the process, as "Personal change is the prerequisite to organizational change... organizational transformation occurs one individual at a time."[28]

CONCLUSION

The presence of fluctuations, instability, and disorder signals the formidable challenge that confronts public sector managers during the change process. These processes are neither surprising nor unexpected, because public agencies function in a nonlinear environment fraught with uncertainty, chaos, and unintended consequences.

The process of change may present agencies with a seemingly insurmountable challenge. Notwithstanding, both management and other employees must have the discipline to facilitate emerging procedures and structures. A successful transformed public agency would benefit employees and clientele in several ways. Nutt and Backoff [29] articulate that such agency would be able to serve a greater variety of clients in several new ways and improve the efficacy of the agency's operations.

REFERENCES

1. Simon, H.A. *Administrative Behavior: A Study of Decision-Making Processes in Administrative Organization,* 3rd Ed.; The Free Press: New York, 1976.
2. Denhardt, R.B. *Theories of Public Organization*; Wadsworth, Inc.: Belmont, CA, 1984.
3. Starling, G. *Managing the Public Sector,* 5th Ed.; Harcourt Brace and Company: Orlando, FL, 1998.
4. Simon, H.A. *Administrative Behavior: A Study of Decision-Making Processes in Administrative Organizations,* 3rd Ed.; The Free Press: New York, 1976.
5. Allison, G.T. *Essence of Decision: Explaining the Cuban Missile Crisis*; Little, Brown and Company: Boston, MA, 1971.
6. Allison, G.; Zelikow, P. *Essence of Decision: Explaining the Cuban Missile Crisis,* 2nd Ed.; Addison-Wesley Educational Publishers Inc.: New York, 1999.
7. Stevenson, M.K.; Busemeyer, J.R.; Naylor, J.C. Judgment and Decision-Making Theory. In *Handbook of Industrial and Organizational Psychology,* 2nd Ed.; Dunnette, M.D., Hough, L.M., Eds.; Consulting Psychologists Press: California, 1990; 283–374.
8. Edwards, W. The theory of decision making. Psychol. Bull. **1954,** *51,* 380–417.
9. Allison, G.; Zelikow, P. *Essence of Decision: Explaining the Cuban Missile Crisis,* 2nd Ed.; Addison-Wesley Educational Publishers Inc.: New York, 1999.

10. Janis, I.L.; Mann, L. *Decision Making: A Psychological Analysis of Conflict, Choice, and Commitment*; The Free Press: New York, 1977.

11. McCormick, J. The wisdom of Solomon. Newsweek **1987**, **August 17**, *110*, 62–63.

12. Bendor, J.; Hammond, T.H. Rethinking Allison's models. Am. Polit. Sci. Rev. **1992**, **June**, *86* (2), 300–320.

13. Przeworski, A. *Democracy and the Market: Political and Economic Reforms in Eastern Europe and Latin America*; Cambridge University Press: New York, 1991.

14. March, J.G.; Simon, H.A. *Organizations*; Wiley: New York, 1958.

15. George, J.M.; Jones, G.R. *Organizational Behavior: Understanding and Managing*; Addison-Wesley Publishing Company: New York, 1996.

16. Simon, H.A. *Administrative Behavior: A Study of Decision-Making Processes in Administrative Organizations,* 3rd Ed.; The Free Press: New York, 1976.

17. Lindblom, C.E. The science of muddling through. Public Adm. Rev. **1959**, *19* (2), 78–88.

18. Tarter, C.J.; Hoy, W.K. Toward a contingency theory of decision making. J. Educ. Adm. **1998**, *36* (3), 212–228.

19. True, J.L. Avalanches and incrementalism: Making policy and budgets in the United States. Am. Rev. Public Adm. **2000**, **March**, *30* (1), 3–18.

20. True, J.L. Avalanches and incrementalism: Making policy and budgets in the United states. Am. Rev. Public Adm. **2000**, **March**, *30* (1), 3–18. Retrieved January 3, 2002 from EBSCOhost Full Display on-line database on the World Wide Web: http://ehostvgw12.epnet.com/ehost.asp?

21. Kiel, L.D. *Managing chaos and complexity in government: A new paradigm for managing change, innovation, and organizational renewal*; Jossey-Bass Inc.: California, 1994.

22. Jurow, S. Change: The importance of the process. Educom Rev. **1999**, **Sept./Oct.**, *34* (5), 60, 1 p. Retrieved August 22, 2001 from EBSCOhost Full Display on-line database on the World Wide Web: http://ehostvgw12. epnet.com/ehost.asp?

23. Limerick, D.; Passfield, R.; Cunnington, B. Transformational change: Towards an action learning organization. Learn. Organ. **1994**, *1* (2), 29–40. Retrieved January 3, 2002 from EBSCOhost Full Display on-line database on the World Wide Web: http://ehostvgw12.epnet.com/ehost.asp?

24. Edelman, L.F.; Benning, A.L. Incremental revolution: Organizational change in highly turbulent environments. Organ. Dev. J. **1999**, **Winter**, *17* (4), 79. Retrieved July 27, 2001 from ProQuest on-line database on the World Wide Web: http://proquestmail@bellhowell. infrolearning.com.

25. Dyck, B. Understanding configuration and transformation through a multiple rationalities approach. J. Manag. Stud. **1997**, **September**, *34* (5), 793–823. Retrieved January 3, 2002 from EBSCOhost Full Display on-line database on the World Wide Web: http://ehostvgw12.epnet.com/ehost.asp?

26. Sastry, M.A. Problems and paradoxes in a model of punctuated organizational change. Adm. Sci. Q. **1997**, **June**, *42* (2), 237–275. Retrieved July 27, 2001 from ProQuest on-line database on the World Wide Web: http://proquestmail@bellhowell.infrolearning.com.

27. Porras, J.I.; Robertson, P.J. Organizational Development: Theory, Practice and Research. In *Handbook of Industrial and Organizational Psychology,* 2nd Ed.; Dunnette, M.D., Hough, L.M., Eds.; Consulting Psychologists Press: Paola Alto, CA, 1992.

28. Backer, T.E. Managing the human side of change in VA's transformation. Hosp. Health Serv. Adm. **1997**, **Fall**, *42* (3), 433–459. Retrieved July 27, 2001 from ProQuest on-line database on the World Wide Web: http://proquestmail@ bellhowell.infrolearning.com.

29. Nutt, P.C.; Backoff, R.W. *Facilitating Transformational Change*; The Journal of Applied Behavioral Science, **1997**, *33* (4), 490–508. Retrieved July 27, 2001 from ProQuest on-line database: http://proquestmail@bellhowell. infrolearning.com.

Decision Making, Open System and Nonequilibrium

Keith Carrington
St. John's University, Jamaica, New York, U.S.A.

INTRODUCTION

Making decisions is a normal part of our daily routine. Most of our decisions are made with very little processing or reviewing of alternatives and their consequences. While we make most decisions singularly, we, however, do not act as individual decision makers on all matters affecting our life. There are instances when we make decisions as members of a group. Whether we are involved in the decision-making process as individuals or members of a group, many of the decisions we make have far-reaching consequences.

Decision making is an important organizational function. It is important to public sector organizations because of their important social function. In organizations, individuals and groups make decisions. Many of these decisions not only affect the lives of the agency's clientele but also determine the organization's viability. Not long ago, decision making in organizations was considered the domain of the upper echelon. This notion has since been dispelled with the realization that workers at all levels are involved in the decision-making process. At the lower levels of an organization, decisions are made routinely about operational and other job-related issues. At the upper echelon, however, decision making takes on an additional element as managers deal with complex problems that require a high level of expertise.

Decision making is a "rational, deliberate, purposeful action, beginning with the development of a decision strategy and moving through implementation and appraisal of results."[1] The process consists of three important elements: intelligence, design, and choice. Intelligence involves scanning the environment and arriving at a decision point. The second element is design, which involves developing alternative courses of action. Finally, choice is selecting the alternative with the best chance of success.[2]

Many types of decisions are made in organizations. These decisions can be placed into two categories: programmed and nonprogrammed decisions. Programmed decisions are made in response to recurring, predictable problems. Decision makers respond to recurring problems by automatically implementing performance programs worked out beforehand (see Fig. 1). Performance programs are standard procedures of behavior that employees

follow. An organization may have several performance programs, as some problems may recur. Many programmed decisions evolve from nonprogrammed decisions implemented to deal with problems that occurred earlier.[2–4] These programs are not "written in concrete," and should be reviewed to determine when changes might be necessary.

There are advantages to using programmed decisions. First, time is not wasted searching for information to develop responses to problems that are predictable and recur frequently. Second, these decisions allow the decision maker to respond quickly to threats or problems from the environment, which, if not resolved promptly, could lead to negative consequences. Third, programmed decisions allow decision makers to implement specifically designed strategies, thereby avoiding errors in the decision-making process.

Nonprogrammed decisions are the second type of decisions. These decisions address novel, unstructured, complex, and nonprogrammable programs encountered for the first time.[2–4] This type of decision making requires superior skills and expertise. Decision makers follow particular steps that may include: identifying the problem; collecting information; examining alternatives and consequences; selecting a course of action; implementing the decision; and evaluating.

Framing a strategy to address a novel problem is not an easy task. Two points are worth mentioning. First, decision makers must accurately identify the problem, which would make the underlying causes unambiguous. This minimizes errors in framing and selecting an appropriate response. Second, decision makers must know the upper and lower limits of the decision. According to Sorenson[5] and Starling,[6] the upper limits are as follows:

1. The limits of permissibility (Is it legal? Will others accept it?).
2. The limits of available resources.
3. The limits of available time.
4. The limits of previous commitments.
5. The limits of available information.

The lower limit of a decision "refers to what, at least, must occur for the problem to be solved."[6] The lower limits inform the decision maker of the necessary factors

Encyclopedia of Public Administration and Public Policy
DOI: 10.1081/E-EPAP 120010679

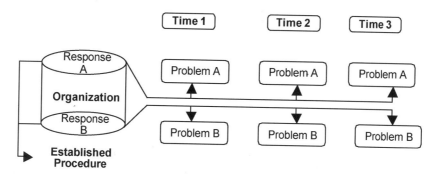

Fig. 1 Programmed decision response to recurring problems.

that must be present for the decision to address the problem or situation identified.

There are several decision-making models, which give decision makers an array of choices. A few of the models are listed below:

1. Incrementalism.
2. The Rational Actor Model.
3. The Organizational Process Model.
4. Government Process Model.
5. The Administration Model (see *Decision making, Incrementalism and Transformational Change* for a discussion of these models).

No model has been proffered as the "one best" model for decision making, and the use of a model does not guarantee success. The best model would be the one that resolves the problem, and it may comprise elements from several models. Adhering steadfastly to one approach to make a decision may preclude the successful resolution of a problem. Tarter and Hoy[1] remind us,

> None of the models is a substitute for reflective thinking. None should be used rigidly as to prevent the recognition of an elegant solution in search of a problem ... When models are depicted in diagrams or schemata, it is tempting to view them as lock-step procedures to follow blindly. This is wrong as seeing all decision making as so idiosyncratic as to deny patterns.

Many of the models provide a theoretical approach to making decisions. Many scholars and practitioners propound that some models project a "cookie cutter" approach to decision making, and many of their features have very little applicability to real-world decision making. The lesson for decision makers is that while the models provide guidelines, there are differences in how decisions are made in the real world. This criticism is not sounding the death knell for the models, as several of their premises are used in real-world decision making.

Real-world decision making offers decision makers several important lessons. First, government's most important decisions are made by groups of people and not individual decision makers working alone. Second, decision making is not a completely rational process. Third, people involved in the decision-making process possess different levels of analytical skills. Fourth, there are real limitations to applying strict analytical methods to all aspects of any problem.[6]

While Simon advocated rationality in the decision-making process, Allison and Lindblom's work shifted the focus to the influence of environmental factors on the decision-making process. This shift showed organizations not as isolated units concerned with only internal factors, but entities subject to the influence of the environment.[7]

OPEN SYSTEMS

The open-system perspective has some of its roots in the intellectual ferment that emerged shortly after World War II. The works of von Bertanffy[8] fostered interest in open systems by showing that systems theory could be applied to many entities, including organizations.[9] The system's perspective views an organization as a complex entity with several intertwined and interconnected elements that continuously interact with the environment.[10] Open-systems organizations are "systems of interdependent activities linking shifting coalitions of participants; the systems are embedded in—dependent on continuing exchanges with and constituted by—the environments in which they operate".[9] An open-systems organization not only has interchanges with the environment but also needs the vital interchanges to maintain its viability.[11]

Organizations are open systems because of their energetic input–output system, interaction, and dependence on the external environment. Organizations were not always considered open systems. Before the application of the open-systems perspective, social scientists used one of two approaches to examine social structures. First, they regarded the structures as closed systems and applied the laws of physics and ignored environmental factors. The second approach endowed a self-determining concept to the structures and attributed their functionality to some magical purposiveness.[12] In a closed system, each part contributes to the overall working of the organization, the primary concern is efficiency, and the agency is considered insulated from environmental influences. The organization then is in full control and therefore focuses on functionality. Taylor's scientific management and Weber's concept of bureaucracy are examples of such systems.[7,9,13]

In contrast to closed systems, where structures were thought to be relatively self-contained and independent, the open-systems perspective views the organization as acutely dependent upon the external environment. The organization has continuous exchanges with the environment. It uses the energy and materials from the environment to produce goods and services that are delivered to its clientele. Such organizations are susceptible to challenges and uncertainties, as managers do not possess full knowledge of the factors that could influence the organization's functions or have the ability to predict and control the factors that can influence the organization.[12]

Notwithstanding the perilous environments that are fraught with formidable challenges, the open-systems organization continues its relationship with the environment, which is crucial to its survival. This interaction can facilitate organizational adaptation and change. Failure to change can lead to an organization's demise. Neumann Jr.[14] articulates that the major challenge facing modern organizations is how they could effectively adapt to their rapidly changing environments. He argues that modern organizational structures have been devised throughout history to meet the demands of the increasingly complex external environments, and expounds:

> As with species that fail to adapt to changes in their environmental niches, so too nonadaptive organizations do not survive. The key to coping with external environments generally requires that the created structures of the organizations be compatible with the existing dynamics of the external world. Such a fundamental requirement should be intuitive, but in practice, many organizations appear not to understand this necessity.

Trist and Emery[15] concur that some type of adaptation or evolution is necessary for an organization to survive in an increasingly turbulent environment. They believe that the evolution to open systems benefits the organization. Heckman[16] also agrees that adopting an open system "maximizes the flexibility and adaptive potential of all its members . . .," thereby allowing the organization to sustain itself in a turbulent and challenging environment.

How can a complex organization adapt and sustain itself in an unpredictable environment? Philip Selznick's[17] study of the Tennessee Valley Authority (TVA) provides insights into some of the methodologies employed to deal with environmental threats. His work on the TVA outlined an open-systems approach to organizational analysis. The analysis emphasized the importance of the relationships between the organization and its environment. The study highlights the intricate system of relationships, which is important to an organization's stability and continuity. These relationships emerge as organizations endeavor to meet their needs and handle numerous problems.

One focus of the study was on the major strategic decisions to deal with threats in the environment. The mechanism used to handle environmental threats was co-optation, which safeguarded the organization and built relationships with social forces in the environment. For example, the TVA leadership co-opted the agricultural leadership—a threat from its environment—into its policy-making structure. The goal of this strategic move was to glean support for the organization's policies. Despite the benefits that could redound through the open-systems approach, many organizations attempt to operate in a closed system. This choice may be foolhardy, as organizations pursuing such isolation never achieve their goals.

NONEQUILIBRIUM

One view of organizations is that they operate in a state of equilibrium for a very long period, where activities would be consistent with their dictates and structures. Public sector agencies are seen by some as examples of organizations striving to maintain equilibrium through stability. Some scholars regard stability and equilibrium as the "normal" and preferred conditions of organizations.[18] Stability does not prevent change. Occasionally, punctuated change is made incrementally to maintain equilibrium. Some believe that the quest for equilibrium is dysfunctional and could lead to an organization's demise.

An opposing view is that organizations function under nonequilibrium conditions, and due to the environmental threats, are constantly adapting to sustain themselves. Nonequilibrium conditions are seen as prerequisites for an organization's growth and adaptation.

Limerick et al.[19] stated that the field has seen stable, incremental change and rapid organizational change. They reconcile the two types of changes by proffering Gould's model of "punctuated equilibrium." He stated:

> Speaking most generally, our usual concept of time and history, abetted by traditional gradualism, views change as continuous and intrinsic, and structure as a temporary

incarnation of the moment. The alternative view, the basic vision underlying catastrophism, if you will, sees stable structure and organization as the usual state of things, and change as a rare and disruptive event provoking rapid shifts from one configuration to another. I believe that we are now witnessing, in field after field, a growing recognition of this punctuational style for change at all scales (cited in Limerick et al.).

This perspective advocates that there are long periods of equilibrium punctuated by short periods of nonequilibrium, which resulted in the reconfiguration of organizations. Some believe that equilibrium and nonequilibrium conditions are interrelated.[19]

Not all scholars and practitioners support the concept of punctuated change. Many believe that the unpredictable environment creates the nonequilibrium conditions in which organizations operate. Many suggest that nonequilibrium conditions prevail in an unpredictable, uncertain and, according to Doyle,[20] ''an unforgiving and, at times even hostile environment.'' These conditions, which are fraught with pitfalls, compel organizations to change. Arthos[21] articulates that nonequilibrium conditions have emerged as one of the natural features of open systems, and the nonequilibrium conditions encourage ongoing attempts to transform organizations. These transformational change attempts are made frequently; however, most of these attempts are rejected.[22]

The equilibrium paradigm no longer holds firmly in the public sector. Practitioners and scholars now acknowledge the nonlinear nature of public sector organizations and the instability and turbulence these organizations confront.[18] These conditions present a formidable challenge to public agencies in their quest to deliver services. Government agencies are open systems, as they extract (taxes and fee) and release energy (services) through interaction with the environment. There may be demands from citizens and employees for a different method of service delivery. These pressures may force the organization to develop a novel service delivery.[23]

The nonequilibrium perspective views the public administration environment in two ways. First, the environment comprises a mosaic of organizations at different stages of their evolution. This montage contains declining, self-regulating, and extremely unstable organizations; the latter may experience symmetry breaks and novel reconfigurations. The second view holds that the intrusion of politics on administration can enhance instability, which may lead to symmetry-breaking behavior. He argues against the politics/administration dichotomy, because politics may be needed to push public sector organizations beyond stability. Consequently, politics and administration must be inexorably linked.[18] The nonequilibrium conditions in which public sector organizations function demands continued renewal and change to

remain viable. To ensure survival, it is necessary for organizations to change to continue operations in a nonlinear environment.

NONEQUILIBRIUM THEORY

Change is an accepted feature of organizations, and knowledge of the change process is important to practitioners and scholars. It is, therefore, important that the explanatory models used should be appropriate to bring to light invaluable lessons. Incremental and equilibrium models are still being used to explain how organizations change to adapt to their environment. However, these models give only a variation on the issue. Due to the nonequilibrium conditions and chaos organizations encounter while interacting with the environment, these models do not properly explain the change process. These models have failed to encompass the complexity of development of social systems and do not ''incorporate those instances when wholesale, dramatic system changes occur''.[18]

The inability of models to explain the changes that occur highlights the need for a new approach. Kiel[18] proffers nonequilibrium theory, which he believes would provide an in-depth understanding of the evolutionary nature of the ''process of change in which instability, disorder, and unpredictability serve as the central features in the development of new forms organization and complexity.'' In addition, the theory gives insights into the change process leading to new configurations and can complement incremental models, thereby elucidating the entire evolutionary processes in systems relevant to public administration.

CONCLUSION

The cataclysmic events of September 11, 2001, underscore the unpredictable and perilous environmental conditions that can befall public and private sector organizations. The fallout from the events has affected all sectors. This has demonstrated several important lessons. First, organizations cannot isolate themselves from their environments. Even if they are not affected directly, ripple effects from turbulence in their environments could have an impact on an organization's overall performance. Second, although the September events are not typical of the environments in which organizations operate, they indicate that organizations would always face uncertainties and challenges. Third, change and adaptation must be a feature of organizations if they are to survive and remain viable in nonequilibrium conditions.

Many may argue that an open-systems organization is better equipped to deal with environmental threats. An advantage a decision maker has in an open systems organization is that he or she can use several methods to achieve the organization's goals; which is a defining characteristic of open systems.[12] Kast and Rosenzweig[24] argued that the dichotomization of systems has led to the belief that open systems are good, and closed systems are bad. They, however, believe that most social organizations are "partially open" and "partially closed," and that both approaches could be used under certain circumstances.

REFERENCES

1. Tarter, C.J.; Hoy, W.K. Toward a contingency theory of decision making. J. Educ. Adm. **1998**, *36* (3), 212–228. Retrieved January 4, 2002 from EBSCOhost Full Display on-line database on the World Wide Web:http://ehostvgw12.epnet.com/ehost.asp?
2. Simon, H.A. *The New Science of Management Decision*; Harper & Brothers Publishers: New York, 1960.
3. Browne, M. *Organizational Decision Making and Information*; Ablex Publishing Corporation: Norwood, NJ, 1993.
4. George, J.M.; Jones, G.R. *Understanding and Managing Organizational Behavior*; Addison-Wesley Publishing Company: New York, 1996.
5. Sorenson, T.C. *Decision Making in the White House*; Columbia University Press: New York, 1963.
6. Starling, G. *Managing the Public Sector*, 5th Ed.; Harcourt Brace College Publishers: New York, 1998.
7. Denhardt, R.B. *Theories of Public Organization*; Wadsworth, Inc.: Belmont, CA, 1984.
8. von Bertanffy, L. *General System Theory: Foundations, Developments, Applications,* Revised Ed.; George Braziller: New York, 1968.
9. Scott, W.S. *Organizations: Rational, Natural, and Open Systems*; Prentice Hall: Upper Saddle River, NJ, 1998.
10. Shafritz, J.M.; Ott, J.S. *Classics of Organizational Theory*, 3rd Ed.; Brooks/Cole Publishing Company: Pacific Grove, CA, 1992.
11. Swanson, D. Dysfunctional conglomerates: An explanation provided by linking ontological individualism to social relationships within an open system. Behav. Sci. **April 1992**, *37* (2), 139, 14 pp. Retrieved from Retrieved August 8, 2001 from EBSCOhost Full Display on-line database on theWorld Wide Web:http://ehostvgw12.epnet.com/ehost.asp?
12. Katz, D.; Kahn, R.L. Organizations and the System Concept. In *Classics of Organization Theory*, 3rd Ed.; Shafritz, J.M., Ott, J.S., Eds.; Brooks/Cole Publishing Company: Pacific Grove, CA, 1992; 270–280.
13. Navatorava, V.N.; Crompton, J.L. A revised conceptualization of marketing in the context of public leisure services. J. Leis. Res. **2000**, *33* (2), 160–185. Retrieved August 22, 2001 from ProQuest on-line database on the World Wide Web:http://proquestmail@bellhowell.infrolearning.com.
14. Neumann, F.X., Jr. Organizational structures to match the new information-rich environments: Lessons from the study of chaos. Public Prod. Manage. Rev. **September 1997**, *21* (1), 86–100. Retrieved from Retrieved January 4, 2002 from EBSCOhost Full Display on-line database on the World Wide Web:http://ehostvgw12.epnet.com/ehost.asp?
15. Trist, E.L.; Emery, F.E. The causal texture of organizational environments. Hum. Relat. **1965**, *18*, 21–32.
16. Heckman, F. Designing organizations for flow experiences. J. Qual. Partic. **March 1997**, *20*, 2. Retrieved from Retrieved January 4, 2002 from EBSCOhost Full Display on-line database on the World Wide Web:http://ehostvgw12.epnet.com/ehost.asp?
17. Selznick, P. *TVA and the Grass Roots*; Harper & Row: New York, 1949.
18. Kiel, L.D. Nonequilibrium theory and its implications for public administration. Public Adm. Rev. **1989**, *49*, 544–551. Retrieved October 8, 2001 from ProQuest on-line database on the World Wide Web:http://proquestmail@bellhowell.infrolearning.com.
19. Limerick, D.; Passfield, R.; Cunnington, B. Transformational change; Towards an action learning organization. Learn. Organ. **1994**, *1* (2), 29–40. Retrieved from Retrieved January 4, 2002 from EBSCOhost Full Display on-line database on the World Wide Web:http://ehostvgw12.epnet.com/ehost.asp?
20. Doyle, M. Organizational transformation and renewal: A case for reframing management development? Personal Rev. **1995**, *24* (6), 6–18. Retrieved from Retrieved January 4, 2002 from EBSCOhost Full Display on-line database on the World Wide Web:http://ehostvgw12.epnet.com/ehost.asp?
21. Arthos, J. Locating the instability of the topic places: Rhetoric, phronesis and neurobiology. Commun. Q. **Summer 2000**, *48*, 3. Retrieved October 4, 2001 from ProQuest on-line database on the World Wide Web:http://proquestmail@bellhowell.infrolearning.com.
22. Dyck, B. Understanding configuration and transformation through a multiple rationalities approach. J. Manag. Stud. **1997**, *34* (5). Retrieved from Retrieved January 4, 2002 from EBSCOhost Full Display on-line database on the World Wide Web:http://ehostvgw12.epnet.com/ehost.asp?
23. Kiel, L.D. *Managing Chaos and Complexity in Government: A New Paradigm for Managing Change, Innovation, and Organizational Renewal*; Jossey-Bass: San Francisco, 1994.
24. Kast, F.E.; Rosenzweig, J.E. General Systems Theory: Applications for Organization and Management. In *Classics of Organization Theory*, 3rd Ed.; Shafritz, J., Ott, J.S., Eds.; Brooks/Cole Publishing Company: Pacific Grove, CA, 1992; 294–307.

Decision Making, Rational

E. J. Woodhouse

Rensselaer Polytechnic Institute, Troy, New York, U.S.A.

D

INTRODUCTION

In everyday life, an action is considered rational to the extent that it embodies good sense, including logic, proportionality, and appropriate fit with its context. In the mid-twentieth century, however, the term "rational decision making" came to be appropriated by systems theory, multiattribute utility analysis, and other hypercognitive approaches to figuring out what to do in complex situations. This article summarizes aspects of that specialized usage but also points to many other traditions of political thought that contribute to understanding the requisites for reasoned social choice.

Complex, ideologically contested choices typify governmental decision making, and analysis alone cannot determine how to cope sensibly with such situations. Calculation can assist in negotiating viable policy, but cannot take the place of ordinary reasoning and political deliberation. Hence, fairer and wiser governance depends on improved political processes more than on better analysis, and I argue for reappropriating the term "rational" so as to recapture its underlying spirit and refocus on the political.

This article analyzes aspects of that usage in the context of other traditions of thought bearing on reasoned social choice. I argue for reappropriating the term "rational" so as to recapture its original spirit.

CALCULATION AS PART OF POLITICS

In everyday usage, the term "rational" typically contrasts a reasoned mode of thought or action with one that is "irrational," in the sense of being unreasonably distorted by emotion, bias, or ideology. Thus, a housing bureaucrat asks others in his profession: "Is our only choice between 'solutions based on cool, rational decision-making by the experts' and solutions based on the 'passions' of a mobilized mass movement?" His answer, of course, is that "Rational decision-making in the production and rehabilitation of affordable housing is not incompatible with community organizing and direct action."[1] Likewise, working within a commonsensical meaning of the term is a professor at the Royal Military Academy in Brussels, Belgium, advocating what he calls "rational military

decision making," choices that are "both ethical and efficient."[2]

The first systematization of rational decision making in political science was Dahl and Lindblom's *Politics, Economics, and Welfare*, which drew on a long tradition of political thought recognizing that "Discussion is perhaps the oldest and most universal process for facilitating rational calculation in social action." They analyzed "an extensive variety of social processes that facilitate rational calculation," including two contrasting approaches to reducing the number and complexity of variables: quantification and delegation.[3] Sensible collective action, they were saying, depends on a diverse combination of methods, some analytic and some social, and these methods typically intertwine, as when tasks are delegated to experts.

More generally, a variety of social science scholarship clarifies barriers facing intelligent collective action while illuminating possibilities for circumventing or lowering those barriers. Building on the old saying attributed to Clement Atlee, "He who controls the agenda controls the meeting," research on agenda setting arguably attacks one of the most important barriers to intelligent governance.[4–6] Even more fundamental than governmental agenda setting are the psychological, sociocultural, and political processes by which people come to frame how they think about issues.[7,8] If the attack on Pearl Harbor inherently constituted an act of war, then launching World War II against the Japanese was a foregone conclusion, and there merely remained a few details about how to do it. In contrast, if international relations theorist Bruce Russett was correct in determining that Pearl Harbor did not constitute a clear and present danger to U.S. national security, then a much wider array of options might usefully have been considered.[9] Framing is key.

Social and political psychologists who study conflict resolution and group and organizational choice observe situational factors leading to patterned, less-than-intelligent behaviors such as groupthink.[10] Among the approaches offered to ameliorate problems that are complex and ill-structured and which change as problem solving advances, there is "double-loop learning." This emphasizes learning to change underlying values and assumptions[11] by interacting with others to induce questioning of one's "theory of action,"[12] resulting in better

Encyclopedia of Public Administration and Public Policy
DOI: 10.1081/E-EPAP 120010886

acceptance of failures and mistakes, yielding a more realistic approach to problem solving.[13,14] Much of the voluminous literature on organizations bears on improving their functioning and, hence, on rational decision making.

ENTER HYPERRATIONALITY

The mix of analysis and politics assumed in the bulk of social science scholarship on decision making is not well reflected in the treatments of decision theory with which the label "rational" has been most closely associated for the past several decades. Hyperrational decision approaches attempt to describe and sometimes prescribe how individuals (or groups making a joint decision) do and should choose among alternatives in accord with their preferences and understandings.

The basic elements of utility theory were initiated long ago by Bernoulli,[15] Bentham,[16] and Pareto,[17] and translated in the mid-twentieth century to the goal of maximizing "expected utility." That sounds sensible, but operationalizing the intention turns out to be pretty difficult, as some critics recognized quite early.[18] Step one in figuring out the expected utility of an action typically is to multiply the probability of a predicted outcome by the utility of that outcome. Because most political actions produce multiple outcomes, step two is to add the utilities of all the outcomes. That sounds cumbersome, but it is not too bad until one realizes that political participants hardly ever really know the probabilities or the utilities, which begins to undermine one's confidence in the whole operation. The hyperrationalists are smart folks, of course, so they have partial responses to these problems; at bottom, however, the dividing line between the hyperrationalists and most social thinkers is that the majority just does not buy the basic story that utility maximization is possible or that it can be achieved via calculation.

von Neumann and Morgenstern's[19] work on game theory sometimes is considered a starting point for contemporary formal decision theory, but attention to ways of dealing with risk and uncertainty go back much farther through Charles Knight to earlier economists, including Marshall. Luce and Raiffa[20] popularized the term "decision theory," and Raiffa[21] formalized a workable approach to "decision analysis" on which continuously refined work continues on topics such as revealed probabilities and the structure of individual utility functions.[22] Cost–benefit, risk–benefit analysis and probabilistic risk assessment were offshoots, the latter focusing on probabilistic analysis of risky endeavors, such as nuclear power plants.[23]

Rational decision advocates often attempt to break choices down into a series of steps: define the problem, identify criteria, weight the criteria in terms of their relative importance, generate alternatives, rate each alternative on each criterion, and "compute the optimal decision."[24] There may have been a time when some analysts were naïve enough to assume this process unproblematic, but most now recognize lots of problems with it. Because human memory and other cognitive capacities are so limited, we proceed by bounded rationality, meaning we tend to focus on just one or two criteria instead of the full range that might be sensible.[25] Criteria are tough to compare, and relative importance depends on the situation: lower taxes are attractive, but at the expense of driving science teachers into industry? How often does one actually know the probability that a given action will have a given effect? And what about unintended consequences?

Emotion and interpersonal cuing tend to be extremely important to most humans, and trying to squeeze it all out of decision choices actually can lead to counterproductive outcomes. Thus, probabilistic risk analysis was deployed with great skill at high expense by nuclear power advocates, but many people just did not feel comfortable with giant power plants that could suffer even a small risk of catastrophic meltdown.[26] Even economists are increasingly questioning their field's conventional assumptions about human choice.[27,28] Thus, it no longer is weird to read in the *Journal of Economic Literature* that:

> Because we are social animals, the collective behavior of humans must be understood in terms of the cultural forces at work. World views, mores, taboos, and sanctions are among the social influences that shape and guide our behavior, so much so that characterizing our activities as "choice" and "decision making" is often inappropriate. This is no less true in market settings than it is elsewhere.[29]

Behavioral Decision Theory or Heuristic Judgment Theory is generally regarded as a more realistic approach to understanding human choice, in part, because it is based on empirical observation of the guidelines and heuristics people actually use when they make decisions.[30] For example, when particular images are highly "available" cognitively (World Trade Center collapse, shark attack, fire), people's thinking will be more influenced than when dangers are less vivid (flood, radon in the basement, stress from gradually accumulating sleep deprivation). Individuals, groups, and organizations depart rather significantly from the choices experts say would be most in line with real-world probabilities.[31] We have weak capacities for estimating probabilities and general cognitive limits for processing information.[32] Simon[33] argued that making a choice that is good enough, satisficing, usually makes more sense than trying to optimize; and in everyday practice, this certainly is how most humans and their organizations behave (when they behave sensibly, which, of course, is far from routine). The psychology-based approach, therefore, is more helpful in understanding real life than are the various cognitive approaches derived from conventional economic assumptions about "rational man"; but the psychological approach also promises a good deal less than does rational choice (for a direct comparison, see Ref. [34]).

RATIONAL CHOICE

Differing substantially from these policy-analytic endeavors is Rational Choice Theory, founded in part by Arrow,[35] Downs,[36] Buchanan and Tullock,[37] and Olson.[38] Practitioners of rational choice are generally concerned with understanding rather than with prescription and focus more on political behavior than on the substance of public policy. But, their approach was the most prestigious and rapidly growing part of political science in the last quarter century, colonizing many subfields of the discipline by drawing on economists' simplifying assumptions about human behavior. So, one cannot speak of rational decision making without taking rational choice theory into account.

Rational choice begins with simple assumptions about individuals having incentives to maximize income, economize on time, and otherwise get what they want, and it attempts from this microfoundation to develop understandings of why people and institutions function as they do in politics. Blending with game theory in some hands (e.g., Ref. [39]), analysts attempt to show why most of what happens in politics is "rational." For example, whereas most observers of Congress perceive many different factors influencing assignments of legislators to committees, rational choice theorists try to demonstrate an underlying cause: committee assignments maximize the probability of policy outcomes that suit the majority of legislators in each party.[40]

Despite widespread professional admiration for the theoretical rigor, most social thinkers find the assumptions used so simpleminded as to undermine the believability of the claims. Moreover, practitioners of rational choice have devoted far more effort to refining their theorems than to empirical tests of their ideas.[41]

COPING WITH UNCERTAINTY AND DISAGREEMENT

Another way to tell the story of the "rational-comprehensive" approach in decision theory is to emphasize not its intellectual but its cultural roots.[a] The receptivity to

<hr>

[a]This section is drawn largely from Ref. [42].

calculation as a substitute for political interaction stems from its compatibility with the mastery tradition in western thought: Techniques to conquer uncertainty have long been popular, manifested in the physical sciences and engineering as well as in religion.

Lindblom systematized and effectively debunked the folk theory of rational-comprehensiveness in "Muddling Through" and subsequent work, showing that rational-comprehensive aspirations make impossible demands for information, causal theory, time, and other resources.[43–45] For example, as Alice Rivlin put it, "Little progress has been made in comparing the benefits of different social action programs," and "little is known about how to produce more effective health, education, and other social services."[46]

Fortunately, although there is no way to calculate the "correct" approach to a complex policy issue or to analytically set the agenda or to even define what "the problems" are, political participants declare what they consider the high-priority problems, and they propose solutions. Such proposals are never proven superior to other possible problem definitions, agendas, and policy options, but fortunately, proof is unnecessary, because action is undertaken when a working majority reaches agreement.

Can mere agreement really be considered an intelligent way to run a society? To evaluate that, one needs some way of judging what constitutes an "intelligent" political process. No one has a definitive set of criteria for that, but many people might look for at least the following:

1. That concerns moderately or strongly held by any sizeable number of people are taken into account in some nontrivial way.
2. That reasonable tradeoffs are made among conflicting values.
3. That, insofar as feasible, policy actions take into account available information about social problems and opportunities, performance of existing programs, costs, and other relevant matters.

Although no political system is presently designed to achieve these elements of intelligent policy making nearly as well as can be envisioned, it turns out that negotiations and other adjustments among political partisans can often achieve a measure of all of these goals. How? Consider some of the ways partisans are likely to think about making and responding to policy proposals:

1. In crafting a proposal, partisans will tend to look for ways to get what they want without stirring up adverse responses or retaliations from others. So, the search for agreement simultaneously becomes a method of taking diverse views into account.
2. Knowing that they will need allies when putting forth their own proposals, others are disposed to grant what

proposers ask, unless there is some good reason not to do so. Thus, a bias toward action is built into the system: I will help you get what you need, if you will help me get what I need.

3. Those with initial objections have strong motivation to come up with counterproposals, ones that will allow them to join with the original proposer in seeking a mutually beneficial outcome.

4. The need to win agreement keeps demands within the sphere likely to be considered "reasonable" or intelligent by most of those whose agreement is needed.

5. Moderation likewise is encouraged, because those putting forth a proposal will be wasting their own scarce time, energy, and other resources if they cannot win agreement; and, even if eventually winnable, immoderate proposals may not be worth the effort and the favors used in the process.

Thus, working for their private gain and for their vision of the public interest, partisans interact with each other in ways that often converge toward fairly sensible outcomes. The need to achieve agreement leads to policy making that, to some degree, aims for the three goals of responsiveness to public sentiment, sensible trade-offs, and attention to relevant information.

These interactions can be thought of as substituting politics for analysis, because no one really "understands" the social problem that is being ameliorated, inasmuch as the participants each hold somewhat different definitions of the problem. Alternatively, political interaction can be said to achieve a form of understanding that cannot be produced through analysis alone. Because understanding is generally sought as a means to improved action, whenever a working majority agrees on a new or revised policy, that policy can be thought of as embodying a new understanding. This accords with one definition of the term understanding: a shared agreement.[42]

It is not clear that anyone in the field now really advocates rational-comprehensive techniques as the primary method of approaching complex public issues, but various scholars dissatisfied with incrementalism tried to formulate second-best approaches seeking to preserve some of the aims of comprehensive analysis, such as making sure that important priorities are not overlooked.[47–49] Despite all the attention to incrementalism and to Simon's work on satisficing, despite the fact that most policy scholars got the point, those who understand analysis as an adjunct to politics perhaps have not done as well as the hyperrationalists at advancing a systematic program of conceptually and empirically refined research.

However, one strand of qualitative decision theory has built a research program around the fact that social problem solving ordinarily proceeds through trial-and-error learning. How can policy analysts help partisans figure

out how to make the inevitable errors less damaging and how to learn from them more rapidly? Three of the main pitfalls in ordinary trial-and-error learning are as follows: 1) a policy trial may produce unbearably costly outcomes; 2) policy moves may retain too little flexibility, preventing errors from being corrected readily; and 3) learning about errors may be very slow. More intelligent trial and error would feature strategies for making errors less costly, for building in greater flexibility, and for speeding up the learning process.[26,42]

Even in highly uncertain endeavors, it is often possible to partly foresee and protect against some of the worst risks, as the National Institutes of Health did in requiring early biotechnology research to be conducted in special laboratories, sealing in potentially dangerous new organisms.[50] To prevent policies from becoming deeply enmeshed in implementers' careers and otherwise resistant to change, in framing policy moves, partisans and analysts can improve their odds of success by developing policy options that can be altered fairly readily, should unfavorable experience warrant. For example, flexibility is higher when a policy's costs are borne gradually, allowing expenditures to be redirected as learning develops. NASA's space shuttle illustrates the problem: A launch regime relying on expendable rockets would have been much easier to revamp.[51,52]

Flexibility also can be enhanced by phasing in a policy during a learning period, a common practice in business; by experimenting in a limited geographical area or for a delimited client base; by conducting simultaneous trials of two or more alternative approaches; by using an existing bureaucracy instead of creating a new, dedicated organization with permanent staff; and by many other tactics.[53–55]

The research on intelligent trial and error exemplifies a much broader body of policy-oriented scholarship aimed at understanding how to make collective action more intelligent without the simplifying assumptions typically necessitated by the hyper-rational approaches. The spirit of that endeavor is captured by Andrews'[56] concept of "humble analysis."

CONCLUSION

In sum, rational decision making is a sprawling topic not defined by any simple, bounded set of literature. The term is contested, with hyperrationalists influenced by economics tending to win disproportionate (but often unfavorable) attention from policy intellectuals and from participants in policy processes. Critics of cost–benefit analysis, game theory, and other purely analytical techniques have been on the defensive for several decades, in part because their techniques are much fuzzier and more difficult to teach and deploy.

But, the critics' intellectual case is convincing: analysis simply cannot be substituted for politics, and virtually no one really argues otherwise. As Johan Olsen put it, hyperrationalists "suggest an approach that assumes away most of the complexity of political actors, the organized settings within which they operate, and institutional change, rather than make a serious effort to understand that complexity."[57]

For the future, it is safe to assume that one basic challenge will continue to confront those who care about bringing greater intelligence to bear in social problem solving. The potential intelligence of democracy primarily requires that social institutions and processes be arranged so that interaction among diverse persons can find areas of agreement that take into account a great many considerations bearing on each choice. This partially substitutes for rational calculation and partly uses analysis in the service of partisan goals. Yet, those who exercise political and economic authority generally are far more willing to utilize narrow techniques for improving efficiency than they are to improve and redefine effectiveness by listening to social scientists calling for social–organizational changes to broaden the sphere of negotiation and otherwise strengthen the decision-making process.

Hence, "the troubled attempt to understand and shape society" goes to the heart of power relations in contemporary civilization and is by no means a purely academic dispute.[8] The quest for more intelligent or "rational" collective decision making goes well beyond the terrain conceivably covered by rational choice, cost–benefit, multiattribute utility theory, and other logico-quantitative techniques. Such techniques usually are not aimed at how issues are framed, and they are not aimed at many other factors that actually matter when policy negotiations and impositions are going on; hence, the analytic techniques sometimes called "rational decision theory" actually are most helpful when located within the much broader universe of social thought pertaining to intelligent choice. Rethinking rational decision making to make relevant a broader swath of scholarship in public policy, political science, and social thought more generally probably is essential for narrowing the substantial discrepancy between aspiration and achievement in moving toward the potential intelligence of democracy.

REFERENCES

1. Davis, J.E. *Rational Decision Making to Balance Ideological Extremes*; National Housing Institute, Shelterforce Online, March/April 1994; 1.
2. Van Damme, G.C. Course syllabus. **2001**, 1 (http://www. usafa.af.mil/jscope/JSCOPE00/VanDamme00.html, 9/30/01).
3. Dahl, R.A.; Lindblom., C.E. *Politics, Economics, and Welfare*; Harper and Brothers: New Jersey, 1953.
4. Cobb, R.W.; Elder, C.D. *Participation in American Politics: The Dynamics of Agenda-Building*; Allyn and Bacon: Boston, 1972.
5. Rochefort, D.A.; Cobb, R.W. *The Politics of Problem Definition: Shaping the Policy Agenda*; University Press of Kansas: Lawrence, KS, 1994.
6. Cobb, R.W.; Ross, M.H. *Cultural Strategies of Agenda Denial: Avoidance, Attack, and Redefinition*; University Press of Kansas: Lawrence, KS, 1997.
7. Edelman, M. *The Symbolic Uses of Politics*; University of Illinois Press: Urban, IL, 1964.
8. Lindblom, C.E. *Inquiry and Change: The Troubled Attempt to Understand and Shape Society*; Yale University Press: New Haven, 1990.
9. Russett, B.M. *No Clear and Present Danger: A Skeptical View of the U.S. Entry into World War II*; Harper and Row: New York, 1972.
10. Janis, I.L.; Mann, L. *Decision Making*; Free Press: New York, 1977.
11. Argyris, C. *Increasing Leadership Effectiveness*; Wiley: New York, 1976.
12. Argyris, C.; Schon, D. *Theory in Practice*; Jossey-Bass: San Francisco, 1974.
13. Argyris, C. *On Organizational Learning*; Blackwell: Cambridge, MA, 1993.
14. Schon, D.A.; Argyris, C. *Organizational Learning II: Theory, Method, and Practice*; Addison-Wesley, Reading: MA, 1996.
15. Kendall, M.G. Daniel Bernoulli on maximum likelihood. Biometrika **1961**, 48, 1–18.
16. Bentham, J. *Principles of Morals and Legislation*; Oxford University Press: Oxford, 1823.
17. Pareto, V. *Manuel d'Economie Politique*; Marcel Giard: Paris, 1927.
18. Edwards, W. The theory of decision making. Psychol. Bull. **1955**, *41*, 380–417.
19. von Neumann, J.; Morgenstern, O. *Theory of Games and Economic Behavior*, 3rd Ed.; Princeton University Press: Princeton, NJ, 1953.
20. Luce, R.D.; Raiffa, H. *Games and Decisions*; Wiley: New York, 1957.
21. Raiffa, H. *Decision Analysis: Introductory Lectures on Choices Under Uncertainty*; Addison-Wesley: Reading, MA, 1968.
22. Viscusi, W.K.; Evans, W.N. Estimation of revealed probabilities and utility functions for product safety decisions. Rev. Econ. Stat. **Feb. 1998**, *80*, 28–33.
23. Crouch, E.A.C.; Wilson, R. *Risk/Benefit Analysis*; Ballinger: Cambridge, MA, 1982.
24. Bazerman, M.H. *Judgement in Managerial Decision Making*, 5th Ed.; Wiley: New York, 2002.
25. Simon, H.A. A behavioral model of rational choice. Q. J. Econ. **1955**, *69*, 99–118.
26. Morone, J.G.; Woodhouse, E.J. *The Demise of Nuclear Energy? Lessons for Intelligent Democratic Control*

of Technology; Yale University Press: New Haven, 1989.

27. Sen, A. Social choice theory: A re-examination. Econometrica **1977**, *45*, 53–89.

28. Arrow, K.J. Rationality of Self and Others in an Economic System. In *Decision Making: Alternatives to Rational Choice Models*; Zey, M., Ed.; Sage: Newbury Park, CA, 1992; 63–77.

29. Harvey, J.T. Heuristic judgment theory. J. Econ. Issues **Mar. 1998**, *32*, 47–64.

30. *Judgment Under Uncertainty: Heuristics and Biases*; Kahneman, D., Slovic, P., Tversky, A., Eds.; Cambridge University Press: Cambridge, 1982.

31. Dawes, R.M. *Rational Choice in an Uncertain World*; Harcourt Brace Jovanovich: New York, 1988.

32. Rappoport, L.; Summers, D. *Human Judgment and Social Interaction*; Holt, Rinehart and Winston: New York, 1973.

33. Simon, H.A. *Administrative Behavior: A Study of Decision-Making Processes in Administrative Organization*; Macmillan: New York, 1947.

34. Hogarth, R.M.; Reder, M.W. *Rational Choice: The Contrast Between Economics and Psychology*; University of Chicago Press: Chicago, 1986.

35. Arrow, K.J. *Social Choice and Individual Values*; Yale University Press: New Haven, 1951.

36. Downs, A. *An Economic Theory of Democracy*; Harper and Row: New York, 1957.

37. Buchanan, J.M.; Tullock, G. *The Calculus of Consent: Logical Foundations of Constitutional Democracy*; University of Michigan Press: Ann Arbor, MI, 1962.

38. Olson, M. *The Logic of Collective Action*; Harvard University Press: Cambridge, 1965.

39. Brams, S.J. *Rational Politics: Decisions, Games, and Strategy*; Academic Press: Boston, 1985.

40. Kiewiet, R.D.; McCubbins, M.D. *The Logic of Delegation*; University of Chicago Press: Chicago, 1991.

41. Green, D.P.; Shapiro, I. *Pathologies of Rational Choice: A Critique of Applications in Political Science*; Yale University Press: New Haven, 1994.

42. Lindblom, C.E.; Woodhouse, E.J. *The Policy-Making Process*, 3rd Ed.; Prentice Hall: Englewood Cliffs, NJ, 1993.

43. Lindblom, C.E. The science of 'muddling through'. Public Adm. Rev. **1959**, *19*, 78–88.

44. Braybrooke, D.; Lindblom, C.E. *A Strategy of Decision: Policy Evaluation as a Social Process*; Free Press of Glencoe: New York, 1963.

45. Lindblom, C.E. *The Intelligence of Democracy*; The Free Press: New York, 1965.

46. Rivlin, A.M. *Systematic Thinking for Social Action*; Brookings Institution: Washington, DC, 1971; 7.

47. Dror, Y. Muddling through: Science or inertia? Public Adm. Rev. **1964**, *24*, 153–157.

48. Etzioni, A. Mixed-scanning: A 'third' approach to decision-making. Public Adm. Rev. **1967**, *27*, 385–392.

49. Dryzek, J. Complexity and rationality in public life. Polit. Studies. **1987**, *35*, 424–442.

50. Morone, J.G.; Woodhouse, E.J. *Averting Catastrophe: Strategies for Regulating Risky Technologies*; University of California Press: Berkeley, 1986.

51. Logsdon, J. The decision to develop the space shuttle. Space Policy **1986**, *2*, 103–119.

52. Brunner, R.D.; Byerly, R., Jr. The space station programme: Defining the problem. Space Policy **1989**, *6*, 131–145.

53. Collingridge, D. *Technology in the Policy Process: The Control of Nuclear Power*; St. Martin's Press: New York, 1983.

54. Collingridge, D. *Management of Scale: Big Organizations, Big Technologies, Big Mistakes*; Routledge: New York, 1992.

55. Woodhouse, E.J.; Collingridge, D. Incrementalism and the Future of Political Decision Theory. In *An Heretical Heir of the Enlightenment: Science, Politics, and Policy in the Thought of Charles E. Lindblom*; Redner, H., Ed.; Westview: Boulder, 1993.

56. Woodhouse, E.J.; Weiss, A. Reframing incrementalism: A constructive response to the critics. Policy Sci. **1993**, *25*, 255–273.

57. Andrews, C.J. *Humble Analysis: The Practice of Joint Fact-Finding*; Praeger: Westport, CT, 2002.

58. Olsen, J.P. Garbage cans, new institutionalism, and the study of politics. Am. Polit. Sci. Rev. **2001**, *95*, 191–198.

Deontology

James R. Heichelbech
University of Colorado at Denver, Denver, Colorado, U.S.A.

INTRODUCTION

Deontology refers to any approach to ethics that emphasizes obligation or duty. The most notable deontologists are Immanuel Kant in the eighteenth century and John Rawls in the twentieth century.[1,2] Deontological theories are typically contrasted with utilitarian theories. Deontology differs from utilitarianism insofar as it specifically excludes consequences as a basis for moral judgment, whereas utilitarianism claims that *only* consequences can serve to ground morality. The practical manifestations of deontology generally focus on principles and obligations, with attention to compliance and enforcement.

ADVANTAGES AND DISADVANTAGES OF DEONTOLOGY

The advantages of deontology are usually found in its intuitive appeal, as many people expect morality to concern principles and obligations. In this respect, the results of deontological thinking are perceived as theoretically well grounded and practically useful. Deontology also seems quite compatible with rights-based ethics, as one is obligated to respect the rights of others. However, this is not to say that deontology and rights always produce the same results. For example, there are obligations that might not have corresponding rights, such as keeping a generous promise.

Deontological approaches to ethics have been criticized in numerous ways. They offer a ''thin'' conception of morality, some argue, as they focus on rationality to the exclusion of other human qualities, such as emotion. Responses to these criticisms range from defenses of traditional theories to development of hybrid theories.

KANT

Historically, the most prominent deontologist has been Immanuel Kant, whose work remains central, if difficult reading for anyone interested in principle-oriented ethics. Although the *Groundwork of the Metaphysic of Morals* is only a small part of Kant's work on moral theory, and not the central work at that, it is what most academics intend when they refer to Kant's ethics. A brief overview of the *Groundwork*, therefore, will suffice as a description of Kant's deontological theory as it is typically characterized.

The primary goal of the *Groundwork* is to discover the supreme principle of morality. According to Kant, a principle of morality must carry with it absolute necessity, for nothing else, he argues, is adequate to the task of grounding obligation. Numerous concepts are particularly important for understanding his attempt to meet this challenge—*a good will, duty, autonomy,* and the *categorical imperative.*

Kant begins the *Groundwork* by explaining that nothing is good without qualification, except a *good will.* A good will is good through its willing alone, not through the resulting consequences. Furthermore, a good will is unqualified in this way insofar as it is determined solely by the motive of *duty,* for it is only through the motive of duty that a will is capable of obligating itself. Acting from duty requires acting from principle alone.

Autonomy is a property that a will has in virtue of its capacity for acting from duty, for being a law unto itself. An autonomous will is free in the sense that it determines the principle of its own volition apart from all natural interests or causes. Because only an autonomous will can determine itself, only such a will is capable of acting from duty. Because it is self-legislation that creates obligation, only a will that is self-legislating can fulfill an obligation. Only an autonomous will, therefore, can be good.

The *categorical imperative* is the practical expression of the principle of morality. It is a command of reason concerned only with its own form and the principle from which it follows, not with the action itself or the results. There are two specific formulations that are more frequently mentioned. First, *act only on that maxim through which you can at the same time will that it should become a universal law.* Second, *act in such a way that you always treat humanity, whether in your own person or in the person of any other, never simply as a means, but always at the same time as an end.* One who is moral must necessarily will in accordance with the categorical imperative. However, even a conscious effort to act according to the categorical imperative does not guarantee moral success. One can never know whether one in fact has a good will.

Encyclopedia of Public Administration and Public Policy
DOI: 10.1081/E-EPAP 120010925

RAWLS

In *A Theory of Justice*, John Rawls described what he calls "justice as fairness," which consists of principles chosen from an "original position" of rational deliberation. He argued that principles of social justice concern the basic structure of society through the arrangement of major social institutions. Justice as fairness requires principles that "free and rational persons concerned to further their own interests would accept in an initial position of equality as defining the fundamental terms of their association."[2]

From this initial position, or original position, principles of justice are chosen from behind a "veil of ignorance," without knowledge of anyone's place in society or natural abilities. Rawls argued that two principles in particular would be chosen: 1) "each person is to have an equal right to the most extensive basic liberty compatible with a similar liberty for others;" and 2) "social economic inequalities are to be arranged so that they are both (a) reasonably expected to be to everyone's advantage, and (b) attached to positions and offices open to all."[2]

Justice as fairness is deontological for a few reasons. First, Rawls' account of justice fits within the social contract tradition, placing emphasis on the importance of *agreement* as a necessary condition of principles that can obligate, just as Kant claimed that moral principles must be self-legislated. A second reason is that Rawls himself labeled it as such. Because justice as fairness is not a teleological theory, such as utilitarianism, it is by definition deontological. Specifically, justice as fairness "does not interpret the right as maximizing the good."[2] "The original position," Rawls said, can be viewed as "a procedural interpretation of Kant's concept of autonomy and the categorical imperative."[2] Whereas utilitarianism values the satisfaction of all desires, justice as fairness accepts principles without knowledge of more particular interests.

DEONTOLOGY IN PRACTICE

Practical manifestations of deontology reflect the emphasis on obligations and principles. Although the principles are usually not explicitly self-legislated, they are typically considered principles that every rational agent would choose or should choose. It is this aspect that lends the weight of moral obligation. Deontologically grounded principles are typically directed toward basic concerns about the dignity and equality of persons. They frequently have the aim of preserving rational decision-making processes as well. Codes of conduct, regulations concerning financial conflicts of interest, and other sorts of "principle-oriented" efforts strive to clarify what is acceptable and what is not.

Deontology is a useful concept for administrators insofar as it helps to clarify the nature of administrative ethics. Traditionally, ethics in U.S. government has revolved around constitutionally based prohibitions. The deontological character of public administration consists of obligations that correspond to various rights, such as those mentioned in the U.S. Declaration of Independence—life, liberty, and the pursuit of happiness. Such "inalienable" rights obligate us in the strongest sense. However, the specific duties described in the U.S. Constitution tend to be negative. That is, government is prohibited from infringing on specific rights, such as free exercise of religion. Duties of public administration, therefore, tend to be indirect and prohibitive.

Two specific examples of this form of administrative deontology are programs directed by the U.S. Office of Government Ethics and the handling of compliance issues within human resources management. The Office of Government Ethics works to educate government employees about various obligations, most of which concern impartiality and the proper use of position. Through specific rules that prohibit or restrict such things as gifts and honoraria, these obligations help to preserve the integrity of public sector agencies, which are in turn an important piece of democratic decision making.

As important as expressions of democratic decision making are the various laws governing employment practices. The compliance issues encountered by human resource specialists are deontological, both in the sense that they concern obligations and in the sense that they concern the basic structure of the work environment, one that free and rational persons would choose.

Despite the solid grounding in negative duties, there is a growing trend within public administration toward positive duties. Whereas traditional duties have been correlates of rights, public administrators are more frequently thinking as professionals, for whom duties emerge from a sense of integrity and responsibility. Evidence of this trend is clearly visible in the American Society of Public Administration Code of Ethics, with its emphasis on personal integrity and professional excellence. There is a greater sense now than in the past that obligations must be self-imposed and principles are developed beyond external authority. In this sense, public administration is becoming more genuinely deontological.

REFERENCES

1. Kant, I. *Groundwork of the Metaphysic of Morals*; Paton, H.J., Ed.; Harper Torchbooks: New York, 1964.
2. Rawls, J. *A Theory of Justice*; Harvard University Press: Cambridge, MA, 1971; pp. 11, 30, 60, 256.

Development Policy

Lawrence S. Graham
University of Texas, Austin, Texas, U.S.A.

INTRODUCTION

Development policy is the general term used to capture the dynamics and the processes of purposive change focused on creating the conditions for economic growth, technological change, and human development. There is growing consensus that, although economic growth centered in markets and measured in terms of increases in gross national product (GNP) is indispensable, it is not a sufficient condition to bring about improvements in the human condition in such a way that human development can occur. Although the human development concept embraces numerous different indices, it is generally defined as the process of enlarging people's choices in terms of securing human rights, guaranteeing their basic necessities, and enabling them to improve the quality of their own lives. Linked to this shift toward thinking of development in more humane terms are initiatives involving empowerment, participation, equity, and sustainability. In this debate over how to both engender economic growth and increase the capacity of people in all nations and communities to improve their conditions of life, the tasks remain daunting.

Although problems of poverty, ethnic and cultural conflict, and inequities in income distribution and in opportunities to improve conditions of life continue to present obstacles, advances have been made in setting priorities for the development programs and projects that comprise development policy. In the midst of thousands of reports and publications related to development, the annual publication of the World Bank's World Development Report (WDP) and the United Nations Development Programme's Human Development Report (HDR) are primary sources of information and valuable documents to consult in understanding the changing agendas that dominate the discourse on development. As a consequence, in exploring development issues, reference to the Human Development Index (HDI) and awareness of the range of indicators used for this index are as important as discussions of GNP, tables surveying economic growth, and understanding the economic and social indicators used to measure development on a worldwide basis. Especially useful documents are the WDP and HDP reports for 2000, issued at the turn of the century, which reflect the changing concepts and increased understanding of issues involved in development policy.

LINKING PUBLIC ADMINISTRATION AND POLICY WITH DEVELOPMENT

There is a relevant public administration and policy literature that reflects changing perceptions of the issues linked to development over the last half century. Although there was an earlier literature on civil service systems in Western Europe published in the 1930s, generally comparative concerns in public administration and policy date back to the 1960s, to the formation of the Comparative Administration Group (CAG), under the leadership of Fred W. Riggs, with funding from the Ford Foundation. Despite criticism of the CAG's publications and Riggs' work on the ecology of public administration in developing countries on the grounds that they were excessively theoretical, they generated a new body of scholarship, centered largely in South and East Asian experience, which called attention to the very different ethos surrounding public administration in the developing countries. Names that stand out in this literature are William J. Siffin, John Montgomery, Ralph Braibanti, Ferrel Heady, and Milton J. Esman. Many of these scholars responded to the critique of excessive theorizing in the CAG by emphasizing that the endeavor they were embarked on was development administration, explaining the conditions in the national bureaucracies of the developing countries that worked against development initiatives. What was needed, they emphasized, was a more relevant public administration, capable of responding to the issues they had confronted in programs and projects linked to economic development, social change, and improvement in such diverse areas as agriculture, public health, and education. Sources summing up this debate and the evolution of this field into what has become know as comparative and development administration are works authored or edited by Heady, Esman, and Farazmand.

Although the public administration literature that is international in its perspective and identified with a professional school orientation has continued to focus on the Third World across the years, an important parallel is to be found in the comparative policy work of political scientists such as Peters; Heidenheimer, Heclo, and Adams; Aberbach, Putnam, and Rockman; and Freeman. Essentially European in its concerns, as this literature has evolved, it has focused more generally on the industrialized countries and the transformation of these societies through changing technologies, immigration policy, and social welfare.

Both perspectives on public administration and policy in the developed and the developing countries, however, have undergone considerable evolution, as the issues of development and change in the modern world have become more complex. In the public administration field, in addition to evolving perspectives on comparative and development administration, the impact of business administration can be traced in the literature on public management and the emergence of a distinctive development management literature (with its own particular concerns with public management in developing countries and the techniques and skills public managers need for their work in government and civil society, in postindustrial and industrializing societies). More recent concerns, in the shift toward policy and process in development work, are to be found in the policy reform literature. The best way to capture these developments is to consult the work of Brinkerhoff and Crosby.

Yet another path taken in the public administration and policy field, which falls within the purview of development policy, is that centered on institutional analysis and development. Derived from the rational choice institutionalist literature, the evolution of this line of thinking about how to better confront development dilemmas is best reflected in Ostrom's work. The themes dominating this writing concern the need for precise, operational concepts and applications in policy analysis that focus on thinking of institutions as rules that over time structure politics, policy, and action, and have a direct impact on political and administrative behavior in various national settings, be they Asian or Western European. Ostrom's work in development policy is explicit in how it lays out the various incentives and disincentives that influence policy in such areas as common property resource management. Issues concerning communal grazing, irrigation systems, fisheries, and forestry services, and how to retain a common set of rules and expectations center on the use of these resources in such a way that they can be sustained over time without destroying them. Another area of activity involves policy issues concerning questions of infrastructure development and maintenance—for example, the use of simple and complex market arrangements, centralized management and control initiatives, decentralized policy incentives, and polycentric management schemes. These latter, more complex schemes aim at providing more dynamic mixes of centralization (to provide more effective coordination and control of development initiatives) and decentralized programmatic initiatives (to encourage wider citizen participation and greater involvement of the users of public services) in maintaining roads, sufficient water supply, and sanitation and waste systems.

CONCLUSION

The most important point to be made about development issues in public administration and policy is the convergence that has been occurring in the contemporary world in its concern with issues related to economic growth, the maximization of social capital, and sustainable conditions of life. Although there are obviously enormous differences between the most technologically advanced countries and the least developed societies and economies, we can no longer comfortably focus on the shift to knowledge-based industries in the new economies of the more advanced countries, to the exclusion of the enormous problems in public health, poverty, and deficiencies in education that confront those societies, which remain apart from the market economies and levels of living that have accompanied the affluence generated in the First World, as opposed to the poverty and hardships characteristic of the Third World. The confluence of both developments is foremost among the challenges to be faced in responding to the enormous changes occurring in science and technology, in the economy, and in society, and in confronting the conflicts and tensions present when these two worlds intersect. No document sums up more effectively this convergence in development policy (with its emphasis on the need to reconcile security concerns with those of development in a world that no longer can separate issues of development from those of underdevelopment) than the European Commission's May 2001 report, *The European Union's Role in Promoting Human Rights and Democratisation in Third World Countries*. This report adopts the language of development policy and focuses on human development as the basis for promoting human rights globally, and creating more open societies and economies.

FURTHER READING

Aberbach, J.D.; Putnam, R.D.; Rockman, B.A. *Bureaucrats and Politicians in Western Democracies*; Harvard University Press: Cambridge, 1981.

Brinkerhoff, D.; Crosby, B. *Managing Policy Reform: Concepts and Tools for Decision-Makers in Developing and Transitioning Countries*; Kumarian Press: West Hartford, CT, 2001.

Communication from the Commission to the Council and the

European Parliament. The European Union's Role in Promoting Human Rights and Democratisation in Third Countries. European Commission: Brussels (COM [2001] 252 final, 8 May 2001.

Esman, M.J. *Management Dimensions of Development: Perspectives and Strategies*; Kumarian Press: West Hartford, CT, 1991.

Handbook of Comparative and Development Administration, 2nd Ed.; Farazmand, A., Ed.; Marcel Dekker: New York, 2001.

Nations of Immigrants: Australia, the United States, and International Migration; Freeman, G., Jupp, J., Eds.; Oxford University Press: New York, 1992.

Heady, F. *Public Administration: A Comparative Perspective*; Prentice Hall: Englewood Cliffs, NJ, 1966 (with numerous revisions and expansions up through the 1980s).

Heidenheimer, A.J.; Heclo, H.; Adams, C.T. *Comparative Public Policy: The Politics of Social Choice in Europe and America*; St. Martin's Press: New York, 1975.

Ostrom, E. *Governing the Commons: The Evolution of Institutions for Collective Action*; Cambridge University Press: New York, 1990.

Ostrom, E. Institutional Rational Choice: An Assessment of the Institutional Analysis and Development Framework. In *Theories of the Policy Process*; Sabatier, P.A., Ed.; Westview Press: Boulder, CO, 1999.

Ostrom, E.; Schroeder, L.; Wynne, S. *Institutional Incentives and Sustainable Development: Infrastructure Policies in Perspective*; Westview Press: Boulder, CO, 1993.

Peters, B.G. *Comparing Public Bureaucracies: Problems of Theory and Method*; University of Alabama Press: Tuscaloosa, AL, 1988.

United Nations Development Programme. *Human Development Report 2000*; Oxford University Press, 2000.

World Bank. *World Development Report 1999/2000: Entering the 21st Century*; Oxford University Press: New York, 2000.

Discipline and Dismissal

Steven W. Hays

University of South Carolina, Columbia, South Carolina, U.S.A.

INTRODUCTION

Discipline and dismissal comprise the human resource management processes by which organizations seek to correct deviations from acceptable conduct, and to rid themselves of individuals who are unable or unwilling to comply with reasonable standards of performance. Discipline is an ongoing responsibility of every manager, all of whom are expected to identify problems arising from employee behavior and introduce corrective measures. The application of discipline is not necessarily a negative process, in that the ultimate objective of a disciplinary procedure should be to provide employees with proactive guidance on how to improve their deficiencies. Dismissal, in contrast, should occur only when a worker has committed an offense that is so serious that it demands immediate action, or has proven to be unable to perform at an acceptable level after being provided with ample opportunity to address performance shortcomings.

THE GOVERNMENTAL CONTEXT OF DISCIPLINE AND DISMISSAL

Unlike conditions that prevail in much of the private sector, public managers confront numerous additional constraints when imposing discipline or undertaking dismissal actions against workers. Nonunionized private employees have few recognized rights in their employment. They serve "at will," meaning that they can be hired or fired with or without a substantive cause. In contrast, civil servants enjoy a considerable number of protections from any "adverse action" that is pursued by a supervisor. Because of the fear that political factors might contribute to their mistreatment or termination, public employees typically cannot be sanctioned without careful attention to numerous procedural, legal, and constitutional guidelines. In legalistic terms, this means that public workers retain certain property and liberty interests in their employment that require extreme caution on the part of supervisors seeking their punishment or termination.

In brief, civil servants are entitled to due process whenever faced with a disciplinary action that substantially threatens their job status, such as a demotion, suspension, or termination. Due process potentially includes

many factors, but the most basic requirements are as follows:[1]

1. Managers must abide by the human resource management procedures that are in place; any requirements included in a policy manual, employee handbook, or other document might be interpreted in court as an "implied contract."
2. Any adverse action must be based on a job-related reason or cause; employees cannot be sanctioned for actions or behaviors that do not influence their job performance in some negative fashion.
3. Employees are protected by all relevant antidiscrimination legislation; disciplinary or termination actions are forbidden if they are motivated by discriminatory intent involving a person's race, religion, ethnicity, age, sex, disability, or other protected categories.
4. Supervisors cannot ignore constitutional protections during disciplinary proceedings; employees retain all constitutional rights to free speech, assembly, and other liberties, unless the exercise of those rights severely impinges on the agency's ability to deliver public services effectively.
5. Any adverse action that is conducted in an "outrageous" manner or that is contrary to "public policy" is illegal. Outrageous actions include those that are conducted in a harmful, crass, and embarrassing manner (e.g., a highly public tongue-lashing), whereas violations of public policy occur when punishment is based on malice, bad faith, or is contrary to statutory requirements. For instance, employees cannot be fired in retaliation for filing sexual harassment charges or worker's compensation claims, nor can they be punished for complying with a legal obligation (e.g., testifying under subpoena against the employer).

Despite these restrictions on discipline and dismissal, the widespread perception that civil servants "can't be fired without an act of God" is seriously exaggerated. In most jurisdictions, the necessary procedures are in place for effective employee discipline, provided that supervisors play by the rules. Another important development in recent years has been the impact that the reinvention movement has exerted on employee protections. The "merit systems" of many states have been abolished or

Encyclopedia of Public Administration and Public Policy
DOI: 10.1081/E-EPAP 120010778

weakened, a phenomenon that generally reduces employees' ability to challenge the personnel decisions of their superiors. Many of the traditional systems of employee protection—such as multiple avenues of appeal and unreasonable restrictions on managerial discretion—have been dismantled. For these reasons, there is a clear and distinct trend toward exposing civil servants to greater risks of being disciplined and/or terminated for misconduct or poor performance.[2]

PROGRESSIVE DISCIPLINE PROCEDURES

Whatever their legal status in challenging supervisory actions, public servants are like any other group of workers. Most are well intentioned and industrious, yet there are always some (hopefully only a few) who are ''problem employees.'' The presence of such individuals in the organization has multiple repercussions. It has been estimated that a poorly performing worker will consume at least 10 times more of the manager's time than any (or all) of the competent employees. Clearly, the best way to address this crisis is to avoid it in the first place. That is, a properly functioning human resource management system should weed out most of the misfits before they are hired. Likewise, mentoring systems, careful background checks, and the effective use of probationary periods are helpful ways of solving potential problems before they become acute. Only after an employee has successfully completed a probationary period—usually 1 calendar year—does that individual acquire legal rights to challenge adverse personnel actions. But once that threshold has been successfully crossed, public managers need to exercise care and tact in the handling of employees whose performance is subpar.

A Nonpunitive Focus

The use of a progressive discipline procedure is generally considered to be an effective means of responding to problem employees in contemporary public agencies. These procedures are based on the premise that discipline ought to have a positive rather than a punitive focus. The underlying ethos is to provide the offending worker with notice that a problem exists. Once the performance dilemma has been identified, the requisite steps to resolve the situation should then be articulated. Thus, supervisors have the obligation to confront workers with their complaints and to delineate the specific reasons why they are displeased. Especially in this era of worker empowerment, managers also are expected to involve the subordinate in the problem-solving process. This might be accomplished by discussing the problem with

the worker, allowing them to suggest appropriate responses. A poorly performing individual may need additional training or simply the reality check that comes with a confrontation from the boss. In other cases, a detailed work improvement plan may need to be established. The basic point is that no worker can be expected to remedy a deficiency until she has been notified that the problem exists and then provided with feedback on what constitutes acceptable behavior.

Nonpunitive approaches to employee discipline are believed to create fewer tensions between managers and workers, and therefore have a greater likelihood of use and success. Research has also demonstrated that managers need to be trained in the technical and behavioral aspects of disciplinary actions.[3] In addition to increasing the manager's self-confidence, training improves their appreciation for the legal and emotional pitfalls that surround employee discipline. Another noteworthy characteristic of the nonpunitive approach is that, if it is followed carefully, it will withstand most legal challenges by disgruntled employees. Perhaps the most oft-cited explanation for worker grievances against their supervisors is that they were ''surprised'' by the discipline that was invoked. A regularized system of meeting and discussing performance problems reduces the frequency of such complaints.

Consistency Through Procedural Guidance

Another possible pitfall in the application of discipline is the potential for treating employees arbitrarily or differentially. That is, one worker might be punished for a minor infraction, whereas other employees committing the same offense are ignored. If this phenomenon occurs (which it often does), the sanctioned employee can successfully challenge the disciplinary action on the grounds that they have been singled out for punishment. The essential issue is that employees must be treated in a consistent fashion or else the entire disciplinary scheme is threatened. Although certainly not a panacea, the prescribed response to this dilemma is to provide employees and supervisors with a comprehensive list of infractions and the sanctions that will be imposed for each incident. These progressive discipline procedures are usually inserted in employee handbooks, and consist of lengthy lists of violations accompanied by the punishment that will be invoked for the first, second, and third offenses. For instance, tardiness might be countered with a verbal warning in the first instance, a written warning on the second occurrence, and a formal reprimand on the third occurrence. More serious offenses, such as stealing or sleeping on the job, might call for immediate termination for the first or second offense.

Benefits of a Written Procedure

The existence of a written procedure fulfills three important purposes. First, it constitutes a form of prior notice to employees concerning the norms of acceptable and unacceptable conduct. This makes it more difficult for a worker to allege that they "didn't know" that a particular behavior (e.g., making personal telephone calls on agency time) was forbidden. Second, the procedure contributes to the organization's effort to ensure that workers are treated consistently under the same set of circumstances. A clear delineation of appropriate sanctions essentially constitutes a disciplinary template that ought to be applied uniformly. (No one would be naïve enough to assume that such procedures always result in consistent treatment, but at least their presence provides supervisors with guidance in pursuit of that elusive goal.) Finally, the creation and dissemination of a list of prescribed conduct strengthens the agency's hand in complying with a number of legal expectations concerning the handling of its workforce. One notable example is sexual harassment. Prior to the last decade or so, concise agency standards concerning the punishment for various types of sexual misconduct were rare. Now, with the inclusion of expansive sexual harassment provisions in the agencies' progressive discipline codes, the organizations are able to demonstrate a proactive posture toward eliminating such conduct. This does not exonerate them from liability if they fail to act, but it does demonstrate to judges and juries that they have taken steps to avoid problems and to punish transgressors.

DISMISSAL: THE ULTIMATE SANCTION

When positive efforts to correct employee misconduct fail, the agency is confronted with a narrow range of unpleasant choices. The honorable, but often most difficult, response is to initiate formal termination proceedings. This requires that the supervisor be able to document the performance or behavioral deficiencies, and be prepared to spend considerable time justifying and defending their actions in the event that the employee files a grievance. This occurs with the prior knowledge that the supervisor's conduct will be exposed to as much scrutiny as that of the offending worker. Supervisors must be able to demonstrate adequate reasons (job related) for their actions, and to show that they followed all applicable procedures and treated the employee fairly. Dismissal also requires, of course, the necessity for a face-to-face session

in which the decision is explained to the employee. Because this is a messy and time-consuming process, terminations in government are far less common than in the private sector. On average, private employers terminate about 8% of their workforces annually, whereas dismissal rates in government hover below 1%.[4]

There is little mystery about what happens to public employees who deserve to be terminated but who avoid formal dismissal actions. Too often, the agency's response is either to ignore the inappropriate conduct, or to deal with it in a more proactive yet underhanded fashion. Common responses include promoting the bad employee "up and out of the way," providing a glowing letter of recommendation so as to pawn the worker off on another agency, or to transfer them to a position that carries no responsibility (so-called "turkey farm" jobs). These are age-old "solutions" to the problem employee puzzle, but clearly represent inadequate (even dishonest) responses that are unfair to everyone involved.

Fortunately, the number of successful terminations in public agencies is likely to increase over time in response to the reduction in employee protections that is occurring as part of government reinvention. A related phenomenon is the increased use of alternative dispute resolution techniques, such as mandatory mediation and perhaps even binding arbitration. By reducing the number of appeals and expediting the review process, reformers hope to increase government's ability to rid itself of inept and corrupt employees. As such, there is a discernable move away from highly formalized litigation that is time consuming, expensive, and intimidating to all concerned. The only downside of this trend is the possibility that some innocent and conscientious civil servants might be sacrificed as procedural protections are reduced. In the eyes of most reformers, however, this is a risk that they are willing to take.

REFERENCES

1. Tidwell, R. Employment at will: Limitations in the public sector. Public Pers. Manage. **1983**, *12* (3), 293–304.
2. Walters, J. Who needs civil service? Governing Magazine **1997**, *10* (8), 17–21.
3. Belohlav, J.; Popp, P. Making employee discipline work. Pers. Adm. **1983**, *23* (3), 22–24.
4. Hays, S. Employee Discipline and Removal: Coping with Job Security. In *Public Personnel Administration: Problems and Prospects,* 3rd Ed.; Hays, S., Kearney, R., Eds.; Prentice Hall, 1995; 145–161.

Diversity

Sonia M. Ospina
James F. O'Sullivan
New York University, New York, New York, U.S.A.

INTRODUCTION

Public agencies have the mandate to consider the plurality of values, concerns, and voices of the larger population in their work, as well as to include a wide variety of citizens in their workforce. When diversity is pursued as an organizational objective, more efficient management and the democratic values of responsiveness and representation in public administration are both said to be better achieved.

Workforce diversity emphasizes functioning with employees with differences in personality, work style, and the visible manifestations of social diversity, such as gender and ethnicity, and using those differences to better fulfill the organization's mission. According to the literature, increased workforce diversity in public organizations provides many benefits. These benefits include increased production capacity and organizational flexibility, contributions to fairness in the workplace, greater compliance with personnel regulations, increased representation and responsiveness among members of the bureaucracy, and more grassroots support for agency programs and policies. Also, the organization may enhance its reputation and, as a result, be able to attract and keep the best employees.

Unresolved diversity problems, it has been shown, often deflect employee energy and attention from performance, with a consequent loss of productivity, and can cause an organization to lose valued employees. Critics of diversity management sometimes argue that achieving diversity requires an organization to compromise on the quality of its employees or services, but merit should not be an issue if job attributes are well defined and staffing practices are not limited by stereotypes.

Diversity management in the public sector, as in any organization, is a multidimensional challenge that requires permanent and focused managerial attention. Proponents of diversity management suggest that organizations must be able to realistically diagnose the status of their organization to determine the right strategies for diversity management, and several schema have been developed for that purpose.

WORKFORCE DIVERSITY IN PUBLIC ORGANIZATIONS: A NEW IMPERATIVE

The shifts from an industrial to an information-based society and to a service economy have radically challenged assumptions about how to best organize tasks and people. They have also raised demands for organizations to innovate their production functions and to use more diverse talents. Different work arrangements, flatter organizational structures designed around teams and networks, and more permeable boundaries for intra- and interorganizational cooperation have produced a new complexity in work operations. A diverse workforce—in both functional and social terms—becomes a prerequisite for large organizations in both the private and public sectors to manage their turbulent environment.

Workforce diversity has, indeed, become recognized as an imperative for organizational competitiveness and effectiveness,[1,2] and diversity management is increasingly becoming a principle of human resources (HR) management.[3] Today, state-of-the-art management literature in both public and private sectors views workforce diversity not as a problem to be managed away but as a requirement of organizational effectiveness.[2] Traditional affirmative action and equal employment opportunity efforts are no longer viewed as sufficient in themselves to manage today's workforce effectively, even though they may still be an important component of the agenda.

Increased workforce diversity in public organizations, according to the literature, results in ethical, legal, HR management and organizational benefits.[4] Ethically, diversity contributes to fairness in the workplace, and helps to create economic opportunity and reduce social inequality. Legal and policy benefits include greater compliance with personnel regulations, increased representation and responsiveness among members of the bureaucracy, and increased grassroots support for agency programs and policies. Human resource benefits are an enhanced agency reputation and the resulting ability to attract and keep the best employees, while promoting creative approaches to work. Organizational benefits are substantial, including increased internal capabilities, grea-

Encyclopedia of Public Administration and Public Policy
DOI: 10.1081/E-EPAP 120010771

ter organizational flexibility and ability to address change and fluidity in organizational design, and decreased discrimination litigation. These claims appear repeatedly in normative and empirically based literatures.

Diversity challenges are compounded in public agencies by specific pressures they face as organs of government. The government environment in the United States is characterized by a changing workforce, declining confidence in government, reduced budgets, downsizing at the federal level, higher demands for productivity, and proposals for alternative approaches to public service, including contracting out and privatization.[5] In this context, two broad diversity demands affect contemporary public personnel systems. One is the demand for increased performance, whereby diversity becomes a performance requirement; the other is a legitimization demand, in which workforce diversity is a tool to address the political and ethical mandates for a bureaucracy that is representative of the citizenry. Combined, these two demands produce a strong incentive to pursue and manage workforce diversity effectively.

The published literature on diversity is large but limited. In a literature review of diversity, Wise and Tschirhart[6] found 106 empirical studies of the outcomes of diversity, published between 1961 and 1998 in peer-reviewed academic journals. Thousands of other papers related to diversity and diversity management were published in the same 37 years, but they were mainly descriptive, reviewed ideological or policy perspectives on diversity, or presented survey findings on attitudes toward aspects of diversity. The authors also found that the generalizability of published empirical studies was limited because experimental populations or simulated work situations were most often used in the research. Moreover, published papers tended to be authored by business and psychology professors, with the result that public management issues around diversity were not well addressed. Starting in the 1990s, however, the authors found that scholarly research on diversity began to appear regularly in highly ranked public policy and public personnel journals.

CLARIFYING THE NATURE OF DIVERSITY

There is no single common usage of the concept of diversity in the organizational literature.[7,8] Simple definitions of diversity most often equate it with variety. Diversity can be studied at a societal level or within particular institutions. Applied to organizational life, there are at least three categories of diversity related to performance and strategy. These are structural or functional diversity (differences based on organizational functions and tasks such as administrative vs. operational), business

diversity (differences in markets, products, and services), and workforce diversity (different types of employees).[9] At the most general level, Gentile[2] suggested that in the United States, diversity has become a code word to discuss issues related to how various types of difference impact individuals' and groups' life experiences.

Most of the diversity management literature focuses on workforce diversity.[8,10] Workforce characteristics can range from attributes directly related to work or tasks such as differences in skills, to those that are social in nature and—in theory—only indirectly related to work, such as gender. There are several types of workforce diversity. Occupational diversity (e.g., locksmiths vs. teachers), professional diversity (e.g., nurses aides vs. registered nurses), and social diversity. The latter refers to variations in the characteristics that identify a person with a social category (e.g., male vs. female). The interdependencies among types of workforce diversity create situations that must be managed (e.g., the experience of a male doctor is different from that of either a female doctor or a male nurse).

The organizational challenges of diversity are based on the existence of documented patterns of exclusion from society's resources along social identity lines. The existence of clusters of jobs occupied by individuals with similar social traits often unrelated to the job, which experts call job segregation, or clusters of persons in occupations and professions who belong to the same identity group, which is called occupational segregation, are well documented.[11,12] These realities produce differential opportunity in processes and outcomes for members of different identity groups, and thus reproduce inequality.[13]

SOCIAL DIVERSITY

Research suggests that the salience of an attribute is often socially and historically constructed.[7,13,14] Social markers include gender, race, ethnicity, religion, sexual orientation, physical ability, and age, as well as family, economic, educational, and geographic backgrounds and status. Some scholars distinguish visible from invisible social dimensions;[15] others also consider behavioral attributes associated with functional diversity, such as differences in learning, communication, and work styles. Combined, these social attributes produce the "social types" that make up an organization's workforce,[4] and determine its particular diversity challenges.

For several reasons, social diversity offers the hardest challenges to managers. Social identity involves both self-definition and attributes perceived by others.[1] Also, categorizing individuals on the base of a single identity attribute is usually considered detrimental because the parts of peoples' identities occur simultaneously (e.g., a "typical" Latino employee may be a member of certain religion, could be gay or straight, or may have a disability not readily apparent to the naked eye). Tough diversity dilemmas emerge from these social dynamics, and from the interactions between social and functionally related identities (e.g., occupation or position in the organization).

The empirical literature to date does not offer much assistance on dealing with multiple identities. Wise and Tschirhart[6] concluded that findings about the impact or management of diversity within one group of employees are not generalizable to other groups. They also find that diversity related to educational attainment, work experiences, and tenure with an organization were less studied, and disability was largely absent, as compared with studies of sex, ethnicity/race, and age.

BROAD AND NARROW DIVERSITY MANAGEMENT STRATEGIES

Two distinct approaches have characterized the theory and practice of managing workforce diversity. In the world of practice, a broader definition of workforce diversity emphasizes differences in personality, work style, and visible manifestations of social diversity. In contrast, a narrower definition focuses on social exclusion of what the United States law calls "protected classes," that is, women, racial and ethnic minorities, persons with disabilities (and in some jurisdictions, but not all, gay, lesbian, bisexual, and transgender individuals).

The broader approach places diversity within a context that expands beyond representation and compliance of the law. The narrower approach focuses on efforts to redress existing patterns of inequality and to reduce disparities in the future. Thomas (1991) argued that both approaches are necessary: without rigorous "narrow" efforts to recruit and promote persons not part of the dominant social group, no "new faces" would enter the organization or managerial ranks. However, without a "broad" organizational focus to make the organization a welcoming place to all, the original effort would go to waste. In this sense, the broad and narrow approaches are complementary.

The distinction also appears in the diversity management literature. Work focusing on the practice of managing diversity is normative and emphasizes the broad definition. Empirical research on issues of diversity in the workplace tends to concentrate on specific dimensions that suggest a narrow approach, such as examining the representation of specific populations or the impact of diverse membership on performance. The distinction

stems from the historical development of diversity efforts, from ideological battles fought in that process, and from the way research has followed practice in this area.

In the United States, following the Civil Rights Act of 1964 and the Equal Employment Opportunity Act of 1972, diversity in the workplace was originally measured by counting the number of employees that fit into each of the desired categories. As a result, diversity management is frequently confused with affirmative action. However, since the mid-1960s, three distinct phases of diversity management have evolved. First, affirmative action and equal employment opportunity (EEO) employment policies sought to increase the representation of minorities and women in many areas of employment and to reduce discriminatory practices. Then, as persons from different backgrounds entered, organizations started to try to change their workplace culture via awareness courses and celebrations of diverse characteristics. These activities, known as "valuing diversity," were often isolated from organizational strategy or job needs, however. Later, a new type of effort, known as "managing diversity," started to link changes in work practices to workforce diversity. These new approaches combine solving organizational problems and addressing justice concerns. This points to the need to consider both the ethical and practical drives underlying diversity management. In theory, the phases occur sequentially within the life cycles of organizations, but in practice most organizations will use parts of all three phases simultaneously.

In a final iteration of this development, "diversity management" has become the preferred term, mixing aspects of the narrow and broad approaches. Gilbert et al.[16] defined diversity management as a managerial principle used to make HR decisions and implement practices that create greater inclusion of all individuals into both formal programs and informal social networks. Meyerson and Fletcher[17] referred to diversity management as a "persistent campaign of incremental changes that discover and destroy the deeply embedded roots of discrimination" (see Ref. 17, p. 131).

ETHICAL AND PRACTICAL MOTIVATIONS FOR DIVERSITY MANAGEMENT

The diversity literature highlights ways in which diversity makes good business sense. Public sector scholars promoting the value of diversity have followed this lead under the assumption that managers take pragmatic arguments more seriously than ethical arguments. It is true that the costs of not attending to workforce diversity can be high. Unresolved diversity problems can deflect employee energy and attention from performance toward justice and fairness issues with a consequent loss of productivity. Poor diversity management can cause the organization to lose good employees and therefore incur the expenses of recruiting and training their replacements, as well as potentially diverting financial and human resources to deal with litigation or to pay punitive damages.[4,18] But there are also compelling reasons to stress the ethical underpinnings of diversity.

Diversity management is based on the normative assumption that diversity is a value, and that its management requires a commitment to social inclusion and therefore equality. In this sense, diversity refers to the degree to which there is a variety of attributes (including social, cultural, functional) within a particular structure of governance (be it organizational, sectorial, societal), and the extent to which this variety is distributed at all levels of the structure. Equality, in turn, refers to the extent to which opportunities, resources, information, and power are distributed across diverse individuals and groups within a particular structure of governance. Lack of social diversity and patterns of organizational inequality usually go hand in hand.

Gilbert et al.[16] highlighted the relevance of ethics in diversity by reviewing three ethical principles that support successful diversity initiatives. The first principle is the *Golden Rule*: if you want to be treated fairly, treat others fairly. The second is the *Disclosure Rule*: you must be comfortable with decisions after asking whether you would mind if others became aware of them. The third is the *Rights Approach*, which assumes that people should have the ability to freely choose what they will do with their lives.

Even when the motivation to address the diversity challenge is not ethical, these ethical principles contribute to its successful implementation. Abiding by the first rule, successful diversity programs are inclusive and provide fair treatment to all employees. The openness needed to administer diversity programs responds to the second rule. Diversity management addresses the third rule by allowing people to choose opportunities according to their interests and abilities. If these diversity principles are removed, Gilbert et al.[16] argued, diversity initiatives will collapse. Critics of diversity management may argue that achieving diversity requires a trade-off between equity, merit, and diversity. Such trade-offs, however, contradict theoretical definitions of diversity. Merit is not at question if attributes of the job and staffing practices are not limited by societal expectations or stereotypes. Equality means that every one qualified to do the job is allowed to do it.

Managers implementing diversity initiatives need to expect some friction even under the most favorable circumstances. The performance and representation requirements for increased diversity in the public workplace

generate interpersonal, organizational, and political challenges that require direct managerial attention. Williams and O'Reilly[7] argued that although diversity increases the opportunity for creativity and the quality of group work, it also increases the likelihood of group conflict, member dissatisfaction, turnover, and failure in the implementation of ideas. Hence, as a ''double-edge sword'' diversity ''requires careful and sustained attention to be a positive force in enhancing performance'' (see Ref. 7, p. 120). It requires careful diagnosis and designing an agenda that is part of a broader framework to enhance organizational performance.

DIVERSITY MANAGEMENT FRAMEWORKS

Proponents of diversity management suggest that organizations must be able to realistically diagnose the status of their organization to determine the right strategies for diversity management. Cox[1] developed a helpful typology to assess an organization's distance from achieving the goal of diversity. The ''monolithic organization'' comprises mostly similar employees, and the culture rewards only those who conform to the norms of the dominant group. In such an organization, a person with a language accent may not be promoted as fast as others providing similar input and ideas into the organization's processes. Next, ''the plural organization'' has a mixed group of employees, but the systems and culture remain dominated by one group. Women who have advanced through the bureaucracy but receive fewer promotions at the higher levels may have hit a ''glass ceiling'' because predominantly masculine features such as assertiveness continue to be seen as the necessary values for success. In all monolithic and some plural organizations, informal communications, networks, and key decision-making bodies are closed to nondominant employees. Cox's third organizational type is the ''multicultural'' organization, in which differences are viewed as potential organizational assets. In these organizations, inclusion and fairness are important values, and this is reflected in the demographic composition of the workforce at all levels.

Locating the organization along the ''diversity continuum'' (between discriminatory and nondiscriminatory, from monolithic, to plural, to multicultural) can help managers to identify methods to pursue their diversity strategy. Ospina[4] proposed that organizations must differentiate among four consecutive managerial tasks: *considering*, *pursuing*, *managing*, and *maximizing* diversity, depending on the organization's place in the diversity continuum. To overcome the monolithic organization, managers first start by *considering* diversity, that is becoming aware of the costs and benefits of maintaining a monolithic workforce. In *pursuing* diversity, they look for strategies to attract and recruit a diverse workforce, usually starting with EEO initiatives. Once the organization opens up to a more diverse workforce, becoming more plural in nature, leaders find ways to ensure that policies and practices support all employees, thereby *managing* diversity. Finally, managers use diversity strategically to add value to the organization strategic goals by supporting the unique contributions each organizational member of their multicultural workforce brings, independent of their background, thus *maximizing* diversity. As an organization achieves multiculturalism, diversity management also requires looping constantly among these tasks over time, so that the diversity challenge never stops.

In their diversity management framework, Thomas and Ely[19] differentiated existing approaches to diversity according to the underlying philosophy of the managers involved. Managers pursuing efforts based exclusively in a diversity philosophy seeking proportional representation expect all employees to assimilate to the dominant culture (Thomas and Ely call this the *discrimination and fairness* paradigm). Other managers pursue efforts that acknowledge the strategic function of diversity to target minority consumer groups. In this approach, diverse employees are not allowed to integrate their unique features to the larger organization, but instead are valued only because of their potential to interact effectively with clients of similar backgrounds (Thomas and Ely call this the *access and legitimacy* paradigm). Finally, in organizations where the *learning and efficiency* diversity paradigm is espoused, employees are not pegged to market niches, but are encouraged to use their diverse backgrounds to enhance productivity and to create new opportunities for the organization. These organizations are said to value innovation, creativity, and diversity in problem solving and decision making, independent of each employee's social identity.

Cox's organizational typology, Ospina's developmental tasks, and Thomas and Ely's philosophies represent valuable frameworks to provide guidance to managers in implementing a diversity agenda. The underlying assumption is that diversity is an organizational imperative, not just a managerial choice. For this reason, the responsibility for diversity management must, in a large organization, be shared. Program managers are responsible for developing and implementing the goals of the organization. Personnel managers, in turn, are responsible for the design and maintenance of HR systems that support both the successful execution of the organization's mission and programs that sustain a diversity philosophy. In partnership, personnel and program managers ensure that the diversity challenge is woven into the organizational goals, its systems and functions, and overall managerial decisions, so that eventually diversity be-

comes embedded in all practices and routines of the organization.[18]

DIVERSITY, PUBLIC PERSONNEL MANAGEMENT, AND CIVIL SERVICE

The functional and political requirements for diversity in public agencies take place in a climate where many are questioning the traditional institution of civil service. Originally implemented to increase rationality in public employment, today civil service is often viewed as an obstacle to attaining the flexibility required for organizational adaptation. In addition, some argue that many systems have failed to address problems of social exclusion, political favoritism, and lack of social representativeness in public service.[13] Although there is no consensus around these claims, there is a generalized call for reforming public employment institutions to ensure they accomplish their role in a democratic society.[20] Diversity management must be included in any discussion of civil service reform.

Although civil service systems can provide general guidelines to ensure diversity, the specifics of diversity management fall within the purview of each agency because every organization is unique. Ultimately, diversity management in the public sector, as in any organization, is a complex and multidimensional challenge that requires permanent and focused managerial attention. Some civil services do not function well (e.g., where patronage and corruption still predominate in spite of the system), whereas in others the system is functional but has produced exclusionary practices and outcomes. Moreover, in civil service contexts, diversity issues may complicate the managerial requirements to balance contradictory pressures for employee protection and stability required for professionalizing public employment, and demands for accountability and transparency to make public service more efficient.

In this context, a thorough diagnosis to assess workforce diversity problems includes an analysis of the system as a whole, as well as audits of each agency the system regulates. Relevant questions include the extent to which a civil service system promotes both effectiveness and multiculturalism, diversity of the workforce in the entire jurisdiction and its component agencies, and the trade-offs associated with introducing systemwide strategies to promote multiculturalism versus incremental changes to address agency-level diversity problems. Answering these questions and designing a reform strategy are tasks that require collaboration among actors of the several jurisdictions regulating public employment and managers who need to make decisions to satisfy performance requirements at the agency level.

Ultimately, all stakeholders must strive to design a system of public employment where:

- Opportunities in hiring, compensation, promotion, and personal development are available to all employees across jobs and levels.
- Access to information and networks in an organization are available to all employees across jobs and levels.
- Every employee believes they are treated as a unique individual whose multiple identities and abilities are respected and appreciated for their potential contributions to the organization. In turn, employees see each other and themselves as valuable members of a working community, while still comfortable with and proud of their identities.
- The right policies, systems, and processes exist to ensure the agency's ability to attract, retain, and develop employees with diverse backgrounds.
- Members of the community can see themselves reflected and represented in the workforce that serves them.

In this context, the envisioned workplace is characterized by an organizational climate and an HR management system in which employee diversity becomes a "normal" condition of organizational life.

DIVERSITY AS A WIDER ISSUE FOR PUBLIC ADMINISTRATION AND PUBLIC POLICY

The list of topics to be included in a full discussion of diversity in public administration and public policy is constantly expanding and cannot be limited to workforce considerations alone. The requirement for diversity in public organizations is rooted in both efficiency and the democratic values of responsiveness and representation in public administration. Public agencies have the mandate to represent in their workforce a wide variety of citizens, as well as consider the plurality of values, concerns, and voices of the larger population. Social movements have challenged traditional patterns of exclusion in the most important institutions of society, and it is no surprise that the same happens in work institutions and public employment.

Although the diversity literature has primarily focused on workforce diversity and diversity management, these topics are not isolated from broader discussions about topics such as multiculturalism and participatory democracy. Scholars of deliberative democracy seek to acknowledge and incorporate different viewpoints in public policy formation. The need for broad representation in democratic decision making and policy implementation

makes diverse participation in the policy process a priority for these authors.[21] Stafford[22] went even further, arguing that the assumptions and analytical tools used in policy analysis are the product of historical and ongoing processes that exclude certain groups of society, and are therefore not representative enough to serve as the foundation for truly democratic policy decisions. Participatory policy making therefore implies the need for managing diversity among the citizenry and not just the workforce.

If public organizations are viewed as part of the implementation stage of public policy, both workforce variety and diversity in decision making are of concern to all interested is a democratic society. Writers from all points of the political spectrum invoke diversity considerations in most contexts of governance. No current scholar presently forecasts the end of this discussion.

REFERENCES

1. Cox, T., Jr. *Cultural Diversity in Organizations: Theory, Research and Practice*; Berrett-Koehler: San Francisco, CA, 1993.
2. Gentile, M. *Managerial Excellence Through Diversity: Text and Cases*; Waveland Press: Prospect Hills, IL, 1996.
3. Mathews, A. Diversity: A principle of human resource management. Public Pers. Manage. **1998**, *27* (2), 175–185.
4. Ospina, S. Realizing the Promise of Diversity. In *Handbook of Public Administration*; Perry, J., Ed.; Jossey Bass: San Francisco, CA, 1996; 441–459.
5. Berman, E.M.; Bowman, J.S.; West, J.P.; Van Wart, M. *Human Resource Management in Public Service: Paradoxes, Processes and Problems*; Sage Publications, Inc.: Thousand Oaks, CA, 2001.
6. Wise, L.R.; Tschirhart, M. Examining empirical evidence on diversity effects: How useful is diversity research for public sector mangers. Public Adm. Rev. **2000**, *60* (5), 386–394.
7. Williams, K.Y.; O'Reilly, C.A., III. Demography and Diversity in Organizations: A Review of 40 Years of Research. In *Research in Organizational Behavior*; JAI Press Inc.: Greenwich, CT, 1998; Vol. 2, 77–140.
8. Schneider, S.K.; Northcraft, G.B. Three social dilemmas of workplace diversity in organizations: A social identity perspective. Human Relat. **1999**, *52* (11), 1445–1467.
9. DeLuca, J.; McDowell, R. Managing Diversity: A Strategic "Grass Roots" Approach. In *Diversity in the Workplace: Human Resources Initiatives*; Jackson, S.E., et al., Eds.; Guilford Press: New York, 1992; Vol. 1, 227–247.
10. Jackson, S.; Stone, V.; Alvarez, E. Socialization Amidst Diversity: Impact of Demographics on Work Team Oldtimers and Newcomers. In *Research in Organizational Behavior*; Cummings, L., Straw, B., Eds.; JAI Press: Greenwich, CT, 1999; Vol. 15.

11. Tomaskovic-Devey, D. *Gender and Racial Inequality at Work: The Sources and Consequences of Job Segregation*; ILR Press: Ithaca, NY, 1993.

12. Guy, M. *Women and Men of the States: Public Administrators at the State Level*; M.E. Sharpe, Inc.: New York, 1992.

13. Ospina, S. *Illusions of Opportunity: Employee Expectations and Workplace Inequality*; Cornell University Press: Ithaca, NY, 1996.

14. Williams, R.E. *Hierarchical Structures and Social Value: The Creation of Black and Irish Identities in the United States*; Cambridge University Press: New York, 1990.

15. Mor Barak, M.E. Beyond affirmative action: Toward a model of diversity and organizational inclusion. Adm. Soc. Work **2000**, *23* (3–4), 47–68.

16. Gilbert, J.A.; Stead, B.A.; Ivancevich, J.M. Diversity management: A new organizational paradigm. J. Bus. Ethics **1999**, *21* (1), 61–76.

17. Meyerson, D.E.; Fletcher, J.K. A modest manifesto for shattering the glass ceiling. Harvard Bus. Rev. **2000**, *78* (1), 126–136.

18. Ospina, S.; O'Sullivan, J.F. Working Together: Meeting the Challenges of Workforce Diversity. In *Public Personnel Administration: Problems and Prospects,* 4th Ed.; Hays, S., Kearney, R., Eds.; Prentice Hall: Englewood Cliffs, NJ, 2003; 238–255.

19. Thomas, D.A.; Ely, R.J. Making differences matter: A new paradigm for managing diversity. Harvard Bus. Rev. **1996**, *74* (5), 79–90.

20. Klinger, D.; Lynn, D. Beyond civil service: The changing face of public personnel management. Public Pers. Manage. **1997**, *26* (2), 157–173.

21. Weeks, E. The practice of deliberative democracy: Results from four large-scale trials. Public Adm. Rev. **2000**, *60* (4), 360–372.

22. Stafford, W. In *Multiculturalism and Public Administration*, Presentation at the National Association of Schools of Public Affairs and Administration Annual Conference, Raleigh, NC, Oct. 17, 1997.

Economic Development, Citizen Participation and

Terry F. Buss
Florida International University, Miami, Florida, U.S.A.

F. Stevens Redburn
U.S. Office of Management and Budget, Washington, District of Columbia, U.S.A.

Marcela Tribble
Florida International University, Miami, Florida, U.S.A.

Thomas Jefferson once pointed out that if the people appeared not enlightened enough to exercise their control of government, the solution was not to take away the control but to "inform their discretion by education." The cooperative processes that are springing up around the country are doing just that, giving to large numbers of citizens a new comprehension of the complexity involved in government decisions, out of which has got to come a heightened appreciation of, and tolerance for, the necessary work of government. If these processes work, if they spread, if they become an indispensable part of government at all levels, we may take it as a sign that we, as a people, have moved up a grade in democracy's school. It holds out the hope that, eventually, the United States will be ready for self-government.

—William Ruckelshaus,
Restoring Public Trust in Government,
National Academy of Public Administration,
November 15, 1996

INTRODUCTION

The 1990s witnessed an increased interest among policy makers, scholars, and advocates in expanding and deepening citizen participation processes, particularly in community and economic development activities. The Bush Administration, early in its tenure, philosophized about the idea of a "citizen-centric" government. The Clinton Administration, under the leadership of Vice President Al Gore, worked on numerous citizen participation initiatives as part of its "reinventing government" program. Scholars, most notably, Robert Putnam, in books such as *Bowling Alone*,[1] called attention to the decline in civil society. Redburn and Buss, in their monograph, *Modernizing Democracy*, called attention to the power of new information technology and the Internet to engage citizens in public life in more sophisticated

ways, and outlined a program to accomplish this goal. Advocates, such as the Orton Family Foundation, have invested heavily in the development and marketing of software—*CommunityViz*—to improve the quality of citizen deliberations on community and economic development policy and programming (www.communityviz. com). Representatives from neighborhood groups, the planning profession foundations, think tanks, and universities met in Tampa in January 2002 to form a national association to raise the visibility of and expand opportunities for citizen participation in building communities (www.PlaceMatters.com). Hundreds of web sites on citizen participation now dot the Internet landscape (e.g., www.democracyinnovations.org).

This article first examines reasons why many want to deepen and expand citizen participation processes. Next, it looks at mandates requiring citizen participation processes at the local level, especially those that are part of public programs for economic and community development. Then the article discusses different modes of citizen participation, evaluating the advantages and disadvantages of each. The entry concludes with an overview of the issues in the design and administration of citizen participation processes intended to support community and economic development.

WHY DEEPEN AND EXPAND CITIZEN PARTICIPATION?

Influential Movements

Political theorists—Robert Dahl, Charles Lindblom, Mancur Olson, William Riker, Anthony Downs, and Alexis D'Tocqville, to name a few—have long been interested in citizen participation as a requisite for democracy. There is no single source for the explosive rise in

Encyclopedia of Public Administration and Public Policy
DOI: 10.1081/E-EPAP 120010205

interest in citizen participation, especially in community and economic development. But we suspect that five independent, although interrelated, forces are at work: a renewed interest in democracy, likely arising out of efforts to assist former Soviet Bloc countries in their transition away from communism; a concerted effort, now world-wide, to "devolve" government as close to the people as possible; the "reinventing government" movement, almost single-handedly launched by David Osborne in his books, *Laboratories of Democracy*[2] and *Reinventing Government*;[3] anticorruption and civil society movements promoted by multilateral and bilateral aid organizations in the Third World; and interest in collaborative shared decision-making models of government inspired separately in business management and public administration leadership literatures (e.g., Refs. [4] and [5]).

American experts, helping to rebuild societies in Russia, its former republics, and Eastern Europe, not only engaged in serious thinking about how to build democracy and economic reconstruction in these countries, but they also called into question how democratic countries in the West really were. The Open Society Institute, based in Budapest, Hungary, and funded by the Soros Foundation, is a think tank devoted to issues of democracy, particularly citizen involvement in redirecting local economies Eastern Europe and Russia (see www.osi.hu). The World Bank, United Nations, and other multilaterals, not to mention efforts across the United States, have extensive programs to decentralize government, devolving power to local people. Microcredit programs targeted at poor neighborhoods and villages as a community/economic development tool is but one example.[6] Anticorruption is a major thrust of World Bank development policy. The World Bank Institute offers a technical assistance and training program—specializing in fiscal decentralization and economic development—to empower local decision making on public expenditures (see www.worldbank.org). The reinventing government movement, a descendent of past "good government" and reform movements, is a focus of a National Academy of Public Administration's Alliance for Redesigning Government in its efforts to build capacity for community development (see www.alliance.napawash.org). The Pew Trust has in place a nationwide project, the Civic Entrepreneur Initiative, to promote local leadership (see www.pew-partnership.org).

Goals

The rationales offered by these five sources of new interest in citizen participation illustrate the diversity of motives and perspectives from which it can be argued that citizen participation processes ought to be expanded and deepened.

Making democracy more democratic

In democratic theory, popular sovereignty refers to the capacity of a people for independence and self-government. Modern American democracy boasts, according to Schattschneider, only a "semisovereign" people, dependent on an expansive, paternalistic political elite intent on reducing deliberative forms of participation.[7] Expanding and deepening citizen participation is a way to make democracy more democratic—that is, direct, deliberative, and participatory. As Thomas Jefferson so aptly stated, "[there is] no safer depository of the ultimate power of society but the people themselves."

Redefining power structures

For some, increasing citizen participation among selected underrepresented groups is a way to redistribute power.[8] The Administrative Procedure Act of 1946 required federal agencies to submit their proposed regulations to public review for the first time. The Housing Act of 1954 expanded participation for the general public by requiring agencies to appoint citizen advisory committees as a prelude to undertaking community development activities. In the 1960s, civil rights legislation enfranchised many Black voters and struck down legal barriers to participation. The Johnson Administration's "War on Poverty" programs under the Equal Opportunity Act of 1964, at the same time, briefly challenged many existing power structures, supporting emergent local organizations with federal funds in an effort to create "maximum feasible participation." Community action agencies, still functioning today, gave many poor people "voice" in local development efforts. The decades following saw the empowerment of groups concerned about local issues, including for our purposes, environmental, planning, zoning, and land use. Citizen participation occurred first through litigation, then through legislation and executive order, requiring nearly all federal agencies to facilitate citizens' input. Executive Order 12898, *Federal Actions to Address Environmental Justice in Minority Populations and Low-Income Populations*, for example, mandates meaningful participation and access for minorities to resolve issues such as toxic waste dump location decisions.

Enhancing credibility

Many believe that governments that reach out to citizens will likely gain credibility from greater openness, transparency, and responsiveness. When government is credible, citizens will support government programs, projects, or initiatives. Today, much social science research finds a public increasingly alienated and disconnected from government at all levels. Less than one-half of registered voters have bothered to show up at the polls since the 1960s. According to monthly "tracking polls" conducted by Harvard's Shorenstein Center on the Press, Politics, and Public Policy, less than one-half of voters, when asked in the months preceding the 2000 campaign, thought about or discussed the campaign. Reengaging alienated citizens is a challenge to those who seek to restore government's credibility.

Managing conflict and building consensus

If everyone agreed on public issues, there might not be a need for government. Because people do not agree, citizen participation processes may be useful in either building consensus or resolving conflict.[9–12] The 1980s brought an increased focus on "stakeholders," and precipitated efforts to get those most affected by public policy to at least be consulted and at most to have a say on outcomes. Analysts soon discovered that involving stakeholders in public decisions was perhaps a necessary condition, but not a sufficient one for developing consensus. Involving stakeholders who disagreed with one another often caused more rather than less problems for public officials. For example, in the U.S. Northwest, farmers wanting to divert water for irrigation, Native Americans desiring to fish depleted waters, environmentalists seeking a primeval environment, and developers promoting development all came into conflict over future economic development of a river region. Where disagreements tended to be intense, as say with environmental issues, new methods for resolving disputes and mediating disagreement were tried. The Environmental Protection Agency (EPA) recognized the need to create an office of conflict resolution.

Feedback

The most sought-after product of citizen participation and the least controversial is the opportunity it affords to allow citizens to provide valuable input on how programs or policies should be crafted, how well they work, and how they might be improved. The notion is that citizens as consumers are best positioned to answer these questions. A major development in this area is the citizen satisfaction survey in which government asks a representative group of citizens formally for feedback on services, in the same way that businesses do. Many community development agencies, for example, periodically survey citizens to gain insight into their needs and expectations.

Accountability

Accountability of public officials for the decisions they make and the services they provide is a major goal of citizen participation processes. If citizens have a say in government, they can influence decisions more frequently and more specifically than simply voting in elections. Public officials who know that citizens are engaged will likely make better decisions.

MANDATED CITIZEN PARTICIPATION PROCESSES

At the federal, state, and local level, few mandates compel local public officials to engage extensively in promoting and using citizen participation processes. Those mandates that do have the force of law are limited, discretionary, and flexible. Transportation planning in Oregon State and economic and community development planning at the Department of Housing and Urban Development (HUD) are illustrative.

Oregon has a long history of citizen participation mandates.[13] In the 1970s, Oregon created the Land Conservation and Development Commission (LCDC) specifically to create the "opportunity for citizens to be involved in all phases of the [transportation] planning process" (p. 7). In 1990, LCDC and the Oregon Department of Transportation developed the *Transportation Planning Rule*, which put even more responsibility on agencies to elicit citizen input. Over time, citizens in Oregon have developed high expectations of government at all levels. Many professionals believe that Oregon leads the nation in citizen participation applications.

Department of Housing and Urban Development's Community Development Block Grant (CDBG) program, a $4.4-billion flexible funding source for community and economic development projects in 50 states and more than 1000 local "entitlement communities," administered by the Office of Community Development and Planning (www.hud.gov). The *Code of Federal Regulations* [24 CFR 91.105] requires a strategic plan—"the Consolidated Plan"—that includes a citizen participation component allowing citizens to help in developing, amending and evaluating CDBG projects. People with low and moderate incomes, particularly those living in slums or blighted areas, represent a special focus. Entitlement communities must take "whatever actions are appropriate to encourage the participation of all their citizens, including minorities and non-English-speaking persons, as well as persons with disabilities." Entitlement communities must hold at least two public hearings annually, one hearing must be scheduled to allow citizens to participate in plan development. Entitlement communities meet publication requirements by publishing a plan summary in a general circulation newspaper and by making copies of the plan available at libraries, government agencies, and public places. Entitlement communities must follow their citizen participation plans, but amendments are permitted as long as public comment is invited. Citizen participation requirements cannot restrict the responsibility or authority of an entitlement community for the development and execution of its plan.

At the local level, few communities mandate specific citizen participation processes, except for hearings on budgets, land use planning, and the like. Most citizen participation activity is mandated by either federal or state law or regulation.

MODES OF CITIZEN PARTICIPATION

A panoply of options exists to satisfy citizen participation requirements under law or because they are considered desirable in themselves (see, e.g., Ref. [14]).

Referendum, Initiative, Recall

At the state and local level, the oldest and perhaps the most basic form of citizen participation is a vote in a general or special election. Citizens typically vote on the performance or expected performance of candidates for public office. In rarer cases, citizens may be asked to pass or defeat referendums or initiatives on issues—citizens may unite to put their own issues on ballots—that have policy implications. Only 21 states have both a referendum and initiative option, 2 have initiatives only, 3 referendums only, and 18 neither option (www.iandrinstitute. org). Or they may vote elected officials out of office—recall—before their terms are up. Although elections are at the heart of democracy, they do not allow citizens to participate except by giving thumbs up or down. Some argue that the referendum process has been largely co-opted by monied interests able to influence electoral outcomes through sheer spending.[15] In any case, elections may be a necessary condition of citizen participation in democracy, but are not sufficient in any sense. They also are not terribly relevant in community and economic development locally where most activities are project based and not the proper object of elections.

Hearings

Public hearings are the most common form of citizen participation in practice, at least locally. Virtually every unit of local government must hold hearings when plans are developed, projects are approved or amended, or budgets are proposed or revised. In many cases, federal, state, and local units of government may mandate hearings. Department of Housing and Urban Development requires hearings on its Consolidated Plan, states require a hearing on matching funds tied to federal fun-

ding, and local governments may require hearings on federal and state funding allocated to the local budget, for example. Although the most frequently used form, hearings could be the least effective vehicle for citizen input. Typically, hearings are poorly attended and citizen comment is likely not representative, even when millions of proposed expenditures on economic and community development funding are at stake. Hearings are also risky for public officials because they are impossible to control—anyone can say just about anything, all before the mass media. Most officials can recount horror stories about how an angry citizen unexpectedly derailed a "safe" project in a hearing. The setting encourages posturing and discourages dialog and new thinking. For most hearings on economic and community development projects, public officials do not want fully developed projects changed or rejected in final stages after a great deal of effort has been expended. Perhaps this is why public officials view hearings as a pro forma requirement to get out of the way.

Advocacy Group Influence

Since the 1960s scholars (e.g., David Truman's, *The Governmental Process*) have pointed out that interest groups have come to dominate citizen participation processes, usually around a narrow set of issues or programs that directly concern their members. For instance, directors of state-level community development agencies, such as the Council for State Community and Economic Development Agencies, lobby HUD on community and economic development issues, on everything from lead abatement in housing projects to management information systems used in reporting block grant expenditures. Although advocacy group input is important—these groups often have the expertise and information necessary to make good policy decisions—they may dominate citizen participation processes so much so that the process becomes lopsided. At HUD, for example, only two groups are mandated to be included through outreach in citizen participation processes in HUD's CDBG grant—labor unions and the disabled community. All other groups must rely on their own devices to be heard.

Surveys and Focus Groups

Increasingly, communities are turning to surveys and focus groups as a preferred mode of citizen input (e.g., Ref. [16]). Surveys, by telephone, mail, e-mail, group distribution, or in person, afford policy makers the opportunity to elicit large amounts of information from representative groups of people at relatively low cost. Their disadvantage is that they are highly structured and not especially rich in the information they produce. Focus groups—small groups of people whose interaction yields rich information—often supplement survey information as a mode of input. An issue with surveys and focus groups is that they have become a kind of barometer used by public officials in decision making. In other words, decision makers decide based on trends in polls and focus groups. However, polls and focus group data may tap fickle opinions that can vary greatly in a short period of time. This is the case in Boston's $15-billion "Big Dig" transportation/economic development project since the 1990s (www.bigdig.com). Public opinion support ebbed and flowed as bridges, highways, and tunnels appeared, while neighborhoods were disrupted; billions in cost overruns were reported; and dust, noise, and water pollution become commonplace.

Meetings/Workshops/Retreats

Meetings, workshops, and retreats are increasingly popular as ways to involve citizens in governmental decision making. These modes are most often used to gather information from citizens or provide them with it, greatly limiting their utility. Even so, these methods are especially useful in economic development where maps, models, and other visual aids are necessary.

Neighborhood/Community/Citizen Advisory Boards

Some communities formalize citizen input into programs or policy areas by creating special boards that offer input into planning processes. Boards do not have decision-making authority (these should not be confused with zoning or planning boards, which do have authority to make decisions). Boards typically strive to be representative of communities or neighborhoods by including one or more "stakeholders" from each group likely to be affected. The problem with boards is that they cannot really be representative of neighborhoods, except in some nominal way. Board members also tend to have different values than either elected officials or the general public.[17]

Group Facilitation

Group facilitation modes have been around for decades, but seem to be enjoying a renaissance in the last few years.[18] Most methods have in common that citizens are chosen to participate in a process over time in which they reach consensus on problems and solutions (see Table 1 for a list of large group process methods). Public officials may participate in groups as members. The latest innovations in group methods have to do with increasing dramatically the number of participants to give their deliberations more credibility and to increase diversity of

Table 1 Examples of large group process methods

Method	Web site
Citizen juries	www.jefferson-center.org
Collaborative input	www.ci.eugene.or.us/news/cisp
Shared decisions	www.ci.eugene.or.us/news/cisp
Open space technology	www.marwww.marand.si/business
Future search	www.futuresearch.net/fsis.htm
Appreciative inquiry	www.pancultural.com

opinion. A shortcoming of group methodologies is that on the whole they have never undergone widespread scientific evaluation: What works and why? Are group methods superior to other methods? Its unclear whether the numerous techniques available are really different or just boast different "brand names."

Complex Voting/Computers/Internet

E-government is a high priority at the federal level, as well as at state and local agencies. At present, e-government focuses on the development of web sites to disseminate information to the public and e-mail links to elicit citizen feedback.[19] Fourteen counties in northwestern Georgia, for example, linked together in the Growth Management Initiative web site to provide a forum on growth/antigrowth issues in a project funded by the Appalachian Regional Commission (www.arc.gov). Although common, these methodologies do not yet take full advantage of new technology. High-speed computers, sophisticated decision-making software, and Internet access could revolutionize citizen participation processes. Citizens working at terminals, for instance, could participate in inexpensive sophisticated simulations and decision-making games and activities.[20] However, even this method of citizen participation can be problematic. No matter how simple or user friendly, some individuals may be excluded as participants.

CITIZEN PARTICIPATION PROCESSES IN ACTION

Despite the varied options available to public officials to improve access to government, there is wide variation among communities in the extent to which they promote citizen participation opportunities. We believe that most communities offer minimal options; consider HUD's programs. As required by law, all entitlement communities must have at least two hearings related to the Consolidated Planning process. Many communities create citizen advisory boards, composed either of neighborhood residents or community representatives, including advocacy groups, citizen groups, nonprofit agencies, and the like. Many communities conduct surveys or focus groups to elicit citizen input. These can take many forms, ranging from narrow attempts to identify specific needs to more global looks at community development issues. Judging from HUD's Best Practice Awards program in the recent past, the latter activities are uncommon enough to enjoy the status of "best practices" (see HUD web site, "Blue Ribbon Practices in Community Development").

Richmond, California, for example, received a citation for best practice in citizen participation, stated as:

> The City undertook a number of activities to expand and enhance citizen participation in the Consolidated Planning process. The City formed a Consolidated Plan Advisory Task Force that was made up of citizens, including Public Housing Authority residents and members of neighborhood councils. The Task Force reviewed drafts of the Plan and provided suggestions for improving the document. In addition, the staff of the Task Force brought together an interdepartmental working group and a variety of other agencies.

Columbus, Ohio's efforts under CDBG, by contrast, are exemplary. They distributed 10,000 surveys, door hangers, and fliers. They visited dozens of nonprofit, social service agencies, and public places (e.g., shopping malls) to elicit input. They set up community information hotlines; held numerous community forums, inviting citizens to attend by letter invitation; sent out direct mailings; and provided information to the mass media.

ISSUES

Because citizen participation is not straightforward in any sense, the following issues will always be of concern.

Defining Stakeholders

Most modes of citizen participation depend on targeting certain kinds of stakeholders who will participate. But how should "stakeholders" be defined? An obvious way is to determine who is most affected by development activity, then bring them to the table. Who is most affected is always relative. Is it persons directly or indirectly affected? Are those who are slightly affected but intense considered, and consequently some will be excluded or included "inappropriately" in the process? Are taxpayers who will be asked to pay the bill stakeholders? Is impact enough or should it take into account severity of impact? The list of qualifications is endless. Once defined, how should stakeholders be identified? Should stakeholders those in certain demographic groups (e.g., age, race, lan-

guage, ethnicity, income), residents of an area, or both. Definitions lead to more or less inclusion or exclusion. For example, HUD encourages communities to establish neighborhood strategy areas to address the needs of the poor. However, there are few areas with relatively large homogenous populations. Rather there is usually a mix of low- and moderate-income people, and even high-income people occasionally, all with a "stake" in development.

Decision-Making Authority

Many advocates want to see citizen participation processes have more "teeth" when it comes to implementation,[21] but this is a double-edged sword. Why should citizens participate if their deliberations are not taken seriously? The other side of the coin is that elected and appointed officials are in office to make decisions. If they do badly, then citizens might vote them out. Laws and customs requiring citizen participation processes greatly favor the latter. An untenable situation exists when citizens devote inordinate amounts of time to providing input only to find it rejected. Some public officials desire to change this. In Seattle, Mayor Paul Schell inaugurated his "city of choices" initiative in which citizens provide early input on economic and community development issues that are then implemented by the city. Public officials gave citizens in Eugene, Oregon, control over small grants for community/economic development as a start in citizen empowerment.

Bad Advice

Public officials often eschew citizen participation processes because they want to avoid bad advice, especially publicly given. Although this seems reasonable on its face, it denies citizens their right to be heard—often and vociferously. It also is highly paternalistic, assuming that elites are much more likely to be "right." An emerging trend in this field is the notion that public officials are unreasonably afraid of the public mostly because these officials have not received the training necessary to manage citizen participation processes effectively or to their advantage. Bramson advocates training public officials in the art and science of engaging citizens in a dialog, under the assumption that public officials have unfounded fears about engagement that might be overcome through learning and training.[22]

Necessity to Triangulate Methods

Importantly, although there are numerous ways to engage citizens in the workings of government, employing only a handful of methods is not sufficient to fulfill the requirements of democracy. Different methods reach only selected people, but equally important, different methods when applied to the same people sometimes yield differing results. A survey and focus group methodology applied to residents of a neighborhood can easily produce different, perhaps conflicting, results. The dilemma for public officials is what methods to choose and how to interpret results. The best approach is to engage in as many methods as possible then reconcile disparate results where appropriate by bringing in additional information or consulting experts, or gathering additional input. However, this can be expensive and time consuming, not to mention complicated.

E-government

E-government, even in its most sophisticated and technologically advanced aspects, for many tends to be viewed as another way to facilitate citizen input. Although this is the case, e-government, according to columnist Neal Peirce, should not be considered a convenience, but rather a way to personalize government and make it more responsive, even for people of little wealth or influence.[23] Viewed in this way, it could become essential as an expression of a properly functioning government. However, it will take considerable effort to move from convenience to responsiveness.

Planning v. Participation

Some argue that citizen participation and planning processes are in continual tension, so much so that the former is the Achilles heel of the latter.[24] Citizen participation improves democratic processes, while planning mostly involves negotiation; relies on formal processes, while planning is much more informal; and is inclusive and routinized, while planning is selective, changing, and flexible. Citizen participation is, by definition, transparent, while planning may occur, for legitimate reasons, behind closed doors. The implication is that effective citizen participation may lead to ineffective planning.

Evaluation

In spite of mandates for and the prevalence of citizen participation activities across the United States, few have ever been formally evaluated (e.g., Ref. [25]). In part, public officials do not see the need to evaluate citizen participation processes, believing that investing in evaluation reduces funding available for programs, and may not want to know what works and what does not. These arguments against evaluation are unfounded. Evaluation can help to determine what works and what does not so that funding from all sources can be better

spent. If performance-based management, grounded in goals, objectives, and outcomes is meaningful for program implementation, then evaluation of citizen participation processes would be critical in determining all phases of the policy process—design, implementation, evaluation, and feedback.[26,27] Most federal funding and a great deal of state funding allows for and encourages expenditures for administrative costs, including evaluation generally and citizen participation specifically. Communities spend a lot on administration: why not channel it into evaluation. Public officials may not want to be held accountable, but if they are not, change will likely not occur. Citizen participation is the engine of change and must be done effectively—good or bad.

Inappropriate Citizen Input

Some argue that a few policy issues defy any rational use of citizen participation processes. These issues tend to be those that are complex, time sensitive, secret, or proprietary. The EPA exempts many of its policy issues from citizen input because administrators do not believe that people are sophisticated enough to understand the science and that people in any case would not have sufficient time to review and absorb documents necessary to acquire the scientific knowledge. The Defense Department, State Department, Federal Bureau of Investigation, Central Intelligence Agency, and numerous other agencies may exclude citizen involvement because of the sensitive nature of the policies (e.g., war and peace) being deliberated. All agencies may face time pressures on some policies (e.g., natural disasters) that preclude public comment. Aside from national security issues, exempting citizens for expediency's sake from input is likely overstated.

Promoting the Idea of Citizen Participation

Assuming that expanding and deepening citizen participation opportunities is desirable, who should take the lead in making it reality? Foundations and government agencies can fund demonstration projects to draw attention to the issue (www.pew-partnership.org). Universities, foundations, advocacy and professional groups, and government can publish best practice information for wide dissemination (e.g., www.hud.gov). Federal agencies can provide grantees, say under CDBG, with incentives to undertake citizen participation activities. Federal agencies or Congress could expand regulations to require greater participation opportunities. Perhaps what is also needed is a national, federally funded organization charged with promoting citizen participation nationwide. It is ironic that no such agency now exists, considering that America is a beacon for democratic practices, yet itself has a considerable way to go. The U.S. funds such an agency—Institute of Peace—for countries in transition, but not for our own country (www.usip.org).

CONCLUSION

Citizen participation is essential in any democracy, but must continue to be nurtured. Renewed interest in citizen input makes this a propitious time to experiment with methods to expand and deepen opportunities for citizens to interact with their government on economic and community development issues, and also other agendas. With computers, software, and the Internet the options are limitless, but a concerted effort in government and the public must occur.

REFERENCES

1. Putnam, R. *Bowling Alone: The Collapse and Revival of American Community*; Simon and Schuster: New York, 2001.
2. Osborne, D. *Laboratories of Democracy*; Harvard Business School Press: Cambridge, MA, 1990.
3. Osborne, D. *Reinventing Government*; A Plume Book: New York, 1993.
4. Seifter, Economy and Hackman, **1997**.
5. Chrislip, D.; Larson, C. *Collaborative Leadership*; Jossey-Bass: San Francisco, 1994.
6. Snow, D.; Woller, G.; Buss, T.F. *Microfinance and Economic Development Policy*; Nova: New York, 2001.
7. Schattschneider, J. *Semi-Sovereign People*; Thompson Publishing: New York, 1997.
8. Cortner, H. *Public Involvement*; Institute for Water Resources, US Corps of Army Engineers: Alexander, VA, 1993.
9. Madigan, D., et al. *New Approaches to Resolving Public Disputes*; National Institute for Dispute Resolution: Washington, DC, 1990.
10. Susskind, L.; Field, P. *Dealing with an Angry Public*; The Free Press: New York, 1996.
11. Susskind, L.; Cruikshank, J. *Breaking the Impasse*; Basic Books: New York, 1987.
12. Susskind, L., et al. *Consensus Building Handbook*; Sage: Thousand Oaks, CA, 1999.
13. Federal Highway Administration. *Public Involvement at Oregon Department of Transportation*; US Department of Transportation: Washington, DC, 1997.
14. Office of Intergovernmental and Public Accountability. *How to Design a Public Participation Program*; US Department of Energy: Washington, DC (undated).
15. Gerber, E. *The Populist Paradox*; Princeton University Press: Princeton, NJ, 1999.
16. The Leadership Initiative. *Strategic Planning For Community Development*; Department of Economic Development and Finance, State of North Dakota: Bismark, ND, 2001.
17. Redburn, F.S.; Buss, T.F.; Foster, S.; Binning, W. How representative are mandated citizen participation processes? Urban Aff. Q. **1980**, *15* (3), 345–352.
18. Group Methods for Whole Systems Change. *Public Organization Review*; Bramson, R.A., Buss, T.F., Eds.; 2002; *in press.*
19. Buss, T.F.; Redburn, F.S. Information Technology and Governance. In *Sound Governance*; Farazmand, A., Ed.; Marcel Dekker: New York, 2002.
20. Redburn, F.S.; Buss, T.F. *Modernizing Democracy*; Brookings Institution: Washington, DC, 2002.
21. Advisory Council on Intergovernmental Relations (ACIR). *Citizen Participation*; ACIR: Washington, DC, 1979.
22. Bramson, R.A. *Public Dialogue*; Union Institute: Cincinnati, 2000.
23. Peirce, N. *E-government: Not Just Convenience*; Alliance for Redesigning Government (www.alliance.napawash.org): Washington, DC, 2000.
24. Benveniste, G. *Mastering the Politics of Planning*; Jossey-Bass: San Francisco, 1989.
25. Office of Policy. *Stakeholder Involvement and Public Participation at the U.S. EPA*; Environmental Protection Agency: Washington, DC, 2001.
26. Council for Urban Economic Development. *Performance Monitoring: Achieving Performance Excellence in Economic Development*; Author: Washington, DC, 1998.
27. Department of Public Instruction. *Community Education Tool Kit*; Author, State of Wisconsin: Madison, WI (undated).

Economic Development, Community Organizations and

Herbert J. Rubin
Northern Illinois University, DeKalb, Illinois, U.S.A.

INTRODUCTION

In conventional economic development programs, locales rely upon a variety of incentives to compete with one another to attract upscale office, research, and commercial properties to downtowns and to suburban commercial, industrial, and research parks. As a consequence of these economic development efforts, public wealth is transferred to established firms, while the economic needs of older, industrial, inner-city neighborhoods already harmed by structural changes in the economy are neglected.[1,2] Scholars and activists argue that an alternative approach toward economic development—one in which concerns with social equity, of helping the poor and poor neighborhoods—predominates.[3,4]

Unfortunately, the administrative complexities of implementing equity economic development within disadvantaged neighborhoods can be daunting. Projects tend to be small, provide little publicity for elected officials, and are undertaken in the neighborhoods with which most public officials are least familiar. In addition, in inner-city neighborhoods, individuals face numerous social problems that complicate the efforts to bring about economic repair.

To bring about equity in economic development, activist scholars suggest following a "community option in urban policy" through which "local services and redistributive subsidies, along with decision-making authority and accountability, might be decentralized... from public to community-based organizations."[5] With the community option, the public sector is not directly involved in programs of neighborhood repair, but instead it facilitates those economic development efforts chosen by community members and implemented by community-based development organizations (CBDOs). Such an approach can succeed. The National Congress for Community Economic Development, the trade association for CBDOs, notes that community organizations have already developed 71 million square feet of commercial and industrial space, lent $1.9 billion to business enterprises, and created 247,000 full-time jobs mostly benefiting poor communities and their residents.[6]

TYPES OF CBDOs

Community-based development organizations are organizations responsible to a neighborhood or constituency group of disadvantaged individuals, usually but not always incorporated as nonprofits, whose stated mission is to economically improve neighborhoods of deprivation in ways that benefit current residents and individuals in need. A wide array of community-based development organizations undertake equity economic development work.

Many *neighborhood organizations* and *block associations* include economic development efforts as part of their ongoing community organizing efforts. These nonprofit and volunteer organizations encourage city hall to provide infrastructure repairs or to increase services (e.g., garbage pickup, frequency of public transit) needed to retain existing businesses in the neighborhoods, join coalitions to advocate for neighborhood projects, and encourage the formation of specialized organizations that focus on economic development work. In several progressive cities, government have worked with neighborhood planning organizations to obtain citizen input into economic development efforts. In Minneapolis, for instance, neighborhood organizations are responsible for the local plans that city line agencies follow in their renewal efforts. In Boston, the Dudley Street Neighborhood Initiative has prepared for its own neighborhood and city redevelopment plan. In several dozen other locales, comprehensive community initiatives (CCIS) set up by foundation–city–neighborhood partnerships to coordinate social programs, housing efforts, and infrastructure renewal to improve the community environment in ways that will create jobs or attract businesses.[7]

In contrast to neighborhood organizations, planning groups, CCIs, community development corporations (CDCs), and community development financial institutions (CDFIs) focus their entire efforts on economic development and housing projects. Community development corporations are community-based organizations that undertake capital-intensive, physical development projects, such as building affordable housing, setting up commercial properties, and promoting industrial renewal.

Encyclopedia of Public Administration and Public Policy
DOI: 10.1081/E-EPAP 120010705

Although most of their work focuses on housing renewal, many CDCs also act as neighborhood economic developers. Community Development Corporations are structured as nonprofits that can receive grant money, but are also chartered as quasicapitalistic organizations that can participate in commercial, housing, and industrial development work. Community development corporations can become stock holders, partners, or owners in for-profit ventures; acquire debt; and manage firms. In addition, CDCs act as a neighborhood business advocates, run training programs that help people to improve their job skills or learn how to set up a business. To complement their efforts in housing and economic development, CDCs collaborate with social service agencies to help individuals combat personal, family, or economic problems that limit their economic activities.[6] Another cluster of community-based-organizations, CDFIs, focus their efforts on providing capital needed for economic renewal within poor neighborhoods. The array of CDFIs include community credit unions, community venture capital development funds, community development banks, and microenterprise funds that collectively act as financial intermediaries within poor neighborhoods.[8]

PHILOSOPHIES OF COMMUNITY-BASED DEVELOPMENT

How do the efforts of community-based development organizations differ from those of conventional economic developers? To begin, the work of CBDOs is guided by a shared organic theory[9] that promotes the idea that economic development is about empowering the poor, not merely about doing projects. Redevelopment projects initiated by CBDOs explicitly attempt to increase social equity in ways that benefit those most in need. Promoting dead end, unskilled jobs does not bring about social equity; neither do high-tech projects that displace the poor and gentrify the neighborhoods. Instead, in their efforts to make sure that the poor benefit from economic development efforts, a CBDO would set up a training program to prepare community members for the skilled positions offered by firms that are helped by the CBDOs. For instance, in Kansas City, a CBDO helped a telephone company to set up a back office facility in an inner-city neighborhood that employed community members who received the training necessary to upgrade their skills to the level needed by the company.

As a second component of the organic theory, CBDO-sponsored economic development projects are intended to increase capital flow within poor neighborhoods. When firms that expand in the neighborhood hire community members, wages earned are recycled as employees purchase goods in locally owned stores. Community-based

development organizations have helped to develop supermarkets in neighborhoods that lacked convenient and affordable shopping, insisting that the supermarkets both train and employ community members. Or, a CBDO might assist a local business that provides insulation to homes, enabling community members to save money on utility money, money that is exported from the community, and to spend it in neighborhood stores.

Third, economic development is not done in isolation but instead becomes part of broader, programs of holistic social repair. Efforts to improve schools or provide day care are incorporated within the broader economic development agenda. Without better schools, employees are not prepared for jobs; for single mothers to be able to leave home and work, day care is needed. Women are more likely to be victims of poverty than are men, so many CBDOs establish programs to aid female entrepreneurs obtain capital or learn how to convert a skills or talents into a microenterprise business. Because businesses fear crime; crime watch and antidrug programs become part of the CBDO's broader economic development agenda. The housing build by CDCs creates a stable residential environment for the poor, while luring back the working class. In turn, the residents of the new, affordable housing form a market that encourages commercial ventures to return to the neighborhood. In regional efforts, CBDOs join with environmentalists to promote smart-growth programs that restore inner-city communities, helping community residents and reducing urban sprawl.[10]

TECHNIQUES OF COMMUNITY-BASED ECONOMIC RENEWAL

In guiding the economic renewal of poor neighborhoods, CBDOs follow five overlapping approaches that vary from directly sponsoring entrepreneurial, capitalistic projects to community-organizing efforts meant to pressure government not to abandon poor communities.

As entrepreneurial capitalistic investors, CBDOs themselves establish profit-making enterprises, usually those supplying goods or services lacking within poor communities. In undertaking such efforts, the CBDO will first obtain public or foundation support to pay for the social costs of remediation—acquiring and repairing an abandoned property, cleaning up a brownfield, removing abandoned vehicles. Then, with the land improvements accomplished, the CBDO will by itself or in partnership with conventional firms develop a commercial project on the restored site. For instance, the Kansas City CDC rehabilitates abandoned inner-city sites, one so derelict that it was used as a set for a postatomic war movie, and then builds inner-city shopping malls often owned and managed by the CDC itself. In a disadvantaged Newark neighborhood, New Communities Corporation (in partnership with a grocery chain) built a full-service super market on a previously derelict lot; other CBDOs have started firms to process and recycle waste materials found in the older industrial neighborhoods into usable products. People in poor communities are consumers of social and medical services for which they often have to leave the neighborhood to receive. Community-based development organizations, such as Bethel in Chicago, will set up social service agencies—medical clinics, for instance, that provide needed services within the community while also training community members to work in these agencies. As social service providers, such CBDOs themselves become a major community employer. As quasicapitalists investor, CDFIs endeavor to expand the capital available in poor communities, setting up development banks that directly invest in neighborhood projects or forming community development credit unions that allow community members both to deposit their earnings and to receive loans.

With catalytic economic development projects, CBDOs encourage government to provide the incentives that enable for-profit firms to expand their efforts within neighborhoods of need. For instance, as neighborhood shopping strips disappeared, poor communities found themselves devoid of economic centers that provided needed goods and services and symbolized economic vitality. Acting as chambers of commerce, CBDOs form business investment districts that obtain public resources to restore such shopping strips. Community-based development organizations have initiated transportation-oriented development projects (TODs) in which government is pressured to improve a transit node and, in doing so, rebuild in ways that encourage stores to locate near this high traffic generator. By setting up industrial or commercial incubators, CBDOs catalyze economic renewal. In incubator projects, a CBDO obtains a subsidy to convert an older building, often an abandoned industrial plant, into affordable space for start-up firms, both from the neighborhood itself and those that will employ community members. At times, funds are even available to hire a successful business person to act as a mentor for start-up companies. In other catalytic efforts, CBDOs help to form worker cooperatives in which individuals learn skills, market products, and collectively own their firms. In Alaska, for instance, indigenous people have set up a Musk Ox Cooperative to process and sell the exotic wool of that Arctic animal.[11] Community development financial institutions provide loans (that mainstream financial institutions refuse to make available) to conventional entrepreneurs willing to invest in neighborhoods of need, while revolving loan funds are established to provide the small amount of seed capital required to set up microenterprises. Community-based development organizations will teach neighborhood capitalists how to prepare business plans and pro formas that can then be used in obtaining investment capital, while introducing them to loan officers at banks.

Most CBDOs recognize that to repair the economic damage in poor communities, efforts are needed to expand social and human capital. Poor people often lack both training and capital to start a business or to obtain the specialized education needed for better employment. To encourage this expansion in human capital, CBDOs link training and education efforts to individual development account programs (IDAs). While community members further their education or undertake apprenticeship training, money is put aside for them in an escrowed account. On completion of the training, people receive the lump sums to be used as investment capital either in a business or in further education. Individuals from poor communities lose wealth by being victimized by exploitative predatory lenders. Community development financial institutions establish financial literacy programs, teaching people how to negotiate the increasingly complicated financial system and to avoid losing their limited capital to unscrupulous lenders.

Community-based development organizations expand social capital by linking people to each other. Appalachian Center for Economic Networks (ACENET) in Appalachian Ohio set up flexible manufacturing networks that linked small manufacturers, designers, and marketers to promote products, while Esperanza Unida in Milwaukee brought together older experienced community members to train unemployed youth as mechanics. In Chicago, the Jane Addams Resources Corporation responds to requests by neighborhood companies to help workers the companies already employ to update the skills needed to enable the companies to survive in a changing economy.[12] After the major change in the mid-1990s in welfare laws, CBDOs expanded their efforts to provide training and job access to the welfare poor. For instance, in Texas, Project Quest run by a CBDO provides potential employees with the specific training requested by firms, virtually guaranteeing future work.[13] Social service agencies can expand needed social capital. For instance, day care, especially services that are open during the irregular shifts that the poor are forced to work, create jobs within the community for those who provide the service, while allowing others to take jobs away from home. Increased neighborhood pride also expands social capital. Several CBDOs have initiated projects that celebrate a community's culture, such as the Jazz Museum and Black Baseball Museum established by a CBDO in Kansas City.

As advocates for neighborhood economic development, CBDOs provide an assertive voice that speaks for the economic needs of poor communities. Community-based development organizations set up "early warning systems" to shout out to the public sector when established businesses threaten to leave inner-city neighborhoods, often because of the lack of city services. Community-based development organizations join with local labor alliances, such as in the Calumet Project in Indiana, to pressure companies not to abandon poor neighborhoods.[11] Community-based organizations such as BREAD in Columbus, Ohio, pressure city officials to set up transit centers that enable those from the inner city to commute to suburban jobs.[10]

Working in citywide coalitions, CBDOs advocate for first-source hiring programs that mandate that companies that receive public subsidies must hire community members, often people trained by the CBDO. In living wage campaigns, CBDOs join with other community activists to insist that no public dollars be provided to firms unless the companies pay wages that at least match the family poverty level. Advocacy coalitions such as Chicago's Neighborhood Capital Budget Group have brought together CBDOs and neighborhood activist organizations to campaign to ensure that neighborhoods, not just downtown, receive funds for infrastructure repairs.

GOVERNMENT POLICIES IN SUPPORT OF CBDOs

How can public policies and the actions of public officials be redirected to help the community-based development in this movement? To begin, public officials must recognize that heavily subsidized, grandiose, downtown projects do little to help the poor. Instead, they must accept that economic development is about creating social redress and that CBDOs play a crucial part in bringing about economic equity.

Public subsidies to establish economic development trust funds can help to pay for the seed money for projects in poor communities, as does capital to set up revolving loan funds. In poor communities, land ends up in public ownership because of tax forfeitures. The public sector can donate this land to CBDOs for economic development work, but before doing so paying for the remediation that many of these brownfields require. In places such as in the Dudley neighborhood in Boston[2] or in Chicago during the progressive Mayor Washington administration, government delegated authority to community groups for planning, land use, and zoning, and seed money for start-up firms,[14] enabling communities to better control their own development. Local government salaries must recognize that CBDOs rarely make sufficient profit to pay for their core operating expenses (e.g., salaries of ongoing employees, office space) and should use community development block grant, or tax increment financing funds, to provide a substantial proportion of the core operating expense of CBDOs.

National policies, too, could be introduced or enhanced to help the community economic development movement. The Office of Community Services in the Department of Health and Human Services administers a small grant program that provides capital investments to neighborhood economic development projects that have leveraged a significant private sector investments. This program must be continued and expanded. Public funding helps to pay the administrative costs of CDFIs, and enables these financial intermediaries to work on the smaller, overhead-intensive, investment projects needed to stimulate neighborhood business growth. Federal programs such as the New Markets Tax Credit that provide tax credits that encourage both for-profits and CBDO–for-profit partnerships to invest in poor communities need to be expanded. Most important, federal regulators must enforce the Community Reinvestment Act (CRA) that mandates banks to reinvest in poor communities, both for housing and economic development projects. New federal regulations are needed that require the increasing array of nonbank financial institutions to provide capital to communities of need.

Recognizing that they need help, activists within the community redevelopment movement, working with foundations, have set up support organizations that provide technical assistance and political advocacy for community developers. These organizations include trade associations, technical assistance providers, financial intermediaries, training academies, specialized consultants, and accounting and legal firms that concentrate on community renewal programs, and increasingly include academic institutions that offer programs in community redevelopment. Expanded public funding of these support organizations would dramatically increase the knowledge available on community economic development.

REFERENCES

1. Imbroscio, D. *Reconstructing City Politics: Alternative Economic Development and Urban Regimes*; Sage Publications: Thiousand Oaks, CA, 1997.

2. Bright, E. *Reviving America's Forgotten Neighborhoods: An Investigation of Inner City Revitalization Efforts*; Garland Publishing: New York, NY, 2000.

3. Rubin, H. Partnering with the poor: Why local government should work with community-based development organizations to promote economic development. Int. J. Public Adm. **2000**, *23* (9), 1679–1709.

4. Krumholz, N. Equitable approaches to local economic development. Policy Stud. J. **1999**, *27* (1), 83–95.

5. Clavel, P.; Pitt, J.; Yin, J. The community option in urban policy. Urban Aff. Rev. **1997**, *32* (4), 435–458.

6. Rubin, H.; Rubin, I. *Community Organizing and Development*, 3rd Ed.; Allyn and Bacon: Boston, MA, 2001.

7. Meyer, D.; Blake, J.; Caine, H.; Pryor, B. *On the Ground with Comprehensive Community Initiatives*; The Enterprise Foundation: Columbia, MD, 2000.

8. www.cdfi.org/what.cdfi.html (accessed July 30, 2001).

9. Rubin, H. *Renewing Hope Within Neighborhoods of Despair: The Community-Based Development Model*; State University of New York Press: Albany, NY, 2000.

10. Kalinosky, L.; Desmond, K. *Smart Growth, Better Neighborhoods: Communities Leading the Way*; National Neighborhood Coalition: Washington, D.C., 2000.

11. www.grass-roots.org (accessed 3/14/2000).

12. Pitcoff, W. Developing workers: Community-based job training brings families out of poverty. Shelterforce **1998**, *xx* (6)10–13, 28.

13. Harrison, B.; Weiss, M. *Workforce Development Networks: Community-Based Organizations and Regional Alliances*; Sage Publications: Thousand Oaks, CA, 1998.

14. Mier, R. *Social Justice and Local Development Policy*; Sage Publications: Newbury Park, CA, 1993.

Economic Development, Financing

William L. Waugh, Jr.
Georgia State University, Atlanta, Georgia, U.S.A.

INTRODUCTION

Economic development is a policy priority for most local, regional, and central governments. Economic development is a means to reduce unemployment, increase tax bases, leverage other resources from the community, and curry public favor and support. When economic development slows, stagnates, or declines, it has an adverse effect on the community and political and economic leaders are held responsible. Therefore, the competition for new and expanding businesses can be intense and economic development programs may include a broad range of incentives to lure firms from other communities and to cultivate new firms locally. Financing economic development is a crucial concern and one that raises fundamental issues concerning who should pay for government programs, and how much should and can be invested.

DIRECT AND INDIRECT FINANCING

The financing of economic development programs may be direct in terms of investments of public monies in specific firms or sites, or indirect in terms of encouraging private sector investment. To some extent, there is an expectation that economic development will be guided and funded by those who reap the most direct benefit, private firms and individuals. However, governments guide choices and invest public resources to ensure that economic development serves the best interests of the community. In fact, many governments have pursued development with little consideration given to the social and economic impact on their communities, but such unfocused approaches are much less common today. To increase the likelihood of appropriate or desired kinds of development, communities typically offer incentives to locate, relocate, or expand in their communities. Incentive programs may include economic or financial incentives, along with other kinds of incentives. Financial incentives provide direct or indirect support. For example, governments may invest public monies in specific businesses as low-interest loans, or they may invest monies in training and infrastructure thereby permitting firms to use their money for other purposes.

The unavailability of adequate financing has been a major impediment to economic development in many jurisdictions. As a private sector issue, financing has largely focused on the cultivation of venture capital when traditional financing (i.e., bank loans) is unavailable. As a public sector issue, the financing of economic development has been through direct and indirect means. Governments have invested public monies directly in economic development efforts (e.g., providing loans to new and expanding businesses and providing access to pools of money such as public pension funds). They have also invested indirectly—offering tax abatements to reduce the financial burden of property and other taxes; issuing bonds to finance infrastructure and facilities; providing grants usually for specific purposes, such as training; assisting with debt financing, such as providing loan guarantees to help reduce interest rates; and offering more direct financial assistance in exchange for royalty payments.[1]

Revolving Loan Funds

One of the most direct means of financing economic development with public money is to create a revolving loan fund. Loans are made available for start-ups, expansions, and other needs. As loans are repaid, the money is returned to the fund and made available for new businesses.

Loan Guarantee Programs

Rather than making money available through a public loan program, governments can provide guarantees to banks and other financial institutions that loans made to businesses locating in an industrial park or enterprise zone will be repaid even if the firm fails. Loan guarantee programs are useful when traditional lenders consider the risk of business failure too high for them.

TAX INCENTIVES

Tax incentives have been one of the more popular means of encouraging economic development, and they are widely assumed to have a significant impact on the site selection and/or expansion decisions of businesses. The popularity of tax incentives has characterized local and

Encyclopedia of Public Administration and Public Policy
DOI: 10.1081/E-EPAP 120010689

state development programs for several decades, despite the number of studies that demonstrate their marginal impact. Tax incentives generally take three forms: 1) broad-based incentives; 2) targeted incentives; and 3) selectively applied incentives. The broad-based incentives are offered to any and all businesses that choose sites within a jurisdiction, make particular investments, or provide jobs of a particular kind or number. The government offers tax credits, exemptions, and/or deductions in exchange for investment, new jobs, research and development, and/or depreciation of equipment and/or other assets. Targeted incentives are offered for specific kinds of firms, such as firms choosing to locate in areas of high unemployment or in free enterprise zones or so-called high-tech or manufacturing firms. Communities may attempt to lure ``clean'' industries, such as movie making, hospitality or tourism, research, and education.[2–4]

Property Tax Abatements

For local governments, in particular, property tax abatements can provide substantial financial relief for new businesses. Local governments generally do not have the financial wherewithal to create revolving funds and to make large investments in infrastructure and human resources, but they do have authority to levy property taxes. Reducing or eliminating property taxes for a period of time, sometimes for 10 or more years, can be a significant incentive for new businesses.[5] State laws may also permit exemptions from inventory taxes through the establishment of ``free ports.''

Also, economic development authorities, such as community development corporations, can purchase sites and build facilities and lease them to firms without the firms being liable for property taxes. They can also assist in securing loans for start-up and other needs, provide technical assistance, and act as an intermediary in dealing the regulatory agencies.

Tax Increment Financing

Tax increment financing has been a popular means of funding economic development because it is essentially a product of that development. Additional property taxes that result from the development in an enterprise zone or development district are paid to the general-purpose (town or city or county) government or special-purpose (school district) government and placed into a fund to finance improvements to the zone or district.[6,7]

Industrial Revenue Bonds

The broadly focused approach has been characterized by the use of incentives, such as industrial revenue bonds,

subsidies for compliance with pollution control regulations, property tax abatements, loan guarantees, accelerated depreciation of business assets, and corporate income tax exemptions.[8]

Free Enterprise Zones

In the 1980s, ``free enterprise zones'' were the fashion and many still exist in the United States. ``Free enterprise zone'' programs are characterized by the designation of an area for development and the provision of various incentives for businesses locating within the zone. Property tax abatements, public investments in infrastructure improvements and job training, increased police protection, loan guarantees, tax credits for hiring residents of the zone, and other benefits are offered to lure businesses to the zone and to reward those that remain.

INDIRECT PUBLIC INVESTMENT

Infrastructure Improvements

To some extent, public investment in infrastructure, including the creation of industrial and research parks, provide indirect financing for economic development. The investments can reduce start-up and operating costs to business and can facilitate growth.

Technical Assistance Programs

Programs to provide technical assistance with marketing, export regulations, and other crucial capacities, and management training to improve internal operations, may also be considered indirect financing. Such programs increase the likelihood of success and, thereby, increase the likelihood of funding by banks and other venture capital sources.

Land Banks

Some cities have created land banks to assist firms in acquiring properties for development. Abandoned, tax delinquent, donated, and transferred properties are put into the land bank. The bank assures that the titles are clarified, waives tax liability, and sells the property to developers. The land bank can be used to put together parcels for large development projects, such as manufacturing plants and condominium complexes. The bank can reduce the cost of property to developers and facilitate the process of land acquisition by assuring that large parcels can be acquired without having to deal with many different property owners.[9]

LEVERAGING PRIVATE FINANCING

Perhaps the most obvious and less risky approach to economic development is through leveraging private investment. Economic development can be financed through the encouragement of traditional bank financing and through foundation grants. Community commitment to development can increase the likelihood of success among participating firms. Banks and foundations may judge that the community commitment will increase the likelihood of success. Similarly, government officials and private entrepreneurs can cultivate venture capital from private investors.

Community Improvement Districts

Private investment is also encouraged through the creation of community improvement districts. Development within the districts is facilitated by public–private arrangements and funded directly by a system of self-taxation. Public investment is generally in the form of enhanced public services, including public safety, and infrastructure improvements.[10]

CONCLUSION

The trend is toward broad incentive packages that are responsive to the needs of both the community and the participating firms. In the state of Georgia, for example, the state offers job tax credits, investment tax credits, retraining tax credits, child care tax credits, sales tax exemptions, and freeport (property) tax exemptions.[11] The stakes are high in economic development efforts. There is much risk in direct investments of public money because of the high failure rate of new firms and at least some risk in indirect investments in such things as infrastructure improvements that may be firm- or industry-specific because firms may choose to leave for reasons beyond the control of the local government. In short, communities may be left with millions of dollars in bond debt for improvements that the next firm may not find useful or desirable. To address that problem, Ledebur and Woodward suggested that governments evaluate development incentives carefully and assure that they are cost effective. When firms do not live up to their responsibilities, governments should be prepared to reduce or eliminate public subsidies for nonperformance.[12]

The trend has also been toward more creative forms of financing to overcome constitutional and statutory limits on taxing, spending, and borrowing (debt) authority. Local governments have few sources of revenue and limited political autonomy, except in some larger cities and counties. State governments, too, have limits on how they can raise and spend revenues. The use of general obligation bonds may be severely limited, and there is tremendous political opposition to new taxes regardless of their purpose. These are the constraints within which economic development authorities operate.[13]

REFERENCES

1. Hill, E.W.; Shelly, N.A. An Overview of Economic Development. In *Financing Economic Development: An Institutional Response*; Bingham, R.D., Hill, E.W., White, S.B., Eds.; Sage Publications: Newbury Park, CA, 1990; 13–28.
2. Waugh, W.L., Jr.; Waugh, D.M. Baiting the hook: Targeting economic development monies more effectively. Public Adm. Q. **Summer 1988**, *12*, 216–235.
3. Dewar, M.E. Tax Incentives, Public Loans, and Subsidies: What Difference Do They Make in Nonmetropolitan Economic Development. In *Financing Economic Development*; Bingham, R.D., Hill, E.W., White, S.B., Eds.; Sage Publications: Newbury Park, CA, 1990; 40–54.
4. Ihlanfeldt, K.R. Ten Principles for State Tax Incentives. In *Approaches to Economic Development*; Blair, J.P., Reese, L.A., Eds.; Sage Publications, 1999; 68–84.
5. Hy, R.J.; Waugh, W.L., Jr. *State and Local Tax Policies*; Greenwood Press: Westport, CT, 1995; 219–221.
6. Bland, R.L. *A Revenue Guide for Local Government*; International City Management Association: Washington, D.C., 1989.
7. Paetsch, J.R.; Dahlstrom, R.K. Tax Increment Financing: What It Is and How It Works. In *Financing Economic Development*; 82–98.
8. Rasmussen, D.W.; Benedict, M., Jr.; Ledebur, L.C. Evaluating state economic development incentives from a firm's perspective. Bus. Econ. **May 1983**.
9. Hy; Waugh. *State and Local Tax Policies*; Greenwood Press, 1995; 226–227.
10. Hy; Waugh. *State and Local Tax Policies*; 225–226.
11. Ihlanfeldt. *Ten Principles for State Tax Incentives*; 77–79.
12. Ledebur, L.C.; Woodward, D.P. Adding a Stick to the Carrot: Location Incentives with Clawbacks, Rescissions, and Recalibrations. In *Approaches to Economic Development*; Blair, J.P., Reese, L.A., Eds.; Sage Publications: Newbury Park, CA, 1999; 61–66.
13. Schoettle, R.P. What Public Finance Do State Constitutions Allow. In *Financing Economic Development*; 57–74.

Economic Development, Governance Issues in

Kuotsai Tom Liou
University of Central Florida, Orlando, Florida, U.S.A.

INTRODUCTION

This article examines the importance of governance in the process of economic development. The article first provides a literature review about the role of government in promoting economic development and the major issues emphasized in recent government reform projects. Then, the focus is on three policy changes and issues related to the topic of governance and economic development: 1) regulatory reform; 2) privatization policy; and 3) decentralization policy. To conclude discussions about the continuing arguments about the role of government, the increasing importance of local governments, and the contribution of nongovernmental or nonprofit organizations in economic development are presented.

OVERVIEW

Government has traditionally played an important role in the process of economic development. From the perspective of public policy analysis, the importance of government to economic development is primarily based on three interrelated roles, functions, or activities. First, government plays a pivotal policy role in identifying and formulating important development policies and programs to promote economic growth and social change. Next, government serves a critical managerial role in assuring the successful institutional development and reform to implement many identified development policies and programs. Last, government provides a supporting role in maintaining positive and stable political and social environments to provide the opportunity and time for the success of development policies and programs.

The study of governance is important to economic development researchers and policy makers. For researchers, the challenge is to systematically collect objective data from different countries and regions to test, verify, or create various development concepts, strategies, and theories. For policy makers, the challenge is to consider different environmental factors in their countries and to design an appropriate model of governmental intervention through the analysis of many development theories, strategies, and experiences. The interaction of researchers and policy makers is critical to the success of economic

development because of the significant consequence of negative development results.

THE ROLE OF GOVERNMENT IN ECONOMIC DEVELOPMENT

The important role of government in the modern economic system has been well recognized and accepted in the literature of public finance, development economics, and political economy. For example, with regard to specific government functions and activities in the market economy, Adam Smith emphasized three duties of the government (state): 1) protecting the society from violence and invasion by other societies; 2) establishing an exact administration of justice; and 3) erecting and maintaining certain public works and institutions.[1] From the public finance perspective, Musgrave and Musgrave promoted three functions of government: 1) the allocation of social and other goods that the market will not of itself provide; 2) the equitable distribution of income and wealth; and 3) the stabilization of unemployment and control of inflation.[2] Stern summarized the related literature by identifying five different arguments for governmental intervention in the economy. They were as follows: 1) a concern for market failure (arising from sources such as externalities, public goods, and imperfect information); 2) a concern to prevent or reduce poverty and improve income distribution; 3) the assertion of a right to certain facilities or goods (e.g., education, health, and housing); 4) the importance of paternalism (e.g., relating to education, pensions, and drugs); and 5) the rights of future generations (e.g., concerns about the environment).[3]

The issue of state or government involvement in economic growth has been further emphasized and debated in the literature related to economic development. The issue of debate is not whether a state or government should be involved in economic development but what the appropriate role of government might be in promoting growth and development. For example, according to the underdevelopment thesis of dependency theory, the problems of many less-developed countries (LDCs) are related to a situation in which these countries downgraded the central role of their governments in the development process to a dependent and responsive entity. These

Encyclopedia of Public Administration and Public Policy
DOI: 10.1081/E-EPAP 120010688

governments have no autonomy in policy making and implementation, and especially, they respond to the interests of foreign capital at the expense of their national interests.[4,5]

The neoclassical arguments of development emphasize the role of foreign trade and investment and the importance of a free market in stimulating competition during the development process.[6–9] They claim that the problems of LDCs result from extensive government intervention in promoting import-substitution policies that limit the scope of industrialization. They argue that one of the major factors contributing to the success of East Asia's newly industrialized countries is the adoption of export-oriented policies that encourage the process of technological adaptation and entrepreneurial maturation. They recognize the role of state in the process of development but emphasize a passive and limited role of government in such activities as maintaining stability and providing physical infrastructure.

Statist arguments of development, however, indicate that the successful experience of newly industrialized countries is related not only to the operation of the free market but also to the active role of government in directing public and private resources to change the structure of their economy.[8,10–12] For example, many of the successful newly industrialized countries emphasize a general incentive policy to encourage the accumulation of production factors (tax measures, research and development) and an industrial targeting policy to promote the growth of particular industries (e.g., subsidizing credit or import protection).

In its study of Asian economic growth, the World Bank indicated that the high-performing Asian economies were successful in getting the basics right, including a stable macroeconomy, superior accumulation of physical and human capital investment, effective and secure financial systems, limiting price distortions, openness to foreign technology, and assurance of agricultural development policies.[13] In addition, the governments of the high-performing Asian economies have also intervened, systematically and through multiple channels, to promote development, including targeting and subsidizing credit to selected industries, protecting domestic import substitutes, subsidizing declining industries, establishing and financially supporting government banks, establishing firm-and industry-specific export targets, and developing export marketing institutions.

Considering both the market and state arguments, Aoki, Kim, and Fujiwara promoted a market-enhancing view, which emphasized the role of government policy to facilitate or complement private-sector coordination.[14] They maintained that the previous approaches viewed the market and government as the only alternative and as mutually exclusive substitutes, and that the market-

enhancing approach stressed the mechanisms whereby government policy is directed at improving the ability of the private sector to solve coordination problems and overcome other market imperfections. One example of the mechanisms is the important role of government–private-sector intermediaries (e.g., deliberation councils, national wages council) in facilitating information change to avoid possible market coordination failures and in realizing an efficient allocation of credit under the condition of information asymmetry.

Many studies of economic structure adjustments in developing countries and economic reforms or transitions in postsocialist nations also address the issue of governmental involvement in economic development. With regard to structural adjustments, for example, researchers emphasize the importance of the administrative and political functions of the state in the successful implementation of an adjustment program or a reform policy.[15,16] Similarly, many studies of economic transitions in postsocialist countries emphasize the issue of stabilization in the process of economic transformation and identify the important role and involvement of government to assure the success of the transition.[17–20]

Comparing the reform experience in China and Eastern European countries, for example, most of the studies point out that one of the major factors contributing to China's success is the gradual reform approach and stable environment emphasized by the Chinese government. Specifically, Liou identified five major roles of government in the process of China's post-Mao economic reforms, including: 1) government as a promoter of economic growth (i.e., formulating and implementing growth policies); 2) government as a manager of the economy (i.e., managing fiscal and monetary policies); 3) government as a distributor of income (i.e., distributing resources between different regions and among different social groups); 4) government as a regulator of industry (i.e., regulating for social and economic reasons); and 5) government as a protector of citizens and business (i.e., protecting citizens and business from foreign attacks as well as criminal and illegal activities).[21]

CHANGES IN REGULATION, PRIVATIZATION, AND DECENTRALIZATION POLICIES

To assure the success of economic growth, many researchers of economic development recognized the importance of an efficient and ethical public management system in developing and implementing sound development policies and programs, as well as the need to reform the public sector to overcome many unethical and inefficient bureaucratic dysfunctions and problems.[15,16,22] To achieve these goals, recent reform policies have emphasized not only reforms or changes of the civil service system, public budgetary system, and state-owned enterprises, but also restructuring and adjustment policies in market liberalization, privatization, deregulation, and decentralization. The policy measures emphasized in recent government reforms have broadened the traditional concerns of improving management and operational issues in public organizations to a new focus on good governance for successful development. The policy changes of regulatory reform, privatization, and decentralization are furthered explained as follows.

Regulatory Reform

Public policy researchers have noticed that governments often pursue their policy objectives through regulation policies and use them to replace traditional public finance instruments.[23] Government regulation refers to any attempt by the government to control the behavior of citizens, corporations, or subgovernments.[24] Regulation may consist of such categories as economic regulation, social regulation, and administrative regulation.[25,26] Economic regulation focuses on direct government intervention in corporations and market decisions, such as pricing, competition, and market entry or exit. Social regulation is related to government protection of citizen and social values, such as health, safety, the environment, and social cohesion. Administrative regulation has to do with government formalities and paperwork. The instruments used in these regulation policies include, for example, laws, orders, and rules issued by all levels of government.[26]

The pervasive use of regulation and the growth of regulatory cost have resulted in many suggestions for regulatory reforms. The purpose of regulatory reform is to improve the quality of regulations in terms of enhancing performance, reducing costs, or finding alternative policy tools. The reform activities range from revising a single regulation to scrapping and rebuilding an entire regulatory system (policies, processes, and institutions). Deregulation is part of the overall regulatory reform, which refers to complete or partial elimination of regulation in a sector to improve economic performance.[26]

With regard to economic development, regulatory reforms are especially useful in promoting economic growth, firm competitiveness, and consumer welfare. Reform activities for industry development focus on the removal of such barriers or burdens as rigidities, disincentives, and market distortions, and the promotion of competition, entrepreneurship, technological innovation, productivity, structural adjustment, and other important market issues. Reforms that emphasize the increase of the transparency and the reduction of red tape and paperwork are also valuable for investors and ordinary citizens because of the time saved on information communication and collection.[26]

Privatization Policy

The second major policy change in governance is the increase of privatization policies emphasized by policy makers in developed and developing countries. The word "privatization" has been used in many different ways in relation to pubic-sector reforms. In the broadest sense, it refers to a whole range of reformative actions designed to subject administrative activity to the disciplines of the marketplace; in other cases, it may be specialized as acts of selling government-owned enterprises, assets, or shareholdings (see Refs. [27–29]). In the United States, policy makers and public managers emphasize the use of privatization policy to deal with the problem of fiscal retrenchment (due to such changes as tax revolt, "Reaganomics," etc.) and continued service demand. Privatization policies consist of such options as contracting out (outsourcing), franchising, local (service) shedding, public–private partnerships, grants, subsidies, vouchers, asset divestment, competitive contracting, volunteer services, and total privatization.

The arguments for privation policies are based on some beliefs, such as government should not provide services or products when these services or products are available in the private market; government is better when it is smaller; private firms are more efficient than government agencies; and private managers are better than public administrators. Specifically, privatization policy offers such advantages as improving government operations, meeting short-term project needs, lowering the costs involved in service delivery, adjusting for resource limitations, and improving service quality.[30] The potential problem associated with privatization policy is the increasing dangers of sector blurring and the twilight zone,[31,32] where individuals fall into a situation in which they will receive less than optimal treatment as citizens receiving services from government or as customers from private firms. It is believed that substantial benefits and significant values and protections may be lost in the transition from government to the private sector.[30,32,33]

Finally, privatization policy has also been emphasized in many developing or economic-transforming countries.[34–37] For these countries, privatization policy is closely related to the policy of reforming state-owned enterprise (SOE). As a part of economic liberalization measures, privatizing SOE is designed to improve the operation of SOE (maximizing benefits, reducing cost, or enhancing effectiveness) and to reduce the role of government in the market economy. Privatization of SOE consists of such measures as contracting out, restraining and redeveloping labor, denationalizing and disinvesting, imposing budgetary constraints, promoting marketization, and introducing competition.

Decentralization Policy

The last major change in governance is the importance of decentralization policies in many developed and developing countries.[38–40] In the United States, decentralization policies were emphasized as a result of the huge federal budget deficit, the cutback of federal aid, and the Reagan federalism philosophy. In many developing countries, decentralization policies were adopted because of the emphasis on structural adjustment policies by international assistance organizations (the World Bank and the International Monetary Fund). The structural adjustment policies call for, among other things, decentralization of national government administration and reduction of the central government's control over or intervention in the economy.[41,42]

Decentralization has been defined as the transfer of responsibility for planning, management, and the raising and allocation of resources from the central government and its agencies to field units of government agencies; subordinate units or levels of government; semiautonomous public authorities or corporations; area-wide, regional, or functional authorities; or nongovernmental private or voluntary organizations.[43] Researchers have debated the advantages and problems of the decentralization policy.[38–40] On the one hand, they recognize that advantages of decentralization policy include emphasizing administrative responsiveness, increasing political participation, and promoting democratic principles.[38–40] On the other hand, they notice that decentralization policy may generate such problems as increasing disparities among regions, jeopardizing economic and social stability, affecting administrative efficiency.[44] They maintain that these problems may result from the lack of resources and information at the local level, and the low administrative skills, training, and educations among local public employees.

To implement decentralization policy, it is important for policy makers to consider the decentralization from a comprehensive strategic planning perspective. The strategic planning perspective emphasizes important policy components, such as understanding political, social-economic, and institutional environments of central and local governments; analyzing constraints and opportunities of these governments; considering policy scope and nature; developing an action plan of decentralization; and focusing on capacity building and empowerment. The component of capacity building is especially important, as it includes such areas as institutional, personnel, fiscal, and information capacity building.

CHALLENGES AND IMPLICATIONS

The previous review of the role of government and policy changes provides the background information for the following discussion of major challenges in the study of governance and economic development. Three issues are especially important here: 1) the continuing arguments about the role of government; 2) the increasing role of local government; and 3) the contributions of nongovernmental or nonprofit organizations.

The Continuing Argument for the Role of Government

Economic development researchers are continually debating the role of government, especially governmental intervention, in the process of economic development. The market approach of development emphasizes the role of international trade and investment and the importance of a free market in stimulating competition during the development process. The statist approach stresses the active role of government in directing public and private resources to change the structure of their economy. A third market-enhancing approach considers advantages of the market and the state approaches and promotes the role of government policy to facilitate or complement private-sector coordination and overcome other market imperfections. Many of the theoretical arguments of these approaches are mainly based on the Asian development experience, especially the performance of the high-performing Asian economies.

The recent experience of the Asian financial crisis has not resolved the different arguments about the issue of governance. The causes of and cures for the Asian financial crisis are directly or indirectly related to the government policy and managerial activities that are important to economic development.[45–49] On the one hand, political leaders and governmental officials have been questioned about such problems as excessive governmental intervention, lack of sound regulation and supervision of financial sectors, as well as unethical and illegal government–business connections. On the other hand, suggestions to resolve financial crisis also call for governmental action in strengthening central banks; establishing a prudent banking regulation system; and reforming administrative, political, and legal systems.

In sum, government continues to play an important role in the process of economic development. The challenges for policy makers are not only to understand different arguments of governance but also to design their own development model, which considers the balance of public and private sectors and the trade-off between market and government failure. In other words, they have to promote some specific development policies to coordinate resources in public and private sectors in order to deal with market failure problems and to compete in the global economic system. The development model or policies must consider the unique strengths and weaknesses of their own economic systems and overcome many problems and weaknesses of the system.

The Importance of Regional or Local Governments

The impact of decentralization policy and other changes in governance policy has resulted in the increasing role of regional (or state) and local governments in promoting economic development programs and activities. In the United States, state and local governments have expanded their efforts in economic development policies and programs to deal with fiscal problems and new challenges.[50–55] On the one hand, local governments have experienced continuing fiscal difficulties and challenges, such as the increasing difficulties in raising adequate revenues (because of the impact of tax revolts) and the increasing demand for public services (because of the cutback of federal social programs). On the other hand, local officials have become actively involved in economic development promotion activities, because they recognized many business development opportunities resulting from changes in the advancement of communication technology and the globalization of the world economy. The formal change refers to the development of telecommunication systems and web-based Internet services, which significantly reduce the barriers of time and distance among business communities. The latter change has to do with the end of the Cold War and the development of many postsocialist countries, which provides additional businesses and markets for local economy growth.

Researchers of regional economic development have supported the involvement of state and local governments in promoting business development. For example, Bartik used the market failure approach to explain the importance of a regional economic development policy.[56] This approach has strengths, such as allowing a wise use of government resources, because it focuses on what private markets are unable to do, and leading to goals that are measurable in the common currency of dollar benefits. The limitations of the market failure approach consist of the lack of precise information about the magnitude of some nonmarket benefits, no consideration of distributional effects of regional economic development policies, and overlooking the benefits and costs of one region's policies in relation to other regions. In the absences of federal government involvement, however, Bartik believed that encouraging regional governments to pursue regional efficient policies is likely, on average, to increase the efficiency of the national economy.[56]

The economic development strategies emphasized by state and local governments vary depend on the environment of their communities and the different goals of their economic development plan. In general, four types of development strategies have been adopted: 1) subsidizing traditional inputs such as capital (e.g., direct loans and loan guarantees, tax-example bond financing, development corporations), land (e.g., land banking, site development provision), and labor (e.g., low cost/mass production, and high quality/lean production); 2) lowering political costs of doing business, including tax abatements and incentives and limitations on the regulatory environment; 3) promoting entrepreneurial activities of market development (e.g., export promotion, research, and dissemination) and business services (e.g., policy planning, research and development support and consortia); and 4) developing attractive social amenities (e.g., arts, environment) and improving distressed areas (e.g., enterprise zones).[57] All of these strategies are directly or indirectly based on or related to policy or managerial issues of governance.

The Contribution of Nongovernmental or Nonprofit Organizations

Many market-oriented policy changes, such as deregulation and privatization, have resulted in the rise and contribution of nongovernmental or nonprofit organizations in the delivery of public goods and services.[58–62] In many developing countries, policy makers emphasize the development of these organizations as service providers because of their proximity to the persons served (establishing a long-term relationship with the communities); their cost-effectiveness (using volunteers and relying on donations); and their flexibility, innovativeness, dedication, and responsiveness.[58–62]

With regard to economic development, researchers have recognized the important contribution of these organizations to economic growth and social development. For example, in the United States, Rubin emphasized the importance of community-based development organizations (CBDOs) to promote economic development.[63] As neighborhood-based nonprofit organizations, CBDOs help many distressed communities to receive financial support, build affordable housing, provide job-related training activities, and create many employment opportunities. Similarly, Bhatt and Tang[64] examined the development of group-based microfinance to promote economic development in many developing countries. Recognizing many problems associated with developmental finance in developing countries, they pointed out the contributions of group-based lending programs to help the poor generate income and employment opportunities as well as to encourage grassroots participation and empowerment in disadvantaged communities.

Despite their popularity, many nongovernmental or nonprofit organizations experience problems such as lacking managerial skills, facing uncertain financing and erratic regulation, encountering fragmentation and no coordination, and falling short on standards of transparency and accountability. To overcome these problems, researchers emphasized the importance of forming partnerships between public development agencies, nongovernmental organizations, and private voluntary organizations on the one hand, and investing in capacity and institution building on the other hand to improve the effectiveness of their organization management.[63]

CONCLUSION

Government continues to plan an important role in the process of economic development. This article has reviewed major literature related to governance and economic development and examined major policy changes in deregulation, privatization, and decentralization. The scope of recent policy changes emphasizes not only structural or process changes within the governance system but also the interaction between government and market. The market-oriented reform policies have significant impact on future economic development programs. The importance of local governments and the contribution of nonprofit or nongovernmental organizations to economic development will certainly change the traditional arguments related to the issue of governance and economic development. Future research on new changes of these organizations will contribute to the overall literature of economic development.

REFERENCES

1. *Adam Smith: An Inquiry into the Nature and Causes of the Wealth of the Nations*; Cannan, E., Ed.; University of Chicago Press: Chicago, 1976.
2. Musgrave, R.A.; Musgrave, P.B. *Public Finance in Theory and Practice,* 3rd Ed.; McGraw Hill: New York, 1980.
3. Stern, N. Public policy and the economics of development. Eur. Econ. Rev. **1991**, *35* (2/3), 241–254.
4. Bodenheimer, S. Dependency and imperialism. Polit. Soc. **1971**, *1*, 327–357.
5. Dos Santos, T. The structure of dependence. Am. Econ. Rev. **1970**, *60*, 213–236.
6. *Foreign Trade and Investment: Development in the Newly Industrializing Asian Economies*; Galenson, W., Ed.; University of Wisconsin Press: Madison, WI, 1985.
7. Haggard, S. *Pathways from the Periphery: The Politics of Growth in the Newly Industrializing Countries*; Cornell University Press: Ithaca, NY, 1990.
8. Wade, R. East Asia's economic success: Conflicting perspectives, partial insights, shaky evidence. World Polit. **1992**, *44*, 270–320.
9. *Governing the Market: Economic Theory and the Role of Government in East Asian Industrialization*; Princeton University Press: Princeton, NJ, 1990.
10. Johnson, C. *MITI and the Japanese Miracle*; Stanford University Press: Stanford, NJ, 1982.
11. Ho, S. South Korea and Taiwan: Development prospects and problems in the 1980s. Asian Surv. **1981**, *21*, 1175–1196.
12. Lin, C.Y. *Latin America vs. East Asia: A Comparative Development Perspective*; M.E. Sharpe: New York, 1989.
13. World Bank. *The East Asian Miracle: Economic Growth and Public Policy*; Oxford University Press: New York, 1993.
14. *The Role of Government in East Asian Economic Development: Comparative Institutional Analysis*; Aoki, M., Kim, H.-K., Okuno-Fujiwara, M., Eds.; Clarendon Press: New York, 1997.
15. Haggard, S.; Webb, S.B. What do we know about the political economy of economic reform? World Bank Res. Obs. **1993**, *8*, 143–168.
16. Rondinelli, D.A.; Montgomery, J.D. Managing economic reform: An alternative perspective on structural adjustment policies. Policy Sci. **1990**, *23*, 73–93.
17. Fisher, S.; Gelb, A. The process of socialist economic transformation. J. Econ. Perspect. **1991**, *5*, 91–105.
18. Fisher, S.; Sahay, R.; Vegh, C.A. Stabilization and growth in transition economies: The early experience. J. Econ. Perspect. **1996**, *10*, 45–66.
19. Liou, K.T. Strategies and lessons of China's post-mao economic development. Policy Stud. Rev. **1999**, *16*, 183–208, (Spring).
20. Liou, K.T. *Managing Economic Reforms in Post-Mao China*; Praeger: Westport, CT, 1998.
21. Liou, K.T. The role of government in economic development: The Chinese experience. Int. J. Public Adm. **1998**, *21*, 1257–1983.
22. Summers, L.H.; Thomas, V. Recent lessons of development. World Bank Res. Obs. **1993**, *8*, 241–254.
23. Tanzi, V. Fiscal Policy for Growth and Stability in Developing Countries: Selected Issues. In *Government Financial Management: Issues and Country Studies*; Premchand, A., Ed.; International Monetary Fund: Washington, DC, 1990; 15–27.
24. Meier, K.J. *Regulation: Politics, Bureaucracy, and Economics*; St. Martin's Press: New York, 1985; 1.
25. Buchholz, R.A. *Business Environment and Public Policy: Implications for Management and Strategy,* 4th Ed.; Prentice Hall: Englewood Cliffs, NJ, 1992.
26. OECD. In *Regulatory Reform: Overview of OECD's Work*; 1998; Paris. http://www.oecd.org/subject/regreform.
27. de Ru, H.J.; Wettenhall, R. Progress, benefits and costs of privatization: An introduction. Int. Rev. Adm. Sci. **1990**, *56*, 7–14.

28. Drucker, P.F. *The Age of Discontinuity*; Harper and Row: New York, 1969.

29. Savas, E.S. *Privatization in the Public Sector*; Chatham House: Chatham, NJ, 1982.

30. Donahue, J.D. *The Privatization Decision: Public Ends, Private Means*; Basic Books: New York, 1989.

31. Bozeman, B. *All Governments Are Public: Bridging Public and Private Organizational Theories*; Jossey-Bass: San Francisco, CA, 1987.

32. Moe, R.D. Exploring the limits of privatization. Public Adm. Rev. **1987**, *47*, 453–460.

33. Sullivan, H.J. Privatization of public services: A growing threat to constitutional rights. Public Adm. Rev. **1987**, *47*, 461–467.

34. *Privatization in Less Developed Countries*; Cook, P., Kirpatrick, C., Eds.; St. Martin's Press: New York, 1988.

35. Cowan, G.L. *Privatization in the Developing World*; Greenwood Press: New York, 1990.

36. Dinavo, J.V. *Privatization in Developing Countries: The Impact on Economic Development and Democracy*; Praeger Press: Westport, CT, 1995.

37. *Alternatives for Delivering Public Services: Toward Improved Performance*; Savas, E.S., Ed.; Westview Press: Boulder, CO, 1977.

38. *Decentralization and Development: Policy Implementation in Developing Countries*; Chemma, G.S., Rondinelli, D.A., Eds.; Sage Publications: Beverly Hills, CA, 1983.

39. Rondinelli, D.A.; McCullough, J.S.; Johnson, R.W. Analyzing decentralization policies in developing countries: A political-economy framework. Dev. Change **1989**, *21*, 513–530.

40. Samoff, J. Decentralization: The politics of interventionism. Dev. Change **1990**, *21*, 513–530.

41. Please, S. The World Bank: Lending for Structural Adjustment. In *Adjustment Crisis in the Third World*; Fineberf, R.E., Kallab, V., Eds.; Transaction Books: New Brunswick, NJ, 1984; 83–98.

42. Nellis, J.; Kikerri, S. Public enterprise reform: Privatization and the world bank. World Dev. **1989**, *17*, 659–672.

43. Rondinelli, D.A.; Nellis, J.R. Assessing decentralization policies in developing countries: A case for cautious optimism. Dev. Policy Rev. **1986**, *4*, 3–23.

44. Prudhomme, R. The dangers of decentralization. World Bank Res. Obs. **1995**, *10* (2), 201–220.

45. Dolven, B. Hang looser. Far East. Econ. Rev. **1998**, *161* (14), 12–14.

46. Granitsas, A. Going for gold. Far East. Econ. Rev. **1998**, *161* (14), 10–12.

47. Goldstein, M. *The Asian Financial Crisis: Causes, Cures, and Systemic Implications*; Institute for International Economics: Washington, DC, 1998.

48. International Monetary Fund. The Asian crisis: Causes and cures. Finance Dev. **1998**, *35* (2), 18–21.

49. Sender, H.; Lumpur, K.; Lee, C. Rotten to the core. Far East. Econ. Rev. **1998**, *161* (14), 14–16.

50. Blakely, E.J. *Planning Local Economic Development: Theories and Practice,* 2nd Ed.; Sage Publications: Thousand Oaks, CA, 1994.

51. Eisinger, P.K. *The Rise of the Entrepreneurial State: State and Local Economic Development Policy in the United States*; University of Wisconsin Press: Madison, WI, 1988.

52. Levy, J.M. *Economic Development Programs for Cities, Counties and Towns,* 2nd Ed.; Praeger: New York, 1990.

53. Luke, J.S.; Ventriss, C.; Reed, B.J.; Reed, C.M. *Managing Economic Development: A Guide to State and Local Leadership Strategies*; Jossey-Bass: San Francisco, CA, 1988.

54. *Economic Development Strategies for State and Local Governments*; McGowan, R.P., Ottensmeyer, E.J., Eds.; Nelson-Hall: Chicago, 1993.

55. Reese, L.A. The role of counties in local economic development. Econ. Dev. Q. **1994**, *8*, 28–42.

56. Bartik, T.J. The market failure approach to regional economic development. Econ. Dev. Q. **1990**, *4*, 361–370, (November).

57. Clark, C.; Montjoy, R. Globalization and the Revitalizaiton of U.S. Economic Competitiveness: Implications for Economic Development Policy. In *Handbook of Economic Development*; Liou, K.T., Ed.; Marcel Dekker: New York, 1998; 169–170.

58. Carroll, T.F. *NGOs: The Supporting Link in Grassroots Development*; Kumarian Press: West Hartford, CT, 1992.

59. Clark, J. *Democratizing Development: The Role of Voluntary Organizations*; Kummarian Press: West Hartford, CT, 1991.

60. Fisher, J. *Nongovernments, NGOs and the Political Development of the Third World*; Kumarian Press: West Hartford, CT, 1998.

61. *Bureaucracy and the Alternatives in World Perspective*; Henderson, K., Dwivedi, O.P., Eds.; Macmillan: London, 1999.

62. *NGOs, New Paths to Democratic Development in Latin America*; Reilly, C., Ed.; Lynne Rienner: Boulder, CO, 1995.

63. Rubin, H.J. Economic partnering with the poor: Why local governments should work with community-based development organizations to promote economic development. Int. J. Public Adm. **2000**, *29*, 1679–1709.

64. Bhatt, N.; Tang, S.Y. Group-Based Micro Finance and Economic Development. In *Handbook of Economic Development*; Liou, K.T., Ed.; Marcel Dekker: NY, 1998; 115–138.

Economic Development, Immigration, Self-Employment and

Marcela Tribble
Terry F. Buss
Florida International University, Miami, Florida, U.S.A.

INTRODUCTION

Immigration for decades has interested economists, sociologists, and historians, at least in part because America is a nation of immigrants. Only recently has immigration attracted much attention from economic development researchers, policy makers, and practitioners. Even though immigration is a huge economic policy issue in America, little solid empirical evidence exists to inform debate, and the information that does exist tends to be contradictory. Yet there is enough information available to cobble together insights around the following questions:

- Immigrants arrive in the United States from around the world: which groups are likely to become entrepreneurial and why?
- Immigrants affect local economies in various ways—good and bad: what are these effects, and why do they occur?
- What are the policy implications facing local economic development decision makers?

We focus mostly on self-employment among immigrant groups because this is central to economic development. We do not address the importance of immigrants to the labor force—immigrants are critical in filling jobs in lesser skilled and, in some cases, higher skilled occupations—because this is another policy domain, better addressed elsewhere. Before discussing these questions, we provide an overview of trends in immigration.

IMMIGRATION TO AMERICA

Commentators have christened the decade of the 1990s as the *Second Great Migration*, the first occurring at the turn of the twentieth century.[1] In the past decade, about 9 million legal immigrants arrived, a number unprecedented since the early 1900s when 8.8 million migrants came to America. In fiscal year 2000 alone, the Immigration and Naturalization Service (INS) legally admitted 849,807

immigrants into the United States. The number of foreign born, according to the 2000 Census, is now 31,107,889, or 11.1% of the population. If children of immigrants born in the United States are included, the immigrant population becomes 20.4%. Immigrants account for 37% of U.S. population growth, 50% if calculations include their American-born children.

States receiving most immigrants in 2000 were California (217,753), New York (106,061), Florida (98,391), Texas (63,840), New Jersey (40,013), Illinois (36,180), and Massachusetts (23,483). Immigrant groups tend to migrate to places having large populations from similar cultures. Chinese cluster in California and New York; Cubans and Haitians in Miami; Indians, Filipinos, and Salvadorians in California; and Mexicans in California, Texas, Arizona, and Florida. U.S. Census data show that 95% of immigrants live in urban areas, and that 65% live in just 10 cities, probably because immigrants receive a better reception in cities, can access more services, and have better opportunities.

Immigrants come from all over the world, but some countries contribute a much greater share. In 2000, Mexico (173,919), China (45,652), Philippines (42,474), India (42,046), Vietnam (26,747), Nicaragua (24,029), El Salvador (22,578), and Cuba (20,831) were major contributors. This represents a substantial shift away from European and Canadian origins, where economies are in good shape, toward Latin American and Asian countries, where prosperity is limited.

Of those admitted to the United States in 2000, few (189,357) reported having an occupation. But 94% of working-age immigrants were in the labor force, as compared with 91% of natives. Some 28%, or 237,841 immigrants, were 19 years of age or younger, making them on average much younger than the native population. One-half (54.4%) of all immigrants were married. About one-third arrived with less than a high school education, but 29% had a college degree. Those with no occupation, no family, and little education will have difficulty becoming self-employed.

Anywhere from 7.1 to 8.5 million immigrants are illegal aliens. Two-fifths entered the United States le-

Encyclopedia of Public Administration and Public Policy
DOI: 10.1081/E-EPAP 120010204

gally, lost their legal status, and remained here as illegals. About one-half of illegals are Mexicans. Illegal aliens will find it much more difficult to find work, let alone successful self-employment.

WHO BECOMES SELF-EMPLOYED?

Self-Employment Theory

From an economic development perspective, one would want to know why some groups become productive members of communities through self-employment, whereas others arriving in the United States do not. There are three widely invoked models to explain immigrant new business formation—*middlemen minority*,[2] *ethnic enclave*,[3] and *reactive cultural*[4] theory—all of which focus on *supply-side*, meaning those who produce goods and services, and comparisons of intergroup differences.[4]

Middlemen minority theory holds that some immigrants enter majority society only for commercial reasons where they serve as middlemen between well-off producers with goods to sell and poorer consumers desiring to buy them. They remain isolated or detached from majority society because they eventually intend to return home. Korean grocers in Los Angeles, for example, are middlemen between white producers and distributors of produce and poor African Americans in distressed neighborhoods. Ethnic enclave theory asserts that successful immigrant entrepreneurs tend to locate in clearly bounded geographic areas where their culture, language, networks, access to labor and capital, and vertically and horizontally integrated markets give them a comparative economic advantage over those in the larger economy. Cubans, once densely concentrated in Miami's "Little Havana," served as a model of this characterization. Reactive cultural theory (and its predecessor, cultural theory) emphasizes trust, solidarity, and mutuality among immigrant groups who pool capital for investment in small businesses, and coordinate social and economic activities. Japanese immigrants to America in the years prior to World War II used ethnic solidarity and ethnic resources to establish and manage small businesses.[5]

Although these theories persist in professional and popular literature, they have been roundly criticized, and even debunked (e.g., Refs. [5]). Middlemen theory overlooks the fact that many immigrants do not intend to return home. Ethnic enclaves cannot explain how immigrants initially started businesses, seemingly only explaining what happened much later in the business formation process when resources had already become available. In addition, researchers have found few, if any,

ethnic enclaves, because economies are much more diverse, less spatially isolated, and less integrated than this narrow model suggests. Cultural theory overemphasizes cultural solidarity, failing to take into account class differences among immigrants. Upper-class immigrants have access to scarce resources, especially capital, not available to everyone in that culture. Cuban refugees fleeing Castro's regime in 1959–1960 were well off, whereas Mariel Boatlift refugees, composed of many criminals and institutionalized populations, of the 1980s were much less prosperous. The former groups took over Miami's economy; the latter were left out.

The most convincing explanation for successful entrepreneurship is that immigrants to the United States, or anywhere else for that matter, must possess the capacity either to create wealth themselves (or to obtain work that allows them to be independent or to eventually become so), and they must locate at or migrate to a place that provides economic opportunities. Successful immigrants are those whose capacity matches opportunity—*interactionism* theory.[4,6] Taiwanese, having math, computer, and engineering skills, came to America to participate in the "dot.com" revolution.

Other theories try to explain why immigrants become self-employed. The two leading contenders have yet to gather convincing empirical support, although both persist in the literature.[7] One is the *blocked mobility* theory—that immigrants facing discrimination or barriers in labor markets are forced into self-employment as the only alternative to unemployment or welfare. Discrimination takes many forms—racial, linguistic, cultural, and religious. But this cannot explain why larger numbers (9 in 10) succeed as workers, and why some immigrants facing barriers never break out. The other is the *predisposition* theory—that some groups are predisposed to self-employment because they were highly entrepreneurial in their home countries and desire to continue the tradition. But this theory cannot account for such phenomenon as the success of recent Eastern European and Russian immigrants who had no business start-up experience.

Ethnic Businesses

A study by Razin and Light[4] shed light on ethnic self-employment in 16 of the largest metropolitan areas. The rate of self-employment was highest in Sunbelt and western metropolitan regions characterized by economic and cultural diversity: Miami, Los Angeles, San Francisco, San Diego, and Seattle. Lowest rates were in declining manufacturing regions: Detroit, Cleveland, Chicago, and Philadelphia, and in the nation's capital, Washington, DC. Immigrant self-employed, as a percentage of the immigrant population, are prevalent in central cities, 10.3%; suburbs, 12.5%; and nonmetro areas, 7.9%.

The higher the rate of self-employment among immigrants, the higher the rate of self-employment overall in the labor force; that is, entrepreneurial places breed entrepreneurial behavior across a wide spectrum. Similarly, the higher the level of immigrant self-employment, the higher the level of income within immigrant groups.

Greeks and Koreans were consistently self-employed in cities across the country. Other "conspicuously" self-employed groups include Middle Eastern and North Africans, among them Iranians and Israelis. Dutch, Hungarian, Czech, and Polish self-employed are dispersed nationwide. Some immigrant groups dominate selected cities. Cubans monopolize Miami, probably more than any other immigrant group controls an American city.

The least entrepreneurial seem to be people from the Caribbean and Philippines. Mexican and Puerto Rican immigrants have lower levels of self-employment, but some argue that they are undercounted because they work in the underground economy as street vendors, handy men, gardeners, babysitters, and the like.[8] But many analysts would reject these activities as they do not really represent self-employment, but causal, part-time labor.

Capacity for Self-Employment

Factors affecting self-employment capacity are generally well-known and apply to immigrant populations. Immigrants having business experience, appropriate skills or education, access to networks (e.g., professional, family, or groups) able to provide support, values or cultural attributes contributing to wealth creation, and access to capital tend to have a greater propensity for successful self-employment.

English

The ability to speak English and its relationship to self-employment has not been studied. Findings for the labor force may generalize to the self-employed, but they are mixed; some finding English language to be a major factor, others not so. Generally, those who speak English improve their earnings over non-English speakers, while those in jobs not requiring English or those living in areas not dominated by English speakers are somewhat less affected.[9] It is likely that speaking a language that fits requirements of the market is an important factor and that being bilingual cannot hurt business prospects. Generally, as time passes, immigrants master some English and their children tend to have much less difficulty. There is, of course, a continuing debate in this country about how and when to immerse immigrant children in an English-only curriculum.

Education

Education is the foundation for success in most societies.[9] Those with an American education or its equivalent tend to do better than those not so fortunate, at least in the American market. For example, it is no accident that a high proportion of Indians immigrating to the United States are physicians or have PhDs; their skills are in demand.

Family ties

For immigrants, family is a major factor in the success of small- or microbusiness development. Family-owned businesses with no paid employees account for more than three-fourths of all immigrant enterprises.[10]

The family can be viewed as a network of obligations that embodies the social, economic and cultural investments made prior to immigration, and that immigrants draw on and continue to invest in during the process of adaptation. The family endows each of its members with the backing of collectively-owned capital, a credential that entitles members to credit.... Thus, the family comprises a social network that can be effectively harnessed to achieve collective goals.

It is also the case that married people are much more likely to operate businesses than single people. But as immigrant businesses continue to develop or advance, family resources (e.g., financial, information, and counsel) tend to decline precipitously over time.[5]

Social capital

After the family, ties with the broader ethnic community become important. These networks, referred to as *social capital*, are sources of business information, including markets, supplies, and opportunity. These networks, often discussed in the context of enclaves, are powerful resources. Networks, for example, so dominate business relationships that they even affect *intracommunal transfers* of businesses. One study in Los Angeles found that Koreans tended to sell their businesses to Koreans, and Hispanics to Hispanics, even though other native buyers were available.

Start-up capital

Obtaining start-up capital is an issue for most businesses.[11] Immigrants largely obtain start-up or expansion capital from friends, relatives, or acquaintances. Capital obtained is generally in small amounts. Once businesses begin to grow, immigrants seek funding from formal sources (e.g., banks, investors), often their countrymen. Capital may originate overseas or locally. In a study of Taiwanese entrepreneurs, 57% reported obtaining start-up capital from their homelands.[12] In a study of Korean entrepreneurs, researchers found that Korean suppliers extended credit terms, lower prices, and easy access to information.[5] Successive waves of Cubans fleeing Castro's government were offered *character loans*—no collateral required—by wealthy Cuban immigrant bankers who were willing to invest in refugees.[13] Indian entrepreneurs in high-tech centers (e.g., Silicon Valley in California, Route 128 in Boston) are highly organized into self-employed networks that can raise millions for new business startups.[11]

Market Opportunity

To be successful, ethnic entrepreneurs must be able to take advantage of market opportunities—*demand-side* factors. This translates into concentrated economic activity, economic linkages, and globalization.

Economic sector

Ethnic self-employed, regardless of where they originate from, are likely to start restaurants or drinking places. These places serve fellow immigrants and natives with a penchant for ''foreign'' cuisine. Also, construction companies are popular in most areas. Many worked construction in their home country or acquired skills as laborers, often unskilled, in this country. Many are non-union shops, making them less costly and more competitive. But some immigrant groups specialize, often quite successfully. Taiwanese and Indians dominate, given their relatively small numbers, the high-tech, info-tech, hardware and software, and communications industries, nationally and internationally (see sections below). These cultures produce people with math, computer, and engineering skills. They come to the United States, receive even more specialized education, then start up or work for high-tech firms.

Linkages

Just as some immigrants exploit networks to enhance their capacity domestically, *transnational networks* or *communities*—cross-border business relationships—have opened up markets considerably over the past few decades.[14] Saxenian studied immigrant entrepreneurs in California's high-tech region, Silicon Valley. She found that one-half of Chinese and Indian immigrants set up subsidiaries, joint ventures, subcontracts, and/or other business operations in their home country. Half of those starting new businesses did so with two or more co-

founders from their home countries. So prevalent are Chinese entrepreneurs in Monterey Park, California, who travel incessantly on business that they have been dubbed ''astronauts.'' Similarly, Chinese immigrants in Queens are widely known to have raised capital for businesses from contacts in Hong Kong and Taiwan.

Globalization

Globalization's effects on local economic development and immigration are only just now beginning to be understood.[15] One factor facilitating international migration is the *liberalization*—removing barriers—of trade. Labor is free to move in search of job opportunities as economies open up. In advanced economies, governments have an interest in opening up their markets to imports from less advanced economies. This allows poorer countries to create wealth through exports that in turn allows them to accept imports *and* keeps workers at home, gainfully employed. The North American Free Trade Agreement (NAFTA) of 1993 between Mexico, Canada, and the United States was an attempt to remove most trade barriers and in the process stem the tide of immigration.

WHAT ARE THE IMPACTS?

Local policy makers want to know how immigrant economic activity affects economic development and how social factors affect economies. In spite of the increasing prevalence of immigrant populations in America, both positive and negative consequences of immigrant economic activity are little supported by solid research, greatly misunderstood or misrepresented, and highly controversial.

Economic Development Impacts

Immigrant entrepreneurs create jobs, build wealth (both private and public), pay taxes, build communities and local economies, and help needy relatives back home. But some also displace native-born Americans; exploit workers from their own culture; participate in the hidden, illegal, or underground economy; and engage in criminal behavior and corruption, in the process retarding community building. It is important not to stereotype people. No group is entirely positive or negative, and we suspect that most people contribute positively whether they are immigrants or natives. It is also important not to exaggerate contributions, either positive or negative.

Growth

At the macro level, recent immigrants increased the value of U.S. gross domestic product (GDP) from $6 billion to $20 billion, depending on the study.

Even though relatively modest as a proportion of a multitrillion dollar economy, the amount that immigrants have contributed to economic growth is a matter of controversy in the literature, in part having to do with who should be considered an immigrant? Many studies consider foreign-born people living in the United States to be immigrants, but their American-born children to be natives. Other studies include, or at least do not explicitly exclude, second and even third generations of immigrant parents in the growth calculation, arguing that subsequent generations would not have been entrepreneurial but for their parents.

In 1997, using narrow definitions, self-employment was equally prevalent among natives, 11.8%, and recent immigrants, 11.3%. Immigrants are neither more nor less likely to be self-employed than natives. Using somewhat broader definitions, according to the U.S. Small Business Administration (SBA), between 1988 and 1998 numbers of self-employed Asians rose by 56.5%, Hispanics by 30.1%, and Whites by 1.1%. Whites account for 90.4% of self-employed people. The growth in self-employment of 3.9% nationwide, then, is based on immigrant, as broadly defined, small-business activity.

Data, over time and across generations, show that immigrants contribute significantly to the economy. The SBA estimates that in 1997, Asian self-employed people generated $275 billion in revenues and employed 1,917,244 workers, whereas Hispanics produced $184 billion and employed 1,492,773 workers. Like most small businesses, the lion's share, 87%, of immigrant businesses employ 10 workers or less. Some immigrant groups contribute economically despite their small numbers. In a study of Silicon Valley high-tech firms, Saxenian[14] found that 24% had either Chinese or Indian executives. About 2000 firms were managed by Chinese entrepreneurs and another 774 firms by Indians. These companies had $16.8 billion in sales and employed 58,000 workers. Companies averaged between $200,000 and $300,000 in sales per employee.

In spite of their contributions to economies, immigrant economic activity has been criticized by some observers.

Remittances

Remittances are transfer payments made by immigrants living in the United States to relatives living in their country of origin. Some critics worry over money being sent overseas. A report on President Bush's visit to Miami in May 2002 by National Public Radio estimated that Cuban exiles in South Florida send about $500 million to Cuba annually. Castro's government receives more money from remittances than from exports of sugar and nickel, and net payments for tourism. The Inter-American Development Bank estimates that immigrants will send about $300 billion home over the next 10 years. The World Bank estimates that Latin America and the Caribbean receive about $15 billion in remittances annually.

According to the World Bank, immigrants earning less than $20,000 annually send as much as $3000 home each year. Remittances slow economic progress for those compelled to send money home. But the longer immigrants remain in the United States, the less likely they are to continue sending money home.

Some consider the decline in U.S. foreign aid to developing countries in recent years to be more than compensated for by remittance transfer payments. Ironically, according to studies by the World Bank, remittances do not reach very poor people; those better off tend to receive transfer payments. As a consequence, remittances and foreign aid may not be a comparable trade-off.

Self-employment activity in transnational communities yields important economic development benefits for developing countries that may in turn benefit America. Residents of Ticuani, Mexico, for example, needed a new town water system, a facility their local government could not provide.[16] Residents petitioned relatives in Brooklyn who in turn formed a committee, referred to as a *home town association*, to raise funding, referred to as a *community remittance*, for the water plant. Provision of the new water plant only occurred because of the continued linkage between Mexican-American entrepreneurs and villagers. Potential positive benefits of transfer payments are that future business development ties may be forged, but such linkages have not been studied.

NAFTA

Critics of NAFTA argue that immigration has not abated and that jobs have been lost in America. Although accurate figures are unavailable, as many as 1 million U.S. jobs, actual and potential, may have been eliminated to NAFTA since the 1990s.[15] Job loss went relatively unnoticed because of the unprecedented growth in the American economy over the decade. Nonetheless, some communities and states felt NAFTA job loss much more than other.

Intergroup competition

Self-employment activity by immigrants might take away opportunities for natives, African Americans being most at risk because they may compete directly with immigrants in some communities. Immigrants working together to erect barriers prevent natives from firmly competing. Fairley and Meyer,[17] in a study of 132 largest metro areas, found that immigrant self-employed appear to displace natives, keeping them from starting new businesses. They found that immigrant self-employed did not displace African Americans overall. But a study by the National Academy of Sciences found some displacement for African Americans living in areas with high concentrations of immigrants. Presence of immigrant self-employed did not affect earnings of natives.

Immigrants might displace or impede self-employment for other immigrants. Having a common language, for example, does not guarantee that economic benefits will accrue. In Miami, although Spanish-speaking Cubans dominate, Spanish-speaking Mexicans and other Latinos have been excluded from the larger Cuban economy for cultural reasons.[18]

Low wages

Since the 1990s, immigrant earnings have steadily declined relative to natives, with natives earning one-third more than immigrants. This is largely because recently arrived immigrants are unskilled and poorly educated compared with their predecessors. Being unskilled, they are forced to work for less. This depresses the wages of native unskilled labor that must compete with immigrants willing to work for less, but drives up wages for skilled workers who become scarcer. It takes about 16 to 20 years for an immigrant to reach wage parity with a native, after controlling on education and English fluency.[1]

Studies are mixed as to whether immigrant self-employed exploit fellow immigrants by paying them low wages. Some argue that immigrants take advantage of recent arrivals because they lack education, language skills, experience, and capital to either make it on their own or to work for higher wages. Where immigrant populations are concentrated, workers become vulnerable to exploitation. Others argue that immigrant workers eventually do as well as natives, and in many cases better (e.g., Taiwanese). In the worse case, highly concentrated areas act as incubators, helping to launch people into better jobs as they acquire skills, and in many cases into self-employment as they accumulate experience and capital. Likely there is some truth in both observations. But it is certain that migrant farm workers, illegal aliens, and unpaid family members may not always prosper in America.

Hidden economy

Many people believe that some immigrant groups are prone to illegal activity, either because they come from a culture that condones such behavior or because they adopt this activity out of necessity. Immigrants, especially illegals, from poor countries may be forced into the *hidden* or *underground* economy just to get a start in America. Miami is awash with "handymen" from Latin America who operate home repair businesses, some quite large, all outside the view of the tax collector and business regulators. Many of these businesses produce

low-quality work. When the supply of cheap labor dried up after the Mariel Boatlift, Cuban entrepreneurs in the garment industry "contracted" with Cuban immigrants to do "homework" for low wages, no benefits, and employment instability.[13]

The hidden economy is large, but there are no good, reliable estimates. And, it is not possible to parcel out underground activity among natives, foreigners and immigrants. One study of the informal economy in Hialeah, Florida, a city with a high concentration of Cuban immigrants, estimated that there was a $300 million off-the-books economy in operation.[13]

Criminal activity

Immigrant populations are "popularly" associated with crime and corruption.[13] *Proposition 187* in California, for example, asserts that the people of California have suffered personal injury and damage caused by the criminal conduct of illegal aliens in the state. In 1999, cities spent about $1.5 billion incarcerating illegal aliens for criminal activity. In Miami, many immigrant businesses are deeply tied to the illegal drug trade, either as fronts for money laundering or as investments by "drug lords" in legitimate businesses. Many consider Miami the drug capital of the world, taking in $50 billion annually. Eventually, illegal drug money ends up in off-shore banks where it cannot be accounted for. In 1979, the Federal Reserve Bank in South Florida had a cash surplus of $3.2 billion, an amount representing 77% of cash surplus nationally. Immigrants from former Soviet block countries have fallen easily into criminal activity. The Russian mafia is now prominent in the United States and indeed worldwide, where they exploit networks once dominated or created by the KGB.

Even though crime among immigrants may be perceived as prevalent, research shows that recent inflows of immigrants have had no effect on crime rates in cities where they are heavily concentrated.[19] Youth born abroad were significantly less likely to be involved in crime than native youth.

Social Impacts

Immigrant economic activity also creates positive and negative social impacts in communities that in turn affect economics.

Ethnic contributions

No one would disagree with the proposition that immigrants have enriched American culture. Indeed, if there is an American culture, then it is an amalgamation of the contributions of disparate ethnic groups. This is a positive legacy, but there are possible negative consequences.

Ethnic conflict

Immigrant populations either dispersed across the country and assimilated, isolated themselves in enclave neighborhoods or communities, or took over communities once dominated by native-born Americans. Cubans in Miami and Taiwanese in Los Angeles are illustrative of the latter. Cuban refugees descended on Miami in 1959, after Castro took over Cuba in a Communist coup. This takeover was followed by the 1980s Mariel Boatlift. Now, in 2002, Cubans make up 30% of the population. Many Cubans chose not to assimilate, maintaining Spanish as the language of business and private life, preserving Cuban culture including preservation of the Santeria religion, and remaining isolated in large enclaves.[13] Taiwanese took over large portions of Los Angeles not by gradually moving from the central cities to better neighborhoods, then to the suburbs, but by leap frogging to the suburbs directly.[12] Their wealth allowed them to bypass the usual migration patterns prevalent among other immigrant groups.

When immigrant populations take over communities, they tend to preserve their own culture sometimes at the expense of those already there. In Miami, Cuban cultural change fostered an *English First* movement whose goal was to quell the rise in Spanish speaking. When that and other counterattacks on Cuban culture failed, Anglos began moving north in large numbers. This in turn caused many Cubans to further eschew assimilation.

Taiwanese immigrants formed "Little Taipei" in Monterey Park, California. Because of their wealth, home and commercial property prices began to skyrocket. Taiwanese were criticized for speculating in land—"The Taiwan Syndrome"—they intend to sell later. This practice has so driven up land prices that high-tech workers cannot afford to live there, creating a labor shortage. Anglos also blame Taiwanese for unplanned development, traffic congestion, and loss of community. Anglo businesses have gradually fled, as have many of its original residents.

It should be noted that the history of the United States is one in which one immigrant group successfully displaces another, either from abroad or internally. In Miami, Jews were replaced by Cubans who are now being replaced by Central Americans. Who knows what group will emerge next?

Ghettos

More often then not, poor immigrants, especially illegals, are forced either into distressed neighborhoods where housing is inexpensive or into more prosperous neighborhoods where multiple families share single-family dwellings. "Little Haiti" in Miami is a poor neighborhood dominated by Haitians and Dominicans. By contrast, the City of Miami Beach, the playground of the idle rich, also houses poor families in single rooms who survive by pooling resources. When the City of Miami faced a fiscal crisis in 1996, officials set out to identify illegal residences and collect taxes.[13] About 4500 illegal residences were found and $2.1 million in property taxes collected. High concentrations of poor people make neighborhoods depressed until they acquire resources either to move on to better accommodations or to revitalize it themselves, a rarer occurrence. But poor neighborhoods are the price societies pay to have inexpensive labor who produce low-cost goods and services.

Costs and Benefits

The problem with cost–benefit studies of immigration is that they are "questimates" with dubious assumptions and scant data yielding conflicting conclusions. Both pro- and anti-immigration advocates cite the same "definitive" National Academy of Sciences (NAS) report as evidence in favor of their conclusions, for example. Overall, NAS estimated that immigrant contributed between $1 billion and $10 billion in benefits to society, while suggesting that they cost $15 billion to $20 billion to taxpayers. In another study by the National Research Council, in 1997, immigrants made tax payments in excess of $80,000 over the cost of services received. When only the first-generation immigrants are taken into account, recent immigrants consume more in services than they pay. Those who are poorly educated and unskilled tended to consume $13,000 more in services than they paid in taxes. About 22% of immigrant households are on welfare, as compared with 15% for natives. Another study looking at gross domestic product (GDP) found that it cost native workers about $72 billion annually or 1% of GDP.[20] The only certainty about costs and benefits is their uncertainty. We agree with the following conclusion:[21] "There may be costs for native workers in America, yet the gains to immigrant workers far outweigh them."

LOCAL POLICY ISSUES

For economic development professionals, like it or not, immigrant populations necessitate a greater role in, or at least an awareness of, national and even international factors (e.g., NAFTA), that now affect local economies. Likewise, greater attention must be devoted to cultural issues, social services, housing, and the like that accompany immigration; areas that have not traditionally been the province of economic development.

Within this broad context, what are the policy implications of immigration, self-employment, and economic development? Economic development professionals basically face the same issues as they would if only natives were involved, but with some twists. Should self-employed people be left to fend for themselves, or should the public sector assist them through technical assistance, training, or lending? If the public sector assists them, should immigrant businesses be targeted, or should they compete for services directly with natives? If immigrants are targeted, should immigrants control the services they receive?

Other articles in this encyclopedia address options for and benefits of facilitating economic development, so they need not be reviewed here. The real issue is targeting. If immigrant businesses represent culturally separate economic activity, then assistance to them must likewise be customized. Training Spanish speakers in English, for example, may not be effective. The best way to customize assistance is to provide funding and resources to ethnic communities and then allow them to meet their own needs. But, self-determination should occur within a broader city- or regionwide economic development strategy, of which an ethnic community is a part.

REFERENCES

1. Orrenius, P.M.; Viard, A.D. The second great migration. Southwest Econ. **2000**, *7*, (3), 1–8. May/June.
2. Bonacich, E. A theory of middleman minorities. Am. Sociol. Rev. **1973**, *38*, 583–594.
3. Portes, A.; Bach, R. *Latin Journey*; University of California Press: Berkeley, 1985.
4. Razin, E.; Light, I. Ethnic entrepreneurs in America's largest metropolitan areas. Urban Aff. Q. **1998**, *33*, 332–360. January.
5. Yoon, I.-J. The changing significance of ethnic and class resources in immigrant businesses. Int. Migr. Rev. **1991**, *25*, 303–331.
6. Waldinger, R.; Aldrich, H.; Ward, R. *Ethnic Entrepreneurs*; Sage: Newbury Park, CA, 1990.
7. Raijman, R.; Tienda, M. Immigrants' Socioeconomic Progress Post 1965. In *The Handbook of International Migration*; Hirschman, C., Ed.; Russell Sage Foundation: New York, 1999; chapter 13.
8. Raijman, R. Mexican immigrants and informal self-employment in Chicago. Human Organ. **2001**, *60* (1), 47–55.
9. Bureau of International Labor Affairs. *The Triennial Comprehensive Report on Immigration*; US Department of Labor: Washington, D.C., 1999.
10. Light, I.; Har-Chvi, H.; Kan, K. Black/Korean Conflict in LA. In *Managing Social Conflicts*; Dunn, S., Ed.; Sage: Newbury Park, CA, 1994; 72–87.
11. Buss, T.F. *Capital, Emerging High Growth Firms and Public Policy*; Praeger: New York, 2001.
12. Tseng, Y.-F. Beyond "Little Taipei." Int. Migr. Rev. **1995**, *29*, 33–58.
13. Franco, A. *The Impact of Miami Cuban Exiles*; Florida International University: Miami, 2001. Dissertation.
14. Saxenian, A.L. *Local and Global Networks of Immigrant Professionals in Silicon Valley*; Public Policy Institute of California: San Francisco, 2002.
15. Scott, R.E. *NAFTA at Seven*; Economic Policy Institute: Washington, D.C., 2001; briefing paper.
16. Portes, A. Global villages. Am. Prospect **1996**, 74–77. March–April.
17. Fairley, R.W.; Meyer, B.D. *Does Immigration Hurt African American Self Employment?*; Northwestern University, Institute for Policy Research: Chicago, 2001.
18. Zsembick, B.A. *The Cuban Ethnic Economy*; Division of Immigration Policy and Research, US Department of Labor: Washington, D.C., 1996. Working Paper # 27.
19. Butcher, K.F.; Piehl, A.M. Cross-city evidence on the relationship between immigration and crime. J. Policy Anal. Manage. **1998**, *17*, 457–494.
20. Davis, D.; Weinstein, D. *Technological Superiority and the Losses from Migration*; Department of Economics, Columbia University: New York, 2002.
21. A price worth paying. Economist **2002**, *364*, 72. June 1.
22. Fairley, R.W.; Meyer, B.D. *The Effect of Immigration on Native Self-Employment*; National bureau of Economic Research: Cambridge, MA, 2000. Working Paper 7561.

Economic Development, Infrastructure and

Robert Krol
California State University, Northridge, Northridge, California, U.S.A.

INTRODUCTION

An economy's infrastructure provides valuable services to private firms and individuals. Infrastructure investment can influence the growth, level, and spatial distribution of economic activity. The bulk of the research since the 1990s has focused on the impact of public capital investment on productivity and overall economic development.

Initial studies suggested that public capital had a large impact on U.S. economic activity. More recent studies found only a modest overall impact on the economy. The low net return to public capital investment reflects diminishing marginal returns to infrastructure construction, the spatial reallocation of economic activity, higher tax rates needed to finance projects, and reductions in agglomeration economies.

This article is organized in the following manner. First, U.S. infrastructure trends are reviewed. What follows is a discussion of how infrastructure influences the economy. Key empirical studies that examine the impact of public capital on the economy are reviewed. Special attention is given to reasons why the estimated net impact in recent studies is so small. Finally, policies to improve the efficiency of infrastructure provision and its use are discussed.

PUBLIC INFRASTRUCTURE TRENDS

This section discusses the composition and trends in the public infrastructure stock of the United States. To get a sense of public infrastructure trends, Fig. 1 provides plots of a quantity index for federal-state & local fixed assets (the public capital stock) from 1960 to 1999. The non-military public capital stock data used in this section includes equipment and software, structures, highways and streets, conservation and development, sewer systems, water supply, and other structures. The data comes from the U.S. Department of Commerce *Fixed Assets and Consumer Durable Goods in the United States.*

Both indices trend upward over this period. The slowdown in federal infrastructure investment occurred in the late 1960s. This coincided with the completion of the interstate highway system. State and local infra-structure accumulation has not slowed significantly over this period.

Table 1 provides information on the composition of nonmilitary government fixed assets for selected years between 1960 and 1999. The shares do not change radically over the period. For the federal government, the exception was equipment and software, which more than doubled over the period. This is no surprise, as the government significantly increased its use of computers, beginning in the late 1980s and continuing into the 1990s. There is a noticeable decline in the federal conservation component over the period. Structures and highway's shares remained fairly stable during this period. The composition of state and local fixed assets appears more stable than for the federal government. Once again, the clear exception is the equipment and software component of state and local infrastructure.

State and local governments own the vast majority of the public infrastructure stock. As shown in Table 1, the federal government owned approximately 18% of total nonmilitary government fixed assets in 1960. By 1999, the federal government's share had declined to roughly 13%.

INFRASTRUCTURE'S IMPACT ON ECONOMIC ACTIVITY

Public infrastructure is made up of public goods typically subject to economies of scale, such as roads, sewage treatment facilities, and water supply systems. Increases in infrastructure can have a significant impact on economic activity in various ways. The effects on output can be direct and indirect.[1] In the case of a direct effect, the infrastructure provides intermediate services to the private sector. For example, a new or wider road can reduce congestion, reducing travel time. Local businesses can now make more deliveries with the same number of trucks and drivers, resulting in higher output. Investments by firms in additional trucks would have produced the same result—an increase in the number of deliveries the firm is capable of making.

The indirect output effect works through the impact of greater infrastructure on the marginal product of private inputs hired by firms. If a complementary relationship

Encyclopedia of Public Administration and Public Policy
DOI: 10.1081/E-EPAP 120010710

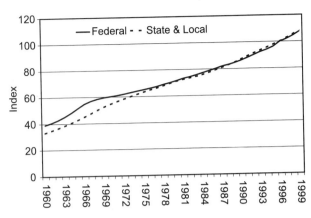

Fig. 1 Public infrastructure stock.

crowds out private capital. It may even reduce economic activity if government is a less efficient provider.

New infrastructure can influence the spatial distribution of economic activity in a region.[2] The building of a new road can cause businesses to relocate to take advantage of lower transportation costs and greater customer flows. The new road raises the marginal product of private inputs near it, creating an incentive for the private inputs to relocate closer to the road. Economic activity increases near the new road, but declines in areas away from the road. In this case, the road provides only localized benefits to firms near the road. As a result of spatial reallocation of economic activity, net output increases little in the region as a whole.

exists between public capital and private inputs, increases in public capital result in a higher marginal product of private inputs. The marginal product of the private inputs rises because they have more public capital to work with in the production process. The higher marginal product of private inputs raises the firm's demand for those inputs. Continuing with the road example, the improved road system makes existing trucks and drivers more productive. As a result, the firm buys more trucks and hires additional drivers, causing the firm's output to rise.

The previous example illustrated a complementary relationship between public and private capital. Alternatively, higher public capital can substitute for private capital, reducing private inputs in production. For example, a city can decide to produce electricity itself, rather than have it produced privately. In this case, public capital

AGGREGATE AND REGIONAL EMPIRICAL STUDIES

This section reviews empirical studies that have played an important role in shaping the literature on infrastructure investment (see Ref. [3] for more details). Much of the research in this area was stimulated by a controversial 1989 study by David Aschauer.[4] Aschauer estimated an aggregate production function for the United States using annual data for the period from 1949 to 1985. He found public capital to have a large positive impact on total factor productivity and the productivity of private capital. In addition, he showed that the slowdown in the accumulation of public capital during the 1970s contributed significantly to the overall decline in U.S. productivity growth during the 1970s and 1980s.

Table 1 Composition of infrastructure stock

	1960	1970	1980	1990	1999
Federal					
Equipment and software	0.057	0.094	0.075	0.108	0.131
Structures	0.513	0.505	0.52	0.516	0.513
Highways and streets	0.027	0.034	0.037	0.034	0.028
Conservation and development	0.397	0.354	0.352	0.321	0.29
Other structures	0.001	0.012	0.015	0.021	0.038
State and local					
Equipment and software	0.016	0.017	0.019	0.029	0.032
Structures	0.604	0.601	0.604	0.605	0.612
Highways and streets	0.249	0.258	0.229	0.214	0.21
Conservation and development	0.001	0.009	0.011	0.012	0.011
Sewer systems	0.047	0.042	0.055	0.054	0.052
Water supply	0.043	0.034	0.036	0.035	0.034
Other structures	0.034	0.038	0.047	0.052	0.05
Federal/total	0.183	0.161	0.146	0.138	0.13

John Tatom[5] questioned Aschauer's results on three counts. First, Aschauer ignored significant time trends in the data; this could lead to a spurious finding of a relationship between public capital and productivity when none is present. Second, Aschauer ignored significant energy price changes that might have affected productivity during the sample period. Tatom found that including energy prices in the model and adding time trends reduced the measured impact of public capital on productivity by one-half. Tatom also provided evidence that some of the variables in the model are not stationary. Because of this, the model should be estimated in first differences. When Tatom estimated the model in first differences, public capital is no longer significant.

John Fernald[6] reexamined the link between public capital and productivity. Fernald used a growth accounting approach to assess the impact of the growth in highway construction on U.S. industry-level productivity growth for the period from 1953 to 1989. He tested whether the increase in the highway capital stock had a disproportional impact on productivity growth in industries that are vehicle intensive. He found this to be true.

His results explained the productivity slowdown in the United States in the 1970s. Road construction was unusually productive before 1973, but not since that time; road construction today provides below normal returns. In other words, building the interstate highway system was exceptionally productive, but a second one would not provide comparable returns.

Rather than focusing on aggregate measures, some researchers began examining the impact of public capital on the economy at the state and local levels. Analysis at the state level increases sample size, improving statistical inference. It also makes sense because decisions and ownership of the public capital stock are primarily at the state and local levels.

Alicia Munnell[7] constructed estimates of state-level public capital to examine the relationship between infrastructure and economic development. Munnell estimated production functions using state level data for the period 1970 to 1986. She found that a 1% increase in a state's public capital stock raises per-capita real gross state product by 0.15 of a percent point. This estimate is smaller than some aggregate results, but is statistically significant.

Munnell's results were challenged by Holtz-Eakin[8] and Krol.[9] Both researchers pointed to the fact that Munnell failed to control for unobserved differences in state production functions. Ignoring these differences can significantly bias estimates of public capital productivity. Both Holtz-Eakin and Krol found that once unobserved production function differences are controlled for, public capital is generally no longer a significant determinant of productivity. These results question the widespread view

that large increases in state infrastructure investment are an important source of state economic development.

Morrison and Schwartz[10] focused on the manufacturing sector, examining the impact of additional infrastructure investment on regional manufacturing costs. Estimating cost functions for regions of the United States for the period from 1970 to 1987, they found that additional public capital significantly lowers manufacturing costs in all regions. An additional $1 million worth of infrastructure lowered manufacturing costs by about $160,000 to $180,000 per year. But a positive marginal product is not enough in and of itself to justify additional investment; there must be a positive net return after the costs of financing the investment are considered.

Tax and Spatial Issues

The studies discussed in the previous section indicate that additional infrastructure investment will lead to only modest increases in productivity and output. Three factors contribute to muting the net affect of public capital on productivity and output. First, financing additional infrastructure can result in higher taxes and interest rates. Second, new infrastructure causes economic activity to be reallocated, resulting in small net regional increases in output. Third, because new highways lower transportation costs, spatial density falls, reducing agglomeration economies.

New infrastructure projects must be financed through taxation or borrowing. Taxes levied on private economic agents distort decisions, resulting in a less efficient allocation of resources. In addition, the higher taxes raise the cost to businesses in the economy. The higher costs due to greater taxation can offset the lower production costs associated with the benefits of additional infrastructure.

Borrowing funds in capital markets to finance an infrastructure project can raise interest rates (interest rate effects are likely to be modest in global capital markets). As in the tax example, this raises business costs that can offset the benefits derived from additional infrastructure. In both cases, the net effect on business costs and production may be close to zero.

Morrison and Schwartz,[10] and Seitz,[11] found evidence to support this conclusion. Morrison and Schwartz found the annual benefits to businesses from additional public investment (lower costs) to be less than the annual marginal costs of funds in most years. Seitz found any increase in manufacturing employment resulting from additional infrastructure to be offset by the negative employment effects of the higher taxes.

The spatial reallocation of resources that results from the construction of a new highway was examined Chandra and Thompson.[2] They investigated this relationship for nonmetropolitan counties with new highway constructed during the period between 1969 and 1993. Rather than estimating a production function, they instead estimate a county earnings function, controlling for national, regional, and local factors that influence economic activity.

They find that the construction of a new highway in a county draws economic activity away from adjacent counties. Earnings in counties where the highway was constructed rise relative to counties that do not receive a new highway. Total earnings are 6% to 8% higher in the long run in the counties that get a new highway. Total earnings fall 1% to 3% in adjacent counties. Services and retail rise 5% to 8% in the county with the new highway and fall 8% to 11% in the adjacent county. They conclude the net effect of the new highway is about zero.

Boarnet[12] confirmed this result, looking at California counties during the period from 1969 to 1988. He found negative spillovers in the case of the construction of new highways. He found the construction of a new highway to be positively related to within-county output, but negatively related to adjacent-county output. These two studies confirmed the idea that highway construction provides mostly localized benefits, with limited aggregate effects.

Furthermore, the construction of a new highway can reduce productivity because it can lower the benefits derived from agglomeration economies. By lowering transportation costs, the incentive for businesses to locate near one another falls. As a result, firms are in less of a position to capture the local geographic externalities that arise with agglomeration economies.

Ciccone and Hall[13] found that if you double employment density in a state, average labor productivity rises by 6%. This supports the link between density and productivity. Haughwout[14] found lower benefits to densely populated urban areas from highway construction. This result links highway construction and the associated lower transportation costs to reduced agglomeration economies. It appears that highway construction can reduce agglomeration economies, which lowers productivity and output growth.

Improving the Provision of Infrastructure

This section examines how infrastructure policy reforms can improve the efficiency associated with the construction and use of highways. Highways and roads represent one of the largest civilian public capital goods in the United States. Winston,[15] and Boarnet and Haughwout,[16] discussed how changing the way we finance and price our highways and roads can lead to large net welfare gains. These policy reforms would also moderate the demand for additional highway construction.

Highway construction is financed primarily using funds from the Federal Highway Trust Fund. In most cases, 80% of the funds used to build a new highway come from the federal government. The justification for the federal government's major role in financing highways was the presence of significant spillover benefits captured by individuals living outside the area where a road is built. However, the studies discussed in the last section indicated that highway benefits tend to highly local.[2,12] As a result, a case can be made for the elimination of federal financing of highway construction (repealing the federal gas tax and refunding the Highway Trust Funds to state and local governments).

Federal financing raises concerns because it introduces biases toward excessive highway construction. Federal funds focus primarily on construction, rather than maintenance. Funding programs ignore the higher return to road maintenance, compared with the low return on road construction. The reason for this bias is believed to be political. Voters reward elected officials for opening a new spur of a highway, but tend to take regular maintenance to an existing road for granted.

In addition, Boarnet and Haughwout[15] pointed out that financing new highway projects with pooled tax revenues results in noneconomic projects being funded. In many cases, the local benefits individuals capture from a new road exceed local costs. However, this does not make the project economic because the local benefits are often less than the total cost of building the road. As a result, total welfare is reduced when the road is built using federal funds. Instead, if local decision makers are required to finance their own roads, only those that can pass a full cost–benefit analysis will be constructed.

Congestion on many urban highways creates political pressure to build more roads. This approach has done little to solve the congestion problem. Congestion indicates the price of using the highway is too low. An alternative to the costly "build your way out of congestion" approach is to move to an efficient pricing system. More efficient use of existing highways would significantly reduce the need for additional highway construction.

Today, in the United States, a flat gas tax is used to finance highways. This tax does not solve peak-load congestion problems, nor does it accurately reflect the pavement wear associated with using roads. Instead, a toll can be levied directly on users of the highway. Efficient tolls are higher during rush hours. This gives drivers an incentive to take into account the longer commuting time associated with increasing highway congestion. Tolls can be administered electronically to minimize the inconvenience of payment for road users. The potential net welfare gain from imposing congestion tolls in the United States was estimated to be almost $4 billion per year in 1998 dollars.[17]

Not only can highway construction be offset by cheaper maintenance spending, but also maintenance expenditures can be lowered by a tax that reduces highway damage. The current gasoline tax worsens highway wear and tear by trucks. Because the tax is on a per-gallon basis, trucks are built using fewer axles to improve mileage. However, highway damage depends on weight per axle, not total vehicle weight. As a result, the current tax system leads to greater highway damage then one based on a toll system that factors in weight per axle.[15]

Road maintenance can also be forestalled by building thicker roads and highways. Winston[15] argued that the adoption of efficient pricing and building thicker roads has a benefit-to-cost ratio of 4. This suggests that these reforms are economic and would result in a net improvement in welfare, if implemented.

On a less optimistic note, Winston[17] argued that entrenched special interest groups, the construction industry, and public employee unions make serious transportation policy reform unlikely. The only way to get the needed reform is to privatize the construction, operation, and maintenance of the transportation system. He argued that market incentives are the only way to correct for government failure, and to improve the efficiency and quality of service.

CONCLUSION

In this article, I have argued that public infrastructure has both direct and indirect effects on the marginal products of private inputs. If the relationship between public and private inputs is complementary, public capital investment can raise productivity, employment, and output. When public and private inputs are substitutes, the impact of additional public capital on output is weaker.

The empirical evidence suggests that additional public infrastructure has only a modest impact on economic activity. The small impact is the result of diminishing marginal returns to public capital, the spatial reallocation of economic activity, higher taxation to finance the project, and reductions in agglomeration economies.

With respect to highways, many observers have pointed to alternatives to costly highway construction. Net welfare can be increased by using congestion pricing, setting user fees that more accurately reflect road damage, building thicker roads, and by using cost–benefit analysis in project evaluation.

REFERENCES

1. Tatom, J.A. Should government spending on capital goods be raised? Federal Reserve Bank of St. Louis Review **1991**, *73* (2), 3–15.
2. Chandra, A.; Thompson, E. Does public infrastructure affect economic activity? Evidence from the rural interstate highway system. Reg. Sci. Urban Econ. **2000**, *30* (4), 457–490.
3. Krol, R. Public Infrastructure and Economic Development. In *Handbook of Economic Development*; Liou, K.T., Ed.; Marcel Dekker: New York, 1998.
4. Aschauer, D.A. Is public expenditure productive? J. Monet. Econ. **1989**, *23* (2), 177–200.
5. Tatom, J.A. Public capital and private sector performance. Federal Reserve Bank of St. Louis Review **1991**, *73* (3), 3–15.
6. Fernald, J.G. Roads to prosperity? Assessing the link between public capital and productivity. Am. Econ. Rev. **1999**, *89* (3), 619–638.
7. Munnell, A.H. How Does Public Infrastructure Affect Regional Economic Performance. In *Is There a Shortfall in Public Capital Investment*; Munnell, A.H., Ed.; Federal Reserve Bank of Boston: Boston, 1990.
8. Holtz-Eakin, D. Public-sector capital and the productivity puzzle. Rev. Econ. Stat. **1994**, *76* (1), 12–21.
9. Krol, R. Public infrastructure and state economic development. Econ. Dev. Q. **1995**, *9* (4), 331–338.
10. Morrison, C.J.; Schwartz, A.E. State infrastructure and productive performance. Am. Econ. Rev. **1996**, *86* (3), 1095–1111.
11. Seitz, H. Infrastructure, industrial development, and employment in cities: Theoretical aspects and empirical evidence. Int. Reg. Sci. Rev. **2000**, *23* (3), 259–280.
12. Boarnet, M.G. Spillovers and the locational effects of public infrastructure. J. Reg. Sci. **1998**, *38* (3), 381–400.
13. Ciccone, A.; Hall, R.E. Productivity and the density of economic activity. Am. Econ. Rev. **1996**, *86* (1), 54–70.
14. Haughwout, A.F. State infrastructure and the geography of employment. Growth Change **1999**, *30*, 549–566, (Fall).
15. Winston, C. Efficient transportation infrastructure policy and pricing. J. Econ. Perspect. **1991**, *5* (1), 113–127.
16. Boarnet, M.G.; Haughwout, A.F. Do highways matter? Evidence and policy implications of highways influence on metropolitan development. Discussion Paper, The Brookings Institution Center on Urban and Metropolitan Policy. **2000**, 1–30.
17. Winston, C. Government failure in urban transportation. Fisc. Stud. **2000**, *21* (4), 403–425.

Economic Development, International

Cal Clark
Auburn University, Auburn, Alabama, U.S.A.

INTRODUCTION

Issues of international development have given rise to two important sets of policy debates over the postwar era. The first involves how to best promote national development. During the second half of the twentieth century, several distinct stages evolved, beginning with a consensus that was followed by a series of heated debates. Economic development practices in the United States constitute the second major policy domain linked to international development. Until the 1980s, economic developmental strategies with the United States had little concern or connection with international development, but this has changed radically since then, both because globalization has had a major impact on the American economy and because there is growing recognition of parallels in the central issues and dilemmas. The policy debate in the United States has not been as fractious as disputes over international economic development, but competing perspectives are easy to discern at both the national and state-local levels. As the twenty first century opens, economic development policy remains contentious both within the United States and at the international level. In America, in particular, the current policy trajectories appear to be somewhat contradictory.

INTERNATIONAL ECONOMIC DEVELOPMENT STRATEGIES

For the first two decades of the postwar era, there was general consensus that economic development in the form of industrialization was highly desirable and that the economic, social, and political dimensions of development were generally reinforcing. By the late 1960s, this *modernization approach* was strongly challenged by *dependency theory*, which argued that the capitalist economic relations advocated by the dominant paradigm actually prevented and perverted development in much of the world.[1,2] The strident debate between these two schools of thought waned during the 1980s, when economic failure in the Soviet bloc and many statist economies discredited the dependency approach. Rather than resulting in a new consensus, though, controversy soon broke about between

advocates of laissez-faire economics and of the developmental state model.[3] Gradually, the two sides in this debate moved toward each other; however, before another consensus could be declared, a new central controversy about international economic development erupted between advocates and critics of "globalization."[4,5]

The modernization theory of the 1950s and 1960s assumed that the western path to industrialization was the universally valid and only one to development and prosperity and, thus, advocated that the developing world simply follow this tried-and-true formula—primarily the replication of western economic and political institutions (e.g., capitalism and democracy) and the replacement of traditional societies and cultures by "modern values," which would promote this economic and political change. While the modernization approach advocated westernization and capitalism, its "developmental economics" generally presumed that the state had to play a leading role in economic development. This is consistent with the work of Alexander Gerschenkron,[6] who argued that the state generally had to play a much stronger role in late-developing, as opposed to early-developing, countries. The "catch-up" nature of industrialization in late developers, according to Gerschenkron, required the rapid massive accumulation of capital for infrastructure and capital-intensive industries (e.g., steel) that was simply beyond the capabilities of private entrepreneurs in nations such as Germany and Russia in the late nineteenth and early twentieth centuries, not to speak of the many extremely poor Third World nations after World War II.

In terms of economic development itself, the nature of industrialization itself has changed dramatically during the nineteenth and twentieth centuries in terms of what industry was the most advanced or "technological driver"—first textiles, then iron and steel, then automobiles, and most recently high-tech and advanced electronics. Fig. 1 sketches an overview of how these changes in leading industry constitute an *S* curve in terms of increases in productivity and gross national product (GNP)—the curve in Fig. 1 is viewed (at least by economists) as looking like an *S*. In traditional agricultural economies, productivity increases are of necessity relatively small, but productivity and consequently GNP growth "take off"[7] once industrialization starts. The

Encyclopedia of Public Administration and Public Policy
DOI: 10.1081/E-EPAP 120010699

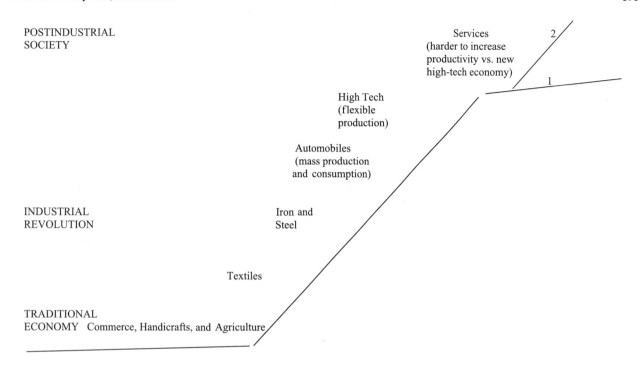

Fig. 1 Changes in leading economic activity and the S-curve of productivity and GNP growth. Line signifies rate of annual GNP and productivity growth. Line 1 represents conventional theory; line 2 represents the theory of the new economy. (From Ref. [9], p. 155.)

first big jump is into light industry (e.g., textiles and shoes), heavy industry creates another surge in productivity, and the high-tech sector constitutes the top of the manufacturing ladder. Conventionally, it was assumed that the growth of the tertiary or service economy that succeeds industry in this model would result in decelerating productivity gains and economic growth; and growth in the advanced industrial societies did indeed slow noticeably once they reached a "mature" level of development, as indicated by line 1 in Fig. 1. However, the recent surge in the high-tech and information industries has led to the argument that these new technologies have generated another upswing in productivity and growth (denoted by line 2 in Fig. 1) that has been labeled the "new economy."[8]

By the late 1960s, however, the continuing impoverishment of much of the Third World indicated that development was far from as simple and automatic as the modernization school was wont to assume. Thus, the emergence of a contending approach is easy to understand. In contrast to the modernization focus on factors internal to a nation or society that determined whether it would take advantage of the potentialities of capitalism, dependency theory concluded that the workings of the global capitalist economy itself was responsible for the absence of development in the Third World.

According to this paradigm, capitalism generates market imperfections or market power, which corporations in the industrial "core" could use to create unchallengeably high "entry barriers" to economies in the "periphery" that prevented their participation in the more desirable and profitable economic activities. This economic power, moreover, was buttressed by international class alliances between industrialists in the core and reactionary elites in the periphery.

Dependency theory lost much of it vitality during the 1980s, however, due to escalating economic problems in various nations whose governments tried to steer their economies. In particular, the 1980s witnessed the collapse of state socialism due in large part to its profound economic inefficiencies, the deteriorating economic performance of most Western welfare states where large government bureaucracies came to be increasingly viewed as drags on economic vitality, and the widespread blame of inept and corrupt governments for the many economic crises in the Third World.

The winding down of the debate between the dependency and modernization schools produced two very different theoretical reactions that, in turn, set off a new debate about the political economy of development. From one perspective, the numerous problems with statist economic policies around the world led logically and rapidly to a strong assertion of the efficacy of laissez-faire or neoclassical economics. Evidently, at least to the neo-classicists, the economy was an autonomous and self-sustaining sector of social life. What had caused the crisis of the 1970s and early 1980s was that too many other politically determined objectives that undercut economic efficiency had been attached to it. Consequently, laissez-faire economics became something of an orthodoxy in many parts of the "development community"—among economists, political leaders in the industrialized world, aid donors (e.g., the World Bank and International Monetary Fund), and many reformers in the Third World itself. Although economic problems in most of the world pointed toward the "magic of the marketplace," the most dynamic and successful region in the global economy (i.e., East Asia) pointed in exactly the opposite direction because of the strong state leadership therein promoting economic upgrading by aggressive "industrial policy." Thus, the advocates of laissez-faire were soon under strong challenge from the proponents of the "developmental state model." The cleavage between the laissez-faire and developmental state models, in essence, can be viewed as a splintering of the original consensus in modernization theory that capitalism and state economic leadership could be combined productively. Rather, one side in this debate believed that the market should rule, while the other side stressed the importance of a nation's industrial policy. During the 1990s, the two sides seemed to be moving toward each other as there appears to be an emerging pragmatism in development studies that recognizes that the old consensus of modernization theory was overly simplistic, and seeks to overcome the trade-offs and contradictions between the market and the state.[3]

This does not mean that a new consensus is growing about international economic development, however. In fact, a new sharp controversy erupted in the late 1990s, this time between the advocates and critics of globalization or the rapidly growing economic interdependence (i.e., trade and capital flows, and the activities of multinational corporations) across national borders that has marked the late twentieth century.[5,10] Both the scholarly and popular discussion of globalization are quite polarized. For some, globalization suggests that the new millennium (the twenty first century) will actually live up to its name with greater prosperity in many nations, less hierarchic relations in the business world, the spread of democracy in an historic "third wave," and many fewer threats to world peace in a "global village." Conversely, others view globalization as the primary driving force behind alarmingly regressive change. In particular, they cite the growing inequality and social turmoil in the developed world, the exploitation of developing nations, and the subversion of indigenous cultures and values by "coca-cola capitalism," all stemming from the decreased ability of governments to protect the public interest from corporate policy.[4] Although far from being resolved, the debate over globalization highlights Joseph Schumpeter's key insight that economic development involves "creative destruction."[11] New industries arise but only as old ones are destroyed, creating massive "costs of adjustment" and social turmoil. Certainly, the faster pace of "creative destruction" associated with globalization is creating a massive challenge for many governments.

ECONOMIC DEVELOPMENT POLICY IN THE UNITED STATES

Since the 1980s, the growing exposure of the U.S. economy to international competition, popularly termed globalization, has brought momentous changes affecting the American economy, society, and lifestyles. In the economic realm, globalization has forced a substantial change in the U.S.'s production structure. In particular, many of the nation's basic economic sectors in light and heavy industry are being forced to relocate "off shore" due to international competition. However, fortunately for the United States, they are being replaced by a "new economy" tied to high-tech industries and advanced services. Consequently, economic development policy, especially at the state and local levels where it is primarily practiced, is coming under strong challenge to respond to this industrial restructuring.

The social and economic changes associated with globalization have certainly been substantial and, in some ways, unsettling. In the 1950s and 1960s, the United States clearly had the most productive and competitive economy in the world based on mass production techniques of standardized goods. During the 1970s and 1980s, in contrast, America's leading economic position came under challenge for two interconnected reasons. First, the transportation and communications revolutions made it easier to locate mass production factories away from the existing industrial centers to take advantage of lower wages. Second, affluence made consumers increasingly eager to buy more specialized and higher-quality goods than the traditional mass production techniques could fashion. The recession of the early 1990s, in particular, raised fears about America's ability to retain its industrial leadership and prosperous lifestyle. By the mid-1990s, however, many U.S. corporations had responded quite well to this challenge, reorganizing themselves to promote high-quality and high-tech production, and moving into advanced and sophisticated service industries. In fact, by most indices, the United States has regained the lead in global competitiveness. Still, this transformation from an Industrial Age to an Information Age economy has done little, if anything, to help many of the communities and workers who had depended on the traditional industries for their well-being.[5,10,12–14]

The governmental response to the challenge of globalization differed dramatically between the national and state-local levels. The United States has long had a tradition or public philosophy of limited government, which has resulted in a government that is smaller and weaker than almost any other country in the developed world.[15] This laissez-faire tradition, therefore, militated against a turn to industrial policy to help reinvigorate the nation's international competitiveness and manage the considerable transformation of the American economy that was under way. In fact, the federal government took quite limited action. In ironic contrast, however, almost all state and many local governments made an explicit commitment to promoting their communities' economic development, in almost polar opposition to the laissez-faire approach of national policy. This is ironic because the federal government is seen as more liberal than most state and local ones and, thus, would be expected to pursue more interventionist economic policies.[16]

State and local economic development activities and programs span a wide gamut, although two principal types or strategies can be discerned, as summarized in Table 1. The first represents the traditional strategy of attracting new investment by lowering the cost of doing business in a given locality by either subsidizing the traditional inputs used by firms (e.g., capital, land, labor) or by limiting the "political costs" of doing business (i.e., minimizing taxes and regulation). Because these incentives were generally targeted at large mass production industries, the strategy of using them came to be called (somewhat sarcastically) "smoke-stack chasing." The other, newer strategy, which might be termed "promoting entrepreneurship," seeks to stimulate business expansion and creation by developing new markets, by providing services that enhance business operations (e.g., human capital development, support for research and development), or by offering a community with attractive amenities.[9,17–21]

An initial "wave" of state-local economic activism began in the years before World War II and continued for the first decade or so after the war. The central thrust of this wave was a drive by poorer and less industrial regions, primarily the South, to catch up with the more affluent parts of the nation. It focused on the conventional strategies of subsidizing business inputs and lowering political costs. The South's ability to lure industry from the Northeast and Midwest proved so successful by the 1950s that the old industrial heartland decided to fight fire

Table 1 Changing models of state-local economic development policy

	Smoke-stack chasing	Promoting entrepreneurship
Theory of growth	Growth is promoted by lowering the factor costs of production by government subsidies of capital and land and by low taxes.	Growth is promoted by discovering, expanding, developing, or creating new markets for local goods and services.
Focus of efforts	1. Stimulate relocation of large, established firms. 2. Government supports low-risk enterprises. 3. Any firm is a suitable target for aid.	1. Stimulate new and small business formation and expansion. 2. Government nurtures high-risk enterprises and activities. 3. Use strategic criteria for aid.
Desirable firms	Large existing ones	New start-ups, small firm, high tech, environmentally friendly
Desirable labor force	Low-cost labor	Skilled and flexible
Primary government contribution	Low-cost land and tax subsidies	Access to advanced technology and finance capital
Government's role	Government should follow and support private decisions about where to invest, what businesses will be profitable, and what producers will sell—basically laissez-faire	Government should help to identify investment opportunities for the private sector (i.e., new markets, products, and industries)—movement to create public–private partnerships
Location assets	Comparative advantage based on physical assets	Comparative advantage from social and environmental amenities
Market focus	Local and regional	National and international

Source: From Ref. [9], p. 173.

with fire by emulating the South's locational incentives. By the early 1960s, the Northeast and Midwest had matched, if not surpassed, the South in incentive policies. A new wave in state and local economic development policy commenced during the 1970s and 1980s in response to the growing economic stress generated by America's shift in the global economy and by the declining amounts of federal aid. Traditional locational incentives assumed a major role in this offensive, but there was turn to "promoting entrepreneurship" strategies, in large part because globalization was luring most of the "smoke stacks" out of the country altogether. This change in development strategy did not turn out to be necessarily permanent, as the recession of the early 1990s brought a renewed emphasis on competitive "smoke-stack chasing."[9,18,21–24]

AN UNCERTAIN FUTURE

The policy issues outlined in the last two sections remain unsettled as the twenty first century opens. Controversy over the potential good or evil of globalization, symbolized perhaps by the "Battle in Seattle" (i.e., the 1999 protests against the WTO meeting in Seattle), has long passed the cottage-industry stage and displays no signs of reaching resolution. Globalization, moreover, has certainly been a double-edged sword in regard to its impact on the United States, as the new technologies that are driving it both undercut the nation's position in traditional industries and create the foundation for a new economic surge in the high-tech and advanced services sectors, in line with the image of "creative destruction." On the one hand, the emergence of the "new economy" of the Information Age represents extremely good news for America. There is "life after manufacturing," and the strong performance of the U.S. economy for most of the 1990s demonstrates the vitality and growth of these new industries. On the other hand, the "destructive" half of creative destruction is far too great to be ignored either. Many workers and communities that prospered in the Industrial Age have proved incapable of adjusting to the "new economy," creating increasing social and economic inequality for a significant segment of the population.[4,5,13,25]

In terms of policy, the commitment of the United States to a relatively small government and laissez-faire policies has created a paradox for reacting to the challenges of globalization. Business is able to be flexible and innovative, allowing the United States to become the world leader in most of the emerging Information Age industries. However, the country is constrained in its attempts to improve education, build new infrastructure,

and retrain workers whose skills have become obsolete, all vital tasks for retraining competitiveness at the top of the international product cycle. Furthermore, the absence of federal industrial policy means that states and communities often enter into stiff competition for business investment in a game in which the rules are undefined, creating what has been called "the new civil war,"[26] leaving some analysts worried that state and local governments may be dangerously undercutting their resources, as well as their ability to respond to the challenge of the Information Age.[22]

REFERENCES

1. Caporaso, J.A.; Levine, D.P. *Theories of Political Economy*; Cambridge University Press: Cambridge, 1992.
2. Randall, V.; Theobald, R. *Political Change and Underdevelopment: A Critical Introduction to Third World Politics*; Duke University Press: Durham, NC, 1985.
3. Clark, C.; Roy, K.C. *Comparing Development Patterns in Asia*; Lynne Rienner: Boulder, CO, 1997.
4. Clark, C. Globalization: Schizophrenic Scenarios and the Need for Creative Crossdressing in U.S. Policy. In *Visions of the 21st Century: Social Research for the Millennium*; Schoenhals, M.; Behar, J., Eds.; Global Publications of the State University of New York: Binghamton, NY, 2001; 151–166.
5. Friedman, T.L. *The Lexus and the Olive Tree*; Farrar, Strauss, Giroux: New York, 1999.
6. Gerschenkron, A. *Economic Backwardness in Historical Perspective: A Book of Essays*; Harvard University Press: Cambridge, 1962.
7. Rostow, W.W. *The Stages of Economic Growth: A Non-Communist Manifesto*; Cambridge University Press: Cambridge, 1960.
8. Atkinson, R.D.; Court, R.H.; Ward, J.M. *Technology, Innovation, and New Economy Project*; 2000, www.neweconomyindex.org.
9. Clark, C.; Montjoy, R. Globalization and the Revitalization of U.S. Economic Competitiveness: Implications for Economic Development Policy. In *Handbook of Economic Development*; Liou, K.T., Ed.; Marcel Dekker: New York, 1998; 151–182.
10. Gilpin, R. *The Challenge of Global Capitalism: The World Economy in the 21st Century*; Princeton University Press: Princeton, 2000.
11. Schumpeter, J.A. *Capitalism, Socialism, and Democracy*, 3rd Ed.; Harper & Row: New York, 1950.
12. Piore, M.J.; Sabel, C.F. *The Second Industrial Divide: Possibilities for Prosperity*; Basic Books: New York, 1984.
13. Thurow, L.C. *Building Wealth: The New Rules for Individuals, Companies, and Nations in a Knowledge-Based Economy*; HarperCollins: New York, 1999.

14. Womack, J.P.; Jones, D.T.; Roos, D. *The Machine that Changed the World: The Story of Lean Production*; MacMillan: New York, 1990.

15. Kingdon, J.W. *America the Unusual*; St. Martin's Press: New York, 1999.

16. Graham, O.L., Jr. *Losing Time: The Industrial Policy Debate*; Harvard University Press: Cambridge, 1992.

17. Bingham, R.D.; Mier, R. *Theories of Local Economic Development: Perspectives from Across the Disciplines*; Sage: Newbury Park, CA, 1993.

18. Brace, P. *State Government and Economic Performance*; Johns Hopkins University Press: Baltimore, 1993.

19. Bradshaw, T.K.; Blakely, E.J. What are 'third wave' state economic development efforts? From incentives to industrial policy. Econ. Dev. Q. **1999**, *13* (3), 229–244.

20. Clarke, S.E.; Gaile, G.L. *The Work of Cities*; University of Minnesota Press: Minneapolis, 1998.

21. Eisinger, P.K. *The Rise of the Entrepreneurial State: State and Local Economic Development Policy in the United States*; University of Wisconsin Press: Madison, 1988.

22. Brace, P. Economic development policy in the American states: Back to an inglorious future? In *Globalization's Impact on State-Local Economic Development Policy*; Clark, C., Montjoy, R., Eds.; Nova Science: Huntington, NY, 2001; 91–109.

23. Cobb, J.C. *The Selling of the South*; Louisiana State University Press: Baton Rouge, 1982.

24. Kanter, R.M. *World Class: Thriving Locally in the Global Economy*; Simon & Schuster: New York, 1995.

25. Smith, H. *Rethinking America: A New Game Plan from the American Innovators: Schools, Business, People, Work*; Random House: New York, 1995.

26. Watson, D.J. *The New Civil War*; Praeger: Westport, CT, 1995.

Economic Development and Organization

C. Fred Baughman
*University of Central Florida–Daytona Beach,
Daytona Beach, Florida, U.S.A.*

INTRODUCTION

A new trend within the economic development profession is the reconsideration of the organizational form of local economic development agencies. Recently, the Fort Wayne–Allen County Economic Development Alliance was established as a partnership between the City of Fort Wayne, Allen County, and the Greater Fort Wayne Chamber of Commerce. Before its creation, each of the three entities had its own economic development staff.[1] This is an example, therefore, of governmental and private sector agencies combining to form a public/private partnership.

However, not all recent reorganizations have been in that direction. The local elected officials in Volusia County, Florida, withdrew their financial support from the existing public/private partnership (Enterprise Volusia, Inc.). Instead, Volusia County is going to create an in-house economic development department. Because of concern by the private sector in regards to the public sector's ability to accomplish effective business recruitment, three of the local chambers of commerce within Volusia County have also formed an alliance to perform business attraction activities. This is an example, consequently, of a public/private partnership being split into separate governmental and private sector economic development entities.

HISTORICAL PERSPECTIVE

Historically, the source of funding has played an important role in the type of economic development activities within a community. Due to federal funding, many local planning offices were involved in the preparation of economic development planning documents in the late 1970s. Economic development committees were established to prepare Overall Economic Development Programs (OEDP) funded by the U.S. Economic Development Administration. In addition, again because of the availability of federal funding, many local governments were involved in urban renewal efforts that improved the real estate of communities.

However, the actual implementation of business recruitment efforts, in order to create new local jobs, was normally the role of the chamber of commerce (private sector). Other nonprofit organizations were formed to take advantage of programs from the U.S. Small Business Administration. Communities began, therefore, to form revolving loan programs as incentives for development, oftentimes targeted to minority- and women-owned businesses.

As federal funds became scarce for economic development activities, the trend was toward the creation of public/private partnerships, where both entities have a stake in local economic development efforts. The public and private sectors would provide funding for the economic development activities, however, the percentage of the contribution from the sectors was different in various organizations.

Currently, local economic development organizations can be divided into three categories: public sector agencies, private sector organizations, and public/private partnerships.[2] No matter which form of economic development entity is established, each will have its own advantages and disadvantages. The local community must decide which form fits best with local needs.

PUBLIC SECTOR AGENCIES

Some communities believe that economic development is most effective when accomplished by an agency that is an integral part of local government (city or county). The public sector agency model of economic development organization is unique in that it is funded and directed entirely by the public sector. The local elected politicians provide the policy direction for economic development. In addition, through the annual budget process, they appropriate the available funds for economic development efforts. The economic development staff that carries out the required activities is composed of government employees that report directly to the local elected officials.

Advantages of the Public Sector Agency

Secure source of funding

There is a more secure source of funding for economic development efforts. This source might come from the

Encyclopedia of Public Administration and Public Policy
DOI: 10.1081/E-EPAP 120010690

general fund of the local government. Other communities have established impact fees to support economic development. The State of Indiana allows its counties to create an Economic Development Income Tax (EDIT). No matter what the source of the funds, economic development staffs in governmental agencies are not expected to be involved in fund-raising activities.

Proximity to decision makers

Most financial incentives in economic development projects come from the public sector. If the economic development organization is a governmental agency, then it is much closer to the decision makers that will commit those incentive dollars.

Interdepartmental cooperation

Similar to being closer to incentive decision makers, the staffs of public sector economic development agencies work closely with other governmental departments. Many times, an economic development deal will require the cooperation of other departments for permit approvals or infrastructure improvements.

Citizen participation

Another advantage of public sector economic development agencies is the legal requirement for citizen participation. This requirement ensures that the economic development staff is not acting in a manner contrary to the overall vision of the community.

Disadvantages of the Public Sector Agency

Timing of economic development projects

Many local officials are elected to two-year terms. Consequently, those local elected officials focus on programs with quick results. However, economic development is not an activity that normally produces benefits in a fast time frame. From the time that an economic development staff begins talking to a business prospect until that business makes a locational decision can typically be from two to four years. Therefore, local elected officials creating an economic development agency, and making annual budget appropriations, might not see a successful economic development project during their term in office. It is commonly believed that local elected officials oftentimes support those activities that get them reelected. David Osborne and Peter Plastrik, in their book, *Banishing Bureaucracy*, indicate that leaders of the future are going to have to be committed, ''willing to stick it out...willing to invest the time it takes to communicate

their vision; and if they can prove themselves...they can succeed.''[3] There is no guarantee that economic development efforts can produce desired results in the short run—elected leaders are going to have to take a long-term perspective.

Political infighting

Another disadvantage of public sector economic development agencies is the local infighting between political organizations. For example, if the leadership of a local city is politically different than the leadership of the county, then there might not be the cooperation required for a successful economic development program by either entity. In addition, the infighting within a political organization can have just as serious consequences. The lack of political leadership can be a large disadvantage for a public sector economic development agency.

Inefficient government structure

An inefficient government structure can also be a disadvantage. As stated earlier, an advantage of the public sector agency was its closeness to decision makers. However, if the organizational structure of the government does not allow for this proximity, then the advantage is no longer realized. Therefore, economic development staffs should not be buried in an umbrella department. In addition, it should be recognized that the motivating factors of planning staffs and economic development staffs are very different. While both groups should pursue smart and managed growth, the economic development staff will normally be promoting growth, and the planning staff will normally be constraining growth.

Governmental bureaucracy can be a limiting factor to the success of economic development efforts. The saying ''time is money'' is never more true than in the area of economic development. Business prospects expect, and require, the immediate turnaround of information and decisions. Any delay in the opening of a new business is an opportunity cost to that company.

Public disclosure requirements

A further disadvantage of a public sector economic development agency is public disclosure requirements. These are commonly known as ''Sunshine Laws.'' The overall concept of sunshine laws is positive in its belief that the activities of government should be conducted in the public view. However, most business prospects demand confidentiality during the early stages of the economic development process. For labor and market reasons, it is important for them that information of their potential relocation does not become public. The sunshine laws place a public sector economic development agency in an uncomfortable position.

Ability to attract professional staff

The final disadvantage of the public sector agency is its ability to attract and retain competent economic development professionals. This constraint might be because of the pay level of other city staff members or just of the legal structure of the human resources procedure required of governmental entities.

PRIVATE SECTOR ENTITIES

As stated above, early in the formation of the economic development profession, most business recruitment activities were done by the local chamber of commerce. In some communities, the chamber of commerce is still the focal point for economic development. The private sector entities obtain their leadership, agenda, and funding entirely from private enterprise. Oftentimes, this leadership is composed of real estate brokers, attorneys, bankers, accountants, and small business owners. Not surprisingly, these individuals see a direct potential business benefit from successful economic development efforts.

Advantages of the Private Sector Entities

Freedom from governmental legal constraints

The first advantage of the private sector organization is its freedom and the fact that it is not constrained by the many legal structures of local government. Those constraints might be procurement procedures, personnel regulations, sunshine laws, and others. Another related advantage is the private sector's ability to recruit and compensate talented economic development professionals.

Not part of the government organization

By being outside the governmental structure, the private sector organization can often act as an ombudsman during the economic development process. If a project gets held up in government "red-tape," then the private sector organization can use steps to remedy the problem without worrying about hurting the feelings of government employees. This type of organizational entity does not require the government to "police" itself.

Able to respond quickly

As stated above, timing is often critical in economic development activities. In many cases, the private sector

will respond more quickly and is more efficient than the public sector. As Osborne and Plastrik state, "The problem with government monopolies is that they have no real reason to improve their performance."[4]

Disadvantages of the Private Sector Entities

Responsiveness to community sentiment

One of the disadvantages of the private sector organization is that it can be less responsive to the community sentiment for economic development.

Conflicts of Interest

Another disadvantage is that the private sector leadership might have a conflict of interest when it comes to economic development projects. Even though a project might be a benefit and create many well-paid jobs for the community, some private sector leaders might not support the project because of the competition it creates for their own labor force needs.

Secure funding sources

The final disadvantage of the private sector economic development organization is that the funding stream is less secure. Rather than a dedicated source of funds, most private sector organizations rely upon fund-raising for their budgetary needs. Consequently, a staff hired for economic development expertise can spend a considerable amount of time instead on organizational fund-raising activities.

PUBLIC/PRIVATE PARTNERSHIP

The public/private partnership is the form of organizational structure most recently preferred by many communities for economic development activities, because it can combine the advantages of the public sector agency and the private sector organization. As the name implies, the public/private partnership is a collaborative effort of the public and private sectors. It is estimated that over 80% of current organizations have a board of directors comprised of members from the public (government) and private sectors.[5]

Advantages of the Public/Private Partnership

Vehicle for communication

One of the main advantages of the public/private partnership is that it provides a vehicle for the interaction between local government officials and leaders in the private sector. This may be one of the few opportunities within the community for this type of interaction to occur. Consequently, the public/private partnership has the opportunity to maximize the powers of the public and private sectors.

Broader base of funding

Economic development activities are becoming more expensive. Funding of the public/private partnership normally comes from both sectors but can be contributed at different percentages. The specific strengths and weaknesses of the local community will assist in establishing that ratio for the organization. However, less time will be spent on fund-raising than in a fully private sector organization.

Need for confidentiality

As stated earlier, the economic development prospect often requires total confidentiality in regards to its interest in a potential relocation. Because of "sunshine laws," the government entities are not able to provide this needed service. As a result, the prospect will many times communicate with a public/private partnership much earlier in the process than it would with a strictly public sector organization.

Disadvantages of the Public/Private Partnership

Multiple sources of responsibility

The primary disadvantage of the public/private partnership is that the economic development staff may be forced into a position of reporting to multiple "bosses."

Project coordination

Another disadvantage is that unless all the entities involved in the partnership trust the process, there may be charges of leads being steered to certain locations. The professional staff will need to establish a lead-sharing procedure and rely heavily upon it.

CONCLUSION

As stated earlier, every type of organizational structure will have advantages and disadvantages. Again, the individual strengths and weaknesses of every community will be important in determining the economic development organizational structure that is most effective. A recent

article comparing the St. Paul model (public sector agency) to the Philadelphia model (public/private partnership) in conclusion stated, "We think the quasi-public corporation, with its legal flexibility and combination of public and private resources, offers the broadest range of powers and the strongest opportunity for coordination between the public and private sectors. Although independent to some degree, it also recognizes its responsibilities to both sides—to the private sector in creating a favorable business climate and to the public sector in creating job opportunities and improving the city's tax base."[6]

In general, therefore, the trend is toward the public/private partnership because of its ability to contribute the advantages of the public sector agency and the private sector organization while minimizing the disadvantages of both. Dr. David Kolzow recently concluded, "the advantages of teamwork in the local economic development process are becoming increasingly apparent in the face of changing economic trends, budget constraints, and the growing need for the combined resources of the private and public sectors. Communities in which the public and private sector band together to form economic development teams through an organization structured as a public–private partnership are more likely to experience effective actions and successful results."[7]

REFERENCES

1. http://theallianceonline.com/index2.htm (accessed August 2001).
2. Whitehead, W.; Ady, R. *Organizational Models for Economic Development, Practicing Economic Development,* 3rd Ed.; Koepke, R., Ed.; American Economic Development Council Education Foundation: Rosemont, IL, 1996; 41.
3. Osborne, D.; Plastrik, P. The Culture Strategy. In *Banishing Bureaucracy: The Five Strategies for Reinventing Government*; A Plume Book, a member of Penguin Putnam, Inc.: New York, NY, 1998; 296.
4. Osborne, D.; Plastrik, P. The Consequences Strategy. In *Banishing Bureaucracy: The Five Strategies for Reinventing Government*; A Plume Book, a member of Penguin Putnam, Inc.: New York, NY, 1998; 130.
5. Whitehead, W.; Ady, R. *Organizational Models for Economic Development. Practicing Economic Development,* 3rd Ed.; Koepke, R., Ed.; American Economic Development Council Education Foundation: Rosemont, IL, 1996; 41–42.
6. Knack, R.; Bellus, J.; Adell, P. Setting Up Shop for Economic Development. In *Economic Development in Local Government*; Kemp, R., Ed.; McFarland & Company, Inc.: Jefferson, NC, 1995; 44.
7. Kolzow, D. *Public/Private Partnership: The Economic Development Organization of the 90s. Practicing Economic Development,* 3rd Ed.; Koepke, R., Ed.; American Economic Development Council Education Foundation: Rosemont, IL, 1996; 47.

Economic Development, State Government Administration of

Keith Boeckelman
Western Illinois University, Macomb, Illinois, U.S.A.

INTRODUCTION

Throughout much of U.S. history, economic development has been a critical state function. Activity in this area dates to colonial times, when states first began to offer land grants, loans, and tax exemptions to subsidize industry.[1] During the nineteenth century, states used massive infrastructure investments, such as the Erie Canal, to foster growth. After a post-Civil War period of federal dominance in the economic realm, development issues reemerged as a concern for state policy makers during the twentieth century. Since the 1970s, economic development issues have been at or near the top of most states' policy agendas. Three approaches to economic development, known as the first, second, and third waves, characterize the contemporary era. Each is summarized and evaluated below. Following this discussion, current state efforts are examined and future trends are speculated.

It is easier to describe the various approaches to economic development than it is to determine exactly what states are doing in this area or whether their efforts have the desired impact. The fact that many programs exist off budget, use intergovernmental grants, or operate through public–private partnerships complicates description. Evaluating the results of economic development programs is also notoriously difficult. States have open economies subject to a large number of national and international variables. Isolating the impact of policies on the economy is therefore a tricky proposition. In addition, factors that supposedly affect economic development, such as labor costs, are in turn affected by levels of economic development, making it difficult to ascertain what is causing what. These complications can frustrate both elected officials and practitioners in their efforts to develop coherent and effective policies.

FIRST-WAVE ECONOMIC DEVELOPMENT POLICIES

First-wave economic development efforts, also referred to as the "supply-side approach" or "locational policies," adopt a business recruitment model. These policies try to entice manufacturing plants to locate in a state by reducing taxes, wage rates, construction and infrastructure expenditures, or other costs. Tax incentives are the most common and widely publicized first-wave policies. They typically excuse businesses from corporate income or property taxes, or reduce levies on firms that engage in economically beneficial activities, such as buying new equipment or creating jobs in the state.[2] Other common first-wave programs include industrial development bonds, right-to-work laws, and enterprise zones. State or local governments use the former to finance the construction or purchase of industrial buildings. Right-to-work laws forbid closed-shop provisions thus weakening the collective bargaining power of unions in order to depress wage rates. Finally, enterprise zones target various tax and other incentives to putatively depressed parts of a state.

Southern states pioneered first-wave policies, beginning in the 1920s.[3] At about the same time, these states began to create economic development agencies to spearhead business recruitment efforts. By the late 1970s, however, economic difficulties in the Northeast and Midwest led to a nationalization of first-wave policies. This trend was perhaps most evident in the rivalry to attract foreign auto plants, such as Volkswagen, Mitsubishi, and Mercedes Benz. The competition for jobs in lean economic times led to a climate of desperation where incentive programs escalated into an "arms race" as states matched and exceeded the deals their neighbors offered.[4]

The impact of first-wave economic development policies has been a matter of substantial debate, particularly with respect to the question of whether tax policies affect a state's economy. The answer seems to depend, at least in part, on research methodology. Studies based on interviews of corporate decision makers suggest that tax incentives play a negligible role in determining where businesses locate.[5] At best, taxes may determine which states are eliminated from contention in the early stages of the decision-making process. For the finalists in the location sweepstakes, however, factors such as transportation and labor costs become more important in determining which state ultimately wins.[6]

Econometric studies, however, show a more significant role for tax policy. Overall levels appear to be especially important, although targeted incentives matter in some instances, according to this research. Specifically, high tax rates are likely to reduce employment, gross state product,

Encyclopedia of Public Administration and Public Policy
DOI: 10.1081/E-EPAP 120011021

manufacturing investment, and the number of business locations. Tax incentives are most important in affecting where capital-intensive manufacturers move.[7] Yet, the number of jobs affected by tax policy is usually rather small.

Any analysis of incentive programs must also note that they often distort a state's tax system by treating similar businesses unequally, because some receive breaks while others do not. Furthermore, they are regressive because profitable companies receive the majority of concessions. In addition, widespread use of incentive programs complicates tax administration, as laws are likely to change more frequently. Tax incentives can also have negative consequences that spill over a state's borders and create a negative-sum game for the nation as a whole. In other words, the money that states spend attracting businesses are a waste of national resources because the plants would locate somewhere in the United States anyway. Thus, if all states increase incentives to respond to the competitive "arms race," they not only lose revenue but they also do not create new competitive advantages.

Economic development programs that focus on labor costs, such as right-to-work laws, affect plant location decisions, particularly for those firms that do not need to be near specific markets or suppliers.[6] Obviously, however, such policies attract relatively low-wage jobs. Existing studies suggest that enterprise zone programs tend to target businesses that would operate in the area anyway, and rarely hire neighborhood residents.[8] Evaluations of industrial bond programs show that about 60% of the projects they fund would have occurred anyway.[2]

SECOND-WAVE ECONOMIC DEVELOPMENT POLICIES

Second-wave policies, also sometimes known as "demand-side" or "entrepreneurial" approaches, began to appear in the 1980s. They emerged due to concerns about the cost and effectiveness of tax incentive programs, as well as the perception that the jobs created by first-wave initiatives were of low quality. These programs emphasize nurturing existing local businesses and promoting entrepreneurial activity, rather than trying to attract companies from outside the state. Resembling Japanese-style industrial policy, at least superficially, the state government's role can include targeting investment to specific regions and industries or fostering public–private partnerships.

Specific examples of second-wave policies include high-technology initiatives, venture capital efforts, and export development programs. High-technology programs have two basic goals. Some focus on promoting hi-tech jobs in general because officials view this sector as having great potential for growth. Other initiatives attempt to preserve the viability of existing industries through technological improvements. Texas' Advanced Research Program and Advanced Technology Program are examples of the first type, while the Ben Franklin Partnership in Pennsylvania typifies the second approach. Many states administer their high-technology programs through public research universities in order to draw on the expertise of science and engineering faculty.

Venture capital programs provide loans to small, entrepreneurial businesses that may not have access to funds through traditional methods. State pension funds often serve as a source of capital for such programs. Export development initiatives assist firms in developing export markets overseas. About 40 states maintain offices abroad to administer these programs. A few states have also tried to bolster economic performance by restructuring labor–management relations or targeting industries outside the high-technology realm, but these programs have been less widely adopted.

Because they are of more recent vintage, there are fewer independent evaluations of second-wave policies than of the first wave. Existing studies suggest that high-technology business incubator programs that provide space and shared services, such as secretarial and accounting assistance, are effective. Export development initiatives appear to have a greater direct economic impact than do venture capital efforts or university-based technology programs.[9] The public–private partnerships that many states have created to administer second-wave policies raise unique accountability issues. For example, it is not clear whether such entities must obey "freedom of information" or "sunshine" laws that govern more typical state agencies.[10]

THIRD-WAVE ECONOMIC DEVELOPMENT POLICIES

Doubts about the effectiveness of both first- and second-wave policies led to a new approach beginning in the early 1990s. "Third-wave" initiatives reflect a retreat from direct economic management in favor of more general "capacity-building" activities. Specifically, states began to offer different programs and to organize them in new ways. Programmatically, the third wave emphasizes fundamentals, such as infrastructure, educational improvements, and job training. Organizationally, this approach favors giving nonprofits some responsibility for economic development administration and cutting back on direct state spending. It also emphasizes greater coordination between state and local governments, and among officials in a particular region.[11] Studies of the impact of third-wave policies suggest that funding highway infrastructure raises state incomes, but not necessarily employment levels, while educational spending has little impact.[12] The organizational innovations associated with the third wave are difficult to measure and evaluate.[11]

402

STATE ECONOMIC DEVELOPMENT POLICY TODAY AND IN THE FUTURE

The appearance of a new wave of economic development policies does not necessarily wash away its predecessors. Thus, most states use program elements of all three approaches discussed in this article. As noted, measuring levels of state commitment to the various waves of economic development is difficult, in part because so much activity occurs off budget. Nevertheless, it appears that states devote the greatest amount of resources to first-wave programs, which continued to grow at least through the 1990s.[13] This continuing dominance reflects two political advantages that the later approaches to economic development cannot match. First, supporters of first-wave efforts are often powerful business interest groups. By contrast, second-wave policies such as technology initiatives tend to have few organized beneficiaries, while they foster opposition from labor unions who see few program benefits accruing to relatively uneducated production workers. Second, it is easy for the public to draw a causal connection between a tax incentive followed by a plant location, while the benefits of second- or third-wave policies are rarely as visible.

Despite their continued popularity, there have been increasing concerns about the possible misuse of first-wave programs, especially tax incentives. State officials fear that the arms race mentality results in temptations to "give away the store" by offering packages that exceed job benefits. For example, Alabama's offered about $300 million to entice Mercedes Benz to come to the state at a cost per job of about $200,000 for the 1500 positions created. In addition, states have little recourse when companies receiving incentives fail to deliver on the promised job benefits.

States have adopted various policies in response to these concerns. Perhaps the most common are "clawback laws" that require companies to pay back all or part of incentive packages if the promised number of jobs do not materialize. States are often unwilling to enforce such provisions, however, particularly if they run the risk of antagonizing local industries who are in financial trouble. Meanwhile, the general public is largely oblivious to the cost of tax incentives, perhaps because they are not part of the normal budget process. In fact, many states do not know how much they spend on incentives.[2] Another, albeit less used, alternative to protect the public interest is to require cost–benefit analyses before offering incentives. Finally, some states have adopted "nonaggression pacts," whereby they collectively agree to limit their use of incentives. These agreements have usually failed, however, with some pacts lasting only a few months. Efforts to get the federal government to intervene to deescalate the incentive arms race have also been unsuccessful.

Even during the robust economic times of the late 1990s, state interest in economic development did not appear to wane. Thus, it is unlikely to do so in the current, more uncertain, climate. It is not clear if states will stick with existing strategies, or opt for new approaches leading to a fourth wave of activity. Some have suggested that the next logical step for state economic development policy is to address economic inequality issues.[14] One example of this approach would be to integrate technology development programs with efforts to train former welfare recipients for new jobs. A few states already use their economic development agencies to implement the Temporary Assistance for Needy Families program associated with the 1996 welfare reform law. Getting involved in redistributive policy brings political headaches that economic development officials may want to avoid, however, so it is not clear how far this trend will go.

REFERENCES

1. Brace, P. *State Government and Economic Performance*; Johns-Hopkins Univ. Press: Baltimore, 1993.
2. Buss, T.F. The effect of state tax incentives on economic growth and firm location decisions: An overview of the literature. Econ. Dev. Q. **2001**, *15* (1), 90–105.
3. Cobb, J. *The Selling of the South*; University of Illinois Press: Urbana, 1993.
4. Wilson, R.H. *States and the Economy*; Praeger: Westport, CT, 1993.
5. Donahue, J.D. *Disunited States*; Basic Books: New York, 1997.
6. Schmenner, R.; Huber, J.C.; Cook, R.L. Geographic differences and the location of new manufacturing facilities. J. Urban Econ. **1987**, *21* (1), 83–104.
7. Wasylenko, M. Taxation and economic development: The state of the economic literature. N. Engl. Econ. Rev. **1997**, 37–52, March/April.
8. Porter, M. New strategies for inner-city economic development. Econ. Dev. Q. **1997**, *11* (1), 11–27.
9. Bingham, R.E.; Bowen, W.M. The performance of state economic development programs. Policy Stud. J. **1994**, *22* (3), 501–513.
10. Fulton, W. The business of bringing in business. Governing **1996**, *9*, 92, October.
11. Bradshaw, T.K.; Blakely, E.J. What are third wave state economic development efforts? From incentives to industrial policy. Econ. Dev. Q. **1999**, *13* (3), 229–244.
12. Fisher, R.C. The effects of state and local public services on economic development. N. Engl. Econ. Rev. **1997**, 53–65, March/April.
13. Chi, K.S.; Leatherby, D. *State Business Incentives: Trends and Options for the Future*; Council of State Governments: Lexington, 1997.
14. Bozeman, B. Expanding the mission of state economic development. Issues Sci. Technol. **2000–2001**, *17*, 33–36, Winter.

Economic Efficiency

Brian E. Dollery
University of New England, Armidale, New South Wales, Australia

Joe L. Wallis
University of Otago, Dunedin, New Zealand

INTRODUCTION

Economic efficiency is defined in three main ways in economic discourse. First, technical or productive efficiency refers to the use of resources in the technologically most efficient manner. Obtaining the maximum possible output(s) from a given set of inputs, or technically efficient production, was first defined with precision by Farrell[1] and approximates what laypeople commonly conceive of as "best practice" in production. A somewhat looser term, covering the social and technological dimensions of productive activity, was subsequently developed by Leibenstein[2] and took the name "X-inefficiency." Leibenstein[2] argued that although X-inefficiency (sometimes also termed organizational slack) derives primarily from a lack of motivation by productive agents, factors such as the incomplete specification of labor contracts, incomplete knowledge of production functions, and the lack of complete markets for some inputs, including market information, can also explain the existence of X-inefficiency. The second measure of economic efficiency, known as allocative efficiency, refers to the efficient distribution of productive resources among alternative uses so as to produce the optimal mix of output. In the jargon of economics, under conditions of "perfect competition," the optimal output mix arises through consumers responding to prices that reflect the true costs of production, or "marginal costs." Allocative efficiency thus involves an interaction between the productive capacity and consumption activity of society. Dynamic or intertemporal efficiency represents the third way of defining economic efficiency. The notion of dynamic efficiency can be traced to Joseph Schumpeter's[3] emphasis on innovation and his argument that the perfectly competitive conditions of allocative and productive efficiency were not necessarily the most conducive to long-term innovation and economic growth. In contrast to productive efficiency and allocative efficiency, dynamic efficiency is a much less precise concept with no universally agreed upon formal definition. In general terms, dynamic efficiency refers to the economically efficient usage of scarce resources through time, and thus, it embraces allocative and productive efficiency in an intertemporal dimension.

BACKGROUND INFORMATION

Economics is said to be founded on the acultural and ahistorical principle of relative scarcity. In this sense, relative scarcity characteristically refers to the universal relationship between limited means and unlimited wants representative of the human condition. Available means or resources are thus scarce relative to the various ends to which they can be devoted, which necessarily implies economizing in the allocation and use of scarce resources. If means were unlimited, or human wants limited, then efficiency in the use of resources would not be necessary. But, given the pervasive existence of relative scarcity in the real world, the efficient employment of limited productive means to fulfill unlimited consumption wants becomes a critical issue. It is thus clear that the concept of efficiency plays a central role in economic analysis and economic discourse.

Interaction between "rational maximizing economic agents" occurs within the context of exchange relationships, with the market mechanism acting as the basic coordinating structure. Although economics focuses on voluntary interaction in exchange relationships, it is important to emphasize that other coordinating mechanisms coexist with exchange relationships in human society. Kenneth Boulding,[4] in his *Ecodynamics*, distinguishes between three broad groups of social organizers. First, the "threat system," based on interaction of the type "you do something I want, or I will do something you do not want," underlies the existence of organized government, thus providing for the existence and enforcement of property rights and other legal entitlements and obligations. Second, the "integrative system" embraces such things as love and hate, altruism, affection, and so forth, and consequently, generates social structures like the family, community, and nation, which serve to foster and legitimize the operations of the threat and

Encyclopedia of Public Administration and Public Policy
DOI: 10.1081/E-EPAP 120010874

exchange systems. Finally, and in direct contrast to the threat system, the "exchange system" is based on mutual gain epitomized by interaction of the type "you do something for me, and I will do something for you." Exchange or market relationships are thus premised on the twin notions of voluntarism and mutual benefit.

Given the historical existence of market interaction involving the voluntary transfer of property rights between buyers and sellers, economic theory must explain why exchange relationships arise and endure. In essence, it is argued that rational maximizing economic agents exchange property rights through the market mechanism, because they benefit from such exchange. Mutual benefits occur due to the gains from trade accruing to all market participants as a consequence of the law of comparative advantage. The law of comparative advantage holds that individuals, firms, and nations can raise their incomes by specializing in that sphere of economic activity where they possess a greater degree of relative (and not absolute) efficiency, and by exchanging property rights for the output of other economic agents specializing in areas where they, in turn, possess a greater degree of relative efficiency.

While microeconomic theory is centrally concerned with the behavioral implications of the universal existence of relative scarcity, microeconomic policy focuses on measures designed to reduce the extent of scarcity and to alter the burden of scarcity among members of society. Put differently, microeconomic policy seeks to diminish the degree of relative scarcity by improving economic efficiency and to redistribute the burden of scarcity by modifying income differences between individuals. For example, the program of privatization in the United Kingdom, public sector reform in New Zealand, and airline deregulation in Australia represent cases of efficiency—enhancing microeconomic policies. By way of contrast, federal government efforts aimed at the equalization of the financial capacities of the various provinces and territories in Canadian fiscal federalism, drought relief programs in South Africa, and unemployment benefit systems in Western Europe, are instances of microeconomic policy interventions directed at redistributing the burden of scarcity among different individuals and groups in society. Thus, whereas microeconomic theory attempts to explain how markets work, microeconomic policy deals with how well markets can work.

Economic efficiency is defined in the following three main ways in economic discourse.

PRODUCTIVE EFFICIENCY

First, technical or productive efficiency refers to the use of resources in the technologically most efficient man-

ner. Obtaining the maximum possible output(s) from a given set of inputs, or technically efficient production, was first defined with precision by Farrell[1] and approximates what laypeople commonly conceive of as "best practice" in production. A somewhat looser term, covering the social and technological dimensions of productive activity, was subsequently developed by Leibenstein[2] and took the name "X-inefficiency." Leibenstein[2] argued that although X-inefficiency (sometimes also termed organizational slack) derives primarily from a lack of motivation by productive agents, factors such as the incomplete specification of labor contracts, incomplete knowledge of production functions, and the lack of complete markets for some inputs, including market information, can also explain the existence of X-inefficiency.

Regardless of whether we accept productive efficiency or the broader concept of X-inefficiency, this notion of economic efficiency is insufficient, because the efficient production of goods does not consider the consumption desires of society. It is pointless to produce goods efficiently if people would rather consume some other combination of goods. Accordingly, additional measures of economic efficiency are necessary.

ALLOCATIVE EFFICIENCY

The second measure of economic efficiency, known as allocative efficiency, refers to the efficient distribution of productive resources among alternative uses so as to produce the optimal mix of output. In the jargon of economics, under conditions of "perfect competition," the optimal output mix arises through consumers responding to prices that reflect the true costs of production, or "marginal costs." Allocative efficiency thus involves an interaction between the productive capacity and consumption activity of society.

Historically, economic theory has been chiefly concerned with allocative efficiency, and only in recent times, has attention been focused on productive or X-efficiency. Perhaps the main reason for this is the central position traditionally occupied by the perfectly competitive model in neoclassical theory. Under perfect competition, market forces ensure an absence of X-inefficiency, because, with decreasing returns, firms must produce at the minimum point of long-run average cost. Any producer that exhibits X-inefficiency will thus not pass the "survival of the fittest" test.

A major accomplishment of economic theory resides in the establishment and refinement of the properties of allocative efficiency. Two approaches to the problem of allocative efficiency have been developed.

Pigouvian Approach

First, the partial equilibrium or Marshallian approach represents the primary method of studying particular markets in isolation. This technique examines the equilibrium conditions in a single market on the assumption that the prices of all other commodities and factors of production are given. It is evident that a partial equilibrium approach does not allow for feedback effects between markets. In practice, the partial equilibrium or Marshallian approach is especially suitable for markets with output that is not a significant item in total expenditure or highly substitutable for any other single commodity.

In terms of the Marshallian approach, the conditions for allocative efficiency were first specified by Pigou.[5] In essence, Pigou argued that allocative efficiency occurred when the benefit to society of consuming some good or service exactly equaled its cost to society. In technical language, allocative efficiency for private goods occurs where marginal social benefit equals marginal social cost; that is, no divergence between private and social benefits and costs exists. In intuitive terms, this means that the resultant price and quantity accurately reflect the degree of relative scarcity for this good or service.

Paretian Approach

The second major approach to the problem of allocative deficiency is the general equilibrium or Walrasian approach, which examines equilibrium conditions in all markets simultaneously. Because all markets are analyzed at the same time, interrelationships between markets and feedback effects occupy a central position in the general equilibrium approach.

Whether a partial or general equilibrium approach should be employed depends largely on the problem at hand. For instance, if the primary concern is a proposed policy change that has a direct impact on many sectors of the economy simultaneously, then a general equilibrium approach is clearly appropriate. An example of this kind of problem would be the introduction of, or modifications to, general sales tax. On the other hand, if the main concern was a proposed policy change that has a direct effect on only one sector, then a partial equilibrium analysis would probably suffice. Excise taxes on items such as cigarettes and liquor constitute examples of this type of problem.

In terms of the general equilibrium or Walrasian approach, the conditions for allocative efficiency are somewhat more complex. In fact, allocative efficiency in the general equilibrium context requires the simultaneous concurrence of three conditions. First, economic efficiency in production must occur such that no intersectoral reallocation of resources can increase the output of any economic good without decreasing the output of some other economic good. In economic jargon, this means that the marginal rates of technical efficiency of input factors must be equal in all production sectors at current factor market prices. Second, economic efficiency in consumption must occur such that no interpersonal reallocation of commodities can increase the well-being (or utility) of some consumer without decreasing the well-being of some other consumer. In technical terms, the marginal rates of substitution for all goods and services must be equal for all consumers at prevailing market prices. And finally, overall economic efficiency in production and consumption requires an optimal conformity between economic efficiency in production and economic efficiency in consumption, such that a change in the composition of output cannot increase the utility (or satisfaction derived from consumption) of some consumer without decreasing the utility of some other consumer. In technical language, a given set of market-determined prices will equal the marginal rate of transformation in production and the common marginal rates of substitution in consumption. If these three conditions are met, then society is said to have achieved high-level optimality in the sense that allocative efficiency occurs in all spheres of economic activity.

Walrasian general equilibrium is said to be Pareto efficient in the sense that it is impossible to improve anyone's welfare by altering production or consumption without impairing someone else's welfare. The concept of Pareto efficiency derives from the work of Vilfredo Pareto,[6] in his 1906 *Manual of Political Economy*, and forms the basis of much of contemporary welfare economics. A central proposition of neoclassical welfare economics holds that if all prices are market determined, then a Pareto-efficient general equilibrium will ensue. In other words, the operation of competitive markets in a capitalist economy automatically ensures that allocative efficiency will occur in all markets. No corrective intervention by governments can improve upon this outcome, because it is already Pareto efficient.

DYNAMIC OR INTERTEMPORAL EFFICIENCY

Dynamic or intertemporal efficiency represents the third way of defining economic efficiency. The notion of dynamic efficiency can be traced to Joseph Schumpeter's[3] emphasis on innovation and his argument that the perfectly competitive conditions of allocative and productive efficiency were not necessarily the most conducive to long-term innovation and economic growth. In contrast to productive efficiency and allocative efficiency, dynamic efficiency is a much less precise concept with no universally agreed upon formal definition. In general terms, dynamic efficiency refers to the economically efficient usage of scarce resources through time, and thus, it embraces allocative and productive efficiency in an intertemporal dimension. Sometimes, the concept of dynamic efficiency is given more specific meaning in the literature. For instance, the macroeconomic debate on the optimal rate of saving, or the decision to postpone some part of current consumption to a future date, has been referred to as intertemporal efficiency. Similarly, the comparative institutions approach, often associated with New Institutional Economics, focuses on the efficiency of alternative institutional arrangements at exhausting the welfare gains attendant upon exchange relationships.[7]

REFERENCES

1. Farrell, M.J. The measurement of productive efficiency. J.R. Stat. Soc. **1957**, *120* (Part III), 253–282.
2. Leibenstein, H. Allocative v. X-efficiency. Am. Econ. Rev. **1966**, *56* (2), 394–407.
3. Schumpeter, J.A. *Capitalism, Socialism and Democracy*; Allen and Unwin: London, 1943.
4. Boulding, K.E. *Ecodynamics*; Sage: New York, 1978.
5. Pigou, A.C. *The Economics of Welfare*; Macmillan: London, 1920.
6. Pareto, V. *Manual of Political Economy*; Girard and Briere: Paris, 1906.
7. Vira, B. The political coase theorem: Identifying differences between neoclassical and critical institutions. J. Econ. Issues **1977**, *31* (3), 761–789.

Economic Theories of Public Leadership

Brian E. Dollery
University of New England, Armidale, New South Wales, Australia

Joe L. Wallis
University of Otago, Dunedin, New Zealand

INTRODUCTION

The concentration of the operational authority over public organizations in the hands of chief executives (CEs) is a striking feature of the new public management (NPM) that has emerged from about two decades of public sector reform in English-speaking nations. This article is concerned with the extent to which the new-styled CEs should be expected to exercise leadership and management.

NEW PUBLIC MANAGEMENT AND ORGANIZATIONAL LEADERSHIP

Although there are variations in the way NPM has been applied in different countries, it generally moves away from a traditional, highly prescriptive, administrative framework by emphasizing the importance of "hands-on" professional management and the "freedom to manage," the introduction of performance appraisal with explicit performance standards, and a greater use of output controls with their stress on results rather than procedures.

The restructuring required to implement these doctrines has often been radical as large bureaucratic structures have been broken up into "single-objective, trackable and manageable units"[1] within which it is easier to match resources to defined tasks and to shift from controlling input to monitoring output. This reflects a fundamental realignment of the core administrative values that are embodied in organizational design. According to Hood,[1] the quest to implement the doctrines of NPM may advance what he calls the "sigma-type" cluster of administrative values that highlight "economy" and "parsimony," even where this makes it more difficult to realize "theta-type" values of "honesty" and "fairness," and "lambda-type" values of "security" and "resilience."

Numerous researchers have pointed out that NPM has been influenced as much by economic theories as by management theories. For example, Hood[1] argued that the core doctrines of NPM are derived from a "marriage of two different streams of ideas"—economics, especially new institutional economics and public choice theory, with their emphasis on contractual solutions to agency problems in the public sector, and "managerialism," with its emphasis on a "professional management" that is "portable," "paramount," "discretionary," "central," and "indispensable."

The compatibility of these two streams stems from the way economic contractualism seeks to depoliticize the CE's role so that they can be "freed to manage" through the application to public organizations of "best practices" developed in the private sector. If economic theory sees the public sector as a vertical chain of principal–agent relationships, then the goal of NPM-style reforms is to delineate accountability for "outcomes," "outputs," and "inputs." This process has been carried furthest in New Zealand where the State Sector Act of 1988 made Cabinet ministers accountable for "outcomes" so that they would have to contract with specific agents, including the CEs of government departments, to supply the "outputs" they deemed necessary to achieve these "outcomes." The CEs could then be made accountable for the delivery of these outputs, but given the discretion to manage their inputs and delivery mechanisms in the manner they deemed to be most efficient. Through successive funding cuts it was hoped that these CEs would be placed under relentless pressure to save costs by restructuring their organizations.

The staff redundancies in the organizations being restructured have often been substantial. However, the costs incurred by redundant staff, in retraining for and seeking new jobs, and by the state, in providing them with income support while they are unemployed, are typically not internalized by the CEs of the restructured organizations. These officials are more likely to take into account the transaction costs involved in establishing the contractual and accounting systems designed to make them accountable for the efficiency with which they deliver specified "outputs." To rationalize the restructuring required to implement NPM, they can draw on both

Encyclopedia of Public Administration and Public Policy
DOI: 10.1081/E-EPAP 120010878

economic theories and managerialism to argue that a shift to NPM enables their organizations to potentially realize "productivity gains" with a net present value that exceeds these transactions costs.

Managerialism does, however, differ from economic theories in terms of the way it relates these productivity gains to the quality of leadership exercised by the CEs responsible for transforming public organizations according to NPM principles. Although economists have traditionally neglected the study of leadership, managerialists have been able to draw from extensive studies in management and organizational behavior that have identified leadership as having a significant impact on organizational performance, particularly during periods of discontinuous organizational change.[2]

In surveying this literature, Bryman[3] pointed out that there as many definitions as there are theories of organizational leadership. This is because leadership is a multifaceted phenomenon so that the definition can often do no more than highlight the aspects of the phenomenon that the subsequent theorizing sets out to elaborate. We recognize this by advancing a definition of leadership that brings together the political and social aspects that are the subject of a range of other leadership theories. We then show how economic theory can be modified to explain the social influence aspect. We then argue, by way of conclusion, that there is a need to look beyond economics to explain the irreducibly political dimension of leadership in order to assess the contractualist view that the role of the CE should be depoliticized.

THEORIZING FROM DEFINITIONS OF LEADERSHIP

Many writers on organizational leadership seek to define this phenomenon in a way that distinguishes it from "management." Two aspects of leadership are often highlighted. The first is reflected in the oft-quoted slogan that "management is about doing things right while leadership is about doing the right thing." This focuses on the judgment-making aspect of leadership. To exercise leadership in these terms, a CE must make judgments that affect the direction of an organization's development. Interpretive studies of leadership[4] stress the political dimension of this judgment-making process. They depict leaders as making these judgments through their involvement in the multidimensional processes of social interaction through which acceptable meanings of issues, events, and actions are created and sustained.

Second, many writers conceive leadership as a distinctive type of social influence relationship. To lead is to influence, guide, engage a following, and build their commitment to realize a particular vision. According to Tichy and Devanna,[5] leadership involves pulling an organization into the future "by creating a positive view of what the organization can become and simultaneously providing emotional support for individuals during the transition process."

For CEs to be said to be exercising leadership in this way, they must be striving to influence the intrinsic and not just the extrinsic motivation of actual and potential followers. As CEs, they will be in a position to exercise "reward power" by using extrinsic rewards to induce subordinates to perform the tasks they set them, or "coercive power" by administering a set of extrinsic penalties for noncompliance with their directions. They cannot be said to be exercising leadership per se if they choose to exercise only these forms of power. Leadership more essentially involves influencing the intrinsic motivation of followers, through processes of "internalization" when they amplify values and beliefs that are shared by both leaders and followers, and "identification" when they engage in behaviors that reinforce and strengthen the sense of personal identification and loyalty that followers place in them.

Comparative studies have often found these processes to be more advanced in private than in traditional public organizations. For example, a Canadian study by Zussman and Jabes[6] found that the percentage of middle managers who reported that their chief executive officers provided leadership in these ways was significantly lower in public organizations than private organizations, and that the level of public service leadership falls off much more rapidly as one goes down the organization than is the case in the private sector. The implication of these studies is that the implementation of NPM may give the CEs of public organizations the opportunity to close this "leadership gap" by adopting private sector best practices.

In this article, we attempt to elaborate a definition of leadership that brings both its political and social influence aspects together. Accordingly, we propose that a CE can be said to be exercising leadership when this official makes judgments about the direction in which an organization should be moving in a way that engages the hopes of its members to a degree that induces them to strive together to move the organization in this direction. We also propose that economic theory can only make a contribution to understanding this concept of leadership if it is initially assumed that the judgment about organizational direction has already been made. This assumption can later be relaxed when we consider the implications the judgment-making process has for the politics–administration dichotomy.

THE ENACTMENT PROCESS

Once leaders have made a judgment about the direction in which they want to steer the organization, they will need to engage its members by calling them together, at all levels of the organization, to consider how they are to enact their leaders' judgment and advance their quest. This enactment process can therefore set in motion interactions that can take the form of "expression games." According to Goffman,[7] these involve "senders" who express themselves in particular ways and "receivers" who take in and react to such expressions, forming an impression of the "senders." The expression games generated by the enactment process can give participants the opportunity to express the hope they have placed in the leader's quest.

The CEs of large public organizations will typically only be able to engage directly in such expression games in interactions that bring together actors at higher levels of the organization. These interactions can, however, serve two functions. First, they can give the CEs the opportunity to model the behavior they expect of "followers." Second, they can give other participants the opportunity to identify themselves as such followers. A "follower" in this context is someone whose hopes are aligned with those of the leader. To a varying degree, such followers can look to the leader to strengthen their hopes. The leaders can also look to those followers who leave an impression of their trustworthiness to reproduce these expression games in interactions at lower levels of the organization.

Through the reproduction of these expression games, the enactment process may be accompanied by a diffusion of leadership and a development of a following at all these levels. To understand why this may have a significant impact on the organization's culture and performance, we need to examine the motivational effect of the hopes that are evoked and influenced through this process.

AN ECONOMIC THEORY OF HOPE AND LEADERSHIP

The traditional reluctance of economists to study the social influence aspect of leadership may have been based on the perception that, in seeking to influence followers, leaders are trying to change their preferences. The study of leadership would therefore seem to be out of bounds

to the majority of economists who subscribe to the convention that economic analysis should either 1) take the preferences of individuals as given and not look inside the "black box" within which they are formed and transformed; or 2) assume that they are stable and explain apparent preference change in terms of adjustments in the shadow prices of inputs in household production functions.[8]

However, attempts have been made by Hermalin[9] and Casson[10] to analyze how leaders can influence followers by inducing them to internalize the externalities of their discretionary effort decisions. Hermalin[9] argued that situations of asymmetric information may ironically give leaders the opportunity to alleviate the weak incentives followers have to supply effort to a team when they cannot be compensated according to their individual contributions. In these situations, leadership by example may be interpreted as a signal that leaders have better information about the value of effort devoted to their common activity so that "the harder the leader works, the harder the followers work."

This model is, to some extent, complemented by an earlier one[10] in which the effect on individual utility functions of the emotions of shame and guilt followers experience when they fail to internalize effort externalities, is susceptible to "moral manipulation" through rhetoric the leader addresses to the group as a whole. Casson went on to show how leaders can compare the net benefits of raising the intensity of moral manipulation with those associated with more intense monitoring in a group in which individuals have varying "moral sensitivities."

In our view, neither model lays an adequate foundation to explain how CEs can influence the hopes that followers place in their quest to move the organization in a particular direction. The general approach Elster[11] recommended in his article, "The Emotions and Economic Theory," may be more helpful in this regard. Elster basically argued that economists should reject this simple cost–benefit approach to modeling the effect of the emotions on behavior in favor of one, derived from cognitive dissonance theory, that views an emotion as a particular type of action tendency engendered by antecedent beliefs and the investment of emotional energy.

This perspective may explain why the members of an organization who have focused their hopes on advancing a quest to realize a particular vision may have an action tendency to interact in a way that reinforces their beliefs and enhances their emotional energy. These hopes will be based on beliefs that the advancement of the quest is "neither impossible nor inevitable" and that it is "worthwhile" or "important" in the sense that it is worthy of pursuit in a special way incommensurable with other goals.

If one cannot hope without holding a belief in the worth and possibility of advancing the quest that is the object of hope, it would seem that to hope is to locate oneself in a "space of questions" about both these beliefs and the authenticity of one's claims to hold them. These questions may give rise to a dissonance that can only be alleviated by engaging in interactions with actors who can both supply clearer, more articulate reasons for holding the beliefs that trigger hope and opportunities to authenticate these beliefs by striving to advance the quest in which this hope is placed. Leader–follower relationships will thus emerge in groups where one person, the leader, plays a focal role in supplying such "reasons" and "opportunities."

The extent to which the process of enacting the judgments of a CE engages the hopes of an organization's members may thus be gauged in terms of the way it draws leader–follower groups into a network that penetrates every level of the organization. To understand how the expression games pursued in such groups can enhance the capacity of their members to supply effort toward advancing the CE's quest, it may be helpful to refer to Collins'[12] theory of "Emotional Energy as the Common Denominator in Rational Social Action."

Collins focuses on the reinforcement and strengthening of emotional energy that occurs when "interaction rituals" (IRs) pass thresholds of "boundedness" and "density." Leader–follower expression games may pass the threshold of boundedness when they give participants the opportunity to express an observable "passion" to advance shared hopes. Where such interactions also pass the "threshold of density" such that the participants are close enough for a sufficient period of time to ensure that they can be moved by one another's passion, the participating group's focus of attention and common emotional mood is likely to go through a short-term cycle of increase and mutual stimulation until a point of emotional satiation is reached. The interaction will leave each participant with an "energetic afterglow" that "gradually decreases over time" so that individuals have an incentive to reinvest their emotional energy in subsequent interactions. It may therefore accumulate across IRs so that "an individual may build up a long-term fund of confidence and enthusiasm by repeated participation in successful IRs."[12]

The leader–follower expression GAMES that are set in motion during an enactment process may thus significantly boost the emotional energy reserves of followers throughout the organization. This concept of leadership differs from that advanced by Hermalin and Casson in that it emphasizes the influence of leadership on the capacity rather than the willingness of an organization's members to supply effort in excess of that for which they can be monitored and compensated. As economic theories, all three concepts tend to ignore the complexities involved in the irreducibly political process of judgment making. The implications of this neglect in assessing the leadership role of CEs must be considered by way of conclusion to this article.

CONCLUSION: THE POLITICAL DIMENSION OF PUBLIC SECTOR LEADERSHIP

The process that is resolved when a CE makes a judgment about organizational development would seem to involve the type of "autonomous politics" that, according to Barber,[13] characterizes occasions when "some *action* of *public* consequence becomes *necessary* and when men must thus make a *public choice* that is *reasonable* in the face of *conflict* despite *the absence of an independent ground*" (original emphasis). Moreover, to the extent that this judgment sets in motion an enactment process than transforms the culture of an organization by focusing the hopes of its members on advancing a particular quest, it would seem that there is an irreducibly political dimension to the leadership that steers this process.

This is because there are likely to be competing perspectives on the appropriate culture for a public organization and no independent grounds for judging between them. It would therefore not be reasonable for a CE to make a judgment in this regard without striving to appreciate the divergent perspectives different stakeholders bring to this issue and giving them an adequate opportunity to make case for the values, interests, and perspectives they are seeking to advance.

Significantly, the tenure of a CE may become unsustainable, particularly where they are not entitled to a renewal of fixed-term contracts, when these judgments erode their relations of trust with portfolio ministers. These relationships are likely to be based on mutual impressions of reasonableness. They are clearly more personal and less "arms length" than typical contractual relationships. The view that contractualist reforms of NPM can revive the traditional politic–administration dichotomy therefore seems to break down in the analysis of the leadership role of the CEs of public organizations. This role cannot be exercised outside a political relationship of mutual trust between these CEs and their principals. The political dimension of organizational leadership in the public sector must thus ensure it has to be collectively supplied.

REFERENCES

1. Hood, C.A. Public administration for all seasons? Public Adm. **1991**, *69* (1), 3–19.
2. Bass, B. *Bass and Stogdill's Handbook of Leadership*; Free Press: New York, 1990.
3. Bryman, A. *Leadership and Organisation*; Routledge and Kegan Paul: London, 1986.
4. Kay, R. Leadership and Voluntary Organizations. In *Voluntary Agencies: Challenges of Organization and Management*; Billis, D., Harris, M., Eds.; Macmillan: London, 1996.
5. Tichy, N.; Devanna, M. *The Transformational Leader*; John Wiley and Sons: London, 1986.
6. Zussman, D.; Jabes, J. In *Perceptions of Leadership: A Comparison Between Government and Business Organization*, Paper Presented at RIPA Conference on Government and the Private Sector, Canterbury 1988.
7. Goffman, E. *The Presentation of Self in Everyday Life*; Anchor Books: New York, 1959.
8. Stigler, G.; Becker, G. De Gustibus Non Est Disputandum. Am. Econ. Rev. **1977**, *67* (2), 76–90.
9. Hermalin, B. An economic theory of leadership. Am. Econ. Rev. **1998**, *88* (5), 1188–1206.
10. Casson, M. *Economics of Business Culture: Game Theory, Transactions Costs and Economic Performance*; Clarendon Press: London, 1991.
11. Elster, J. Emotions and economic theory. J. Econ. Lit. **1998**, *36* (1), 47–74.
12. Collins, R. Emotional energy as the common denominator of rational social action. Ration. Soc. **1999**, *5* (2), 203–220.
13. Barber, B. *Strong Democracy: Participatory Politics for a New Age*; University of California Press: Los Angeles, 1984.

Economics, Transaction Cost

Glenn A. Daley
RAND Graduate School, Santa Monica, California, U.S.A.

INTRODUCTION

Transaction cost economics (TCE) is the study of how markets and organizations are affected by the costs of creating and maintaining economic relationships, apart from the production costs of goods and services. The initial concept of TCE was formulated by Ronald H. Coase in 1937,[1] but only developed into a distinct field of study since the early 1970s, in the works of Oliver E. Williamson[2] and others. It has become a cornerstone of the new institutional economics. Starting with the study of transaction costs as economic phenomena, TCE has developed into a broad discipline for the study of governance in organizational and social terms, not just traditionally economic terms.[2]

THEORY OF TCE

It is obvious that transaction costs affect economic choices. However, there is disagreement among economists about the generalizations of TCE regarding organizational and institutional effects. There are also difficulties in defining transaction costs precisely and measuring their aggregate level in a firm or in the national economy. Thus, TCE is a developing field of study; its proponents continue working to refine the theory, test it empirically, and apply it to a widening variety of economic and organizational phenomena.

In a nutshell, the theory of TCE is that firms and other organizations, as well as social institutions and modes of governance, represent various adaptations to the existence of transaction costs. Further, TCE claims that the characteristics of transactions deeply affect the types of governance used in organizations and in society. This provides insight into economic behavior that is not easily explained within the models of classical economics, showing that seemingly inefficient practices might actually perform efficiency-promoting functions in a transaction cost framework. This approach has been applied to phenomena as diverse as contracting for uncut diamonds and theater bookings,[3] the behavior of illicit drug dealers,[4] and even vote trading in the U.S. Congress.[5]

In his essay, Coase asked why firms exist at all, given the classical concept that economic efficiency is best achieved through the market pricing mechanism.[1] A firm is characterized by the fact that it suspends the market pricing mechanism for its own internal relationships, while depending on the market in its external relationships. But what advantage is gained by suspending the market pricing mechanism internally? Why are these particular relationships internalized, whereas others are kept external? The classical notion of economies of scale does not adequately answer these questions. It is conceivable that even a large-scale production technology could be adopted by a "virtual" firm consisting solely of independent contractors, using rented capital equipment, and engaging in competitive market transactions with each other on a daily basis. We almost never see this happen, though, and the question is why not?

Coase's answer was that there are costs to using the market pricing mechanism. A firm can reduce these costs through internalization and integration, producing a certain good or service in-house rather than buying it in the market. This raises another question: If internalization reduces costs, why isn't everything produced by one giant firm? The answer is that integration brings its own penalties, such as increased costs of coordination and supervision, various other kinds of overhead, and the loss of flexibility due to maintaining a permanent workforce instead of hiring contractors by the day. Thus, what matters is finding the level of internalization that minimizes the net of transaction, integration, and production costs. As in much of economics, the emphasis is on comparing alternative choices at the margin, the "differential" transaction costs of a particular organizational structure or mode of governance, as compared with feasible alternatives.

The field of TCE currently faces a broad agenda of empirical research, both to measure different types of transaction costs and to test specific predictions of the theory. Because it is impossible to observe the costs of an alternative not chosen, it has been difficult to quantify differential transaction costs; much of the published literature consists of case studies rather than quantitative studies. But there is an increasing body of quantitative studies with fruitful results.

One such study by Masten, Meehan, and Snyder[6] showed that organization costs represented about 14% of total costs for the acquisition of components by a naval shipbuilder, that internalization of the work currently performed by subcontractors would increase internal

Encyclopedia of Public Administration and Public Policy
DOI: 10.1081/E-EPAP 120011011

organization costs by about 70%, and subcontracting work currently performed internally would result in market organization costs almost triple the current costs. This suggests that the firm has found an optimal level of internalization. This study also confirmed that variations in the cost and governance characteristics of transactions were associated with the level of internalization of those transactions. The researchers found that integration decisions were motivated more by their effects on internal organization costs than by their effects on market mechanism costs. This empirical result supports a broader view of TCE as including not only direct market costs, but also all costs associated with alternative modes of organization.

WHAT ARE TRANSACTION COSTS, AND WHY DO THEY OCCUR?

The classical microeconomic model focuses on production costs—the capital, labor, and raw materials that go into creating goods and providing services. In contrast, transaction costs include the costs of locating and evaluating goods, buyers, and sellers; the costs of negotiating and making contracts; and the costs of monitoring and enforcing the terms of contracts over time. The idea of a transaction cost is easily seen in examples such as brokerage and banking fees, sales commissions, and the expense of hiring attorneys to review contracts. However, the concept also includes costs incurred in the process of creating and maintaining alternative arrangements for the governance of transactions.

Whereas classical economics treats management costs as a high-level labor input to production, TCE treats management and other integration costs as the costs of internal transactions. Integration costs (i.e., internal transaction costs) are distinct from the more obvious category of market-related transaction costs, and attempts have been made to measure them independently. But both categories must be considered. Internal transaction costs, including management, are substitutes for market costs; in other words, they are the costs of choosing integration rather than the market pricing mechanism as a mode for organizing economic activities. Thus, transaction costs are any costs that arise from the need to create and govern economic relationships between parties, whether they result directly from transactions or indirectly from the type of structure adopted to govern transactions.

Bounded Rationality and Opportunism

In the classical model, a transaction is a simple event. Both buyer and seller know everything they need to know. The choice of trading partners is based on price alone, but because competition forces the price to be the same for everyone, all sellers are interchangeable, and all buyers are interchangeable. Every good is purchased in separate transactions, with no bundling or tying together of goods. There are no linkages between transactions across time; tomorrow's purchase depends only on tomorrow's price and not on the terms of today's transaction. Both parties can specify exactly what they want from the exchange, and observe instantly whether it is satisfied. The transaction is concluded as money and goods change hands, so there is no need for enforcement after the fact. Due to all these features, the transaction is frictionless and costless.

These assumptions are clearly unrealistic for numerous reasons, but transaction cost economists emphasize two key problems. First is the fact that people are limited in their ability to know and control every detail necessary to achieve their intended outcomes. Where the classical model assumes human rationality, the new approach assumes only *bounded rationality*, a term introduced by Herbert Simon[7] to indicate human fallibility in the context of rational intentions. Many transactions result in unsatisfactory outcomes because the parties cannot predict the future, know all the relevant facts, and control every detail; knowing this, buyers expect vendors to provide customer service departments, warranties, and return policies.

The second problem is that people tend to take advantage of situations for their own benefit, especially any ambiguity in the terms of an agreement or any lack of observation by the other parties to an agreement. This tendency is called *opportunism*. It includes fraud, deception, and misconduct, but it also includes the many subtle ways that people find to manipulate transactions for their own self-interest. An example is an employment relationship where employees are tempted to shirk responsibilities whenever a supervisor is not looking and an employer is tempted to pressure employees to work additional hours without claiming overtime.

These problems have been addressed to some extent by accommodating new assumptions into the classical model, leading to what is called the neoclassical model. For instance, instead of assuming that the buyer knows what is being purchased and receives it without risk, we say that the buyer has expectations about the utility to be received and adjusts demand in light of the risk. The new model also accommodates asymmetric information, where one of the parties cannot observe all relevant information about the good. Examples include quality in the case of a complex good such as a used car, performance in the case of a service such as auto repair, and responsible behavior in the case of insured risks such as driving safety. Problems such as these are labeled *adverse selection*—the effect of unobserved information on market choices prior to the transaction—or *moral hazard*—the effect of unobservability on behavior after the transaction.

The neoclassical approach emphasizes structuring the terms of a transaction in advance so as to obtain the best expected return considering these risks. In employment and other performance contracts, the approach of structuring incentives to motivate the optimal response from other parties is called the *principal–agent* model. For example, an employment contract may include both a fixed wage and a variable bonus contingent upon the output of a work team; the bonus places part of the risk of nonperformance on the employee, and thus creates an incentive not to shirk.

According to TCE, these elements of the neoclassical approach still do not solve many aspects of the problems of bounded rationality and opportunism, and inadequately describe the ways in which people adapt to these problems in the real world. Asymmetric information models address some but not all the difficulties of *observing* the performance of a contract. However, they do not address the difficulty of *specifying* the performance of a contract. Many economic relationships, such as construction contracts, depend on highly complex and uncertain plans for the future. In other cases, such as personal services, the expected outcome may be a highly subjective experience. In such cases, it may not be possible—or affordable—for a buyer to specify in perfect detail what would constitute the expected outcome of the transaction.

Incomplete Contracts

A contract that specifies every possible detail of its fulfillment and how that fulfillment will be recognized, so that there is no room for opportunism or unanticipated error, is called a *complete* contract. All other contracts are *incomplete*. It is obvious that we seldom do business using complete contracts. The purchase of a simple object that can be inspected at the time of the sale, perhaps an apple or a greeting card, is based on an unwritten complete contract. But where there are hidden qualities, even in something as simple as a bottle of soda or an article of clothing, we rely not on the completeness of contracts but on other aspects of the relationship. We consider such factors as our familiarity with the vendor, our recognition of a commercial brand, and our trust in the truth of labels. Even a lengthy contract for a major industrial project cannot specify every eventuality; rather, it specifies a *process* for resolving unspecified issues during the life of the contract. In TCE, such dispute resolution processes, truth-in-labeling regulations, commercial brands, and ongoing vendor relationships are recognized as substitutes for complete contracts.

Contracts become even more complex and costly when they are connected to other transactions. This is clear when different goods must interact, such as computer hardware and software; critical elements of one contract may depend on the fulfillment of other contracts with different parties, multiplying the consequences of bounded rationality and opportunism. There is also interconnectedness in multiple transactions with the same partner. When a transaction is repeated many times, uncertainty is reduced and the contract becomes a matter of mutual understanding, making it costly to switch vendors even to obtain a lower price. The terms of contracts may be modified on the basis of expectations about later transactions, while the terms of subsequent contracts may be altered due to previous experiences, so that a transaction becomes part of a pattern of favors granted or withheld over time. Thus, the transacted price of a good or service can deviate considerably from the market price.

Asset Specificity

Another characteristic of transactions, closely related to the above characteristics of complexity and repetition, is called *asset specificity*. It describes the degree to which a good, service, vendor, or employee cannot be interchanged with other goods, services, vendors, or employees. At one level of specificity, semiconductor fabricating equipment cannot be interchanged with metalworking machine tools; at an even higher level, the dies used in manufacturing a firm's proprietary product cannot be exchanged with dies from other firms. With regard to employment contracts, an accountant cannot be interchanged with a mechanic. An accountant with many years of experience in a firm has knowledge that cannot be replaced even by hiring another accountant from outside. Furthermore, the accountant with such inside knowledge is more valuable to this particular employer than he or she would be to a different employer.

Clearly, the higher the degree of asset specificity, the greater the mutual dependence between the parties to a transaction. In such a dependent relationship, one or both of the parties would lose value by switching partners, and thus has an incentive to maintain the relationship. Because people are forward looking and rational, but aware of bounded rationality and opportunism, they will form contracts to balance the potential cost of losing such relationships with the ongoing costs of maintaining the relationships. Both of these costs are high where asset specificity is high; both are low where asset specificity is low. Thus, the employment contract for a high-level systems engineer with knowledge of proprietary technologies involves higher transaction costs, and more complex organizational arrangements, than the contract for a janitor.

GOVERNANCE AND ORGANIZATIONS

As a result of bounded rationality and opportunism, we generally recognize that we cannot depend on commitments others make or expect others to depend on commitments we make. There are social settings where a person's word is taken as a dependable bond, but closer study reveals that members of such communities depend on cultural norms or institutions and their ongoing relationships with each other to guarantee these commitments. People use diverse and creative methods to establish the credibility of commitments in advance, perhaps by making visible, irreversible investments or by setting up structural impediments to opportunistic mind changing. These methods often involve behavior that does not fit well into a competitive market model. Identifying such nonmarket guarantees of commitments in our society is one of the major contributions of TCE and new institutional economics.

The neoclassical approach focuses on the incentives and uncertainties in the contract itself, and emphasizes the design of the contract prior to its adoption. It assumes that people attempt to solve the problems of uncertainty and motivation in the terms of the contract. However, even under carefully structured incentives, there will be incomplete contracts and windows for opportunism. The neoclassical model assumes that contracts are well specified and can be enforced in courts of law. Where even this remedy breaks down and the parties cannot find a way to make satisfactory enforceable contracts, there must be some kind of market failure. There will be no agreement and thus no market; or there will be an agreement with externalities in which some part of the burden of noncompliance falls on parties without their consent, and thus not captured within the agreed-upon price.

However, the TCE model acknowledges the incompleteness of contracts, placing them in the context of ongoing economic relationships. Thus, in addition to the incentive structure of the contract, it examines the nature of the ongoing relationship and describes how the contract is governed over time. Clearly, resolving conflicts through the courts is expensive, and most of the time we use less costly arrangements or institutions, such as personal negotiation, mediation, and arbitration. Within a community of individuals or interacting organizations, much governance can be carried out through social influence, reputation effects, and informal rewards and punishments. Within a firm, governance of internal transactions can be carried out through direct supervision with explicit power to reward and punish.

In fact, one of the defining characteristics of a firm is the degree of control it has over its assets and its employees.[8] This control is largely free from oversight by the legal system, much more so than in the case of external market transactions. This brings us back to Coase's initial question about the existence of firms. Now we can say that firms provide a structure for governance that is an alternative to the market system and the legal system. Internalization

occurs when the total of transaction costs, including integration costs, governance costs, and the potential costs of unfulfilled contracts, can be reduced by bringing transactions inside the firm's control.

Although it focuses on the transaction, TCE provides a powerful tool for the analysis of organizations. A firm is not just a contract, it is a long-term organizational structure for making and governing contracts, one of the many types of arrangement available. In contrast to the principal–agent approach that focuses on designing a contract to optimize its expected outcomes, the TCE approach shows that the very choice of the organizational structure in which contracts are embedded is an adaptation to the incompleteness of contracts. This adaptation can be understood as optimizing the expected net of transaction costs, integration costs, governance costs, and the costs of unfulfilled contracts over a long-term sequence of many transactions.

Such adaptations are not limited to the polar extremes of hierarchical firm versus competitive market. Many large firms are not strictly hierarchical in practice; the study of management control systems provides insights into the practical task of governing transactions within firms to obtain the motivational advantages of market competition and incentives without losing the cooperative and transaction cost advantages of hierarchical organization.[9] There is a broad range of hybrid types of governance combining various elements of hierarchical integration and competitive market pricing. Claude Menard[10] outlined how labor arrangements in organizations may vary between quasimarkets and direct hierarchies, with other forms in between, depending on the nature of the transactions, especially their uncertainty and asset specificity.

In addition, different types of adaptation occur at different stages in the same contract. Before a long-term contract is awarded, the process of obtaining competitive bids is essentially a market process; at that stage, the bidders are more or less interchangeable, and asset specificity has not yet become a concern. Where there are enough bidders and enough opportunities for them to compete, the price for the contract as a package will be determined by a market pricing mechanism. In what is called the *fundamental transformation*, the situation changes after the contract is awarded, and the winning bidder establishes an asset-specific long-term relationship requiring nonmarket forms of governance. This transformation clearly happens with large industrial contracts, and to a lesser extent when employees are hired. But transactions such as commodity purchases that lack the characteristics of uncertainty, complexity, and asset specificity do not go through the transformation; they remain governed by the market pricing mechanism and conform more closely to the standard economic models.

PUBLIC ADMINISTRATION AND PUBLIC POLICY IMPLICATIONS

Efficiency in Government

Transaction cost economics suggests that government agencies, as well as firms, are significantly molded by transaction cost effects. Government agencies can be viewed as governance arrangements for public goods transactions, an especially necessary type of governance because of the high incentives for opportunism, called "free riding" in this context. Public sector governance is also affected by asset specificity; many of the human skills and physical assets employed by government could not be interchanged with private sector skills and assets without some loss of value. In public administration, the creative use of marketlike incentives where appropriate can help to make agencies more efficient, but these must be tempered by awareness of the TCE reasons that markets do not work for all types of transactions.

In an era of government reform, devolution, and downsizing, it pays to study how outsourcing and governance decisions are made in the private sector. Major changes in the structure and practices of government organizations inevitably bring about changes in transaction costs. Identifying these costs, and comparing them between existing arrangements and alternative proposals, can make an important contribution to the evaluation of reorganization plans.

Efficiency in Markets

In classical and neoclassical welfare economics, a competitive market equilibrium is regarded as the gold standard of economic efficiency. In this view, any organizational arrangements, social institutions, or economic practices that interfere with or fall short of such an outcome must to that extent be inefficient. For example, the traditional view of antitrust policy has been that unfamiliar or nonstandard business practices must be anticompetitive in intent or effect, and thus inefficient. However, TCE has shown in theory and in several empirical studies of utility markets[10] that surprising and unusual forms of business relationships, hard to account for with standard economic models, can often be explained and justified as efficiency-promoting adaptations to transaction costs and the need for governance of complex long-term relationships. Where this is true, prohibiting such practices through antitrust regulation might increase costs to the consumer, not the effect intended by the regulators.

The theoretical and empirical task of applying TCE to various contexts is unfinished. But the antitrust example indicates that at least some apparent market failures are actually adaptations to transaction costs. This suggests that policy makers should consider the economic functions served by existing institutions and relationships, which can then be taken into account in proposing or evaluating government interventions that might alter transaction cost structures.

However, government investments in public goods and externalities that reduce everyone's transaction costs may contribute more to the general welfare than interventions in such apparent market failures. Transactions take place in the context of a society's legal system, its information infrastructure, and its regulatory and tax burdens on business firms. Thus, policies that might increase transaction efficiency across the board include dispute resolution alternatives in the legal system, improved communication and access to information through technology such as the Internet, simplifications of reporting requirements for businesses, programs to retrain workers displaced by economic and technological change that makes their specific skills unneeded. In general, this approach suggests that consumer and business policies should—wherever possible—reduce rather than increase the uncertainty of transactions, and increase rather than reduce the flexibility of parties to govern their own contracts.

REFERENCES

1. Coase, R.H. The nature of the firm. Economica. **November 1937**, *IV*, 386–405.
2. Williamson, O.E. *The Mechanisms of Governance*; Oxford University Press: New York, 1996.
3. Kenney, R.; Klein, B. The economics of block booking. J. Law Econ. **1983 October**, *26*, 497–540.
4. Turvani, M. Illegal Markets and New Institutional Economics. In *Transaction Cost Economics: Recent Developments*; Menard, C., Ed.; Edward Elgar: Cheltenham, UK, 1997; 127–148.
5. Weingast, B.R.; Marshall, W.J. The industrial organization of congress; or, why legislatures, like firms, are not organized as markets. J. Polit. Econ. **1988**, *96* (1), 132–163.
6. Masten, S.E.; Meehan, J.W.; Snyder, E.L. The costs of organization. J. Law Econ. Organ. **Spring 1991**, *7* (1), 1–25.
7. Simon, H. Theories of Bounded Rationality. In *Decision and Organization*; McGuire, C.B., Radner, R., Eds.; American Elsevier: New York, 1972; 161–176.
8. Williamson, O.E. Hierarchies, Markets and Power in the Economy: An Economic Perspective. In *Transaction Cost Economics: Recent Developments*; Menard, C., Ed.; Edward Elgar: Cheltenham, UK, 1997; 1–29.
9. Anthony, R.N.; Govindarajan, V. *Management Control Systems,* 9th Ed.; Irwin McGraw-Hill: New York, 1998.
10. Menard, C. Internal Characteristics of Formal Organizations. In *Transaction Cost Economics: Recent Developments*; Menard, C., Ed.; Edward Elgar: Cheltenham, UK, 1997; 30–58.

Education Policy

Frederick M. Hess
Joleen R. Okun
University of Virginia, Charlottesville, Virginia, U.S.A.

INTRODUCTION

Education policy includes the world of elementary and secondary, postsecondary, and early childhood education. It involves measures ranging from organization of traditional schooling to the setting of college tuition to the provision of programs intended to help nurture preschoolers. In this sense, education policy is the public policy area in which American government is most heavily invested. In 2001, all levels of government—federal, state, and local—spent well in excess of $647 billion on educational provision. Approximately 60% of this amount is devoted to providing K–12 schooling, which serves 33.5 million children, while the remaining 40% of these funds are used to support college and university programs.

During the late 1990s and through 2002, the American public consistently listed education as one of its top two or three national concerns. This marked a sharp break with the nation's past, as schooling (and, by extension, education policy) had traditionally lagged near the bottom of the public's policy concerns. Education began to gain increased attention in the mid-1980s, and it began to move up the list of prominent public concerns during the late 1980s and early 1990s.

EDUCATION POLICY

The substance and shape of U.S. education policy has shifted radically over the course of the nation's history. Government involvement in educational provision was haphazard until the late nineteenth century, and systematic public provision of both K–12 schooling and higher education only took on their contemporary form during the first half of the twentieth century. Before that time, schooling remained primarily a locally funded and locally governed service that rarely attracted significant policy attention. Schools were only standardized at the state level, as sustained federal involvement in higher education did not begin until after World War II and did not begin in K–12 or preschool education until the launch of the Great Society programs in the mid-1960s. In fact, the U.S. Department of Education was not created until 1979. Given the scope and largely decentralized nature of public schooling, affecting change is often difficult. This is especially evident in light of the fact that the United States currently has over 15,000 local school districts and 50 state boards of education that coordinate their efforts with the Department of Education.

Brief History of Education Policy

From the nation's founding, education occupied a central place in the imagination of America's leaders. Founders like Benjamin Rush and Thomas Jefferson championed the importance of an educated citizenry, calling for a system of public schools and the creation of state-supported higher education. Throughout the colonial period and the early nineteenth century, however, education policy consisted of little more than the state supplying land for school houses and a small amount of money to support the operation of grammar schools.

The first important move toward what can more conventionally be understood as ''education policy'' was Horace Mann's crusade as President of the Massachusetts Board of Education (1837–1849) to reform the state's schools, enhance the caliber of teachers, and increase the level of instruction. Much of the support for Mann's effort, and for similar efforts elsewhere, was inspired by a desire to ''Americanize'' the new waves of immigrants populating the United States at that time. In fits and starts, such efforts proceeded across the nation in the latter half of the nineteenth century, as state after state adopted compulsory education programs that required children to attend at least some grammar school. Between 1890 and 1940, these measures were developed into an ongoing commitment to nearly universal education. The population of students attending school and graduating from the K–12 system grew at a dramatic rate, partially propelled by state provisions for compulsory attendance. Although the first such law was passed in 1853, it was not until the turn of the century that an overwhelming majority of states had enacted such legislation.

During this time period, the federal government slowly began to increase its involvement in education policy.

Encyclopedia of Public Administration and Public Policy
DOI: 10.1081/E-EPAP 120011073

This began in 1862, when Congress passed the Morrill Act, a provision that earmarked land to support the construction of public universities across the nation. The act marked the first time the federal government sought to involve itself directly in schooling or education. At the K–12 level, the first significant federal efforts would not occur until 1917, when Congress provided fiscal incentives for vocational education in the form of the Smith–Hughes Act.

Different Forms of Education Policy

Education policy serves a broad range of student needs, encompassing much of a broader role outside traditional K–12 schooling and higher education. In the twentieth century, the federal government began to further address the needs of discrete populations by implementing new programs. Those detailed have been among the most popular and widely cited examples of such interventionism.

Early childhood

The federal government made its first foray into preschool education by establishing the Head Start program for disadvantaged preschool children under the Economic Opportunity Act of 1964. Aimed initially only at poor children, its purpose was to organize programs that would prepare preschool children for elementary school. Money was appropriated through the Office of Economic Opportunity, which made individual grants to cities and other localities to set up Head Start centers. In 1969, the program was transferred to the Department of Health and Human Services. It was later extended to children above the poverty level, whose parents, however, had to pay according to their income.

Special education

It was not until the late 1960s that education policy addressed the equalization of student opportunity throughout the United States. A new concern for persons with disabilities was addressed by the Johnson administration. The watershed in the development of these programs was the federal government's landmark legislation in 1975, entitled the Education for All Handicapped Children Act (EAHCA), which was incorporated into a new law, the Individuals with Disabilities Education Act (IDEA) of 1990. In 1997, Congress reauthorized and amended IDEA, expanding the purpose of the law to emphasize outcome measures for preparing disabled children for

employment and independent living rather than that of merely requiring access to public education.

Changing Governmental Role in Education Policy

The federal government initially served a distributory, rather than a regulatory, role in the American educational system. From the early nineteenth century, Congress issued state land grants to provide for common schools. In conjunction with the federal requirement that all states draft a constitution, this was the only role the federal government played in the establishment and administration of state-run school systems.

Education occupied a prominent place in state constitutions, yet schools were largely locally run. Many voters were distrustful of strong, centralized authority during the nineteenth century and resisted moves toward further state control. Throughout this era, educators sought to replace haphazard standards of teacher training and certification, supervision, and curriculum by consolidating school districts and extending state authority over public education. These efforts led primarily to symbolic efforts that were not standardized throughout the state educational system.

However, with the advent of the Progressive era in the early 1900s, greater standardization was achieved. School leaders used state laws to bureaucratize and centralize public schools. This push for change relied heavily on professional expertise rather than lay participation in decision making. Educators and their allies contended that a modern system of education demanded increased consolidation, standardization, and centralization. In light of this, state legislators enacted such changes in spite of public preference for a more locally run educational system. At this time, schools became more heavily bureaucratized, with state-mandated provisions for curriculum, teacher status, administrative organization, and consolidation.

Shift to centrally dictated outcomes, but increased operational freedom

One of the central reforms in education policy throughout the 1990s was a standards movement, which was implemented as states and school districts sought to enhance student achievement. Although earlier reform movements were characterized by either a "top-down" (i.e., mandates) or "bottom-up" (i.e., local control) approach, standards-based reform combines both approaches to enable states and districts to define the focus and expectations for educational outcomes and to hold educators accountable for meeting these aims. This paradigm involves both a set of clearly defined student performance goals for schools to strive toward (usually content standards), and an accountability system that provides a set of incentives for schools or districts to achieve the standards and accompanying penalties for failing to move toward them (rewards and sanctions). Yet, it also provides districts and schools with greater autonomy to make decisions that they believe will improve instruction and student outcomes. Policy makers recognize that instructional improvement needs to be motivated and developed at the school and classroom level, and they are developing ways to give schools and teachers increased autonomy to make decisions that affect student learning.

New Trends in Education Policy

Accountability

Since the 1990s, a growing number of states have created comprehensive accountability systems designed to increase student learning in public schools. These accountability systems are based on ''high-stakes'' standardized testing of a state curriculum. Local educators face consequences based on how well their students do on these exams. They receive rewards for good student performance and are subject to interventions to rescue children from low-performing schools. This shift toward comprehensive accountability systems includes set goals for student achievement, specific outcome measures for these goals, incentives for educators who yield good student outcomes, and interventions for students who may be underperforming in so-called failing schools.

State policy makers have been reluctant to extend a great deal of flexibility to districts, and are increasing using high-stakes testing to measure student outcome and guide curricular decisions. States for many years have been accumulating testing requirements that their legislatures, state officials, or local administrators have chosen. As these outcome measures continue to be widely used in a growing number of states, assessment has been inextricably aligned with the centralized testing of student achievement with standardized instruments. Student performance goals were made more explicit so that testing could be more precisely focused, and efforts were made to align curricula with the testing.

School choice

As accountability measures are increasingly being used to determine how well public schools are serving students, the issue of providing parents with options to ensure enhanced achievement has also taken flight. During the 1990s, school choice has become a pervasive topic in education policy, as over two-thirds of state legislatures passed provisions allowing the establishment of charter schools.

In 1994, federal charter school legislation was passed that exempts these institutions from state and local regulations that inhibit flexible management, yet provides that these schools be guided by public control. A charter school possesses much greater autonomy than a traditional public school. Charter schools are free from many district, state, and union regulations or requirements, including those governing curriculum, teaching methods, contracting for services and facilities, and the hiring of personnel. In exchange, charter schools are held accountable for student performance. Yet, although charter schools have moved to a national forum as a form of school reform, this movement has developed in different ways and at varying rates at the state and local level. The federal government has had only a limited role in the development of charter schools, leaving state charter legislation broad and varied. Such measures may constrain who is eligible to obtain a charter, how many such schools may operate, and to what measures of accountability these schools will be responsible.

A less widely implemented and more ardently contested method of school choice has been the proposed use of vouchers to allow parents to more actively guide their children's education and provide more options to those who could otherwise not afford private schooling. This means of school choice involves encouraging open competition within the school system so that schools are held directly accountable for meeting students' needs. Proponents argue that giving parents a tax credit and allowing them to use it to dictate their child's school of choice allows both schools the opportunity to change to attract students, and parents and students the opportunity to decide what educational opportunity best suits their needs. Voucher plans range from public plans, which would allow students to attend schools according to either inter- or intradistrict regulations to private plans, which would allow students to attend private or parochial schools.

Home schooling

A trend antithetical to the historical growth of compulsory schooling for all children has grown increasingly prominent. In the latter part of the 1990s, state legislatures increasingly amended state compulsory attendance laws to permit home schooling. Regulations on attendance, curriculum, and other requirements vary from state to state, as home schooling became increasingly popular in the first years of the twenty-first century. The Department of Education estimated in 2001 that over 500,000 students were currently home schooled in the United States.

420

Tuition support/HOPE scholarship

The 1997 Taxpayer Relief Act provided two major provisions, which make pursuing higher education less financially burdensome, the Hope Scholarship Credit and the Lifetime Learning Credit. The Hope Scholarship Credit allows taxpayers to claim up to $1500 per student for each of the first 2 years of study at an approved institution of higher learning. The Lifetime Learning Credit applies to those who are beyond the first 2 years of higher education or pursuing part-time enrichment to improve or upgrade their job skills. This provision provides families with a 20% tax credit for the first $5000 of tuition and fees through 2002, and for the first $10,000 thereafter.

CONCLUSION

The field of education policy has become a much more varied, contested process. New initiatives prove to play out differently among various states, as the government attempts to better serve the educational needs of children in the United States. The current direction appears to be toward enhanced accountability for certain outcomes, while retaining a greater degree of choices for parents and students. The system of public education has grown from a provincial, nonmandated institution to a wide-ranging system that nearly every American experiences on a multitude of levels throughout their lives.

FURTHER READING

Alexander, K.; Alexander, D.M. *American Public School Law*, 5th Ed.; Wadsworth Group: Belmont, CA, 2001.

Linn, R.L.; Herman, J.L. *Standards-Led Assessment: Technical and Policy Issues in Measuring School and Student Progress*; CSE Technical Report 426, National Center for Research on Evaluation, Standards, and Student Testing (CRESST), Center for the Study of Evaluation, Graduate School of Education and Information Studies, University of California: Los Angeles, 1997.

National Center for Education Statistics. *NAEP 1996 Trends in Academic Progress*; Campbell, J.R., Voelkl, K.E., Donahue, P.L., Eds.; U.S. Department of Education: Washington, DC, 1997. NCES 97-985.

Pipho, C. Standards, assessment, accountability: The tangled triumvirate. Phi Delta Kappan **1997**, *78* (9), 673–674.

Education, State Administration of Primary and Secondary

Thomas C. Sutton
Baldwin-Wallace College, Berea, Ohio, U.S.A.

INTRODUCTION

The administration of primary and secondary public education in the United States is conducted primarily by state governments in conjunction with local school districts. All states with the exception of Hawaii employ the structure of local school districts as the direct administrators of public primary and secondary education. Local administration of public schools dates back to the seventeenth-century New England colonies, where communities would collect a property tax for the purpose of hiring a ''tutor'' to teach the children of the village and surrounding farms. The importance of public education has been emphasized by states since the Declaration of Independence, evidenced by the inclusion in all 50 state constitutions of a clause stipulating that the state government is responsible for ensuring the provision of a system of public education. The constitutional provision for each state established the legal responsibility of state governments for ensuring the effective administration of public education, either directly or through local school districts.[1]

State involvement in public education has grown significantly during the twentieth century, driven in part by public calls for improvements to public education. With education being viewed as a key element of both civic engagement in a democratic society and as the basis for skill training necessary for gainful employment in a rapidly changing economy, American society has made many demands on school districts. New policy developments and mandates such as integration, the development of special education services for students with physical and learning disabilities, vocational education, improving curriculum and facilities, and increasing teacher preparedness have been developed usually as initiatives of state legislatures and administered through state departments and boards of education.

STATE AND LOCAL ADMINISTRATIVE STRUCTURES

Although local school districts usually predate the formation of states and state constitutions, they are considered to be legal extensions of state authority. State administration of primary and secondary public education (herein referred to as public education) begins with the granting of charters allowing the formation of geographic units as school districts. School district boundaries conform with either county or municipal boundaries. School district residents elected representatives to a board of education, which is responsible for oversight of all administrative concerns of the district, including financial management, personnel, facilities, curriculum, and student conduct. School boards range in number from 3 to as many as 15 members who serve on a voluntary basis (some large municipal districts provide a small stipend) and are usually elected at large. Boards of education hire a superintendent who acts as the primary administrator of the district, and who in turn is responsible for hiring building principals; teachers; service staff, such as custodians, bus drivers, and secretaries; and supporting administrative staff to handle district finances, curriculum, and personnel issues.[2]

Paralleling the local district model, states created boards of education responsible for the oversight of public education. State boards range from elected members representing state districts and at large seats to entities appointed by governors and legislators, to mixed boards of elected and appointed members. State boards oversee a state superintendent of public instruction who may be appointed by the board and/or the governor, or may be elected. The state superintendent directs a state department of education that is responsible for administering all state public education mandates, policies, and finances. Occasionally, such departments will have authority for a specific program removed due to concerns of accountability by legislators. An example of this is Ohio, which began a significant program of state funding for local school facility construction and repair in 1997, with the creation of a separate School Facilities Commission that reported directly to the governor and the state legislature.[3]

Despite the somewhat unique structure within state government, it is often the governor rather than the board of education and/or superintendent who is the most prominent advocate for public education, especially in periods of reform. Governors of southern states took the lead in the 1980s, seeking to improve teacher compensation and training and school curriculum in the wake of the 1983 ''Nation at Risk'' report issued by the National Commission on Excellence in Education. A second effort

Encyclopedia of Public Administration and Public Policy
DOI: 10.1081/E-EPAP 120011028

at reform was led by the National Governors Association in 1991, with its issuance of "Goals 2000," a set of benchmarks for student achievement and preparedness endorsed by President Bush as the blueprint for national policy priorities in public education.[4]

At times, other statewide offices are involved in public education administration. State auditors may become involved through periodic examination of school district finances and intervention in districts with systems that are weak or in crisis. State attorneys general have often served as the lead defense counsel for states that have been sued for issues ranging from integration to provision of special education programs to school finance inequities. Secretaries of State oversee implementation of local elections and levy votes through county election boards, while lieutenant governors are often given responsibility for oversight of special education initiatives related to safety, such as reducing school violence and services for juvenile delinquents.

State legislatures play an important role in public education administration through their growing involvement in policy development and evaluation. State legislatures have passed statutes stipulating exact credit and course distribution requirements for high school diplomas; required degrees, coursework, internships, and testing for teachers and administrators; and mandatory proficiency testing as a graduation requirement, along with the formulas for state aid to local school districts. The activist role of governors and state legislatures is an important reason why state school boards and departments of education have been relegated to largely passive roles as implementers of policy.

SCHOOL FUNDING

School districts are funded through two primary sources: property taxes and state aid. Historically, property taxes served as the primary source of income for districts. Currently, the percentage of funding from property taxes ranges from 40% in Michigan and Kentucky to 70% in New Hampshire, Wyoming, and Vermont.[5] Property taxes are levied as millage, which is a unit equaling one-tenth of one cent on each dollar of assessed property value. States allow a minimum of between 10 and 20 mills to be levied by districts without voter approval. Additional millage requires voter approval and is usually for a specific period of time, requiring periodic renewal votes. The rapid rise of property values in the 1970s led to a property tax revolt by voters exemplified by California's Proposition 13, which froze property taxes and required voters to approve all new increases, including changes to adjust for inflation. As a result, districts in states such as California, New York, and Ohio frequently

have new tax levies on the ballot that are necessary to pay for cost increases due to inflation rather than for improvements to the district's educational capacity.[6]

States use various funding formulas to supplement local property taxes. The most common is the foundation aid formula, which attempts to guarantee a minimum per-pupil spending level for every district, adjusted for variations in local cost-of-doing-business factors. A few states use a foundation grant program, which provides flat grant amounts of varying levels determined by the size and property wealth of a district, as opposed to attempting to establish a minimum spending floor for every student.[7]

The basis of funding in property taxation inevitably results in fiscal disparities between districts with low and high tax capacity and property wealth. These disparities have persisted despite growing levels of state aid, with districts in some states having as wide as a $10,000 difference in spending per pupil between the poorest and richest public school districts. As a result, school districts began suing states in state courts, alleging that such disparities violated state constitutional guarantees of accessible public education. In 1973, the *San Antonio v. Rodriguez* case was appealed to the U.S. Supreme Court, seeking a ruling on whether funding disparities violated the due process and equal protection clauses of the Fourteenth Amendment. The court ruled that public education is not a guaranteed right under the U.S. Constitution, sending such cases back to state courts. Since the San Antonio decision, 38 states have experienced school finance litigation, with 23 state supreme courts ruling systems of school funding to be in violation of state constitutional provisions for accessible public education.[8] Cases in some states have dragged on for years through multiple appeals and rehearings.

Urban school districts face special funding challenges. Higher poverty rates produce low residential property values as well as a higher percentage of students with special social and educational needs, incurring higher costs than suburban districts. Added to these factors are the higher costs of urban areas, the presence of strong teacher and service worker unions that drive up wage levels, all compounded by the endemic inefficiency of large administrative bureaucracies that are part and parcel of large urban districts.[2] A few of the school funding litigation cases have specifically focused on the needs of urban districts, in particular, the New Jersey case of *Abbott v. Burke* (1985).[9]

CURRICULUM AND PERSONNEL

States are responsible for setting standards for school district curriculum, teacher, and administrator certification, and are often also involved in oversight of facilities. Curriculum is determined by state standards that mandate a set number of courses in each discipline at the secondary school level necessary to obtain a high school diploma. Primary school curriculum is usually measured by student achievement benchmarks for each grade, such as achieving literacy by fourth grade and arithmetic proficiency by fifth grade. Secondary level (grades 7–12) course credit is measured in Carnegie Units, which are determined by the number of minutes a course meets each week during the four quarters of a school term. States also set the number of days schools must meet each academic year, usually ranging from 175 to 200 days. Districts in many states determine start and end dates, as well as holiday schedules. States will allow a set number of cancelled days, beyond which days a district is closed must be made up by extending the school year or shortening vacation periods (a particularly nagging problem for northern state districts with frequent snowstorms).

States also administer certification for teachers and school administrators. Teachers are required to have a minimum of a Bachelor's degree in education, combined with field-specific coursework in the disciplines the teacher will be using in their career. Most states have shifted from permanent certification to certificates for periods of between 5 and 10 years, requiring teachers to achieve additional professional development to obtain continued certification. Professional development usually takes the form of graduate-level coursework. When combined with district pay schedules that pay incentives to earn graduate degrees, the result is that a majority of career teachers now hold Master's degrees in education. Administrators are usually drawn from teacher ranks. They are also required to earn a Master's degree or graduate certificate in education administration before becoming administrators. Education subfield degree specializations include special education, reading instruction, gifted and talented education, vocational education, counseling, curriculum development, and management.[2]

Personnel issues include an impending shortage of teachers and administrators. High job stress, lower compensation than in other fields with equivalent educational requirements, and negative public perceptions of public education have contributed to the shortage, and are issues requiring response in order to effectively recruit and retain future teachers and administrators.

STUDENT ACCESSIBILITY AND SERVICES

Public schools are much more accessible than ever before. In 1954, the *Brown v. Board of Education* decision ushered in 30 years of desegregation orders applied to local school districts throughout the United States. Al-

though desegregation successfully tore down the system of separate and unequal schools within school districts, the success of tactics such as busing, mandatory student assignments to buildings, and magnet schools is mixed. Demographics of urban districts changed rapidly, leading to the situation in most urban areas of poorer urban districts with a majority of minority students surrounded by predominantly white, middle-class, suburban districts. As a result, providing strong public education to students who need it most continues to be a major challenge, compounded by the reflected demographic changes in state legislatures, which are less interested in spending more tax dollars on failing schools with fewer constituents.

Federal funding tied to mandates for provision of special education combined with the Americans with Disabilities Act of 1991 constitutes a mandate to states and local districts to provide special education to all eligible students. Such services are expensive, and are often not adequately funded by state and federal dollars. States usually operate a formula aid program that sends funding to local districts based on how many students require special education services. School district resources have been stretched in recent years by implementation of the philosophy of ''mainstreaming,'' which requires that special needs students receive services while attending regular classes with nonspecial needs students, rather than being taught in separate, specialized classrooms.

ISSUES OF ACCOUNTABILITY

Since the early 1990s, schools and teachers have been under increasing scrutiny over issues of accountability. State legislatures have responded by requiring proficiency testing at various levels of primary and secondary education. Many states require passing a high school proficiency test, usually taken in the ninth or tenth grade, to earn a high school diploma. A major concern has arisen over the social promotion of students who fail to achieve grade-level skill development, but are advanced with their age peers. States are experimenting with proficiency tests in the primary grades to measure literacy and math skill attainment. Students who fail these tests receive extra instruction or summer school, or may be held back until passing the tests.

Proficiency testing has been controversial. Proponents see testing as a way of uniformly measuring and guaranteeing minimum standards for student achievement, thus avoiding the stories of illiterate high school graduates. Opponents argue that proficiency testing limits curriculum, with teachers focusing on ''teaching to the test.'' Others are concerned that proficiency tests disproportionately affect minority students in urban districts. President George W. Bush included proficiency testing at every grade level through tenth grade as a major component of his education reform package. The Bush plan is to provide incentives and support to help schools with low test passage rates to improve, but to remove the funding if a school district fails to show improvement after 3 years.

Critics of failing urban school districts advocate the use of vouchers and charter schools as ways to introduce competition into public education. Proponents believe that public schools will improve if faced with losing students and funding to private schools. Vouchers are public dollars given to poor families to use to pay for private school tuition. Voucher programs have been in place since the late 1990s in Milwaukee, Wisconsin; Cleveland, Ohio; and Florida.[10] The use of public dollars to fund education at religious schools prompted a legal challenge under the First Amendment. The Cleveland voucher program will be heard by the U.S. Supreme Court during the 2001–2002 term. Charter schools are private schools chartered by the state for specialized education that are often exempted from regulations governing school districts, to encourage innovative curricula and teaching. Rather than paying for individual tuition at private schools, states subsidize the expenses of the entire charter school. Although appealing as a form of school choice, charter school evaluations in Ohio and other states have shown mixed results in terms of improving student achievement.

REFERENCES

1. Kirp, D.L.; Driver, C.E. The aspirations of system reform meet the realities of localism. Educ. Adm. Q. **1995**, *31*, 589–612.
2. Chance, W. *The Best of Educations: Reforming America's Schools in the 1980's*; The MacArthur Foundation: Chicago, 1986.
3. Browning, R.G. *School Funding Policy Recommendations. Unpublished Report to the Ohio School Funding Task Force*; State of Ohio: Columbus, OH, 1997.
4. Education Commission of the States *The Progress of Education Reform*; Education Commission of the States: Denver, CO, 1996.
5. DeBartolome, C.A.M. What determines state aid to school districts? A positive model of foundation aid as redistribution. J. Policy Anal. Manage. **1997**, *16*, 32–47.
6. Gionocchio, J.S.; Hamilton, H.D. Fiscal Policymaking by Plebiscite: Local Tax and Bond Referenda in Ohio, *Political Behavior and Public Issues in Ohio*. Gargan, J.J., Coke, J.G., Eds.; Kent State University Press: Kent, OH, 1972.
7. Enrich, P. Leaving equality behind: New directions in school finance reform. Vanderbilt Law Rev. **1995**, *48*, 101–194.
8. Evans, W.N.; Murray, S.E.; Schwab, R.M. Schoolhouses, courthouses, and statehouses after *Serrano*. J. Policy Anal. Manage. **1997**, *16*, 10–31.
9. Odden, A. School finance reform in Kentucky, New Jersey, and Texas. J. Educ. Financ. **1993**, *18*, 293–317.
10. Chubb, J.E.; Moe, T.M. *Politics, Markets and America's Schools*; The Brookings Institution: Washington, D.C., 1990.

Efficiency

Hwang-Sun Kang
Seoul Development Institute, Seoul, Republic of Korea

INTRODUCTION

This article introduces the concept of efficiency and discusses the validity of the concept being used as the primary criterion of performance measurement in the public sector. From Wilson, the father of public administration in 1887 to Osborne and Gaebler, advocates of reinventing government in 1992, efficiency has been said to be the first ideology of public administration. Wilson pinpointed the role of government: government should be able to implement delegated tasks from the legislature. Efficiency is defined as the ratio of outputs to inputs. It describes the cost of resources used for an activity to achieve given outputs. This entry shows how the formula applies to prevalent management techniques such as cost−benefit analysis and data envelopment analysis. This entry introduces an argument related with efficiency. When a public policy is analyzed based on the ideology of efficiency, it is questionable if government performance could be measured by the definition of efficiency. Although the definition emphasizes final outputs of government activity, many scholars hold that it is extremely difficult to measure the final facet of government activities. It is neither desirable nor reasonable to measure government performance based on economic (monetary) efficiency. This article holds that there are two kinds of efficiency: technical efficiency and social efficiency. When government performance is evaluated based on the rationale of efficiency, those two concepts should be considered.

DEFINITION OF EFFICIENCY

From Wilson, the father of public administration in 1887, to Osborne and Gaebler, advocates of reinventing government in 1992, efficiency has been said to be the first ideology of public administration. Wilson pinpoints the role of government: government should be able to implement delegated tasks from the legislature. A motto of reinventing government: "Cost Less and Work Better," also represents the underlying idea of the definition of efficiency.

Efficiency is defined as the ratio of outputs to input. It describes the cost of resources used for an activity to achieve given outputs. Here, it should be noted that the numerator of the formula of efficiency should be the final outputs of government activity. For instance, "caseload per worker" is not an efficiency measure, because caseloads are not outputs.[1]

Fig. 1 describes the definition of efficiency and its relationship with effectiveness. Ammons[2] illustrated some examples of efficiency measures, indicating the difference from other related definitions (Table 1).

MANAGEMENT TOOLS BASED ON EFFICIENCY

Although the basic logic of efficiency is simple, it is the ultimate idea of many management techniques used in the public sector. Cost−benefit analysis that is one of the most traditional techniques of public-policy analysis is based on the simple formula of efficiency. Activity-based management skill imported from the private management arena is also using efficiency as its basic logic.

Another powerful skill newly emerging in the public sector, data envelopment analysis (DEA), adopts efficiency as its basic logic. Interestingly, DEA introduces a new term related to efficiency: relative efficiency. The DEA determines a nonparametric best practice frontier and then measures efficiency relative to that frontier. Thus, DEA is also called "frontier analysis." DEA method does not use any statistical inferences, rather, it is a mathematical programming technique developed by the operational research arena focusing on business firms and not-for-profit organizations to find a best practice unit among multiple units (decision-making units). DEA has many advantages:[3]

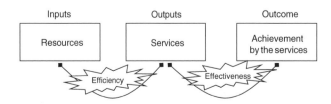

Fig. 1 Relationship between efficiency and effectiveness.

Encyclopedia of Public Administration and Public Policy
DOI: 10.1081/E-EPAP 120010906

Table 1 Examples of four representative measures of government performance

Municipal function	Workload measure	Efficiency measures	Effectiveness measures	Productivity measures
City clerk	Number of sets of city council meeting minutes prepared	Employee hours per set of city council minutes prepared	Percentage of city council minutes approved without amendment	Percentage of city council minutes prepared within 7 days of the meeting and approved without amendment
Library	Total circulation	Circulation per library employee	Circulation per capita	Circulation per 1000
Meter repair	Number of meters repaired	Cost per meter repair	Percentage of repaired meters still functioning properly 6 months later	Cost per properly repaired meter (i.e., total cost of all meter repairs within 6 months)
Personnel	Job application received	Cost per job application processed; cost per vacancy filled	Percentage of new hires and promotions successfully completing probation and performing satisfactorily 6 months later	Cost per vacancy filled successfully (i.e., employee performing satisfactorily 6 months later)

Source: From Ref. [2].

- DEA can handle multiple input and multiple output models.
- It does not require an assumption of a functional form relating inputs to outputs.
- Decision-making units are directly compared against a peer or combination of peers.
- Inputs and outputs can have different units. For example, X1 could be in units of lives saved and X2 could be in units of dollars without requiring an a priori trade-off between the two.

ARGUMENT RELATED TO EFFICIENCY

There is an argument related with efficiency. When a public policy is analyzed based on the ideology of efficiency, it is questionable if government performance could be measured by the definition of efficiency. Although the definition emphasizes final outputs of government activity, many scholars hold that it is extremely difficult to measure the final facet of government activities. Especially, it is neither desirable nor reason-able to measure government performance based on economic (monetary) efficiency.

Considering this argument, it is necessary to expand the definition of efficiency. There are two kinds of efficiency in the social science arena: technical efficiency and social efficiency.

Technical efficiency refers to the general meaning of efficiency that indicates the rates of inputs to outputs. In contrast, social efficiency discusses not only economic (monetary) efficiency but also social relevance of a government activity. Even if a government activity is implemented efficiently economically, the government activity should be interpreted on whether it is compatible with social needs (social ideology or social relevance).

REFERENCES

1. Berman, E. *Productivity in Public and Nonprofit Organizations*; Sage Publication Inc.: Thousand Oaks, CA, 1998.
2. Ammons, D. *Municipal Benchmarks*, 2nd Ed.; Sage Publication Inc.: Thousand Oaks, CA, 2001.
3. http://www.emp.pdx.edu/dea/wvedea.html.

Electronic Government

Mary Maureen Brown
*The University of North Carolina at Charlotte,
Charlotte, North Carolina, U.S.A.*

INTRODUCTION

Electronic government (e-gov) refers to government's use of technology, particularly web-based Internet applications, to enhance the access to, and delivery of, government services to citizens, business partners, employees, and other government entities. Electronic government activities focus on three forms of interactions: Government to Citizen, Government to Business, and Government to Government. Within each of these interaction domains, four types of activities typically take place. The simplest type of activity is to provide information over the Internet. Under this scenario, public agencies employ the Internet to distribute information such as school closing notices, public hearing schedules, issue briefs, or regulatory notifications. The second type of activity allows two-way communications between the agency and the citizen, a business, or another government agency. These web pages allow users to engage in dialog with agencies—users can post queries, comments, or requests to the agency, regardless of time of day or day of week. Gaining in complexity, the third form of activity that takes place over the Internet involves conducting transactions. Some governments have begun to port transaction-based services to the web, allowing users the opportunity to access agency services 24 hours a day, 7 days a week. Some of the more common transaction-based activities include:

Procurement	Interagency payments	Employee leave requests
Joint tax filing	Vehicle registration	Worker's compensation
File business taxes	Apply for licenses	Birth/death certificates
Marriage licenses	Divorce decrees	Criminal background checks
Request license plates	Register to vote	School enrollment
Pet licensing	Change of address forms	Electronic fund transfers
Travel expense reimbursement vouchers		

The final form of activity that takes place over the web centers on governance. Online polling, voting, and campaigning are just some of the ways governments are attempting to increase citizen involvement in the political process.

Despite the noted benefits, the implementation and maintenance of online service delivery efforts can encounter formidable challenges. The deployment of web-based services requires an extraordinarily complex combination of technical, organizational, economic, human, and political factors. Some of the areas that dominate discussions pertaining to digital government include better methods of information technology management, models for electronic public service transactions and delivery systems, and avenues for citizen participation in democratic processes. Other topics such as secure and controlled access to timely, accurate, and authoritative public records are central to any web-based initiative. Data quality, willingness to share data across organization boundaries, and threats to privacy and security all serve to stymie digital government benefits.

TECHNOLOGICAL COMPONENTS

Governments connect to the Internet by establishing services with an Internet service provider (ISP). The citizen then accesses the government web site via their ISP subscription. Citizens gain access to all the online services a government might provide on these servers via a single entry screen known as a "portal." A portal is a "single face" where citizens can conduct "one-stop shopping" for their government needs. Portals allow organizations to aggregate and share content—information, services, and applications with customers, partners, employees, and suppliers. Portals are often organized by topic area rather than bureaucratic function and often incorporate various levels of government. For example, in the "my vehicle" section, citizens may find all information pertaining to vehicles—from driver's licensing, to vehicle registration, to traffic citations. In designing a portal, attention should be given to content, presentation, density, and color

DOI: 10.1081/E-EPAP 120011052

schemes. Above all, web sites should be easy to navigate and users should not have to follow more than three links to find the information for which they are looking.

Software Applications

As mentioned earlier, governments employ online services in four ways: 1) to disseminate information; 2) to promote communication; 3) to conduct transactions; and 4) to facilitate governance. A standard design includes a firewall server, a web server, a transaction server, and a database server. Depending on how they choose to employ online services, the following applications may be needed to establish online government services.

1. Electronic payment systems allow the government agency to collect fees and levy taxes for services such as business licensing, vehicle registration, or refuse collection. Electronic payment systems differ in their approach to how they collect fees. Some software systems allow credit card transactions, some electronic checking, and others provide a digital cash approach. Initiatives are also underway to allow tax payers to pay for services via automated teller machine accounts. When deciding which payment scheme (or schemes as the case might be) to employ, careful consideration must be given to confidentiality, integrity, and authentication issues.

2. Commerce server software provides numerous features pertaining to product information, shopping carts, shopper information, order initialization, shipping charges, taxes, payments, and receipts. Commerce server software allows citizens to easily conduct one or more transactions in one visit. This software tracks the transactions and provides a final summary and checkout process for the citizen.

3. Web server software allows citizens to request information and serves up the pages as requested. The server software controls the storage and retrieval of documents and their transfer; it is also responsible for encryption and authentication. Moreover, the software will have incorporated communication programs that allow it to communicate over the Internet. The software packages range in price according to functionality. The software should be simple to configure, as well as easy to administer and manage on a daily basis. Performance is critically important. The software must be capable of receiving hundreds of thousands of transactions per day.

4. Web browser software allows citizens to connect with servers to access any number of web pages, and to follow links from document to document or page to page. Browser software acts as a link between the user and the Internet or online service. The browser will contact the online service and send a request for information or for a web page. The browser then receives the information, usually in the form of a page, and displays it on the user's computer. Browsers often include plug-ins, which are software programs that are needed to display images, hear sounds, or run animation sequences.

5. Transaction server software is often referred to as online transaction processing (OLTP) software. Its basic duty is to process data according to the rules established by an organization. It passes requests from the web server on to the database server. The transaction server confirms orders, sends a request for payment, and captures payment information. It also takes responsibility for adding, deleting, and modifying orders. The transaction server runs the programs that tell the database server how to handle the data. Because OLTP systems are designed for high volume, the underlying data will change on a minute-by-minute basis. Online transaction processing software captures the day-to-day e-government operations by capturing data about basic business processes and events. Many users concurrently access the database to insert, retrieve, update, and delete individual records. Data are stored in operational databases to meet these transactions. This software is designed for a high volume of small transactions. The focus of these systems is on performing reliably under heavy transaction loads. These systems support day-to-day operations, and are designed to be performance sensitive and to work well under repetitive routine transactions. Because they are not designed for analytical purposes, they do not generate decision-based information well.

6. Firewall server software controls the flow of traffic between two or more networks. The firewall is usually placed between the government network and an external network such as the Internet or a partner's network. Firewalls monitor access to and from specific networks. These systems can protect against viruses, intrusions, and other unauthorized system access.

Hardware Solutions

Internet-based solutions are built on the client/server concept. The client/server concept incorporates a number of computer devices that "serve" or "host" or "operate" an installed software application. For the most part, each server will "host" only one application. The hosting of only one application per server allows activities on the other servers to continue while one is taken out of service for maintenance or repair. Hence, loss of services is kept to a minimum with the client/server model. In short, depending on the type and number of online services the agency will be providing and the number of citizens that will be accessing the services, a separate computer server will probably be required for each of the fore-mentioned software applications.

For the most part, computer servers only differ in three major ways. They differ in their processing speed, their storage capacities, and the speed of their data input–output transporting mechanisms. In determining the hardware requirements for designing the servers, the following issues should be carefully considered:

- *Performance*: The ability to perform numerous operations or to handle a large workload without requiring extensive modifications.
- *High reliability*: The ability to run without a non-recoverable failure for long periods of time.
- *Service/support*: Maintainability and ease-of-use considerations, such as the ability to remove and replace a component (e.g., fan, disk drive, power supply) without having to shut down the system or cause processing functions to stop.
- *Storage*: The storage capacity, both in terms of raw space (i.e., how many gigabytes) and the number of disk drives a server can support inside the chassis.
- *Redundancy*: Whether a given component (e.g., fan, power supply, network interface card, disk drive) has a backup and a fail-over mechanism; redundancy is a method for improving system reliability and availability.
- *Interoperability*: The ability for the different hardware components to interconnect and communicate seamlessly. Software and hardware incompatibilities continue to create difficulties in deploying technology initiatives.

INTERNET ACCESS AND INTERNET SERVICE PROVIDERS

Much as freeways are networks of roads designed to transport people from one location to the another, networks provide the opportunity for data to travel from one location to the next. The Internet is often defined as a highly connected virtual highway that allows data to pass from person to person, organization to organization, and country to country. Data are able to make these cross-country or international trips because the Internet has standardized on a common protocol of data definitions. To communicate effectively, everyone that transfers data via the Internet adheres to the TCP/IP (transfer communication protocol/Internet protocol) protocols.

Governments, businesses, and citizens gain access to the Internet by subscribing with a locally affiliated ISP. The ISP charges a flat monthly rate for their connection, which usually includes their fee and the cost of a dedicated line from your location to their nearest facility or point-of-presence for connection to the Internet. The dedicated line is typically provided by the local telephone company, and most ISP's make these arrangements for their customers.

Today's backbone consists of high-speed fiber-optic lines. The number of "hops" the data make as they are routed from the government to the backbone will affect the speed at which data are delivered to the citizen. The more computers in between the ISP and the backbone, the slower the connection. When contemplating establishing a subscription with an ISP, several issues should be considered. The ISP should also incorporate numerous security mechanisms to protect the data from unauthorized access and destruction. The ISP should also provide written guarantees on levels of service and technical support. Also, inquire about financial and technical background, and ask about expansion capabilities.

Reliability and speed are two critical issues to consider when deciding on an ISP service agreement. An ISP should provide performance guarantees regarding their uptime or availability. In essence, the ISP should be able to guarantee that their services will be available 99.9% of the time.

Bandwidth refers to the speed with which content can be delivered to the end user. Internet service providers typically provide a range of choices on how the government might connect to the Internet, and the choices will vary according to speed, user load, and cost. Some users connect to the Internet over ISDN telephone lines with connection speeds of 128 Kbps. Telephone companies are offering digital subscriber line connections, which deliver at speeds approximating 1.5 Mbps. Likewise, some cable companies offer high-speed cable access in the 10 Mbps range. Government agencies often link to ISPs with dedicated telephone connections such as T3 lines (deliver at speeds of 45 Mbps), T1 lines (1.5 Mbps), or fractional T1 services (256 Kbps to 1.5 Mbps). The decision as to how much bandwidth is required is based on the number of users that will access the system and the types of services the government wants to deliver.

It is important to keep in mind that many of the citizens will be connected to their ISP by way of dial-up telephone lines. Most consumers connect to the Internet over telephone modems with speed ranges from 14.4 Kbps to 256 Kbps. Because these connections are slow, web design efforts should account for users employing slower dial-up connections.

Although much attention has been dedicated to Internet activity, government agencies also deploy services using an intranet or extranet approach. In theory, the only difference between the Internet and an intranet or extranet is how the data are routed. With an Internet, the data travel the "open roads" via the high-speed backbone. With intranets and extranets, data are more confined and do not access the backbone. With intranets, data remain within the organization's network. With extranets, data leave the internal network and travel to outside organizations via dedicated lines. It would not be uncommon for a single government agency to maintain an intranet, an extranet, and also a public Internet.

In summary, as decisions are made regarding the various technical alternatives that a government agency might employ in developing their online service, overarching concerns should always center around system performance issues pertaining to:

- *Scalability*—The system should be capable of handling increasing numbers of users without any disruption to service.
- *Flexibility*—The system must provide a broadly configurable array of hardware and software devices that do not require major reinstallations as enterprise requirements change.
- *Compatibility*—The system must meet expandable configuration requirements, as well as standard industry specifications, to protect future application investment.
- *Manageability*—The system should not demand excessive management time and effort for maintaining online operations.
- *Availability*—The system must be capable of sustaining tens to hundreds of thousands of processing transactions with minimal wait time or downtime.
- *Security*—The system must incorporate an appropriate level of security to prevent unauthorized access to data.
- *Total cost of ownership*—An amalgam of the fully configured system price, including installation, setup, training, infrastructure costs, downtime costs, and ongoing maintenance.

THE POLICY ARENA

Much attention must be given to developing the underlying policy framework that will support online services. Most policy discussions center on issues pertaining to security, privacy, and ethics. However, attention must also focus on substantive, or field/profession-specific, policy issues. As organizations migrate from the first three channels to the fourth channel, substantive policies related to the actual operation that is being automated may require modification. Nonetheless, this section focuses on policies related to security, privacy, and ethics.

Security

Public agencies are particularly vulnerable to three types of security threats. The illicit modification, destruction, or exposure of data can create serious consequences—jeopardizing not only privacy rights, but inappropriate data access can threaten the safety of citizens. Overriding concerns regarding the moral, legal, and ethical ramifications of security breaches have forced many public managers to take a more risk-averse route, imposing serious limitations on computer information-sharing capabilities.

Unfortunately, as mentioned, the sharing of departmental data can result in the deletion, modification, circulation, and theft of important organizational data. Stallings defined four broad categories of data attacks. Interruption occurs when assets of the system (i.e., certain data elements) are destroyed or become unavailable for use, and interception occurs when an unauthorized party gains access to an information asset.

Conversely, modification relates to tampering with the data, and fabrication occurs when an unauthorized party inserts counterfeit objects or data into the system. According to Icove et al., the motives for these attacks are based on entertainment value, or financial or personal gain.[1] The results of these penetrations can be serious, and can result in the corruption or disclosure of information, theft of data, or denial of system services. All these threats expose the organization to severe repercussions. Legal liability, as well as the erosion of public confidence that results from an agency's inability to ensure data security, has widespread societal implications.

Public key cryptography is touted as a potential solution to the security problem. This involves securing data with two keys—one is used to encrypt (scramble) the message, and the other is used to decrypt (unscramble) the message. A key is used to encrypt the message prior to its being sent, and a corresponding key is used to decrypt the message once it has received. In its simplest form, each person in the transaction has a pair of keys— one private and one public. The public key is made available for public access (e.g., to friends, colleagues, etc., or to anyone who might want to send the individual a confidential message). Employing encryption application software such as "pretty good privacy" software, the sender will encrypt the message with the designated receiver's public key. The only way the message can be decrypted is via the receiver's private key, which the receiver keeps confidential. Only the receiver has the private key that is capable of decrypting the message. Thus, files can be encrypted to allow only certain individuals' access to the message content. Interestingly, it is virtually impossible to calculate one key based on knowledge of the other.

Privacy

Privacy is the right to be left alone and the right to be free of unreasonable personal intrusions. Information privacy is the claim of individuals, groups, or institutions to determine for themselves when, and to what extent, information about them is communicated to others. This issue is becoming the most important issue for consumers. Unfortunately, compliance with the Privacy Act of 1974 and its extensions are not simple because the line between legal definitions in ethics is not always clear. Protecting intellectual property on the web is also quite difficult because it is easy and inexpensive to copy and disseminate digitized information. The Organization for Economic Cooperation and Development[2] recommended the following guidelines:

- Personal data should be obtained by lawful and fair means, and with the knowledge or consent of the data subject.
- Personal data collection should be relevant to the purposes for which that data are to be used. To the extent necessary for those purposes, such data should be accurate, complete, and current.
- The purpose of the data collection effort should be specified, and the subsequent use of such data should be only for the stated purpose as agreed to by the individual.
- Personal data should not be disclosed or otherwise used for any purposes other than that which was set forth in the purpose specification, except with the consent of the data subject by the authority of law.
- Personal data should be protected with reasonable security measures to prevent unauthorized access, destruction, modification, or disclosure.
- The data controller should make available information concerning the existence, use, and nature of all personal data that are collected.
- Individuals should have the right to ascertain from a data controller whether the data controller has personal data relating to that individual and should have access to correct the data, as required.

Ethics

Because the increasing use of information technology has created new ethical challenges, many of today's organizations are developing their own code of ethics as a guide

for their members. Mason et al. categorized ethical issues into four domains: privacy, accuracy, property, and accessibility.[3] Privacy relates to the collection, storage, and dissemination of information about individuals.

Data collection principles should focus on collecting only those data that are required to accomplish a legitimate business objective. Collection efforts should not be excessive and should be targeted only toward what is required. All individuals should be allowed to give their consent before data are gathered. However, such consent may be implied from the individual's actions, for example, applications for credit, insurance, or employment.

Accuracy relates to the information's authenticity as it is collected and processed. Steps should be taken to verify the accuracy of the information as it is acquired, processed, stored, and disseminated. Furthermore, the data should be made available to the individual to ensure that they are correct. If there is disagreement about the accuracy of the data, the individual's version should be noted an included with any disclosure of the file. Furthermore, in disseminating information, agencies should provide some indicator as to the accuracy of the information as misleading information can be worse than no information at all.

Property relates to ownership and the issue of intellectual property rights. Organizations need policies concerning who owns what data and how the data are to be employed. To date, many of the issues associated with ownership of electronic data remain under debate. As courts work through the intricacies of ownership, organizations can limit their liabilities by instituting policies pertaining to data ownership rights.

Accessibility relates to the right to access information. All access rights should be based on a legitimate "need-to-know" basis. Public organizations should maintain adequate security practices and procedures.

MANAGEMENT CHALLENGES

Although most public officials appreciate the benefits that e-government solutions can offer, they question their agencies' ability to overcome the hurdles associated with adoption and implementation. A study of state CIOs conducted by NASIRE identified that while funding is always difficult, cultural, organizational, and leadership issues are some of the most significant barriers to adoption. Specifically, the survey revealed that the greatest barriers center on:

- Providing a culture of teamwork, innovation, and change
- Education of executives and managers

- Collaboration and integration efforts
- Skills and expertise
- Diversity and complexity of existing operational processes

These noted concerns demonstrate an overwhelming need to establish a learning environment for coaching, nurturing, and facilitating both the adoption and maintenance of digitally based government services. Specifically, public managers need to be sure to encourage staff to:

- Develop skill sets to understand how to leverage Internet tools.
- Develop mechanisms to ensure responsibility and accountability for planning initiatives.
- Assess impacts as they relate to government outputs and outcomes.
- Understand how program specifications and requirements drive e-government developments.

- Assess impact on *all* citizens.
- Develop and monitor web-based balanced scorecards.
- Develop policies in areas such as security, privacy, electronic payments, standards, investments, digital archiving, encryption, and authentication.

REFERENCES

1. Icove, D.; Seger, K.; VonStorch, W. *Computer Crime: A Crimefighter's Handbook*; O'Reilly & Associates: Sebastopol, CA, 1995.
2. Organization for Economic Cooperation and Development. *Guidelines on the Protection of Privacy and Transborder Flows of Personal Data*; http://www.oecd.org//dsti/sti/it/secur/prod/PRIV-EN.HTM.
3. Mason, R.O.; Mason, F.M.; Culnan, M.J. *Ethics of Information Management*; Sage Publications: Thousand Oaks, CA, 1995.

Enterprise, Public Versus Private

Thomas S. Nesslein
University of Wisconsin–Green Bay, Green Bay, Wisconsin, U.S.A.

E

INTRODUCTION

For the major part of the twentieth century, a key topic of political economy was the question of the appropriate scope of government suppliers of goods and services relative to private suppliers. In the socialist planned economies of the former Soviet Union, Eastern Europe, and China, state enterprises dominated most of the economy. Moreover, a great number of developing countries sought economic growth via state-owned producers in key sectors of the economy. Likewise, in the capitalist welfare states—for example, most northern European countries, the United Kingdom, Australia, and New Zealand—the dominant view was that government enterprises should control the commanding heights of the economy. Typical examples were the railroads, the mining sector, telecommunications, banking and insurance, and key industrial sectors such as chemicals and steel. Of course, the nationalization of education was strongly supported without serious debate. In distinct contrast, in the United States, direct government production was largely limited to major parts of the education sector, the postal system, and local government utilities and services, such as police/fire protection and refuse collection.

Since the mid-1970s, however, radical change in thinking concerning the appropriate scope of direct government production has occurred.[1] The collapse of Communism in Europe has led to massive privatization of formerly state enterprises, and the privatization movement has also taken hold in the capitalist welfare states and spread extensively throughout the developing world. In the United States, serious questions are now being raised with respect to the continued direct government production of education, refuse collection, prisons, housing, mail delivery, and air traffic control, among others.

The widespread enthusiasm for government enterprise, especially during the first 30 years after World War II, seems largely linked to the failures of the market economy during the Great Depression, the apparent success of the Soviet planned economy, and the failure to appreciate the role of market incentives in stimulating innovation. However, advances in economic theory, emerging empirical research, and changing circumstances have greatly weakened the case for direct government provision.

THE DESIRABLE SCOPE OF PUBLIC PROVISION: A MODERN VIEW

What kinds of goods and services should be produced by public enterprises rather than private suppliers?[1] Let us begin by examining the case of benevolent government; that is, we assume that the government's goal is to maximize society's welfare. It is instructive to note then the conditions under which it makes no difference whether production is public or private. In brief, if the government knows precisely what kind of good or service it wants produced, then all the relevant product characteristics can be specified in a contract (or regulation), and production can be contracted out to private suppliers. In such cases, governments may continue to *finance* production (e.g., education), but direct government production is no longer essential. For example, it is often believed that a government postal system is required because the delivery of mail to sparsely populated areas is generally unprofitable. Yet, the government can easily specify in a contract that private firms operating a postal concession must deliver mail to all areas.

Of course, the ability to write perfect contracts and regulations does not often exist. There are many instances where the government cannot precisely and completely specify and enforce all the *quality* dimensions that it deems desirable. In essence, many real world cases involve what may be labeled as *incomplete contracts*. In many cases, the government may desire the supply of specific product characteristics that are impossible to specify and enforce contractually, so-called noncontractible *quality*. For example, the government may be concerned with how well prisons treat inmates, how well schools inculcate character and social responsibility, and how innovative producers are. Consequently, in this view, an important element in choosing between public or private production is how different forms of ownership affect the incentives to deliver the desired noncontractible quality attributes as well as the cost. In this respect, Shleifer[1] stated:

[C]onsider two types of investment incentives: those to reduce costs and those to improve quality or to innovate. When assets are publicly owned, the public manager has relatively weak incentives to make either of these

Encyclopedia of Public Administration and Public Policy
DOI: 10.1081/E-EPAP 120010897

investments, because this manager is not the owner and hence gets only a fraction of the return. In contrast, private regulated contractors have much stronger incentives because, as owners, they get more of the returns on the investment. Which ownership structure is more efficient depends on whether having high-powered incentives to invest and innovate is a good idea.

However, the case against government enterprise is not so clear-cut when private suppliers have strong incentives to reduce cost, and increase profits, by decreases in non-contractible quality. Put differently, in some cases, efficient production may require *soft* incentives. For example, private schools, hospitals, prisons, and so on may have strong incentives to hire less well-trained and qualified workers to reduce labor costs.

Two market forces, however, often attenuate inefficient decreases in noncontractible quality. First, if the product market is reasonably competitive, consumers will shun suppliers making inefficient reductions in noncontractible quality. Second, in many markets, a key element of long-run profitability is repeat sales. In such cases, private suppliers are given strong incentive to avoid actions that increase short-run profitability at the expense of long-run profitability. Finally, it should be noted that private, not-for-profit firms often emerge in a market economy in those instances where soft incentives seem particularly important. In the United States, for example, a large sector of private, not-for-profit hospitals and universities has long existed.

Assuming benevolent government, Shleifer[1] summarized the case against government enterprise as follows:

These considerations point to a rather narrow set of circumstances in which government ownership is likely to be superior. These are the situations in which: 1) opportunities for cost reductions that lead to non-contractible deterioration of quality are significant; 2) innovation is relatively unimportant; 3) competition is weak and consumer choice is ineffective; and 4) reputational mechanisms are also weak. This list gives, in my opinion, a fair sense of how tenuous, in general, is the normative case for government production.

GOVERNMENT FAILURE AND THE CASE FOR PRIVATIZATION

So far, the discussion has assumed a benevolent government seeking to maximize society's welfare. It has now long been recognized, however, that government policies and programs often fail in this respect. In particular, special interest groups in many cases dominate the political process and the political outcomes that emerge

are often a pale reflection of society's general interest. In brief, highly inefficient policies and programs are adopted that to an important extent serve to transfer wealth to politically powerful interest groups. In this respect, government enterprises are often used by the ruling party as a means to increase their political support via above-market wages, excess employment, and outright transfers of wealth. In developing countries, in particular, government monopolies and projects are created expressly to transfer wealth, often to a handful of relatives and key political supporters of the ruling family or party. Shleifer[1] summarized as follows: "In other words, state firms are inefficient not just because their managers have weak incentives to reduce costs, but because inefficiency is the result of the government's deliberate policy to transfer resources to supporters."

Moreover, in a highly nuanced critique of both neoclassical economics and socialist economic planning, Joseph Stiglitz[2] also recognized both a political and economic case favoring privatization. To begin, privatization is seen as a means to weaken the coercive powers of the state and to depoliticize enterprise operations. Moreover, Stiglitz argued that a strong economic case can be made for privatization, but one that goes beyond the standard arguments regarding differences in managerial incentives. Stiglitz stressed three points. First, privatization is seen as enhancing the government's commitment to a competitive economy and to sharply circumscribing enterprise subsidies. Second, incentives are strengthened as privatization increases the likelihood that hard enterprise budget constraints will be substituted for soft budget constraints. Third, a dynamically efficient economy requires hard budget constraints to enhance the economy's "selection mechanism, through which it is decided not only which enterprises survive but which enterprises garner additional resources to expand. Those who cannot meet the market test are weeded out."[2]

COMPARATIVE ENTERPRISE EFFICIENCY: THE EVIDENCE

De Alessi[3] undertook the first major survey of comparative enterprise efficiency within the context of a broader analysis of the economics of property rights. De Alessi concisely examined key empirical studies from the 1960s and 1970s that assess the relative efficiency of government versus private enterprises with respect to water and electric utilities, urban transit, airlines, banks, hospitals, fire prevention services, and refuse collection. De Alessi concluded from his review that strong evidence exists for the superiority of private ownership.

In contrast, three major reviews during the 1980s[4] found little or no difference in efficiency between public and private enterprises. In brief, these studies suggest that differences in enterprise efficiency are overwhelmingly related to the degree of competition faced in the market, not ownership per se. Vining and Boardman[5] labeled this the *primacy of competition versus ownership* argument. In the extreme, the argument implies that in highly competitive markets, without significant distortions, ownership does not matter for enterprise efficiency. More recent evidence strongly counters this view, however.[6]

To begin, Mueller[6] presented a table of some 50 studies examining comparative enterprise efficiency and concisely summarized the cost differences found. In only two studies were government enterprises found to be more efficient. In over 40 studies, government firms were found to be the higher cost producers, generally more than 20% higher, and often 40% to 60% (or more) higher. The case favoring private ownership is further buttressed by several major empirical studies undertaken since the late 1980s.[6] Of particular note are the related studies of Boardman and Vining, and Vining and Boardman.

A key argument made by these authors is that the relatively few studies that show public enterprise superiority, or at least no difference in efficiency, cannot convincingly demonstrate their claim. In brief, these studies compared firms in sectors with characteristics of monopoly, duopoly, and/or heavy regulation, and thus are not relevant to assessing comparative efficiency in a competitive market. In this respect, Vining and Boardman[5] stated:

> Many studies cited ... pertain to sectors where "firms" have geographic monopolies (electric utilities, water, refuse, fire services) and, therefore, do not directly compete with each other. While these studies tell us something about the effect of ownership on performance in noncompetitive, monopoly environments, by definition they cannot inform us about the effect of ownership in competitive environments.

With respect to the empirical evidence, Boardman and Vining[6] used a statistical analysis capable of measuring the independent effect of ownership on comparative enterprise performance. They estimated their model using several measures of profitability and efficiency as related to three enterprise types: state-owned enterprises, mixed enterprises (a hybrid ownership category where the government has retained an equity position), and private enterprises. Their study used data on the 500 largest manufacturing and mining firms from outside the United States as of 1983. After controlling for a range of factors (e.g., firm size, degree of product market competition), Boardman and Vining found that ownership has a substantial independent effect on enterprise profitability and efficiency. For example, on average, state-owned enterprises have a return on equity almost 12% less than comparable private enterprises. Relatedly, two studies using a similar methodology, but focusing on the 500 largest nonfinancial enterprises in Canada (Vining and Boardman) and the 500 largest non-U.S. corporations (Picot and Kaulman), also find credible evidence that state enterprises are less efficient than private enterprises.[6] More recently, Boubakri and Cosset[6] examined changes in the economic performance of 79 enterprises from 21 developing countries that experienced full or partial privatization between 1980 and 1992. They find substantial increases in profitability, operating efficiency, capital investment spending, output, employment level, and dividends following privatization.

CONCLUSION

Since the mid-1970s, a radical change in thinking concerning the appropriate scope of direct government production has occurred. The reorientation has been stimulated in part by advances in economic theory—in particular, the theory of ownership and contracting, a greater appreciation of the link between ownership and innovation for a dynamically efficient economy, and a fuller understanding of the adverse consequences of government ownership. Also playing a role are the increasing competitiveness of market economies and improvements in government contracting and regulation. Finally, much real world experience and a growing body of high-quality empirical research supports the comparative efficiency of private enterprise.

REFERENCES

1. Shleifer, A. State versus private ownership. J. Econ. Perspect. **1998**, *12* (4), 133–150. The following two sections concisely summarize Andrei Shleifer's seminal analysis of the desirable scope of public provision from a modern perspective.
2. Stiglitz, J. *Whither Socialism?*; MIT Press: Cambridge, MA, 1994, 181.
3. De Alessi, L. The Economics of Property Rights: A Review of the Evidence. In *Research in Law and Economics*; Zerbe, R., Ed.; JAI Press: Greenwich, CT, 1980; Vol. 2, 1–47.
4. Borcherding, T.E.; Pommerehne, W.W.; Schneider, F. Comparing the efficiency of private and public production: A survey of the evidence from five federal states. Z. Nationalokon./J. Econ. Theory **1982**, (Supplement 2), 127–156. Millward, R. The Comparative Performance of

Public and Private Ownership. In *The Mixed Economy*; Roll, E., Ed.; Macmillan: London, 1982. Boyd, C.C. The Comparative Efficiency of State-Owned Enterprises. In *Multinational Corporations and State-Owned Enterprises: A New Challenge in International Business*; Negaandhi, A.R., Thomas, H., Rao, K.L.K., Eds.; JAI Press: Greenwich, CT, 1986; 99–184.

5. Vining, A.; Boardman, A. Ownership versus competition: Efficiency in public enterprise. Public Choice **1992**, *73*, pp. 205, 216.

6. Mueller, D.C. *Public Choice II*; Cambridge University Press: Cambridge, England, 1993. Boardman, A.; Vining, A. Ownership and performance in competitive environments: A comparison of the performance of private, mixed, and state-owned enterprises. J. Law Econ. **1989**, *32* (1), 1–33. Vining, A.; Boardman, A. (5), 205–239. Picot, A.; Kaulman, T. Comparative performance of government-owned and privately-owned industrial corporations—Empirical results from six countries. J. Inst. Theor. Econ. **1989**, *145* (June), 298–316. World Bank. *Bureaucrats in Business*; Oxford University Press: London, 1995. Boubakri, N.; Cosset, J. The financial and operating performance of newly privatized firms: Evidence from developing countries. J. Finance **1998**, *53* (3), 1081–1110. Cowie, J. The technical efficiency of public and private ownership in the rail industry: The case of swiss private railways. J. Transp. Econ. Policy **1999**, *33* (3), 241–251. Plane, P. Privatization, technical efficiency and welfare consequences: The case of the cote d'lvoire electricity company (CIE). World Dev. **1999**, *27* (2), 343–360. Ros, A. Does ownership or competition matter? The effects of telecommunications reforms on network expansion and efficiency. J. Regul. Econ. **1999**, *15* (1), 65–92. Scully, G. Reform and efficiency gains in the New Zealand electrical supply industry. J. Product. Analysis **1999**, *11* (2), 133–147.

Entitlements and the Congressional Budget Process

Patrick Fisher
Monmouth University, West Long Branch, New Jersey, U.S.A.

INTRODUCTION

Entitlements are government spending programs for which Congress has set eligibility criteria—age, income, location, occupation, etc. If meeting the criteria, a recipient is "entitled" to the money. Due to the rapid growth of entitlement programs over the past four decades, less than half of the federal budget today is considered "controllable" through the budget process. The fact that entitlements are broadly considered to be relatively "uncontrollable" is somewhat misleading. While Congress cannot control levels of eligibility in the population, it can control such levels under the law (cost of living adjustments, for example). It would be accurate to say, however, that politically, entitlements are relatively uncontrollable. Entitlements are available for a vote, but only if Congress decides to arrange one. Congress can change or repeal any law it passes, and lawmakers can revisit entitlements at any time to reduce or eliminate them.

THE GROWTH ENTITLEMENT SPENDING

Federal entitlement programs range from gigantic ones, such as Social Security and Medicare, to extremely small ones, such as an indemnity program for dairy farmers whose milk is contaminated by chemicals. Some entitlement payment levels, such as for unemployment insurance, are difficult to predict, while others, such as Social Security, are fairly predictable. While most entitlements go to people, some also go to other units of government. The Title XX Social Services block grant, for instance, goes to states based on population.

What makes entitlements different from the other major forms of congressional spending is that they are mandatory; money must be provided until the program is changed by Congress. By contrast, discretionary spending is good only for one year, and Congress has to renew it annually through the appropriations process. Less than a third of the budget during the Kennedy administration, entitlement, and mandatory spending is now more than one-half of the budget. Discretionary spending (for domestic, defense, and international purposes), on the other hand, has gone from making up 63% of federal government expenditures in 1962 down to about a third in 2000

(see Table 1). The tremendous growth of entitlements may be problematic, because entitlements limit the ability of Congress to maneuver in adopting the budget. Congress, therefore, may not be given the flexibility it needs in the budget process. Because most government expenditures are disbursed in long-term authorizations, there is some question about the democratic accountability of the budget process.[1]

ENTITLEMENTS AND THE TRANSFORMATION OF THE CONGRESSIONAL BUDGET PROCESS

Congress has deliberately authorized entitlement spending because it believed that the government should protect certain obligations from yearly political controversy. Members of Congress have some control over annual entitlement spending, but the total changes in any single year are a relatively small part of the entire budget. Over the long run, however, there is the potential for adequate flexibility within the budget for Congress to make significant changes in the composition of the federal budget.[2]

Budgeting is a different process from what it once was. The postwar transformation of federal budgeting from a control process to one oriented toward spending growth has upset the relationship between available resources and demands on the budget. Claims on the budget became stronger when budgeting was an expansionary process, and it has not been easy for Congress to reverse course, as the climate has become more constrained.[3] Budgeting for growth (1950s–1960s) differs from budgeting for stabilization or cutback (1970s–1990s). The expectation of growth makes it easier to please greater numbers of actors, because government can afford to give people what they want. As critics of congressional budgeting argue, this transformed budgetary environment has become a long-term threat to Congress's power of the purse, because Congress had become unwilling, for political reasons, to control mandatory spending.[4]

The budget cannot be completely isolated from the economy—the economy drives the budget. The assumptions on which the budget's prescriptions are based all lie at the mercy of national economic conditions. Beginning

Encyclopedia of Public Administration and Public Policy
DOI: 10.1081/E-EPAP 120010881

Table 1 The growth of entitlement spending: budget expenditures for fiscal years 1962 and 2000

	2000	1962
Entitlements and mandatory spending	55%	31%
Domestic discretionary spending	16%	12%
Defense spending	16%	46%
Interest on the national debt	12%	6%
International discretionary spending	1%	5%

Source: Congressional Budget Office.

in the early 1970s, demands on the budget soared more than resources did. Congress did not foresee in the 1960s that the budget situation would become much more dire as the economy stagnated.[3] Politics and economics combine to shape the varying patterns of activity for the legislators working on the budget.[5] On the one hand, economic goal-setting has often been a frivolous exercise in symbolic politics in the absence of realistic means to achieve goals. Year after year, the most important factor in determining the current year's budget allocations is last year's budget allocations. On the other hand, the establishment of inflexible methods to achieve a goal may simply make other problems worse and threaten the economy.[6] As economic conditions change, so do priorities; legislators need to maintain their ability to respond to varying economic conditions.

THE POLITICAL SIGNIFICANCE OF ENTITLEMENT PROGRAMS

There are good policy reasons for entitlement spending. Entitlements can be an efficient way of the government providing services, and it seems logical that the government may want to avoid the political difficulty of not being able to maintain its promises, regardless of the financial condition of the government, which is, after all, highly reliant on the state of the economy. One prob-

lem with entitlements is that, to a large degree, they go to fund what has been called "middle-class welfare." That is, entitlement benefits are dispensed largely on the basis of criteria other than income (such as age). Programs that require proof of low income to receive benefits are a small proportion of entitlements; more than three-fourths of all entitlement spending (including Social Security and Medicare) is directed toward non-means tested programs, where recipient eligibility is not based on need (see Table 2).

The huge surge in entitlement spending came between 1966 and 1976. During this period, the creation of programs such as Medicare, Medicaid, and food stamps combined with expanded Social Security benefits to provide an enormous boost to entitlement spending. From 1966–1976, entitlements more than doubled in relation to the size of the economy, growing from 5.4% of the GDP to 11.3%, where it leveled until health care costs began driving entitlement costs up again in the 1990s. All together, three entitlement programs—Social Security, Medicare, and Medicaid—make up more than 70% of all mandatory spending.

The rapid growth of entitlements has given them a bad name in some quarters, because they were held to blame for deficits that plagued the federal government through the 1980s and early 1990s. Furthermore, entitlements came to be seen as a means by which the authorization committees could circumvent the appropriations committees. Dramatically increased entitlements spending, without a corresponding willingness to raise taxes, broke the back of the classical budget process.[1]

Conservatives fear that the result of the growth in entitlements will be higher taxes and deficits; liberals fear that entitlements will squeeze out other programs and, if they keep growing, use up future revenue increases. Yet both conservatives and liberals in Congress have been unwilling to confront the growth in entitlements. As a result, as Social Security has been placed politically out of reach and other entitlements get harder to contain, discretionary spending has become a larger part of what

Table 2 The top entitlements

Rank	Program	Expenditures (billion of $)	% of GDP
1.	Social Security	406.0	4.1
2.	Medicare	216.0	2.2
3.	Medicaid	117.4	1.2
4.	Other retirement/disability	87.8	0.9
5.	Farm price supports	30.5	0.3
6.	Unemployment	20.7	0.2
	Total means tested	235.9	2.4
	Total nonmeans tested	793.9	8.1

Source: Congressional Budget Office.

is up for grabs in the short term. This, in turn, has curtailed the power of the appropriations committees. The piece of the budget they control was nearly three-fourths of the budget during the Kennedy Administration; now it is down to little more than one-third of the budget and is dropping.

Some argue that the difficulty in reducing or eliminating entitlements is exactly what the architects of entitlements had intended, and exactly what contemporary Congresses ought to be doing. Entitlement programs dole out benefits automatically so that basic benefits would not be subject to the year-to-year inconsistencies of the appropriations process. Furthermore, entitlements are growing as they were supposed to, especially during a bad economy. The so-called automatic stabilizers such as unemployment insurance and food stamps are designed to pick up the slack during bad economic periods.

Entitlement programs, however, do not always have the effect that their creators intended. Times change, but often, established entitlements are unable to change as new circumstances dictate. A problem with entitlements is that it is much easier to start an entitlement for an apparently needy group than it is to terminate an entitlement after it no longer makes sense. Most subsidy programs, for example, began for the same reason as programs to benefit individuals—that is, they were a response to hardship cases. In their early days, aid was targeted on the basis of an immediate need or a significant national purpose. Over the years, many of these programs, especially in agriculture, lost their focus as conditions changed. Instead of being phased out, many were expanded for political purposes.[7]

Another entitlement that has had unintended consequences is the civil service retirement program, where expenditures are currently skyrocketing. Civil service retirement is subject to its own demographic characteristics: the number of retirees has increased dramatically in recent years because of the large number of civilians on the federal payroll during and following World War II. Furthermore, expenditures will increase more rapidly in the future because of the benefit characteristics of the system. Not only do federal retirees receive relatively generous benefits, but the system encourages early retirement, further adding to the costs for the government and taxpayers.[8]

Some of the largest and most expensive programs in the federal budget, such as Social Security and Medicare, are entitlements that are perceived to be politically hazardous to alter. Social Security, in fact, is called by politicians ''the third rail of American politics''—touch it and die. Given a choice, members of Congress would rather look almost anywhere else for ways to cut spending. Unfortunately, the cost of Social Security and Medicare is rising so fast that they risk crowding out the rest of domestic spending. The political power of Social Security was demonstrated with a House vote in 1994 that called for attacking the deficit by reining in entitlement spending, but with a provision excluding Social Security from any cuts. A move to keep Social Security on the chopping block along with other entitlement programs lost by a resounding vote of 392–37. After this vote, the House then proceeded to vote 424–0 to prohibit any move to increase the Social Security payroll tax to help fill the gap in case entitlement spending ever exceeds preset limits.

The problem remains, however, that it is questionable whether or not the budget can be balanced over the long run without reforming Social Security. Social Security is the largest single spending program in the federal budget, and at a cost of $406 billion in 2000, it accounted for nearly a quarter out of every dollar the federal government spends. Defenders insist that it should remain as it is because it is self-financed by the payroll tax, which is currently running a huge surplus. A problem with this argument is that it leaves the mistaken impression that the biggest program in the budget would not affect the rest of the budget. Critics argue that the sheer size of Social Security makes it a must for any sizeable budget cuts. As the size of the House votes in 1994 show, however, any meaningful cuts in Social Security in the near future are extremely unlikely.

Medicare's political power was demonstrated after Congress passed a Medicare Catastrophic Coverage Act of 1988, which was to be paid for in large part by an income surtax on middle- and high-income beneficiaries. After ugly demonstrations led by those who were going to have to pay the surtax, however, Congress backed down and repealed the measure. Despite Congress' experience with the Catastrophic Coverage Act, there still remains the fact that you cannot control entitlement spending without altering Medicare and Medicaid.

It is doubtful, however, that Medicare (the federal health insurance for the elderly and disabled) and Medicaid (the joint federal-state health program for the poor) can be controlled without overhauling the nation's entire heath system. Because climbing health care costs are expected to increase the deficit significantly as the baby boom generation nears retirement, early in his administration, President Clinton proposed attempting to channel the pressure for continuing deficit reduction into the health care reform debate. Politically, however, Clinton's health care strategy proved to be unsuccessful, and prospects for significant health reform were shattered with the Republican takeover of Congress in 1994. The fact remains, however, that to reduce Medicare and Medicaid effectively, the whole health care system has to be reformed.

Taken together, Medicare and Medicaid are almost as expensive as Social Security. They are also currently by far the fastest growing entitlements. Medicare and Medicaid have been growing at a tremendous rate because of demographics and technology. Demographically, health costs increase as Americans get older; the elderly consume far more health care services than younger people. Medical technology makes health costs more expensive, because it provides doctors and hospitals with more things they can do for patients. Thus, not only are our health costs skyrocketing, but the rising costs are not helping to cover those who need health care the most. The elderly receive a disproportionate share of the federal health insurance, largely because they have a great deal of political power. The budgetary process, therefore, is an inherently weak mechanism for controlling mandatory entitlements such as Medicare and Medicaid.

When the budget is squeezed, as it has been for the past three decades, the easiest place to formulate budget cuts is in the "discretionary spending" portion of the budget. Discretionary spending includes the choices Congress has to fund state–local assistance and federal domestic programs which cover the spectrum of services—discretionary spending represents the money Congress appropriates every year for everything from battleships to Head Start. The constitutional authority that allows Congress to make annual appropriations, however, has been weakened considerably.

Due to the growth of entitlement spending, the sector of government that Congress can readily get to from one year to another is no longer expanding. In fact, during the 1990s, it actually shrunk in real terms. In 1990, Congress put strict limits on appropriations, which have since been tightened even further, imposing a "hard freeze," i.e., not allowing increases to keep up with inflation. That policy kept discretionary spending virtually flat through the rest of the decade. That means that there was not enough money to cover the same value of services the government previously provided, much less expand them. The proliferation of entitlement spending at the expense of discretionary spending may potentially sacrifice the capacity of Congress to build new programs appropriate to changing national needs.

REFERENCES

1. Wildavsky, A.; Caiden, N. *The New Politics of the Budgetary Process,* 3rd Ed.; Scott, Foresman and Company: Glenview, IL, 1997.

2. Leloup, L. *The Fiscal Congress*; Greenwood Press: Westport, CT, 1980.

3. Schick, A. *The Capacity to Budget*; The Urban Institute: Washington, D.C., 1990.

4. Ippolito, D.S. *Hidden Spending*; University of North Carolina Press: Chapel Hill, 1984.

5. Fenno, R. *The Emergence of a Senate Leader: Pete Domenici and the Reagan Budget*; CQ Press: Washington, D.C., 1991.

6. Leloup, L. A Fiscal Policy and Congressional Politics. In *Congressional Politics*; Deering, C.J., Ed.; Brooks/Cole: Pacific Grove, CA, 1989; 262–283.

7. Pascall, G. *The Trillion Dollar Budget*; University of Washington Press: Seattle, 1985.

8. Anderson, A.G. A Civil Service Pay and Retirement. In *Entitlement Issues in the Domestic Budget*; Weicher, J., Ed.; American Enterprise Institute: Washington, D.C., 1985; 34–56.

Environmental Ethics

Christine M. Reed
University of Nebraska at Omaha, Omaha, Nebraska, U.S.A.

E

INTRODUCTION

Environmental ethics is a branch of applied philosophy that addresses arguments about the value of nature. The literature in environmental ethics is voluminous, reflecting various philosophical traditions and therefore different ways of approaching such questions as whether the source of value in "nature" is objective, or socially and culturally constructed; whether value in nature is human centered (anthropocentric) or centered outside the sphere of human welfare (nonanthropocentric); and whether value in nature "for itself" is based on the interests and/or rights of individual animals, or on the preservation of species and ecosystems as a whole.

THE INTRINSIC VALUE OF NATURE

In *Respect for Nature*, Paul Taylor[1] assumed a non-anthropocentric stance when he argued that it is possible for a human to *take an animal's standpoint* and to make objective (moral) judgments about what is good for a nonhuman. One of the most important contributions made by the field of environmental ethics to public administration and policy is the argument for intrinsic value in nature, the argument that nature has value in itself and not for its instrumental value to humans. A familiar form of the intrinsic value argument locates the source of value in the objective properties of nature. Value and scientific (especially ecological) facts are closely related, according to those who write from a nonanthropocentric position, and external nature is a source of moral authority.[2] The objective ecological reference point for restoration of the landscape is nature as it existed prior to human cultivation, and the ethical duty is to return an ecosystem to a point where it can evolve independently of further human support.[3]

AESTHETIC VALUE IN NATURE

Another source of intrinsic value are "nonnatural" properties that are systematically dependent on natural properties, but are comprehended through moral intuition rather than through sensory faculties. The preferences or judgments of the valuer have no bearing on the question of intrinsic value.[4] This form of argument supports the preservation of natural landscapes, simply because a beautiful world has intrinsic value. An extension of this argument is that the natural landscape is more beautiful (than an artistic representation of that landscape) because aesthetic qualities exist more fundamentally in the natural objects making up the natural landscape than in the painting depicting them.[5] The aesthetic qualities associated with natural beauty are nevertheless similar to those attributed to art objects: environments that are magnificent and rich, that present the viewer with new ways of perceiving, that have cultural significance because of a connection with the past, and that challenge the way people live or think.[6]

ENVIRONMENTAL PRAGMATISM

Some theories about value in nature try to reconcile anthropocentric and nonanthropocentric approaches by articulating arguments for a "weak anthropocentrism," a point of view that typically emerges from philosophical pragmatism and rejects the idea that the locus of value is *either* in human consciousness *or* in an independent nature. One example is the distinction between individual (human) "felt preferences" for commodities that are satisfied by a market transaction versus "considered preferences" that reflect human value formation arising from the experience of natural objects.[7] A second example of weak anthropocentrism views human understandings of nature as culture-laden linguistic descriptions or metaphors that reflect the human experience of nature, rather than nature as an external reality.[8] A third contribution of environmental pragmatism is the idea of the "mixed community" or shared social world of humans and animals. Human language originates, at least in part, from interaction with nature and from natural sounds and patterns.[9,10]

ENVIRONMENTAL ETHICS AND POLITICAL VALUES

Linking environmental ethics to public administration and policy means going beyond arguments for valuing nature

Encyclopedia of Public Administration and Public Policy
DOI: 10.1081/E-EPAP 120005558

441

and developing arguments for political systems that are compatible with respect for nature. Therein lies the challenge. The major problem of environmental ethics (i.e., the appropriate relationship between people and the natural world) must also address the relationship between political and environmental values. From one perspective, there is a potential conflict between justice for humans and preservation of nature. Arguments in environmental ethics for valuing the biotic community over individual animals *could* (it is feared by some) be extended to advocate sacrificing human rights for the sake of preserving endangered species. From another perspective, however, there is a synergy between respect for people and respect for nature and the potential to improve outcomes for both.[11]

Ecological Rationality

One way to resolve the potential value conflict between the interests of human society and nature is to broaden the definition of (economic) rationality to include ecological values. Agricultural policy, for example, is ecologically rational when it promotes farming practices that meet the basic survival and social needs for all present and future human generations, while also maintaining the overall integrity of ecosystems.[12] Respect for people and nature improves outcomes for both when, for example, forests in Third World countries are protected from clear-cutting to support the fast food market. A policy to prevent clear-cutting would preserve the biodiversity of the forest, thereby supporting its long-term health *and* allow nearby villages to maintain their local subsistence economies and escape desperate poverty.[11]

Green Reason

A second way to balance environmental and political values is to maintain concern for processes of governance that are legitimate because they are based on principles of justice, while extending the moral community to include nonhumans. "Green reason" is an extension of the ideal of communicative rationality to nonhumans.[13] It involves defining nonlinguistic beings as capable of intersubjective communication. It also insists that freedom from domination and distortion in human-to-human discourse be extended to interaction with nature. Just as the policy agenda is often dominated by a few powerful interest groups, so too are human representations of the world privileged via-à-vis representations from other marginal positions, especially animal species.[14] Thus, extending communicative reason to make it truly egalitarian and free from the distortions of political power entails the inclusion of nonhumans as well as human. Communicative rationality is not democratic if it discriminates against nonhuman species ("speciesism") by assuming that only human linguistic representations are privileged in discourse communities.

Reconstructing Human Relationships with Nature

A third approach to balancing environmental and democratic values challenge the appeal to nature as an external source of moral authority, but also rejects the idea of social interaction with a nature that is "other" than us. Instead nature is what humans have constructed through their own social practices. Nature has value precisely because it is shaped by cultural practices and is therefore our responsibility.[15] The primary ethical responsibility is to be aware of nature as a social construction and to make human relationships with the natural world more just and accountable.[16] Preservation of wild nature is an anachronism because "nature" as a reality independent of human or cultural intervention no longer exists. Lamenting the end of nature is an excuse for failing to take responsibility for what society has constructed in both figurative and literal senses of the term. The blurring of the boundaries between the spheres of nature and culture is manifest in the fact that no wilderness areas are left in the United States, apart from some remote areas of Alaska. We are now custodians of a managed world and responsible for all its life forms.[17]

Civic Environmentalism

The term "civic environmentalism" means that a community has organized on its own, rather than in response to federal mandates, to protect its environment. It refers to a process of local, communal self-reflection and recognition that certain environmental hazards, such as "nonpoint" source pollution of streams and rivers, are created over time by the social practices of an entire community.[18] The policy tools for reducing nonpoint source pollution, managing solid waste disposal, and protecting ecosystems include citizen education and participation in changing collective lifestyles. Environmental ethics and democratic values come together when citizens are motivated by civic virtue to become engaged in the political and ecological welfare of their communities.

Public Obligations to Future Generations

The final example of an approach to linking environmental ethics to public administration and policy is concern for intergenerational equity: what are the obligations of public officials and society as a whole to make policy decisions in the present that protect life in the future? One answer is to extend the thought experiment of John Rawls and to imagine people behind a "veil of ignorance" who are establishing procedures for a just society, and who do not know either their economic and social status in society or their place in history. Under those conditions, people will agree to rules of social justice that consider the welfare of future generations.[11] The scope of intergenerational ecological problems, such as global warming and loss of biodiversity, involves public administration and policy at the international level, as well as intervention in the private market, to regulate in favor of future generations.[19]

CONCLUSION: EXPLORING THE LINKAGES

Environmental ethics is a relatively new field, originating in the 1970s. Nevertheless, it has led to the publication of a major journal, *Environmental Ethics*, as well as numerous books on the subject. An encyclopedia entry can only introduce the reader to the essential concepts and arguments, and provide a detailed bibliography of key books for those who want to pursue the topic further. This article has summarized several key approaches to balancing environmental and political values; however, the vast majority of work in environmental ethics makes various philosophical arguments for valuing nature without examining the implications for political values such as individual rights and social equity. Conversely, one reason for the dearth of writing about environmental ethics in public administration and policy is that it poses "significant challenges to mainstream ideas of the ideal society. Public administration tends to focus on how to make society work better, not how to make fundamental alterations."[20] Linking environmental ethics to public administration and policy will therefore require ongoing dialog between the disciplines.

REFERENCES

1. Taylor, P. *Respect for Nature: A Theory of Environmental Ethics*; Princeton University Press: Princeton, 1986.
2. Rolston, H.R. *Environmental Ethics: Duties to and Values in the Natural World*; Temple University Press: Philadelphia, 1988.
3. Attfield, R. Rehabilitating Nature and Making Nature Habitable. In *Philosophy and the Natural Environment*; Attfield, R., Belsey, A., Eds.; Cambridge University Press: Cambridge, 1994; 45–57.
4. Elliot, R. *Faking Nature: The Ethics of Environmental Restoration*; Routledge: London, 1997.
5. Hargrove, E. *Foundations of Environmental Ethics*; Prentice Hall: Englewood Cliffs, 1989.
6. Thompson, J. Aesthetics and the value of nature. Environ. Ethics **1995**, *17*, 291–305, (Fall).
7. Norton, B. Environmental ethics and weak anthropocentrism. Environ. Ethics **1984**, *6*, 131–147, (Summer).
8. Harlow, E.M. The human face of nature: Environmental values and the limits of nonanthropocentrism. Environ. Ethics **1992**, *14*, 27–42, (Spring).
9. Midgley, M. *Animals and Why They Matter*; The University of Georgia Press: Athens, 1983.
10. Weston, A. *Back to Earth: Tomorrow's Environmentalism*; Temple University Press: Philadelphia, 1994.
11. Wenz, P.S. *Environmental Ethics Today*; Oxford University Press: New York, 2001.
12. Aiken, W. Ethical Issues in Agriculture. In *Earthbound: New Introductory Essays in Environmental Ethics*; Regan, T., Ed.; Random House: New York, 1984; 247–288.
13. Dryzek, J.S. Green Reason: Communicative Ethics for the Biosphere. In *Postmodern Environmental Ethics*; Oelschlaeger, M., Ed.; State University of New York Press: Albany, 1995; 101–118.
14. Hayles, N.K. Searching for Common Ground. In *Reinventing Nature? Responses to Postmodern Deconstruction*; Soule, M.E., Lease, G., Eds.; Island Press: Washington, D.C., 1995; 47–63.
15. Vogel, S. *Against Nature: The Concept of Nature in Critical Theory*; State University of New York Press: Albany, 1996.
16. Cronon, W. Introduction: In Search of Nature. In *Uncommon Ground: Rethinking the Human Place in Nature*; Cronon, W., Ed.; W.W. Norton & Company: New York, 1996; 23–56.
17. Borgmann, A. The Nature of Reality and the Reality of Nature. In *Reinventing Nature? Responses to Postmodern Deconstruction*; Soule, M.E., Lease, G., Eds.; Island Press: Washington, D.C., 1995; 31–45.
18. John, D. *Civic Environmentalism: Alternatives to Regulation in States and Communities*; Congressional Quarterly Press: Washington, D.C., 1994.
19. Frederickson, H.G. Can public officials correctly be said to have obligations to future generations? PAR **1994**, *54* (5), 457–464.
20. Luton, L. Symposium–ecological philosophy and public administration theory: Is an ecocentric public administration possible? Introduction. ATP **2001**, *23* (1), 7–9.

Environmental Pollution Control, State Government Administration of

A. Hunter Bacot
The University of North Carolina at Charlotte, Charlotte, North Carolina, U.S.A.

INTRODUCTION

Since 1980, state governments have assumed much responsibility for environmental program administration. Administrative responsibilities of states for pollution control policies are crucial to national environmental initiatives to prevent or contain pollution. Therefore, the management of pollution control policies is conducted primarily by states, and environmental affairs continue to be national priorities that rely on states for administration and implementation.

Environmental administration in the United States is generally distinguished according to media—air, water, and waste are the three generally accepted environmental arenas. Concerning pollution control, states enjoy significant latitude for monitoring and enforcement of air and water pollution control policies. National air and water regulations delegate administrative responsibilities to states based on each state's ability to perform these regulatory functions.[a] State environmental agencies given responsibility for implementing administrative and enforcement provisions of national air and water policies have primacy [i.e., the state has primary responsibility for environmental management in the state, although the Environmental Protection Agency (EPA) oversees state management]. To date, nearly every state has full or partial authority from the EPA to control air and water pollution within their respective borders.

Three national legislative efforts (and subsequent reauthorizations)—the Clean Air Act (CAA), the Clean Water Act (CWA), and the Safe Drinking Water Act (SDWA)—provide states with much of the responsibility for regulating air and water pollution. This delegation of authority is examined in this article. Major provisions of air and water legislation, the degree to which states assume control of the administration of these legislative acts, and how well states fare in controlling pollution are also reviewed.

DELEGATING REGULATORY AUTHORITY TO STATES FOR POLLUTION CONTROL

States having primacy over environmental policies and programs must meet criteria established by the EPA to manage pollution control within their borders. The EPA has ultimate authority over all pollution control programs in the United States, and thus approves whether states are able to manage their own environmental situations. To acquire primacy status from the EPA, states must adhere to guidelines of the EPA (as stated in acts governing pollution) and receive the agency's approval for managing pollution control programs.

The CAA, CWA, and SDWA provide significant administration and implementation responsibilities to states for air and water pollution control. To demonstrate the capacity to enforce national laws within their borders, states initially submit required biennial reports to the EPA discussing state environmental laws, which cannot be less stringent than the national laws, and how these laws support national environmental legislation. States must demonstrate to the EPA the ability to accept many of the permitting, administrative, and enforcement provisions contained in national laws.

To demonstrate an ability to accept environmental management responsibilities (i.e., to attain primacy), states must submit state implementation plans to the EPA. State implementation plans explain to the EPA how state regulations serve national interests with regard to environmental pollution control. State implementation plans are involved, providing detailed explanations about a state's ability to oversee environmental management programs and policies within its borders. They include information about pollution control legislation, state agency information, due process procedures (hearings, comment periods, appeals, etc.), enforcement capabilities, etc. The EPA must approve the state implementation plan, or it can authorize the state to administer environmental policies on a limited or partial arrangement until approval of the state's state implementation plan is granted. Full authorization or delegation gives states full control of environmental programmatic responsibilities. In the year 2002, most states had primacy for most major environmental programs (see Table 1).

---

[a]In addition to the public laws detailing these responsibilities, much of the following discussion draws generally from a host of excellent sources discussing the administration of environmental programs (see Refs. [1–11]).

Encyclopedia of Public Administration and Public Policy
DOI: 10.1081/E-EPAP 120011046

Table 1 State pollution control status for selected air and water acts

Primacy status	Selected air acts (number of states)					Selected water acts (number of states)		Selected drinking water acts (number of states)	
	NSPS	NES HAPS	PSD	Title V	NSR	NPDES	P	PWSS	WPP
Full program delegation or authorization	40	39	14	17	0	38	31	49	15
Partial program delegation or authorization	8	9	3	0	1	4	0	0	0
Program delegation or authorization is approved, pending, or in interim status	1	2	33	28	43	0	1	0	21
Not delegated or not subject to delegation	1	0	0	5	6	8	18	1	14

Notes: For the CAA: State-delegated responsibilities for the **CAA** includes state authority to administer the following components of the act, and include the New Source Performance Standards (NSPS; deals with emission standards performance testing and compliance), National Emission Standards for Hazardous Air Pollutants (HAPS), Prevention of Significant Deterioration (PSD; ensures that areas subject to provisions of the National Ambient Air Quality Standards are not declining), Title V Operating Permit authority, New Source Review (ensures continued compliance with air standards according to air standards permitting base on best available control technology). For the CWA: State-delegated administrative responsibilities for the **CWA** includes state authority to administer the National Pollution Discharge Elimination System (NPDES; governs point source discharges) and pretreatment programs for publicly owned treatment works facilities (P; governs effluents treated at treatment plants before discharge, and directed at nonpoint source treatment). For the SDWA: Safe Drinking Water Act (SDWA; governs drinking water quality),which is a separate act from the CWA, has delegable components for ensuring water quality for consumption; here we are interested in ensuring safe drinking water and water supply, which are specified in the SDWA as the Public Water System Supervision (PWSS; publicly operated water systems) and the Wellhead Protection Program (WPP; protects public water supply wells from contaminants).
Source: Author, Refs. [19] and [20].

Upon acquiring authorization to administer their own programs, states and the EPA remain partners in pollution control. The EPA supports states through the administration of millions of dollars in grants, and provides additional assistance to states through research, technology, and technical support. If states fail to adhere to pollution control strategies stated in their state implementation plans, the EPA can rescind state authorization for administering environmental programs (which rarely occurs). Thus, although most states currently administer their "own" state environmental programs, continuing administration of national initiatives depends on a state's administrative capacity, as so deemed by the EPA, to accept this responsibility.

AIR POLLUTION CONTROL REGULATIONS

Provisions in the CAA, which was originally passed in 1972 and subsequently amended and reauthorized, guide cooperation on policies affecting air quality in the United States. The CAA initially regulated air quality standards of pollutants. CAA amendments furthered air regulations to include air toxins, acid rain, and local air quality attainment, which expanded the agency's responsibility for improving air quality. The original CAA listed only a few contaminants and established national emissions standards for hazardous air pollutants (NESHAP). The NESHAP increased air pollution regulations by addressing commercial and industrial air pollutants (e.g., asbestos, mercury, benzene).

In 1990, subsequent amendments to the CAA increased the roles of states; provisions of the act mandate state participation in the administration of environmental programs. The amendments also require states to prepare state implementation plans (SIPs), which force states to submit to the EPA an "inventory" of their progress in reducing air pollution. Congress also increased the number of regulated pollutants, which, because most states have attained primacy status, gives states additional regulatory and administrative responsibility for air pollution. The amendments also identify new areas of regulation to control releases contributing to acid rain and ozone depletion (among others), define urban nonattainment areas, and identify a host of contaminants, as well as acceptable emission levels for each contaminant.

Generally, states are given reasonable responsibility for establishing acceptable emission levels (in their SIPs). States must account for their performance by tracking emission levels of chemical sources, as well as other new sources identified through increased technological capacity. New emission regulations determine areas that have poor air quality, as well as areas that meet ambient air recommendations (which are established using technologically driven analysis based on "best available technology" or other technological criteria). As technological capacity constantly reveals previously undetectable elements, states that meet their specified standards must continually monitor the status of air pollutants, which is noted in biennial pollution reports required by the EPA.

As is evident in testing standards and monitoring responsibilities, states' assumption of programmatic responsibility for air quality is an arduous assignment. Most states have prospered with program primacy because only a few do not have some program responsibilities delegated (see Table 1). Environmental management of air quality is a continuous, challenging task that is but one of the primary environmental media demanding attention by state environmental agencies.

WATER POLLUTION CONTROL REGULATIONS

An equally demanding area of emphasis for state environmental administrators is surface water quality (e.g., rivers, lakes) and underground water quality (e.g., wellhead protection, aquifers). Like air quality, water quality standards are guided by national legislation—the CWA and its subsequent amendments, and the SDWA—and are generally implemented at the state level. Improved water quality is realized by regulating discharges from industrial, commercial, and municipal (ICM) facilities, as well as nonpoint sources and stormwater systems.

Water quality pollution control is managed by controlling effluents discharged into regulated waters and protecting drinking water sources. Based on treatment standards and effluent lists, states create ambient water quality standards for ICM facilities that discharge conventional pollutants and nonconventional pollutants into surface waters. Conventional pollutants are discharges that deplete or disturb natural elements and/or the balance of elements, whereas nonconventional pollutants are airborne or leachate pollutants that originate elsewhere and migrate or settle in bodies of water and/or area water supplies.

Similar to most laws regulating pollutants, sections of the CWA provide specific guidelines to the EPA for managing water quality and returning programmatic responsibilities to states. States, with EPA oversight, implement most of the provisions set forth in the CWA. Also specified in the CWA are water quality standards based on the type and use of waters—whether recreational, sporting, or serving as a water supply, etc.[b] States classify bodies of water in accordance with standards required for maintaining the classified use. Common classifications of water types and uses organize waters based on exceedances of the specified minimums for stated categories, according to national definitions, as well as designate certain pristine waters as protected.

Drinking water pollution control is another area of significant responsibility for state agencies, and is governed by the SDWA. Drinking water pollution is caused by the contamination of water supplies. Effluents migrating from offsite locations, whether to an aquifer, to wellheads, or generally into the water table, contaminate water supplies. States protect water supplies by establishing standards (based on national standards), distinguishing among source uses (agriculture, drinking water, etc.), and controlling nonpoint threats. Determination of water quality regulations becomes states' responsibility, as water sources, uses, and threats vary widely across states.

The CWA amendments give states responsibility of the permitting process for the National Pollutant Discharge Elimination System (NPDES). The EPA maintained responsibility of pollution discharges until 1987, when responsibility was delegated to states for establishing effluent levels and granting discharge permits. The NPDES regulates direct discharges, or point source discharges into surface waters. National standards guide states in determining allowable discharges and the water quality of water bodies that accept discharges. Facilities discharging effluents into surface waters must have a permit from the state, which grants these facilities permission to discharge effluents into affected surface waters within allowable limits (as established by the EPA).

Over time, states have demonstrated the ability to manage water quality programs. In fact, approximately one-half of the 50 states administer comprehensive water protection programs. Although difficult, states are assuming responsibilities for administering programs to protect and preserve water quality.

---

[b]Categories are classified based on water quality that supports recreational uses by people (class A); ecological integrity and natural habitation (class B); water supplies for public consumption (class C); and industrial, commercial, and agricultural activities (not intended for consumption) (class D).

STATE PROGRESS IN AIR AND WATER POLLUTION CONTROL

From most perspectives, states have succeeded in controlling air and water pollution in the United States. Yet, despite the successes of environmental management in the United States, as Rosenbaum observed, "the nation's air and water remain seriously polluted."[12] Without legislation and policies directed at controlling air and water pollution, however, the situation would likely be much worse. Thus, overall, states' efforts to reduce pollution in our air and water systems are deficient, and although there are improvements in curbing air and water pollution, most improvements are based on seriously limited assessment information.

Under the direction and guidance of the EPA, states have shown progress in cleaning air, water, and drinking water supplies since the 1980s. Air pollution policies enforced by states reveal improvement in air quality throughout the United States. This success in managing pollution is achieved despite regulations governing approximately 200 pollutants, which is a dramatic increase in the number of regulated elements from the original legislation enacted in 1970. Of the six criteria pollutants,[c] each has decreased from 1989 levels. In fact, four of these six pollutants decreased between 25% and 56% (Ref. [13]: Table A-9). There are other areas, namely ozone, in which states continue to encounter difficulty in achieving established reduction goals; another area of special importance to states is air quality in rural areas, which is lagging compared with established goals.[13]

Water quality trends have improved dramatically since 1970, with the enactment of the CWA and subsequent amendments to the act. Improvements in water quality are based on available information, which is woefully inadequate as only approximately one-third of all water bodies have been assessed to determine pollution levels. For example, only 23% of rivers, 42% of lakes, and 32% of estuaries have been assessed to determine surface water quality in the United States.[14] Of water bodies assessed by states, however, there are indications of improvements in water quality. In fact, "states reported that 65 percent of assessed river and stream miles, 55 percent of assessed lake acres, and 56 percent of assessed estuarine square miles fully support the water quality standards states evaluated."[14] As a result, water quality is improving across the states, although this judgment is based on limited information.

Drinking water and groundwater are two other areas involving water quality assessments in states. Although states find overall groundwater quality acceptable, there are measurable problems with contamination from nearby sources, such as underground storage tanks, landfills, septic tanks, etc.[14] Based on state reports, groundwater quality has improved in recent years and continues to support major uses of groundwater resources.[15] As tremendous strides in assessing groundwaters are made, significant deficiencies in coverage remain.[15] Safe drinking water is probably the success story for states aspiring to improve water quality. Although challenged to provide safe drinking water to all citizens, states—armed with provisions of the SDWA—have improved the quality of drinking water since the 1980s.[16] As improvements are made in the "testing, treatment, protection, and provision of drinking water to the public," challenges remain as technology continues to advance the ability to track and detect elements in smaller quantities.[16]

STATE PROGRESS IN MONITORING AND ENFORCEMENT OF POLLUTION CONTROL POLICIES

Although states appear to be making progress in controlling pollution within their borders, the overall picture of states' progress in this area is formidable. States made significant progress in controlling pollution on identified sources or assessed sources. However, because identified or assessed sources comprise only a small percentage of pollution threats, much is not assessed or identified by state agencies charged with managing pollution. It is information about "the unknown" that should concern citizens of each state.

According to the EPA's Office of Inspector General, "air enforcement audits disclosed fundamental weaknesses with state identification and reporting of significant violators of the Clean Air Act."[17] Similar findings plague efforts to control water pollution. Another EPA report submitted "that state enforcement programs could be much more effective in deterring noncompliance with discharge permits and, ultimately, improving the quality of the nation's water."[18] States lag significantly in addressing pollution control problems for all contaminant threats to the nation's air and water. Analysis of state efforts in air and water program enforcement and monitoring suggests states are woefully deficient and, if advances in controlling pollution are to occur, states must improve their efforts, or pollution sources will remain unchecked.

States, therefore, must improve their pollution enforcement and monitoring programs, as well as assessment programs affecting all water bodies and air quality. However, the within-state challenges most states face make improvement extremely difficult and, as a result, unlikely. Most states have improved their pollution control programs

---

[c]Criteria pollutants are carbon monoxide, lead, nitrogen dioxide, ozone, particulate matter, and sulfur dioxide.

dramatically since the 1980s, but these improvements have not kept pace with the increasing program demands required with program primacy. Pollution control for states is proving a Sisyphean task that, despite ample progress, has states struggling to keep up with program requirements.

CONCLUSION

As states continue to cite gains in the quality of air and water by acquiring data necessary to establish current dispositions, more must be known about the true threat of pollution; this is particularly important as information continues to improve knowledge of states' environmental situations. States are continually increasing their capacity to monitor air and water quality, but advances are slow, deliberate, and costly, which imposes considerably on state resources. Accordingly, although states show some success in mitigating pollution, as the analytical capabilities continue to improve with science and technology, states will continually confront new areas of environmental need that commands their attention. More troublesome for states (and citizens) are that many problems remain undetected, and thus may not be recognized until conditions deteriorate to a level unable to support intended uses.[15] As a result, there can be no celebration of state environmental successes, only brief recognition of these successes. The battle to control air and water pollution is daunting and progress in assessment, monitoring, and enforcement must improve dramatically if pollution is to be curtailed and contained.

REFERENCES

1. Advisory Commission on Intergovernmental Relations. *Intergovernmental Decisionmaking for Environmental Protection and Public Works*; USACIR: Washington, D.C., 1992; (A-122).
2. Brownell, F.W. Clean Air Act. In *Environmental Law Handbook,* 14th Ed.; Sullivan, T.F.P., Ed.; Government Institutes: Rockville, MD, 1997; 72–108.
3. Council of State Governments. *Resource Guide to State Environmental Management*; Council of State Governments: Lexington, KY, 1996.
4. Gallagher, L.M. Clean Water Act. In *Environmental Law Handbook,* 14th Ed.; Sullivan, T.F.P., Ed.; Government Institutes: Rockville, MD, 1997; 109–160.
5. Halbleib, W.T. Emergency Planning and Community Right-to-Know Act. In *Environmental Law Handbook,* 14th Ed.; Sullivan, T.F.P., Ed.; Government Institutes: Rockville, MD, 1997; 481–509.
6. Mangun, W.R. Environmental Program Evaluation in an Intergovernmental Context. In *Environmental Program Evaluation: A Primer*; Knapp, G.J., Kim, T.J., Eds.; University of Illinois Press: Urbana, IL, 1998.
7. Nardi, K.J. Underground Storage Tanks. In *Environmental Law Handbook,* 14th Ed.; Sullivan, T.F.P., Ed.; Government Institutes: Rockville, MD, 1997; 360–384.
8. Rabe, B.G. Power to the States: The Promise and Pitfalls of Decentralization. In *Environmental Policies in the 1990s: Reform or Reaction*; Vig, N.J., Kraft, M.E., Eds.; CQ Press: Washington, D.C., 1997; 31–52.
9. Scagnelli, J.M. Pollution Prevention Act. In *Environmental Law Handbook,* 14th Ed.; Sullivan, T.F.P., Ed.; Government Institutes: Rockville, MD, 1997; 510–521.
10. Scheberle, D. *Federalism and Environmental Policy: Trust and the Politics of Implementation*; Georgetown University Press: Washington, D.C., 1997.
11. Williams, S.E. Safe Drinking Water Act. In *Environmental Law Handbook,* 14th Ed.; Sullivan, T.F.P., Ed.; Government Institutes: Rockville, MD, 1997; 196–225.
12. Rosenbaum, W.A. *Environmental Politics and Policy*; CQ Press: Washington, D.C., 2002.
13. US EPA. Office of Air Quality Natl. Air Qual. Emiss. Trends Rep., 1999; (EPA 454/R-01-004, March).
14. US EPA. Office of Water. *Water Quality Conditions in the United States: A Profile from the 1998 National Water Quality Inventory Report to Congress*; 2000; ES-3(EPA-841-F-00-006, June).
15. US EPA. Office of Water. *Environmental Indicators of Water Quality in the United States*; 1996; (EPA 841-R-96-002, June).
16. US EPA. Office of Water. *25 Years of the Safe Drinking Water Act: History and Trends*; 1999; 34 (EPA 816-R-99-007, December).
17. US EPA. Office of Inspector General. *Audit Report Consolidated Report on OECA's Oversight of Regional and State Air Enforcement Programs*; 1998; i (E1GAE7-03-0045-8100244, September).
18. US EPA. Office of Inspector General. *Audit Report Water Enforcement: State Enforcement of Clean Water Act Dischargers Can Be More Effective*; 2001; i (Report No. 2001-P-00013, August).
19. Environmental Council of the States, http://www.sso.org/ecos/, (accessed July/August 2001).
20. Local Government Environmental Assistance Network, http://www.lgean.org/html/stateregs.cfm, (accessed July/August 2001).

Equal Employment Opportunity and Affirmative Action

Norma M. Riccucci
University at Albany, State University of New York,
Albany, New York, U.S.A.

INTRODUCTION

Equal employment opportunity (EEO) is largely viewed as a means to prevent discrimination in the workplace. Title VII of the Civil Rights Act of 1964, for example, as amended, is intended to prevent discrimination on the basis of race, color, religion, gender, and national origin in public and private sector workforces. Affirmative action, however, which emerged in response to pervasive employment discrimination, embodies proactive efforts to redress past discriminations and to diversify the workplace in terms of race, ethnicity, gender, age, physical abilities, and so forth. Affirmative action has been viewed as a legal tool to ensure EEO or diversity (see Table 1 for comparison of the concepts).

EMPLOYMENT DISCRIMINATION AND THE EVOLUTION OF EEO

Although there were a handful of early efforts to combat employment discrimination in our society, it was not until the 1960s that this nation, spurred by racial unrest, was galvanized into taking genuine action to end discriminatory employment practices. In 1964, Title VII of the Civil Rights Act, which is the cornerstone of EEO law in the United States, was passed. Title VII was intended to prevent private sector employers, with 15 or more employees, from discriminating on the basis of race, color, religion, gender, and national origin.[1] Today, there are numerous statutes, executive orders, and policies in place that are intended to combat employment discrimination in the workplace. Table 2 illustrates the major EEO laws and policies that have been advanced since the Reconstruction era. As can be seen, Title VII of the Civil Rights Act was extended to public employers with passage of the Equal Employment Opportunity Act in 1972. It is this act, along with provisions of the U.S. Constitution (e.g., the Fourteenth Amendment) and its enforcing legislation (Sections 1981 and 1983 of The Civil Rights Acts of 1866 and 1871, respectively), that are the primary legal mechanisms geared to protect women and people of color from employment discrimination in the public sector.[2]

As with race, ethnicity, and gender, employers are also prohibited from discriminating against persons on numerous other dimensions or characteristics, including age and ability. For example, the Age Discrimination in Employment Act (ADEA) of 1967 makes it illegal for private businesses to refuse to hire, to discharge, or to otherwise discriminate against an individual between the ages of 40 and 70. The act was amended in 1974 to apply to state and local governments. Age discrimination in federal employment is prohibited by executive order, but additional amendments to the ADEA banned forced retirement for federal employees at any age. Enforcement authority over the ADEA was originally vested in the Department of Labor, but was transferred to the Equal Employment Opportunity Commission as part of the federal civil service reform of 1978.

There are also various laws that prohibit discrimination on the basis of a disability. For instance, the Vocational Rehabilitation Act of 1973, as amended, prohibits discrimination against persons with disabilities. These protections were strengthened by Title I of the Americans with Disabilities Act (ADA) of 1990, which covers private sector employers as well as state and local government employers with 15 or more employees. The federal workforce, which is not protected by the ADA, continues to be covered by the Rehabilitation Act of 1973. An important aspect of the ADA is that it covers persons who are positive for human immunodeficiency virus or who have acquired immune deficiency syndrome.

FROM EEO TO AFFIRMATIVE ACTION

Equal employment opportunity law is considered to be passive in the sense that it requires employers to refrain from discriminating against protected-class members (i.e., those designated for protection by the specific EEO legislation). Affirmative action, however, requires employers to take positive steps toward employing, promoting, and retaining qualified women, people of color, and other protected-class persons (see description of Executive Order 11246, as amended, in Table 2). Not only would this help to rectify past and present discrimination, but it would also help to create "representative bureaucra-

Encyclopedia of Public Administration and Public Policy
DOI: 10.1081/E-EPAP 120010766

Table 1 Comparing EEO and affirmative action

EEO	Affirmative action
Qualitative/Quantitative. Emphasis on preventing or ending discrimination	**Qualitative/Qualtitative.** Emphasis on redressing past discrimination and achieving diverse, representative workforces
Legally driven. Mandated by federal law	**Managerially and legally driven.** Involves voluntarily developed goals and court-ordered programs; common law has defined its legality and constitutionality
Fairness. Seeks to end discrimination and create equal opportunities	**Remedial and compensatory.** Specific target groups benefit as past and present wrongs are remedied
Access model. Model assumes that protected-class persons will be able to access organizations	**Assimilation model.** Assumes that persons and groups brought into the system will adapt to existing organizational norms; can result in ''sink or swim'' atmosphere/environment
Level playing field. Seeks to ensure equal opportunity and access	**Opens doors.** Seeks to affect hiring and promotion decisions in organizations

Source: Adapted from Ref. [1].

cies''—that is, government bureaucracies that are demographically representative of the general populations they serve. Because affirmative action is based on proactive efforts, it has led to myriad lawsuits challenging its legality and constitutionality. In fact, one of the first legal challenges, *Regents of the University of California v. Bakke* (1978),[3] argued that affirmative action resulted in ''reverse discrimination.'' In Bakke, the U.S. Supreme

Table 2 Federal EEO law

Law/policy	Provisions/coverage
Civil Rights Act of 1866, Section 1981	Provides that ''all persons shall have the Same right ... to the full and equal benefit of the laws ... as is enjoyed by white citizens''
Fourteenth Amendment to U.S. Constitution (1868)	Requires all states and their political subdivisions to provide equal protection of the laws to all persons in their jurisdictions
Civil Rights Act of 1871, Section 1983	Prohibits persons acting ''under color of any statute, ordinance, regulation, custom or usage ...''from depriving any citizen or person within the jurisdiction of the United States of any rights, privileges, or immunities secured by the Constitution
Ramspect Act 1940	Prohibits discrimination in federal employment based on race, color, or creed
Executive Order 8802 (1941)	Called for the elimination of discrimination based on race, color, religion, or national origin with the federal service and defense production industries
Civil Rights Act of 1964, Title VII	Prohibits discrimination on the basis of race, color, religion, and national origin
Executive Order 11246, as amended (1965)	Forbids employment discrimination based on race, color, religion, gender, and national origin by federal government and federal contractors and subcontractors, and requires the federal government and contractors to engage in affirmative action to hire and promote persons based on these characteristics
Age Discrimination in Employment Act (ADEA), as amended (1967)	Forbids employment discrimination based on age
Equal Employment Opportunity Act of 1972 (amends Title VII of CRA of 1964)	Extends Title VII protection to state, local, and federal government employees and workers in educational institutions
Vocational Rehabilitation Act of 1973	Prohibits federal government and its contractors from discriminating against persons with disabilities
Vietnam Era Veterans' Readjustment Act of 1974	Requires the federal government and its contractors to promote employment opportunities for Vietnam-era veterans
Americans with Disabilities Act (ADA) of 1990	Forbids private, state, and local government employers from discriminating on the basis of disability
Civil Rights Act of 1991	Overturned several negative U.S. Supreme Court decisions issued in 1989 on EEO and affirmative action; established a Glass Ceiling Commission to study the artificial barriers to the advancement of women and persons of color in the workplace

Court upheld, for the first time, the legality of an affirmative action program, when it ruled in favor of a flexible admissions program of the University's Medical School, which took race into account as a criterion for admissions.

A Snapshot of Affirmative Action Case Law

Overall, the legal status of affirmative action has been so mercurial that its current standing as an employment tool or social policy is often difficult to delineate. That is to say, as new and different judges filter through the various federal and state court systems, the case law is transformed, and ultimately the parameters of affirmative action are altered. However, a brief summary of the case law since passage of the Civil Rights Act of 1991 is presented in Table 3. Passage of the 1991 act was significant because it reversed a series of Supreme Court decisions issued in 1989 that severely restricted the use of affirmative action. As Table 3 shows, without a definitive ruling on the merits of affirmative action from the U.S. Supreme Court, a hodgepodge of rulings are being issued by U.S. Appeals Courts, where some circuit courts are upholding affirmative action programs and others are not.

Perhaps the most important legal developments around affirmative action as of this writing include the following cases: *Hopwood*,[4] Piscataway,[5] *Smith*,[6] and *Lesage*.[7] In *Hopwood v. State of Texas* (1996), for example, the U.S. Supreme Court let stand a decision by the U.S. Court of Appeals for the Fifth Circuit. The Fifth Circuit Court in *Hopwood* struck down the constitutionality of an affirmative action program at the University of Texas's Law School aimed at increasing the number of African–American and Mexican–American students. In effect, the Fifth Circuit's ruling called into question the continued validity of the High Court's 1978 *Bakke* ruling. Because the Supreme Court did not rule on the merits of the case, the *Hopwood* ruling, at least for now, governs the three states comprised by the Fifth Circuit—Texas, Louisiana, and Mississippi.

In another critical case, *Taxman v. Piscataway Township Board of Education* (1996), the school board in this New Jersey district was forced to lay off teachers because of budget problems. In an effort to maintain racial diversity in its teaching staff, the school board dismissed Sharon Taxman, a white teacher, rather than the equally qualified African–American teacher, Debra Williams, the only person of color in the Business Department out of 10 other teachers. Both had accrued an equal amount of

Table 3 Chronology of legal actions around affirmative action since the 1990s

1991	Civil Rights Act passed. Restores affirmative action to its pre-1989 legal status.
1995	*Adarand v. Peña* (115 5. Ct. 2097). U.S. Supreme Court rules that the Equal Protection Clause of the Fifth Amendment requires that racial classifications used in federal set-aside programs must undergo strict scrutiny analysis.
1995	*In re Birmingham Reverse Discrimination Employment Litigation* (115 S. Ct. 1695). U.S. Supreme Court let stand without comment, a decision by the U.S. Court of Appeals for the Eleventh Circuit (20 F.3d. 1525, 1994) that invalidated a promotion plan aimed at promoting African–American firefighters to the position of lieutenant.
1995	*Claus v. Duquesne Light Company* (115 S. Ct. 1700). U.S. Supreme Court let stand, without comment, a decision by the Third Circuit Court (46 F. 3d 1115, 1994) of Appeals, that awarded a white engineer for a utility company $425,000 in damages because, according to the court, he was ''passed over'' in favor of an African American for promotion to a managerial job.
1996	*Hopwood v. State of Texas* (1996 WL 227009). U.S. Supreme Court let stand a ruling by the U.S. Court of Appeals for the Fifth Circuit (78 F. 3d. 932) that struck down the constitutionality of an affirmative action program at the University of Texas Law School.
1996	President Clinton suspends, for a minimum of 3 years, all federal set-aside programs.
1997	*Taxman v. Piscataway Township Board of Education* (91 F.3d 1547, 1996) is dropped from the U.S. Supreme Court's calendar because parties settled. Thus remains the 1996 opinion of U.S. Court of Appeals for the Third Circuit: the goal of achieving or maintaining diversity cannot be a justification under Title VII of the Civil Rights Act, as amended, for a race-based employment decision.
1999	*Lesage v. Texas* (120 S. Ct. 467). U.S. Supreme Court throws out a reverse discrimination suit filed under the Equal Protection Clause of the Fourteenth Amendment against the University of Texas' Department of Education.
2000	*Smith v. University of Washington* (2000 U.S. App. LEXIS 31160, 9th Cir.). Relying on the *Bakke* ruling, the Ninth Circuit Court of Appeals upholds a race-based affirmative action program for admissions, stating that a properly designed and operated race-conscious admissions program would not be in violation of Title VI or the Fourteenth Amendment.

seniority. Taxman filed suit, claiming that her rights under Title VII of the Civil Rights Act of 1964, as amended, had been violated. The appeals court examined whether Title VII permits the use of affirmative action to promote racial diversity. As the trial proceeded, Taxman was rehired by the school board, so reinstatement was not an issue.

The U.S. Court of Appeals for the Third Circuit in *Taxman* struck down the affirmative action program ruling that the goal of achieving or maintaining diversity cannot be a justification for a race-based employment decision under Title VII of the Civil Rights Act. The U.S. Supreme Court agreed to hear an appeal to the case, but before the case went before the High Court, the parties settled. Taxman received $186,000 in the settlement, with her lawyers receiving $247,500. Thus, the Third Circuit's opinion stands and the High Court did not have the opportunity to issue a ruling on the merits of the case. The Third Circuit covers the following districts: Delaware, New Jersey, Pennsylvania, and the Virgin Islands.

In contrast with the *Hopwood* and *Piscataway* decisions is the Ninth Circuit Appellate Court ruling in *Smith v. University of Washington* (2000), where the appeals court upheld an admissions policy at the University of Washington's Law School that takes race into account. In *Smith*, three white applicants to the law school sued for the school's use of affirmative action in admissions decisions. Similar to the *Bakke* case, the applicants claimed that they were denied admissions to the law school because racial preferences were granted to people of color. Race was considered as one of several diversity factors in making admissions decisions. In upholding the admissions policy, the Ninth Circuit Court in *Smith* (2000: 1201) stated that because "*Bakke* has not been overruled by the Supreme Court.... Justice Powell's opinion [in *Bakke*] remains the law." The districts covered by the Ninth Circuit include Alaska, Arizona, California, Hawaii, Idaho, Montana, Nevada, Oregon, Washington, Guam, and the Northern Mariana Islands.

Another important case as of this writing is *Lesage v. Texas* (1998). In this case, Lesage, an African immigrant of Caucasian descent, applied for admission to a PhD program in the Education Department of the University of Texas at Austin. Of the 233 applications received, about 20 students were admitted to the program. Lesage was not admitted, but 1 person of color out of the 20 was offered admission. Lesage discovered that race was a factor at some stage in the admissions review process and filed a "reverse discrimination" suit, claiming that his rights under the Equal Protection Clause of the Fourteenth Amendment had been violated.

Although the district court ruled against Lesage in favor of the university, the Fifth Circuit Appellate Court reversed the lower court's decision, stating that the university violated Lesage's constitutional rights by "reject-ing his application in the course of operating a racially discriminatory admissions program" (*Lesage*, 1998: 222). It may be recalled that it was the Fifth Circuit that struck down the affirmative action program at the University of Texas in *Hopwood*; thus, its decision in *Lesage* was somewhat anticipated.

The U.S. Supreme Court, however, in a surprising decision, reversed the judgment of the appeals court (*Lesage*, 1999). Although the court did not decide whether the university's admissions process was discriminatory, it ruled that the Court of Appeals erred in its judgment that it was "irrelevant" as to whether Lesage would have been admitted to the university in the absence of an affirmative action program. Referring to one of its earlier decisions, the Supreme Court stated that an employer could "defeat liability by demonstrating that if would have made the same decision absent the forbidden consideration" (*Lesage*, 1999: 468). This suggests that public employers and universities can avoid liability in constitutional challenges to their affirmative action programs by demonstrating that they would have made the same decision (e.g., to hire or admit a person of color) without the affirmative action program.

In sum, the contours of affirmative action law continue to be reshaped by the courts. However, it should further be noted, that some lower courts continue to uphold the use of affirmative action programs. In addition, the U.S. Supreme Court, pursuant to its *Lesage* (1999) decision, has said that public employers can mount certain constitutional defenses of their affirmative action programs.

THE FUTURE OF EEO AND AFFIRMATIVE ACTION

Although it is unlikely that EEO laws would be repealed at this point in time, the degree to which courts are willing enforce the laws can vary. Indeed, as the U.S. Supreme Court continues to promote its policy of "federalism," whereby the court upholds the sovereignty rights of the states, protecting them from unnecessary or unwarranted intrusion by the federal government, severe restrictions have been placed on state workers' ability to sue their state in federal court for federal EEO violations. In two recent cases, *Kimel v. Florida Board of Regents* (2000)[8] and *Garrett v. the University of Alabama*, (2001),[9] the U.S. Supreme Court, for the first time, held that the ADEA and the ADA, respectively, were inapplicable to the states. In effect, state workers can file suit against state governments, but only if the state agrees to be sued and only under the state's EEO law. These laws tend to be weaker, less effective, and narrower in scope. For example, state disability laws tend to be much less rigorous than the ADA around reasonable accommodations. The future of affirmative action also rests with the courts. However, it is important to note that given the demographic shifts in the United States, as well as public employers' continued efforts to develop diversity programs, public sector workforces are becoming more diverse. Thus, despite court rulings, employers, whether through diversity efforts or affirmative action programs, seem unwilling to abandon their efforts to diversify their workplaces.

REFERENCES

1. Rosenbloom, D.H. *Federal Equal Employment Opportunity*; Praeger Publishers: New York, 1977.
2. Riccucci, N.M. *Managing Diversity in Public Sector Workforces*; Westview Press: Boulder, 2002.
3. Regents of the University of California v. Bakke, 438 U.S. 265 (1978).
4. Hopwood v. State of Texas, 78 F. 3d. 932 (1996); cert. denied, Thurgood Marshall Legal Society v. Hopwood, 518 U.S. 1033 (1996).
5. Taxman v. Piscataway Township Board of Education, 91 F.3d 1547 (3rd Cir. 1996).
6. Smith v. University of Washington, 2 F. Supp. 2d 1324 (W.D. Wash. 1998); aff'd, 233 F.3d 1188, (9th Cir. 2000).
7. Lesage v. Texas, A-96-CA-286, 1997 (unpublished); rev'd, 158 F.3d 213 (1998); rev'd and remanded, 120 S.Ct. 467 (1999).
8. Kimel v. Florida Board of Regents, 528 U.S. 62 (2000).
9. Garrett v. the University of Alabama, 193 F.3d 1214 (11th Cir. 1999); cert. granted, University of Alabama at Birmingham Bd. of Trustees v. Garrett, 529 U.S. 1065 (2000); Board of Trustees of the University of Alabama v. Garrett, ____ U.S. ___, 121 S.Ct. 955 (2001).

Ethics, Feminist Perspective on

Dana Burr Bradley
The University of North Carolina at Charlotte,
Charlotte, North Carolina, U.S.A.

INTRODUCTION

Since at least the 1980s, feminist philosophers and ethicists have been debating new ground in ethical theory. Feminist ethics criticizes the normative analysis of issues and concepts concerning right action, the qualities of humanitarian good, and social justice. Many different versions of feminist ethics exist, and eight major strains of feminist theory (liberal, Marxist, radical, psychoanalytical, socialist, ecological, phenomenological, and postmodern)—each with its own epistemology, ontology, and ethical implications—have been identified.[1]

DOMINANT THEMES OF FEMINIST ETHICS

Feminist ethics criticizes the gender blindness and biases that characterize much of traditional ethical theory. For example, traditional ethics has tended to assume a public–private dichotomy, according to the primary characteristics considered to be part of the "moral point of view "of universality and impartiality, that corresponds implicitly to institutions and activities dominated by men. This has led to the questioning by feminist philosophers of the opposition between reason and emotion presumed by much traditional ethical theory. In response, the field has offered important accounts of the role of emotions in moral reason.

Feminist ethics has developed new theories and concepts that are more gender sensitive, and has worked to conceptualize issues of right action, social justice, and the human good from out of the more gendered experience of diverse groups of women. Each major strain of thought—liberal, Marxist, radical, psychoanalytical, socialist, and postmodern—attempts to address the causes and solutions its framework identifies for the subordination of women.

Liberal Feminist Thought

Liberal feminist theory traces its roots to Wollstonecraft's *A Vindication of the Rights of Woman*[2] and in Mill's *The Subjection of Women*.[3] In this paradigm, it is cultural constraints that hinder women from competing fully in the public world. Traditional society excludes women from law, politics, medicine, and so forth because they are believed to be less capable. Therefore, liberal feminists endeavor to change this situation by insisting that women be accorded the same educational and occupational opportunities as men.

Marxist Feminist Thought

Marxist feminist thought promulgates that it is impossible to secure genuine equal opportunity within a class-based society. Private ownership of the means of production is responsible for an inegalitarian class system. A communist system must replace a capitalist system to ensure that no one would be economically subordinate to anyone else. Thus, men and women would be economic equals.

Radical Feminist Thought

Radical feminist thought, like Marxist feminist thought, stands in contrast to liberal feminist paradigms. Radical feminists believe that the patriarchal system so oppresses women that it cannot be reformed. Therefore, the legal, economic, political, social (the family), and cultural (church) institutions associated with a patriarchal system must be eliminated. In contrast to Marxists feminists, radical feminists insist that men, not capitalism, are women's primary oppressors.

Psychoanalytical Feminist Thought

Psychoanalytical feminists also focus on gender and sexuality, but in a different way than that of radical feminists. This theoretical orientation seeks to explain differences in male and female sexuality by using Freudian-based analyses of infant or childhood experiences. Psychoanalytical feminists seek to rewrite the Oedipal drama by promoting dual parenting and dual career by heterosexual couples. This paradigm views the raising of children by both men and women as essential to promoting the universality of human values. Following this precept, children would no longer view the values of authority and autonomy as male the values of love and dependence as strictly female.

Encyclopedia of Public Administration and Public Policy
DOI: 10.1081/E-EPAP 120011059

Socialist and Postmodern Feminist Thought

The liberal, Marxist, radical, and psychoanalytical perspectives are not the only ones offering paradigms for feminist ethics. The socialist feminist perspective tries to weave a coherent ideology from each of the other major perspectives. Juliet Mitchell[4] argued that four structures overdetermine women's existence: production, reproduction, sexuality, and the socialization of children. Woman's status and function in all these components must change if true equality is to be realized by women. Alison Jaggar[5] built upon this perspective by using the concept of alienation to explain how, under a capitalist system, everything and everyone can be both a source of a woman's integration and disintegration as a person. Postmodern feminists have in turn challenged these efforts as ''phallogocentric'' thought and dismissive of the true diversity (from a class, culture, and race perspective) of women.

ETHICS OF CARE

The most famous of the feminist paradigm is the ethics of care first proposed by Carol Gilligan[6]—and pursued and refined by other philosophers[7]—in part as a response to the androcentric ethics of justice model that they view as the traditional approach to framing ethical issues. It is most closely allied with the liberal perspective, drawing upon the importance of culture in framing the experience of woman.

Noting that many feelings are as widely held as valid as rationality, the feminist care framework calls for using the women's perspective in approaching ethical issues by incorporating intuition and emotion along with reason. Feminist moral theory stresses the value of incorporating context, practical considerations, and relationship into one's ethical relationship.[8] In feminist ethics, intimate contexts are seen as important as more global ones, because universal principles do not in actuality apply to all circumstances or individuals. Gillian posited the mother–child relationship as the model for ethical decision making. Key elements include an emphasis on self-sacrifice for the good of the other, a concern for the well-being of the whole person, and a desire to nurture individual development and independence.

Although Gilligan's argument for gender differences received widespread attention, the assertion of systematic sex differences has not held in subsequent research.[9,10] However, the ethics-of-care paradigm offers a contrast to the bureaucratic approach to social policy and public administration. In the latter, focus is on rules, control, formal lines of authority, and ensuring relative uniformity in service delivery. A feminist ethics-of-care paradigm promotes attention to the individual, as well as to family, context, consideration of the uniqueness of the particular individual, and seeking solutions that fit specific circumstances rather than applying standards.

Historically, the success of bureaucratic organizations has been evaluated in terms of their precision, continuity, and technical utility.[11] With its historical emphasis on the abstract agent, public administration leaves little room for emotion, ambiguity, and social relationships.[12] Thus, organizational goals emphasize efficiency and effectiveness, and put less weight on context and relationships.

The traditional approach to public administration and public policy emphasizes a values-neutral perspective, and reliance upon structures and rules. This means that the application of established principles increases the likelihood that decision making is clear and applied in an unbiased manner. The downside to this approach is that strict adherence to rules in decision making may not fully account for the complexity of the problem and tends to discount the needs of marginalized populations.

The feminist ethics-of-care approach provides a different perspective by emphasizing the inclusion of many voices in the decision process. By valuing relationships, the feminist ethics of care connects the decision maker and those affected by the decisions. This leads to a viewing of more complex and contextual factors that are then explicitly incorporated into the decision process. Most important, it stresses the culture of caring along a dynamic continuum.[13]

Feminist care ethics is not a panacea. Because this paradigm encourages the development of caring relationships within the formulation and administration of policy, there is a demonstrable problem with ensuring equality of attention, service, and care. This issue leads to an important ethical question regarding the delivery of services to individuals with established relationships to decision makers over those who are perhaps less well known, but have more pressing needs.

An additional disadvantage to the feminist care approach is that, with its emphasis on meeting individualized needs, it can theoretically be highly labor intensive or time consuming. Issues relating to accountability can also be a drawback. Most programs and services have developed recognizable benchmarks, related to measuring the program's structures or policies. A feminist care approach would challenge this assessment strategy, relying more upon an individualized approach to both service delivery and quality measurement.

Some who have assessed feminist care ethics have argued that, although it may be a powerful ethical approach for one-to-one or community-level issues, it is a less useful guide for public administration or public policy due to its emphasis on the personal and individual contexts, and its concern with individual relationships.[14]

Liedtka[15] described a caring organization as one in which networks of ongoing personal relationships are formed by "connected selves." Derived from concepts in feminist ethics, she suggested caring organizations are ones that focus on persons, are ends in themselves instead of a means to profits, are essentially personal, and are growth enhancing for the members by developing people to their full capacities. Liedtka, and Dobson and White,[16] suggested that organizations that exhibit these caring tendencies will have better economic performance than organizations based on other foundations. Dobson and White specifically suggested that a caring organization will be a place where trust will flourish because trust is required for personal relationships: "One needs to be trusting if one sees oneself as interdependent and connected."[16]

The feminist ethics paradigm, with its focus on contextual sensitivity, flexibility, client autonomy, and individuality, adds important elements to debates in public administration or public policy. Health care, in particular, with its current emphasis on productivity, concern for market dynamics, and a disconnect between decision making and patient input, would benefit from incorporating a feminist ethics perspective.

CONCLUSION

Bringing feminist ethical theory to reflect on specific social policies and on the development of public administration theories is productive for both theory and practice by raising important questions for each. Do feminist ethical critiques and positive concepts suggest directions for policy other than those currently on the public agenda? A feminist approach to policy and administration asks about the differences between men and women that "so-called neutral" policy evaluation has failed to highlight. Normative approaches to the gendering of policy often reveal the need for more contextual applications of principles and methods for understanding the plural identities that characterize most people's lives. Such normative approaches also tend to show that simple alternative between formalized equality and special treatment, and/or

allowing or forbidding actions often do not adequately address feminist policy issues.

REFERENCES

1. *Feminism and Philosophy*; Tuana, N., Tong, R., Eds.; Westview Press: Boulder, CO, 1995.
2. Wollstonecraft, M. *A Vindication of the Rights of Women*; Poston, C.H., Ed.; W. W. Norton: New York, 1975; reprint.
3. Mill, J.S. The Subjection of Women. In *Essays on Sex Equality*; Rossi, A.S., Ed.; University of Chicago Press: Chicago, 1970; 184–185.
4. Mitchell, J. *Psychoanalysis and Feminism*; Vintage Books: New York, 1975.
5. Jaggar, A.M. *Feminist Politics and Human Nature*; Rowman and Allanheld: Totowa, NJ, 1983.
6. Gilligan, C. *In a Different Voice: Psychological Theory and Women's Development*; Harvard University Press: Cambridge, 1982.
7. Hoddings, N. *Caring: A Feminine Approach to Ethics and Moral Education*; University of California Press: Berkeley, CA, 1984.
8. Held, V. *Feminist Morality: Transforming Culture, Society and Politics*; University of Chicago Press: Chicago, IL, 1983.
9. Jurkiewicz, C.L.; Massey, T.K., Jr. The influence of ethical reasoning on leader effectiveness: An empirical study of nonprofit executives. Nonprofit Manag. Leadersh. **1998**, *9* (2), 173–186.
10. Walker, L. Sex Differences in Moral Reasoning. In *Handbook of Moral Behavior and Development, Vol. 2: Research*; Jurtines, W., Gewirtz, J., Eds.; Erlbaum: Hillsdale, NY, 1991.
11. Dill, A. Defining needs, defining systems: A critical analysis. Gerontologist **1993**, *33*, 453–460.
12. Stivers, C. Toward a feminist perspective in public administration. Women Polit. **1990**, *10* (4), 49–55.
13. Tronto, J.C. *Moral Boundaries: A Political Argument for an Ethic of Care*; Routeledge: New York, 1993.
14. Carse, L.A.; Nelson, H. Rehabilitation Care. Kennedy Inst. Ethics J. **1996**, *6* (1), 19–35.
15. Liedtka, J.M. Feminist morality and competitive reality: A role of an ethic of care? Bus. Ethics Q. **1996**, *6* (2), 182–194.
16. Dobson, J.; White, J. Toward the feminine firm. Bus. Ethics Q. **1995**, *5* (3), 463–478.

Ethics, Governance Structures

Carole L. Jurkiewicz
Louisiana State University, Baton Rouge, Louisiana, U.S.A.

INTRODUCTION

Organizational theorists, researchers, and practitioners have increasingly recognized the importance of ensuring behavioral compliance with ethical standards through a governance structure.[1] A governance structure refers to an ethics infrastructure that contains the tools, systems, and conditions for motivating and enforcing high standards of conduct.[2] These can take many forms, but all include systematized policies and procedures to impartially monitor compliance with an ethical code, ethical mission, or other form of articulated standards of conduct. Generally, the governance structure operates as a separate entity with an organizational hierarchy that protects it and the people working on behalf of it from repercussions of those it may necessarily investigate and discipline. The scope of its oversight can be organization-wide or focused on specific departments. Within its purview, it has the authority to create and enforce policies regarding the conduct of individuals from the highest to lowest levels of authority and responsibility. Effective governance structures are believed to reduce the number of ethical violations,[3] strengthen organizational culture[4] and managerial accountability,[5] and enhance public trust in government.[6]

The framework of governance structures assumes that a broad-based approach is most effective in ensuring compliance behaviors;[7] policies and processes are thus targeted simultaneously to people, structure, and technology. Although the concept is rooted in the arguments of Friedrich[8] and Finer,[9] the theoretical foundations of governance structures can be traced to the early literature on organizational design[10] and change.[11] This systems approach was first alluded to as a method for moderating ethical behavior in public administration as early as 1955.[12] In 1978, efforts to elaborate upon and refine governance structures garnered institutional legitimacy with the establishment of both the U.S. Office of Government Ethics (see http://www.usoge.gov) and the Office of Inspectors General (see http://www.ignet.gov/). Calls for substantive innovation in governance structures continue, notably with Truelson's argument for institutional controls;[11] the emphasis on establishing appropriate ethical climates[4,13] and systematized values;[14] and the introduction of transparency systems.[15] One of the most active areas of implementation and innovation is currently in municipal governments in Europe and Africa (see http://www.oecd.org/).

FRAMEWORK OF ETHICS GOVERNANCE STRUCTURES

The necessary underpinning of governance structures is to ensure that the ethical standards are clearly communicated and understood.[16,17] This includes dissemination of materials, training, updating information as appropriate, and creating accountability systems. Efforts are made to reinforce the importance of this message to the same degree in all levels of the organization.[18] In addition to articulating the standards, specifying the repercussions of violating these standards in terms of organizational policies and legal frameworks is essential. Although laws are inflexible and generally fall short of specifying desired behaviors, they are important safety nets in governing structures.[2] Accountability mechanisms should provide adequate control, while allowing for reasonable flexibility. Ethical wrongdoing is frequently contributed to by too many and by rules that are too complex and difficult to comprehend and follow, even for those whose intentions are to do so.[2] Employees should understand what is expected of them in terms of ethical behavior, in terms of the scope of their decisional boundaries, and in terms of consequences if those standards are violated. Disciplinary sanctions typically range from warnings and reprimands to financial penalties and dismissal. Disciplinary measures are expected to be timely, fairly enforced, and open to public scrutiny. It is sometimes advisable to involve external institutions in cases involving individuals or issues that may be particularly intractable.

It is expected that the ethical standards communicated should be demonstrated and reinforced by officials in both their day-to-day activities, the reputation they strive to uphold, and the policies they support on behalf of the organization. Implicit and explicit commitment to ethics should be evidenced in both the spirit and the letter of their management philosophies.[3] Particular attention is generally given to issues relating to the use of official information and public resources, receiving gifts or benefits,

Encyclopedia of Public Administration and Public Policy
DOI: 10.1081/E-EPAP 120010932

and interactions crossing the public–private sector boundaries. More detailed oversight is generally given to individuals in positions that are historically more susceptible to corruption, such as procurement and human resources.[19] Such oversight may include regulations and guidelines specific to these functions, stricter controls, and regular redeployment. Managers' decision-making processes, financial interests, and potential conflicts of interest should be transparent, and available for public scrutiny facilitated by democratic processes and with legislative oversight.[20] This pattern of openness, referred to as transparency systems,[15] becomes increasingly important as one ascends the hierarchy. The importance of disclosure systems, as well as a free and independent media, are essential elements in the governance structure.

Mechanisms for detection and independent investigation of wrongdoing need to be reliable, consistently employed, and subject to the same ethical standards to which the employees themselves are being held.[21] In addition, citizens and employees should be made aware of their rights and obligations if they are a witness to wrongdoing or if they are being pressured to participate in behaviors that violate the ethical standard. Generally, the obligation involves formal legislation or organizational rules that require reporting of misconduct.[2] Tangential concerns involve ensuring confidential methods of communication are in place, and it is clear to whom the employee should turn in such a circumstance. Safeguards to protect the whistleblower from negative repercussions from revealing such wrongdoing are of course integral to such efforts.[22]

FUTURE DIRECTIONS IN GOVERNANCE STRUCTURES

Integration of governance structures with other organizational functions and externally with professional associations represent an area of growing interest. An overview of these various initiatives provides insight into the extent to which governance structures are integral to successful management of ethics in public administration, although no organization currently evidences all these in union.

Anticipating and avoiding ethical problems by inclusion of governance structures in organizational and departmental strategic planning sessions, change initiatives, and reform efforts[19] is an initiative gaining widespread support. Voice is thus given to considerations of the ethical consequences of policy or priority changes as part of the planning process. This integrates governance structures in the early stages of programs and can save resources in preventing unethical outcomes through careful planning. Shifting legislation, increasing public demands and lobbying activities, shifts in public–private sectors

relationships,[23] and changes in procurement procedures are some examples of conditions that warrant ethical scrutiny in the planning phases.[24]

The structure of the organization or department itself can be conducive to ethical or unethical behavior and as such is a focus of governance moving toward the future.[7] Reporting relationships, accessibility to people and information, confidentiality issues, resource distribution, privacy, and special needs are all areas affected by the physical structure. Approaching the layout and organization of a department in the planning of additions or remodeling, and routinely assessing how the environment affects the communication patterns and flow of work through the system can provide keys to areas of needed intervention.[25] Instances of wrongdoing are analyzed in terms of where the individuals who violated the standards were physically located. Perhaps more or less privacy is needed in that area, or more secure locks or other arrangements need to be provided. Organizational structure is viewed as a preventive measure of governance structures.

Creating human resource policies and procedures that reinforce and reward ethical behavior is another new area of focus in the governance process. Communicating expectations for ethical performance in the job description, recruiting literature, the interview process, and new employee information packets is emphasized. Incorporating these behavioral expectations in measurable form in employee performance reviews and in exit interviews[26] is equally important in reinforcing the type of ethical behavior expected in the workplace. Individuals selected for rewards or promotions are those who represent in practice and philosophy the ethical standards supported by the organization.[26] Offering organizational rewards for outstanding skill in managing the ethical aspects of public service is another method of reinforcing desired behaviors. At the core of effective preventive elements of governance structures is to create outcomes for being ethical that outweigh those for being unethical.[27] Of course in organizations where corruption is rampant, enforcement is more important in the short run, but in organizations where instances of misconduct are minimal, prevention is a more valuable method of governance. Prevention purportedly is less expensive in the long term, has a more positive impact on the culture of public service, and reduces cynicism toward corrupt public service by a civil society.[28]

More broadly within the human resource function, attention to confidentiality of records, guarded access to employee and insurance information files, equanimity of treatment in evaluating applications and training managers on the ethics of interviewing and hiring protocol are given equal attention. The way in which an employee is recruited, hired, and socialized into an organization or department establishes a self-governing standard that can supplement the institutions' ethical governance measures.[29] Monitoring of electronic and voice communications is an increasingly common form of governance activity.[30,31] Employees are generally made aware of this policy and practice upon employment, and are asked to sign a statement acknowledging familiarity with this policy. It is also important to review personnel policies and procedures annually, and to report the assessment's findings publicly as part of the transparency structure.[32] The effort spent in this regard represents the balance between prevention and enforcement; sound governance policies include both.

An independent ethics forum is another form of effective governance. Such forums are generally informal luncheon sessions that meet regularly on a weekly or biweekly basis, depending on interest. Invitations to attend are distributed via an intranet messaging system or through memos. Attendance is voluntary, and a culture of open discussion is established whereby ideas or concerns related to ethical issues faced on the job or in theory are put on the table for discussion. All attendees have an equal voice in discussing the issue, generally with an unbiased facilitator present. No records are kept of the meeting and those attending are asked to keep all conversations confidential, a request enforced through organizational sanctions. Attendance by individuals up and down the hierarchy is encouraged, and having representation from the highest levels of management offers validation and perceived importance to the group. This also demonstrates that ethical issues occur at all levels in various forms, and knowing that individuals are not isolated in such occurrences has been shown to facilitate their seeking external advice and supporting transparency systems. A culture of openness is established and safeguarded. Such forums allow for individuals to practice the language of ethical discussion, become aware of the complex issues that usually surround a concern, and provide practice in resolving and addressing ethical dilemmas that carries over into daily practice. These interactions tend to instill confidence in attendees that they can deal with a seemingly insurmountable ethical challenge and that there are objective methods in doing so. These forums are not intended to absolve managers, departments, or organizations from ethical oversight, but rather to act in concordance in support of their efforts.

Phone and electronic hotlines for whistleblowers are a relatively new development in supporting governance measures. These are generally monitored by an outside agency or organization that does not trace the source of the information and passes along the information with all identifying traces removed. If a reward system is in place to encourage whistleblowing, this agency generally provides a code number to the informant. The information

along with the code number is reported to the organization. If, after investigating the issue and determining it was a legitimate concern, the reward is made available at a bank where the informant need only present the pre-assigned code, with no other identifying information. Notice of the award is posted in company newsletters or on web sites, and the informant usually has 6 to 12 months to claim it. The outside agency chosen for this initiative must be monitored for strict confidentiality compliance procedures. There is some debate over the efficacy of such hotlines,[33] and results are inconclusive.

Professional associations or unions are another element in establishing governance structures for ethical behavior. The ethical codes they develop and support, the importance given a standing ethics committee, and the strength with which they communicate and enforce professional ethical standards can work in concert with intraorganizational systems governing ethical behavior. However, tensions can result over a conflict between association codes of ethics and governmental codes of ethics. This is often the case with bar associations' codes regarding confidentiality, although attorneys working for the federal government are obligated to protect government interests over such individual obligations. Effective role modeling can evolve from these opportunities to share ideas in professional forums. Training by ethics professionals external to the organization frequently occurs at such meetings and can be a valuable aspect of membership supported by the institution. Individuals can be asked to share these materials upon their return, becoming in turn recognized for their enhanced expertise in a specific area.

Internal controls such as annual or semiannual reviews leading to recommendations for improving management processes or procedures can directly inform the organization and general public of steps to strengthen governance structures. The goal of governance structures is to keep public servants accountable for their actions and to remove opportunities for ethical compromises to occur. Independent scrutiny such as legislative reviews, regular management audits, inspectors general or ombudsman investigations, and specific judicial and ethics reviews are increasingly popular methods of oversight.[28]

Governance structures themselves are most often subject to independent scrutiny as a monitor of their due process and compliance with the same ethical standards they are charged to enforce. Bias, regardless of whether intentional, can be revealed by overt reviews for fairness and objectivity, as well as audits of the process and procedures for handling complaints. External reviews not only instill confidence in the governance structure by those subject to them, but they also encourage double-loop learning on the part of those charged with ethical oversight. As a consequence, they are more likely to review their own behavior and the patterns in that behavior and adjust accordingly, knowing that authoritative others will be viewing their actions from that framework.[34,35]

REFERENCES

1. Truelson, J.A. New Strategies for Institutional Controls. In *Ethics Frontiers in Public Management*; Bowman, J.S., Ed.; Jossey-Bass: San Francisco, CA, 1991; 225–242.
2. Organisation of Economic Co-operation and Development. In *Ethics and Corruption*; 2001. http://www.oecd.org/puma/ethics/infras.htm.
3. Jurkiewicz, C.L. The trouble with ethics: Results from a national survey of healthcare executives. HEC Forum **2000**, *12* (02).
4. Menzel, D.C. The Ethics Factor in Local Government: An Empirical Analysis. In *Ethics and Public Administration*; Frederickson, H.G., Ed.; M.E. Sharpe: Armonk, NY, 1993; 191–204.
5. Foster, G.D. Legalism, moralism and the bureaucratic mentality. Public Pers. Manage. **1981**, *10*, 93–97.
6. Garment, S. *Scandal: The Culture of Mistrust in American Politics*; Time Books: New York, 1991.
7. Cooper, T. *The Responsible Administrator*; Jossey-Bass: San Francisco, CA, 1998; 4.
8. Friedrich, C.J. Public policy and the nature of administrative responsibility. Public Policy **1940**, *1*, 3–24.
9. Finer, H. Administrative responsibility in democratic government. PAR **1941**, *1* (3), 335–350.
10. Weber, M. *The Theory of Social and Economic Organizations*; Free Press: New York, 1947.
11. Lewin, K. *Field Theory in Social Science*; Harper & Row: New York, 1951.
12. Wood, R.C. Ethics in government as a problem in executive management. PAR **1955**, *15* (1), 1–7.
13. Bruce, W.M. Ethics Education in Municipal Government: It Does Make a Difference. In *Teaching Ethics and Values in Public Administration Programs*; Bowman, J., Menzel, D., Eds.; State University of New York Press: New York, 1998; 231–249.
14. Van Wart, M. *Changing Public Sector Values*; Garland Reference Library of Social Science, Garland: New York, 1998; Vol. 1045.
15. Gilman, S. Realignment and Public Sector Ethics: The Neglected Management Problem in the New Public Administration; Organisation of Economic Co-operation and Development, 2001. http://www.oecd.org/puma/ethics/symposium/gilman.htm.
16. Hejka-Ekins, A. Teaching ethics in public administration. Public Adm. Rev. **1988**, *48*, 885–891. (September/October).
17. Darley, J.M. How Organizations Socialize Individuals into Evildoing. In *Codes of Conduct*; Messick, D.M., Tenbrunsel, A.E., Eds.; Russell Sage Foundation: New York, 1996.
18. Bruhn, J.G. Being good and doing good: The culture of professionalism in the health professions. Health Care Manag. **2001**, *19*, 47–58.
19. Lewis, C.W. *The Ethics Challenge in Public Service*; The Jossey-Bass Public Administration Series; Jossey-Bass: San Francisco, CA, 1991.
20. Hays, S.W.; Gleissner, R.R. Codes of ethics in state government: A nationwide survey. Public Pers. Manage. **1981**, *10*, 48–58.
21. Adams, J.S. Inequity in Social Exchange. In *Advances in Experimental Social Psychology*; Berkowitz, L., Ed.; Academic Press: New York, 1965; 2.
22. Bowman, J.S. Whistle-blowing in the public service: An overview of the issues. Rev. Public Pers. Adm. **1980**, *1* (1), 15–27.
23. Goodman, J.B.; Loveman, G.W. Does privitization serve the public interest? Harvard Bus. Rev. **1991**, *69*, 28.
24. Jurkiewicz, C.L.; Thompson, C.R. Conflicts of interest: Organizational vs. individual ethics in healthcare administration. J. Health Human Serv. Adm. **2000**, *23* (1), 100–123.
25. Daft, R.L. *Organization Theory and Design*; South-Western College Publishing: Cincinnati, OH, 1998; 6.
26. Jurkiewicz, C.L.; Giacalone, R.A. Healthcare administrative ethics in a global context. J. Public Aff. Inf. **2001**, *5* (3), 1–18.
27. Klingner, D.E.; Nalbandian, J. *Public Personnel Management*; Prentice Hall: Upper Saddle River, NJ, 1998.
28. Organisation of Economic Co-operation and Development. *Building Public Trust: Ethics Measures in OECD Countries*; 2000, PUMA Policy Brief No. 7. http://www.oecd.org/puma/.
29. Chao, G.T.; O'Leary-Kelly, A.M.; Wolf, S.; Klein, H.J.; Gardner, P.D. Organizational socialization: Its content and consequences. J. Appl. Psychol. **Oct., 1994**, *79* (5), 730–744.
30. Prince, M. Employers should establish clear rules on e-mail. Bus. Insur. **2001**, *35* (19), 25.
31. Scott, A. No privacy in the workplace. Intern. Aud. **2001**, *58* (3), 15–16.
32. Carter, M. *Complete Guide to Ethics Management: An Ethics Toolkit for Managers*; Wallace and Pekel: London, 1999.
33. Moody, M.S.; Serepca, B. Inspector general hotlines: Have they been good? At what cost? What is lost? J. Public Inquiry **1998**, *4* (1), 9–12.
34. Argyris, C.; Schoen, D.A. *Organizational Learning II*; Addison-Wesley: Reading, MA, 1996.
35. Jurkiewicz, C.L.; Knouse, S.B.; Giacalone, R.A. When an employee leaves: The effectiveness of clinician exit interviews and surveys. Clin. Leadership Manage. Rev. **2001**, *15* (2), 97–100.

Ethics in Organizations, Implementation of

Evan M. Berman
University of Central Florida, Orlando, Florida, U.S.A.

INTRODUCTION

Organizations undertake many activities that aim to increase the ethical conduct of employees and to ensure that ethical principles are reflected in their programs and policies. Although no organization can prevent isolated incidents of unethical conduct, much can be done to systematically improve ethical conduct, thereby increasing stakeholder trust and, in some instances, protecting organizations from legal or moral culpability. The following discusses major elements of an ethics implementation strategy.

RECENT DEVELOPMENT OF ETHICS IMPLEMENTATION EFFORTS

Concern for ethics in public administration greatly increased during the post-Watergate period in the late 1970s. Although initially focused on individual ethics (specifically, criminal acts), efforts soon led to the passage of new or more stringent ethics laws. Many of these new laws focused on conflict of interest situations that involve the acceptance of gifts, employment (limiting "revolving door" and lobbying practices for those who recently left a government office), and financial disclosure. The federal government and many states established or increased their government ethics office to oversee the implementation of ethics laws.[1]

During the late 1970s and early 1980s, many observers also called for an aspirational ethics strategy that aimed to promote public-sector values. This aspirational strategy complements the legal strategy that focuses on minimizing wrongdoing. During the late 1980s, many organizations began to develop or emphasize codes of ethics that identified their aspirational values. Typically, codes of ethics discuss organizational values related to democratic governance, the public interest, personal and professional integrity, having respect for others and a constructive attitude, transparency and inclusiveness in decision making, and effective and efficient services.

Despite the growing importance of ethics in the 1980s, few organizations had a well-defined ethics implementation strategy in place. Merely having a code of ethics does not guarantee ethical conduct. During the 1990s, codes of conduct were developed that detailed specific conduct that should or should not occur. Training was increasingly used to communicate these standards to employees and to help them address a broad range of common but ethically troubling workplace situations. Facilitation was also used to help groups of employees develop their own codes of ethics and conduct. In some organizations, ombudsmen were also used. Today, these tools are beginning to be integrated with other, established practices, such as hiring and leadership, to provide a systematic ethics implementation strategy that involves assessment, training, and reinforcement.

ETHICS ASSESSMENT

If the purpose of ethics implementation is to increase ethical conduct, or support existing ethical conduct, then managers need to know the current state of ethics in their organizations. An ethics climate survey is a systematic, written survey that probes existing employee knowledge of ethics standards, as well as the presence of conduct that may be ethically troublesome. Such a survey supplements managers' subjective assessment that may be based on their intuition and the unethical acts of a few. Typically, all employees or a sample of employees are asked to voluntarily participate in an ethics climate survey. At this time, climate surveys are diagnostic, only; they have not been psychometrically validated against a broad sample of organizations. The results of ethics climate surveys can also be used as an element of training (below), when results are discussed with work groups.

For example, employees are asked to evaluate the following questions on a seven-point Likert scale that ranges from Strongly Agree–Strongly Disagree (Ref. [2]. This instrument contains 43 items):

"Employees maintain the same ethical standard even when no one is watching."
"My supervisor encourages me to act in an ethical manner."
"My department has a defined standard of integrity."

Encyclopedia of Public Administration and Public Policy
DOI: 10.1081/E-EPAP 120010935

"You can rely on the accuracy of the organization's information about what will or will not happen."

"Members of my department have not misused their positions to influence the hiring of their friends or relatives in government."

IMPLEMENTING ETHICS THROUGH LEADERSHIP

Many studies support that top leaders are examples of moral conduct for others in organizations. When top leaders are seen to espouse the highest values of virtue, and are strong advocates that these values are adopted by others and incorporated into decisions and organizational systems (such as human resource management), then ethical conduct is readily promoted. Conversely, the popular expression "rot starts at the top" identifies the corrupting impact of top leaders on organizational culture when ethics is not espoused in word and deed. When top managers are perceived as getting away with or condoning wrongdoing, then calls for increased ethical conduct by others ring hollow and will have little impact.

It is currently believed that top leaders should develop ethics priorities for their organization. These include a variety of standards and specific actions, such as regarding client relations, program development, accounting, financial disclosure, personal responsibility, and so on. The above ethics climate survey can assist top managers in deciding which ethics items should be priorities. When top managers make ethics standards important priorities for lower managers, a cascading effect occurs when lower managers advocate the same standards in their units, setting examples for their employees and supervisors. This effect is reinforced by informal and formal structures of accountability; for example, managers may be asked to ensure that specific ethical conduct is discussed with employees, or that certain ethical standards be reflected in program decisions.

. For example, one such way in which ethics is promoted is by making ethics a criterion in hiring and promotion. The background check of candidates includes questions about their ethics judgment and examples of exemplary ethical behavior and ethical misconduct, if any. During job interviews, candidates are given scenarios for analysis that involve matters of ethics, such as potential conflicts of interest (for example, accepting minor gifts). They may also be asked about their support for ethics training and other implementation activities and their experience with making ethics a priority in their units. Such ethical standards and practices in hiring increase the likelihood of obtaining candidates with ethical behavior. Disseminating these standards sends a signal to existing employees who hope for promotion that ethics is an important priority for their organization.[3]

ETHICS TRAINING

In recent years, many professional associations published new ethics training materials for their members. These materials included seminar training manuals, ethics readers, and ethics self-tests in paper and electronic formats (for example, CD-ROM). Ethics training is one of several ways through which top leaders indicate their commitment to ethics. The purpose of many training packages is to increase ethical behavior through new insight and understanding. Ethics training is typically conducted in small groups, which promote insight through feedback and participation by all. Ground rules typically include that everyone should participate, and that comments stay in the room, which promotes confidentiality.[2]

Ethics training efforts typically begin with a definition of ethics as a standard of conduct. A code of ethics and conduct captures the important standards of an organization. Then, a distinction between ethical and legal conduct is made. For example, leaving work a few minutes early each day is legal but unethical. The importance of ethical conduct is linked to heightened trust, morale, and productivity. Cases are widely used to highlight the complexity of many ethical dilemmas, to discuss proper ways of dealing with ethical complexity, and to heighten awareness for unethical temptations and various warning signs (for example, "no one will ever know..." or "I deserve a little extra...").

For example, trainees are asked to discuss the following situation. A very competent employee of the agency has quietly been using agency resources, including office supplies, copies, phone, vehicles, and health supplies, to operate a small, private business. Over a period of several years, this has resulted in the misuse of several thousands of dollars in agency resources. Is there an ethical problem? What should you do?[4] This case is often adapted in the following way: What if a competent worker has used office supplies for incidental, personal use. Is there an ethical problem? What should you do?

Ethics training not only teaches employees to identify and deal with ethically compromising situations, it also provides them with a general framework for dealing with ethical issues. Typically, such frameworks begin with fact gathering, preparing a statement of ethical principles, preparing a statement of legal issues (if any), identifying consequences, examining options, and analyzing of options.

REINFORCEMENT

Ethics is reinforced by providing feedback to employees about their conduct. Feedback can be used to reinforce the ethics priorities of organizations. Theories of motivation suggest that the impact of feedback on behavior is most effective when feedback is perceived as being swift, certain, and significant. Two types of feedback are distinguished: feedback that aims to eliminate (discourage) unethical behavior, and feedback that aims to encourage ethical behavior.

Many public organizations have officials and bodies whose job includes investigating wrongdoing. Federal agencies often have Inspectors General (IG) who provide a broad range of audits, include those relating to fraud and abuse. IGs operate independently of agency executives. Many states have Ethics Commissions whose job is to oversee the implementation of ethics laws and to investigate allegations of ethical wrongdoing. The U.S. Office of Government Ethics oversees the implementation of ethics laws in the federal government and provides regulatory and compliance information to agencies; many large federal agencies have their own ethics offices. Collectively, IGs, Ethics Commissions, and Government Ethics Offices might be thought as "ethics police." In addition, some agencies have ombudsmen who also oversee ethics complaints, and many professional associations provide ethics advice and sometimes investigate ethics complaints against their members.

Consensus exists that ethics policing is only somewhat effective in reinforcing ethics. Although the work of IGs and Ethics Commissions on individual cases typically is thorough in its fact finding and unbiased in its conclusions, ethics policing is neither swift nor certain. Many complaints take years to investigate. The number of complaints, and those that are investigated, are quite small. Investigations are often limited to allegations of legal wrongdoing. Thus, the presence of an ethics police does not appear to be much of a deterrent force for those inclined to commit unethical acts. Rather, the rigor with which individual organizations deal with unethical acts may be a greater deterrent. When managers pursue allegations and take a proactive stance in their investigations, the effect on conduct may be more certain.

Similarly, managers can reinforce positive ethical behavior by acknowledging and rewarding it. This can be done formally and informally. In some organizations, performance appraisals now include a category that allows managers to reward such behavior. Ethical actions can also be the basis for evaluating employee performance awards. In addition to these formal sanctions, managers can also informally acknowledge ethical conduct to individuals. Recognition is likely to be more effective when it is timely, certain, and significant.

IMPLEMENTING ETHICS IN SPECIAL SITUATIONS

Many work situations involve special attention to ethics, a few of which are discussed below. Readers interested in ethics applications in their areas can contact their professional associations which sometimes have publications or training materials relevant to ethics. They can also obtain information from the references below and from Internet sites that deal with ethics.

Law enforcement, for example, involves concerns for the rights of alleged offenders and their victims. This has received heightened interest in the wake of publicity related to wrongdoing. Those in police custody deserve to be treated with respect and dignity, regardless of race and alleged crime. Law enforcement also raises concern about bribery and criminal wrongdoing by officers. Prolonged exposure to criminal activity can have a corrupting impact on those who come in contact with it. Thus, ethics implementation in law enforcement requires the development of ethical standards that deal with these problems, and implementation through training, policing, reinforcement, and top leadership.[5]

Health care settings require consideration for patient rights. Patients may be quite vulnerable financially, emotionally, and physically when they seek treatment. Ethical treatment of patients requires full and timely disclosure of diagnosis and medical options. Doctors have an obligation to avail patients of their options, including second opinions. Then, nursing of patients requires attention to various side effects of treatments, including emotional consequences.[6]

City management has its own unique challenges. It is increasingly common for public organizations to employ both spouses, which may be necessary when recruiting scarce talent. This raises issues regarding supervision and promotion, especially when one of the spouses is the city manager. City management also involves ethical challenges of dealing with elected officials, such as requests for personal services. In this regard, ethics training of elected officials is now increasingly mandatory for newly elected officials.[3]

Finally, in some developing countries, corruption and graft have become accepted ways of dealing with government officials. This is furthered by extraordinarily low compensation structures for public officials. Ethics implementation in these settings requires not only an increase in ethics policing but also greater transparency in the interactions of employees and citizens. This is achieved through, for example, increased job rotation as well as publication (transparency) of exemptions of delinquent taxes and regulatory requirements that often are the object of graft and corruption.[7]

INTERNET RESOURCES

A variety of ethics-related web sites are available. A good starting point is the Ethics Section of the American Society for Public Administration at http://www.aspanet. org or http://www.niu.edu/~tp0dcm1/aspa/ethicsec/index. htm. The Ethics Section Newsletter, *Ethics Today*, regularly publishes a list of ethics-related web sites (see, for example, the Winter 2000 issue, pp. 4–5). Some useful web sites are as follows (all accessed June 8, 2001):

Ethics Officer Association: http://www.oea.org.

Ethics Updates (Material for Instructors and Students): http://ethics.acusd.edu/index.html.

International City/County Management Association: http://www.icma.org.

Federal Inspectors General: http://ignet.gov.

Freedom to Care (Ethics in Policing): http://www. freedomtocare.org/page24.htm.

Organization for Economic Cooperation and Development, Anti-Corruption Unit: http://www.oecd.org/ daf/nocorruption/index.htm.

National Institutes of Health: http://ethics.od.nih.gov/.

State of Wisconsin Ethics Board: http://ethics.state.wi.us/.

U.S. Department of Defense Standards of Conduct Office: http://www.defenselink.mil/dodgc/defense_ethics/ index.html.

U.S. Office of Government Ethics: http://www.usoge.gov.

REFERENCES

1. *Handbook of Administrative Ethics*; Cooper, T., Ed.; Marcel Dekker, 2001.
2. International City/County Management Association. *Ethics in Action*; ICMA, 1999; 86–88.
3. *The Ethics Edge*; Berman, E., West, J., Bonczek, S., Eds.; ICMA, 1998; 227–236.
4. Mertins, H.; Bruke, F.; Kweit, R.; Pops, G. *Applying Standard and Ethics in the 21st Century*; American Society for Public Administration, 1998.
5. Kleinig, J. *The Ethics of Policing*; Cambridge University Press, 1996.
6. Spencer, E. *Organization Ethics in Health Care*; Oxford University Press, 2000.
7. Organization for Economic Cooperation and Development. *No Longer Business As Usual: Fighting Bribery and Corruption*; OECD, 2000.

Ethics in Public Administration, Teaching of

Donald Menzel
Northern Illinois University, DeKalb, Illinois, U.S.A.

E

INTRODUCTION

The teaching of ethics in public administration is a multifaceted and often controversial enterprise. It is multifaceted because the field of public administration ranges broadly within and across organizations, nations, and cultures. It is often controversial because there is little agreement on what to teach and how to teach ethics. Indeed, some persons believe that ethics cannot be taught to others in a traditional class or course context. Rather, the best that can be hoped for is to teach *about* ethics. Still, there is widespread view among practicing public administrators and educators in the United States and abroad that an ethical public service is essential to a well-functioning democracy. According to this view, the teaching of ethics to men and women who occupy positions of public trust should and must be pursued, regardless of the arguable outcomes.

ETHICS AND PUBLIC OFFICE HOLDING

''When a man assumes a public trust, he should consider himself a public property,'' President Thomas Jefferson admonished. Yet, there are legions of stories in various countries where these words have fallen on deaf ears. In Jefferson's age, it was often believed that men of character were the essential foundation for building a democratic and just society. Today, it has become abundantly clear that, although character qualities are important among the men and women who conduct the nation's public affairs, they have not proven to be reliable qualities.

President John F. Kennedy, in a message to Congress on April 27, 1961, also recognized the importance of recruiting men and women of sound character to public office when he said, ''the ultimate answer to ethical problems in government is honest people in a good ethical environment.'' Furthermore, we ''must develop in all government employees an increasing sensitivity to the ethical and moral conditions imposed by public service.'' In other words, recruiting honest people to public service is highly desirable, but is not enough. Thus, we have here a statement about teaching ethics—it should increase a person's ''sensitivity to the ethical and moral conditions imposed by public service.'' This is not so arguable, and it

is doable; that is, it does not get mired in the quandary of teaching character traits that could presumably change one's character.

SENSITIVITY AND AWARENESS TEACHING

A sensitivity and awareness approach to the teaching of ethics in public administration has followed two primary paths. The first path is legalistic and is often reflected in state-level ethics commissions that provide advice and instruction to state and local public employees and elected officials on the ''dos and don'ts'' of state ethics laws. Such laws typically emphasize conflicts of interest, financial disclosure, and confidentiality of information. This ''how to stay out of trouble'' approach is also embraced by the U.S. Office of Government Ethics. The bad news about this approach is that it is often reduced to the level of ''if it's not illegal, it's okay!'' This approach, as John Rohr aptly reminded us in *Ethics for Bureaucrats*,[1] is the ''low road'' to public service ethics.

The second path is semilegalistic in its focus on professional codes of ethics or agency rules of acceptable behavior. At the professional association level, for example, nearly every public service association has adopted a code of ethics that its members are expected to support. Two professional associations are illustrative in this regard—the American Society for Public Administration (ASPA) and the International City/County Management Association (ICMA). The ASPA is a 10,000-member organization consisting primarily of educators, students, and public employees drawn from local, state, and federal agencies, as well as members of nonprofit associations. The ASPA code, which was adopted in 1984, identifies five key principles: 1) serve the public interest; 2) respect the Constitution and the law; 3) demonstrate personal integrity; 4) promote ethical organizations; and 5) strive for professional excellence. Members who violate the Code can be expelled from ASPA, but there has been a noticeable absence of such actions taken (see http://www.aspanet.org/).

The ICMA is a 7500-member organization consisting primarily of practicing public managers in cities and counties in the United States and abroad (e.g., Ireland, Australia). The ICMA code dates to 1924, and provides

Encyclopedia of Public Administration and Public Policy
DOI: 10.1081/E-EPAP 120010941

specific guidance on acceptable and unacceptable behaviors of local government managers. For example, it is deemed unethical for a city manager to leave the management post with less than 2 years' service, unless there are extenuating circumstances such as severe personal problems. It is also viewed as unethical for a city manager to publicly endorse a commercial product that a vendor might sell to a city. The ICMA actively enforces the code with a half-dozen or more members sanctioned nearly every year for violations (see http://www.icma.org/go.cfm).

Agency rules that define acceptable behaviors and practices of public employees are common place among local governments in the United States. In Kansas City, Missouri, for example, the *Ethics Handbook* issued to all city employees asserts that it is unacceptable behavior to spend several hours a week of city time to download Internet information on a relative's medical condition (see http://www.kcmo.org/index.htm). In California, many local governments place restrictions on their employees receiving gifts. In San Diego (http://www.sannet.gov/), for example, employees ''shall not accept gifts, gratuities, or favors of any kind which might reasonably be interpreted as an attempt to influence their actions with respect to city business.'' The Town of Los Gatos' (http://www.los-gatos.org/) administrative regulations are even more restrictive. For example, one rule states that ''no employee shall accept money or other consideration or favor from anyone other than the town for any reason.''[2]

The teaching of ethics based on codes or administrative rules of behavior such as those above stress the contents of the codes or the rules themselves, which unfortunately can sometimes become ends themselves. The teaching of codes and rules are often conducted by training personnel within a governmental agency, management consultants, and college and university instructors, especially those in graduate degree granting programs that prepare men and women for public service careers.

TEACHING MORAL REASONING

Another approach to the teaching of ethics in public administration is moral reasoning. This approach, which is prominently advocated by Terry L. Cooper in successive editions of *The Responsible Administrator*,[3] presumes that one can learn to reason through a difficult moral or ethical dilemma. Stated differently, learning how to be ethical in public service is just that—a learning process that, when reality sets in, can be applied with desirable outcomes.

The reasoning process set forth by Cooper puts the accent on decision making through ethical reflection based on the interplay of moral rules, ethical principles, self-appraisal, and justification. His ethical decision-making model is shown in Fig. 1. At the heart of this exercise is what Cooper calls exercising one's moral imagination to sort through right or wrong decision outcomes.

Another proponent of teaching ethical decision making is Carol W. Lewis who, in *The Ethics Challenge in Public Service*,[4] presents the reader with a problem-solving guide. This guide engages the learner with real and hypothetical decision-making scenarios, self-assessment tools, and questions that stimulate ethical reflection. It contends that neither the ''low'' road of compliance nor the ''high'' road of integrity are realistic guides for

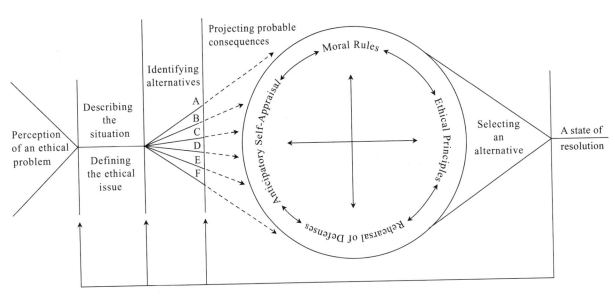

Fig. 1 Ethical decision-making model.

navigating the often stormy political and bureaucratic environments of public service. Rather, it is necessary to develop a two-pronged, systematic approach that incorporates both the path of compliance with formal standards and the path of individual integrity. She labeled this approach the "fusion route" to meeting the ethics challenge in public service.

How does one learn to engage in moral reasoning? Related, how can ethical decision making be taught? The answer here is practice, practice, practice. That is, one can learn how to reason and make ethical decisions by practicing; the learner can engage himself with decision dilemmas and work through them. A teacher of ethics can use decision-making scenarios and small-group processes to help the learner practice ethical decision making and acquire skill in doing so. This approach has much in common with virtue ethics espoused by Aristotle in the Age of Antiquity. Aristotle believed that one could only acquire a virtue by engaging in virtuous acts. But, he was wise to add, one does not acquire a virtue by engaging in foolhardy acts. Jumping into a lion's cage to acquire the virtue of courage is not what he had in mind!

LEADERSHIP AND EXEMPLAR TEACHING

A third approach to the teaching of ethics in public administration centers on leadership and exemplars in public service. This approach has had a time-honored tradition in the U.S. military academies and is increasingly reflected in the curricula of professional public administration graduate schools that award the Masters' of Public Administration degree. Some schools, such as the LBJ School of Public Affairs at the University of Texas, have established (2001) a Center for Ethical Leadership, which they believe will attract men and women who have a strong desire for public service leadership responsibilities (see http://www.utexas.edu/lbj/research/leadership/).

The study of leadership, of course, is rather wide reaching, and includes business, industry, political, and educational sectors. Interestingly, however, the study and teaching of administrative leadership has been problematic as Larry Terry notes in *Leadership of Public Bureaucracies*.[5] Several factors have contributed to this situation—the complexity of modern public organizations including the growing interdependency of private and public sector organizations, the antibureaucratic ethos that permeates American politics, and the challenge of distinguishing administrative leadership from political leadership.

Nonetheless, there is increasing attention given to this important subject and in linking it to the behavior of exemplars such as those found in Terry Cooper and Dale Wright's edited volume *Exemplary Public Administrators*.[6] Their book examines the life and career histories of nearly a dozen public administrators who have successfully resolved challenging ethical dilemmas. Students and teachers who use this material are able to discuss the life histories and experiences of these exemplars, relate them to their own life experiences, and therefore engage in ethical self-reflection.

In summary, Table 1 illustrates the key features of the three approaches to the teaching of ethics discussed above.

TEACHING FUTURE PUBLIC SERVANTS

The teaching of ethics in public administration described above, and other approaches detailed in James S. Bowman and Donald C. Menzel's book *Teaching Ethics and Values in Public Administration Programs*,[7] are promising beginnings. That more effort and results are needed is without dispute. Perhaps most revealing are the findings reported by Paul C. Light in his book *The New Public Service*.[8] Light conducted a study of the graduates of the nation's leading public policy and administration pro-

Table 1 Approaches to teaching of ethics in public administration

	Sensitivity and awareness	Moral reasoning	Leadership
Focus	Moral choice among right vs. wrong behavior	Deliberation, self-examination, decision making	Moral choice among right vs. wrong and right vs. right behavior
Substance	Rules, standards of conduct, conflicts of interest	Dilemmas, trade-offs, experience, learning	Observation and modeling
Purpose	Behavioral and legal compliance, obedience	Personal integrity, responsibility	Norm setting and following behavior
Illustrations	U.S. Office of Government Ethics and professional association codes	Cooper, Lewis	U.S. Military Academies—Oliver North's congressional testimony

Source: Adapted from Ref. [4].

grams (e.g., Syracuse, Kansas, University of Southern California, University of Michigan, Harvard). These graduates, regardless of current sector of employment (government, nonprofit, private), placed "maintaining ethical standards" at the top of the list of skills considered important for success in their current job. At the same time, when asked if their school was helpful in teaching skills that would enable one to maintain ethical standards, most rated their education as insufficient. In fact, Light reported that this gap between how helpful a school is in teaching ethics and how important ethics is to one's job success was the largest of all skills listed, including such important skills as "budgeting and public finance," "doing policy analysis," "managing motivation and change," and "managing conflict."

In 1989, the National Schools of Public Affairs and Administration (http://www.naspaa.org/), through its Commission on Peer Review and Accreditation, incorporated language in its accreditation standards (4.21) to the effect that graduates should be able "to act ethically." Standard 4.21 has encouraged schools to put into place ethics courses or otherwise demonstrate that they are teaching ethics across the curriculum. This tightening up of the standards is promising, but evidence regarding the outcome is skimpy. A survey conducted in 2001 by the author of more than 80 of the 143 accredited programs in the United States found that many ($n = 32$) schools have increased the emphasis placed on ethics in their curriculum, but the majority ($n = 44$) have not. Some schools claim they have not increased their emphasis because they are already giving considerable attention to ethics—a claim that is difficult to validate. A sizeable majority of schools ($n = 59$) believe that Standard 4.21 is sufficient, although some express concern about its implementation and enforcement by the Commission on Peer Review and Accreditation. Only a handful of schools claim that they have developed outcome measures of their graduates ability "to act ethically."

In conclusion, the teaching of ethics in public administration is a diverse, dynamic, and challenging enterprise that could be described as a "cottage" industry. However, there is evidence that this industry will grow in the decade ahead in both the United States and internationally. A chapter in an edited volume by Terry L. Cooper, *Handbook of Administrative Ethics*,[9] tracked the emergence of administrative ethics as a field of study in the United States since the 1950s and leaves little

doubt that more, not less attention will be devoted to the teaching of ethics in public administration.

Internationally, there is also considerable movement as emerging Third World democracies struggle for economic and political independence, and as nations like Russia attempt to shake loose from the vice of corruption and embrace the rule of law. The United Nations (UN) has also increased its efforts to lend a helping hand. *Public Service in Transition*,[10] a report prepared by the UN Division of Public Economics and Public Administration, emphasized "the critical importance of probity and integrity" of governments worldwide to conduct the public's business. The UN has also developed an impressive web site called UNPAN (http://www.unpan.org/), which provides valuable advisory and training resources that can be drawn on for the teaching of ethics in public administration (see also http://www.unpan.org/training-professionalism.asp). The teaching of ethics in public administration is a robust and future-shaping enterprise.

REFERENCES

1. Rohr, J. *Ethics for Bureaucrats*; Marcel Dekker, Inc.: New York, 1978; 352.
2. Simmons, C.W.; Roland, H.; Kelly-DeWitt, J. *Local Government Ethics Ordinances in California*; California State Library, California Research Bureau: Sacramento, CA, March 1998.
3. Cooper, T.L. *The Responsible Administrator*, 4th Ed.; Jossey-Bass Publishers: San Francisco, 1998; 278.
4. Lewis, C.W. *The Ethics Challenge in Public Service*; Jossey-Bass Publishers: San Francisco, 1991; 228.
5. Terry, L.D. *Leadership of Public Bureaucracies*; Sage Publications, Inc.: Thousand Oaks, CA, 1995; 207.
6. *Exemplary Public Administrators*; Cooper, T.L., Wright, N.D., Eds.; Jossey-Bass Publishers: San Francisco, 1992; 352.
7. *Teaching Ethics and Values in Public Administration Programs*; Bowman, J., Menzel, D., Eds.; State University of New York Press: Albany, NY, 1998; 352.
8. Light, P.C. *The New Public Service*; The Brookings Institution: Washington, D.C., 1999.
9. *Handbook of Administrative Ethics*, 2nd Ed.; Cooper, T.L., Ed.; Marcel Dekker, Inc.: New York, 2001; 763.
10. United Nations, Division for Public Economics and Public Administration. *Public Service in Transition*; United Nations: New York, 1999; 164.

Ethics and Public Policy

Amy K. Donahue
University of Connecticut, Storrs, Connecticut, U.S.A.

INTRODUCTION

Ethical questions surrounding the substance and application of public policy arise daily, as a cursory review of newspapers and news broadcasts readily demonstrates. In a single week in 2001, for example, the questions of whether the government should fund research that uses human genetic material, how to allocate tax refunds, whether to invest in building a national missile defense system, and whether to allow oil exploration in a wildlife refuge all competed for attention as part of the national policy agenda. Such issues are inherently ethical because they turn on normative choices—trade-offs among multiple values, judgments about how to interpret complex data, and decisions that distribute power and resources. In short, interactions between ethics and public policy are at once ubiquitous and complex.

DEFINITIONS

Public policy and ethics are each vast and disparate realms of scholarship and practice that defy concise definition. Nonetheless, some broad characterization of these concepts and the linkages between them is warranted and useful.

Public Policy

Broadly speaking, public policy comprises the development and outcomes of government decisions. It is fundamentally concerned with three kinds of decisions: first, what problems exist in society?; second, when should government intervene to solve them?; third, how should it intervene?; or, as Harold Lasswell said in 1936, public policy is about deciding "who gets what, when, and how."[1] As commonly used, the term "public policy" has several variants. It can refer to the outputs or outcomes of government processes—that is, the substance of what government does, rather than the way it makes decisions—noting also that what government intends to do is different from what it actually does. Alternatively, it can connote the general framework of authoritative rules that guide government activities, including but not limited to legislation. Finally, it may mean a program of action designed to achieve a specified goal or purpose that often involves all levels of government and formal as well as informal actors.[2]

Public policy fulfills an array of societal objectives. Among the most important functions of policy are the reconciliation of conflicting claims on scarce resources (accomplished by establishing incentives for cooperation or collective action that would be irrational absent government intervention, or by providing direct services or benefits to citizens), the prohibition of behavior unacceptable under reigning societal norms, the protection of individual and group rights, and the promotion of activities that are essential or important to governance. To meet these objectives, policy is created in a vast array of substantive realms that distribute and redistribute resources and regulate behavior.

Public policy is generated through a complex series of negotiated activities collectively known as the policy-making process. This process is how society validates claims about resource and power needs—how it decides which needs are real and legitimate, and what approach it should take to resolving them. This is particularly salient because government policy is generally believed to be about collective interests, but needs are almost always experienced individually. In a sense, policy politics is about defining individual needs collectively, as "public" needs.[3]

Generally, the policy-making process incorporates policy formulation, implementation, and the subsequent effects of policy. An important point is that the process must also account for the range of factors that affect whether policy decisions and their social effects are consistent with popular preferences. In other words, public policy cannot be separated from the environment in which it is made. There are two important dimensions and effects of the environment to consider. First, the political and ideological context must be acknowledged. These are fundamentally important because they define what forms of policy are acceptable and whether they can garner enough support to be implemented. Second, a whole array of socioeconomic factors affects whether a policy can achieve its desired outcomes. These contingencies bear on how ethical principles can be defined and applied in the context of public policy making.

Encyclopedia of Public Administration and Public Policy
DOI: 10.1081/E-EPAP 120010940

Ethics

Ethics receives treatment in several entries in this volume that clarify others of its aspects. With respect to public policy, ethics refers to moral reasoning and behavior by policy makers and other stakeholders in the public policy system. Ethics enters this system because all public policies express value judgments by allocating resources, entitlements, and authorities. As Swain and Duke explained, "ethics concerns things about which individuals have behavioral choices. Those choices have social consequences."[4]

The exercise of ethics in policy making proceeds from an array of philosophic traditions—most generally, deontological theories and teleological theories. Generally, deontological approaches are more classical and are concerned with the moral legitimacy of the policy process. These approaches tend to yield rules that prescribe proper behavior for decision makers and are meant to be universally applied. Along these lines, some in the field take a deontological view, under which ethics refers to the system of moral conventions that direct conduct. This perspective gives rise to published codes of ethics, available for an array of professional associations and public agencies, that influence the nature of public policy by guiding the behavior of policy makers.

Teleological approaches, in contrast, are focused on the goodness of consequences, rather than the character of the process that caused them. This view permits decision makers discretion in the application of moral rules to account for contingencies that affect the achievement of desirable outcomes. The literature of public administration commonly exhibits a teleological bent whereby actors weigh policy alternatives according to the net utility (or satisfaction) they generate. This is most evident in the frequent references to benefit–cost analysis as an appropriate rational basis for making normative policy decisions.

In practice, neither deontology nor teleology offers fully apposite guidance under all circumstances, and elements of both typically enter policy-making activities. Policy makers thus may employ broad ethical princi-

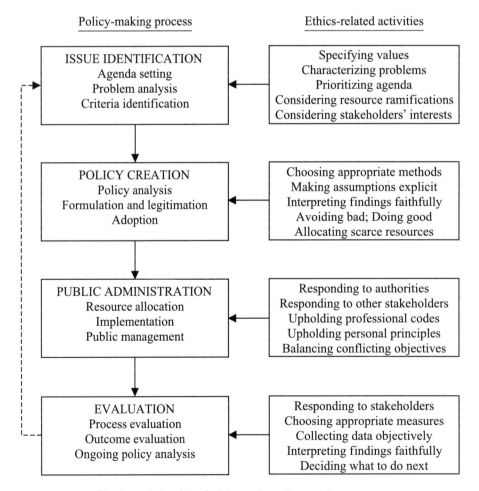

Fig. 1 Relationship of ethics to the policy-making process.

ples—or even specific rules of conduct—but make exceptions when these principles and rules are inconsistent or policy outcomes can be improved.[5] The impracticality of rigid conventions has prompted several scholars to characterize the nature of ethics in practice as evolutionary. Here the professional responsibilities of actors in the policy process are defined over repeated application to generate what Cooper termed an "operational ethic."[6] Similarly, Tong saw public actors as developing (or in need of developing) a personal moral perspective that upholds a chosen set of ideals[7] —a compass, rather than a rule book.

ETHICS IN THE POLICY-MAKING PROCESS

Most scholars agree that public policy making involves an iterative staged process, and most agree what the stages generally are, although how exactly they are delineated varies somewhat. Each stage poses a forum for value-based debate and thus an opportunity for ethical dilemmas to arise. Generally, the main stages and the ethical considerations each raises are (see Fig. 1):

1. *Issue identification.* Public officials and nongovernmental actors care about a broad range of matters. During issue identification, this list is narrowed to an agenda, or the set of concerns policy makers seek to address. In other words, issue identification is the process by which policy makers recognize specific problems, decide that government can and should address them, and initiate the development of focused solutions. Ethics bears on issue identification because alternative sets of values offer different conceptualizations of the public interest and thus suggest different public policy objectives. Moreover, how policy issues are characterized at this stage of the policy process later shapes the nature of solutions sought and the commensurate distribution of resources that results from execution of these solutions. Further, the particular values on which a policy agenda is based prompt the use of certain criteria for assessing the value of benefits and costs that will accrue from a given policy over other possible criteria.

2. *Policy creation.* This phase starts with policy analysis, a mechanism by which the range of possible alternative solutions to a problem is identified and analyzed in terms of their monetary and nonmonetary benefits and costs. Then, an alternative is chosen and a policy is drafted that specifies what objectives are sought and how things will be done to reach them. Political considerations often modify the proposal to make it acceptable (known as the process of legitimation). The policy is then adopted, most commonly

as law, but executive orders, rules, regulations, and court orders are also possible. Ethics enters the public policy process at this stage because all policy fundamentally involves the distribution of resources, which are finite. This scarcity forces policy makers to make choices that trade off between what Rohr characterizes as the two key activities of ethics: preventing bad and promoting good.[8] Ethics is also an important dimension of analysis where the choice of research methods, and the interpretation of data and findings, involve a series of judgments that profoundly influence how policy makers understand the ramifications of each policy alternative.

3. *Public administration.* Once adopted, the public bureaucracy usually takes over to implement the chosen policy—to put it into action. Implementation may proceed according to a rigid program that explicitly and rationally lays out procedures to forestall cooptation of the process, or it may be freely structured to permit policy improvements and more flexible response to contextual realities.[2] Regardless of how carefully or loosely defined the process, implementation typically involves a long series of activities and a multitude of actors; thus, there are many points at which there may be pressure to modify the policy from its original design. As a result, public administrators are repeatedly confronted with ethical dilemmas in the course of implementation. This may occur for a host of reasons, including that the stated policy goals are vague, obscured, or forgotten; stakeholders seek to substitute their own objectives or to intervene to halt or alter implementation; unforeseen technical difficulties arise that require adjustment; new information about policy effects arises as implementation progresses; multiple internal and external authorities have conflicting expectations; or there are overlapping jurisdictions and authorities that must be resolved.

4. *Evaluation.* Once implemented, it remains to decide if the policy worked—in other words, to determine the extent to which it produced its intended consequences, and whether there were any unintended ones. Frequently (even usually), policies fall short of their objectives, often because of ambiguous goals, ignorance about how to reach those goals, adversarial political conditions, or poor measures of success. Thus, evaluation also helps to uncover why policies do not wholly meet the agendas of those who designed them. There are hundreds of types of evaluation that essentially fall into two big categories: process evaluation looks at the extent to which implementation comports with prescribed guidelines, and outcome evaluation looks at the extent to which a policy achieved a positive change in the problem being addressed. Ethical concerns arise during evaluation

because evaluation fundamentally depends on measurement, a tricky business that involves resolving what measures should be used, whether it is possible to measure everything that matters, and the extent to which observed effects were within the government's control.

ETHICS AND POLICY ANALYSIS

The bearing of ethics on analysis deserves specific comment because the central objective of policy analysis is to improve public policy, an inherently normative target. Policy analysis directly intervenes in the policy-making process at several junctures. It is the set of formal methods by which public problems, their various alternative policy solutions, and the outcomes of chosen solutions are understood. Often these methods attempt objectivity—that is, they involve systematically gathering data, employing reliable methods to analyzing it, and choosing the best possible option according to specified criteria. Yet, the reality that emotions, values, beliefs, capabilities, and other mitigating contingencies enter into any diagnostic process means that policy analytical endeavors have embedded nonrational components that challenge their ostensible objectivity.

Over time, the field of policy analysis has undergone dramatic transformation to contend with the role of values in social scientific study. Policy analysis first emerged as a self-conscious discipline in response to the demands of the Planning, Programming, and Budgeting System in the Department of Defense after Word War II. These origins engendered a rationalist analytical approach that presumed that logical reasoning and scientific methodologies could yield optimal decisions. The field matured as its role expanded throughout the branches and levels of government, as well as beyond the public sector, so that policy analysts were asked to respond to a diverse set of demands and decision makers across society.[9] With such diversity came recognition of the role of values as an important influence on the

policy analytical and policy-making process. As Dunn noted, "The same policy-relevant information may be interpreted in markedly different ways, depending on the assumptions contained in the frame of reference, theory, or ideology of policy analysts and other policy stakeholders."[10]

Inevitably, disagreements about values arise in the policy process. Some argue that because values claims cannot be demonstrated empirically, and merely communicate preferences, they cannot enter rational debate. Others, however, hold that policy debates and analysis can and should be founded on explicit statements of ethical rules and moral principles, although debates about the legitimacy of value choices can only be resolved politically. Sound contemporary policy analysis thus attempts to use evidence and logic to choose the most favorable alternatives, but recognizes that public policy decisions cannot be divorced from the ideologies, politics, values, or environment in which these decisions are set, or from the moral perspective of those who make them. Thus, policy analysis and ethics should go hand in hand. As Brown explained, "ethics helps us identify assumptions we hold in common with others, and discard noncrucial assumptions at variance with those of others. It therefore helps us identify areas of consensus."[11] We can therefore identify where empirical research will not improve a given decision process because remaining disputes are over values.[5]

ETHICAL BEHAVIOR BY POLICY MAKERS

Finally, a word about the behavior of those who practice policy making. One reason that ethics is central to the public policy process is that citizens expect decision makers who are in the privileged position to analyze, make, and implement policy to "do the right thing." In other words, as Tong explained in her discussion of ethical behavior by policy experts, with privilege comes a requirement for trustworthiness.[7] Even analysts, who may not wield final decision-making authority, have po-

Table 1 Internet resources

Organization	Web site
American Society for Public Administration Section on Ethics	www.niu.edu/~tp0dcm1/aspa/ethicsec/index.htm
Journal of Power and Ethics: An Interdisciplinary Review	www.spaef.com/JPE_PUB/index.htm
Public Integrity	www.niu.edu/~tp0dcm1/PI/index.htm
International Institute for Public Ethics	www.iipe.org
Association for Practical and Professional Ethics	www.php.indiana.edu/~appe/home.html
Ethics Updates	www.ethics.acusd.edu/index.html
U.S. Office of Government Ethics	www.usoge.gov/

wer derived from their presumed expertise and thus have some responsibility for policy consequences.

This requirement can be onerous when a public official is asked to serve numerous constituents with varying needs, consider the implications of policy for third parties (present now and in future generations), evaluate data and findings susceptible to alternative interpretations, and balance conflicting values. On top of these demands, Weimer and Vining argued that policy makers and analysts must also uphold their own moral principles—as they explain it, individuals must be true to their own personal conception of "the good society."[12] In short, the broad and common teleological perspective in public policy requires public officials to weigh these demands simultaneously, and to manage continuously outcomes, circumstances, and values throughout the policy process. This multiplicity of constraints on behavior creates what Frankena called a "conflict of duties."[13]

Many organizations and associations have developed codes of ethics designed to prescribe behavior in ways that assist actors in managing conflicts of values, objectives, and interests (Table 1). Such sets of rules are difficult to apply universally and are subject to individual interpretation, but they can provide guidelines for how to handle common ethical dilemmas. They also serve as the formal representation of consensus within a particular agency or field about the goals or ideals to which members aspire and the standards of conduct that all agree constitute professional behavior. Moreover, as Patton and Sawicki argued, the exercise of developing ethical codes has utility because it can help to clarify moral principles and shed light on ethical dilemmas, and because it helps to keep policy makers conscious of the ethical choices at hand.[5]

REFERENCES

1. Lasswell, H.D. *Politics: Who Gets What, When, How*; McGraw-Hill Book Company, Inc.: New York, 1936.
2. Gerston, L.N. *Public Policy Making: Process and Principles*; M. E. Sharpe, Inc.: Armonk, NY, 1997; 6–8, 95–119.
3. Stone, D. *Policy Paradox: The Art of Political Decision Making*; W. W. Norton and Company: New York, 1997; 99–103.
4. Swain, J.W.; Duke, M.L. Recommendations for research on ethics in public policy from a public administration perspective: Barking dogs and more. Int. J. Public Adm. **2001**, *24* (1), 126.
5. Patton, C.V.; Sawicki, D.S. *Basic Methods of Policy Analysis and Planning*, 2nd Ed.; Prentice Hall: Englewood Cliffs, NJ, 1993; 37, 39–42.
6. Cooper, T.L. *The Responsible Administrator: An Approach to Ethics for the Administrative Role*; Associated Faculty Press, Inc.: Port Washington, NY, 1982; 12.
7. Tong, R. *Ethics in Policy Analysis*; Prentice Hall: Englewood Cliffs, NJ, 1986; 81–105.
8. Rohr, J.A. *Ethics for Bureaucrats*; Marcel Dekker, Inc.: New York, 1978; 6–7.
9. Radin, B.A. *Beyond Machiavelli: Policy Analysis Comes of Age*; Georgetown University Press: Washington, D.C., 2000; 9–54.
10. Dunn, W.N. *Public Policy Analysis: An Introduction*, 2nd Ed.; Prentice Hall: Upper Saddle River, NJ, 1994; 126.
11. Brown, P.G. Ethics and education for the public service in a liberal state. J. Policy Anal. Manage. **1986**, *6* (1), 62.
12. Weimer, D.L.; Vining, A.R. *Policy Analysis: Concepts and Practice*, 3rd Ed.; Prentice Hall: Upper Saddle River, NJ, 1999; 45–47.
13. Frankena, W.K. *Ethics*; Prentice Hall: Englewood Cliffs, NJ, 1963; 2.

Executive Leadership in Local Government

James H. Svara
North Carolina State University, Raleigh, North Carolina, U.S.A.

INTRODUCTION

Executive leadership is a complex topic in local government because of uncertainty about the scope of this type of leadership and variation in the officials to which it is assigned. This is especially true in the United States, where different forms of government are used in local governments. In simplest form, the topic encompasses the leadership provided by persons in the highest positions in the governmental structure who have responsibility for discerning the preferences of citizens and mobilizing popular support for policies, for developing proposals for what government will do, and for directing the work of the government. The citizen dimension might be considered beyond the scope of a type of leadership that is associated with activity within the governmental and organizational structure. Connection with the citizenry is, however, essential to democratic governance and creates the foundation for the internal executive functions.

Handling some or all the executive responsibilities falls to mayors (and their equivalents in counties) in all governments and in many governments to appointed chief administrators as well. Although it is natural to associate executive leadership with one person who has responsibilities that range from the electoral to the managerial aspects of leadership, in local government, executive leadership broadly defined is commonly shared more or less widely. In view of this division of leadership functions, the discussion is presented in three sections that deal with mayors who are elected executives, nonexecutive mayors, and appointed executives. For simplicity, and in recognition that the preponderance of the literature on leadership in local government has focused on cities, terms from city as opposed to county or other types of government are used to refer to the officials.

The division of responsibility depends largely on the form of government and, within mayor–council cities, on whether there is a chief administrator present in the governmental structure.[a] Largely excluded from the discus-

sion are weak-mayor council forms in which executive functions are spread across a number of offices and boards in city government and small-town mayor-council governments in which executive functions are shared and there is sharing of tasks between elected officials who do a lot of the work of city government and part-time staff. Connecting with citizens and mobilizing popular support for proposals is the responsibility of the mayor in all forms of government. Policy leadership (i.e., determining the purpose and policies of the government) is the responsibility of the mayor with approval of council in mayor–council cities, the mayor with advice of chief administrative officer (CAO) and approval of council in mayor–council–CAO cities, and the mayor, council, and city manager in council–manager cities. Finally, administrative leadership or directing the administrative apparatus and work of the staff is handled by the mayor, mayor and CAO, or the city manager, depending on the form of government.

Most cities have one executive and one mayor, but the two offices are not necessarily combined.[1] Cities that use the mayor–council form of government vest all or some executive powers in the elected mayor, who is the political head of city government, the driving force in setting policy, and in charge of the administrative organization. The executive mayor with full powers ultimately has authority of hiring and supervising staff, formulating and (after approval by the council) expending the budget, and directing the organization, subject to the limitations set by the city charter. If the city has a chief administrator, some administrative functions are delegated to this official. In council–manager cities, the city manager—an executive appointed by the city council—makes a major contribution to policy making and exercises administrative powers. Managers have extensive contact with citizens, are somewhat attentive to popular preferences, and have subtle influence on public opinion. Still, city managers do not get directly involved in mobilizing public opinion or shaping public support, unless instructed by the council to do so (e.g., seeking to secure votes in a bond referendum approved by the council). Council–manager cities also have a mayor who is the political head of the government and presides over the city council, but usually has no powers other than those available to other members of the council.

---

[a]Largely excluded from the discussion are weak-mayor council forms in which executive functions are spread across a number of offices and boards in city government and small-town mayor-council governments in which executive functions are shared and there is sharing of tasks between elected officials who do a lot of the work of city government and part-time staff.

Encyclopedia of Public Administration and Public Policy
DOI: 10.1081/E-EPAP 120010840

ELECTED EXECUTIVE MAYORS

The mayor–council form of government is based on separation of powers with authority divided between the executive and the legislature. The strong mayor–council version of this form has separation of powers between a mayor with extensive powers and integrated administrative control over staff, and the elected legislative body. The lines of authority for all or most departments of city government lead to the mayor's office.

In contrast, the council is confined to a more limited role in strong mayor–council cities. Even in policy making, the council is heavily dependent on the mayor for proposals and information, and it can be checked by the mayor's veto power. The mayor also occupies a favorable position for mobilizing public opinion in support of proposals. The council, however, must approve policies and can override vetoes, so there is the potential for the council to overrule the mayor if there is a large (i.e., veto-proof) like-minded majority on the council in opposition to the mayor, or for deadlock between the executive and legislature if a narrow majority opposes the mayor.

The checks and balances in mayor–council cities affect how officials relate to each other and the freedom of mayoral action. Because the purpose of offsetting powers is to permit one set of officials to hold the other in check, it is common for conflict to arise in the relationship between the mayor and the council.[2] The conflict may concern policy preferences and priorities, administrative performance, and the extent of independent executive authority assigned to the mayor. Separation of powers can allow the departments of city government to play the mayor and council off against each other and develop their own base of constituency support that produces greater autonomy vis-à-vis the mayor.[3] Strong mayors have the potential to blend the dimensions of leadership. They can tap organizational resources and mobilize public support to advance their political agenda. The executive can face the challenges of overcoming council resistance or opposition and recalcitrance from city departments, but may be able to use threats or inducements to win support.

In the political science literature, the ideal mayor in mayor–council cities is an innovator (also called an entrepreneur) who provides creative solutions to problems and pyramids resources to increase the ability to build coalitions and gain leverage over other actors.[4,5] This mayor is effective at both initiation and implementation of policies and programs. Leadership is fashioned from a combination of formal and informal resources. The former are part of the governmental structure and official policies of city government. The latter are derived from personal characteristics or the political process. Formal resources available to mayors remain fairly constant over time, but each incumbent differs in their ability to make the best use of these resources. Still, some important informal resources, for example, support from a political party, have been declining over time.

The terms "strong" and "weak" mayor refer to the level of authority assigned to the mayor, but there is no "pure" strong or weak mayor form. Strong and weak mayors are arrayed along a continuum. The key formal powers, which may be assigned to the executive or divided among a number of officials, are appointment of department heads, developing the budget, directing the administrative departments, and veto of council actions. The mayor's authority varies widely. Beyond the organizational leadership resources that are derived from appointment of department heads, control of other appointments can augment the mayor's leverage, and patronage appointments can reinforce party organizational cohesion and support. Most mayors, however, do not directly control large numbers of city government jobs. Civil service protection of most positions limits the jobs a mayor can dispense. Court cases since the 1980s have limited the ability of elected officials to remove, promote, or transfer staff for partisan reasons, unless employees are directly involved in providing advice on policy strategies, as opposed to policy implementation.[6]

A 1991 survey conducted by the International City Management Association measures the variation in mayoral authority within the mayor–council form of government.[7] In cities over 100,000 in population, two-thirds of the mayors develop the budget, and approximately 90% appoint department heads and have veto power. In cities under 50,000, the likelihood that the mayor possesses these powers decreases with declining population. Mayor–council governments of most moderately large to large cities generally correspond to the strong mayor–council form, whereas medium-size mayor–council cities are divided between strong and weak mayoralties. Small cities with the mayor–council form approximate the weak mayor–council form of government.

The formal resources of the mayor's office provide only part of the explanation of effective mayoral leadership. Even in mayor–council cities, informal resources are extremely important. Mayors such as the first Richard Daley in Chicago[8] and Richard Lee in New Haven[9] were noted for their ability to convert a formally weak position into one of strength. Support from a political party or community elites, strong popular backing, and a host of private backers indebted for jobs, favors, contracts, and recognition can give mayors the added political clout that can be helpful in dealings with the council and their own administration to get ideas accepted and acted upon.

Several trends in American politics have reduced these informal resources of the mayors and made it more difficult for mayors to use their influence. First, the declining strength of political parties and the increasing independence of voting behavior by citizens remove a force that mayors could use to bind together office holders and secure support for the mayor's program. Second, there has been a splintering and thinning of power elites resulting from the breakup of large corporations, takeover of local firms by national and international concerns, increased competition and downsizing, and the move of companies to the suburbs. Third, the proliferation of interest groups and the political organization of neighborhoods have increased the range and diversity of organizations operating in local politics. Fourth, council members are more diverse in their characteristics, more activist in their orientation, and less likely to accept the leadership of the mayor out of deference to the mayor's power or common party loyalty. All these changes in city politics make it more difficult for the mayor to lead effectively. The new openness of the local electoral process and the individualism of persons elected to office diffuse the concentration of power needed for governing the city.[10]

The mayor's performance is also affected by individual characteristics—experience; personal or occupational financial and staff support; personal attributes, such as charisma, reputation, wisdom, and commitment to the job (time, resources, energy expended); and effectiveness in dealing with the media. These factors determine how well and how fully the mayor fills the position, and how creatively the mayor exploits both formal and informal resources. The charismatic or adroit weak mayor may be able to win substantial support from the community and wring more advantage from limited powers than others have done. Ferman argued that "effective political skills" are the critical factor for strong mayoral leadership.[11]

Effective leadership by the mayor is critical in the mayor–council city. Without it, the offsetting powers of the mayor and council can produce policy stalemate and administrative departments can resist change. The performance of mayors can be judged by their effectiveness on two dimensions: initiating policies, and getting policies implemented. The various types of mayors can be classified using this approach. If the mayor is a *caretaker* with no goals, the city will drift and be reactive when problems occur. If the mayor is a *reformer* or policy initiator but poor at getting things done or a *broker* who can arrange compromise but has a weak policy agenda, city government will lack a key element of leadership. This form functions best when the mayor is an *innovator* who can help to provide a clear direction for city govern-

ment and ensure that city departments are focused on accomplishing the goals of elected officials.

Nonexecutive Mayors in Council–Manager Cities

The council–manager form is based on the unitary model of organizing government. The council ultimately possesses all governmental authority, and executive authority is assigned to the city manager. There is no separation of powers or checks and balances in the system, although the form provides for specialization of roles. The council and mayor occupy the overtly political roles in government, set policy, and select the city manager who is continuously accountable to the council. The manager provides policy advice and recommendations to the council, and directs the administrative apparatus. Within this broad division of functions, there is considerable sharing, which this form of government promotes. The city manager also provides policy leadership in helping to frame the agenda of concerns that the council considers, and has latitude in the way that policy goals are converted into programs and services. The council, in contrast, has the potential to oversee the administrative performance of the city through appraisal of how the manager is doing specifically (and whether the manager will continue in office) and its ability to secure information about the performance of administrative staff in general.

The mayor is typically the presiding officer of the council and has no formal powers different from those of other council members, except for the veto power in 13% of council–manager cities. Mayors, directly elected in 62% of these cities,[12] can be an important source of policy guidance and coordination of participants, although they rarely exercise any administrative authority. Thus, mayors in council–manager cities are not executives. They have close interaction, however, with the appointed executive and potentially affect the city manager's performance and influence.[13] It is useful, therefore, to examine the roles of this kind of mayor as an official who helps to bridge the relationship between the appointed executive and the council.

The ideal mayor in council–manager cities is a facilitator who promotes positive interaction and a high level of communication among officials in city government and with the public, and who also provides guidance in goal setting and policy making.[14] This type of leadership is well suited to the conditions of the council–manager city in which cooperative relationships among officials are common and the city manager provides support to the elected officials to whom the manager is accountable. Effective leadership by this kind of mayor improves the working relationships among officials, makes the form of government function more smoothly, and increases the involvement of elected officials in setting policy.

Typically, the mayor in the council–manager city is formally the presiding officer and serves as ceremonial head of the government. In addition, mayors may provide coordination and communication that helps to link the representative leadership of the council and the executive leadership of the manager. Finally, mayors may provide policy leadership and guide the work of the council. These roles are mutually reinforcing and are filled concurrently.

Facilitative leadership does not depend on a superior power position. There are resources available in the council–manager form and within the incumbent as a person to develop leadership in the areas of coordination and policy guidance. The strategic location occupied by the mayor in the center of communication channels to the council, the city manager and staff, and the public provides the foundation for effective leadership. Mayors with a clear conception of the job who use personal resources skillfully are more likely to be able to take advantage of this resource.

There is variation in the nature and scope of leadership, depending on how well the roles that make up the office are filled. Those who do not fill even the traditional roles (e.g., being an ineffective presiding officer who allows the council to flounder in meetings) could be called a *caretaker*, whereas those who fill these roles well but attend to no other are *symbolic heads*. Both the *coordinator* and *director* create an atmosphere that promotes cohesion and communication among officials and strengthens the capacity of the council to identify problems and make decisions. The coordinators, however, are not strongly associated with a policy agenda of their own, even though they contribute to fashioning and acting on an agenda as part of the council. The directors are associated with a distinctive policy agenda, although this agenda incorporates to a greater or lesser extent the views of other officials. The coordinators are effective at developing a sense of cohesion and purpose in their cities and at strengthening the policy-making process. They are not themselves, however, active policy initiators. They are more process oriented than policy oriented. The director-type mayors create an agenda in the sense that they take the initiative to put it together and their own ideas are central to it. Other officials and the public recognize this contribution and view the director mayor as a policy initiator.

In sum, although these mayors lack formal powers over other officials, they occupy a strategic location in the communication channels with the council, the manager, and the public. The moderately effective mayor goes beyond ceremonial leadership to provide effective coordination and communication and, thus, affect how the manager as executive is connected and interacts with the city council. The director-type, highly effective mayor also helps to develop a common set of goals with wide council support that provide a framework within which the manager as executive can operate.

CITY MANAGERS AND ADMINISTRATORS

The city manager is the executive officer with extensive authority for directing staff, formulating and (after approval by council) expending the budget, and controlling operations. The manager is appointed by the council without approval by voters and serves at the pleasure of the council without term. The manager is typically the only staff member hired by the council (in some cities, the city attorney and/or clerk are selected by the council as well); all other employees are hired under the authority of the manager. The norm of the system is for elected officials to respect the insulation of staff from "political" interference.

The structure of council–manager government promotes cooperative relationships among officials. Because the ultimate control over city government lies with the council, there is less likelihood of power struggles between the council and the manager. The council and the manager do not compete for the same "rewards" from public service. Elected officials seek public support and reelection, whereas managers are concerned about how the council assesses their work and their standing and respect in their profession in order to have the option for advancement by moving to another city. Furthermore, city managers have a professional commitment to helping the council accomplish its goals; if they do not, they can be replaced. To be sure, tensions can emerge among elected officials or between them and the staff. The important difference from mayor–council governments is that, with no separation of powers, officials do not have to deal with structural factors that lead to conflict, and positive relationships are common. The approach to leadership taken by the city manager in the council–manager form can be different than that of executive mayors operating in a separation-of-powers setting.

The city manager as executive in council–manager cities is extensively involved in the policy formation aspect of executive leadership and responsible for directing the administrative organization. They are also community leaders. To an extent not found at other levels or in other forms of government, city managers along with other local government-appointed executives, such as school superintendents and directors of public authorities, are both general policy leaders and organizational directors. City managers do not report to an elected executive or go through political appointees in developing policy recom-

mendations for elected officials; they report on performance directly to the governing board. Because of their
close working association with the residents of the
communities they serve, they have a special obligation
to value community leadership, as well as to preserve and
protect the democratic quality of the political process as a
whole. Unlike the elected executive, city managers are
accountable to the entire governing board and are expected to provide leadership from a professional perspective.
This does not mean that the city manager is not involved
in politics, but rather that this involvement should be
guided by professional considerations and standards.

City managers are potentially involved in a wide range
of activities. City managers have commonly been shown
to be active contributors to policy formulation, and they
are responsible for directing the administrative organization.[15] In addition, they advise the elected officials on a
range of topics. Analysis of the extent to which top administrators are policy innovators, advisers to elected officials, and administrators has revealed consistency and
variation.[16] Most city managers (85%) are active as policy innovators. One-half combine this role with emphasis
on administrative functions, and one in eight combine it
with high involvement in advising elected officials. Over
20% are highly active across the board. The minority
(about one in six) who are not active in policy innovation
are not very involved in the other roles either. Thus,
appointed executives tend to be actively and more or less
broadly engaged in the governmental process.

City council members generally give city managers
high ratings on their performance. In the national survey
of council members in cities over 25,000 in population
mentioned earlier, over 80% of the respondents agreed
that the council and city manager have a good working
relationship and that the manager does a good or very
good job of accomplishing the goals established by the
council.[17] Over 70% feel that the manager is doing at
least a good job in providing the council with sufficient
alternatives for making policy decisions and sufficient
information to assess the effectiveness of programs and
services. Furthermore, 83% gave a high rating to the
manager for improving efficiency, and 87% gave this
rating for maintaining high standards of personal conduct
for self and for staff.

In over one-half of the mayor–council cites over 2500
in population, there is a CAO[b] or city administrator. The
scope of the position and the duties depend on what
responsibilities are assigned in the charter or by the
officials who appoint the CAO. These usually include
authority over implementation of programs, day-to-day

administrative concerns, and budget formulation, as well
as playing an advisory role in developing other policy
recommendations. It has been common to assume that the
CAO is appointed by the mayor, derives their influence
from the mayor, and operates within the orbit of the
mayor.[18] In a 2001 survey, in cities with a population of
2500 or more, 44% of the CAOs are appointed by the
mayor with the approval of the city council, and another
39% are chosen by the city council.[b] In only 16% of the
cities is the CAO appointed by the mayor alone, although
direct mayoral appointment is found in approximately
two-fifths of the cities over 100,000 in population. When
appointed by the mayor, the CAO serves at their
"pleasure" and turnover is high, especially when a new
mayor comes into office. When appointed or approved by
the council, the CAO is similar in characteristics to the
city manager.

Chief administrative officers are also supposed to bring
management expertise to city government and can manifest the same characteristics as city managers. In general, however, the CAO is more likely to be recruited
from within the city in which they serve and selected by
the mayor for reasons other than professional qualifications, although the CAO may have extensive training as
well as experience.[19] City managers are somewhat more
likely to be "careerists" who have served in other cities
and aspire to move to "better" positions elsewhere. In a
1997 survey of city administrators, approximately one-
fourth of the top administrators in both major forms of
government are recruited from within the city, although
the percentage of CAOs recruited from the city in which
they serve increases with greater city population. If
recruited from another local government, city managers
are more likely than city administrators to have served as
the chief administrator or as the assistant manager (51%
vs. 36%) in their previous post. However, 17% of CAOs
come from the private sector compared with 8% of the
city managers.[20]

When appointed by the mayor, the CAO is the agent of
the mayor and has power proportionate to their responsibility to the mayor. The CAO is valued as the mayor's
most active troubleshooter. The scope of the position and
the duties depend on what the mayor assigns. The CAO's
status is ambiguous because mayors have difficulty giving
the CAO sufficient power to bring professionalism to the
administration of city government, and CAOs have difficulty winning the confidence of the mayor. Often, mayors and department heads bypass the CAO in their
dealings with each other. Thus, the CAO's subordination
to the mayor compromises their policy and executive
leadership. However, when the CAO is appointed or
approved by the council, which is more common in
smaller cities, this official follows the lead of the entire
council. These CAOs are similar to city managers in their

---

[b]Calculations by authors of data from *Form of Government Survey 2001*;
International City/County Management Association, Washington, DC.

values and orientation. Still, CAOs tend to stay in their position a shorter time than city managers. In the 1997 survey of city managers and CAOs, the average number of years in the current positions is 6.9 years for city managers and 6.5 years for CAOs. In cities over 50,000, the tenure drops to 6.4 for council–manager cities and 4.3 years for mayor–council cities. In comparison to managers, CAOs are not as upwardly or geographically mobile.

CONCLUSION

City managers are executives and city administrators are partial executives who bring a wide range of professional considerations to the discussion of city government policies and practices. By raising professional considerations in policy discussions, city managers help to ensure a balanced approach to policy decisions.[c] By acting out of commitment to strategic goal setting, ethical standards, and sound management, city managers also promote proactive policy making, as well as fairness and efficiency in the delivery of services and the use of organizational resources. These contributions can be combined with those of the mayor as elected executive or the mayor as shaper of the context for the appointed administrator to create a blend of political and professional leadership in the executive functions in local government.

REFERENCES

1. Svara, J.H. The Embattled Mayors and Local Executives. In *American State and Local Politics: Directions for the 21st Century*; Weber, R.E., Brace, P., Eds.; Chatham House: New York, 1999; 139–165. Portions of this article come from this chapter.

2. Svara, J.H. *Official Leadership in the City: Patterns of Conflict and Cooperation*; Oxford University Press: New York, 1990; 97–105, ch. 2.

3. Yates, D. *The Ungovernable City*; MIT Press: Cambridge, 1977.

4. Cunningham, J.V. *Urban Leadership in the Sixties*; Schenkman Publishing Company: Cambridge, 1970.

5. George, A.L. Political leadership in American cities. Daedalus **1968**, *97*, 1194–1217 (Fall).

6. *Managing Local Government*; Bingham, R.D., Ed.; Sage: Newbury Park, 1991; 79–80.

7. Renner, T.; DeSantis, V. Contemporary Patterns and Trends in Municipal Government Structures. In *Municipal Year Book 1993*; International City/County Management Association: Washington, 1993; 57–69.

8. Banfield, E.C. *Political Influence*; The Free Press: New York, 1961.

9. Dahl, R.A. *Who Governs?* Yale University Press: New Haven, 1961. Wolfinger, R.E. *The Politics of Progress*; Prentice-Hall: Englewood Cliffs, 1974.

10. Ehrenhalt, A. *The United States of Ambition*; Random House: New York, 1991.

11. Ferman, B. *Governing the Ungovernable City*; Temple University Press: Philadelphia, 1985; 202–205.

12. Adrian, C.R. Forms of City Government in American History. In *Municipal Year Book 1982*; International City/County Management Association: Washington, 1982; 10.

13. Mouritzen, P.E.; Svara, J.H. *Leadership at the Apex: Politicians and Administrators in Western Local Governments*; University of Pittsburgh Press: Pittsburgh, 2002; 216–217.

14. Svara, J.H.; Associates. *Facilitative Leadership in Local Government*; Jossey-Bass Publishers: San Francisco, 1994.

15. Newell, C.; Ammons, D.N. Role emphasis of city managers and other municipal executives. Public Adm. Rev. **1987**, *47*, 246–252.

16. Mouritzen, P.E.; Svara, J.H. *Leadership at the Apex: Politicians and Administrators in Western Local Governments*; University of Pittsburgh Press: Pittsburgh, 2002; 112–115.

17. Svara, J.H. *A Survey of America's City Councils*; National League of Cities: Washington, 1991; 81.

18. Hogan, J.B. *The Chief Administrative Officer*; University of Arizona Press: Tucson, 1976.

19. Hogan, J.B. *The Chief Administrative Officer*; University of Arizona Press: Tucson, 1976. Nelson, K.L. Assessing the CAO position in a strong-mayor government. Natl. Civic Rev. **2002**, *91* (Spring), 41–54.

20. Svara, J.H. U.S. City Managers and Administrators in a Global Perspective. In *Municipal Year Book 1999*; International City/County Management Association: Washington, 1999; 25–33.

---

[c]For example, should a new recreation center go into a neighborhood in which residents have organized to pressure officials to select their area or into a neighborhood where the need is the greatest?

Federal Subsidies for New Entrepreneurial High-Growth Firms

Terry F. Buss
Florida International University, Miami, Florida, U.S.A.

INTRODUCTION

Only 3% to 5% of small firms account for three-fourths of jobs created in the United States.[1] Not only do these high-growth firms create jobs, but they also are much less likely than other small businesses to fail; create considerably more wealth in the form of profits, sales, and value; pay higher wages and offer greater employee benefits; are much more likely to export products and services; and invest more in research and development (R&D). These firms also outperform the Fortune 500 companies.

Many observers believe that for every one that succeeds, many more potential and emerging high-growth firms that are worthy investment opportunities never start up or die prematurely because capital needs at earliest stages of development are unmet. For economists, capital gaps occur when worthy business opportunities go unfunded even though capital is available in the economy overall. Capital is unavailable, inaccessible, insufficient, costly, or in improper form (e.g., debt versus equity).

Believing that some potential and emerging high-growth firms worth investing in lack needed capital, some observers argue that federal action—potentially including tax incentives, subsidies, loans, equity, spending, regulation, and/or geographic reallocation—is necessary to address private capital market failure. Indeed, existing federal economic development programs are based on this market failure premise.

This article reviews empirical evidence on, and economic theory about, possible capital gaps affecting potential and emerging high-growth firms:

- During long-term, sustained growth in the 1990s, the preponderance of evidence suggests that capital gaps do not seriously affect high-growth firm formation and development.
- Some regions attract less outside capital or produce less capital from local investors because these regions lack requisite industrial clustering and resource concentration, characteristic of regions infused with early stage investment, and produce fewer or much less attractive investment opportunities. This is not a capital gap because large numbers of worthy investment opportunities do not appear to be left unfunded.
- Some technology-based ventures—because of high R&D and startup costs, high risk, lengthy product development time, scarcity of information about potential markets, and lack of management experience on the startup team—may have difficulty accessing early stage capital. Financing these firms sometimes requires highly sophisticated, specialized, experienced, knowledgeable investors, typically venture capital fund managers, former executives in the industry, or corporations in the field.

WHAT IS A HIGH-GROWTH FIRM?

High-growth firms are those that experience rapid employment growth, usually at least 10% to 20% annually over a 5-year period. High-growth firms do not necessarily create or employ new technologies in starting up. Many well-known high-growth firms—Staples, Office Max, Office Depot, Walmart, Starbucks, Planet Hollywood, and even high-tech companies such as Amazon.com—do not use new technologies. Rather, they employ existing delivery systems in more efficient ways to meet consumer demand. High-growth companies do not need to be manufacturers. Neither are they exclusively high-technology or technology-based firms. Using Dun & Bradstreet national data for 1997, analysts discovered that all net growth in jobs derived from the service sector. In the economy as a whole, only 1 in 50 firms can be classified as high tech. High-growth firms are found in every industrial sector.

Potential high-growth firms are those in the idea, seed, or R&D stage of development. Emerging high-growth firms are those starting up or in early stages of development. Most analysts exclude firms created through mergers and acquisitions from discussions of potential or emerging high-growth firms. These activities combine workforces, rather than creating new jobs from scratch, and in any case, are not considered to be as early stage.

An earlier version of this publication was presented to the U.S. Congress as a report from the Economics Division, Congressional Research Service, U.S. Library of Congress.

Encyclopedia of Public Administration and Public Policy
DOI: 10.1081/E-EPAP 120015700

Mergers and acquisitions are none the less important because they create increased funding for earliest stage firms. Large high-tech firms may reduce R&D investment, preferring to acquire it from fledgling firms, rather than develop it in-house.

Entrepreneurs, here, are people who start, or are in the process of starting, what they hope will be a high-growth firm, rather than a small business. Entrepreneurs use new methods in production or service delivery, or create new products, processes, or services. They are not small business operators.

HOW ARE HIGH-GROWTH FIRMS CAPITALIZED?

Capital flowing to high-growth firms is segmented into overlapping niches. Financing depends on levels of risk and expected return on investment, whether firms require equity or debt capital, and the role the startup entrepreneur(s) play in management.

Insider investors—the entrepreneur, friends, relatives, and acquaintances—typically are *the* major source of investment at seed, startup, and early stages. Entrepreneurs with capital are willing to take chances on their ideas; others close to them either have confidence in the entrepreneur's ability to pay them back or make their investment profitable, or are willing to gamble on the prospect. At these earliest stages, potential and emerging high-growth firms, generally require modest amounts of capital.

Angel investors are the second most important source of investment at earliest stages. Angel investors are wealthy individuals who invest in new ventures in exchange for equity. Their role in capital markets for some firms at least is best compared to baseball analogy. They function as a farm team—preparing firms for venture capital investment and eventual public ownership. Angels invest an average of $60,000 to $85,000 in a firm in exchange for equity. Angels often invest in consortia, averaging $660,000 per firm. There may be as many as 250,000 angels, investing about $10 billion in 30,000 firms annually, but estimates vary widely because there is no reliable way to count them.

High net worth individuals are generally much wealthier than angel investors and do not take an active role in growing businesses. They allow either venture capital firms or management to grow businesses. High net worth individuals may invest directly, usually from $5 million to $50 million, in private placements in ventures without venture capital intermediaries.

Venture capital flows to seed or startup stage ventures, but only in relatively modest amounts. Venture capital refers to capital invested through venture capital firms (actually managed funds) by large institutional inves-

tors—pension funds, university endowments, or banks; corporations; or high net worth individuals. There is no comprehensive source of data on venture capital fund investments. Rather, individual brokerage houses and research firms track some funds but not others. There is also some overlap in tracking by different sources. Venture capital firms not only experience high returns on investment at later stages, but they also experience comparable, although lower, returns at earlier stages. Many venture capital firms generally balance out their portfolios with early- and later-stage investments. In recent years, some venture capital firms have even begun to specialize in early stages, investing as little as $5000. Perceptions that venture capital does not flow to seed and R&D stage ventures are unfounded. At issue here is the amount of capital available from venture capitalists and number of ventures capitalized.

Initial public offerings (IPOs) generally do not capitalize potential or emerging high-growth firms. They usually capitalize young, but proven firms, trying to reach a new stage of accelerated growth for which large amounts of capital are required. The average IPO is about $50 million.

Bank and finance company debt financing does not typically flow to early stage high-growth firms. Risks are too high, investment amounts are too small, and returns are too low. Researchers have recently observed that finance companies appear to be willing to take greater risks on startups than banks. Reasons for this have yet to be established. But even in those relatively rare cases when banks and finance companies do lend to earliest stage firms, capital may not be sufficient, sometimes causing firms to fail. Banks and finance companies do not lend at anywhere near the magnitude of angel or venture capital firms. As such, ventures requiring large amounts, but relying instead on commercial and industrial (C&I) loans, may find themselves undercapitalized and at risk of failure.

Even though commercial loans are rare for earliest stage ventures, entrepreneurs may use personal debt instruments to capitalize businesses indirectly. Second mortgages, home equity loans, borrowing against Keogh retirement accounts or insurance policies, and credit cards are commonly used. Entrepreneurs may also use consumer loans to purchase automobiles, computers, and homes for use in businesses. Entrepreneurs may have access to large amounts of capital not taken into account when only examining private equity or commercial loans.

There are three other sources of capital used by early stage firms: corporate venturing, strategic alliances, and trade credit. Corporate venturing occurs when a parent company spins off an independent firm, with the parent capitalizing the venture. Employees of the parent firm are paid or encouraged to create the new venture. Strategic alliances are joint ventures or partnerships where one firm, having capital, partners with a startup to exploit a market, manufacture a product, or deliver a service. Strategic partners invest about $250,000 on average. Trade credit is widely used, but not well documented for potential high-growth firms. Suppliers, distributors, or consumers offer credit, usually as extended payment terms, to new ventures to get them started.

Once firms emerge at early stage, later-stage venture capital, as well as bank and finance company loans, tend to become more readily available. Also at this stage, many firms receive financial help from trade credits. However, insider finance remains the major source of capital for the vast majority of firms. Entrepreneurs invest their own capital or retained earnings when they are able to make sales. In some cases, entrepreneurs may sell a prototype and use the income—retained earnings—to reinvest in a better model. Friends and relatives provide capital, as do angels.

An important point about financing early-stage high-growth firms is that some investors bring not only capital, but also expertise to ventures—they are value-added investors. Angels and venture capitalists typically have extensive experience in markets, industry, and management, allowing them to actively participate not only in capital formation, but also in firm development. Angels mostly invest in entrepreneurs with whom they are comfortable and concern themselves less with markets, whereas venture capital firms often control entrepreneurs and concern themselves more with markets. Having an equity position in the firm empowers them to participate in its management. In the case of angels, most invest in firms near their homes, facilitating their active participation in new ventures. Empirical research confirms importance of this guidance and expertise to entrepreneurs. Corporate spin-offs and strategic alliances also are value-added investments. Banks and finance companies, mutual funds, bond traders, stock brokers, and high net worth investors are only minimally value-added investors, relying on the track record of the firm established over time, disclosure required by regulatory agencies, and/or value of pledged collateral.

ARE THERE CAPITAL GAPS?

The preponderance of empirical research, analysis, and opinion in the 1990s suggests that overall, insider, informal, and formal capital markets function well. Surveys of entrepreneurs in businesses generally, and high-growth firms particularly, reveal that capital formation was not a problem. A review—based on surveys of entrepreneurs, business associations, and bankers, along with analyses of lending data—by the Board of Governors of the Federal Reserve System of capital availability nationally concluded that capital formation was not a significant problem. Business magazines across the United States generally report that the economy is flooded with capital. Venture capital funds over the past few years have invested record amounts of capital in early stage, including seed and R&D, firms. Because some observers believe significant capital gaps exist, even in the face of the evidence above, it is useful to take a closer look at empirical research undergirding this conclusion.

There may be some confusion about problems entrepreneurs have in raising capital versus the lack of capital available for investment in worthy business opportunities. Entrepreneurs typically spend a great deal of time searching for and then obtaining capital. This poses a problem in that entrepreneurs do not obtain capital right off the bat. However, the grueling process of obtaining capital is necessary to help entrepreneurs test the viability of their ideas in the market. As they get turned down by investors, they learn more and more about their idea: that it likely will be commercially viable or not. This process protects entrepreneurs from wasting their own resources—time and money—and those of investors. A major function of capital markets, then, is not only to provide capital, but also to ferret out investments, worthy and unworthy. The tough process of capital formation is not a capital gap because it does not concern a shortage of capital for worthy ideas.

One reason capital formation may not be a problem at early stages is that, for most ventures, only small amounts of capital are required to develop an idea, start up, and begin production. One-half of *Inc.* magazine's top 500 fastest-growing new small businesses in America were seeded with less than $50,000, one-fourth with less than $5000. A Coopers & Lybrand study of fast-growing new firms found that median startup capital was $82,300. Because the vast majority of high-growth firms do not need massive infusions of capital, issues of formal venture capital availability are important to a relatively small number of firms, a finding supported below.

Evidence concerning impact of earliest-stage venture capital on firm growth, rather than startup, appears mixed. One study found that entrepreneurs who were denied venture capital believed that their businesses grew more slowly as a result. Other studies show that firms with venture capital backing grew faster than those without it. However, surveys of entrepreneurs with venture capital backing report that although they had venture capital, it was not critical in helping their firms to grow. These survey results can be interpreted in several ways. It may be that venture capital fund managers are good at picking the most promising high-growth potential firms, with the result that they grow faster than nonventure-backed firms, which may be less desirable choices. This is consistent with the fact that venture capital firms spend a great deal of resource evaluating prospective deals before they invest. Another explanation may be that venture capital is not so important to growth as the value-added investment and management control that—through equity—venture capitalists bring to emerging high-growth firms. Entrepreneurs in venture capital-backed firms clearly do not distinguish between the finance and knowledge that venture capitalists bring to new enterprises. Human capital may be more important than finance.

Empirical evidence cited above on startup capital and earliest-stage venture capital only concerns successful, proven firms. What can be said about firms that were intended to be high-growth ventures, but never started up because of insufficient capital? Virtually nothing can be said, at least directly. It is easy to identify entrepreneurs with ideas who failed early on for want of capital, but impossible to determine whether their ventures would have attained high growth or whether they would have been viable. If firms initially denied capital eventually start up and succeed, then one might argue that they are not victims of capital gaps by definition. Analysis here is concerned with entrepreneurs who never start.

One way of getting at the issue of unmet capital needs versus noncapital-related failure, at least indirectly, is to look at how existing high-growth firms are capitalized at earliest stages. Numerous studies show that the vast majority of entrepreneurs obtained insider or informal capital, and, to some extent, angel investment, but typically not venture capital funds or other forms of private equity. Because of their age and size, they also did not access public equity or debt. Therefore, if existing high-growth firms did not typically rely on sources other than insider and perhaps some angel capital, then it is unlikely that there is a large, unmet need for formal capital investment at earliest stages. Entrepreneurial failure to start up in most cases must relate to noncapital issues, such as poor business ideas or poor management skills or capacity.

It is also important to reemphasize that venture capital represents a small proportion of earliest-stage investment, compared with insider and angel capital. Yet, venture capital seems to receive much more attention than insider and angel capital investment. Venture capital investment has become highly visible in the press, whereas insider and angel finance remain a private activity. Shortage of venture capital and capital gaps are not equivalent issues.

Another line of argument in the literature is whether the very existence of federal and state venture capital programs suggests prevalence of capital gaps for potential or emerging high-growth firms. It is argued that entrepreneurs accessing these federal and state programs have been turned down by private investors and have insufficient insider or informal capital to start up. This seems to show that successful businesses funded by publicly

subsidized programs represent investment opportunities missed by private capital markets. The Small Business Administration's Small Business Investment Company (SBIC), for example, funded household names in the computer industry in their formative stages—Intel, Cray, and Apple. In short, existence of public programs reinforces the perception of capital gaps at earliest stages.

However, many economists offer other possible interpretations. Public programs do not generally capitalize businesses at seed or startup stages, and only a few address earliest stages.[a] Audits by the Inspector General's Office, for example, showed that SBICs judiciously avoid earliest-stage financing even when subsidized to take on increased risk.[2] In this respect, publicly subsidized programs are like formal capital markets. Most important, economists argue that many publicly subsidized firms

---

[a]Consider three very different federal programs as examples. SBICs are widely replicated in OECD countries and represent the largest venture capital program in the United States (see Ref. [2]). Ostensibly, the program's intent is to encourage investments in pioneer firms, not just traditional ventures, in filling capital gaps left by private capital markets. Yet, in a report on SBIC best practices by SBA's Office of the Inspector General, the OIG found that the most successful—that is, profitable, and not at risk of failure—SBICs invested in later stage companies, especially leveraged buyouts, and avoided seed or startups altogether. Further, successful SBICs only invested in firms with an established market niche. Investments made in early-stage companies with speculative markets had relatively low success rates. Therefore, even though SBICs, as financial intermediaries, are backed by government guarantees to encourage debt and equity investment in riskier ventures, SBIC managers still tend to make investment decisions as do private venture capitalists. When they act differently, they risk going out of business, even with government backing.

In the high-tech field consider the federal Advanced Technology Program (ATP) (see Ref. [3]). Advanced Technology Program provides funding, matched by private investment to companies or firms in consortia of universities, businesses, and government laboratories for the development of generic technologies with broad application. Advanced Technology Program funds high-risk development *past the basic research stage*, but not yet ready for commercialization. In addition, ATP also specifies as a qualification: the past performance of the company or joint venture members in carrying out similar kinds of efforts successfully, including technology applications (consideration of this factor in the case of a startup company or new joint venture takes into account the past performance of key people in carrying out similar kinds of efforts). Only 37% of awardees of ATP grants were small businesses (see Ref. [4]). A study by GAO found that public funding crowded out private investment in R&D, contrary to the legislative intent of the program (see Ref. [5]). See also Refs. [6] and [7] for positive and negative assessments of federal technology-based programs for high-growth firms.

The SBA 7(a) loan guarantee program. 7(a) is a loan guarantee program for institutional lenders extending credit to new (no older than 6 months) and existing small businesses, which were turned down for credit using normal business channels (see Ref. [8]). Earliest stage ventures are clearly not represented in the 7(a) program. Only about one-fourth of 7(a) loans even go to new businesses. There is no requirement that borrowers have high-growth potential ventures or innovative products, technologies, or processes.

could have accessed private capital (even though they were turned down by private investors or lenders), but were attracted to lower capital costs afforded by public programs.[b] In its study of Advanced Technology Program, for example, the General Accounting Office (GAO) found that this federal program was for many firms the first choice of funding, rather than an alternative source once having been turned down by private capital.[8] To the extent that this is so, publicly subsidized capital programs displace or crowd out private funds that would have been invested were it not for subsidies.[10]

Although federal programs do not appear to reach earliest stage high-growth ventures, they do, however, reach ventures pursuing earliest stage technologies, processes, or products. This distinction is often overlooked or ignored in evaluating federal program outcomes.

Researchers also find that many state-funded venture capital programs across the United States have been unsuccessful, and many are being defunded.[11] State-funded programs rarely submit to independent evaluation, but studies generally find job creation claims to be overblown. Many claim greatest success in job retention, raising the question of whether programs are subsidizing jobs that would have been maintained without public funding or keeping alive firms that ought to die or shrink. State venture capital programs, presumably tailored to needs of local business, likely would be more in demand were capital gaps really so prevalent for high-growth firms.[c] Some analysts conclude that state venture capital programs exist mostly in response to other states: existence of a program in one state is perceived as a competitive disadvantage by adjacent states, so they too adopt one.[13] This draws into question whether capital market failure exists. So these programs are created not so much to stimulate new development as they are to channel firms that would have started up anyway into selected locations.

The argument that federal and state programs may not be addressing real capital gaps is supported by empirical research suggesting that venture capital firms, angels, and banks have excess capital to lend, but are not offered viable investment opportunities. Venture capitalists, for example, only fund 3% to 5% of the 200 to 500 (in some cases more) finance proposals most receive annually; this after they spend a great deal of time evaluating the entrepreneur's capacity to grow a company and market opportunity. Economists refer to this as preinvestment due diligence. Venture capital firms often retain consultants and experts to evaluate products. It is not unusual for a venture capital firm to pay consultants to take a product apart to see how it was made and whether it can be mass

produced for profit. Of the 3% to 5% pursued, most will not pan out. Venture capital fund returns, including the more than $1 billion annually invested in earliest stage firms, are three times higher than publicly traded stock on average, but venture capital returns have three times the standard deviation above or below the average than the average for publicly traded stock. The implication: some venture capitalists receive high returns on investments, whereas many others fail miserably. Venture capitalists also refer viable projects to other venture capital firms when they are unable to fund them, and in numerous cases, venture capitalists counsel entrepreneurs in how to make their business plans marketable. Many venture capital firms, not interested in an idea themselves, will help an entrepreneur to prepare a business plan for another venture capital firm's consideration, sometimes in exchange for equity. Venture capital firm practices suggest that entrepreneurial proposals receive wide consideration in the market.

The notion that good ideas are not plentiful is borne out in studies about why venture capitalists and angels, for that matter, reject investment proposals from would-be high-growth entrepreneurs. The two major reasons for rejection are 1) there is no demonstrated market for the product, and 2) the entrepreneur has insufficient management capacity to grow the firm. A common problem in potential and emerging high-growth, technology-based firms is that they were started by scientists or technicians who lack management, marketing, and entrepreneurial skills.

A final line of argument concerns study methodology. Most researchers examine whether capital formation was a problem for entrepreneurs starting high-growth firms. Study results mostly show that for entrepreneurs capital formation is difficult, and rightly so, as observed above. However, studies fail to ask whether the entrepreneur merely desired more capital or really needed it, and whether the entrepreneur eventually raised money in another way or found ways around the difficulty. When these additional factors are explored, capital gaps among entrepreneurs seem to be more perceptual than real.

In sum, empirical evidence suggests that capital gaps for potential and emerging high-growth firms are not a significant problem in today's economy, at least not significant enough to warrant federal intervention.

ARE THERE REGIONAL DISPARITIES?

Empirical studies suggesting regional capital gaps abound. Regions, states, and rural economies differ markedly in amount of capital available locally or attracted from outside for investment in earliest-stage potential high-growth firms. Regions differ with respect to rates of startup, employment generation, and industrial sectoral

---

[b]Research on this point is legion (see Refs. [6,9]).
[c]Some analysts take a more positive view of state-funded venture capital programs. See for example, Ref. [12].

growth. Research focuses either on venture capital investment or prevalence of high net worth individuals, likely because both are easier to track. Angel investment, because it is not publicly monitored or regulated, is virtually impossible to track. Studies look at the amount of venture capital attracted to high-growth regions per firm or per capita, and compare this with the region in question. The difference between what a region has now and could have if it performed like a high-growth counterpart is regarded as the capital gap. Studies of high net worth individuals and angels examine census data showing number of individuals with high incomes in the region and investments made. These are then compared with other regions to discern capital gaps.

Many regional studies finding capital gaps conclude that regions either have local investors—venture capitalists, angels, or high net worth individuals—who are not interested in local investment, or they have insufficient numbers of local investors. In the former, capital flows out of the region and is not replaced by sufficient inflows, in the latter there is a shortage of capital. The same studies tend to rely on studies reviewed in the previous section to support the notion that worthy opportunities for investment are plentiful, but are not capitalized.

Regional studies are problematic because they rely on research and inferences about the prevalence of unfunded worthy investment opportunities seemingly suffering from the same problems already presented in the preceding sections. If the analysis above holds, then it is not likely that there are large numbers of worthy unfunded investments in most regions. Analysts, then, may be misperceiving or overestimating potential high-growth firm opportunities available for investment.

Critics question whether methodologies employed in such regional research actually reveal capital gaps on the investment side. Criticism differs for venture capital, angels, and high net worth investors.

Venture Capital

Concerning venture capitalists, venture capital is attracted to a region from investors across the United States and internationally because ventures in the region present the best investment alternatives—highest return adjusted for risk. Risk is assessed on information that venture capitalists hold about entrepreneurs and that markets entrepreneurs propose to exploit. Venture capitalists have expertise in industries in which they invest and in the markets these industries serve, and are adroit at evaluating entrepreneur capacity to grow a company. Successful initial venture capital investments attract subsequent investment to a region, a kind of herd effect. What undercapitalized regions lack, then, is not only the best investment opportunities compared with others, but also agglomeration of

ventures working in similar industrial sectors, professionals with expertise in these industries—bankers, lawyers, marketing professionals, technicians, scientists, and engineers—educational facilities, especially universities producing research and graduates for industry, and so on. It is unlikely that venture capitalists will extensively invest in regions without this supportive infrastructure.

Consider Route 128 in Boston. This corridor is or was home to hundreds of high-tech companies with household names, Digital Equipment, Lotus Development, Wang, and Data General. It is served by dozens of venture capital funds and some of the largest emerging growth company funds, such as that offered by Fidelity Investments. It boasts of MIT and Harvard, not to mention Brandies, Tufts, Boston University, and Boston College, whose professors, scientists, and students spawn hordes of new high-tech, high-growth companies annually. In addition, there are countless consulting firms and businesses supporting these ventures. Such clustering in turn attracts entrepreneurs and high-tech workers. Only a handful of regions in the United States can boast of this concentration of resources in high-tech. This leads some critics to argue that in addition to lacking viable business ideas, capital does not flow to some regions to potential high-growth firms because they lack the supportive infrastructure, not just money.

Angel Investors

However, not all investment is made by venture capital funds, angels play a substantial role. Concerning angel investors, critics argue that angels, like venture capitalists, are also knowledgeable investors, having experience in industries in which they invest and living near their workplaces so that they can take an active role in operating a company. Angels know about markets, but their main focus for investment is their potential relationship with entrepreneurs. Also, the literature suggests that many angels invest not only to profit, but also as a kind for recreation. In short, they receive both monetary and psychological rewards from investment. If local opportunities for investment do not include both dimensions, then angels may not be interested. Capital gaps can only exist if potential angels elect not to invest in local opportunities that are at least as profitable as others. Because angels usually invest close to home and take part in businesses, it is unlikely that other regions would attract them as investors who will take an active role in companies. Some studies tend to look at people with the same income or worth as angels as potential investors. But wealth alone is not an indicator of the capacity of individuals to make investments in risky ventures. Again, it is not capital that is at issue, it is expertise and participation that separate angels from comparably wealthy people.

High Net Worth Investors

Critics argue that high net worth investors, like venture capitalists, invest in opportunities representing the best investment adjusted for risk. Capital, then, flows across the United States. Unlike venture capitalists and angels, high net worth investors do not tend to take an active role in assessing investments or operating companies. More important, they invest millions at a time and are generally not interested in directly investing small amounts of capital in emerging businesses. They tend to leave oversight and due diligence to intermediaries—either venture capital fund managers or brokerage firms. So research looking at prevalence of high wealth individuals, critics argue, is misdirected because their money is intermediated by investment firms. Investment firms, then, are the issue, not the wealthy. So, it does not matter whether high net worth investors are themselves present or absent from a region.

Other evaluations suggest that some regional studies may be measuring perceptions of capital gaps that cannot be supported. In a survey of economic development practitioners in Alabama, Maine, Minnesota, and Washington, for example, the GAO found that 66% and 77%, respectively, believed that credit and equity gaps existed to a great or very great extent, for startup businesses, but somewhat less for expanding businesses at 26% and 33%, respectively.[14] However, when GAO asked practitioners to provide empirical evidence to support their conclusions, none was forthcoming.

In evaluating the regional capital gap literature, it is important to consider evaluations of public programs. One critical study examined firm performance data for participants in the federal Small Business Innovation Research (SBIR) program,[d] comparing them with a control group of firms not participating in the program.[18] Overall, SBIR participants outperformed nonparticipants in sales and employment growth. At first blush, it appears that capital gaps were closed by publicly subsidized programs. However, SBIR participants, located in areas with low concentrations of private venture capital and sparse industrial clustering, had less in sales and employment growth compared with SBIR participants in regions with concentrations of venture capital and industry clustering. It might also be the case that SBIR investors do a better job of picking winners in supportive economies than in less supportive economies. Yet, this exception might prove the rule: perhaps SBIR investors in less supportive economies find it difficult to adequately evaluate merging high-growth firms because of the lack of supportive infrastructure.[17] This also tends to confirm the impression that factors other than capital availability influence business location.

One thing on which nearly all analysts agree is that rural areas have sufficient access to capital generally, but are underserved by equity investors, angels, or venture capital. There are insufficient numbers of entrepreneurs to attract outside investors and relatively few local investors. Consequently, investment opportunities in rural areas are somewhat less likely to come to fruition locally. The perception is that entrepreneurs who take their ideas to cities, where capital is more readily available, face high transaction costs—costs of finding investors or lenders—and high rejection rates because they are not known to investors or lenders.

The rural capital gap for equity investment may be overstated. A study of all Initial Public Offerings (IPOs) from 1970 to 1995, broken down by urban and rural areas showed that 10% of IPOs—measured in amounts invested and numbers of firms—were for rural firms.[19] In addition, more than one-half of rural IPOs were backed by venture capital, while less than one-half of urban firms had this backing. Rural IPOs performed as well as urban ones, as measured by stock price and return on investment. Venture capital and IPO investment does flow to many rural areas. How can this be reconciled with the fact that rural areas lack investors locally, industrial concentrations, and supportive infrastructure? The answer is that entrepreneurs actually do find investors and support in regional financial centers—Minneapolis, Denver, Houston, and the like—contrary to perceptions. Capital markets function well for emerging high-growth firms as long as they are near urban centers, which most appear to be.[e] This research also tends to call into question prevalence of barriers in linking investors and entrepreneurs in rural areas rather than capital gaps.

ARE THERE TECHNOLOGY-BASED SECTOR DISPARITIES?

Empirical studies on capital gaps for emerging high-growth firms have not definitively resolved the issue of capital availability for technology-based companies, but

---

[d]For an overview of this program, see Refs. [15,16]. The SBIR Program's intent is to stimulate technological innovation, use small businesses to meet federal R&D needs, foster participation by minorities and disadvantaged people, and increase commercialization of innovations. Research on the program finds that it, like ATP discussed above, also crowds out private funding using public subsidies. In addition, the fact that firms tend to receive repeat awards draws into question whether SBIR is reaching startup entrepreneurs. See especially, Ref. [17].

[e]There are about 2000 rural counties in the United States. The lion's share of these are federal conservation lands, and sparsely populated and remote farming, ranching, and mining regions. Much of the rural population lives in counties adjacent to metropolitan areas. See Ref. [20].

there is evidence that is suggestive, either from limited empirical investigations, or more often from anecdotal evidence and case studies. In exhaustive, independent reviews of research and venture capital programs in western, industrialized countries by the Bank of England and Organization for Economic Cooperation and Development (OECD) [21,22]—along with extensive Congressional testimony,[f] reports from the *1995 White House Conference on Small Business*, and others [24,25]—most observers concluded that technology-based, high-technology, and biotechnology-based (hereafter, referred to as technology-based firms) potential and emerging high-growth firms, although they pass through the same growth stages as other ventures, have more specialized capital formation needs and are more likely to experience capital gaps. Like other firms, technology-based firms depend heavily on insider capital in earliest stages. Exceptions, of course, are spin-offs from existing corporations. But capital needs of technology-based firms tend to be much higher than other businesses starting up. Technology-based companies often require access to expensive equipment and materials during seed and R&D earliest stages. Entrepreneurs in these companies may take years to develop and test a product to see if it even works. Once it works, then more time is required to determine whether it can be manufactured at a reasonable profit. Large amounts of capital over the long-term, required at seed or R&D stages by some ventures, are sometimes not available from insider and informal sources. Angels and venture capitalists—having large amounts of capital, invested at high risk, over an extended period—may be the only source of finance for some ventures. Angels and venture capitalists often invest in rounds—first, second, and third—as entrepreneurs increasingly demonstrate the viability of their ideas. Because this process can take years before investors profit, angel and venture capital is often called ''patient capital.'' Once they mature, technology-based companies begin to resemble other businesses in their capital needs.

A peculiarity of technology-based firms is that they tend to be started by technicians—engineers, programmers, or scientists—who have a single product to market, have little or no management experience, and may lack capacity to grow a company. Having a single product or application makes it difficult for investors because all the ventures eggs are in one basket. Most emerging high-growth firms are single-product dominated or use a single application. Dell Computers, for example, the best performing high-tech stock of the 1990s found a competitive advantage in the computer industry: selling directly to customers while avoiding a middleman. Dell Computers

did not innovate new technologies across several product lines. This greatly increases investment risk, turning away potential investors. Technicians, having little management experience, further increase risks, if they try to grow the business themselves without seeking professional help. Because technicians may be reluctant to give up firm management, they greatly reduce the pool of investors likely to be interested in their venture.

Even though angels and venture capitalists may be the investors of last resort for technology-based firms, entrepreneurs may not have access to these investors. Angels and venture capitalists tend to specialize in certain technologies where they have expertise. Some good investments may not be of interest to all potential investors. Angels and venture capitalists, with expertise in certain technologies, may not have time to evaluate or participate in the opportunity. Entrepreneurs and investors may be unable to find one another to close a deal. Or, angel and venture capitalists, having to work closely with entrepreneurs they fund, may not like their prospective business partners so they reject a deal.

Although capital formation for technology-based ventures may be subject to the influences above, research that moves beyond this to identify what kinds of firms experience capital gaps, why difficulties occur, and to what extent there are problems is lacking, and ought to be a priority for future study. As it stands now, the doubtful existence of capital gaps generally still seems to apply in the high-tech area.

CONCLUSION

Because most new jobs are created by a small number of emerging high-growth small companies, some observers are calling for government intervention in capital markets to reduce capital gaps, causing emerging high-growth firms to grow too slowly and potential high-growth firms from failing early on.

Empirical evidence suggests that capital markets, including formal and informal investors, work well, and that overall capital gaps are not problematic for potential and emerging high-growth firms. Capital gaps might emerge in the future during severe economic downturns, as they have in the past.

Evidence about capital gaps for regions and technology-based firms, is not conclusive. Some regions have greater concentrations of capital for potential and emerging high-growth firms than others, but this may have more to do with the prevalence and quality of investment opportunities and the requisite industrial clustering and financial infrastructure that stimulates and sustains investment, than with capital unavailability. Some technology-based firms appear to experience capi-

---

[f]See, for example, Ref. [23].

tal gaps, because of the peculiarities of how these firms typically grow and are financed, but there is little evidence to support or refute the notion that there is a widespread capital gap problem for large numbers of high-tech firms.

It appears that the case for federal intervention to correct capital market failure for emerging and potential high-growth firms has not been made.

REFERENCES

1. Birch, D.L. *Hot Industries*; Cognetics, Inc.: Boston, 1998.
2. U.S. Delegation to the OECD The U.S. Experience. *Best Practice Policies for Small and Medium-Sized Enterprises*; Organization for Economic Cooperation and Development: Paris, 1997; 45–58.
3. U.S. Library of Congress, Congressional Research Service, *Advanced Technology Program*; October 8, 1998; CRS Report 95-36 SPR.
4. Technology Administration. *ATP*; National Institute of Standards, April 1996; 20NIST-ATP-96-2.
5. GAO. *Measuring Performance*; General Accounting Office: Washington, D.C., April 10, 1997; T-RECD-97-130.
6. *Investing in Innovation: Creating a Research and Innovation Policy That Works*; Branscomb, L., Keller, J.H., Eds.; MIT Press: Cambridge, MA, 1998.
7. Cohen, L.; Noll, R. *The Technology Pork Barrel*; Brookings Institute: Washington, D.C., 1991.
8. GAO. *A Comparison of SBA's 7(a) Loans and Borrowers with Other Loans and Borrowers*; GAO, September 1996; RCED-96-222.
9. Economic Research Service. *Credit in Rural America*; Agricultural Economic Report, ERS, U.S. Department of Agriculture: Washington, D.C., April, 1997; Vol. 749.
10. Irwin, D.; Klenow, P.J. *High Tech R&D Subsidies*; National Bureau of Economic Research: Cambridge, 1994#4974. Haynes, G.W. A Comparison of Borrowers with SBA and Other Loan Guarantees, U.S. Small Business Administration, Contract Report, June 1993. Study raises questions on SBIR, Physiologist, **1995**, *38*, 148. Corporate welfare or funding godsend, Scientist, **1997**, *11*. See Ref. [6].
11. Eisinger, P. State venture capitalism, state politics, and the world of high-risk investment. Econ. Dev. Q. **May 1993**, *7*, 131–139. Florida, R.; Smith, D.F. Venture capital, innovation and economic development, Econ. Dev. Q., **November 1990**, *4* (4), 345–360. For an inventory of federal/state programs, see, Coburn, C.; Bergland, D. *A Compendium of State and Federal Cooperative Technology*. Battelle: Columbus, 1995 and for a review see U.S. Library of Congress, Congressional Research
   Service. *Technology Development: Federal-State Issues*. CRS Report 96-958 SPR, November 22, 1996, by W. Schacht.
12. Bygrave, W.D.; Timmons, J.A. *Venture Capital at the Crossroads*; Harvard Business School Press: Boston, MA, 1992.
13. Jenkins, J.C.; Leicht, K. Direct action by the subnational state. Soc. Probl. **August 1996**, *43* (3), 306–326. Fosler, R.S. State Strategies for Business Assistance. In *Growth Policy in the Age of High Technology*; Schmandt, J., Wilson, R., Eds.; Unwin: Boston, 1990.
14. GAO. *Rural Development: Availability of Capital for Agriculture, Business and Infrastructure*; GAO: Washington, D.C., May 1997; RCED-97-109.
15. U.S. Library of Congress, Congressional Research Service. In *SBIR Program*; Schach, W.H., Ed.; September 11, 1998; CRS Report 96-402 SPR.
16. GAO. *Federal Research*; GAO: Washington, D.C.: 1998; RCED-98-132.
17. Wallsten, S.J. *Rethinking the Small Business Innovation Program*; Branscomb, L., Keller, J.H., Eds.; MIT Press: Cambridge, MA, 1998.
18. Lerner, J. *The Government as Venture Capitalist*; National Bureau of Economic Research: Cambridge, 1996; #5753.
19. Brophy, D.J. Developing Rural Equity Capital Markets. *Financing Rural America*; Federal Reserve Bank of Kansas City: Kansas City, April 1997; 159–172.
20. Economic Research Service. *Understanding Rural America*; Agriculture Information Bulletin, U.S. Department of Agriculture, February 1995; Vol. 710.
21. Bank of England, The Financing of Technology-Based Small Firms. London: Bank of England, 1997.
22. Organization for Economic Cooperation and Development (OECD). Venture Capital and Innovation. Paris: OECD, 1997.
23. Committee on Banking, Finance and Urban Affairs, U.S. House of Representatives Hearing Before the Subcommittee on Economic Growth and Credit Formation. *Availability of Financing for High-Technology Companies*; November 16, 1993; 103rd Congress, First Session, Serial no. 103-99.
24. Carnegie Commission on Science, Technology and Government. *Science, Technology and the States in America's Third Century*; New York, September, 1992. Westhead, P.; Storey, D.J. Financial constraints on the growth of high technology firms in the United Kingdom. Appl. Financ. Econ. **1997**, *7*, 197–201. Moore, B. Financial Constraints to the Growth and Development of Small High Technology Firms. In *Financing Small Firms*; Hughes, A., Storey, D.J., Eds.; Routledge: London, 1994. Oakey, R. *High Technology New Firms: Variable Barriers to Growth*; Paul Chapman: London, 1995. Ref. [25].
25. Majewski, S.E. Using Strategic Alliance Formation. Berkeley, CA: University of California, 1997, working paper.

Federalism in "Homeland Security" and Crisis Management

Alethia H. Cook
David J. Louscher
The University of Akron, Akron, Ohio, U.S.A.

INTRODUCTION

Responding to a domestic act of terrorism in the United States will be a major challenge for coordinated federal, state, and local response. The word "will" in the preceding sentence was used intentionally instead of "would." There is general agreement among federal, state, and local governments, as well as the defense community, that the terrorist threat is a question of when, not if, a strike will occur. The Oklahoma City bombing and the World Trade Center bombing brought this harsh reality to the forefront for many in government and academia who were studying terrorism. The rest of the country was made painfully aware of the threat on 11 September 2001 when terrorists hijacked four planes and flew them into the World Trade Center towers, the Pentagon, and a field in Pennsylvania. In spite of these many warnings, the nation is woefully unprepared to meet this critical challenge, particularly if the terrorist act is something other than a conventional explosive.

The concept of federalism, so important in the American political system, itself will be one of the critical challenges. Local authorities who are witnessing the devastation wrought by an act of terrorism in their own backyards will understandably be reluctant to turn over responsibilities for dealing with the crisis to state and federal level entities. Federal organizations are interested in protecting evidence and the crime scene in the interest of catching the perpetrator, as well as assisting the local government with recovering from the event. These potentially conflicting goals may create tensions between the different government agencies at different levels. Response to an intentional biological contamination may be even more complex than for a chemical or conventional strike.

While the nation has been making efforts to improve preparedness, two distinct problems remain that threaten to undermine effective response. The first is that the majority of the effort to improve readiness has been made at the federal level. This is problematic as the response to terrorism, whether it is chemical, biological, nuclear, radiological, or conventional, is necessarily a local event. The police, firemen, emergency management services (EMS), hospital personnel, and other first responders that will be tasked with dealing with the impact of such an event are the ones that need the resources to improve preparation. The second major problem with preparedness is that most of the preparation efforts have focused on either a chemical, nuclear, or conventional attack. Although these threats are important, they are not the only ones faced. Because the nature of the events are so different, increasing preparedness for chemical response will not help deal with a biological attack. The impact of federalism on these two challenges to preparedness, public administration, and effective response are the focus of this article.

FEDERAL PREPARATION FOR A LOCAL CRISIS

There is no question that the United States has been working to improve its response capabilities. In particular in the aftermath of September 11, extensive efforts to better train, equip, organize, and manage response have been a focus of government. What is in question, however, is whether the resources that are being expended are being used in an efficient and effective manner. As demonstrated on Fig. 1, there is a lot of funding being spent at the federal level, with little money reaching the first responder. There is no centralized coordination for the expenditure of this money or for training and preparation.[1] This is problematic as there are over 40 government agencies playing an active role in homeland defense.[2] According to Warren Rudman, "[t]he United States stands in dire need of stronger organizational mechanisms for homeland security. It needs to clarify accountability, responsibility, and authority among the departments and agencies with a role to play in this increasingly critical area."[3]

One of the major efforts undertaken by the federal government has been the establishment of 27 National Guard Weapons of Mass Destruction Civil Support Teams. These teams are trained and equipped by the federal government, but will be deployed under the control of governors in the state where the event has occurred. They

Encyclopedia of Public Administration and Public Policy
DOI: 10.1081/E-EPAP 120011033

489

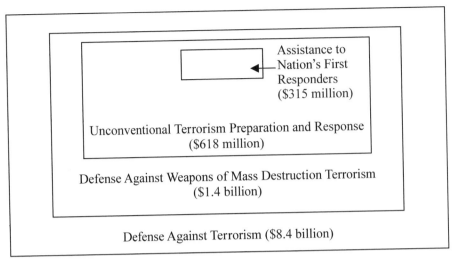

Fig. 1 Breakdown of the federal budget to combat terrorism, 2000. (Adapted from Ref. [5].)

train regularly and have access to state-of-the-art communications equipment.[4] Although the National Guard teams are a valuable asset, an argument can be made that the funding could have been spent to equip first responders rather than a federal level team that will take time to deploy. According to one critic, "2333 hospitals or fire stations could be out fitted with decontamination capabilities for the cost of standing up one National Guard Civil Support team. If the total 1999 budget for these National Guard teams had been used thusly, 49,800 local facilities could have been armed for decontamination."[5]

This situation places the burden on local responders to determine where the federal resources are and how they can get them quickly in case of an emergency. Without this kind of arrangement in place, it does not matter how much the federal government spends on preparedness. If the local-level entities cannot rapidly get equipment, vaccines, and other resources, the terrorist strike will have a much more devastating impact on the local community.

Federal organizations are engaged in outreach activities aimed at informing local responders about the resources available to them and providing training. This task is more complex than it would seem. The event itself will dictate who the responsible local authorities will be. As a result, the federal organizations need to get their information out to all local fire, police, health, and infrastructure officials that may be relevant to a terrorist strike. Because of this complexity, major cities have received the majority of contact with and training from the federal government, leaving smaller communities seriously unprepared.[6]

An additional problem with this federal training is that once the exercise is over, there is no follow-on training or regular practice of the techniques for effective response. Furthermore, there are no standardized ways of assessing the quality of response.[5] The implications of these pro-

blems are significant. It is unreasonable to expect first responders to learn more effective response if they are trained only once, are not given adequate feedback on their performance, and do not have the opportunity to learn from their mistakes.

Local authorities clearly need to be better trained to identify and respond to a terrorist event when one occurs. The implications of this federalism problem are significant. Money, training, and cooperation have to be spread among the levels of government if the United States hopes to mount a successful response. The problems of coordinating the levels of government will fall within the tasking of the new Department of Homeland Security. It will be responsible for making the country more prepared to respond to catastrophic terrorism. One of its major challenges will be to find a more effective pattern of funding, training, and organization to overcome the paradox of federal level preparations for local level events. Although there is a definite response role for the federal government, it will not be first on the scene of a terrorist strike, nor is it likely to be the most important element of any response. A careful reassessment of the nation's response spending priorities should be undertaken to correct these problems and put resources in the hands of those tasked with first response. However, before that can be done, government must gain a better understanding of the complexity of response.

FAILURE TO PREPARE FOR BIOLOGICAL EVENTS

As mentioned above, different types of threats confronting the United States require distinctly different types of response. In the event of a chemical or conventional attack, there is an identifiable moment that the attack occurs. If a bomb goes off, responders know when it went off, they mobilize their resources to mount an effective response, arrive on the scene, struggle to mitigate the impact of the attack, and then turn the victims over to the medical community. The majority of the efforts underway to improve preparedness have focused on this kind of event.[7]

However, a biological attack will present itself very differently. This was demonstrated in the Anthrax attacks in 2001, when those exposed to the agent became ill over an extended period of time. Biological agents can take anywhere from 2 to 14 days to incubate and become symptomatic. Victims who are exposed to the agent may circulate among the general population during this time without being aware that they have been infected. Depending on the type of agent and the way it is transmitted, those who have been exposed may be spreading the disease within the community. To detect this kind of event, the public health system will have to recognize that an epidemic is underway. The faster the agent used is identified, the lower will be the casualty rate from the event. Each day that the event goes unreported is another day that the victims are infecting others. The problem is exacerbated by the fact that the public health providers must be able to identify the difference between a naturally occurring event and one that is intentional.

Effective response to a biological event, therefore, requires that local-level health providers be aware of the symptoms of the major potential biological warfare agents so that they can identify these diseases quickly (Table 1). They must also understand the ways in which a naturally occurring event is likely to differ from a terrorist strike. Finally, health care providers must be ready and able to report suspicious diseases to a system that can help to identify infection patterns. Although cases of a disease may cluster in a small community if the agent was dis-

tributed locally, it may be that the agent is distributed in a way that will initially manifest as a few cases that are widely spread.

Some analysts believe that the government is overreacting to the threat of biological terrorism. They argue that biological agents are difficult to grow in quantities necessary to disseminate them widely and that effective delivery of the agent is incredibly difficulty.[9] The anthrax attacks seem to support this argument as the agent was deployed in an inefficient manner and caused relatively limited casualties. However, fanatical terrorists may allow themselves to be infected with an agent, become contagious, and board an international flight; infecting the other passengers on each leg of the flight and effectively spreading the disease around the world.[7]

This is where the concept of federalism will complicate response. Although diseases will initially be reported the local level, with patients going to their doctors or to an emergency room, identifying the extent of the terrorist act may rely on a national or even international coordination of medical information. The Centers for Disease Control and Prevention (CDC) in the United States issues guidelines to American hospitals for those diseases they must report so that outbreaks can be identified. However, many biological agents have flu-like symptoms and it may not immediately be clear to physicians that they are dealing with something other than the common flu. Furthermore, a widespread epidemic may be difficult to identify as patients arrive at different hospitals but no real trend seems to be present until much later. Every day the spread of the disease goes unrecognized, the potential impact of the event increases exponentially. Communication about disease diagnoses is key.

This poses a significant problem for many local health systems that are consistently underfunded. A survey revealed that many local systems do not have access to e-mail and the Internet, and may even still have ro-

Table 1 Critical biological agents

First-tier agents	Second-tier agents	Third-tier agents
Anthrax	Brucellosis	Hantaviruses
Botulism	Cholera	Multidrug-resistant tuberculosis
Ebola	E. coli	Nipah virus
Junin (Argentine hemorrhagic fever)	Epsilon toxin	Tickborne hemorrhagic fever
Lassa fever	Equine encephalomyelitis	Tickborne encephalitis viruses
Marburg	Glanders	Yellow fever
Plague	Ricin	
Smallpox	Salmonella	
Tularemia	Shingella	

Note: First-tier agents are easy to employ, spread easily, and have high mortality rates; second-tier agents are moderately easy to employ and have low mortality; and third-tier agents are available, easy to produce and disseminate, and the potential for high mortality.
Source: Adapted from Ref. [9].

tary phones.[7] They are not networked in any meaningful way aside from their communications with the CDC. As such, the CDC may be the first to pick up on a local epidemic because hospitals may not be able to effectively communicate about their patients' symptoms. These problems exist in spite of significant efforts on the part of the Department of Health and Human Services and the CDC to help local entities build their response capacities.[5]

Another major problem that will be confronted by public health care officials is the panic that will likely occur among the local population. Again, a biological event will be different from a chemical or conventional attack. If someone bombs a building or releases a chemical agent in a subway, citizens who were not in those areas can be relatively certain that they were not affected. If a disease begins to spread, people will begin to worry that they have been exposed. Mass numbers of generally healthy individuals, or people with flu-like symptoms, may converge on hospitals and doctors' offices seeking medical attention. The Anthrax attacks provided evidence of this problem, with mailrooms closed around the country and sales of Cipro (the antibiotic for treating Anthrax) being sold on the internet to people who had been nowhere near the known cases of exposure. In any biological attack, local-level officials will need help in containing the panic and dealing with the influx of patients. Communication will also be important in this effort. Notifying the public about the threat, the way in which the disease is transmitted, the symptoms of the illness, and where to seek treatment will be critical to controlling the public's reaction. Calming public fears will be a serious challenge facing local authorities. This is an issue rarely covered by training exercises that are focused on chemical or conventional terrorism.

These problems generated by the federal nature of the American system must be overcome in order to have more effective response capabilities. Policy makers need to rethink the focus of national efforts to increase preparedness so that resources can be expended in ways that assist first responders in performing their roles. More attention needs to be paid to the unique nature of biological terrorism or a major epidemic so that those kinds of problems can be detected and contained as quickly as possible. Without these changes in U.S. policy, a major terrorist strike will have an unacceptably large impact on the society and may undermine public faith in government.

REFERENCES

1. Neus, E. Bioterrorism: How real is the threat? USA Today **1999, October 27**, 1. See also NGB report: No one WMD ready. Natl. Guard **1999**, *53* (10), 13–14.
2. Holzer, R. Homeland security bill aims to coordinate agency roles. Def. News **2001**, *16* (12), 12.
3. Rudman, R.B. *Statement Before the House Committee on Government Reform*; March 27, 2001.
4. Garamone, J. *Guard Teams to Combat Weapons of Mass Destruction*; www.defenselink.mil/specials/destruction/Garamone.ltr.html (accessed March 29, 2001).
5. Smithson, A.E.; Levy, L. *Ataxia: The Chemical and Biological Terrorism Threat and the U.S. Response*; The Henry L. Stimson Center: Washington, D.C., 1999.
6. Stanton, J. U.S. homeland defense policy mired in competing interests. Natl. Def. **2001**, 10–13.
7. Nesmith, J. Nation ill-prepared for warfare against germs. Palm Beach Post **1998, August 31**, 1A+.
8. Kahn, A.S.; Morse, S.; Lillibridge, S. Public-health preparedness for biological terrorism in the USA. Lancet **2000**, *356*, 1179–1182.
9. Sokolski, H. Rethinking bio-chemical dangers. Orbis **2000**, *44* (2) 207–219 and Tucker, J. Chemical and biological terrorism: How real a threat. Curr. Hist. **2000**, 147–153.

Feminism and Chaos Theory

Mary Ann McClure
John Jay College of Criminal Justice, New York, New York, U.S.A.

INTRODUCTION

Contemporary chaos theory explains phenomena traditional science cannot and reveals hidden order in the apparent random behavior of, among other things, business cycles, epidemics, and insect populations. It also provides a vision of nature that challenges the notion of nature central to traditional science. In its concept of nature and methodology, chaos theory parallels the efforts of contemporary feminists to reshape traditional understanding of scientific inquiry. Both feminist philosophers of science and chaos theory presume a methodology that attends to difference, is nonreductionistic, attributes agency to nature, and conceives of inquiry as fallible.

Traditional science makes a claim to being objective. The scientist who pursues objectivity seeks a context-free knowledge that aspires to be omniscient, fully formalizable, and unbiased and disinterested. What connects these characteristics is the key concept of detachment. Objectivity as detachment means the separation of the knowing subject from the object of knowledge. Objectivity depends upon clear and distinct boundaries between the self and the world. Thus, in the act of trying to gain objective knowledge, the scientific mind separates itself from nature.

THE FEMINIST CRITIQUE OF TRADITIONAL SCIENCE

Feminist epistemologists have examined the concept of scientific objectivity in terms of its claim to value-neutrality and in its association with masculinity, where the ''masculine'' denotes a cognitive style rather than a biological category. They have traced the historical origins of the concept of objectivity to the emergence of the Newtonian paradigm in the sixteenth and seventeenth centuries, when the new science of that day demanded new concepts of nature and inquiry. Newtonian science was struggling against the older medieval view that held nature to be an alive organism and part of God's domain. Seeking a new concept of nature, modern science reconceptualized nature as dead and thus passive and inert—like a machine—in a fixed and determinate universe.

Feminist philosophers of science have argued that this conceptual framework of modern science is fundamentally gendered. Attributes such as objectivity, detachment, and abstract thinking that are attributed to science are also stereotypically masculine. The achievement of scientific knowledge, identified as a specifically male way of knowing, demands not only the separation from, but the domination and control of nature and of female human nature in particular. Thus, the feminist project becomes one of rethinking the concept of objectivity and, once again, reimagining our concept of nature.

SCIENCE AS FALLIBLE

If traditional objectivity claims omniscience, feminist philosophers of science, such as Sandra Harding, advocate a ''stronger'' sense of objectivity in which knowledge is understood to be fallible.[1] Evelyn Fox Keller and Donna Haraway seek alternative framings of biological and physical theories in which scientific knowledge is modeled on a dialogue that remains open-ended and does not seek closure. For Keller and Haraway, rational knowledge is less a set of facts or theories than a process. This notion of scientific inquiry as a process places emphasis upon on the act of revision, in which we encounter the limits of our control of the natural world. To understand is not merely to know a set of facts about nature but to possess the skill of being open to the experience of limitations.

The move from scientific inquiry having the potential for omniscience to its being understood as inherently limited and fallible is best captured by Keller's distinction between order and law in nature. A law-like nature fits the demand of traditional objectivity which calls for a total correspondence between theory and reality. Nature that is law-like can be captured best by the language of science–mathematics. In contrast, when Keller understood nature as being orderly, she conceived of the order in nature as being more complex than any law that the human understanding will ever invent. Theory can never provide a complete representation of reality, because nature will always remain more abundant than our representations. Nature is characterized by an a priori

Encyclopedia of Public Administration and Public Policy
DOI: 10.1081/E-EPAP 120010682

complexity that will inevitably confound the capacity of the human inquirer.[2]

Similarly, chaos theory seeks to find patterns and connections, while jettisoning the requirement that the patterns must be ruled by law-like necessity. Researchers, fascinated by the development of chaotic motion, look for regularities, using computer graphics to identify and explore ordered patterns that would otherwise be buried in reams of computer output. But, there is a difference between searching for patterns and searching for laws. These researchers studying chaotic motion realize that the patterns they discern will not have a unique evolution or act predictably.

Traditional science has been based upon the power to predict and control, but chaos theory asserts that when systems become chaotic, science no longer has this ability. The defining characteristic of chaos theory is a sensitivity to initial conditions, such that for chaotic systems, we will never be able to measure the initial conditions accurately enough to get an accurate prediction. It is inherently impossible, because if the initial configuration of a chaotic system is changed even slightly, its future behavior is altered radically.

It is far better to consider chaos theory as a search for order, a concept broader—as Keller pointed out—than the concept of law. The determinate randomness of chaotic systems can be better understood as conforming to a sense of order rather than law, because we are studying behavior that has intrinsic causes, that is, it is orderly, but remains irregular and unpredictable. Thus, chaos theory by challenging the notion of scientific omniscience validates the insight of feminist epistemologists that scientific knowledge is inherently fallible.

NATURE AS AGENT

The Newtonian vision of the world as a clockwork mechanism implies that physical matter is inert and dead. Feminist epistemologists argue that this metaphor of the world as a machine has functioned as a justification for power over and domination of nature. To move beyond a notion of knowledge as power and of power as domination, feminist philosophers of science have attempted to restore agency to nature. Thus, it becomes important for Keller that nature not be bound by the necessity of law but be understood as generative and resourceful. She argues that Noble Laureate Barbara McClintock's work on genetic transportation was possible because McClintock had a belief in the resourcefulness of the natural order. Her discovery of the capacity of organisms to reprogram their own DNA points to the existence of forms of order more inventive than those we had previously envisioned.[3]

Haraway also suggests that we grant the status of agent to the objects in the world. She speaks of the world as having a sense of humor and as resisting being reduced to mere resource. To express a concept of nature that eludes being completely captured by the human imagination, she appropriates the metaphor of the coyote trickster of Native American legend. We keep pursuing the wily coyote all the time, knowing that it will inevitably get the better of us.[4]

Chaos theory also finds nature to be generative and resourceful. If the Newtonian paradigm reduced nature's complexity and simplified it into predictable, law-like behavior, chaos would allow for an understanding of nature rich in disorder and surprise. Even though a chaotic system is deterministic, we cannot predict what it is going to do next; this indeterminacy can make for resourcefulness. For example, the chaotic path of a prey in flight can be used to evade a predator.

ATTENDING TO DIFFERENCE

The model of scientific law in the Newtonian paradigm is based on a universalism in which difference disappears. In contrast, feminist epistemology advocates a methodology that is sensitive to difference and that makes difference intelligible rather than making it disappear as a mere anomaly to a general rule. Keller notes that for McClintock, the discovery of anomalous kernels of corn pointed, not to disorder or unlawfulness, but to a larger system of order that is not reducible to a single law. Similarly, Haraway's concept of "situated knowledges" reflects a commitment to pluralism and difference. Knowledge that is situated demands the participation of as many perspectives as possible and recognizes that the answers that come out of a plurality of perspectives can never be reduced to unity.

In the same manner, chaos theory by designating disorder to be complex information makes difference meaningful. Researchers in human physiology are now looking to the chaotic dynamics of the body to better diagnose and predict illness. Epileptic seizures and heart attacks were once understood to be rhythmic disorders in contrast to healthy, ordered rhythms. Now physiologists believe that chaos provides a healthy flexibility to the heart and brain. And in fact, healthy systems are characterized by innate variability, while impaired systems are marked by a transition to more ordered, less complicated states. Investigators are beginning to think that, contrary to accepted belief, healthy bodies do not seek homeostasis but rather that chaos is the natural way to put together the systems of the body.[5]

Researchers are learning, therefore, that a lot of useful information can be attained by attending to the variability of a system as well as to its stable order. Chaos theory by alerting scientists to attend to difference validates the feminist insistence that difference matters and that discoveries come out of a plurality of perspectives that can never be reduced to a unity.

NONREDUCTIONISM

The method of the Newtonian model is reductionistic. To understand how a clock works, you break it down into its parts, study each element individually, and reassemble it to understand the whole. Study of the individual unit is more important than the study of constituent interactions. Keller argued that scientific techniques contribute to and are product of the ideology of a culture. She analyzed how the reductionist model when applied to biology reinforces values stereotypically associated with masculinity: individuality, autonomy, competition, and dominance. Both population genetics and mathematical ecology, for example, give precedence to competition over cooperative interactions. Genes are understood to be inherently selfish. And when the existence of cooperative behavior is acknowledged, it is reidentified as "cooperative competition."[6] In genetics, DNA is understood to be a "master" molecule that encodes and transmits all instructions for cellular development.

Chaos theory helps undermine the methodology of reductionism. It privileges qualification over quantification and recursive symmetries over individual units. In the Newtonian paradigm, a scientific theory without quantification was not a theory, but for dynamic systems, quantification is frequently not possible. Instead, qualitative understanding is achieved by studying what the whole looks like as it moves through changes by watching the activity of a strange attractor. To study turbulence or a fractal, it is necessary to assume that the part is the whole rather than to make the reductionist assumption that the whole is the sum of its parts.

To conclude, chaos theory has opened up a space within scientific inquiry for a notion of knowledge that is fallible, for a restoration of agency to nature, and for a methodology that attends to difference and that moves beyond reductionism. And in so doing, chaos theory represents the revisioning of nature and scientific inquiry sought by feminist epistemologists.

REFERENCES

1. Harding, S. *Whose Science? Whose Knowledge?*; Cornell Univ. Press: Ithaca, NY, 1991; 138–163.
2. Keller, E. *Reflections on Gender and Science*; Yale Univ. Press: New Haven, CT, 1985; 75–176.
3. Keller, E. *A Feeling for the Organism: The Life and Work of Barbara McClintock*; W. H. Freeman: New York, 1983; 121–138.
4. Haraway, D. *Simians, Cyborgs, and Women: The Reinvention of Nature*; Routledge: New York, 1991; 183–202.
5. Poole, R. Is it healthy to be chaotic? Science **1989**, *243*, 604–607.
6. Keller, E. *Refiguring Life: Metaphors of Twentieth-Century Biology*; Yale Univ. Press: New Haven, CT, 1995; 99–118.

Financial Emergencies

Jane Beckett-Camarata
Kent State University, Kent, Ohio, U.S.A.

INTRODUCTION

Financial emergencies in U.S. local governments are an ongoing, significant, and complex public policy issue for legislators, state, and local officials and citizens. For our purposes, a financial emergency is defined as a formal legal declaration by a state government of local government financial default. Such formal legal declarations are in response to a local government's negative account imbalances (e.g., general fund imbalances); that is, the inability to provide basic services; the inability to meet payroll, service debt, pay vendors, or pay retirement fund obligations; or the inability to meet its significant financial obligations.

Financial (fiscal) emergencies have serious negative consequences for the local government, the community, the region, and the state. The end result of a financial emergency is reduced services, lower quality of life, and a threat to the physical infrastructure and safety. Each state has its own unique way of dealing with inadequate local government fiscal conditions. However, most attempt to address these inadequacies through a four-stage fiscal health/financial emergency continuum. The four stages in the continuum are 1) fiscal health, 2) fiscal watch or monitoring, 3) fiscal stress, and 4) fiscal emergency. Local governments with fiscal emergencies must develop and implement strategies for eliminating the actual fiscal emergencies as well as the causes. Inadequate fiscal conditions at the local level are a problem for the state as a whole as well as for the local community. Most states have laws that govern fiscal emergencies. For example, the cities of Miami, Florida, and Washington, DC, have been in a state of public receivership. The financial management of both cities was handed over to public boards until fiscal integrity was restored. In the cast of Washington, DC, a Memorandum of Agreement between the District of Columbia Financial Responsibility and Management Assistance Authority conveys back to the Mayor of Washington, DC, control over operations, but retains statutory oversight responsibilities.

In addition to state laws governing fiscal emergencies, local governments can file for bankruptcy under Title 9 of the U.S. Bankruptcy Code. If a local government files for bankruptcy under Title 9 and the state is silent on the filing, it is tantamount to authorizing the municipality to file under federal bankruptcy law.[1] Bankruptcy applies only to instances for which there has been a formal filing of a bankruptcy petition under Chapter 9 of the Federal Bankruptcy Act (www.accessgpo.gov). To file a bankruptcy petition, the government must declare itself insolvent. Either a general-purpose local government or a special district can file this petition. Orange County, California, filed for bankruptcy because of unsound investment practices.

State-authorized eligibility to file for bankruptcy under Title 9 is a Tenth Amendment issue that is central to bankruptcy proceedings.[1] Georgia, for example, prohibits municipalities from filing and Pennsylvania requires prior state permission. Other states expressly and specifically grant municipalities the authority to file for bankruptcy.

THE FISCAL HEALTH/FISCAL EMERGENCY CONTINUUM

A local government's fiscal health can be viewed as part of a four-stage fiscal health/fiscal emergency continuum (Fig. 1). The term fiscal emergency represents stages two, three, and four of this continuum, with each succeeding stage representing a declining level of fiscal health and adequacy. For example, a local government in stage one is in sound fiscal health. In stage two, the locale is showing early signs of fiscal problems such as general fund account imbalances. In stage three, the fiscal concerns are much more significant in that the locale not only has a general fund imbalance, but is also unable to provide adequate basic services to its community. In stage four, in addition to the items in stage three, they cannot meet payroll, service debt, pay vendors, pay retirement fund obligations, or meet other significant financial obligations. Stage four is a true fiscal emergency.

ANALYZING FISCAL HEALTH

Over the past several years, the regularity of financial emergencies in several states has confirmed the need for an effective system to provide taxpayers, creditors, managers, and legislatures, and others with timely notice of

Encyclopedia of Public Administration and Public Policy
DOI: 10.1081/E-EPAP 120010738

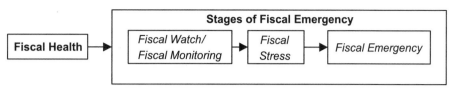

Fig. 1 Fiscal health/fiscal emergency continuum.

the situation. In most instances, financial constraints, coupled with financial reports (both internal and external) of the local governments, did not provide information as to the nature of the fiscal problems until it was too late. In spite of improvements in financial reporting, fiscal emergencies continue to occur. Preventing fiscal emergencies requires an ongoing system of financial monitoring that can provide a warning of fiscal problems that may affect the community.

Credit Analysis

Credit agencies (e.g., Moody's, Standard and Poor's) examine both *structural* and *budgetary* factors, such as 1) economic, 2) financial, 3) debt, and 4) administrative/political. Standard and Poor's emphasizes debt factors (25). Moody's emphasizes the issuer's economic base.[2] However, both Moody's and Standard and Poor's examine factors in each of the four groups. The ratings are viewed as one indicator of long-term financial condition. For example, Moody's Aaa rating indicates a city is likely in better financial position than a city with a Baa rating (the lowest *investment grade* rating). Further, ratings assigned to general obligation (GO) bonds often apply to all GO bonds of the same issuer.

A local government's fiscal health is its ability to meet its financial obligations as they become due and to deliver fundamental public services to its residents. One way that fiscal health can be assessed is by analyzing a local government's fiscal health over time. In addition to looking at the changes in financial indicators of fiscal health and relationships among indicators, environmental factors such as community needs and resources, economic conditions, political culture, intergovernmental constraints, and natural disasters and emergencies largely determine revenue capacity and demand for services. The way in which a local government responds to environmental demand and changes in the environment is a major factor in determining how environmental factors are translated into fiscal health.

State Government Analysis

There are various ways to analyze fiscal problems. A municipality in Ohio, for example, may fail certain policy criteria for fiscal emergency at year-end, but correct its fiscal situation in time to avoid state control. For example, existence of any year-end emergency criteria is not a fiscal emergency if the emergency criteria do not exist at the time of the fiscal emergency audit.[3] Ohio policy requires calculations at the prior year-end at the time of the fiscal emergency audit. Although the Ohio fiscal emergency policy delineates fiscal emergency, it is silent on the causes. It is also silent on fiscal emergency prevention strategies. The Ohio fiscal emergency policy is primarily intended as a remedial action to restore a local government's fiscal soundness. The Ohio State Auditor declares that a particular local government has a fiscal emergency. The State Auditor may initiate a review based on problems through its audit function of the state, or the governor, mayor, or presiding officer of the local government can request a fiscal emergency analysis.

Ratio Analysis

An important part of analyzing fiscal health is the use of ratios. Ratios help management and external users proactively understand the local government's strengths and weaknesses. A better understanding of strengths and weaknesses can lead to corrective action before a fiscal emergency occurs. In financial statement analysis, ratios are used to compare numbers taken from the financial statements. For instance, knowledge about how much a local government had in assets compared with current liabilities may be desired. If the Town of Bainbridge, for instance, had $61,900 in current assets compared with its current liabilities of $14,000, the comparison is done by dividing one number by the other. If we divide $61,900 by $14,000, the result is 4.4. This means that there are 4.4 dollars of current assets for every one dollar of current liabilities. This would be referred to as a ratio of 4.4 to 1 or simply a ratio of 4.4. This ratio is called a *current ratio*.

Ratios are used because the comparison between two numbers generates information that is more useful than either or both of the numbers separately. If we know that the town has $61,900, that does not tell us whether it has adequate short-term resources to meet its obligations. Knowing that we have 4.4 dollars of liquid assets for each dollar of short-term liabilities tells us much more about the relative safety of the organization. Each local government has to develop its own set of useful ratios about the its fiscal health. For example, the ratio of total revenues to total expenditures indicates the relationship of inflow from revenues to outflow for expenditures; a high ratio is viewed as positive.

In addition to evaluating ratios, the stability, flexibility, and diversity of revenue sources; budgetary control over revenues and expenditures; adequacy of insurance protection; level of overlapping debt; and growth of unfunded employee-related benefits. Socioeconomic and demographic trends should also be analyzed, including trends in employment, real estate values, retail sales, building permits, population, personal income, and welfare. Much of this information is contained in the statistical section of the Comprehensive Annual Financial Report (CAFR), if the local government prepares a CAFR.

Operational Definitions

There are two basic *operational* definitions of fiscal emergencies: 1) *structure*, and 2) *budget*. The *structural* definition outlines a fiscal emergency in terms of the *external* constraints that are placed on the local government's fiscal health by the local economy (its economic base) and by the population demographic structure. The *budget* definition characterizes fiscal emergencies in terms of internal *budget* actuality. That is, the inability of local governments to balance their budgets, regardless of the causes of the problem. For example, fiscal mismanagement can cause a *budgetary* fiscal emergency, as well as sudden changes in local revenues (loss of major taxpayer or intergovernmental aid) or change in community needs (e.g., a catastrophe or sudden growth).

Legal Definitions

Within the budgetary category, there are legal definitions for three categories of budgetary fiscal problems. For example, in Ohio, the state auditor declares 1) *fiscal watch/fiscal monitoring*; 2) *fiscal stress*; and 3) *fiscal emergency, under the following conditions*:

1. *Fiscal watch/fiscal monitoring.* This status is declared to provide early warning to local governments whose finances are approaching fiscal stress. Local governments are monitored by the state when a deficit exists in the General Fund or other funds and when such deficit exceeds one-twelfth of total General Revenue Funds. It is declared when any one of the following factors exist:
   - All accounts that are due and payable from the General Fund for more than 30 days, less the year-end balance of the General Fund exceeds one-twelfth of the General Fund budget for the year.

- All accounts that are due and payable from all funds for more than 30 days, less the year-end balance in these funds, exceeds one-twelfth of the available revenue for the preceding fiscal year from these funds.
- Total deficit funds, less the total of any balances in the General Fund and in any special fund that may be transferred to meet such deficits, exceeds one-twelfth of the total General Fund budget for that year and the receipts to those deficit funds during that year (other than transfers from the General Fund).
- Money and marketable investments, less outstanding checks, less total positive fund balances of general fund and special funds, exceeds one-twelfth of the total amount received during the preceding fiscal year.

2. *Fiscal stress.* This status is declared when and one of the fiscal watch/fiscal monitoring factors are present, and there is an inability to fund service delivery needs and requirements because of a decrease in resources and an increase in demands for resource utilization.

3. *Fiscal emergency.* This status is declared when, in addition to fiscal stress conditions, there is a failure to meet significant financial obligations. This classification includes cases in which governments have failed to meet principal and interest payments on their debt; failed to meet payrolls, pay vendors, or pay retirement fund obligations; or failed to meet other significant financial obligations. In most instances, these emergencies are confirmed by the state declaring the local government in a financial emergency.[3]

CAUSES OF FISCAL EMERGENCIES

There are five broad *causes* of fiscal emergencies:

1. Socioeconomic decline (i.e., "regional or national forces, principally economic and demographic, that have weakened city tax bases and strained local services")
2. Local political factors largely relating to disproportionate demands for public services from specific groups or from unions, changing electoral coalitions that call for increased government spending to reward the partners of winning coalitions, and local political cultures that are supportive of different levels of public spending
3. Government growth through inevitable dynamics of bureaucratic expansion, giving rise to increased expenditures
4. Poor fiscal management practices
5. State policies limiting revenue and expenditures[4]

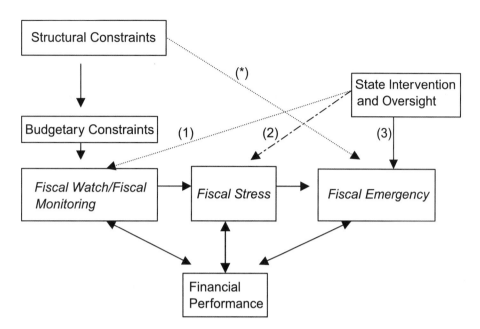

Fig. 2 Fiscal emergency model. (*) Unique catastrophic environmental occurrence; (1) minimal informal monitoring; (2) extensive informal monitoring; (3) formal intervention and oversight.

The first cause relates to the *structural* definition of fiscal problems, as discussed above. The last four relate to the *budgetary* definition of fiscal problems also discussed above.

Some cities are candidates for fiscal emergencies because some local government managers take a short-term view, surviving each fiscal year by ''getting by'' or short-run tactics that may detract from the local government's long-term fiscal integrity. Although they cannot correctly be described as having financial mismanagement, two types of shortcomings still exist. First, it is difficult to determine a local government's vulnerability to a fiscal emergency from its published budget, balance sheet, and income and expense statements without also being familiar with its local policies and accounting method. Second, comparison of operating revenues and expenditures is also challenging if there is no capital budget, or if there are numerous operating funds.

Inferences drawn from the both the literature and state fiscal emergency laws might suggest the following interrelationships (Fig. 2).

VISIBLE SIGNS OF FISCAL EMERGENCIES

Some visible signs of a fiscal emergency are:

1. A decline or inadequate growth in revenues relative to expenditures
2. Declining property values

3. Declining economic activity (e.g., increasing unemployment, declining retail sales, declining building activity)
4. Erosion of capital plant, particularly infrastructure
5. Increasing levels of unfunded pension and other post-employment obligations
6. Inadequate capital expenditures

Signs such as these, especially if several exist simultaneously, may indicate a potential fiscal emergency unless the local government takes immediate action to increase revenues or decrease spending. The typical sign of a fiscal emergency is fund deficits. There are three fundamental explanations for municipal fund deficits: 1) increased costs associated with state mandated (funded and unfunded) programs; 2) local plant closings; and 3) decreased income tax base.[5] Mandates, which are typically new unfunded programs or procedures, approved by a state legislature or Congress and implemented at the local level, contribute to fund deficits. Many of these unfunded mandates relate to health care for the indigent population, the administration of the court system, the administration of the prison system, the education system, and the mental health system.

Fund deficits are affected by other constraints placed on municipal governments. For example, municipalities confronting a declining tax base may be unable to raise additional revenue in the short run because of state laws limiting tax increases, bond indebtedness, or the use of special revenue mechanisms. In addition, some states such as Ohio are overly reliant on local income taxes, which are adversely affected by local plant closings.

Taxing powers have a central role in fiscal emergencies. Taxing powers are important because their applicability defines different credit instruments, including general obligation bonds. Taxing powers may be constrained by tax-and-expenditure limitations. Some local tax-and-expenditure limitations have been on the books for decades. The ostensible purpose behind statewide tax-and-expenditure limitations on local jurisdictions is often enforcing governmental economy; the structure, rather than the size, appears more likely to be affected, and the long-term outcome is the centralization of the state-local fiscal system. In some instances, a tax increase may be counterproductive to the community because it is also accompanied by a reduction in services. In the case of Bridgeport, Connecticut, unless the city increased services without increasing property taxes, it would suffer property value losses, job flight, loss of businesses, and a fall-off of middle-class residents. Municipalities are in competition with their surrounding suburbs; therefore, a high proportion of relocatable retail and service-sector jobs and businesses will leave.

Measures associated with loss of financial flexibility include 1) the proportion of own source revenues dedicated to matching funds; 2) the percentage of expenditures funded from grant funds; 3) the debt burden indicated by the ratio of general obligation long-term indebtedness to municipal population or the ratio of debt service payments to total own-source revenues; 4) the budget overruns indicated by the year-end expenditures over the original budget; 5) the ratio of the legally authorized tax rate over the current tax rate; and 6) the proportion of municipal expenditures allocated for covering mandates.[6]

STATE FINANCIAL RECOVERY LAWS

States respond to signs of a fiscal emergency through the use of fiscal recovery laws. In Ohio, the fiscal emergency law is primarily intended to restore a local government's fiscal soundness through the use of a fiscal commission and state auditor oversight. The Ohio State Auditor is responsible for certifying that a particular local government has a fiscal emergency. The state auditor may initiate a review based on problems through its audit functions of the state or the governor, mayor, or presiding officer of the local government can request a fiscal emergency analysis.

State Oversight Commission

Once the state auditor has determined that a fiscal emergency exists, the governor appoints a Financial Planning and Supervision Commission to work with the local government. The commission has eight members:

1. State Treasurer
2. Director of the State Office of Budget and Management
3. For municipalities, the mayor and presiding officer of the local government legislative authority
4. For counties, the president of the Board of County Commissioners and the county auditor
5. For townships, a member of the board of township trustees and the county auditor
6. Three appointed members chosen out of five names provided to the governor by the mayor and presiding officer of municipal legislative authority, or by the county board of commissioners or board of township trustees. These individuals must be residents of the declared government (by home or office address) with at least 5 years private sector business/financial experience.[3]

Responsibilities of a State Oversight Commission

In Ohio, for example, the Oversight Commission is responsible for approving a financial recovery action plan to essentially eliminate fiscal emergency conditions, balance the budget, and avoid future deficits and market long-term obligations. The mayor, board of commissioners, or board of trustees must submit the plan to the commission within 120 days of its first meeting. The commission can either accept or reject the plan. The above officials then have 30 days to resubmit a plan, and the process is repeated until a plan is accepted.

The Oversight Commission has far-reaching authority to 1) review all revenue and expenditure estimates to ensure a balanced budget; 2) require the government (by ordinance or resolution) to maintain monthly levels of expenditures and encumbrances consistent with the financial plan; 3) approve and monitor expenditure and encumbrance levels; 4) approve the amount and purpose of any debt issues; 5) make and enter into all contracts and agreements necessary to the performance of its duties; and 6) make recommendations for cost reductions or revenue increases to carry out the financial plan.

All financial transactions require commission review and approval. The commission reviews the local government's budgets, tax levy ordinances, and appropriation measures. It approves the purpose and amount of any debt obligation. It also serves as an adviser on the structure and terms of debt obligations, on methods to increase revenues, and on ways to reduce costs.

The use of a commission or board forces fiscal discipline on the municipality and typically represents state control over financial performance. A commission or board, by having state representation, provides leverage in remedying the problem and holds the local officials accountable for restoring fiscal health.[7] To accomplish its work, a commission needs such extensive oversight. Municipalities in financial emergency must comply with the commissions' requirements. Municipalities under financial emergency must also comply with certain legal requirements. In Ohio, as noted above, the municipality must present its financial plan to the commission within 120 days of its first meeting. The plan must include the municipality's proposals for eliminating all fiscal emergency conditions and deficits, paying all overdue bills, restoring fund moneys, balancing the budget, and regaining the ability to market long-term general obligation bonds. Also included is an action plan for carrying out the plan and preventing a new fiscal emergency from arising in the future. Failure to submit a timely financial plan results in an automatic spending restriction in the general fund. The spending ceiling is 85% of general fund expenditures for that month in the preceding year. Fiscal discipline imposed by commissions usually results in managing within existing resources and not increasing the tax rate.

The Oversight Commission assists the municipality in developing sound financial practices to prevent future financial problems. The change in practices requires an improvement in the local government's internal capacity to identify and manage fiscal problems before they escalate. The local government must have a decision-support system that provides adequate and timely data for management decision making. It must also have accountability at each level of government.

ADDRESSING FISCAL EMERGENCIES

Local governments respond to fiscal emergencies by using several different strategies. First, they immediately tighten fiscal controls. Many use short-term strategies such as freezing/cutting the workforce and non-workforce expenditure reductions. Long-term strategies, the key to sound financial management, include putting more clarity and order into the local government's fiscal process and initiating an economic development program. This means 1) revising the budget formulation process, 2) controlling expenditures, 3) ensuring that an economic development program is in place and is maximized, and 4) initiating productivity and efficiency programs.

The local government response to the fiscal emergency should have a positive impact on its fiscal health. In New York, like Ohio, a municipality in financial emergency must prepare a multiyear financial plan for approval by the commission. These multiyear plans allow local decision makers to decide service allocations, but within revenue estimates and spending plans monitored by the commission.

Termination of the State Oversight Commission

To end state supervision, Ohio municipalities, for example, must comply with the following:

- An effective financial accounting and reporting system is being implemented with expected completion within 2 years.
- All fiscal emergency conditions have been or are in the process of being eliminated, and no new emergency conditions have occurred.
- The financial recovery plan objectives are being met.
- The entity has a 5-year financial forecast that the State Auditor determines is "nonadverse."[3]

Other Fiscal Emergency Oversight

In Florida, the tests for meeting a municipal fiscal emergency are similar to those in Ohio, but the governor has the discretion to design a response to the local problem. The Florida Statute allows the Florida governor's office to informally consult with officials regarding the appropriate steps necessary to rectify the problem.[8] New Jersey's laws are similar to Ohio and Florida, but in New Jersey discretion resides in a board rather than the governor.[7]

New York State operates on a case-by-case basis, and a state law dictates the response to each particular fiscal emergency. In Pennsylvania, the head of the Department of Community Affairs appoints a department employee or a consultant as the coordinator of the municipality in fiscal emergency. The Pennsylvania Municipalities Financial Recovery Act (Act 47) governs fiscal emergencies. The act provides a range of grants local governments in fiscal emergency, including:

1. *Shared Municipal Services*: Grant funds are provided to promote cooperation between neighboring municipalities enabling various functions to be provided more efficiently and effectively.
2. *Local Government Capital Projects Loan Program.* Provides low-interest loans (2%) to municipalities (under 12, 000 in population) to assist with the purchase of equipment and facilities.
3. *Land Use Planning and Technical Assistance Program*: Provides grants to municipalities, counties, and other units of local government for multimunicipal

planning efforts that further the sound land-use initiatives.

4. *Regional Police Assistance Grant Program*: Provides grants for the start up of consolidated police departments for a period of up to 3 years.

5. *Floodplain Land Use Assistance Program*: Provides reimbursement for 50% of the eligible expenses connected with a municipality preparing, enacting, and implementing or administering floodplain management regulations.[9]

CONCLUSION

Fiscal emergencies are a significant and complex public policy issue because such emergencies have serious negative consequences for local government, community, region, and the state. A fiscal emergency can lead to low quality of life and to reduced services. Fiscal emergencies are a state problem as well as a local problem. Each state has its own unique way of dealing with the emergency, although there are four generic fiscal strategies for eliminating fiscal emergencies. These strategies generally operate through state laws governing fiscal emergencies. As discussed above, states generally respond to fiscal emergencies by oversight through the use of Fiscal Emergency Laws and oversight boards.

The State Fiscal Emergency Laws used in Ohio, for example, in aiding municipalities' experiencing fiscal problems appear to have a positive effect on long-term local government financial performance.[5] What was once a financial "last resort" has become to some degree a less exceptional, more acceptable political option for assisting local governments in restoring fiscal health. Proactively preventing financial problems is the joint responsibility of states, local governments, and citizens. State legislative bodies are responsible for sound fiscal policies for the government they serve. Oversight bodies such as fiscal emergency oversight boards have responsibility for monitoring and, in some cases, establishing the fiscal policies of governmental units for which they have oversight responsibility.

REFERENCES

1. Lewis, C.W. Municipal bankruptcy and the states. Urban Aff. Q. *30* (1).
2. Lynch, T.D. *Public Budgeting in America*; Prentice Hall: Englewood Cliffs, 1995.
3. State of Ohio Website. www.st.oh.gov.
4. Pammer, W.J. *Managing Fiscal Stress in Major American Cities*; Greenwood Press: New York, 1990.
5. Beckett-Camarata, J. *Understanding Ohio Fiscal Emergencies*; 2001, Unpublished Manuscript.
6. Wilson, E.R.; Kattelus, S.C.; Hay, L.E. *Accounting for Governmental and Nonprofit Entities*; McGraw-Hill-Irwin: New York, 2001.
7. Hildreth, W.B. Financial Emergencies. In *International Encyclopedia of Public Policy and Administration Eds*; Westview Press, 1998; (2) (D–K).
8. State of Florida Website. www.st.fla.gov.
9. Commonwealth of Pennsylvania Website. www.inventpa.com.

Financial Resource Management in Local Government

Kenneth A. Klase
The University of North Carolina at Greensboro, Greensboro, North Carolina, U.S.A.

INTRODUCTION

Financial resource management in local government involves a multitude of techniques and approaches focused on the financial management of resources to accomplish local government aims. Financial resource management occurs within diverse local government environments that profoundly influence it. Decision making in the local government fiscal system is shaped by the underlying local social and economic conditions, the formal authority structure of the local government, and by other stakeholders in the decision-making process. Fig. 1 shows the relevant factors involved and the interrelationships among factors in the process of decision making in local government financial resource management, including social and economic factors (community needs and resources); formal authority structure (degree of local government autonomy or home rule granted in state-local relations, especially with respect to financial management decision making); interest groups and other government agencies (political strategies developed and coalitions formed around particular issues). All these factors define the specific political and organizational environment, ultimately affecting financial decisions and outcomes.[1]

STRATEGIC MANAGEMENT AND MANAGEMENT CONTROL

Although an environment such as that described above places constraints on the potential goals and strategies of local governments, local government financial resource management is most successful when performed within a strategic management context. Resource management provides the critical link between formulation of goals and objectives in a strategic planning process and the actual performance of local government activities. Local government is concerned about the effective allocation of public resources to carry out plans, strategies, and programs. Financial management is involved in the acquisition of resources and in the tracking of performance, resulting from the allocation of financial resources used to satisfy the demands of constituents within financial constraints. Thus, financial resource management focuses on planning for achievement of desired results, implementation of those plans, and taking appropriate actions to control results so they conform to the plans. What has actually occurred must be determined, and then these actual outcomes must be reported through the financial reporting process.[2–4]

These aspects of financial resource management are accomplished through the management control process. Management control occurs through a management control structure consisting of responsibility centers (e.g., program structures or service units) working toward the accomplishment of specific objectives. The management control process involves determining appropriate programming or activities to address strategic goals and strategies; budget preparation of a budget plan for implementing program objectives; operations and measurement in which resources are consumed and actual results attained; and reporting and evaluation where accounting and other information is summarized, analyzed, and reported. The information from reporting is used to help achieve local government goals by controlling current operations, evaluating operating performance, and performing program evaluation.[5]

FINANCIAL MANAGEMENT FUNCTIONS

Basic functions common to financial management emphasize control, cost management, and planning. These functions include accounting and control mechanisms, allocation and management of existing resources through cost management, and long-term financial planning techniques for assessing the long-term needs of the organization and for acquiring the needed resources. Figure 2 illustrates the principal financial management functions in local government and their emphases. Accounting and financial reporting emphasize control. Functions emphasizing cost management include cost allocation and cash management. Planning is emphasized by the functions of operations budgeting, capital budgeting, and debt admin-

Encyclopedia of Public Administration and Public Policy
DOI: 10.1081/E-EPAP 120010848

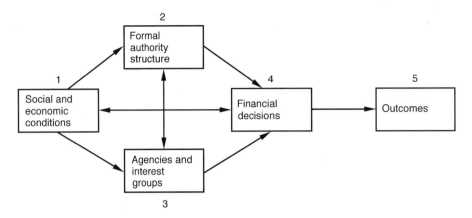

Fig. 1 A model of local government financial resource management. (*Source*: Ruchelman, Leonard I. "The Finance Function in Local Government." In Aronson, J. Richard and E. Schwartz, eds. *Management Policies in Local Government Finance*, 3rd edition. Washington D.C.: ICMA, 1987, p. 23.)

istration. It is the individual functional components of financial management described in Fig. 2 that enable financial resource management to be accomplished and the management control process to function. These es-

sential tools for managing public resources include appropriate mechanisms for accounting control and reporting of financial information, rational procedures for allocating resources and controlling costs, and

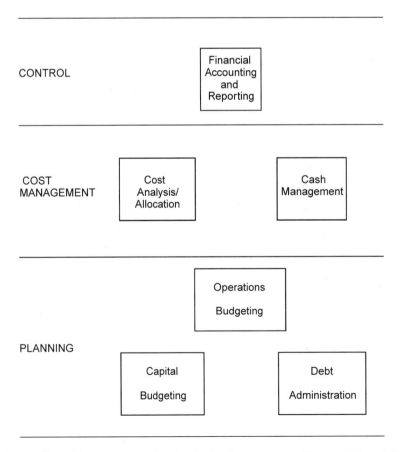

Fig. 2 Emphasis of principal financial management function in local government. (*Source*: Adapted from Steiss, Alan Walter. *Financial Management in Public Organization*, Brooks/Cole Publishing Company: Pacific Grove, CA, 1989, exhibit 1–1, p. 5.)

techniques for assessing long-term needs and for acquiring needed resources.[6]

Accounting and Financial Reporting

Financial accounting control systems are important components of financial resource management because of their role in record-keeping and financial control functions. They are important not only for financial record-keeping and external reporting, but also because accounting serves as the basis for management planning, decision making, and control. Financial accounting is concerned with the results of fiscal transactions and the resulting financial position of the local government. Generally accepted accounting principles (GAAP) are the rules, guidelines, or accounting conventions used for reporting on financial transactions and creating an organization's financial statements so that they fairly represent the organization's financial position and results of operations. For state and local governments, GAAP are established by the Governmental Accounting Standards Board (GASB), an authoritative body associated with the Financial Accounting Standards Board, which determines GAAP primarily for private sector organizations; both are private sector organizations that promulgate accounting standards for accounting professionals.[7] Traditionally, GAAP has required fund accounting as the primary mechanism for control of governmental activities. Under fund accounting, resources are segregated into individual funds according to designated purposes, and reporting is performed within the fund structure. The major categories and fund types used in state and local fund accounting include the following:

- *Governmental funds* used to account for general government operations. Generic fund types classified as governmental include the *General Fund* for all resources not required to be accounted for in another fund; *Special Revenue Fund* to account for resources legally or administratively restricted for specific purposes; *Capital Projects Funds* used to account for resources restricted for major capital outlays; *Debt Service Funds* to account for resources used to repay principal and interest on general-purpose long-term debt.
- *Proprietary funds* used to account for government activities similar to commercial activities in the private sector. *Enterprise funds* are used to account for operations financed and operated similar to a business enterprise (e.g., public utilities), and *internal service funds* are used to account for operations that provide goods or services to other departments on a cost reimbursement basis (e.g., motor pool, data processing, or print shop).

- *Fiduciary funds* used to account for assets held by government in a trust or agent capacity, including *agency funds, pension trust funds, expendable and nonexpendable trust funds.*

To accomplish financial accounting and reporting of fiscal transactions in local government for these fund types, what is measured and when it should be measured must be determined. The spending measurement focus emphasizes spending or the financial flow of funds by reporting only current assets and liabilities, and the difference between them or what is available to be spent in the current accounting period. In contrast, the capital maintenance measurement focus reports on all assets and liabilities (short and long term), and the difference between them or the capital or equity of the fund. Accounting principles require that a different basis of accounting be used to determine what transactions should be recognized for reporting purposes, depending on measurement focus differences between fund types. The modified accrual basis of accounting emphasizes a financial flow or spending measurement focus, records revenues when they are measurable and available, and records expenditures when they are measurable and incurred (to be paid from current resources). Because a financial flow or spending focus applies, fixed assets are an operating expenditure and only accounted for as a general fixed asset, accounting for depreciation (representing the orderly write off of some portion of the value of fixed assets used up in producing a product or service) is optional, and long-term debt is handled as a general liability rather than a liability of a specific fund. The accrual basis of accounting emphasizes a capital maintenance or equity focus, records revenues when measurable and earned (service has been provided), and records expenses when measurable and incurred (liability created). Because a capital maintenance focus applies, fixed assets are an asset of the specific fund where purchased, depreciation is an expense for the fund-owning fixed assets, and long-term debt is a liability of the specific fund where issued. Thus, measurement focus and consequent basis of accounting depend on fund type: governmental funds and fiduciary funds with a spending or flow of funds measurement focus are accounted for under modified accrual accounting, whereas proprietary funds and fiduciary funds with a capital maintenance measurement focus are accounted for under accrual accounting.[8]

Accounting changes for state and local government accounting and reporting under GASB Statement 34 have added to this model of fund accounting additional requirements for comprehensive entity reporting by local governments. Implementation of changes by local governments are being phased in according to the size of annual revenues for the local government, but will be fully implemented by 2003. The changes in reporting requirements are being implemented to enhance the understandability and usefulness of financial reports to various users who often find fund accounting complex and unintelligible. The new requirements focus on moving from reporting separately for different types of funds to reporting for the entity as a whole through two governmentwide statements (Statement of Net Assets, essentially an accrual accounting Balance Sheet and Statement of Activities, essentially an accrual accounting Operating Statement) as part of the basic financial statements for the government. In addition, governments are also required to continue fund financial statements. Perhaps most useful to users of the basic financial statements, local governments are required under the GASB 34 changes to provide a management's discussion and analysis section and other required supplementary information, including a comparison of actual results with authorized budgets. These interpret the financial statement information in a more understandable manner for users.[2,9–11]

Cost Allocation and Cash Management

The cost analysis/allocation and cash management functions in financial resource management emphasize cost management, as shown in Fig. 2. Cost management depends on information available from accounting control systems. Local government accounting systems do not generally generate good cost data, given the financial flow measurement focus of governmental fund types. Consequently, local governments engage in cost analysis/allocation. Analysis of costs is used to forecast short- and long-term needs, and provides input to cash management decision making and long-term financial planning. Cost accounting approaches attempt to determine the full costs of local government service delivery and to assign accountability for costs to the appropriate local government responsibility center. Through cost analysis, costs can be classified as direct (costs directly associated with a specific purpose) or indirect (costs associated with more than one activity and not able to be traced directly to any one of the activities). Cost allocation involves allocating indirect costs or overhead using some basis of allocation (e.g., number of square feet that a cost center occupies) to specific cost centers to arrive at a more accurate measurement of the full costs (direct plus allocated indirect) for those cost centers. In addition, determination of fixed and variable costs can enable differential cost analysis for alternative decision making.[6,12]

Cash management also emphasizes cost management and is concerned with short-term cash flow management, cash mobilization, and investment. Short-term cash flow management involves ensuring that adequate cash resources are available in a timely manner when needed for current operations to avoid cash shortages. Many organizations prepare a cash budget, usually indicating month by month how much cash is forecasted to be received or paid. The most difficult problem is accurately estimating receipts. Forecasted deficits in cashflow require borrowing, while surpluses allow for short-term investments to be made. Cash management also involves cash mobilization as a technique to assemble funds and make them more readily available for investment. Cash mobilization is accomplished through accelerating receivables (reduction of time delays in collecting receivables or deposit float) and controlling disbursements (especially delaying cash outflows through disbursement procedures and consolidated concentration accounts). Cash is mobilized to maximize investment return on temporary cash balances. The principal factors considered in selecting appropriate investment options for public funds are safety/risk, liquidity/marketability, maturity, and yield. Appropriate investments for local governments are often confined to certificates of deposit, U.S. Treasury bills, other federal agency securities, and state investment pools. Interest earned on investments is an important benefit of good cash management, but safety and liquidity of cash assets have to be balanced against possible yield.[6,13,14]

Operations Budgeting

The operations budgeting component of financial resource management emphasizes planning as depicted in Fig. 2, but is traditionally viewed as a control mechanism to ensure legal compliance and accountability through appropriation to specific objects of expenditure linked to budgetary accounting. The most common operating budget format in local government, the line item budget, appropriates funds to specific line items in this fashion and is oriented toward controlling expenditures in accordance with fiduciary accountability. Significant management and planning capacity can be incorporated into the operations budgeting process where performance and program budgeting formats and approaches are used. The performance budget is organized around tasks, activities, or direct output performed. It emphasizes expenditure by workload or activity and unit costs by activity. Performance budgets have a management orientation because they emphasize efficiency in performance, maximizing unit output per unit input of resources. The program budgeting format emphasizes effectiveness by relating expenditures to public goals through its organization by programs. It focuses on achievements, outcomes, or final products as a result of its planning orientation and links results to strategic planning goals. Financial resource management in local government can be enhanced by incorporating elements of these approaches where they help to focus on efficiency in the utilization of resources and effectiveness in accomplishing desired goals and objectives. Thus, the operations budget can become a planning tool that helps local government to achieve strategic planning goals.[15–19]

Capital Budgeting and Debt Administration

Capital budgeting in local government emphasizes long-term capital facilities planning and programming. It differs from operations budgeting in focusing on long-term, nonrecurring projects that are of high value and are financed from other than operating budget revenues, usually debt financing. The capital budgeting process depends on assessment and forecasting of community needs, evaluation and ranking of capital projects to address those needs over a period of time, and determination of the financial capacity of the community to pay for capital improvements. It results in a capital improvement program (CIP) for a 5- or 6-year period by scheduling capital projects in priority order over the period. The first year of the 5- or 6-year CIP becomes the next year's capital budget.[6,15,20]

Debt administration associated with capital financing requires establishing appropriate debt policy (in particular, no issuance of debt with a maturity longer than the useful life of the project). It also involves determining the structure and design of debt to be issued: type of security—general obligation bond debt backed by full faith and credit vs. limited liability revenue bond debt backed by revenue to be generated from the project; term to maturity of the bond—either term or serial with multiple maturities; and call provisions before maturity. The borrowing costs of bond issuance is affected by a local government's bond rating, an assessment of creditworthiness or risk to potential purchasers for a particular bond issue as determined by commercial rating firms. Because the marketing and long-term administration of bond debt is problematic for local governments, bonds are usually sold to an underwriting firm that purchases the entire issue and resells it at a profit to investors.[6,15]

CONCLUSION

Financial resource management in local government is constrained by its environment, but nonetheless is a means for accomplishing strategic management. Through management control, the component functions of financial management enable goals and objectives from strategic planning to be linked to actual results. The component functions of financial management accomplish these ends through their emphasis on financial management's core values: control, performance (efficiency), and planning (effectiveness).

As a dynamic process, financial management in local government is continually changing. This is evident in the dramatic changes in accounting and financial reporting standards that will have significant impacts on local governments. It is evident in the increased emphasis on cost analysis to use resources more efficiently. It is also evident in the increased emphasis in operations budgeting on performance and program approaches to incorporate strategic planning to achieve planned results, and thus to enhance local government effectiveness and accountability. All these changes are further evidence of the continuing influence of the core values that component functions of financial management emphasize.

REFERENCES

1. Ruchelman, L.I. The Finance Function in Local Government. In *Management Policies in Local Government Finance*, 3rd Ed.; Aronson, J.R., Schwartz, E., Eds.; ICMA: Washington, D.C., 1987; 23.
2. Finkler, S.A. *Financial Management for Public, Health, and Not-for-Profit Organizations*; Prentice Hall: Upper Saddle River, NJ, 2001; pp. 21, 370–371.
3. Bryant, S. Strategic management: Developing and realizing a strategic vision. Public Manage. **Oct. 1997**, *79*, 28–32.
4. Berry, F.S. Innovation in public management: Adoption of strategic planning. Public Adm. Rev. **July/August 1994**, *54*, 322–330.
5. Anthony, R.N.; Young, D.W. *Management Control in Nonprofit Organizations*, 6th Ed.; Irwin/McGraw-Hill: Boston, MA, 1999; 3–23.
6. Steiss, A.W. *Financial Management in Public Organizations*; Brooks/Cole Publishing Company: Pacific Grove, CA, 1989; pp. 1–4, 8–25, 53–120, 169–224.
7. Antonio, J.F. Role and future of the governmental accounting standards board. Public Budg. Finance **Summer 1985**, *5* (2), 30.
8. Glick, P.E. *How to Understand Local Government Financial Statements: A User's Guide*; GFOA: Chicago, IL, 1986.
9. Governmental Accounting Standards Board (GASB), Statement No. 34 of the Governmental Accounting Standards Board. *Basic Financial Statements—and Management's Discussion and Analysis—for State and Local*

Governments; Financial Accounting Foundation: Norwalk, CT, 1999.

10. Crain, G.W.; Bean, D.R. What users think of the new reporting model for governments: The results of the GASB's focus group sessions. Gov. Finance Rev. **February 1998**, *14*, 9–12.

11. Gauthier, S. GASB reporting model exposure draft. Gov. Finance Rev. **June 1997**, *13*, 60–61.

12. Brown, R.E.; Sprohge, H.-D. Government managerial accounting: What and where is it? Public Budg. Finance **August 1987**, *7* (3), 35.

13. Mattson, K.; Hackbart, M.; Ramsey, J.R. State and corporate cash management: A comparison. Public Budg. Finance **Winter 1990**, *10* (4), 18–27.

14. Petersen, J.E. Managing and investing public money. Governing **March 1993**, *6*, 43–54.

15. Mikesell, J. *Fiscal Administration: Analysis and Applica-*
tions for the Public Sector, 5th Ed.; Harcourt Brace & Company: Fort Worth, TX, 1999; pp. 181, 223–261, 533–567.

16. Allen, J.R. The uses of performance measurement in government. Gov. Finance Rev. **August 1996**, *12*, 11–15.

17. Clifford, C. Linking strategic planning and budgeting in Scottsdale, Arizona. Gov. Finance Rev. **August 1998**, *14* (4), 9–14.

18. Gross, J. NACSLB recommended budget practices: What they are and how to use them. Gov. Finance Rev. **1998**, *14* (3), 9.

19. Thompson, F. Mission-driven, results-oriented budgeting: Fiscal administration and the new public management. Public Budg. Finance **Fall 1994**, *14* (3), 90.

20. Forrester, J. Municipal capital budgeting: An examination. Public Budg. Finance **Summer 1993**, *13* (2), 85–101.

Financial Statement Analysis

Martin Ives
New York University, New York, New York, U.S.A.

INTRODUCTION

Financial statements communicate to readers the financial position and operating results of an entity. The statements array the numerous day-to-day economic transactions and events in such a way that readers can make informed decisions about the entity and assess its accountability. Financial statement analysis involves using the statements, the related notes, and the auditor's opinion to develop information about an entity's profitability, financial viability, and accountability. A more comprehensive analysis (sometimes called financial condition analysis) of state and local governments can be made by also taking account of certain economic and demographic data, to determine an entity's ability to meet its short- and long-term financial obligations to creditors and others, as well as its service obligations to the citizenry.

USERS AND USES OF FINANCIAL STATEMENT ANALYSIS

Persons both internal and external to a particular entity may make use of financial statement analysis. (When prescribing financial reporting standards, accounting standards-setters generally consider the needs of external users, because internal users have ready access to whatever information they need.) Users of financial statement analysis include a governmental entity's elected and appointed officials; officials of oversight governments; managers and trustees of not-for-profit entities; donors and potential donors; citizens and citizen advocate groups; providers of goods and services, including employee unions; and financial resource providers and their representatives (e.g., banks, municipal debt-rating agencies, insurers of municipal debt).

Financial statement analysis leads the user not only to assess financial position, and results of operations and accountability, but also to act on the information obtained. For example, a manager or trustee may decide that the data provide early warning of a deteriorating financial position, and therefore act to shore up the entity's fi-

nances. These are some specific concerns an analyst might have when analyzing financial statements:

- To determine the likelihood of the entity's ability to pay its short-term obligations, such as tax anticipation notes and amounts due to vendors and employees.
- To determine the likelihood of the entity's ability to pay its long-term obligations, such as long-term bonds and pensions.
- To see if the entity's margin of revenues over expenses provides a sufficient cushion to weather economic downturns, finance certain expenditures, or meet contingencies.
- To ascertain the composition of an entity's revenues and expenses (e.g., the portion of revenues obtained from sales taxes or the portion of expenses used for program, rather than administrative, purposes).
- To determine what portion of an entity's resources may be used for general or unrestricted purposes, rather than being restricted for specific purposes by law or donor requirement.

CONTENTS OF FINANCIAL STATEMENTS

Generally, the starting point for financial statement analysis is a thorough reading of the statements, the accompanying notes, and the auditor's opinion. The formats and titles of financial statements prepared by governmental and not-for-profit entities (including not-for-profit hospitals) are somewhat different, but the kinds of data they convey are similar. This section contains a brief description of the contents of the various types of financial statements and the related notes. (Accounting standards-setters have required many changes in financial reporting during the past few years, some of which were in the process of implementation at this writing.)

Governmental and not-for-profit entities generally use fund accounting. Each fund is a separate fiscal and accounting entity, established for the purpose of carrying on specific activities in accordance with laws, regulations, and restrictions. Recent changes in both governmental and not-for-profit financial reporting standards place emphasis on the entity as a whole, rather than on individual funds or fund types. Governmental financial reporting standards now require two levels of reporting, a governmentwide level (which distinguishes between governmental and business-type activities) and a fund level (where the focus is on major funds). Not-for-profit entity reporting standards require reporting on the entity as a whole, but permit entities to provide data by fund type in external financial reports if they want to do so. Within their entitywide reporting, not-for-profit entities are required to report year-to-year changes in net assets by net asset classification; namely, unrestricted, temporarily restricted by donors, and permanently restricted by donors.

The most common financial statements prepared by governmental and not-for-profit entities fall into these general categories:

- Statement of financial position (or statement of net assets, or balance sheet)
- Statement of operations (or statement of activities, or statement of revenues, expenditures/expenses, and changes in fund balances)
- Cash flow statement

In addition, depending on the circumstances, some not-for-profit entities may prepare a statement of functional expenses and a statement of changes in net assets.

Statement of Financial Position

A statement of financial position provides information about an entity's assets, liabilities, and net assets at a point in time. When considered together with the notes to the financial statements and other data, the statement of financial position helps the analyst assess the entity's liquidity, financial flexibility, and ability to meet both its financial and service obligations. Assets and liabilities appearing in the statement of financial position are organized generally in order of liquidity, that is, in terms of nearness to being converted to cash or nearness to being paid. Sometimes, the assets and liabilities are grouped based on whether they are current or noncurrent; the term "current" meaning the expectation that the assets will be converted to cash or consumed in operations in the next year and that the liabilities will be paid off in the next year.

The net asset section of the statement of financial position—that is, the difference between assets and liabilities—is segregated as between unrestricted and restricted. (Use of resources in a governmental entity may be restricted by law or by creditors; use of resources in a not-for-profit entity may be restricted by donors.) Re-

sources classified as unrestricted may be used for any purpose consistent with the entity's functions.

Statement of Operations

The statement of operations, when used with the related notes and other data, provides information to help users evaluate the entity's financial performance during a period. It shows the composition of the various types of revenues and expenses, and how revenues were used in providing programs or services. There are some differences in format and emphasis among financial statements prepared for governmental entities, not-for-profit entities in general, and not-for-profit hospitals.

Governmentwide operating statements, prepared on the full accrual basis of accounting, show the relative financial burden each governmental function places on its taxpayers. The statements do this by reporting the expense of each function net of revenues (e.g., charges for services and operating grants from other governments) directly related to the function. Taxes, other general revenues, special items, and extraordinary items are then deducted from the sum of the net expenses of all functions to show the change in net assets for the year. (Special items, sometimes called "one-shots," are transactions within the control of government that are either unusual in nature or that do not occur frequently.) The change in net assets provides a measure of the extent to which the year's revenues financed the services provided by the government.

Governments must also report operating statements for each major fund. There is likely to be more than one set of fund-level statements because those statements are prepared on the modified accrual basis of accounting for governmental funds and the full accrual basis for proprietary funds. After considering the revenues, expenditures, other financing sources, and special items in the governmental fund statements, the result is the net change in fund balances. By definition, governmental fund accounting focuses on short-term revenues and expenditures; also, other financing sources may contain nonrevenue inflows. Therefore, the analyst must use these statements with care.

The statement of activities prepared by not-for-profit entities shows the changes in net assets by net asset class (unrestricted, temporarily restricted, and permanently restricted) and in total. This statement shows major revenue sources (e.g., contributions, fees, investment income) for each net asset class. Because reporting standards require that all expenses be reported in the unrestricted class of net assets, the amount of net assets released from restriction for use in operations is also shown. To help analysts to assess an entity's service efforts, not-for-profit entities report expenses by functional classification, such as major classes of program services and supporting activities. Not-for-profit entities classified as voluntary health and welfare organizations must report expenses both by major function and by natural classification (e.g., salaries, rent, utilities).

Not-for-profit hospitals follow the same reporting standards as other not-for-profit entities. Those concerned with hospital financial reporting, however, believe it is important for hospitals to have a clear bottom line measuring financial performance. They therefore recommend using two activity statements, a statement of operations, and a statement of changes in net assets. In the statement of operations, the caption excess of revenues over expenses provides the analyst with a useful performance indicator.

Cash Flow Statement

An entity could report an excess of revenues over expenses in the statement of operations because it uses the full accrual basis of accounting, yet experience financial difficulties because a shortage of cash. The cash flow statement shows the factors that result in cash inflows and outflows, and thus provides a useful link to the other financial statements.

Notes to Financial Statements

Because the financial statements themselves do not provide a complete picture of financial position and results of operations, they are accompanied with notes. The notes are considered necessary to fair presentation and are an integral part of the financial statements. Sometimes, accounting standards-setters permit disclosures to be made either on the face of the financial statements or in the notes. The notes provide useful details on such matters as significant accounting policies, contributions, restrictions, contingencies, pension plans, and financing arrangements.

Other Data

You can sometimes find information for financial analysis purposes within the entity's financial report, but outside the statements and the accompanying notes. For example, new reporting standards require state and local governments to prepare a Management Discussion and Analysis (MD&A) to precede the financial statements. The MD&A provides condensed financial information derived from the governmentwide statements, comparing the current year with the previous year. An accompanying analysis of the government's financial position and results of operations helps financial statement users assess whether the entity's financial position improved or deteriorated as a

result of the year's operations. The analysis must also include a discussion of significant variations between budgeted and actual amounts, as well as currently known reasons for variations that are expected to affect future services or liquidity. Important economic factors that significantly affected operating results for the year must also be discussed.

A more complete analysis of a state or local government's financial condition requires using data outside the financial statements, such as economic and demographic data. This data may be found elsewhere in the entity's financial report; more often, the analyst will need to get the data from a unit of the government being studied, or from another governmental agency such as the U.S. Bureau of the Census or U.S. Bureau of Economic Analysis. Economic and demographic data helpful in financial condition analysis includes population, full value of taxable real property, personal income, unemployment rates, and poverty rates.

FINANCIAL STATEMENT ANALYSIS METHODOLOGY

After studying the financial statements and the related notes, the analyst uses various tools and methods to analyze and interpret them. Time-series analysis and comparative analysis provide the basic methodology. Effective financial statement analysis also requires conversion of financial and other data into forms that facilitate the time-series and comparative analyses. These forms include ratios, percentage change information, common size analysis, and location quotient determination. There are limits, however, to what one can do with the individual bits of information derived from each aspect of the analysis. A few ratios may suffice for some purposes; for example, if the analyst wants to know only the present composition of the entity's expenses. If the analyst wants to draw conclusions about the long-term financial viability of a governmental entity, however, many matters (including data outside the financial statements) must be examined. Financial statement analysis (and the broader financial condition analysis) is an art, not a precise science.

Basic Methodology—Time-Series and Comparative Analysis

Time-series analysis and comparative analysis are the most basic methods of financial statement analysis. Time-series analysis looks at changes within an entity over time to see if conditions have improved or deteriorated. Time-series analysis requires a minimum of 2 years, and financial statements generally report financial position and results of operations both for the current and the previous year. In assessing a state or local government's financial condition, time-series analysis covers a period of at least 5 years. Time-series analysis is useful in drawing conclusions about changes in an entity's financial position and results of operations. It suffers, however, from the lack of a reference point outside the entity that allows the analyst to interpret the overall implications of the changes.

Comparative analysis provides that external reference point. It provides data so one may compare conditions within an entity either to a peer group of similar entities or to generally accepted norms or rules of thumb developed over the years by analysts. Care must be taken in developing a reference group for comparison purposes because data may be distorted by such factors as differences in mission, size, location, and mix of population served. Thus, a peer group might include hospitals of generally similar bed size and that perform similar functions; also, governments of the same type, performing similar functions, of roughly similar size, and within the same state. For example, an analyst might compare financial data of a village with, say, 10 villages of roughly similar population in the same state.

Norms or rules of thumb, often developed by municipal bond rating agencies, are sometimes available for comparison purposes. Although having a reference point allows the analyst to draw inferences about the entity under study, using comparative data also has some limitations that need to be recognized. It is possible, for example, for the reference group itself to suffer from the same problems experienced by the entity under study. Also, a rule of thumb may be based on data that includes an excessive number of entities operating under conditions not similar to the entity under study.

Conversion of Data to More Useful Forms

To make time-series and comparative data useful, financial data contained in financial statements must be converted to a useful form. A simple form of data conversion is the percentage change from an earlier period to the current period. Another form of data conversion, the location quotient, is obtained by using the number for the entity under study as the numerator and the reference group number as the denominator. When used in time-series analysis, the location quotient readily reveals the direction of the data element for the entity under study relative to the reference group. Converting certain financial data to per capita information (e.g., to compute property tax revenues or education expenditures per resident) also facilitates comparison with a peer group.

Common size analysis also facilitates financial statement analysis over time and in relation to other entities

because it converts all numbers to percentages of the whole. Thus, for example, if the total expenses of a not-for-profit entity are calculated as 100%, the amount reported for administrative and fund raising expenses might be, say, 28% of the total. By itself, that percentage might not be meaningful. However, if that percentage was 24% last year and if similar not-for-profit entities report an average of 20%, the percentage change from last year and the location quotient relative to the peer group might cause the analyst to raise questions.

The most significant tool in financial statement analysis is the use of ratios. Ratios compare one data element in a financial statement with another data element in a financial statement or with an economic or demographic data element. By converting financial and other data to a ratio, you can gain insights not previously evident. Further, ratios make it possible to track data over time and to compare it with other entities. For example, it is difficult to draw conclusions by noting that accounts receivable are $90,000 in the statement of financial position and that revenues are $405,000 in the statement of operations. When those numbers are considered together, however, and converted to ratios, you find that it takes an average of 80 days to collect the receivables (calculation simplified by using 360 days in a year). Comparing that number with last year's number of, say, 75 days and an industry norm of, say, 60 days, allows the analyst to reach conclusions and to raise appropriate questions.

FINANCIAL STATEMENT ANALYSIS RATIOS

Some of the more common ratios developed as a result of financial statement analysis are shown in the ensuing paragraphs. To assess the overall financial condition of an entity, it is necessary to consider the implications of these and other ratios and factors. Some of these ratios are applicable both to governments and to not-for-profit entities (including not-for-profit hospitals), whereas others are unique to particular types of entities. In the sections that follow, calculations unique to government are designated as (G).

Liquidity Ratios

Liquidity ratios (sometimes called cash solvency ratios) provide information on the ability of an entity to meet its short-term obligations, such as payroll, bills for supplies that have been received, and payments on borrowings coming due in the near future. Paying short-term obligations requires using cash currently on hand and other current assets that will be converted to cash in time to pay the bills.

Commonly developed liquidity ratios compare cash and cash equivalents, as well as other current assets, with current liabilities. These ratios are referred to either as the current ratio or the quick ratio, depending on the extent to which current assets other than cash and cash equivalents are included in the numerator.

In computing the quick ratio, cash equivalents are included with cash because they are short-term, highly liquid investments that are readily convertible to known amounts of cash and are so close to maturity (having had an original maturity of 3 months or less) that there is little risk of loss in value. Some analysts add other short-term, highly liquid investments and receivables when computing the quick ratio. State and local government analysts often do not, however, because current liabilities are generally due to be paid in 30 days whereas current assets other than cash and cash equivalents may not be readily convertible to cash in time to pay bills. A quick ratio of 1.0 is a generally accepted norm, but a ratio of less than 1.0 does not necessarily mean the entity is illiquid. For example, large cash inflows (e.g., next year's property taxes) may flow in during the first month of the next fiscal year, reducing the need for maintaining a quick ratio of 1.0.

$$\text{Current ratio} \quad \frac{\text{Current assets}}{\text{Current liabilities}}$$

$$\text{Quick ratio} \quad \frac{\text{Cash} + \text{Cash equivalents*}}{\text{Current liabilities}}$$

*sometimes, other current assets are added

Another perspective on cash liquidity, often used by not-for-profit hospitals and other entities, can be obtained by calculating the number of days' cash on hand. This ratio tells the analyst how long the entity can continue to pay its bills without further cash inflows. It may also reveal that the entity has excessive cash, which might be better used to acquire new facilities and equipment.

Days' cash on hand

$$\frac{\text{Cash} + \text{Cash equivalents} + \text{short term invest.}}{\text{Cash needs per day*}}$$

*Total operating expenses less bad debts and depreciation, divided by 365

The speed with which receivables are converted to cash is a significant indicator of both liquidity and efficiency. The quicker the receivables can be converted to cash, the less cash and other assets an entity needs for

paying current obligations; also, the quicker the excess cash can be converted to interest-paying assets. Receivables liquidity ratios may be expressed and calculated somewhat differently by governmental and other not-for-profit analysts, but they yield the same results.

Days' revenue in receivables

$$\frac{\text{Net patient accounts receivable}}{\text{Net patient service revenue}/365}$$

Property tax receivable rate (G)

$$\frac{\text{Real property taxes receivable}}{\text{Real property tax revenues}}$$

Tax collection delinquency (G)

$$\frac{\text{Uncollected current year real property taxes}}{\text{Current year real property tax levy}}$$

Long-Term Financial Flexibility Ratios

Long-term financial flexibility ratios provide evidence of the entity's ability to meet its long-term financial and service obligations. These ratios help answer questions such as: Is the entity likely to have sufficient resources to pay its long-term debts, including bonded debt, pension obligations, and postemployment health care obligations? Does it have the capacity to issue new debt to meet its current and future capital needs? Some ratios are calculated differently for state and local governments than for not-for-profit entities, but the concepts are similar.

The most common measures of debt burden in government relate the outstanding long-term debt to a base that is useful in measuring the entity's ability to pay the debt. Calculations of debt burden relate the entity's outstanding debt to its population, full value of taxable real property, and personal income. These denominators are not shown on the face of financial statements, but the information may be elsewhere in the financial report. In calculating the numerator, the analyst should include general obligation debt, lease-purchase debt, debt incurred through specially created agencies, and a share of the overlapping debt from governments that tax its citizens from the same tax base. Analysts also generally do not include self-supporting debt in the total debt. Trend analysis, peer group comparisons, and rules of thumb are particularly important in assessing the implications of these ratios.

Debt burden (G)

$$\frac{\text{Long-term debt}}{\text{Population or full value of taxable real property}}$$
or personal income

Counterpart debt burden measures for not-for-profit entities relate debt to the entity's equity, the notion being that the greater the ratio, the more difficult it will be for the entity to increase its borrowings to finance capital needs. Analysts use several variations of this ratio. The numerator always includes long-term debt and may include other forms of debt. The denominator may be either total assets or net assets. Again, trends and peer group comparisons help in interpreting the ratios.

Debt-to-equity ratio $\dfrac{\text{Long-term debt (or total debt)}}{\text{Total assets (or net assets)}}$

Closely related to the debt burden indicators are the debt service (interest and principal) burden indicators. Obviously, the greater the debt service burden, the less the amount of resources that is available for program services. State and local government analysts use the ratio of total debt service to total revenues. The general rule of thumb here is that 10% is moderate and 15% is high, but peer group comparisons provide a better basis for assessment. Not-for-profit entity analysts focus on debt service coverage; that is, the number of times the total debt service is covered by the revenues, or the number of times the interest on the debt is covered by the revenues.

Debt service burden (G)

$$\frac{\text{Total debt service}}{\text{Total revenues}}$$

Debt service coverage

$$\frac{(\text{Revenues} - \text{Expenses}) + \text{Depreciation} + \text{Interest}}{\text{Principal payment} + \text{Interest expense}}$$

Times interest earned

$$\frac{(\text{Revenues} - \text{Expenses}) + \text{Interest expense}}{\text{Interest expense}}$$

Where pensions are a significant element of an entity's expenses, the extent of the funding of the pension system has a bearing on the ability of the entity to meet its long-term obligations to its employees. The most common measures of pension funding adequacy are the funded status (ratio of pension assets to the pension obligation—a required disclosure in government financial reporting) and the ratio of pension assets to pension benefit expenditures (a useful measure if the funded ratio is not available).

Funded ratio

$$\frac{\text{Pension fund assests available for benefits}}{\text{Pension benefit obligation}}$$

Pension payout coverage

$$\frac{\text{Pension fund assets available for benefits}}{\text{Pension benefits paid last year}}$$

Operating Results Ratios

Ratios that depict operating results are sometimes called budgetary solvency ratios by governmental entity analysts or profitability ratios by not-for-profit entity analysts. The most common operating results ratio is similar to the return on sales (net income divided by sales) ratio found in business enterprise. Although neither governments nor not-for-profit entities operate for the purpose of making profit, they need to at least break even for the year. Depending on the entity, they may also need to achieve a reasonable excess of revenues over expenses to meet future economic downturns, to cover contingencies, and to finance capital needs.

Depending on the format of the operating statement, the names of the numerator and the denominator may be somewhat different for the various types of entities. For example, the numerator may be the excess of revenues over expenses, the increase in net assets, or the increase in unrestricted net assets. The denominator may be the total revenues and other financing sources or the total revenues, gains, and other support. In any event, the governmental analyst, in particular, must take care to eliminate (or to separately consider) one-shot resource inflows from borrowings, unusual financing arrangements, or other special items so as not to distort the operating results for a particular year.

Operating surplus or Operating margin

$$\frac{\text{Excess of revenues over expenses (or expenditures)}}{\text{Total revenues, gains, and other support*}}$$

*or Total revenues and other financing sources

Those who analyze state and local government financial statements are particularly concerned with cumulative results of operations and the resulting fund balance. This is because fund balance provides a cushion against future budgetary problems caused by economic downturns or emergency expenditure needs. A rule of thumb is that unreserved fund balance of 2% to 8% of revenues is adequate. The fund balance ratio of entities with relatively volatile revenue structures (where a large part of the tax base consists of income and sales taxes) should be at the higher end of the range.

$$\text{Budgetary cushion (G)} \quad \frac{\text{Total unreserved fund balance}}{\text{Total revenues}}$$

In addition to the overall operating results, those who analyze governmental financial statements focus on trends in the composition of revenues and expenditures. This is because increases in tax rates for a particular revenue source may weaken the ability of the entity to raise rates in the future. Increases in certain expenditures may indicate particular social and economic problems that need to be addressed. Those who analyze not-for-profit entity statements may be interested in the portion of the entity's resources that is spent on program activities versus nonprogram activities, such as administrative and fund-raising expenses.

$$\text{Program service ratio} \quad \frac{\text{Program expenses}}{\text{Total expenses}}$$

Economic and Demographic Data

Analysis of the financial condition of governments requires consideration not only of data from the financial statements, but also of certain economic and demographic data that cannot be obtained from the financial statements. Generally, more current economic and demographic data are available for states, counties, and large cities than for other units of government. Assessing the financial condition of state and local governments requires

consideration of trends in such matters as population, poverty, property values, personal income, unemployment rates, and business activity.

The ability of a governmental entity to finance future expenditures arising out of previous commitments depends heavily on the strength of its economy. Therefore, one concerned with assessing a governmental entity's financial condition must look not only to financial indicators, but also to such matters as a growing property tax and income base resulting from new residential and commercial construction, as well as a strong employment base.

Time-series analysis and peer group analysis (using percentage changes and location quotients) are the commonly used methods for assessing economic and demographic data. Other ratios based on economic and demographic data may also be developed to help assess financial condition. For example, analysts may calculate an entity's tax bite (the portion of a governmental jurisdiction's total personal income used to pay property and other taxes) to indicate its ability, relative to other jurisdictions, to raise future taxes.

FURTHER READING

Berne, R.; Schramm, R. *The Financial Analysis of Governments*; Prentice-Hall: Englewood Cliffs, NJ, 1986.

Finkler, S. Financial Statement Analysis. In *Financial Management for Public, Health, and Not-for-Profit Organizations*; Prentice-Hall: Upper Saddle River, NJ, 2001.

Groves, S.; Valente, M. *Evaluating Financial Condition—A Handbook for Local Government*; ICMA: Washington, D.C., 1994.

Ives, M.; Schanzenbach, K. *State and Local Government Financial Condition Analysis and Management*; Sheshunoff Information Services, Inc.: Austin, TX, 2000.

Fiscal Federalism

William Duncombe
Syracuse University, Syracuse, New York, U.S.A.

INTRODUCTION

Fiscal federalism describes the division of fiscal resources and responsibilities among levels of government. Fiscal federalism is not just confined to countries with a federalist form of government, but can exist in any country where both central and local governments are assigned power over resource allocation and revenue-raising decisions.[1] A brief review of theories and research on fiscal federalism is first presented. Then the concepts of fiscal federalism are discussed, by examining some recent changes in intergovernmental fiscal relations in the United States.

THEORIES OF FISCAL FEDERALISM

Theories of fiscal federalism develop a framework for deciding which level of government should provide a particular government service, with which sources of revenue, and what fiscal relationships should exist between them. Public finance economists, who have written extensively on this topic, emphasize that economic criteria, such as allocative and productive efficiency, should be used in making these decisions.[2] Allocative efficiency refers to matching the type and level of government service provision with the demands of citizens, and productive efficiency is achieved when the maximum output is produced for a given budget.

Assignment of Functions

In his seminal work on fiscal federalism, Wallace Oates offered a convincing case for division of service responsibilities across levels of government.[1] His framework for assignment of functions is based on the assumption that people and resources can flow freely across borders of local governments, but not across national boundaries. The economic functions of government can be divided into three major categories—stabilization, distribution, and allocation. Each function entails responsibilities, which may be best administered at a particular level of government.

Stabilization involves using monetary and fiscal policies to maintain employment, economic growth, and price stability. Macroeconomic functions of government are best performed at the federal level, in part, because of the need for central control of the banking system and money supply. Also, the mobility of resources across local government borders greatly weakens the influence that any particular local government can have in the short run on economic growth within its borders.

Distribution describes the role government can play in assuring a socially desired distribution of resources across individuals within a country. It is generally argued that redistributive programs are best implemented by central governments, with a supplemental role for regional governments, such as states and provinces. Mobility across local government borders limits the ability of local governments to offer significantly better social services than neighboring governments. Evidence suggests that recipients of these services are mobile and will move to locations where services are better.[3] Turning these social services over exclusively to local governments may promote a ''race to the bottom'' as local governments lower social services to encourage low-income households to move to a different community.[4]

Allocation and production of socially desired goods and services remains the principal role of government. According to Oates' *correspondence principle* the size of the government providing a service should be the smallest government, which includes all the beneficiaries of the service.[1] National government should provide only those services, such as defense, immigration, and national transportation systems, that benefit a national constituency. Regional governments should specialize in services that have significant benefits extending beyond local boundaries, such as pollution control, corrections, and higher education. The remaining services should be decentralized to the local government level.

Local governments, by representing a smaller constituency, can best match government services to local citizen preferences, improving allocative efficiency. In addition, monitoring government performance is easier for citizens in smaller governments, which should also lead to improved productive efficiency. These efficiency benefits of smaller governments must be balanced against the potential cost savings from economies of scale for certain types of services, and the additional costs of running a number of smaller governments.[1]

Encyclopedia of Public Administration and Public Policy
DOI: 10.1081/E-EPAP 120010845

The efficiency advantages of decentralization could be enhanced by competition among local governments as households "vote with their feet" by choosing local governments with the best tax and service package.[5] However, interjurisdictional competition over tax rates and services levels may lead to an underprovision of some public services.[3] In an attempt to attract business, local governments may cut taxes and services not valued by business to levels below that desired by citizens in the community. The efficiency impact of competition may depend in part on whether the government is attempting to attract business or mobile households looking for the optimal mix of taxes and services.

Assignment of Taxes

An equally important part of an intergovernmental fiscal system is deciding which taxes are best suited for use at national and subnational levels of government.[3] Key tax criteria include minimizing efficiency losses from the tax and enhancing vertical equity. In general, the larger the private sector response to avoid the tax, the larger the efficiency loss. Enhancing vertical equity involves designing tax systems that impose tax burdens on individuals in line with their ability to pay. In particular, we want to generally avoid regressive taxes, where taxes as a percent of income are higher for low-income households than high-income households.

Assuming mobility of resources within a country, subnational governments will have difficulty using progressive taxes. Any attempt to impose higher tax rates on upper-income individuals or owners of businesses could lead them to relocate to a local government with a more favorable tax climate. This mobility will increase the efficiency losses of the tax and reduce potential revenues. Instead, an ideal local tax system from an efficiency standpoint would involve the use of either user charges for services rendered, or taxes on relatively immobile tax bases.[2] The most obvious example of the latter would be a property tax on unimproved land, which is completely immobile. Although property taxes and user charges may create relatively small efficiency losses, they are generally considered to be regressive and slow-growing sources of revenue.

The potential regressivity and inelasticity of local taxes suggests the need for the national government (and to a lesser degree, states and provinces) to use progressive taxes, which are responsive to economic growth. Income taxes, in particular, match these criteria, because they are tied directly to personal income changes, and they can be implemented with a progressive tax rate structure. General sales taxes are also responsive to economic changes, but can be regressive unless necessities, such as food and clothing, are removed from the tax base.

Intergovernmental Aid

Intergovernmental grants represent a key tool in the design of an intergovernmental fiscal system. The most efficient division of functions across governments may involve assigning many of the most important and costly functions to subnational governments. Yet, optimal tax policy indicates that some of the largest and fastest-growing revenue sources should be at the national or regional level. The "vertical imbalance" between central revenues and local expenditures can be addressed through the distribution of revenues from the central government to local governments in the form of intergovernmental grants. Besides resolving the "vertical imbalance problem," intergovernmental grants can be used by the central government to encourage local governments to increase their provision of services that have benefits beyond the boundaries of the local government.[6] For example, local governments are often responsible for environmental infrastructure, such as waste treatment plants and solid-waste disposal facilities. Because the effects of water pollution will literally flow outside the boundaries of the local government, central governments can encourage local governments to improve waste treatment by providing grants. In addition, grants can be used to adjust for differences between local governments in their ability of finance public services. The largest grant programs in most state governments in the United States are to local school districts, and are used in part to equalize the fiscal capacity of these districts to finance education services.

The design of intergovernmental aid systems involves decisions over several dimensions. First, should the grant be targeted to the provision of specific services or resources, commonly called categorical grants, or should unconditional grants be provided to supplement general revenues (also called revenue sharing)? Another choice is whether the grant should be a lump-sum transfer of resources to a local government or in the form of a price change. By agreeing to match local contributions in the form of a matching grant, central governments can effectively lower the price for local governments to provide particular services. A third design decision is whether the grant is distributed by a predetermined formula (formula aid) or requires the local government to formally apply to receive funds (project grants).

Ideally, grant design should match the objectives of the grant. If the grant is to be used primarily to stimulate an increase in local spending on a particular service, then the grant should generally be a categorical open-ended matching grant. Whether the grant should be distributed by formula or through a project application depends on the complexity of the service being provided, and whether there are concerns about local capacity to use the funds effectively. If the grant is going to be used primarily to correct for horizontal inequities across governments, then a noncategorical, lump-sum formula grant is preferred, with the formula carefully designed to adjust for differences in fiscal capacity and costs across local governments.[7] If the grant is being used primarily to compensate local governments for using smaller, less elastic revenue sources, then noncategorical grants distributed roughly in proportion to the central government revenue collected in the local government might be justified. General revenue sharing (GRS), passed in 1972 under the Nixon Administration, was the only major attempt by the U.S. federal government to develop a general grant to address vertical imbalance problems. General revenue sharing was eliminated in 1986 by another Republican president, Ronald Reagan.

FISCAL FEDERALISM IN THE UNITED STATES

Recent Trends

In general, the intergovernmental fiscal system described above closely mirrors the division of fiscal responsibilities in the United States. The empirical evidence suggests that, for many government functions, fiscal federalism and the correspondence principle seem to be operative. Local governments, for example, tend to provide goods and services, such as public safety, housing, and re-

Table 1 Government expenditures by function in the United States by level of government, 1992 (percent of total expenditures)

Function	Total	Federal	State	Local
General expenditure	74.7	70.2	87.3	86.9
National defense and international relations	14.1	23		
Postal service	1.8	2.9		
Space research	0.5	0.9		
Education and libraries	14.1	3.2	30.1	36.8
Social services and income maintenance	13.7	13.1	29.6	12.2
Transportation	3.5	1.7	7.7	5.6
Public safety	3.8	0.7	4.2	8.8
Environment and housing	6.1	6.1	2.5	9.6
Government administration	2.7	1.3	3.7	4.7
Interest on general debt	10.2	13.1	3.5	4.6
Other	4.2	4.2	6	4.5
Utility and liquor store	3.4		1.4	11.4
Insurance trust	21.8	29.8	11.3	1.6

Source: U.S. Bureau of the Census, *Compendium of Government Finance*, 1992 Census of Governments, Table 1.

Table 2 Major revenue sources in the United States by level of government, 1996 (percent of total revenue)

Revenue source	Total	Federal	State	Local
Intergovernmental revenue	14.8	0.2	22.9	33.7
General revenue from own sources	59.9	64.5	56.8	54.6
Taxes	45.9	53.7	43.3	33.7
Property	6.3	0.0	1.0	24.8
Individual income	22.0	37.5	13.8	1.7
Corporation income	5.7	10.0	3.0	0.3
Sales and gross receipts	9.7	4.8	21.3	5.3
Other	2.2	1.4	4.1	1.5
Charges and miscellaneous revenue	14.0	10.9	13.5	20.9
Utility and liquor store revenue	2.3	0.0	0.7	8.5
Insurance trust revenue	23.0	35.3	19.6	3.3

Source: U.S. Bureau of the Census, *Statistical Abstract of the United States, 2000*, Table 494.

creation whose benefits are somewhat limited by jurisdictional boundaries. However, several of the major services provided by local government, particularly education, wastewater treatment, and solid waste extend beyond local borders. State governments are involved with goods benefiting larger groups of individuals, such as transportation, corrections, and higher education. Contrary to the theory, states are major providers of distributive programs in social services and health. The federal government is clearly responsible for national public goods, such as defense and foreign affairs, and has funded major social and income support programs in the past (Table 1).

In terms of assignment of revenues, the general pattern across levels of governments also fits recommendations. The federal government generally taxes the most mobile and elastic sources of revenue—corporate and personal income. Given that corporations are often mobile across state boundaries, the federal government should be the principal user of this tax. The federal government also receives significant revenue in the form of payroll taxes for social insurance programs (social security). State governments rely most heavily on personal income and sales taxes. For both types of taxes, mobility across borders could be a problem, but only for residents and consumers living near state borders. As recommended by theory, local governments are heavy users of property taxes and user charges and fees (Table 2).

The general trend in fiscal federalism in the United States is toward increasing state and local government

Table 3 Trends in federal grants to state and and local governments in the United States

| | Federal grants as a percent of | | |
Year	State-local revenues	Federal outlays	Gross domestic product
1950	13.7	5.3	0.8
1955	13.1	4.7	0.8
1960	19.1	7.6	1.4
1965	20.4	9.2	1.6
1970	26.3	12.3	2.4
1975	33.7	15.0	3.2
1980	38.3	15.5	3.3
1985	27.9	11.2	2.6
1990	25.0	10.8	2.4
1995	31.0	14.8	3.1
2000	29.3	15.9	2.9

Source: U.S. Office of Management and Budget. *The Budget of the United States for Fiscal Year* 2002, Tables 12.1 and 15.1.

reliance on federal grants. Since the 1970s, total federal aid has represented roughly 3% of gross domestic product, and has grown from 5.3% of total federal outlays in 1955 to 16% in 2000 (Table 3). From 1950 to 2000, federal grants as a percentage of state-local revenues increased from 13.7% to nearly 30%. State-local reliance on federal aid peaked in 1980, when federal aid represented close to 40% of state-local revenue. Although federal aid to states and local governments declined in the early 1980s, by the early 1990s, its importance to state and local revenues began to increase again. Despite several attempts by Republican presidents to increase the use of block grants since the 1970s, categorical grants continue to dominate federal aid. In 1995, estimates suggest that nearly 90% of all federal aid to states and local governments took the form of categorical grants (Table 4).

Table 5 provides information on the changing functional composition of federal grants since 1965. Transportation-related grants have decreased in importance, whereas health related grants—Medicaid, in particular—have increased dramatically as a percent of total federal aid. Postwar federal investments in the national interstate highway system represented significant portions of federal aid prior to 1965, but they have diminished as the system nears completion. Transportation grants dropped from 38% of federal aid in 1965 to 15% in 2000. Despite federal funding increases for environmental infrastructure in the 1970s, federal investments in state and local infrastructure have plainly lost ground to other priorities. In inflation-adjusted dollars, federal spending on state and local environmental infrastructure dropped from $6.5 billion in 1980 to $2 billion by 1996.[8] In

contrast, federal grants devoted to health, income security, and employment and training increased from 48% of total federal aid in 1965 to 75% in 2000. Clearly, the distributive function of the federal government is crucially important in the current intergovernmental fiscal system.

Devolution and Block Grants

The most important current reforms in fiscal federalism involve the incorporation of more flexible, block grant-style federal aid mechanisms, with increased "devolution" of program responsibility to state governments. The bulk of federal aid, as well as the focus of most reforms, was that portion of the social safety net that was jointly financed by federal and state governments, namely Aid for Families with Dependent Children and Medicaid. In 1996, President Clinton signed the Personal Responsibility and Work Opportunity Reconciliation Act (PRWOR), which includes substantial reforms for federal and jointly funded income support programs. A critical component of the reform is a shift from an open-ended matching formula to a block grant for Temporary Aid for Needy Families (TANF), which replaces the 30-year-old AFDC program. Under the new law, the federal block grants require states to impose strict time limits for individual TANF benefits, as well as stringent work requirements.[8]

The official justification for moving to state block grants has traditionally been to provide states with more flexibility in designing and administering their programs. Locating income support programs in the states may improve program design and efficiency through state experimentation. In addition, there may be allocative efficiency gains associated with enabling citizen

Table 4 Composition of federal aid types, percent of total dollar outlays, 1975–1995

Year	General purpose	Broad based	Categorical
1975	14.1	9.2	76.7
1979	12.3	14.7	73.0
1981	7.2	10.6	82.2
1984	7.0	13.3	79.7
1987	1.9	12.1	86.0
1989	1.9	10.4	87.6
1991	1.4	10.8	87.8
1993	1.1	10.6	88.3
1995	1.0	10.0	89.0

Source: Advisory Commission on Intergovernmental Relations. 1995. *Characteristics of Federal Grant-in-Aid Programs to State and Local Governments.*

Table 5 Changes in functional composition of U.S. federal grants to state and local governments (percent of total federal aid)

Function and fund group	1965	1970	1980	1985	1990	1995	2000
National defense	0.3	0.2	0.2	0.1	0.1	0.1	0.2
Energy	0.1	0.1	0.1	0.2	0.5	0.5	0.3
Natural resources and environment	1.7	1.8	1.7	5.0	5.9	3.8	3.0
Agriculture	4.7	2.9	2.5	0.5	0.6	2.3	1.1
Transportation	37.6	31.6	19.1	11.3	14.2	16.1	14.9
Community and regional development	5.9	4.5	7.4	9.1	7.1	4.9	3.3
Education, training, employment, and social services	9.6	20.0	26.7	26.4	23.9	16.8	18.0
Health	5.7	9.0	16.0	16.3	17.2	23.1	30.1
Income security	32.2	27.8	24.1	17.7	20.2	25.7	26.7
Veterans benefits and services	0.1	0.1	0.1	0.1	0.1	0.1	0.1
Administration of justice			0.2	0.7	0.6	0.1	0.4
General government	2.1	2.0	2.0	12.4	9.4	6.5	1.8

Source: U.S. Office of Management and Budget. *The Budget of the United States for Fiscal Year* 2002, Table 12.2.

preferences to be more closely reflected in state spending decisions. Whether the potential efficiency gains from state administration of welfare programs will materialize is an area of substantial debate.[3] However, block grants have also commonly been used to cut federal aid to states.

These reforms constitute fundamental shifts in the design of federal aid to support the social safety net and will undoubtedly have a significant impact on the spending behavior of states. Devolving redistributive social programs from the federal government to state governments runs counter to theories of fiscal federalism that suggest such programs should be operated at the national level. Because PRWOR eliminates the price subsidy offered through the matching grant formula, state spending in this area could drop substantially in the coming years.[4] Spending decreases on welfare programs could be exacerbated by competitive pressure between states to keep tax rates low by cutting social services.

The actions of the federal government in the United States to devolve functions to state and local governments pose several challenges to conventional theories of fiscal federalism. The federal government has drastically cut back funding for state and local environmental infrastructure even though the benefits from these facilities clearly extend beyond state and local borders. The devolution of key programs in the social safety net to state governments risks competition among subnational governments that could lead to an underprovision of these services. It seems inevitable that state and local

governments will come under intensified fiscal pressures as the economy slows down over the next decade. The ability of these subnational governments to maintain their core infrastructure and the social safety net with diminished federal support will indicate whether it is time to write a new chapter in fiscal federalism.

REFERENCES

1. Oates, W.E. *Fiscal Federalism*; Harcourt Brace: New York, 1972.
2. Bird, R.M. Threading the fiscal labyrinth: Some issues in fiscal decentralization. Nat. Tax J. **1993**, *46* (2), 207–227.
3. Oates, W.E. An essay on fiscal federalism. J. Econ. Lit. **1999**, *37* (3), 1120–1149.
4. Brueckner, J.E. *Welfare Reform and the Race to the Bottom: Theory and Evidence*; Institute of Gov. and Public Affairs, U. Illinois, 1998; WP 64.
5. Tiebout, C. A pure theory of local expenditures. J. Polit. Econ. **1956**, *64*, 416–424.
6. Duncombe, W.D.; Johnston, J.M. Intergovernmental Fiscal Relations: Revisions and Reforms. In *The White House and the Blue House: Government Reform in the United States and Korea*; Cho, Y.H., Frederickson, H.G., Eds.; University Press of America: New York, 1997; 271–309.
7. Gramlich, E.M. A policymaker's guide to fiscal decentralization. Nat. Tax J. **1993**, *46* (2), 229–235.
8. Ladd, H.F.; Yinger, J. *America's Ailing Cities: Fiscal Health and the Design of Urban Policy*; Johns Hopkins Univ. Press: Baltimore, MD, 1989.

Fiscal Transparency

A. Premchand
Consultant, Irvine, California, U.S.A.

F

INTRODUCTION

The content of fiscal transparency has evolved over years. The cumulative developments in this area are expected to provide an overview on the wisdom, faithfulness, and economy in the use of resources, in the provision of services, and in securing macroeconomic stability. Despite the efforts of international financial institutions to strengthen fiscal transparency, about one-third of the world's population does not have full access to information on the fiscal operations of public bodies. More efforts are indicated to expand the scope of fiscal information and to establish bodies of oversight. What remains to be achieved is significant and urgent.

HISTORY OF FISCAL TRANSPARENCY

The contours of fiscal transparency and its content were shaped over the years by two distinct trends—a desire to make the public officials accountable for their actions, and the political arithmetic of the times reflecting the concerns of the financial class and their interest in investing money in instruments of indebtedness. The evolution of fiscal transparency to date can be analyzed in terms of five stylized stages. During the first stage, the concerns of financial accountability of the monarchs and the concerns of an active society seeking a role in the utilization of public money—a feature associated with the Athenian state in the pre-Christian era—dominated the fiscal scene. The concern of the king was the preservation of the wealth of his own domain, and this required him to devise ways and penalties that would have the effect of preventing his officials from stealing. Writing more than 2000 years ago, a prime minister of a small North Indian kingdom cautioned his king to "Look well to the Treasury, for it is the key to all." Variants of these approaches were followed in China, and this subsequently became the main feature of the Cameralist school associated with European kingdoms during the Middle Ages. The emphasis in a monarchy was on transparency that was intended for only one person, viz. King, and his audit agency. The concerns were the same in the development of the Athenian state, where there was explicit recognition, amongst others, by Aristotle, of the risks associated with handling of large sums of money by

officials and the need for systematic accounts that would illumine the whole area.[1,2]

In the second stage, there emerged an investing class, and the political and financial arithmetic associated with their investments in government during seventeenth-century England had an impact on the content of fiscal transparency. A continuous engagement in wars depleted the British Treasury and made it dependent on private sources of financing raised through borrowing. The investing class was, however, keen to have detailed accounts of fiscal transactions of the government so that the financial health of the government could be ascertained. As these accounts were not forthcoming, the investors resorted to the appointment of their own staff to undertake independent compilation of accounts. In due course, however, this had the effect of government appointing its staff and led to the emergence of accountants as a class in government. The overall development of a new nexus between governments and their investing public contributed to the colonization of the state by financial interests.[3,4] During this stage, the need for transparency received wider acceptance, although it was seen primarily as that of the investing class.

During the third stage, reflecting the gradual development of the legislative institutions and their powers to review the "wisdom, faithfulness and economy" with which parliamentary grants were spent, efforts were made to appoint a Commission of Accounts and a Commission on Audit (a predecessor of audit as practiced now), culminating in the establishment of a permanent national audit agency to review the use of approved financial resources. This stage emphasized that transparency was not an end in itself but was a means for the legislature to ensure accountability of the government and its officials. What was however, within the domain of the legislature, was also within the reach of the public. These British practices, were in due course, replicated in the British commonwealth countries and variations of their approach were introduced in others. A result of these efforts was the explicit recognition of the need for fiscal transparency as a feature of a democratic government.

The fourth stage represents the more recent experience of governments, particularly since the 1950s. The growth of the welfare state, as well as the steady expansion in the size of governments and the range of activities undertaken

Encyclopedia of Public Administration and Public Policy
DOI: 10.1081/E-EPAP 120010719

by them, contributed to an inexorable growth in expenditures and, over the years, to growing fiscal deficits and crisis. The emergence of fiscal crisis contributed to the erosion of the public trust in government and to greater demands for the involvement of the public, along with its legislative institutions, in shaping their own fiscal destiny. It was suggested that improvements in governance required the empowerment of the community and its participation, whenever possible, in the formulation of policies. In turn, this implied that there should be greater fiscal transparency so that the community recognizes where it is and determines where it should go. The idea of improved governance came to be dependent on the reality of fiscal transparency.

The fifth stage reflects the series of financial crises in the 1990s that had a substantive impact on the emerging market countries. These countries, dependent on capital inflows, were highly vulnerable to sudden changes in market perceptions (i.e., perceptions of the investing class) and their destabilizing effects. Preventive action, aimed at forestalling the crises, or at a minimum, reducing the intensity, required the strengthening of the fiscal system, and enhancement of fiscal transparency. Such transparency was aimed at correcting the information asymmetries and associated belief systems. Cumulatively, the result is that extensive fiscal transparency has become an essential feature of governments. The content of fiscal transparency has not, given the diverse developments, however, been articulated coherently, except to some extent by international financial institutions.[5,6]

Objectives

Reflecting the various influences in the mutation of fiscal transparency, the objectives sought to be achieved comprise three groups:

- *Stewardship of resources*: Governments should provide data on the state of finances, for the past, present, and the future so that the community can make its own assessment about the viability of the policy stance, including the preventive actions taken or contemplated to reduce or avoid financial market failures. This requires that the information be comprehensive, including all activities, as well as contingent liabilities, on a consistent basis. The data must comply with specified standards.
- *Adequacy of the fiscal machinery*: Information is needed on the various aspects of tax administration, expenditure management, lending and borrowing operations, sales and purchase operations, and management of the financial portfolio. Efforts in this regard are aimed, in part, to restore the credibility of the public management systems and to assure the community of

the continuing effective functioning of the fiscal machinery. As an integral part of this effort, attention paid to ensuring the due process, prevention of opportunities for corruption, and the smooth working of the accountability channels associated with legislative or other forms of social action is revealed to the public.
- *Decision-making approaches*: There should be a window of opportunity for the community to be informed about the decision-making approaches behind the fiscal policies sought to be pursued. The window should enable an understanding, even as decisions are made (and not after they have been made) on the main components of fiscal policy—pursuit of macroeconomic stability, effective performance in the delivery of services, and pursuit of economy and efficiency.

These objectives aim at the complete fulfillment of fiscal transparency and, to that extent, go beyond the guidelines issued by international financial organizations. The guidelines issued by these organizations place more emphasis on the legal framework (intended more for international audiences), linkages with macroeconomic trends and policies, operational procedures, dissemination of fiscal data, and channels of accountability with legislatures. Correspondingly, less focus is laid on the adequacy of the fiscal machinery and delivery of services, aspects that are of critical importance to the community.

Content of fiscal information

The fiscal information provided to the public and the arrangements for transparency have their roots in the government accounting system, which is a homogeneous source of supply. The users of the information are, however, varied and the heterogeneous groups that include the community, legislatures, market analysts, investors, policy makers, external donors, and others. Information aimed at meeting these diverse requirements is provided through various channels. The features of the information supplied are shown, in detail, in Table 1.

Uses and limitations

The demands for additional information on government fiscal operations have grown during recent years. Along with these demands, the capacity of government has also increased severalfold, to meet them. To a large extent, this has been facilitated by the application of computer technology to government transactions, transforming a long drawn-out, slow, and often tedious process into a quick and often cost-effective way of using information for policy making. Notwithstanding the assiduous efforts to

(*Text continues on pg. 528*)

Table 1 Fiscal transparency: components, instruments, and features

Functional area	Instruments	Features
I. Structures and policy spheres (a) Structures • Functions and fiscal responsibilities of central, state, and local governments • Transfers from the central government to the state and local government; where revenue collections are decentralized, states, regions, or provinces may make transfers to the central government	• These are, in general, specified in the constitution and associated legal framework. • These transfers may be specified in the Constitution. Annual transfers determined with reference to legal criteria may be shown in the budget documents; where budgets are not available to the public (see below), the quantum of these transfers and their utilization may not be known.	• In federal types of countries, the financial relationships among these levels tend to be complex. • The experience of federal types of countries shows that these transfers, including devolution of resources, are determined in a quasijudicial process; the findings, as distinct from proceedings, are made public. • Experience of unitary governments is far more diverse; the details are contained in the budget documents (and are specifically shown as transfers), while in a few cases, they remain obscure.
• Autonomous bodies of the central governments	• These bodies have, in general, their own budgets, and the extent of dependence on government is shown therein.	• Access to these documents is problematic and dependent on the laws governing the autonomous bodies.
• State-owned enterprises	• Enterprises are obligated, in most cases, to publish their annual balance sheets and accounts. Their budgets, where the activities tend to be commercial, are not made public. The main instruments of transparency are the accounts and the periodic reports published by them. These reports may be more frequent where there is a high degree of dependence on the capital markets.	• Their accountability to the legislatures differs very widely: • The accounts and associated reports may not specify the costs of noncommercial objectives that the enterprises follow at the behest of governments. Moreover, subsidies given by governments may not have the specific end use, given the fungibility of resources, indicated by governments.
• Relationship with central bank/monetary authority and other public financial institutions	• These relationships are usually specified in the form of a law, inter-alia, indicating the tasks and responsibilities of the institutions in the management of public debt. The financial institutions publish their annual accounts and other reports that are within the public domain.	• Although the accounts are available, the quasifiscal accounts or activities undertaken by them may not be fully shown. Standards in this regard are evolving, and it is likely that more detailed information will be available on the quasifiscal activities.
• Relationships with the corporate private sector	• In most cases, the patterns of government equity ownership and the responsibility of governments in regard to regulation are specified in law (e.g., Companies Act). In some cases, regulation may be enforced through autonomous agencies.	• Laws and associated guidelines are generally matters that can be enforced through judicial means. In some countries, however, the ownership patterns are both highly complex and opaque.

(Continued)

Table 1 Fiscal transparency: components, instruments, and features (*Continued*)

Functional area	Instruments	Features
(b) Relationships with legislatures	• The patterns vary among countries. Broadly, there are three types of legislatures 1) where legislatures have the dominant role, 2) where the executive has the dominant role, and 3) where legislatures do not have any role in terms of annual management of finances, except that they are kept informed on all key aspects. In several countries, there is a framework of delegated legislation within which the executive wing of the government has powers to levy taxes, duties, fees, etc., and to spend the proceeds. • Legislatures are provided with medium-term fiscal strategy, development plans, medium-term budgets, annual budgets, and supplementary budgets. All these documents are in the public domain.	• The usefulness of the documents prepared by governments to determine the current fiscal status and its viability varies considerably among countries. In some countries, budgets are not available to the public; instead, summaries of the main features are presented.
(c) Primary fiscal instruments	• The range of fiscal instruments has expanded over the years. In addition to the annual budget intended for purposes of legislation, several documents seeking to provide background information are provided. These include multiyear rolling budgets and other documents referred to above. The most important instrument continues to be the budget. To serve the purposes of transparency, budgets are required to be: • *Comprehensive*, covering all transactions, including foreign aid, proceeds of taxation, gross spending, gross borrowing and lending, and gross buying and selling. • As *integral part* of the above and reflecting the full status of finances, data on extrabudgetary accounts, quasifiscal activities, tax expenditures, guarantees provided, and consequent contingent liabilities are also needed;	• Although all countries have budgets, their features vary considerably. • In many cases, large chunks of expenditures may be organized in the form of extrabudgetary activities or as quasifiscal activities. This feature limits the usefulness of the main budget. More significantly, in the absence of data on guarantees and related contingent liabilities, the community may not have the data to assess critically the current status of government finances and their sustainability.

Table 1 Fiscal transparency: components, instruments, and features (*Continued*)

Functional area	Instruments	Features
(c) Primary fiscal instruments	• *On a gross basis* to avoid misleading conclusions, expenditure offsets, etc., are to be avoided. • *On an accounting basis*, that reflects the cash position as well as liabilities. • A *classification* of government transactions into a functional program, as well as economic types, to illustrate the broad purposes of expenditures.	• In general, many budgets are organized on a gross basis, but a frequent resort to netting is also common. • Most budgets are organized on a cash basis. During recent years, attempts have been initiated to introduce forms of accrual budgeting. • Patterns of classification vary considerably among countries. Different practices are in vogue for budgets and for international reporting. Categories such as defense remain, for the most part, opaque.
II. Fiscal management (a) Objectives	• The range of instruments includes fiscal responsibility legislation, medium-term rolling framework, and development plans. These documents provide the essential context within which the annual budget serves as the most important fiscal instrument.	• During recent years, some countries, such as Argentina, Brazil, etc., have—following the experience of Australia and New Zealand—enacted fiscal responsibility legislation indicating the broad goals of fiscal policy.
(b) Consolidated budget	• The budget and its supplementary instruments seek to reflect the totality of government finances within a country. Because regional/state/provincial budgets have an important role, they need to be consolidated for the country as a whole.	• In unitary forms of government, budgets reflect the total picture. In federal types, however, the lower levels of government formulate their own budgets. In several countries, these are consolidated, usually after a lag, and made available to the public. Even here, the budgets of local governments (county and city governments), being too many, may not be included in the consolidation exercise.
(c) Macroeconomic framework	• The purposes of the annual budget reflect the times. To facilitate an understanding of this crucial element in fiscal policy, assumptions about the growth in the economy, exchange rate, inflation rate, aggregate demand factor, and estimated capital flows are indicated.	• The actual experience in this regard varies considerably. In most cases, the macroeconomic framework may not be explicit. In some cases, autonomous research organizations may publish them as a part of their studies. Objectives, where indicated, tend to be too general and may not constitute a strategy.
(d) Annual policy making	• The annual budget, being the main vehicle, is expected to indicate the following: • New policies to address the problems in the economy. As an integral part of this effort, new outlays are distinguished from continuing policies.	• The approaches to annual budget vary among countries, depending on the role of the legislature. • Although new policies are highlighted, the expenses associated with them and their continuing financial implications may not be adequately analyzed.

(Continued)

Table 1 Fiscal transparency: components, instruments, and features (*Continued*)

Functional area	Instruments	Features
(d) Annual policy making	• Changes in revenue policies including changes in tax expenditures.	• Tax expenditures, guarantees, and changes in lending policies do not, in general, receive specific focus in the documents.
	• Changes in lending policies. • Policies aimed at deficit containment including austerity management.	• Deficit reduction has been a dominant theme during recent years. Austerity management, however, may not be specified in detail to prevent lobbying by interest groups.
	• Changes in public debt patterns, including maturity.	• Although data on outstanding domestic and foreign debt are provided, their holders and maturity patterns—in particular, in the area of foreign debt—may not be indicated in detail.
	• Changes made in delivery of services and expenditure benefits. • Identification of high-risk areas (e.g., foreign aid).	• Expenditure benefits have not received adequate attention until recently. • Risk areas and associated efforts at risk management remain, where undertaken, at a nascent stage.
	• Some of these areas may be made public before the presentation of the annual budget, through public announcements, white papers, and sessional documents.	
(e) Detailed objectives of departments and agencies	• The objectives to be achieved during a fiscal year are to be stated in detail in each agency budget.	• Objectives, where indicated, tend to be too general and may not constitute a strategy.
(f) Performance orientation	• The agency budgets should also indicate the achievements, in terms of delivery of services, expected during the fiscal year. This constitutes an important vehicle for full accountability. As an integral part of this data on cost–service–quality linkages are sought to be provided.	• Performance budgeting in governments has had a chequered career. During recent years, there has been a revival of some aspects of this system. Many countries have yet to implement this.
(g) Pursuit of efficiency and economy	• Agency budgets are also expected to indicate the specific efforts made to achieve economy and efficiency.	• To a large extent, this remains to be fulfilled.
(h) Changes in supporting administrative infrastructure	• Governments announce, through annual budgets, changes made in the tax collection machinery, expenditure management, and debt management. In tax administration, the effort is to augment the legal specification of the tax basis, while reducing the administrative discretion in its application. In expenditure management, the intent is to facilitate internal financial operations of the spending agencies.	• In tax administration, the major area of darkness continues to be the use of discretionary powers by tax officials and related rent-seeking behavior. In expenditure management, procurement and related contracting remain, as noted below, less transparent. Debt transactions also remain, in some cases, shrouded in secrecy.

Table 1 Fiscal transparency: components, instruments, and features (*Continued*)

Functional area	Instruments	Features
(h) Changes in supporting administrative infrastructure	• In debt management, the instruments seek to provide more information on the currency of debt, separation of interest from principal, etc.	
III. Implementation of budgets	• Notwithstanding differences of degree, several stages of policy implementation are common to all countries. These include the following: • Phased release of budgetary authority • Organized cash management that facilitates a linkup with debt management • Award of contracts, procedures for tendering and contracting • Procedures to ensure budgetary outcome as intended • Specification of performance measures	• Several of the activities enumerated are usually considered as "in-house" activities and, as such, may not be open to the public. The primary issue for the community is whether there is adequate machinery empowered to deal with these aspects and whether the machinery is working effectively. In practice, the most controversial area is the award of contracts. The range of contracts has widened considerably and now includes services such as day care centers. These contracts may not, in several cases, be in the public realm. Specification of performance is still at a nascent stage. The budgetary outcome may, in some cases, be technically managed through the accumulation of payment arrears.
IV. Accounting and reporting	• The accounting system is intended to ensure that the tasks inherent in the stewardship of money are being handled. It should therefore specify 1) the basis-cash, accrual, etc., 2) the procedures for payment and budget monitoring, and 3) the compilation of periodic and year-end accounts. Accounts provide the data for the past, whereas the budget contains the present and projected trends.	• Emphases on procedures vary. In general, however, accounting systems are designed to handle the tasks enumerated. During recent years, however, significant leakages have become common. These relate to the exclusion of off-budget accounts, guarantees, contingent liabilities, quasifiscal activities, and tax expenditures.
		• Periodic reports on the status of government finances are now being released by several countries in conformity with the desire of the international financial institutions to publish standardized fiscal data. Intra-year trends may however, be significantly different from the year-end outcome as developments in the last quarter have a unique pace.
Administrative reports	• Fiscal and other agencies are required to issue annual reports illustrating their activities. These agencies include the tax collection machinery.	• These documents, which vary enormously in content and coverage, are in the public domain in most countries.
V. Evaluation	• Government activities are evaluated by their own agencies to gain experience in the utilization of resources.	• Evaluation is limited in most governments and, where conducted, may not always be available to the public.

(*Continued*)

Table 1 Fiscal transparency: components, instruments, and features (*Continued*)

Functional area	Instruments	Features
VI. Audit	• There should be adequate arrangements for an independent audit agency to verify the appropriation accounts and carry out accountancy, financial, and performance audits.	• Although many countries have independent audit offices, their effective contribution is dimmed by their limited purview (policy matters are excluded) and lack of firm legislative arrangements for a review of the findings.
VII. Independent standards	• Standards are specified for the maintenance of accounts and audit. Similar arrangements exist in some countries (e.g., Sweden) for rating the overall financial management systems, including tax collection machinery.	• Accounting standards for government are evolving and, as a result, more governments may have them in the future.
VIII. Legislative review	• Submission of the budget, consideration of new policies or changes in the existing ones, and annual accounts provide several opportunities to the legislature to exercise the traditional control of purse.	• In practice, the power of the legislatures vary considerably. Even where endowed with requisite powers and instruments, they may not exercise them in view of the party discipline and related procedural limitations.

improve the coverage and content of fiscal transparency, from the user's point of view, several problem areas remain to be addressed.

In the current situation, approximately one-third of the world's population has little access to the budget details and, thus, to the fiscal policies that have a profound and continuing impact on their lives. People living in centrally planned countries such as China, Vietnam, or quasi monarchies like the Gulf Kingdoms, and similarly placed governments receive few budget details. This is in stark contrast to the former Soviet Republics, which have made a quantum jump, in a short period, to the establishment of fiscal transparency as in other democracies.

The transactions of government and the structure of their portfolios have changed during recent years. In several cases, central governments have become funding and policy agencies, while the operations are conducted by the other levels of government, as well as by nongovernmental organizations and the corporate sector. Information in regard to the latter tends to be brief, where provided, and aggregative in nature. To the extent that these shadow governments are not fully covered the usefulness of data on fiscal operations tends to be reduced.

Fiscal transparency does not yet take the community into confidence in the realm of public policy making. In taxation, concerns of secrecy, with regard to defense, concerns of security, have contributed to a large degree of opaqueness (North American Treaty Organization countries have begun efforts to provide more information on defense costs). Similarly, little information is available about the effectiveness of the fiscal machinery (see Ref. 7, for a discussion of the limitations of audit and legislative control).

The data provided are mostly intended to meet the requirements of the investing class and do not go far in illuminating the fiscal status for the common man. The language of data is generally complex and, without the aid of a professional interpreter, may not be clear to the general public. The community's preference is for analytical data, rather than the voluminous raw data about operations.

Fiscal transparency, unaccompanied by channels of public accountability,[2] is not likely to be effective. In many cases, however, these channels remain to be effective; thus, more remains to be achieved.

REFERENCES

1. Premchand, A. *Effective Government Accounting*; International Monetary Fund: Washington, 1995.
2. Premchand, A. Public Financial Accountability. In *Governance, Corruption and Public Financial Management*; Schiavo-Campo, S., Ed.; Asian Development Bank: Manila, 1999; 145–192.
3. Brewer, J. *The Sinews of Power, War, Money and the English State, 1688–1783*; Alfred K. Knopf: New York, 1989.
4. Ferguson, N. *The Cash Nexus: Money and Power in the Modern World, 1700–2000*; Basic Books: New York, 2001.
5. International Monetary Fund. *Code of Good Practices on Fiscal Transparency. Declaration of Principles*; Washington, 1998.
6. International Monetary Fund. *Code of Good Practices on Fiscal Transparency*; Washington, 2001.
7. Premchand, A. *Control of Public Money*; Oxford University Press: New Delhi, 2000.

Forms of Government

Victor S. DeSantis
Bridgewater State College, Bridgewater, Massachusetts, U.S.A.

F

INTRODUCTION

The legal relationships between states and local governments are extremely complex and vary widely from state to state. Local governments, herein used to describe municipalities and counties, are legally considered to be creatures and agents of state government and, as such, subordinate to that state. All power and autonomy that local governments possess are granted to them through state action, and that power can be enhanced and rescinded. This legal principle is referred to as Dillon's Rule and dates back to the late 1800s.

State law, as well as a region's political culture and traditions, affects the selection of a local government's organizational structure. Although three levels of state law establish the parameters of local government autonomy—the state constitution, the state legislature (in the form of statutes), and state charters—many forms of government issues are specifically addressed in state charters. Charters are the legal mechanism that states use to recognize the existence of local governments and generally provide detail on the local government organization, powers, and responsibilities. Charters may be proffered by legislation and chosen by the jurisdiction or, in the case of home-rule jurisdictions, drafted and approved locally by citizens. Much like a state constitution, charters enumerate the basic purposes and tasks of local governments, the selection and powers of local officials, the authority and process for passing local ordinances or bylaws and, finally, the basic structures or forms of municipal and county government.

MUNICIPAL FORMS OF GOVERNMENT

There are five general forms of municipal government found in the United States today. These are the mayor–council, council–manager, commission, town meeting, and representative town meeting forms. Although each form retains distinct structural characteristics, it appears that there has been a modest, but consistent, movement since the mid-1980s toward council–manager forms of government, and away from mayor–council and commission forms. Specifically, research indicates that there has been a general convergence of the different forms over the past several decades that is especially apparent

between the mayor–council and council–manager systems.[1–3] In addition to the overall movement toward the council–manager model, other less noticeable but important changes in the structures of local government have also surfaced.[4,5] First, an increasing percentage of communities with mayor–council or town meeting forms have hired chief administrative officers to assist with the day-to-day operations of the government. Second, these chief administrative officers have increased their budgetary and appointment powers relative to the elected officials. Finally, a decreasing percentage of municipalities report giving their mayor a veto power over council actions.

The 1996 national Municipal Form of Government survey, conducted by the International City/County Management Association (ICMA), indicated that the majority of American cities operate under the mayor–council or council–manager form. The 1996 ICMA survey data show that 51.9% of responding communities used the council–manager form, whereas another 31.9% used the mayor–council form. The remaining survey respondents used the commission, town meeting, or representative town meeting forms, or were unsure of their specific categorization.[4]

Mayor–Council

The mayor–council form of government (Fig. 1) is most prevalent in the nation's larger cities and smaller jurisdictions. In this form, there is usually a legislative body, the city/town council, and a separately elected chief executive, the mayor. The actual titles afforded to the legislative body and executive official vary widely and are usually based on long-standing local or regional tradition. There are generally two types of mayor–council government, the "strong mayor" and "weak mayor" models. The substantive difference between these types depends on the administrative duties and power given to the mayor.

The strong mayor form of government centralizes the administrative powers in the hands of the popularly elected mayor, while vesting the legislative function in the elected council. In this form, the mayor has the authority to prepare and control the administration of the budget, appoint and remove department heads, preside over council meetings, and set the council agenda. The strong mayor may also have a veto power over council

Encyclopedia of Public Administration and Public Policy
DOI: 10.1081/E-EPAP 120010838

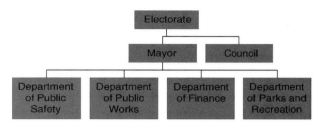

Fig. 1 Model of the typical mayor–council form of government.

actions. Supporters of a strong mayor government argue that a strong mayor provides leadership to a community while being held responsible to citizens for their actions. Also, a strong mayor may be better able to exercise political power in bigger cities to bring together large and diverse interest groups.

Increasingly, strong mayors are also opting to appoint a chief administrative officer for the city who serves at their pleasure to focus on the details of day-to-day government administration, such as budget preparation and personnel management. This arrangement frees mayors to concentrate more on their roles out of city hall and in the community, and also increases their ability to deal on policy matters and agenda setting.

The weak mayor system is the older of the two mayor models, resulting from the traditional American distrust of strong executive power. The weak mayor is often selected from among the council members, instead of being elected directly by the people. The weak mayor generally has limited appointment and budgetary authority and does not have veto power over council. This system is also characterized by its decentralized and fragmented nature, with multiple department heads and other local officials directly elected by the community. The weak mayor form of government is the more commonly used in the United States, especially in smaller communities.

The dawn of the twentieth century was an important watershed period for municipal government in the United States, most specifically for the traditional mayor council model of government. Across the nation, political bosses and machine politics were the norm in many larger cities. Although the newly formed National Municipal League first supported the strong mayor form in 1898 in an effort to decrease the power of political machine bosses, this effort was short lived. Further efforts at reforming the structure and process of local government in reaction to the widespread corruption and inefficiency surfaced during this period, which became popularly known as the Progressive Era. At the core of this ''good government'' movement were the upper middle-class residents that had grown tired of the powerful political machines and the immigrant groups keeping them in power.[6] Their speci-

fic agenda included numerous election reforms and the promotion of more efficient and professional government through civil service systems, competitive bidding practices, and forms of municipal government that provided for an apolitical appointed (rather than elected) executive. These reform efforts led to experiments with the commission and council–manager forms of government.

Commission

Cities and towns with the commission form of government provide for a full centralization of power in the elected council to make policy and direct the executive operations of the local government. Each elected commissioner serves as a member of the legislative body and is also elected to lead one or more administrative departments. This form continues to decline and is currently found in only a few communities nationwide.

In 1900, in response to a disastrous hurricane and flood that crippled the city of Galveston, the Texas governor appointed a set of five businessmen (later elected by the community) to handle the policy and administrative functions of the community. Supporters of this model believed that this plan was a positive step toward improving local government because it unified all power in the hands of a board of commissioners. Many of the good government reformers, themselves from the business community, began promoting the commission form, and it was adopted widely over the next decade.[7] However, one of the weaknesses of the commission form that began to surface was that it fragmented administrative functions and was too unwieldy. Reformers later latched on to the idea of the council–manager form, a hybrid of the strong mayor and commission forms of government.

Council–Manager

Another form of municipal government that grew out of the Progressive Era is the council–manager form (Fig. 2). Council–manager government combines the strong political leadership of elected officials with the strong

Fig. 2 Model of the typical council–manager form of government.

managerial leadership of an appointed professional manager. This form of government rests the policy-making power in the hands of the elected legislative body. A professional manager serving at the pleasure of the elected body is charged with day-to-day administration of the government. The manager commonly has the authority to direct administrative operations, appoint administrative officers, prepare and administer the budget, and advise the council on matters of policy.

Although many council–manager forms of government have a popularly elected mayor, many of the mayors in this form are selected from among the membership of the legislative body. These mayors have restricted powers that are generally limited to presiding over council meetings and making appointments to boards or commissions. Mayors are part of the council and vote as regular members, although they have little or no veto power. Proponents of the council–manager form of government argue that this structure allows supervisory and administrative responsibility to be centralized in one individual. This allows the individual's expertise and knowledge of administrative activities to be developed, while vesting all power in an elected governing body to promote representative democracy.

The council–manager form is actually a hybrid of two previous government structures: the strong mayor and commission. In an effort to improve on the decentralized and fragmented commission form, Richard S. Childs and other local government reformers proposed a plan that combined the commission form with a strong administrative element, concentrating all administrative powers in the form of a single professional manager. This became the council–manager plan and, in 1915, the National Municipal League revised its model city charter to reflect this new form of government.[7,8]

Town Meetings

The town meetings of New England are often considered to be one of the last modern-day examples of direct democracy in action. This distinction comes from the mass public meetings, in which any registered voter of the jurisdiction may attend, speak, and vote on various policy, administrative, and budgetary issues. The town meeting process as practiced in New England can be traced back to the Massachusetts Bay Colony of the late 1620s[9] and is currently found only in the New England states of Maine, Massachusetts, New Hampshire, Vermont, Rhode Island, and Connecticut. However, in recent decades, the prevalence and operation of town meeting forms of government have experienced substantial tension and change.

The limited empirical evidence on town meetings indicates a growing trend toward abandoning open town meetings in favor of an elected town council or estab-

lishing a representative town meeting government.[10] The representative town meeting involves the voters selecting a limited number of citizens to represent them and vote at town meetings. All citizens may attend and participate in the debate, but only the duly elected representatives may actually vote. Other New England communities have adopted a more incremental change by hiring full-time professional chief administrative officers, in addition to the open town meeting process.

Under the town meeting form of government, the town meeting is considered the local legislative body with the authority to pass ordinances and bylaws, and raise and appropriate funds. Each town with this form generally holds one annual town meeting and may also hold as many additional meetings (called special town meetings) as deemed necessary to carry out the town's business. A warrant (from the term "warning") is issued to townspeople stating the date, time, place, and itemized agenda for annual and special town meetings. An elected moderator presides over the town meeting and has wide latitude in directing the debate and conducting business.

During the remainder of the year, the elected board (usually called selectmen) of three or five members is charged with running the daily operations of the town. Boards of selectmen carry out many appointing, financial, and licensing responsibilities granted to them by the town meeting. Many towns have added the position of chief administrative officer to assist the board in their administrative roles on an ongoing basis. These chief administrative officers serve at the pleasure of the board of selectmen and have their duties prescribed by board action or a town meeting bylaw.

COUNTY FORMS OF GOVERNMENT

As units of local government, counties have historically been considered administrative arms of state government and operate with more constraints than their municipal counterparts. In most areas of the United States, this means that counties operate with less local autonomy or "home rule" authority and have their operations and structures dictated substantially by state law. There are three general forms of county government found in the United States today. These are the commission, council–administrator, and council–elected executive forms. Although the reform movement for county government came later in the twentieth century than the municipal reform movement, there has been modest improvement, especially over the last few decades. Many of these efforts have been aimed at improving and streamlining county operations and providing for greater professional leadership. Research points to increased usage of the council–administrator and council–elected executive forms.

Indeed, the overall trend toward professional management in counties can be seen by the ever-increasing number of counties, even with the traditional form, that provide for a position of chief administrative officer.[11]

Commission

The commission or plural executive form of government in counties is the oldest and most traditional organizational structure. A central governing board characterizes it with members usually elected by district. Although various names exist for this board, among the favorite are the board of commissioners or supervisors and the county court. Most often, the board selects one of its members as the presiding officer. Members of the governing board may act as department heads, but this is not a defining characteristic as in the municipal commission model. The governing boards share administrative and, to an extent, legislative functions with independently elected officials: the clerk, the treasurer, the sheriff, the assessor, the coroner, and others. Generally, no single administrator oversees the county's operations. In some counties with the commission form, the structure includes an official (generally full time), such as the county judge, who is independently elected at-large to be the presiding officer of the governing board. As noted previously, many disadvantages associated with the commission form stem from the usual lack of a chief administrator to provide more professionalism, executive leadership, and accountability.

Council–Administrator

The council–administrator form of government for counties is similar to the council–manager form for cities, but three distinct variations are identifiable. In its strongest variation, the council–administrator form provides for an elected county board or council and an appointed administrator. The county board adopts ordinances and resolutions, adopts the budget, and sets policy. The administrator, appointed by the board, has responsibility for budget development and implementation, the hiring and firing of department heads, and recommending policy to the board. In some counties, where a weaker version of the council administrator plan is in place, the administrator usually has less direct responsibility for overall county operations and less authority in hiring and firing, and may consult with the board on policy issues.

Council–Elected Executive

The third form of county government is the council–elected executive form. This system has two branches of government—legislative and executive—and more clearly resembles the strong mayor form of city government.

Here, the county council or board assumes responsibility for county policies, adopts the budget, and audits the financial performance of the county. The elected at-large executive is considered the chief elected official of the county and often has veto power, which can be overridden by the council. The executive prepares the budget, carries out the administration of the county operations, appoints department heads (usually with the consent of the council), and suggests policy to the governing board. In addition, this official carries out appropriations, ordinances, and resolutions passed by the board and generally acts as the chief spokesperson for the county. When the executive is considered the chief political spokesperson, the executive often delegates the administrative responsibility for the daily county operations to a chief administrator. This form, along with the council–administrator form, has begun to receive more popular support over the past few decades and push counties forward in their quest for modernization.

REFERENCES

1. Renner, T. Elected Executives: Authority and Responsibility. In *Baseline Data Report*; International City Management Association: Washington, DC, 1988; Vol. 20 (3).
2. Boynton, R.P.; DeSantis, V.S. Form and Adaptation: A Study of the Formal and Informal Functions of Mayors, Managers, and Chief Administrative Officers. In *Baseline Data Report*; International City Management Association: Washington, DC, 1990; Vol. 22 (1).
3. Frederickson, H.G.; Johnson, G.A. The adapted American city: A study of institutional dynamics. Urban Aff. Rev. **2001**, *36*, 872–884, (July).
4. Renner, T.; DeSantis, V.S. Municipal Forms of Government: Issues and Trends. In *The Municipal Year Book 1998*; International City/County Management Association: Washington, DC, 1998.
5. Hansell, W. Is it time to reform the reform. Public Manage. **1998**, *80*, 15–16, (December).
6. Renner, T.; DeSantis, V.S. Contemporary Patterns and Trends in Municipal Government Structures. In *The Municipal Year Book 1993*; International City/County Management Association: Washington, DC, 1993.
7. Nolting, O. *Progress and Impact of the Council–Manager Plan*; Public Administration Service: Chicago, IL, 1969.
8. Stillman, R.J. *The Rise of the City Manager*; University of New Mexico Press: Albuquerque, NM, 1974.
9. Zimmerman, J.F. The New England Town Meeting: Pure Democracy in Action? In *The Municipal Year Book 1984*; International City Management Association: Washington, DC, 1984.
10. DeSantis, V. *Open Town Meetings in Massachusetts: Issues and Evaluation*; Institute for Regional Development: Bridgewater, MA, December 1997; Vol. 97 (2).
11. DeSantis, V. County Government: A Century of Change. In *The Municipal Year Book 1989*; International City Management Association: Washington, DC, 1989.

Game Theory

Michael A. Kelley
Pittsburg State University, Pittsburg, Kansas, U.S.A.

INTRODUCTION

Game theory is a mathematical approach to individual decision making that employs games as paradigms of rational decision-maker interactions. Used to study a variety of social, economic, and political issues, such as arms races, legislative coalition formation, military strategy, regulative public policy, voting behavior, and even aspects of marriage, game theoretic models delineate those decisions actors should make when confronted with competing policy alternatives or decision consequences. Far from seeing games as trivial, game theorists posit that game decisions exhibit the same rules or forces that drive more complex political and other social interactions and outcomes. After all, games, like politics, involve player moves and interactions, selection of strategies with specific consequences, and, at times, coalition formation, all predicated on a desire to maximize individual player interests.

POSITIVE POLITICAL THEORY AND THE RATIONALITY ASSUMPTION

Intrinsic to game theory is the idea that individual decisions are rational, i.e., individuals are engaged in purposeful action directed at ordered goal attainment. Positive political theory asserts that individuals order their goals when engaged in public choice, choosing to maximize their expected utility and preferring to win or gain rather than lose or fail to gain when there are real conflicts of interest. Indeed, enforced policy choices by government are the result of socially expressed, ordered, and calculated preferences for particular policies. The idea of rationality and the resulting regularity in human behavior explicates a positive science of politics that encourages the confrontation of assertion with experimentation and tests of validity.

Game theory, which employs games as abstractions of real-world situations and assumes player rationality, assigns specific mathematical payoffs to decision situations. It delineates the appropriate strategy rational players will pursue given a particular game and given that players maximize gains and limit losses when confronted with a decision or problem. There is the fur-

ther expectation that other players in the game will behave similarly in order to maximize their own individual utility, when there are competing policy alternatives. Games, thus, are heuristic devices in that they simplify reality based on particular assumptions in order to provide insights into human conduct.

Game theory involves decision problems, where there are at least two parties, and players must choose among competing decision alternatives with particular consequences, consistently order their preferences based on decision consequences and where the consequential interaction of player choices can be specified mathematically. Example 1 exemplifies these points and illuminates the assumption of rationality.

Example 1

"Polluter versus Regulator"

Polluter

	Delay (A)	Comply (B)
Intensive (A*)	8; -8 (A*; A)	5; -5 (A*; B)
Less Intense (B*)	1; -1 (B*; A)	3; -3 (B*; B)

Regulator (row labels at left)

In this situation, the regulator confronts a polluter with a set of new rules. Row A* provides for more intensive regulative monitoring, with positive payoffs (fines collected from polluter) of at least five units, and this is the regulator's dominant strategy in this game (payoff is always higher than another choice, i.e., $8 > 3$ and $5 > 1$); while row B* involves less monitoring and would permit more cheating by the polluter. The polluter, wanting to avoid cleanup costs, must choose between meeting the rules (column B) or choosing a strategy (column A) of doing only what is required after legal action. Polluter's choice is column B in this zero-sum game (what one player gets, the other loses), because the polluter wants to limit losses and assumes that a rational regulator will choose row A* to maximize the fines collected. With this choice, at most, polluter will lose five and could lose only three units, if the regulator fails to act rationally and selects row B*. The rational result would be a payoff of

Encyclopedia of Public Administration and Public Policy
DOI: 10.1081/E-EPAP 120010802

+5 units to the regulator and −5 units to the polluter (A*B), but polluter avoids the −8 units consequence by pursuing a rational strategy of compliance.

EXAMPLES OF GAME SITUATIONS

Game theory is not only a mathematically based science of decision problems, it also is a classification scheme for games. As surrogates, games must reflect the complexity of real-world decision situations. Games are classified by the number of players (2...n) and the types of outcomes (typically, zero-sum and nonzero-sum). Each game in the resulting game classification matrix has its own particular set of rules, which explain expected player choice relative to specified outcomes.

Two-Person, Zero-Sum Games

As seen in Example 1's highly conflictual situation, whatever one player wins, the other player loses, interests are diametrically opposed, player payoffs add to zero, and both antagonists possess perfect information about the consequences of their actions. Exemplified by wartime strategy, decisions in this game are based on the "worst-case assumption" or the idea that each player will seek maximal advantage. Assuming the worst, a *minimax* strategy, where regulator seeks to minimize the maximum amount of harm to interests in the face of Regulator's *maximin* choice of maximizing its minimum gain. In the example, a *minimax* strategy leads to the saddle point or optimal solution of A*B or 5, −5 (the payoff that is a row minimum and a column maximum), in that this is the best that either player can do, given that each opponent is rational. In a zero-sum, two-person game there is always at least one pair of optimal strategies (if there is more than one set of optimal strategies, players are indifferent to any particular pair), hence, there is always a solution to the game.

Two-Person, Nonzero-Sum Games

In these games, player interests are not diametrically opposed but rather have some shared interest in avoiding particular outcomes. An oft-used example of this game is the "Prisoner's Dilemma." As Example 2 illustrates, two prisoners charged with the same serious crime are separated and cannot communicate. The prosecutor can convict both of them of a minor crime but must get at least one of them to inform on the other in order to solve a more serious charge. During the interrogation, the pro-

secutor informs the separated prisoners that the one who informs will be set free, and the other will spend 15 years in jail. If both cooperate and remain silent, they both spend 2 years in jail, while if they both inform on each other, they will each spend 7 years in jail. Which strategy should be pursued is the salient question, i.e., to maximize one's payoff or a strategy of trusting the other to remain silent. Prisoner 1's maximizing strategy would be such that: B*A > A*A and B*B > A*B, hence, his rational strategy is to inform. Prisoner 2 rationally understands that A*B > A*A and B*B > B*A and also chooses to inform. Pursuit of individual rationality results in a 7-year prison sentence for each prisoner (B*B). On the other hand, they would have served only 2 years each (A*A), if they could trust each other to remain silent. The dilemma exists, because the rational choice of payoff maximization and the fear of the consequences of the other cheating results in a lower payoff than an alternative approach of trust, hence, the "Prisoner's Dilemma." This "game" is often used to describe why arms races occur even when cooperation would provide for a more satisfactory outcome for both parties.

Example 2

"Prisoners Dilemma"

Prisoner 2

	Quiet (A)	Informs (B)
Quiet (A*)	A*; A 2; 2	A*; B 15; 0
Informs (B*)	B*; A 0; 15	B*; B 7; 7

Prisoner 1 (Quiet A*, Informs B*)

N-Person, Zero-Sum Games

In these games, the zero-sum rules apply, but the distinction is that the winners are members of a coalition whose gain equals the losses suffered by those outside of the winning coalition, and where players can reach private agreements about the division of the spoils (side payments). The game's characteristic function (how much each possible coalition of actors can receive by acting in concert) will determine the game's outcome. Players taking into account the characteristic function will form coalitions that they believe are only large enough to win and which maximize their individual gains. This aspect of a game helps explain why it is so difficult to form and maintain "grand" legislative coalitions (see Example 3), because players can win more of the finite rewards if they form smaller coalitions. Indeed, empirical observation of grand alliance structures in domestic and international politics demonstrates that "grand" coalitions tend to

Example 3

"Size Principle and Legislative Coalitions"

In this simple game (where the characteristic function is either 1 or 0), the parties in a legislature want to control the government in order to appoint ministers but must form a coalition in order to win. Legislative strengths of the parties are as follows:

Party A = 45%
Party B = 20%
Party C = 25%
Party D = 10%

The minimum winning coalitions (there is no majority if a member is subtracted) are AB, AC, AD, and BCD. It is possible to further refine the results by noting that A probably prefers AD to the other possibilities, because B and C will be more demanding, given their relative legislative strengths. D also prefers AD, because it will share the win with only one coalition partner or the smallest number of players. The AD coalition is the one likely to emerge, if there are no ideological or information problems that lead to larger than minimal winning coalitions.

form in times of crisis or discontinuity and then devolve into competing parties or smaller coalitions when the crisis has passed.

N-Person, Nonzero-Sum Games

This game is most relevant to political and administrative decision making, the central aspect of which is coalition formation, where the benefits of cooperation outweigh those of maximizing individual utility. In these games, where constant communication occurs over many different decisions, cooperation can bring positive payoffs, while noncooperation provides no increase in individual utility. In the N = 4 example (Example 4), the question is, when will an individual support a fee, if the levy will generate a desired public value twice as great as the total costs to the individual players. While each person would prefer to receive benefits at no cost, because there is communication, players are more likely to prefer to win something than pursue an individually rational strategy that would result in no individual benefit. After all, players prefer to win something than forego winning at all. A coalition will form if the players receive a benefit or there is no cost associated with receiving the public good.

Example 4

"Community Good"

Agree	Individual Cost	Total Cost	Community Good	Individual Benefit	Individual Gain	Cell
Yes—4 No—0	$40 $0	$160	$320	$80	$40	A
Yes—3 No—1	$40 $0	$120	$240	$60	$20 $60	B
Yes—2 No—2	$40 $0	$80	$160	$40	$0 $40	C
Yes—1 No—3	$40 $0	$40	$80	$20	-$20 $20	D
Yes—0	$0				$0	E

The most likely result is Cell C. In Cell E, no one gains anything; while in D, it is unlikely that a single player will solely finance the public good. On the other hand, there is a benefit to defect (compare individual gain in Cell B and Cell A) from the grand coalition. However, if a player can convince just one other person of the levy's value, there is no cost relative to the received and desired benefit (Cell C). A minimal coalition can be formed to acquire the desired good, provided it is profitable (or does not cost) the players.

536

CONCLUSION

The idea that individuals are rational gives social scientists a powerful mechanism with which to understand various forms of political and social decision making. The theory of games assumes that decisions are not randomly derived but rather are arrived at through a process where each player seeks to maximize positive rewards relative to costs in situations when there are competing perspectives. Games, with their specified outcomes relative to particular decision problems, permit decision-making theorists to look at real decisions in a predictive or evaluative mode. The predictive mode allows for the delineation of a strategy relative to an expressed set of ordered goals, with the presumption that rationality compels particular procedures and results. On the other hand, the evaluative approach infers from actual decisions the goals which must have existed under the rationality assumption to lead to the particular result. Games are not perfect analogies to real-world decision making, yet the use of games allows us to test to see if decision makers behaved in a purposeful and ordered fashion to maximize individual utilities.

FURTHER READING

Bartos, O.J. *Simple Models of Group Behavior*; Columbia University Press, 1967.

Hamburger, H. *Games as Models of Social Phenomena*; W.H. Freeman and Company, 1979.

Rapoport, A. *N-Person Game Theory*; University of Michigan, 1973.

Rapoport, A. *Two-Person Game Theory*; University of Michigan, 1973.

Riker, W.H. *The Theory of Political Coalitions*; Yale University Press, 1962.

Riker, W.H.; Ordeshook, P.C. *An Introduction to Positive Political Theory*; Prentice-Hall, 1973.

The Study of Coalition Behavior; Groennings, S., Kelley, E.W., Leiserson, M., Eds.; Holt, Rinehart, and Winston 1970.

Gender Bias, Ethical Analysis of and in Public Policy

J. J. Hendricks
April Hejka-Ekins
California State University, Stanislaus, Turlock, California, U.S.A.

INTRODUCTION

The content of this entry defines and discusses gender bias, the theories that have been central in its exposure and analysis, ethical implications, and the effect of gender bias in public policy. The theories discussed are elaborated upon as they affect the public service and its mission. Gender bias is an increasingly recognized topic with significant ramifications for citizens and public-sector employees. There are enormous ethical implications issuing from the way in which the legitimate needs of citizens are disproportionately recognized in policies and disproportionately served programmatically as a result of gender. In this entry, the ethics of care and the postmodern structural critique are presented. Both critiques are highly relevant to public administration. Finally, thoughts on attempts to present alternative feminist policy delivery systems are discussed.

GENDER DEFINED

Although often treated synonymously, gender is to be distinguished from the biological category sex, which is used to denote femaleness and maleness. Both sex and gender have come under increasing scrutiny as categories. They have been subjected to criticism as essential, therefore natural, categories. Gender is a dichotomous typology, which is socially constructed through the many processes that pervade a culture. Through the creation of the social types, female and male, humans are divided into categories, and traits and roles deemed appropriate for males and females are assigned to each. Traditionally, in patriarchal societies, males are assigned traits such as strength and competitiveness, while females are assigned traits such as docility and the capacity to nurture. These traits are assigned differently in various cultures, an example being the hijras of India, men who adopt female dress and behavior.[1]

GENDER ROLES AND BEHAVIORAL NORMS

Gender roles are the behavioral sets that accompany the assignment of gender to the categories of male or female. Members of society are socialized to display the appropriate behaviors assigned their gender roles. Although these learned roles may vary somewhat in different contexts, for example, in the workplace or in the home, expectations for both genders are remarkably durable and affect interactions in all contexts—the family, the educational setting, and the workplace—to one degree or another. Given the establishment of contexts as the domains of males, for example, combat and business, or females, for example, the home and professions such as social work and nursing, these contexts take on the behavioral norms associated with an assigned gender. In addition, much work is segregated by gender, which means that structural as well as behavioral norms are gendered.

THEORETICAL CRITIQUE

Gender and sex have been subjected to heavy criticism. Sex as a biological phenomenon is a great deal more plastic than popular culture allows.[2] This is important to a discussion of gender, as biological determinism is often used to support the essential nature of males and females and the established gender categorizations. Biological determinism is the claim that sex determines behavioral outcomes.

Gender as a construct has been heavily criticized by all schools of feminist thought. One of the most recent and influential schools of thought, postmodern feminist critique, originates in a number of sources, but the work of Jacques Derrida is often utilized in constructing an argument. In Derrida's critique of modernism, reality is first divided into oppositional categories (either/or, black/white, male/female, public/private). One opposition is subsequently elevated and privileged, and one is devalued by comparison.[3] Using Derrida's method of deconstruction, feminist theorists deconstruct the binary opposition of male/female and the subsequent assignment of these categories to either the public or private arena. Thus, bias enters the picture.

Gender bias can be defined as the privileging of males over females and things masculine over things feminine. Black feminist scholars have revised feminist

Encyclopedia of Public Administration and Public Policy
DOI: 10.1081/E-EPAP 120011077

criticism to include the unequal positions of women of color. Patricia Hill Collins, for example, has developed a matrix of domination, in which a more complex hierarchical positioning that includes the intersection of gender and race is presented. This intersection would incorporate an analysis of the devaluing women of color experience doubly, due to both white privilege and male privilege.[4]

STREAMS OF ETHICAL ANALYSIS

As a reaction to gender bias, two streams of ethical theory and analysis have emerged. One stems from the feminine school of thought, which advocates that an ethic of care needs to be valued by society and incorporated into organizational norms and institutional processes. A second stems from postmodern feminist theorists who critique the structure and arrangement of male-dominated organizations. Both schools attempt to eliminate gender bias through different approaches.[5]

THE FEMININE ETHIC OF CARE

As compiled by Scranton and Rainney, the literature indicates that the feminine ethic of care was first articulated by Carol Gilligan in 1982 as a reaction against what she considered to be the gender-biased theory of Lawrence Kohlberg, who advocated that justice is the primary ethic in decision making. Kohlberg constructed a six-stage model of moral development, based on notions of universality, abstract reasoning, and individual rights, while relegating the value of caring to stage three in his schema. In response, Gilligan criticized Kohlberg for discounting the importance and complexity of the value of caring, asserted that the moral development of women is based on a different voice—an orientation of caring—and proposed a morality of care and responsibility. Other feminine theorists, such as Noddings, Tonto, and Chodorow, critiqued the exclusion of care as an essential aspect of gender bias and advocated for its acknowledgement and primary inclusion in all aspects of social and organizational life.[5]

THE POSTMODERN CRITIQUE

However, research studies by Kanter, Derry, and Stewart and Sprintall have shown that the ethic of care is not expressed by women in male-dominated organizations. Indeed, because no value differences could be found among men and women, it appears that in order to succeed, women are forced to adapt to the demands of the gendered organizational structure and culture in which they work. As a result, postmodern feminist ethicists critique male-dominated organizations by showing how the structure of hierarchy and the cultural values of aggression and competitiveness suppress the expression of care by women who strive to be successful in organizations.[5] Kathy Ferguson maintained that the subordinate position of women in public life rests upon the increasingly bureaucratic nature of modern society. In this description, large-scale bureaucracy as a masculinist form of organization with a propensity toward conformity, control, and anonymity, systematically renders the voices of women as workers and clients silent, as well as any alternative vision of collective life.[6] The recent work of Camilla Stivers discussed the materially different organizational reality and dissonant professional roles of women relative to men as civil servants.[7] At the same time, Ferguson and Stivers exposed the contradiction that while bureaucracies in structure, culture, and practice are discriminatory toward women and hamper their full expression, the ethos of serving the public good renders the public workforce and its clientele "feminized" and devalued in the thinking of society.

PRESCRIPTIONS FOR CHANGE ISSUING FROM ETHICAL ANALYSIS

It is not difficult to see how devalued notions of the feminine in society affect the ethic of care within the fabric of organization and society. It is also not difficult to find ways in which to demonstrate alternative approaches to organizational life. Two responses to ameliorate gender bias have emerged from the feminine ethic of care within organizational life to transform male-dominated organizational structure and culture. Feminine theorists advocate for the inclusion of the ethic of care within organizational life to transform male-dominated institutions. For example, Helgeson described how women who reach the top levels of management are more willing to express the care ethic and implement feminine values, while Rosner suggested that women's management style tends to be more inclusive, more flexible, and more supportive than men.[5] By legitimizing the feminine care ethic, these theorists are trying to persuade the male-dominated power elite that inclusion of the care ethos in organizational structure and culture will improve work life and organizational effectiveness, while simultaneously uplifting the status of women. The second response by feminist theorists and activists is to reject gender-biased institutions and create feminist organizations that reflect a more organic, decentralized form and culture of values that include respect, equality, diversity, open communication, collaboration, creativity, and consensus. Ferree and Martin documented a wide range of organizations that have been effective on a global level. Women envision these organizations as embodying a transformative process that provides a moral framework for expressing such values as nurturance, democracy, and empowerment.[8]

POLICY IMPLICATIONS

One question that arises from these two women's movements to counter gender bias is the extent to which the feminine ethic of care and the creation of feminist organizations affect public policy and the public sector. In actuality, the devaluing of the position of women in the public sector interacts with the inequitable implementation of public policies to continue the concrete effects of gender bias. This actuality rests on a gendered philosophical and structural foundation, which initially excluded women.

GENDER BIAS IN THE FOUNDING DOCUMENT

The United States Constitution as the founding social contract on which public policy in the United States rests has been incisively criticized by MacKinnon for its exclusion of the standpoint of women citizens in the deliberation, articulation, and implementation of policy.[8] This absence of the voices of women's issues from the binary construction of the socially constructed public spaces of men and the domestic spaces of women, was termed "the doctrine of separate spheres."

THE GENDERED NORMATIVE ORDER

Gendered institutions and constructed realities result in a view of public policy in which the feminine as a devalued category affects the "taken-for-granted" nature of the lived experience of citizens. Many of the gendered ways in which resources are allocated are viewed as normal and not questioned. Assertions of inequitable relations and policy distribution must do battle with the normative views of the established order. These views are legitimized by the institutional belief systems of, for example, religious and economic theories extant in society.

IMPACT OF GENDER BIAS REVEALED

The numerous arenas in which policy analyses detail inequitable distribution of resources by gender as well as by gender intersecting with race, preclude elaborate or substantial documentation, given the scope of this entry. A broad overview presents a grim and inequitable picture. Occupational and wage distribution exhibits gross inequity. Poverty and welfare are increasingly manifest among women, spawning the term "the feminization of poverty." Sociologist Margaret Anderson indicated that in 1997, 31.6% of all female-headed households lived below the official poverty line.[9] The callousness of the "taken-for-granted reality" of the American public is illustrated by the common term, "welfare queen." Such terms are not harmless, but affect political realities and the policies consistent with such views, i.e., "workfare." Work that is traditionally performed by women is excluded from that which produces a wage. Women in the workforce continue to earn around 74% the income of men. Workplace environments have been addressed above but must be included when addressing violence against women. The incidence of women's sexual harassment has remained at just below 50% since the policy guidelines were articulated in 1980. Costs to individuals, women as a group, and employers are many, serious, and economically very high.[10] Domestic violence and incest seem impervious to policies and criminal statutes directed toward them. Women's health and reproduction issues continue to be defined largely by men who dominate science, medicine, and policy-making institutions. In issues such as war and peace, women's concerns are largely missing. While 14% of the officers in the military are women, gender segregation persists.[9] As a gendered institution characterized by violence, aggression, and force, military values legitimize violence and sexual aggression in war. From the incidence of gender bias, one can only conclude that gendered institutions are to date impervious to efforts to ameliorate them or their effects. To overcome this tendency toward the status quo will take great and enduring effort.

CONCLUSION

One insight seems particularly important to note. Feminist organizations that resist cultural norms of gender bias have proliferated both inside and external to the public service over the past 30 years. They serve the purpose of providing alternative structural arrangements, as examples of what might be desirable to achieve. Though valuable in this way, they do not significantly impact the power inequities in public policy that act to structure and control women's lives. Their successes are striking but in no way create the change that the public is led to believe exists in the average women's daily lived existence. In fact, they often function to address and remediate the most blatant violent examples of gender discrimination, masking the common realities. This conclusion is not meant to devalue or downplay the heroic and enduring efforts of feminists to act over time on behalf of women. However, until changes in consciousness and power occur, the ill effects of gender bias will remain unabated.

Resources:

Activist Organizations and Research:

Gender Watch: http://gw.softlineweb.com/.
Feminist Majority on Line: http://www.feminist.org/.
V-Day, http://www.vday.org/index2.cfm.
Women of Color and Women Worldwide: http://www-sul.stanford.edu/depts/ssrg/kkerns/wcolor. html.

Journals:

Feminista!: http://www.feminista.com/.
Hypatia: http://www.csupomona.edu/~hypatia/.
Yale Journal of Law and Feminism: http://www.yale.edu/lawnfem/law&fem.html.

REFERENCES

1. Ward, M. *A World Full of Women,* 2nd Ed.; Allyn and Bacon: Massachusetts, 1999; 82.
2. Fausto-Sterling, A. *Myths of Gender: Biological Theories About Women and Men*; Basic Books, 1992.
3. Derrida, J. *Margins of Philosophy*; Bass, A. Trans.; University of Chicago Press: Chicago, 1984.
4. Collins, P. *Black Feminist Thought: Knowledge, Consciousness and the Politics of Empowerment,* 2nd Ed.; Routledge: New York, 2000; 18.
5. Scranton, A.; Rainney, M. Gender Differences in Administrative Ethics. In *Handbook of Administrative Ethics*; Cooper, T.L., Ed.; Marcel Dekker, Inc.: New York, 2001; 555.
6. Ferguson, K.E. *The Feminist Case Against Bureaucracy*; Temple University Press: Philadelphia, 1984.
7. Stivers, C. *Gender Images in Public Administration: Legitimacy and the Administrative State*; Sage Publications, Inc.: Newbury Park, CA, 1993.
8. MacKinnon, C. *Feminism Unmodified: Discourses on Life and Law*; Harvard University Press: Cambridge, MA, 1987.
9. Anderson, M. *Thinking About Women: Sociological Perspectives on Sex and Gender,* 5th Ed.; Allyn and Bacon: Boston, MA, 2000; pp. 137, 308.
10. Petrocelli, W.; Repa, B.K. *Sexual Harassment on the Job: What It Is and How to Stop It,* 4th Ed.; Nolo: Berkeley, CA, 1999.

Generally Accepted Accounting Principles

Catherine L. Staples
Randolph-Macon College, Ashland, Virginia, U.S.A.

G

INTRODUCTION

Generally accepted accounting principles (GAAP) are the minimum standards or rules organizations must follow in determining what financial information should be included in the general-purpose financial statements and how the information should be presented. These basic guidelines form the basis around which financial statements are created.

WHO ESTABLISHES GAAP?

The primary organizations responsible for setting accounting standards are the Governmental Accounting Standards Board (GASB), the Financial Accounting Standards Board (FASB), and the Federal Accounting Standards Advisory Board (FASAB). For state and local governments, GAAP is established primarily by the GASB, while the FASAB serves as the main standard-setting body for the federal government. All other entities, including nongovernmental not-for-profits, follow guidance established by the FASB.

Of the three, FASB and GASB are considered parallel organizations. That is, they perform the same function, standard setting, but for different types of entities. In addition, oversight responsibility for both boards lies with the same private-sector organization, the Financial Accounting Foundation (FAF), whose primary responsibilities include appointing the seven members of each of the two boards and providing considerable financial support for the operating expenses of both.

Federal governmental agencies apply accounting and reporting standards recommended by the FASAB. This relatively new organization was created in 1990 and consists of nine members, six of whom must come from prescribed federal agencies such as the Congressional Budget Office or the Department of Defense. Standards issued by the FASAB are evaluated and approved by the U.S. General Accounting Office, the U.S. Department of the Treasury, and the U.S. Office of Management and Budget prior to the final issuance of a statement.

Although the GASB, FASB, and the FASAB are the main standard-setting bodies, other organizations, such as the American Institute of Certified Public Accountants (AICPA) and the Securities and Exchange Commission (SEC), also provide guidance on accounting and financial issues. This guidance may be considered GAAP if no formal statements have been issued on the topic. Widely recognized industry practices and accounting textbooks are also considered potential sources of GAAP.

OBJECTIVES OF ACCOUNTING AND FINANCIAL REPORTING

The development of GAAP is based upon a foundation of financial accounting objectives or goals. This foundation guides standard setters in their formation of the specific details for a statement and is based upon the primary purpose for the creation of an entity's financial statements. For instance, federal, state, and local governments are concerned with accountability to citizens, while for-profit organizations need to provide information to creditors and investors.

Accountability is the focal point of the accounting objectives for state and local governments. In particular, GASB's Concepts Statement No. 1, *Objectives of Financial Reporting*, purported that the basic function of a set of financial statements is to "justify the raising of public resources and the purposes for which they are used."[1] Consequently, state and local government financial reports should be used primarily to compare actual financial outcomes with the legally adopted budget, appraise the financial condition and results of operations, and ensure compliance with applicable legal or contractual requirements. Governments must be accountable to several groups of stakeholders, including citizens, legislative bodies, oversight officials, investors, and creditors.

The FASB established accounting objectives with the focal point being the provision of useful information to users. FASB's Statement of Financial Accounting Concepts No. 1, *Objectives of Financial Reporting by Business Enterprises*, described the three main objectives as follows: 1) provide information about economic resources, claims to resources, and changes in resources and claims; 2) provide information useful in assessing the

Encyclopedia of Public Administration and Public Policy
DOI: 10.1081/E-EPAP 120010723

amount, timing, and uncertainty of future cash flows; and 3) provide information useful in making investment and credit decisions.[2]

The FASAB issued Statement of Federal Financial Accounting Concepts No. 1, *Objectives of Federal Financial Reporting*, detailing four objectives, which focused on accountability. Financial statements prepared by federal government agencies should be based upon the objectives of budgetary integrity, operating performance, stewardship, and systems and controls.[3] A federal government agency's compliance with applicable budgets, laws, and regulations is the focus of the objective budgetary integrity in reporting, while the objective of operating performance suggests the importance of evaluating and reporting an entity's service efforts, costs, and accomplishments. The remaining objectives also reflect a need for accountability over a government's operations and its financial systems and controls.

THE HIERARCHY OF GAAP

As shown, a variety of reference sources are available to finance officers, including official pronouncements of the FASB, GASB, and the FASAB, pronouncements and practice guides from other organizations, such as the SEC and the AICPA, and even accounting textbooks. Given this variety, how does a finance officer decide which rule, practice, or pronouncement should predominate? The AICPA, in Statement on Auditing Standards No. 69, "*The Meaning of Present Fairly in Conformity with Generally Accepted Accounting Principles in the Independent Auditor's Report*," provided finance officers with guidelines to use in determining when a set of rules takes precedence over all the others.[4] Table 1 shows the hierarchy that should be followed in the selection process for state and local governments and for nongovernment organizations. An amendment to SAS No. 69, SAS No. 91, *Federal GAAP Hierarchy*, provides a hierarchy for federal governmental entities as illustrated in Table 2.[5] In all three cases, Level 1 sources, which primarily include official pronouncements of the governing board, take precedence over all other possible GAAP sources. If no Level 1 source is available, Level 2 sources are consulted, then Level 3, Level 4, and, finally, Level 5.

In each case, official pronouncements from the governing organizations take precedence over those issued by other organizations. For instance, state and local governments must follow relevant GASB pronouncements, unless specifically approved by GASB. If no pronouncements exist on the subject, other sources, including FASB pronouncements, can be utilized.

Table 1 GAAP hierarchy summary

State and local governments	Nongovernmental entities
1. GASB Statements and Interpretations; AICPA and FASB pronouncements if made applicable to state and local governments by the GASB	1. FASB Statements and Interpretations, APB Opinions, and AICPA Accounting Research Bulletins
2. GASB Technical Bulletins; AICPA Industry Audit and Accounting Guides and Statements of Position if made applicable to state and local governments by the GASB	2. FASB Technical Bulletins, AICPA Industry Audit and Accounting Guides, and AICPA Statements of Position
3. Consensus positions of the GASB Emerging Issues Task Force (when created); AICPA Practice Bulletins if made applicable to state and local governments by the AICPA	3. AICPA Practice Bulletins and consensus positions of the FASB Emerging Issues Task Force
4. Implementation guides published by the GASB staff; widely recognized and prevalent industry practices of state and local governments	4. AICPA accounting interpretations, "Qs and As" published by the FASB staff, as well as industry practices widely recognized and prevalent
5. Other accounting literature, including GASB Concepts Statements; FASB Concept Statements; AICPA Issues Papers; International Accounting Standards Committee Statements; pronouncements of other professional associations or regulatory agencies; AICPA Technical Practice Aids, and accounting textbooks, handbooks, and articles	5. Other accounting literature, including FASB Concepts Statements; APB Statements; AICPA Issues Paper; International Accounting Standards Committee Statements; GASB Statements, Interpretations, and Technical Bulletins; pronouncements of other professional associations or regulatory agencies; AICPA *Technical Practice Aids*; and accounting textbooks, handbooks, and articles

SOURCE: SAS No. 69, The meaning of present fairly in conformity with generally accepted accounting principles in the independent auditor's report.

Table 2 Federal GAAP hierarchy

1. FASAB Statements and Interpretations plus AICPA and FASB pronouncements if made applicable to federal governmental entities by a FASAB Statement or Interpretation

2. FASAB Technical Bulletins and the following pronouncements if specifically made applicable to federal governmental entities by the AICPA and cleared by the FASAB: AICPA Industry Audit and Accounting Guides and AICPA Statements of Position

3. AICPA Accounting Standards Executive Committee (AcSEC) Practice Bulletins if specifically made applicable to federal governmental entities and cleared by the FASAB and Technical Releases of the Accounting and Auditing Policy Committee of the FASAB

4. Implementation guides published by the FASAB staff and practices that are widely recognized and prevalent in the federal government

5. Other accounting literature, including FASAB Concepts Statements; FASB Concepts Statements; GASB Statements, Interpretations, Technical Bulletins, and Concepts Statements; AICPA Issues Papers; International Accounting Standards of the International Accounting Standards Committee; pronouncements of other associations or regulatory agencies; AICPA *Technical Practice Aids*; and accounting textbooks, handbooks, and articles

SOURCE: SAS No. 91, Federal GAAP hierarchy.

EXAMPLES OF GAAP FOR STATE AND LOCAL GOVERNMENTS

The following sections describe a few of the accounting rules and regulations considered GAAP for state and local governments.

Fund Accounting

Because accountability is a key component in government financial reporting, state and local governments are strongly encouraged to use funds in the accounting for resources. Used to demonstrate compliance with legal and contractual requirements, a fund is a separate accounting and fiscal entity with a self-balancing set of accounts from which financial statements can be prepared. Because the use of funds provides for more control over resources, most state and local governments utilize more than one fund, depending upon the source and use of those resources. Essentially, each fund maintains its own set of accounting records, interacting with other funds whenever appropriate. Further, because each fund maintains a separate set of accounts, each fund also generates its own set of financial statements.

Three main categories of funds exist: governmental, proprietary, and fiduciary. Which fund a government uses is determined by the source and use of the resources involved. Governmental funds are utilized for basic government activities financed primarily from taxes and intergovernmental grants. Proprietary funds are for business-type activities that generate most resources through the collection of user fees. Fiduciary funds account for resources held by the government, or its agent, in trust for a third party.

Resource flows for the basic operations of state and local governments are accounted for in a governmental fund. In particular, the majority of the resources are accounted for in the general fund, a subfund of the governmental funds. Typically, the general fund is the largest and most active of all funds. For some small governments, it could be the only fund utilized. General fund resources that have been legally restricted for specific purposes typically are accounted for as a special revenue fund, another subfund of the governmental funds. A government that provides services to the public at large and charges a fee for the services could account for the resources in an enterprise fund, a subfund of the proprietary funds. A separate enterprise fund would be used for each "business," maintaining increased control and responsibility over the fund's resources. An agency fund, a subfund of the fiduciary funds, may be used to account for sales tax monies collected by a city for the state government. Soon after the monies go into the fund, they are transferred out to the state government.

Modified Accrual Accounting

Because governments are concerned with how resources are consumed, and not the bottom line, the basis for accounting for those resources differs from that of for-profit organizations. For-profit organizations utilize full accrual accounting that requires an entity to recognize revenue when it has been earned, that is, when the related goods and services have been provided. The revenues also must be measurable, i.e., the amount of the revenue is known. In addition, full accrual accounting requires the recognition, or recording, of an expense, whenever a cost is incurred that helps to generate revenue. This provides for an appropriate matching of revenues and expenses in the financial statements and results in a measurement of income for a specified period.

Under modified accrual accounting, revenue recognition follows that of full accrual accounting, with one major caveat. In addition to being earned and measurable, revenue must be available to finance expenditures of the current fiscal period. GASB Statement No. 33, *Accounting and Reporting for Nonexchange Transactions*, stated "available means collectible within the current period or soon enough thereafter to be used to pay liabilities of the current period."[6] Full accrual accounting only requires a reasonable assurance that the cash will be collected, while modified accrual accounting provides greater assurance that the cash will be available to pay liabilities when they come due. So how does a government interpret "available"? GASB only provided a specific definition of "available" for property tax revenues. Existing standards, in particular, GASB Interpretation No. 5, *Property Tax Revenue Recognition in Governmental Funds*, provided that if property taxes are collected more than 60 days after the end of the fiscal year, they may not be recognized in that fiscal year, because they cannot be used to pay the current liabilities.[7] They must be recognized in the year of the collection. Because no specific guidelines exist for other types of revenues, some governments have established time periods such as 30 days, 60 days, or longer for their recognition.

The recognition of expenses also differs under modified accrual accounting. For instance, governmental funds following modified accrual accounting recognize expenditures, not expenses. Expenditures are defined as decreases in net current financial resources, such as cash, while expenses are a reduction in overall net assets, such as the depreciation of a building or the use of supplies. Existing standards require the recognition of an expenditure when cash is paid out or when a liability has been incurred for goods or services received. For instance, if a local government buys a new fire truck, whether with cash or on credit, an expenditure is recognized immediately. An asset may be recorded but in a separate fund from the expenditure. A for-profit organization would recognize an asset and then expense a portion of the cost each year for the remainder of the truck's economic useful life.

The Governmental Reporting Entity

Many state and local governments are affiliated with independent legal entities that provide them with essential services the governments do not provide for themselves. For instance, a local government may determine a need for a wastewater treatment plant. Once it is established, the governing board could choose to operate the plant as an integral part of the government and account for it as an enterprise fund. Recall that an enterprise fund is a government business that charges a fee for its services. Under this approach, any debt entered into by the plant would affect the debt levels of the whole government—not just the treatment plant. If the wastewater treatment plant was established as an independent legal entity, however, and incurred its own debt, the direct financial effect on the primary government may be minimal.

Obviously, a plant treated as an enterprise fund would be included in a government's financial statements. But what about the independent legal entity? If the entity was established by the government, should the plant be included as part of the government's financial statements? GASB Statement No. 14, *The Financial Reporting Entity*, was issued to help resolve potential problems of this type, and it specified criteria for determining what economic entities should be included in a reporting entity.[8]

Specifically, a financial reporting entity consists of a primary government and any component units associated with that primary government. GASB No. 14 defines a primary government as "any state government or general purpose local government (municipality or county)."[8] A component unit is a legally separate government for which the primary government is financially accountable or an organization whose relationship with the primary government is such that if it were excluded from the primary government's financial statements, they would be misleading and incomplete.

Once a component unit has been determined to be part of the reporting entity, GASB No. 14 also provides criteria as to how it should be included in the financial statements. Depending upon the relationship between the two entities, a component unit is blended into or discretely presented on the financial statements of the primary government. A very close relationship between the two entities results in a set of blended financial statements. A superficial evaluation of the blended statements would not suggest the existence of a component unit, because the financial information of the component unit is fully integrated into the data of the primary government. The financial data for a discretely presented component unit, however, is reported on the face of the financial statements in a separate column from the primary government's information with a total column used to indicate the overall effect of the two consolidated entities.[8]

The Financial Reporting Model

In June 1999, GASB issued what many consider to be one of the most important statements in the history of governmental accounting. GASB Statement No. 34, *Basic Financial Statements—and Management's Discussion and Analysis—for State and Local Governments*, radically changed the way financial statements for state and local governments are presented.[9] Previously, governments prepared individual financial statements for each fund category. With the implementation of GASB No. 34, governments still prepare fund financial statements, but government-wide statements also must be generated. Government-wide statements are designed to give users an overview of the financial position of the government by consolidating the governmental and business-type activities into a statement of net assets and a statement of activities. In addition, these statements must be presented using full accrual accounting, while fund-based financial statements follow full or modified accrual accounting, depending on the fund. Because the governmental financial information is presented using both the full accrual and modified accrual bases of accounting, a reconciliation between the two is required to be presented.[9]

GASB No. 34 also dramatically changed how a government reports its infrastructure, which is defined as long-lived capital assets such as bridges, roads, and tunnels that have economic useful lives significantly longer than most other capital assets. Previously, governments were not required to report this information in their financial statements. The adoption of GASB No. 34, however, results in the inclusion of infrastructure on a government's financial statements. Because many governments may not have maintained accurate records of the cost of their infrastructure, GASB No. 34 allows the use of estimates for retroactive reporting of infrastructure. New assets must be reported at actual cost.[9]

In addition, governments must record depreciation for their infrastructure on the government-wide financial statements. Two options for depreciation exist. First, a government may record depreciation in a manner similar to other capital assets—over a fixed period of time using a method such as straight-line depreciation. Each year, depreciation expense and accumulated depreciation would be recorded for the infrastructure. Or, a government may choose to use the modified approach to infrastructure reporting. Essentially, if a government chooses the modified approach, it chooses not to depreciate. However, the government is committed to the maintenance of accurate, up-to-date inventory records of its infrastructure and is committed to preserving the assets at a prescribed condition level. Any expenditures made to extend the life of the infrastructure would be charged to expense and recognized in the period incurred.[9]

CONCLUSION

In simple terms, GAAP is a set of rules for reporting financial information. Whether for a governmental, nonprofit, or a for-profit entity, financial statements prepared following GAAP provide users with assurances as to the reliability of the information and give preparers some guidelines to follow in the creation of those reports.

REFERENCES

1. GASB Concepts Statement No. 1. *Objectives of Financial Reporting*; Govermental Accounting Standards Board, 1987.
2. FASB Statement of Financial Accounting Concepts No. 1. *Objectives of Financial Reporting by Business Enterprises*; Financial Accounting Standards Board, 1978.
3. Statement of Federal Financial Accounting Concepts No. 1. *Objectives of Federal Financial Reporting*; Federal Accounting Standards Advisory Board, 1993.
4. AICPA Statement on Auditing Standards No. 69. *The Meaning of Present Fairly in Conformity with Generally Accepted Accounting Principles in the Independent Auditor's Report*; American Institute of Certified Public Accountants, 1992.
5. AICPA Statement on Auditing Standards No. 91. *Federal GAAP Hierarchy*; American Institute of Certified Public Accountants, 1999.
6. GASB Statement No. 33. *Accounting and Financial Reporting for Nonexchange Transactions*; Govermental Accounting Standards Board, 1998.
7. GASB Interpretation No. 5. *Property Tax Revenue Recognition in Governmental Funds—An Interpretation of NCGA Statement 1 and an Amendment of NCGA Interpretation 3*; Govermental Accounting Standards Board, 1997.
8. GASB Statement No. 14. *The Financial Reporting Entity*; Govermental Accounting Standards Board, 1991.
9. GASB Statement No. 34. *Basic Financial Statements—and Management's Discussion and Analysis—for State and Local Governments*; Govermental Accounting Standards Board, 1999.

Global Ethics and Corruption

Leo W. J. C. Huberts
Vrije Universiteit, Amsterdam, The Netherlands

INTRODUCTION

Corruption, ethics, and integrity have become important issues in the practice and theory of politics and public administration. This has led to more awareness and knowledge of the ethical or moral dimension of politics and the causes of and solutions for corruption in politics and administration at the national as well as the international levels. Elements of that knowledge and awareness to be discussed include the meaning of concepts, such as corruption, ethics, and integrity; the content of the moral dimension (the values at stake); the causes of (the level of) corruption in different nations; the solutions proposed to curb corruption and to safeguard integrity; and the initiatives by international actors that aim to contribute to that purpose.

CORRUPTION, ETHICS, AND INTEGRITY

Clarity about concepts like corruption, ethics, and integrity is important, certainly when it concerns public debate, policy making, and theory development on an international level.[1–3]

Public corruption is often defined as involving behavior on the part of officials in the public sector, whether politicians or civil servants, in which they improperly and unlawfully enrich themselves, or those associated with them, by misusing the public power entrusted to them. A brief definition is the abuse of public office for private gain. Corruption, then, is a specific type of violation against the moral norms and values for political and administrative behavior. *Ethics* refer to the collection of values and norms, functioning as standards or yardsticks for assessing the integrity of one's conduct. The moral nature of these principles refers to what is judged as right, just, or good (conduct). Values are principles or standards of behavior that should have a certain weight in choice of action (what is good to do or bad to omit doing). Norms state what is morally correct behavior in a certain situation. Values and norms guide the choice of action and provide a moral basis for justifying or evaluating what we do.

Public integrity denotes the quality of acting in accordance with the moral values, norms, and rules accepted by the body politic and the public. A number of integrity violations or forms of public misconduct can be distinguished: corruption including bribing, nepotism, cronyism, and patronage; fraud and theft; conflict of interest through assets, jobs, or gifts; manipulation of information; discrimination and sexual harassment; improper methods for noble causes (using immoral means to achieve moral ends); the waste and abuse of resources; and private time misconduct.

In this framework, corruption is a type of integrity violation; however, "corruption" is often also used as the umbrella concept, covering all or most types of integrity violation or unethical behavior.

VALUES AND NORMS TO BE PROTECTED

There are numerous attempts to sum up the basic values that might be seen as constituting public-sector ethics.[4,5] A well-known ethical framework for public officials was developed in the United Kingdom by the Committee on Standards in Public Life chaired by Lord Nolan.[4] The Nolan Committee sketched "Seven Principles of Public Life." Holders of public office should decide because of the public interest; private interests or obligations to outside individuals and organizations should have no influence (selflessness and integrity). They should make choices on the basis of merit (objectivity); they are accountable for their decisions and actions (accountability); and they should be as open as possible (openness and transparency). Holders of public office have a duty to declare any private interests and resolve possible conflicts of interest (honesty). They should promote and support these principles by leadership and example (leadership). The Nolan values have been discussed and used in many contexts, for example by the Committee of Independent Experts that reported on fraud, mismanagement, and nepotism in the European Commission of the European Union in 1999 (leading to the resignation of the whole commission in March 1999). Many of the values mentioned can also be found in the codes of conduct of governmental organizations as well as in the United Nations International Code of Conduct for Public Officials. The latter contains a set of basic standards of integrity and performance expected from public officials, with "wide acceptance on the basis of experience acquired in various countries." The code includes general principles: public

Encyclopedia of Public Administration and Public Policy
DOI: 10.1081/E-EPAP 120010933

officials shall act in the public interests, function efficiently and effectively, in accordance with the law and with integrity, and shall be attentive, fair, and impartial. The code also contains rules concerning conflicts of interest and disqualification, disclosure of assets, acceptance of gifts and other favors, confidential information, and political activity.

Discussion

An important question is always how important the values actually are for the people working in the organizations with often impressive mission statements and codes of conduct. When politicians tell researchers that honesty and openness are among the values that are most important for their work, this, of course, does not mean these indeed are the central values in actual political decision making.

In the code of the United Nations, values such as efficiency and effectiveness are added to the values more often associated with "moral" values and norms like honesty, selflessness, openness, and accountability. The relationship between these two sets of values has long been a topic in the international political as well as scientific debate. The dominant view in the global discussion nowadays is that state corruption undermines state efficiency and that good governance is a precondition for financial support and developmental aid. On the national level, a comparable view is dominant, although research shows that anticorruption policies and regulation can also harm efficient and credible government.

Another subject to be mentioned is the relationship between the core values of the public and the private realm. How do public- and private-sector values relate to one another? The answer is not an easy one. In the literature, contradictory visions exist. On the one hand, there is the thesis that public and business sector ethics share basic values and norms (as integrity, honesty, and efficiency).[6] On the other hand, there is the opposite view that stresses that there is a fundamental conflict between the moral foundations of politics and commerce and that organizations will sink in "functional and moral quagmires...when they confuse their own appropriate moral system with the other."[7] Warnings against the confusion of morals often lead to doubts about practices from the commercial world when these practices are to be applied in the public sector.

EXTENT OF THE PROBLEM IN A GLOBAL CONTEXT

Empirical research by social scientists on the extent of public corruption and fraud is, by definition, complicated. Corruption is crime without a (recognizable) victim, and the corruptor and the corrupted benefit from secrecy. Most empirical data, therefore, concern criminal cases involving corruption: what has been discovered, investigated, prosecuted, and convicted can most easily be counted. Additionally, information has been collected on opinions on the extent and seriousness of the corruption problem. The most famous research has been done by Göttingen University and Transparency International. Since 1995, a corruption perception index (CPI) is published, based on the perceptions of the degree of corruption as seen by businesspeople, risk analysts, and the general public. Some countries have the reputation of being very corrupt, and as might be expected, most of these are developing countries like Nigeria and Indonesia

Table 1 Corruption perceptions index—transparency international, 2001 (10 highly clean–1 highly corrupt)

Country	2001 CPI score
Least Corrupt Countries	
Finland	9.9
Denmark	9.5
New Zealand	9.4
Iceland	9.2
Singapore	9.2
Sweden	9.0
Canada	8.9
Netherlands	8.8
Luxembourg	8.7
Norway	8.6
Most Corrupt Countries	
Bangladesh	0.4[a]
Nigeria	1.0
Uganda	1.9
Indonesia	1.9
Kenya	2.0
Cameroon	2.0
Bolivia	2.0
Azerbaijan	2.0
Ukraine	2.1
Tanzania	2.2
Other Countries	
United Kingdom	8.3
United States	7.6
Japan	7.1
South Africa	4.8
Brazil	4.0
China	3.5
India	2.7

[a]Transparency International adds that the Bangladesh data should be viewed with extra caution.
Source: Transparency International and Göttingen University, http://www.gwdg.de/~uwvw (August 2001); also: http://www.transparancy.org/documents/cpi/2001 (27 June 2001).

Table 2 Corruption perceptions index, 1988–2000 (10 highly clean – 1 highly corrupt)

	1988–1992	**1996**	**1998**	**2000**	**2001**
Sweden	8.7	9.1	9.5	9.4	9.0
Australia	8.2	8.6	8.7	8.3	8.5
United Kingdom	8.3	8.4	8.7	8.7	8.3
United States	7.8	7.7	7.5	7.8	7.6
Japan	7.3	7.1	5.8	6.4	7.1
Brazil	3.5	3.0	4.0	3.9	4.0
China	4.7	2.4	3.5	3.1	3.5
India	2.9	2.6	2.9	2.8	2.7
Indonesia	0.6	2.7	2.0	1.7	1.9
Nigeria	0.6	0.7	1.9	1.2	1.0

Source: Transparency International and Göttingen University, http://www.gwdg.de/~uwvw (August 2001).

or transitional (Eastern European) states like the Ukraine. Northern European countries are perceived as being among the less corrupt (Table 1).

The image of countries appears to be rather stable. Once a reputation for corruptness is established, it takes time and efforts to change (Table 2).

Corruption in Business and Government

Corruption research often is research on public-sector corruption. This suggests that the problem is more prominent in government than in business. However, this idea needs to be questioned.

First, it is clear that corruption involves a corruptor and a corrupted. Many bribe givers are business organizations. In business, the possibility of profit is often more important than integrity and ethics, which until recently, was supported by governments of industrialized countries (the costs of bribes have long been tax deductible).

The Transparency International Bribe Payers Survey concerns the willingness of companies from leading exporting states to pay bribes to public officials to win or retain business. It shows that companies from countries like China, South Korea, Taiwan, Italy, and Malaysia are most likely to pay bribes. Additionally, the survey shows that the scores for countries like the United Kingdom, the United States, and Japan are lower than the corruption scores for the countries. Bribing a foreign official seems more acceptable than bribing at home.

Second, survey research shows that corruption experts in higher-income countries differ from their colleagues in poorer countries concerning the prominence of corruption in the public and private sectors. Respondents from the lower-income countries think corruption is much more prominent in the public sector, while

experts from higher-income countries find the opposite to be the case.

CAUSES OF CORRUPTION

Research shows that a conglomerate of social, economic, political, organizational, and individual causal factors are important to explain cases of public corruption and fraud in a country.[2,8,9]

Among the more important political causes are the values and norms of politicians and civil servants and their commitment to public integrity, the organizational quality of the public sector (working conditions, control, and auditing), the relationship between the state and the business sector, and a number of social factors (e.g., the presence of organized crime and the content of social norms and values).

These factors are important to explain the corruption in higher- and lower-income countries, but an ample explanation also has to take into account the differences between these countries. A number of factors related to developmental problems are of crucial importance to lower-income countries.[10] Economic failure and poverty, poor conditions for human development (schooling, health), and corruption are interrelated. For example, it is clear that low salaries and bad working conditions in the public sector can be disastrous for the possibility and the willingness to behave ethically.

For countries going through a process of privatization, liberalization, and democratization, the period of transition offers extra possibilities for corruption.[8,10] It takes time to establish a more stable political and economic system that is able to curb corruption.

SOLUTIONS AND THEIR EFFECTIVENESS

It is always necessary to relate anticorruption strategies to characteristics of the actors involved (and the environments in which they operate). There is not one concept and program of good governance for all countries and organizations, there is no "one right way."[10,11] There are many initiatives, and most are tailored to specific contexts; societies and organizations will have to seek their own solutions.

Yet, they can learn from the experiences of others and the international search for practices based on serious and well-evaluated programs. There are examples of organizations and societies that succeeded in radically curbing corruption. Hong Kong's Independent Commission Against Corruption is often presented as an example for other countries. This city managed to curb the corruption that was prevalent in the 1960s.[11]

Concepts and programs like National Integrity Systems (Transparency International), The Ethics Infrastructure (OECD), and A Framework for Integrity (World Bank) offer numerous methods and institutions to curb corruption and promote integrity.[1,12–15] The main elements are summarized.

The overall *goals* should include development strategies that yield benefits to the nation as a whole, including its poorest and most vulnerable members, and not just to well-placed elites. Additionally, it is important that public services be efficient and effective and that government function under law, with citizens protected from arbitrariness (including abuses of human rights).

Many institutions and activities are important in the struggle against corruption. Leadership counts—the research is unanimous on this. Embodying the political will to fight corruption, leaders set the tone through their policies and the examples they present. In the political system, parliament as representative of the people and watchdog of political power is at the center of the struggle to attain and sustain good governance and to fight corruption. An independent, impartial, and informed judiciary holds a central place in the realization of just, honest, open, and accountable government. The public service is important for its services as well as for the protection of the public decision-making process (including the system of public procurement, often vulnerable because of its opportunities for corruption). Integrity is a crucial element of professionalism. People should be given a feeling of pride in their work and that deviance undermines the core of the profession.

A powerful anticorruption device also is the simple establishment of sound financial management practices, including a timely and efficient accounting system combined with punctual, professional review by internal and independent auditors. Important institutions are also an effective Auditor-General as a watchdog over financial integrity and the credibility of reported information, an ombudsman who can recommend improvements to procedures and practices and act as an incentive for public officials to keep their files in order, and Independent Anticorruption Agencies to raise awareness among the public, to stimulate prevention, and to detect and investigate corruption cases. The availability of resources, their independence from management, and the availability of mechanisms of transparency and accountability are important factors for the success of these institutions. Of importance is a judicious balance between positive and negative social control. An extreme accent on control can be extremely counterproductive. An anticorruption campaign in New York City fostered its own pathology of excessive rules and procedures, paralysis of decision making, and the undermining of quality.[16] To safeguard integrity presupposes that attention is being paid to group and organizational culture (norms, values, and perceptions), including training and education in ethical dilemmas and the development of codes of conduct.

Additionally, it is important that the media and civil society play a role. Information and public awareness (the "right to know"), are linked inextricably to accountability, the central goal of any democratic system of government. The principal vehicle for taking information to the public is an independent and free media. The role for civil society must be to claim and defend its own values and not leave this integral function to those in power.

INTERNATIONAL AND SUPRANATIONAL INITIATIVES

Nowadays, a lot of attention is being paid to corruption and ethics in international fora. Anticorruption congresses and conferences with thousands of participants are no exception. Conventions and treaties have been prepared, signed, and implemented, in international relations, conditions of good governance have become an important topic. Governments are more aware of the importance of their national integrity system. Many global and international initiatives are worth mentioning.

The United Nations' General Assembly Resolution on Corruption in 1997 reaffirmed its concern at the seriousness of the corruption problem and adopted the International Code of Conduct for Public Officials. The resolution recommended that member states use the code as a tool to guide their efforts against corruption.[10] In 2001, the foundations for a United Nations Convention Against Corruption were discussed in The Hague at the Second Global Forum on Fighting Corruption and Safeguarding Integrity. Within the United Nations, the Development Program approaches the issue of corruption as a governance problem, and it has made the minimization of corruption central to achieving the organization's overall purpose of alleviating poverty and attaining social and people-centered sustainable development.[10]

In line with political developments, major international financial and economic institutions like the World Bank and the International Monetary Fund have made corruption their topic. The World Bank changed its policies in 1996, and the cancer of corruption is seen as a crucial problem for economic development. Its "Pillars of National Integrity" are interdependent and include the rule of law, sustainable development, and quality of life. Corruption and fraud have become important topics within bank-financed projects as well as in the country assistance strategies and country lending considerations.[10,15]

The Organization for Economic Co-Operation and Development, with 29 member states, representing the industrialized world, has made anticorruption initiatives and ethics and integrity policies an important aspect of its work.[13,14] The concepts of an "Ethics Infrastructure" summarizes OECD's view with core elements of political commitment, workable codes of conduct, professional socialization mechanisms, an ethics coordinating body, supportive public service conditions (decent working conditions), an effective legal framework, efficient accountability mechanisms, and an active civil society. The OECD supports its pleas with research and analysis on the ethics measures of its member countries. In the international arena, the OECD's main contribution has been the 1997 OECD Convention on Combating Bribery of Foreign Public Officials in International Business Transactions. The Convention was signed by all member countries and came into force in 1999. Its main achievement is that it made bribing a foreign public official a criminal offense in many countries (while in the past, this bribe was even tax deductible in several of the OECD countries).

Transparency International, based in Berlin, is a nongovernmental international organization against corruption with branches in roughly 70 countries. It favors a holistic approach to a national integrity system.[1,12] Although each country or region is unique in its own history and culture, its political system, and its stage of economic and social development, similarities exist, and experience and lessons are often transferable. Transparency International proposes a National Integrity System as a comprehensive method of fighting corruption. It comprises eight pillars (public awareness, public anticorruption strategies, public participation, watchdog agencies, the judiciary, the media, the private sector, and international cooperation) which are interdependent. Every 2 years, Transparency International organizes the International Anti-Corruption Conference (IACC).

The mentioned initiatives are part of a more general trend toward anticorruption policies, as, for example, is also shown by the Organization of American States (Inter-American Convention Against Corruption), the European Union, the Council of Europe (and its Group of States Against Corruption *GRECO*), the Global Coalition for Africa, and the International Chamber of Commerce.[10,14–15]

Criticism

Corruption, ethics, and integrity have become more important topics in international and national political, economic, and social forums, but this does not mean there exists an overall consensus on concepts, causes, and policies. Criticism can still be heard on a number of subjects.

First, there is the question of which interests are best served by the anticorruption initiatives.[2,10] Optimists see it as a win–win situation: the interests of multinational corporations are served as well as the interests of the peoples of developing countries. Others argue that initiatives of institutions like the World Bank and the International Monetary Fund contribute to the development in the direction of a global free market capitalism and that globalization of that type harms the poor and powerless.

Second, there is the contradiction between the general policy frameworks of, for example, the World Bank, and the notion that there is no "one right way." Countries are confronted with demands coming from the frameworks, and the room to adapt to national circumstances is limited.

This is related to a third comment. How much consensus is possible and desirable on the ethics of politics and administration? Many frameworks suggest that ethics is universal and based on global consensus. Others argue, however, that the frameworks reflect the values and norms of only a small part of the world.[3,15] More knowledge of the values and norms reflected in non-Western political and social thought and practice would be useful to come to a more precise picture.

CONCLUSION

A last remark concerns our knowledge of the extent of corruption in countries and the effectiveness of anticorruption methods and strategies. Most proposals and frameworks are based on experiences and knowledge of anticorruption practitioners and not on scientific evaluation. Although scientific knowledge has increased (as journals such as *Public Integrity* and *Crime, Law and Social Change* show), more comparative research will be necessary to come to more reliable conclusions on the effectiveness of strategies and methods. The same applies to our knowledge of the extent and mechanisms of bribery and corruption in countries.

INTERNET RESOURCES

a. Council of Europe (http://www.coe.int) and its program against corruption and organized crime: http://www.legal.coe.int/economiccrime; and the Group of States Against Corruption:http://greco.coe.int.

b. European Commission (http://europa.eu.int) and its codes of conduct: http://europa.eu.int/comm/codesofconduct/index_en.htm.

c. Independent Commission Against Corruption of Hong Kong: http://www.icac.org.hk; and New South Wales Australia: http://www.icac.nsw.gov.au.

d. International Monetary Fund: http://www. imf.org.

e. Organization of American States' (http://www.oas.org) anticorruption efforts, including model laws and Inter-American Convention Against Corruption.

f. Organization for Economic Co-operation and Development's (http://www.oecd.org) anti-corruption program for business and the public sector, and its general library.

g. Transparency International (http://www.transparency.org), *The TI Source Book*, and, with Göttingen University, the Internet Center for Corruption Research (http://www.gwdg.de/~uwvw/icr_head.htm), including Transparency Internatinal's *Corruption Perception Index*.

h. The UK Committee on Standards in Public Life: http://public.standards.gov.uk.

i. The United Nations (http://www.un.org) and http://magnet.undp.org for the Programme for Accountability and Transparency of the United Nations Development Programme.

j. The U.S. Office of Government Ethics (http://www.usoge.gov) on international developments in ethics (programs).

k. The World Bank's (http://www1.worldbank.org) public-sector program (http://www1.worldbank.org/publicsector/anticorrupt) and links.

ACKNOWLEDGMENT

I am very grateful for the assistance and suggestions offered by Professor Carol Lewis.

REFERENCES

1. Doig, A.; McIvor, S. *Transparency International, The National Integrity System. Concept and Practice. A Report by Transparancy International (TI) for the Global Forum II on Fighting Corruption and Safeguarding Integrity*; Transparency International: Berlin, 2001.

2. *Political Corruption. A Handbook*; Heidenheimer, A.J., Johnston, M., Levine, V.T., Eds.; Transaction Publishers: New Brunswick, 1989; 1016 pp.

3. *Coping with Corruption in a Borderless World. Proceedings of the Fifth International Anti-Corruption Conference*; Punch, M., Kolthoff, E., van der Vijver, K., van Vliet, B., Eds.; Kluwer Law and Taxation Publishers: Deventer, 1993; 172 pp.

4. Cooper, T.L., Ed.; *Handbook of Administrative Ethics*; Marcel Dekker: New York, 2001.

5. *Public Sector Ethics. Finding and Implementing Values*; Sampford, C., Preston, N., Bois, C.-A., Eds.; The Federation Press: Annandale and Routledge, London, 1998.

6. Lawton, A. *Ethical Management for the Public Services*; Open University Press: Buckingham, 1998.

7. Jacobs, J. *Systems of Survival. A Dialogue on the Moral Foundations of Commerce and Politics*; Hodder & Stoughton: London, 1992.

8. *Political Corruption*; Heywood, P., Ed.; Blackwell: Oxford, 1997; 250 pp.

9. Klitgaard, R. *Controlling Corruption*; University of California Press: Berkeley, 1988.

10. UNDP United Nations Development Programme. *Corruption and Integrity Improvement Initiatives in Developing Countries*; UNDP: New York, 1998; 174 pp.

11. Huberts, L.W.J.C. Anticorruption strategies: The Hong Kong model in international context. Public Integrity **2000**, 2 (3), 211–228.

12. Pope, J. *Confronting Corruption: The Elements of a National Integrity System (TI Source book 2000)*; Transparency International: Berlin, 2000; 364 pp. (also at http://www.transparency.org).

13. OECD Organizaton of Economic Co-operation and Development. *Trust in Government. Ethics Measures in OECD Countries*; OECD: Paris, 2000; 329 pp.

14. OECD Organizaton of Economic Co-operation and Development. *No Longer Business as Usual. Fighting Bribery and Corruption*; OECD: Paris, 2000; 276 pp.

15. *Korruption im internationalen Geschäftsverkehr. Bestandsaufnahme. Bekämpfung. Prävention*; Pieth, M., Eigen, P., Eds.; Luchterhand: Neuwied, Kriftel, 1999; 735 pp.

16. Anechiarico, F.; Jacobs, J.B. *The Pursuit of Absolute Integrity. How Corruption Control Makes Government Ineffective*; University of Chicago Press: Chicago, 1996; 274 pp.

Governance Networks

Robert Agranoff
Indiana University, Bloomington, Indiana, U.S.A.

Michael McGuire
University of North Texas, Denton, Texas, U.S.A.

INTRODUCTION

Governance networks refer to formal and informal structures comprised of representatives from governmental and nongovernmental agencies working interdependently to jointly formulate and implement policies and programs, usually through their respective organizations. These networks are a function of "differentiated polities," characterized by institutional and functional specialization. They bring the nonprofit and for-profit sectors together with government in a number of policy arenas, including economic development, health care, criminal justice, human services, information systems, rural development, environmental protection, biotechnology, transportation, and education. The activities of governance are purposeful efforts to guide, steer, control, or manage, in which public and private actors do not act separately but in conjunction, operating as a network. Governance refers to the patterns that emerge from the governing activities of the actors, e.g., coregulation, costeering, coproduction, cooperative management and public–private partnerships.[1,2]

EXAMPLES OF A GOVERNANCE NETWORK

Three different types of governance networks demonstrate the range of collaborative activities undertaken. First, Sematech, an acronym for semiconductor manufacturing technology, is a public–private development partnership involving the Defense Advanced Research Projects Agency of the U.S. Department of Defense and 14 information technology manufacturers, who jointly invest equal amounts of money in basic research and development designed to restore U.S. leadership in the computer chip industry. Sematech has focused its efforts on a prototype chip fabrication plant that leads to the high-tech equipment that serve as a testing venue for new American precompetitive technologies. The research and development effort improves the competitive stance of all partners. This approach has allowed all of the potentially competing partners to remain involved and invested, and

it indirectly serves the Defense Department's needs for research and development.

Second, a less formal set of governance networks operate in Michigan in order to create the "Gold Collar" jobs needed to emphasize strategic priorities in advanced manufacturing, information technology, and life sciences. Implemented by its state agency, the Michigan Economic Development Corporation, a number of strategic alliances have been created with the automotive industry, information technology companies, pharmaceutical research centers, medical centers, university research centers, engineering schools, and others. In addition, the state agency staff promotes eight industry cluster roundtables (e.g., automotive, food products, forest products) designed to identify common problems and opportunities, recommend policy and regulatory changes, share and develop technology, promote technical assistance, and forge other new working relationships.

Third, the Applegate Partnership of southern Oregon and northern California is a locally organized watershed governance network that promotes ecologically and financially responsible resource management. The partnership involves industry, conservation organizations, public natural resource agencies, and residents working together on land management efforts through community involvement and education. Applegate's "signature" project involved the development of a GIS system that integrated BLM, U.S. Forest Service, and county tax lot information.

BACKGROUND AND CONCEPTS

There are many forces that have led to the emergence of governance networks. One important factor is the changing nature of work from labor-based production and services to the integration of knowledge-based symbolic–analytic work, which places greater value on human capital. The basic challenge is that knowledge is specialized and must be integrated collaboratively to solve many problems, a core issue in change management. As a result, government agencies, once thought to be the monopolistic holders of key information and expertise relating to public

Encyclopedia of Public Administration and Public Policy
DOI: 10.1081/E-EPAP 120010870

Table 1 Iowa's rural policy academy: a governance network in action

Network actors	Antecedent programs	Academy aims	Key strategic areas	Sequence of activities	Highlights of results
1. Academy team.	-Rural Enterprise Fund	-Bottom-up rural development	-Business development: agricultural and electrical, nonelectrical machinery; 14 industry sectors identified	-Formation of team	-Increases in Agriculture Enterprise Fund to foster linkages with commodity groups, support livestock production policy network
-Iowa Department of Economic Development (DED) Rural Coordinator	-Infrastructure Planning	-Foster inter-agency and interorganiza-tional cooperation with existing programs—partnerships are key	-Agriculture: new production and marketing technology while addressing food safety and environmental protection; value-adding businesses	-Identification of key strategic issues	-Extension Service project on livestock facility retrofitting
-Director Iowa Department of Management and Budget Representative, Regional Councils	-Tourism Welcome Centers	-Focus on existing problems and future demands	-Health care: maintaining a viable rural health care system through partnerships between the state, private sector, and local leaders	-Workshop retreat: review public and private programs; analyze existing needs and program gaps; set priorities; explore alternative strategies; examine potential coordina-tion efforts	-Increased technology transfer funding
-Director, Iowa Agricultural Development Authority	-Rural Main Street	-State govern-ment's role is increasingly that of a facilitator and catalyst for action, rather than that of a direct and sole provider of a service	-Community leadership: assisting rural communities to develop local leaders and organizations designed to improve their growth and services	-Subsequent team meetings to sift issue areas and draft strategic documents	-Enhanced Rural Enterprise Fund
-Iowa Hospital Association Director	-Rural business incubators	-Comprehensive strategy with stakeholder involvement and support	-Government services/infrastruc-ture: maintain services that are sufficient to pro-mote growth; local governments taking innovative actions to better serve resi-dents and control their own destinies	-Five issue areas are identified and stakeholder work-groups are identified and developed for each area	-Rural leadership program shift to county community leadership clusters and linkages
-Area Devel-opment Group	-Rural leadership development	-Creation of an implementation plan		-Second retreat to refine the five issue areas	-Funding for major rural infrastructure assessment

(Continued)

Table 1 Iowa's rural policy academy: a governance network in action (*Continued*)

Network actors	Antecedent programs	Academy aims	Key strategic areas	Sequence of activities	Highlights of results
-Iowa Cooperatives Bankers' Association	-Agricultural diversification	-Legislative submission, incorporation in the governors budget, enactment		-Work groups meet to conduct environmental scan and to draft policy statements	-Task Force on "Government of the Future" with the focus on collaborative services and regional institutions authorized
-Federal–State Cooperative Extension Service	-Marketing efforts	-Program development by DED, Department of Public Health, Extension Service, regional centers, and many nongovernmental organizations		-Two days of focus group sessions held on each issue area, involving 25 to 30 persons per group	-Funding of plastics technology and graphic arts centers to promote small business networks
-Four legislators, two from each house, each party -Consultant/ facilitator (former legislator)	-Office of Rural Health -Regional trade and business centers (16)			-Drafting of final strategy -Introduction of strategic elements into state budget and legislative proposals	-Internet marketing consortium launched -Training program for rural bankers on nonagriculture lending
2. Work group representatives	-Technology transfer foundation				-Entrepreneurship development materials for Iowa schools
-State agency program heads	-Lottery funds for environmental projects				-Establishment of pilot community health system in one rural county
-Federal agency (USDA, SBA, EDA) staff located in Iowa	-Quality and productivity enhancement coalition				-Public–private task force on retention of health professionals
-General farm organizations (FarmBureau, Prairie Fire)	-Road funds to support economic development				
-State agricultural commodity organizations -Iowa State University, School of Planning and Design, School of Agriculture, Extension Service	-Fiber optic telecommunication system				

Source: From Iowa Rural Policy Academy.

issues, now only possess some of the information needed to solve problems.

A second factor is the changing nature of government. The twentieth century was a time of growth of welfare states and, consequently, government agencies and programs at national and subnational levels. The government took on more and more problems and created many new policy arenas. As public efforts grew, however, it became apparent that the government could not garner the resources, investments, expertise, or commitments needed to solve all public problems. Networks involving several organizations became one of a number of collaborative efforts to try to approach some of society's "wicked problems," or challenges that could not be handled by dividing them in simple pieces, in isolation from one another.[3] A related factor is the idea that government should not only collaborate or partner but also should take on more of a developmental or steering role, promoting, regulating, and encouraging various types of nongovernmental activity and operations. This philosophy has, in many fields, unfolded in the 1980s and 1990s, and it has led to greater variety in government–nongovernmental organizational interaction.

A number of academic research streams have also confirmed the importance of governance networks. The urban politics work of Clarence Stone on regime theory is perhaps most seminal. In his study of urban power, he concludes that in a fragmented, world where power, resources, knowledge, and the other means to solve problems are dispersed among many individuals and organizations, "the issue is how to bring about enough cooperation among disparate community elements to get things done—and to do so in the absence of an overarching command structure or a unifying system of thought." Governance is the power to combine the necessary elements toward a result, that is, the capacity to assemble and use needed resources for a policy initiative.[4]

Intergovernmental researchers have also recognized the importance of public and nonpublic networks, often operating in complex and overlapping fashions,[5,6] and in many ways, changing the traditional role of governments and their links with nongovernmental organizations[7] and with the various tools and strategies that lead to different public–private configurations.[8] A study by Radin and associates demonstrates how federal–state–private councils in rural development have recommended many program changes and demonstration approaches in governance.[9] In the same vein, research on economic development at the state and local levels has demonstrated how these governments enhance their economies by stimulating private sector action, engaging in partnerships with such organizations as chambers of commerce and industry groups, and working together on developmental policies in human resource development, technology advancement, and global marketing.[10–12] Finally, research in the environmental policy area also demonstrates

that new solutions to such problems as nonpoint source pollution (e.g., agricultural chemicals), estuary restoration, and forest management can be approached by formally and informally convening government agencies, conservation advocacy groups, industry representatives, land developers, and the scientific community into joint decision bodies.[13,14]

HOW GOVERNANCE NETWORKS OPERATE

How do governance networks function? Table 1 provides a live example of a formal effort to enhance rural development policy in Iowa. It was called a Rural Policy Academy, because it was part of a program of that name sponsored by the National Governor's Association. A small team guided the effort, led by two state officials, but it also involved several statewide nongovernmental organizations involved in agriculture, health, and economic development. Early in the process, the Academy added four state legislators as a means of enhancing its political support. The network brought in dozens of other stakeholders through its work groups in each of the five areas it chose to emphasize strategically. The Academy built upon some 14 existing state rural development programs, using a strategic planning approach that was designed from the start to influence policy and be implementable through state government and several nongovernmental stakeholders.

Through a series of retreat-workshops, the Iowa Academy identified the five core areas of emphasis: business development, agriculture and agribusiness, health care, community leadership, and government services and infrastructure. After the key issues were identified, subsequent retreats by the core team reviewed programs, set priorities, and drafted a strategic document. From there, the network was expanded in each of the five strategic areas to include the technical work groups comprised of a broadened group of stakeholders. Those groups ultimately developed a set of policy statements. These draft policy statements were discussed by sets of 25- to 30-person focus groups, who represented even more rural development stakeholders. Finally, the refined proposals were introduced into the state budget and into legislative proposals.

The results of the Academy effort were mixed, because the State of Iowa was facing a budget shortfall during the year of completion. Nevertheless, over a dozen program expansions and new programs were ultimately adopted, including enhancing various forms of venture capital, creating several new production networks and consortia, and redirecting other programs. Most important, many of these programs were implemented outside of state government, for example, the pilot rural health system, the Internet marketing consortium, the bankers training, and the rural leadership program. The Iowa Rural Policy

Academy demonstrates the concrete actions involved in solving public problems by governance networks.

GOVERNANCE NETWORK MANAGEMENT

Despite the prevalence of governance networks, less is known about how they are managed, because so much of the focus in public administration has been on the hierarchical governmental organization. A few important approaches can nevertheless be advanced. The overriding concern is that networks are not hierarchical and, thus, are not bound by legal authority or by the normal rules and procedures that bind single organizations. Moreover, the importance of knowledge or possession of some other resource, like financing or implementation ability, makes the administrative playing field different than that of a public bureaucracy.

It appears that network actors follow a sequence of activities that is different from the usual planning, organizing, staffing, directing, and so on. The process usually begins with *activation*, or identifying participants and stakeholders and tapping the disparate skills, knowledge, and resources. Then, *framing* follows, which is the process establishing and influencing the operating rules of the network, influencing the governance structures prevailing values and norms, and altering the perceptions of the participants. Next comes the *mobilizing* actions, involving getting the various governance stakeholders to sense a strategic purpose and to establish a common set of objectives. Finally, there are the *synthesizing* activities, that is, the acts of creating the environment and enhancing the conditions for favorable decisions related to the strategic purpose of the network.

Working in a network is behaviorally different than working in an organization. Instead of ''motivation,'' various forms of shared learning processes are key, which come from interagency task group development and lead to jointly arrived at solutions. Under normal circumstances, decisions are deliberative, creative, and group derived, as organization representatives shed some of their ideologies and personal ''baggage'' in order to forge redefined problems, a mutual course of action, a multiorganization implementation technology, and diversified methods of resource acquisition. Some argue that these processes are held together by a generally held belief in the overall purpose of the network, whereas others point to the importance of social capital, which is the stock or built-up reservoir of good will that flows from different interests and organizations working together for mutual productive gain. It is also widely recognized that trust, the obligation to be concerned with others' interests, is an important ingredient in network behavior.

The presence of collective decision making and shared learning does not mean that issues of power are absent in governance networks. Coequality is a principle that is often professed in networks but is hard to maintain. Beyond the facade of trust and collaboration, stronger partners may be able to take advantage of weaker partners. Some actors sit in positions where their knowledge, financial resources, organization position, or legal authority alters the balance of power. On the other hand, a governance network working together and making reasonable proposals can accrue a great deal of power to create new strategies and policies that carry the support of a wide range of organizations.[15]

''METAGOVERNMENT''

Operating in governance networks is obviously changing the nature of government organizations, at least in regard to that portion of its activities that relate to policies and programs that are shared with other organizations. Foremost, public agencies, or their representatives, become partners with other organization representatives in examining problems, establishing strategies, and formulating policy responses. Often, the public organization actor serves as the convener, but once the process begins, this person becomes one among many participants. Second, the public agency representative does not have nearly the monopoly or the corner on technical expertise that previous public administrators possessed. Many stakeholders, e.g., scientists, organizational researchers, interest groups, and advocacy groups, bring needed knowledge and information to the governance table. Third, resources are more dispersed. In the past, the government agency possessed the major allocation or appropriation needed to launch a program, and money (and indirectly control) was dispensed through a chain of agencies, public and nonpublic. Today, the resources are more dispersed throughout the network, as government increasingly tries to use its role in governance to leverage investments by a host of nongovernmental organizations.

Fourth, program implementation occurs through many of the same organizations that were involved in formulating strategies and policies. As government has taken on more of a guidance role, and has encouraged nongovernmental investments, the carrying out function is no longer exclusively through an intergovernmental chain of public organizations but involves a variety of grantees, contractees, and collaborating partners. Finally, some analysts have argued that this renders the government agency unimportant, powerless, and a bystander to a series of private actions. Governance networks change the role of government in democratic systems. Government agencies are not, however, marginal players in the multiple organization process. They remain important actors, because they continue to possess a legitimacy to approach public problems and policy solutions, retain important legal authority to set rules and norms, continue to contribute financial resources to programs, and retain some of the needed subject matter and scientific knowledge needed to approach problems. Government agencies are almost always key partners in governance networks.

It is important to note that the notion of democratic accountability may need to be reconceptualized in the light of multiorganizational decision making that lies largely outside of the formal organs of representative government.[16] There is no obvious principal or agent in network governance and no exigent authority to steer the activities of the network in harmony with elected officials. Interaction between civil servants and representatives of private interest groups, other governmental layers, and implementing organizations makes it hard for representative bodies to influence policy. Network governance may force a shift from concerns with hierarchical accountability to notions of responsibility, responsiveness, and the fostering of democratic ideals. Because an hierarchical control orientation is problematic for collaborative structures, some steps can be taken to maintain the flexibility of collaboration while ensuring accountability.[17] For example, collaborative processes can be developed as supplemental to, not exclusive of, normal decision-making processes. The activities of networked arrangements could be reviewed by independent, ostensibly objective, sources. Additionally, collaborative decision making can strive toward achieving agreed-upon performance measures that capture the intent of policy objectives, and the home agencies of collaborative decision makers can monitor and evaluate the network's progress toward achieving the desired objectives.

FUTURE OF GOVERNANCE NETWORKS

The future will put these collaborative decision structures at the core of organized efforts. Knowledge is an increasingly important resource, a new capital that resides in human resources or knowledge workers, who will continue to need some form of collective that will bring them together. Knowledge is nonhierarchical, in that if it is required for a situation, professional performance needs to be applied, regardless of organizational position, social status, or possession of wealth. As a result, portable knowledge application plus rapid access to information can and has led to the disintegration of large-scale organizations into more flexible structures, such as the identified partnerships, joint ventures, alliances, and other governance structures. In the future, several different types of organizations are expected to interlock along these lines. These trends will also accelerate the need for greater study of the new forms of organizing and operating. As Peter Drucker maintains, "Despite all the present talk of 'knowledge management,' no one yet really knows how to do it."[18] Finally, these structures will increasingly be used to deal with social problems. David Korten concludes that knowledge and reformation

have provided powerful new collective intelligence that can be used to master social and institutional discovery and innovation through problem solving.[19]

G

REFERENCES

1. Kooiman, J. Social-Political Governance. In *Modern Governance: New Government–Society Interactions*; Kooiman, J., Ed.; Sage: London, 1993; 1–2.
2. Rhodes, R.A.W. *Understanding Governance: Policy Networks, Governance, Reflexivity and Accountability*; Open University Press: Buckingham, 1997.
3. O'Toole, L.J. Treating networks seriously: Practical and research-based agendas in public administration. Public Adm. Rev. **1997**, *57* (1), 46.
4. Stone, C. *Regime Politics*; University Press of Kansas: Lawrence, KS, 1989; 227.
5. Agranoff, R.; McGuire, M. Multi-network management: Collaboration and the hollow state in local economic policy. J. Public Adm. Res. Theory **1998**, *8*, 67–91.
6. Meier, K.J.; O'Toole, L.J. Managerial strategies and behavior in networks: A model with evidence from U.S. public education. J. Public Adm. Res. Theory **2001**, *11* (3), 271–294.
7. Mandell, M. Community collaborations: Working through network structures. Policy Stud. Rev. **1999**, *16* (1), 42–64.
8. McGuire, M. Collaborative policy making and administration: The operational demands of local economic development. Econ. Dev. Q. **2000**, *14*, 276–291.
9. Radin, B.A.; Agranoff, R.; Bowman, A.O'M.; Buntz, G.G.; Ott, S.J.; Romzek, B.S.; Wilson, R.H. *New Governance for Rural America: Creating Intergovernmental Partnerships*; University Press of Kansas: Lawrence, KS, 1996.
10. Clarke, S.E.; Gaile, G.L. *The Work of Cities*; University of Minnesota Press: Minneapolis, 1998.
11. Eisinger, P. *The Rise of the Entrepreneurial State*; University of Wisconsin Press: Madison, 1988.
12. Fosler, R.S. State economic policy: The emerging paradigm. Econ. Dev. Q. **1992**, *6* (2), 3–13.
13. John, D. *Civic Environmentalism*; Congressional Quarterly Press: Washington, D.C., 1993.
14. Wondolleck, J.M.; Yaffee, S.L. *Making Collaboration Work: Lessons from Innovation in Natural Resource Management*; Island Press: Washington, D.C., 2000.
15. Agranoff, R.; McGuire, M. Big questions in public network management research. J. Public Adm. Res. Theory **2001**, *11* (3), 295–326.
16. Hirst, P. Democracy and Governance. In *Debating Governance*; Pierre, J., Ed.; Oxford University Press: Oxford, 2000; 13–35.
17. Wondolleck, J.M.; Yaffee, S.L. *Making Collaboration Work: Lessons from Innovation in Natural Resource Management*; Island Press: Washington, D.C., 2000.
18. Drucker, P.F. The next society. Economist **Nov. 3 2001**, *28*, 16.
19. Korten, D.C. *Getting to the 21st Century: Voluntary Action and the Global Agenda*; Kumarian Press: West Hartford, CT, 1999; 214–221.

Government Failure, Theory of

Thomas S. Nesslein

University of Wisconsin–Green Bay, Green Bay, Wisconsin, U.S.A.

INTRODUCTION

In *The Wealth of Nations* (1776), Adam Smith presented the basic case for the comparative efficiency of a capitalist market economy. According to Smith, within a competitive economy, an *invisible hand* turns self-interest toward the common good. The modern counterpart of Adam Smith's invisible hand conjecture is the so-called *Fundamental Theorem of Normative Economics*. Using highly sophisticated mathematics, economists such as Kenneth Arrow and Gerald Debreau were able to prove that under certain conditions—albeit highly restrictive—a perfectly competitive economy will result in an efficient allocation of resources.[a]

In the twentieth century, however, economists began to investigate seriously under what specific conditions a market economy might fail to achieve efficient resource allocation. Modern textbooks present a fairly standard list of market failures. Markets are argued to fail in the following key ways: 1) monopoly; 2) collective goods (e.g., national defense, the legal system, etc.); and 3) externalites or external effects (e.g., pollution). More recently, the theory of market failure has been extended to include the ubiquitous problem of costly information and incomplete markets.[2] This broader more refined analysis of market failure suggests a potential role for government to improve the efficiency of, for example, major insurance markets and capital markets. To date, most undergraduate textbooks, however, have yet to incorporate this broader analysis of market failure.

Theories of market failure are without doubt an important analytic framework for helping policy analysts discern potential government policies that may improve the efficiency of the economy. However, the application of market failure theory is an incomplete, and sometimes invalid, guide to efficient public policy making. In brief, for much of the twentieth century, there was a strong tendency by policy analysts to simply assume away the

possibility of government failure. In essence, policy interventions were implicitly assumed to be perfectly implemented by a benevolent, all-knowing, and all-powerful entity called "Government." This point was stressed initially by members of the Chicago School of Political Economy, such as Ronald Coase,[3] George Stigler, Milton Friedman, and Harold Demetz. Demetz[4] presented a concise but particularly cogent argument in this respect:

> The view that now pervades much public policy economics implicitly presents the relevant choice as between an ideal norm and an existing "imperfect" institutional arrangement. This *nirvana* approach differs considerably from a *comparative institution* approach in which the relevant choice is between alternative real institutional arrangements. In practice, those who adopt the nirvana viewpoint seek to discover discrepancies between the ideal and the real and if discrepancies are found, they deduce that the real is inefficient. Users of the comparative institution approach attempt to assess which alternative real institutional arrangement seems best able to cope with the economic problem; practitioners of this approach may use an ideal norm to provide standards from divergences are assessed for all practical alternatives of interest and select as efficient that alternative which seems most likely to minimize the divergence.

INEFFICIENCIES OF POLITICAL INSTITUTIONS: A FEW ILLUSTRATIONS

Criticism of the market failure paradigm as the sole guide to policy interventions stimulated many scholars, in particular, members of the so-called *public choice* school, to examine the question of government failure. Rather than assuming that political actors generally pursue the public interest or common good, public choice analysts posit that political actors have their own agendas and generally seek their self-interests. They then employ the analytic tools of economics to explain the outcomes of the political process and governmental institutions. The public choice literature has many books and articles on the causes and consequences of a large range of government failures.[5–11] Often, analysts, in particular, textbook authors, simply present an unorganized listing

---

[a]The Fundamental Theorem of Normative Economics establishes that a competitive economy will result in a Pareto-efficient allocation of resources. That is, the competitive price mechanism will lead to adjustments such that it is not possible to reallocate resources in any way that will increase the satisfaction of one party without decreasing the satisfaction of some other party (Ref. [1]).

Encyclopedia of Public Administration and Public Policy
DOI: 10.1081/E-EPAP 120010876

of what they believe to be important reasons for government failure. A modest improvement in this respect, perhaps, is to relate key government failures to deficiencies in one of the three fundamental structures of all social choice mechanisms, whether market or nonmarket, namely, the *decision-making* structure, the *information* structure, and the *incentive* structure.

To begin, in a competitive market economy, consumers are able to channel their preferences to producers and make them effective, via their dollar votes in the marketplace. Each consumer, within the limits of their budget, can purchase exactly the quantity and quality of goods and services they desire. Absent market failures, the decentralized decision-making structure of a market economy results in efficiency, i.e., resources are allocated to those lines of production that maximize society's net benefit.

In contrast, the use of a more centralized social decision-making mechanism, namely, collective or political choice mechanisms, often presents major problems in efficiently channeling the preferences of voters and making these choices effective. One method for making social choices is via direct democratic referendum, where the preferences of 50 plus 1 of the voters decide the issue. Clearly, a key problem of a majority decision-rule is that the preferences of a lukewarm and small majority may dominate the preferences of an intense minority. For example, perhaps a majority of voters in a school expenditure referendum are willing to pay a small increase in taxes per year, whereas a large minority may actually desire a significant decrease in taxes. Such a situation may easily lead to an inefficient level of school spending and taxation because of the inability of a majority voting rule to account for the intensity of voter preferences.

Of course, in modern democracies, the bulk of collective decisions are not made by referenda but by elected representatives. Perhaps the central problem of representative government is that the outcomes of the political process often fail to reflect society's general interest, and instead, they reflect the interests of organized groups (i.e., so-called *special interests*). Often, these organized interest groups seek legislation that makes wealth transfers to them at the expense of society in general, the classic example being tariff and other trade barriers protecting favored industries from more efficient foreign competitors.

The basic reasons for inefficient special interest legislation are straightforward. First, for most voters, the cost in time, effort, and money of being well-informed on a large number of public policy issues is large relative to the benefits to them. Consequently, it is rational for most voters to remain uninformed on most policy questions. Obviously, voter ignorance greatly impedes the monitoring of their political representatives. Second, self-interested political representatives generally place a high priority on getting reelected in order to continue to enjoy the perquisites of political office. Finally, the influence of special interest groups is greatly increased, because organized interest groups have the means and incentive to be the primary providers of political funding. It is not difficult to see that in political systems where the political funding is paramount to elector success and where the perquisites of political office are exceedingly large, special interest legislation will be especially pervasive.

A second major cause of government failure relates to information deficiencies on the part of voters. Two basic sources of information deficiencies are the following. Again, a fundamental problem is that it is rational for the bulk of voters to be uninformed on most political issues. Greatly compounding this inherent problem is the fact that self-interested politicians have strong incentive to structure policies and programs so as to systematically exaggerate potential benefits while concealing the true social costs. For example, in the United States, the Social Security pension system is financed by a payroll tax on workers and a mandated matching employer contribution. Yet, economists generally agree that workers actually bear the full burden of financing Social Security, as the employer contribution results in a corresponding reduction in wages in the long run.

A final major source of government failure relates to the large range of incentive problems. Much of government activity is accomplished via government agencies and enterprises. Analysts have long noted that public-sector managers confront a set of incentives that generally undermines efficient performance. In particular, government agencies and firms fail to be disciplined by the threat of bankruptcy or outside takeover, while at the same time, soft budget constraints provide incentive for increased expenditure and a lack of cost consciousness. Compounding basic incentive problems is another, often overlooked, cause of public-sector inefficiency noted by Shleifer:[12] "In other words, state firms are inefficient not just because their managers have weak incentives to reduce costs, but because inefficiency is the result of the government's deliberate policy to transfer resources to supporters."

TOWARD A THEORY OF GOVERNMENT FAILURE

While numerous, rather narrow, articles have been produced examining various aspects of government failure, "few writers have tried to synthesize this literature to construct a theory of government failure that parallels that of the market."[13] The major exceptions are studies by Wolfe,[5–11] Le Grand,[13] and Vining and Weimer.[14]

While each of these studies provide valuable insights toward the development of a theory of government failure, to date, no complete and fully adequate theory of government failure exists. Dollery and Worthington[15] provided an excellent concise critique of the government failure literature. Three key general criticisms made by them[15] are as follows:

> [I]n at least two respects extant public choice theory does not provide policymakers with a conceptual analogue of the market failure paradigm to inform public policy decisions. Firstly, the public choice approach is positive, and not a normative, theory of government processes, and thus cannot provide an idealised or optimal vision of policy intervention against which actual government behaviour can be compared, in the same way as welfare economics furnishes the theory of market failure with a yardstick to evaluate real-world markets. And secondly, public choice theory is premised on the behavioural posulate of *homo economicus* and follows methodological individualism, which may not always capture the full intricacies of politicised policy environments. . .[Finally,] effective policy analysis requires a general theory of organisational failure, rather than conceptually distinct theories of market failure and nonmarket failure. This has been recognised by Williamson (1989) who has argued that ''. . .all forms of organization, not just markets, need to be assessed comparatively. . ..''

MARKET FAILURE VERSUS GOVERNMENT FAILURE

What is to be done, then, to aid the policy analyst in making policy choices in a world of imperfect markets and imperfect government? Le Grand's approach[12] appears to be one potentially useful path to follow. In brief, Le Grand attempted to provide a more general policy analysis by focusing on the three basic ways that governments intervene in a market economy and then assessed these three interventions in terms of efficiency and equity criteria. Le Grand provided a concise and basic analytical discussion of direct government *provision*, *taxation* and *subsidy*, and *regulation*. To be of much use for policy making, however, a more extensive theoretical development is needed. For example, a more precise and refined theoretical analysis of the optimal scope of government and private provision is now available to be incorporated into Le Grand's analytic framework.[2,16]

Perhaps even more important is the increased production of high-quality empirical research that carefully assesses real-world market outcomes relative to real-world outcomes of various forms of political allocation. As several writers on government failure have noted: The

choice between markets and political allocation is ultimately an empirical question. One prominent example is the rapidly growing, improved empirical research concerning the privatization of state-owned enterprises.[17,18] Another good example is the improved comparative research of alternative housing systems, where major differences in performance can now be discerned between market-oriented housing systems and various *planning* systems.[19,20]

REFERENCES

1. Arrow, K.; Debrue, G. Existence of an equilibrium for a competitive economy. Econometrica **1954**, *22*, 265–290.
2. Stiglitz, J. *Whither Socialism?* MIT Press: Cambridge, MA, 1994.
3. Coase, R. The problem of social cost. J. Law Econ. **1960**, *3* (1), 1–44.
4. Nesslein, T. Housing: The Market Versus the Welfare State Model Revisited. Urban Studies. **1988**, *25* (1), 94–108.
5. Gwartney, J.; Stroup, R. *Economics: Private and Public Choice,* 8th Ed.; The Dryden Press: New York, 1997.
6. Ekelund, R.; Tollison, R. *Economics: Private Markets and Public Choice,* 6th Ed.; Addison-Wesley: New York, 2000.
7. Wolf, C. A theory of nonmarket failure. J. Law Econ. **1979**, *22*, 107–139.
8. Wolf, C. *Markets or Government: Choosing Between Imperfect Alternatives*; MIT Press: Cambridge, MA, 1988.
9. Weimer, D.; Vining, A. *Policy Analysis: Concepts and Practice*; Prentice Hall: Engelwood Cliffs, NJ, 1992.
10. Mitchell, W.; Simmons, R. *Beyond Politics: Markets Welfare, and the Failure of Bureaucracy*; Westview Press: Boulder, CO, 1994.
11. Adachi, Y. Inefficiencies in public policies. J. Comp. Policy Anal. **1999**, *1* (2), 225–236.
12. Shleifer, A. State versus private ownership. J. Econ. Perspect. **1998**, *12* (4), 142.
13. Le Grand, J. The theory of government failure. Br. J. Polit. Sci. **1991**, *21*, 423.
14. Vining, A.; Weimer, D. Government supply and government production failure: A framework based on contestability. J. Public Policy **1991**, *10* (1), 1–22.
15. Dollery, B.; Worthington, A. The evaluation of public policy: Normative economic theories of government failure. J. Interdiscip. Econ. **1996**, *7* (8), 27–39.
16. Shleifer, A. State versus private ownership. J. Econ. Perspect. **1998**, *12* (4), 133–150.
17. Vining, A.; Boardman, A. Ownership versus competition: Efficiency in public enterprise. Public Choice **1992**, *73*, 205–239.
18. World Bank. *Bureaucrats in Business*; Oxford University Press: London, 1995.
19. Nesslein, T. *Housing: The Market Versus the Welfare State Model Revisited*; Urban Studies, 1988.
20. Angel, S. *Housing Policy Matters: A Global Analysis*; Oxford University Press: London, 2000.

Governors as Chief Administrators, The Changing Role of

H. Edward Flentje
Wichita State University, Wichita, Kansas, U.S.A.

INTRODUCTION

The independently elected chief executive represents a unique American contribution to modern democratic governance. The role of such executives including presidents, governors, and mayors among others in the administration of U.S. governments has evolved dramatically over the course of U.S. history. In the early days of the nation, distrust of government and executive power limited the scope of government and severely restrained the authority granted to elected executives. The progressive movement at the beginning of the twentieth century initiated an enlargement of executive powers, including gubernatorial powers, and this trend has continued in ebbs and flows to the present day. Today, governors—more than any other state officials—are held politically accountable for directing the administration of state government.

BACKGROUND

In its purest form, the role of governor as chief administrator is founded on progressive-era ideals; that is, the public interest in administering state government may best be served through rule of law, hierarchical structures, division of labor, specialized competence, and the insulation of administration from politics.[1] Rule of law, including written rules and regulations promulgated to interpret the law, assures that administration will be conducted within the bounds of the law. Hierarchical structures unify administration and centralize executive control. Hierarchy also provides the rationale for extending executive control. Division of labor rationalizes executive functions by purpose or process and guides executive reorganization. Specialized competence calls for selection of administrative personnel based on considerations of merit, such as education, experience, and expertise. Insulating administration from politics assures that administration will be conducted free of political influence and corruption by narrow special interests. These ideals provide a model of the "one best way" to conduct gubernatorial administration and give guidance to the governor's role as chief administrator.

This model of gubernatorial administration has been applied in state governments at different times and stages,

often in fits and starts, throughout the twentieth century. Application of the model received preeminence with the emergence of the modern governorship in the last half of the century. Larry Sabato, who described this transformation of the U.S. governorship as "Goodbye to Goodtime Charlie," found governors serving between 1950 and 1975 to be "younger and better educated" with preparation for office "more thorough and appropriate" than ever before. Within the executive sphere, these governors were successful not only in "orchestrating constitutional revisions and reorganizations but also in consolidating and fortifying their control of administration." Most institutional obstacles formerly in the way of governors "have been dislodged and swept away." Governors gained "appointive powers where it really matters, at the top-levels of state government... [T]he strengthening of the executive budget and other planning and management tools have consolidated the control of the chief executive over state administration." As a result, fewer of this modern new breed of governors "are being defeated because of political and administrative incompetency."[2]

Governors in this period became evangelistic in asserting their role as chief administrator of state government. For example, interviews of 15 former governors who served their terms between 1965 and 1979 saw the managerial role to be "the most important facet of the office." The governors interviewed were emphatic, for example: Edwards of South Carolina: "... The management role is really where the meat of the Governor's office is.... Without management, you have practically no leg to stand on." Exon of Nebraska: "To me, that's number one—being a good manager...more important, I think, than programs or anything else." Rampton of Utah: "...if a Governor is going to do his job, he has got to be the manager." Walker of Illinois: "What counts is management...we have to get the Governors to concentrate on management." Wollman of South Dakota: "...if a Governor doesn't devote a high percentage of his time—over half of his time—just to executive management functions, he is really missing the boat." Each governor interviewed emphasized the governor's role as manager from his own perspective; none denigrated its import.[3]

During this period, the same exuberance for the governor's administrative role permeated the work of the governors' vehicle for collective action, the National Governors' Association (NGA). This enthusiasm was transmitted to new governors by NGA through biennial seminars and through *Governing the American States: A Handbook for New Governors*. Over half of the NGA handbook is dedicated to guiding governors on topics such as office organization and management, staff development, selection of cabinet officials, policy and budget development, time management, and reorganization, among other topics. The volume prescribes guidelines for relating to cabinet members, avoiding staff-line conflicts, and keeping records within the governor's office. The chapter on reorganization states that "reorganization is usually a high priority" and outlines reorganization actions "to increase the Governor's executive authority and management capacity," such as expanding the governor's appointment power, reducing the number of statewide officials chosen by popular election, eliminating fixed terms of office for cabinet members, ensuring appointees serve at the pleasure of the governor, and eliminating boards and commissions that operate state agencies.[4]

POLITICS OF GUBERNATORIAL ADMINISTRATION

The idealized view of gubernatorial administration shapes the governor's role as chief administrator but reflects some degree of political naiveté. Governors conduct their administrative role through the exercise of administrative powers, such as the power of appointment, fiscal power, the power of organization, and the power of command. Most state constitutions provide for administrative powers that are *separate*, yet *shared* between the governor and legislature. A governor's unique constitutional status and independent political base allow the exercise of administrative powers separately from and independently of the legislature. The open-ended constitutional language defining the powers of chief executives gives governors an advantage in the exercise of administrative power. However, administrative powers are shared in the sense that a legislature may also act in the administrative sphere if it so chooses—a situation that makes the exercise of administrative powers competitive and interdependent. Further, as executive powers have expanded, the legislature's capacity for oversight of state administration has also increased.

Gubernatorial exercise of administrative powers also immerses a governor in bureaucratic politics. According to one observer, state bureaucracies "tend to be creatures of habit, inflexible, and enmeshed in the process of administering ongoing programs. Around them emerge a complex of interest groups and legislative supporters, all committed to the survival and growth of extant bureaus and their programs."[5] These triangular alliances of state bureaus, organized clientele groups, and legislative friends represent potent forces in U.S. politics and a formidable challenge to gubernatorial direction of state bureaucracies. Any governor who takes seriously his role as chief administrator can expect to contest toe-to-toe with the iron triangles of state bureaucratic politics. In sum, state constitutional frameworks and state politics place the governor's role as chief administrator squarely in the political realm, which may be seen more clearly by examining the primary administrative powers.

POWER OF APPOINTMENT

The power most fundamental to the role of governor as chief administrator is the power of appointment—the power to hire and to fire executive officials. Other administrative powers in large measure flow from the power of appointment. The legislature may share in the appointment powers by enacting legislation that: 1) removes positions from gubernatorial appointment through the creation of independent boards and commissions or independently elected offices; 2) limits gubernatorial removal by placing certain administrative positions under civil service status or giving them terms of office; 3) requires legislative confirmation of gubernatorial nomination to certain positions; 4) establishes specific statutory criteria for appointment to certain positions; or 5) enacts such restrictions in some combination. Constitutional provisions may also restrict gubernatorial powers of appointment, but constitutional and statutory restraints are slowly being removed. In 1955, for example, 337 state officials elected independently from the governor headed state agencies in the 50 states; as of 1994, that number had declined to 260, a decrease of 23%.[6]

The active exercise of appointment powers also has political ramifications for governors.[a] Governors making key administrative appointments based on considerations of specialized competence, managerial skill, education, and experience may cause antagonism within their state party organizations. For example, retaining a competent agency head from a prior administration of the opposing party may offend partisans in the governor's party. Merit-based appointments to cabinet positions may preclude the use of patronage in those departments and, if appointees are recruited from out of state or from outside state service, irritate current state employees. More difficult

---

[a]Numerous references to the political difficulties encountered by individual governors in exercising administrative powers follow and may be found in various sources, including Refs. [3,5,7–9].

politically than selection is the removal of key officials. According to one former governor, ''Nothing can bedevil an administration more than weaknesses among appointees.'' According to another, ''If they're bad, you get more minuses for their being really bad than you get pluses out of their being good.''[3] Outright firing of a department head in order to change policy direction in a department may unify clientele groups, loyal bureaucrats, and legislative allies to protest gubernatorial action and, if a replacement is not quickly in place, lead to political havoc wrought by a runaway bureaucracy.

FISCAL POWER

The power of the purse—the power of governors to direct or substantially influence levels of state spending and revenue raising—is essential to the governor's role of chief administrator. While state constitutions grant legislatures primary powers over taxing and spending, the fiscal powers of governors evolved significantly during the twentieth century. Through statutory assignment, governors and their appointees now dominate budget making, that is, recommending an annual plan for expenditures, revenues, and year-end balances. Governors may also enforce their fiscal recommendations through use of veto powers—outright veto of appropriations bills, line-item vetoes, or the threat of vetoes. While legislatures jealously guard their control over power of the purse through more detailed line items, appropriation riders, ''veto-proof'' appropriation bills, and various mechanisms designed to oversee expenditures, governors and their appointees have substantial discretion to shape spending decisions once appropriations are authorized. A number of governors also have statutory authority to exercise spending discretion among line items, impound funds, or make mid-year spending reductions when revenue falls short of projections or for other statutory purposes. Further, state statutes often grant executive agencies ''off-budget'' fiscal powers, such as raising various fees and charges, accepting nonstate funds, and issuing debt, among others, and these powers are susceptible to gubernatorial control or influence.

A governor's struggle with the legislature for control over power of the purse has political consequences. For example, between 1951 and 1975, 21 incumbent governors were evicted from office through elections in which the key issue was a tax initiative of the governor.[2] Governors can survive a general tax increase, but the survivors list is a short one. On the expenditure side, most studies of state budgetary processes show a contest of competing interests—clientele groups, agency advocates, legislative spokesmen, and other political interests. This contest promotes decision rules for the budget process

that do not seriously question existing operations of state agencies. Governors who want to enter this fray and seek substantial fiscal change will be required to expend considerable political capital, and even then, they may be faced with embarrassing budgetary defeats. Another political bugaboo for most governors is the necessity to recommend periodic salary adjustments for state employees that will likely be perceived as too little on one side and too much on the other. Those governors seeking to reward managerial performance may also be stalemated by the egalitarian instincts of legislatures to spread limited salary funds to more employees at the lower end of the salary schedule and reduce compensation for managers.

POWER OF ORGANIZATION

The power of organization—the power to create and abolish offices and to assign and reassign purposes, authorities, and duties to these offices—is critical to the governor's role as chief administrator, for it may be used to confer organizational status and give certain public purposes, programs, and constituencies higher priority and visibility than others. The legislature holds primary authority to create state offices and prescribe duties and responsibilities for such offices and, therefore, shares substantially in the power of organization, but gubernatorial powers of organization are on the increase. In 1955, only two states granted governors such powers, but as of 1994, 23 states granted governors authority to initiate executive reorganization subject to some form of legislative review.[6] Moreover, within the bounds of state statutes and appropriations, most governors and their appointees have broad discretion in exercising the power of organization, for example, in establishing a cabinet and mechanisms to coordinate major state agencies, reorganizing administrative operations within agencies, creating gubernatorial task forces and study commissions, and assigning supplementary duties of gubernatorial priority to certain offices, among others. The gubernatorial power of organization may be applied to achieve policy objectives or for purposes of management.

Gubernatorial action in the organizational arena commonly runs into direct and immediate conflict with the iron triangles of bureaucratic politics, and many reorganization proposals can be found in the political graveyards of state government. Most often, exercise of the power of organization will be vigorously opposed by elements in the legislature, by interest groups, from within the bureaucracy, or by a combination of these forces. Such actions will likely be denounced as a ''power grab'' or as attempts to import the ideas of out-of-state experts and associations. The politics of reorganization are well summarized by the late Robert Bennett, former governor of Kansas:

> ...during the election campaigns there wasn't a candidate of either party...that didn't proclaim loud and clear that he was for reorganization, he was going to abolish unneeded activity, he was going to merge...duplicating departments, he in fact was going to streamline government. In the abstract, it is without a doubt, one of the finest and one of the most palatable theories ever espoused by a modern day politician. But in practice...it becomes the loss of a job for your brother or your sister, your uncle or your aunt. It becomes the closing of an office on which you have learned to depend for a small portion of your municipal economic sustenance. It becomes the doing away with an activity that is of personal economic benefit to you although it may be of little benefit to others. So there may in many instances be more agony than anything else in this reorganization process.[10]

POWER OF COMMAND

The power of command—the power of a governor to order the actions of executive officials—is also shared with the legislature and, therefore, varies from state to state.[11] Most state constitutions grant governors explicit or implied powers in the form of the "supreme executive power," the power to "faithfully execute the laws," and the power to "require information in writing from the officers of the executive department." On the other hand, the authority to create state offices and prescribe the duties and responsibilities of state offices resides with the legislature. Precedents at state and national levels generally authorize the elected chief executive to direct the official actions of any agency head subject to the chief executive's power of appointment. In other words, the discretionary acts of an agency head are subject to command by the governor and enforced, if necessary, through the power of removal. Further, because most state statutes grant agency heads broad authority to define state programs, specify program purposes, and implement those programs, gubernatorial command may encompass not only the individual acts of agency heads but also their discretionary authority to issue rules and regulations. Gubernatorial orders may take the form of verbal instructions, executive orders, proclamations, reorganization orders, memoranda, and various other policy directives. The legislature may seek to limit the scope of gubernatorial command by prescribing an agency head's duties with more specificity or by removing an agency head from appointment by the governor or through statutory mechanisms providing for legislative oversight of executive rule making.

Gubernatorial commands may generate political liabilities, for example, in issuing directives that narrow program purposes and exclude potential beneficiaries. Directing personnel on a day-to-day basis may be unproductive. According to former governor Pryor of Arkansas, a governor "will spend almost as much time keeping his staff and his cabinet and the people around him happy as he does keeping his constituency happy."[3] Governors are also thrust into resolving battles among and between staff and agency personnel that ultimately result in deflated egos. Directing an agency to do something it is reluctant to do may lead to bureaucratic foot dragging and attempts to emasculate the directive. Or, directing an agency to turn down a federal grant may generate interest group pressure to reverse the governor's decision. Another approach to the power of command is to delegate, but delegation too has political impact. A governor who delegates may be viewed as a weak manager by agency personnel and by the public but ultimately will be held politically accountable for problems that occur under delegation.

In sum, the role of governor as chief administrator is conducted in the political arena, and the exercise of administrative power requires an investment of political capital. Although administrative action frequently has more impact than legislative action, governors have come to recognize the political costs of investing time and resources in the administrative role. Says former governor Walker of Illinois: "Nobody cares...whether you're actually managing state government...It's not a political plus...In terms of getting votes or a better image or a better reputation, you'd better spend your time somewhere else."[3] Another assessment similarly concludes:

> ...the substantive success of the Governor's efforts at management improvement could not be translated into votes, for there was little, if any, real political support for effective management. Unlike almost any other area of state policy, there was no major constituency to whom management improvement was a salient issue. Indeed the situation was quite the contrary, as most organized interest groups pushed for objectives which militated against good management.[10]

EMERGING TRENDS IN GUBERNATORIAL ADMINISTRATION

At the start of the twenty-first century, new directions in gubernatorial administration are emerging—shaped in part by progressive-era ideals evident from the start of the twentieth century and in part by political realities experienced throughout the past century. Governors today have wider latitude than ever before in determining the character of their governorship and specifically in performing the role of chief administrator of state government. Emerging trends suggest that governors may determine their governorship and administrative role around three distinct patterns, discussed below.[b]

First, *a governorship should be balanced in its attention to policy and administration.* In the modern governorship, a governor should attend to two primary and roughly equivalent roles, which are as chief administrator and chief policy maker in state government. As chief administrator, a governor is held politically accountable for the administration of state government and advances those long-standing progressive-era ideals that give order and value to management in state government. Effective gubernatorial management should be conducted through sophisticated delegation to essential components of gubernatorial administration, specifically, gubernatorial staff, executive budget staff, and cabinet officers. A governor should reinforce the core values and distinctive contribution expected of these administrative components. Gubernatorial staff should assure focus on the governor's policy priorities. Executive budget staff should enforce the governor's fiscal policy priorities. Cabinet officers should manage major state functions and represent the administration to the primary constituencies of state government.

Second, *a governorship should focus on policy and political strategy.* In the modern governorship, a governor should focus on policy and political strategy essential to achieving gubernatorial policy priorities. The governor should practice "hands-off" management, and management of state government should be a secondary concern of the governorship. Gubernatorial appointees should be oriented foremost to gubernatorial policy, and administrative actions should be assessed in terms of their contribution to the policy agenda and political resources of the governor. State bureaucracies are expected to implement public policies.

Third, *an entrepreneurial governorship should commit to reinventing state government through competition and individual choice.* In the modern governorship, a governor should exercise entrepreneurial leadership to reinvent government, take risks in stimulating the economy, and advance free market competition and individual choice. The governor's attention should be focused on steering the state; the rowing functions of state government should be delegated, decentralized, diffused, or privatized. Competition should be injected into the delivery of state services, and those delivering services should be held accountable to their customers. State bureaucracies should be required to compete for service delivery with private and nonprofit organizations. Wherever possible, public–private partnerships should be encouraged, and authority for state services should be diffused and decentralized.

REFERENCES

1. Flentje, H.E. State Administration in Cultural Context. In *Handbook of State Government Administration*; Gargan, J.J., Ed.; Marcel Dekker, Inc.: New York, 2000; 80–86.
2. Sabato, L. *Goodbye to Good-Time Charlie*; D.C. Heath & Co.: Lexington, MA, 1978; pp. 90, 107–118, 207–208.
3. Center for Policy Research, National Governors' Association. In *Reflections on Being Governor*; National Governors' Association: Washington, DC, 1981; pp. 67, 104–105, 128, 169, 184, 231, 243–244, 266, 284.
4. Center for Policy Research, National Governors' Association. *Governing the American States: A Handbook for New Governors*; National Governors' Association: Washington, DC, 1978; 204.
5. Connery, R.H.; Benjamin, G. *Rockefeller of New York: Executive Power in the Statehouse*; Cornell University Press: Ithaca, NY, 1979; 153.
6. Beyle, T.L. Enhancing executive leadership in the states. State Local Gov. Rev. **1995**, *27* (1), 19–21.
7. Weinberg, M.W. *Managing the State*; MIT Press: Cambridge, MA, 1977.
8. Rosenthal, A. *Governors and Legislatures: Contending Powers*; CQ Press: Washington, DC, 1990.
9. *Governors on Governing*; Behn, R.D., Ed.; National Governors' Association: Washington, DC, 1991.
10. *Selected Papers of Governor Robert F. Bennett: A Study in Good Government and Civics Book Politics*; Flentje, H.E., Ed.; Center for Urban Studies, Wichita State University: Wichita, KS, 1979; pp. 259, 264.
11. Bernick, E.L.; Wiggins, C.W. The governor's executive order: An unknown power. State Local Gov. Rev. **1984**, *16* (1), 3–10.
12. Adamany, D. Successful hands-off management. J. State Gov. **1989**, *62* (4), 140–146.
13. *Making Government Work: Lessons from America's Governors and Mayors*; Andrisani, P.J., Hakim, S., Leeds, E., Eds.; Rowan and Littlefield: Sanham, MD, 2000.
14. Cox, R., III. The Management Role of the Governor. In *Gubernatorial Leadership and State Policy*; Herzik, E.B., Brown, B.W., Eds.; Greenwood Press: New York, 1991; 55–71.
15. Flentje, H.E. Clarifying purpose and achieving balance in gubernatorial administration. State Gov. **1989**, *62* (4), 161–167.
16. Hebert, F.T. Governors as Chief Administrators and Managers. In *Handbook of State Government Administration*; Gargan, J.J., Ed.; Marcel Dekker, Inc.: New York, 2000; 107–126.
17. Osborne, D. *Laboratories of Democracy*; Harvard Business School Press: Boston, 1990.
18. Osborne, D.; Gaebler, T. *Reinventing Government*; Addison-Wesley: Reading, MA, 1992.

---

[b]These patterns are summarized from a variety of sources, primarily from Refs. [12–18].

Grievance Procedures and Administration

Lisa B. Bingham
Tina Nabatchi
Indiana University, Bloomington, Indiana, U.S.A.

INTRODUCTION

This chapter describes the basics of the grievance procedure. It provides a discussion of several theoretical perspectives used in grievance procedure research, and reviews literature on grievance initiation, processing, decisions, and outcomes. Then, a brief discussion about grievances and organizational performance is provided. Finally, the grievance mediation, a recent innovation in the grievance procedure is examined.

THE GRIEVANCE PROCEDURE

The grievance procedure has received significant attention from scholars and practitioners as a critical component of the labor–management relationship. There are substantial variations in the scope of the grievance procedure from contract to contract and across the public and private sectors. The definition of a grievance is subject to the terms of the collective bargaining agreement or contract. In its broadest conception, a grievance is any employee complaint about an employment relationship. In a grievance procedure, a grievance is a *written* allegation by employees that management has in some way violated their contractual rights. Grievances generally allege some breach, violation, misinterpretation, or misapplication of language in the collective bargaining agreement, often with regard to wages and hours, discharge and discipline, safety and health, insurance benefits, seniority, leaves of absence, promotions, vacations, management rights, and union rights.[1–3] Although there is variation across the private and public sectors, the basic issues brought to arbitration in the two sectors are similar. The primary difference between the public and private sectors appears to be with the prevalence of certain categories of grievances. For example, termination, suspension, or disciplinary actions resulting from drug and alcohol use, insubordination, absenteeism and tardiness, and abusive behavior are the highest incidence of cases brought to arbitration in the public sector.[3]

Although there are significant variants, grievance procedures generally move through a series of steps before increasingly higher management authorities, be-

ginning with informal discussion and the writing of a complaint, and ending with arbitration. The overwhelming majority of grievance procedures culminate in binding arbitration, in which an outside neutral third party issues a final decision on the grievance. The common step structure of the grievance procedure is described below.

Informal Step

The first step of any grievance requires the expression of a complaint. The employee, sometimes with the assistance of the union steward, discusses the complaint with the immediate, first-line supervisor. Most contracts encourage this informal step, because it is generally preferable to resolve all disputes as early or as quickly as possible, because parties' positions tend to harden once a grievance becomes formal and written. In this step, many disputing parties settle grievances during informal discussions between the employee and supervisor, and these never enter the grievance process as a formal, written complaint. Unfortunately, these informal grievances are generally not captured in traditional management information systems; therefore, researchers are limited in discovering the true nature and extent of informal grievances in the workplace.

Step One

If the employee and supervisor cannot resolve the dispute informally, then the grievance is submitted in writing, formally becomes a grievance, and technically enters the grievance procedure. Usually, there are time limits within which employees must act. Once the written grievance is filed with the first-line supervisor, a formal written decision must be issued, again within negotiated time limits. If the employee or union is dissatisfied with the step one response, they may appeal the grievance to step two.

Step Two

At step two, the grievance is generally presented to officials higher in the organization. In the public sector, it might move from the immediate supervisor to a de-

Encyclopedia of Public Administration and Public Policy
DOI: 10.1081/E-EPAP 120010789

partment head, or from a school principal to the superintendent of schools. In the private sector, it might move from the immediate supervisor to a plant manager, or to some other designated representatives who are familiar with the contract and with grievance precedent. The officials hear the complaint and render a written decision. The employee or union can still appeal the decision; however, they must usually file the appeal within a stricter and shorter time frame.

Step Three

If a complaint reaches step three of the grievance process, then it likely has precedent-setting ramifications, major cost implications, or broad application within the firm's operation.[4] As such, participants with more authority are brought into the discussion. In the public sector, the grievance might reach a board of police commissioners, school board, city council, personnel board, or other elected multimember public agency. In the private sector, it would reach upper management. Again, the responding official renders a written decision within a limited time frame. This is often the step at which parties call in legal counsel or regional union representatives. The union usually has the sole prerogative to determine which grievances will move beyond this step to arbitration and has an internal union grievance committee for making these decisions.

Step Four

The final step in the grievance procedure is usually arbitration, in which a neutral third party hears both sides of the case and renders a written decision to the appropriate management and union officials. This written decision is usually final and binding, although traditionally, the arbitrator is not bound by precedent. Witness testimonies and documents can be presented as arbitration evidence, and the party initiating the grievance (usually the employee or union) typically has the burden of proof.

THEORETICAL PERSPECTIVES ON GRIEVANCE PROCEDURES

There are several theoretical perspectives used in the scholarly study of grievance procedures. Researchers using *systems theory* examine the connections between several variables and the different stages of grievance procedures, emphasizing a correlation between labor relations and the filing, processing, and settlement and postsettlement outcomes of grievances.[5–10] *Human resource management* theorists suggest that human resource practices that encourage worker participation in work teams, problem solving, and other high-involvement activities can improve grievance procedures and have a positive affect on organizational performance. *Procedural-Distributive Justice* theorists, applying a research framework first used in courtroom settings, argue that organizational decisions will be more readily accepted if the processes by which they are achieved are perceived to be fair.[11,12] Research supports the suggestion that perceptions of the fairness of grievance procedures significantly influence employee perceptions and attitudes toward those grievance procedures.[13,14]

Research based on Hirschman's[15] *exit-voice-loyalty theory* suggests that the grievance procedure is a "voice" mechanism that allows employees to air complaints and issues to management. The theory holds that when provided a "voice" option, employees will be less likely to "exit," or quit the organization. Accordingly, some theorists suggest that employees who file grievances will be less likely to leave their employers than those employees who do not file grievances.[16–18] However, empirical evidence for this theory is mixed. In contrast, other scholars using *organizational punishment–industrial discipline theory* suggest that those involved in grievance activities are significantly more likely to be the subjects of negative postgrievance outcomes, such as retaliation. Empirical support for these propositions is garnered by the fact that "fear of reprisal" is the most frequently cited reason for not using available grievance procedures.[19,20]

DETERMINANTS OF GRIEVANCE INITIATION

There has been extensive research on the determinants of grievance filing. Some researchers have found significant *demographic* differences between grievance filers and nonfilers. For example, researchers have found that grievants tend to be younger and less educated and that minorities tend to file more grievances than Caucasians.[5,21] Similarly, researchers have found that grievance filers are typically younger, with more skilled jobs, higher rates of absenteeism, dispensary visits, and insurance claim filings than non-grievants.[22] Finally, others have found that grievance filers have significantly lower job satisfaction, more negative attitudes toward their supervisors, greater perceived pay inequity, stronger preferences for worker participation in decision making, and lower satisfaction with their unions than nongrievants.[23]

Some researchers have examined the relationship between *management factors* and grievance initiation. Research demonstrates that managerial strictness with regard to performance and disciplinary actions is significantly related to grievance filing rates,[24] as is managerial monitoring of employees.[25] *Union factors* also appear to have an impact on grievance filings. Research shows that the grievance behavior of union stewards is related to company commitment, union commitment, and job satisfaction,[26] and the activity and involvement of union officials in grievance procedures can affect grievance filing rates.[5,24,27] Just as union officials may have an impact on the filing of grievances, so too do grievance filings affect union officials. For example, more favorable grievance outcomes are associated with larger, more supportive constituencies for union stewards,[28] and grievance handling has a significant effect on the probability of being reelected as a union steward, as well as on the percentage of votes obtained in that reelection.[29] Finally, the degree of perceived conflict in the *collective bargaining relationship* is significantly related to grievance filing rates.[28,30] If union–management relations are hostile or confrontational, then grievance procedures may be used more frequently, possibly to increase pressure on management during times of contract negotiation; conversely, a cooperative union–management relationship may have a constructive and productive impact on grievance activity.[31,32] In short, evidence indicates that grievance filing rates are likely to decline given cooperative union–management relationships.

GRIEVANCE PROCESSING, SETTLEMENT, DECISIONS, AND OUTCOMES

Research regarding grievance processing addresses the efficiency of the grievance procedure in resolving disputes quickly and with finality. As such, an important measure of grievance procedure effectiveness has been the rate of grievance resolution in the steps before arbitration or the intervention of some other third-party neutral. Early settlement of grievances is preferable, because grievances tend to become more difficult to settle once they are written and proceed through higher levels of the grievance process. Factors such as early authorization from upper management and union officials to resolve a grievance, and the written presentation of a grievance as opposed to simply an informal discussion, have been correlated with the earlier settlement of grievances.[33]

Typically, an arbitrated case can have one of three settlements: 1) the grieving party can win the case; 2) the grieving party can lose the case; or 3) the arbitration can result in a compromise.[3,26,34] In terms of the settlements decisions, research demonstrates that the longer a grievance is under consideration at any level of the process, the more likely management is to respond favorably.[29] Moreover, some assert that employees can typically expect a favorable grievance settlement, because parties involved in a workplace dispute must usually continue their relationship after the dispute is re-

solved.[32,35] Research comparing public- and private-sector grievance outcomes confirms the following: 1) public-sector employees tend to "win" grievance cases more frequently than their private-sector counterparts; 2) there tend to be fewer discharge cases in the private sector than in the public sector; 3) more suspension and reprimand cases reach arbitration in the private sector than in the public sector; and 4) of grievance cases that resulted in suspension, fewer public-sector cases resulted in long suspensions.[36]

Even though employees can usually expect a favorable settlement, important research using the organizational punishment–industrial discipline theory of grievances suggests that grievants can also face significant unfavorable postsettlement outcomes. For example, in the postgrievance settlement period, grievants tend to have lower performance ratings, promotion rates, and work attendance rates, as well as higher turnover rates.[5] In addition, research has also shown that grievance filers *and* the supervisors against whom the grievances were filed, have significantly higher turnover rates and significantly lower job performance ratings and promotion rates in the immediate postgrievance settlement period than employees who did not file grievances and their supervisors.[21] In short, evidence suggests that employees and supervisors involved in grievance activities face the potential of more workplace retribution than employees and supervisors who are not involved in grievance activity.

GRIEVANCE PROCEDURES AND ORGANIZATIONAL PERFORMANCE

Historically, one impetus for the development of grievance procedures was to help reduce strikes and work stoppages; yet, there are few studies that systematically compare the strike activities of employees with grievance procedures to those without grievance procedures. A study of the coal-mining industry, an industry with historically high strike rates, suggests that strikes were more frequent in those mines where supervisors were perceived as being unable to effectively handle grievances or where disputes could not be resolved locally.[37]

More commonly, research in this area links grievance filing rates to various measures of organizational performance. There is evidence that access to grievance procedures contributes to lower quit rates, which likely helps lower turnover and retraining costs,[17,38] and that employee turnover rates are lower among unionized firms with access to grievance procedures.[39] Other research has shown that high levels of grievance activity are associated with reduced levels of productivity.[39–43] One possible explanation for these findings is that an effective grievance system can help organizations detect current or potential problems and rectify issues and undesirable situations before they develop into larger, more systemic problems.

INNOVATIONS IN GRIEVANCE PROCEDURES: GRIEVANCE MEDIATION

While employment dispute resolution and arbitration are addressed in other chapters in more detail, there are also innovations under way in the collectively bargained grievance procedure. The most notable innovation is the use of grievance mediation. Grievance mediation is an alternative to arbitration and is typically included as an additional step prior to arbitration. In grievance mediation, a third-party neutral assists the union and management parties in negotiating a mutually agreeable and voluntary settlement to the grievance.[44,45] Whereas arbitration is generally seen by unions and employers to be expensive, time-consuming, and overly legalistic,[46] mediation has been shown to have greater cost-effectiveness and result in swifter settlements, while simultaneously ensuring the satisfaction of participants.[32,47,48] Moreover, whereas arbitration is intrinsically adversarial, mediation has more of a cooperative nature that allows greater opportunity for problem solving and collaborative initiatives. Research has generally shown grievance mediation to be an effective alternative to arbitration, resolving more than 80% of mediated grievances, and an efficient alternative to arbitration, resolving grievances more quickly and cheaply.[32,35,49]

CONCLUSION

This chapter provided an overview of the collectively bargained grievance procedure, its structure, a brief review of theories about its function, major themes in the empirical research about that function, and an introduction to grievance mediation as a recent innovation. The grievance procedure is an essential component of the collective bargaining relationship, one that makes the benefits of industrial democracy accessible to the individual employee. It provides employees with a meaningful avenue to exercise voice with regard to workplace concerns. Researchers have learned much about what factors contribute to grievance initiation, how procedures can process grievances most efficiently and effectively, and what grievance procedures produce in terms of decisions and outcomes. However, there is still need for considerably more research, particularly on the systemic impact of grievance procedures on organizational performance.

REFERENCES

1. BNA Editorial Staff. *Grievance Guide*, 10th Ed.; The Bureau of National Affairs, Inc.: Washington, DC, 2000.
2. Richardson, R.C. *Collective Bargaining by Objectives: A Positive Approach*; Prentice-Hall, Inc.: Englewood Cliffs, NJ, 1985.
3. Mesch, D.J.; Shamayeva, O. Arbitration in practice: A profile of public sector arbitration cases. Public Pers. Manage. **1996**, *25*, 119–132.
4. Duane, M.J. *The Grievance Process in Labor-Management Cooperation*; Quorum Books: Westport, CT, 1993.
5. Lewin, D.; Peterson, R.B. *The Modern Grievance Procedure in the United States*; Greenwood Press: Westport, CT, 1988.
6. Knight, T.R. Feedback and grievance resolution. Ind. Labor Relat. Rev. **1986**, *39*, 585–598.
7. Knight, T.R. Toward a Contingency Theory of the Grievance-Arbitration System. In *Advances in Industrial and Labor Relations*; Lipsky, D., Ed.; JAI Press: Greenwich, CT, 1985; Vol. 2, 269–318.
8. Lewin, D. Theoretical Perspectives on the Modern Grievance Procedure. In *New Approached to Labor Unions: Research in Labor Economics*; Reid, J.D., Ed.; JAI Press: Greenwich, CT, 1983; 127–147. Supplement 2.
9. Lewin, D. Empirical measures of grievance procedure effectiveness. Labor Law J. **1984**, *35*, 491–499.
10. Peterson, R.B.; Lewin, D. A Model for Research and Analysis of the Grievance Process. In *Proceedings of the 34th Annual Meeting of the Industrial Relations Research Association*; IRRA: Madison, WI, 1982; 303–312.
11. Greenberg, J. Looking Fair and Being Fair: Managing Impressions of Organizational Justice. In *Research in Organizational Behavior*; Shaw, B.M., Cummings, L.L., Eds.; 1990; Vol. 12, 111–157.
12. Sheppard, B.H.; Lewicki, R.J.; Minton, J. *Organizational Justice*; Lexington: Lexington, MA, 1992.
13. Folger, R.; Greenberg, J. Procedural Justice: An Interpretive Analysis of Personnel Systems. In *Research in Personnel and Human Resource Management*; Rowland, K.M., Ferris, G.R., Eds.; JAI Press: Greenwich, CT, 1985; 141–183.
14. Fryxell, G.E.; Gordon, M.E. Workplace justice and job satisfaction as predictors of satisfaction with union and management. Acad. Manage. J. **1989**, *32*, 851–866.
15. Hirschman, A.O. *Exit, Voice, and Loyalty*; Harvard University Press: Cambridge, MA, 1970.
16. Bemmels, B. Exit, Voice, and Loyalty in Employment Relationships. In *The Human Resource Management Handbook*; Lewin, D., Mitchell, D.J.B., Zaidi, M.A., Eds.; JAI Press: Greenwich, CT, 1997; 245–259.
17. Rees, D.I. Grievance procedure strength and teacher quits. Ind. Labor Relat. Rev. **1991**, *45*, 31–43.
18. Freeman, R.B.; Medoff, J. *What Do Unions Do?* Basic Books: New York, 1984.
19. Lewin, D. Dispute resolution in a nonunion firm: A theoretical and empirical analysis. J. Confl. Resolut. **1987**, *31*, 465–502.

20. Boroff, K. Measuring the Perceptions of the Effectiveness of a Workplace Complaint Procedure. In *Advances in Industrial and Labor Relations*; Sockell, D., Lewin, D., Lipsky, D., Eds.; 1991; 207–235.

21. Lewin, D.; Peterson, R.B. Behavioral outcomes of grievance activity. Ind. Relat. **1999**, *4*, 554–576.

22. Labig, C.E.; Greer, C.R. Grievance initiation: A literature survey and suggestions for future research. J. Labor Res. **1988**, *9*, 1–27.

23. Allen, R.E.; Keaveny, T. Factors differentiating grievances and non-grievants. Hum. Relat. **1985**, *38*, 519–534.

24. Labig, C.E.; Helburn. Union and management policy influences on grievance initiation. J. Labor Res. **1986**, *7*, 269–284.

25. Kleiner, M.M.; Nicklesburg, G.; Pilarski, A. Monitoring, grievances, and plant performance. Ind. Relat. **1995**, *34*, 169–189.

26. Dalton, D.R.; Todor, W.D. Antecedents of grievance filing behavior: Attitudes/behavioral consistency and the union steward. Acad. Manage. J. **1982**, *25*, 158–169.

27. Bemmels, B.; Reshef, Y.; Stratton-Devine, K. The roles of supervisors, employees, and stewards in grievance initiation. Ind. Labor Relat. **1991**, *45*, 15–30.

28. Meyer, D.; Cooke, D. Economic and political factors in formal grievance resolution. Ind. Relat. **1988**, *27*, 318–335.

29. Meyer, D. The political effects of grievance handling by stewards in a local union. J. Labor Res. **1994**, *15*, 33–52.

30. Dastmalchian, A.; Ng, I. Industrial relations climate and grievance outcomes. Ind. Relat. **1990**, *45*, 311–324.

31. Ury, W.; Brett, J.; Goldberg, S. *Getting Disputes Resolved: Designing Systems to Cut the Cost of Conflict*; Jossey-Bass Publishers, Inc.: San Francisco, CA, 1989.

32. Feuille, P. Dispute Resolution Frontiers in the Unionized Workplace. In *Workplace Dispute Resolution: Directions for the Twenty-First Century*; Gleason, S.E., Ed.; Michigan University Press: East Lansing, MI, 1997; 17–55.

33. Davy, J.A.; Stewart, G.; Anderson, J. Formalization of grievance procedures: A multi-firm and industry study. J. Labor Res. **1992**, *13*, 307–316.

34. Mesch, D.J.; Dalton, D.R. Arbitration in practice: Win, lose, or draw? Hum. Resour. Prof. **1992**, *44*, 37–41.

35. Feuille, P. Grievance Mediation. In *Employment Dispute Resolution and Worker Rights in the Changing Workplace*;

36. Mesch, D.J. Grievance arbitration in the public sector: A conceptual framework and empirical analysis of public and private sector arbitration cases. Rev. Public Pers. Adm. **1995**, 22–36, Fall.

37. Brett, J.M.; Goldberg, S.P. Wildcat strikes in bituminous coal mining. Ind. Labor Relat. Rev. **1979**, *32*, 465–483.

38. Spencer, D.G. Employee voice and employee retention. Acad. Manage. J. **1986**, *29*, 488–502.

39. Ichniowski, C.; Lewin, D. Grievance Procedure and Firm Performance. In *Human Resources and the Performance of the Firm*; Kleiner, M.M., Block, R.N., Roomkin, M., Salsburg, S.W., Eds.; Industrial Relations Research Association: Madison, WI, 1987; 159–193.

40. Ichniowski, C. The effects of grievance activity on productivity. Ind. Labor Relat. Rev. **1986**, *40*, 75–89.

41. Katz, H.C.; Kochan, T.A.; Gobeille, K. Industrial relations performance, economic performance, and the effects of quality of working life efforts: An interplant analysis. Ind. Labor Relat. Rev. **1983**, *37*, 3–17.

42. Katz, H.C.; Kochan, T.A.; Weber, M. Assessing the effects of industrial relations and quality of working life efforts on organizational effectiveness. Acad. Manage. J. **1985**, *28*, 509–527.

43. Norsworthy, J.R.; Zabala, C.A. Worker attitudes, worker behavior, and productivity in the U.S. automobile industry, 1959–76. Ind. Labor Relat. Rev. **1985**, *38*, 544–557.

44. Moore, C. *The Mediation Process*, 2nd Ed.; Jossey-Bass Publishers, Inc.: San Francisco, CA, 1996.

45. Connors, E.K.; Bashore-Smith, B. Employment dispute resolution in the United States: An overview. Can.-U.S. Law J. **1991**, *17*, 319.

46. Goldberg, S.B. The mediation of grievances under a collective bargaining contract: An alternative to arbitration. Northwest. Univ. Law Rev. **1982**, *77*, 270–315.

47. Goldberg, S.B.; Brett, J.M. An experiment in the mediation of grievances. Mon. Labor Rev. **1983**, *106*, 23–30.

48. Brett, J.M.; Goldberg, S.P. Grievance mediation in the coal industry: A field experiment. Ind. Labor Relat. Rev. **1983**, *37*, 49–69.

49. Feuille, P. Why does grievance mediation resolve grievances? Mediat. J. **1992**, *8*, 131–146.

Eaton, A.E., Keefe, J., Eds.; Industrial Relations Research Association: Champaign, IL, 1999; 187–217.

Groups and Their Properties

Claus Langfred
Washington University, St. Louis, Missouri, U.S.A.

INTRODUCTION

Groups are an inherent part of human social organization and have relatively recently been heavily incorporated into modern organizations in the form of work groups and teams. Groups have many important features that affect their performance and dynamics, and while they are prized for the performance benefits they have compared to the same number of individuals, they can also be a source of inefficiency, conflict, and errors.

As a general rule, effective groups require three things. First, the group must have the knowledge, skills, and abilities (KSAs) necessary to perform the task. Not every member of a group needs to have all of the KSAs for the group to succeed, but the group collectively must have them. Second, motivation and willingness to expend effort toward the group's goal is necessary. If group members are not interested in performing the task, it matters little whether they are able to or not. The converse is also true: no matter how motivated or enthusiastic members of a group are, the group will not succeed without the necessary KSAs. Third is the communication and coordination necessary to carry out the task. Many groups fail in this third category and often do not understand why. These are the three minimum requirements for groups to be effective and successful.

DEFINITION AND TYPES OF GROUPS

A work group (or team) is a collection of individuals who see themselves, and are seen by others, as a social entity and who are embedded in one or more larger social systems. They are interdependent (to some degree) in their tasks and often manage relationships with people external to the group. While most agree with the basic definition by Hackman,[1] some researchers feel that ''team'' connotes more than ''group,'' describing a group with relatively more commitment and cohesion, in addition to a greater task focus.

Teams can be subdivided into various categories and typologies, such as parallel, project, cross-functional, management, and others. While such distinctions separate them on the basis of task, it is not clear that they distinguish groups from teams. As a general rule, the terms group and team can be used interchangeably with little loss of meaning. This article focuses on the small group or team, typically ranging in size from as little as three or four people up to as many as 20 people.

POPULARITY AND PREVALENCE OF GROUPS

The use of work teams has rapidly grown in the United States, with an estimated half of all employees currently working in team situations. Work groups and teams have become critical to organizational effectiveness, and their use has become pervasive in modern organizations. The use of teams and groups ranges from the production floor to the executive suite and covers activities from heart surgery to fire fighting and from dog food manufacturing to space exploration. Teams are used by social service agencies, in the military, and in hospitals, and in schools and universities. It is difficult to identify a field of human endeavor in which groups and teams have not become commonplace. Even in a relatively specialized and individual field like academia, we find groups represented in permanent and temporary committees, departments, and for administrative tasks.

With the increased adoption of groups and teams by a wide range of firms and organizations, and as the use of groups and teams in organizations continues to increase, researchers and practitioners focused their attention on understanding the dynamics, design, and effectiveness of teams. As the use of teams has increased, so has the variety of different team designs. The use of self-managing, empowered, or autonomous groups and teams has increased dramatically in recent decades. Of Fortune 1000 firms, about two-thirds use self-managed work teams, and practically all use employee participation groups of some sort.

CHARACTERISTICS OF GROUPS

Group size is one of the most obvious of group characteristics, and it affects groups in many ways. The ideal group size is between four and eight people. When a group becomes too large, it is more difficult to effectively

Encyclopedia of Public Administration and Public Policy
DOI: 10.1081/E-EPAP 120010859

coordinate the behavior of group members, and the group starts to divide into smaller subgroups and cliques. Larger groups are more susceptible to various motivational problems, such as free riding and social loafing. If a group is too small, on the other hand, many benefits of groups can be lost, and conflict and polarization are more likely.

The structure of a group can vary widely and refers to the way a group is organized and how various positions in the group relate to one another. Well-established groups will have a much more developed and rigid structure than newly formed groups. Characteristics like roles, status, norms, cohesion, and interdependence are part of a group's structure.

Diversity refers to the variation among group members on a variety of dimensions, such as background, education, nationality, ethnicity, age, gender, etc. If the task of the group involves decision making, problem solving, or creative tasks, diversity allows the group to perform better and with greater accuracy and quality. However, if the group's task is highly interdependent and requires considerable coordination, then diversity can interfere with its ability to perform effectively. While a group with little diversity, and hence few differences, can coordinate and communicate effectively, it cannot be as effective at problem solving and decision making. The benefits or costs of diversity are thus dependent on the task and other characteristics of the group.

Roles are the expected behaviors associated with a given position within a group. Members of a group will generally occupy different social roles. Some roles are formal and may be externally imposed, while others are less formal and may emerge over time. Group members may hold multiple roles, and roles may even be switched or interchanged within a group. Different social roles are usually associated with different degrees of status, which affect group dynamics insofar as members with higher status may have more influence or may be less susceptible to group norms or pressure.

Group norms are the general rules and expectations for appropriate behavior that are accepted by the group. Norms can be explicit, or they can be implicit and emerge over time. Norms generally develop quickly and often have a strong influence on member behavior. Groups are effective at enforcing behavior to conform to the norms in the group, particularly in cohesive groups. The more cohesive a group, the better it is at enforcing conformity to group norms.

Cohesion is the extent to which group members feel a part of the group and wish to remain in the group. Generally, the more cohesive a group, the more loyal and committed group members are to the group. Cohesion can be good or bad, in that high cohesion in a group means it is good at enforcing norms, regardless of what those

norms are. If the group is interested in and motivated toward high performance, this is desirable, but it is quite detrimental if the group is motivated toward other goals, interfering with high performance. Effective teams generally are characterized by high cohesion combined with performance-oriented norms.

Interdependence is the degree to which coordination between individuals in the group is necessary for successful task attainment. Depending on the nature of the task, interdependence can be described as pooled, reciprocal, or sequential.[2] The interdependence in a group dictates the extent to which coordination and communication are required in the group and is one of the defining and most crucial characteristics of a group. A highly interdependent group with high coordination requirements clearly is different from a group in which close coordination among group members is not necessary for group goals to be realized.

While leadership has long been known to exert a strong influence on group effectiveness, few general conclusions can be drawn about leadership. Depending on organizational contexts—such as the immediate task environment, resources, time pressures, interdependence, diversity, personalities and attitudes of group members, and other factors—different leadership styles may be appropriate to the situation. Under some conditions, an empowering and inclusive leadership style may yield the best results, whereas under other conditions, a directive and dictatorial leadership style may be most effective.

Autonomy has received a lot of attention in recent years, as the prevalence of self-managing teams, autonomous work groups, and empowered teams has increased dramatically. Granting autonomy to groups can lead to better group performance, because groups and group members are closer to the task and, thus, are able to make more accurate task-related decisions than a more "distant" supervisor. However, the increased coordination and communication required for group decision resulting from increased autonomy can also lead to process losses, so while the potential of autonomy is great, the implementation of it is difficult. Autonomy also raises the issue of striking a balance between the amount of autonomy that individual group members have and the amount of autonomy the group as a whole has—another difficult management decision.

Finally, an important characteristic of a group is the stage of its life cycle. Groups, like people, often have a specific life span. They are created at some point, they go though a period of learning and maturation, and they become mature groups. While some groups replenish themselves indefinitely through member turnover, others may end. Where a group is in its life cycle also has implications for dynamics and performance. Young groups are busy developing norms and communication systems and will not be able to perform as well as mature groups. A mature group, on the other hand, might be stable and cohesive but may suffer from problems of conformity, polarization, and other biases in decision making and problem solving.

BENEFITS OF GROUPS

Some of the benefits of groups are obvious, as a group of people can accomplish things that the same number of individuals cannot. Given effective coordination, groups achieve many feats that are completely outside the scope of the same number of individuals. Groups with high degrees of task interdependence particularly demonstrate this, such as a military assault team or a surgical team involved in a complicated heart procedure.

As groups make decision or solve problems, they are generally more accurate than the average group member and often as accurate as even the best group member. The group decision is much more than just a simple aggregation of individual decisions, involving active discussion and evaluation of ideas, viewpoints, and alternatives. This process of information sharing and interaction, and even conflict and disagreement, generates better decisions.

Often, disagreements lead to novel solutions or alternative viewpoints that increase the quality of decisions. Having a dissenting minority opinion in a group has been found to cause more complex and rich discussion of issues. In this sense, limited conflict in a group contributes to a higher quality of decisions. By the same logic, the amount of diversity in the group also leads to more creative outcomes, which can be further facilitated by a wide variety of existing group decision-making techniques.

Groups, through such characteristics and cohesion and strong norms, can also increase commitment and motivation to a task, such that a group may expend a lot more effort and energy on a task than the same number of individuals. In military organizations, morale and esprit de corps is deliberately encouraged and reinforced so that units will be more motivated and will not give up on difficult tasks, where otherwise, individuals might lose motivation. This is one of the greatest strengths of groups, the social identification that can be generated, and is a method by which members of a group may be much more motivated toward a goal than a comparable number of individuals.

A more "hard-wired" variation of this motivational effect that membership in a group may have on individual members is the phenomenon of social facilitation. Social facilitation is the effect that the "mere presence" of others has on performance.[3] When other people are present, individuals tend to perform better or work harder. The theory is more complex, and disagreement exists as to the mechanisms and details of the phenomenon, but it is indisputable that the presence of other group members affects the effort level of an individual.

Another aspect of the strong social interactions that can improve group and team performance over that of the same number of individuals is trust. Along with strong cohesion and norms, highly effective teams are characterized by high levels of trust within the team and toward the team leader or supervisor. In the context of a team, particularly a highly interdependent team, trust is much more likely to develop than in an independent group of individuals.

Thus, a stable and cohesive team consisting of relatively interdependent people, who share performance-oriented norms and trust one another, and who possess the KSAs, motivation, and communication skills to accomplish their goal, will be far more effective than the same number of individuals working toward the same goal. In some cases, the individuals will not be able to accomplish the goal, and in others they will simply perform at a much lower level.

POTENTIAL HAZARDS OF GROUPS

While a variety of benefits to groups are outlined above, there are also aspects of group dynamics that can hurt performance. It is important to note that in the balance, the benefits of groups far outweigh the hazards (hence, the widespread use in modern organizations), but some hazards exist and can lead to poor performance and dysfunction. Understanding and recognizing these limitations is therefore important in order to avoid them. Some benefits of groups, like strong group identity and competition, can become potential problems if not managed, and these are discussed as well.

One of these potential limitations is process loss. Because groups need to coordinate the activities of members (depending on the amount of task interdependence in the group), inefficient coordination and communications can harm performance. In the extreme case, performance can be extremely poor, and process loss can outweigh any benefits of the group, as group members spend too much time trying to communicate and coordinate rather than working.

Groups can also suffer motivation losses, among individual group members or the group as a whole. Social loafing is a phenomenon where individuals decrease their effort level as the size of the group increases.[4] The effect is strongest when tasks are simple and additive or when individual effort is not easily identifiable but can be minimized when individual effort is accurately identifiable or when tasks are sufficiently involving.

Another motivational problem that occurs is free riding, which occurs when a member of a group exerts less effort and lets others in the group do more of the work. Free riding is somewhat more deliberate than social loafing and occurs when people perceive their efforts to be dispensable. In other words, if an individual believes that the group will succeed regardless of his efforts, he will be less likely to work hard. In general, groups with high task interdependence are less susceptible to extensive free riding, as are groups in which individual effort is more easily identifiable.

Free riding and social loafing can lead to other motivation losses, namely, those based on equity theory. If other group members perceive that some in the group are free riding off their efforts, they tend to lessen their effort level to reduce the perceived inequity of "carrying" the free rider. This loss of motivation has been called the "sucker effect"[5] and is a conscious and deliberate behavior. It is important to note that much as it appears that free riding can lead to a downward performance spiral, it is unlikely in cohesive groups with strong performance norms. It is more likely in groups of a temporary nature or in groups in which norms and trust have not fully developed.

Conformity effects are powerful in groups.[6] In general, people tend to conform to the group (even when they know it is wrong) when they face a unanimous group, the judgment is difficult, they value or admire the group, their deviation is easily identifiable, or they are scared. On the other hand, people conform to the group less when they have great confidence in their expertise on the issue, they have high status in the group, they are strongly committed to their initial view, or they do not like or respect the group. This is generally a good thing, in that conformity allows groups to be unified and decisive in their action, but it has a potential downside in that creativity can be stifled, and group decision making can be superficial or even erroneous.

Such pressure to conform or not to express a different view is the central component of the groupthink phenomenon,[7] in which valuable information is ignored or not even raised during discussion. The best examples of groupthink are in foreign policy, such as the Bay of Pigs invasion, Argentina's decision to invade the Falkland islands, or the escalation of the Vietnam War under Lyndon Johnson, suggesting that a crisis atmosphere contributes to the problem.

Groups can also become more polarized in opinions or behavior than the individual group members were originally. This effect occurs when group members share an underlying agreement. When this is the case, group discussion often leads to group consensus around a more extreme viewpoint than the one originally held by the group members. Group polarization is sometimes also discussed as *risky shift* in groups, in which group discussion leads to riskier decisions than individual group members'

decisions. Again, like conformity, this can be a good thing as well as a bad thing, depending on circumstances.

The risk of disagreement and conflict is, of course, a risk in any social group. While a solitary individual working on a task has no potential for conflict, groups, by definition, run the risk of conflict. Even though some disagreement and dissent contributes to better and more complex decisions, too much disagreement can obviously lead to conflict that interferes with the coordination and stability in the group, and ultimately harms performance. While a potential threat, a stable group with members that possess good communication skills is relatively immune to such destructive levels of conflict.

Groups that exist in an environment with other groups, which is the case in most organizations, also suffer from a number of perceptions and behaviors that appear to be ingrained in humans. One of these effects is in-group favoritism and out-group discrimination. Group members tend to favor their own group and discriminate against other groups, in terms of allocating resources or rewards. This effect, called the minimal group paradigm, can even be triggered by creating groups based on insignificant and arbitrary differences[8] and is, thus, quite powerful when applied to existing groups that differ on significant and salient dimensions. Individuals perceive members of their own group to be more varied and individually distinct (in-group heterogeneity) and perceive members of other groups as being more similar to one another and having less variation (out-group homogeneity). It is worth noting that this is again only a *potential* hazard. Having groups with a strong identity and commitment to the group over other groups is generally a positive trait that will contribute to cohesiveness and trust.

Groups can also become quite competitive and aggressive toward one another, leading to intergroup conflict, especially when competing for scarce resources or when incompatible goals exist.[9] Many groups in large organizations will be competing with other groups for resources, rewards, and other forms of recognition, and conflict can intensify effects such as perceptions of out-group homogeneity. When managed, this is a great source of motivation and energy for groups, and group identification combined with competitiveness can spur greater performance. Some of the greatest team performance is created in the context of intense competition with other teams. Very beneficial to organizations, this only becomes a potential problem if it is allowed to spin out of control and become destructive and nonperformance oriented.

CONCLUSION

Groups are a pervasive and inescapable aspect of life in modern organizations, and understanding and managing them is crucial to overall organizational performance. While groups can easily outperform the same number of independent individuals, it is important to be aware of potential limitations, related to process and coordination, as well as to motivational and social psychological effects, that can interfere with the considerable benefits of groups and teams.

REFERENCES

1. Hackman, J.R. Designing Work for Individuals and for Groups. In *Perspectives on Behavior in Organizations*; Hackman, J.R., Ed.; McGraw-Hill: New York, 1983; 242–256.

2. Thompson, J.D. *Organizations in Action*; McGraw-Hill: New York, 1967.

3. Zajonc, R.B. Social facilitation. Science **1965**, *149*, 269–274.

4. Latane, B.; Williams, K.; Harkins, S. Many hands make light the work: The causes and consequences of social loafing. J. Pers. Soc. Psychol. **1979**, *37* (6), 822–832.

5. Kerr, N.L. Motivation losses in task-performing groups: A social dilemma analysis. J. Pers. Soc. Psychol. **1983**, *45*, 819–828.

6. Asch, S.E. Opinions and social pressure. Sci. Am. **1955**, *193* (5), 31–35.

7. Janis, I.L. *Victims of Groupthink*; Houghton Mifflin: Boston, 1972.

8. Tajfel, H. *Human Groups and Social Categories: Studies in Social Psychology*; Cambridge University Press: Cambridge, England, 1981.

9. Sherif, M.; Harvey, O.J.; White, B.J.; Hood, W.R.; Sherif, C.W. *Intergroup Cooperation and Competition: The Robbers Cave Experiment*; University Book Exchange: Norman, OK, 1961.

Health Care Finance in the Twenty-First Century

Judith J. Kirchhoff
Long Island University, Brooklyn, New York, U.S.A.

INTRODUCTION

In the early years of the twenty-first century, it is fair to say that changes in the financing and delivery of health care services have led to a health care delivery system far different from the fragmented delivery by independent, unconnected service units characterizing most of the twentieth century. A health delivery system or integrated network offering a continuum of prepaid managed medical care is now the norm, covering 75% of the U.S. insured population.[1] The term "managed care" has come to refer to organized networks of service delivery providing or arranging provision of a continuum of services to a defined population.[2] In organizational terms, a managed care system "seeks vertical integration,"[1] a state of control by administrative decision.

The shift to widespread adoption of managed health care in the United States can be traced to 1973, when the U.S. federal government promoted competition as a method to slow health care cost inflation deriving from the launch of Medicare and Medicaid in 1967.[3] Under the 1973 law, widely referred to as the HMO Act,[4] federally qualified health maintenance organizations (HMOs) could require employers with more than 25 employees to offer an HMO option. This gave employers, and their employees, choices of health plans beyond the traditional indemnity insurance that had prevailed until then.

Growth of managed health plans initially was slow but gained momentum as the 1970s gave way to the 1980s and 1990s.[5] More health plans drew members away from indemnity insurance plans using lower premiums and broader coverage as enticements. Managed health plans' were able to lower member premiums by shfting from provider-set fees to negotiated contracts involving volume discounts.

At the same time, continuing escalation of health care costs led to higher numbers of uninsured or underinsured citizens, 40 million citizens on average in the mid-1990s.[6] This number is much smaller than the 54 million people who lacked insurance coverage for at least one month (1993) and the 67 million who lacked coverage at some point during the two-year period 1992–1993.[5]

Because the average number of citizens without insurance increased to an estimated 44 million by 1999,[7] it is likely that the dynamic numbers have increased as well. It

should be noted that underinsurance involves, to the extent permitted by law, exclusions for preexisting conditions, services not covered, absence of catastrophic coverage, insurance deductibles and copayments, gaps in medicare coverage, and lack of long-term care coverage.[5] One particularly probematic form of underinsurance occurs for individuals who reach benefit limits while still needing care;[8] such individuals often become dependent on government health care and income support, if the condition is debilitating.

In the early 1990s, the Clinton Administration proposed universal health care coverage through a complex system of "managed competition" to control costs.[9,10] Though the Clinton proposal failed to become legislation, it energized the private sector into aggressive pursuit of alternatives, resulting in a pronounced shift to managed health plans.[11]

Health care finance at the dawn of the twenty-first century can be understood in terms of decision choices of participants in the health care system and payment mechanism incentives.

PARTICIPATION DECISIONS AND FINANCING

Health plans are entities providing health care services at a fixed monthly premium for a specific period of time. Employees join health plans through their employers, who pay a fixed premium per employee for a specified benefits package for a specific period of time, usually one year. The health plan selects providers and negotiates price, volume, and payment method, which may vary depending on the type of provider. The health plan "manages" members and delivery of care using administrative tools and analytical processes. Providers include primary care physicians and specialists, inpatient and outpatient services, labs and imaging centers, pharmacies, therapists, and home health organizations.[12] Patients are health plan members who access care through in-plan providers or, at extra personal cost, out-of-plan providers.

Employers are the dominant purchasers of health care coverage for their employees.[6] Taxpayers, through government purchasers, finance Medicare for the elderly and other eligible patients, Medicaid for the eligible poor,

Encyclopedia of Public Administration and Public Policy
DOI: 10.1081/E-EPAP 120010756

care for the Armed Forces and their dependents, eligible veterans, American Indians, children and the working poor, and other eligible populations.[13] More recently, the 1997 federal State Children's Health Insurance Program (SCHIP) provided strong incentives to states to expand health care coverage for children in families with incomes of less than 200% of the U.S. poverty level but higher than Medicaid eligibility levels.[14] By the end of 2001, the program provided coverage for three million children.

In transactions with health plans, employers are motivated to keep their expenditures for health care coverage low, choosing health plans offering benefits that attract and keep good employees while minimizing employer health care expenses. Some employers drop coverage for their employees if premiums increase too much.[15] Employees participate in health care coverage costs to the degree of their contributions to premium payments and the amount of co-pays to health providers.

For example, a relatively young and healthy single employee may perceive little need for health care coverage and participate only to the degree required, effectively gambling on remaining well and accident-free. Other employees may have conditions requiring continuous or expensive medical care, or family members with such conditions. These employees know that they will use more benefits than they pay for, and are grateful that they have coverage at all.

Government purchasers, because they are purchasing for large numbers, have great leverage in negotiating prices. Indeed, the federal government prospectively sets prices as one strategy for estimating cost outlays. The ability to estimate is limited, because Medicare and Medicaid are entitlement programs for their eligible populations, meaning all who are eligible may enroll, and all who enroll are entitled to all medically indicated approved services.[16] Thus, demand for approved services ultimately determines government expenditures for these programs in any given year.

Health plans seek profitability, that is, revenues greater than expenditures. Health plan ''products'' are benefit packages sold for the ''monthly premiums'' that employers pay and health plans use to pay providers and other operating costs. More generous benefit packages carry higher potential costs for the health plan and require higher premiums. Federal and state mandates require some types of coverage, and others are left to the health plan's discretion. Health plans calculate annual premiums using actuarial data, i.e., members' demographic characteristics and historical health care utilization data. Plan profitability depends in part on skilled forecasting of members' service utilization and in part on setting premium rates high enough to be profitable without discouraging membership in the plans.

In order to meet these goals, health plans seek control of plan members' health care utilization decisions through financial incentives, for example, co-payments and charges for out-of-network care. If the plan member seeks in-plan provider network care, one co-payment applies. Out-of-network providers carry a higher co-payment. Staff model health plans restrict access to staff providers and others only as authorized by the staff providers.[1]

Changes in health plan membership take place annually during an open enrollment period. Employers may elect to discontinue coverage for all employees if premium costs increase too much, a choice many have exercised in recent years. Or, a large employer may move to self-funding health care costs, that is, become self-insured. Governments cannot eliminate health benefits to eligible recipients without legislative authorization. Plan members can change health plans but may not withdraw from at least minimum coverage by their employer. Health plans may elect not to offer coverage to an employer or membership categories, for example, the elderly, as some health plans have opted to do. In addition to federal regulation, many states regulate health plan choices about offering and withdrawing coverage, among other practices.[4]

Employers and employees, governments, and health plans also can seek to limit their risks by limiting benefits offered (services covered), shifting more costs to others, or, in the case of governments, by limiting eligibility for the entitlement. Health plans also have the option, with constraints already mentioned, of limiting benefits or raising premium rates, both at the risk of encouraging employers to respond by self-insuring, searching for less costly health plans, or eliminating coverage. Employee options are limited by employer decisions about coverage. The employee may seek another employer, buy additional coverage through an outside source, or, if a spouse also has employer-sponsored coverage, elect to be covered under the spouse's plan.

MANAGED CARE FINANCIAL INCENTIVES

The financial incentives used by health plans profoundly affect the way health care services are delivered. The goal of the health plan in these transactions, as already noted, is profitability, which depends in part on the ability of the health plan to control expenditures to providers and internal operating costs. Controlling expenditures to providers requires managing utilization of care by plan members and delivery of care by providers.[17] In their efforts to manage providers and patients, health plans employ incentives designed to reduce the amount, frequency, and intensity of services delivered by providers and used by patients[18] and to shift risk to members and providers.

Financial incentives vary by provider type. Capitated rates are most frequently used with primary care physicians (PCPs).[19] PCPs are "gatekeeper" physicians who control access to the rest of the medical care system. Capitation pays per member per month fees for each enrollee registered with a provider. The capitated payment is designed to cover medical care within the practitioner's scope of practice and often includes routine lab tests and specialist referrals. Capitated payments make provider forecasts of plan member utilization extremely important.

For care outside the PCPs scope of practice, PCPs refer to specialists under another financial mechanism that often links additional PCP revenue to number of referrals. A percentage of PCP capitation revenue may be "withheld" to create a pool of funds used to pay specialists.[19] Alternatively, the cost of specialists may come directly out of the PCP's capitation income.[19]

In the first case, whatever is "saved" by minimizing the use of specialists is shared by the plan's PCPs at the end of the contract year. Those with fewer referrals often earn the largest share of the pool. Some states regulate such revenue-sharing practices. In the second case, the PCP may make significant "profit" if many enrollees seek no care during the year, but the PCP is at risk of substantial losses if some patients have high specialty medicine costs. PCPs must carry stop-loss insurance to cover for such situations.[20]

Some services are "carved out" of the capitation payment system, as are certain kinds of care, for example, mental health services[19] and expensive but relatively infrequent procedures like neurosurgery and cardiac surgery.

Capitation rates base health plan expenditures and PCP revenues on number of enrollees. Health plans can forecast expenditures, and physicians can forecast their annual revenues from the plan based on the number of plan members they serve.[20] Total physician revenues will be calculated from the number of plans accepted and the number of enrollees from each plan. Total health plan expenditures to each physician also are settled for the contract year based on members enrolled in the PCP's practice. Members can change PCPs freely within a health plan's provider list, and health plans manage such changes carefully, because plans do not want to pay two PCPs for the member who changes from one PCP to another. The capitated payment follows the member from the "losing" physician to the "gaining" physician.

Discounted fees and prospectively set case rates are contract payment mechanisms commonly used for hospitals and other providers. Discounted fees simply pay a set amount for the service. For example, a physical therapist may charge $90 for a service unit, and the health plan may pay $60. The economic incentive for the physical therapist is to shorten the service unit time of $60 patients. A case rate bundles services into an identifiable episode of care reimbursed at a flat fee. Medicare's diagnostic-related groups are perhaps the most familiar type of case rate[21] for inpatient care.

For outpatient care, Resource Based Relative Value Units are a form of case rate.[19] Discount and case rate contracts may involve negotiations between payers and providers over the amount of the discount from charges (providers' regular price) and assumptions used in setting case rates or global fees for specified categories of members or care episodes.

Revenues are more difficult to forecast with discounted fees and case rates, because they are based on service units rather than a fixed number of patients or episodes of care. Case rates incorporate assumptions about episode duration and procedures.[19]

Health plan internal operations are controlled by executive decisions and management of employees. Internal operations of health plans constitute administrative costs. Health plans have marketing and sales functions, processing and paying enrollee medical care claims functions, and provider and patient relations functions. Marketing and sales functions are related to selling benefits packages to employers, medical care claims are a payment function, and provider and patient relations are new health plan management functions associated with controlling the amount of care provided.

Health plan operations management includes developing provider networks to deliver medical services to enrollees; negotiating prices with provider representatives or providers; precertifying procedures; coordinating benefits for enrollees with separate coverage; managing individual episodes of care; reviewing patient utilization, physician diagnosis and treatment patterns, and hospital lengths of stay; encouraging enrollees to undergo preventive tests; ensuring good relationships with providers and enrollees; and monitoring provider and patient satisfaction.[22]

These activities are replicated in provider organizations to fulfill health plan reporting requirements and to generate management information for complex contract decisions.[23] This adds administrative costs to providers' operations. At the same time, federal and state governments add regulatory complexity, requiring physicians and hospitals to provide more and better documentation to prevent fraud and ensure quality care at reasonable cost.[24] Additionally, increasing amounts of quality information about health plans is available to assist employers in making coverage decisions, but studies show that it is rarely used.[25] All of these functions add administrative costs to health care service delivery in the United States, costs incorporated into the sales, premium, expenditure cycle described herein.

In summary, the health care system at the turn of the twenty-first century is far different from that which dominated for much of the twentieth century. The health care system is rapidly becoming organized and managed by profit-making health care plans using financial incentives that spread costs and risks among the participants. At this point in time, however, it cannot be said that managed health care is less costly or more efficient. After a short period of declining inflation in health care costs, costs to all participants are on the rise again.

REFERENCES

1. Folland, S.; Goodman, A.; Stano, M. Managed Care. In *The Economics of Health and Health Care*; Prentice-Hall: Upper Saddle River, NJ, 2001; 248–280.
2. Kovner, A.R. Health Maintenance Organizations and Managed Care. In *Jonas and Kovner's Health Delivery in the United States*, 6th Ed.; Kovner, A.R., Jonas, S., Eds.; Springer: New York, 2001; 279–306.
3. Patel, K.; Rushefsky, M.E. Health Care Policy in the United States. In *Health Care Politics and Policy in the United States*, 2nd Ed.; M. E. Sharpe: Armonk, NY, 1999; 25–54.
4. Pozgar, G.D. Managed Care and Organizational Restructuring. In *Legal Aspects of Health Care Administration*; Aspen: Gaithersburg, MD, 1996; 615–653.
5. Bodenheimer, T.S.; Grumbach, K. Access to Health Care. In *Understanding Health Care Policy, A Clinical Approach*; McGraw Hill: New York, 2002; 15–32.
6. Folland, S.; Goodman, A.; Stano, M. The Organization of Health Insurance Markets. In *The Economics of Health and Health Care*; Prentice-Hall: Upper Saddle River, NJ, 2001; 227–247.
7. Fershein, J.; Sandy, L.G. The Changing Approach to Managed Care. In *To Improve Health and Health Care 2001*; Isaacs, S.L., Knickman, J.R., Eds.; Robert Wood Johnson Foundation: Princeton, NJ, 2001; 77–100.
8. Billings, J. Access to Health Care Services. In *Jonas and Kovner's Health Delivery in the United States*, 6th Ed.; Kovner, A.R., Jonas, S., Eds.; Springer: New York, 2001; 401–438.
9. Maxwell, J.; Temin, P. Managed competition versus industrial purchasing of health care among the Fortune 500. J. Health Polit. Policy Law **2002**, *27* (1), 5–30.
10. Starr, P. *The Logic of Health Care Reform*; Penguin Group Publications: New York, 1994.
11. Loomis, C.J. The real action in health care. Fortune **1994, July 11**, 149–154.
12. Kovner, C.; Salsberg, E.S. The Health Care Work Force. In *Jonas and Kovner's Health Delivery in the United States*, 6th Ed.; Kovner, A.R., Jonas, S., Eds.; Springer: New York, 2001; 64–115.
13. Patel, K.; Rushefsky, M.E. Health Care Policy in the United States. In *Health Care Politics and Policy in America*; M. E. Sharpe: Armonk, NY, 1999; 25–54.
14. Bodenheimer, T.S.; Grumbach, K. Paying for Health Care. In *Understanding Health Care Policy, A Clinical Approach*; McGraw Hill: New York, 2002; 5–14.
15. Thorpe, K.E.; Knickman, J.R. Financing for Health Care. In *Jonas and Kovner's Health Care Delivery in the United States*, 6th Ed.; Springer: New York, 2001; 32–63.
16. Patel, K.; Rushefsky, M.E. Medicaid Health Care for the Poor. In *Health Care Politics and Policy in America*; M. E. Sharpe: Armonk, NY, 1999; 55–94.
17. Shimshak, D.G.; DeFuria, M.C.; DiGiorgio, J.J.; Getson, J. Controlling Disenrollment in Health Maintenance Organizations. In *Managed Care, Strategies, Networks and Management*; Brown, M., Ed.; Aspen: Gaithersburg, MD, 1994; 231–238.
18. Bodenheimer, T.S.; Grumbach, K. Mechanisms for Controlling Costs. In *Understanding Health Care Policy, A Clinical Approach*; McGraw Hill: New York, 2002; 89–103.
19. Zelman, W.N.; McCue, M.J.; Millikan, A.R. Alternative Payment Systems and Provider Cost. In *Financial Management of Health Care Organizations*; Blackwell: Malden, MA, 1998; 342–370.
20. Bodenheimer, T.S.; Grumbach, K. Capitation Payment in Managed Care. In *Understanding Health Care Policy, A Clinical Approach*; McGraw Hill: New York, 2002; 44–52.
21. Patel, K.; Rushefsky, M.E. Health Care Cost Containment. In *Health Care Politics and Policy in the America*; M. E. Sharpe: Armonk, NY, 1999; 162–195.
22. Duncan, W.J.; Ginter, P.M.; Swayne, L.E. *Strategic Management of Health Care Organizations*, 2nd Ed.; Blackwell: Cambridge, MA, 1995.
23. Bodenheimer, T.S.; Grumbach, K. Reimbursing Health Care Providers. In *Understanding Health Care Policy, A Clinical Approach*; McGraw Hill: New York, 2002; 33–43.
24. Sparrow, M. *License to Steal: Why Fraud Plagues America's Health Care System*; Westview Press: Boulder, CO, 1996.
25. Patel, K.; Rushefsky, M.E. The Triumph of Incrementalism. In *Health Care Politics and Policy in America*; M. E. Sharpe: Armonk, NY, 1999; 292–339.

Health Care Organizations, Managing

Grant T. Savage
The University of Alabama, Tuscaloosa, Alabama, U.S.A.

Julie W. Robinson
Tuscaloosa Research and Education Advancement Corporation, Tuscaloosa, Alabama, U.S.A.

INTRODUCTION

The United States has experienced major changes in the way health care is delivered and coordinated, making the task of managing these organizations both complex and uncertain. Therefore, top managers need not only the traditional skills of communication, leadership, planning, and organizing, but also conflict, stakeholder, and strategic management skills. This article provides a current snapshot of the health care industry, trace its history, and note current trends in health care management. It concludes by noting the need to expand managerial competencies, as well as the vision of what health care organizations can accomplish.

A CURRENT SNAPSHOT OF THE HEALTH CARE INDUSTRY

Hospitals are no longer the dominant centers for health care delivery. Ambulatory, home health, and long-term care facilities represent significant rivals. Moreover, managed care organizations, for-profit corporations, and the government exert significant influence on the industry. Ambulatory care services have grown and expanded with advances in medical technology. These advances also are making it possible for home health agencies to provide care to more patients. At the same time, managed care and government programs have significantly reduced reimbursements, and hospitals have integrated with other care providers, creating organized delivery systems and networks. Long-term care has also been transformed, with assisted living centers having been built at a rapid pace. Fig. 1 shows the major players that influence the health service delivery sector.

Buyers

Employers, state and federal governments, and insurers are buyers of health services. Because of cost containment pressures from buyers, health care providers have reduced staff and sought economies of scale through mergers and acquisitions.[1] Addressing patient safety and quality expectations of buyers is a major challenge for health care providers.

Suppliers

Suppliers include the pharmaceutical, medical, and durable goods and devices that enable health care organizations to provide services. Suppliers are declining in number. Competition, rising costs, and consolidation have encouraged this trend.[1]

Substitutes

Alternative and complementary medicine is gaining greater acceptance and use by health care consumers. Complementary and alternative medicine is defined as "diagnosis, treatment and/or prevention which complements mainstream medicine by contributing to a common whole, by satisfying a demand not met by orthodoxy or by diversifying the conceptual frameworks of medicine."[2] Many people have turned to alternative or complementary treatments such as acupuncture, chiropractic, and herbal remedies out of frustration with traditional medicine.

New Entrants

Long-term care facilities—in particular, assisted living centers and web-enabled home health—are just two of the emerging entrants in the health care industry. Assisted living centers provide a combination of housing, support services, and limited health care. As of 2000, more than 1 million Americans were living in assisted living residences.[3] Assisted living, a consumer-driven sector of the health care industry, appeals to the healthiest segment of those in long-term care, with the sickest and least capable patients concentrated in nursing homes. Web-enabled home health is further accentuating this trend, as

Encyclopedia of Public Administration and Public Policy
DOI: 10.1081/E-EPAP 120010762

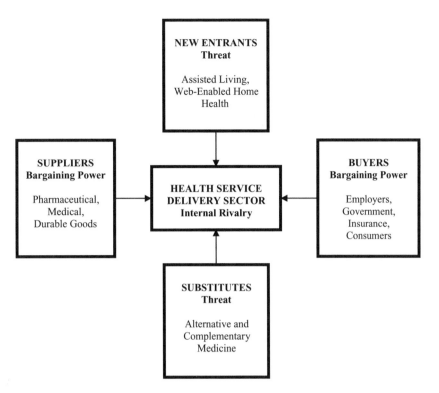

Fig. 1 Market forces model.

telemedicine allows chronically ill patients to be monitored at a distance.

BRIEF HISTORY OF HEALTH CARE ORGANIZATION AND MANAGEMENT

Before the advent of hospitals, health care was a private matter, delivered in the patient's home. The services of private physicians, midwives, and nurses were obtained when needed and financially feasible. Chemists sold medications or ''tonics.'' Health care has since centralized, decentralized, and is now integrated (Table 1).

Centralization of Care

Hospitals in the United States began with the almhouses and pesthouses of the 1700s.[4] Local governments established these facilities to feed and shelter the orphaned, homeless, elderly, disabled, and chronically or mentally ill, and they provided health care as a secondary function. Hospitalization carried with it the stigma of disgrace.

During the Industrial Revolution in the United States, medical technology and training and the desire to standardize medical education all aided in the demand for and the subsequent development of hospitals. As medical technology, such as anesthesia and the X-ray, grew so did the demand by physicians for facilities with the capabilities to practice these advanced techniques.[4] Neither the physician's home nor the home of a patient was now equipped to diagnose and practice medicine.

Along with medical advancements came the need to standardize medical education and training. In 1910, Abraham Flexner lead a study of medical education. The Flexner Report sparked systematic efforts to standardize medical education.[4] Apprenticeships with practitioners gave way to hands-on experience in a facility with the capabilities to train students in the most advanced medical technology. Hospitals became not only places of care, but also teaching, research, and training facilities. During the early twentieth century, most administrators were physicians or clergymen who often followed the preferences of local physicians. Most hospitals centralized power at the executive level, much like a university. The competencies necessary to manage included internally focused communication, leadership, organizing, and planning skills.

World War II contributed to the development of hospitals as not-for-profit institutions. Americans began

Table 1 Organizational phases

Organizational phase	Period		
Centralization of care	1850 to 1899 • Development of the Pennsylvania Hospital • Growth of medical and caring professions • Introduction of public health	1900 to 1964 • Beginning of advances in medical technology, training, knowledge and standardization of medical education • Formation of insurance plans • Hill-Burton Act	1965 to 1970 • Creation and expansion of Medicare and Medicaid • Growth in health services and medical specialization
Decentralization of care	1971 to 1980 • Shift from inpatient to outpatient care begins • Beginning of cost containment efforts by insurers and government • For-profit hospital chains emerge	1983 to 1985 • Medicare prospective payment system enacted and implemented • Managed care gains market share • Growth in joint ventures between hospitals and physicians	1986 to 1990 • Freestanding ambulatory care facilities double • Many rural and secondary hospitals close • Hospitals diversify to counter market competition
Integration of care	1990s • Integrated Delivery Systems emerge as a result of consolidation, mergers, and acquisitions	1996 • Over 55% of U.S. hospitals report being in an alliance	1999 • 72% of hospitals reported being in an alliance

organizing care for mentally and physically wounded veterans. The number of skilled and technical workers increased in hospitals, and management's role became one of creating an environment where health care professionals could do their job, as opposed to controlling the workplace.[5] Moreover, employers began paying for health insurance. The federal government had placed wage and price controls on war industries, so employers used health coverage for recruitment and retention.[6]

Direct federal involvement in hospitals began in 1947. The Hill-Burton Act was intended to fund the construction of hospitals in rural areas, but amendments extended it to provide grants that matched the funds generated by a community.[4] The federal government's involvement continued to grow in the mid-1960s with the creation of Medicare and Medicaid. These programs, along with employer-sponsored health insurance, increased the demand for hospital-based health services. Top managers of hospitals were referred to as administrators, and often had either clinical or accounting backgrounds.[7] By the

1970s, hospitals were the center of medical activity, and the administrator's duties had become increasingly complex. Managerial competencies included not only communication, leadership, organizing, and planning skills, but also increasingly skills in conflict management and external relations.

Decentralization of Care

The 1980s and 1990s gave rise to the professionalization of health care management. Hospital administrators were now referred to as chief executive officers (CEOs). The majority of CEOs were educated—as they are today—at the master's degree level in health services administration.[8] A shift from inpatient care to outpatient care also occurred during the 1980s. Reimbursement incentives, continued medical advances, and the introduction of managed care were three factors that prompted the shift.

The enactment of the Medicare prospective payment system (PPS) in 1983 resulted in hospitals being paid a "predetermined amount for Medicare inpatients based on diagnosis-related groups (DRGs)."[9] The PPS encouraged hospitals, physicians, and health care entrepreneurs to enter the ambulatory care arena. Ambulatory care takes place in various locales including urgent care centers, physician offices, hospital emergency rooms, and patients' homes. Increasingly, ambulatory care services are often the patient's first point of contact in the health care delivery system.[10] This new form of medical practice required a new style of management practice. The traditional administrator who managed internal affairs now had to focus outward and compete for patients based on quality *and* on cost. Business skills gained currency, as assuming financial risk for the care provided, contracting with physicians, and marketing services were added to the already complex duties of the health care manager.[11]

Moreover, medical technology permitted sophisticated procedures to be delivered in ambulatory rather than inpatient facilities.[12] Between 1980 and 1990, the American Hospital Association reported that the number of freestanding ambulatory care facilities doubled.[10] Many diagnostic and therapeutic procedures, as well as treatment, do not necessitate overnight stays, which plays to patients' preferences for accessible, convenient, and prompt care.

Finally, the growth of managed care expanded the ambulatory care sector. The financial incentive to provide care in an outpatient setting was a natural fit with the managed care philosophy of using gatekeepers to reduce costly hospitalization. As health care consumers continue to be vocal in their demands and medical technology continues to advance, the market for ambulatory care will increase.

Integration of Care

The 1990s were a decade of vertical and horizontal integration in the health care industry. To integrate in the health care industry means to bring together practitioners, hospitals, health plans, employers, and patients.[13] Under this strategy, repetitive services are eliminated and the expense of technology is consolidated in an effort to streamline health care delivery. The increasing cost of delivering health care and patient's demands for convenient "one-stop shopping" were two of the drivers for integrated delivery systems (IDSs). In 1996, over 55% of America's hospitals were reported to be in an alliance;[14] in 1999, that number rose to 72%.[15]

Hospitals first ventured into horizontal integration. *Horizontal* integration consists of alliances between separate hospitals in an effort to become more efficient by creating economies of scale. *Vertical* integration is the merger and/or acquisition of health care providers at different positions along the continuum of care to improve efficiency and coordinate care across the entire organization.[14] An IDS combines vertical and horizontal integration so managers have accountability at every level.[5] Chief executive officers, departmental managers, and entry-level managers all must manage the expectations of stakeholders. Significantly, management competencies expanded from managing an organization to managing a network of services and alliances.[16]

CURRENT TRENDS IN HEALTH CARE

The delivery of health services will continue to be buffeted by change (Fig. 2). Forces for change include advances in information and medical technology, increased governmental regulation, growing consumerism, and aging demographics. Health care executives will have to manage conflicting values as they face pressures to contain costs while maintaining access and improving quality. Management trends addressing cost and quality concerns include the use of continuous quality improvement (CQI), population health management, and information technology.

CQI

Less than stellar results with static, quality assurance programs led to the health care industry's experimentation with total quality management (TQM), typically called CQI. Continuous quality improvement builds on traditional assurance methods, emphasizing all three of Donabedian's criteria: structure, process, *and* outcomes. CQI looks for improvement *opportunities*. Three practices distinguish CQI from previous quality assurance models: consumer-focus, systems thinking, and statistical quality control methods.

Continuous quality improvement recognizes the rise in health care consumerism.[17] As consumers are becoming more knowledgeable about their health and health care delivery, they are demanding better care, better information, and better coordination of their care. The definition of quality of care has broadened in response to these social changes and now includes patient–provider interaction, the setting in which care is given, and quality of life.[18]

"Customers," in CQI terms, are those people affected by a product or process, including both internal and external customers.[19] External customers are patients, benefactors, payers, or purchasers of health care services.

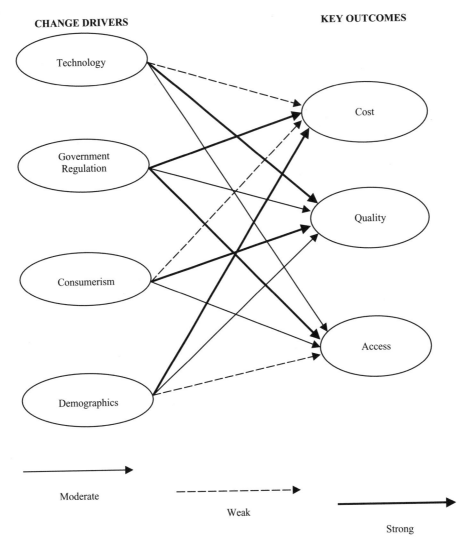

Fig. 2 Factors for change. (From Ref. [1].)

Health care providers, their colleagues, or other departments and services within the organization are internal customers. Continuous quality improvement encourages the development and use of methods to discover consumer needs and expectations.

"Systems thinking" recognizes that processes are interrelated.[19] Continuous quality improvement avoids personal blame and focuses on the managerial and professional processes associated with an outcome.[17] Continuous quality improvement involves each person associated with the process in the problem identification or quality opportunity phase *and* the actual redesign process. It encourages each member of the organization to see the process through to the end and consider the "big picture."

Quality circles and improvement teams that were popular in the 1970s and 1980s encouraged the use of sta-

tistical tools, but CQI requires these fact-based decision-making tools.[17] Employees as well as managers, study possible causes and brainstorm systemwide solutions, requiring personnel educated in statistical analysis and control processes. "The use of data-based management and scientific principles to the clinical and administrative processes that produce patient care is what CQI is all about."[17]

Population Health Management

Population health management refers to the change in focus from caring for individual illnesses to encouraging the wellness and health of a population. An ideal system would deliver comprehensive and personalized preventive through tertiary care, while guiding and tracking patients through a continuum of services.[14] Some health systems are now providing primary through tertiary care, as well as home and long-term care. More specifically, population health management relies on the evidence-based practices of catastrophic care, demand, disease, disability, and lifestyle.[21]

These five forms of population health management have varying foci and benefit different stakeholders. Lifestyle management emphasizes reducing health risks and preventing illnesses by targeting a relatively healthy population, such as young employees. Demand management concentrates on consumer requests and inquiries for medical care services, supplying advice, counseling, and referrals to appropriate providers, thus lowering the costs and improving the efficiency of care seeking. Disease management focuses on individuals with chronic conditions, such as diabetes, congestive heart failure, or asthma, coordinating the services needed for these specific diseases. Catastrophic care management centers on providing health services for individuals with catastrophic illnesses or injuries, such as acquired immune deficiency syndrome or stroke patients. Disability management focuses on reducing injuries, preventing job-related illnesses, and managing employee disabilities. All health population management approaches add value by reducing costs and improving the quality of care.[21]

Information Technology

Information technology (IT) is a valuable resource for CQI and population health management efforts. Information technology provides the foundation for the flow, storage, and analysis of data, converting it into usable information for making operational and strategic decisions.

More important, IT has the potential to radically transform the health care industry, improving quality and access while minimizing costs. Telemedicine demonstrates IT's benefits. Radiology, for example, is a common application within telemedicine that Medicare now covers. The managed care industry quickly saw the opportunity to contain costs through IT. By deploying IT, health service organizations can improve clinical outcomes, ensure patient safety, and streamline administrative tasks. However, without industrywide standards, the full benefits of IT cannot be realized.[20]

Indeed, both population health management and CQI require a robust information infrastructure.[22,23] Without an information infrastructure that connects all providers, insurers, third-party administrators, and employer/payers, effective disease and other population health management measures are much less efficient. At the same time, the coordination of care that results from establishing health networks is also more effective and efficient when an information infrastructure connects primary, secondary, and tertiary providers within and across communities.

CONCLUSION

Health care managers face the challenge of developing and managing delivery organizations that are internally complex, and involve external networks of other providers. Health care executives must manage conflicting values among internal stakeholders, while also managing complex strategic alliance relationships. Relational and strategic competencies, as well as abilities in managing technology, quality improvement, and population health are now prerequisites for health system CEOs. As health system managers develop information infrastructures, manage population health, and improve internal quality processes and outcomes, they begin to achieve a community health care management focus. The challenge for health care executives is both to articulate a vision, and to master the skills needed for managing these complex and emergent organizational forms.

REFERENCES

1. Savage, G.T.; Campbell, K.S.; Patman, T.; Nunnelley, L.L. Beyond managed costs. Health Care Manage. Rev. **2000**, *25* (1), 93–108.
2. Ernst, E. The role of complementary and alternative medicine. Br. Med. J. **2000**, *321*, 4.
3. Assisted Living Federation of America. **2002**. What is Assisted Living? [On-Line]. Available: http://www.alfa.org/public/articles/details.cfm?id=96.
4. Haglund, C.L.; Dowling, W.L. The Hospital. In *Introduction to Health Services*, 4th Ed.; Williams, S.J., Torrens, P.R., Eds.; Delmar Publishers, Inc.: Albany, NY, 1993; 134–159.
5. Kovner, A.R.; Neuhauser, D. *Health Services Management*; Health Administration Press: Chicago, 2001.
6. Knight, W. *Managed Care*; Aspen Publishers: Gaithersburg, MD, 1998.
7. Wolper, L.F.; Pena, J.J. History of Hospitals. In *Health Care Administration*, 3rd Ed.; Wolper, L.F., Ed.; Aspen Publishers: Gaithersburg, MD, 1999; 391–400.
8. McConnell, C. The changing face of health care management. Health Care Manag. **2000**, *18* (3), 1–17.
9. Hosking, J.E. Planning Health Care Facilities and Managing the Development Process. In *Health Care Administration*, 3rd Ed.; Wolper, L.F., Ed.; Aspen Publishers, Inc.: Gaithersburg, MD, 1999; 237–256.
10. McGuire, J.P. Ambulatory care services continue to grow. Healthc. Financ. Manage. **1994**, *48* (11), 10–12.
11. Nelson, R.A. The Role of the Medical Group Manager. In *Ambulatory Care Management and Practice*; Barnett,

A.E., Mayer, G.G., Eds.; Aspen Publishers: Gaithersburg, MD, 1992.

12. Barr, K.W.; Breindel, C.L. Ambulatory Care. In *Health Care Administration*, 3rd Ed.; Wolper, L.F., Ed.; Aspen Publishers: Gaithersburg, MD, 1999; 431–466.

13. McBride, S.H. Integration: Key to surviving managed care? Dermatol. Times **1995**, *6* (4), 43–48.

14. Barber, J.B. Evolution of an integrated health system: A life cycle framework. J. Healthc. Manag. **1998**, *43* (4), 359–377.

15. Friedman, L. Why integrated health networks have failed. Frontiers of Health Services Management **2001**, *17* (4), 3–54.

16. Savage, G.T.; Roboski, A.M. Integration as Networks and Systems: A Strategic Stakeholder Analysis. In *Advances in Health Care Management*; Fottler, M.D., Savage, G.T., Blair, J.D., Eds.; JAI Press: New York, 2001; Vol. 2, 37–62.

17. McLaughlin, C.P.; Kaluzny, A.D. *Continuous Quality Improvement in Health Care*; Aspen Publications: Gaithersburg, MD, 1999.

18. Donabedian, A. Commentary on some studies of the quality of care. Health Care Financ. Rev. **1987**, December; Spec No: 75–85.

19. Kongstvedt, P.R. *Essentials of Managed Health Care*, 4th Ed.; Aspen Publishers: Gaithersburg, MD, 2001.

20. van der Reis, L. The idea behind information systems. San Francisco Medicine **1996**, *69*, 70.

21. McAlearney, A.S. Population Health Management in Theory and Practice. In *Advances in Health Care Management*; Savage, G.T., Blair, J.D., Fottler, M.D., Eds.; JAI Press: New York, 2002; Vol. 3, 117–158.

22. Feifer, C.; Ornstein, S.M.; Nietert, P.J.; Jenkins, R.G. System supports for chronic illness care and their relationship to clinical outcomes. Top. Health Inf. Manag. **2001**, *22* (2), 65–72.

23. Payton, F.C. How a community health information network is really used. Commun. ACM **1999**, *42* (12), 85–90.

Health Care Settings, Change in

R. Wayne Boss
University of Colorado at Boulder, Boulder, Colorado, U.S.A.

Mark L. McConkie
University of Colorado at Colorado Springs, Colorado Springs, Colorado, U.S.A.

H

INTRODUCTION

Health care organizations are unique. Hospitals, for example, are different from other organizations in both the private and public sectors, and their differences make the management of change much more difficult. In contrast to industrial firms, for example, hospitals have the following characteristics:

- They tend to be more vitally important to society.
- They have more highly differentiated, specialized, and complex organizations.
- They contain four major power groups (physicians, nurses, administrators, and boards of trustees) with different interests, poor communication, and weak linkages.
- They are dominated by one power group (physicians) who are socialized as professionals, assume cosmopolitan roles, and function autonomously and independently from the rest of the organization.
- They produce personal, unique services with an unusually strong emphasis on quality.
- They have vague goals, produce results that are difficult to measure, and show little standardization among organizations.
- They tend toward random delivery of services with little organizational control.
- They are less adaptable to planned change, because so much of the energy is devoted to adapting to the external environment.
- They provide fewer incentives for effective management, primarily because effective management is not highly valued by the physicians.
- They experience greater and more complex levels of intraorganizational interdependence among professionals and nonprofessionals.
- They need many highly trained and technically competent professionals with related but often mutually exclusive skills and expertise.
- They are staffed by personnel who are often unwilling to take risks and try new modes of delivery.

- They are paid for good intentions and programs, rather than for their products and results.
- They are subject to government regulation that has an immediate and far-reaching impact on the industry, particularly in terms of reimbursement patterns.
- They are often controlled by insurance companies that make reimbursement decisions (in terms of the amount of reimbursement and the services for which the hospital will be reimbursed), and determine from what institutions patients can receive treatment. This takes the decision for health care services out of the hands of the physicians and puts them into the hands of bureaucrats and administrators.
- Their personnel populations have reached almost a crisis point because of increased demands for services (due to the aging population) and the decreased numbers of people entering the health care field.
- They are far more interdependent, to the point that it is impossible for some departments to deliver services to patients without the cooperation of many other departments. Indeed, if one department, such as the pharmacy, fails to do its job, it can practically close down the entire organization (Adapted from Ref. 1, pp. 15–16). Given these differences, many consultants and health care administrators find the process of change difficult to manage. However, the research indicates that significant changes can take place when those involved in the change process pay attention to the unique characteristics of health care organizations.

ORGANIZATION DEVELOPMENT

The typology used here comes from an Organization Development (OD) perspective. Although the definitions of OD vary significantly, the most widely accepted is that given by Beckhard: "Organization development is an effort that is planned, organization wide, and managed from the top to increase organization effectiveness and health through planned interventions in the organi-

Encyclopedia of Public Administration and Public Policy
DOI: 10.1081/E-EPAP 120011084

zation's processes, using behavioral science knowledge."[2] OD has a long-range focus. It is designed to improve an organization's health, efficiency, and effectiveness in effecting change, reaching decisions, and taking advantage of the full potential of the organization's most valuable resource: its people. In short, OD applies behavioral science knowledge to facilitate change, to build skills in people, and to resolve problems, whether personal, interpersonal, intragroup, intergroup, or organizational (see Ref. 1, p. 18).

THE ACTION RESEARCH MODEL

The basic approach of most OD practitioners is to use the action research model, a data-based, problem-solving model designed to replicate the scientific method of inquiry (for a general discussion of action research, see Ref. 3). The specific steps in the action research model include data collection from individuals and groups within the organization, feedback of the data to the organization personnel, problem diagnosis, and action planning and interventions within the system. Once the interventions have been completed, additional data are collected and fed back to the client system, problems are diagnosed, and additional action planning of subsequent interventions takes place. Thus, implementation of the action research model involves a cycle of interactions designed to provide immediate feedback to the client on the status of problems within the system. Action research, therefore, implies a meaningful link between research and action and connotes action based on valid information. It is important to realize that each phase of the action research model constitutes a clear intervention into the client system (Ref. 4, p. 260).

OD INTERVENTIONS

The term "OD interventions" refers to a range of structured activities designed to resolve problems and enable personnel to develop and maintain healthy organizations. These methods and techniques can be implemented by the client and the consultant and constitute an evolving array of methods and techniques, based on the diagnosis of the problems and the needs of the client system.

Although few OD projects include all possible intervention activities, the following constitutes a generally agreed upon set of definitions for the major types of OD interventions.

- *Team building*: Activities designed to enhance the effective operation of system teams.

- *Intergroup activities*: Activities designed to improve effectiveness of interdependent groups. They focus on joint activities and the output of groups considered as a single system rather than as two subsystems.

- *Survey-feedback activities*: Although related directly to the diagnostic process described above, these activities tend to become an ongoing process in the organization. Data collection activities, in the form of questionnaire surveys of the target population and interviews with key personnel, take place on a regular basis. The data are analyzed, problem areas are identified by the organization's leadership, and action plans are developed to deal with problems related to the total organization. The data are then shared with the organization's personnel in department or division meetings, and specific action plans are formulated for problems that relate to the specific units.

- *Education and training activities*: Activities designed to improve skills, abilities, and knowledge of individuals. The activities may be directed toward technical skills required for effective task performance or may be directed toward improving interpersonal competence. The activities may be directed toward leadership issues, responsibilities and functions of group members, decision making, problem solving, goal setting, planning, and so on.

- *Technostructural or structural activities*: Activities designed to improve the effectiveness of the technical or structural inputs and constraints affecting individuals or groups. The activities may take the form of experimenting with new organization structures and evaluating their effectiveness in terms of specific goals or devising new ways to bring technical resources to bear on problems. Structural interventions are defined as the broad class of interventions or change efforts aimed at improving organization effectiveness through changes in the task, structural, and technological subsystems. Included in these activities are certain forms of job enrichment, management by objectives, collateral organizations, and physical settings interventions.

- *Sociotechnical systems*: Activities designed to focus simultaneously on the technical systems and the social systems of the organization. Such activities often involve the restructuring of work methods, rearrangements of technology, or the redesign of organizational social structures. The objective is to maximize the "fit" between the technical system and the human system. Often, the implementation of sociotechnical systems involves the creation of work teams or autonomous work groups, which are responsible for a specific product or output. The concept, originally developed in London at the Tavistock Institute of Human Relations, has had broad applications in mines and factories in England and the Scandinavian countries. Successful sociotechnical interventions have also been reported in joint United Auto Workers-General Motors plants in the United States.

- *Process consultation*: Activities on the part of the consultant to assist the client in perceiving, understanding, and acting upon process events that occur in the client's environment. Specific emphasis is placed on the human processes that occur at the individual, interpersonal, and intergroup levels. These processes include communications, group problem solving and decision making, the functional roles of group members, group norms and group growth, leadership and authority, and intergroup processes. Because organizations are made up of networks of people, with these processes continually occurring between them, the objective of process consultant activities is to help the client gain the skills to understand, diagnose, and manage such processes effectively.

- *Third-party consultation*: Activities conducted by a skilled third party, which are designed to resolve problems regarding interpersonal or substantive issues and help those parties deal effectively with their conflict. Such interventions involve conflict resolution in superior–subordinate and peer relationships. Among the substantive issues are disagreements over policies and procedures, different conceptions of roles, and competition for scarce resources. The interpersonal issues often involve feelings of anger, distrust, fear, scorn, resentment, or rejection.

- *Coaching and counseling activities*: Activities that involve the consultant or other organization members working with individuals to help them define learning goals; learn how others see their behavior; and learn new modes of behavior to see if these help them to better achieve their goals. A central feature of this activity is the nonevaluative feedback given by others to an individual. A second feature is the joint exploration of alternative behaviors.

- *Life and career planning activities*: Activities that enable individuals to focus on their life and career objectives and how they might go about achieving them. Structured activities lead to production of life and career inventories, discussions of goals and objectives, assessment of capabilities, needed additional training, and areas of strength and deficiency.

- *Planning and goal-setting activities*: Activities that include theory and experience in planning and goal setting, utilizing problem-solving models, and the like. The goal of all such activities is to improve these skills at individual, group, and organization levels (see Ref. 4, pp. 262–265).

A MODEL FOR CHANGE

Golembiewski provided a model of organizational change that has proven effective in a number of different settings. Specifically, to introduce change into simple systems, he suggested include the following:

1. Move slowly.
2. Implement one innovation at a time.
3. Precede each step with ample warning.
4. Accompany each step by a statement of reasons and benefits.
5. Offer maximum opportunities to participate.
6. Provide outlets for inevitable hostilities.

Occasionally, harsh or dramatic changes are desirable; sometimes it is the only way to facilitate change. When the manager feels it practically necessary or morally defensible to so induce change, that manager simply will neglect the above list. Even then, however, the manager can expect a low probability of success and should anticipate much time and effort sweeping up afterwards.

A comparable list of steps for changing complex more systems is less straightforward or complete. At least fragmentarily, then, the managerial change agent intent on affecting a complex system should keep such general guidelines in mind:

1. Changes in any subsystem often require changes in other systems.
2. Changes at any one level of organization often require changes at the level above and below.
3. Change is usefully begun where stresses exist.
4. Planning any change should involve formal and informal organizations.
5. The higher the level at which change begins, the greater the chances of success.[5]

Given the complex nature of health care organizations, change agents in hospitals do well to adhere to the guidelines suggested for complex systems, particularly given the highly interdependent nature of health care organizations. For example, the leaders of an outpatient surgery department in a major medical center decided to move the nurses' station from one side of a room to the other. This change directly impacted 29 other departments.

THREE CASE STUDIES

Given the challenges currently facing health care, one would expect it to prove a fertile field for applying OD technology. Consider, for example, the following applications of OD technology to a variety of different health care settings (materials in this section is adapted from Ref. 1, pp. 1–2):

Lincoln Hospital's Operating Room

Lincoln is a 400-bed for-profit hospital and medical center located in the southwestern United States. Lincoln had long had trouble with egotistical and dictatorial physicians who constantly threatened to take their patients elsewhere if their demands were not met. Historically, the hospital administration had catered to these doctors, even firing nurses who had alienated particular physicians.

Mary, the OR director for 13 years, had a reputation as being a conservative, strong-willed, strict constructionist who would brook no deviations from hospital rules. Don, the incoming chief of surgery, was an outspoken critic of the hospital. Nurses and administrators feared his sharp tongue, quick temper, and critical disposition, but Mary was not the least bit intimidated by his behavior, and the two had openly clashed on numerous occasions. Faced with the new broom's need to make a difference, Don openly declared that his major goal for his first year as chief of surgery was to have Mary fired.

One year later, following multiple OD interventions, Mary had successfully completed her 14th year as OR director. Not only did she and Don trust each other, but the two had engineered some major changes in the surgical services area, including a decrease in the turnover rate among surgical nurses from 40% to zero, a resolution of the difficult problem of scheduling operations for a group of prima donna surgeons, and a significant decrease in physicians' verbal abuse of nurses.

Manchester Nursing Services Division

Manchester hospital and medical center is a 300-bed for-profit facility located in the northwestern United States. Although all of Manchester's 900 employees generally felt frustrated with the problems facing the organization, low morale was most pronounced in the 500-employee nursing services division. Several factors contributed to the nurses' dissatisfaction: the decentralization of nursing management, enormous technical and managerial problems for the new managers; an almost 100% turnover among head nurses; mistakes in filling key management positions; distrust for the administration; and physician abuse. The nurses felt unappreciated, undervalued, and powerless in dealing with the administration and with the physicians, and the turnover rate among nurses had fluctuated between 30 and 40% for the previous four years.

Three years later, the Manchester nursing services division achieved significant improvements in organization climate and group effectiveness. The turnover rate among nurses dropped from over 32% the year before the OD project started to 5.8% the third year. This decrease in turnover saved Manchester over $1.5 million during the three-year period.

City Hospital and Medical Center

City Hospital is a 250-bed denominational hospital and medical center with 850 employees, located in a fast-growing southeastern city. After holding his position for 10 years, the hospital's administrator had run into trouble with the medical staff, the employees, and the corporate board, and had left for a hospital in a different region.

The new administrator inherited several serious problems: a lack of effective leadership, ineffective communication, poor decision making, an absence of planning, a hostile medical staff, a poor public image, dissatisfied nurses, an employee population that felt overworked, underrewarded, and burned out, and serious financial problems (to the point that the hospital had recorded its first financial loss in over 50 years).

Three years later, the number of City Hospital employees in the advanced stages of burnout had decreased by 31%. Net revenue as a percent of gross revenue (profits) showed double-digit increases, and market share had increased by 6.3%. Days of revenue in gross accounts receivable were down by 18.9 days, for an increase in revenue of approximately $2,835,000 during the three years. In addition, employee turnover dropped from over 25% to 4%. By the most conservative estimates, the hospital had saved over $2 million in recruitment costs for registered nurses alone during the three-year period.

ESSENTIALS FOR SUCCESS

The purpose of OD is to improve an organization's effectiveness in making decisions, accomplishing its missions, and in reaching the full potential of its people. Successful OD efforts will simultaneously create a regenerating system characterized by trust, openness, a flow of accurate information, freedom for individuals to grow and develop, and a minimal interpersonal risk or perceived threat. Under such conditions, minimal resistance to change is generated, and a high level of collaboration is ensured (material in this section is adapted from Ref. 1, pp. 102–105).

Of course, not all OD efforts attain these objectives. Often, the project is doomed to failure simply because many essential elements of effective change are missing. A successful OD project will include the following variables:

1. Commitment of the chief executive officer.
2. Cultural preparedness in the organization.
3. Realistic expectations about the success of the project.
4. Internal tension and pain.
5. Involvement of other people in positions of power.
6. Development of internal resources.
7. Methods for holding people accountable.
8. A competent consultant.
9. A clear psychological contract between the CEO and the consultant.
10. Technically competent supervisors.

Commitment of the Chief Executive Officer

The CEO is the single most important person in the change effort, largely because the CEO controls the reward structure, which in turn, controls individual behaviors. Two further examples illustrate this point.

First, 37 top-level administrators in seven criminal justice agencies participated in a 6-day confrontation team building meeting. Thirty-three were members of six natural teams or organizational family groups. The remaining four comprised a cousin group from a seventh organization. Cousin group members represented four different departments in a state agency. No two members reported to the same supervisor. The major variable among the six natural teams was that only one team met with its CEO. Although the natural team with the CEO showed significant improvement between the before and after scores on standard organization climate measures, the five leaderless teams, the cousin group, and a comparison group showed no statistically significant change.

Second, a seasoned hospital administrator retained a consultant and launched a major OD effort. During the next two years, the consultant worked closely with the administrator, his administrative council, and department managers to resolve problems, open channels of communication, enhance cooperation, and increase organizational effectiveness. Hospital personnel, however, perceived the administrator's behavior to be incongruent with the values of openness, honesty, and candor that he had professed to espouse. They saw him as deceitful and manipulative and felt that OD was a gimmick. Two years after the project began, the consultant quit; six months later, the administrator was fired.

Within two months, a new administrator was appointed. He immediately hired the same consultant and began another 2-year OD effort, with the same people and

the same objectives. Both projects were characterized by the following:

• The same consultant was employed.
• The consultant used the same approach.
• The consultant spent approximately the same number of days in the organization each year.
• The organization experienced little turnover, and there was none among the administrative council level.
• The general approach to hospital work was the same.

The only major difference was the person who served as administrator. Data collected at the start of the first OD effort, 2 weeks before the administrator was fired, and 2 years after the new chief was hired, showed that the organization retrogressed between the first and second data collections but improved significantly in organizational climate and leader effectiveness by the time of the third collection.[6]

The results of these and other studies suggest that the CEO is the single most important factor in determining the success or failure of an OD effort. Without the CEO's total support, the potential for a successful OD project is questionable at best; if that support is marginal, the OD project should not be started at all.

Cultural Preparedness

To achieve lasting change, an organization must be culturally prepared; that is, its employees' psychological energies must be directed toward achieving, not sabotaging, the organization's goals. Below a certain threshold of organizational health, successful OD efforts are impossible. Important elements of cultural preparedness include interpersonal trust among employees, their willingness to resolve problems, their willingness to be held accountable, and their psychological health.

Interpersonal Trust

Trust is essential to organizational effectiveness. People who trust each other are significantly more effective in group problem solving than people who do not. The degree to which people trust one another determines the degree to which they will communicate honestly, share relevant information, try to control others, and permit others to influence their own behavior and decisions. The level of interpersonal trust at the outset of an OD project is typically an accurate indicator of the potential success of the effort. If trust has degenerated below a minimum level, the consultant or manager must scrap the project or replace the offensive party. Without minimal trust, the chances of successful changes are practically zero.

A Willingness to Resolve Problems

Organization development, by definition, involves problem solving. Those involved must be willing to resolve their problems or change cannot take place. For example, in one client organization, the line personnel had major conflicts with their supervisors. During the diagnostic phase of the project, the consultant interviewed all the parties, but 60% of the line personnel refused even to sit down in the same room with their supervisors and discuss the problems. Under such circumstances, the objectives of OD could not be achieved; only power-oriented, win–lose behavior would have resolved problems.

A Willingness to be Held Accountable

Effective managers are not only able to hold employees accountable but also willing to be held accountable themselves. Competent people generally appreciate such responsibility. Incompetent people, on the other hand, resist it, because it exposes their weaknesses and inabilities.

Psychological Health

Although psychological health is relative, people must have a minimum level to resolve conflict effectively. Without it, supportive confrontation is difficult. If most of the members of a group need intense therapy, rational problem solving is impossible.

Realistic Expectations

Everyone involved in an OD project must understand at the outset that it is a long-range project requiring a substantial investment of time and energy. It took time to create the problems, and they should not expect those problems to be resolved quickly. Realistic expectations can prevent the anxiety, frustration, and tension associated with most change efforts.

Internal Tension and Pain

Any successful OD project results from recognizable discomfort, tension, and pain. Without a felt need for change, particularly among the administrators, no change can occur. Organizational change efforts have a high probability of success only when the individuals involved have been experiencing internal stress.

Involvement of People in Power

Change efforts, where possible, should start with top-level administrators but must involve the informal (natural) leaders of the rank and file. Their support and cooperation can mean the difference between success and failure.

The Development of Internal Resources

Internal resources must be developed to ensure that the organization remains healthy after the consultant leaves. Without such resources, it remains dangerously dependent on the external consultant. This resource development can take two forms: intense managerial training and educational programs can build managerial competence throughout the leadership; or a few employees can be trained as internal change agents. For the latter, areas of emphasis should at least include process consultation, conflict management, team building, data gathering, problem diagnosis, and personnel training.

Methods for Holding People Accountable

Effective managers must be able to hold people accountable for the fulfillment of their responsibilities. One method used in the studies reported in this book is the personal management interview. Regular meetings between supervisor and subordinate provide opportunities for sharing information, training, building technical skills, dealing with interpersonal issues, and holding employees accountable. Notes of each meeting are kept, and action items are reviewed during subsequent meetings to ensure followup.

A Competent Consultant

Although many changes can be effected by resources within the organization, the objectives of OD generally require the help of someone outside it. Obviously, caution should be exercised in selecting that person. A client–consultant relationship, like a marriage, requires a great deal of interdependence and trust. The CEO should consider whether the consultant has the professional skills necessary to help diagnose and solve the problems and the interpersonal skills necessary for a trusting and open relationship with company personnel. The CEO should thoroughly interview consultants and check with their previous clients, especially those in similar organizations.

A Clear Psychological Contract Between the CEO and the Consultant

It is absolutely essential that the consultant and the CEO reach a clear understanding about all aspects of their relationship before the consultant enters the system.

They must spell out the client's expectations of the consultant and OD effort, the consultant's expectations of the client, the problems to be solved, the phases of the project, and the parameters within which the consultant and client will work. Such a psychological contract prevents misunderstandings and difficulties during the OD project.

Technically Competent Supervisors

Although not so central as the other essentials, the technical competence of the supervisors, especially the top administrators, is a major factor in successful change efforts. This factor is particularly important in occupations with a high degree of interdependence and personal risk. When subordinates put their destiny in the hands of someone else, the technical competence of the critical others is essential.

CONCLUSION

The factors listed above do not include all of the variables that may contribute to an effective change effort; and most consultants can cite cases where change ef-

forts were successful in the absence of one or more of these conditions. Ignoring any of these essentials, however, will greatly hamper the change effort and substantially decrease the prospects of achieving the objectives of OD.

REFERENCES

1. Boss, R.W. *Organization Development In Health Care*; Addison-Wesley: Reading, MA, 1989; 15–16.
2. Beckhard, R. *Organization Development: Strategies and Models*; Addison-Wesley: Reading, MA, 1969; 9.
3. French, W.L.; Bell, C.H. *Organization Development*, 5th Ed.; Prentice-Hall: Englewood Cliffs, NJ, 1995; 137–154.
4. Boss, R.W. Organization Development: A Vehicle for Improving the Quality of Work Life. *Handbook of Organization Management*; William Eddy, W.B., Ed.; Marcel Dekker Inc.: New York, 1983; 260.
5. Golembiewski, R.T. *Perspectives on Public Management*; F.E. Peacock Publishers: Itasca, IL, 1967; 35–36.
6. Boss, R.W.; Golembiewski, R.T. Do you have to start at the top? The chief executive officer's role in successful organization development efforts. J. Appl. Behav. Sci. *31* (3), 259–277.

Home Rule

Dale Krane
The University of Nebraska at Omaha, Omaha, Nebraska, U.S.A.

INTRODUCTION

Home rule refers to the authority of a local government to make and implement a policy decision without first obtaining specific permission from a superior tier of government. In the United States, home rule is defined legally as the authority of a local government to exercise those powers granted by the state legislature, except where the exercise of a power would violate state law or the state constitution. Embedded in the idea of home rule is an important aspect of democracy and citizen sovereignty—policy decisions affecting a locality ought to be made by the citizens and officials of the locality. Of course, cities, counties, and other forms of local government exist within a larger framework of state governments and are expected to accommodate their actions to the interests of other localities as well as the state government. This is especially the case when the effects of a local decision "spill over" into another jurisdiction. Home rule, therefore, is a critical dimension of state–local relations in the United States, and as such, varies among the 50 states in terms of the types and extent of discretionary authority available to local governments. In some states, local governments possess little or no autonomy from state government control, while in other states, local governments exercise a broad range of policy making in areas such as their structure, functions, finances, and administration. The result of this interstate variation is that the capacity of local governments to act in ways desired by their residents or to solve problems in a manner congruent with local conditions depends directly on the degree of home rule possessed by local governments in a particular state.

CREATURES OF THE STATE

The U.S. Constitution, while it contains numerous specific statements on the relationship between the national government and state governments, is silent on the place of local governments in the federal framework. The absence of any constitutional language referring to local governments means that the position and powers of local governments have been left to decisions by the states. Instead of granting local governments substantial authority and capacity, states have acted to make local governments legally inferior jurisdictions.

In contrast to the federal relationship between the national and state governments, American local governments exist and function as units of government under the hierarchical control of state government. A local government, be it a municipality, a county, a special district, or a public authority, may act only in areas and in ways specified by state government. American legal theory, at least since the late 1860s, has held that local governments are "the creatures of state government." Any action or means not permitted by state government is prohibited. If any doubt exists as to which level of government has the authority to act, this doubt must be resolved in favor of the state government. Furthermore, the existence and continuation of a local government rests with state government.

This "creatures of the state" theory of local government authority was promulgated in a precedent-setting decision by the Iowa Supreme Court in 1868. In the case of the *City of Clinton v. Cedar Rapids and Missouri Railroad Company*, Judge John F. Dillon ruled that municipalities "owe their origin to, and derive their powers and rights wholly from the [state] legislature," and, therefore, are "mere tenants at will of the legislature." This decision became known as Dillon's Rule, and after it was upheld by the U.S. Supreme Court in 1903 and again in 1923, it has served as the principal legal opinion governing state–local relations.[1]

Since the promulgation of Dillon's Rule, the legal interpretation of home rule has become relatively standardized around the country. While the idea of home rule implies vigorous local government autonomy and self-determination, generally, state courts have held that local governments have only as much freedom and authority to govern their own affairs as the state, through its constitution and statutory laws, chooses to give to local governments. Unfortunately, Dillon's Rule "often is interpreted improperly by observers who conclude the Rule centralizes all exercisable authority in the state legislature and local governments possess very limited discretionary authority. What these observers fail to recognize is the fact that the state legislature is free to grant broad discretionary powers to local governments and several have done so."[2] That many state govern-

Encyclopedia of Public Administration and Public Policy
DOI: 10.1081/E-EPAP 120010836

ments have granted substantial discretionary authority to local governments is an important trend that flies in the face of prevailing legal theory. In fact, the over-time accretion of significant powers by local governments has altered and even negated Dillon's Rule in many states. So, it is important not to view the legal position of local governments as exactly the same in all 50 states.

THE HOME RULE MOVEMENT

Dillon's Rule settled the question of the balance of powers between state and local governments in favor of state government. Other reformers who believed in more independence for local governments argued for a different solution to the question of just what was the proper balance of state and local government authority. These reformers campaigned to enact state constitutional changes that would permit cities to write and amend their own charters. This reform strategy was known as the Home Rule Movement and originally sought to end the interference of local state legislative delegations in municipal affairs by creating municipal charters for local governments. Eventually, the Home Rule Movement became associated with the idea of broad grants of local government autonomy.

In the 1840s and 1850s, local delegates to state legislatures used their position to write statutes that permitted the local legislative delegation to interfere in municipal decisions. So-called "local privilege" legislation often led to battles between the city council and the local legislative delegation. This state–local conflict sometimes provoked the state legislature to transfer control of certain activities of municipal government (e.g., police protection) to state-appointed officials. These laws became known as "ripper laws." Beginning in the 1850s, some states such as Ohio and Iowa acted to prohibit "local privilege" legislation and to grant a modest degree of home rule to cities. But the state courts followed the "creatures of the state" theory, so reformers had to push for constitutional changes that altered the state–local relationship.[3]

After the Civil War, those who sought to provide cities with constitutional protections from state legislative abuse understood that it would be impossible to obtain grants of substantive powers to cities without also conferring on cities the power to write their own charters. When Missouri wrote its 1875 constitution, it included the first-ever state constitutional provision to permit the drafting of municipal charters. Several other states soon followed Missouri and gave positive grants of authority to municipalities via various forms of general enabling laws and the option for home rule charters. By 1912, constitutional language in the 13 states shared the common feature of establishing home rule through the use of a locally drafted charter that was to be ratified by local voters or by the city council.[4]

Advocates of home rule benefited from an association with the Progressive reformers who sprung up on the Great Plains after the Civil War. The Progressive Movement's emphasis on business-like government became the vehicle for further efforts to reform government after World War I, and the home rule idea continued to spread. In the 1920s, "Good Government" associations such as the National Municipal League disseminated model constitutional provisions which included home rule ideas. By 1937, 21 states had adopted some form of home rule charter authority.

The Home Rule Movement in its campaign for municipal and county charters raised the crucial question of "where was the line between state and local powers to be drawn?" New York State in 1923 tried to answer this question with a constitutional amendment that included a long list of items regarded as "local," and thus, would be under local government control. Other states also adopted this strategy to enumerate "local affairs," because this approach was thought to clarify the line between state and local interests, and as a consequence, would reduce the number of lawsuits initiated after the adoption of a home rule charter. This enumeration of a local affairs solution to state–local relations suffered from the inflexibility of constitutions. Once the list of state versus local powers was written into the state constitution, it was difficult to amend. State courts soon faced numerous lawsuits over whether some activity such as public health, street repair, or liquor licenses was a matter of local or state affairs. Finding a clear line was frustrating, and many state supreme courts found it easier to continue to adhere to Dillon's Rule.[5]

The American Municipal Association, forerunner to the National League of Cities, hired Dean Fordham in 1952 to devise a new model of state–local relations. He proposed a plan in which a state legislature would permit municipalities to write a charter with a broad list of powers. This new charter would allow municipalities to supersede special state laws and many general laws applicable to municipal corporations. In its essence, the Fordham "devolution of powers" plan proposed a reversal of Dillon's Rule. Instead of the position that municipalities may exercise only those powers explicitly granted to them, municipalities under Fordham's plan could act unless explicitly prohibited by state law. This model of home rule authority is sometimes referred to as "legislative home rule." Several states have adopted this model.[6]

Home rule for county government also made progress after World War II. In 1945, Missouri made home rule charters available to its largest counties, and Washington enacted county home rule in 1948. By the end of the 1960s, county home rule had been established in 15 states. By the mid-1990s, 37 states (of the 47 states with viable counties) provided for some form of county home rule.

THE COMPLEXITY OF HOME RULE

Most treatments of home rule discuss the topic from a legal perspective. Yet, home rule refers to the actual discretion local officials exercise over various dimensions of local government. Usually, the powers granted by states to municipal or county governments are placed in three main classes: 1) governmental powers, which include the authority to enact ordinances, levy taxes, and exercise police powers; 2) corporate powers, which include the ability to enter into contracts, buy and sell property, and sue as well as be sued; and 3) proprietary powers, which allow local governments to own and operate commercial enterprises such as a utility. Which of these three classes of powers is granted to which type of local government varies from state to state.[7]

The history of the Home Rule Movement shows that proponents of more local government authority focused their efforts primarily on amending state constitutions in order to create charters, or lists of power and authority possessed by a local government. The earliest charters typically provided local residents with the opportunity to select their own form of government (e.g., mayor–council, council–manager, or commission form). While the first charters granted by state governments were limited to the structural features of local government, over time, home rule advocates convinced state legislatures to broaden the scope of municipal (and county) charters to include other dimensions of local government. As state legislatures found that "local affairs" consumed more and more legislative time, state legislatures increasingly assigned responsibility for designated policy areas to local governments or permitted local governments more discretion over certain public functions. Likewise, state legislatures, often responding to demands from local government officials, granted more authority over administrative and financial matters to local governments. In recent years, states have even granted significant new authority to allow local governments to pursue economic growth.

All of these changes in the scope and types of discretionary authority that local governments possess and exercise demonstrate that a legal perspective to home rule is a narrow view of home rule. Any portrayal of local government authority that continues to paint a picture of local governments as "creatures of the state" ignores the changes that have occurred in the relationship between state and local governments since 1970. Just as state governments modernized their structures and administration, so too have they enhanced the authority of local governments to make choices across a wide range of important activities. The litmus test of local government autonomy is discretion over fiscal matters. While it is true that states have continued to impose certain constraints on local fiscal authority, primarily restrictions on the use of the property tax, it is also true that many states have diversified the types of revenue sources local governments may choose to tap. Furthermore, states have granted local governments more discretion in how they spend their resources. As long as a legal lens is used to study home rule, the description will miss the complexity of the state–local relationship, and thus, miss much of the actual behavior of local governments.[8]

CURRENT STATUS OF HOME RULE

Despite the enlargement of local government discretion during the last half of the twentieth century, the actions of state legislatures have often been negated by state courts that have been reluctant to overturn Dillon's Rule. Since 1970, however, several states have acted to redefine the scope of local government authority. Illinois, for example, modified the devolution-of-powers model by moving in the direction of the enumeration strategy that had been tried during the "good government" era. That is, the Illinois constitution set forth complex decision rules related to the establishment of home rule, the writing and adoption of charters, the specific areas of local affairs including powers to regulate health, safety, morals, and welfare, and powers to tax and incur debt. Equally important, the Illinois constitution went to the heart of Dillon's Rule by telling state legislators and judges how to interpret the list of local powers—"the powers and functions of home rule units shall be construed liberally." By contrast, non-home-rule units and limited purpose governments (e.g., special districts, townships) "shall have only powers granted by law."[9]

The Illinois approach is significant, because it established a new model of home rule—the "liberal construction" model. By sorting out the list of local powers and stating them in language that the state courts and the legislature had to follow, Illinois lawmakers specified the conditions under which the state government could preempt a local government charter. If the specified conditions did not exist or pertain, then the state government (legislature or courts) could not preempt actions taken by a local government. Other states copied the Illinois language in recent revisions of their constitutions. The Alaska constitution is direct: "...a liberal construction shall be given to the powers of local government

<u>**No Home Rule**</u>   n = 9

Alabama, Connecticut, Idaho, Indiana, Nebraska,
Nevada, New Hampshire, Virginia, West Virginia

<u>**Constitutional Home Rule Charter**</u>   n = 22

Arizona, Arkansas, Colorado, Florida, Georgia, Hawaii*,
Iowa, Kentucky, Maine, Maryland, Massachusetts, Minnesota,
Missouri, New York, Oklahoma, Oregon, Pennsylvania,
Rhode Island, South Dakota, Tennessee, Texas, Utah

<u>**Legislative Home Rule Charter**</u>   n = 6

California, Delaware, Mississippi,
North Carolina, Vermont, Washington

<u>**Liberal Construction**</u>   n = 13

Alaska, Illinois, Kansas, Louisiana, Michigan,
Montana, New Jersey, New Mexico, North Dakota,
Ohio, South Carolina, Wisconsin, Wyoming

*Hawaii does not have municipalities; four counties constitute local government.
Source: Author's review of state chapters in (Ref. 11).

Fig. 1   Municipal home rule, by type.

units…'' and ''[a] home rule borough or city may exercise all legislative powers not prohibited by law or by charter.'' Amendments to constitutions in Colorado, Louisiana, Montana, and New Jersey also added similar language.[9]

The usual classification of the home rule authority found in the 50 states identifies three distinct models of local government authority: 1) Dillon's Rule states where no home rule exists; 2) home rule charter states where cities and often counties may adopt a charter with specific powers; and 3) ''devolution of powers'' states where local governments may act unless something is specifically prohibited.[10] A fourth model of ''liberal construction'' should be added to these three different distributions of authority between state and local governments. This fourth model would include states where constitutional language has been written so as to instruct the state courts to interpret broadly the authority of local governments.

A recent compilation of the status of home rule in the 50 states describes in detail the variation in local government discretionary authority.[11] Fig. 1 classifies state governments by the type of home rule available to municipal governments. Only nine states currently restrict their municipalities to a narrow interpretation of Dillon's rule. In 22 states, the state constitution provides

for the drafting of home rule charters by municipal governments. Six states make home rule power available to municipalities via grants by the state legislature. Thirteen states have adopted some version of the ''liberal construction'' approach to home rule. Other than those states in the first category [no home rule], the other 41 states permit municipal governments to exercise various combinations of discretionary authority, most typically discretion over the form of local government and over functional responsibilities. About a dozen states also grant their municipalities some degree of fiscal discretion. The existence of this considerable degree of variation in the extent and types of authority available to local governments means that local governments in many states are no longer ''creatures of the state,'' but rather, these local governments are increasingly becoming ''partners of the state'' in the provision and delivery of services to citizens.

REFERENCES

1. Frug, G.F. The city as a legal concept. Harvard Law Rev. **1980**, *93* (6), 1059–1154.

2. Liebschutz, S.F.; Zimmerman, J.F. Fiscal Dependence and Revenue Enhancement Opportunities for Local Governments in the United States. In *Future Challenges of Local Autonomy in Japan, Korea, and the United States: Shared Responsibilities Between National and Sub-National Governments*; Horie, F., Nishio, M., Eds.; National Institute for Research Advancement: Tokyo, 1997; 186–207.

3. Zimmerman, J.F. *State-Local Relations: A Partnership Approach*, 2nd Ed.; Praeger Publishers: Westport, 1995.

4. McBain, H.L. *The Law and the Practice of Municipal Home Rule*; Columbia University Press: New York, 1916.

5. Alderfer, H.F. *American Local Government and Administration*; MacMillan: New York, 1956.

6. Fordham, J.B. *Local Government Law: Text, Cases, and Other Materials*; Foundation Press: Brooklyn, 1949.

7. Martin, D.L. *Running City Hall: Municipal Administration in America*, 2nd Ed.; University of Alabama Press: Tuscaloosa, 1990.

8. Krane, D. Local Government Autonomy and Discretion in the United States. In *The Challenge to New Governance in the Twenty-First Century: Achieving Effective Central-Local Relations*; Hoshino, S., Fosler, R.S., Eds.; The National Institute for Research Advancement and The National Academy of Public Administration: Tokyo, 1999; 267–298.

9. Krane, D.; Rigos, P.; Hill, M., Jr. Introduction. In *Home Rule in America*; Krane, D., Rigos, P., Hill, M., Jr., Eds.; CQ Press: Washington, D.C., 2001; 1–22.

10. Weeks, J.D.; Hardy, P.T. The Legal Aspects of Local Government. In *Small Cities and Counties: A Guide to Managing Services*; Banovetz, J.M., Ed.; International City/County Management Association: Washington, D.C., 1984; 25–41.

11. Krane, D.; Rigos, P.; Hill, M., Jr. Appendix: Home Rule Across The Fifty States. In *Home Rule in America*; Krane, D., Rigos, P., Hill, M., Jr., Eds.; CQ Press: Washington, D.C., 2001; 471–491.

Human Relations Management Theory

Gerald T. Gabris
Northern Illinois University, DeKalb, Illinois, U.S.A.

H

INTRODUCTION

Human relations management theory encompasses a rich and diverse tradition of models, techniques, research findings, and ideas that often trace their roots back to the Hawthorne Experiments conducted during the late 1920s. Researchers implementing experiments at the Hawthorne plant of Western Electric (in Cicero, IL) placed two groups of employees doing the same work into separate rooms. One group was treated as the control, and the second was exposed to various experimental stimuli such as increased lighting, decreased lighting, rest pauses, and so on. The researchers, F.J. Roethlisberger of Harvard and W.J. Dickson of Western Electric management, expected the experiments to lead to different levels of performance for the experimental group.

This thinking was in vogue for the day, where classical organization theory conceived the organizational system as a mechanism that could be manipulated or readjusted to affect employee performance. To the amazement of the researchers, both groups increased their performance. Subsequent analysis of these unexpected results led Roethlisberger and Dickson to conclude that the experimental design was problematic, which allowed extraneous factors to enter the design that led to these unanticipated results.[1]

What happened was that employees in the control and experimental groups were treated as special. They were given attention by management, separated from other employees, and encouraged to perform. The fundamental lesson that emerged from this early research suggested that employees who are given attention by management, who are treated as special, and who perceive their work as significant can become highly motivated and thus become more productive. While this insight today may seem rather commonsensical, back then, it was novel. Employees were not conceived as special but rather as expendable cogs in a machine who either performed their work or were terminated. The need to motivate employees to perform better was not part of the managerial equation at this point in time.

Needless to say, the results of the Hawthorne Experiments, once the reasons for them were better understood by managers and academicians, served as a springboard for a panoply of new theories and approaches to management.

This new way of thinking that gained impetus in the 1930s and 1940s can be broadly labeled "human relations management." Subsequent research and theory development in the 1950s and 1960s provided further conceptual grounding to this management school of thought to a point where today, using human relations techniques and models is considered an almost taken-for-granted skill that effective managers have mastered. This essay will provide a brief snapshot of the kinds of human relations theories that have emerged over the years by discussing their commonalities and areas of difference. But first, we will endeavor to define this rather broad approach to management by identifying its core values.

HUMAN RELATIONS MANAGEMENT DEFINED

In fairness, there is no simple, all-encompassing definition for the human relations school of thought. Nonetheless, there are certain values and themes that tend to permeate the theories, techniques, and models connected with this way of thinking. These can be stated as follows.

Human relations management acknowledges the centrality of the employee as one of the important and, indeed, perhaps most important strategic factors within the organization.[2] Here, it is management's responsibility to treat employees with respect, dignity, and value in order to motivate and develop the full performance potential of employees. Often, but not always, this involves utilizing employees in decision making, expanding job responsibilities, delegating authority, and increasing employee autonomy, all aimed at maximizing an employee's perception of self-worth. In other words, by striving to satisfy the higher pyschological needs of their employees, organizations find that employees exhibit better performance and commitment to organizational goals and needs. Both win. On balance, employees are considered mature, self-directed individuals who will perform high-quality work if given the chance. Supervisors are expected to avoid rigid and overbearing invasive control methods and to rely more on coaching, mentoring, and participative styles.

Encyclopedia of Public Administration and Public Policy
DOI: 10.1081/E-EPAP 120010872

This broad description of human relations management incorporates elements of many different models and theories. All tend to support and affirm the concepts highlighted above. At this point, we will briefly consider several seminal contributions to human relations theory and how these ideas have become part of the day-to-day vernacular of public administration.

THE OHIO STATE UNIVERSITY STUDIES

In the 1950s, researchers at Ohio State were striving to finding a balance between tasks and relationships insofar as to how managers dealt with their subordinates. Much of this was based on the Leader Behavior Description Questionnaire (LBDQ).[3] Later, Stogdill[4] condensed this work into the concepts of "initiating structure" and "consideration." The importance of this research involves its emphasis on structure and human relationships that effective managers need to master. Managers who solely stress structure, tasks, and production will not be as effective as managers who also strive to motivate employees by appealing to their human needs and emotions. What the Ohio State research was finding, was that the most effective managers blended and balanced an emphasis on task structure with consideration of the human needs of their subordinates. In short, effective managers needed to appeal to the higher psychological needs of employees.

Although now considered passé, the work of Abraham Maslow[5] provided perspective on this point. Maslow's "hierarchy of needs" made the case that what really motivates people the most is not basic, extrinsic, physical needs, but instead, higher psychological needs such as esteem and actualization. These are intrinsic. Managers should keep this in mind when trying to motivate employees. Strategies that only emphasize physical and extrinsic factors may satisfy basic needs for a short while but will not likely cultivate deeper motivational drives that keep employees going when they are not closely supervised.

DOUGLAS MCGREGOR'S THEORY X AND THEORY Y

Douglas McGregor's *The Human Side of Enterprise* captured, perhaps better than most "human relations theories," the basic core of this particular notion.[6] This model dichotomized management style into two basic strategies called "theory X" and "theory Y." This simple duality builds on Maslowian motivation theory

and points out that if given the chance, most employees will become reasonably productive because they want to, not because they are forced to.

Theory X assumes employees are only motivated by basic needs and, consequently, have relatively little motivation to grow and mature in their work environment. Theory X suggests that most employees are naturally lazy, docile, indolent, and incapable of performing complex tasks without direct supervision. Thus, supervisors need to utilize a variety of "control" techniques to keep employees in line so they have little option other than to comply with managerially determined objectives.

Theory Y provides an alternative model based on quite different assumptions. Here, employees are understood to be motivated by higher psychological needs. Employees want to grow, to be given challenging tasks, and to take on new responsibilities. By providing a work environment that enables employees to meet these higher needs, the organization not only satisfies the goals of the employee but also motivates the employee to a higher level of performance in achieving organizational objectives. Theory Y suggests that most employees want to work hard, and want to experience challenging jobs, but all too often, are treated like children and thus conform to the lower expectations placed upon them. Based on these concepts, McGregor concluded that by humanizing management, we create better employees and better organizations. This is the normatively correct path to follow.

BLAKE AND MOUTON: THE MANAGERIAL GRID

A somewhat related yet conceptually distinct theory developed by Robert Blake and Jane Mouton is referred to as the "managerial grid".[7] These authors provided a more practical application of the Ohio State Studies' concepts of "initiating structure" and "consideration." The managerial grid consists of two simple axis. The vertical axis measures "concern for people," while the horizontal axis measures "concern for results." A nine-point scale measures each axis, creating a grid.

Blake and Mouton then labeled specific grid intersects with benchmark descriptors to facilitate how a person's score on their leadership questionnaire could be interpreted. For example, managers who have a high concern for results but a low concern for people (1, 9) are labeled "authority compliance" managers. Those concerned with people and not interested in results (9, 1) are called "country club" managers. The best managers in all situations are those who evidence a simultaneous concern for people and results (9, 9), and they are referred to as "team" managers. This is the kind of management system to which all organizations should aspire.

RENSIS LIKERT AND
THE HUMAN ORGANIZATION

Rensis Likert, a researcher at the University of Michigan, wrote a book in 1961 that further expanded our knowledge of human relations in organizations.[8] As a survey researcher, Likert surveyed large numbers of employees in many different organizational settings. He is the developer of the "profile of organizational characteristics" survey questionnaire that serves as the basis for his theory and data.

Based on expansive data, Likert divided organizations into four systems. These were as follows:[9]

System 1—Exploitative authoritarian.
System 2—Benevolent authoritarian.
System 3—Consultative.
System 4—Participative group.

Each system is composed of several factors, such as motivation techniques, supervisory style, incentive systems, and so on. Likert referred to these as managerial systems, because how an organization scores on one factor is predictive of how they score on other factors. Hence, organizational factors are interrelated parts. What Likert found was that most organizations score somewhere between systems 1 and 2 on average, but that when asked where they would like to be, most organizations respond systems 3 or 4. Thus, he infers that system 4, participative group, must be normatively the best, because that is where employees want to be if they can, almost all of the time.

In a vein similar to McGregor and Blake and Mouton, Likert made a strong case that humanizing the organization by increasing participation, expanding communications, appealing to higher psychological needs, and increasing responsibility contributes to the responsible freedom of employees and, therefore, should stimulate higher performance. As a consequence, organizations may wish to incorporate human relations management philosophy into their repertoire, not simply out of altruism but out of self-interest.

CONTINGENCY MANAGEMENT THEORY:
HERSEY AND BLANCHARD

This essay will provide one final twist on the human relations perspective. Some scholars suggest that style of management is contingent on the situation, and that perhaps there is no one best way to manage all of the time. Paul Hersey and Ken Blanchard[10] utilized the same axis descriptors as Blake and Mouton, but they came to quite different conclusions. Their vertical axis is labeled "relationship" behavior, and the horizontal axis is labeled "task" behavior. How one scores on their Leadership Effectiveness Adaptiveness Description (LEAD) survey determined where one would be placed on their grid.

Hersey and Blanchard suggested that in some cases, employees are immature or ignorant on how to perform certain tasks. Here, participation makes little sense. Supervisors should simply tell the employees what to do. They call this S1 or "telling" management. Sometimes, employees may not know how to perform a task, but there is a need for them to work together cooperatively. Here, an S2 or "selling" style of management would be better. Alternatively, employees may know how to perform a task or have high task maturity, but they need to build relationships to work cooperatively on a project. In this case, an S3 or "participative" style might work best. Finally, if employees know how to perform a task, and they do not need to work with others to get it done, then a supervisor should use an S4 style or simply "delegate" the work.

The point is that Hersey and Blanchard realized that supervisory style and approach are somewhat contingent on conditions at work. They felt that a human relations approach may be useful at times but not necessarily in all situations. This approach represents a more sophisticated approach to understanding how human relations theory might be utilized in public organizations. It is a tool, an approach that encourages more flexibility and adaptativeness, in contrast to the earlier models discussed.

CONCLUSION

Human relations management is alive and well today. We probably take it for granted in most of the organizations we work in and for. Bosses today who exude little regard for people are typically considered old-fashioned autocrats who, due to insecurity, strive to bully people around. It is not surprising that in research conducted by Jay Hall[11] that asked employees to rate their favorite supervisor and to specify their behavioral traits, those who received the highest "management achievement quotients" or MAQs (one's hierarchical rank divided by chronological age) were those who practiced human relations management. Human relations management has become an ingrained assumption about how we should manage public organizations. While it may at times be difficult to define, you can tell it when you see it.

REFERENCES

1. Roethlisberger, F.; Dickson, W. *Management and the Worker*; Harvard University Press: Cambridge, MA, 1947.
2. Barnard, C. *The Functions of the Executive*; Harvard University Press: Cambridge, MA, 1935.
3. Hemphill, J.; Coons, A. Development of the Leader Behavior Description Questionnaire. In *Leader Behavior: Its Description and Measurement*; Stogdill, R.M., Coons, A.E., Eds.; Ohio State University Bureau of Business Research: Columbus, OH, 1957.
4. Stogdill, R.M. *A Handbook of Leadership: A Survey of Theory and Research*; The Free Press: New York, 1974.
5. Maslow, A. *Motivation and Personality*; Harper and Brothers: New York, 1954.
6. McGregor, D. *The Human Side of Enterprise*; McGraw-Hill: New York, 1960.
7. Blake, R.; Mouton, J. *The Managerial Grid*; Gulf Publishing: Houston, TX, 1964.
8. Likert, R. *New Patterns of Management*; McGraw-Hill: New York, 1961.
9. Likert, R. *The Human Organization*; McGraw-Hill: New York, 1967.
10. Hersey, P.; Blanchard, K. *Management of Organizational Behavior*; Prentice-Hall: Englewood Cliffs, NJ, 1982.
11. Hall, J. To achieve of not to achieve: The manager's choice. Calif. Manage. Rev. **1976**, *18* (4), 5–18.

Human Resource Management

Stephen E. Condrey
University of Georgia, Athens, Georgia, U.S.A.

INTRODUCTION

The field of public human resource management has endured a tumultuous, yet challenging decade, with the emergence of reforms such as outsourcing, privatization, decentralization, reinventing government, new public management, and the like. At the center of these reform activities has been the call for human resource management to become a relevant and viable partner in the actual management of public organizations.

In a sense, human resource management is always in a state of reform—competing values such as responsiveness, economy, efficiency, and social equity play an important role in shaping the field. Lynn and Klingner noted that as the profession has evolved, so too has the role of the human resource manager:

> (H)istorical traditions emphasize the technical side of personnel management, with less emphasis on policy-related analytical work, relationships with outside organizations, and decision making among conflicting values...A more contemporary view emphasizes different activities and relationships...For example, the modern personnel director might be called upon to prepare cost-benefit analyses of alternative pay and benefit proposals related to collective bargaining with employees in the solid waste department. At the same time, he or she might also be asked to evaluate the cooperative feasibility, productivity, and cost of privatizing or contracting the entire function out, thus making the collective bargaining analysis obsolete.[1]

Human resource managers must adapt to these changes in the profession, all the while implementing effective and responsive human resource management systems in their organizations. In *Human Resource Management in Public Service*, Berman, Bowman, West, and Van Wart defined human resource management as "a titanic force that shapes the condition in which people find themselves...From deciding how individuals will be recruited to how they are then compensated, trained, and evaluated, human resource administration has a significant, even definitive effect on the careers of all employees."[2]

OVERVIEW

Human resource management affects individual employees and their internal calculus as to whether and to what extent they will contribute toward organizational goals. Collectively, the system of human resource management present within an organization will positively or negatively affect the internal functioning of the organization and ultimately the quality of services it delivers to its clients (citizens).

This article is divided into two sections. The first section briefly discusses significant elements of an effective system of human resource administration. The second section provides a listing of reference sources in the field.

DESIGNING AN EFFECTIVE HUMAN RESOURCE SYSTEM

What makes an effective system of human resource management? While there is no simple answer to this question, it is nonetheless a critical issue to be explored. Indeed, an effective system of human resource management can enhance every area of administrative operations. Likewise, an ineffective or nonresponsive human resource management system can hinder administrative performance and have debilitating effects on an organization's climate, its performance, and its ability to attract and retain a quality workforce.

The following eight elements can be combined to help develop an effective public human resource management system:

- Systematic and meaningful employee involvement.
- Competitive compensation and benefits system.
- Responsive position classification system.
- Professional human resource management staff.
- Political and bureaucratic support.
- Integral part of the organization's management infrastructure.
- Aggressive employee recruitment and professional selection techniques.
- Effective and systematic training and development activities.

While this is a nonexhaustive listing, it begins to bring substance to the concept of an effective human resource management system. Following is a brief discussion of each of these elements.

Encyclopedia of Public Administration and Public Policy
DOI: 10.1081/E-EPAP 120010795

Table 1 Selected public human resource management reference sources

Texts:	
Human Resource Management in Public Service: Paradoxes, Processes, and Problems (Sage, 2001)	Berman, Bowman, West, and Van Wart
Public Personnel Management: Contexts and Strategies (Prentice Hall, 2002)	Klingner and Nalbandian
The New Public Personnel Administration (F. E. Peacock Publishers, 2000)	Nigro and Nigro
Readers:	
Public Personnel Administration: Problems and Prospects (Prentice Hall, 2002)	Hays and Kearney
Public Personnel Management: Current Concerns, Future Challenges (Longman Publishing, 1997; 3rd edition, 2002)	Ban and Riccucci
Radical Reform of the Civil Service (Lexington Books, 2001)	Condrey and Maranto
Handbooks:	
Handbook of Human Resource Management in Government (Jossey-Bass, 1998)	Condrey
Handbook of Public Personnel Administration (Marcel Dekker, 1994)	Rabin
Journals:	
Review of Public Personnel Administration (Sage Publications)	Section on Personnel Administration and Labor Relations, American Society for Public Administration
Public Personnel Management (IPMA)	International Personnel Management Association
Web Sites	
Sectional on Personnel Administration and Labor Relations	www.spalr.org
International Personnel Management Association	www.ipma.org
Review of Public Personnel Administration	www.roppa.org
Society for Human Resource Management	www.shrm.org
National Association of State Personnel Executives	www.naspe.net
United States Equal Employment Opportunity Commission	www.eeoc.gov

Systematic and meaningful employee involvement in human resource decisions and processes can build the trust and support necessary for employee buy-in concerning organizational mission and goals. Additionally, a competitive compensation and benefits system will help attract and retain a quality workforce. An effective compensation system is predicated upon a flexible and responsive system of job classification. The classification system should assure "equal pay for equal work," while also providing mechanisms to recognize professional growth and development through the use of career ladders or broadbanding.

Necessary to any effective human resource management system is professional staff devoted individually or collectively to various aspects of the personnel system. Additionally, the organization's political and bureaucratic leadership must be committed to a professional human resource management system and allow adequate funding for its development and maintenance. As a corollary to the above, human resources should be viewed as an integral part of the organization's management infrastructure. This entails the human resource management staff having input into important general management concerns. Because three-quarters of most public organization's budgets are personnel related, it makes good managerial sense to involve the human resource staff in managerial decisions.

An aggressive system of recruitment and selection can help an organization recruit quality employees into the organization. Coupled with professional selection techniques such as assessment centers, an effective recruitment and selection program can build and strengthen an organization. Finally, effective and systematic training and development activities can further enhance organizational capacity.

DISCUSSION

Taken individually, each of the areas discussed above will not result in an outstanding human resource management department or function. Collectively, however, they signal a human resource department that is attuned to the needs of the organization's employees, its management purpose, and the citizens it serves. Building an effective human resource management system cannot be accomplished overnight; it requires internal competence and external support. As such, it is necessarily an incremental process, whereby major actors in the organization (governing body, management, and employees) gain confidence and respect in the human resource department and its ability to facilitate an effective and responsive system of personnel management. Those seeking an effective human resource system should not look to the latest management fad or "quick fix," but rather concentrate on the proper resources (monetary and human) and buy-in of the organization's major stakeholders.

SOURCES AND RESOURCES

Table 1 lists various resources for those interested in further information concerning human resource management. The table lists texts, readers, handbooks, journals, and web sites that should prove useful. While not exhaustive, this listing should provide a sound starting point for discovering further information about public human resource management.

CONCLUSION

This article has provided a brief introduction to the challenging and evolving field of human resource management in public organizations. It is hoped that the reader will refer to the reference sources herein as a roadmap for further study in the field.

ACKNOWLEDGMENTS

The author is grateful to Jason Fleury, Linda Seagraves, and Jared Gilstrap of the Carl Vinson Institute of Government for research and technical assistance in preparing this article.

REFERENCES

1. Lynn, D.B.; Klingner, D.E. Beyond Civil Service: New Roles and New Tools for Public Personnel Managers. In *Radical Reform of the Civil Service*; Condrey, S.E., Maranto, R., Eds.; Lexington Books: Lanham, MD, 2001; 198–199.
2. Berman, E.M.; Bowman, J.S.; West, J.P.; Van Wart, M. *Human Resource Management in Public Service: Paradoxes, Processes, and Problems*; Sage Publications: Thousand Oaks, CA, 2001; xvi.

FURTHER READING

Condrey, S.E. *Handbook of Human Resource Management*; Jossey-Bass: San Francisco, 1998.

Human Resource Management for Productivity

Seok-Hwan Lee
University of Illinois at Springfield, Springfield, Illinois, U.S.A.

INTRODUCTION

Human resource management for productivity refers to a comprehensive strategy that is designed to achieve productivity improvement by managing human resources in public organizations. Although productivity improvement in the public sector is also comprehensive both in concept and scope, it is possible to define productivity improvement in human resource management. From a perspective of effective human resource management, productivity is defined as the production of a series of efforts that encourage public employees to work hard in an efficient manner.

In addition, because productivity improvement is affected by various factors, ranging from top management support to feedback and correction on budget management decisions, productive human resource management requires human resource managers to pay special attention to four major elements in an open system perspective.

SELECTION AND COOPERATION AMONG RELATED AGENCIES: RIGHT PEOPLE, RIGHT TIME, AND RIGHT PLACE

Productive human resource management must start with recruiting the best and brightest. Because certain negative images (for example, corruption, red tape, and buffoonery) about public services and adverse circumstances prevail among citizens, attracting highly qualified people into the public sector may be harder than into the private sector. However, streamlined and flexible selection procedures can provide effective tools to hire highly talented people at the right time and at the right place.

Structured Application Forms

A structured application form that is focused on specific selection criteria and competencies provides an agency with a major head start in the short-listing stage of the recruitment process. Application forms must be tailored to a specific competency model that reflects agencies' professional needs.

Effective Cooperative Systems Among Related Agencies

So often, ineffective cooperation systems among related agencies hinder hiring agencies from carrying out their recruitment plan. Given that productive human resource management must be focused on the premise of "right people, right time, and right places," a lack of effective cooperation and the failure to eliminate unnecessary involvement by related agencies will delay the process and cause hiring agencies to lose the opportunity of having highly qualified and talented people in the competitive market.

Effective cooperation can benefit from using Internet technology that enables related agencies to communicate important information in a timely manner. Internet technology can certainly make a streamlined recruitment process possible by cutting time and costs, as well as raising an agency's ability to locate and identify qualified people in the market.

Continuous Recruitment Process

Flexibility in recruitment is essential to attract viable candidates from the limited pool. Furthermore, diversification of public employees will also be facilitated by continuous recruitment. Whenever there is a job vacancy, an agency should be able to hire the right people immediately. The longer the gap between vacancy and replacement, the more likely an agency is to lose competitiveness.

In an effective continuous recruitment process, hiring department managers will submit a "request to recruit" to the human resource department and develop a written rationale that the availability of qualified candidates is limited. The approval notice must be made as soon as possible.

Professional Needs and Process Needs: Shared Responsibility

A streamlined and flexible recruitment process also encourages greater strategic use of the agencies' people, as well as a better balance between the professional needs of employees and the process needs of the agencies.[1] When

Encyclopedia of Public Administration and Public Policy
DOI: 10.1081/E-EPAP 120010915

there is a need for human resources, the recruitment process requires both the human resource department and related departments to work together. The reason is that working together not only helps to identify whose qualification would most fit a specific department's need, but it also facilitates budgetary approvals to create the position in a timely manner.

In addition, although the human resource department is in charge of the whole recruitment process, it is also important to have related department managers involved in the process. Department managers can assist the recruitment effort through disseminating letters or announcements to colleagues in the field and soliciting similar assistance from current employees to attract the best-qualified people.[2] Therefore, shared responsibility among departments is a necessary first step for a streamlined recruitment process.

NEED FOR CONTINUOUS EDUCATION AND TRAINING

Productivity also depends on those who have appropriate knowledge, skills, and abilities (KSAs). As missions and environments change, KSAs become outdated. Therefore, organizations must continually renew their human resources.[3] Training is critical to improving performance and reduces the likelihood of employee obsolescence in a changing environment. Staff training and development efforts are important to achieving manpower plans, as well as to improving competencies of individuals. Successful continuous training and development programs that require all members to actively participate typically include providing:

- An opportunity for employees to meet on a regular basis, thus enhancing team spirit
- A forum for discussion of problems encountered on the job
- A means of continuous reinforcement of the core mission of the organization
- Valuable information for use on the job
- Necessary tools and feedback for personal development

IDENTIFYING MULTIPLE MOTIVATIONAL BASES

Perhaps, motivating employees to work hard is the most important job of human resource managers. Because pro-

ductive organizations depend heavily on productive workforces, it is essential to identify employees' motivational bases and encourage them to work at their peak. Among other motivational bases, organizational commitment has been said to be the key to enhancing productivity in any organization. The importance of employee commitment is found in its relationship to performance and productivity. Much of the literature on organizational commitment finds that commitment to organization is positively associated with job satisfaction, motivation, and attendance, and negatively related to such outcomes as job performance, absenteeism, and turnover.[4,5] It should be noted, however, that employees could also be differentially committed to occupations, top management, supervisors, co-workers, and customers.[6,7]

Among other foci of commitment, commitment to a supervisor is an important motivational base for increasing individual performance. Because extrinsic rewards controlled by one's supervisor are a major means for directing and reinforcing managerial and executive behavior,[8] those committed to their supervisor are likely to be motivated to improving productivity. It is also possible to expect that where a teamwork-based organizational culture prevails, people are likely to be committed to their work group, thereby increasing their willingness for group-based performance. Therefore, human resource managers should realize that employees' motivational bases are different from individual to individual. This indicates that simply focusing on how to enhance organizational commitment (commitment to organization) may not guarantee a high level of individual performance and productivity.

Productivity improvement so often requires innovative behaviors among employees. Existing literature points out that innovation in the public sector is a function of strong leadership, openness, freedom, and public service spirit. However, because innovation often requires risk-taking behaviors among employees, many public employees are not inclined to suggest innovative ideas, even if they have some ideas that may help to improve productivity in the workplace. From such a point of view, this study assumes that employee trust, along with employee commitment, is the key to encouraging innovative behaviors among employees.

On a general level, employee trust is defined as an expectancy of positive outcomes that one can receive based on the expected action of another party in an interaction characterized by uncertainty. In the meantime, employee commitment is defined as employees' psychological attachments to their workplaces. It has also been said that the level of trust increases that of employee commitment. Therefore, to encourage innovative behaviors among employees, it is essential to have a high level of trust, thereby increasing the level of commitment.

This study argues that previous research has mainly centered on a unidimensional approach to both employee trust (organizational trust) and employee commitment (organizational commitment), and that distinguishing among different dimensions of trust and commitment will help to explain variations in innovative behaviors above and beyond those that are explained by both organizational trust and organizational commitment. In this regard, this study proposes that both employee trust and commitment are multidimensional constructs.

As for employee trust, employees can differentially trust their supervisor, their co-workers, and their organization. Each dimension of trust also has three subdimensions: competency trust, work-related trust, and family-related trust. With reference to employee commitment, employees can also be differentially committed to their supervisor, co-workers, and organization.

ORGANIZATIONAL JUSTICE

Productive human resource management should be able to deal with various issues associated with workplace and personal life. It is the employers' responsibility to maintain a working environment free from discriminatory harassment. Any form of unlawful discrimination, including harassment based on race, color, religion, gender, national origin, age, disability, or any other characteristic protected by applicable law, is strictly prohibited.

Employee Assistance Program

Crises in employees' personal lives obviously affect their performance at work. When organizations help employees to overcome these problems, they can improve employee morale and loyalty and avoid incurring costs to the organization.[1] The Employee Assistance Program (EAP) can help employees with the challenges of balancing work and personal life. The EAP is designed to provide easy access and assistance with resolution for a wide variety of personal issues, such as alcohol and drug abuse, financial counseling, and domestic and workplace violence. The EAP directors must be able to coordinate the EAPs offered by the organization or by contract providers, as a response to personal employee problems that become workplace issues.[3] An effective EAP requires easy access to professional, confidential service 24 hours per day, 7 days per week, on either phones or Internet sites.

Due Process

The Fifth and Fourteenth Amendments to the Constitution ensure that the state and national government cannot deprive individuals of life, liberty, or property, except by established judicial procedure. These due process clauses provide the people with several means for the procedural protection of their fundamental rights from arbitrary administrative action. Its ultimate goal is to secure the fairness in a feasible and reasonable way.

Due process in the legislative rule-making setting probably requires a fair-minded administrative official and adequate advance notice of the content of the rule to permit compliance. However, the agency that chooses to develop its substantive policies through case-by-case adjudication must conduct itself, in each case, so as not to violate the applicable procedural due process requirement that courts have defined for varying adjudicative situations.

In this regard, the adjudicative action does require the due process, such as a hearing, because:

1. The government action is not general and affects a relatively small number of persons.
2. The immediate effect on the class is significant and direct.
3. The government action is directed at specific person.

In the meantime, legislative action does not require due process. The characteristics are as follows:

1. The government action is general and affects equally all persons within the class.
2. Immediate effect on the class is significant but indirect.
3. The government action is not directed at a specific person.
4. The government action is "general determination dealing only with the principle" on which all assessments are based.

CONCLUSION

From an open system perspective, productivity improvement requires comprehensive efforts, ranging from internal top management support to feedback from citizens. Among others, effective utilizations of human resources are crucial for productivity improvement.

An organization without human commitment is like a person without a soul: skeleton, flesh, and blood may be able to consume and to exert, but there is no life force. Government desperately needs life force.[9] Thus, recognizing and responding to emergent human resource management demands is directly connected to improving productivity in public organizations.

Productive organizations are humane and show genuine concern for meeting employees' needs. Productive human resource management in the twenty-first century is the management that focuses on balancing both employees' and the organization's needs.

REFERENCES

1. Holzer, M.; Callahan, K. *Government At Work: Best Practices And Model Programs*; Sage: Thousand Oaks, CA, 1998.
2. Hickman, G.R.; Lee, D. *Managing Human Resources in the Public Sector: A Shared Responsibility*; Harcourt College: Orlando, FL, 2001.
3. Klingner, D.E.; Nalbandian, J. *Public Personnel Management: Context and Strategies*, 4th Ed.; Prentice Hall: Upper Saddle River, NJ, 1998.
4. Mathieu, J.E.; Zajac, D.M. A review and meta-analysis of the antecedents, correlates, and consequences of organizational commitment. Psychol. Bull. **1990**, *108*, 171–194.
5. Balfour, D.L.; Wechsler, B. Organizational commitment: Antecedents and outcomes in public organizations. Public Prod. Manage. Rev. **1996**, *19*, 256–277.
6. Becker, T.E. Foci and bases of commitment: Are they distinctions worth making? Acad. Manage. J. **1992**, *35*, 232–244.
7. Reichers, A.E. A review and reconceptualization of organizational commitment. Acad. Manage. Rev. **1985**, *10*, 476–485.
8. Perry, J.L.; Wise, L.R. The motivational bases of public service. Public Adm. Rev. **1990**, *50*, 367–373.
9. Minzberg, H. Managing government, governing management. Harvard Bus. Rev. **1996**, *74*, 75–83.

Human Resources Administrators in State Government, Changing Roles of

Curtis R. Berry
Shippensburg University, Shippensburg, Pennsylvania, U.S.A.

INTRODUCTION

Numerous challenges and expectations confront human resources administrators in state government today. The "devolution" of governmental responsibilities by the federal government has shifted increased responsibility for domestic policy to the states. A sluggish economy has created, in several states, intense budgetary pressures and the need to cut expenditures or impose tax increases. Terrorist threats and workplace violence increasingly make the headlines and contribute to increased anxiety in the workplace. Today more than ever state personnel agencies are experiencing increased pressure to provide effective, meaningful, and timely assistance to agencies of state government.

GROWTH IN STATE BUREAUCRACIES

In May 2002, the seasonally adjusted number of persons employed by the 50 states totaled some 4,930,000. Increases in state employment levels were recorded in 9 of the 11 years between 1990 and 2000 and by 10.2% between 1991 and 2000. These increases, however, were not evenly distributed across the 50 states or among agencies or programs within the states. Between October 1990 and April 2000, 36 states experienced a net increase in full- and part-time employment, with 26 states experiencing growth of 10% or greater and six states experiencing growth of 20% or more in their level of employment. Since the fall of 2001, numerous states experienced fiscal stress brought on by the recession (and the events of September 11, 2001). Commentators were once again focusing on the phenomena late hired, first fired and the implications that it holds for minority and female employment (Table 1).[1,2]

ORGANIZATION OF STATE PERSONNEL AGENCIES

With the exception of Texas, all states have a centralized personnel function, although significant differences exist in their structure and scope. In 47 states, a single personnel office has primary responsibility for most activities associated with the personnel function. In some, one or more functions (e.g., labor relations or appeals of adverse actions) may be assigned to a separate organization. Some offices have responsibility for serving only state agencies or departments; other have additional responsibilities for educational institutions and/or local government administrative units. Two states, Pennsylvania and California, divide responsibilities associated with directing the state merit system into separate agencies. In about one-half of the states, the personnel function operates as a stand-alone administrative entity, whereas in the remaining states it functions as a division of a larger administrative structure, such as an Office of Administration. The chief personnel official in most states (26) is selected by the governor; officials in 15 states are appointed by the department head of the agency in which the personnel office is located; in the remaining states, a personnel board makes the appointment. Finally, the number of employees the office is responsible for ranges from about 10,000 in New Hampshire to 188,000 in New York.[3–5]

FUNCTIONS OF THE CENTRAL PERSONNEL AGENCY

Functions of the central personnel agencies alone or shared with operating agencies included activities such as recruitment, test development and administration, issuing hiring rules, classification and compensation administration, labor–management relations, and appeals of personnel actions. The range of functions and roles handled by the central personnel agency in the states is shown in Table 2.

Recruitment

Recruitment of personnel is a vital function with central personnel agency normally developing and disseminating recruitment literature, and maintaining a pool of applicants certified for appointment for the various state agencies, educational institutions, and local governments served by the office. The Internet has substantially in-

Encyclopedia of Public Administration and Public Policy
DOI: 10.1081/E-EPAP 120011023

Table 1 State government employment growth (decline), 1990–2000

State	No. of state employees 1990	No. of state employees 2000	Percentage change	No. per 10,000 population 1990	No. per 10,000 population 2000	Percentage change
1 Kentucky	84,177	86,756	3.06	228	214	− 6.14
2 Arizona	60,674	77,372	27.52	165	150	− 9.09
3 Idaho	22,818	28,993	27.06	227	224	− 1.32
4 Texas	258,905	305,957	18.17	152	146	− 3.95
5 Utah	43,012	58,689	36.45	250	262	4.80
6 Missouri	86,507	110,243	27.44	169	197	16.57
7 Hawaii	57,595	67,184	16.65	520	554	6.54
8 Washington	112,110	139,936	24.82	230	237	3.04
9 Colorado	68,854	79,546	15.53	209	184	− 11.96
10 Louisiana	99,572	113,456	13.94	236	253	7.20
11 Connecticut	66,939	74,942	11.96	204	220	7.84
12 Arkansas	49,245	59,954	21.75	209	224	7.18
13 Mississippi	52,854	60,402	14.28	205	212	3.41
14 North Dakota	20,081	20,541	2.29	314	319	1.59
15 Delaware	24,878	27,330	9.86	374	348	− 6.95
16 North Carolina	122,535	142,791	16.53	185	177	− 4.32
17 Florida	180,597	202,883	12.34	140	126	− 10.00
18 Pennsylvania	150,008	149,753	− 0.17	126	121	− 3.97
19 New Hampshire	21,011	24,395	16.11	189	197	4.23
20 California	389,805	434,856	11.56	131	128	− 2.29
21 Georgia	123,249	136,908	11.08	190	167	− 12.11
22 Ohio	171,742	176,694	2.88	158	155	− 1.90
23 South Carolina	87,724	92,621	5.58	252	230	− 8.73
24 Tennessee	91,811	93,706	2.06	188	164	− 12.77
25 Alabama	92,124	95,841	4.03	228	215	− 5.70
26 Oregon	62,221	67,791	8.95	219	198	− 9.59
27 Indiana	106,536	104,667	− 1.75	192	172	− 10.42
28 West Virginia	39,407	39,085	− 0.82	220	216	− 1.82
29 Oklahoma	78,006	87,807	12.56	248	254	2.42
30 Montana	22,807	24,046	5.43	285	266	− 6.67
31 Virginia	141,309	142,469	0.82	228	201	− 11.84
32 New Mexico	51,535	53,012	2.87	340	291	− 14.41
33 South Dakota	17,300	16,588	− 4.12	314	219	− 30.25
34 Rhode Island	24,274	24,291	0.07	242	231	− 4.55
35 Iowa	62,445	63,330	1.42	225	216	− 4.00
36 Minnesota	84,898	79,982	− 5.79	194	162	− 16.49
37 Wyoming	12,679	13,506	6.52	279	273	− 2.15
38 Nevada	21,705	25,752	18.65	181	128	− 29.28
39 Kansas	57,824	53,381	− 7.68	233	198	− 15.02
40 Nebraska	35,751	36,002	0.70	227	210	− 7.49
41 New Jersey	125,430	146,480	16.78	162	174	7.41
42 Alaska	25,021	26,011	3.96	455	414	− 9.01
43 Vermont	14,743	14,276	− 3.17	261	234	− 10.34
44 Illinois	170,438	167,761	− 1.57	149	135	− 9.40
45 Maine	26,659	24,692	− 7.38	217	193	− 11.06
46 Michigan	177,721	172,515	− 2.93	191	173	− 9.42
47 New York	305,475	275,780	− 9.72	170	145	− 14.71
48 Maryland	101,522	95,523	− 5.91	212	180	− 15.09
49 Massachusetts	107,901	105,623	− 2.11	179	166	− 7.26
50 Wisconsin	90,367	75,399	− 16.56	185	140	− 24.32
Year average	1990	2000		1990	2000	
	No. of state employees	No. of state employees	Percentage change	No. per 10,000 population	No. per 10,000 population	Percentage change
	90,056	95,950	6.55	225.74	212.26	− 5.97

Source: Adapted from Refs. [43] and [44].

Table 2 Functions and responsibilities of central personnel agencies in the states

- Establishes minimum qualifications
- Merit system testing
- Provides HRIS
- Human resources planning
- Classification
- Position allocation
- Compensation
- Recruitment
- Selection
- Performance evaluation
- Position audits
- Personnel function audit of agencies
- Employee assistance and counseling
- HR development
- Training
- Employee health and wellness programs
- Affirmative action
- Labor and employee relations
- Collective bargaining/labor negotiations
- Grievance and appeals
- Alternative dispute resolution
- Employee incentive programs
- Productivity systems
- Conducts employee attitude surveys
- Dependent care
- Workers' compensation
- Group health insurance
- Deferred compensation
- Drug and alcohol testing
- Retirement
- Employee promotions
- Provide budget recommendations to the legislature

Source: Adapted from Ref. [14].

creased the potential audience of their recruiting efforts in recent years. Central personnel agencies' web sites linked to their state's "Home Page," as well as nationally focused web sites, such as "U.S. Government Info/Resources/Jobs in State Government: State Employment and Job Openings Web Sites," "State Job Search," and "State Government Jobs," to name a few, have opened up an unparalleled audience for state recruitment efforts in the twentyfirst century.[6–8]

Test Development and Administration

Decentralized testing and assessment of applicants has been widely discussed; however, it generally remains the responsibility of the central personnel office. Although Wisconsin has received a lot of attention for decentralizing testing, the actual extent of that decentralization is somewhat limited. Test development and

validation is a highly technical, time-consuming, and expensive endeavor. It must be undertaken in a manner consistent with the requirements of federal civil rights laws, as well as specific and perhaps unique requirements of the agencies being served. In addition, the "client" agency may assist in developing procedures or standards used by panels who conduct oral interviews of applicants for vacant positions. The central personnel agency has responsibility for certifying test results and applying the veteran's bonus points to passing test scores of qualifying applicants. Finally, civil service lists of "eligibles for appointment" must be continually updated.[3]

Hiring Process Constraints

Political choices play a significant role in the policies associated with hiring employees. Hiring constraints include the desire for a socially representative bureaucracy at a time when there is a backlash against the use of affirmative action, which for some implies "reverse discrimination." Popular initiatives, legislation, or gubernatorial executive orders have restricted or banned the use of affirmative action, causing states to rethink their strategies for achieving a workforce representative of the society it serves. Many have adopted policies that are less aggressive or threatening to the interests of majority group males, effectively stunting efforts to achieve a representative workforce in the short term. Today, the focus is on "workforce diversity," a concept open to interpretation as to meaning and extent of effort in pursuing a representative bureaucracy.[9–11]

Another hiring constraint can be found in statutory rules mandating reliance on the so-called "Rule of 3." A number of jurisdictions have sought ways to expand the pool of persons eligible for consideration through interviews. States have expanded the pool of applicants under consideration by adopting a "Rule of 5" (e.g., Alaska, Kentucky, Maryland, Nevada, South Carolina); a "Rule of 6" (Maine); a "Rule of 7" (Washington), a "Rule of 10" (Alabama, Arkansas, Idaho, Ohio, Oklahoma, West Virginia); or a "Rule of 15" (Delaware, Missouri). In Connecticut and Kansas, anyone who passes the examination may be interviewed. In some states, agencies may hire applicants based on the specific requirements of the position.[3]

"Veterans' preference" systems represents yet another major constraint on the hiring process used by agencies to fill vacancies. Typically, the preference entails awarding of "bonus points" to the test scores of qualifying veterans. At least 42 states award bonus points of 2, 5, or 10 points to qualifying veterans. Disabled veterans or veterans with service/combat-connected disabilities may receive bonus points of 10, 15, or 20 points, depending on the state in which they are seeking employment. At least seven states have an ''absolute preference'' in the appointment of personnel.[3,12]

Position Classification

Classification is typically a function that the central personnel agency shares with operating agencies or those who contract with it for services. The number of separate classifications found in a state can be enormous, with some 6169 existing in New Jersey in the mid-1990s. Several factors contribute to this situation. States with large workforces responsible for a multitude of activities typically have larger numbers of classes. Growth in the number of classes is also linked to ''grade creep'' and efforts to circumvent the restrictive nature of the compensation plan linked to the classification system. The frequency with which the overall system undergoes a comprehensive updating significantly affects the number of classifications. Finally, absolute veterans' preference may cause agencies to prepare narrow position descriptions and classification specifications to mitigate against the negative impact such systems have on sound personnel selection procedures.[12,13]

Managing the Compensation Plan

Revisions to the compensation plan require that the agency address several important concerns. It must carefully consider how many steps or levels will exist in the plan. An appropriate balance must be struck between longevity and qualifications. Further, if employees are guaranteed step increases plus cost of living adjustments during their career with the organization, they may become complacent. Consequently, the organization needs to prudently consider how much of a percentage change there should be between increments in the salary plan. Generally, the larger the increments, the more time an employee should remain within a pay grade.[9,14]

To minimize the future implications of negotiated compensation increases, the agency may seek payment of a one-time only ''bonus'' to employees in lieu of an increase in the base pay structure. Such a strategy allows management to claim that it has addressed the needs of employees to keep pace with inflation in a particular year, but without making the long-term commitment of modifying the base. By limiting growth in the base, the employer's related expenses for social security, Medicare, pensions, health and welfare benefits, and the like are held constant at the current level. Employee unions will likely resist proposed bonuses because future compensation levels and other benefits are not positively enhanced or adjusted to keep pace with inflation.[15]

Controlling Benefit Costs and Increasing the ''Value'' of Benefits

Employers are increasingly asking employees and/or their unions to choose between improvements in salary/wage levels or preserving existing benefits and minimizing the shift to employee contributions (e.g., higher deductibles or copayments) or reductions in levels of coverage. Imposing higher deductibles represents a significant cost containment strategy. The greater the deductible, the lower the premium the employer and/or employee pays. Another tool involves use of an offset, which represents a benefit paying something less than 100% of the lost income or expense replacement. Coordination of benefits has become commonplace and entails ascertaining if a scheduled payment can be reduced or rejected because it is covered by a spouse's plan. Finally, a coinsurance/copayment benefit provision in which the employee generally must pay a fixed percentage of the cost of service provided by a benefit on each occurrence of use is another significant cost containment mechanism.[16,17]

''Cafeteria benefits'' programs allow employees to personalize the range of benefits and levels of coverage contained in their compensation packages. ''Flexible spending accounts'' represent yet another option to assist employees in tailoring a benefits program to meet their unique needs. This form of ''cafeteria benefits'' allows an employee to set aside ''pretax'' dollars into a specific fund for recurring or routine medical, dental, and dependent care expenses. Funds are then deducted from the account to pay the incurred expenses. The principle advantage of these accounts is that neither income nor social security taxes are paid on the funds set aside.[16,18]

Early Retirement Incentives and Cost Savings

Early retirement incentives and ''window'' periods have been created to enable employees to separate from the personnel system prior to the normal retirement age, with fewer years of service than normally required to qualify for full pension entitlements and/or with ''bonus'' credits allowing the retiree to enjoy a higher monthly pension. In considering such a strategy, several issues must be considered in determining its appropriateness. First, determining which employees are to be targeted and how the incentive will affect their decision to leave the system. Second, deciding whether the objective is to permanently eliminate positions or merely replace more ''expensive,'' older personnel with younger, less expensive ones. Additional administrative expenses and resources associated with implementing the early retirement effort must also be anticipated and accounted for.

Finally, these incentives may not yield the cost savings expected when initially considered. Careful analysis must be undertaken to avoid a situation in which, rather than producing substantial financial savings, the effort ends up haunting the jurisdiction for years to come and creates nearly insurmountable barriers to future early retirement incentive efforts.[14,19,20]

Labor Relations and Collective Bargaining

Collective bargaining rights for state employees exists in some 28 states plus the District of Columbia. Strikes by public employees are strictly prohibited, with severe penalties imposed in the event of an illegal strike or job action in all but 13 states that authorize a "limited right to strike." The central personnel agency may bear responsibility for contract negotiations with a number of separate bargaining units (and unions), representing a wide range of employees, negotiating in succession, with each attempting to gain a better deal than the one arrived at previously by other units. Once negotiated, the office advises line agencies on matters related to the implementation and enforcement of the "master" collective bargaining agreement in a wide array of units that may have local agreements or "side letters," which have an impact on the bargaining relationship.[21–24]

Appeals of Adverse Actions

Adverse action appeals may be handled through administrative reviews in the operating agency and/or the central personnel agency. When the facts are in dispute, hearings before an impartial decision-maker leads to factual determinations and recommendations for resolution. These "preliminary" determinations are subject to final review by the agency head and/or merit protection panel operating in the jurisdiction. Critics of the merit system cite the amount of time and documentation necessary to terminate public employees which appears to be generally low. Delays are often a function of a backlog of cases and the inability to schedule hearing until months after petitions are filed. Requests for continuances by one or both of the parties and the need for multiple hearing dates may also push back the final decision date.[3,12,25]

Outsourcing and Privatization

Privatization efforts in the state government can range from "modest"—such as reliance on clerical employees provided by a temporary employment service while a permanent employee is on maternity or military leave—to private sector construction and lease back of facilities, to construction, staffing, and operation of correctional facilities. Appropriate administrative controls need to be developed prior to implementation of privatization initiatives. Promised savings should be closely scrutinized to ensure that they are real and that private delivery of such services are not more expensive than the public systems they replace. Additional staff may have to be hired and trained to draft complex contracts that cover the specific services for which government is seeking private sector bids. Poorly crafted requests for proposal and contract language may result in vendors delivering far less than what advocates of privatization expected. Contract compliance officers must be employed to monitor and oversee the implementation of contracts to ensure that government is getting that for which it has paid. Agencies need to develop tools to effectively and accurately measure performance, and account for all relevant costs to realistically determine if tax dollars are being saved and the public is being served better.[26]

Preserving Merit System Principles

The federal government has been a driving force behind the implementation of merit-oriented personnel systems in state government. Today, such standards are set forth for recipients of grants-in-aid. The standards cover recruitment and selection of personnel, promotions, equitable compensation, access to training opportunities, continued employment based on adequate performance, identification of prohibited partisan abuses, and fair treatment in all aspects of personnel administration.[12]

Beginning in 1976, a trilogy of U.S. Supreme Court cases,[27–29] addressing "freedom of association" protections began to have a profound impact on the manner in which elected officials and political appointees carry out or influenced the process of staffing and maintaining bureaucracy. These decisions make it essential for personnel departments to clearly identify those positions that are legitimately policy making in character and are therefore among those organizational slots that may be properly filled on the basis of political sponsorship.

A final factor restricting political sponsorship or spoils patronage are the standards for imposing discipline in collective bargaining agreements. Such agreements often cover persons occupying nonmanagerial positions that were once the prize to be claimed after the election was won. Contracts specifically limit dismissals to a "just cause" determination subject to appeal through the grievance procedure culminating in binding arbitration. These provisions coupled with the union's "Duty of Fair Representation" create a powerful incentive to challenge the legitimacy of terminations, which smack of patronage dismissals.[19,30,31]

Several steps can be taken to minimize organizational exposure to judicial challenges on the basis of alleged patronage employment practices. The personnel agency should develop and disseminate clear statements concerning patronage practices and nepotism in the workplace. Such pronouncements should clearly state the organization's commitment to "neutral competency." Positions which are nonpolicy making should be clearly identified, and the organization should state its commitment to identifying qualified personnel for such vacancies.[32]

EMPLOYEE RELATIONS ISSUES CONFRONTING THE CENTRAL PERSONNEL AGENCY

Nepotism and Workplace Romances

Nepotism policies prohibit relatives and spouses from being employed in the same organization, the same office, or in a supervisor–subordinate relationship. Such policies exist to protect the "merit principle" by preventing the appointment of employees on the basis of family connection rather than competence. In addition, such policies are intended to prevent the potentially disruptive consequences that may arise when married couples work together. Restrictive policies may adversely affect the employment opportunities of dual career couples. Organizations may minimize inequities created by such policies by clearly defining the family relationships [i.e., spouses (including "partners or companions"), children, parents, brothers, sisters, blood relatives] covered by the policy. The policy should then stipulate that these persons are not be permitted to work in the same department, under the direct line of supervision of each other (first and second line), or be involved in decisions affecting each other in areas involving compensation, benefits, promotion, performance appraisal, etc.[33,34]

Personnel offices have also increasingly had to deal with employees who date one another or who cohabit. Promulgating policies that balance the employer's legitimate interest and concern in maintaining an efficient and effective workplace while respecting an employees right to privacy is problematic. Office romances may undermine employee morale if coworkers believe a colleague is receiving special treatment as a result of their relationship with a superior. The employer has legitimate concerns about the possibility of the romance turning sour and the subordinate employee raising allegations that they are being sexually harassed or punished for ending the relationship. Nonfraternization policies will not prevent office romances from developing, but well-thoughtout policies can minimize the negative potential of such relationships for the organization.[35,36]

Sexual Harassment Policy

The central personnel agency must develop and promulgate specific policies that assist organizations to identify

and root out sexual harassment whenever it arises in the workplace. Central personnel offices should, in consultation with employee representatives, develop and disseminate to all agencies, departments, and bureaus under its jurisdiction a clear and unequivocal policy against all forms of sexual harassment. Education and training programs for supervisors and managers are a key component in the success of the program. All employees should be informed of what constitutes harassment, their right to raise the issue, and how they may file a complaint. An in-house grievance or complaint procedure, with appropriately trained individuals to hear and investigate fully and fairly all claims of sexual misconduct, should be developed. Staff responsible for conducting the investigation should be sensitized to the special aspects of sexual harassment cases. Investigators should listen and take complaints seriously. Immediate steps should be taken to stop the harassment and rectify any wrongs that have been documented. When the evidence warrants, transfers, training and education or disciplinary action should be directed against persons engaging in harassing conduct.[37,38]

Addressing Violence in the Workplace

Various steps can be taken to minimize threats to employees in the workplace. The personnel office must develop and promulgate a comprehensive policy on workplace violence that provides clear direction to agencies. Included would be information that helps employees to identify the warning signs that an employee, former employee, client, or vendor is potentially violent. The policy should also provide direction to employees to help them to minimize personal threats they may encounter and to deescalate potentially violent situations. In addition, the policy should provide a detailed reporting mechanism to document and communicate to superiors threats or incidents that employees observe, receive, or encounter on the job. Finally, a "zero tolerance" policy with respect to employees bringing weapons to the workplace should be adopted, which includes a provision for a "measured response."[39,40]

Potential threats to the workplace may be addressed by preemployment background checks on prospective employees and inquiries about prior incidents of violence from previous employers. Persons with a history of workplace threats or violence obviously should not be employed if a potential for similar behavior in the future exists. In addition, the central personnel agency, in consultation with those responsible for facilities management should evaluate security measures and use of barriers, security devices, etc., to minimize threats to employees.[39,40]

Qualified Immunity/Civil Suits for Damages

Central personnel offices are responsible for disseminating clear statements to all personnel that violating the constitutional or statutory rights of public employees, agency clients, or persons incarcerated or subject to the authority of the state's paroling authority is intolerable. If employees knew or should have reasonably known that the actions taken were in violation of someone's rights, they may be found liable for damages. Employees should receive appropriate training regarding their job-related actions that may create legal liability. In the current legal environment, employees enjoy what might be characterized as ''qualified immunity.'' As such, if a violation of protected rights occurs, they may be sued personally for actual and punitive damages associated with rights violated. When allegations arise regarding employee involvement in violations of protected rights, the employer should conduct an independent internal investigation to determine if any of its policies or rules were violated that might subject the employee to discipline or discharge.[41,42]

THE INTERNET: MASTERING AN EMERGING RESOURCE

The Internet has the promise of making it considerably easier for the agency to fulfill its mission. Recruitment efforts, for example, can and have been enhanced as agencies post information about position vacancies, civil service position announcements, testing requirements, submission of applications, and the like. Test development and validation efforts have the potential for significant improvement due to the ability to have nearly instantaneous access to information from operating agencies, professional associations, personnel agencies in other states, and the federal government. The central personnel agency staff has instant access to information from federal databases, and professional counterparts in other states without ever having to telephone anyone or send a written request for information. As the knowledge explosion continues, the Internet affords personnel agencies a low cost means of keeping pace with available information.

REFERENCES

1. Bureau of Labor Statistics, Bureau of Labor Statistics Data. *Nonfarm Payroll Statistics from the Current Employment Statistics, National Employment, Hours, and Earnings, Seasonally Adjusted: State Government*; U.S. Department of Labor: Washington, D.C., 1998. http://146.142.4.24/cgi-bin/surveymost, 7-13-98, 12:43 PM.

2. Bureau of Labor Statistics, Bureau of Labor Statistics Data. *Table B-1 Employees on Nonfarm Payrolls by Industry*; U.S. Department of Labor: Washington, D.C., 2002. http://www.bls.gov/news.release/empsit.t11.htm, 6-12-02, 1:29 PM.

3. Sheibley, L.B. *Survey of Other States: Decentralization of Personnel Functions*; Pennsylvania Civil Service Commission: Harrisburg, PA, October 21, 1997.

4. National Association of State Personnel Executives. *State Personnel Office: Roles and Functions*, 3rd Ed.; The Council of State Governments: Lexington, KY, 1996.

5. Council of State Governments. *The Book of the States, 1996–1997 Edition, Volume 31*; The Council of State Governments: Lexington, KY, 1996.

6. *U.S. Gov Info/Resources, ''State Government Job Resources''*; @ http://usgovinfo.about.com/blstjobs.htm, 6-12-02, 1:49 PM. Copyright © 2002 About, Inc.

7. *Employment Spot, ''State Job Search''*; @ http://www.employmentspot.com/state/, © 2001, StartSpot Mediaworks, Inc., 6-12-02 @ 2:55 PM.

8. *The Internet Job Source, ''State Government Jobs''*; @ http://www.statejobs.com/gov.html) 6-12-02 @ 2:45 PM.

9. Sylvia, R.D.; Meyer, C.K. *Public Personnel Administration*, 2nd Ed.; Wadsworth Publishing Company, Inc.: Belmont, CA, 2002.

10. *Public Personnel Management: Current Concerns, Future Challenges*, 3rd Ed.; Ban, C., Riccucci, N.M., Eds.; Addison, Wesley Longman, Inc.: New York, NY, 2002.

11. Ridge, T., Governor Commonwealth of Pennsylvania. *Executive Order 1996–9, Equal Employment Opportunity*; Office of Administration, Governor's Office, Commonwealth of Pennsylvania: Harrisburg, PA, December 20, 1996.

12. PA Legislative Budget and Finance Committee. *Study on Civil Service Reform: Pursuant to Senate Resolution 1977–14*; PA Legislative Budget and Finance Committee: Harrisburg, PA, April 1998.

13. States Update Personnel Systems. *State Trends Bulletin*; April/May 1995; Vol. 1 (3), pp. 1, 6–7.

14. Klingner, D.E.; Nalbandian, J. *Public Personnel Management: Contexts and Strategies*, 4th Ed.; Prentice-Hall, Inc.: Englewood Cliffs, NJ, 1998.

15. Mayer, D.F. *Comments of Dr. Donald F. Mayer, Chairperson Negotiating Team, 1998*; Association of Pennsylvania State College and University Faculties, June 1998.

16. McCaffery, R.M. *Employee Benefit Programs: A Total Compensation Perspective*; PWS-Kent Publishing Company: Boston, MA, 1988.

17. Rosenbloom, J.S.; Hallman, G.V. *Employee Benefit Planning*, 2nd Ed.; Prentice-Hall, Inc.: Englewood Cliffs, NJ, 1986.

18. Henderson, R.I. *Compensation Management: Rewarding Performance*, 4th Ed.; Reston Publishing Company: Reston, VA, 1985.

19. *Handbook of Public Personnel Administration*; Rabin, J., Vocino, T., Bartley Hildreth, W., Miller, G.J., Eds.; Marcel Dekker, Inc.: New York, NY, 1995.

20. PA Public Employee Retirement Commission. *Feasibility of Early Retirement Incentives in the Public Sector*; Public Employee Retirement Commission, Commonwealth of Pennsylvania: Harrisburg, PA, March 1995.

21. Kearney, R.C.; Carnevale, D.G. *Labor Relations in the Public Sector*, 3rd Ed.; Marcel Dekker, Inc.: New York, NY, 2001.

22. Public Employee Department, AFL-CIO. *Public Employees Bargain for Excellence: A Compendium of State Labor Relations Laws*; Public Employee Department, AFL-CIO: Washington, DC, 1997.

23. Kenyon, C.F. *Comments of related to personnel and collective bargaining issues within the Commonwealth of Pennsylvania*; Spring 1998.

24. Office of Administration, Bureau of Personnel. *Pay Plan 1996: M525.2*; Commonwealth of Pennsylvania, Office of Administration, Bureau of Personnel: Harrisburg, PA, July 12, 1996.

25. Ridge, T., Governor Commonwealth of Pennsylvania. *Governor's Annual Workforce Report 2001*; Governor's Office, Commonwealth of Pennsylvania: Harrisburg, PA, 2001.

26. U.S. General Accounting Office. *Report to the Chairman, House Republican Task Force on Privatization: Privatization: Lessons Learned by State and Local Government*, GAO/GGD-97-48; U.S. General Accounting Office, Washington, D.C., March 1997.

27. *Richard J. Elrod, et al. v. John Burns, et al.*; 427 U.S. 347, 96 S. Ct. 2673; 49 L. Ed. 2d 547; 1976 U.S. LEXIS 109; 1 BNA IER CAS 60 (1976).

28. *Peter Branti, as Public Defender of Rockland County v. Aaron Finkel and Alan Tabakman*; 445 U.S. 507; 100 S. Ct. 1287; 63 L. Ed. 2d 574; 1980 U.S. LEXIS 4; 1 BNA IER CAS 91 (1980).

29. *Cynthia Rutan, et al., v. Republican Party of Illinois, et al.*; 497 U.S. 62, 110 S. Ct. 2729; 111 L. Ed. 2d 52; 1990 U.S. LEXIS 3298; 58 U.S.L.W. 4872; 5 BNA IER CAS 673 (1990).

30. Act 1970-195, The Public Employee Relations Act, 43 PA Statutes Annotated, Section 1101.101 et seq.

31. Elling, R.C. Bureaucracy—Maligned Yet Essential. In *Politics in the American States: A Comparative Analysis*, 6th Ed.; Gray, V., Jacob, H., Eds.; Congressional Quarterly Press: Washington, D.C., 1996.

32. PA Legislative Budget and Finance Committee. *PA Turnpike Commission Performance Audit: Issues Related to Turnpike Organization, Management and Operations: Report II*; PA Legislative Budget and Finance Committee: Harrisburg, PA, July 1997.

33. Tompkins, J. *Human Resource Management in Government*; HarperCollins College Publishers: New York, N.Y., 1995.

34. PA Fish and Boat Commission, (March 27, 1995). *Nepotism Policy, Memo to all Managers and Supervisors*, from Executive Director, Pete Colangelo, PA Fish and Boat Commission, Harrisburg, PA.

35. Winning, E.A. *Romance in the Workplace*; E.A. Winning Associates: Walnut Creek, CA, 1998, http://www.ewin.com/articles/romance.htm, 8-11-98. @ 10:54 AM.

36. Levine, Daniel. S. (1995). *Dangerous Liaisons: Why Your Employer Wants To Tell You With Whom You Can Sleep And Why They Probably Don't, Disgruntled Feature*; 1995; Vol. 1, No. 4. http://www.disgruntled.com/love.html (June 15, 1998 @9:48 AM).

37. Greenbaum, M.L., Arbitrator/Mediator and former President Society of Professionals in Dispute Resolution, Essex, MA. Sexual Harassment in the Workplace. In *Presentation at the 14th Annual Summer Program of the American Arbitration Association, Ogunquit, Maine*; July 20, 1992.

38. U.S. Merit Systems Protection Board. *Sexual Harassment in the Federal Workplace: Trends, Progress, Continuing Challenges*; U.S. Merit Systems Protection Board: Washington, D.C., November 1997.

39. Williams, H.A.H. Violence in the workplace: A reality for men and women. Calif. Labor Employ. Law Q. **Spring 1997**, (http://www.calbar.org/2sec/3lab/labs7-11.htm 6-25-98 @ 1:50 PM.

40. Defense Personnel Security Research Center for the Private Sector Liaison Committee of the International Association of Chiefs of Police. *Combating Workplace Violence—Guidelines for Employer's and Law Enforcement*; The International Association of Chiefs of Police: Alexandria, VA, 1995. http://www.amdahl.com/ext/iacp/ps1c1.toc.html 6-25-98 @12:32 PM.

41. Rosenbloom, D.H.; Carroll, J.D.; Carroll, J.D. *Constitutional Competence for Public Managers: Cases and Commentary*; Peacock Publishers, Inc.: Itasca, IL, 2000.

42. *Bryce Harlow and Alexander Butterfield v. A. Earnest Fitzgerald*; 457 U.S. 800, 102 S. Ct. 2727, 73 L. Ed. 2d 396 (1982).

43. PA Legislative Budget and Finance Committee. *1992 Statistical Digest*; PA Legislative Budget and Finance Committee: Harrisburg, PA, 1992.

44. PA Legislative Budget and Finance Committee. *2001 Statistical Digest*; PA Legislative Budget and Finance Committee: Harrisburg, PA, 2001.

Human Resources Management in Local Government

J. Edward Kellough
University of Georgia, Athens, Georgia, U.S.A.

INTRODUCTION

In the broadest sense, human resources management encompasses everything connected with the management of people in organizations. More specifically, it is that area of activity associated with the recruitment, selection, training, compensation, and discipline of employees. These functions are central to effective management; in the public sector, which is heavily labor intensive, that significance is magnified. Furthermore, in local governments, jurisdictional size and the nature of certain public services provided will shape the context of human resources management in important ways. Small local governments, for example, may lack the capacity necessary for in-house delivery of critical human resource management functions, and in some locations where the legal environment is permissive, public employee unions play an important role in shaping the nature of human resource management policies. Some local government services, including police and fire protection, have long histories of union activity.

FUNCTIONS IN HUMAN RESOURCES MANAGEMENT

Employee Selection

One of the most significant human resources management functions is employee selection. Obviously, it is in the interest of local governments, or any organization, to select employees who are capable and well qualified. In the public sector, of course, a responsibility to the citizenry makes that objective even more imperative. Typically, public jurisdictions structure selection processes through merit systems designed to ensure that employees and applicants for employment are screened on the basis of their ability to perform the jobs at issue. The focus of activity is on open competitive examinations of qualifications. Examinations may be written or nonwritten, and may include assessments of job knowledge, skills, abilities and, in certain instances, physical capabilities. Often, the selection process in-

volves a combination of several examination techniques. Individuals who pass an examination are certified as eligible for employment and have their names placed on a list or register in descending order by examination score. Those selected for employment are required to come from the top of the list. In many jurisdictions, rules will limit selection to among the top three (or four or five) on the register.

Of course, the integrity of selection processes organized in this fashion depends in large part on the validity of the examinations used. In this context, validity refers to the extent to which the examination used actually measures job qualifications. The most widely used approach to assessing examination validity is based on the notion that an examination for selection should reflect job content and should do so proportionately. For example, an examination for a clerical position might assess a job candidate's word processing skills, provided that the job requires word processing as part of its ordinary activity. It is not unusual for smaller local governments to use examinations developed and validated by consultants or other larger public organizations, given the limited resources often available in smaller jurisdictions.

Job Analysis, Job Evaluation/Classification, and Compensation

Job analysis, job evaluation/classification, and compensation are also major human resources management functions. Job analysis is the process of systematically examining and determining job content. The purpose is to identify the tasks and activities involved in a particular job, the amount of time devoted to specified tasks, and the kinds of knowledge, skills, and abilities required to perform the job effectively. Once this information, is collected, it may be used to inform selection procedures and the construction of examinations, employee performance appraisal systems, and compensation decisions. Questionnaires completed by employees and supervisors, employee interviews, and direct observation are a few of the techniques used to collect data on job content. The information is organized and presented in a formal written

Encyclopedia of Public Administration and Public Policy
DOI: 10.1081/E-EPAP 120010847

document known as a job description, which specifies the nature of the job, the various tasks involved, and the qualifications required.

Once job descriptions are developed, jobs may be compared with one another so that the relative value of each may be determined. This is known as job evaluation, or sometimes as job classification. It is based on the assumption that an employee's rank within an organization should be determined by the nature of the job or position held—a concept known as rank in job. The most common approach to job evaluation is one in which jobs are assessed based on the presence or absence of a set of specific job characteristics or factors. Typical job factors used, include knowledge, skills, contacts with other employees, responsibility for materials and equipment, working conditions, and physical effort required. The factors are weighted and various levels of each are identified. Points are then assigned to each level of each factor, and jobs are then assigned points on the basis of the presence in the jobs of the specified levels of each factor. Once points are assigned to a job on the basis of each factor, a summary score is then developed by adding the factor scores. The summary scores or point totals are then assumed to represent the relative value of jobs analyzed.

After job evaluation is completed and a determination has been made regarding the relative value of the jobs in an organization, the stage is set for the development of a compensation or pay structure. An underlying purpose here is to ensure that employees are treated fairly with respect to compensation. This objective will require that employees with different jobs be paid differently and employees with similar jobs be paid similarly. Jobs that have been determined to have lower relative values will be paid less that those that have higher values. In this manner, the compensation structure, which is usually based on the identification of specific pay grades, will provide equity internally among employees within an organization. It is also important, however, that an organization achieve what is known as external equity, which is the idea that employees be paid fairly relative to what employees in other organizations are paid. Obviously, this objective requires that the organization collect and analyze salary information from the labor market within which it operates.

Clearly, job analysis, job evaluation, and compensation are based on complex and time-consuming processes. Significant skill is necessary to properly complete these functions. Again, smaller local governments may not always have the resources in terms of skilled staff members who can perform these functions. There is an industry of private consultants available, however, to assist in the provision of these services, and

smaller jurisdictions may turn to them for such assistance. It is true, though, that consultant's services are often very expensive; as a result, human resources functions associated with job analysis and evaluation are sometimes not adequately performed in small governments. Large municipalities and urban county governments are usually in a much stronger position to take advantage of professional human resources services, either from well-known consulting firms or from professionals employed in their own human resources management staffs.

LOCAL GOVERNMENT FRAMEWORK

The legal framework within which local government human resources management occurs is also extremely important. As is the case in any public sector setting in the United States, constraints imposed on government by the Constitution significantly influence the nature of human resources practices in local government. In particular, the constitutional guarantee of equal protection of the laws found in the Fourteenth Amendment will restrict the government's ability to draw distinctions among employees and may be particularly important in limiting the nature of affirmative action programs used within selection ad promotion systems. Constitutional requirements of due process also significantly shape human resources policies, especially in terms of adverse actions taken against employees. Due process requires, for example, notice and a hearing prior to the dismissal of most (although not all) local government employees. Employees' First Amendment rights to freedom of speech and association must also be protected.

State law also provides further limitations on the operation of human resources management practices in local government settings. States may mandate specific kinds of procedures or practices, and of course, these laws can vary considerably from one state to the next. A good example is provided by laws governing the operation of public employee unions in local governments. Some states permit collective bargaining on a range of issues, including salary and benefits, whereas other states prohibit bargaining in any form with unions and their representatives.

CONCLUSION

In sum, human resources management in local government is a dynamic field. Although the core functions associated with the effective management of human resources are the same in all jurisdictions, the manner in which those functions are carried out varies considerably, depending on the size of local governments and the availability of resources. Variation across the sates in the legal framework as specified in state law will also determine the nature of local government human resources practices.

FURTHER READING

Ban, C.; Riccucci, N.M. *Public Personnel Management: Current Concerns, Future Challenges*, 3rd Ed.; Longman: New York, 2002.

Berman, E.M.; Bowman, J.S.; West, J.P.; Van Wart, M. *Human Resource Management in Public Service: Paradoxes, Processes, and Problems*; Sage Publications: Thousand Oaks, CA, 2001.

Buford, J.A.; Lindner, J.R. *Human Resource Management in Local Government*; Southwestern Publishers: Cincinnati, 2002.

Daley, D.M. *Strategic Human Resources Management: People and Performance Management in the Public Sector*; Prentice Hall: Upper Saddle River, NJ, 2002.

Gatewood, R.D.; Field, H.S. *Human Resource Selection*, 4th Ed.; The Dryden Press: Fort Worth, TX, 1998.

Hays, S.W.; Kearney, R.C. *Public Personnel Administration: Problems and Prospects*, 4th Ed.; Prentice Hall: Englewood Cliffs, NJ, 2002.

Shafritz, J.M.; Rosenbloom, D.H.; Riccucci, N.M.; Naff, K.C.; Hyde, A.C. *Personnel Management in Government: Politics and Process*, 5th Ed.; Marcel Dekker: New York, 2001.

Human Rights, Ethical Analysis of and in Public Policy

Cyrus Ernesto Zirakzadeh
University of Connecticut, Storrs, Connecticut, U.S.A.

INTRODUCTION

Today, politicians and political activists of different partisan bents and ideological leanings cite ''human rights'' as a warrant for extraordinary action. Protesters sometimes justify civil disobedience on the grounds that they are protecting or promoting human rights. Citing the need to punish violators of human rights, superpowers sometimes intervene in other states' affairs and, on occasion, inflict economic boycotts, war, and other forms of suffering on foreign populations.

Of course, protesters, nation states, and other political actors sometimes are mistaken, insincere, and dishonest when they declare that are acting to protect or promote human rights. Still, human rights are cited often enough to merit an investigation into its meaning. What do we mean when we sincerely talk about human rights? What are the implications of human rights for public policy?

DUAL CHARACTER OF HUMAN RIGHTS

''Human rights'' is a compound concept with philosophical and political connotations.

The concept is partly rooted in a Western tradition of moral philosophy—sometimes called the natural-rights tradition—that stretches back at least as far as the ancient Greeks. This tradition derives moral prescriptive judgments from a presumption that underneath the flux of daily life, a timeless natural order exists independently of humans' preferences and wishes. One element of the timeless order is a fixed human nature.

According to Aristotle, systematic observation of the world reveals that humans are a distinctive species. Among all animals, humans are uniquely able to make reasoned judgments about competing values and about right and wrong behavior. Human-rights philosophers since Aristotle have contended that this choice-making characteristic of human beings is self-evidently valuable and should be protected by all governments. Moreover, its protection ought to outweigh competing government duties, except under truly extraordinary circumstances, such as military invasion. In the language of contemporary human-rights philosophers, human rights normally

should ''trump'' all competing political interests, values, and goals.

The notion of human rights has another connotation that arises from often blood-drenched histories of political struggles against tyranny. For many political observers and scholars, ''human rights'' refers to those quasi-constitutional arrangements that have been established to minimize the danger of arbitrary and violent action by rulers against the ruled. Here, the concept is closely connected to specific civil rights and legal processes, such as rule of law and the principle of habeas corpus. A government's ''human-rights record'' refers to the government's palpable treatment of citizens and to the citizens' practical rights to dissent and contest.

The choice-making and antityrannical connotations of human rights are equally true. Neither meaning is false, and one is not superior or more important than the other. The two meanings are, in a sense, different sides of the same conceptual coin. The philosophic meaning celebrates opportunities for individuals to be creative. The legalist tradition celebrates constraints on the power of the state.

HUMAN RIGHTS AS THE OPPORTUNITY TO MAKE CHOICES

Many natural-rights and human-rights philosophers, such as Jack Donnelly, H. L. A. Hart, and Ronald Dworkin, used evocative phrases, such as treating people as ''ends in themselves'' or as ''subjects, and not objects,'' to convey their public-policy orientations. Such pithy mottos assume that all humans are supremely valuable because of their capacities to establish goals, to dream of alternative conditions, and to deliberate about and prioritize aims. Stated differently, the policy implications of human rights arise from the assumptions that humans are meaning-creating creatures who are capable of choice, and that this creative, self-directing capacity should not be curtailed except for extraordinary reasons. Therefore (argue human-rights philosophers), public policy should be guided foremost by the principle that each person should be as free as possible to choose how to dispose of time, energy, and other possessions. Any government that infringes on its citizens' opportunities to be auto-

Encyclopedia of Public Administration and Public Policy
DOI: 10.1081/E-EPAP 120011079

nomous (or self-directing) must demonstrate that such actions are needed to protect citizens from a clear, immediate danger of significant proportions. Otherwise, the government's infringement is illegitimate, and citizens have the right to defy, rebel, and (if necessary) overthrow political authorities.

Some human-rights advocates, such as Milton Friedman and Ayn Rand, make almost no further recommendations about legitimate government action. In effect, they say that a government should resemble the proverbial night watchman, whose sole task is to insure that enough peace exists within the community for individual residents to pursue their private dreams. On strictly human-rights grounds, a government should not enforce or implement a particular theory of economic justice on citizens, because this may limit individuals' opportunities to reason morally for themselves. Perceiving the laissez-faire implications of human rights for public policy, Karl Marx criticized the concept's celebration of greed, competitiveness, and self-concern.

Some political philosophers and theorists, however, have deduced more ambitious lists of government responsibilities from the working assumption that all humans are endowed with a capacity to choose. These authors argue that the capacity to choose requires that the government directly or indirectly promote specific social and economic conditions.

One condition that is frequently cited in the human-rights literature is economic security. Some writers believe that without protection from hunger, homelessness, and joblessness, a person cannot have the peace of mind needed to reflect carefully and systematically on values, options, and priorities. Donnelly, for one, argued that governments in advanced capitalist societies must assure all citizens a minimum standard of living (including minimum levels of education, health care, and housing), although Donnelly denied that there need be either a strict equality of condition among all citizens or state ownership of the means of production. In Donnelly's opinion, the exercise of human choice presupposes, whenever possible, an extensive but never totalitarian welfare–capitalist order (akin to the social democratic practices of northern Europe).

Some human-rights philosophers contend that because of contemporary sexual stereotyping, the development of the moral reasoning capacity of human beings requires that the state regulate gender relations and extinguish popular prejudices that may deter some citizens from aggressively defining and pursuing their own goals. Martha Nussbaum, for instance, contended on human-rights grounds that a government should protect its gay and lesbian citizens from housing discrimination, from exclusion from the military, and from daily verbal harassment—hardly a laissez-faire agenda. Arati Rao similarly

argued on human-rights grounds that it is the government's responsibility to protect women from the internalization of feelings of worthlessness and inferiority, and that this may require governmental monitoring of and intervention in citizens' conventionally understood "private affairs"—for example, aggressive enforcement of laws against marital rape.

Donnelly's, Nussbaum's, and Rao's policy recommendations illustrate how the philosophic assumptions of human rights need not lead to the set of laissez-faire policy prescription envisaged by Friedman, Rand, and Marx. The number and kinds of public-policy recommendations that human-rights advocates draw depend in large part on their implicit theories of psychological growth. Broadly speaking, the larger the number of social preconditions that one considers necessary before citizens are emotionally ready to exercise their independent judgments to choose, the larger will be the number of the duties that one wants a government to undertake in the name of promoting human rights.

HUMAN RIGHTS AS THE MINIMIZATION OF TYRANNY

Unlike the philosophic approach to human rights that deduces political prescriptions from a mental vision of all humans as choice makers, Edmund Burke, in the late eighteenth century, championed a historical approach to appreciating rights. He argued that rights should not be viewed mathematically, as logical deductions from timeless principles. Instead, rights should be viewed as the outgrowth of collective experience in overcoming concrete dangers, tyranny in particular. Rights are those arrangements that have been demonstrated to protect groups and individuals from significant political harm.

According to Burke and the later followers of his historical approach, human rights are a logically messy collection of pragmatic rules of thumb that have been tested in actual political struggles and that have been shown to be valuable in constructing ramparts against authoritarianism and illegal rule. Perhaps the first collection of guidelines was the Magna Charta, which in 1215 prohibited the English King from capriciously convicting and punishing subjects. Since 1215, documents outlining proper restrictions on the state have become more commonplace across the globe and also have gradually grown longer. Consider the 1689 English Bill of Rights that specified limits to the King's authority to suspend laws, keep a standing army, and tax subjects. The U.S. Constitution's Bill of Rights (adopted in 1791) similarly enumerated several bulwarks against tyranny, such as citizens' right to bear arms.

Many historically oriented students of human rights believe that the 1948 United Nations' Universal Declaration of Human Rights marked a turning point in the evolution of these quasi-legal documents. Unlike previous documents, the Universal Declaration broadened the concept of tyranny to include social conditions that deprive human beings of different forms of happiness and respect. Later twentieth-century documents, such as the 1993 Vienna Declaration and Programme of Action, continued the practice of seeing social, and not just governmental, threats to personal freedom.

The Universal Declaration of Human Rights did not only explicitly prohibit cruel and unusual punishment by governments and their use of torture. It also proclaimed that dignified work, motherhood, free elementary education, the opportunity to participate in trade unions, and periodic holidays with pay are "human rights" that, if not politically protected and promoted, may compel people to engage in "rebellion against tyranny and oppression." Article 23 proclaimed that "everyone has the right to work" and a right to "free choice of employment," to "just and favorable conditions of work," to "just and favourable remuneration insuring for himself and his family an existence worthy of human dignity." Article 24 added that "everyone has the right to rest and leisure, including reasonable limitation of working hours and periodic holidays with pay." According to Article 25, "Everyone has the right to a standard of living adequate for the health and well-being of himself and of his family, including food, clothing, housing and medical care and necessary social services."

Some critics of the Universal Declaration, the Vienna Declaration, and other similarly worded twentieth-century documents say that these proclamations are little more than laundry lists composed by dewed-eyed reformers, and that the lists are for the most part disconnected from the concrete problems of tyranny that made earlier human-rights doctrines so important. After all, is it obvious that the absence of periodic holidays with pay is a form of tyranny and oppression that must be eradicated immediately? What about the absence of free elementary education?

Another common criticism is that these twentieth-century lists are disconnected from practical sensitivity to the constraints and possibilities posed by historical conditions. How can everyone be assured of "dignified work," in any nontrivial sense of the phrase, given the inevitability of monotonous and servile service-sector jobs even in the wealthiest of nations? And when we look outside the industrialized West, do these proclamations amount to much more than pie-in-the-sky thinking? Can decent housing and modern health services be provided for all citizens in most African and Asian countries, to take but one example?

Brian Barry is among the scholars who are wary of the usefulness of recent lists of human rights. He has openly wondered whether the conventional notion of human rights has drifted so far from the original antityrannical concerns of the Magna Charta that the notion now is little more than shorthand for a particular group's image of desirable social relations—a topic on which opinions differ and about which there are no authoritative "right answers." Barry, moreover, found most of the specific rights listed in the Universal Declaration of Human Rights to be obscure and to be too vaguely stated to be useful even in debates. Barry mused that the cryptic statement in the Universal Declaration about everyone having a right to an "adequate" standard of living might mean no more than that the state is obligated to keep citizens at least barely alive. Any serious declaration of human rights ought to explain what grand phrases mean, insisted Barry. Otherwise, the declaration can have no practical, prescriptive force.

Maurice Cranston, going a step beyond Barry's critique, has argued that even if we give the current lists of human rights clear, substantive meaning, we soon will discover that the concept has become wildly utopian and therefore meaningless. Can we truly expect (Cranston asked) that impoverished nations in Africa and Asia will in the foreseeable future provide free elementary education to everyone? Where will money for teachers' salaries and professional training come from? What about school buildings, books, and electricity? Similarly, "special care and assistance" to mothers and "periodic holidays with pay" will seem utterly impossible goals as soon as we try to give these entitlements some concrete meaning.

Cranston may have a point. Can universal paid holidays, employment security for everyone, and "just and favourable remuneration" (to mention just a few provisions found in the Universal Declaration) be guaranteed to all residents in any major country, including those with the most prosperous, industrialized, and rapidly growing national economies of our day?

But, Cranston could also be wrong. One might, after all, believe in a more optimistic theory of economics and argue that sufficient economic resources already exist to meet almost all the social demands that the Universal Declaration of Human Rights enumerates. Donnelly, for example, has insisted that today, economic surpluses are adequate to realize the social rights listed in the Universal Declaration. The failure to secure these rights reflects a lack of political will, not a shortage of economic wherewithal (or so Donnelly contended).

A somewhat different line of criticism of the current political–historical notions to human rights draws on Sir Isaiah Berlin's seminal distinction between positive and negative freedom. A negative freedom (or negative right) refers to a person's freedom not to be interfered with, to be left alone. As an example, consider the freedom to pray to the god of one's choice without pressure from the state. Negative freedom is, Berlin maintained, valuable, because it allows for idiosyncrasy, originality, and creativity. A positive freedom (or positive right) refers to the opportunity to affect the external world and thus master one's fate. Consider the freedom to petition a government official or to vote. Critics, such as Cranston, sometimes argue that recent declarations of human rights improperly mix negative and positive freedoms. This mixture is confusing, because it combines two different postures toward political rule: one highly critical and oppositional, and one highly supportive and almost supplicating. The notion of human rights pushes one, paradoxically, toward wanting to hem in the state and wanting to enlarge its powers. How can one derive a coherent and consistent view of public policy when one's basic attitude toward government is so bipolar?

Finally, many commentators have noted that the long list of rights that currently comprise human-rights documents fail to address the messy question of prioritizing policy claims. Of the many proclaimed rights in existence, which should the government take more seriously when conflicts in rights inevitably occur? Article 26 of the Universal Declaration of Human Rights, for example, states that all levels of education are to include a specific ethical curriculum that "promotes understanding, tolerance and friendship among all nations, racial or religious groups, and shall further the activities of the United Nations for the maintenance of peace." But, Article 26 in the same document states, "parents have the prior right to choose the kind of education that shall be given to their children." What if parents wish to teach their children to be wary and critical of the beliefs and practices of other nations, racial groups, or religious groups? Consider the following two hypothetical cases. What should happen if Catholic parents in southern California do not want their child to be exposed to the Islamic ideas of nearby Iranian-Americans, or Amish parents in Ohio do not want their child to be exposed in school to the more agnostic and materialistic values of nearby city dwellers? Which of these two rights governing education of children—the right to learn religious tolerance or the right of parents to choose the kind of education that their children will receive—takes precedence?

Similar questions arise when we juxtapose the human right to "own property alone" (Article 17) with the long list of employees' human rights to a livable wage, to job security, to a paid holiday, and to dignified treatment in a healthy workplace (Articles 23–25). Which, if any, of these rights is to be privileged—the rights of business owners to use their property as they see fit or the rights of employees to particular wages, holidays, and styles of work?

PUNISHMENT OF RADICAL EVIL

One policy area where the notion of human rights has been applied with minimal conceptual criticism or confusion involves what the late legal philosopher Carlos Santiago Nino called the punishment of "radical evil." This phrase refers to large-scale acts of government violence against unarmed people, such as the Nazis' enslavement and extermination of millions of Jews, homosexuals, gypsies, and ethnic minorities; the "Young Turks" massacre of one-third of Turkey's Armenian population in 1914; and the Argentine military's torture and murder of thousands of students, lawyers, journalists, and peasants during the 1960s and 1970s. Regardless if one adheres to the philosophic understanding of human rights or the political understanding, such acts seem to be unquestionable violations of human rights on a large scale. What policy response is appropriate?

Nino, Hannah Arendt, and some other political philosophers and theorists have concluded that reasonable assessments of proper punishment are hard to reach, partly because it is difficult to determine who should be held responsible for atrocities on a such a scale: the soldiers who are expected in times of war to carry out orders without question; the bankers and industrialists who financially backed the tyrannies and therefore might be considered as complicit in the atrocities; or just a handful of top government officials who signed the orders to murder? Moreover, how does one determine the proper punishment for perpetrators of radical evil—what punishment could ever be commiserate with the scale of the inhumanity of the act? Lastly, because acts of radical evil usually are formally legal—that is, when the despicable violence was carried out, the perpetrators scrupulously adhered to the letter of existing laws and seldom technically violated them—how do outsiders who want to punish someone for the crime against human rights avoid charges of arbitrarily imposing one country's moral standards upon others? How can one reconcile the rule of law, which denies the legitimacy of ex post facto laws, with conscientious concern for human rights?

A few famous human-rights trials, such as the 1945–1946 Nuremberg trial of Nazi leaders, have been undertaken since World War II. Although Nino and Arendt were outraged by the Nazis' violence (Arendt died before the Argentine trial was held in the 1980s), both were greatly troubled, because at times, the victors seemed to arbitrarily impose their own standards of justice and openly trample on legal principles. Arendt and Nino were further troubled, because an unusually large number of local onlookers (other than members of the victims' families) appeared disinterested in the course of the trials. Arendt and Nino reported that if anything, many citizens of Germany and Argentina expressed admiration for the perpetrators of radical evil because of their atypically high status and material wealth. Conversely, most local citizens expressed little outrage over the fate of the victims of radical violence, especially when the victims were poor, gypsies, or belonged to some other socially stigmatized group.

The apparent disinterest of local populations during trials of radical evil raises troubling questions about the extent to which the moral concept of human rights is held worldwide and among all social strata. Although some human-rights advocates, such as Donnelly and Dworkin, insist that arguments about human rights carry considerable weight among policy makers and citizens at large, the observations of Arendt and Nino suggest otherwise. Could it be that in the current pecking order of political goals and social values, the concept of human rights is not as highly placed as Donnelly and Dworkin contended?

Whether in the foreseeable future human rights will become more influential in domestic or foreign policy making depends in part on whether political theorists can satisfactorily answer current questions about conceptual vagueness, resolve debates about the social preconditions for human choice, address concerns about the economic practicality of twentieth-century human rights, and solve puzzles about prioritizing the many rights that human-rights documents currently proclaim. Perhaps if the meaning of the concept becomes more refined and its policy implications less ambiguous, the importance of human rights will become more salient to both government officials and everyday citizens.

FURTHER READING

Arendt, H. *Eichmann in Jerusalem*; Viking Press: New York, 1963.

Barry, B. *Political Argument*; The Humanities Press: New York, 1965.

Berlin, I. *Two Concepts of Liberty*; Clarendon Press: Oxford, 1958.

Burke, E. *Selected Writings and Speeches*; Doubleday: Garden City, 1963.

Cranston, M. *What Are Human Rights?* Basic Books: New York, 1964.

Donnelly, J. *The Concept of Human Rights*; St. Martin's Press: New York, 1985.

Dworkin, R. *Taking Rights Seriously*; Harvard University Press: Cambridge, 1970.

Friedman, M. *Capitalism and Freedom*; University of Chicago Press: Chicago, 1962.

Hart, H.L.A. Are there any natural rights? Philos. Rev. **1955**, *64*, 175–191.

Marx, K. On the Jewish Question. In *The Marx-Engels Reader*, 2nd Ed.; Tucker, R.C., Ed.; W. W. Norton and Company, Inc.: New York, 1978; 26–52.

Nino, C.S. *Radical Evil on Trial*; Yale University Press: New Haven, 1996.

Nussbaum, M.C. Lesbian and Gay Rights. In *The Philosophy of Human Rights*; Hayden, P., Ed.; Paragon House: St. Paul, 2001; 574–597.

Rand, A. *Atlas Shrugged*; Penguin Putnam Inc.: New York, 1957.

Rao, A. Right in the Home: Feminist Theoretical Perspectives on International Human Rights. In *The Philosophy of Human Rights*; Hayden, P., Ed.; Paragon House: St. Paul, 2001; 505–525.

The English Bill of Rights. In *The Human Rights Reader*; Laqueur, W., Rubin, B., Eds.; Temple University Press: Philadelphia, 1979; 104–106.

The Magna Charta. In *The Human Rights Reader*; Laqueur, W., Rubin, B., Eds.; Temple University Press: Philadelphia, 1979; 102–104.

The Universal Declaration of Human Rights. In *The Human Rights Reader*; Laqueur, W., Rubin, B., Eds.; Temple University Press: Philadelphia, 1979; 197–201.

The Bill of Rights of the United States of America. In *The Philosophy of Human Rights*; Hayden, P., Ed.; Paragon House: St. Paul, 2001; 347–349.

Vienna Declaration and Programme of Action. In *The Philosophy of Human Rights*; Hayden, P., Ed.; Paragon House: St. Paul, 2001; 641–649.

Human Subjects Research, U.S. Public Policy and

Patricia M. Alt
Marcie Weinstein
Towson University, Towson, Maryland, U.S.A.

INTRODUCTION

While the benefits of scientific research on humans have been considerable, it has also raised many ethical questions, most notably about the treatment of the people participating in the research. Public policy makers have tended to produce regulations governing the conduct of human subject research in the aftermath of scandal. In the United States today, federal regulations apply only to research using certain types of public funds or in institutions that choose to apply them to all their activities. Pressure is growing for a uniform system of protection for human research participants.

BRIEF HISTORY OF HUMAN SUBJECT RESEARCH POLICY

One of the most notorious examples of policy making in crisis was the Nuremberg War Crime Trials, conducted at the end of World War II, which resulted in the drafting of the Nuremberg Code as a set of international standards for judging physicians and scientists who had performed biomedical experiments on concentration camp prisoners. The World Medical Association's Declaration of Helsinki, issued in 1964, further elaborated on these principles. The United States only developed strict policies about human subject protection in research when information about exploitation of subjects in this country became public knowledge in the 1960s and 1970s, painfully exemplified by the famous Tuskegee Syphilis Study. Signed into law in 1974, the National Research Act (PL 93-348) charged the Department of Health, Education and Welfare (HEW) with codifying its human subject protection policies into federal regulations. It also created the National Commission for the Protection of Human Subjects of Biomedical and Behavioral Research, whose charge was to identify the basic ethical principles that should underlie the conduct of research involving human subjects, and to develop guidelines to assure that research is conducted in accordance with those principles. The Commission issued the Belmont Report in 1978, identifying three basic ethical principles, which when applied by scientists, subjects, and reviewers, were intended to provide an analytical framework for the resolution of ethical problems. In 1979, HEW [renamed the Department of Health and Human Services (DHHS)] started the revision of the 1974 regulations and gave final approval in 1981 to 45 CFR 46, referring to Title 45, Part 46 of the Code of Federal Regulations, Protection of Human Subjects.[1,2]

The principles discussed in the Belmont Report are *respect for persons*, which requires the acknowledgement of individual autonomy and the protection of individuals with diminished autonomy; *beneficence*, which translates into "do no harm," seeking to maximize potential benefits and minimize potential harms; and *justice*, referring to fairness in distribution of research benefits and burdens, so that no one group unduly bears the costs, while other groups unduly reap the benefits.[2] These three principles form the basis for six norms of scientific behavior that the Belmont Report mandated for the ethical conduct of research, and they are summarized below:[3]

- Valid research design: The researcher must use a valid design that takes into account relevant theory, methods, and prior findings; design is selected to minimize risks.
- Competence of researcher: The researcher must have the necessary skills and experience to carry out all procedures; the researcher is responsible for training all other investigators; and the researcher is responsible for guaranteeing appropriate facilities for safe implementation.
- Identification of consequences: The researcher must provide subjects with an assessment of benefits and risks, taking care to establish a favorable balance of benefits to risks; the researcher must respect privacy and ensure confidentiality.
- Selection of subjects: The researcher must offer additional protections to vulnerable populations and enroll them only in minimal risk studies; the researcher must use fairness in enrolling subjects so that no groups are unduly burdened and no groups are excluded who may benefit.
- Voluntary informed consent: The researcher must obtain consent beforehand that must be obtained freely after the subject is fully informed, has the opportunity to ask questions, and demonstrates comprehension;

Encyclopedia of Public Administration and Public Policy
DOI: 10.1081/E-EPAP 120011061

consent means that explicit agreement is reached, and it can be withdrawn at any point during the study.

- Compensation for injury: The researcher is responsible for what happens to subjects and is required by federal law to inform subjects of possible compensation; compensation is not required.

The 45 CFR 46 regulations require institutions that receive federal funds and conduct research involving human participants to establish Institutional Review Boards (IRBs) for the purpose of protecting the rights and welfare of human research subjects. Specific requirements govern the composition and operation of IRBs; they must be composed of a minimum of five members, and their membership should be sufficiently diverse to guarantee expertise in a broad range of scientific, and also ethical, considerations. Racial and cultural diversity must be considered, as well as community representation.

Researchers submit their research protocols to their institution's IRB prior to conducting research, and IRBs use the following criteria to evaluate whether the proposals appropriately safeguard the rights and welfare of subjects:

- Is the study design consistent with sound scientific principles and ethical standards?
- Have all risks to subjects been minimized, including their right to privacy and confidentiality of participation?
- Are risks to participants reasonable relative to anticipated benefits and the importance of the potential knowledge generated?
- Is subject selection equitable? If subjects are drawn from vulnerable populations, such as children, pregnant women, and prisoners, are additional appropriate safeguards built in? Are questions of undue influence and coercion considered?
- Are all necessary elements of voluntary informed consent present? Is the consent form written in language that would be understandable to a layperson? Are subjects apprised of all of their rights as a research subject, such as the right to withdraw without penalty?
- Does the study design make adequate provisions to ensure the safety of subjects during their participation, and to modify protocols as appropriate, including discontinuation?
- Are adequate provisions in place to safeguard the data at study conclusion to protect subjects' rights to privacy and confidentiality?[4]

IRBs are responsible not only for the prospective review of all research involving human participants but also for the ongoing review of each approved research protocol, at least annually. In an initial review, an IRB may approve a study protocol, may approve the protocol contingent upon modifications requested from the Board,

may declare a study exempt from IRB approval if specific criteria are met, or may deny approval. An IRB has the responsibility to modify, suspend, or terminate an ongoing study that is not being conducted in accordance with its initial requirements or that poses serious risk to subjects.

While institutionally based IRBs provide oversight and assurances of human subject protection in their respective facilities, the Office for Human Research Protections (OHRP), which was formerly called the Office for Protection from Research Risks (OPRR), is the body responsible for broadly overseeing the implementation of 45 CFR 46 at the federal level. Housed in the Office of the Secretary, DHHS, the OHRP also provides guidance on ethical issues related to biomedical and behavioral research. Similarly, the U.S. Department of Education has federal regulations governing the protection of human subjects, known as 34 CFR 97, and provides oversight through the Grants Policy and Oversight Staff (GPOS). In fact, a number of federal agencies have their own policies and regulations for human subject protection, and while they maintain their individual oversight functions and regulations specific to vulnerable populations, there is substantial similarity among them. In 1981, 17 federal departments and agencies adopted a common set of regulations known as the Federal Policy for the Protection of Human Subjects, or "Common Rule." The "Common Rule" is based on the ethical principles and standards outlined in the Belmont Report. The "Common Rule" was reissued in 1991, without change, and was again endorsed by the federal agencies it governs. However, not all federally funded human subjects research is covered by those agencies. Although the "Common Rule" has provided for essential safeguards, changes to the policies and procedures for human subject protection are often encouraged to increase overall flexibility and ability to adapt to emerging ethical and scientific issues.[5]

IRBs have the mandate to educate researchers about human subject protection and will, therefore, work with researchers to design or revise protocols in order to include the necessary safeguards. Some IRBs have begun requiring proof from investigators that they have been trained in the responsible conduct of research (RCR), which includes not only human subjects protection but also plagiarism, animal protection, etc. The Office of the Inspector General, in a series of 1998 reports, found that investigators had inadequate knowledge of their responsibilities toward human subjects.[6] The National Institutes of Health now require investigators to have had basic human subjects ethics training in order to be considered for grant funding. However, the Public Health Service's Office of Research Integrity policy requiring broader RCR training of all investigators was suspended indefinitely during 2001, following a Congressional request that it be reviewed further.[7] There is no common standard among federal agencies regarding investigator training in human subject research or RCR at this time.

The National Bioethics Advisory Committee (NBAC) issued a draft report called ''Ethical and Policy Issues in Research Involving Human Participants'' in December, 2001, just as it disbanded. This report advocates the creation of a centralized National Office of Human Research Oversight (NOHRO) to supervise all federal and private studies. The ''Common Rule'' does not currently apply to private, non-federally funded studies, but the committee pointed out the tremendous growth in privately funded research, particularly pharmaceutical, and argued that it should be held accountable to the same standards.[8,9] The proposed centralized office would also eliminate other problems associated with the ''Common Rule,'' including the difficulty and confusion in enforcing 15 sets of regulations without a single authority overseeing uniform protections. The ''Common Rule'' is considered inflexible and unable to adapt to emerging ethical and scientific issues.[8] However, there is also fear that creating a centralized oversight agency will stifle research creativity, as the NBAC report calls for the NOHRO to have ''final authority for enforcement,'' although that ''function should be shared with federal departments, institutions, and accrediting bodies.''[8] Upon the expiration of the NBAC's charter in November, 2001, President George Bush created a successor President's Council on Bioethics, with a similar mission. It is unclear whether any of the NBAC's recommendations will be pursued by this group, or whether it will focus more on ''hot'' political issues such as stem cell research.

Another pressure on research with human participants is coming from the gradual implementation of the Health Insurance Portability and Accountability Act of 1996 (HIPAA). While compliance with the privacy regulations is not required until April, 2003, debate over their impact on medical research has been raging since the law was passed. As an outgrowth of nationwide concern over the privacy of medical information, HIPAA's main concern is not with human subjects research. However, the regulations most likely will make research using medical records much more cumbersome. In order to protect individuals' rights to control access to their medical records, these regulations establish much stricter guidelines for access to personal records than the ''Common Rule'' has required. The Biotechnology Industry Organization and the Association of American Medical Colleges are among the groups arguing that the rules for eliminating identifying information are going to make the use of medical records much less meaningful.[10] However, it can also be argued that the public's increased concern for privacy needs to be reflected in the IRB system, and in all aspects of human subjects research. As George Annas stated, ''Public support of medical research is really a function of public trust. Providing meaningful protection of the privacy of medical records in research is an important goal in its own right

and will also increase public trust in the entire medical-research enterprise.''[10]

Additional human research policy issues have been raised by governmental and private agencies.[5,9] Frequently heard are concerns that IRBs are not supplying adequate oversight and are often pressured to review and approve protocols quickly. Several well-known cases of ethical violations in medical research resulting in serious adverse incidents have instigated repeated calls for heightened scrutiny and tighter regulation. A review by the General Accounting Office, among others, concluded that IRBs face serious shortages of staff and financial resources, undermining their ability to provide sufficient oversight to assure human subject protection.[5] Other reports discussed the changing climate in medical research, which current regulations are inadequate to address, such as multisite research, conflicts of interest arising from privately sponsored research, new issues related to protection of vulnerable populations, and underrepresentation of women and children in research studies.[8,9]

The Children's Health Act of 2000 required that DHHS and FDA regulations for research with children be brought into agreement. It also required further study of the adequacy of IRB protection for children in clinical trials. As a result, the DHHS and the FDA issued new regulations during 2001 about the appropriate use of vulnerable populations in studies. While seeking to protect these populations, they are also seeking to ensure their representation in studies, so that the results will be applicable to all groups of the population.[11]

In addition, policy questions continue to arise about the appropriate balance between gathering information for public health purposes and for research. Should different privacy and informed consent standards apply if a county Health Department is gathering information while investigating an epidemic or potential bioterrorism than if it is ''only'' gathering the information to produce generalizable knowledge? How do we differentiate between public health practice and research, other than by the original intent of the data gathering?[12] And, what about the concept of ''group risk,'' which would call for IRBs to review research for its possible negative policy consequences for a protected group (such as Native Americans), as well as for the individual research subjects?[13]

Finally, a perplexing policy question concerning the ethical principle of justice in human subject protection has received some attention. Whereas justice was initially intended primarily as protection for vulnerable groups easily exploited in subject recruitment, a differing view looks at justice in terms of access to clinical trials for vulnerable groups. Since the paradigm began shifting in the late 1980s and early 1990s, there has been a growing belief that research can offer real benefits, and the focus on potential benefits has started to override the focus on potential risks. A classic example occurred in the HIV/AIDS community, which demanded opportunities to participate in studies of experimental drugs and protested limited enrollment in these studies, claiming injustice due to the lack of access to potential research benefits. Some cancer studies have produced similar results. The implications for human subject protection from a policy perspective concern the appropriate balance between protection from risk and access to benefits, the potential loss of distinction between research and treatment, and the adequacy of current informed consent standards.[1]

CONCLUSION

Recognizing that many of our most important scientific discoveries and medical advances have resulted from the participation of human subjects in research, the United States continues to evolve its policies for the protection of those human participants. In the process, policy makers are seeking to balance the benefits of the research, to participants and to the world, against potential risks to each individual participant. Our policies seek to maintain the rights of all citizens to be treated ethically in the pursuit of science. To that end, current regulations, promulgated at the federal and state levels, and implemented at the local and institutional levels, aim to provide for the safety and protection of human subjects in research. Because scientific inquiry is a dynamic process, policy makers are attempting to ensure that regulations keep pace with the research they are charged to oversee. Most recently, this has included an emphasis on such areas as medical privacy rights, new genetic technologies and therapies, increased concern for the rights of children, and more stringent review of IRB operations.

REFERENCES

1. Mostroianni, A.; Kahn, J. Swinging on the pendulum: Shifting views of justice in human subjects research. Hastings Cent. Rep. **2001**, *31* (3), 21–28.
2. The National Commission for the Protection of Human Subjects of Biomedical and Behavioral Research, The Belmont Report: Ethical Principles and Guidelines for the Protection of Human Subjects of Research; United States Department of Health, Education and Welfare, 1979; http://ohrp.osophs.dhhs.gov/humansubjects/guidance/belmont.htm.
3. Sieber, J.E. *Planning Ethically Responsible Research: A Guide for Students and Internal Review Boards*; SAGE Publications, Inc.: Newbury Park, CA, 1992.
4. United States National Institutes of Health. *Guidelines for the Conduct of Research Involving Human Subjects at the National Institutes of Health*; National Institutes of Health, 1995; http://ohsr.od.nih.gov/guidelines.php3. (Accessed February 2002).
5. U.S. General Accounting Office. In *Scientific Research: Continued Vigilance Critical to Protecting Human Sub-*

jects; US General Accounting Office: Washington, DC, March, 1996; Publication GAO/HEHS-96-72.
6. Yessian, M. Reflections from the Office of the Inspector General. In *Institutional Review Board: Management and Function*; Amdur, R., Bankert, E., Eds.; Jones & Bartlett: Sudbury, MA, 2002; 9–12.
7. Pascal, C. RCR Requirement Suspended; United States Department of Health and Human Services, Office of Research Integrity, 2001; http://ori.hhs.gov/html/programs/congressionalconcernsresponse.asp.
8. Appel, J.M. Research guidelines: Changes urged. J. Law Med. Ethics **2001**, *29*, 103–112.
9. Moreno, J.; Caplan, A.L.; Wolpe, P.R. Updating protections for human subjects involved in research. J. Am. Med. Assoc. **1998**, *280*, 1951–1958.
10. Annas, G. Medical privacy and medical research—Judging the new federal regulations. N. Engl. J. Med. **2002**, *346*, 216–220.
11. Nelson, R. Research Involving Children. In *Institutional Review Board: Management and Function*; Amdur, R., Bankert, E., Eds.; Jones & Bartlett: Sudbury, MA, 2002; 383–388.
12. Speers, M. Epidemiology/Public Health Research. In *Institutional Review Board: Management and Function*; Amdur, R., Bankert, E., Eds.; Jones & Bartlett: Sudbury, MA, 2002; 424–427.
13. Freeman, W.; Romero, F. Community Consultation to Evaluate Group Risk. In *Institutional Review Board: Management and Function*; Amdur, R., Bankert, E., Eds.; Jones & Bartlett: Sudbury, MA, 2002; 160–164.

FURTHER READING

Internet Resources on Human Subjects Research

Association of American Medical Colleges: http://www.aamc.org.
Biotechnology Industry Organization: http://www.bio.org.
National Bioethics Advisory Commission Report: http://www.bioethics.georgetown.edu/nbac.
President's Council on Bioethics: http://www.bioethics.gov.
U.S. Department of Health and Human Services, Public Health Service, National Institutes of Health, Office of Human Subjects Research: http://ohsr.od.nih.gov.
U.S. Department of Health and Human Services, Office of the Inspector General: http://www.hhs.gov/oig.
U.S. Department of Health and Human Services, Office of the Secretary, Office for Human Research Protections: http://ohrp.osophs.dhhs.gov.
U.S. Department of Health and Human Services, Public Health Service, Office of Research Integrity: http://ori.dhhs.gov.
U.S. Food and Drug Administration: http://www.fda.gov/oc/ohrt/irbs/.
U.S. General Accounting Office: http://www.gao.gov.
U.S. Veterans Administration, Office of Research Compliance and Assurance: http://va.gov/orca.
World Medical Association: http://www.wma.net.

Impasse Resolution Procedures

Gary E. Roberts
The University of Memphis, Memphis, Tennessee, U.S.A.

INTRODUCTION

The collective bargaining process frequently results in an impasse, an inability to reach an agreement on one or more issues under dispute between labor and management. The objective of this article is to describe the various impasse resolution strategies typically employed to resolve labor disputes as well as their respective strengths and weaknesses (Table 1).

The exact timing of a formal impasse declaration varies according to federal, state, or local labor laws. In some situations, there are well-defined dates to reach an unaided settlement, after which an impasse must be declared. In other settings, the law is silent or ambiguous as to when an impasse must be declared and is left to the discretion of labor and management based upon their bargaining history and prevailing practice (how labor and management customarily resolve disputes). An impasse can also be declared at any time in the bargaining process when the differences between the parties are of such a magnitude that future negotiations are deemed hopeless.

Once an impasse is reached, there are a variety of impasse resolution procedures to aid labor and management in overcoming their differences. They include mediation, fact finding, arbitration, and their variants, such as med-arb. The federal government and 38 states have legislation supporting some type of impasse resolution procedure, with mediation being the most common (36), followed by fact finding (33) and arbitration (30).[1]

FUNDAMENTAL LABOR RELATIONS PRINCIPLES

A fundamental tenet of the collective bargaining process is that the most equitable settlement is crafted by the parties. As such, impasse resolution techniques are designed to encourage both parties to reach a voluntary agreement before the imposition of a settlement by a strike or lockout or through the actions of a third party such as the government. Strikes are permitted in the private sector, but only 11 states permit public employees a limited right to strike.[1] Strikes impose serious costs on labor and management while disrupting production and service delivery to the public.

A common misconception regarding labor disputes is that when parties reach an impasse, they disagree over many issues. In most cases, labor and management dissent over a few key bargaining areas. The specific disagreement areas that trigger an impasse vary dramatically from one situation to another, but certain subject areas prompt more disputes than others. The most frequently contested area entails wages and other compensation practices such as longevity pay, merit pay, and employee benefits. Common nonmonetary issues include disputes over job security, such as outsourcing, promotion practices, and working conditions, among others.

MEDIATION

When a stalemate is reached, the typical first dispute resolution technique employed is mediation. A mediator is a neutral third party who attempts to restart direct talks between labor and management to facilitate a voluntary settlement. Full-time mediators employed by federal and state governments receive specialized training and are certified by professional organizations. The expertise of ad hoc mediators varies significantly, and their use has uncertain, and sometimes negative, outcomes. There is no formula for success as a mediator given the multitude of variables that influence any single impasse situation. General personality traits associated with success include problem-solving ability, tact, diplomacy, patience empathy, and clear communication skills.[2]

Mediators employ three strategies based upon their analysis of the situation.[3] A reflexive approach entails meeting the parties separately to develop an understanding of the disputed issue(s), the parties' positions on each issue, how each side views the other, and identification of the actors with the power to approve or reject a settlement. The nondirective approach attempts to create a climate more conducive to reaching a settlement and to help labor and management become more effective at crafting an agreement. This frequently entails an educational process in which the mediator outlines the causes and consequences of an extended bargaining impasse. In addition, a mediator may suggest potential solutions or trial balloons that provide novel means for solving the impasse. For example, if the major issue at dispute is a

Encyclopedia of Public Administration and Public Policy
DOI: 10.1081/E-EPAP 120010792

Table 1 Advantages and disadvantages of impasse resolution procedures

Procedure	Advantages		Disadvantages	
Mediation	1.	Flexibility	1.	Scarcity of skilled mediators
	2.	Encourages creativity	2.	Absence of finality
Fact finding	1.	Increases pressure for settlement	1.	Absence of finality
	2.	Formal record maintained	2.	High economic cost
Conventional arbitration	1.	Finality, no strike	1.	High administrative cost
	2.	Decisions are usually binding	2.	Chilling and narcotic effects
			3.	High settlement costs
			4.	"Split-the-difference" tendency
			5.	Delegation of budgeting authority
Final offer arbitration	1.	Finality, no strike	1.	High administrative cost
	2.	Decisions are usually binding	2.	Chilling and narcotic effects
	3.	Reduces rate of unreasonable offers	3.	Chance of unreasonable settlements
			4.	Delegation of budgeting authority

wage increase, the mediator may suggest greater employer pension contributions in lieu of a large salary increase. The final strategy is a directive approach, in which the mediator takes an active role to craft a settlement. This is accomplished by directly proposing a settlement and pressuring the parties to agree, in essence, taking control of the process. A mediator may use one or all of these approaches during the course of a negotiation, depending on the skill, motivation, and external factors such as economic or political conditions.

The advantages of mediation include its flexibility, economy, lack of a written record thereby encouraging creativity, the ability to educate inexperienced parties, and adherence to the voluntary settlement principle.[1] The desirable characteristics of mediation can be a serious liability in other situations. For example, the absence of a terminal process makes the outcome of mediation uncertain, because the mediator cannot force a settlement. For mediation to be effective, the mediator needs to be skilled and experienced, qualifications that are in scarce supply.

FACT FINDING

The next level of impasse resolution is fact finding, which is more common in the public than the private sectors. Fact finding is a formal, quasi-judicial process in which a single fact finder or a panel of fact finders hears one or two days of formal testimony from labor and management on the disputed issues. A transcript of the hearings is sometimes produced. States such as Florida mandate that a collective bargaining impasse situation culminate in fact finding, while in other states, fact finding is voluntary

upon the agreement of both parties. There is significant variability in how the fact-finding session is conducted. Some fact finders engage in mediation prior to issuing a decision by informally meeting with the parties and encouraging a voluntary settlement, while others take a more legalistic approach and simply hear the case. There is significant variation in the outcomes of fact finding in terms of the recommendations and the degree of public scrutiny. In some instances, fact finders offer no formal recommendations, while in others, detailed recommendations are issued. Clearly, fact finding absent a formal recommendation differs little from mediation. In terms of public review, in some instances, fact-finding decisions are public record and are widely publicized in the media, while in other settings, the recommendations are not released to the public. There is disagreement on the value of public disclosure, with proponents arguing the force of public opinion encourages a settlement, while other observers claim that most labor disputes command little public interest except in a strike situation.[1]

What criteria does a fact finder use to make decisions? Typical criteria include wage comparability in the local labor market area, the organization's fiscal health and ability to pay, changes in the cost of living, local labor market conditions, and prevailing practice (what most other employers provide or mandate) in terms of working conditions and work rules.

What are the main advantages of fact finding? Fact finding provides an opportunity for parties to reflect on their positions and reduce tensions and anger. It also provides additional negotiating time and can provide "cover" for one or both parties to make concessions that would result in considerable resistance or controversy if a settlement was voluntarily reached. Skilled fact finders can mediate the dispute, resulting in a voluntary settlement during negotiations. The negative aspects of fact finding revolve around its absence of finality given its voluntary nature. Empirical studies of fact-finding effectiveness have found mixed results with relatively low settlement rates after the issuance of a reward.[1]

ARBITRATION

Binding arbitration is the final common impasse resolution technique. Our focus is on interest arbitration, which entails issuing a decision on the terms of a collective bargaining contract, versus grievance arbitration, which addresses disputes over the interpretation of an existing contract. However, grievance arbitration disputes can enter interest arbitration decisions if they become part of an effort to change or reinterpret the contract. For example, if there are numerous grievances on forced overtime provisions, one or both parties may reach an impasse over contractual language changes. The main benefit of binding arbitration is the closure provided and its avoidance of a strike or lockout. In states with binding arbitration, the incidences of strikes are reduced when compared to statutory prohibitions.[1]

Arbitration is mandated by legislation for certain categories of public safety employees, such as police and firefighters in states such as Pennsylvania, while in other circumstances, the parties may voluntarily agree to the use of binding arbitration as the terminal conflict resolution procedure. Successful arbitrators are typically highly educated professionals such as lawyers and college professors. There is a professional organization of labor arbitrators, The American Arbitration Association (AAA), that certifies the qualifications of arbitrators and provides lists of its members to those interested in employing the service of an arbitrator. The most experienced arbitrators conduct the majority of arbitration hearings given labor and management's interest in having a skilled and seasoned neutral with a proven track record hear their case. Arbitration awards are published by commercial publishers, thereby providing an opportunity for labor and management to research an arbitrator's case history. Unions and management strive to select arbitrators that issue fair, balanced, and well-reasoned decisions.

Larger employers and unions may have a panel of arbitrators hear their case, while smaller employers typically select a single representative. In some industries, union and management contract with an arbitrator to be the exclusive third-party neutral to hear interest and grievance arbitration cases. The advantage of having the same arbitrator is the increased knowledge and understanding gained by the arbitrator regarding the industry, bargaining history, and economic conditions surrounding the collective bargaining environment. There are a variety of approaches in arbitrator selection. A common strategy is to request a list of names from the AAA, typically 10 arbitrators. Management and labor alternately strike off names until the required number of arbitrators is left.

Most arbitration hearings are conducted in a quasi-judicial manner with sworn testimony, transcripts, and cross-examination permitted. Frequently, union and management are represented by attorneys. Each side presents detailed evidence supporting its position along with voluminous documentation from research studies, prior arbitration decisions, and records of the collective bargaining process that demonstrate the intent and meaning of the respective parties. After hearing the details of the case, the arbitrator issues a written and binding decision. As is the case in most collective bargaining situations, the issues at dispute are limited, narrowing the scope of the arbitrator's decision. In most cases, the only appeal of an arbitration ruling is to the courts, but the standard of review is high in many states and requires a violation of the authorizing statute or a procedural or due process error. Courts are reluctant to overturn an arbitration decision absent a compelling and unremediable error that damages one or both parties and clearly violates case or statutory law.

CONVENTIONAL ARBITRATION

There are several variants to the arbitration process. Conventional arbitration permits the arbitrator wide discretion in crafting a settlement. This places a heavier burden on the arbitrator's analytical and legal reasoning skills. For example, if the union is asking for a 10% wage increase and management is offering 5%, the arbitrator operating under a conventional arbitration process could split the difference (a 7.5% raise). If the information submitted warrants a different wage increase from a simple compromise, the arbitrator is free to settle on an alternate figure usually supported by a detailed economic or equity justification. Arbitrators vary in their inclination to mediate, as some encourage the parties to settle voluntarily even after the hearing is conducted and before a ruling is issued, while others make no attempt to reconcile the bargaining positions. There is a variant of arbitration that formally incorporates mediation into the arbitration process and is called med-arb. The parties choose a mediator, and if a settlement cannot be reached, the mediator assumes the arbitrator's role.[1]

As with fact finding, arbitrators typically utilize well-defined decision rules in making awards. These include wage and benefit comparability, fiscal impact on the employer including the ability to pay, and industry or sector prevailing practice regarding working conditions and work rules. Union and management typically present detailed wage and benefit surveys to support their contention that their proposals are reasonable. Detailed budgetary information on revenue and expenditures supports fiscal capacity and impact arguments. The financial impact of the settlement on staffing and service levels is another common information source.

FINAL OFFER ARBITRATION

Conventional binding arbitration has been criticized for permitting arbitrators to simply split the difference and not consider the broader economic or policy considerations. If the union believes that the arbitrator will compromise, they are more likely to present a large wage increase and hope that the arbitrator will provide half of a much larger ''loaf.'' This compromise may impose serious financial burdens on the employing organization.

As such, states such as New Jersey have instituted a variant of conventional arbitration, final offer arbitration.[4] In final offer arbitration, the arbitrator must select the complete package of labor and management with no alternations. The theory behind the final offer approach is that the threat of having the other parties' package selected in total reduces the incentive to present unreasonable proposals and have the arbitrator select a compromise position. A variant of the final offer by package approach is a final offer arbitration on an issue-by-issue basis. Each side presents their final offers on each disputed issue, and the arbitrator must select the union's or management's final proposal without alternation. Hence, the final offer by issue approach provides more flexibility for the arbitrator and reduces the probability of forcing an arbitrator to choose between final offers that contain unreasonable demands from both sides. For example, in the typical final offer approach, management could demand an unreasonable benefits reduction, while the union package could contain a huge wage increase. This enhanced flexibility, however, reduces the deterrent impact of having the arbitrator reject your complete proposal and select the other side's.

ARBITRATION CRITIQUES

Arbitration is attacked on a number of fronts. The first critique is the cost involved. Direct costs include the fees charged by arbitrators, research and proposal development costs, the costs of presenting the proposal, and the time spent analyzing and interpreting the final settlement. Complex arbitration cases can run into the tens of thousands of dollars.

Another arbitration critique is that the process illegally delegates budgetary authority to an unaccountable third party, an arbitrator. Adherence to arbitration awards can require tax increases, service cutbacks, or layoffs that are not approved by the electorate or the legislative branch. Based upon this illegal delegation of authority argument, several states forbid binding arbitration. Related to this is the argument that arbitrators place excessive weight on wage and benefit comparability without a complete analysis of the municipality's fiscal health and ability to finance a settlement. Several New Jersey arbitration awards were overturned in court when arbitrators placed excessive weight on comparability, thereby imposing costly settlements on municipalities that were fiscally stressed.[4] The aggregate research on the wage impact of arbitration indicate only modest gains in mean salary levels.[1]

A second critique is that arbitration, on average, favors unions, as arbitrators are more concerned about alienating unions which represent multiple bargaining units across a given geographic area than single employers who are less likely to share information. However, most arbitrators possess a clear incentive to issue balanced awards in order to maintain their credibility. The available empirical evidence indicates relative balance between labor and management in terms of wins and losses in arbitration.[1]

A third critique is that the availability of arbitration radically reduces the incentive of labor or management to settle voluntarily. There are two variants of this dysfunctional effect. The first is the ''chilling effect'' in which arbitration attenuates the motivation of the parties to settle earlier in the collective bargaining process given the absence of a strike or lockout threat. The second drawback is the ''narcotic effect,'' which occurs when one or both parties perceive that they have a greater chance of success in achieving their collective bargaining goals through arbitration than through traditional collective bargaining. Hence, the rate of arbitration use increases dramatically over time. Empirical evidence on the chilling and narcotic effects are mixed, however, with strong regional differences.[1]

Other less common impasse resolution strategies include labor–management committees composed of neutral representatives from labor, management, and the community. The committee members are appointed by the governor based upon nominations by the respective stakeholders. Another strategy is a public referendum, or letting the public vote on issues at an impasse. This strategy manifests several disadvantages, including the difficulty in communicating complex bargaining issues, lack of voter interest and education on the issues, the expense and delays associated with the voting process, and an increase in political posturing.[1]

CONCLUSION

The primary goal of impasse resolution is to reduce the number of strikes and lockouts in order to preserve labor peace, safeguard service delivery, and protect the public interest. Voluntary settlement of collective bargaining disputes is the desired outcome, but given the many factors that mitigate against voluntary settlements, impasse resolution procedures are a necessary safeguard. The central objective is to assist the parties in clarifying their basic interests so a reasonable compromise can be crafted. Mediation and fact finding are nonbinding impasse resolution procedures, while arbitration and its variants impose finality to the collective bargaining process.

REFERENCES

1. Kearney, R.C. *Labor Relations in the Public Sector,* 2nd Ed.; Marcel Dekker, Inc.: New York, 1992.
2. Simkin, W.E. *Mediation and the Dynamics of Collective Bargaining*; BNA Books: Washington, D.C., 1971; as cited in Ref. [1].
3. Kressel, K. Labor Mediation: An Exploratory Survey. In *Public Sector Labor Relations: An Analysis and Readings*; Feuille, P., Kochan, T.A., Eds.; Thomas Horton and Daughters: Glen Ridge, NJ, 1977; 252–272, as cited in Ref. [1].
4. Roberts, G.E.; McGill, J. New Jersey interest arbitration reform act: A third year assessment. Rev. Public Pers. Adm. **2000**, *20* (3), 28–42.

Incrementalism, Budgetary

Carol W. Lewis
University of Connecticut, Storrs, Connecticut, U.S.A.

INTRODUCTION

Incrementalism is an approach to decision making in general and to budgeting in particular. It is used in descriptive and explanatory variants and may refer to the decision-making process or outputs from the process. This perspective relies upon established roles, decision rules, and shared expectations; it broadly divides budgeting into the base and relatively small changes or marginal adjustments; decision making is characterized by a process of "successive limited comparison"; and politics is the dominant explanatory variable.

DEFINITION

Aaron Wildavsky initially described budgeting as incremental, meaning that it is "based on last year's budget with special attention given to a narrow range of increases or decreases." The focus is on "relatively small increments to an existing base" and a "small number of items over which the budgetary battle is fought".[1] The literature of public administration and public budgeting include numerous definitions.[2–4] One definition sees incrementalism as:

> ...a theory of the budgetary process proposing that policy makers give only limited consideration to small parts of the budget and arrive at decisions by making marginal adjustments in last year's budget...participants [in different roles] make decisions through a process of bargaining and negotiation.... The budget as a whole is not considered.... Instead, participants make marginal changes on an already existing base.[5]

There are four central ingredients to budgetary incrementalism. The first is that change is marginal and occurs by small steps. The second ingredient is the base, which answers the question: Change from what? Wildavsky defined the base as the "general expectation among the participants that programs will be carried on at close to the ongoing level of expenditures" and operationalized the concept using appropriations.[1] As a result, "[t]he largest determining factor of the size and content of this year's budget is last year's budget. Most of the budget is a product of previous decisions".[1] (His illustrations include standard items, long-range commitments, mandatory programs, and sacred cows.) He stated the following:

> The previous year's budget, the largest part of which is composed of continuing programs and prior commitments, is usually taken as a base needing little justification.... Attention is normally focused on a small number of incremental changes, increases and decreases, calling for significant departures from the established historical base of the agency concerned.[6]

The idea of *fair share* is the third ingredient and invokes open, pluralist decision making moderated by participants' shared expectation of short-term proportionality and longevity. All players anticipate sharing in the action (increases or decreases) and returning again to compete for resources in future budget cycles. This concept is operationalized by budget share, the relative size of the budget going to a program or agency.[1] As a result, incremental budgeting is often depicted as limiting the scope and intensity of competition. Illustratively, *A Citizen's Guide to the Federal Budget*, a federal resource published annually for the general public, lays out major categories of spending according to the budget share of each.[7]

The fourth and last ingredient is roles, of which there are two main types: program advocate or promoter and resource guardian or naysayer. Roles are especially important because, with incrementalism, which relies upon politics as an explanatory factor, decisions are seen as outcomes from negotiations and accommodations among a stable group of players, including the chief executive, bureaucrats, professional budgeters, legislators, and others. Long-term relationships and, therefore, strategy develop as players come back to the process in each budget iteration.

Participation, like roles, is believed to hold down competition in the process. "Whatever else they may be, budgets are manifestly political.... Participants in budgeting...drastically simplify their task by concentrating on the relatively small portion of the budget that is politically feasible to change".[6] As a political perspective on decision making, incrementalism:

> assumes that political pluralism, limited rationality, and time and resources pressures on public administrators are

Encyclopedia of Public Administration and Public Policy
DOI: 10.1081/E-EPAP 120010979

significant constraints on decision making. Consequently, administrators typically can take only small steps toward some general policy objective.... The test of the desirability of a decision tends to measured in terms of political support or opposition, rather than cost-effectiveness or scientific analysis.[4]

INTELLECTUAL FOUNDATIONS

Formative contributions to incremental decision making were made by Herbert A. Simon and Charles E. Lindblom. It is ironic that incrementalism, developed by economists and strongly influenced by psychology as well as economics, emphasizes the political aspects of decision making. One budgeting textbook asserts, "The most important characteristic of the muddling through or incrementalism approach as applied to budgeting is its emphasis on the proposition that budgetary decisions are necessarily political".[8]

In his *Administrative Behavior* published in 1947, Simon emphasized observable behavioral factors and decision-making processes over the rationalist precepts, structures, and norms associated with the preceding orthodox perspective on administration.[9] He argued that, because of cognitive limits, external developments, and other constraints, decision makers operate within *bounded rationality*. In 1958, James G. March and Simon introduced a new word to the vocabulary of administration: *satisficing*.[10] This refers to the "process of finding a decision alternative that meets the decision maker's minimum standard of satisfaction.... Agencies must satisfice by accepting partial solutions rather than pursue illusory, perfect, or optimal solutions".[2]

In his now classic article, "The Science of 'Muddling Through'," first published in 1959, Lindblom built upon these ideas about cognitive limits and decision-making strategies.[11] "The incrementalist paradigm he advanced is uniquely comprehensive, including elements of pluralism, satisficing, bounded rationality, organizational drift, limited cognition, and decentralized authority".[2] Lindblom's central thesis is that there are two distinct varieties of decision making. One he calls the rational-comprehensive or root method, and the second, the successive limited comparisons or branch method.[12] The latter "assumes that a historic chain of decisions exists which the administrator can use as a basis for future choices".[2] Accordingly, "public administrators pragmatically select from among the immediate choices at hand the most suitable compromise that satisfies the groups and individuals concerned" and actual decision making is incremental, "for small steps are always taken to achieve objectives, not broad leaps and bounds".[12] Lindblom revisited his view of "muddling though" in a 1979 article.[13]

The foremost scholar of budgetary incrementalism, Aaron Wildavsky applied the concepts associated with Simon and Lindblom specifically to budgetary decision making with the publication in 1964 of the first edition of his *Politics of the Budgetary Process*.[1] Much of the literature in public administration and in budgeting for the next two decades was devoted to examining incremental decision making empirically and theoretically.

IMPACT

One reason for incrementalism's profound influence is that it criticized and ultimately outweighed the faith in rationalism and progress that had dominated public administration since the latter part of the nineteenth century. As the predominant model of decision making and particularly budgetary decision making, the incremental model of decision making has been applied to federal, state, and local governments in the United States and to other governments around the world.[14–16] "Incrementalism has been the favored political approach to public budgeting in the United States".[4] Indeed, it served as the conceptual core of budgetary decision making; its basic concepts and writings were routinely featured in texts, scholarly collections, and dictionaries.[2] Lindblom's "The Science of 'Muddling Through'" is familiar to every student and scholar in public administration and Aaron Wildavsky's *Politics of the Budgetary Process*, once the single most widely used text in the field, went through many editions since its initial publication in 1964.

CRITIQUE

Incrementalism quickly came under fire for analytic biases, scientific shortcomings, and normative implications ascribed to it. A wide-ranging and influential critique written by Lance LeLoup concluded that its "self-fulfilling nature renders incrementalism nearly useless for social science theory".[14] Another critique acknowledged that incrementalism is "intuitively and experientially appealing," but with a "lure" attributable to "the chaos in human behavior" rather than to its meeting epistemological standards.[17] At least nine major criticisms have been leveled at incrementalism as a decision-making theory or heuristic model.

1. Incrementalism is associated with bias toward stability and conservatism.[3,14] Wildavsky asserts, "Once enacted, a budget becomes a precedent; the fact that something has been done once vastly increases the

chances that it will be done again. Since only substantial departures from the previous year's budget are normally given intensive scrutiny, an item that remains unchanged will probably be carried along the following year as a matter of course".[1] The thrust, then, is this: the best predictor of an agency's budget request is history. Of course, stability is anticipated only in the short term, because annual reiterations allow for rapid change, albeit in small steps, compounded over a few years. Lindblom's 1979 response to this criticism was that "incrementalism in politics is not, in principle, slow moving. It is not necessarily, therefore, a tactic of conservatism. A fast moving sequence of small changes can more speedily accomplish a drastic alteration of the status quo than can an only infrequent major policy change".[13]

2. In much of the research, aggregation is at high levels that smooth change at the agency or governmental level and mask underlying changes in programs. Variance analysis is a standard tool in budget analysis and is often included in Comprehensive Annual Financial Reports. Variance analysis at as low a programmatic or organizational level as possible yields a more accurate count. Variance is calculated by disregarding positive and negative signs and simply adding together *all* changes from the prior base. An increase of $150,000 in one program and a cut of $150,000 in another in the same agency do not cancel each other out, but rather sum to a $300,000 variance or change.

3. Predictive power in effect is sacrificed in favor of descriptive accuracy, because incrementalism fails to link decision-making dynamics to specific budgetary results. One slant on this issue is that incrementalism addresses only a small part of what budgeting entails. Surely, demand is a factor weighing on the budget in a politically responsive system, where projected changes in the use of a service or good such as public parks may translate into changes in spending. However, there are numerous other factors pressing on budgets that cannot be directly attributable to current decision makers. In fact, a great proportion of governmental budgets are settled before decision makers even get to work. Debt service on long-term debt incurred by previous decision makers is a legal obligation that current budgets must honor; the same is true of accrued liabilities such as pensions and other personnel benefits. Multiyear labor and service contracts and economic conditions such as inflation, unemployment, gross domestic product, and personal income may generate changes in prices and needs as, for example, reflected in the eligibility pools for entitlement programs. (The public is most familiar with the Consumer Price Index at http://stats.bls.gov/

cpihome.htm.) Demographic and other social changes (e.g., age structure, household formation) affect services from schools to public safety to elderly services and public works. Changes in programs and services that are required by law (or *mandated*) may mean changes in service levels, beneficiary eligibility, and benefits. (Some changes may be intergovernmental mandates that are addressed at http://www.cbo.gov/cost.html.) Courts also may mandate program changes with significant budgetary impact on, for example, prison conditions or services for the mentally ill. Many of these changes substantially reduce decision-making discretion over a given fiscal year's budget, and budget outputs are pushed by factors other than incremental decision making. This critique suggests that, while incrementalism is an accurate depiction of a small-to-trivial part of the budget, it fails to address the major factors influencing budgetary outputs.

4. The value or size of marginal change is not specified, although Wildavsky used plus or minus 10% of the prior year's appropriation. Lindblom argued, "Where the line is drawn is not important so long as we understand that size of step in policy making can be arranged on a continuum from small to large".[13] Specific variables defined in terms of clearly empirical referents are necessary if research is to be understood, replicated, and useful.

5. The major explanatory variable, the base, shares the problem of specificity. Scholarly work features differing concepts of the base, which may refer to prior year's appropriation or current services. Current services refers to the resources necessary to continue programs at the prior year's level and often allows for inflation, changes in law, and other factors.

6. Incrementalism focuses on expenditures to the exclusion of revenue decisions and outcomes, which limits its usefulness for understanding decision making in jurisdictions in which the budget must be balanced.

7. Incrementalism's application to decision processes or budgetary outputs or both fosters confusion between them.

8. Incrementalism fails to meet the generally accepted criteria of a scientifically valid model as specified in items three, four, and five, above.

Today, incrementalism is in disrepute among some scholars. For example, Irene Rubin argued that the norms of moderation and fairness have diminished, because transparency and long-term relationships have diminished.[18] Incrementalism is deemed inadequate in several major respects as a *theory* that explains and predicts outputs from budget processes.

CURRENT USAGE AND SIGNIFICANCE

Incrementalism is still an important influence on the practice and understanding of budgetary decision making. General texts on public administration, texts on public budgeting, and collections of works considered classics in these fields continue to address incrementalism.[3,4,12,19]

Explanatory incrementalism is no longer "the dominant theory of budgeting" it was a quarter of a century ago.[14] On the other hand, its descriptive, process-oriented form remains a useful device by which to portray routine budgetary decision making for many—*but by no means all*—budget decisions in many jurisdictions. While noting that "budget processes are complex and vary widely among states" in its 1999 report on state legislative budget procedures, the *National Conference of State Legislatures* categorizes a majority of the states as relying predominantly upon a "traditional/incremental" budget approach (and more, if legislatures such as Delaware, Illinois, and Massachusetts that combine this with another approach are included).[20] As Wildavsky noted, there is "nothing to be gained by ignoring overwhelming evidence or the observation of everyday life".[1]

The information provided and its presentation guide attention in particular directions and trigger particular analytic concerns.[21] It is especially important that an incremental mode of decision making is built into many of the basic budget documents, because the "way in which budgetary questions are framed has a great deal to do with the outcomes of contests for public dollars".[4] (Many state and city budget documents are available online via jurisdictions' home pages and see also the listings under Internet Resources.)

Four signs suggest that descriptive incrementalism as an analytic orientation is practiced at least to some extent. All four point to process, not outputs or outcomes. These signs include the following: 1) historical spending arrayed in columns alongside the current requests, as shown in the *State of Washington's spreadsheets on expenditures history, the New York City Mayor's proposed budget for fiscal 2002* with financial summaries and fire department data, and the summary schedule of spending in *A Citizen's Guide to the Federal Budget for Fiscal 2002*; 2) the concept of current services as a point of departure for decision making, as illustrated by Section 1 of the *State of Washington's operating budget instructions* for fiscal years 1999–2001; 3) an emphasis on change, as in many budget messages and narratives that highlight new priorities and initiatives, as shown in the budget highlights for the *Illinois State Police* in the executive budget proposed for fiscal 2002; and 4) special detail on and scrutiny of new spending. *Connecticut's legislative Office of Fiscal Analysis* noted in its description of budget formulation that agencies are "required to present a current services budget plan and a separate list of pro-

grammatic options if changes in expenditures or revenues are requested." And, Sections 5 and 6 of the *State of Washington's operating budget instructions* illustrate justification requirements.

Conventional formats display figures from prior years, the base, alongside figures for the current cycle. Some jurisdictions specify that the base is defined in terms of current services, meaning that budget requests allow for inflation, changes in law, and other factors. Change, expressed in percentages or dollars, is the decision-making focus in many budget documents; the executive's budget message and summary narratives and schedules usually lay out proposed changes in detail. Instruction forms sent to the agencies at the beginning of budget preparation commonly require more elaborate justification of proposed changes than of ongoing operations; as a result, under ordinary circumstances, most of the base goes largely unexamined, and new competitors for the always scarce resources are relatively disadvantaged.

INTERNET RESOURCES

1. U.S. federal budget process—*A Citizen's Guide to the Federal Budget, Budget of the United States Government*: http://www.access.gpo.gov/usbudget. Federal offices and agencies:

    a. Office of Management and Budget: http://www.whitehouse.gov/OMB.
    b. Bureau of Labor Statistics: http://www.bls.gov/.
    c. Bureau of the Census and its *Statistical Abstract*: http://www.census.gov/.
    d. Bureau of Economic Analysis: http://www.bea.doc.gov.
    e. General Accounting Office: http://www.gao.gov.
    f. Congressional Budget Office: http://www.cbo.gov.

2. State budgets and finances: http://www.census.gov/govs/www/state.html. National Conference of State Legislatures: http://www.ncsl.org. Tax Foundation: http://www.taxfoundation.org/.

3. State and local links: http://lcweb.loc.gov/global/state/stategov.html.

4. Professional associations:

    a. Governmental Accounting Standards Board: http://www.rutgers.edu/Accounting/raw/gasb/index.html.
    b. Government Finance Officers Association: http://www.gfoa.org.
    c. National Association of State Budget Officers: http://www.nasbo.org.

d. Association for Budgeting and Financial Management of the American Society for Public Administration: http://www.fpac.fsu.edu/abfm.

e. American Association for Budget and Program Analysis: http://www.aabpa.org.

REFERENCES

1. Wildavsky, A. *The Politics of the Budgetary Process,* 2nd Ed.; Little Brown: Boston, 1974; pp. xiii, 3, 13, 15, 17.

2. Chandler, R.C.; Plano, J.C. *The Public Administration Dictionary*, 2nd Ed.; ABC-CLIO: Santa Barbara, CA, 1988; pp. 28, 123, 128, 144, 145, 154, 156.

3. Henry, N. *Public Administration and Public Affairs,* 7th Ed.; Prentice Hall: Upper Saddle River, NJ, 1999; 355.

4. Rosenbloom, D.H.; Goldman, D.D. *Public Administration: Understanding Management, Politics, and Law in the Public Sector,* 4th Ed.; McGraw-Hill: New York, 1998; pp. 32, 312, 318, 576.

5. LeLoup, L. *Budgetary Politics,* 4th Ed.; King's Court Communications: Brunswick, OH, 1986; 13.

6. Wildavsky, A.; Hammond, A. Comprehensive versus incremental budgeting in the department of agriculture. Adm. Sci. Q. **1965**, *10* (3), pp. 322, 323.

7. Office of Management and Budget. In *A Citizen's Guide to the Federal Budget for Fiscal 2002*; U.S. Government Printing Office: Washington, D.C., 2001; Chapter 2, on-line at *A Citizen's Guide to the Federal Budget.*

8. Lee, R.D., Jr.; Johnson, R.W. *Public Budgeting Systems,* 6th Ed.; Aspen: Gaithersburg, MD, 1998; 19.

9. Simon, H.A. *Administrative Behavior,* 2nd Ed.; Free Press: New York, 1957; originally published in 1947.

10. March, J.; Simon, H.A. *Organizations*; John Wiley and Sons: New York, 1958.

11. Lindblom, C.E. The science of "muddling through". Public Adm. Rev. **1958**, *19*, 79–88.

12. Stillman, R.J., II. *Public Administration: Concept and Cases,* 7th Ed.; Houghton Mifflin: Boston, 2000, pp. 223, 224.

13. Lindblom, C.E. Still muddling, not yet through. Public Adm. Rev. **1979**, *39* (6), 517–525.

14. LeLoup, L. The myth of incrementalism: Analytical choices in budgetary theory. Polity **1978**, *x* (4), pp. 488, 492, 509.

15. Rickards, R.C. How the spending patterns of cities change: Budgetary incrementalism reexamined. J. Policy Anal. Manag. **1984**, *4* (1), 56–74.

16. Ezzamel, M. Organization Change and Accounting: Understanding the Budgeting System in the Organizational Context. In *Organization Studies*; European Group for Organizational Studies, 1994; (#213), on-line at http://www.ptg.djnr.com/ccroot/asp/publib/story.

17. Wanat, J. Bases of budgetary incrementalism. Am. Polit. Sci. Rev. **1974**, *68* (3), 1221.

18. Rubin, I.S. *The Politics of Public Budgeting,* 3rd Ed.; Chatham House: Chatham, NJ, 1997.

19. Shafritz, M.J.; Russell, E.W. *Introducing Public Administration,* 2nd Ed.; Longman: New York, 2000; pp. 52, 451.

20. National Conference of State Legislatures. In *Legislative Budget Procedures: A Guide to Appropriations and Budget Processes in the States, Commonwealths and Territories*; 1999; (May) on-line at http://www.ncsl.org.

21. Schick, A. The road to PPB, the stages of budget reform. Public Adm. Rev. **1966**, *26*, 243–258.

Information Systems

Mary Maureen Brown
Piper S. Charles
The University of North Carolina at Charlotte,
Charlotte, North Carolina, U.S.A.

INTRODUCTION

An information system (IS) can be defined as a set of interrelated components, such as hardware, software, policies, communications, users, and data, that collects, manipulates, stores, and disseminates data and information that support the business activities of the users. As the public continues to place pressure on government to provide services cheaper, better, and faster, public managers have sought ways to streamline their operations to achieve those objectives and improve services. Information systems are the support mechanism to enhance and improve an organization's ability to carry out its primary mission and achieve its organizational goals. Through the use of information systems, government operations can be conducted more quickly, accurately, and efficiently. In addition, information systems permit government agencies to make a wide range of information available to the public, as well as conduct business electronically. By the end of 2000, nearly 40 million Americans were doing business with the government electronically.[1]

Strategic information management is the process by which top agency officials and line managers plan, direct, and evaluate the use of information and information systems to help accomplish their programmatic objectives. Organizations need accurate, reliable, and timely information for strategic planning, identifying objectives, improving productivity, and facilitating service delivery. Technology is becoming the vehicle from which accurate, reliable, and timely information is produced to achieve organizational goals.

Government agencies can leverage the strengths of information systems to achieve efficiencies and operational gains, such as eliminating duplication and process bottlenecks, streamlining processes, increasing productivity, broadening the range and scope of service delivery, improving analysis and decision-making capabilities, enabling coordination of processes across distances and functions, reducing complexity, and adding value for the customer.

TYPES OF INFORMATION SYSTEMS

There are several types of information systems: office information systems, transaction processing systems, management information systems, decision support systems, expert systems, executive information systems, and geographic information systems.

Office Information System

An office information system improves workflow and communications among employees in an organization. The software supports activities such as word processing, spreadsheets, databases, presentations, e-mail, scheduling, and web browsing. It may even include voicemail, fax, scanner, and videoconferencing from the desktop computer.

Transaction Processing System

A transaction processing system collects and processes data on a routine basis, generally performing the same transactions on large amounts of data. The strength of these systems is their ability to process large amounts of data quickly and repetitively. Examples of transaction processing systems are a payroll system, utility billing system, or a computer-aided dispatch system for fire and police.

Management Information System

A management information system (MIS) is a system designed to support the information needs of managers to make decisions and solve problems within the organization. A management information system has the ability to analyze data and provide timely, accurate, and meaningful information in the form of reports. For example, a utility billing MIS system might produce reports to indicate high water usage in the summer months that managers may

Encyclopedia of Public Administration and Public Policy
DOI: 10.1081/E-EPAP 120010805

need to react to, or identify water leakage based on unusual water usage. Water usage information can be useful for planning water line expansions or additions. Likewise, the police department can use MIS systems to examine call for service data to assist in resource deployment and to identify problem areas with repeat calls for service.

Decision Support System

A decision support system (DSS) is used more in business than in public organizations. A decision support system is used to provide a greater level of detailed information to support a particular decision. A DSS is able to handle large amounts of data from internal and external sources to support the problem-solving process. For example, some coastal jurisdictions are looking to decision support systems to determine the best time and method for evacuating coastal residents in the event of a hurricane. The DSS can calculate a number of factors, such as number of residents affected; characteristics of the hurricane, such as its rate of approach, wind speed, size, and potential for damage; available roads; and other factors to assist emergency management authorities in determining the best plan for evacuation.

Executive Information System

An executive information system (EIS) is similar to a decision support system designed to assist the decision-making process of the executive. An executive information system will often present the data in the form of charts and graphs to indicate pattern and trends and other statistics to assist the executive in developing strategic plans for the future activities and direction of the organization.

Expert System

An expert system is an information system that collects and stores the knowledge of human experts, draws conclusions from complex relationships, and provides the reasoning used to arrive at a suggested decision. The expert system can assist less-experienced users through the decision-making process. The expert system has two components: the knowledge base and inference rules. The knowledge base is the collection of human knowledge, and the inference rules are a set of business rules applied to the knowledge base to generate a suggested solution or decision. Expert systems are seen in the medical field to assist doctors in diagnosing diseases based on a patient's particular set of symptoms. A unique feature of the expert system is its ability to capture human expertise that can be shared with other less-experienced users.

Geographic Information System

A geographic information system (GIS) can take data in tabular form that is associated with a location and present that data in a graphical format on a predrawn map. An example of the use of a GIS is in local area planning, where a map can indicate various zoning classifications over the county map. This geographic representation of data can aid managers and planners in developing zoning policy and future area development plans. Police departments often utilize GIS to identify areas of concentrated crimes, called "hot spots," or to identify patterns of crimes occurring in particular locations. Geographic identification aids police in developing tactics to address specific crime problem locations.

COMPUTER LITERACY VERSUS INFORMATION LITERACY

In order for the public manager to be able to develop appropriate information systems, the public manager must be computer literate as well as information literate. Computer literacy is the knowledge and understanding of hardware components, communications and networks, programming languages, and software applications, such as databases. Information systems literacy includes not only knowledge of computer technology but also the broader scope of what data and information are required by the organization's personnel and the customers in order to achieve organizational mission and goals. This includes how to find information, how to analyze the information, as well as how to use the information effectively. Understanding how to apply the various types of information systems within the organization to obtain maxmum use of available data is the essence of information literacy. Knowledge management is the ability to derive knowledge from data and information to be applied to provide solutions to future business problems.

SYSTEMS DEVELOPMENT

Systems development is the process of creating, developing, or modifying information systems to support agencies' missions and goals. The systems development life cycle (SDLC) is a set of activities developed to assist and guide the development of information systems. The SDLC provides several steps, such as planning, analysis, design, implementation, maintenance, and review.

The Clinger–Cohen Act of 1996 set requirements for performance-based and results-oriented decision making for all major developments of information technology at the federal level. Investments in information systems and technology can have a significant impact on an organization's performance but only when they are well managed and focused on supporting the organization's mission. A key goal of the Clinger–Cohen Act is for agencies to establish mechanisms to ensure that information system projects contribute in a measureable way to improved mission performance and are implemented in a reasonable time frame and at a reasonable cost.

These mechanisms include the first stage of selection: developing a portfolio of information system projects; identifying the costs, benefits, and risks associated with the projects; determining priorities; and selecting those projects that should be funded for the near future, based on how well the projects support the goals of the organization. The second stage involves controlling of the project and ensuring that the projects deliver the expected benefits on time and within budget. The third stage is the evaluation of projects and the use of the lessons learned in the next selection stage.[2]

CHALLENGES AND OBSTACLES

The implementation of information systems in the public organization brings several challenges for the public executive. The public manager must ensure that strategic goals, information, and technology are integrated into common organizational procedures, ensure that effective management strategies are applied to all information technology adoption efforts, and ensure that everyone on the project is involved in risk management.

However, public managers are faced with obstacles often unique to public organizations. Although IT implementation is considered a high-risk endeavor in public and private sectors, the obstacles to successful implementation in the public sector tend to be greater for several reasons:

1. Public managers often are not motivated to implement large technology projects. Rarely does a public manager receive any incentive, monetary or otherwise, for a successful technology implementation that results in significant productivity gains. However, the public manager is fully exposed to public criticism if the system fails in any number of categories. As a result, public managers tend to be conservative with technology implementation, relying on only proven technology.
2. Agency executives often do not have a clear line of authority for information system implementation.

Often, their decisions must comply with existing laws, budget appropriations, legislative mandates, and a host of other political influences. Further, many agency executives have tenure that is short-lived, compared to the relatively long life cycle of system implementation.
3. Government agencies and programs are influenced by a number of stakeholders who often have competing interests and goals. The act of balancing and mediating these competing interests often stifles the creativity and implementation of information systems.
4. Most government agencies budgets are developed on an annual basis. The uncertainty of the future availability of funds to continue an information system project implementation as well as support and maintain the project after implementation hinders the ability of public managers to plan and implement information systems successfully. In addition, budgets and policy or program mandates are often legislated separately and may not correlate with each other.
5. Public agencies have more intangible and diverse goals and objectives with efficiency that is harder to measure. They provide services on the basis of public interest rather than services exchanged in the economic market.
6. The procurement mechanisms for government are cumbersome and time-consuming. While designed to maintain integrity and fairness in government acquisitions, the competitive procurement processes are often a source of problems and delays. These delays create additional complications for the procurement of technologies that are constantly changing.[3,4]

SECURITY, PRIVACY, AND ETHICS

Security, privacy, and ethics are additional issues that must be considered during the development and management of public agency information systems. Security pertains to the protection of the components of information systems from loss, damage, or unauthorized access. Computer viruses and hackers are two examples of security breaches that can damage information systems or allow unauthorized access to and exposure of confidential information about citizens. System failure, electrical power loss or power surges, as well as the physical security of equipment from tampering, theft, or damage from natural disasters can place information systems at risk.

Public agencies collect a wealth of information on individuals. Privacy refers to the right of these individuals to control or restrict the collection, storage, or dissemination of personal data without their knowledge or consent.

This issue surfaced recently when several state departments of motor vehicles were said to be selling drivers' license information to third parties in order to earn revenue to ease strained budgets. Many citizens have a strong interest in who gains access to personal information contained in records retained by public agencies.

Ethical issues are of concern in not only how the information collected and retained by public agencies is used but also in the accuracy of the information. One example involves a man whose identity was ''stolen'' by another man who lives in another state. The other man has an extensive arrest record, and the man whose identity was stolen nearly lost a job opportunity because of his ''arrest record.'' The problem is in placing responsibility on a particular agency for data accuracy and developing procedures for ensuring data accuracy. Unfortunately, in this case, the ''victim'' was unable to correct this inaccuracy, and the national crime computer still shows an arrest history for him. Other ethical issues involve the appropriateness of supervisors to monitor employee use of the Internet, or track their whereabouts during work hours via the use of electronic key cards.

CONCLUSION

Information systems can provide accurate, reliable, and timely information to public agency managers to support the achievement of the agency missions and goals. In addition, information systems can be used to facilitate the delivery of services to the public (see the article *Electronic Government*).

REFERENCES

1. National Partnership for Reinventing Government. *Access America: E-Gov*; 2001 Available at: http://govinfo.library.unt.edu/npr/initiati/it/index.html.
2. United States General Accounting Office. *Assessing Risks and Returns: A Guide for Evaluating Federal Agencies' IT Investment Decision-making*; 1997.
3. Rainey, H.G. *Understanding and Managing Public Organizations*, 2nd Ed.; Jossey-Bass: San Francisco, 1997.
4. Dawes, S.; Kelly, K.; Anderson, D.; Bloniarz, P.; Cresswell, A. *Making Smart IT Choices: A Handbook*; Center for Technology in Government: Albany, 1996.

Innovation and Public Policy

Stuart S. Nagel (Deceased)
University of Illinois, Urbana, Illinois, U.S.A.

INTRODUCTION

The purpose of this article is to discuss some aspects of the relations between public policy and creativity. There are basically two kinds of relations in this context. One set deals with how public policy can help stimulate creativity. The other set of relations deals with how creativity can be helpful in improving public policy.

On public policy as a stimulant to creativity, this article briefly discusses policies that relate to politics, economics, socialization, and psychology. On creativity in improving public policy, this article briefly describes pushing, facilitating, and pulling factors. It also discusses sources of policy goals and policy alternatives. It further discusses concepts that are useful in arriving at win–win public policies.

Win–win policies are alternatives that can enable conservatives, liberals, and other major viewpoints to all come out ahead of their best initial expectations simultaneously. Win–win is also called superoptimizing or doing better than the previous best of all major groups.

There are basically five steps to win–win policy analysis:

1. What are the major goals of conservatives, liberals, or other major groups who are disputing what policy should be adopted for a given policy problem?
2. What are the major alternatives of those groups for dealing with the policy problem?
3. What are the relations between each major alternative and each major goal? In their simplest form, these relations can be expressed in terms of a minus sign (relatively adverse relation) and a plus sign (relatively conducive relation) and a zero (neither adverse nor conducive relation).
4. What new alternative is there that might be capable of:

    a) Achieving the conservative goals even better than the conservative alternative.
    b) Simultaneously capable of achieving the liberal goals even more than the liberal alternative. Whatever new alternative meets these two criteria is a win–win alternative or a superoptimum solution (SOS).

5. Is the proposed win–win alternative capable of getting over various hurdles that frequently exist? These hurdles may be political, administrative, technological, legal, psychological, and economic in random order. Win–win solutions should also consider how to upgrade workers and firms that may be displaced by downsizing due to increased productivity, free trade, defense conversion, immigration, merit treatment, labor utilization, creativity, and related factors.

PART ONE: PUBLIC POLICY IN STIMULATING CREATIVITY

The following political, economic, sociological, and psychological institutions or ways of doing things in a society are conducive to innovative and effective public policy making. This includes public policies that can enable conservatives, liberals, and other major viewpoints to come out ahead of their best initial expectations simultaneously, i.e., superoptimum or win–win solutions.

Political Methods

Competitive political parties

This is a key facilitator, because the out-party is constantly trying to develop policies (including possibly SOS policies) in order to become the in-party. The in-party is also busy developing new policies in order to remain the in-party. New policies are developed largely as a result of changing domestic and international conditions, not just for the sake of newness. Without the stimulus of an out-party, the in-party would have substantially less incentive to be innovative. More important, without the possibility of becoming the in-party, the out-party would lose its incentive to be innovative. More innovation generally comes from the out-party than the in-party (all other factors held constant), including the possibility of SOS innovations.

Encyclopedia of Public Administration and Public Policy
DOI: 10.1081/E-EPAP 120011053

Better policy analysis methods and institutions

SOS solutions are likely to be facilitated by policy analysis methods that deal with multiple goals, multiple alternatives, missing information, spreadsheet-based decision-aiding software, and a concern for successful adoption and implementation. Better policy analysis institutions refer to training, research, funding, publishing, and networking associations. These institutions can be part of the activities of universities, government agencies, and independent institutes in the private sector. The extent to which these policy institutions deal with superoptimizing analysis will make them even more relevant to facilitating SOS solutions.

Economic Policies

Competitive business firms

Competition among political parties may be essential for facilitating SOS public policy. Competition among business firms may be essential for facilitating a prosperous economy and a prosperous world through international business competition. Numerous examples can be given of nations that failed to advance and collapsed due largely to a one-party system, such as the former Soviet Union. Likewise, numerous examples can be given of business firms that failed to advance and virtually collapsed due largely to lack of substantial competition, such as the American steel industry. The American automobile industry has not collapsed, but it failed to develop small cars, cars that resist style changes, safer cars, less expensive cars, and more durable cars in comparison to the international competition that was not taken seriously until almost too late.

Well-targeted subsidies and tax breaks

In the context of superoptimum solutions, this tends to mean subsidies and tax breaks that increase national productivity and international competitiveness. Such subsidies and tax breaks are the opposite of handouts that provide a disincentive to increased productivity on the part of welfare recipients or big business. Good targeting in this regard especially refers to upgrading skills and stimulating technological innovation and diffusion. A dollar invested in those kinds of subsidies is likely to pay off many times over without necessarily having to wait very long for the results.

Increased national productivity

All these facilitators are important. Economists might rightfully consider increased national productivity to be especially important. It leads to an increased gross national product or national income, which means an increased tax base to which the tax rate is applied. If increased productivity increases the tax base, then tax rates can be lowered and still produce more tax money for well-targeted subsidies that produce further increases in national productivity. These increases, however, are not an end in themselves. The increased national income can facilitate finding and implementing SOS that relate to employment, inflation, agriculture, labor, business, poverty, discrimination, education, families, the environment, housing, transportation, energy, health, technological innovation, government structures, government processes, world peace, international trade, and every other public-policy field. In other words, with more money and resources available, SOS solutions are facilitated, but SOS solutions often draw upon creativity that is associated with doing much better on relevant goals with constant or decreasing resources.

Sociology: Childhood Socialization

Risk-takers get generated from about age 0 to 5 in little children, depending on whether they are allowed to take chances or are treated in such a way that they never come in contact with anything that might hurt them. There is certainly a need for encouraging more experimentation on the part of children, within reason. More rebelliousness, more of the kind of trying out to see what will happen if you push your food off the highchair onto the floor without being punished for doing so, to see if the bowl will break or not. That does not necessarily mean that you jump off the third-story porch to see if your head will break.

Liberals have a lot of trouble talking about socialization, because it sounds like brainwashing people. It can be done in a brainwashing way, or it can be done in a way that encourages children to think things out for themselves to some extent. An example might be telling children not to discriminate on the basis of race or gender, as contrasted to setting up a situation where they more creatively reason that discrimination is undesirable. Such a situation might involve the teacher calling for volunteers to erase the blackboard and virtually everyone volunteers. The teacher says we cannot have so many people erasing the blackboard, and we might therefore just pick the African-American girls. She then asks for reactions and alternative suggestions. She thereby stimulates creativity and possibly an implicit understanding of such concepts as merit treatment, sharing benefits, sharing costs, having a minimum benefit threshold, having a maximum cost threshold, and other such ideas without using those words.

In the SOS context, this refers to creating a frame of mind that causes adults to do what is socially desired, because the alternative is virtually unthinkable. This can be contrasted with a less effective emphasis on deterrence, whereby socially desired behavior is achieved through threats and bribes. Examples include childhood socialization to reduce adult behavior that is violent, alcoholic, drug addictive, and hostile toward constitutional rights.

Psychology of SOS Solutions

Innovative risk taking

This is an important SOS facilitator, because many SOS solutions involve technological fixes. In order to develop new technologies, many people usually had to risk substantial amounts of money, time, effort, and other resources. There may have been a strong possibility that it would have all been wasted. An SOS society needs more people who are willing to take such chances. Classic examples include Marie and Pierre Curie who sacrificed about 30 years of work plus their health to develop radium and thus radioactivity, which is part of the basis for nuclear energy. Thomas Edison frequently not only risked his resources but also his reputation by announcing inventions before he had developed them in order to give himself an ego risk as a stimulus to quickly inventing what he falsely said he had already done.

Sensitivity to opportunity costs

This means trying through socialization or an appropriate incentive structure to get decision makers to be more sensitive to the mistake of failing to try out a new idea that might work wonders, as contrasted to being so sensitive to sins of commission rather than omission. Both wrongs are undesirable. One can, however, say that a police officer who wrongly beats a suspect is doing less harm to society than a president who wrongly fails to adopt a new health care program that could save numerous lives or a new education program that could greatly improve productivity and the quality of life. A person who is sensitive to opportunity costs tends to say "nothing ventured, nothing gained," whereas an insensitive person tends to say "nothing ventured, nothing lost." We need more of the former in order to facilitate the generating, adopting, and implementing of SOS.

SOS combination of pessimism and optimism

This does not mean a balance or a compromise between being pessimistic and being optimistic. It means being 100% pessimistic or close to it regarding how bad things are and how much worse they are going to get unless we actively do something about them, including developing SOS solutions. It simultaneously means being 100% optimistic or close to it regarding how good things can get in the future if we vigorously work at them, including

developing SOS. This is in contrast to those who say the present is wonderful and needs little improvement. It is also in contrast to those who say the present may be wonderful or not so wonderful, but some invisible hands or automatic forces of Adam Smith, Karl Marx, or God will automatically improve the future.

Constantly seeking higher goals

This list of societal facilitators is in random order. Some of the items overlap or interact, but it is better to overlap than leave gaps in this context. It is appropriate perhaps to have the last facilitator relate to constantly seeking higher goals. Traditional goal seeking leads to compromises. Worse, it can lead to one side trying to win 100% and the other side losing 100%, but the war, strike, litigation, or other negative dispute resolution leads to both sides losing close to 100%. Obviously, seeking higher goals is more likely to result in higher goal achievement than seeking lower goals, including SOS goal achievement. The counterargument sometimes made is that higher goals lead to frustration because of the gap between goals and achievement. There may be more frustration in fully achieving low goals that provide a low quality of life when others are doing better. High societal goal seeking (including SOS) is facilitated by all of the above factors, but it is a factor in itself, because high goal seeking tends to become a self-fulfilling prophecy.[a]

PART TWO: CREATIVITY FOR IMPROVING PUBLIC POLICY

Pushing, Facilitating, and Pulling Toward Innovative Public Policy

A useful way of organizing ideas for stimulating creativity is in terms of pushing factors, facilitators, and pulling factors. That three-part organization comes from Frederick Jackson Turner's analysis of the causes of people moving west in the 1800s. The pushing factors included undesirable aspects of the East, such as overcrowding, lack of jobs, and debts. Facilitating factors included wagon trails, railroads, river systems, and other means of transportation. Pulling factors included attractions in the West, such as free land and business opportunities.

In this context, the pushing factors include other people and commitments. The facilitators include relevant literature, working style, and multicriteria decision making. The pulling factors include the rewards that go to successful imagination. The rewards here emphasize

---

[a]On public policy in stimulating creativity, see Ref. [1]. Also see Refs. [2,3].

intellectual rewards, partly because the article is based on experience in academic and government activities, where monetary rewards are not as great as they are in business. The reader can adjust the ideas, however, to fit other contexts besides the academic and governmental contexts.

Pushing factors

Other People as Pushing Factors. Talk with someone else about generating alternatives. Trying to explain alternative ways of achieving something with an audience listening stimulates more ideas than talking or thinking to one's self. Put one's head together with someone else who is trying to come up with ideas. The interaction of two or more people trying to generate ideas tends to work better than one person alone. Have contact with stimulating colleagues via correspondence, conventions, informal campus relations, or other on-the-job relations. Work with graduate students and undergraduates to develop dissertations, seminar papers, and term papers.

Work with different people to provide a variety of interaction. Arrange to be asked questions by people with a variety of orientations, including sincere inquiry, skepticism, cynicism, and even a touch of malice. Try to operate in an interdisciplinary environment for a great variety of perspectives. Apply one's creative ideas to see what happens in practice.

Commitments as Pushing Factors. Accept a commitment to write an article, a book chapter, or a conference paper on how to deal with a policy problem. That is likely to generate new alternatives. Teach in those fields in which one wants to generate policy alternatives. Take on obligations to coauthor articles, chapters, or papers.

Take on obligations to do consulting work that involves generating alternatives. Prepare grant proposals. Arrange for competitive situations as a stimulus to developing new ideas.

Facilitators

Literature. Consult the literature in the field. There may be lots of alternatives already suggested. There are some software checklists that might be worth trying, such as "Trigger" published by Thoughtware and the "Idea Generator" published by Experience in Software, Inc., 2039 Shattuck Avenue, Suite 401, Berkeley, CA 94701. Keep up with the newest ideas in various policy fields. Read provocative literature. Know the general literature in the fields in which one is interested.

Read some of the literature on creativity, including the list of references attached to this article. Have theoretical frameworks that can serve as checklists and prods for developing alternatives. Be familiar with the methods of knowing, including how to inductively generalize, how to deduce conclusions, how to determine what authorities hold, and how to do sensitivity analysis. Think about ways of generating ideas like this article or adding to this article.

Working Style. Talk out loud about the possible alternatives. Dictating is better than thinking in generating ideas. Delegate work to others in order to have more time to think. Have a pencil and paper handy at all times or dictating equipment to write or dictate ideas that come to one's mind before they are lost. Schedule time periods for creative development and idea implementation. The more time periods the better. Occasionally travel in order to provide a variety of environments.

Multicriteria Decision Making. Try listing some alternative, even if one only has in mind one or two alternatives to begin with. Merely trying to generate a list tends to result in more items being listed than one originally had in mind, or thought one had in mind. After generating some alternatives, then list some criteria for evaluating them. That will lead to more alternatives. After generating alternatives and criteria, then generate some relations between the alternatives and criteria. That will lead to more alternatives. After generating alternatives, criteria, relations and initial conclusions, then do various forms of sensitivity analysis designed to determine what it would take to bring a second-place or other-place alternative up to first place. That may generate still more alternatives.

If there is a situation in which there are two conflicting sides, each one favoring a different alternative, look to see what kind of alternative could maybe satisfy the goals of both sides. Also look to the possibility of a compromise alternative that will partially satisfy each side if it is not possible to find an alternative that will fully satisfy both sides. Then, observing how the alternatives score on the criteria, ask how each alternative can be improved. Try to convert the alternatives, criteria, relations, tentative conclusions, and sensitivity analysis into a publishable table with notes. That may generate new alternatives.

Pulling factors: rewards

Be motivated to want to generate alternatives. Arrange to be in situations where one is rewarded for generating alternatives, such as recognition, grants, publishing opportunities, graduate students, consulting opportunities, etc. Nonintellectual rewards can also be arranged for. These might include money, power, love, food, sleep, pure recreation, etc. Operate in a permissive environment that encourages experimentation and new ideas. The earlier one can get into such an environment the better, preferably starting at birth.

Some people use heredity as an excuse for not being creative. In both areas, there is a substantial range in which each person can operate. If one is more determined, then one can operate closer to the top (rather than the bottom) of one's inherited range. Creativity is probably less a matter of heredity than intelligence is. It is more susceptible to the kind of pushing, facilitating, and pulling factors mentioned above. Thus, one can more easily arrange to be a more creative person than one can arrange to be a brighter person by seeking more favorable occurrences of those factors. Doing so can be rewarding, as well as produce the kinds of rewards mentioned above. The broader rewards accrue not only to the individual, but also to the many potential beneficiaries of individual creativity. It is an ability well worth stimulating by society and by one's self.[b]

Sources of Goals and Alternatives

Public-policy evaluation can be defined as the determination of which various governmental policies or decisions are best for achieving a given set of goals in light of the relations between the alternative policies and the goals and various constraints and conditions.

This definition emphasizes four key elements in public-policy evaluation:

1. A set of goals to be achieved within various normative constraints.
2. A set of alternative policies or combinations of policies that could be relevant to achieving the goals.
3. A set of relations between the policies and the goals.
4. The drawing of a conclusion from those goals, policies, and relations as to which policy or combination is best.

Where do these goals, policies, and relations come from? The answer includes four main possibilities:

1. Authority: one or more persons, books, articles, or other reliable sources of information regarding the relevant goals, policies, or relations.
2. Statistical or observational analysis: the analyzing of specific instances in order to generalize what the goals, policies, or relations might be.

3. Deduction: the drawing of a conclusion from premises that have been established from authority, observation, and intuition.
4. Sensitivity analysis: the guessing of the goals, policies, or relations and the determination of what effect, if any, the guessed values have on the final decision regarding which policy is best.

The four basic sources can be subclassified in various ways. For example, authority can be meaningfully discussed in terms of expert authority and general public opinion. Authority could also be contemporary or historical. Observation can be impressionistic or systematic, including statistical. Deductive approaches can be based on intuitively accepted premises or on empirically validated premises. Sensitivity analysis is threshold analysis in which we want to know the break-even point, above which we should take one course of action, and below which we should take another.

Authority

Consulting authorities, rather than establishing the goals, feasible policies, or relations in a policy evaluation with original data or reasoning, can be a big time saver. Traditional social science tends to downplay introspective information-gathering methods, in contrast to nonobtrusive methods. In policy evaluation, however, perhaps more consultation with insiders is needed in order to obtain more meaningful information about relationships than can be obtained from the limited and questionable data records that are available.

Who constitutes an authority on goals, policies, or relations? The answer depends on the subject matter. The Supreme Court is an authority, for example, on what goals are legitimate in satisfying the right-to-counsel clause of the Sixth Amendment to the Constitution. The Court has said that saving money is not an appropriate goal, but that saving innocent persons from being convicted is. If, however, the issue is not where right to counsel should be provided but rather how it should be provided, then saving money is an appropriate goal. For this issue, the goals of a county board would be relevant, because it generally appropriates money to pay court-appointed lawyers to represent the poor. Such goals might include satisfying local lawyers while minimizing expenditures. The board might, therefore, decide on a salaried public defender system, rather than on a less expensive but less politically feasible assigned counsel system or a less legally feasible volunteer system. For other policy problems, the key authorities might be legislative opinion, public opinion, the head of an administrative agency, or the like.

---

[b]On pushing, facilitating and pulling toward innovative public policy, see Ref. [4].

Statistical observation

Statistical analysis is the most systematic form of inducing generalizations from many instances or observations. It is generally used for establishing relations, rather than for establishing goals or feasible policies. Statistical analysis can, however, be useful in establishing goals or weights for the goals, whenever the goals, rather than being ultimate, are instrumental for achieving higher objectives.

Accounting is a variation on statistical analysis. Like statistical analysis, it involves aggregating data, but accounting data is generally more precise than statistical analysis that is based on averages or the fitting of curves to scattered data points. A public opinion survey is not a variation on statistical analysis in the context of the typology of sources used in this article. Rather, it is a form of consulting authority in which the authority is the general public or a special segment of it. A statistical analysis (as a distinct source of information on goals, policies, or relations) involves a cross-tabulation, an analysis of the variation between averages, or a regression-equation analysis. These forms of statistical analysis involve determining a relation that is relevant to weighting goals, deciding which policies are feasible to choose among, or relating a policy to a goal.

Deduction

Deduction involves arriving at a conclusion from premises that have been established by way of authority, empirical validation, prior deduction, or intuition. The more acceptable the premises are, the more acceptable the conclusions should be, assuming the conclusions have been validly deduced from the premises. Deduction is especially helpful where there is no authority and no empirical data for determining the information desired.

It is important to note that deductively analyzing premises may lead to an alternative policy that might be missed if one only relies on authority or statistical analysis. Authority is often not very creative in foreseeing problems, and statistical analysis is incapable of dealing with policies that have never been adopted.

Sensitivity analysis

In policy evaluation, sensitivity analysis is a useful source of information about goals, policies, and relations when authority, statistics, and deduction do not provide clear answers regarding them. Sensitivity or threshold analysis enables one to determine how much room for error there is in weighting the goals, listing the policies, or measuring the relations. Often, the controversy over precision in these matters is wasted, because within the range in which the controversy occurs, the overall conclusion as to which policy or combination is best is still the same. Sensitivity analysis also enables the policy evaluator to convert difficult questions about goals, policies, and relations into relatively easy questions, such as, "Is a given weight, policy, or relation above or below some threshold?" rather than, "What is the exact weight, policy score, or relation?"

In using sensitivity analysis to determine a set of feasible policies, we have to distinguish between a method that will provide a set of policies from which we can choose, rather than a method designed to arrive at an optimum policy. All four sources of information can be used to arrive at feasible policies or an optimum policy.

Intuition

Intuition is closely related to sensitivity analysis as a source of goals, policies, and relations. Sensitivity analysis frequently involves determining how different guessed values affect the optimizing conclusions. Intuition is also a form of guessing or basing estimates on strong feelings. Goals are sometimes accepted intuitively rather than being justified in terms of authority, statistics, or higher premises. This is especially so if the goals are general or near-ultimate goals, rather than instrumental. Policies may often be suggested as a result of a flash of insight, which is the case with hypotheses in traditional social science research. Although it is not generally respectable in social or policy science to arrive at relations through intuition, one can repeatedly guess at a relation until the reasonable possibilities have been exhausted and then see how these guesses affect the optimizing conclusions. One may find that it is unnecessary to be any more scientific than that, because all the reasonable guessed values may yield the same conclusion as to which policy is best.

Ultimately, all goals and relations depend on intuition. Goals can be justified by appeal to authority, statistics, or deduction. However, how does one justify the authority, the dependent or goal variable in a statistical analysis, and the basic premises in a deductive analysis? One can likewise ask for a justification of these justifications. In policy evaluation, one usually has an overall goal that is accepted intuitively, such as promoting the greatest happiness for the greatest number or satisfying the decision makers. Likewise, one can ask, why does policy X cause goal Y? The answer might be that there is a Z variable between X and Y which is caused or increased by X, and which in turn, causes or increases Y. One can then ask, why does X cause Z, and why does Z cause Y? At each stage of the causal regress, one tends to move further away from substantive policy and social science toward natural science and metaphysics. Ultimately, the question becomes, how do we know there is an X or a Y? That is, how do we know there is such a thing as a congressional statute or an American population that has social-indicator characteristics? In other words, on a philosophical level, we have to accept some empirical reality, such as the existence of the world. Fortunately for most policy evaluation, the goals in dispute are seldom ultimate goals, but rather instrumental goals that can be justified in terms of authority, statistics, or deduction. Similarly, the relations are seldom, if ever, metaphysical; rather, they can also be explained in a satisfactory, non-philosophical way in terms of authority, statistics, and deduction.

We can conclude from this analysis of the sources of goals, policies, and relations in policy evaluation that there are a variety of sources that can be systematically classified. We can also conclude that perhaps policy evaluation should be making more use of the variety of sources available. Unfortunately, certain disciplines tend to overlook some sources at the expense of others. Law and political science seem to rely heavily on authority as a source, especially legal authority. Psychology and sociology may rely too heavily on statistical analysis, which tends to overemphasize variables that are easily measurable and policies that need to be adopted before they can be evaluated. Economics and engineering often rely too heavily on deduction, especially mathematical modeling, which sometimes involves unrealistic or incomplete premises. By working with a combination of authority, statistics, and deduction, one provides a form of triangulation that increases the likelihood of arriving at more meaningful goals–weights, policies, and relations.

There is no need to argue over which source between authority, statistics, and deduction is the most desirable. Authority is clearly a big time saver if an accessible and respected authority is involved. Deduction enables one to draw conclusions about goals, policies, and relations without having to gather original data, but instead by synthesizing already known information. Statistical analysis constitutes a more ultimate, but more difficult, form of proof. In any concrete policy evaluation situation, the best source depends on the subject matter and what is to be done with it. If the policy evaluation involves constitutional policy, an appeal to Supreme Court authority may be most relevant. If it involves the effects of a strike in the coal industry on another segment of the economy, a deductive input–output model may be the preferable type of analysis. If it concerns the trade-off problem of inflation and unemployment, a time-series statistical analysis may be especially appropriate in relating inflation and unemployment to suicide rates, to the percentage of the two-party vote that goes to the incumbent party, or other social indicators.

We can also conclude that sensitivity of threshold analysis is a useful tool in policy evaluation, because even with authority, statistics, and deduction, it may still not be possible to arrive at precision in weighting goals, measuring policies, or determining relations. Sensitivity analysis enables one to determine whether increased precision is needed. It is only needed if the range of unclearness on a goal–weight, a policy, or a relation happens to encompass a threshold value. Thus, if the range of unclearness on a goal–weight or a relation is between 20 and 30, but the threshold value of the goal–weight or the relation is 10, then one can forget about clarifying the unclearness if one is mainly concerned with determining which policy is best. If, however, the threshold value is 26, then one should seek additional information from authority, statistics, and deduction to determine whether the actual value is above or below 26.

The purpose of this article has been to discuss the sources of goals, policies, and relations in policy evaluation. The article represents a synthesis of reasonable common sense, at least as a matter of hindsight. That is what good policy evaluation should be, namely, codified common sense. For thousands of years, many human beings have been making effective and efficient decisions. What decision science and policy science should now try to do is to capture the essence of what these good decision makers have done implicitly. Less naturally competent decision makers can then improve their decision-making or policy-evaluating skills.[c]

A Typology Toward Win–Win Public Policy

There are about 14 different ways of arriving at win–win superoptimum solutions, whereby conservatives, liberals, and major viewpoints can all come out ahead of their best initial expectations simultaneously. The list could be used as a checklist to prod one's mind into thinking of solutions to specific problems.

More resources to satisfy all sides

Expanding Resouces. An example might include well-placed subsidies and tax breaks that would increase national productivity and thus increase the gross national product and income. Doing so would enable the tax revenue to the government to increase, even if the tax rate decreases. This would provide for a lowering of taxes, instead of trying to choose between the liberal and conservative ways of raising them. It would also provide

---

[c]On sources of goals and alternatives toward innovative public policy, see Ref. [5].

for increasing domestic and defense expenditures, instead of having to choose between the two.

Third-Party Benefactor.
Some situations involve a third-party benefactor that is usually a government agency. An example is government food stamps, which allow the poor to obtain food at low prices, while farmers receive high prices when they submit the food stamps they have for reimbursement. Another example is rent supplements, which allow the poor to pay low rents, but landlords receive even higher rents than they would otherwise expect.

More efficiency in achieving goals

Setting Higher Goals.
An example of setting higher goals than what was previously considered the best while still preserving realism might include the Hong Kong labor shortage with unemployment at only 1%. Hong Kong is faced with the seeming dilemma of having to choose between foregoing profits (by not being able to fill orders due to lack of labor) and opening the floodgates to mainland Chinese and Vietnamese (in order to obtain more labor). An SOS might involve adding to the labor force by way of the elderly, the disabled, and mothers of preschool children. It also would provide more and better jobs for those who are seasonally employed, part-time employed, full-time employed but looking for a second job, and full-time employed but not working up to their productive capacity.

Decreasing Causes of Conflict.
An example of removing or decreasing the source of the conflict between liberals and conservatives, rather than trying to synthesize their separate proposals, would be concentrating on having a highly effective and acceptable birth control program to satisfy proponents and opponents of abortion, because abortions would then seldom be needed. Another example would be concentrating on a highly effective murder-reduction program to satisfy proponents and opponents of capital punishment. Such a murder-reduction program might emphasize gun control, drug medicalization, and reduction of violence socialization.

Redefining the Problem.
Quite often, a highly emotional controversy between liberals and conservatives may be capable of being resolved beyond the best expectations of each side through the approach of redefining the problem. They may be arguing over how to deal with a problem that is relatively unimportant in terms of achieving their goals, as contrasted to a more important problem on which they might be likely to get mutually satisfying agreement. This involves seeing beyond a relatively superficial argument to the higher-level goals that are endorsed by liberals and conservatives, although possibly not to the same relative degree.

Increasing Benefits and Decreasing Costs.
There are situations where one side can receive big benefits but the other side incurs only small costs. An example is in litigation, where the defendant gives products that it makes. The products may have high market value to the plaintiff, but low variable or incremental cost to the defendant, because the defendant has already manufactured the products or can quickly do so.

Early Socialization.
The socialization matter could be discussed across every field of public policy. If one is going to have a superoptimum society, then it is important what kinds of attitudes children have with regard to discrimination, poverty, world peace, crime, education, consumer–merchant relations, labor–management relations, free speech, and fair procedure. One could even say that the key purpose, or a key purpose of public policy, is to provide for a socialization environment in which children have socially desired attitudes on every field of public policy. If that is done properly, then a good deal of the problems of what policies to adopt will take care of themselves, because the need for public policy will be lessened. If children, for instance, are imbued with more of the idea of judging each other in terms of their individual characteristics rather than in terms of ethnic characteristics, then we have less need for public policies dealing with racism, because there is likely to be a lot less racism.

Technological Fix.
The second level of insight is to communicate a recognition that such SOS are realistically possible and not just conceptually possible. A good example relates to the ozone problem and the use of fluorocarbons in hair sprays and other aerosol containers. As of about 1985, such devices represented a serious threat to depleting the ozone layer, thereby causing a substantial increase in skin cancer throughout the world. The solution was not to rely on an unregulated marketplace, which normally provides almost no incentives to manufacturers to reduce their pollution. The solution was not regulation or prohibition, which tends to be evaded, is expensive to enforce, and is enforced with little enthusiasm given disruptions that might occur to the economy. The most exciting aspect of the solution (although the problem is not completely solved) was the development of new forms of spray propellant that are less expensive for manufacturers to use and simultaneously not harmful to the ozone layer.

This kind of solution tends to be self-adopting, because manufacturing firms, farmers, and others who might otherwise be polluting the environment now have an important economic incentive to adopt the new low-polluting methods, because they reduce the expenses of the business firm. This approach requires substantial research and substantial government subsidies for research and development as contrasted to paying the polluters not to pollute, which is even more expensive and often not so effective, because they may take the money and pollute anyhow. The business firms generally do not have capital for that kind of research and development, or the foresight or forbearance which public policy and governmental decision making may be more capable of exercising. This includes international governmental decision makers, as well as those in developing nations.

Contracting Out. As for how the SOS operates, it involves government ownership, but all the factories and farms are rented to private entrepreneurs to develop productive and profitable manufacturing and farming. Each lease is renewable every year, or longer if necessary to get productive tenants. A renewal can be refused if the factory or farm is not being productively developed, or if the entrepreneur is not showing adequate sensitivity to workers, the environment, and consumers.

As for some of the advantages of such an SOS system, it is easier not to renew a lease than it is to issue injunctions, fines, jail sentences, or other negative sanctions. It is also much less expensive than subsidies. The money received for rent can be an important source of tax revenue for the government to provide productive subsidies elsewhere in the economy. Those subsidies can be used especially for encouraging technological innovation–diffusion, the upgrading of skills, and stimulating competition for market share, which can be so much more beneficial to society than socialistic or capitalistic monopolies. The government can more easily demand sensitivity to workers, the environment, and consumers from its renters of factories and farms than it can from itself. There is a conflict of interest in regulating oneself.

International Economic Communities. An exciting new development with regard to international interaction to deal with shared policy problems is the international economic community (EC). It involves a group of countries agreeing to remove tariff barriers to the buying and selling of goods among the countries as a minimum agreement to constitute an EC. The agreement may also provide for removal of immigration barriers to the free flow of labor, and removal of whatever barriers might exist to the free flow of communication and ideas. The European Economic Community is a good example, but other examples are developing in North America, Africa, Asia, and East Europe.

The alternative of having an economic community does well on the conservative goal of preserving national identity, because no sovereignty is lost in an IEC, as contrasted to the sovereignty that is lost in a world government or a regional government. The IEC may also add to the national stature of the component parts by giving them the increased strength that comes from being part of an important group. Thus, France may have more national stature as a leader in the European Economic Community than it has alone.

Likewise, the alternative of having an economic community does well on the liberal goal of promoting quality of life in terms of jobs and consumer goods. Jobs are facilitated by the increased exporting that the IEC countries are able to do. Jobs may also be facilitated by free movement to countries in the EC that have a need for additional labor. Consumer goods are facilitated by the increased importing that the EC countries are able to do without expensive tariffs.

More combinations of alternatives

Big Benefits on One Side, Small Costs on the Other. An example of this kind of SOS is the case of growers versus farmworkers in Illinois. The essence of the solution is that the growers agree to deposit $100,000 to begin an employee credit union. Depositing $100,000 costs nothing to the growers, because it is insured by the federal government and can be withdrawn after an agreed-upon time period, possibly even with interest. The $100,000, however, serves as the basis for the beginning of an economic development fund that enables the workers through real estate leveraging to obtain a mortgage for building over $500,000 worth of housing as a big improvement over their current housing. The existence of the credit union also enables them to avoid having to get advances from the growers, which generates a lot of friction as a result of alleged favoritism in giving and collecting the advances. There are other elements involved, too, such as new grievance procedures and reports regarding compliance with other rules governing the working conditions of migratory labor. The essence of the solution, though, is that both sides come out ahead of their original best expectations.

Combining Alternatives. An example of combining alternatives that are not mutually exclusive is combining government-salaried legal-aid attorneys with volunteer attorneys. Doing so could give the best of public-sector and private-sector approaches to legal services for the poor. Another example is combining tax-supported higher education plus democratic admission standards with contributions from alumni and tuition plus merit standards. Doing so results in universities that are better than pure government ownership or pure private enterprise.

Developing Multifaceted Packages. One can develop a package of alternatives that would satisfy liberal and conservative goals. An example is pretrial release, where liberals want more arrested defendants released prior to trial, and conservatives want a higher rate of appearances in court without having committed a crime while released. The package that increases the achievement of both goals includes better screening, reporting in, notification, and prosecution of no-shows, as well as reduction of delay between arrest and trial.

Sequential SOS. We can put the land reform example in with sequential SOS. The current verbalization does not say anything about encouraging the landless peasants to subsequently upgrade their skills to be able to take on nonagricultural work or to upgrade the skills of their children. We could change the SOS definition to say simultaneously or sequentially. One drawback is that there is subjectivity and favoritism as to which alternative goes first. Simultaneity has an air of equality and equity; doing it sequentially may be essential in terms of developing feasibility. It is not so feasible to do various alternatives or goals simultaneously.[d]

CONCLUSIONS

Public policies that tend to stimulate creativity are those that relate to the following:

1. Competitive political parties.
2. Better policy analysis methods and institutions.
3. Competitive business firms.
4. Well-targeted subsidies and tax breaks.
5. Increased national productivity.
6. Childhood socialization.
7. Innovative risk-taking.
8. Sensitivity to opportunity costs.
9. Combination of pessimism and optimism.
10. Seeking higher goals.

Some of these stimulants are part of the culture, not just official or unofficial public policy.

Factors that stimulate innovative improvements in public policy include:

1. Pushing factors, including other people and commitments.
2. Facilitators, including literature, working style, and multicriteria decision making.
3. Pulling factors or rewards.

4. Consulting authorities as a source of policy goals and alternatives.
5. Statistical observation.
6. Deduction.
7. Sensitivity analysis or experimenting.
8. Intuition.
9. More resources to satisfy all sides in win–win policy.
10. More efficiency for achieving goals in win–win policy.
11. More combinations of alternatives in win–win policy.

It is hoped that this article will help build some bridges between people interested in creativity innovation and people interested in improving public policy.[e]

REFERENCES

1. Win–Win Societal Facilitators. In *Super-Optimum Solutions and Win–Win Policy: Basic Concepts and Principles*; Nagel, S., Ed.; Greenwood-Quorum, 1997.
2. The Economic Process of SOS Solutions. In *The Policy Process and Super-Optimum Solutions*; Nagel, S., Ed.; Nova Science, 1994.
3. The Psychology–Sociology of SOS Solutions. In *The Policy Process and Super-Optimum Solutions*; Nagel, S., Ed.; Nova Science, 1994.
4. Multiple Alternatives and Criteria with Discrete Choices. In *Evaluation Analysis with Microcomputers*; Nagel, S., Ed.; JAI Press, 1989.
5. Sources of Goals, Policies, and Relations. In *Public Policy: Goals, Means, and Methods*; Nagel, S., Ed.; St. Martins, 1984.
6. Nagel, S. *Creativity and Public Policy: Generating Super-Optimum Solutions*; Ashgate, 1999.
7. *Creativity: Being Usefully Innovative in Solving Diverse Problems*; Nagel, S., Ed.; Nova Science Publishers, 2000.

FURTHER READING

Austin, J. *Chase Chance and Creativity: The Lucky Art of Novelty*; Columbia University Press, 1978.
Baker, S. *Your Key to Creative Thinking: How to Get More and Better Ideas*; Harper & Row, 1962.

---

[d]On a typology toward win–win public policy, see Ref. [6].

[e]On creativity and public policy in general, see the quarterly journal called *Creativity Plus*. It is a journal of the Policy Studies Organization and the Creativity Plus Association. Both are headquartered at the Everett–Dirksen–Adlai Stevenson Institute for International Policy Studies, 711 Ashton Lane South, Champaign, Illinois 61820. Also see Ref. [7].

Brookfield, S.D. *Developing Critical Thinkers: Challenging Adults to Explore Alternative Ways of Thinking and Acting*; Jossey-Bass, 1991.

Buffington, P.W. Strokes of genius. Sky **February 1987**, 121–125.

Campbell, D. *Take the Road to Creativity and Get Off Your Dead End*; Center for Creative Leadership, 1985.

Coogan, W.H.; Woshinsky, O.H. *The Science of Politics: An Introduction to Hypothesis Formation and Testing*; University Press of America, 1982.

De Bono, E. *Lateral Thinking: Creativity Step by Step*; Harper Colophon Books, 1973.

De Bono, E. Thinking in America: The lost art. Crit. Intell. **October 1994**, 3–9.

Dogan, M.; Pahre, R. *Creative Marginality: Innovation at the Intersections of Social Sciences*; Westview Press, 1990.

Harman, W.; Rheingold, H. *Higher Creativity: Liberating the Unconscious for Breakthrough Insights*; G. P. Putman's Sons, 1984.

Harriman, R. Creativity: Moving beyond linear logic. Futurist, **August 1984**, 17–20.

Nierenberg, G.I. *The Art of Creative Thinking*; Barnes & Noble, 1996.

Nuernberger, P. Mastering the creative process. Futurist, **August 1984**, 33–36.

Osborn, F. *Applied Imagination: Principles and Procedures of Creative Problem-Solving*; Charles Scribner's Sons, 1963.

Parnes, S.J. Learning creative behavior: Making the future happen. Futurist, **August 1984**, 30–32.

Quester, G.H. Creativity and bureaucracy: The search for success. Futurist, **August 1984**, 27–29.

Rosenfeld, R.; Servo, J.C. Business and creativity: Making ideas connect. Futurist, **August 1984**, 21–26.

Rothenberg, A. *The Emerging Goddess: The Creative Process in Art, Science, and Other Fields*; University of Chicago Press, 1990.

Stein, M.I.; Heinze, S.J. *Creativity and the Individual: Summaries of Selected Literature in Psychology and Psychiatry*; Free Press of Glencoe, 1960.

Tatsuno, S.M. Japan's move toward creativity. GAO J. **Summer 1990**, 13–18.

Technology is changing basic structure of education. News Rep. **Summer 1993**, 2–5.

Waitley, D.E.; Tucker, R.B. How to think like an Innovator. Futurist, **May–June 1987**, 9–15.

Weinstein, B. *20 Ways to be More Creative in Your Job*; Simon & Schuster, 1983.

Inventory Management

Ronald John Hy
University of Central Arkansas, Conway, Arkansas, U.S.A.

INTRODUCTION

Sound inventory management is designed to save money by minimizing inventory costs. Inventories are items—such as building materials, office supplies, and chemicals, to name a few—that are used to produce products and/or services. Managing inventories efficiently is important because inventories are among the largest nonwage expense of most public and nonprofit agencies.[1]

Inventory management saves money by purchasing as inexpensively as possible the optimal number of needed items so that they are always readily available, but in an amount that minimizes storage and holding costs. Having a sufficient number of items readily available, therefore, must be balanced against the cost of storing and holding items.

Inventory management requires:

- Preparing specifications, obtaining competitive bids, negotiating, and receiving items
- Buying specific items
- Monitoring the deterioration, obsolescence, storing, issuing, theft, handling, interest, and insurance of items
- Overseeing the storage and holding costs of items.

The most common mistakes made by inventory management are:[2]

- Stocking too many items
- Stocking items which are seldom, if ever, needed
- Failing to balance purchasing cost and storage costs
- Failing to consider the full cost of holding inventories

Sound inventory management, then, controls costs and thereby saves money by determining the number or amount needed to be readily available, while keeping storage cost to a minimum. Inventory management also contributes to the availability of working capital, which refers to the organization's short-term or current assets (e.g., cash, short-term marketable securities, accounts receivable, and inventories). Spending as few dollars as needed on inventory allows an agency to spend more money on products and/or services, to invest more money for future use, or to pay off current debts.

VALUING INVENTORIES

In terms of accounting, inventory usage either is first-in, first-out (FIFO) or last-in, first-out (LIFO). With FIFO, the oldest items in the inventory are used first. With LIFO, the newest items in the inventory are used first. Using one of these two systems is necessary because each item in an inventory is not labeled individually. Thus, when similar items have been purchased at different prices, which frequently is the case, the price of each particular item may not be readily known, just the price of a group of items. For example, if the purchasing department buys a chemical at $5 an ounce at one time and $6 an ounce at another, it probably does not know which chemicals were purchased at $5 and which were bought at $6 because in storage the two shipments are ordinarily mixed together. Purchasing, however, surely knows how many chemicals were bought at $5 and how many were bought at $6. Therefore, to keep track of costs the agency has to use a consistent policy, either FIFO or LIFO. A consistent, systematic policy is the only way to keep an accurate record of actual inventory costs.

Under FIFO, the first item leaving the inventory is costed at the newest price in the inventory. Consequently, the value of the inventory at any point in time is determined by the most recent cost of the item. Under LIFO, the first item leaving the inventory is priced at the most oldest price in the inventory. In inflationary periods, using the higher-priced item has a decided advantage over using the lower-priced item because the most expensive items are used first and the least expensive items are held in inventory. Last-in, first-out pricing lowers the value of the inventory over time. Consequently, not as much money is tied up in inventory, and the inventory cost is less. Last-in, first-out pricing also allows the agency to increase reimbursable costs.[3]

Besides lowering costs and saving money, inventory management keeps inventories amply stocked. Because the time lag between ordering and receiving some items is sometimes substantial in terms of money, time, and even life, it is important that these items be available for immediate use. An agency cannot always project with certainty the number of items that will be needed at any given time. Therefore, to meet the demand and ensure the

Encyclopedia of Public Administration and Public Policy
DOI: 10.1081/E-EPAP 120010806

continuation of services, inventories must be kept suitably stocked. If a sufficient number of cast iron pipes and fittings are not readily available, then water lines cannot be fixed even when personnel are available to work on the lines. A sufficiently stocked inventory will prevent such discontinuities from occurring.

COSTING INVENTORIES

Given the need to minimize inventory cost, an agency must decide on the optimal number of items to keep in inventory. Inventory management relies on various formulas that are based on certain assumptions of future behavior, as well as common sense and experience.[4] Inventory cost consists of purchasing cost, order cost, carrying cost, overstock cost, and stock-out cost. The inventory formulas discussed in the following sections are taken from Breman, Kukla, and Weeks.[5]

Purchasing Cost

Purchasing cost is the price paid for each item. This expense is essential. Even though an agency has little control over the price it pays for items (the price is set by the seller), it can reduce the purchase cost by buying in large enough quantities to qualify for a discount. The timing of the order, as well as its specifications and bidding procedures (when applicable), also influence the price of items. As a result, the price of any item should always be considered to some extent variable and negotiable.

The purchasing cost formula is:

Purchasing cost $= PN$

where:

P = price of each unit.
N = number of units purchased annually.

Order Cost

Order cost is direct expenses incurred when purchasing items, expenses such as writing specifications, letting and analyzing bids, preparing order forms, and receiving items. This cost normally is minimal, especially when items are standard and purchasing processes routine. However, first-time, unstandardized orders do increase the order cost. The order cost, unlike the purchasing cost, varies with the number of orders placed, not the size of the order. Therefore, the order cost component of the inventory cost encourages large and fewer orders.

The order cost formula is:

Order cost $= (D/Q)O$

where:

D = number of units purchased annually.
Q = size of the order.
O = average cost of placing an order.

Carrying Cost

Carrying cost is the expense involved in holding items in the inventory. This cost actually consists of two elements: opportunity costs and storage costs. Opportunity costs are incurred when the organization spends money purchasing and holding items for inventory, instead of spending the money for something else that will reduce its operating cost (e.g., new equipment). Opportunity costs occur when an agency foregoes the opportunity to buy something other than inventory in favor of stocking the inventory. Generally, the greater the inventory cost, the greater the opportunity costs.

Besides opportunity costs, carrying cost includes storage costs, which are incurred when organizations, as they must, properly store, insure, secure, and otherwise protect their inventory. Storage costs tend to be positively related to the size of the inventory. As with opportunity costs, the larger the inventory, the larger the storage costs.

The carrying cost formula is:

Carrying cost $= HQ + IP(Q/2)$

where:

H = storage cost per unit, determined in much the same manner as rates are fixed.
Q = size of the order, usually the maximum number of items stored at any given time.

$IP(Q/2)$ = opportunity cost,

where:

I = interest.
P = price per unit.
$Q/2$ = average inventory holdings.

Overstock Cost

Overstock cost is the expense of holding unused or unneeded items in the inventory. This cost consists of surplus carrying costs and perishable costs. Surplus carrying costs exist when items are purchased for use in a particular time period, but are not used during that period. Thus, an agency is forced to pay an unexpected carrying cost for the surplus items until they can be used. Overstocking, therefore, contributes to an increase in the carrying cost.

The second element of overstock cost is perishable costs. Although perishable costs do not apply to most public and nonprofit agency inventories, they do to some, especially foodstuffs and chemicals. If an agency overstocks and is unable to use a chemical before the expiration date, it incurs a cost similar to that of a tomato that must be discarded.

The overstock formula is:

Overstock cost $= [HQ + IP(Q/2)] + S$

where:

$HQ + IP(Q/2) =$ carrying cost.
$S =$ perishable costs.

Stock-Out Cost

Stock-out cost is the expense incurred when there is an insufficient supply of a needed item. Keeping the stock-out cost minimal increases the inventory cost. This trade-off, however, is almost mandatory when avoiding stock-out is critical. Generally, public and nonprofit agencies seldom, if ever, experience this cost. They generally compensate by keeping substantial inventories on hand.

In summary, inventory cost (IC) is based on the following components:

$$IC = PN + (D/Q)O + [HQ + IP(Q/2)$$

$$+[[HQ + IP(Q/2)] + S]$$

When using this formula, one should keep in mind that, according to Breman, Kukla, and Weeks, about 15% of inventory items represents 70% of the inventory value.[5] Another 15% represent approximately 25% of the inventory value. The remaining 70% of the items account for only 5% of the inventory value. By concentrating on the 30% of the items representing 95% of the inventory and ignoring the rest, one can more readily and systematically estimate cost factors.

REFERENCES

1. Hy, R. *Financial Management for Health Care Administrator*; Quorum Books: New York, 1989; 119.
2. Lynch, T. *Public Budgeting in America*; Prentice-Hall: Englewood Cliffs, NJ, 1979; 295.
3. Lusk, E.; Lusk, J. *Financial and Managerial Control: A Health Care Perspective*; Aspen: Rockville, MD, 1979; pp. 102–107, 125.
4. Lynch, T. *Public Budgeting in America*; Prentice-Hall: Englewood Cliffs, NJ, 1979; 295.
5. Berman, H.; Kukla, S.; Weeks, L. *The Financial Management of Hospitals*; Health Administration Press: Ann Arbor, MI, 1974; pp. 261, 268.

Job Classification

Lyn Holley
University of Nebraska at Omaha, Omaha, Nebraska, U.S.A.

INTRODUCTION

This article begins with a summary description of job classification, then situates job classification within a context of organizing to accomplish work, and discusses the management functions supported by job classification and the roles in classification played by executives, managers, and job classifiers. It discusses "scientific classification," the impact of different frames of reference (i.e., different employers and different criterion measures) on classification, and describes various job classification techniques. It discusses job classification as a vehicle for both micromanagement and public accountability. Finally, it concludes that job classification codes provide information vital to management of work in circumstances ranging from the stabilizing civil services of African and Central American nations, to the rapidly reconfiguring teams of the "new" Western public workforce.

DEFINITION

Job classification is the process of identifying codes that represent the type and level of work assigned to a particular job. Its classification code locates the work of a job in relation to the work of the other jobs within a defined frame of reference. Classification codes identify which jobs are considered to be equivalent in type or level of work assigned. Its classification code links a job to a pay range, qualifications needed to do the job, and many other administrative requirements and laws.

One example of a classification code is "Counseling Psychologist, GS-0180-11." In the U.S. federal government frame of reference, many jobs have this classification code. Jobs with the same classification code are considered equivalent in respect to the type and level of work assigned to the job. Jobs with the same code have the same minimum qualifications requirements and are in the same pay range.

Different levels of work have different codes. For example, the job classification code, "Counseling Psychologist, GS-0180-09" indicates a job at a lower level of work than "Counseling Psychologist, GS-0180-11." A job at level "09" has a lower pay range than a job at level "11." A level of work such as level "11" or level "09" may cut across many different occupations. For example, the "Counseling Psychologist, GS-0180-11" code is different from the "Information Technology Specialist (Systems Administration), GS-2210-11" code, even though "11" indicates the same level of work in both occupations.

Job classification is used in the United States by the federal government, all state governments, and virtually all local governments.[1] Large and medium-size private organizations use job classification. Different employers use different classification systems. Government job classification systems tend to be more detailed than private sector job classification systems. Many types or levels of government work have no effective counterpart in the private sector—law making and law enforcement are two examples. Pay for these jobs cannot be compared directly with pay in the private labor market. Setting pay levels for these jobs in relation to the private sector labor market is achieved by establishing the relationship of these jobs to other government jobs having private sector counterparts.

Despite its widespread application, job classification is not widely understood. Most managers and employees are aware of job classification only as a seemingly arbitrary limitation on pay or staffing flexibility.

ORGANIZING WORK

To plan, coordinate, or direct work, a way to estimate and track the type and amount of human resources needed to produce desired results is necessary. Public officials or contractors who manage people directly require some means for distinguishing the knowledge, skills, and abilities needed to produce desired results, identifying persons who have those attributes, and communicating about the work of the job. The realities of the relevant labor market, law, and employees' perceptions of fairness all pressure managers to pay people appropriately in relation to others. Public expectations of accountability require agency heads and legislators or boards to be able to ensure pay ranges are justified and defensible. Job classification codes are an essential element in accomplishing all these functions.

Encyclopedia of Public Administration and Public Policy
DOI: 10.1081/E-EPAP 120010767

Job classification systems are composed of classification codes and rules for how to match work and jobs with classification codes. Classification rules govern how jobs are sorted by type of work (e.g., as Secretary or Nurse) and level of work (e.g., as trainee, journeyman, or expert). The codes label each type of work and level of work. Different job classification systems have different sets of rules and codes.

One of the results of applying a job classification system is an outline of the work of an organization. The traditional organization chart of a unit may show only job titles and numbers of similar jobs. Some job classification is necessary to assign titles to jobs such that similar jobs have the same job titles. Assigning the same job titles to similar jobs makes it possible to count the jobs in each job title and show the numbers of jobs on the chart. Job titles allow organizations to interface in a general way with the labor market. The U.S. government supports economic development, record keeping, and workforce research by providing systems of standard job titles and occupational codes for hundreds of different types of work.[a]

Job titles are one level of job classification "code." The more precise the "coding" of work into types and levels, the more comprehensive the information on the organization chart about each job. For example, the classification code "Counseling Psychologist GS-0180-11" includes much information in addition to the job title. It links the job (or jobs) with that code to specific pay tables and directives about pay, in this case, to pay range 11 in the General Schedule (GS). Its classification code also links the job to specific classification standards. The classification standards include information about the nature of the Counseling Psychologist occupation, 0180, and explain how jobs are classified in that occupation at the 11 level. The classification code links the job to standards, studies, and directives about qualifications needed to carry out the work, and to specific procedures for hiring or selecting people to fill the job. The classification code also links the job to laws, regulations, or handbooks outlining other administrative requirements, such as eligibility of the incumbent of the job for various types of overtime or for inclusion in the union bargaining unit. Finally, the classification code links the job to the employer and employee records of work, and staffing or personnel records and reports.

[a]The Standard Occupational Classification System (SOC) classifies occupations on the basis of work performed and required skills, education, and training or credentials. Each occupation is assigned to only one group at the lowest level of the occupation. The SOC issued in Fall 1998 blends previous industry- or worked-based classification systems (e.g., the SIC, Standard Industrial Classification System) with previous skills and worker attributes-based systems (e.g., the DOT, Dictionary of Occupational Titles).

Job classification is not needed in very small organizations where the mission statement is often adequate for communicating about work. Division of work within the organization (e.g., a team of research scientists, a family farm) can be fluid and informal. The "job" of each person in the organization can emerge from the requirements of each new day. However, if the family farmers seek to recruit a Farm Equipment Repair Specialist, they will have to define a "job" to interface with the labor market, locate people with the skills needed, identify appropriate pay, and communicate with applicants about duties to be assigned and work expected.

Larger organizations have more interchange with the external labor market. In larger organizations, relationships are more contractual than familial, and require more formal record keeping. In larger organizations, different laws and regulations apply. Larger organizations are characterized by division and specialization of labor, and require some means for summarizing and combining information about many jobs. Job classification meets these and other needs of larger organizations.

FUNCTIONS SUPPORTED BY JOB CLASSIFICATION

Job classification is a function of the management of work carried out by people. Job classification facilitates movement of people to and among jobs. As it is used in the United States, job classification helps employers to find people and people to find employers on the basis of the work of the job, rather than on another basis such as kinship, ethnicity, or propinquity. Each paragraph in this section describes a management function to which job classification is fundamental.

Estimating, Tracking, and Fulfilling Human Resources Requirements

The concept of "job" is the basis for estimating human resources costs and requirements. "Job" is a unit of analysis for work; it is used to estimate how many of what kind of people are needed to achieve desired results and to specify how many of what kind of people should be hired or let go. A "job" exists apart from its incumbent.

Identifying the type and level of work in a job is essential to accessing a work-based internal or external labor market. Job titles and further classification codes for type and level of work link the work of the job to qualifications required, and suggest the type and level of work assigned. Job descriptions communicate the work of the job in more detail.

Managing and Planning Work

Distribution of work is guided by job classification. Job descriptions record decisions made about the typical flow of work in an organization, and the typical work of each employee. Supervisors assign and employees accept work within this framework of prior agreement. At higher management levels, classification codes guide assignment of additional or new work (e.g., programs, projects). Classification codes identify the location and number of jobs with qualifications relevant to the new or additional work [e.g., Information Technology Specialists (Systems Administrators)]. The U.S. federal government can access this information for the million or so jobs covered by its central classification system.

Comparing Pay

The concept of "job" is fundamental to most methods for comparing pay. Comparing one person's pay with another person's pay has little meaning in the labor market or in court, unless both persons are doing substantially similar work. Work is usually considered "substantially similar" if both persons incumber jobs with the same classification codes.

Appraising Performance

To appraise the performance of individual employees or to set standards for performance, it is necessary to establish a basis for comparison. Where work performance is the basis for comparison, job classification identifies which types of work are comparable. Comparing the work performance of a secretary with the work performance of an electrical engineer is as inappropriate as comparing circles with squares. Although both a secretary and an electrical engineer might have the same performance rating (e.g., "acceptable"), deciding in each case whether the incumbent has met acceptable work standards requires comparison with work standards of the appropriate occupation.

Comparing Unit Productivity

Comparing productivity of organization units requires a way to represent the types of work performed by the units and levels of resources available in the units. If Unit E carries out engineering aspects of environmental cleanup and Unit L carries out legal aspects of environmental cleanup, direct comparison of their work performance is inappropriate. Although both units might have the same performance rating (e.g., "meets plan"), the process of deciding in each case if the unit has "met plan" to a greater or lesser extent than another unit requires com-

parison with comparable units. Comparing comparable units further requires some way to take into account differences in resources available to each unit. Comparing Unit E with a unit also performing engineering aspects of environmental cleanup (Unit E2) requires some consideration of resources available in each unit. It may be that Unit E has operated with 50% of its engineer positions vacant, whereas Unit E2 has had no vacancies. It may be that Unit E has had only one supervisor or senior worker for every eight engineers, whereas Unit E2 has had three. It may be that Unit E has 30% of its engineer positions filled at the trainee level, whereas Unit E2 engineers all are at full proficiency. Job classification provides the codes necessary to identify similar units, and within units, to sort out types and levels of resources (jobs) required and available. Job classification codes outline particular configurations of resources and types of work, and support comparison and evaluation of effectiveness of various ways of organizing work.

Identifying Incumbent Rights and Entitlements

The classification of each job links the job with laws, regulations, agency guidance, and precedents that determine the eligibility of its incumbent for inclusion in a union bargaining unit; vs. Fair Labor Standards Act of 1938 overtime; merit pay pools; and, particular retirement, health, or paid leave benefits.

Keeping Records of Work and Employment

Job classification codes link records of hiring, paying, and appraising employees and key the records to laws, regulations, and guidance in effect at specific times.

To fully consider the impact of changing a job classification system, executives and experts need to consider all the ways in which job classification supports management.

EXECUTIVES, MANAGERS, AND JOB CLASSIFIERS

Classification is fundamental to management decisions about what type of people to hire, how much to pay them, which employees are eligible for union membership, how to distribute rewards, and how to report and explain staffing and pay to company executives, regulators, and the courts.

Private sector executives supported by classification experts select job classification techniques, the criterion for the relationships between jobs, and the coverage of job classification used by their organization. Executives use the information provided by job classification to control costs, account for expenditures, plan work, and allocate resources. In the public sector, the legislature typically makes these executive decisions.

Many public sector executives and, in both sectors, many managers are aware of job classification only as a restraint on whom they can hire and how much they can pay. Job classification specialists are the messengers who bring to managers the "bad news" about controls imposed at executive levels. The tension between the responsibilities of job classification specialists and managers sometimes generates an adversary relationship.

Job classification specialists are expert in applying the rules of the job classification system used by their employer. Job classification specialists must often certify job classification decisions before the decisions are implemented. Making an exception to the system for one manager almost inevitably evolves into an "exception" for all managers. In the federal system and several others, the job classification specialist is bound by the ethical implications of classification rules with a basis in law.

Job classification specialists typically classify jobs in many different occupations. Developing the ability to gather and understand enough information about a particular job to classify it in the time available requires years of training and experience.

The process of job classification is being simplified by a trend toward using less specific classifications, more generic job descriptions, and electronic access to classification resources such as standards, examples of job descriptions, and decision support software. Some government agencies have delegated responsibility to managers for classifying their own subordinate positions. In those circumstances, the role of job classification specialist becomes one of providing expert advice and training, updating electronic resources, or auditing decisions made by managers.

SCIENTIFIC CLASSIFICATION

Classification is a necessary step in dealing with large amounts of information of all kinds. Ancient Egyptians classified, recorded, and analyzed the behaviors of the Nile River to interface more effectively with nature. Family farms classify income and expenses to more effectively interface with lenders or tax collectors. Modern organizations classify work to interface with external labor markets, as well as coordinate management of their internal workforces.

Early in the twentieth century, progressive reformers in the United States sought to address government corruption by instituting a merit system for some government jobs.[2] Duties and responsibilities of each job covered by a merit system are typically specified and recorded in a job description. Qualifications required to do the work are specified and selection of personnel is based on qualifications required to do the work. Pay is set in relation to the work of the job. Job classification is necessary to compare pay for a job with the pay for similar jobs in the labor market, and to compare pay of one job with pay of another job in the same organization. The Classification Act of 1923 established a classification system in the federal government, which modified and expanded by successor acts, now applies to about 1 million federal jobs.

Achievements of the physical sciences have generated much enthusiasm for scientific methods. Job classification methods echo methods of the physical sciences and, by virtue of establishing systematic procedures for inquiry and analysis of jobs, have been called "scientific."

Classification, however, is more judgmental than chemistry. Chemists observe elements objectively and classify the elements with precision into categories of objective phenomenon, such as the categories in the Periodic Table of Elements. Job classifiers observe work objectively, however, the classification system itself is a product of past and present values and circumstances, not a description of physical facts. Rather than a Periodic Table of Elements, the fundamental criterion of a job classification system is a hierarchy of jobs or job elements. The hierarchy consists of level relationships considered necessary for legitimacy of the classification system in a particular context. It is this hierarchy of jobs or job elements that any job classification system must reliably reproduce and rationalize. This hierarchy is the criterion used to develop the job classification system.

Within occupations, different levels or hierarchies of work reflect aspects valued more (e.g., the work of training others) and aspects valued less (e.g., working at a trainee level). Between and among occupations, differences depend on customary groupings of skills and knowledges in the labor market and the educational system. Present groupings of skills and knowledges reflect how past occupations responded to opportunities and accidents of history. On the early Western frontier, the occupation of barber may have included the duties of dentist. When the occupation of barber separated into the two specialized occupations of barber and dentist, salaries of the specializations reflected what was valued more (dentistry) and what was valued relatively less (barbering) by labor markets past and present. Within a specific frame of reference, job classification can systematically, predictably, and rationally replicate the hierarchy of values expressed in the criterion of the job classification system applied.

Results of job classification reflect values embedded in the selection of the job classification criterion, techniques, and coverage. Some societies, labor markets, or employers may value services of fully proficient barbers above those of fully proficient dentists. In those societies or labor markets, job classification systems would place jobs of fully proficient barbers in a higher pay range than jobs of fully proficient dentists.

Every job classification system rests on a criterion measure that embodies values. In the United States, the values typically echo those of the external labor market as it is experienced and interpreted by the employer at the time the classification criterion is chosen and the job classification system is established. In the mid-1970s, an interest in pay equity emerged and prompted some discussion of universal job evaluation systems. The idea of a universally applied classification criterion never gained solid support in the United States. Relevant laws and judicial rulings have typically defined the standard for acceptable pay equity practice as the fair and consistent use by an employer of any professionally designed job classification system.[3]

Job classification is presented in many personnel manuals as an objective, even scientific, process for determining job worth. This presentation is only a partial truth. Job classification is, in essence, a systematic way of identifying correct relationships among jobs. The correctness of the relationships, however, is based on custom and culture as reflected in the criterion used to develop the job classification system. Correctness is not based on some physically verifiable fact or on a scientifically established theoretical model. Like budget, the scientific component of job classification is the "science" of management.

JOB CLASSIFICATION TECHNIQUES

Different techniques of job classification involve codes, forms, and formats that appear to be very different. Differences in codes, forms, and formats generate different jargon, and each requires mastery of a different vocabulary. However, if the same criterion is used, application of any of the techniques to the same job information should produce about the same job relationships and job structure. Consider, for example, the criterion of salary in the relevant labor market, and consider two different classification systems based on this criterion—a system using benchmark whole job comparison, and a system using point factor evaluation. Formats, forms, and codes for classifying jobs under the two systems appear to be very different. However, classification of a group of jobs using the benchmark whole job comparison should produce about the same job structure as classification of the same group of jobs using the point factor evaluation system. The two systems look different, but are fun-

damentally the same because both are based on the same criterion.

However, if the same type of classification system (e.g., a point factor system) is developed for two organizations, but each organization uses a different *criterion*, the job structure resulting from classification may be different. If organization A uses the judgment of occupational experts as a criterion and organization B uses the labor market, and if a group of occupational experts gives "knowledge" more weight than does the relevant labor market, fully proficient librarian jobs may be above fully proficient secretary jobs in the structure of organization A and below fully proficient secretary jobs in organization B, despite both organizations having used the same job classification technique.

Although different criteria may produce different job structures, the dynamics of the culture and the labor market influence all criteria toward conformity and stabilize long-term job relationships. Cultural values are shared by groups of experts within an occupation and by different employers, and also by legislators in state governments or the U.S. Congress. These shared values influence views of the legitimacy of a job hierarchy. Criteria express values, and values are slow to change. Within occupations, level relationships are stable. Fully proficient barbers have been paid more than barbers in training, at least since Medieval Europe.

Among occupations, however, relationships are less stable. Relationships among occupations are more likely to change in response to economic influences, especially in the short term. For example, a limited supply of electricians in an area of high demand could drive the market value of electricians above the market value of accountants. Responding to the opportunity for higher pay, trained electricians may be attracted from other areas or people may take training to become electricians and, over time, electricians may be oversupplied in that area, electrician wages may stop rising, and accountants may resume their previous place in the labor market hierarchy. Organizations that hire from the labor market or periodically adjust wages of employees to the labor market must adjust to changes in occupational relationships. Because most market changes are temporary fluctuations, it is often more appropriate to make temporary salary adjustments than to change a job classification system. The federal government's criterion measure for the classification system covering about 1 million white-collar jobs is expressed in legislation (Chapter 51 of Title 5, United States Code). The federal government adjusts to temporary market effects by paying "special rates" to certain occupations in certain areas. However, some of the market changes endure and require changes in the job classification systems to interface effectively with the labor market.

Other things being equal, if the criterion measure is the same, any or all the techniques applied to the same job information should produce about the same structure of jobs. Understanding the role of the criterion is key to evaluating how accurately a job classification system is reflecting its criterion, considering the currency and appropriateness of the criterion, and distinguishing between the need for temporary or fundamental change in a job classification system. Each of the following techniques of job classification can be used to produce job structures consistent with a criterion measure chosen by an organization. A single criterion measure can apply to all occupations, as in the case of the federal government system for classifying white-collar occupations, or to a smaller group of occupations, such as technical occupations.

Classifying Whole Jobs and Classifying Jobs Factor by Factor

Each of the following techniques may be used to classify a "whole job" or to classify a job factor by factor. Each job has a potentially limitless number of factors that could be considered in deciding its classification. Each technique listed below typically provides guidance as to whether to use whole job or factor-based classification. The advantages of whole job classification include its simplicity and flexibility. The disadvantages of whole job classification include the potential for inconsistency in classifying jobs due to the flexibility for each classifier to consider different factors or to weigh the same factors differently.

In both whole job and factor-based classification, consistency can be improved by having more than one classifier classify the job independently and subsequently reconciling their classification decisions, or by developing guidance for classifying each group of jobs.

Factor-based classification identifies and limits the number of factors to be considered in classifying jobs. The advantages of factor-based classification include improved consistency in classifying jobs by guiding and limiting what is considered. Disadvantages of factor-based classification systems include the costs of producing more specific guidance particularly in respect to how evaluations of factors of a job are to be combined to decide the overall classification of a job. A further advantage of factor-based classification is the more detailed information it provides—at the level of specific job factors rather than at the level of the whole job. This specific, factor-level information, however, comes at a price—factor-based classification standards are more costly to develop and classification of record-keeping requirements is more extensive.

Ranking

Jobs are classified by being ranked in relation to each other by a group of raters who can credibly rate the jobs in the organization. Advantages of this technique include potential for less paperwork associated with classification and development of the job classification system at minimal cost. A disadvantage is that it is only as credible and defensible as the raters; further, the number of jobs that can be ranked effectively by any group of raters is limited, and only the original raters can classify jobs. This type of system may not be sustainable over time.

Benchmark Job Classification Standards

Jobs are classified by reference to standards. The standard is composed of descriptions of actual jobs that exemplify each level of work. Advantages of this technique include the potential for less paperwork associated with classification of jobs that match benchmarks, that the benchmarks can be applied by as many people as are trained to use them, and the ease of communicating about classification of jobs that match benchmarks. A disadvantage of this technique is that it is only as credible as the process used to rank the benchmark jobs; also, jobs not matching the benchmarks may be difficult to classify. This technique is most efficient for occupations in which there is not much variation of work within levels, such as most blue-collar work in the trades.

Narrative Job Classification Standards

Jobs are classified by reference to standards consisting of narrative descriptions and examples of work at selected levels. There is usually a standard for each major occupational group of jobs. Standards are often prefaced by a section giving general information about the occupation and describing features of work important in distinguishing one level within the occupation from another. Advantages of this technique include the potential for application of the standards by as many people as are trained to use them; the standards are typically general and can be applied to large numbers of jobs. These typically general standards allow flexibility for classifiers to weigh unique features of each job. The language distinguishing levels of work is explicit, and can be challenged and refined; the standards provide a uniform basis for communicating about classification of work in an occupation. Disadvantages of the narrative standards technique include the potential for inconsistency due to diverse interpretations of the general language describing each level of work in the occupation and that the system is expensive to develop. Systems using narrative standards typically generate large files because documenting a classification decision requires addressing how the work of the job was compared with all the factors assessed in deriving classification of the job.

Points-Based Job Classification

Jobs are classified with reference to standards that are narrative descriptions explaining and exemplifying "points" in a range of point values. Although points may be used to express or combine multiple judgments of whole jobs, points almost always are associated with factor-based job classification systems. Advantages and disadvantages of the points-based job classification technique parallel those of narrative job classification. In factor-based systems, points restrict flexibility in judging the relative value of different aspects of work. Restricting flexibility improves consistency of ratings. For example, the work of a historian might match a higher level in respect to knowledge than in respect to authority. If the points for knowledge have greater weight in the overall classification, the job might be classified at the level of its knowledge. If the points for authority have greater weight, the job might be classified at the lower level. In narrative standards, points are not included, which gives whoever classifies the job more flexibility in determining which of the two levels was more appropriate for the historian.

Finally, the fundamental nature of all job classification techniques is to guide the process of observation and decision making. Job classification is largely a judgmental process. Like personality, each job is unique. To classify a job requires reduction of the job to elements used in a particular classification system, and identifying the "best" match between the job and the appropriate classification standard. It is not surprising that different people sometimes reach different conclusions about the same job.

JOB CLASSIFICATION PROCESS

Classifying a job is the process of assigning to the job codes that represent the type and level of work assigned to the job. "Counseling Psychologist GS-0180-11" is an example of a classification code. Job classification codes include by reference a great deal of information indicating the type and level of work, the qualifications characterizing a job, and the terms and conditions of the employment arrangement.

For the different job classification techniques discussed, the elements of the job classification process are essentially the same. Initially, the work assigned to the job is described. Although the job incumbent is usually consulted, supervisors usually control description of work assigned and may draft the description. A second-line supervisor must usually approve the description.

Classifying the job is the middle step of the process. A job classification specialist, a manager, a panel of peers, a consultant may be responsible for matching the work of the job with the appropriate classification codes.

Job classification decisions usually require additional clearances and approvals before new classification codes are assigned to a job. Assigning new classification codes may affect other systems supported by job classification. For example, if a job has grown to a higher classification level, necessary clearances may be obtained and its incumbent may be promoted to a higher pay range. Some personnel systems require open competition for the "new" job at the higher level. If classification of a job reveals that new duties assumed are "confidential management duties," a decision may be made to withdraw the job from a union bargaining unit, triggering subsequent dealings with the union. When informed about the impacts of impending changes in classification codes, management in some systems has the opportunity to alter assigned duties so classification codes do not change in ways that have undesired consequences.

Finally, classification activity, reasoning, and outcomes are documented. Requests for classification review may be frequent, and documenting classification activity helps to manage and monitor the work of classifying jobs. Documenting classification reasoning permits detection of errors in observation or classification, and promotes consistency and perceived fairness by making transparent the basis for judgment. Changes in classification codes may trigger changes in other areas such as pay, training requirements, or bargaining unit membership. Even when classification codes remain the same, when a job description has changed, performance standards may have to be updated.

MICROMANAGEMENT AND ACCOUNTABILITY

Job classification is, in its essence, an information system. As such, it has functioned as part of management systems for controlling personnel expenses and practices. The information made available by job classification can be a vehicle for micromanagement by the U.S. Congress, state legislatures and other governing bodies, chief executives, budget directors, and others. Through job classification and its linkages to pay, staffing, and other types of practices, executives can dictate and monitor, among other things, exactly how many jobs will be available to do work, how much each job can be paid, and minimum qualifications required for each job. Managers and workers frequently chafe under the added demands and limitations of these types of top-down administrative controls.

However, job classification is a key instrumentality of government accountability. The merit system for the U.S. civil service initiated by the Pendleton Act of 1883 was an antidote to government corruption.[2] Job classification is at the heart of any merit system.[4] Reformers in the early 1900s saw job classification as a means for controlling patronage abuses. The work of government jobs would be defined, and the work of campaigning and soliciting campaign contributions would not be done on the public payroll. Only those qualified would be hired, and the qualifications required would be based on the work to be performed. Pay levels would be related to work performed, and jobs assigned equal work would be in the same pay range. In 1923, the U.S. government passed the Classification Act, which is the foundation of classification processes and approaches still used in the U.S. federal civil service.[5]

The importance of job classification to public accountability is supported by its association with the emergence of merit systems in Central American governments following periods of political corruption.[6] The new Draft Charter for Public Service in Africa implies adoption of merit systems for career civil service jobs and pay consistent with work—functions that are implemented and monitored using job classification codes.[7]

MANAGING THE NEW WORKFORCE

Since the mid-1980s, management delayering and team-based rationalization has reduced the number of middle-income jobs in the United States and restructured much of the workforce.[8] The new type of flatter, nonunionized, flexible workforce can be reorganized at almost Internet speed into different team configurations. Any given team may include both management and nonmanagement members, both public and private sector members, both contingent and permanent employees, and both part- and full-time employees.

To the extent governments can simply "buy" services in the marketplace without regard to wage equity, credentialed qualifications, or other personnel rules, governments may simply specify the product desired. The challenge of managing work in this new environment would in that way be passed on to contractors or teams agreeing to deliver the product. Whether it occurs inside or outside government organizations, management of work in the new environment requires even more information than managing work in traditional structures. Developing a bid, distributing work among teams, and

assigning resources to teams requires some method of estimating amount of work. Recruiting from the labor market and making up teams requires identifying qualifications needed for jobs, matching qualifications with work, and matching work to be done with the "going rate" in the relevant labor market. Differentially rewarding teams for productivity requires some way of identifying comparable teams.

Job classification codes are the language of the information needed to manage and coordinate the new type of workforce, much as they have been for the traditional workforce. Traditional processes for providing the information, however, need to be improved to meet new demands. Flexibility of some linkages characterizing traditional civil service personnel systems might be increased. Some governments are considering "pay banding." Also called "grade banding," this type of system increases the number of levels of work covered in each pay range, thus decreasing the precision of job classification and possibly loosening the linkage of pay to the external labor market. Another approach would be to consider relaxing the linkage between level of work and level of qualifications in the manner of U.S. military systems, which permit assignment of persons to jobs classified at levels above or below the person's level of qualifications and experience. Another approach to increased flexibility is breaking large interlinked groups of occupations into subgroups. The U.S. government linkage of all white-collar occupations to the same classification criterion, for example, might be examined to determine feasibility of breaking occupations into smaller categories, each with a distinctive criterion, such as the professional, administrative, technical, and clerical categories widely used in the private sector.

CONCLUSION

Job classification is widely used in both public and private sectors. It is an important part of merit systems throughout the United States and around the world, and it is a practice now poised on the brink of rapid change.

REFERENCES

1. Henry, N. *Public Administration and Public Affairs,* 8th Ed.; Prentice Hall: New Jersey, 2001; 249.
2. Ingraham, P.W. *The Foundation of Merit: Public Service in American Democracy*; The Johns Hopkins University Press: Baltimore, 1995.
3. Risher, H.; Wise, L. Job Evaluation. In *New Strategies for Public Pay*; Risher, H., Fay, C.H., Eds.; Jossey-Bass, Inc.: San Francisco, 1997; 98–124.

4. Dubnick, M.J.; Romzek, B.S. *American Public Administration: Politics and the Management of Expectations*; MacMillan Publishing Company: New York, 1991.

5. Holley, L.M.; O'Connell, J.R. Job Classification. In *New Strategies for Public Pay*; Risher, H., Fay, C.H., Eds.; Jossey-Bass, Inc.: San Francisco, 1997; 76–97.

6. Klingner, D.E.; Nalbandian, J. *Public Personnel Management,* 4th Ed.; Prentice Hall: New Jersey, 1998.

7. Hon. Hage Geingob and Ministerial Working Group. Draft Charter for the Public Service in Africa (Windhoeck Agreement). In *Annex of Background and Synopsis of the Draft Charter for the Public Service in Africa*; United Nations Secretariat, 27 March 2000; ST/SG/AC.6/2000/L.3. Also see http://www.unpan.org and select What's New, then select Windhoeck. Articles 15 and 19.

8. Snyder, D.P. Future Pay: Reinventing Compensation for the Information Age. In *ACA News*; American Compensation Association: Scottsdale, AZ, October/November 1994; Vol. 1, 17–20.

FURTHER READING

Society for Human Resources Management web site, which responds to a search for "job classification" with topical information having a private sector focus. Members of the society have access to more information than nonmembers. http://shrm.org.

Standard Occupational Code (SOC) System User Guide; http://www.bls.gov/soc/socguide.htm.

U.S. DOL ETA Dictionary of Occupational Titles, 4th Ed.; 1991. This is an archived copy of the final edition of this useful classification that originated in the 1930s to support the work of the U.S. Employment Service. http://www.oalj.dol.gov/libdot.htm.

U.S. federal job classification standards, guidance for application, and other related material: http://www.opm.gov and select classification.

U.S. professional association of job classification specialists. http://www.classandcomp.org.

Judicial Ethics

David A. Yalof
University of Connecticut, Storrs, Connecticut, U.S.A.

INTRODUCTION

Our nation's judicial system rests on the theory that a neutral and competent arbiter of disputes (the judge) provides the most effective means of resolving legal disputes among competing parties. Judges are responsible for defining each party's legal rights and responsibilities, allocating resources, and supervising the actions of public officials, among other tasks. In carrying out these duties, the willingness of each judge to respect and honor the judicial office as a public trust is considered fundamental to the success of the system; if members of the judiciary are not held to the highest standards of integrity and independence—or if there is even an appearance of impropriety in their actions—confidence in the judicial system may break down.

For well over a century, much attention has been paid to the ethical conduct of lawyers, who must balance the duty to provide zealous representation of their clients with their sometimes conflicting responsibilities as officers of the Court. Considerably less attention—scholarly or otherwise—has been paid to judicial ethics. In court, judges may be held to even higher standards of integrity than those to which lawyers or other participants in the process normally are held. Outside of court, a judge may still be held to exceedingly high standards of honesty and propriety, as private actions may also reflect on the judge's capacity to perform judicial functions with impartiality. Although judges certainly can (and often do) maintain some personal opinions on broad legal issues, the premise that judges can nevertheless be open minded and impartial regarding the specific legal issues and parties that come before them remains a bedrock principle of our legal system.

EXAMPLES OF ETHICAL DILEMMAS FACED BY JUDGES

Ethical considerations inevitably play a part in many of the decisions made by judges during their tenure on the bench. Unfortunately, the rules and laws that guide judicial conduct only go so far in specifying detailed responses to every possible situation a judge may face. For example, what role can a judge play in participating in public affairs when not actually presiding over court? To maintain the appearance of propriety, a judge probably should avoid actively campaigning for political candidates or assisting in raising funds for political campaigns. But what about public service activities that call (at least in part) upon a judge's expertise in interpreting facts and the law? In 1946, Justice Robert Jackson temporarily stepped down from his position on the United States Supreme Court to serve as the federal government's chief prosecutor at the Nuremberg War trials. Immediately after President John Kennedy was killed in November of 1963, Chief Justice Earl Warren of the U.S. Supreme Court accepted President Lyndon Johnson's appointment to chair the commission investigating the circumstances that led to President Kennedy's assassination. On a lesser scale, local court judges are often asked to serve on various boards and committees in their home communities. Under what circumstances might such extra-judicial political activities compromise a judge's independence, or at least create the appearance of impropriety?

Financial conflicts of interest pose another ethical minefield for judges. Normally, we would expect judges to disqualify themselves from presiding over cases whenever their impartiality might be "reasonably" questioned. But what does the phrase "reasonably" entail? One judge was replaced in litigation involving the Exxon Corporation when his wife inherited less than one–one billionth of the stock of that company. Another judge stepped down from an antitrust case, because a family member owned less than 10 shares in one of the 2000 corporate parties involved in the litigation. Over 30 years ago, a federal appellate judge (Clement Haynsworth) was denied an appointment to the U.S. Supreme Court, largely because while serving on the corporate board of the Carolina Vend-A-Matic Corporation ("CVAC"), he had supervised a case involving a second company whose parent entity held $50,000 worth of contracts with CVAC. When is a financial conflict significant enough that it requires a judge to recuse himself from all matters related to the conflict?

A third area of judicial ethics concerns on-the-bench judicial decision making that may, under certain circumstances, constitute an abuse of power. When a judge commits a legal error, it is generally a matter for legal appeal, rather than a question of judicial misconduct. Still,

Encyclopedia of Public Administration and Public Policy
DOI: 10.1081/E-EPAP 120012958

some errors are so egregious (and perhaps deliberate) that they might be considered unethical, provoking calls for sanctions against the judicial offender. Judges have occasionally been disciplined for disposing of cases summarily without allowing an opportunity for even minimal adversary proceedings. One judge was sanctioned for coercing parties into disposing of their cases out of fear or intimidation. Judges cannot make inappropriate comments that demonstrate bias or insensitivity to the parties before them. In general, judges are required to administer justice through a faithful and competent application of the law. Yet when do judicial decisions cross the line from mere error into an improper use (or even outright ''abuse'') of power?

The above examples barely scrape the surface of potential judicial misconduct. Once assuming judicial office, an individual must be prepared to navigate through a maze of ethical considerations, most of which are accompanied by ambiguous instructions and heavily qualified guidelines.

HISTORY OF JUDICIAL ETHICS

Prior to the 1960s, judicial misconduct in the United States was addressed almost exclusively through formal removal procedures, whether by impeachment, a bill of address passed by a legislature, or recall by the people. Because such remedies are quite extreme and cumbersome, they were only rarely utilized. (Legislatures may have also been wary of how frequent threats of removal might hamper judicial independence.) Consequently, many cases of judicial misconduct went unaddressed or ignored for much of our nation's history.

At least some of the blame for this state of inaction lay with the legal profession's governing body, the American Bar Association (ABA). The ABA's lone attempt at formulating standards of judicial ethics proved an almost total failure: the original ''Canons of Judicial Ethics'' (promulgated by the ABA in 1924) were universally criticized as amounting to mere statements of ''moral posturing'' that provided little guidance in answering difficult questions of judicial ethics.

Beginning in the 1960s, however, the federal government and various state governments began to adopt new mechanisms for disciplining judicial misconduct. Their efforts focused on the adoption of formal codes of judicial misconduct and the creation of official judicial conduct organizations authorized to investigate and discipline judges. Finally in 1972, the ABA promulgated a new Model of Judicial Conduct to replace the mostly ignored Canons it had formulated almost a half-century earlier. In less than two decades, the 1972 Code was adopted (albeit with minor variations) by 47 states, the District of Co-

lumbia, and the Federal Judicial Conference, which oversees judicial misconduct in federal courts. In 1990, a revised Model Code was adopted, and in the decade that followed, an additional 23 states adopted this new version of the code, which featured the use of gender-neutral language and other minor alterations. To date, 49 of 50 states have adopted some version of one or the other of these codes. (The lone holdout has been Montana, which created its own set of rules of judicial conduct.)

THE CODE OF JUDICIAL CONDUCT

Both the Model Code of Judicial Conduct promulgated in 1972 and the 1990 revised version of the code set forth the same basic standards that govern judicial conduct in and out of the nation's courts. Although the codes are intended to provide a framework for disciplinary agencies to regulate conduct, they provide no basis for civil liability or criminal prosecution.

In both versions, Canon 1 requires judges to ''uphold the integrity and independence of the judiciary.'' It is in every sense the ''philosophical backdrop'' of the entire document; the other provisions of the code give substance to Canon 1.

Canon 2 requires judges to ''avoid impropriety and the appearance of impropriety'' in all of their activities. In the 1990 version of the code, Canon 2 admonishes judges to adhere to the most broadly accepted norms of social conduct in three specific ways:

- A judge must ''respect and comply with the law'' and shall act in a manner that ''promotes public confidence in the integrity and impartiality of the judiciary.''
- A judge cannot allow personal or political relationships to influence ''judicial conduct or judgment'' and cannot lend the prestige of the office to advance the private interests of others, whether by conveying the appearance of favoritism or by testifying voluntarily as a character witness.
- A judge may not hold membership in ''any organization that practices invidious discrimination on the basis of race, sex, religion or national origin.''

Because a judge's actions often come under intense public scrutiny, the code specifically imposes burdens that separate a judge from ordinary citizens. According to the official ABA commentary accompanying Canon 2, the test for ''appearance of impropriety'' is whether the conduct would ''create in reasonable minds a perception that the judge's ability to carry out judicial responsibilities with integrity, impartiality and competence is impaired.'' Under this provision, judges are encouraged to disqualify themselves whenever they maintain a formal financial interest, personal relationship, or any other type of interest in the parties, litigation, or subject matter at hand. Informal appearances matter as well. (Consistent with Canon 2, at least one judge was disqualified for sitting at a lunch table with counsel during breaks, even though there was no evidence of any inappropriate discussion.)

Canon 3 of both codes provides that judges should perform the duties of their office "impartially and diligently." Those duties include numerous adjudicative and administrative responsibilities, disciplinary responsibilities, and self-disqualification whenever the circumstances of the situation demand it.

The drafters of the 1990 Code of Judicial Conduct combined former Canons 4, 5, and 6 of the 1972 code into one Canon 4 that deals comprehensively with off-the-bench conduct. This new Canon 4 specifically prohibits judges from participating in extra-judicial activities that may cast doubt on their capacity to judge impartially, demean the judicial office, or interfere with the proper performance of judicial duties. Canon 4 does *not* restrict judges from engaging in various avocational activities (writing, lecturing, teaching, etc.); serving as a nonlegal officer or advisor for an agency dedicated to the improvement of law, or as a part of a nonprofit educational, religious, or charitable organization; or managing family financial affairs. But, judges are restricted from taking on extra-judicial assignments in government that are unrelated to the general improvement of law; engaging in business dealings that may be perceived as exploiting the judge's position on the bench; receiving improper gifts or loans; and serving as a fiduciary in proceedings that might come before him. A judge may not practice law, except in an unpaid manner to draft or review documents for a family member.

Finally, Canon 5 of the 1990 code essentially reinstitutes Canon 7 of the 1972 code, which orders judges to "refrain from inappropriate political activity." Judges are admonished to avoid active participation in political organizations and must resign from judicial office upon becoming a candidate for a nonjudicial government position. As a candidate for judicial office, a sitting judge must "maintain the dignity appropriate to judicial office" while he is campaigning; thus, the judge cannot personally raise funds for office, even if subject to a public election. And, a judge cannot even speak to a political gathering until becoming a formal candidate for election. This final canon has been a source of some controversy, as judges seeking reelection have had to wrestle with the demands of a hard-fought campaign for office. Specifically, how does a judge defend positions on the campaign trail, while at the same time "maintaining the appropriate dignity" of the judicial office? Certainly, candidates for judicial office enjoy some leeway in criticizing opponents, but such criticism should not bring the judge's impartiality into question. As the reporter for the drafting committee of the original code explained, this complicated set of rules amounts to a set of "compromises between political reality and the aim of maintaining the appearance of judicial impartiality."[a]

PROCEDURES FOR DISCIPLINING JUDGES

Along with the proliferation of federal and state judicial ethics codes patterned after the Model Code, numerous new judicial conduct organizations were established in the middle part of the twentieth century to consider legitimate accusations of judicial misconduct and to supervise the application of judicial ethics provisions to offending judges.

In 1960, California became the first state to create a permanent state commission responsible for regulating judicial conduct, and other states quickly followed suit. By the early 1980s, all 50 states and the District of Columbia maintained organizations with the authority to investigate and prosecute judges for misbehavior. Unlike in earlier periods, outright removal was not the only penalty available to public authorities; most of these organizations enjoyed the power to impose or recommend sanctions ranging from simple admonishment to temporary suspensions, as well as removal.

To oversee judicial misconduct in the federal judicial system, Congress in 1980 passed the Judicial Councils Reform and Judicial Conduct and Disability Act, which created judicial councils in each federal circuit charged with reviewing complaints against judges and, where appropriate, ordering sanctions. As with state commissions, these judicial councils can impose a range of sanctions under the act; however, Congress specifically withheld power from such councils to remove a federal judge outright from office, on the theory that Congress enjoys the authority to remove duly appointed federal judges by impeachment under the Constitution.

Although early critics of judicial misconduct commissions and councils feared they would pose a serious threat to judicial independence, the structure of the system acts to allay any such fears. In each jurisdiction, judges play a role at every step of the process (in some states, judges actually comprise a majority of the commission's membership). Moreover, decisions rendered by such commissions are appealable to another judicial court, transforming the process into a system of "self-regulation" in which threats to judicial independence carry little credence.

[a]Jeffrey Shaman, Steven Lubet and James Alfini, eds., *Judicial Conduct and Ethics, Third Edition.* (New York: Matthew Bender, 2000), p. 365 (quoting E.W. Thode, *Reporter's Notes To the Code of Judicial Conduct* (1973), p. 96.)

In addition to the formal sanctions available to a judicial commission or council, Congress and individual state legislatures can also remove judges accused of certain specified levels of misconduct. Under the federal Constitution, a majority of the House of Representatives can impeach federal officers (including judges) for "Treason, Bribery, or other High Crimes and Misdemeanors"; the Senate then enjoys the sole power to try the judge on the impeachment charges and remove the judge from office if found guilty by a two-thirds majority. Most state constitutions refer to "criminal activity," "serious malfeasance," or "gross incompetence" as possible grounds for impeachment.

Although the procedures governing systems of judicial discipline vary widely from state to state, there are at least two general categories of systems currently in place. Forty-one states and the District of Columbia have adopted a "one-tier system," in which a panel composed of judges, lawyers, and even some nonlawyers handles every aspect of the process, from the filing of complaints to the prosecution of charges, the conduct of hearings, and the issuing of a formal recommendation on sanctions. Some states require that the state's highest court actually impose the sanctions; in other states, the panel may impose sanctions directly. Nine states feature a "two-tiered system" in which a panel investigates and prosecutes formal charges, but an entirely separate panel actually adjudicates the charges and makes a final disposition.

No matter which system is utilized, judicial conduct councils and commissions function as the equivalent of noncriminal investigatory bodies in which discovery occurs and procedural due process rights (including the right to counsel) must be provided. The records of all such proceedings are generally kept confidential, although many commissions at least provide for disclosure to the judge of the identity of the complainant and any witnesses.

CONCLUSION

Just as ethical standards applicable to lawyers must evolve as circumstances in the legal profession and the court system change, so are standards of judicial ethics shaped by shifting circumstances affecting the selection, performance, and extra-judicial activities of judges. Today, judges participate in a myriad of activities in their local communities; much of that participation might have seemed imprudent as recently as a few decades ago. To stay relevant, the Canons of judicial ethics must therefore be flexible enough to react to these real-world changes, and yet stable enough so that they may provide useful reference points for judges who must rely on them for guidance on a continuing basis. Clearly, an interested observer looking for the most up-to-date understandings and interpretations of judicial ethics would be well-advised to look beyond the language and commentary of the Canons of Judicial ethics. Specifically, a number of Internet sources may be helpful in this regard, including web sites associated with the American Bar Association (http://www.abanet.org/home.html); the Federal Judicial Conference (http://www.uscourts.gov/judconf.html); and the American Judicature Society (http://www.ajs.org/ethics1.html). Additionally, one should actively consult web sites administered by each individual state's judicial system, which may feature links to state variations on the Model Code, as well as to state judicial opinions interpreting various provisions on judicial ethics.

FURTHER READING

American Bar Association. In *Model Code of Judicial Conduct*; American Bar Association: Chicago, 1998.

Boutrous, T., et al. *State Judiciaries and Impartiality: Judging the Judges*; National Legal Center for the Public Interest: Washington, D.C., 1996.

Eastland, T., et al. *Ethics in the Courts: Policing Behavior in the Federal Judiciary*; National Legal Center for the Public Interest: Washington, D.C., 1990.

Lubet, S. *Beyond Reproach: Ethical Restrictions on the Extrajudicial Activities of State and Federal Judges*; American Judicature Society: Chicago, 1984.

Shaman, J., et al. *Judicial Conduct and Ethics,* 3rd Ed.; LEXIS Law Publishing: Charlottesville, VA, 2000.

Volcansek, M. *Judicial Misconduct: A Cross-National Comparison*; University Press of Florida: Gainesville, FL, 1996.

Judicial Independence

Ian Greene
York University, Toronto, Ontario, Canada

INTRODUCTION

A key feature of jurisdictions that practice the rule of law is an independent judiciary. This principle means that judges must be in a position, and also perceived by the public to be in a position, to make judgements about the cases before them as impartially as possible. Any attempts to influence a judge's decision outside of the rules of the courtroom are violations of judicial independence, whether from elected politicians, public servants, or private interests. Illicit attempts to influence judges might be direct, such as bribes, threats, or a telephone call from a government official. Indirect breaches of judicial independence might take the form of manipulations of the salaries or working conditions of judges who fail to tow a particular line, or they might involve exploitation of the administrative arrangements or structures of courts with the intention of swaying judicial decisions. Imprudent practices by interest groups, politicians, or the media might also threaten judicial independence.

DEVELOPMENT OF JUDICIAL INDEPENDENCE

Judicial independence evolved along with the struggle for the rule of law. The victors in the Glorious Revolution in England in 1688 had fought for the supremacy of Parliament and its laws over arbitrary decrees by the monarch, and they also demanded an independent judiciary to apply the law evenhandedly. Judicial independence was officially recognized in 1701 in the Act of Settlement, which guaranteed security of tenure for superior court judges of the central courts and protected judicial salaries from tampering by the executive. Prior to 1688, however, there had been a number of attempts to further the cause of the supremacy of the law and judicial independence. In 1329, the Statute of Northampton "declared that no royal command shall disturb the course of the common law, and that if such a command is issued, the judges shall ignore it."[1] Because judges served at the pleasure of the monarch, however, their desire to keep their judicial appointments and their income often outweighed their resolve to decide independently. Nevertheless, the growing popularity of the ideal of judicial independence some-

times restrained monarchs from removing independently-minded judges.[2]

After 1688, the major theoretical defense of the idea of an independent judiciary was provided by John Locke, who argued for "indifferent" judges to settle disputes about the application of the law so that the law would "not be varied in particular Cases, but [there should be] one Rule for the Rich and Poor, for the Favourite at Court, and the Country Man at Plough." For Locke, it was particularly important for members of the government to be subject to the equal application of the law, so that no one would be "a judge in his own case."[3]

MECHANISMS FOR PROTECTION OF JUDICIAL INDEPENDENCE

The two means for protecting judicial independence in the Act of Settlement were appointment of central superior court judges for life during good behavior and the establishment of judicial salaries by Parliament. Prior to this time, judicial appointments had been at pleasure, meaning that the monarch could remove judges whose decisions he or she disagreed with. "During good behaviour" meant that judges could only be removed by a joint address of both houses of Parliament, and then only because of behavior inappropriate for a judge (such as accepting a bribe, consistently failing to attend at court hearings, or a serious lapse in morals). There has been only one serious attempt to remove a central court judge since 1714, and that was with regard to a judge accused of accepting bribes in the nineteenth century.[4]

THE AMERICAN REVOLUTION AND THE SEPARATION OF POWERS

It is ironic that the principles of judicial independence that progressive Britons had struggled so hard to achieve near the beginning of the eighteenth century were not applied to the colonies. The failure of the colonial authorities to institute judicial independence was one of the grievances that led to the American revolution. The framers of the 1789 constitution were familiar not only with the arguments of John Locke but also with those of William

Encyclopedia of Public Administration and Public Policy
DOI: 10.1081/E-EPAP 120010827

Blackstone and Montesquieu. Blackstone described the separation of powers that had developed between the judiciary and the other branches of government.[5] Montesquieu, writing in the mid-eighteenth century, attributed the apparent success of the English system of government in preserving liberty to the separation of governmental powers into the legislative, executive, and judicial branches.[6] He seemed unaware of the development of cabinet government in the United Kingdom about that time, which fused the executive and legislative branches, while continuing to treat the judiciary as a separate branch, more or less. The separation of the judiciary from the other two branches of government has never been as complete in the United Kingdom as in the United States For example, the Lord Chancellor is both a cabinet minister and the head of the judiciary, and the law lords of the House of Lords constitute the final court of appeal. In the United Kingdom as in some other Commonwealth countries, constitutional conventions, or principles of appropriate behavior, limit the intermingling of the judiciary with the other branches of government, and are a major safeguard of judicial independence.[1]

The theory of the separation of powers was adopted by constitutional framers in the United States Adams wrote, "The judicial power ought to be distinct from both the legislative and executive and independent upon both, so it may be a check upon both.[7]" According to Madison, "The accumulation of all powers, legislative, executive, and judiciary, in the same hands...may justly be pronounced the very definition of tyranny.[8]" And Hamilton, referring to Montesquieu, argued that "liberty...would have everything to fear from [the judiciary's] union with either of the other departments. ..."[9,10]

The result of the constitutional debates was Article 3 of the U.S. Constitution, which describes the "judicial power of the United States." Article 3 was intended to be "a pillar of the separation of powers designed to provide genuine judicial independence.[11]" In Article 3, we see the two mechanisms for protecting judicial independence developed by the Act of Settlement, security of tenure, and establishment of judicial salaries: "The Judges, both of the supreme and inferior courts shall hold their Offices during good Behavior, and shall at stated Times, receive for their Services, a Compensation, which shall not be diminished during their Continuance in Office." Federally appointed judges may be removed through impeachment by the House of Representatives and conviction by the Senate. Article 3 does not apply to the State judiciaries, which have developed their own methods for protecting judicial independence. These usually include safeguards for judicial salaries to prevent arbitrary tampering and security of tenure during fixed terms (renewable by appointment or election) and sometimes during appointments to retirement.

Between 1803 and 1989, seven federally appointed judges were impeached and convicted, and six others were impeached. Six of those convicted were District Court judges, and one was a Commerce Court judge. The reasons for the convictions included loose morals, frequent drunkenness, conviction for serious criminal charges such as tax evasion or perjury, or accepting bribes. A judge was convicted in 1862 for supporting the Confederate side in the Civil War.[a]

Every liberal democracy claims to have an independent judiciary, as well as administrative tribunals which, although not often possessing the same guarantees of judicial independence as judges, nevertheless, are intended to decide the issues that come before them impartially. Judicial independence often has constitutional status and safeguards, although constitutional safeguards are neither a necessary nor a sufficient condition for judicial independence. The test for judicial independence is the degree to which judges feel they can decide impartially, without undue influence from outside the courtroom.

THREATS TO JUDICIAL INDEPENDENCE

Peter Russell has suggested that the threats to judicial independence can be sorted into four categories: structural, personnel, administrative, and direct.[12] To this list can be added a fifth category: societal.

Structural

Even if courts have constitutional protection, legislatures can often alter the size and the jurisdiction of courts. If such alteration occurs as an attempt to influence the judges' decision making, then judicial independence becomes an issue. Perhaps the most famous example of a structural threat to judicial independence was President Franklin Roosevelt's proposed legislation to increase the number of judges on the Supreme Court by six in 1937. The plan was a reaction to the fact that the Court had struck down 16 New Deal laws in a little over a year. The six new positions would have allowed Roosevelt to appoint additional judges more sympathetic to the New Deal. Although the New Deal was popular, Roosevelt's attempt to erode judicial independence was not, and Roosevelt withdrew the controversial legislation. In the end, after one of the conservative judges changed his mind about the New Deal legislation, and after Roosevelt had a chance to appoint a judge, the Court stopped striking down the New Deal laws.[11]

---

[a]Nine other judges resigned before they could be formally impeached (Ref. [11]).

The transfer of jurisdiction away from a court or tribunal so that a government can reduce the caseload of judges appointed by a different government, or the re-organization of a court to make redundant the jobs of judges unpopular with the government, are also examples of the structural threats to judicial independence that occasionally occur even in liberal democracies.[13]

Personnel

Personnel issues focus around hiring, promotion, remuneration, and firing. The three systems of judicial selection are appointment by the government (either through partisan or nonpartisan procedures), acceptance into a career judiciary through competitive examinations (as in many civil law jurisdictions), and popular election, as in many U.S. States. The nonpartisan appointment method and the competitive examination method are the most compatible with the promotion of judicial impartiality and, therefore, independence, while popular election (especially when combined with periodical subsequent confirmation elections) may pose the greatest risk.

The system of judicial promotions may leave open the possibility that judges may be rewarded for pursuing a particular ideological line in their decision making. In Canada, although judicial selection advisory committees have helped to promote more non-partisan systems for judicial appointment to the trial level in most jurisdictions, the federal cabinet's rational for elevating trial judges to the appellate level remains shrouded in secrecy. And in Japan, it may be that lower court judges hoping for a promotion tend to adopt the ideological orientation of the judicial elite responsible for making judicial promotions.[14]

It is well established that independent judges cannot have their salaries reduced except during times of economic crisis, and judges must not be treated more harshly than others on the public payroll during such periods. How to determine judicial salary increases is a more thorny issue. It is not easy to conduct salary negotiations between the judiciary and the executive in a way that avoids the appearance of violating judicial independence. In 1997, the Canadian Supreme Court declared that judicial independence requires the creation of independent judicial compensation commissions to recommend adjustments of judicial salaries on a triennial basis. The Court required governments to be prepared to demonstrate that the recommendations of the commissions were given serious consideration.[b] This decision has raised the ques-

tion of whether judges can sometimes exaggerate the scope of judicial independence in order to protect professional autonomy interests unrelated to judicial impartiality. Whether administrative tribunals and Justices of the Peace also require compensation commissions is a hot topic currently being litigated in Canada.

Independent judges cannot be removed because their decisions are unpopular or because of alleged errors in their reasoning, but only when it has been demonstrated through an impartial process that the judge is not capable of undertaking judicial duties fairly and impartially. In 2001, Zimbabwean President Robert Mugabe encouraged state officials and veterans supporting his cause to threaten the safety of several Supreme Court judges who had found that the government's seizure of farms owned by whites was illegal. The result was the resignation of three judges, paving the way for new appointments who then declared the seizures lawful.[c] A less blatant example of an attempt to pressure a judge to resign is the parliamentary enquiry established to consider allegations against a radical judge on Australia's High Court in 1986.[13]

Administrative

Administrative practices in the courts have the potential to erode judicial independence in a number of ways. For example, prosecutors may be in a position to manipulate the case scheduling system so as to get the cases they are most concerned about before judges with a reputation of being sympathetic to prosecution arguments. Those who control the court's budget may use this power to reward judges who favor the administration's ideology by providing more prestigious working conditions. Worries by judges about the potential abuse of power by the executive branch caused the federal judiciary in the United States to push for and eventually achieve judicial control over court administration in 1939. The result is that the machinery of federal court administration is controlled by committees of judges. Although this system has advanced judicial independence in some ways, the disadvantage is that the courts may not be in a better position than before to obtain a reasonable budget allocation. As well, judges may not be as skilled in administration as those employed by the executive branch.[15] In Canada, the Supreme Court has declared that in order to protect judicial independence, judges must have control over the case scheduling system, the assignment of judges to cases, and court sittings.[16] The Court was not persuaded that judicial control over other aspects of court administration was necessary to protect judicial independence.

---

[b]Reference re Remuneration of Judges of the Provincial Court of Prince Edward Island, [1997] 3 S.C.R., 1.

[c]Mugabe seized lands lawfully, court says. *National Post*, Dec. 5, 2001, A12, quoting from *Agence France-Presse* and *The Daily Telegraph*.

Threats to judicial independence can also come from within the judiciary. Chief judges who want the puisne judges to favor a particular ideological stance might, for example, reward compliant judges with more conference travel. On appellate courts, there is the danger that a chief justice might arrange panels so as to increase the likelihood of a particular outcome.

Direct

Direct threats to judicial independence can be blatant, such as attempts to bribe judges or to intimidate them with physical threats. The public criticism of judicial decisions by elected politicians may also threaten judicial independence, because judges cannot defend themselves through entering into a public debate without impugning their impartiality. As liberal democracies mature, however, conspicuous attempts to influence, judges become infrequent. More subtle illicit contacts can, however, be just as damaging. Often, these more abstruse attempts to influence judges take the form of an informal chat or telephone call between a judge and an elected politician or senior administrative official, during which the judge is lobbied to handle a case in a particular way. This kind of contact with a judge represents undue influence, because it might result in an unfair advantage to the party attempting to influence the judge.

Societal

Societal threats to judicial independence include sensationalist media coverage of judicial proceedings or decisions, and demonstrations in front of courthouses that are intended to attract media attention and pressure judges to decide cases in a particular way. Judges in liberal democracies generally do not regard scathing critiques of their decisions in academic journals as a threat to judicial independence, because the writers are usually well-informed about legal issues, and academic analysis is regarded almost as a form of continuing legal education for judges. However, if media criticism is out of context, or seriously unbalanced, this can affect the judge's public reputation and family life. Because of judicial independence, judges may not enter into public debate to defend their decisions. Some judges fear that a conscious or unconscious desire to avoid being pilloried in the media might affect the judicial reasoning process.[17] On the other hand, if judges have security of tenure, their salaries may not be tampered with, and they are administratively secure, it is questionable whether societal threats to judicial independence are sometimes more perceived than real.

CONCLUSION

Judicial independence consists of arrangements to ensure that judges are in a position in which they feel they can decide cases as impartially as practically possible. The impartial application of the law is an important principle of liberal democratic government. Arrangements established to protect judicial independence usually include security of tenure until retirement or during a fixed term, the prohibition of tampering with judicial salaries to influence judicial decision making, and providing judges with control over administrative matters that can have an important impact on judicial decision making.

Regardless of the safeguards built into the law or the constitution to protect judicial independence, those wishing to influence judicial decisions outside of the regular courtroom process will attempt to find ways to interfere with judicial independence. Therefore, procedures designed to protect judicial independence need to evolve in order to meet new threats and challenges. Enhancing the protection mechanisms for judicial independence, however, needs to proceed cautiously, lest judicial independence is allowed to encroach on the rightful domains of executive and legislative independence. For example, when judges decree that judicial compensation commissions are constitutionally required to protect judicial independence, have they overstepped the boundaries of judicial independence? More generally, an activist judiciary that imprudently strikes down legislation on constitutional grounds puts judicial independence at risk.

All liberal democracies struggle with the question of the degree to which courts should control their own administrative apparatus in order to promote judicial independence. This issue is particularly important in jurisdictions like the United States that adhere to a strict separation of powers doctrine.[18] On the one hand, administration—including courts administration—is arguably the responsibility of the executive branch. On the other, executive administration of the courts can be abused so as to endanger judicial independence. However, courts that control their own administration machinery always encounter judicial independence concerns when dealing with budgetary and labor relations issues. As with many administrative conundrums, there are no perfect solutions, and intrastate and international comparisons of attempted resolutions of these issues is always enlightening.

REFERENCES

1. Pucknett, T.F.T. *A Concise History of the Common Law*, 3rd Ed.; Butterworth and Co.: London, 1940; 45.
2. Lederman, W.R. The independence of the judiciary. Can. Bar Rev. **1956**, *34*, pp. 769, 1139.

3. Locke, J. *Second Treatise on Government*; Library of Liberal Arts: New York, 1952; 51c. 1690.

4. Stevens, R. Judicial Independence in England: A Loss of Innocence. In *Judicial Independence in the Age of Democracy: Critical Perspectives from Around the World*; Russell, P.H., O'Brien, D.M., Eds.; University Press of Virginia: Charlottesville, 2001; 155–172.

5. Blackstone, W. *Commentaries on the Laws of England,* 3rd Ed.; John Exshaw: Dublin, 1768; 269.

6. Montesquieu. *The Spirit of the Laws,* Rev. Ed.; Colonial Press: New York, 1900; 151–160.

7. Adams, J. On Government. In *The Works of John Adams*; Adams, C.F., Ed.; Little, Brown: Boston, 1856; Vol. 4, pp. 181, 198.

8. Madison, J. The Federalist No. 47. In *The Federalist: or, The New Constitution*; Hamilton, A., Madison, J., Jay, J., Eds.; Dent: London, 1961.

9. Hamilton, A. The Federalist No. 78. *The Federalist.*

10. Wheeler, R. *Judicial Administration: Its Relation to Judicial Independence*; National Center for State Courts: Williamsburg, VA, 1988.

11. Abraham, H.J. The Pillars and Politics of Judicial Independence in the United States. In *Judicial Independence in the Age of Democracy*; Russell, P.H., O'Brien, D.M., Eds.; pp. 25–36.

12. Russell, P.H. Toward a General Theory of Judicial Independence. In *Judicial Independence in the Age of Democracy*; Russell, P.H., O'Brien, D.M., Eds.; 1–24.

13. Williams, J.M. Judicial Independence in Australia. In *Judicial Independence in the Age of Democracy*; Russell, P.H., O'Brien, D.M., Eds.; 173–193.

14. O'Brien, D.M.; Ohkoshi, Y. Stifling Judicial Independence from Within: The Japanese Judiciary. In *Judicial Independence in the Age of Democracy*; Russell, P.H., O'Brien, D.M., Eds.; 37–61.

15. Fish, P.G. *The Politics of Federal Judicial Administration*; Princeton Univ. Press: Princeton, NJ, 1973.

16. Valente v. The Queen, [1985] 2 S.C.R., 673.

17. Greene, I.; Baar, C.; McCormick, P.; Szablowski, G.; Thomas, M. *Final Appeal: Decision-Making in Canadian Courts of Appeal*; Lorimer: Toronto, 1998.

18. Vile, M.J.C. *Constitutionalism and the Separation of Powers,* 2nd Ed.; Liberty Fund Inc.: Indianapolis, IN, 1998.

Judicial Selection and Merit Selection

Cole Blease Graham, Jr.
University of South Carolina, Columbia, South Carolina, U.S.A.

INTRODUCTION

Based on the principle of dual sovereignty, there are parallel court systems in America—one for the federal or national system and one for each of the 50 states. Generally, these courts are at three levels—an entry level called circuit or district, an intermediate or appeals level, and a final or supreme court. Complementing these general civil and criminal and review courts are specialty courts, such as a regulatory agency court or a court that deals with a single problem such as bankruptcy, as well as courts of lesser or preliminary jurisdiction such as magistrates.

The United States Constitution establishes the process through which the President and Senate select judges for the United States Supreme Court. Congress initiates legislation to create and design all other federal courts. Similarly, individual state constitutions define each state's court system and the roles of the executive and legislative branches or local governments in selecting judges. Reformers have advocated a merit plan for judicial selection to replace the more traditional electoral processes within the states. A merit plan is based on more defined criteria for the qualifications of a judge.

OVERVIEW

When thinking about courts, it is easy to focus on the prominence of the persons or parties on trial and to overlook the fact that courts are really managed by lawyers who are guided by judges. Lawyers have to be guided through court proceedings by judges to create a written record which is respected by other lawyers and by higher courts. A judge must have a sufficient legal background to direct the operation of a court credibly. The American Bar Association (ABA), long an advocate of merit selection, has proposed professional qualifications instead of political party membership as the preferred basis for judicial selection. In addition, the ABA argues that judges should have solid personal attributes such as "superior self-discipline" and "moral courage."[1] The ABA also promotes standards for evaluating the performance of a sitting judge for any needed disciplinary measures and the development of continuing education programs.

MERIT CONCEPT

The merit concept is applied more vigorously in countries where the judiciary is treated as a separate, civil service profession.[2] In such instances, judges are selected by higher entry qualification standards, such as exceptionally high student grades, success in special examinations, and completion of additional training requirements. A judge's career moves up to more demanding jurisdiction and responsibility based on positive evaluations by higher-level justices rather than by elections or executive appointment. One exception in a civil service system for judges is a constitutional court to which a Parliament may elect some proportion of the judges, even then usually from among already qualified judges and for a limited term.

JUDICIAL SELECTION

Judges in the American federal system are appointed by the President and confirmed by the Senate. The advice and consent clause of the United States Constitution has the intent of promoting an independent, highly professionalized federal judiciary without advancing a specific political ideology or political party. It is nonetheless a highly politicized process.[3,4] Except for Supreme Court justices, the senior Senator of the President's party from the state in which the vacancy occurs or a new judgeship is created typically controls the appointment. Most federal judges have been members of the same political party as the President who nominated them.

Before confirmation by the Senate, a presidential nomination is reviewed by the Senate Judiciary Committee. The committee will not act until it has received the ABA report on each nominee, a tradition that began in the mid-twentieth century. Each potential nominee gets a questionnaire and returns it in 3 to 4 weeks. The ABA committee evaluates integrity, competence, and judicial temperament and rates each as "well qualified," "qualified," and "not qualified." In March, 2001, the George W. Bush administration discontinued reliance on the ABA report before announcing its nominations and, instead, decided to rely on the advice of the Federalist Society.[5]

The political reputation of a judicial nominee often predetermines the outcome of the selection process.

Encyclopedia of Public Administration and Public Policy
DOI: 10.1081/E-EPAP 120010829

Lately, a "blue-slip" policy has emerged in which an individual senator, often, but not always from the home state of a nominee, may veto confirmation.[6] This practice stalls confirmation of judicial nominees. Critics fear that the integrity of federal courts is threatened by a growing number of judicial vacancies, delays in filling them, and a decrease in legislative respect that may lead to mediocre compromise selections and reduced performance.

States use five approaches to judicial selection: popular election by party (partisan); election without regard for party (nonpartisan); legislative election; merit selection; and gubernatorial appointment.[7] Following the "common man" ideals of Jacksonian democracy that promote the qualifications of the ordinary citizen for government positions, 39 states elect state supreme court justices, and many also elect appeals court judges. Election advocates believe voters should express their preference, and that the ballot box is the best means to select a qualified judiciary.

Judicial candidates in partisan contests must finance their campaigns, make speeches at political rallies, and take positions on issues just like other candidates. Often, campaigns become heated, and candidates are negatively attacked for previous actions as a lawyer or prosecutor, such as defending a drug dealer, or for decisions in previous experience as a judge that may be portrayed as too soft on crime. The ABA Code of Judicial Conduct discourages aggressive partisanship by recommending against discussion of legal issues in partisan campaigns. Challenges by judicial candidates to the ABA ban or other ethical restrictions are often sustained on a First Amendment right to free speech argument.

In June, 2002, the Supreme Court of the United States struck down a canon of judicial conduct adopted by the Minnesota Supreme Court to bar candidates for judicial offices from publicly stating their views on controversial legal or political issues. The nation's highest court cited two reasons for its action. First, it found that the challenged canon violated the First Amendment of the U.S. Constitution, which protects the content of speech. Second, it decided that this canon infringed upon a category of speech protected by this amendment; namely, the right of judicial candidates to express publicly their qualifications for such offices [*Republican Party of Minnesota v. White*, 536 U.S.-(2002)].

Nonpartisan elections select candidates without party identification or the participation of a political party in an effort to reduce negative politics or party influence. It is arguable that nonpartisan elections do not achieve the ideals of reformers for an independent judiciary when compared to elections based on party.[8] Both approaches to popular election of judges are criticized for low rates of voter participation, increased costs of campaigning, and the tendency of incumbents to be reelected continuously. Where judges are elected on a less-than-statewide basis, for example, a state circuit or district judge, the Voting Rights Act of 1965 has been increasingly applied by federal officials to the electoral process if racial discrimination may be present.

Reform of popular election of judges has focused significantly on campaign finance. In February, 2002, the ABA recommended public financing for judicial elections as a way to reduce the fund-raising burden on candidates, the potential influence of contributors, and suspicious criticism of the fairness of courts. Although 14 states provide some level of public financing, recent campaigns have become more expensive and more combative. In a study initiated by merit system appointment advocates, it was found that spending in state supreme court elections doubled from 1994 to 1998 and increased another 60+% in 2000 to total over $45 million.[9]

Among opponents of public financing are business interests which may be adversely affected by court decisions. Some interest groups issue reports on candidates as a way to influence voter decisions. In 2002, the United States Chamber of Commerce and the Business Roundtable launched an effort—the Litigation Fairness Campaign—to raise and direct campaign financing to influence judicial elections in states where previous outcomes in tort litigation in business liability has hurt the business community.

Legislative election remains in only two states—South Carolina and Virginia—where a majority vote of legislators selects a judge. These two former English colonies perhaps continue the tradition of legislative action to offset the potential impact of executive appointment authority or the fear of popular elections. A recent reform is the addition of a preview panel to recommend the qualifications of candidates rather than have candidates appeal directly to the legislature. Legislative voting outcomes show an overwhelming tendency to elect candidates who have previously served in the legislature. Opponents of this approach to selection argue that serving as a judge is very different from legislative service, and that public accountability is reduced by insider pressures for legislative conformity.

About half the American states use a merit selection plan. The typical plan is called the Missouri Plan after the state that first adopted the ABA reform recommendations. It typically involves four steps. First, a nominating commission composed of judges, bar association representatives, and citizens is established. It is typically nonpartisan or attempts to represent both parties equally. Second, the nominating commission generates a list of candidates, conducts hearings or investigations on them, picks three names from the long list, and forwards the names with accompanying information to the governor. Third, the governor appoints one to the judgeship. Fourth, at the next general election, the governor's appointee is confirmed for a full term or rejected.

Some variations occur within the states, as the elements of a Missouri merit selection plan are combined differently. For example, in California, the governor goes first by sending a nomination to a commission on judicial appointments made up of the Chief Justice, an appellate judge, and the Attorney General. If the commission approves, a candidate takes office until the next general election, at which time, the candidate is voted on for a 12-year term. New Mexico features nomination by a commission and appointment by the governor. But, for a full term, the nominee must run in the next general election on a partisan basis and in the subsequent general election on a nonpartisan basis.

Gubernatorial appointment as an exclusive process for judicial selection is used in five states. It is an example of checks and balances between two branches of government. The popularly elected executive reflects the will of the people in designating judges who then act independently of the executive. Critics inject that there may be more politics than meets the eye, because a governor's selection may reflect political considerations more than judicial qualifications. The potential for executive political influence is expanded even more, because governors often appoint individuals to fill vacancies before elections or a merit system commission can act, thus giving a specific candidate the benefit of incumbency.

CONCLUSION

The President and the U.S. Senate have played key roles in judicial selection in federal courts during the more than 200-year history of the nation. Recently, political controversies, often sharply divisive, have made this process more contentious and delayed filling some vacancies. Presidential nominations have become less reliant on the influential role of the ABA. Senatorial advice and consent decisions have diminished senatorial courtesy by giving

greater leeway to an individual Senator's ability to veto a presidential nomination.

About half the American states select judges based on merit principles of professionalism as a way to soften what may be called the unnecessary politicization of the courts through campaigns and elections. Advocates of judicial elections maintain that political campaigns give voters substantive choices and enhance the accountability of judicial performance. Many states now include campaign finance reform as a way to orient popular judicial elections toward merit selection concerns.

REFERENCES

1. American Bar Association. *Standards Relating to Court Organization*; American Bar Association: New York, 1974; 43–44.
2. Murphy, W.F.; Pritchett, C.H.; Epstein, L. *Courts, Judges, and Politics: An Introduction to the Judicial Process*, 5th Ed.; McGraw Hill: Boston, 2002; 137–138.
3. Giles, M.W.; Hettinger, V.; Peppers, T. Picking federal judges: A note on policy and partisan selection agendas. Polit. Res. Q. **2001**, *54* (3), 623–641.
4. Yalof, D.A. *Pursuit of Justices: Presidential Politics and the Selection of Supreme Court Nominees*; University of Chicago Press: Chicago, 1999.
5. Palmer, E. Senate GOP backs down from dispute over handling of nominees. Congr. Q. Wkly. Rep. **2001**, *59* (23), 1360–1361.
6. Taylor, S., Jr. Judicial selection: Compromise on ideology, not quality. Natl. J. **2001**, *23* (19), 1379–1380.
7. Bowman, A.O'M.; Kearney, R.C. The Judiciary. In *State and Local Government*, 5th Ed.; Houghton Mifflin: Boston, 2002; 249–256.
8. Hall, M.G. State supreme courts in American democracy: Probing the myths of judicial reform. Am. Polit. Sci. Rev. **2001**, *95* (2), 315–330.
9. Stone, P.H. The blitz to elect business-friendly judges. Natl. J. **2002**, *34* (7), 480.

Index